Borland®
Delphi™ 6 Developer's Guide

Steve Teixeira and Xavier Pacheco

201 West 103rd St., Indianapolis, Indiana, 46290 USA

Borland®
Delphi™ 6 Developer's Guide

Copyright © 2002 by Sams Publishing

International Standard Book Number: 0-672-32115-7

Library of Congress Catalog Card Number: 2001086071

Printed in the United States of America

First Printing: October 2001

04   03   02   01   4 3 2 1

Trademarks

Warning and Disclaimer

EXECUTIVE EDITOR
Michael Stephens

ACQUISITIONS EDITOR
Carol Ackerman

DEVELOPMENT EDITOR
Tiffany Taylor

MANAGING EDITOR
Matt Purcell

PROJECT EDITOR
Christina Smith

PRODUCTION EDITOR
Rhonda Tinch-Mize

INDEXER
Sharon Shock

PROOFREADER
Harvey Stanbrough

TECHNICAL EDITOR
John Ray Thomas
Tom Theobold

TEAM COORDINATOR
Pamalee Nelson

MEDIA DEVELOPER
Dan Scherf

INTERIOR DESIGNER
Anne Jones

COVER DESIGNER
Aren Howell

PAGE LAYOUT
Octal Publishing, Inc.

Contents at a Glance

Table of Contents

PART VI   Internet Development   1047

22   ASP Development   1049

Foreword

"Delphi 6—two years in the making; a lifetime of productivity."

I have been happily employed at Borland for more than 16 years now. I came to work here, in the summer of 1985, to 1) be a part of the new generation of programming tools (the UCSD Pascal System and command line tools just weren't enough), 2) help improve the process of programming (maybe even leaving a little more time for our families and friends), and 3) help enrich the lives of programmers (myself included). We been innovating and advancing developer technology for the past 18 years. I enjoy being a part of this great worldwide Borland community.

Turbo Pascal 1.0 changed the face of programming tools forever. It set the standard in 1983. Delphi also changed the face of programming once again. Delphi 1.0 focused on making object-oriented programming, Windows programming, and database programming easier. Later versions of Delphi focused on easing the pain of writing Internet and distributed applications. Even though we've added a host of features to our products over the years and written pages of documentation and megabytes of online help, there's still more information, knowledge, and advice that is required for developers to complete successful projects.

How do you top the award winning and universally praised Delphi 5? Didn't Delphi 5 already simplify the process of building Internet and distributed applications while also improving the productivity of Delphi programmers? Could the Delphi team push themselves again to meet the demands of today's and tomorrow's developers?

The Delphi team spent more than two years listening to customers, seeing how developers were using the product, looking at the pain points of programming in the new millennium. They focused their efforts on radically simplifying the process of developing next generation e-business Web applications, XML/SOAP based Web Services, B2b/B2C/P2P application integration, cross-platform applications, distributed applications including integration with AppServer/EJBs, and Microsoft Windows ME/2000 and Office 2000 applications.

Steve Teixeira and Xavier Pacheco have done it again. They have crafted their developer's guide so that you can take advantage of the depth and breadth of Delphi 6 programming.

I've known Steve Teixeira (some call him T-Rex) and Xavier Pacheco (some call him just X) for years as friends, fellow employees, speakers at our annual conference, and as members of the Borland community.

Previous versions of their developer's guides have been received enthusiastically by Delphi developers around the world. Here now is the latest version ready for everyone to enjoy.

Have fun, learn a lot. Here's hoping that all of your Delphi projects are enjoyable, successful, and rewarding.

David Intersimone (David I)

Vice President, Developer Relations

Borland Software Corporation

davidi@borland.com

About the Lead Authors

Steve Teixeira is the Director of Core Technology at Zone Labs, a leading creator of Internet security solutions. Steve has previously served as Chief Technology Officer of ThinSpace, a mobile/wireless software company, and Full Moon Interactive, a full-service e-business builder. As a research and development software engineer at Borland, Steve was instrumental in the development of Delphi and C++Builder. Steve is the best-selling author of four award-winning books and numerous magazine articles on software development, and his writings are distributed worldwide in a dozen languages. Steve is a frequent speaker at industry conferences and events worldwide.

Xavier Pacheco is the President and CEO of Xapware Technologies Inc, a software development and consulting company with a purpose of accelerating visions. Xavier is a frequent speaker at industry conferences and is a contributing author for Delphi periodicals. Xavier is an internationally known Delphi expert and member of Borland's select group volunteers—TeamB. He is the best-selling author of four award-winning books that are distributed worldwide in a dozen languages. Xavier lives in Colorado Springs with his wife Anne and children Amanda and Zachary.

About the Contributing Authors

Bob Swart (also known as Dr.Bob—www.drbob42.com) is a UK Borland Connections member and an independent technical author, trainer, and consultant using Delphi, Kylix, and C++Builder based in Helmond, The Netherlands. Bob writes regular columns for *The Delphi Magazine*, *Delphi Developer*, *UK-BUG Developer's Magazine*, as well as the DevX, TechRepublic, and the Borland Community Web sites. Bob has written chapters for *The Revolutionary Guide to Delphi 2*, *Delphi 4 Unleashed*, *C++Builder 4 Unleashed*, *C++Builder 5 Developer's Guide*, *Kylix Developer's Guide*, and now *Delphi 6 Developer's Guide* (for Sams Publishing).

Bob is a frequent speaker at Borland and Delphi/Kylix related seminars all over the world, and writes his own training material for Dr.Bob's Delphi Clinics (in The Netherlands and the UK).

In his spare time, Bob likes to watch video tapes of *Star Trek Voyager* and *Deep Space Nine* with his 7-year old son Erik Mark Pascal and 5-year old daughter Natasha Louise Delphine.

Dan Miser is an R&D Project Manager for the DSP group at Borland, where he spends most of his time researching emerging technologies. Dan also worked on the Delphi R&D team where his responsibilities included DataSnap development. Dan's major focus is finding ways to allow information to be shared across boundaries, and this has allowed him to work with a variety of distributed computing technologies, including MIDAS, SOAP, DCOM, RMI, J2EE, EJB, Struts, and RDS. He has also been involved with promoting Delphi by being a contributing author to the Delphi Developer's Guide series, acting as a technical editor, writing magazine articles, participating on the Borland newsgroups as a member of TeamB, and being a speaker at BorCon on topics such as COM and MIDAS.

David Sampson is an R&D engineer in the Borland RAD Tools Group and is responsible for the CORBA integration into the RAD products. He is long time Pascal, Delphi, and C++ developer, and is a frequent speaker at the Borland Developer's Conference. He lives in Roswell, GA with his wife and enjoys hockey, Aikido, and helping his wife with her pack of Basenjis.

Nick Hodges is a Senior Development Engineer with Lemanix Corporation in St. Paul, MN. He is a member of Borland's TeamB and a long time Pascal and Delphi developer. He serves on the Borland Conference Advisory Board, is a frequent speaker at the conference, and is a frequent writer for the Borland Community Site. He lives in St. Paul with his wife and two children and enjoys reading, running, and helping his wife homeschool their two children.

Ray Konopka is the founder of Raize Software, Inc. and the chief architect for CodeSite and Raize Components. Ray is also the author of the highly acclaimed Developing Custom Delphi Components books and the popular "Delphi by Design" column, which appeared in *Visual Developer Magazine*. Ray specializes in user interface design and Delphi component development, and is a frequent speaker at developer conferences around the world.

Dedication

This book is dedicated to the victims and heroes of September 11, 2001.

Thanks to my family, Helen, Cooper, and Ryan. Without their love, support, and welcome distractions, I'd likely never be able to finish a book, and I'd almost certainly go crazy trying.

—Steve

Thanks to my family, Anne, Amanda, and Zachary. Your love, patience, and encouragement, I cherish.

—Xavier

Acknowledgments

We need to thank those who, without whose help, this book would never have been written. In addition to our thanks, we also want to point out that any errors or omissions you find in the book are our own, in spite of everyone's efforts.

We'd first like to offer our enormous gratitude to our contributing authors, who lent their superior software development and writing skills to making *Delphi 6 Developer's Guide* better than it could have been otherwise. Mr. Component himself, Ray Konopka, wrote the excellent Chapter 13, "CLX Component Development." DataSnap guru Dan Miser pitched in by writing the brilliant Chapter 21, "DataSnap Development." Well-known CORBA expert, David Sampson, contributed Chapter 19, "CORBA Development." Thank you also to Robert "Dr. Bob" Swart, for bringing his considerable talents to bear on Chapter 22, "ASP Development." Last (but certainly not least!), Web wizard Nick Hodges is back in this edition of the book in Chapter 23, "Building WebSnap Applications."

Another large round of thank-yous to our technical reviewers (and all around great guys), Thomas Theobald and John Thomas. These guys managed to squeeze in their duties as uber-technical reviewers among their day jobs of helping Borland create great software.

While writing the Delphi Developer's Guide series, we received advice or tips from a number of our friends and coworkers. These people include (in alphabetical order) Alain "Lino" Tadros, Anders Hejlsberg, Anders Ohlsson, Charlie Calvert, Victor Hornback, Chuck Jazdzewski, Daniel Polistchuck, Danny Thorpe, David Streever, Ellie Peters, Jeff Peters, Lance Bullock, Mark Duncan, Mike Dugan, Nick Hodges, Paul Qualls, Rich Jones, Roland Bouchereau, Scott Frolich, Steve Beebe, and Tom Butt. We're certain there are others whose names we can't recall, and we owe you all a beer.

Finally, thanks to the gang at Pearson Technology Group: Carol Ackerman, Christina Smith, Dan Scherf, and the zillions of behind-the-scenes people whom we never met, but without whose help this book would not be a reality.

Tell Us What You Think!

As the reader of this book, *you* are our most important critic and commentator. We value your opinion and want to know what we're doing right, what we could do better, what areas you'd like to see us publish in, and any other words of wisdom you're willing to pass our way.

As an executive editor for Sams Publishing, I welcome your comments. You can fax, e-mail, or write me directly to let me know what you did or didn't like about this book—as well as what we can do to make our books stronger.

Please note that I cannot help you with technical problems related to the topic of this book, and that due to the high volume of mail I receive, I might not be able to reply to every message.

When you write, please be sure to include this book's title and authors' names as well as your name and phone or fax number. I will carefully review your comments and share them with the authors and editors who worked on the book.

Fax: 317-581-4770

E-mail: feedback@samspublishing.com

Mail: Michael Stephens
         Executive Editor
         Sams Publishing
         201 West 103rd Street
         Indianapolis, IN 46290 USA

Introduction

You hold in your hands the fifth edition in the *Delphi Developer's Guide* series, and the product of literally thousands of man-hours over more than seven years of programming, writing, and refinement. Xavier and Steve were members of the original Delphi team at Borland, and this work is the outlet through which they can share their fifteen-plus years of combined experience developing software in Delphi. In *Delphi 6 Developer's Guide*, we have striven to hold true to the spirit that has made the Delphi Developer's Guide series perhaps the world's most read Delphi books and two-time winner of the Delphi Informant Reader's Choice award. This is a book by developers, for developers.

The intent of *Delphi 6 Developer's Guide* is to supplement and build on the Delphi Developer's Guide series. Ideally, we would have loved to include all the updated content form *Delphi 5 Developer's Guide* and all the new content in one book, but *Delphi 5 Developer's Guide* was already thick enough to stretch the technical limitations of modern book binding. In order to provide enough space to give proper coverage of the entire Delphi 6 feature set, we opted to publish a new book with new information.

Delphi 6 Developer's Guide contains a number of all-new chapters, many chapters that have been significantly enhanced from previous editions, and some of the favorite topics from *Delphi 5 Developers Guide*. The information in *Delphi 5 Developer's Guide* will not be lost, however. On the CD accompanying this book, you will find the entire contents of *Delphi 5 Developer's Guide*, with each chapter in a separate PDF file. On the inside front cover, we have also included the table of contents for *Delphi 5 Developer's Guide* so you can know at a glance where to find that programming tidbit. The end result for you, the reader, is essentially two books in one.

Delphi 6 Developer's Guide is divided into six sections. Part I, "Development Essentials," provides you with the foundation knowledge necessary to be an effective Delphi developers. Part II, "Advanced Techniques," highlights some common advanced development issues, such as threading and dynamic link libraries. Part III, "Database Development," discusses the many faces of Delphi's data access layers. Part IV, "Component-Based Development," takes you through the many manifestations of component-based development, from VCL to CLX to packages to COM and the Open Tools API. Part V, "Enterprise Development," is intended to give you the practical knowledge necessary to develop enterprise-grade applications with technologies such as COM+, CORBA, SOAP/BizSnap, and DataSnap. Finally, Part VI, "Internet Development," demonstrates the development of Internet and wireless applications in Delphi.

Who Should Read This Book

As the title of this book says, this book is for developers. So, if you're a developer, and you use Delphi, you need to have this book. In particular, however, this book is aimed at three groups of people:

- Delphi developers who are looking to take their craft to the next level.
- Experienced Pascal, C/C++, Java, or Basic programmers who are looking to hit the ground running with Delphi.
- Programmers who are looking to get the most out of Delphi by leveraging some of its more advanced and sometimes least obvious features.

Conventions Used in This Book

The following typographic conventions are used in this book:

- Code lines, commands, statements, variables, program output, and any text you see on the screen appear in a computer typeface.
- Anything that you type appears in a bold computer typeface.
- Placeholders in syntax descriptions appear in an italic computer typeface. Replace the placeholder with the actual filename, parameter, or whatever element it represents.
- Italics highlight technical terms when they first appear in the text and sometimes are used to emphasize important points.
- Procedures and functions are indicated by open and close parentheses after the procedure or function name. Although this isn't standard Pascal syntax, it helps to differentiate them from properties, variables, and types.

Within each chapter, you will encounter several Notes, Tips, and Cautions that help to highlight the important points and aid you in steering clear of the pitfalls.

You will find all the source code and project files on the CD-ROM accompanying this book, as well as source samples that we could not fit in the book itself. The CD also contains some powerful trial versions of third-party components and tools.

Delphi 6 Developer's Guide Web Site

Visit our Web site at http://www.xapware.com/ddg to join the *Delphi Developer's Guide* community and obtain updates, extras, and errata information for this book. You can also join the mailing list for our newsletter and visit our discussion group.

Getting Started

People sometimes ask what drives us to continue to write Delphi books. It's hard to explain, but whenever we meet with other developers and see their obviously well used, book marked, ratty looking copy of *Delphi Developer's Guide*, it somehow makes it worthwhile.

Now it's time to relax and have some fun programming with Delphi. We'll start slow but progress into the more advanced topics at a quick but comfortable pace. Before you know it, you'll have the knowledge and technique required to truly be called a Delphi guru.

Development Essentials

PART

I

IN THIS PART

Programming in Delphi

IN THIS CHAPTER

This chapter is intended to provide you with a high-level overview of Delphi, including history, feature sets, how Delphi fits into the world of Windows development, and general tidbits of information you need to know to be a Delphi developer. And just to get your technical juices flowing, this chapter also discusses the need-to-know features of the Delphi IDE, pointing out some of those hard-to-find features that even seasoned Delphi developers might not know about.

This chapter isn't about providing an education on the very basics of how one develops software in Delphi. We figure you spent good money on this book to learn new and interesting things—not to read a rehash of content you can already find in Borland's documentation. True to that, our mission is to deliver the goods: to show you the power features of this product and ultimately how to employ those features to build commercial-quality software. Hopefully, our backgrounds and experience with the tool will enable us to provide you with some interesting and useful insights along the way. We feel that experienced and new Delphi developers alike will benefit from this chapter (and this book!), as long as new developers understand that this isn't ground zero for a Delphi developer. Start with the Borland documentation and simple examples. Once you've got the hang of how the IDE works and the general flow of application development, welcome aboard and enjoy the ride!

The Delphi Product Family

Delphi 6 comes in three flavors designed to fit a variety of needs: Delphi 6 Personal, Delphi 6 Professional, and Delphi 6 Enterprise. Each of these versions is targeted at a different type of developer.

Delphi 6 Personal is the entry-level version. It provides everything you need to start writing applications with Delphi, and it's ideal for hobbyists and students who want to break into Delphi programming on a budget. This version includes the following features:

- Optimizing 32-bit Object Pascal compiler, including a variety of new and enhanced language features.

- Visual Component Library (VCL), which includes over 85 components standard on the Component Palette.

- Package support, which enables you to create small executables and component libraries.

- An IDE that includes an editor, debugger, form designer, and a host of productivity features.

- IDE enhancements such as visual form inheritance and linking, object tree view, class completion, and Code Insight.

- Full support for Win32 API, including COM, GDI, DirectX, multithreading, and various Microsoft and third-party software development kits (SDKs).
- Licensing permits building applications for personal use only: No commercial distribution of applications built with Delphi 6 Personal is permitted.

Delphi 6 Professional is intended for use by professional developers who don't require enterprise development capabilities. If you're a professional developer building and deploying applications or Delphi components, this product is designed for you. The Professional edition includes everything in the Personal edition, plus the following:

- More than 225 VCL components on the Component Palette
- More than 160 CLX components for cross-platform development between Windows and Linux
- Database support, including DataCLX database architecture, data-aware VCL controls, dbExpress cross-platform components and drivers, ActiveX Data Objects (ADO), the Borland Database Engine (BDE) for legacy connectivity, a virtual dataset architecture that enables you to incorporate other database types into VCL, the Database Explorer tool, a data repository, and InterBase Express native InterBase components
- InterBase and MySQL drivers for dbExpress
- DataCLX database architecture (formerly known as MIDAS) with MyBase XML-based local data engine
- Wizards for creating COM/COM+ components, such as ActiveX controls, ActiveForms, Automation servers, property pages, and transactional components
- A variety of third-party tools and components, include the INDY internet tools, the QuickReports reporting tool, the TeeChart graphing and charting components, and NetMasters FastNet controls
- InterBase 6 database server and five-user license
- The Web Deployment feature for easy distribution of ActiveX content via the Web
- The InstallSHIELD MSI Light application-deployment tool
- The OpenTools API for developing components that integrate tightly within the Delphi environment as well as an interface for PVCS version control
- NetCLX WebBroker tools and components for developing cross-platform applications for the Internet
- Source code for the Visual Component Library (VCL), Component Library for Cross-platform (CLX), runtime library (RTL), and property editors
- License for commercial distribution of applications developed with Delphi 6 Professional

Delphi 6 Enterprise is targeted toward developers who create enterprise-scale applications. The Enterprise version includes everything included in the other two Delphi editions, plus the following:

- Over 300 VCL components on the Component Palette
- BizSnap technology for creating XML-based applications and Web services
- WebSnap Web application design platform for integrating XML and scripting technologies with Web-based applications
- CORBA support for client and sever applications, including version 4.0x of the VisiBroker ORB and Borland AppServer version 4.5
- TeamSource source control software, which enables team development and supports various versioning engines (ZIP and PVCS included)
- Tools for easily translating and localizing applications
- SQLLinks BDE drivers for Oracle, MS SQL Server, InterBase, Informix, Sybase, and DB2
- Oracle and DB2 drivers for dbExpress
- Advanced tools for building SQL-based applications, including SQL Explorer, SQL Monitor, SQL Builder, and ADT column support in grid

Delphi: What and Why

We're often asked questions such as "What makes Delphi so good?" and "Why should I choose Delphi over Tool X?" Over the years, we've developed two answers to these types of questions: a long answer and a short answer. The short answer is *productivity*. Using Delphi is simply the most productive way we've found to build applications for Windows. Of course, there are those (bosses and perspective clients) for whom the short answer will not suffice, so then we must break out the long answer. The long answer describes the combined qualities that make Delphi so productive. We boil down the productivity of software development tools into a pentagon of five important attributes:

- The quality of the visual development environment
- The speediness of the compiler versus the efficiency of the compiled code
- The power of the programming language versus its complexity
- The flexibility and scalability of the database architecture
- The design and usage patterns enforced by the framework

Although admittedly many other factors are involved, such as deployment issues, documentation, third-party support, and so on, we've found this simple model to be quite accurate in explaining to folks why we choose Delphi. Some of these categories also involve some amount of subjectivity, but that's the point; how productive are *you* with a particular tool? By rating a tool on a scale of 1 to 5 for each attribute and plotting each on an axis of the graph shown in Figure 1.1, the end result will be a pentagon. The greater the surface area of this pentagon, the more productive the tool.

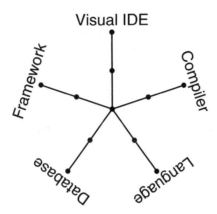

FIGURE 1.1
The development tool productivity graph.

We won't tell you what we came up with when we used this formula—that's for you to decide! Let's take an in-depth look at each of these attributes and how they apply to Delphi as well as how they compare with other Windows development tools.

The Quality of the Visual Development Environment

The visual development environment can generally be divided into three constituent components: the editor, the debugger, and the form designer. Like most modern *rapid application development (RAD)* tools, these three components work in harmony as you design an application. While you're working in the form designer, Delphi is generating code behind the scenes for the components you drop and manipulate on forms. You can add additional code in the editor to define application behavior, and you can debug your application from the same editor by setting breakpoints, watches, and so on.

Delphi's editor is generally on par with those of other tools. The CodeInsight technologies, which save you a lot of typing, are probably the best around. They're based on compiler information, rather than type library info like Visual Basic, and are therefore able to help in a wider variety of situations. Although the Delphi editor sports some good configuration options, I would rate Visual Studio's editor as more configurable.

Recent versions of Delphi's debugger have finally caught up with the debugger support in Visual Studio, with advanced features such as remote debugging, process attachment, DLL and package debugging, automatic local watches, and a CPU window. Delphi also has some nice IDE support for debugging by allowing windows to be placed and docked where you like during debugging and enabling that state to be saved as a named desktop setting. One very nice debugger feature that's commonplace in interpreted environments such as Visual Basic and some Java tools is the ability to change code to modify application behavior while the application is being debugged. Unfortunately, this type of feature is much more difficult to accomplish when compiling to native code and is therefore unsupported by Delphi.

A form designer is usually a feature unique to RAD tools, such as Delphi, Visual Basic, C++Builder, and PowerBuilder. More classical development environments, such as Visual C++ and Borland C++, typically provide dialog editors, but those tend not to be as integrated into the development workflow as a form designer. Based on the productivity graph from Figure 1.1, you can see that the lack of a form designer really has a negative effect on the overall productivity of the tool for application development.

Over the years, Delphi and Visual Basic have engaged in a sort of tug-of-war of form designer features, with each new version surpassing the other in functionality. One trait of Delphi's form designer that sets it apart from others is the fact that Delphi is built on top of a true object-oriented framework. Given that, changes you make to base classes will propagate up to any ancestor classes. A key feature that leverages this trait is *visual form inheritance* (VFI). VFI enables you to dynamically descend from any of the other forms in your project or in the Gallery. What's more, changes made to the base form from which you descend will cascade and reflect in its descendants. You'll find more information on this feature in the electronic version of *Delphi 5 Developer's Guide* on the CD accompanying this book in Chapter 3, "Application Frameworks and Design Concepts."

The Speediness of the Compiler Versus the Efficiency of the Compiled Code

A speedy compile enables you to develop software incrementally, thus making frequent changes to your source code, recompiling, testing, changing, recompiling, testing again, and so forth: a very efficient development cycle. When compilation speed is slower, developers are forced to make source changes in batch, making multiple modifications prior to compiling and adapting to a less efficient development cycle. The advantage of runtime efficiency is self-evident; faster runtime execution and smaller binaries are always good.

Perhaps the best-known feature of the Pascal compiler upon which Delphi is based is that it's fast. In fact, it's probably the fastest high-level language native code compiler for Windows.

C++, which has traditionally been dog-slow in terms of compile speed, has made great strides in recent years with incremental linking and various caching strategies found in Visual C++ and C++Builder in particular. Still, even these C++ compilers are typically several times slower than Delphi's compiler.

Does all this compile-time speed mean a tradeoff in runtime efficiency? The answer is, of course, no. Delphi shares the compiler back end with the C++Builder compiler, so the efficiency of the generated code is on par with that of a very good C++ compiler. In the latest reliable benchmarks, Visual C++ actually rated tops in speed and size efficiency in many cases, thanks to some very nice optimizations. Although these small advantages are unnoticeable for general application development, they might make a difference if you're writing computation-intensive code.

Visual Basic is a little unique with regard to compiler technology. During development, VB operates in an interpreted mode and is quite responsive. When you want to deploy, you can invoke the VB compiler to generate the EXE. This compiler is fairly slow and its speed efficiency rates well behind Delphi and C++ tools. At the time of this writing, Microsoft's next iteration, Visual Basic.NET, is in beta and promises to make improvements in this area.

Java is another interesting case. Top Java-based tools such as JBuilder and Visual J++ boast compile times approaching that of Delphi. Runtime speed efficiency, however, often leaves something to be desired because Java is an interpreted language. Although Java continues to make steady improvements, runtime speed in most real-world scenarios lags behind that of Delphi and C++.

The Power of the Programming Language Versus Its Complexity

Power and complexity are very much in the eye of the beholder, and this particular category has served as the guidon for many an online flame war. What's easy to one person might be difficult to another, and what's limiting to one might be considered elegant by yet another. Therefore, the following is based on the authors' experience and personal preferences.

Assembly is the ultimate power language. There's very little you can't do. However, writing even the simplest Windows application in assembly is an arduous and error-prone venture. Not only that, but it's sometimes nearly impossible to maintain an assembly code base in a team environment for any length of time. As code passes from one owner to the next to the next, design ideas and intents become more and more cloudy, until the code starts to look more like Sanskrit than a computer language. Therefore, we would score assembly very low in this category because, although powerful, assembly language is too complex for nearly all application development chores.

C++ is another extremely powerful language. With the aid of really potent features such as pre-processor macros, templates, operator overloading, and more, you can very nearly design your own language within C++. If the vast array of features at your disposal are used judiciously, you can develop very clear and maintainable code. The problem, however, is that many developers can't resist overusing these features, and it's quite easy to create truly horrible code. In fact, it's easier to write bad C++ code than good because the language doesn't lend itself toward good design—it's up to the developer.

Two languages that we feel are very similar in that they strike a very good balance between complexity and power are Object Pascal and Java. Both take the approach of limiting available features in an effort to enforce logical design on the developer. For example, both avoid the very object-oriented but easy-to-abuse notion of multiple inheritance in favor of enabling a class to implement multiple interfaces. Both lack the nifty but dangerous feature of operator overloading. Also, both make source files first-class citizens in the language rather than a detail to be dealt with by the linker. What's more, both languages take advantage of power features that add the most bang for the buck, such as exception handling, Runtime Type Information (RTTI), and native memory-managed strings. Not coincidentally, both languages weren't written by committee but rather nurtured by an individual or small group within a single organization with a common understanding of what the language should be.

Visual Basic started life as a language designed to be easy enough for programming beginners to pick up quickly (hence the name). However, as language features were added to address shortcomings over the years, Visual Basic has become more and more complex. In an effort to hide the details from developers, Visual Basic still maintains some walls that must be navigated around in order to build complex projects. Again, Microsoft's next-generation Visual Basic.NET is making significant changes in this area, albeit at the expense of backward compatibility.

The Flexibility and Scalability of the Database Architecture

Because of Borland's lack of a database agenda, Delphi maintains what we feel to be one of the most flexible database architectures of any tool. Out of the box, dbExpress is very efficient (although at the expense of advanced functionality), but the selection of drivers is rather limited. BDE still works and performs relatively well for most applications against a wide range of data sources, although it is being phased out by Borland. Additionally, the native ADO components provide an efficient means for communicating through ADO or ODBC. If InterBase is your bag, the IBExpress native InterBase components provide the most effective means to communicate with that database server. If none of this provides the data access you're looking for, you can write your own data-access class by leveraging the abstract dataset architecture or purchase a third-party dataset solution. Furthermore, DataCLX makes it easy to logically or physically divide, into multiple tiers, access to any of these data sources.

Microsoft tools logically tend to focus on Microsoft's own databases and data-access solutions, be they ODBC, OLE DB, or others.

The Design and Usage Patterns Enforced by the Framework

This is the magic bullet or the holy grail of software design that other tools seem to be missing. All other things being equal, VCL is the most important part of Delphi. The ability to manipulate components at design time, design components, and inherit behavior from other components using object-oriented (OO) techniques it a critical ingredient to Delphi's level of productivity. When writing VCL components, you can't help but employ solid OO design methodologies in many cases. By contrast, other component-based frameworks are often too rigid or too complicated.

ActiveX controls, for example, provide many of the same design-time benefits of VCL controls, but there's no way to inherit from an ActiveX control to create a new class with some different behaviors. Traditional class frameworks, such as OWL and MFC, typically require you to have a great deal of internal framework knowledge in order to be productive, and they're hampered by a lack of RAD tool-like design-time support. Microsoft's .NET common library finally puts Microsoft on the right track in terms of component-based development, and it even works with a variety of their tools, including C#, Visual C++, and Visual Basic.

A Little History

Delphi is, at heart, a Pascal compiler. Delphi 6 is the next step in the evolution of the same Pascal compiler that Borland has been developing since Anders Hejlsberg wrote the first Turbo Pascal compiler more than 17 years ago. Pascal programmers throughout the years have enjoyed the stability, grace, and, of course, the compile speed that Turbo Pascal offers. Delphi 6 is no exception—its compiler is the synthesis of more than a decade of compiler experience and a state-of-the-art 32-bit optimizing compiler. Although the capabilities of the compiler have grown considerably over the years, the speed of the compiler has remarkably diminished only slightly. What's more, the stability of the Delphi compiler continues to be a yardstick by which others are measured.

Now it's time for a little walk down memory lane, as we look at each of the versions of Delphi and a little of the historical context surrounding each product's release.

Delphi 1

In the early days of DOS, programmers had a choice between productive-but-slow BASIC and efficient-but-complex assembly language. Turbo Pascal, which offered the simplicity of a structured language and the performance of a real compiler, bridged that gap. Windows 3.1 programmers faced a similar choice—a choice between a powerful-yet-unwieldy language such as C++ and an easy-to-use-but-limiting language such as Visual Basic. Delphi 1 answered that call by offering a radically different approach to Windows development: visual development, compiled executables, DLLs, databases, you name it—a visual environment without limits. Delphi 1 was the first Windows development tool to combine a visual development environment, an optimizing native-code compiler, and a scalable database access engine. It defined the phrase *rapid application development (RAD)*.

The combination of compiler, RAD tool, and fast database access was too compelling for scads of VB developers, and Delphi won many converts. Also, many Turbo Pascal developers reinvented their careers by transitioning to this slick, new tool. Word got out that Object Pascal wasn't the same as that language we had to use in college that made us feel like we were programming with one hand behind our backs, and many more developers came to Delphi to take advantage of the robust design patterns encouraged by the language and the tool. The Visual Basic team at Microsoft, lacking serious competition before Delphi, was caught totally unprepared. Slow, fat, and dumb, Visual Basic 3 was arguably no match for Delphi 1.

The year was 1995. Borland was appealing a huge lawsuit loss to Lotus for infringing on the 1-2-3 "look and feel" with Quattro. Borland was also taking lumps from Microsoft for trying to play in the application space with Microsoft. Borland got out of the application business by selling the Quattro business to Novell and targeting dBASE and Paradox to database developers, as opposed to casual users. While Borland was playing in the applications market, Microsoft had quietly leveraged its platform business to take away from Borland a vast share of the Windows developer tools market. Newly refocused on its core competency of developer tools, Borland was looking to do some damage with Delphi and a new release of Borland C++.

Delphi 2

A year later, Delphi 2 provided all these same benefits under the modern 32-bit operating systems of Windows 95 and Windows NT. Additionally, Delphi 2 extended productivity with additional features and functionality not found in version 1, such as a 32-bit compiler that produces faster applications, an enhanced and extended object library, revamped database support, improved string handling, OLE support, Visual Form Inheritance, and compatibility with 16-bit Delphi projects. Delphi 2 became the yardstick by which all other RAD tools are measured.

The year was 1996, and the most important Windows platform release since 3.0—32-bit Windows 95—had just happened in the latter part of the previous year. Borland was eager to make Delphi the preeminent development tool for that platform. An interesting historical note is that Delphi 2 was originally going to be called *Delphi32*, to underscore the fact that it was designed for 32-bit Windows. However, the product name was changed before release to Delphi 2 to illustrate that Delphi was a mature product and avoid what is known in the software business as the "1.0 blues."

Microsoft attempted to counter with Visual Basic 4, but it was plagued by poor performance, lack of 16-to-32-bit portability, and key design flaws. Still, there's an impressive number of developers who continued to use Visual Basic for whatever the reason. Borland also longed to see Delphi penetrate the high-end client/server market occupied by tools such as PowerBuilder, but this version didn't yet have the muscle necessary to unseat such products from their corporate perches.

The corporate strategy at this time was undeniably to focus on corporate customers. The decision to change direction in this way was no doubt fueled by the diminishing market relevance of dBASE and Paradox, and the dwindling revenues realized in the C++ market also aided this decision. In order to help jumpstart that effort to take on the enterprises, Borland made the mistake of acquiring Open Environment Corporation, a middleware company with basically two products: an outmoded DCE-based middleware that you might call an ancestor of CORBA and a proprietary technology for distributed OLE about to be ushered into obsolescence by DCOM.

Delphi 3

During the development of Delphi 1, the Delphi development team was preoccupied with simply creating and releasing a groundbreaking development tool. For Delphi 2, the development team had its hands full primarily with the tasks of moving to 32 bit (while maintaining almost complete backward compatibility) and adding new database and client/server features needed by corporate IT. While Delphi 3 was being created, the development team had the opportunity to expand the tool set to provide an extraordinary level of breadth and depth for solutions to some of the sticky problems faced by Windows developers. In particular, Delphi 3 made it easy to use the notoriously complicated technologies of COM and ActiveX, World Wide Web application development, "thin client" applications, and multitier databases architectures. Delphi 3's Code Insight helped to make the actual code-writing process a bit easier, although for the most part, the basic methodology for writing Delphi applications was the same as in Delphi 1.

This was 1997, and the competition was doing some interesting things. On the low end, Microsoft finally started to get something right with Visual Basic 5, which included a compiler to address long-standing performance problems, good COM/ActiveX support, and some key new platform features. On the high-end, Delphi was now successfully unseating products such as PowerBuilder and Forte in corporations.

Delphi lost a key member of the team during the Delphi 3 development cycle when Anders Hejlsberg, the Chief Architect, decided to move on and took a position with Microsoft Corporation. The team didn't lose a beat, however, because Chuck Jazdzewski, long time co-architect was able to step into the head role.

Delphi 4

Delphi 4 focused on making Delphi development easier. The Module Explorer was introduced in Delphi, and it enabled you to browse and edit units from a convenient graphical interface. New code navigation and class completion features enabled you to focus on the meat of your applications with a minimum of busy work. The IDE was redesigned with dockable toolbars and windows to make your development more convenient, and the debugger was greatly improved. Delphi 4 extended the product's reach into the enterprise with outstanding multitier support using technologies such as MIDAS, DCOM, MTS, and CORBA.

This was 1998, and Delphi had effectively secured its position relative to the competition. The front lines had stabilized somewhat, although Delphi continued to slowly gain market share. CORBA was the industry buzz, and Delphi had it and the competition did not. There was a bit of a down-side to Delphi 4 as well: After enjoying several years of being the most stable development tool on the market, Delphi 4 had earned a reputation among long-time Delphi users for not living up to the very high standard for solid engineering and stability.

The release of Delphi 4 followed the acquisition of Visigenic, one of the CORBA industry leaders. Borland changed its name to *Inprise* in an effort to better penetrate the enterprise, and the company was in a position to lead the industry to new ground by integrating its tools with the CORBA technology. To really win, CORBA needed to be made as easy as COM or Internet development had been made in past versions of Borland tools. However, for various reasons, the integration wasn't as full as it should have been, and the CORBA-development tool integration was destined to play a bit part in the overall software-development picture.

Delphi 5

Delphi 5 moved ahead on a few fronts: First, Delphi 5 continued what Delphi 4 started by adding many more features to make easy those tasks that traditionally take time, hopefully enabling you to concentrate more on what you want to write and less on how to write it. These new productivity features include further IDE and debugger enhancements, TeamSource team development software, and translation tools. Second, Delphi 5 contained a host of new features aimed squarely at making Internet development easier. These new Internet features include the

Active Server Object Wizard for ASP creation, the InternetExpress components for XML support, and new MIDAS features, making it a very versatile data platform for the Internet. Finally, Borland built time into the schedule to deliver the most important feature of all for Delphi 5: stability. Like fine wine, you cannot rush great software, and Borland waited until Delphi 5 was ready before letting it out the door.

Delphi 5 was released in the latter half of 1999. Delphi continues to penetrate the enterprise, whereas Visual Basic continues to serve as competition on the low end. However, the battle lines still appear stable. Inprise brought back the Borland name but only as a brand. The executive offices went through some turbulent times, with the company divisionalized between tools and middleware, the abrupt departure of CEO Del Yocam, and the hiring of Internet-savvy CEO Dale Fuller, who refocused the company back on software developers.

Delphi 6

Clearly the primary theme of Delphi 6 is compatibility with Borland's Kylix development tool for Linux. To this end, Borland developed the new Component Library for Cross-Platform (CLX), which includes VisualCLX for visual development, DataCLX client data-access components, and NetCLX Internet components. Applications written using only the CLX library and portable RTL elements will easily port between the Windows and Linux operating systems.

The new dbExpress set of components and drivers is one of the biggest breakthroughs to come out of the effort for Linux compatibility because it finally provides a real alternative for the BDE, which has really begun to show its age in recent years.

A secondary theme of Delphi 6 is essentially to embrace all things XML. This includes XML for database applications, Web-based applications, and SOAP-based Web services. Delphi developers have the tools they need to fully embrace the industry-wide trend toward XML, which provides great benefits in terms of applications that function across the traditional boundaries of different development tools, platforms, databases, and across the Internet.

Of course, in addition to all these improvements and additions, Delphi 6 brings the normal host of improvement you've come to expect between product versions in core areas like VCL, the IDE, the debugger, the Object Pascal language, and the RTL.

The Delphi IDE

Just to make sure that we're all on the same page with regard to terminology, Figure 1.2 shows the Delphi IDE and calls attention to its major constituents: the main window, the Component Palette, the toolbars, the Form Designer, the Code Editor, the Object Inspector, Object TreeView, and the Code Explorer.

Toolbars

Object TreeView   Main Window   Form Designer   Component Palette

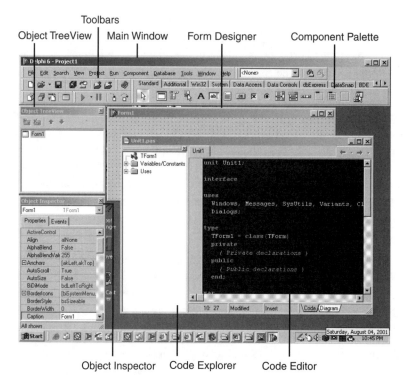

Object Inspector   Code Explorer   Code Editor

FIGURE 1.2

The Delphi 6 IDE.

The Main Window

Think of the *main window* as the control center for the Delphi IDE. The main window has all the standard functionality of the main window of any other Windows program. It consists of three parts: the main menu, the toolbars, and the Component Palette.

The Main Menu

As in any Windows program, you go to the main menu when you need to open and save files, invoke wizards, view other windows, modify options, and so on. Most items on the main menu can also be invoked via a button on a toolbar.

The Delphi Toolbars

The toolbars enable single-click access to some operation found on the main menu of the IDE, such as opening a file or building a project. Notice that each of the buttons on the toolbars offer a *tooltip* that contain a description of the function of a particular button. Not including the Component Palette, there are five separate toolbars in the IDE: Debug, Desktops, Standard,

PROGRAMMING
IN DELPHI

View, and Custom. Figure 1.2 shows the default button configuration for these toolbars, but you can add or remove buttons by selecting Customize from the local menu on a toolbar. Figure 1.3 shows the Customize toolbar dialog box. You add buttons by dragging them from this dialog box and drop them on any toolbar. To remove a button, drag it off the toolbar.

FIGURE 1.3
The Customize toolbar dialog box.

IDE toolbar customization doesn't stop at configuring which buttons are shown. You can also relocate each of the toolbars, the Component Palette, or the menu within the main window. To do this, click the raised gray bars on the left side of the toolbars and drag them around the main window. If you drag the mouse outside the confines of the main window while doing this, you'll see yet another level of customization: The toolbars can be undocked from the main window and reside in their own floating tool windows. Undocked views of the toolbars are shown in Figure 1.4.

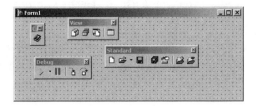

FIGURE 1.4
Undocked toolbars.

The Component Palette

The Component Palette is a double-height toolbar that contains a page control filled with all the VCL components and ActiveX controls installed in the IDE. The order and appearance of pages and components on the Component Palette can be configured via a right-click or by selecting Component, Configure Palette from the main menu.

The Form Designer

The Form Designer begins as an empty window, ready for you to turn it into a Windows application. Consider the Form Designer your artist's canvas for creating Windows applications; here is where you determine how your applications will be represented visually to your users. You interact with the Form Designer by selecting components from the Component Palette and dropping them onto your form. After you have a particular component on the form, you can use the mouse to adjust the position or size of the component. You can control the appearance and behavior of these components by using the Object Inspector and Code Editor.

The Object Inspector

With the Object Inspector, you can modify a form's or component's properties or enable your form or component to respond to different events. *Properties* are data such as height, color, and font that determine how an object appears onscreen. *Events* are portions of code executed in response to occurrences within your application. A mouse-click message and a message for a window to redraw itself are two examples of events. The Object Inspector window uses the standard Windows *notebook tab* metaphor in switching between component properties or events; just select the desired page from the tabs at the top of the window. The properties and events displayed in the Object Inspector reflect whichever form or component currently has focus in the Form Designer.

Delphi also has the capability to arrange the contents of the Object Inspector by category or alphabetically by name. You can do this by right-clicking anywhere in the Object Inspector and selecting Arrange from the local menu. Figure 1.5 shows two Object Inspectors side by side. The one on the left is arranged by category, and the one on the right is arranged by name. You can also specify which categories you would like to view by selecting View from the local menu.

One of the most useful tidbits of knowledge that you as a Delphi programmer should know is that the help system is tightly integrated with the Object Inspector. If you ever get stuck on a particular property or event, just press the F1 key, and WinHelp comes to the rescue.

The Code Editor

The Code Editor is where you type the code that dictates how your program behaves and where Delphi inserts the code that it generates based on the components in your application. The top of the Code Editor window contains notebook tabs, where each tab corresponds to a different source code module or file. Each time you add a new form to your application, a new unit is created and added to the set of tabs at the top of the Code Editor. The local menu in the Code Editor gives you a wide range of options while you're editing, such as closing files, setting bookmarks, and navigating to symbols.

FIGURE 1.5

Viewing the Object Inspector by category and by name.

TIP

You can view multiple Code Editor windows simultaneous by selecting View, New Edit Window from the main menu.

The Code Explorer

The Code Explorer provides a tree-style view of the unit shown in the Code Editor. The Code Explorer allows easy navigation of units in addition to the ability to easily add new elements or rename existing elements in a unit. It's important to remember that there's a one-to-one relationship between Code Explorer windows and Code Editor windows. Right-click a node in the Code Explorer to view the options available for that node. You can also control behaviors such as sorting and filtering in the Code Explorer by modifying the options found on the Explorer tab of the Environment Options dialog box.

The Object TreeView

The Object TreeView provides a visual, hierarchical representation of the components placed on a form, data module, or frame. The tree displays the relationship between individual components, such as parent-child, property-to-component, or property-to-property relationships. In addition to being a means to view relationships, the Object TreeView also serves as a convenient means to establish relationships between components. This can be done most easily by dropping one component from the palette or the tree on another in the tree. This will establish the relationship between two components that have a possibility of forming a relationship.

A Tour of Your Project's Source

The Delphi IDE generates Object Pascal source code for you as you work with the visual components of the Form Designer. The simplest example of this capability is starting a new project. Select File, New Application in the main window to see a new form in the Form Designer and that form's source code skeleton in the Code Editor. The source code for the new form's unit is shown in Listing 1.1.

LISTING 1.1   Source Code for an Empty Form

```
unit Unit1;

interface

uses
  Windows, Messages, SysUtils, Variants, Classes, Graphics, Controls, Forms,
  Dialogs;

type
  TForm1 = class(TForm)
  private
    { Private declarations }
  public
    { Public declarations }
  end;

var
  Form1: TForm1;

implementation;

{$R *.dfm}

end.
```

It's important to note that the source code module associated with any form is stored in a unit. Although every form has a unit, not every unit has a form. If you're not familiar with how the Pascal language works and what exactly a *unit* is, see Chapter 2, "The Object Pascal Language," which discusses the Object Pascal language for those who are new to Pascal from C++, Visual Basic, Java, or another language.

Let's take a unit skeleton one piece at a time. Here's the top portion:

```
type
  TForm1 = class(TForm) ;
  private
    { Private declarations }
  public
    { Public declarations }
  end;
```

It indicates that the form object, itself, is an object derived from TForm, and the space in which you can insert your own public and private variables is labeled clearly. Don't worry about what *class*, *public*, or *private* means right now. Chapter 2 discusses Object Pascal in more detail.

The following line is very important:

```
{$R *.dfm};
```

The $R directive in Pascal is used to load an external resource file. This line links the .DFM (which stands for *Delphi form*) file into the executable. The .DFM file contains a binary representation of the form you created in the Form Designer. The * symbol in this case isn't intended to represent a wildcard; it represents the file having the same name as the current unit. So, for example, if the preceding line was in a file called Unit1.pas, the *.DFM would represent a file by the name of Unit1.dfm.

NOTE

A nice feature of the IDE is the ability for you to save new DFM files as text rather than as binary. This option in enabled by default, but you can modify it using the New Forms As Text check box on the Preferences page of the Environment Options dialog box. Although saving forms as text format is just slightly less efficient in terms of size, it's a good practice for a few of reasons: First, it is very easy to make minor changes to text DFMs in any text editor. Second, if the file should become corrupted, it is far easier to repair a corrupted text file than a corrupted binary file. Finally, it becomes much easier for version control systems to manage the form files. Keep in mind also that previous versions of Delphi expect binary DFM files, so you will need to disable this option if you want to create projects that will be used by other versions of Delphi.

The application's project file; is worth a glance, too. A project filename ends in .DPR (which stands for *Delphi project*) and is really nothing more than a Pascal source file with a different file extension. The project file is where the main portion of your program (in the Pascal sense) lives. Unlike other versions of Pascal with which you might be familiar, most of the "work" of your program is done in units rather than in the main module. You can load your project's source file into the Code Editor by selecting Project, View Source from the main menu. Here's the project file from the sample application:

```
program Project1;

uses
  Forms,
  Unit1 in 'Unit1.pas' {Form1};

{$R *.RES}

begin
  Application.Initialize;
  Application.CreateForm(TForm1, Form1);
  Application.Run;
end.
```

As you add more forms and units to the application, they appear in the uses clause of the project file. Notice, too, that after the name of a unit in the uses clause, the name of the related form appears in comments. If you ever get confused about which units go with which forms, you can regain your bearings by selecting View, Project Manager to bring up the Project Manager window.

> **NOTE**
>
> Each form has exactly one unit associated with it, and you can also have other "code-only" units that aren't associated with any form. In Delphi, you work mostly within your program's; units, and you'll rarely edit your project's .DPR file.

Tour of a Small Application

The simple act of plopping a component such as a button onto a form causes code for that element to be generated and added to the form object:

```
type
  TForm1 = class(TForm)
    Button1: TButton;
  private
    { Private declarations }
  public
    { Public declarations }
  end;
```

Now, as you can see, the button is an instance variable of the TForm1 class. When you refer to the button in contexts outside TForm1 later in your source code, you must remember to address it as part of the scope of TForm1 by saying Form1.Button1. Scoping is explained in more detail in Chapter 2.

When this button is selected in the Form Designer, you can change its behavior through the Object Inspector. Suppose that, at design time, you want to change the width of the button to 100 pixels, and at runtime, you want to make the button respond to a press by doubling its own height. To change the button width, move over to the Object Browser window, find the Width property, and change the value associated with Width to 100. Note that the change doesn't take effect in the Form Designer until you press Enter or move off the Width property. To make the button respond to a mouse click, select the Events page on the Object Inspector window to reveal the list of events to which the button can respond. Double-click in the column next to the OnClick event, and Delphi generates a procedure skeleton for a mouse-click response and whisks you away to that spot in the source code—in this case, a procedure called TForm1.Button1Click(). All that's left to do is to insert the code to double the button's width between the begin..end of the event's response method:

```
Button1.Height := Button1.Height * 2;
```

To verify that the "application" compiles and runs, press the F9 key on your keyboard and watch it go!

NOTE

> Delphi maintains a reference between generated procedures and the controls to which they correspond. When you compile or save a source code module, Delphi scans your source code and removes all procedure skeletons for which you haven't entered any code between the begin and end. This means that if you didn't write any code between the begin and end of the TForm1.Button1Click() procedure, for example, Delphi would have removed the procedure from your source code. The bottom line here is this: Don't delete event handler procedures that Delphi has created; just delete your code and let Delphi remove the procedures for you.

After you have fun making the button really big on the form, terminate your program and go back to the Delphi IDE. Now is a good time to mention that you could have generated a response to a mouse click for your button just by double-clicking a control after dropping it onto the form. Double-clicking a component automatically invokes its associated component editor. For most components, this response generates a handler for the first of that component's events listed in the Object Inspector.

What's So Great About Events, Anyway?

If you've ever developed Windows applications the traditional way, without a doubt you'll find the ease of use of Delphi events a welcome alternative to manually catching Windows messages, cracking those messages, and testing for window handles, control IDs, WParam parameters, LParam parameters, and so on. If you don't know what all that means, that's okay; Chapter 3, "Adventures in Messaging," covers messaging internals.

A Delphi event is often triggered by a Windows message. The OnMouseDown event of a TButton, for example, is really just an encapsulation of the Windows WM_xBUTTONDOWN messages. Notice that the OnMouseDown event gives you information such as which button was pressed and the location of the mouse when it happened. A form's OnKeyDown event provides similar useful information for key presses. For example, here's the code that Delphi generates for an OnKeyDown handler:

```
procedure TForm1.FormKeyDown(Sender: TObject; var Key: Word;
Shift: TShiftState);
begin
end;
```

All the information you need about the key is right at your fingertips. If you're an experienced Windows programmer, you'll appreciate that there aren't any LParam or WParam parameters, inherited handlers, translates, or dispatches to worry about. This goes way beyond "message cracking" as you might know it because one Delphi event can represent several different Windows messages, as it does with OnMouseDown (which handles a variety of mouse messages). What's more, each of the message parameters is passed in as easy-to-understand parameters. Chapter 3 gets into the gory details of how Delphi's internal messaging system works.

Contract-Free Programming

Arguably the biggest benefit that Delphi's event system has over the standard Windows messaging system is that all events are contract free. What *contract free* means to the programmer is that you never are *required* to do anything inside your event handlers. Unlike standard Windows message handling, you don't have to call an inherited handler or pass information back to Windows after handling an event.

Of course, the downside to the contract-free programming model that Delphi's event system provides is that it doesn't always give you the power or flexibility that directly handling Windows messages gives you. You're at the mercy of those who designed the event as far as what level of control you'll have over your application's response to the event. For example, you can modify and kill keystrokes in an OnKeyPress handler, but an OnResize handler provides you only with a notification that the event occurred—you have no power to prevent or modify the resizing.

Never fear, though. Delphi doesn't prevent you from working directly with Windows messages. It's not as straightforward as the event system because message handling assumes that the programmer has a greater level of knowledge of what Windows expects of every handled message. You have complete power to handle all Windows messages directly by using the message keyword. You'll find out much more about writing Windows message handlers in Chapter 3.

The great thing about developing applications with Delphi is that you can use the high-level easy stuff (such as events) when it suits you and still have access to the low-level stuff whenever you need it.

Turbo Prototyping

After hacking Delphi for a little while, you'll probably notice that the learning curve is especially mild. In fact, even if you're new to Delphi, you'll find that writing your first project in Delphi pays immediate dividends in the form of a short development cycle and a robust application. Delphi excels in the one facet of application development that has been the bane of many a Windows programmer: user interface (UI) design.

Sometimes the design of the UI and the general layout of a program is referred to as *prototyping*. In a nonvisual environment, prototyping an application often takes longer than writing the application's implementation, or what is called the *back end*. Of course, the back end of an application is the whole objective of the program in the first place, right? Sure, an intuitive and visually pleasing UI is a big part of the application, but what good would it be, for example, to have a communications program with pretty windows and dialog boxes but no capacity to send data through a modem? As it is with people, so it is with applications; a pretty face is nice to look at, but it has to have substance to be a regular part of our lives. Please, no comments about back ends.

Delphi enables you to use its custom controls to whip out nice-looking UIs in no time flat. In fact, you'll find that after you become comfortable with Delphi's forms, controls, and event-response methods, you'll cut huge chunks off the time you usually take to develop application prototypes. You'll also find that the UIs you develop in Delphi look just as nice as—if not better than—those designed with traditional tools. Often, what you "mock up" in Delphi turns out to be the final product.

Extensible Components and Environment

Because of the object-oriented nature of Delphi, in addition to creating your own components from scratch, you can also create your own customized components based on stock Delphi components. For more details on this and other types of components, you should take a look at Part IV, "Component-Based Development."

In addition to allowing you to integrate custom components into the IDE, Delphi provides the capability to integrate entire subprograms, called *experts*, into the environment. Delphi's Expert Interface enables you to add special menu items and dialog boxes to the IDE to integrate some feature that you feel is worthwhile. An example of an expert is the Database Form Expert located on the Delphi Database menu. Chapter 17, "Using The Open Tools API," outlines the process for creating experts and integrating them into the Delphi IDE.

The Top 10 IDE Features You Must Know and Love

Before we can let you any further into the book, we've got to make sure that you're equipped with the tools you need to survive and the knowledge to use them. In that spirit, what follows is a list of what we feel are the top 10 IDE features you must learn to know and love.

1. Class Completion

Nothing wastes a developer's time more than have to type in all that blasted code! How often is it that you know exactly what you want to write but are limited by how fast your fingers can fly over the keys? Until the spec for the PCI-to-medulla oblongata bus is completed to rid you of all that typing, Delphi has a feature called *class completion* that goes a long way toward alleviating the busy work.

Arguably, the most important feature of class completion is that it is designed to work without being in your face. Simply type in part of a class declaration, press the magic Ctrl+Shift+C keystroke combination, and class completion will attempt to figure our what you're trying to do and generate the right code. For example, if you put the declaration for a procedure called Foo in your class and invoke class completion, it will automatically create the definition for this method in the implementation part of the unit. Declare a new property that reads from a field and writes to a method and invoke class completion, and it will automatically generate the code for the field and declare and implement the method.

If you haven't already gotten hooked on class completion, give it a whirl. Soon you'll be lost without it.

2. AppBrowser Navigation

Do you ever look at a line of code in your Code Editor and think, "Gee, I wish I knew where that method is declared"? Well, finding out is as easy as holding down the Ctrl key and clicking the name of the token you want to find. The IDE will use debug information assembled in the background by the compiler to jump to the declaration of the token. Very handy. And like a

Web browser, there's a history stack that you can navigate forward and back through using the little arrows to the right of the tabs in the Code Editor.

3. Interface/Implementation Navigation

Want to navigate between the interface and implementation of a method? Just put the cursor on the method and use Ctrl+Shift+up arrow or down arrow to toggle between the two positions.

4. Dock It!

The IDE allows you to organize the windows on your screen by docking together multiple windows as panes in a single window. If you have full window drag set in your windows desktop, you can easily tell which windows are dockable because they draw a dithered box when they're dragged around the screen. The Code Editor offers three docking bays on its left, bottom, and right sides to which you can affix windows. Windows can be docked side-by-side by dragging one window to an edge of another or tab-docked by dragging one window to the middle of another. Once you come up with an arrangement you like, be sure to save it using the Desktops toolbar. Want to prevent a window from docking? Hold down the Ctrl key while dragging it or right-click in the window and uncheck Dockable in the local menu.

TIP

Here's a cute hidden feature: Right-click the tabs of tab-docked windows, and you'll be able to move the tabs to the top, bottom, left, or right of the window.

---

5. The Object Browser

Delphi 1 through 4 shipped with essentially the same icky object browser. If you didn't know it was there, don't feel alone; many folks never used it because it didn't have a lot to offer. Delphi now comes equipped with an object browser that enables visual browsing of object hierarchies. Shown in Figure 1.6, the browser is accessible by selecting View, Browser in the main menu. This tool presents a tree view that lets you navigate globals, classes, and units and drill down into scope, inheritance, and references of the symbols.

6. GUID, Anyone?

In the small-but-useful category, you'll find the Ctrl+Shift+G keystroke combination. Pressing this keystroke combination will place a fresh new GUID in the Code Editor, which is a real timesaver when you're declaring new interfaces.

FIGURE 1.6

The new browser.

7. C++ Syntax Highlighting

If you're like us, you often like to view C++ files, such as SDK headers, while you work in Delphi. Because Delphi and C++Builder share the same editor source code, one of the advantages to users is syntax highlighting of C++ files. Just load up a C++ file such as a .CPP or .H module in the Code Editor, and it handles the rest automatically.

8. To Do. . .

Use the To Do List to manage work in progress in your source files. You can view the To Do List by selecting View, To Do List from the main menu. This list is automatically populated from any comments in your source code that begin with the token *TODO*. You can use the To Do Items window to set the owner, priority, and category for any To Do item. This window is shown in Figure 1.7, docked to the bottom of the Code Editor.

9. Use the Project Manager

The Project Manager can be a big timesaver when navigating around large projects—especially those projects that are composed of multiple EXE or DLL modules, but it's amazing how many people forget that it's there. You can access the Project Manager by selecting View, Project Manager from the main menu. There are a number of time saving features in the Project Manager, such as drag-and-drop copying and copy and paste between projects.

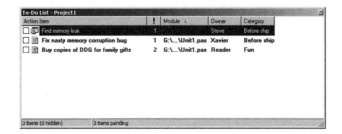

FIGURE 1.7
To Do Items window.

10. Use Code Insight to Complete Declarations and Parameters

When you type **Identifier.**, a window will automatically pop up after the dot to provide you with a list of properties, methods, events, and fields available for that identifier. You can right-click this window to sort the list by name or by scope. If the window goes away before you're ready, just press Ctrl+space to bring it back up.

Remembering all the parameters to a function can be a pain, so it's nice that Code Insight automatically helps by providing a tooltip with the parameter list when you type **FunctionName(** in the Code Editor. Remember to press Ctrl+Shift+space to bring the tooltip back up if it goes away before you're ready.

Summary

By now you should have an understanding of the Delphi 6 product line and the Delphi IDE as well as how Delphi fits into the Windows development picture in general. This chapter was intended to acclimate you to Delphi and to the concepts used throughout the book. Now the stage has been set for the really technical stuff to come. Before you move much deeper into the book, make sure that you're comfortable using and navigating around the IDE and know how to work with small projects.

The Object Pascal Language

IN THIS CHAPTER

This chapter sets aside the visual elements of Delphi in order to provide you with an overview of Delphi's underlying language—Object Pascal. To begin with, you'll receive an introduction to the basics of the Object Pascal language, such as language rules and constructs. Later on, you'll learn about some of the more advanced aspects of Object Pascal, such as classes and exception handling. Because this isn't a beginner's book, it assumes that you have some experience with other high-level computer languages such as Java, C/C++, or Visual Basic, and it compares Object Pascal language structure to that of those other languages. By the time you're finished with this chapter, you'll understand how programming concepts such as variables, types, operators, loops, cases, exceptions, and objects work in Pascal as compared to Java, C/C++, and Visual Basic.

NOTE

When we mention the C language in this chapter, we are generally referring to a language element that exists in both C and C++. Features specific to the C++ language are referred to as C++.

Even if you have some recent experience with Pascal, you'll find this chapter useful because this is really the only point in the book where you learn the nitty-gritty of Pascal syntax and semantics.

Comments

As a starting point, you should know how to make comments in your Pascal code. Object Pascal supports three types of comments: curly brace comments, parenthesis/asterisk comments, and double backslash comments. Examples of each type of comment follow:

```
{ Comment using curly braces }
(* Comment using paren and asterisk *)
// double backslash comment
```

The first two types of comments are virtually identical in behavior. The compiler considers the comment to be everything between the open-comment and close-comment delimiters. For double backslash comments, everything following the double backslash until the end of the line is considered a comment.

NOTE

You cannot nest comments of the same type. Although it is legal syntax to nest Pascal comments of different types inside one another, we don't recommend the practice. Here are some examples:

continues

```
{ (* This is legal *) }
(* { This is legal } *)
(* (* This is illegal *) *)
{ { This is illegal }: }
```

Extended Procedure and Function Features

Because procedures and functions are fairly universal topics as far as programming languages are concerned, we won't go into too much detail here. We just want to fill you in on a few unique or little-known features in this area. Where appropriate, we'll also point out the Delphi version in which various language features appeared to aid in porting or maintaining code compatible between various compiler versions.

Parentheses in Calls

Although it has been in the language since Delphi 2, one of the lesser-known features of Object Pascal is that parentheses are optional when calling a procedure or function that takes no parameters. Therefore, the following syntax examples are both valid:

```
Form1.Show;
Form1.Show();
```

Granted, this feature isn't one of those things that sends chills up and down your spine, but it's particularly nice for those who split their time between Delphi and languages such as C or Java, where parentheses are required. If you're not able to spend 100% of your time in Delphi, this feature means that you don't have to remember to use different function-calling syntax for different languages.

Overloading

Delphi 4 introduced the concept of function *overloading* (that is, the ability to have multiple procedures or functions of the same name with different parameter lists). All overloaded methods are required to be declared with the overload directive, as shown here:

```
procedure Hello(I: Integer); overload;
procedure Hello(S: string); overload;
procedure Hello(D: Double); overload;
```

Note that the rules for overloading methods of a class are slightly different and are explained in the section "Method Overloading." Although this is one of the features most requested by developers since Delphi 1, the phrase that comes to mind is "Be careful what you wish for." Having multiple functions and procedures with the same name (on top of the traditional ability to have functions and procedures of the same name in different units) can make it more difficult to predict the flow of control and debug your application. Because of this, overloading is a feature you should employ judiciously. Not to say that you should avoid it; just don't overuse it.

Default Value Parameters

Also introduced in Delphi 4 were default value parameters (that is, the ability to provide a default value for a function or procedure parameter and not have to pass that parameter when calling the routine). In order to declare a procedure or function that contains default value parameters, follow the parameter type with an equal sign and the default value, as shown in the following example:

```
procedure HasDefVal(S: string; I: Integer = 0);
```

The HasDefVal() procedure can be called in one of two ways. First, you can specify both parameters:

```
HasDefVal('hello', 26);
```

Second, you can specify only parameter S and use the default value for I:

```
HasDefVal('hello');  // default value used for I
```

You must follow several rules when using default value parameters:

- Parameters having default values must appear at the end of the parameter list. Parameters without default values cannot follow parameters with default values in a procedure or function's parameter list.
- Default value parameters must be of an ordinal, pointer, or set type.
- Default value parameters must be passed by value or as const. They cannot be reference (out) or untyped parameters.

One of the biggest benefits of default value parameters is in adding functionality to existing functions and procedures without sacrificing backward compatibility. For example, suppose that you sell a unit containing a revolutionary function called AddInts()that adds two numbers:

```
function AddInts(I1, I2: Integer): Integer;
begin
  Result := I1 + I2;
end;
```

In order to keep up with the competition, you feel you must update this function so that it has the capability for adding three numbers. However, you're loathe to do so because adding a parameter will cause existing code that calls this function to not compile. Thanks to default parameters, you can enhance the functionality of AddInts() without compromising compatibility. Here's an example:

```
function AddInts(I1, I2: Integer; I3: Integer = 0);
begin
  Result := I1 + I2 + I3;
end;
```

Variables

You might be used to declaring variables off the cuff: "I need another integer, so I'll just declare one right here in the middle of this block of code." This is a perfectly reasonable notion if you're coming from another language such as Java, C, or Visual Basic. If that has been your practice, you're going to have to retrain yourself a little in order to use variables in Object Pascal. Object Pascal requires you to declare all variables up front in their own section before you begin a procedure, function, or program. Perhaps you used to write free-wheeling code like this:

```
void foo(void)
{
  int x = 1;
  x++;
  int y = 2;
  float f;
  //... etc ...
}
```

In Object Pascal, any such code must be tidied up and structured a bit more to look like this:

```
Procedure Foo;
var
  x, y: Integer;
  f: Double;
begin
  x := 1;
  inc(x);
  y := 2;
  //... etc ...
end;
```

2

NOTE

Object Pascal—like Visual Basic, but unlike Java and C—is not a case-sensitive language. Upper- and lowercase is used for clarity's sake, so use your best judgment, as the style used in this book indicates. If the identifier name is several words mashed

continues

> together, remember to capitalize for clarity. For example, the following name is
> unclear and difficult to read:
>
>   procedure thisprocedurenamemakesnosense;
>
> This code is quite readable, however:
>
>   procedure ThisProcedureNameIsMoreClear;
>
> For a complete reference on the coding style guidelines used for this book, see the
> electronic version of *Delphi 5 Developer's Guide* on the CD accompanying this book.

You might be wondering what all this structure business is and why it's beneficial. You'll find, however, that Object Pascal's structured style of variable declaration lends itself to code that's more readable, maintainable, and less buggy than other languages that rely on convention rather than rule to enforce sanity.

Notice how Object Pascal enables you to group more than one variable of the same type together on the same line with the following syntax:

```
VarName1, VarName2: SomeType;
```

Remember that when you're declaring a variable in Object Pascal, the variable name precedes the type, and there's a colon between the variables and types. Note that the variable initialization is always separate from the variable declaration.

A language feature introduced in Delphi 2 enables you to initialize global variables inside a var block. Here are some examples demonstrating the syntax for doing so:

```
var
  i: Integer = 10;
  S: string  = 'Hello world';
  D: Double  = 3.141579;
```

> **NOTE**
>
> Preinitialization of variables is only allowed for global variables, not variables that
> are local to a procedure or function.

> **TIP**
>
> The Delphi compiler sees to it that all global data is automatically zero-initialized. When your application starts, all integer types will hold 0, floating-point types will hold 0.0, pointers will be nil, strings will be empty, and so forth. Therefore, it isn't necessary to zero-initialize global data in your source code.

Constants

Constants in Pascal are defined in a const clause, which behaves similarly to the C/C++'s const keyword. Here's an example of three constant declarations in C:

```
const float ADecimalNumber = 3.14;
const int i = 10;
const char * ErrorString = "Danger, Danger, Danger!";
```

The major difference between C constants and Object Pascal constants is that Object Pascal, like Visual Basic, doesn't require you to declare the constant's type along with the value in the declaration. The Delphi compiler automatically allocates proper space for the constant based on its value, or, in the case of scalar constants such as Integer, the compiler keeps track of the values as it works, and space never is allocated. Here's an example:

```
const
  ADecimalNumber = 3.14;
  i = 10;
  ErrorString = 'Danger, Danger, Danger!';
```

> **NOTE**
>
> Space is allocated for constants as follows: Integer values are "fit" into the smallest type allowable (10 into a ShortInt, 32,000 into a SmallInt, and so on). Alphanumeric values fit into Char or the currently defined (by $H) string type. Floating-point values are mapped to the extended data type, unless the value contains four or fewer decimal places explicitly, in which case it's mapped to a Comp type. Sets of Integer and Char are of course stored as themselves.

Optionally, you can also specify a constant's type in the declaration. This provides you with full control over how the compiler treats your constants:

```
const
  ADecimalNumber: Double = 3.14;
  I: Integer = 10;
  ErrorString: string = 'Danger, Danger, Danger!';
```

Object Pascal permits the usage of compile-time functions in const and var declarations. These routines include Ord(), Chr(), Trunc(), Round(), High(), Low(), and SizeOf(). For example, all of the following code is, valid:

```
type
  A = array[1..2] of Integer;

const
  w: Word = SizeOf(Byte);

var
  i: Integer = 8;
  j: SmallInt = Ord('a');
  L: Longint = Trunc(3.14159);
  x: ShortInt = Round(2.71828);
  B1: Byte = High(A);
  B2: Byte = Low(A);
  C: char = Chr(46);
```

CAUTION

The behavior of 32-bit Delphi type-specified constants is different from that in 16-bit Delphi 1. In Delphi 1, the identifier declared wasn't treated as a constant but as a preinitialized variable called a *typed constant*. However, in Delphi 2 and later, type-specified constants have the capability of being truly constant. Delphi provides a backward-compatibility switch on the Compiler page of the Project, Options dialog box, or you can use the $J compiler directive. By default, this switch is enabled for compatibility with Delphi 1 code, but you're best served not to rely on this capability because the implementers of the Object Pascal language are trying to move away from the notion of assignable constants.

If you try to change the value of any of these constants, the Delphi compiler emits an error explaining that it's against the rules to change the value of a constant. Because constants are read-only, Object Pascal optimizes your data space by storing those constants that merit storage in the application's code pages. If you're unclear about the notions of code and data pages, see Chapter 3, "The Win32 API," in the electronic version of *Delphi 5 Developer's Guide* on the CD accompanying this, book.

> **NOTE**
>
> Object Pascal doesn't have a preprocessor as does C. There's no concept of a macro in Object Pascal and, therefore, no Object Pascal equivalent for C's #define for constant declaration. Although you can use Object Pascal's $define compiler directive for conditional compiles similar to C's #define, you cannot use it to define constants. Use const in Object Pascal where you would use #define to declare a constant in C.

Operators

Operators are the symbols in your code that enable you to manipulate all types of data. For example, there are operators for adding, subtracting, multiplying, and dividing numeric data. There are also operators for addressing a particular element of an array. This section explains some of the Pascal operators and describes some of the differences between their Java, C, and Visual Basic counterparts.

Assignment Operators

If you're new to Pascal, Delphi's assignment operator is going to be one of the toughest things to get used to. To assign a value to a variable, use the := operator as you would use the = operator in Java, C, or Visual Basic. Pascal programmers often call this the *gets* or *assignment* operator, and, the expression

```
Number1 := 5;
```

is read either "Number1 *gets* the value 5" or "Number1 *is assigned* the value 5."

Comparison Operators

If you've already programmed in Visual Basic, you should be very comfortable with Delphi's comparison operators, because they're virtually identical. These operators are fairly standard throughout programming languages, so they're covered only briefly in this section.

Object Pascal uses the = operator to perform logical comparisons between two expressions or values. Object Pascal's = operator is analogous to the Java/C == operator, so a Java/C expression that would be written as

```
if (x == y)
```

would be written as this in Object Pascal:

```
if x = y
```

> **NOTE**
>
> Remember that in Object Pascal, the := operator is used to assign a value to a variable, and the = operator compares the values of two, operands.

Object Pascal's "not equal to" operator is <>, and its purpose is identical to C's != operator. To determine whether two expressions are not equal, use this code:

```
if x <> y then DoSomething
```

Logical Operators

Pascal uses the words and and or as logical "and" and "or" operators, whereas Java and C use the && and || symbols, respectively, for these operators. The most common use of the and and or operators is as part of an if statement or loop, as demonstrated in the following two examples:

```
if (Condition 1) and (Condition 2) then
  DoSomething;

while (Condition 1) or (Condition 2) do
  DoSomething;
```

Pascal's logical "not" operator is not, which is used to invert a Boolean expression. It's analogous to the Java/C's ! operator. It's also often used as a part of if statements, as shown here:

```
if not (condition) then (do something);    // if condition is false then...
```

Table 2.1 provides an easy reference of how Pascal operators map to corresponding Java, C, and Visual Basic operators.

TABLE 2.1 Assignment, Comparison, and Logical Operators

Operator	Pascal	Java/C	Visual Basic
Assignment	:=	=	=
Comparison	=	==	= or Is*
Not equal to	<>	!=	<>
Less than	<	<	<
Greater than	>	>	>

TABLE 2.1 Continued

Operator	Pascal	Java/C	Visual Basic
Less than or equal to	<=	<=	<=
Greater than or equal to	>=	>=	>=
Logical and	and	&&	And
Logical or	or	||	Or
Logical not	not	!	Not

The Is comparison operator is used for objects, whereas the = comparison operator is used for other types.

Arithmetic Operators

You should already be familiar with most Object Pascal arithmetic operators because they're generally similar to those used in Java, C, and Visual Basic. Table 2.2 illustrates all the Pascal arithmetic operators and their Java, C, and Visual Basic counterparts.

TABLE 2.2 Arithmetic Operators

Operator	Pascal	Java/C	Visual Basic
Addition	+	+	+
Subtraction	-	-	-
Multiplication	*	*	*
Floating-point division	/	/	/
Integer division	div	/	\
Modulus	mod	%	Mod
Exponent	*None*	*None*	^

You might notice that Pascal and Visual Basic provide different division operators for floating-point and integer math, although this isn't the case for Java and C. The div operator automatically truncates any remainder when you're dividing two integer expressions.

NOTE

Remember to use the correct division operator for the types of expressions with which you're working. The Object Pascal compiler gives you an error if you try to divide two floating-point numbers with the integer div operator or two integers with the floating-point / operator, as the following code illustrates:

continues

```
var
   i: Integer;
   r: Real;
begin
   i := 4 / 3;        // This line will cause a compiler error
   f := 3.4 div 2.3;  // This line also will cause an error
end;
```

Many other programming languages do not distinguish between integer and floating-point division. Instead, they always perform floating-point division and then convert the result back to an integer when necessary. This can be rather expensive in terms of performance. The Pascal `div` operator is faster and more specific.

Bitwise Operators

Bitwise operators enable you to modify individual bits of a given variable. Common bitwise operators enable you to shift the bits to the left or right or to perform bitwise "and," "not," "or," and "exclusive or" (xor) operations with two numbers. The Shift+left and Shift+right operators are shl and shr, respectively, and they're much like the Java/C << and >> operators. The remainder of Pascal's bitwise operators is easy enough to remember: and, not, or, and xor. Table 2.3 lists the bitwise operators.

TABLE 2.3   Bitwise Operators

Operator	Pascal	Java/C	Visual Basic
And	and	&	And
Not	not	~	Not
Or	or	|	Or
Xor	xor	^	Xor
Shift+left	shl	<<	None
Shift+right	shr	>>	None

Increment and Decrement Procedures

Increment and decrement procedures generate optimized code for adding or subtracting 1 from a given integral variable. Pascal doesn't really provide honest-to-gosh increment and decrement operators similar to the Java/C ++ and -- operators, but Pascal's Inc() and Dec() procedures compile optimally to one machine instruction.

You can call `Inc()` or `Dec()` with one or two parameters. For example, the following two lines of code increment and decrement `variable`, respectively, by 1, using the `inc` and `dec` assembly instructions:

```
Inc(variable);
```

```
Dec(variable);
```

Compare the following two lines, which increment or decrement `variable` by 3 using the `add` and `sub` assembly instructions:

```
Inc(variable, 3);
```

```
Dec(variable, 3);
```

Table 2.4 compares the increment and decrement operators of different languages.

> **NOTE**
>
> With compiler optimization enabled, the `Inc()` and `Dec()` procedures often produce the same machine code as *variable_:= variable* + 1 syntax, so use whichever you feel more comfortable with for incrementing and decrementing variables.

TABLE 2.4 Increment and Decrement Operators

Operator	Pascal	Java/C	Visual Basic
Increment	Inc()	++	None
Decrement	Dec()	--	None

Do-and-Assign Operators

Not present in Object Pascal are handy do-and-assign operators like those found in Java and C. These operators, such as `+=` and `*=`, perform an arithmetic operation (in this case, an add and an multiply) before making the assignment. In Object Pascal, this type of operation must be performed using two separate operators. Therefore, this code in Java or C

```
x += 5;
```

becomes this in Object Pascal:

```
x := x + 5;
```

Object Pascal Types

One of Object Pascal's greatest features is that it's strongly typed, or *typesafe*. This means that actual variables passed to procedures and functions must be of the same type as the formal parameters identified in the procedure or function definition. You won't see any of the famous compiler warnings about suspicious pointer conversions that C programmers have grown to know and love. This is because the Object Pascal compiler won't permit you to call a function with one type of pointer when another type is specified in the function's formal parameters (although functions that take untyped `Pointer` types accept any type of pointer). Basically, Pascal's strongly typed nature enables it to perform a sanity check of your code—to ensure that you' aren't trying to put a square peg in a round hole.

A Comparison of Types

Delphi's base types are similar to those of Java, C, and Visual Basic. Table 2.5 compares and contrasts the base types of Object Pascal with those of these other languages. You might want to earmark this page because this table provides an excellent reference for matching types when calling functions in non-Delphi dynamic link libraries (DLLs) or object files (OBJs) from Delphi (and vice versa).

TABLE 2.5 A Pascal-to-Java-to-C-to-Visual Basic 32-bit Type Comparison

Type of Variable	Pascal	Java	C/C++	Visual Basic
8-bit signed integer	ShortInt	byte	char	None
8-bit unsigned integer	Byte	None	BYTE, unsigned short	Byte
16-bit signed integer	SmallInt	short	short	Short
16-bit unsigned integer	Word	None	unsigned short	None
32-bit signed integer	Integer, Longint	int	int, long	Integer, Long
32-bit unsigned integer	Cardinal, LongWord	None	unsigned long	None
64-bit signed integer	Int64	long	__int64	None

TABLE 2.5 Continued

Type of Variable	Pascal	Java	C/C++	Visual Basic
4-byte floating point	Single	float	float	Single
6-byte floating point	Real48	None	None	None
8-byte floating point	Double	double	double	Double
10-byte floating point	Extended	None	long. double	None
64-bit currency	currency	None	None	Currency
8-byte date/time	TDateTime	None	None	Date
16-byte variant	Variant, OleVariant, TVarData	None	VARIANT**, Variant†, OleVariant†	Variant(Default)
1-byte character	Char	None	char	None
2-byte character	WideChar	char	WCHAR	
Fixed-length byte string	ShortString	None	None	None
Dynamic string	AnsiString		AnsiString†	String
Null-terminated string	PChar	None	char *	None
Null-terminated wide string	PWideChar	None	LPCWSTR	None
Dynamic 2-byte string	WideString	String**	WideString†	None
1-byte Boolean	Boolean, ByteBool	boolean	(Any 1-byte)	None
2-byte Boolean	WordBool	None	(Any 2-byte)	Boolean
4-byte Boolean	BOOL, LongBool	None	BOOL	None

†A proprietary Borland C++Builder class that emulates the corresponding Object Pascal type
**Not a language element proper, but a commonly used structure or class

NOTE

If you're porting 16-bit code from Delphi 1, be sure to bear in mind that the size of both the Integer and Cardinal types has increased from 16 to 32 bits. Actually, that's not quite accurate: Under Delphi 2 and 3, the Cardinal type was treated as an unsigned 31-bit integer in order to preserve arithmetic precision (because Delphi 2 and 3 lacked a true unsigned 32-bit integer to which results of integer operations could be promoted). Under Delphi 4 and higher, Cardinal is a true unsigned 32-bit integer.

CAUTION

In Delphi 1, 2, and 3, the Real type identifier specified a 6-byte floating-point number, which is a type unique to Pascal and generally incompatible with other languages. In Delphi 4, Real is an alias for the Double type. The old 6-byte floating-point number is still there, but it's now identified by Real48. You can also force the Real identifier to refer to the 6-byte floating-point number using the {$REALCOMPATIBILITY ON} directive.

Characters

Delphi provides three character types:

- AnsiChar—This is the standard one-byte ANSI character that programmers have grown to know and love.
- WideChar—This character is two bytes in size and represents a Unicode character.
- Char—This is currently identical to AnsiChar, but Borland warns that the definition might change to WideChar in a later version of Delphi.

Keep in mind that because a character is no longer guaranteed to be one byte in size, you shouldn't hard-code the size into your applications. Instead, you should use the SizeOf() function where appropriate.

NOTE

The SizeOf() standard procedure returns the size, in bytes, of a type or instance.

A Multitude of Strings

Strings are variable types used to represent groups of characters. Every language has its own spin on how string types are stored and used. Pascal has several different string types to suit your programming needs:

- AnsiString, the default string type for Object Pascal, is comprised of AnsiChar characters and allows for virtually unlimited lengths. It's also compatible with null-terminated strings.
- ShortString remains in the language primarily for backward compatibility with Delphi 1. Its capacity is limited to 255 characters.
- WideString is similar in functionality to AnsiString except that it's comprised of WideChar characters.
- PChar is a pointer to a null-terminated Char string—like C's char * and lpstr types.
- PAnsiChar is a pointer to a null-terminated AnsiChar string.
- PWideChar is a pointer to a null-terminated WideChar string.

By default, when you declare a string variable in your code, as shown in the following example, the compiler assumes that you're creating an AnsiString:

```
var
  S: string;    // S is an AnsiString
```

Alternatively, you can cause variables declared as string types to be of type ShortString instead using the $H compiler directive. When the value of the $H compiler directive is negative, string variables are ShortString types; and when the value of the directive is positive (the default), string variables are AnsiString types. The following code demonstrates this behavior:

```
var
  {$H-}
  S1: string;  // S1 is a ShortString
  {$H+}
  S2: string;  // S2 is an AnsiString
```

The exception to the $H rule is that a string declared with an explicit size (limited to a maximum of 255 characters) is always a ShortString:

```
var
  S: string[63];    // A ShortString of up to 63 characters
```

The AnsiString Type

The AnsiString (or *long string*) type was introduced to the language in Delphi 2. It exists primarily as a result of widespread Delphi 1 customer demand for an easy-to-use string type without the intrusive 255-character limitation. AnsiString is that and more.

Although AnsiString types maintain an almost identical interface as their predecessors, they're dynamically allocated and garbage-collected. Because of this, AnsiString is sometimes referred to as a *lifetime-managed* type. Object Pascal also automatically manages allocation of string temporaries as needed, so you needn't worry about allocating buffers for intermediate results as you would in C/C++. Additionally, AnsiString types are always guaranteed to be null terminated, which makes them compatible with the null-terminated strings used by the Win32 API. The AnsiString type is actually implemented as a pointer to a string structure in heap memory. Figure 2.1 shows how an AnsiString is laid out in memory.

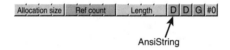

FIGURE 2.1

An AnsiString in memory.

> **CAUTION**
>
> The complete internal format of the long string type is left undocumented by Borland, and Borland reserves the right to change the internal format of long strings with future releases of Delphi. The information here is intended mainly to help you understand how AnsiString types work, and you should avoid being dependent on the structure of an AnsiString in your code.
>
> Developers who avoided the implementation of details of string moving from Delphi 1 to Delphi 2 were able to migrate their code with no problems. Those who wrote code that depended on the internal format (such as the 0th element in the string being the length) had to modify their code for Delphi 2.

As Figure 2.1 illustrates, AnsiString types are *reference counted*, which means that several strings might point to the same physical memory. String copies, therefore, are very fast because it's merely a matter of copying a pointer rather than copying the actual string contents. When two or more AnsiString types share a reference to the same physical string, the Delphi memory manager uses a copy-on-write technique, which enables it to wait until a string is modified to release a reference and allocate a new physical string. The following example illustrates these concepts:

```
var
  S1, S2: string;
begin
  // store string in S1, ref count of S1 is 1
  S1 := 'And now for something... ';
  S2 := S1;              // S2 now references S1.  Ref count of S1 is 2.
  // S2 is changed, so it is copied to its own
  // memory space, and ref count of S1 is decremented


  S2 := S2 + 'completely different!';
```

Lifetime-Managed Types

In addition to `AnsiString`, Delphi provides several other types that are lifetime-managed. These types include `WideString`, `Variant`, `OleVariant`, `interface`, `dispinterface`, and dynamic arrays. You'll learn more about each of these types later in this chapter. For now, we'll focus on what exactly lifetime-managed types are and how they work.

Lifetime-managed types, sometimes called *garbage-collected types*, are types that potentially consume some particular resource while in use and release the resource automatically when they fall out of scope. Of course, the variety of resources used depends on the type involved. For example, an `AnsiString` consumes memory for the character string while in use, and the memory occupied by the character string is released when it leaves scope.

For global variables, this process is fairly straightforward: As a part of the finalization code generated for your application, the compiler inserts code to ensure that each lifetime-managed global variable is cleaned up. Because all global data is zero-initialized when your application loads, each lifetime-managed global variable will always initially contain a zero, empty, or some other value indicating the variable is "unused." This way, the finalization code won't attempt to free resources unless they're actually used in your application.

Whenever you declare a local lifetime-managed variable, the process is slightly more complex: First, the compiler inserts code to ensure that the variable is initialized to zero when the function or procedure is entered. Next, the compiler generates a `try..finally` exception-handling block, which it wraps around the entire function body. Finally, the compiler inserts code in the `finally` block to clean up the lifetime-managed variable (exception handling is explained in more detail in the section "Structured Exception Handling"). With this in mind, consider the following procedure:

```
    procedure Foo;
    var
      S: string;
    begin
      // procedure body
      // use S here
    end;
```

Although this procedure looks simple, if you take into account the code generation by the compiler behind the scenes, it would actually look like this:

```
    procedure Foo;
    var
      S: string;
    begin
      S := '';
      try
        // procedure body
        // use S here
      finally
        // clean up S here
      end;
    end;
```

String Operations

You can concatenate two strings by using the + operator or the Concat() function. The preferred method of string concatenation is the + operator because the Concat() function exists primarily for backward compatibility. The following example demonstrates the use of + and Concat():

```
{ using + }
var
  S, S2: string
begin
  S:= 'Cookie ':
  S2 := 'Monster';
  S := S + S2;   { Cookie Monster }
end.

{ using Concat() }
var
  S, S2: string;
begin
  S:= 'Cookie ';
  S2 := 'Monster';
  S := Concat(S, S2);  { Cookie Monster }
end.
```

> **NOTE**
>
> Always use single quotation marks (`'A String'`) when working with string literals in Object Pascal.

> **TIP**
>
> `Concat()` is one of many "compiler magic" functions and procedures (like `ReadLn()` and `WriteLn()`, for example) that don't have an Object Pascal definition. Such functions and procedures are intended to accept an indeterminate number of parameters or optional parameters, so they cannot be defined in terms of the Object Pascal language. Because of this, the compiler provides a special case for each of these functions and generates a call to one of the "compiler magic" *helper functions* defined in the `System` unit. These helper functions are generally implemented in assembly language in order to circumvent Pascal language rules.
>
> In addition to the "compiler magic" string support functions and procedures, there are a variety of functions and procedures in the `SysUtils` unit designed to make working with strings easier. Search for "String-handling routines (Pascal-style)" in the Delphi online help system.
>
> Furthermore, you'll find some very useful homebrewed string utility functions and procedures in the `StrUtils` unit in the `\Source\Utils` directory on the CD-ROM accompanying this book.

Length and Allocation

When first declared, an `AnsiString` has no length and therefore no space allocated for the characters in the string. To cause space to be allocated for the string, you can assign the string to a literal or another string, or you can use the `SetLength()` procedure, as shown here:

```
var
  S: string;         // string initially has no length
begin
  S := 'Doh!';       // allocates at least enough space for string literal
  { or }
  S := OtherString   // increases ref count of OtherString
                     // (assume OtherString already points to a valid string)
  { or }
  SetLength(S, 4);   // allocates enough space for at least 4 chars
end;
```

You can index the characters of an `AnsiString` like an array, but be careful not to index beyond the length of the string. For example, the following code snippet will cause an error:

```
var
  S: string;
begin
  S[1] := 'a';  // Won't work because S hasn't been allocated!
end;
```

This code, however, works properly:

```
var
  S: string;
begin
  SetLength(S, 1);
  S[1] := 'a';        // Now S has enough space to hold the character
end;
```

Win32 Compatibility

As mentioned earlier, `AnsiString` types are always null-terminated, so they're compatible with null-terminated strings. This makes it easy to call Win32 API functions or other functions requiring `PChar`-type strings. All that's required is that you typecast the `string` as a `PChar`. (Typecasting is explained in more detail in the section "Typecasting and Type Conversion.") The following code demonstrates how to call the Win32 `GetWindowsDirectory()` function, which accepts a `PChar` and buffer length as parameters:

```
var
  S: string;
begin
  SetLength(S, 256);              // important! get space for string first
  // call function, S now holds directory string
  GetWindowsDirectory(PChar(S), 256);
end;
```

After using an `AnsiString` in which a function or procedure expects a `PChar`, you must manually set the length of the string variable to its null-terminated length. The `RealizeLength()` function, which also comes from the `StrUtils` unit, accomplishes that task:

```
procedure RealizeLength(var S: string);
begin
  SetLength(S, StrLen(PChar(S)));
end;
```

Calling `RealizeLength()` completes the substitution of a long string for a `PChar`:

```
var
  S: string;
```

```
begin
  SetLength(S, 256);          // important! get space for string first
  // call function, S now holds directory string
  GetWindowsDirectory(PChar(S), 256);
  RealizeLength(S);           // set S length to null length
end;
```

> **CAUTION**
>
> Exercise care when typecasting a string to a PChar variable. Because strings are garbage-collected when they go out of scope, you must pay attention when making assignments such as P := PChar(Str), where the scope (or lifetime) of P is greater than Str.

2

THE OBJECT PASCAL LANGUAGE

Porting Issues

When you're porting 16-bit Delphi 1 applications, you need to keep in mind a number of issues when migrating to AnsiString types:

- In places where you used the PString (pointer to a ShortString) type, you should instead use the string type. Remember, an AnsiString is already a pointer to a string.
- You can no longer access the 0th element of a string to get or set the length. Instead, use the Length() function to get the string length and the SetLength() procedure to set the length.
- There's no longer any need to use StrPas() and StrPCopy() to convert back and forth between strings and PChar types. As shown earlier, you can typecast an AnsiString to a PChar. When you want to copy the contents of a PChar to an AnsiString, you can use a direct assignment:

```
StringVar := PCharVar;
```

> **CAUTION**
>
> Remember that you must use the SetLength() procedure to set the length of a long string, whereas the past practice was to directly access the 0th element of a short string to set the length. This issue will arise when you attempt to port 16-bit Delphi 1.0 code to 32, bits.

The ShortString Type

If you're a Delphi veteran, you'll recognize the ShortString type as the Delphi 1.0 string type. ShortString types are sometimes referred to as *Pascal strings* or *length-byte strings*. To reiterate, remember that the value of the $H directive determines whether variables declared as string are treated by the compiler as AnsiString or ShortString.

In memory, the string resembles an array of characters in which the 0th character in the string contains the length of the string, and the string itself is contained in the following characters. The storage size of a ShortString defaults to the maximum of 256 bytes. This means that you can never have more than 255 characters in a ShortString (255 characters + 1 length byte = 256). As with AnsiString, working with ShortString is fairly painless because the compiler allocates string temporaries as needed, so you don't have to worry about allocating buffers for intermediate results or disposing of them as you do with C.

Figure 2.2 illustrates how a Pascal string is laid out in memory.

FIGURE 2.2

A ShortString in memory.

A ShortString variable is declared and initialized with the following syntax:

```
var
  S: ShortString;
begin
  S := 'Bob the cat.';
end.
```

Optionally, you can allocate fewer than 256 bytes for a ShortString using just the string type identifier and a length specifier, as in the following example:

```
var
  S: string[45];  { a 45-character ShortString }
begin
  S := 'This string must be 45 or fewer characters.';
end.
```

The preceding code causes a ShortString to be created regardless of the current setting of the $H directive. The maximum length you can specify is 255 characters.

Never store more characters to a ShortString than you have allocated memory for. If you declare a variable as a string[8], for example, and try to assign 'a_pretty_darn_long_string' to that variable, the string would be truncated to only eight characters, and you would lose data.

When using an array subscript to address a particular character in a ShortString, you could get bogus results or corrupt memory if you attempt to use a subscript index that's greater than the declared size of the ShortString. For example, suppose that you declare a variable as follows:

```
var
  Str: string[8];
```

If you then attempt to write to the 10th element of the string as follows, you're likely to corrupt memory used by other variables:

```
var
  Str: string[8];
  i: Integer;
begin
  i := 10;
  Str[i] := 's';  // will corrupt memory
```

You can have the compiler link in special logic to catch these types of errors at runtime by selecting Range Checking in the Options, Project dialog box.

TIP

Although including range-checking logic in your program helps you find string errors, range checking slightly hampers the performance of your application. It's common practice to use range checking during the development and debugging phases of your program, but you should remove range checking after you become confident in the stability of your program.

Unlike AnsiString types, ShortString types aren't inherently compatible with null-terminated strings. Because of this, a bit of work is required to be able to pass a ShortString to a Win32 API function. The following function, ShortStringAsPChar(), is taken from the STRUTILS.PAS unit mentioned earlier:

```
func function ShortStringAsPChar(var S: ShortString): PChar;
{ Function null-terminates a string so it can be passed to functions }
{ that require PChar types. If string is longer than 254 chars, then it will }
{ be truncated to 254. }
begin
  if Length(S) = High(S) then Dec(S[0]); { Truncate S if it's too long }
  S[Ord(Length(S)) + 1] := #0;           { Place null at end of string }
  Result := @S[1];                       { Return "PChar'd" string }
end;
```

> **CAUTION**
>
> The functions and procedures in the Win32 API require null-terminated strings. Do not try to pass a `ShortString` type to an API function because your program will not compile. Your life will be easier if you use long strings when working with the API.

The `WideString` Type

The `WideString` type is a lifetime-managed type similar to `AnsiString`; they're both dynamically allocated, garbage collected, and even assignment compatible with one another. However, `WideString` differs from `AnsiString` in three key respects:

- `WideString` types are comprised of `WideChar` characters rather than `AnsiChar` characters, making them compatible with Unicode strings.

- `WideString` types are allocated using the `SysAllocStrLen()` API function, making them compatible with OLE `BSTR` strings.

- `WideString` types aren't reference counted, so assigning one `WideString` to another requires the entire string to be copied from one location in memory to another. This makes `WideString` types less efficient than `AnsiString` types in terms of speed and memory use.

As mentioned earlier, the compiler automatically knows how to convert between variables of `AnsiString` and `WideString` types, as shown here:

```
var
  W: WideString;
  S: string;
begin
  W := 'Margaritaville';
  S := W;  // Wide converted to Ansi
  S := 'Come Monday';
  W := S;  // Ansi converted to Wide
end;
```

In order to make working with `WideString` types feel natural, Object Pascal overloads the `Concat()`, `Copy()`, `Insert()`, `Length()`, `Pos()`, and `SetLength()` routines and the +, =, and <> operators for use with `WideString` types. Therefore, the following code is syntactically correct:

```
var
  W1, W2: WideString;
  P: Integer;
begin
  W1 := 'Enfield';
```

```
  W2 := 'field';
  if W1 <> W2 then
    P := Pos(W1, W2);
end;
```

As with the `AnsiString` and `ShortString` types, you can use array brackets to reference individual characters of a `WideString`:

```
var
  W: WideString;
  C: WideChar;
begin
  W := 'Ebony and Ivory living in perfect harmony';
  C := W[Length(W)];  // C holds the last character in W
end;
```

Null-Terminated Strings

Earlier, this chapter mentioned that Delphi has three different null-terminated string types: `PChar`, `PAnsiChar`, and `PWideChar`. As their names imply, each of these represents a null-terminated string of each of Delphi's three character types. In this chapter, we refer to each of these string types generically as `PChar`. The `PChar` type in Delphi exists mainly for compatibility with Delphi 1.0 and the Win32 API, which makes extensive use of null-terminated strings. A `PChar` is defined as a pointer to a string followed by a null (zero) value (if you're unsure of exactly what a pointer is, read on; pointers are discussed in more detail later in this section). Unlike memory for `AnsiString` and `WideString` types, memory for `PChar` types isn't automatically allocated and managed by Object Pascal. Therefore, you'll usually need to allocate memory for the string to which it points, using one of Object Pascal's memory-allocation functions. The theoretical maximum length of a `PChar` string is just under 4GB. The layout of a `PChar` variable in memory is shown in Figure 2.3.

TIP

Object Pascal's `AnsiString` type can be used as a `PChar` in most situations, so you should use this type rather than the `PChar` type wherever possible. Because memory management for strings occurs automatically, you greatly reduce the chance of introducing memory-corruption bugs into your applications if, where possible, you avoid `PChar` types and the manual memory allocation associated with them.

PChar

FIGURE 2.3

A PChar in memory.

As mentioned earlier, PChar variables require you to manually allocate and free the memory buffers that contain their strings. Normally, you allocate memory for a PChar buffer using the StrAlloc() function, but several other functions can be used to allocate memory for PChar types, including AllocMem(), GetMem(), StrNew(), and even the VirtualAlloc() API function. Corresponding functions also exist for many of these functions, which must be used to deallocate memory. Table 2.6 lists several allocation functions and their corresponding deallocation functions.

TABLE 2.6 Memory Allocation and Deallocation Functions

Memory Allocated with. . .	*Must Be Freed with. . .*
AllocMem()	FreeMem()
GlobalAlloc()	GlobalFree()
GetMem()	FreeMem()
New()	Dispose()
StrAlloc()	StrDispose()
StrNew()	StrDispose()
VirtualAlloc()	VirtualFree()

The following example demonstrates memory allocation techniques when working with PChar and string types:

```
var
  P1, P2: PChar;
  S1, S2: string;
begin
  P1 := StrAlloc(64 * SizeOf(Char));  // P1 points to an allocation of 63 Chars
  StrPCopy(P1, 'Delphi 6 ');          // Copy literal string into P1
  S1 := 'Developer''s Guide';         // Put some text in string S1
  P2 := StrNew(PChar(S1));            // P1 points to a copy of S1
  StrCat(P1, P2);                     // concatenate P1 and P2
  S2 := P1;                  // S2 now holds 'Delphi 6 Developer's Guide'
  StrDispose(P1);                     // clean up P1 and P2 buffers
  StrDispose(P2);
end.
```

Notice, first of all, the use of SizeOf(Char) with StrAlloc() when allocating memory for P1. Remember that the size of a Char might change from one byte to two in future versions of Delphi; therefore, you cannot assume the value of Char to always be one byte. SizeOf() ensures that the allocation will work properly no matter how many bytes a character occupies.

StrCat() is used to concatenate two PChar strings. Note here that you cannot use the + operator for concatenation as you can with long string and ShortString types.

The StrNew() function is used to copy the value contained by string S1 into P2 (a PChar). Be careful when using this function. It's common to have memory-overwrite errors when using StrNew() because it allocates only enough memory to hold the string. Consider the following example:

```
var
P1, P2: Pchar;
begin
  P1 := StrNew('Hello ');  // Allocate just enough memory for P1 and P2
  P2 := StrNew('World');
  StrCat(P1, P2);          // BEWARE: Corrupts memory!
  .
  .
  .
end;
```

TIP

As with other types of strings, Object Pascal provides a decent library of utility functions and procedures for operating on PChar types. Search for "String-handling routines (null-terminated)" in the Delphi online help system.

You'll also find some useful null-terminated functions and procedures in the StrUtils unit in the \Source\Utils directory on the CD-ROM accompanying this book.

Variant Types

Delphi 2 introduced a powerful data type called the Variant. Variants were brought about primarily in order to support OLE Automation, which uses the Variant type heavily. In fact, Delphi's Variant data type is an encapsulation of the variant used with OLE. Delphi's implementation of variants has also proven to be useful in other areas of Delphi programming, as you'll soon learn. Object Pascal is the only compiled language that completely integrates variants as a dynamic data type at runtime and as a static type at compile time in that the compiler always knows that it's a variant.

Delphi 3 introduced a new type called OleVariant, which is identical to Variant except that it can only hold Automation-compatible types. In this section, we initially focus on the Variant type and then we discuss OleVariant and contrast it with Variant.

Variants Change Types Dynamically

One of the main purposes of variants is to have a variable whose underlying data type cannot be determined at compile time. This means that a variant can change the type to which it refers at runtime. For example, the following code will compile and run properly:

```
var
  V: Variant;
begin
  V := 'Delphi is Great!';    // Variant holds a string
  V := 1;                     // Variant now holds an Integer
  V := 123.34;                // Variant now holds a floating point
  V := True;                  // Variant now holds a boolean
  V := CreateOleObject('Word.Basic'); // Variant now holds an OLE object
end;
```

Variants can support all simple data types, such as integers, floating-point values, strings, Booleans, date and time, currency, and also OLE Automation objects. Note that variants cannot refer to Object Pascal objects. Also, variants can refer to a non-homogeneous array, which can vary in size and whose data elements can refer to any of the preceding data types (including another variant array).

The Variant Structure

The data structure defining the Variant type is defined in the System unit and is also shown in the following code:

```
TVarType = Word;
PVarData = ^TVarData;
{$EXTERNALSYM PVarData}
TVarData = packed record
  VType: TVarType;
  case Integer of
    0: (Reserved1: Word;
          case Integer of
            0: (Reserved2, Reserved3: Word;
                  case Integer of
                    varSmallInt: (VSmallInt: SmallInt);
                    varInteger:  (VInteger: Integer);
                    varSingle:   (VSingle: Single);
                    varDouble:   (VDouble: Double);
                    varCurrency: (VCurrency: Currency);
                    varDate:     (VDate: TDateTime);
```

```
        varOleStr:   (VOleStr: PWideChar);
        varDispatch: (VDispatch: Pointer);
        varError:    (VError: LongWord);
        varBoolean:  (VBoolean: WordBool);
        varUnknown:  (VUnknown: Pointer);
        varShortInt: (VShortInt: ShortInt);
        varByte:     (VByte: Byte);
        varWord:     (VWord: Word);
        varLongWord: (VLongWord: LongWord);
        varInt64:    (VInt64: Int64);
        varString:   (VString: Pointer);
        varAny:      (VAny: Pointer);
        varArray:    (VArray: PVarArray);
        varByRef:    (VPointer: Pointer);
      );
    1: (VLongs: array[0..2] of LongInt);
    );
  2: (VWords: array [0..6] of Word);
  3: (VBytes: array [0..13] of Byte);
end;
```

The TVarData structure consumes 16 bytes of memory. The first two bytes of the TVarData structure contain a word value that represents the data type to which the variant refers. The following code shows the various values that might appear in the VType field of the TVarData record. The next six bytes are unused. The remaining eight bytes contain the actual data or a pointer to the data represented by the variant. Again, this structure maps directly to 'COM's implementation of the variant type. Here's the code:

```
{ Variant type codes (wtypes.h) }

  varEmpty    = $0000; { vt_empty     }
  varNull     = $0001; { vt_null      }
  varSmallint = $0002; { vt_i2        }
  varInteger  = $0003; { vt_i4        }
  varSingle   = $0004; { vt_r4        }
  varDouble   = $0005; { vt_r8        }
  varCurrency = $0006; { vt_cy        }
  varDate     = $0007; { vt_date      }
  varOleStr   = $0008; { vt_bstr      }
  varDispatch = $0009; { vt_dispatch  }
  varError    = $000A; { vt_error     }
  varBoolean  = $000B; { vt_bool      }
  varVariant  = $000C; { vt_variant   }
  varUnknown  = $000D; { vt_unknown   }
//varDecimal  = $000E; { vt_decimal   } {UNSUPPORTED}
                       { undefined  $0f } {UNSUPPORTED}
```

```
   varShortInt = $0010; { vt_i1         }
   varByte     = $0011; { vt_ui1        }
   varWord     = $0012; { vt_ui2        }
   varLongWord = $0013; { vt_ui4        }
   varInt64    = $0014; { vt_i8         }
//varWord64    = $0015; { vt_ui8        } {UNSUPPORTED}

   { if adding new items, update Variants' varLast, BaseTypeMap and OpTypeMap }
   varStrArg   = $0048; { vt_clsid    }
   varString   = $0100; { Pascal string; not OLE compatible }
   varAny      = $0101; { Corba any }
   varTypeMask = $0FFF;
   varArray    = $2000;
   varByRef    = $4000;
```

> **NOTE**
>
> As you might notice from the type codes in the preceding listing, a Variant cannot contain a reference to a Pointer or class type.

You'll notice from the TVarData listing that the TVarData record is actually a *variant record*. Don't confuse this with the Variant type. Although the variant record and Variant type have similar names, they represent two totally different constructs. Variant records allow for multiple data fields to overlap in the same area of memory (like a C/C++ union). This is discussed in more detail in the "Records" section later in this chapter. The case statement in the TVarData variant record indicates the type of data to which the variant refers. For example, if the VType field contains the value varInteger, only four bytes of the eight data bytes in the variant portion of the record are used to hold an integer value. Likewise, if VType has the value varByte, only one byte of the eight is used to hold a byte value.

You'll notice that if VType contains the value varString, the eight data bytes don't actually hold the string; instead, they hold a pointer to this string. This is an important point because you can access fields of a variant directly, as shown here:

```
var
  V: Variant;
begin
  TVarData(V).VType := varInteger;
  TVarData(V).VInteger := 2;
end;
```

You must understand that in some cases this is a dangerous practice because it's possible to lose the reference to a string or other lifetime-managed entity, which will result in your application leaking memory or other resources. You'll see what we mean by the term *garbage collected* in the following section.

Variants Are Lifetime Managed

Delphi automatically handles the allocation and deallocation of memory required of a Variant type. For example, examine the following code, which assigns a string to a Variant variable:

```
procedure ShowVariant(S: string);
var
  V: Variant
begin
  V := S;
  ShowMessage(V);
end;
```

As discussed earlier in this chapter in the sidebar "Lifetime-Managed Types," several things are going on here that might not be apparent. Delphi first initializes the variant to an unassigned value. During the assignment, it sets its VType field to varString and copies the string pointer into its VString field. It then increases the reference count of string S. When the variant leaves scope (that is, the procedure ends and returns to the code that called it), it's cleared and the reference count of string S is decremented. Delphi does this by implicitly inserting a try..finally block in the procedure, as shown. here:

```
procedure ShowVariant(S: string);
var
  V: Variant
begin
  V := Unassigned;  // initialize variant to "empty"
  try
    V := S;
    ShowMessage(V);
  finally
    // Now clean up the resources associated with the variant
  end;
end;
```

This same implicit release of resources occurs when you assign a different data type to the variant. For example, examine the following code:

```
procedure ChangeVariant(S: string);
var
  V: Variant
begin
  V := S;
  V := 34;
end;
```

This code boils down to the following pseudo-code:

```
procedure ChangeVariant(S: string);
var
  V: Variant
begin
  Clear Variant V, ensuring it is initialized to "empty"
  try
    V.VType := varString; V.VString := S; Inc(S.RefCount);
    Clear Variant V, thereby releasing reference to string;
    V.VType := varInteger; V.VInteger := 34;
  finally
    Clean up the resources associated with the variant
  end;
end;
```

If you understand what happens in the preceding examples, you'll see why it's not recommended that you manipulate fields of the TVarData record directly, as shown here:

```
procedure ChangeVariant(S: string);
var
  V: Variant
begin
  V := S;
  TVarData(V).VType := varInteger;
  TVarData(V).VInteger := 32;
  V := 34;
end;
```

Although this might appear to be safe, it's not because it results in the failure to decrement the reference count of string S, probably resulting in a memory leak. As a general rule, don't access the TVarData fields directly, or if you do, be absolutely sure that you know exactly what you're doing.

Typecasting Variants

You can explicitly typecast expressions to type Variant. For example, the expression

```
Variant(X)
```

results in a Variant type whose type code corresponds to the result of the expression X, which must be an integer, real, currency, string, character, or Boolean type.

You can also typecast a variant to that of a simple data type. For example, given the assignment

```
V := 1.6;
```

where V is a variable of type `Variant`, the following expressions will have the results shown:

```
S := string(V);    // S will contain the string '1.6';
// I is rounded to the nearest Integer value, in this case: 2.
I := Integer(V);
B := Boolean(V);   // B contains False if V contains 0, otherwise B is True
D := Double(V);    // D contains the value 1.6
```

These results are dictated by certain type-conversion rules applicable to `Variant` types. These rules are defined in detail in Delphi's Object Pascal Language Guide.

By the way, in the preceding example, it's not necessary to typecast the variant to another data type to make the assignment. The following code would work just as well:

```
V := 1.6;
S := V;
I := V;
B := V;
D := V;
```

What happens here is that the conversions to the target data types are made through an implicit typecast. However, because these conversions are made at runtime, there's much more code logic attached to this method. If you're sure of the type a variant contains, you're better off explicitly typecasting it to that type in order to speed up the operation. This is especially true if the variant is being used in an expression, which we'll discuss. next.

Variants in Expressions

You can use variants in expressions with the following operators: +, =, *, /, div, mod, shl, shr, and, or, xor, not, :=, <>, <, >, <=, and >=.

When using variants in expressions, Delphi knows how to perform the operations based on the contents of the variant. For example, if two variants, V1 and V2, contain integers, the expression V1 + V2 results in the addition of the two integers. However, if V1 and V2 contain strings, the result is a concatenation of the two strings. What happens if V1 and V2 contain two different data types? Delphi uses certain promotion rules in order to perform the operation. For example, if V1 contains the string '4.5' and V2 contains a floating-point number, V1 will be converted to a floating point and then added to V2. The following code illustrates this:

```
var
  V1, V2, V3: Variant;
begin
  V1 := '100'; // A string type
  V2 := '50';  // A string type
  V3 := 200;   // An Integer type
  V1 := V1 + V2 + V3;
end;
```

Based on what we just mentioned about promotion rules, it would seem at first glance that the preceding code would result in the value 350 as an integer. However, if you take a closer look, you'll see that this is not the case. Because the order of precedence is from left to right, the first equation executed. is V1 + V2. Because these two variants refer to strings, a string concatenation is performed, resulting in the string '10050'. That result is then added to the integer value held by the variant V3. Because V3 is an integer, the result '10050' is converted to an integer and added to V3, thus providing an end result of 10250.

Delphi promotes the variants to the highest type in the equation in order to successfully carry out the calculation. However, when an operation is attempted on two variants of which Delphi cannot make any sense, an *invalid variant type conversion* exception is raised. The following code illustrates this:

```
var
  V1, V2: Variant;
begin
  V1 := 77;
  V2 := 'hello';
  V1 := V1 / V2;  // Raises an exception.
end;
```

As stated earlier, it's sometimes a good idea to explicitly typecast a variant to a specific data type if you know what that type is and if it's used in an expression. Consider the following line of code:

```
V4 := V1 * V2 / V3;
```

Before a result can be generated for this equation, each operation is handled by a runtime function that goes through several gyrations to determine the compatibility of the types the variants represent. Then the conversions are made to the appropriate data types. This results in a large amount of overhead and code size. A better solution is obviously not to use variants. However, when necessary, you can also explicitly typecast the variants so the data types are resolved at compile time:

```
V4 := Integer(V1) * Double(V2) / Integer(V3);
```

Keep in mind that this assumes you know the data types the variants represent.

Empty and Null

Two special VType values for variants merit a brief discussion. The first is varEmpty, which means that the variant has not yet been assigned a value. This is the initial value of the variant set by the compiler as it comes into scope. The other is varNull, which is different from varEmpty in that it actually represents the value Null as opposed to a lack of value. This distinction between no value and a Null value is especially important when applied to the field values of a database table. In Part III of this book, "Database Development," you'll learn how variants are used in the context of database applications.

Another difference is that attempting to perform any equation with a variant containing a varEmpty VType value will result in an *invalid variant operation* exception. The same isn't true of variants containing a varNull value, however. When a variant involved in an equation contains a Null value, that value will propagate to the result. Therefore, the result of any equation containing a Null is always Null.

If you want to assign or compare a variant to one of these two special values, the System unit defines two variants, Unassigned and Null, which have the VType values of varEmpty and varNull, respectively.

> ## CAUTION
>
> It might be tempting to use variants instead of the conventional data types because they seem to offer so much flexibility. However, this will increase the size of your code and cause your applications to run more slowly. Additionally, it will make your code more difficult to maintain. Variants are useful in many situations. In fact, the VCL, itself, uses variants in several places, most notably in the ActiveX and database areas, because of the data type flexibility they offer. Generally speaking, however, you should use the conventional data types instead of variants. Only in situations where the flexibility of the variant outweighs the performance of the conventional method should you resort to using variants. Ambiguous data types beget ambiguous bugs.

Variant Arrays

Earlier we mentioned that a variant can refer to a nonhomogeneous array. Therefore, the following syntax is valid:

```
var
  V: Variant;
  I, J: Integer;
begin
  I := V[J];
end;
```

Bear in mind that, although the preceding code will compile, you'll get an exception at runtime because V does not yet contain a variant array. Object Pascal provides several variant array support functions that allow you to create a variant array. Two of these functions are VarArrayCreate() and VarArrayOf().

VarArrayCreate()

VarArrayCreate() is defined in the Variants unit as

```
function VarArrayCreate(const Bounds: array of Integer;
  VarType: Integer): Variant;
```

To use VarArrayCreate(), you pass in the array bounds for the array you want to create and a variant type code for the type of the array elements (the first parameter is an open array, which is discussed in the "Passing Parameters" section later in this chapter). For example, the following code returns a variant array of integers and assigns values to the array items:

```
var
  V: Variant;
begin
  V := VarArrayCreate([1, 4], varInteger); // Create a 4-element array
  V[1] := 1;
  V[2] := 2;
  V[3] := 3;
  V[4] := 4;
end;
```

If variant arrays of a single type aren't confusing enough, you can pass varVariant as the type code in order to create a variant array of variants! This way, each element in the array has the ability to contain a different type of data. You can also create a multidimensional array by passing in the additional bounds required. For example, the following code creates an array with the bounds [1..4, 1..5]:

```
V := VarArrayCreate([1, 4, 1, 5], varInteger);
```

NOTE

The Variants unit was added to the RTL in Delphi 6 because the support for variants was migrated out of the System unit. Among other things, this physical separation of the variant support code helped to smooth compatibility with Borland Kylix and provided the ability to extend variants to support developer-specified data types.

VarArrayOf()

The VarArrayOf() function is defined in the Variants unit as

```
function VarArrayOf(const Values: array of Variant): Variant;
```

This function returns a one-dimensional array whose elements are given in the Values parameter. The following example creates a variant array of three elements with an integer, a string, and a floating-point value:

```
V := VarArrayOf([1, 'Delphi', 2.2]);
```

Variant Array Support Functions and Procedures

In addition to `VarArrayCreate()` and `VarArrayOf()`, there are several other variant array support functions and procedures. These functions are defined in the `Variants` System unit and are also shown here:

```
procedure VarArrayRedim(var A: Variant; HighBound: Integer);
function VarArrayDimCount(const A: Variant): Integer;
function VarArrayLowBound(const A: Variant; Dim: Integer): Integer;
function VarArrayHighBound(const A: Variant; Dim: Integer): Integer;
function VarArrayLock(const A: Variant): Pointer;
procedure VarArrayUnlock(const A: Variant);
function VarArrayRef(const A: Variant): Variant;
function VarIsArray(const A: Variant): Boolean;
```

The `VarArrayRedim()` function allows you to resize the upper bound of the rightmost dimension of a variant array. The `VarArrayDimCount()` function returns the number of dimensions in a variant array. `VarArrayLowBound()` and `VarArrayHighBound()` return the lower and upper bounds of an array, respectively. `VarArrayLock()` and `VarArrayUnlock()` are two special functions, which are described in further detail in the next section.

`VarArrayRef()` is intended to work around a problem that exists in passing variant arrays to OLE Automation servers. The problem occurs when you pass a variant containing a variant array to an automation method, like this:

```
Server.PassVariantArray(VA);
```

The array is passed not as a variant array but rather as a variant containing a variant array—an important distinction. If the server expected a variant array rather than a reference to one, the server will likely encounter an error condition when you call the method with the preceding syntax. `VarArrayRef()` takes care of this situation by massaging the variant into the type and value expected by the server. Here's the syntax for using `VarArrayRef()`:

```
Server.PassVariantArray(VarArrayRef(VA));
```

`VarIsArray()` is a simple Boolean check, which returns `True` if the variant parameter passed to it is a variant array or `False` otherwise.

Initializing a Large Array: `VarArrayLock()` and `VarArrayUnlock()`

Variant arrays are important in OLE Automation because they provide the only means for passing raw binary data to an OLE Automation server (note that pointers aren't a legal type in OLE Automation, as you'll learn in Chapter 15, "COM Development"). However, if used incorrectly, variant arrays can be a rather inefficient means of exchanging data. Consider the following line of code:

```
V := VarArrayCreate([1, 10000], VarByte);
```

This line creates a variant array of 10,000 bytes. Suppose that you have another array (nonvariant) declared of the same size and you want to copy the contents of this nonvariant array to the variant array. Normally, you can only do this by looping through the elements and assigning them to the elements of the variant array, as shown here:

```
begin
  V := VarArrayCreate([1, 10000], VarByte);
  for i := 1 to 10000 do
    V[i] := A[i];
end;
```

The problem with this code is that it's bogged down by the significant overhead required just to initialize the variant array elements. This is because the assignments to the array elements must go through the runtime logic to determine type compatibility, the location of each element, and so forth. To avoid these runtime checks, you can use the VarArrayLock() function and the VarArrayUnlock() procedure.

VarArrayLock() locks the array in memory so that it cannot be moved or resized while it's locked, and it returns a pointer to the array data. VarArrayUnlock() unlocks an array locked with VarArrayLock() and once again allows the variant array to be resized and moved in memory. After the array is locked, you can employ a more efficient means to initialize the data by using, for example, the Move() procedure with the pointer to the array's data. The following code performs the initialization of the variant array shown earlier, but in a much more efficient manner:

```
begin
  V := VarArrayCreate([1, 10000], VarByte);
  P := VarArrayLock(V);
  try
    Move(A, P^, 10000);
  finally
    VarArrayUnlock(V);
  end;
end;
```

Supporting Functions

There are several other common support functions for variants that you can use. These functions are declared in the Variants System unit and are also listed here:

```
procedure VarClear(var V: Variant);
procedure VarCopy(var Dest: Variant; const Source: Variant);
procedure VarCast(var Dest: Variant; const Source: Variant; VarType: Integer);
function VarType(const V: Variant): Integer;
function VarAsType(const V: Variant; VarType: Integer): Variant;
function VarIsEmpty(const V: Variant): Boolean;
```

```
function VarIsNull(const V: Variant): Boolean;
function VarToStr(const V: Variant): string;
function VarFromDateTime(DateTime: TDateTime): Variant;
function VarToDateTime(const V: Variant): TDateTime;
```

The VarClear() procedure clears a variant and sets the VType field to varEmpty. VarCopy() copies the Source variant to the Dest variant. The VarCast() procedure converts a variant to a specified type and stores that result into another variant. VarType() returns one of the varXXX type codes for a specified variant. VarAsType() has the same functionality as VarCast(). VarIsEmpty() returns True if the type code on a specified variant is varEmpty. VarIsNull() indicates whether a variant contains a Null value. VarToStr() converts a variant to its string representation (an empty string in the case of a Null or empty variant). VarFromDateTime() returns a variant that contains a given TDateTime value. Finally, VarToDateTime() returns the TDateTime value contained in a variant.

OleVariant

The OleVariant type is nearly identical to the Variant type described throughout this section of this chapter. The only difference between OleVariant and Variant is that OleVariant only supports Automation-compatible types. Currently, the only VType supported that's not Automation-compatible is varString, the code for AnsiString. When an attempt is made to assign an AnsiString to an OleVariant, the AnsiString will be automatically converted to an OLE BSTR and stored in the variant as a varOleStr.

Currency

Delphi 2.0 introduced a new type called Currency, which is ideal for financial calculations. Unlike floating-point numbers, which allow the decimal point to "float" within a number, Currency is a fixed-point decimal type that's hard-coded to a precision of 15 digits before the decimal and four digits after the decimal. As such, it's not susceptible to round-off errors as are floating-point types. When porting your Delphi 1.0 projects, it's a good idea to use this type in place of Single, Real, Double, and Extended where money is involved.

User-Defined Types

Integers, strings, and floating-point numbers often are not enough to adequately represent variables in the real-world problems that programmers must try to solve. In cases like these, you must create your own types to better represent variables in the current problem. In Pascal, these user-defined types usually come in the form of records or objects; you declare these types using the Type keyword.

Arrays

Object Pascal enables you to create arrays of any type of variable (except files). For example, a variable declared as an array of eight integers reads like this:

```
var
  A: Array[0..7] of Integer;
```

This statement is equivalent to the following C declaration:

```
int A[8];
```

It's also equivalent to this Visual Basic statement:

```
Dim A(8) as Integer
```

Object Pascal arrays have a special property that differentiates them from other languages: They don't have to begin at a certain number. You can therefore declare a three-element array that starts at 28, as in the following example:

```
var
  A: Array[28..30] of Integer;
```

Because Object Pascal arrays aren't guaranteed to begin at 0 or 1, you must use some care when iterating over array elements in a for loop. The compiler provides built-in functions called High() and Low(), which return the lower and upper bounds of an array variable or type, respectively. Your code will be less error prone and easier to maintain if you use these functions to control your for loop, as shown here:

```
var
  A: array[28..30] of Integer;
  i: Integer;
begin
  for i := Low(A) to High(A) do  // don't hard-code for loop!
    A[i] := i;
end;
```

> **TIP**
>
> Always begin character arrays at 0. Zero-based character arrays can be passed to functions that require PChar-type variables. This is a special-case allowance that the compiler provides.

To specify multiple dimensions, use a comma-delimited list of bounds:

```
var
  // Two-dimensional array of Integer:
  A: array[1..2, 1..2] of Integer;
```

To access a multidimensional array, use commas to separate each dimension within one set of brackets:

```
I := A[1, 2];
```

Dynamic Arrays

Dynamic arrays are dynamically allocated arrays in which the dimensions aren't known at compile time. To declare a dynamic array, just declare an array without including the dimensions, like this:

```
var
  // dynamic array of string:
  SA: array of string;
```

Before you can use a dynamic array, you must use the SetLength() procedure to allocate memory for the array:

```
begin
  // allocate room for 33 elements:
  SetLength(SA, 33);
```

Once memory has been allocated, you can access the elements of the dynamic array just like a normal array:

```
SA[0] := 'Pooh likes hunny';
OtherString := SA[0];
```

> **NOTE**
>
> Dynamic arrays are always zero-based.

Dynamic arrays are lifetime managed, so there's no need to free them when you're through using them because they'll be released when they leave scope. However, there might come a time when you want remove the dynamic array from memory before it leaves scope (if it uses a lot of memory, for example) To do this, you need only assign the dynamic array to nil:

```
SA := nil;  // releases SA
```

Dynamic arrays are manipulated using reference semantics similar to AnsiString types rather than value semantics like a normal array. A quick test: What is the value of A1[0] at the end of the following code fragment?

```
var
  A1, A2: array of Integer;
```

```
begin
  SetLength(A1, 4);
  A2 := A1;
  A1[0] := 1;
  A2[0] := 26;
```

The correct answer is 26. The reason is because the assignment A2 := A1 doesn't create a new array but instead provides A2 with a reference to the same array as A1. Therefore, any modifications to A2 will also affect A1. If you want instead to make a complete copy of A1 in A2, use the Copy() standard procedure:

```
A2 := Copy(A1);
```

After this line of code is executed, A2 and A1 will be two separate arrays initially containing the same data. Changes to one will not affect the other. You can optionally specify the starting element and number of elements to be copied as parameters to Copy(), as shown here:

```
// copy 2 elements, starting at element one:
A2 := Copy(A1, 1, 2);
```

Dynamic arrays can also be multidimensional. To specify multiple dimensions, add an additional array of to the declaration for each dimension:

```
var
  // two-dimensional dynamic array of Integer:
  IA: array of array of Integer;
```

To allocate memory for a multidimensional dynamic array, pass the sizes of the other dimensions as additional parameters to SetLength():

```
begin
  // IA will be a 5 x 5 array of Integer
  SetLength(IA, 5,  5);
```

You access multidimensional dynamic arrays the same way you do normal multidimensional arrays; each element is separated by a comma with a single set of brackets:

```
IA[0,3] := 28;
```

Records

A user-defined structure is referred to as a record in Object Pascal, and it's the equivalent of C's struct or Visual Basic's Type. As an example, here's a record definition in Pascal as well as equivalent definitions in C and Visual Basic:

```
{ Pascal }
Type
  MyRec = record
    i: Integer;
```

```
    d: Double;
  end;
/* C */
typedef struct {
  int i;
  double d;
} MyRec;

'Visual Basic
Type MyRec
  i As Integer
  d As Double
End Type
```

When working with a record, you use the dot symbol to access its fields. Here's an example:

```
var
  N: MyRec;
begin
  N.i := 23;
  N.d := 3.4;
end;
```

Object Pascal also supports *variant records*, which allow different pieces of data to overlay the same portion of memory in the record. Not to be confused with the Variant data type, variant records allow each overlapping data field to be accessed independently. If your background is C, you'll recognize variant records as being the same concept as a union within C struct. The following code shows a variant record in which a Double, Integer, and char all occupy the same memory space:

```
type
  TVariantRecord = record
    NullStrField: PChar;
    IntField: Integer;
    case Integer of
      0: (D: Double);
      1: (I: Integer);
      2: (C: char);
  end;
```

NOTE

The rules of Object Pascal state that the variant portion of a record cannot be of any lifetime-managed type.

Here's the C equivalent of the preceding type declaration:

```
struct TUnionStruct
{
  char * StrField;
  int IntField;
  union u
  {
    double D;
    int i;
    char c;
  };
};
```

Sets

Sets are a uniquely Pascal type that have no equivalent in Visual Basic, C, or C++ (although Borland C++Builder does implement a template class called `Set`, which emulates the behavior of a Pascal set). Sets provide a very efficient means of representing a collection of ordinal, character, or enumerated values. You can declare a new set type using the keywords `set of` followed by an ordinal type or subrange of possible set values. Here's an example:

```
type
  TCharSet = set of char;        // possible members: #0 - #255

  TEnum = (Monday, Tuesday, Wednesday, Thursday, Friday);
  TEnumSet = set of TEnum;  // can contain any combination of TEnum members

  TSubrangeSet = set of 1..10; // possible members: 1 - 10
  TAlphaSet = set of 'A'..'z'; // possible members: 'A' - 'z'
```

Note that a set can only contain up to 256 elements. Additionally, only ordinal types can follow the `set of` keywords. Therefore, the following declarations are illegal:

```
type
  TIntSet = set of Integer;  // Invalid: too many elements
  TStrSet = set of string;   // Invalid: not an ordinal type
```

Sets store their elements internally as individual bits, which makes them very efficient in terms of speed and memory usage. Sets with fewer than 32 elements in the base type can be stored and operated upon in CPU registers, for even greater efficiency. Sets with 32 or more elements (such as a set of char–255 elements) are stored in memory. To get the maximum performance benefit from sets, keep the number of elements in the set's base type under 32.

Using Sets

Use square brackets when referencing set elements. The following code demonstrates how to declare set type variables and assign them values:

```
type
  TCharSet = set of char;        // possible members: #0 - #255

  TEnum = (Monday, Tuesday, Wednesday, Thursday, Friday, Saturday, Sunday);
  TEnumSet = set of TEnum;  // can contain any combination of TEnum members

var
  CharSet: TCharSet;
  EnumSet: TEnumSet;
  SubrangeSet: set of 1..10; // possible members: 1 - 10
  AlphaSet: set of 'A'..'z'; // possible members: 'A' - 'z'

begin
  CharSet := ['A'..'J', 'a', 'm'];
  EnumSet := [Saturday, Sunday];
  SubrangeSet := [1, 2, 4..6];
  AlphaSet := [];  // Empty; no elements
end;
```

Set Operators

Object Pascal provides several operators for use in manipulating sets. You can use these operators to determine set membership, union, difference, and intersection.

Membership

Use the in operator to determine whether a given element is contained in a particular set. For example, the following code would be used to determine whether the CharSet set mentioned earlier contains the letter 'S':

```
if 'S' in CharSet then
  // do something;
```

The following code determines whether EnumSet lacks the member Monday:

```
if not (Monday in EnumSet) then
  // do something;
```

Union and Difference

Use the + and - operators or the Include() and Exclude() procedures to add and remove elements to and from a set variable:

```
Include(CharSet, 'a');           // add 'a' to set
CharSet := CharSet + ['b'];      // add 'b' to set
Exclude(CharSet, 'x');           // remove 'z' from set
CharSet := CharSet - ['y', 'z']; // remove 'y' and 'z' from set
```

TIP

When possible, use Include() and Exclude() to add and remove a single element to and from a set rather than the + and - operators. Both Include() and Exclude() constitute only one machine instruction each, whereas the + and - operators require 13 + 6n (where n is the size in bits of the set) instructions.

Intersection

Use the * operator to calculate the intersection of two sets. The result of the expression Set1 * Set2 is a set containing all the members that Set1 and Set2 have in common. For example, the following code could be used as an efficient means for determining whether a given set contains multiple elements:

```
if ['a', 'b', 'c'] * CharSet = ['a', 'b', 'c'] then
  // do something
```

Objects

Think of objects as records that also contain functions and procedures. Delphi's object model is discussed in much greater detail later in the "Using Delphi Objects" section of this chapter, so this section covers just the basic syntax of Object Pascal objects. An object is defined as follows:

```
Type
  TChildObject = class(TParentObject);
    SomeVar: Integer;
    procedure SomeProc;
  end;
```

Although Delphi objects aren't identical to C++ objects, this declaration is roughly equivalent to the following C++ declaration:

```
class TChildObject : public TParentObject
{
  int SomeVar;
  void SomeProc();
};
```

Methods are defined in the same way as normal procedures and functions (which are discussed in the section "Procedures and Functions"), with the addition of the object name and the dot symbol operator:

```
procedure TChildObject.SomeProc;
begin
  { procedure code goes here }
end;
```

Object Pascal's . symbol is similar in functionality to Visual Basic's . operator and C++'s : : operator. You should note that, although all three languages allow usage of classes, only Object Pascal and C++ allow the creation of new classes that behave in a fully object-oriented manner, which we'll describe in the section "Object-Oriented Programming."

> **NOTE**
>
> Object Pascal objects aren't laid out in memory the same as C++ objects, so it's not possible to use C++ objects directly from Delphi (and vice versa). If you are interested in learning more about how this is done, you might want to browse Chapter 13, "Hard-core Techniques," in the electronic version of *Delphi 5 Developer's Guide* on the CD accompanying this book. That chapter shows a technique for sharing objects between C++ and Delphi.
>
> An exception to this is Borland C++Builder's capability of creating classes that map directly to Object Pascal classes using the proprietary `__declspec(delphiclass)` directive. Such objects are likewise incompatible with regular C++ objects.

Pointers

A *pointer* is a variable that contains a memory location. You already saw an example of a pointer in the PChar type earlier in this chapter. Pascal's generic pointer type is called, aptly, Pointer. A Pointer is sometimes called an untyped pointer because it contains only a memory address, and the compiler doesn't maintain any information on the data to which it points. That notion, however, goes against the grain of Pascal's typesafe nature, so pointers in your code will usually be typed pointers.

> **NOTE**
>
> Pointers are a somewhat advanced topic, and you definitely don't need to master them to write a Delphi application. As you become more experienced, pointers will become another valuable tool for your programmer's toolbox.

Typed pointers are declared by using the ^ (or *pointer*) operator in the Type section of your program. Typed pointers help the compiler keep track of exactly what kind of type a particular pointer points to, thus enabling the compiler to keep track of what you're doing (and can do) with a pointer variable. Here are some typical declarations for pointers:

```
Type
  PInt = ^Integer;        // PInt is now a pointer to an Integer
```

```
Foo = record            // A record type
  GobbledyGook: string;
  Snarf: Real;
end;
PFoo = ^Foo;            // PFoo is a pointer to a foo type
var
  P: Pointer;           // Untyped pointer
  P2: PFoo;             // Instance of PFoo
```

> **NOTE**
>
> C programmers will notice the similarity between Object Pascal's ^ operator and C's * operator. Pascal's `Pointer` type corresponds to C's `void *` type.

Remember that a pointer variable only stores a memory address. Allocating space for whatever the pointer points to is your job as a programmer. You can allocate space for a pointer by using one of the memory-allocation routines discussed earlier and shown in Table 2.6.

> **NOTE**
>
> When a pointer doesn't point to anything (its value is zero), its value is said to be `nil`, and it is often called a *nil* or *null* pointer.

If you want to access the data that a particular pointer points to, follow the pointer variable name with the ^ operator. This method is known as *dereferencing* the pointer. The following code illustrates working with pointers:

```
Program PtrTest;

Type
  MyRec = record
    I: Integer;
    S: string;
    R: Real;
  end;
  PMyRec = ^MyRec;

var
  Rec : PMyRec;
begin
  New(Rec);      // allocate memory for Rec
  Rec^.I := 10;  // Put stuff in Rec. Note the dereference
  Rec^.S := 'And now for something completely different.';
```

```
  Rec^.R := 6.384;
  { Rec is now full }
  Dispose(Rec);  // Don't forget to free memory!
end.
```

When to Use New()

Use the New() function to allocate memory for a pointer to a structure of a known size. Because the compiler knows how big a particular structure is, a call to New() will cause the correct number of bytes to be allocated, thus making it safer and more convenient to use than GetMem() or AllocMem(). Never allocate Pointer or PChar variables by using the New() function because the compiler cannot guess how many bytes you need for this allocation. Remember to use Dispose() to free any memory you allocate using the New() function.

You'll typically use GetMem() or AllocMem() to allocate memory for structures for which the compiler cannot know the size. The compiler cannot tell ahead of time how much memory you want to allocate for PChar or Pointer types, for example, because of their variable-length nature. Be careful not to try to manipulate more data than you have allocated with these functions, however, because this is one of the classic causes of an Access Violation error. You should use FreeMem() to clean up any memory you allocate with GetMem() or AllocMem(). AllocMem(), by the way, is a bit safer than GetMem() because AllocMem() always initializes the memory it allocates to zero.

2

THE OBJECT
PASCAL
LANGUAGE

One aspect of Object Pascal that might give C programmers some headaches is the strict type checking performed on pointer types. For example, the variables a and b in the following example aren't type compatible:

```
var
  a: ^Integer;
  b: ^Integer;
```

By contrast, the variables a and b in the equivalent declaration in C are type compatible:

```
int *a;
int *b
```

Object Pascal creates a unique type for each pointer-to-type declaration, so you must create a named type if you want to assign values from a to b, as shown here:

```
type
  PtrInteger = ^Integer;  // create named type

var
  a, b: PtrInteger;       // now a and b are compatible
```

Type Aliases

Object Pascal has the capability to create new names, or *aliases*, for types that are already defined. For example, if you want to create a new name for an Integer called MyReallyNiftyInteger, you could do so using the following code:

```
type
  MyReallyNiftyInteger = Integer;
```

The newly defined type alias is compatible in all ways with the type for which it's an alias, meaning, in this case, that you could use MyReallyNiftyInteger anywhere in which you could use Integer.

It's possible, however, to define *strongly typed* aliases that are considered new, unique types by the compiler. To do this, use the type reserved word in the following manner:

```
type
  MyOtherNeatInteger = type Integer;
```

Using this syntax, the MyOtherNeatInteger type will be converted to an Integer when necessary for purposes of assignment, but MyOtherNeatInteger will not be compatible with Integer when used in var and out parameters. Therefore, the following code is syntactically correct:

```
var
  MONI: MyOtherNeatInteger;
  I: Integer;
begin
  I :=  1;
  MONI := I;
```

On the other hand, the following code will not compile:

```
procedure Goon(var Value: Integer);
begin
  // some code
end;

var
  M: MyOtherNeatInteger;
begin
  M := 29;
  Goon(M);  // Error: M is not var compatible with Integer
```

In addition to these compiler-enforced type compatibility issues, the compiler also generates runtime type information for strongly typed aliases. This enables you to create unique property editors for simple types, as you'll learn in Chapter 12, "Advanced VCL Component Building."

Typecasting and Type Conversion

Typecasting is a technique by which you can force the compiler to view a variable of one type as another type. Because of Pascal's strongly typed nature, you'll find that the compiler is very picky about types matching up in the formal and actual parameters of a function call. Hence, you occasionally will be required to cast a variable of one type to a variable of another type to make the compiler happy. Suppose, for example, that you need to assign the value of a character to a byte variable:

```
var
  c: char;
  b: byte;
begin
  c := 's';
  b := c;    // compiler complains on this line
end.
```

In the following syntax, a typecast is required to convert c into a byte. In effect, a typecast tells the compiler that you really know what you're doing and want to convert one type to another:

```
var
  c: char;
  b: byte;
begin
  c := 's';
  b := byte(c);    // compiler happy as a clam on this line
end.
```

> **NOTE**
>
> You can typecast a variable of one type to another type only if the data size of the two variables is the same. For example, you cannot typecast a Double as an Integer. To convert a floating-point type to an integer, use the Trunc() or Round() functions. To convert an integer into a floating-point value, use the assignment operator:
> FloatVar := IntVar.

Object Pascal also supports a special variety of typecasting between objects using the as operator, which is described later in the "Runtime Type Information" section of this chapter.

String Resources

Delphi 3 introduced the capability to place string resources directly into Object Pascal source code using the `resourcestring` clause. *String resources* are literal strings (usually those displayed to the user) that are physically located in a resource attached to the application or library rather than embedded in the source code. Your source code references the string resources in place of string literals. By separating strings from source code, your application can be translated more easily by added string resources in a different language. String resources are declared in the form of *identifier = string literal* in the `resourcestring` clause, as shown here:

```
resourcestring
  ResString1 = 'Resource string 1';
  ResString2 = 'Resource string 2';
  ResString3 = 'Resource string 3';
```

Syntactically, resource strings can be used in your source code in a manner identical to string constants:

```
resourcestring
  ResString1 = 'hello';
  ResString2 = 'world';

var
  String1: string;

begin
  String1 := ResString1 + ' ' + ResString2;
  .
  .
  .
end;
```

Testing Conditions

This section compares `if` and `case` constructs in Pascal to similar constructs in C and Visual Basic. We assume that you've used these types of programmatic constructs before, so we don't spend time explaining them to you.

The `if` Statement

An `if` statement enables you to determine whether certain conditions are met before executing a particular block of code. As an example, here's an `if` statement in Pascal, followed by equivalent definitions in C and Visual Basic:

```
{ Pascal }
if x = 4 then y := x;

/* C */
if (x == 4) y = x;

'Visual Basic
If x = 4 Then y = x
```

> **NOTE**
>
> If you have an `if` statement that makes multiple comparisons, make sure that you enclose each set of comparisons in parentheses for code clarity. Do this:
>
> ```
> if (x = 7) and (y = 8) then
> ```
>
> However, don't do this (it causes the compiler displeasure):
>
> ```
> if x = 7 and y = 8 then
> ```

Use the `begin` and `end` keywords in Pascal almost as you would use { and } in C and C++. For example, use the following construct if you want to execute multiple lines of text when a given condition is true:

```
if x = 6 then begin
  DoSomething;
  DoSomethingElse;
  DoAnotherThing;
end;
```

You can combine multiple conditions using the `if..else` construct:

```
if x =100 then
  SomeFunction
else if x = 200 then
  SomeOtherFunction
else begin
  SomethingElse;
  Entirely;
end;
```

Using case Statements

The `case` statement in Pascal works in much the same way as a `switch` statement in C and C++. A `case` statement provides a means for choosing one condition among many possibilities without a huge `if..else if..else if` construct. Here's an example of Pascal's `case` statement:

```
case SomeIntegerVariable of
  101 : DoSomething;
```

```
    202 : begin
        DoSomething;
        DoSomethingElse;
      end;
    303 : DoAnotherThing;
    else DoTheDefault;
end;
```

NOTE

The selector type of a `case` statement must be an ordinal type. It's illegal to use nonordinal types, such as strings, as `case` selectors.

Here's the C `switch` statement equivalent to the preceding example:

```
switch (SomeIntegerVariable)
{
  case 101: DoSomeThing(); break;
  case 202: DoSomething();
            DoSomethingElse(); break
  case 303: DoAnotherThing(); break;
  default: DoTheDefault();
}
```

Loops

A *loop* is a construct that enables you to repeatedly perform some type of action. Pascal's loop constructs are very similar to what you should be familiar with from your experience with other languages, so we don't spend any time teaching you about loops. This section describes the various loop constructs you can use in Pascal.

The for Loop

A `for` loop is ideal when you need to repeat an action a predetermined number of times. Here's an example, albeit not a very useful one, of a `for` loop that adds the loop index to a variable 10 times:

```
var
  I, X: Integer;
begin
  X := 0;
  for I := 1 to 10 do
    inc(X, I);
end.
```

The C equivalent of the preceding example is as follows:

```c
void main(void) {
  int x, i;
  x = 0;
  for(i=1; i<=10; i++)
    x += i;
}
```

Here's the Visual Basic equivalent of the same concept:

```
X = 0
For I = 1 to 10
  X = X + I
Next I
```

> **CAUTION**
>
> A caveat to those familiar with Delphi 1: Assignments to the loop control variable are no longer allowed due to the way the loop is optimized and managed by the 32-bit compiler.

The while Loop

Use a while loop construct when you want some part of your code to repeat itself while some condition is true. A while loop's conditions are tested before the loop is executed, and a classic example for the use of a while loop is to repeatedly perform some action on a file as long as the end of the file isn't encountered. Here's an example demonstrating a loop that reads one line at a time from a file and writes it to the screen:

```pascal
Program FileIt;

{$APPTYPE CONSOLE}

var
  f: TextFile;  // a text file
  s: string;
begin
  AssignFile(f, 'foo.txt');
  Reset(f);
  while not EOF(f) do begin
    readln(f, S);
    writeln(S);
  end;
  CloseFile(f);
end.
```

Pascal's while loop works basically the same as C's while loop or Visual Basic's Do While loop.

repeat..until

The repeat..until loop addresses the same type of problem as a while loop but from a different angle. It repeats a given block of code until a certain condition becomes True. Unlike a while loop, the loop code is always executed at least once because the condition is tested at the end of the loop. Pascal's repeat..until is roughly equivalent to C's do..while loop.

For example, the following code snippet repeats a statement that increments a counter until the value of the counter becomes greater than 100:

```
var
  x: Integer;
begin
  X := 1;
  repeat
    inc(x);
  until x > 100;
end.
```

The Break() Procedure

Calling Break() from inside a while, for, or repeat loop causes the flow of your program to skip immediately to the end of the currently executing loop. This method is useful when you need to leave the loop immediately because of some circumstance that might arise within the loop. Pascal's Break() procedure is analogous to C's break and Visual Basic's Exit statement. The following loop uses Break() to terminate the loop after five iterations:

```
var
  i: Integer;
begin
  for i := 1 to 1000000 do
  begin
    MessageBeep(0);          // make the computer beep
    if i = 5 then Break;
  end;
end;
```

The Continue() Procedure

Call Continue() inside a loop when you want to skip over a portion of code and the flow of control to continue with the next iteration of the loop. Note in the following example that the code after Continue() isn't executed in the first iteration of the loop:

```
var
  i: Integer;
begin
  for i := 1 to 3 do
  begin
    writeln(i, '. Before continue');
    if i = 1 then Continue;
    writeln(i, '. After continue');
  end;
end;
```

Procedures and Functions

As a programmer, you should already be familiar with the basics of procedures and functions. A *procedure* is a discrete program part that performs some particular task when it's called and then returns to the calling part of your code. A function works the same except that a function returns a value after its exit to the calling part of the program.

If you're familiar with C or C++, consider that a Pascal procedure is equivalent to a C or C++ function that returns void, whereas a function corresponds to a C or C++ function that has a return value.

Listing 2.1 demonstrates a short Pascal program with a procedure and a function.

LISTING 2.1   An Example of Functions and Procedures

```
Program FuncProc;

{$APPTYPE CONSOLE}

procedure BiggerThanTen(i: Integer);
{ writes something to the screen if I is greater than 10 }
begin
  if I > 10 then
    writeln('Funky.');
end;

function IsPositive(I: Integer): Boolean;
{ Returns True if I is 0 or positive, False if I is negative }
begin
  if I < 0 then
    Result := False
  else
    Result := True;
end;
```

LISTING 2.1 Continued

```
var
  Num: Integer;
begin
  Num := 23;
  BiggerThanTen(Num);
  if IsPositive(Num) then
    writeln(Num, 'Is positive.')
  else
    writeln(Num, 'Is negative.');
end.
```

NOTE

The local variable `Result` in the `IsPositive()` function deserves special attention. Every Object Pascal function has an implicit local variable called `Result` that contains the return value of the function. Note that unlike C and C++, the function doesn't terminate as soon as a value is assigned to `Result`.

You also can return a value from a function by assigning the name of a function to a value inside the function's code. This is standard Pascal syntax and a holdover from previous versions of Borland Pascal. If you choose to use the function name within the body, be careful to note that there is a huge difference between using the function name on the left side of an assignment operator and using it somewhere else in your code. If on the left, you are assigning the function return value. If somewhere else in your code, you are calling the function recursively!

Note that the implicit `Result` variable isn't allowed when the compiler's Extended Syntax option is disabled in the Project, Options, Compiler dialog box or when you're using the `{$X-}` directive.

Passing Parameters

Pascal enables you to pass parameters by value or by reference to functions and procedures. The parameters you pass can be of any base or user-defined type or an open array (open arrays are discussed later in this chapter). Parameters also can be constant if their values will not change in the procedure or function.

Value Parameters

Value parameters are the default mode of parameter passing. When a parameter is passed by value, it means that a local copy of that variable is created, and the function or procedure operates on the copy. Consider the following example:

```
procedure Foo(s: string);
```

When you call a procedure in this way, a copy of string s will be made, and Foo() will operate on the local copy of s. This means that you can choose the value of s without having any effect on the variable passed into Foo().

Reference Parameters

Pascal enables you to pass variables to functions and procedures by reference; parameters passed by reference are also called *variable parameters*. Passing by reference means that the function or procedure receiving the variable can modify the value of that variable. To pass a variable by reference, use the keyword var in the procedure's or function's parameter list:

```
procedure ChangeMe(var x: longint);
begin
  x := 2;  { x is now changed in the calling procedure }
end;
```

Instead of making a copy of x, the var keyword causes the address of the parameter to be copied so that its value can be directly modified.

Using var parameters is equivalent to passing variables by reference in C++ using the & operator. Like C++'s & operator, the var keyword causes the address of the variable to be passed to the function or procedure rather than the value of the variable.

Constant Parameters

If you don't want the value of a parameter passed into a function to change, you can declare it with the const keyword. The const keyword not only prevents you from modifying the value of the parameters, but it also generates more optimal code for strings and records passed into the procedure or function. Here's an example of a procedure declaration that receives a constant string parameter:

```
procedure Goon(const s: string);
```

Open Array Parameters

Open array parameters provide you with the capability for passing a variable number of arguments to functions and procedures. You can either pass open arrays of some homogenous type or constant arrays of differing types. The following code declares a function that accepts an open array of integers:

```
function AddEmUp(A: array of Integer): Integer;
```

You can pass variables, constants, or constant expressions to open array functions and procedures. The following code demonstrates this by calling AddEmUp() and passing a variety of different elements:

```
var
  i, Rez: Integer;
const
```

```
  j = 23;
begin
  i := 8;
  Rez := AddEmUp([i, 50, j, 89]);
```

In order to work with an open array inside the function or procedure, you can use the `High()`, `Low()`, and `SizeOf()` functions in order to obtain information about the array. To illustrate this, the following code shows an implementation of the `AddEmUp()` function that returns the sum of all the numbers passed in `A`:

```
function AddEmUp(A: array of Integer): Integer;
var
  i: Integer;
begin
  Result := 0;
  for i := Low(A) to High(A) do
    inc(Result, A[i]);
end;
```

Object Pascal also supports an `array of const`, which allows you to pass heterogeneous data types in an array to a function or procedure. The syntax for defining a function or procedure that accepts an `array of const` is as follows:

```
procedure WhatHaveIGot(A: array of const);
```

You could call the preceding function with the following syntax:

```
WhatHaveIGot(['Tabasco', 90, 5.6, @WhatHaveIGot, 3.14159, True, 's']);
```

The compiler implicitly converts all parameters to type `TVarRec` when they are passed to the function or procedure accepting the `array of const`. `TVarRec` is defined in the `System` unit as follows:

```
type
PVarRec = ^TVarRec;
  TVarRec = record
    case Byte of
      vtInteger:    (VInteger: Integer; VType:  Byte);
      vtBoolean:    (VBoolean: Boolean);
      vtChar:       (VChar: Char);
      vtExtended:   (VExtended: PExtended);
      vtString:     (VString: PShortString);
      vtPointer:    (VPointer: Pointer);
      vtPChar:      (VPChar: PChar);
      vtObject:     (VObject: TObject);
      vtClass:      (VClass: TClass);
      vtWideChar:   (VWideChar: WideChar);
```

```
       vtPWideChar:  (VPWideChar: PWideChar);
       vtAnsiString: (VAnsiString: Pointer);
       vtCurrency:   (VCurrency: PCurrency);
       vtVariant:    (VVariant: PVariant);
       vtInterface:  (VInterface: Pointer);
       vtWideString: (VWideString: Pointer);
       vtInt64:      (VInt64: PInt64);
  end;
```

The VType field indicates what type of data the TVarRec contains. This field can have any one of the following values:

```
const
  { TVarRec.VType values }
  vtInteger    = 0;
  vtBoolean    = 1;
  vtChar       = 2;
  vtExtended   = 3;
  vtString     = 4;
  vtPointer    = 5;
  vtPChar      = 6;
  vtObject     = 7;
  vtClass      = 8;
  vtWideChar   = 9;
  vtPWideChar  = 10;
  vtAnsiString = 11;
  vtCurrency   = 12;
  vtVariant    = 13;
  vtInterface  = 14;
  vtWideString = 15;
  vtInt64      = 16;
```

As you might guess, because array of const in the code allows you to pass parameters regardless of their type, they can be difficult to work with on the receiving end. As an example of how to work with array of const, the following implementation for WhatHaveIGot() iterates through the array and shows a message to the user indicating what type of data was passed in which index:

```
procedure WhatHaveIGot(A: array of const);
var
  i: Integer;
  TypeStr: string;
begin
  for i := Low(A) to High(A) do
  begin
    case A[i].VType of
```

```
      vtInteger    : TypeStr := 'Integer';
      vtBoolean    : TypeStr := 'Boolean';
      vtChar       : TypeStr := 'Char';
      vtExtended   : TypeStr := 'Extended';
      vtString     : TypeStr := 'String';
      vtPointer    : TypeStr := 'Pointer';
      vtPChar      : TypeStr := 'PChar';
      vtObject     : TypeStr := 'Object';
      vtClass      : TypeStr :=  'Class';
      vtWideChar   : TypeStr := 'WideChar';
      vtPWideChar  : TypeStr := 'PWideChar';
      vtAnsiString : TypeStr := 'AnsiString';
      vtCurrency   : TypeStr := 'Currency';
      vtVariant    : TypeStr := 'Variant';
      vtInterface  : TypeStr := 'Interface';
      vtWideString : TypeStr := 'WideString';
      vtInt64      : TypeStr := 'Int64';
    end;
    ShowMessage(Format('Array item %d is a %s', [i, TypeStr]));
  end;
end;
```

Scope

Scope refers to some part of your program in which a given function or variable is known to the compiler. A global constant is in scope at all points in your program, for example, whereas a variable local to some procedure only has scope within that procedure. Consider Listing 2.2.

LISTING 2.2   An Illustration of Scope

```
program Foo;

{$APPTYPE CONSOLE}

const
  SomeConstant = 100;

var
  SomeGlobal: Integer;
  R: Real;

procedure SomeProc(var R: Real);
var
  LocalReal: Real;
begin
```

LISTING 2.2   Continued

```
  LocalReal := 10.0;
  R := R - LocalReal;
end;

begin
  SomeGlobal := SomeConstant;
  R := 4.593;
  SomeProc(R);
end.
```

`SomeConstant`, `SomeGlobal`, and `R` have global scope—their values are known to the compiler at all points within the program. Procedure `SomeProc()` has two variables in which the scope is local to that procedure: `R` and `LocalReal`. If you try to access `LocalReal` outside of `SomeProc()`, the compiler displays an unknown identifier error. If you access `R` within `SomeProc()`, you'll be referring to the local version, but if you access `R` outside that procedure, you'll be referring to the global version.

Units

Units are the individual source code modules that make up a Pascal program. A unit is a place for you to group functions and procedures that can be called from your main program. To be a unit, a source module must consist of at least three parts:

- A `unit` statement—Every unit must have as its first line a statement saying that it's a unit and identifying the unit name. The name of the unit must always match the file-name. For example, if you have a file named `FooBar`, the statement would be

  `unit FooBar;`

- The `interface` part—After the `unit` statement, a unit's next functional line of code should be the `interface` statement. Everything following this statement, up to the `implementation` statement, is information that can be shared with your program and with other units. The `interface` part of a unit is where you declare the types, constants, variables, procedures, and functions that you want to make available to your main program and to other units. Only declarations—never procedure bodies—can appear in the interface. The `interface` statement should be one word on one line:

  `interface`

- The `implementation` part—This follows the `interface` part of the unit. Although the `implementation` part of the unit contains primarily procedures and functions, it's also where you declare any types, constants, and variables that you don't want to make available outside of this unit. The `implementation` part is where you define any functions or procedures that you declared in the `interface` part. The `implementation` statement should be one word on one line:

```
implementation
```

Optionally, a unit can also include two other parts:

- An `initialization` part—This portion of the unit, which is located near the end of the file, contains any initialization code for the unit. This code will be executed before the main program begins execution, and it executes only once.

- A `finalization` part—This portion of the unit, which is located in between the `initialization` and `end.` of the unit, contains any cleanup code that executes when the program terminates. The `finalization` section was introduced to the language in Delphi 2.0. In Delphi 1.0, unit finalization was accomplished by adding a new exit procedure using the `AddExitProc()` function. If you're porting an application from Delphi 1.0, you should move your exit procedures into the finalization part of your units.

NOTE

When several units have `initialization`/`finalization` code, execution of each section proceeds in the order in which the units are encountered by the compiler (the first unit in the program's `uses` clause, then the first unit in that unit's `uses` clause, and so on). Also, it's a bad idea to write initialization and finalization code that relies on such ordering because one small change to the `uses` clause can cause some difficult-to-find bugs!

The uses Clause

The `uses` clause is where you list the units that you want to include in a particular program or unit. For example, if you have a program called `FooProg` that uses functions and types in two units, `UnitA` and `UnitB`, the proper `uses` declaration is as follows:

```
Program FooProg;

uses UnitA, UnitB;
```

Units can have two `uses` clauses: one in the `interface` section and one in the `implementation` section.

Here's code for a sample unit:

```
Unit FooBar;

interface
```

```
uses BarFoo;

  { public declarations here }

implementation

uses BarFly;

  { private declarations here }

initialization
  { unit initialization here }
finalization
  { unit clean-up here }
end.
```

Circular Unit References

Occasionally, you'll have a situation where UnitA uses UnitB and UnitB uses UnitA. This is called a *circular unit reference*. The occurrence of a circular unit reference is often an indication of a design flaw in your application; you should avoid structuring your program with a circular reference. The optimal solution is often to move a piece of data that both UnitA and UnitB need to use out to a third unit. However, as with most things, sometimes you just can't avoid the circular unit reference. In such a case, move one of the uses clauses to the implementation part of your unit and leave the other one in the interface part. This usually solves the problem.

Packages

Delphi *packages* enable you to place portions of your application into separate modules, which can be shared across multiple applications. If you already have an existing investment in Delphi 1 or 2 code, you'll appreciate that you can take advantage of packages without any changes to your existing source code.

Think of a package as a collection of units stored in a separate DLL-like module (a Borland Package Library, or *BPL file*). Your application can then link with these "packaged" units at runtime rather than compile/link time. Because the code for these units resides in the BPL file rather than in your EXE or DLL, the size of your EXE or DLL can become very small. Four types of packages are available for you to create and use:

- Runtime package—This type of package contains units required at runtime by your application. When compiled to depend on a particular runtime package, your application will not run in the absence of that package. Delphi's VCL60.BPL is an example of this type of package.

- Design package—This type of package contains elements necessary for application design such as components, property and component editors, and experts. It can be installed into Delphi's component library using the Component, Install Package menu item. Delphi's DCL*.BPL packages are examples of this type of package. This type of package is described in more detail in Chapter 11, "VCL Component Building."

- Runtime and Design package—This package serves both of the purposes listed in the first two items. Creating this type of package makes application development and distribution a bit simpler, but this type of package is less efficient because it must carry the baggage of design support even in your distributed applications.

- Neither runtime nor design package—This rare breed of package is intended to be used only by other packages and is not intended to be referenced directly by an application or used in the design environment.

Using Delphi Packages

Package-enabling your Delphi applications is easy. Simply check the Build with Runtime Packages check box in the Project, Options, Packages dialog box. The next time you build your application after selecting this option, your application will be linked dynamically to runtime packages rather than having units linked statically into your EXE or DLL. The result will be a much more svelte application (although bear in mind that you'll have to deploy the necessary packages with your application).

Package Syntax

Packages are most commonly created using the Package Editor, which you invoke by choosing the File, New, Package menu item. This editor generates a Delphi Package Source (DPK) file, which will be compiled into a package. The syntax for this DPK file is quite simple, and it uses the following format:

```
package PackageName

requires Package1, Package2, ...;

contains
  Unit1 in 'Unit1.pas',
  Unit2, in 'Unit2.pas',
  ...;

end.
```

Packages listed in the `requires` clause are required in order for this package to load. Typically, packages containing units used by units listed in the `contains` clause are listed here. Units listed in the `contains` clause will be compiled into this package. Note that units listed here must not also be listed in the `contains` clause of any of the packages listed in the `requires` clause. Note also that any units used by units in the `contains` clause will be implicitly pulled into this package (unless they're contained in a required package).

Object-Oriented Programming

Volumes have been written on the subject of *object-oriented programming (OOP)*. Often, OOP seems more like a religion than a programming methodology, spawning arguments about its merits (or lack thereof) that are passionate and spirited enough to make the Crusades look like a slight disagreement. We're not orthodox OOPists, and we're not going to get involved in the relative merits of OOP; we just want to give you the lowdown on a fundamental principle on which Delphi's Object Pascal Language is based.

OOP is a programming paradigm that uses discrete objects—containing both data and code— as application building blocks. Although the OOP paradigm doesn't necessarily lend itself to easier-to-write code, the result of using OOP traditionally has been easy-to-maintain code. Having objects' data and code together simplifies the process of hunting down bugs, fixing them with minimal effect on other objects, and improving your program one part at a time. Traditionally, an OOP language contains implementations of at least three OOP concepts:

- Encapsulation—Deals with combining related data fields and hiding the implementation details. The advantages of encapsulation include modularity and isolation of code from other code.

- Inheritance—The capability to create new objects that maintain the properties and behavior of ancestor objects. This concept enables you to create object hierarchies such as VCL—first creating generic objects and then creating more specific descendants of those objects that have more narrow functionality.

  The advantage of inheritance is the sharing of common code. Figure 2.4 presents an example of inheritance—how one root object, fruit, is the ancestor object of all fruits, including the melon. The melon is ancestor of all melons, including the watermelon. You get the picture.

- Polymorphism—Literally, *polymorphism* means "many shapes." Calls to methods of an object variable will call code appropriate to whatever instance is actually in the variable.

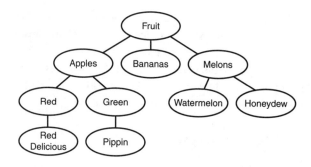

FIGURE 2.4

An illustration of inheritance.

A Note on Multiple Inheritance

Object Pascal doesn't support multiple inheritance of objects as C++ does. *Multiple inheritance* is the concept of a given object being derived from two separate objects, creating an object that contains all the code and data of the two parent objects.

To expand on the analogy presented in Figure 2.4, multiple inheritance enables you to create a candy apple object by creating a new object that inherits from the apple class and some other class called "candy." Although this functionality seems useful, it often introduces more problems and inefficiencies into your code than it solves.

Object Pascal provides two approaches to solving this problem. The first solution is to make one class *contain* the other class. You'll see this solution throughout Delphi's VCL. To build upon the candy apple analogy, you would make the candy object a member of the apple object. The second solution is to use *interfaces* (you'll learn more about interfaces in the section "Interfaces"). Using interfaces, you could essentially have one object that supports both a candy and an apple interface.

You should understand the following three terms before you continue to explore the concept of objects:

- Field—Also called *field definitions* or *instance variables*, fields are data variables contained within objects. A field in an object is just like a field in a Pascal record. In C++, fields sometimes are referred to as *data members*.

- Method—The name for procedures and functions belonging to an object. Methods are called *member functions* in C++.

- Property—An entity that acts as an accessor to the data and code contained within an object. Properties insulate the end user from the implementation details of an object.

2

THE OBJECT
PASCAL
LANGUAGE

> **NOTE**
>
> It's generally considered bad OOP style to access an object's fields directly. This is because the implementation details of the object may change. Instead, use *accessor properties*, which allow a standard object interface without becoming embroiled in the details of how the objects are implemented. Properties are explained in the "Properties" section later in this chapter.

Object-Based Versus Object-Oriented Programming

In some tools, you manipulate entities (objects), but you cannot create your own objects. VBX and ActiveX controls in older versions of Visual Basic are a good example of this. Although you could use these controls in your applications, you couldn't create one, and you couldn't inherit one ActiveX control from another. Environments such as these often are called *object-based environments*.

Delphi is a fully object-oriented environment. This means that you can create new objects in Delphi either from scratch or based on existing components. This includes all Delphi objects, be they visual, nonvisual, or even design-time forms.

Using Delphi Objects

As mentioned earlier, objects (also called *classes*) are entities that can contain both data and code. Delphi objects also provide you with all the power of object-oriented programming in offering full support of inheritance, encapsulation, and polymorphism.

Declaration and Instantiation

Of course, before using an object, you must have declared an object using the `class` keyword. As described earlier in this chapter, objects are declared in the `type` section of a unit or program:

```
type
  TFooObject = class;
```

In addition to an object type, you usually also will have a variable of that class type, or *instance*, declared in the `var` section:

```
var
  FooObject: TFooObject;
```

You create an instance of an object in Object Pascal by calling one of its *constructors*. A constructor is responsible for creating an instance of your object and allocating any memory or initializing any fields necessary so that the object is in a usable state upon exiting the constructor. Object Pascal objects always have at least one constructor called `Create()`—although it's possible for an object to have more than one constructor. Depending on the type of object, `Create()` can take different numbers of parameters. This chapter focuses on the simple case in which `Create()` takes no parameters.

Unlike C++, object constructors in Object Pascal aren't called automatically, and it's incumbent on the programmer to call the object constructor. The syntax for calling a constructor is as follows:

```
FooObject := TFooObject.Create;
```

Notice that the syntax for a constructor call is a bit unique. You're referencing the `Create()` method of the object by the type rather than the instance, as you would with other methods. This might seem odd at first, but it does make sense. `FooObject`, a variable, is undefined at the time of the call, but the code for `TFooObject`, a type, is static in memory. A static call to its `Create()` method is therefore totally valid.

The act of calling a constructor to create an instance of an object is often called *instantiation*.

NOTE

When an object instance is created using the constructor, the compiler will ensure that every field in your object is initialized. You can safely assume that all numbers will be initialized to 0, all pointers to `nil`, and all strings will be empty.

Destruction

When you're finished using an object, you should deallocate the instance by calling its `Free()` method. The `Free()` method first checks to ensure that the object instance is not `nil`; then it calls the object's *destructor* method, `Destroy()`. The destructor, of course, does the opposite of the constructor; it deallocates any allocated memory and performs any other housekeeping required in order for the object to be properly removed from memory. The syntax is simple:

```
FooObject.Free;
```

Unlike the call to `Create()`, the object instance is used in the call to the `Free()` method. Remember never to call `Destroy()` directly but instead to call the safer `Free()` method.

> **CAUTION**
>
> In C++, the destructor of an object declared statically is called automatically when your object leaves scope, but you must manually cause the destructor to be called for any dynamically allocated objects using the delete keyword. The rule is the same in Object Pascal, except that all objects are implicitly dynamic in Object Pascal, so you must follow the rule of thumb that anything you create, you must free. There are, however, a couple of important exceptions to this rule: The first is when your object is owned by other objects, it will be freed for you. The second is reference counted objects (such as those descending from TInterfacedObject or TComObject), which are destroyed when the last reference is released.

You might be asking yourself how all these methods got into your little object. You certainly didn't declare them yourself, right? Right. The methods just discussed actually come from the Object Pascal's base TObject object. In Object Pascal, all objects are always descendants of TObject regardless of whether they're declared as such. Therefore, the declaration

```
Type TFoo = Class;
```

is equivalent to the declaration

```
Type TFoo = Class(TObject);
```

Methods

Methods are procedures and functions belonging to a given object: They give an object behavior rather than just data. Two important methods of the objects you create are the constructor and the destructor methods, which we just covered. You can also create custom methods in your objects to perform a variety of tasks.

Creating a method is a two-step process. You first must declare the method in the object type declaration, and then you must define the method in the code. The following code demonstrates the process of declaring and defining a method:

```
type
  TBoogieNights = class
    Dance: Boolean;
    procedure DoTheHustle;
  end;

procedure TBoogieNights.DoTheHustle;
begin
  Dance := True;
end;
```

Note that when defining the method body, you have to use the fully qualified name, as you did when defining the DoTheHustle method. It's important also to note that the object's Dance field can be accessed directly from within the method.

Method Types

Object methods can be declared, as static, virtual, dynamic, or message. Consider the following example object:

```
TFoo = class
  procedure IAmAStatic;
  procedure IAmAVirtual; virtual;
  procedure IAmADynamic; dynamic;
  procedure IAmAMessage(var M: TMessage); message wm_SomeMessage;
end;
```

Static Methods

IAmAStatic is a static method. The *static* method is the default method type, and it works similarly to a regular procedure or function call. The compiler knows the address of these methods, so when you call a static method, it's able to link that information into the executable statically. Static methods execute the fastest; however, they don't have the capability to be overridden to provide *polymorphism*.

> **NOTE**
>
> Although Object Pascal supports static methods, it doesn't support static data members in the manner of C++ or Java. To achieve the same behavior in Object Pascal, you should use a global variable. You can place the global in the implementation part of the unit if you want it to behave as private data.

Virtual Methods

IAmAVirtual is a virtual method. *Virtual* methods are called in the same way as static methods, but because virtual methods can be overridden, the compiler doesn't know the address of a particular virtual function when you call it in your code. The compiler, therefore, builds a *Virtual Method Table (VMT)* that provides a means to look up function addresses at runtime. All virtual method calls are dispatched at runtime through the VMT. An object's VMT contains all its ancestor's virtual methods as well as the ones it declares; therefore, virtual methods use more memory than dynamic methods, although they execute faster.

Dynamic Methods

IAmADynamic is a dynamic method. *Dynamic* methods are basically virtual methods with a different dispatching system. The compiler assigns a unique number to each dynamic method and uses those numbers, along with method addresses, to build a *Dynamic Method Table (DMT)*. Unlike the VMT, an object's DMT contains only the dynamic methods that it declares, and that method relies on its ancestor's DMTs for the rest of its dynamic methods. Because of this, dynamic methods are less memory intensive than virtual methods, but they take longer to call because you might have to propagate through several ancestor DMTs before finding the address of a particular dynamic method.

Message Methods

IAmAMessage is a message-handling method. The value after the message keyword dictates what message the method will respond to. Message methods are used to create an automatic response to Windows messages, and you generally don't call them directly. Message handling is discussed in detail in Chapter 3, "Adventures in Messaging."

Overriding Methods

Overriding a method is Object Pascal's implementation of the OOP concept of polymorphism. It enables you to change the behavior of a method from descendant to descendant. Object Pascal methods can be overridden only if they're first declared as virtual or dynamic. To override a method, just use the override directive instead of virtual or dynamic in your descendant object type. For example, you could override the IAmAVirtual and IAmADynamic methods as shown here:

```
TFooChild = class(TFoo)
  procedure IAmAVirtual; override;
  procedure IAmADynamic; override;
  procedure IAmAMessage(var M: TMessage); message wm_SomeMessage;
end;
```

The override directive replaces the original method's entry in the VMT with the new method. If you had redeclared IAmAVirtual and IAmADynamic with the virtual or dynamic keyword instead of override, you would have created new methods rather than overriding the ancestor methods. Also, if you attempt to override a static method in a descendant type, the static method in the new object completely replaces the method in the ancestor type.

Method Overloading

Like regular procedures and functions, methods can be overloaded so that a class can contain multiple methods of the same name with differing parameter lists. Overloaded methods must be marked with the overload directive, although the use of the directive on the first instance of a method name in a class hierarchy is optional. The following code example shows a class containing three overloaded methods:

```
type
  TSomeClass = class
    procedure AMethod(I: Integer); overload;
```

```
    procedure AMethod(S: string); overload;
    procedure AMethod(D: Double); overload;
  end;
```

Reintroducing Method Names

Occasionally, you might want to add a method to one of your classes to replace a method of the same name in an ancestor of your class. In this case, you don't want to override the ancestor method but instead obscure and completely supplant the base class method. If you simply add the method and compile, you'll see that the compiler will produce a warning explaining that the new method hides a method of the same name in a base class. To suppress this error, use the reintroduce directive on the method in the ancestor class. The following code example demonstrates proper use of the reintroduce directive:

```
type
  TSomeBase = class
    procedure Cooper;
  end;

  TSomeClass = class
    procedure Cooper; reintroduce;
  end;
```

Self

An implicit variable called Self is available within all object methods. Self is a pointer to the class instance that was used to call the method. Self is passed by the compiler as a hidden parameter to all methods.

Properties

It might help to think of properties as special accessor fields that enable you to modify data and execute code contained within your class. For components, properties are those things that show up in the Object Inspector window when published. The following example illustrates a simplified Object with a property:

```
TMyObject = class
private
  SomeValue: Integer;
  procedure SetSomeValue(AValue: Integer);
public
  property Value: Integer read SomeValue write SetSomeValue;
end;

procedure TMyObject.SetSomeValue(AValue: Integer);
begin
```

```
  if SomeValue <> AValue then
    SomeValue := AValue;
end;
```

TMyObject is an object that contains the following: one field (an integer called SomeValue), one method (a procedure called SetSomeValue), and one property called Value. The sole purpose of the SetSomeValue procedure is to set the value of the SomeValue field. The Value property doesn't actually contain any data. Value is an accessor for the SomeValue field; when you ask Value what number it contains, it reads the value from SomeValue. When you attempt to set the value of the Value property, Value calls SetSomeValue to modify the value of SomeValue. This is useful for two reasons: First, it allows you to present the users of the class with a simple variable without making them worry about the class's implementation details. Second, you can allow the users to override accessor methods in descendant classes for polymorphic behavior.

Visibility Specifiers

Object Pascal offers you further control over the behavior of your objects by enabling you to declare fields and methods with directives such as protected, private, public, published, and automated. The syntax for using these keywords is as follows:

```
TSomeObject = class
private
  APrivateVariable: Integer;
  AnotherPrivateVariable: Boolean;
protected
  procedure AProtectedProcedure;
  function ProtectMe: Byte;
public
  constructor APublicContructor;
  destructor APublicKiller;
published
  property AProperty read APrivateVariable write APrivateVariable;
end;
```

You can place as many fields or methods as you want under each directive. Style dictates that you should indent the specifier the same as you indent the class name. The meanings of these directives follow:

- private—These parts of your object are accessible only to code in the same unit as your object's implementation. Use this directive to hide implementation details of your objects from users and to prevent users from directly modifying sensitive members of your object.

- protected—Your object's protected members can be accessed by descendants of your object. This capability enables you to hide the implementation details of your object from users while still providing maximum flexibility to descendants of your object.

- public—These fields and methods are accessible anywhere in your program. Object constructors and destructors always should be public.

- published—*Runtime Type Information (RTTI)* to be generated for the published portion of your objects enables other parts of your application to get information on your object's published parts. The Object Inspector uses RTTI to build its list of properties.

- automated—The automated specifier is obsolete but remains for compatibility with Delphi 2. Chapter 15 has more details onthis.

Here, then, is code for the TMyObject class that was introduced earlier, with directives added to improve the integrity of the object:

```
TMyObject = class
private
  SomeValue: Integer;
  procedure SetSomeValue(AValue: Integer);
published
  property Value: Integer read SomeValue write SetSomeValue;
end;

procedure TMyObject.SetSomeValue(AValue: Integer);
begin
  if SomeValue <> AValue then
    SomeValue := AValue;
end;
```

Now, users of your object will not be able to modify the value of SomeValue directly, and they will have to go through the interface provided by the property Value to modify the object's data.

"Friend" Classes

The C++ language has a concept of *friend classes* (that is, classes that are allowed access to the private data and functions in other classes). This is accomplished in C++ using the friend keyword. Although, strictly speaking, Object Pascal doesn't have a similar keyword, it does allow for similar functionality. All objects declared within the same unit are considered "friends" and are allowed access to the private information located in other objects in that unit.

Inside Objects

All class instances in Object Pascal are actually stored as 32-bit pointers to class instance data located in heap memory. When you access fields, methods, or properties within a class, the compiler automatically performs a little bit of hocus-pocus that generates the code to dereference that pointer for you. Therefore, to the untrained eye, a class appears as a static variable. What this means, however, is that unlike C++, Object Pascal offers no reasonable way to allocate a class from an application's data segment other than from the heap.

TObject: The Mother of All Objects

Because everything descends from TObject, every class has some methods that it inherits from TObject, and you can make some special assumptions about the capabilities of an object. Every class has the capability, for example, to tell you its name, its type, or even whether it's inherited from a particular class. The beauty of this is that you, as an applications programmer, don't have to care what kind of magic the compiler does to make this happen. You can just take advantage of the functionality it provides!

TObject is a special object because its definition comes from the System unit, and the Object Pascal compiler is "aware" of TObject. The following code illustrates the definition of the TObject class:

```
type
  TObject = class
    constructor Create;
    procedure Free;
    class function InitInstance(Instance: Pointer): TObject;
    procedure CleanupInstance;
    function ClassType: TClass;
    class function ClassName: ShortString;
    class function ClassNameIs(const Name: string): Boolean;
    class function ClassParent: TClass;
    class function ClassInfo: Pointer;
    class function InstanceSize: Longint;
    class function InheritsFrom(AClass: TClass): Boolean;
    class function MethodAddress(const Name: ShortString): Pointer;
    class function MethodName(Address: Pointer): ShortString;
    function FieldAddress(const Name: ShortString): Pointer;
    function GetInterface(const IID: TGUID; out Obj): Boolean;
    class function GetInterfaceEntry(const IID: TGUID): PInterfaceEntry;
    class function GetInterfaceTable: PInterfaceTable;
    function SafeCallException(ExceptObject: TObject;
      ExceptAddr: Pointer): HResult; virtual;
    procedure AfterConstruction; virtual;
    procedure BeforeDestruction; virtual;
    procedure Dispatch(var Message); virtual;
    procedure DefaultHandler(var Message); virtual;
    class function NewInstance: TObject; virtual;
    procedure FreeInstance; virtual;
    destructor Destroy; virtual;
  end;
```

You'll find each of these methods documented in Delphi's online help system.

In particular, note the methods that are preceded by the keyword `class`. Prepending the `class` keyword to a method enables it to be called like a normal procedure or function without actually having an instance of the class of which the method is a member. This is a juicy bit of functionality that was borrowed from C++'s `static` functions. Be careful, though, not to make a class method depend on any instance information; otherwise, you'll get a compiler error.

Interfaces

Perhaps the most significant addition to the Object Pascal language in the recent past is the native support for *interfaces*, which was introduced in Delphi 3. Simply put, an interface defines a set of functions and procedures that can be used to interact with an object. The definition of a given interface is known to both the implementer and the client of the interface—acting as a contract of sorts for how an interface will be defined and used. A class can implement multiple interfaces, providing multiple known "faces" by which a client can control an object.

As its name implies, an interface defines only, well, an interface by which object and clients communicate. This is similar in concept to a C++ `PURE VIRTUAL` class. It's the job of a class that supports an interface to implement each of the interface's functions and procedures.

In this chapter you'll learn about the language elements of interfaces. For information on using interfaces within your applications, see Chapter 15.

Defining Interfaces

Just as all Delphi classes implicitly descend from `TObject`, all interfaces are implicitly derived from an interface called `IUnknown`. `IUnknown`. is defined in the `System` unit as follows:

```
type
  IUnknown = interface
    ['{00000000-0000-0000-C000-000000000046}']
    function QueryInterface(const IID: TGUID; out Obj): Integer; stdcall;
    function _AddRef: Integer; stdcall;
    function _Release: Integer; stdcall;
  end;
```

As you can see, the syntax for defining an interface is very similar to that of a class. The primary difference is that an interface can optionally be associated with a *globally unique identifier (GUID)*, which is unique to the interface. The definition of `IUnknown` comes from the Component Object Model (COM) specification provided by Microsoft. This is also described in more detail in Chapter 15.

Defining a custom interface is straightforward if you understand how to create Delphi classes. The following code defines a new interface called `IFoo`, which implements one method called `F1()`:

```
type
  IFoo = interface
    ['{2137BF60-AA33-11D0-A9BF-9A4537A42701}']
    function F1: Integer;
  end;
```

TIP

The Delphi IDE will manufacture new GUIDs for your interfaces when you use the Ctrl+Shift+G key combination.

The following code defines a new interface, IBar, which descends from IFoo:

```
type
  IBar = interface(IFoo)
    ['{2137BF61-AA33-11D0-A9BF-9A4537A42701}']
    function F2: Integer;
  end;
```

Implementing Interfaces

The following bit of code demonstrates how to implement IFoo and IBar in a class called TFooBar:

```
type
  TFooBar = class(TInterfacedObject, IFoo, IBar)
    function F1: Integer;
    function F2: Integer;
  end;

function TFooBar.F1: Integer;
begin
  Result := 0;
end;

function TFooBar.F2: Integer;
begin
  Result := 0;
end;
```

Note that multiple interfaces can be listed after the ancestor class in the first line of the class declaration in order to implement multiple interfaces. The binding of an interface function to a particular function in the class happens when the compiler matches a method signature in the interface with a matching signature in the class. A compiler error will occur if a class declares that it implements an interface but the class fails to implement one or more of the interface's methods.

If a class implements multiple interfaces that have methods of the same signature, you must alias the same-named methods as shown in the following short example:

```
type
  IFoo = interface
    ['{2137BF60-AA33-11D0-A9BF-9A4537A42701}']
    function F1: Integer;
  end;

  IBar = interface
    ['{2137BF61-AA33-11D0-A9BF-9A4537A42701}']
    function F1: Integer;
  end;

  TFooBar = class(TInterfacedObject, IFoo, IBar)
    // aliased methods
    function IFoo.F1 = FooF1;
    function IBar.F1 = BarF1;
    // interface methods
    function FooF1: Integer;
    function BarF1: Integer;
  end;

function TFooBar.FooF1: Integer;
begin
  Result := 0;
end;

function TFooBar.BarF1: Integer;
begin
  Result := 0;
end;
```

The `implements` Directive

Delphi 4 introduced the `implements` directive, which enables you to delegate the implementation of interface methods to another class or interface. This technique is sometimes called *implementation by delegation*. `Implements` is used as the last directive on a property of class or interface type like this:

```
type
  TSomeClass = class(TInterfacedObject, IFoo)
    // stuff
    function GetFoo: TFoo;
    property Foo: TFoo read GetFoo implements IFoo;
    // stuff
  end;
```

The use of `implements` in the preceding code example instructs the compiler to look to the `Foo` property for the methods that implement the `IFoo` interface. The type of the property must be a class that contains `IFoo` methods or an interface of type `IFoo` or a descendant of `IFoo`. You can also provide a comma-delimited list of interfaces following the `implements` directive, in which case the type of the property must contain the methods to implement the multiple interfaces.

The `implements` directive buys you two key advantages in your development: First, it allows you to perform aggregation in a no-hassle manner. Aggregation is a COM concept pertaining to the combination of multiple classes for a single purpose (see Chapter 15 for more information on aggregation). Second, it allows you to defer the consumption of resources necessary to implement an interface until it's absolutely necessary. For example, say that there was an interface whose implementation requires allocation of a 1MB bitmap, but that interface is seldom required by clients. You probably wouldn't want to implement that interface all the time "just in case" because that would be a waste of resources. Using `implements`, you could create the class to implement the interface on demand in the property accessor method.

Using Interfaces

A few important language rules apply when you're using variables of interface types in your applications. The foremost rule to remember is that an interface is a lifetime-managed type. This means it's always initialized to `nil`, it's reference counted, a reference is automatically added when you obtain an interface, and it's automatically released when it leaves scope or is assigned the value `nil`. The following code example illustrates the lifetime management of an interface variable:

```
var
  I: ISomeInterface;
begin
  // I is initialized to nil
  I := FunctionReturningAnInterface;  // ref count of I is incremented
  I.SomeFunc;
  // ref count of I is decremented.  If 0, I is automatically released
end;
```

Another unique rule of interface variables is that an interface is assignment compatible with classes that implement the interface. For example, the following code is legal using the `TFooBar` class defined earlier:

```
procedure Test(FB: TFooBar)
var

  F: IFoo;
begin
```

```
F := FB;  // legal because FB supports IFoo
  .
  .
  .
```

Finally, the as typecast operator can be used to QueryInterface a given interface variable for another interface (this is explained in greater detail in Chapter 15). This is illustrated here:

```
var
  FB: TFooBar;
  F: IFoo;
  B: IBar;
begin
  FB := TFooBar.Create
  F := FB;  // legal because FB supports IFoo
  B := F as IBar;  // QueryInterface F for IBar
  .
  .
  .
```

If the requested interface isn't supported, an exception will be raised.

Structured Exception Handling

Structured exception handling (SEH) is a method of error handling that enables your application to recover gracefully from otherwise fatal error conditions. In Delphi 1, exceptions were implemented in the Object Pascal language, but starting in Delphi 2, exceptions are a part of the Win32 API. What makes Object Pascal exceptions easy to use is that they're just classes that happen to contain information about the location and nature of a particular error. This makes exceptions as easy to implement and use in your applications as any other class.

Delphi contains predefined exceptions for common program-error conditions, such as out of memory, divide by zero, numerical overflow and underflow, and file I/O errors. Delphi also enables you to define your own exception classes as you may see fit in your applications.

Listing 2.3 demonstrates how to use exception handling during file I/O.

LISTING 2.3 File I/O Using Exception Handling

```
Program FileIO;

uses Classes, Dialogs;

{$APPTYPE CONSOLE}

var
```

LISTING 2.3 Continued

```pascal
  F: TextFile;
  S: string;
begin
  AssignFile(F, 'FOO.TXT');
  try
    Reset(F);
    try
      ReadLn(F, S);
    finally
      CloseFile(F);
    end;
  except
    on EInOutError do
      ShowMessage('Error Accessing File!');
  end;
end.
```

In Listing 2.3, the inner `try..finally` block is used to ensure that the file is closed regardless of whether any exceptions come down the pike. What this block means in English is "Hey, program, try to execute the statements between the `try` and the `finally`. If you finish them or run into an exception, execute the statements between the `finally` and the `end`. If an exception does occur, move on to the next exception-handling block." This means that the file will be closed and the error can be properly handled no matter what error occurs.

> **NOTE**
>
> The statements after `finally` in a `try..finally` block execute regardless of whether an exception occurs. Make sure that the code in your `finally` block doesn't assume that an exception has occurred. Also, because the `finally` statement doesn't stop the migration of an exception, the flow of your program's execution will continue on to the next exception handler.

The outer `try..except` block is used to handle the exceptions as they occur in the program. After the file is closed in the `finally` block, the `except` block puts up a message informing the user that an I/O error occurred.

One of the key advantages that exception handling provides over the traditional method of error handling is the ability to distinctly separate the error-detection code from the error-correction code. This is a good thing primarily because it makes your code easier to read and maintain by enabling you to concentrate on one distinct aspect of the code at a time.

The fact that you cannot trap any specific exception by using the `try..finally` block is significant. When you use a `try..finally` block in your code, it means that you don't care what exceptions might occur. You just want to perform some tasks when they do occur to gracefully get out of a tight spot. The `finally` block is an ideal place to free any resources you've allocated (such as files or Windows resources) because it will always execute in the case of an error. In many cases, however, you need some type of error handling that's able to respond differently depending on the type of error that occurs. You can trap specific exceptions by using a `try..except` block, which is again illustrated in Listing 2.4.

LISTING 2.4   A try..except Exception-Handling Block

```
Program HandleIt;

{$APPTYPE CONSOLE}

var
  R1, R2: Double;
begin
  while True do begin
  try
    Write('Enter a real number: ');
    ReadLn(R1);
    Write('Enter another real number: ');
    ReadLn(R2);
    Writeln('I will now divide the first number by the second...');
    Writeln('The answer is: ', (R1 / R2):5:2);
  except
    On EZeroDivide do
      Writeln('You cannot divide by zero!');
    On EInOutError do
      Writeln('That is not a valid number!');
  end;
  end;
end.
```

Although you can trap specific exceptions with the `try..except` block, you also can catch other exceptions by adding the catchall `else` clause to this construct. The syntax of the `try..except..else` construct follows:

```
try
  Statements
except
  On ESomeException do Something;
else
  { do some default exception handling }
end;
```

> **CAUTION**
>
> When using the `try..except..else` construct, you should be aware that the `else` part will catch *all* exceptions—even exceptions you might not expect, such as out-of-memory or other runtime-library exceptions. Be careful when using the `else` clause, and use the clause sparingly. You should always reraise the exception when you trap with unqualified exception handlers. This is explained in the section "Reraising an Exception."

You can achieve the same effect as a `try..except..else` construct by not specifying the exception class in a `try..except` block, as shown in this example:

```
try
  Statements
except
  HandleException  // almost the same as else statement
end;
```

Exception Classes

Exceptions are merely special instances of objects. These objects are instantiated when an exception occurs and are destroyed when an exception is handled. The base exception object is called `Exception`, and that object is defined as follows:

```
type
  Exception = class(TObject)
  private
    FMessage: string;
    FHelpContext: Integer;
  public
    constructor Create(const Msg: string);
    constructor CreateFmt(const Msg: string; const Args: array of const);
    constructor CreateRes(Ident: Integer); overload;
    constructor CreateRes(ResStringRec: PResStringRec); overload;
    constructor CreateResFmt(Ident: Integer; const Args: array of const);
      overload;
    constructor CreateResFmt(ResStringRec: PResStringRec;
      const Args: array of const); overload;
    constructor CreateHelp(const Msg: string; AHelpContext: Integer);
    constructor CreateFmtHelp(const Msg: string; const Args: array of const;
      AHelpContext: Integer);
    constructor CreateResHelp(Ident: Integer; AHelpContext: Integer); overload;
    constructor CreateResHelp(ResStringRec: PResStringRec;
      AHelpContext: Integer); overload;
```

```
  constructor CreateResFmtHelp(ResStringRec: PResStringRec;
    const Args: array of const;
    AHelpContext: Integer); overload;
  constructor CreateResFmtHelp(Ident: Integer; const Args: array of const;
    AHelpContext: Integer); overload;
  property HelpContext: Integer read FHelpContext write FHelpContext;
  property Message: string read FMessage write FMessage;
end;
```

The important element of the Exception object is the Message property, which is a string. Message provides more information or explanation on the exception. The information provided by Message depends on the type of exception that's raised.

CAUTION

If you define your own exception object, make sure that you derive it from a known exception object such as Exception or one of its descendants. The reason for this is so that generic exception handlers will be able to trap your exception.

When you handle a specific type of exception in an except block, that handler also will catch any exceptions that are descendants of the specified exception. For example, EMathError is the ancestor object for a variety of math-related exceptions, such as EZeroDivide and EOverflow. You can catch any of these exceptions by setting up a handler for EMathError, as shown here:

```
try
  Statements
except
  on EMathError do  // will catch EMathError or any descendant
    HandleException
end;
```

Any exceptions that you don't explicitly handle in your program eventually will flow to, and be handled by, the default handler located within the Delphi runtime library. The default handler will put up a message dialog box informing the user that an exception occurred. Incidentally, Chapter 4, "Application Frameworks and Design Concepts," on the electronic version of *Delphi 5 Developer's Guide* found on the CD accompanying this book will show an example of how to override the default exception handling.

When handling an exception, you sometimes need to access the instance of the exception object in order to retrieve more information on the exception, such as that provided by its Message property. There are two ways to do this: Use an optional identifier with the on ESomeException construct or use the ExceptObject() function.

You can insert an optional identifier in the on `ESomeException` portion of an `except` block and have the identifier map to an instance of the currently raised exception. The syntax for this is to preface the exception type with an identifier and a colon, as follows:

```
try
  Something
except
  on E:ESomeException do
    ShowMessage(E.Message);
end;
```

The identifier (`E` in this case) becomes the instance of the currently raised exception. This identifier is always of the same type as the exception it prefaces.

You can also use the `ExceptObject()` function, which returns an instance of the currently raised exception. The drawback to `ExceptObject()`, however, is that it returns a `TObject` that you must then typecast to the exception object of your choice. The following example shows the usage of this function:

```
try
  Something
except
  on ESomeException do
    ShowMessage(ESomeException(ExceptObject).Message);
end;
```

The `ExceptObject()` function will return `nil` if there is no active exception.

The syntax for raising an exception is similar to the syntax for creating an object instance. To raise a user-defined exception called `EBadStuff`, for example, you would use this syntax:

```
Raise EBadStuff.Create('Some bad stuff happened.');
```

Flow of Execution

After an exception is raised, the flow of execution of your program propagates up to the next exception handler until the exception instance is finally handled and destroyed. This process is determined by the call stack and therefore works program-wide (not just within one procedure or unit). Listing 2.5 illustrates the flow of execution of a program when an exception is raised. This listing is the main unit of a Delphi application that consists of one form with one button on the form. When the button is clicked, the `Button1Click()` method calls `Proc1()`, which calls `Proc2()`, which in turn calls `Proc3()`. An exception is raised in `Proc3()`, and you can witness the flow of execution propagating through each `try..finally` block until the exception is finally handled inside `Button1Click()`.

> **TIP**
>
> When you run this program from the Delphi IDE, you'll be able to see the flow of execution better if you disable the integrated debugger's handling of exceptions by unchecking Tools, Debugger Options, Language Exceptions, Stop on Delphi Exceptions.

LISTING 2.5 Main Unit for the Exception Propagation Project

```
unit Main;

interface

uses
  SysUtils, Windows, Messages, Classes, Graphics, Controls, Forms, Dialogs,
  StdCtrls;

type
  TForm1 = class(TForm)
    Button1: TButton;
    procedure Button1Click(Sender: TObject);
  private
    { Private declarations }
  public
    { Public declarations }
  end;

var
  Form1: TForm1;

implementation

{$R *.DFM}

type
  EBadStuff = class(Exception);

procedure Proc3;
begin
  try
    raise EBadStuff.Create('Up the stack we go!');
  finally
    ShowMessage('Exception raised. Proc3 sees the exception');
  end;
end;
```

LISTING 2.5   Continued

```pascal
procedure Proc2;
begin
  try
    Proc3;
  finally
    ShowMessage('Proc2 sees the exception');
  end;
end;

procedure Proc1;
begin
  try
    Proc2;
  finally
    ShowMessage('Proc1 sees the exception');
  end;
end;

procedure TForm1.Button1Click(Sender: TObject);
const
  ExceptMsg = 'Exception handled in calling procedure. The message is "%s"';
begin
  ShowMessage('This method calls Proc1 which calls Proc2 which calls Proc3');
  try
    Proc1;
  except
    on E:EBadStuff do
     ShowMessage(Format(ExceptMsg, [E.Message]));
  end;
end;

end.
```

Reraising an Exception

When you need to perform special handling for a statement inside an existing try..except block and still need to allow the exception to flow to the block's outer default handler, you can use a technique called *reraising the exception*. Listing 2.6 demonstrates an example of reraising an exception.

LISTING 2.6   Reraising an Exception

```
try              // this is outer block
  { statements }
  { statements }
  ( statements )
  try            // this is the special inner block
    { some statement that may require special handling }
  except
    on ESomeException do
    begin
      { special handling for the inner block statement }
      raise;     // reraise the exception to the outer block
    end;
  end;
except
  // outer block will always perform default handling
  on ESomeException do Something;
end;
```

Runtime Type Information

Runtime Type Information (RTTI) is a language feature that gives a Delphi application the capability to retrieve information about its objects at runtime. RTTI is also the key to links between Delphi components and their incorporation into the Delphi IDE, but it isn't just an academic process that occurs in the shadows of the IDE.

Objects, by virtue of being TObject descendants, contain a pointer to their RTTI and have several built-in methods that enable you to get some useful information out of the RTTI. Table 2.7 lists some of the TObject methods that use RTTI to retrieve information about a particular object instance.

TABLE 2.7   TObject Methods that Use RTTI

Function	Return Type	Returns
ClassName()	string	The name of the object's class
ClassType()	TClass	The object's type
InheritsFrom()	Boolean	Boolean to indicate whether the class descends from a given class
ClassParent()	TClass	The object ancestor's type
InstanceSize()	word	The size, in bytes, of an instance
ClassInfo()	Pointer	A pointer to the object's in-memory RTTI

Object Pascal provides two operators, is and as, that allow comparisons and typecasts of objects via RTTI.

The as keyword is a new form of typesafe typecast. It enables you to cast a low-level object to a descendant and raises an exception if the typecast is invalid. Suppose that you have a procedure to which you want to be able to pass any type of object. This function definition could be defined as

```
Procedure Foo(AnObject: TObject);
```

If you want to do something useful with AnObject later in this procedure, you'll probably have to cast it to a descendant object. Suppose you want to assume that AnObject is a TEdit descendant, and you want to change the text it contains (a TEdit is a Delphi VCL edit control). You can use the following code:

```
(Foo as TEdit).Text := 'Hello World.';
```

You can use the Boolean comparison operator is to check whether two objects are of compatible types. Use the is operator to compare an unknown object to a known type or instance to determine what properties and behavior you can assume about the unknown object. For example, you might want to check to see whether AnObject is pointer-compatible with TEdit before attempting to typecast it:

```
If (Foo is TEdit) then
  TEdit(Foo).Text := 'Hello World.';
```

Notice that you didn't use the as operator to perform the typecast in this example. That's because a certain amount of overhead is involved in using RTTI. The first line has already determined that Foo is a TEdit, so you can optimize the code by performing a traditional typecast in the second line. A traditional typecast generally carries with it no runtime overhead.

Summary

Quite a bit of material was covered in this chapter. You learned the basic syntax and semantics of the Object Pascal language, including variables, operators, functions, procedures, types, constructs, and style. You should also have a clear understanding of OOP, objects, fields, properties, methods, TObject, interfaces, exception handling, and RTTI.

Now that you have the big picture of how Delphi's object-oriented Object Pascal language works, you're ready to move on to more advanced discussions of application frameworks and design concepts.

Adventures in Messaging

IN THIS CHAPTER

Although Visual Component Library (VCL) components expose many Win32 messages via Object Pascal events, it's still essential that you, the Win32 programmer, understand how the Windows message system works.

As a Delphi applications programmer, you'll find that the events surfaced by VCL will suit most of your needs; only occasionally will you have to delve into the world of Win32 message handling. As a Delphi component developer, however, you and messages will become very good friends because you have to directly handle many Windows messages and then invoke events corresponding to those messages.

> **NOTE**
>
> The messaging capabilities covered in this chapter are specific to the VCL and aren't supported under the CLX environment. For more on the CLX architectures, see Chapters 10, "Component Architecture: VCL and CLX," and 13, "CLX Component Development."

What Is a Message?

A *message* is a notification of some occurrence sent by Windows to an application. Clicking a mouse button, resizing a window, or pressing a key on the keyboard, for example, causes Windows to send a message to an application notifying it of what occurred.

A message manifests itself as a *record* passed to an application by Windows. That record contains information such as what type of event occurred and additional information specific to the message. The message record for a mouse button click message, for example, contains the mouse coordinates at the time the button was pressed. The record type passed from Windows to the application is called a TMsg, which is defined in the Windows unit as shown in the following code:

```
type
  TMsg = packed record
    hwnd: HWND;       // the handle of the Window for which the message
                      // is intended
    message: UINT;    // the message constant identifier
    wParam: WPARAM;   // 32 bits of additional message-specific information
    lParam: LPARAM;   // 32 bits of additional message-specific information
    time: DWORD;      // the time that the message was created
    pt: TPoint;       // Mouse cursor position when the message was created
  end;
```

What's in a Message?

Does the information in a message record look like Greek to you? If so, here's a little insight into what's what:

hwnd	The 32-bit window handle of the window for which the message is intended. The window can be almost any type of screen object because Win32 maintains window handles for most visual objects (windows, dialog boxes, buttons, edits, and so on).
message	A constant value that represents some message. These constants can be defined by Windows in the Windows unit or by you through user-defined messages.
wParam	This field often contains a constant value associated with the message; it can also contain a window handle or the identification number of some window or control associated with the message.
lParam	This field often holds an index or pointer to some data in memory. Because wParam, lParam, and Pointer are all 32 bits in size, you can typecast interchangeably between them.

Now that you have an idea what makes up a message, it's time to take a look at some different types of Windows messages.

Types of Messages

The Win32 API predefines a constant for each Windows message. These constants are the values kept in the message field of the TMsg record. All these constants are defined in Delphi's Messages unit; most are also described in the online help. Notice that each of these constants begins with the letters *WM*, which stand for *Windows Message*. Table 3.1 lists some of the common Windows messages, along with their meanings and values.

TABLE 3.1   Common Windows Messages

Message Identifier	Value	Tells a Window That. . .
wm_Activate	$0016	It's being activated or deactivated.
wm_Char	$0102	wm_KeyDown and wm_KeyUp messages have been sent for one key.
wm_Close	$0010	It should terminate.
wm_KeyDown	$0100	A keyboard key is being pressed.
wm_KeyUp	$0101	A keyboard key has been released.
wm_LButtonDown	$0201	The user is pressing the left mouse button.
wm_MouseMove	$0200	The mouse is being moved.
WM_PAINT	$000F	It must repaint its client area.
wm_Timer	$0113	A timer event has occurred.
wm_Quit	$0012	A request has been made to shut down the program.

How the Windows Message System Works

A Windows application's message system has three key components:

- Message queue—Windows maintains a message queue for each application. A Windows application must get messages from this queue and dispatch them to the proper windows.

- Message loop—This is the loop mechanism in a Windows program that fetches a message from the application queue and dispatches it to the appropriate window, fetches the next message, dispatches it to the appropriate window, and so on.

- Window procedure—Each window in your application has a window procedure that receives each of the messages passed to it by the message loop. The window procedure's job is to take each window message and respond to it accordingly. A window procedure is a callback function; a window procedure usually returns a value to Windows after processing a message.

NOTE

A *callback function* is a function in your program that's called by Windows or some other external module.

Getting a message from point A (some event occurs, creating a message) to point B (a window in your application responds to the message) is a five-step process:

1. Some event occurs in the system.
2. Windows translates this event into a message and places it into the message queue for your application.
3. Your application retrieves the message from the queue and places it in a TMsg record.
4. Your application passes on the message to the window procedure of the appropriate window in your application.
5. The window procedure performs some action in response to the message.

Steps 3 and 4 make up the application's *message loop*. The message loop is often considered the heart of a Windows program because it's the facility that enables your program to respond to external events. The message loop spends its whole life fetching messages from the application queue and passing them to the appropriate windows in your application. If there are no messages in your application's queue, Windows allows other applications to process their messages. Figure 3.1 shows these steps.

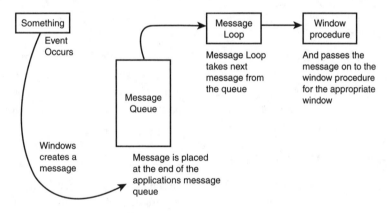

FIGURE 3.1
The Windows Message system.

Delphi's Message System

VCL handles many of the details of the Windows message system for you. The message loop is built into VCL's Forms unit, for example, so you don't have to worry about fetching

3

ADVENTURES IN
MESSAGING

messages from the queue or dispatching them to a window procedure. Delphi also places the information located in the Windows TMsg record into a generic TMessage record:

```
type
  TMessage = record
    Msg: Cardinal;
    case Integer of
      0: (
        WParam: Longint;
        LParam: Longint;
        Result: Longint);
      1: (
        WParamLo: Word;
        WParamHi: Word;
        LParamLo: Word;
        LParamHi: Word;
        ResultLo: Word;
        ResultHi: Word);
  end;
```

Notice that TMessage record has a little less information than does TMsg. That's because Delphi internalizes the other TMsg fields; TMessage contains just the essential information you need to handle a message.

It's important to note that the TMessage record also contains a Result field. As mentioned earlier, some messages require the window procedure to return some value after processing a message. With Delphi, you accomplish this process in a straightforward fashion by placing the return value in the Result field of TMessage. This process is explained in detail later in the section "Assigning Message Result Values."

Message-Specific Records

In addition to the generic TMessage record, Delphi defines a message-specific record for every Windows message. The purpose of these message-specific records is to give you all the information the message offers without having to decipher the wParam and lParam fields of a record. All the message-specific records can be found in the Messages unit. As an example, here's the message record used to hold most mouse messages:

```
type
  TWMMouse = packed record
    Msg: Cardinal;
    Keys: Longint;
    case Integer of
      0: (
        XPos: Smallint;
```

```
    YPos: Smallint);
  1: (
    Pos: TSmallPoint;
    Result: Longint);
end;
```

All the record types for specific mouse messages (WM_LBUTTONDOWN and WM_RBUTTONUP, for example) are simply defined as equal to TWMMouse, as in the following example:

```
TWMRButtonUp = TWMMouse;
TWMLButtonDown = TWMMouse;
```

> **NOTE**
>
> A message record is defined for nearly every standard Windows message. The naming convention dictates that the name of the record must be the same as the name of the message with a *T* prepended, using camel capitalization and without the underscore. For example, the name of the message record type for a WM_SETFONT message is TWMSetFont.
>
> By the way, TMessage works with all messages in all situations but isn't as convenient as message-specific records.

Handling Messages

Handling or *processing* a message means that your application responds in some manner to a Windows message. In a standard Windows application, message handling is performed in each window procedure. By internalizing the window procedure, however, Delphi makes it much easier to handle individual messages; instead of having one procedure that handles all messages, each message has its own procedure. Three requirements must be met for a procedure to be a message-handling procedure:

- The procedure must be a method of an object.
- The procedure must take one var parameter of a TMessage or other message-specific record type.
- The procedure must use the message directive followed by the constant value of the message you want to process.

Here's an example of a procedure that handles WM_PAINT messages:

```
procedure WMPaint(var Msg: TWMPaint); message WM_PAINT;
```

> **NOTE**
>
> When naming message-handling procedures, the convention is to give them the same name as the message itself, using camel capitalization and without the underscore.

As another example, let's write a simple message-handling procedure for WM_PAINT that processes the message simply by beeping.

Start by creating a new, blank project. Then access the Code Editor window for this project and add the header for the WMPaint function to the private section of the TForm1 object:

```
procedure WMPaint(var Msg: TWMPaint); message WM_PAINT;
```

Now add the function definition to the implementation part of this unit. Remember to use the dot operator to scope this procedure as a method of TForm1. Don't use the message directive as part of the function implementation:

```
procedure TForm1.WMPaint(var Msg: TWMPaint);
begin
  Beep;
  inherited;
end;
```

Notice the use of the inherited keyword here. Call inherited when you want to pass the message to the ancestor object's handler. By calling inherited in this example, you pass on the message to TForm's WM_PAINT handler.

> **NOTE**
>
> Unlike normal calls to inherited methods, here you don't give the name of the inherited method because the name of the method is unimportant when it's dispatched. Delphi knows what method to call based on the message value used with the message directive in the class interface.

The main unit in Listing 3.1 provides a simple example of a form that processes the WM_PAINT message. Creating this project is easy: Just create a new project and add the code for the WMPaint procedure to the TForm object.

LISTING 3.1 GetMess—A Message-Handling Example

```
unit GMMain;

interface

uses
  SysUtils, Windows, Messages, Classes, Graphics, Controls,
  Forms, Dialogs;

type
  TForm1 = class(TForm)
  private
    procedure WMPaint(var Msg: TWMPaint); message WM_PAINT;
  end;

var
  Form1: TForm1;

implementation

{$R *.DFM}

procedure TForm1.WMPaint(var Msg: TWMPaint);
begin
  MessageBeep(0);
  inherited;
end;

end.
```

Whenever a WM_PAINT message comes down the pike, it's passed to the WMPaint procedure. The WMPaint procedure simply informs you of the WM_PAINT message by making some noise with the MessageBeep() procedure and then passes the message to the inherited handler.

MessageBeep(): The Poor Man's Debugger

While we're on the topic of beeping, now is a good time for a slight digression. The MessageBeep() procedure is one of the most straightforward and useful elements in the Win32 API. Its use is simple: Call MessageBeep(), pass a predefined constant, and Windows beeps the PC's speaker. (If you have a sound card, it plays a WAV file.) Big

continues

3

ADVENTURES IN
MESSAGING

deal, you say? On the surface it might not seem like much, but MessageBeep() really shines as an aid in debugging your programs.

If you're looking for a quick-and-dirty way to tell whether your program is reaching a certain place in your code—without having to bother with the debugger and break-points—MessageBeep() is for you. Because it doesn't require a handle or some other Windows resource, you can use it practically anywhere in your code, and as a wise man once said, "MessageBeep() is for the itch you can't scratch with the debugger." If you have a sound card, you can pass MessageBeep() one of several predefined constants to have it play a wider variety of sounds—these constants are defined under MessageBeep() in the Win32 API help file.

If you're like the authors and are too lazy to type out that whole big, long function name and parameter, you can use the Beep() procedure found in the SysUtils unit. The implementation of Beep() is simply a call to MessageBeep() with the parameter 0.

Message Handling: Not Contract Free

Unlike responding to Delphi events, handling Windows messages is not "contract free." Often, when you decide to handle a message yourself, Windows expects you to perform some action when processing the message. Most of the time, VCL has much of this basic message processing built in—all you have to do is call inherited to get to it. Think of it this way: You write a message handler so that your application will do the things you expect, and you call inherited so that your application will do the additional things Windows expects.

NOTE

The contractual nature of message handling can be more than just calling the inherited handler. In message handlers, you're sometimes restricted in what you can do. For example, in a WM_KILLFOCUS message, you cannot set focus to another control without causing a crash.

To demonstrate the inherited elements, consider the program in Listing 3.1 without calling inherited in the WMPaint() method. the procedure would look like this:

```
procedure TForm1.WMPaint(var Msg: TWMPaint);
begin
  MessageBeep(0);
end;
```

This procedure never gives Windows a chance to perform basic handling of the WM_PAINT message, and the form will never paint itself. In fact, you might end up with several WM_PAINT messages stacking up in the message queue, causing the beep to continue until the queue is cleared.

Sometimes there are circumstances in which you don't want to call the inherited message handler. An example is handling the WM_SYSCOMMAND messages to prevent a window from being minimized or maximized.

Assigning Message Result Values

When you handle some Windows messages, Windows expects you to return a result value. The classic example is the WM_CTLCOLOR message. When you handle this message, Windows expects you to return a handle to a brush with which you want Windows to paint a dialog box or control. (Delphi provides a Color property for components that does this for you, so the example is just for illustration purposes.) You can return this brush handle easily with a message-handling procedure by assigning a value to the Result field of TMessage (or another message record) after calling inherited. For example, if you were handling WM_CTLCOLOR, you could return a brush handle value to Windows with the following code:

```
procedure TForm1.WMCtlColor(var Msg: TWMCtlColor);
var
  BrushHand: hBrush;
begin
  inherited;
  { Create a brush handle and place into BrushHand variable }
  Msg.Result := BrushHand;
end;
```

The TApplication Type's OnMessage Event

Another technique for handling messages is to use TApplication's OnMessage event. When you assign a procedure to OnMessage, that procedure is called whenever a message is pulled from the queue and about to be processed. This event handler is called before Windows itself has a chance to process the message. The Application.OnMessage event handler is of TMessageEvent type and must be defined with a parameter list, as shown here:

```
procedure SomeObject.AppMessageHandler(var Msg: TMsg;
  var Handled: Boolean);
```

All the message parameters are passed to the OnMessage event handler in the Msg parameter. (Note that this parameter is of the Windows TMsg record type described earlier in this chapter.) The Handled field requires you to assign a Boolean value indicating whether you have handled the message.

You can create an `OnMessage` event handler by using a `TApplicationEvents` component from the Additional page of the Component Palette. Here is an example of such an event handler:

```
var
  NumMessages: Integer;

procedure TForm1.ApplicationEvents1Message(var Msg: tagMSG;
  var Handled: Boolean);
begin
  Inc(NumMessages);
  Handled := False;
end;
```

One limitation of `OnMessage` is that it's executed only for messages pulled out of the queue and not for messages sent directly to the window procedures of windows in your application. Chapter 13, "Hard-Core Techniques," of *Delphi 5 Developers Guide,* which is on this book's CD-ROM, shows techniques for working around this limitation by hooking into the application window procedure.

TIP

`OnMessage` sees all messages posted to all window handles in your application. This is the busiest event in your application (thousands of messages per second), so don't do anything in an `OnMessage` handler that takes a lot of time because you'll slow your whole application to a crawl. Clearly, this is one place where a breakpoint would be a very bad idea.

Sending Your Own Messages

Just as Windows sends messages to your application's windows, you will occasionally need to send messages between windows and controls within your application. Delphi provides several ways to send messages within your application, such as the `Perform()` method (which works independently of the Windows API) and the `SendMessage()` and `PostMessage()` API functions.

The `Perform()` Method

VCL provides the `Perform()` method for all `TControl` descendants; `Perform()` enables you to send a message to any form or control object given an instance of that object. The `Perform()` method takes three parameters—a message and its corresponding `lParam` and `wParam`—and is defined as follows:

```
function TControl.Perform(Msg: Cardinal; WParam, LParam: Longint):
  Longint;
```

To send a message to a form or control, use the following syntax:

```
RetVal := ControlName.Perform(MessageID, wParam, lParam);
```

`Perform()` is synchronous in that it doesn't return until the message has been handled. The `Perform()` method packages its parameters into a `TMessage` record and then calls the object's `Dispatch()` method to send the message—bypassing the Windows API messaging system. The `Dispatch()` method is described later in this chapter.

The SendMessage() and PostMessage() API Functions

Sometimes you need to send a message to a window for which you don't have a Delphi object instance. For example, you might want to send a message to a non-Delphi window, but you have only a handle to that window. Fortunately, the Windows API offers two functions that fit this bill: `SendMessage()` and `PostMessage()`. These two functions are essentially identical, except for one key difference: `SendMessage()`, similar to `Perform()`, sends a message directly to the window procedure of the intended window and waits until the message is processed before returning; `PostMessage()` posts a message to the Windows message queue and returns immediately.

`SendMessage()` and `PostMessage()` are declared as follows:

```
function SendMessage(hWnd: HWND; Msg: UINT; wParam: WPARAM;
  lParam: LPARAM): LRESULT; stdcall;
function PostMessage(hWnd: HWND; Msg: UINT; wParam: WPARAM;
  lParam: LPARAM): BOOL; stdcall;
```

- `hWnd` is the window handle for which the message is intended.
- `Msg` is the message identifier.
- `wParam` is 32 bits of additional message-specific information.
- `lParam` is 32 bits of additional message-specific information.

> **NOTE**
>
> Although `SendMessage()` and `PostMessage()` are used similarly, their respective return values are different. `SendMessage()` returns the result value of the message being processed, but `PostMessage()` returns only a `BOOL` that indicates whether the message was placed in the target window's queue. Another way to think of this is that `SendMessage()` is a synchronous operation, whereas `PostMessage()` is asynchronous.
>
> *continues*

3

ADVENTURES IN
MESSAGING

Nonstandard Messages

Until now, the discussion has centered on regular Windows messages (those that begin with WM_*XXX*). However, two other major categories of messages merit some discussion: notification messages and user-defined messages.

Notification Messages

Notification messages are messages sent to a parent window when something happens in one of its child controls that might require the parent's attention. Notification messages occur only with the standard Windows controls (button, list box, combo box, and edit control) and with the Windows Common Controls (tree view, list view, and so on). For example, clicking or double-clicking a control, selecting some text in a control, and moving the scrollbar in a control all generate notification messages.

You can handle notification messages by writing message-handling procedures in the form that contains a particular control. Table 3.2 lists the Win32 notification messages for standard Windows controls.

TABLE 3.2 Standard Control Notification Messages

Notification	Meaning
Button Notification	
BN_CLICKED	The user clicked a button.
BN_DISABLE	A button is disabled.
BN_DOUBLECLICKED	The user double-clicked a button.
BN_HILITE	The user highlighted a button.
BN_PAINT	The button should be painted.
BN_UNHILITE	The highlight should be removed.
Combo Box Notification	
CBN_CLOSEUP	The list box of a combo box has closed.
CBN_DBLCLK	The user double-clicked a string.
CBN_DROPDOWN	The list box of a combo box is dropping down.
CBN_EDITCHANGE	The user has changed text in the edit control.
CBN_EDITUPDATE	Altered text is about to be displayed.
CBN_ERRSPACE	The combo box is out of memory.
CBN_KILLFOCUS	The combo box is losing the input focus.
CBN_SELCHANGE	A new combo box list item is selected.

TABLE 3.2 Continued

Notification	Meaning
CBN_SELENDCANCEL	The user's selection should be canceled.
CBN_SELENDOK	The user's selection is valid.
CBN_SETFOCUS	The combo box is receiving the input focus.

Edit Notification

EN_CHANGE	The display is updated after text changes.
EN_ERRSPACE	The edit control is out of memory.
EN_HSCROLL	The user clicked the horizontal scrollbar.
EN_KILLFOCUS	The edit control is losing the input focus.
EN_MAXTEXT	The insertion is truncated.
EN_SETFOCUS	The edit control is receiving the input focus.
EN_UPDATE	The edit control is about to display altered text.
EN_VSCROLL	The user clicked the vertical scrollbar.

List Box Notification

LBN_DBLCLK	The user double-clicked a string.
LBN_ERRSPACE	The list box is out of memory.
LBN_KILLFOCUS	The list box is losing the input focus.
LBN_SELCANCEL	The selection is canceled.
LBN_SELCHANGE	The selection is about to change.
LBN_SETFOCUS	The list box is receiving the input focus.

3

ADVENTURES IN MESSAGING

Internal VCL Messages

VCL has an extensive collection of its own internal and notification messages. Although you don't commonly use these messages in your Delphi applications, Delphi component writers will find them useful. These messages begin with CM_ (for *component message*) or CN_ (for *component notification*), and they are used to manage VCL internals such as focus, color, visibility, window re-creation, dragging, and so on. You can find a complete list of these messages in the "Creating Custom Components" portion of the Delphi online help.

A common inquiry is how to detect that the mouse is entered or left a controls space. This can be handled by processing the custom messages CM_MOUSEENTER and CM_MOUSELEAVE. Consider the following component:

```
TSpecialPanel = class(TPanel)
protected
```

```
      procedure CMMouseEnter(var Msg: TMessage); message CM_MOUSEENTER;
      procedure CMMouseLeave(var Msg: TMessage); message CM_MOUSELEAVE;
   end;
…
procedure TSpecialPanel.CMMouseEnter(var Msg: TMessage);
begin
   inherited;
   Color := clWhite;
end;

procedure TSpecialPanel.CMMouseLeave(var Msg: TMessage);
begin
   inherited;
   Color := clBtnFace;
end;
```

This component handles the custom messages by turning the panel white when the mouse has entered the component's surface area and then turns the color back to `clBtnFace` when the mouse leaves. You'll find an example of this code on the CD under the directory `CustMessage`.

User-Defined Messages

At some point, you'll come across a situation in which one of your own applications must send a message to itself, or you have to send messages between two of your own applications. At this point, one question that might come to mind is, "Why would I send myself a message instead of simply calling a procedure?" It's a good question, and there are actually several answers. First, messages give you polymorphism without requiring knowledge of the recipient's type. Messages are therefore as powerful as virtual methods but more flexible. Also, messages allow for optional handling: If the recipient doesn't do anything with the message, no harm is done. Finally, messages allow for broadcast notifications to multiple recipients and "parasitic" eavesdropping, which isn't easily done with procedures alone.

Messages Within Your Application

Having an application send a message to itself is easy. Just use the `Perform()`, `SendMessage()`, or `PostMessage()` function and use a message value in the range of `WM_USER + 100` through `$7FFF` (the value Windows reserves for user-defined messages):

```
const
 SX_MYMESSAGE = WM_USER + 100;

begin
  SomeForm.Perform(SX_MYMESSAGE, 0, 0);
  { or }
  SendMessage(SomeForm.Handle, SX_MYMESSAGE, 0, 0);
```

```
{ or }
PostMessage(SomeForm.Handle, SX_MYMESSAGE, 0, 0);
  .
  .
  .
end;
```

Then create a normal message-handling procedure for this message in the form in which you want to handle the message:

```
TForm1 = class(TForm)
  .
  .
  .
private
  procedure SXMyMessage(var Msg: TMessage); message SX_MYMESSAGE;
end;

procedure TForm1.SXMyMessage(var Msg: TMessage);
begin
  MessageDlg('She turned me into a newt!', mtInformation, [mbOk], 0);
end;
```

As you can see, there's little difference between using a user-defined message in your application and handling any standard Windows message. The real key here is to start at WM_USER + 100 for interapplication messages and to give each message a name that has something to do with its purpose.

> **CAUTION**
>
> Never send messages with values of WM_USER through $7FFF unless you're sure that the intended recipient is equipped to handle the message. Because each window can define these values independently, the potential for bad things to happen is great unless you keep careful tabs on which recipients you send WM_USER through $7FFF messages to.

Messaging Between Applications

When you want to send messages between two or more applications, it's usually best to use the RegisterWindowMessage() API function in each application. This method ensures that every application uses the same message number for a given message.

RegisterWindowMessage() accepts a null-terminated string as a parameter and returns a new message constant in the range of $C000 through $FFFF. This means that all you have to do is call `RegisterWindowMessage()` with the same string in each application between which you want to send messages; Windows returns the same message value for each application. The true benefit of `RegisterWindowMessage()` is that because a message value for any given string is guaranteed to be unique throughout the system, you can safely broadcast such messages to all windows with fewer harmful side effects. It can be a bit more work to handle this kind of message, though; because the message identifier isn't known until runtime, you can't use a standard message handler procedure, and you must override a control's `WndProc()` or `DefaultHandler()` method or subclass an existing window procedure. A technique for handling registered messages is demonstrated in Chapter 13, "Hard-Core Techniques," of *Delphi 5 Developer's Guide*, found on this book's CD-ROM. This useful demo shows how to prevent multiple copies of your application from being launched.

> **NOTE**
>
> The number returned by `RegisterWindowMessage()` varies between Windows sessions and can't be determined until runtime.

Broadcasting Messages

`TWinControl` descendants can broadcast a message record to each of their owned controls—thanks to the `Broadcast()` method. This technique is useful when you need to send the same message to a group of components. For example, to send a user-defined message called um_Foo to all of `Panel1`'s owned controls, use the following code:

```
var
  M: TMessage;
begin
  with M do
  begin
    Message := UM_FOO;
    wParam := 0;
    lParam := 0;
    Result := 0;
  end;
  Panel1.Broadcast(M);
end;
```

Anatomy of a Message System: VCL

There's much more to VCL's message system than handling messages with the `message` directive. After a message is issued by Windows, it makes a couple of stops before reaching your message-handling procedure (and it might make a few more stops afterward). All along the way, you have the power to act on the message.

For posted messages, the first stop for a Windows message in VCL is the `Application.Process Message()` method, which houses the VCL main message loop. The next stop for a message is the handler for the `Application.OnMessage` event. `OnMessage` is called as messages are fetched from the application queue in the `ProcessMessage()` method. Because sent messages aren't queued, `OnMessage` won't be called for sent messages.

For posted messages, the `DispatchMessage()` API is then called internally to dispatch the message to the `StdWndProc()` function. For sent messages, `StdWndProc()` will be called directly by Win32. `StdWndProc()` is an assembler function that accepts the message from Windows and routes it to the object for which the message is intended.

The object method that receives the message is called `MainWndProc()`. Beginning with `MainWndProc()`, you can perform any special handling of the message your program might require. Generally, you handle a message at this point only if you don't want a message to go through VCL's normal dispatching.

After leaving the `MainWndProc()` method, the message is routed to the object's `WndProc()` method and then on to the dispatch mechanism. The dispatch mechanism, found in the object's `Dispatch()` method, routes the message to any specific message-handling procedure that you've defined or that already exists within VCL.

Then the message finally reaches your message-specific handling procedure. After flowing through your handler and the inherited handlers you might have invoked using the `inherited` keyword, the message goes to the object's `DefaultHandler()` method. `DefaultHandler()` performs any final message processing and then passes the message to the Windows `DefWindowProc()` function or other default window procedure (such as `DefMDIProc`) for any Windows default processing. Figure 3.2 shows VCL's message-processing mechanism.

3

ADVENTURES IN
MESSAGING

NOTE

You should always call `inherited` when handling messages unless you're absolutely certain you want to prevent normal message processing.

TIP

Because all unhandled messages flow to `DefaultHandler()`, that's usually the best place to handle interapplication messages in which the values were obtained by way of the `RegisterWindowMessage()` procedure.

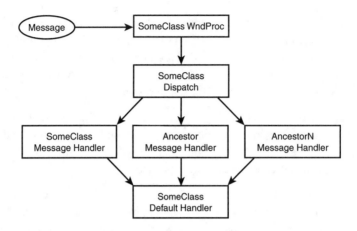

FIGURE 3.2

VCL's message system.

To better understand VCL's message system, create a small program that can handle a message at the `Application.OnMessage`, `WndProc()`, message procedure, or `DefaultHandler()` stage. This project is called `CatchIt`; its main form is shown in Figure 3.3.

FIGURE 3.3

The main form of the `CatchIt` message example.

The `OnClick` event handlers for `PostMessButton` and `SendMessButton` are shown in the following code. The former uses `PostMessage()` to post a user-defined message to the form; the latter uses `SendMessage()` to send a user-defined message to the form. To differentiate between post and send, note that the value 1 is passed in the `wParam` of `PostMessage()` and that the value 0 (zero) is passed for `SendMessage()`. Here's the code:

```
procedure TMainForm.PostMessButtonClick(Sender: TObject);
{ posts message to form }
begin
  PostMessage(Handle, SX_MYMESSAGE, 1, 0);
end;
```

```
procedure TMainForm.SendMessButtonClick(Sender: TObject);
{ sends message to form }
begin
  SendMessage(Handle, SX_MYMESSAGE, 0, 0); // send message to form
end;
```

This application provides the user with the opportunity to "eat" the message in the OnMessage
handler, WndProc() method, message-handling method, or DefaultHandler() method (that is,
to not trigger the inherited behavior and to therefore stop the message from fully circulating
through VCL's message-handling system). Listing 3.2 shows the completed source code for the
main unit of this project, thus demonstrating the flow of messages in a Delphi application.

LISTING 3.2   The Source Code for CIMain.PAS

```
unit CIMain;

interface

uses
  SysUtils, WinTypes, WinProcs, Messages, Classes, Graphics, Controls,
  Forms, Dialogs, StdCtrls, ExtCtrls, Menus;

const
  SX_MYMESSAGE = WM_USER;                   // User-defined message value
  MessString = '%s message now in %s.';  // String to alert user

type
  TMainForm = class(TForm)
    GroupBox1: TGroupBox;
    PostMessButton: TButton;
    WndProcCB: TCheckBox;
    MessProcCB: TCheckBox;
    DefHandCB: TCheckBox;
    SendMessButton: TButton;
    AppMsgCB: TCheckBox;
    EatMsgCB: TCheckBox;
    EatMsgGB: TGroupBox;
    OnMsgRB: TRadioButton;
    WndProcRB: TRadioButton;
    MsgProcRB: TRadioButton;
    DefHandlerRB: TRadioButton;
    procedure PostMessButtonClick(Sender: TObject);
    procedure SendMessButtonClick(Sender: TObject);
    procedure EatMsgCBClick(Sender: TObject);
    procedure FormCreate(Sender: TObject);
```

LISTING 3.2   Continued

```
    procedure AppMsgCBClick(Sender: TObject);
  private
    { Handles messages at Application level }
    procedure OnAppMessage(var Msg: TMsg; var Handled: Boolean);
    { Handles messages at WndProc level }
    procedure WndProc(var Msg: TMessage); override;
    { Handles message after dispatch }
    procedure SXMyMessage(var Msg: TMessage); message SX_MYMESSAGE;
    { Default message handler }
    procedure DefaultHandler(var Msg); override;
  end;

var
  MainForm: TMainForm;

implementation

{$R *.DFM}

const
  // strings which will indicate whether a message is sent or posted
  SendPostStrings: array[0..1] of String = ('Sent', 'Posted');

procedure TMainForm.FormCreate(Sender: TObject);
{ OnCreate handler for main form }
begin
  // set OnMessage to my OnAppMessage method
  Application.OnMessage := OnAppMessage;
  // use the Tag property of checkboxes to store a reference to their
  // associated radio buttons
  AppMsgCB.Tag := Longint(OnMsgRB);
  WndProcCB.Tag := Longint(WndProcRB);
  MessProcCB.Tag := Longint(MsgProcRB);
  DefHandCB.Tag := Longint(DefHandlerRB);
  // use the Tag property of radio buttons to store a reference to their
  // associated checkbox
  OnMsgRB.Tag := Longint(AppMsgCB);
  WndProcRB.Tag := Longint(WndProcCB);
  MsgProcRB.Tag := Longint(MessProcCB);
  DefHandlerRB.Tag := Longint(DefHandCB);
end;

procedure TMainForm.OnAppMessage(var Msg: TMsg; var Handled: Boolean);
{ OnMessage handler for Application }
```

LISTING 3.2   Continued

```pascal
begin
  // check to see if message is my user-defined message
  if Msg.Message = SX_MYMESSAGE then
  begin
    if AppMsgCB.Checked then
    begin
      // Let user know about the message.  Set Handled flag appropriately
      ShowMessage(Format(MessString, [SendPostStrings[Msg.WParam],
        'Application.OnMessage']));
      Handled := OnMsgRB.Checked;
    end;
  end;
end;

procedure TMainForm.WndProc(var Msg: TMessage);
{ WndProc procedure of form }
var
  CallInherited: Boolean;
begin
  CallInherited := True;              // assume we will call the inherited
  if Msg.Msg = SX_MYMESSAGE then     // check for our user-defined message
  begin
    if WndProcCB.Checked then         // if WndProcCB checkbox is checked...
    begin
      // Let user know about the message.
      ShowMessage(Format(MessString, [SendPostStrings[Msg.WParam],
        'WndProc']));
      // Call inherited only if we are not supposed to eat the message.
      CallInherited := not WndProcRB.Checked;
    end;
  end;
  if CallInherited then inherited WndProc(Msg);
end;

procedure TMainForm.SXMyMessage(var Msg: TMessage);
{ Message procedure for user-defined message }
var
  CallInherited: Boolean;
begin
  CallInherited := True;              // assume we will call the inherited
  if MessProcCB.Checked then          // if MessProcCB checkbox is checked
  begin
    // Let user know about the message.
    ShowMessage(Format(MessString, [SendPostStrings[Msg.WParam],
```

LISTING 3.2   Continued

```
        'Message Procedure']));
      // Call inherited only if we are not supposed to eat the message.
      CallInherited := not MsgProcRB.Checked;
    end;
    if CallInherited then Inherited;
  end;

procedure TMainForm.DefaultHandler(var Msg);
{ Default message handler for form }
var
  CallInherited: Boolean;
begin
  CallInherited := True;               // assume we will call the inherited
  // check for our user-defined message
  if TMessage(Msg).Msg = SX_MYMESSAGE then    begin
    if DefHandCB.Checked then          // if DefHandCB checkbox is checked
    begin
      // Let user know about the message.
      ShowMessage(Format(MessString,
        [SendPostStrings[TMessage(Msg).WParam], 'DefaultHandler']));
      // Call inherited only if we are not supposed to eat the message.
      CallInherited := not DefHandlerRB.Checked;
    end;
  end;
  if CallInherited then inherited DefaultHandler(Msg);
end;

procedure TMainForm.PostMessButtonClick(Sender: TObject);
{ posts message to form }
begin
  PostMessage(Handle, SX_MYMESSAGE, 1, 0);
end;

procedure TMainForm.SendMessButtonClick(Sender: TObject);
{ sends message to form }
begin
  SendMessage(Handle, SX_MYMESSAGE, 0, 0); // send message to form
end;

procedure TMainForm.AppMsgCBClick(Sender: TObject);
{ enables/disables proper radio button for checkbox click }
begin
  if EatMsgCB.Checked then
  begin
    with TRadioButton((Sender as TCheckBox).Tag) do
```

LISTING 3.2   Continued

```
  begin
    Enabled := TCheckbox(Sender).Checked;
    if not Enabled then Checked := False;
  end;
end;
end;

procedure TMainForm.EatMsgCBClick(Sender: TObject);
{ enables/disables radio buttons as appropriate }
var
  i: Integer;
  DoEnable, EatEnabled: Boolean;
begin
  // get enable/disable flag
  EatEnabled := EatMsgCB.Checked;
  // iterate over child controls of GroupBox in order to
  // enable/disable and check/uncheck radio buttons
  for i := 0 to EatMsgGB.ControlCount - 1 do
    with EatMsgGB.Controls[i] as TRadioButton do
    begin
      DoEnable := EatEnabled;
      if DoEnable then DoEnable := TCheckbox(Tag).Checked;
      if not DoEnable then Checked := False;
      Enabled := DoEnable;
    end;
end;

end.
```

CAUTION

Although it's fine to use just the `inherited` keyword to send the message to an inherited handler in message-handler procedures, this technique doesn't work with `WndProc()` or `DefaultHandler()`. With these procedures, you must also provide the name of the inherited procedure or function, as in this example:

```
inherited WndProc(Msg);
```

You might have noticed that the `DefaultHandler()` procedure is somewhat unusual in that it takes one *untyped* var parameter. That's because `DefaultHandler()` assumes that the first word in the parameter is the message number; it isn't concerned with the rest of the information being passed. Because of this, you typecast the parameter as a `TMessage` so that you can access the message parameters.

The Relationship Between Messages and Events

Now that you know all the ins and outs of messages, recall that this chapter began by stating that VCL encapsulates many Windows messages in its event system. Delphi's event system is designed to be an easy interface into Windows messages. Many VCL events have a direct correlation with WM_*XXX* Windows messages. Table 3.3 shows some common VCL events and the Windows message responsible for each event.

TABLE 3.3   VCL Events and Corresponding Windows Messages

VCL Event	Windows Message
OnActivate	wm_Activate
OnClick	wm_XButtonDown
OnCreate	wm_Create
OnDblClick	wm_XButtonDblClick
OnKeyDown	wm_KeyDown
OnKeyPress	wm_Char
OnKeyUp	wm_KeyUp
OnPaint	WM_PAINT
OnResize	wm_Size
OnTimer	wm_Timer

Table 3.3 is a good rule-of-thumb reference when you're looking for events that correspond directly to messages.

> **TIP**
>
> Never write a message handler when you can use a predefined event to do the same thing. Because of the contract-free nature of events, you'll have fewer problems handling events than you will handling messages.

Summary

By now, you should have a pretty clear understanding of how the Win32 messaging system works and how VCL encapsulates that messaging system. Although Delphi's event system is great, knowing how messages work is essential for any serious Win32 programmer.

Advanced Techniques

PART
II

IN THIS PART

Writing Portable Code

IN THIS CHAPTER

If you're upgrading to Delphi 6 from a previous version or want to maintain compatibility among Delphi versions, this chapter is written for you. The first section of this chapter discusses general compatibility issues you will face in moving between any versions of Delphi. In the second section, you'll find hints and tips for maintaining compatibility between Delphi on the Win32 platform and Kylix on the Linux platform. The remainder of the chapter highlights the often subtle differences between the various versions and how to take these differences into account in writing portable code or migrating between versions. Although Borland makes a concerted effort to ensure that your code is compatible between versions, it's understandable that some changes have to be made in the name of progress, and certain situations require code changes if applications are to compile and run properly under the latest version of Delphi.

General Compatibility

A number of issues affect general compatibility between the various versions of Delphi, C++Builder, and Kylix. By making yourself aware of the support built into the compiler for writing compatible code, as well as some of the common gotchas, you'll be well on your way to targeting multiple versions from a single code base.

Which Version?

Although most Delphi code will compile for all versions of the compiler, in some instances language or VCL differences require that you write slightly differently to accomplish a given task for each product version. Occasionally, you might need to be able to compile for multiple versions of Delphi from one code base. For this purpose, each version of the Delphi compiler contains a VER*xxx* conditional define for which you can test in your source code. Because Borland C++Builder and Kylix also ships with new versions of the compiler, these edition also contain this conditional define. Table 4.1 shows the conditional defines for the various versions of the Delphi compiler.

TABLE 4.1 Conditional Defines for Compiler Versions

Product	Conditional Define
Delphi 1	VER80
Delphi 2	VER90
C++Builder 1	VER95
Delphi 3	VER100
C++Builder 3	VER110
Delphi 4	VER120
C++Builder 4	VER120

TABLE 4.1 Continued

Product	Conditional Define
Delphi 5	VER130
C++Builder 5	VER130
Kylix 1	VER140
Delphi 6	VER140

Using these defines, the source code you must write in order to compile for different compiler versions would look something similar to this:

```
{$IFDEF VER80}
  Delphi 1 code goes here
{$ENDIF}
{$IFDEF VER90}
  Delphi 2 code goes here
{$ENDIF}
{$IFDEF VER95}
  C++Builder 1 code goes here
{$ENDIF}
{$IFDEF VER100}
  Delphi 3 code goes here
{$ENDIF}
{$IFDEF VER110}
  C++Builder 3 code goes here
{$ENDIF}
{$IFDEF VER120}
  Delphi 4 and C++Builder 4 code goes here
{$ENDIF}
{$IFDEF VER130}
  Delphi and C++Builder 5 code goes here
{$ENDIF}
{$IFDEF VER140}
  Delphi 6 and Kylix code goes here
{$ENDIF}
```

NOTE

If you're wondering why the Delphi 1.0 compiler is considered version 8, Delphi 2 version 9, and so on, it's because Delphi 1.0 is considered version 8 of Borland's Pascal compiler. The last Turbo Pascal version was 7.0, and Delphi is the evolution of that product line.

4

WRITING
PORTABLE CODE

Units, Components, and Packages

The binary format of Delphi compiled units (.dcu files) tends to differ from compiler version to compiler version. This means that if you want to use the same unit in multiple versions of Delphi, you must have either binary units built for that specific compiler version or the source code to those units so that they can be recompiled. Bear in mind that if you use any custom components in your application—your own components or those developed by third parties— you must have the source to these components. If you don't have the version-specific binary or the source code to a particular third-party component, contact your vendor for a version of the component specific to your version of Delphi.

> **NOTE**
>
> This issue of compiler version versus unit file version isn't a new situation and is the same as C++ compiler object file versioning. If you distribute (or buy) components without source code, you must understand that what you're distributing or buying is a compiler-version–specific binary file that will probably need to be revised to keep up with subsequent compiler releases.
>
> What's more, the issue of DCU versioning isn't necessarily a compiler-only issue. Even if the compiler weren't changed between versions, changes and enhancements to core VCL would probably still make it necessary that units be recompiled from source.

Delphi 3 introduced *packages*, the idea of multiple units stored in a single binary file. Starting with Delphi 3, the component library became a collection of packages rather than one massive component library DLL. Like units, packages aren't compatible across product versions, so you'll need to rebuild your packages for each version of Delphi, and you'll need to contact the vendors of your third-party components for version-specific packages.

IDE Issues

Problems with the IDE are likely the first you'll encounter as you migrate your applications. Here are a few of the issues you might encounter on the way:

- Delphi debugger symbol files (RSM) are not always compatible across versions. You'll know you're having this problem when you see the message `"Error reading symbol file."`. If this happens, the fix is simple: Rebuild the application.
- Starting with version 5, Delphi defaults to storing form files in text mode. If you need to maintain DFM compatibility with earlier versions of Delphi, you'll need to save the forms files in binary instead. You can do this by unchecking New Forms As Text on the Preferences page of the Environment Options dialog box.

- Code generation when importing and generating type libraries often changes from version to version. As of Delphi 5, you can customize type-library–to–Pascal symbol name mapping by editing the `tlibimp.sym` file. For directions, see the "Mapping Symbol Names in the Type Library" topic in the online help.

Delphi-Kylix Compatibility

If you endeavor to build applications with any degree of portability between Delphi and Kylix, the most important thing to realize is that VCL is a Windows-specific technology. If you want to build cross platform applications and components, you should use the Component Library for X-platform (CLX), which is currently supported until Delphi 6 and Kylix. CLX is described in greater detail in Chapters 10, "Component Architecture: VCL and CLX," and 13, "CLX Component Development." CLX can be broken down into four major components:

- BaseCLX, which contains the core portions of the component framework.

- DataCLX, which employs the dbExpress technology to provide efficient, lightweight data access and management. dbExpress is described in detail in Chapter 8, "Database Development with dbExpress."

- NetCLX, which provides components and wizards for creating network clients and servers. Perhaps most notably, NetCLX provides a very robust Web development application framework that encompasses and includes the WebBroker technology from previous versions. NetCLX allows targeting of Linux or Windows clients and servers.

- VisualCLX, which provides the cross-platform GUI capability. VisualCLX is externally very similar to VCL, but internally uses Troll Tech's (http://www.trolltech.com) Qt library (as opposed to the Win32 API like in VCL). Qt is a cross-platform GUI framework that enables developers to target a variety of platforms, including Windows and Linux.

When you create a new CLX application using File, New, CLX Application and view the uses clause of the resulting main form unit, you will see a number of unit names beginning with the letter Q, such as `QGraphics`, `QControls`, `QForms`, and so on. These units are similar in content and function to the similarly named VCL units, although they are cross platform.

4

> **NOTE**
>
> Although the current versions of CLX support only Windows and Kylix, it is designed such that it can be extended relatively easily to other platforms. Qt, for example, supports about a dozen different platforms.

Not in Linux

Of course, you won't find the Windows-specific technologies you might have grown to know and love on the Linux platform. This means that technologies such as ADO, COM/COM+, BDE, and MAPI (among others) have no place in a cross-platform application. You should therefore avoid using units such as `Windows`, `ComObj`, `ComServ`, `ActiveX`, and `AdoDb` and platform-specific functions such as any WIn32 API call, `RaiseLastWin32Error()`, `Win32Check()`, and so on. Additionally, there are a number of technologies found in Delphi 6 that aren't available in Kylix 1 but will likely be found in future versions of Kylix. These include DataSnap, BizSnap (SOAP), and WebSnap technologies.

Compiler/Language Features

Although the Delphi and Kylix compilers both target the x86 processor architecture, there are a number of key differences in the compiler that you should be aware of in building portable applications.

LINUX Define

The Kylix compiler defines the `LINUX` conditional, whereas Delphi defines `MSWINDOWS` and `WIN32`, so that you can `IFDEF` your code in order to maintain platform-specific code in a single unit. Such code would like something like this:

```
{$IFDEF LINUX}
  // Linux-specific code goes here
{$ENDIF}
{$IFDEF MSWINDOWS}
  // Windows-specific code goes here
{$ENDIF}
```

PIC Format

The Linux compiler produces executables in Position Independent Code (PIC) format, which is a slight variation on the type of code produced by the Windows compiler. Although this change has little or no effect if you're just writing Pascal code, it can have a dramatic impact on externally linked assembler modules or built-in assembler. Most notably, PIC requires access to all global data to be relative to the EBX register, so the following line in Delphi

```
mov eax, SomeVar
```

would be written for PIC as

```
mov eax [ebx].SomeVar
```

Because of the heavy reliance on the EBX register, PIC also requires that the value of EBX be preserved across function calls and restored prior to external calls. If you want to `IFDEF` your built-in assembly code for PIC and non-PIC, the compiler also defines a <u>PIC</u> conditional for which you can check:

```
{$IFDEF PIC}
  // PIC specific code goes here
{$ENDIF}
```

Calling Conventions

It's worth noting that `stdcall` and `safecall` calling conventions don't exist in Kylix. These directives simply map to the `cdecl` calling convention in Kylix. This is generally only an issue if you have assembly code that depends on parameter order and stack cleanup.

Platform-isms

In general, you should be wary of hard-coding platform-isms, or platform-specifics idioms into your applications. Some items in the vein to keep in mind include

- The notion of drive letters does not exist on Linux.
- The directory separator is a backslash (\) on Windows and a forward slash (/) on Linux. Delphi's `PathSeparator` constant will show you which to use.
- The directory list delimiter is a semicolon (;) on Windows and a colon (:) on Linux.
- UNC pathnames exist only on Windows.
- Avoid depending on platform-specific directories, such as `c:\winnt\system32` or `/usr/bin`.

New Delphi 6 Features

A number of nice additions to Delphi 6, particularly in the language and compiler area, can make application development go more smoothly. However, it's important to bear in mind that employing these features might mean that your code will not compile in earlier product versions.

Variants

Rather than being implemented within the compiler, support for the `Variant` data type has been opened up to support user-installable types. This support is found in the `Variants` unit.

Enum Values

In an effort to achieve greater compatibility with C++, the compiler now supports the assignment of values to elements of an enumerated type, as shown here:

```
type
  TFoo = (fTwo=2, fFour=4, fSix=6, fEight=8);
```

4

$IF Directive

One particular feature that is a long time coming is the addition of the $IF and $ELSEIF directives that allow you to check for defined symbols and to perform Boolean comparisons against constants, as shown here:

```
{$IF Defined(MSWINDOWS) and SomeConstant >= 6}
  // do something
{$ELSEIF SomeConstant < 2}
  // do something else
{$ELSE}
  // if all else fails
{$ENDIF}
```

Potential Binary DFM Incompatibility

The mechanism that saves and loads Delphi forms from stream has been modified, particularly as it relates to high ASCII characters (those higher than 127). Binary DFMs containing high ASCII characters might not be readable in earlier Delphi versions. A workaround would be to use the text version of the form.

Migrating from Delphi 5

Although compatibility between Delphi 5 and 6 is quite good, there are a few minor issues you should be aware of as you make the move.

Writable Typed Constants

The default state of the $J compiler switch (also known as $WRITEABLECONST) is now off, where it was on in previous versions. This means that attempts to assign to typed constants will raise a compiler error unless you explicitly enable this behavior using $J+.

Cardinal Unary Negation

Prior to Delphi 6, Delphi used 32-bit arithmetic to handle unary negation of Cardinal type numbers. This could lead to unexpected results. Consider the following bit of code:

```
var
   c: Cardinal;
   i: Int64;
begin
   c := 4294967294;
   i := -c;
   WriteLn(i);
end;
```

In Delphi 5, the value of i displayed would be 2. Although this behavior is incorrect, you might have code that relies on this behavior. If so, you should know that Delphi 6 has corrected this issue by promoting the Cardinal to an Int64 prior to performing the negation. The final value of i displayed in Delphi 6 is 4294967294.

Migrating from Delphi 4

This section highlights some of the issues you can expect if you're moving up from Delphi 4.

RTL Issues

The only issue you're likely to come across here deals with the setting of the floating-point unit (FPU) control word in DLLs. Prior to version 5, DLLs would set the FPU control word, thereby changing the setting established by the host application. Now, DLL startup code no longer sets the FPU control word. If you need to set the control word to ensure some specific behavior by the FPU, you can do it manually using the Set8087CW() function in the System unit.

VCL Issues

There are a number of VCL issues that you may come across, but most involve some simple edits as a means to get your project on track. Here's a list of these issues:

- The type of properties that represent an index into an image list has changed from Integer to TImageIndex type between Delphi 4 and 5. TImageIndex is a strongly typed Integer defined in the ImgList unit as

  TImageIndex = type Integer;

  This should only cause problems in cases where exact type matching matters, such as when you're passing var parameters.

- TCustomTreeview.CustomDrawItem() added a var parameter called PaintImages of type Boolean. If your application overrides this method, you'll need to add this parameter in order for it to compile in Delphi 5 or higher.

- If you're invoking pop-up menus in response to WM_RBUTTONUP messages or OnMouseUp events, you might exhibit "double" pop-up menus or no pop-up menus at all when compiling with Delphi 5 or later. Delphi now uses the WM_CONTEXT menu message to invoke pop-up menus.

Internet Development Issues

If you're developing applications with Internet support, we have some bad news and some good news:

- The `TWebBrowser` component, which encapsulates the Microsoft Internet Explorer ActiveX control, has replaced the `THTML` component from `Netmasters`. Although the `TWebBrowser` control is much more feature rich, you're faced with a good deal of rewrite if you used `THTML` because the interface is totally different. If you don't want to rewrite your code, you can go back to the old control by importing the `HTML.OCX` file from the `\Info\Extras\NetManage` directory on the Delphi CD-ROM.

- Packages are now supported when building ISAPI and NSAPI DLLs. You can take advantage of this new support by replacing HTTPApp in your uses clause with WebBroker.

Database Issues

A few database issues might trip you up as you migrate from Delphi 4. These involve some renaming of existing symbols and the new DataSnap architecture (formerly called MIDAS):

- The type of the `TDatabase.OnLogin` event has been renamed `TDatabaseLoginEvent` from `TLoginEvent`. This is unlikely to cause problems, but you might run into troubles if you're creating and assigning to `OnLogin` in code.

- The global `FMTBCDToCurr()` and `CurrToFMTBCD()` routines have been replaced by the new `BCDToCurr` and `CurrToBCD` routines (and the corresponding protected methods on `TDataSet` have been replaced by the protected and undocumented `DataConvert` method).

- DataSnap (formerly MIDAS) has undergone some significant changes since Delphi 4. See Chapter 21, "DataSnap Development," for information on the changes and new features.

Migrating from Delphi 3

Although there aren't a great deal of compatibility issues between Delphi 3 and later versions, the few issues that do exist can be potentially more problematic than porting from any other previous version of Delphi to the next. Most of these issues revolve around new types and the changing behavior of certain existing types.

Unsigned 32-bit Integers

Delphi 4 introduced the `LongWord` type, which is an unsigned 32-bit integer. In previous versions of Delphi, the largest integer type was a signed 32-bit integer. Because of this, many of the types that you would expect to be unsigned, such as `DWORD`, `UINT`, `HResult`, `HWND`, `HINSTANCE`, and other handle types, were defined simply as `Integers`. In Delphi 4 and later, these types are redefined as `LongWords`. Additionally, the `Cardinal` type, which was previously a subrange type of `0..MaxInt`, is now also a `LongWord`. Although all this `LongWord` business won't cause problems in most circumstances, there are several problematic cases you should know about:

- `Integer` and `LongWord` are not var-parameter compatible. Therefore, you cannot pass a `LongWord` in a var `Integer` parameter, and vice versa. The compiler will give you an error in this case, so you'll need to change the parameter or variable type or typecast to get around this problem.

- Literal constants having the value of `$80000000` through `$FFFFFFFF` are considered `LongWords`. You must typecast such a literal to an `Integer` if you want to assign it to an `Integer` type. Here's an example:

```
var
  I: Integer;
begin
  I := Integer($FFFFFFFF);
```

- Similarly, any literal having a negative value is out of range for a `LongWord`, and you'll need to typecast to assign a negative literal to a `LongWord`. Here's an example:

```
var
  L: LongWord;
begin
  L := LongWord(-1);
```

- If you mix signed and unsigned integers in arithmetic or comparison operations, the compiler will automatically promote each operand to `Int64` in order to perform the arithmetic or comparison. This can cause some very difficult-to-find bugs. Consider the following code:

```
var
  I: Integer;
  D: DWORD;
begin
  I := -1;
  D := $FFFFFFFF;
  if I = D then DoSomething;
```

Under Delphi 3, *DoSomething* would execute because `-1` and `$FFFFFFFF` are the same value when contained in an `Integer`. However, because Delphi 4 and later will promote each operand to `Int64` in order to perform the most accurate comparison, the generated code ends up comparing `$FFFFFFFFFFFFFFFF` against `$00000000FFFFFFFF`, which is definitely not what's intended. In this case, *DoSomething* will not execute.

TIP

The compiler in Delphi 4 and later generates a number of new hints, warnings, and errors that deal with these types of compatibility problems and implicit type promotions. Make sure that you turn on hints and warnings when compiling in order to let the compiler help you write clean code.

4

WRITING PORTABLE CODE

64-Bit Integers

Delphi 4 also introduced a new type called Int64, which is a signed 64-bit integer. This new type is now used in the RTL and VCL where appropriate. For example, the Trunc() and Round() standard functions now return Int64, and there are new versions of IntToStr(), IntToHex(), and related functions that deal with Int64.

The Real Type

Starting with Delphi 4, the Real type became an alias for the Double type. In previous versions of Delphi and Turbo Pascal, Real was a six-byte, floating-point type. This shouldn't pose any problems for your code unless you have Reals written to some external storage (such as a file of record) with an earlier version or you have code that depends on the organization of the Real in memory. You can force Real to be the old 6-byte type by including the {$REALCOMPATIBILITY ON} directive in the units you want to use the old behavior. If all you need to do is force a limited number of instances of the Real type to use the old behavior, you can use the Real48 type instead.

Migrating from Delphi 2

You'll find that a high degree of compatibility between Delphi 2 and the later versions means a smooth transition into a more up-to-date Delphi version. However, some changes have been made since Delphi 2, both in the language and in VCL, that you'll need to be aware of to migrate to the latest version and take full advantage of its power.

Changes to Boolean Types

The implementation of the Delphi 2 Boolean types (Boolean, ByteBool, WordBool, LongBool) dictated that True was ordinal value 1 and False ordinal value 0. To provide better compatibility with the Win32 API, the implementations of ByteBool, WordBool, and LongBool have changed slightly; the ordinal value of True is now -1 ($FF, $FFFF, and $FFFFFFFF, respectively). Note that no change was made to the Boolean type. These changes have the potential to cause problems in your code—but only if you depend on the ordinal values of these types. For example, consider the following declaration:

```
var
  A: array[LongBool] of Integer;
```

This code is quite harmless under Delphi 2; it declares an array[False..True] (or [0..1]) of Integer, for a total of three elements. Under Delphi 3 and later, however, this declaration can cause some very unexpected results. Because True is defined as $FFFFFFFF for a LongBool, the declaration boils down to array[0..$FFFFFFFF] of Integer, or an array of 4 billion Integers! To avoid this problem, use the Boolean type as the array index.

Ironically, this change was necessary because a disturbing number of ActiveX controls and control containers (such Visual Basic) test BOOLs by checking for -1 rather than testing for a zero or nonzero value.

TIP

To help ensure portability and to avoid bugs, never write code like this:

```
if BoolVar = True then ...
```

Instead, always test Boolean types like this:

```
if BoolVar then ...
```

ResourceString

If your application uses string resources, consider taking advantage of ResourceStrings as described in Chapter 2, "The Object Pascal Language." Although this won't improve the efficiency of your application in terms of size or speed, it will make language translation easier. ResourceStrings and the related topic of resource DLLs are required to be able to write applications displaying different language strings but have them all running on the same core VCL package.

RTL Changes

Several changes made to the runtime library (RTL) after Delphi 2 might cause problems as you migrate your applications. First, the meaning of the HInstance global variable has changed slightly: HInstance contains the instance handle of the current DLL, EXE, or package. Use the new MainInstance global variable when you want to obtain the instance handle of the main application.

The second significant change pertains to the IsLibrary global. In Delphi 2, you could check the value of IsLibrary to determine whether your code was executing within the context of a DLL or EXE. IsLibrary isn't package aware, however, so you can no longer depend on IsLibrary to be accurate, depending on whether it's called from an EXE, DLL, or a module within a package. Instead, you should use the ModuleIsLib global, which returns True when called within the context of a DLL or package. You can use this in combination with the ModuleIsPackage global to distinguish between a DLL and a package.

TCustomForm

The Delphi 3 VCL introduced a new class between TScrollingWinControl and TForm called TCustomForm. In itself, that shouldn't pose a problem for you in migrating your applications

4

from Delphi 2; however, if you have any code that manipulates instances of TForm, you might need to update it so that it manipulates TCustomForms instead of TForms. Some examples of these are calls to GetParentForm(), ValidParentForm(), and any usage of the TDesigner class.

CAUTION

The semantics for GetParentForm(), ValidParentForm(), and other VCL methods that return Parent pointers have changed slightly from Delphi 2. These routines can now return nil, even though your component has a parent window context in which to draw. For example, when your component is encapsulated as an ActiveX control, it might have a ParentWindow, but not a Parent control. This means that you must watch out for Delphi 2 code that does this:

```
with GetParentForm(xx) do ...
```

GetParentForm() can now return nil depending on how your component is being contained.

GetChildren()

Component writers, be aware that the declaration of TComponent.GetChildren() has changed to read as follows:

```
procedure GetChildren(Proc: TGetChildProc; Root: TComponent); dynamic;
```

The new Root parameter holds the component's root owner—that is, the component obtained by walking up the chain of the component's owners until Owner is nil.

Automation Servers

The code required for automation has changed significantly from Delphi 2. Chapter 15, "COM Development," describes the latest process of creating Automation servers in Delphi. Rather than describe the details of the differences here, suffice it to say that you should never mix the Delphi 2 style of creating Automation servers with the more recent style found in Delphi 3 and later.

In Delphi 2, automation is facilitated through the infrastructure provided in the OleAuto and Ole2 units. These units are present in later releases of Delphi only for backward compatibility, and you shouldn't use them for new projects. Now the same functionality is provided in the ComObj, ComServ, and ActiveX units. You should never mix the former units with the latter in the same project.

Migrating from Delphi 1

If you're lucky enough to still be maintaining code that must be compiled and run under both 16 and 32-bit Windows, you have our condolences. There are numerous points of incompatibility between Delphi 1 and later versions, ranging from most of the basic data types to VCL to the Windows API. Because of the relatively small number of developers who continue to maintain and develop 16-bit applications, that information isn't in the text of this book, but you'll find it in Chapter 15 of the electronic copy of *Delphi 5 Developer's Guide* on the CD accompanying this book.

Summary

Armed with the information provided by this chapter, you should be able to migrate your projects smoothly from any previous version of Delphi to Delphi 6. Also, with a bit of work, you'll be able to maintain projects that work with multiple versions of Delphi.

4

WRITING
PORTABLE CODE

Multithreaded Techniques

CHAPTER

5

IN THIS CHAPTER

The Win32 operating system provides you with the capability to have multiple threads of execution in your applications. Arguably the single most important benefit Win32 has over 16-bit Windows, this feature provides the means for performing different types of processing simultaneously in your application. This is one of the primary reasons for upgrading to a 32-bit version of Delphi, and this chapter gives you all the details on how to get the most out of threads in your applications.

Threads Explained

A *thread* is an operating system object that represents a path of code execution within a particular process. Every Win32 application has at least one thread—often called the *primary thread* or *default thread*—but applications are free to create other threads to perform other tasks.

Threads provide a means for running many distinct code routines simultaneously. Of course, unless you have more than one CPU in your computer, two threads can't truly run simultaneously. However, each thread is scheduled fractions of seconds of time by the operating system in such a way as to give the feeling that many threads are running simultaneously.

TIP

Threads aren't and never will be supported under 16-bit Windows. This means that any 32-bit Delphi code you write using threads will never be backward compatible to Delphi 1. Keep this in mind if you still need to develop 16-bit compatible applications.

Types of Multitasking

The notion of *threads* is much different from the style of multitasking supported under 16-bit Windows platforms. You might hear people talk about Win32 as a *preemptive multitasking* operating system, whereas Windows 3.1 is a *cooperative multitasking* environment.

The key difference here is that under a preemptive multitasking environment, the operating system is responsible for managing which thread executes when. When execution of thread one is stopped in order for thread two to receive some CPU cycles, thread one is said to have been *preempted*. If the code that one thread is executing happens to put itself into an infinite loop, it's usually not a tragic situation because the operating system will continue to schedule time for all the other threads.

Under Windows 3.1, the application developer is responsible for giving control back to Windows at points during application execution. Failure of an application to do so causes the operating environment to appear locked up, and we all know what a painful experience that can be. If you take a moment to think about it, it's slightly amusing that the very foundation of 16-

bit Windows depends on all applications behaving themselves and not putting themselves into infinite loops, recursion, or any other unneighborly situation. Because all applications must cooperate for Windows to work correctly, this type of multitasking is referred to as *cooperative*.

Using Multiple Threads in Delphi Applications

It's no secret that threads represent a serious boon for Windows programmers. You can create secondary threads in your applications anywhere that it's appropriate to do some sort of background processing. Calculating cells in a spreadsheet or spooling a word processing document to the printer are examples of situations in which a thread would commonly be used. The goal of the developer will most often be to perform necessary background processing while still providing the best possible response time for the user interface.

Most of VCL has a built-in assumption that it's being accessed by only one thread at any given time. Although this limitation is especially apparent in the user interface portions of VCL, it's important to note that even many non-UI portions of VCL are not thread-safe.

Non-UI VCL

Actually, very few areas of VCL are guaranteed to be thread-safe. Perhaps the most notable among these thread-safe areas is VCL's property streaming mechanism, which ensures that component streams can be effectively read and written by multiple threads. Remember that even very basic classes in VCL, such as TList, are not designed to be manipulated from multiple simultaneous threads. In some cases, VCL provides thread-safe alternatives that you can use in cases where you need them. For example, use a TThreadList in place of a TList when the list will be subject to manipulation by multiple threads.

UI VCL

VCL requires that all user interface control happens within the context of an application's primary thread (the exception is the thread-safe TCanvas, which is explained later in this chapter). Of course, techniques are available to update the user interface from a secondary thread (which we discuss later), but this limitation essentially forces you to use threads a bit more judiciously than you might do otherwise. The examples given in this chapter show some ideal uses for multiple threads in Delphi applications.

Misuse of Threads

Too much of a good thing can be bad, and that's definitely true in the case of threads. Even though threads can help to solve some of the problems you might have from an application design standpoint, they do introduce a whole new set of problems. For example, suppose that you're writing an integrated development environment, and you want the compiler to execute in its own thread so the programmer will be free to continue work on the application while the program compiles. The problem here is this: What if the programmer changes a file that the compiler is in the middle of compiling? There are a number of solutions to this problem, such as making a temporary copy of the file while the compile continues or preventing the user from editing not-yet-compiled files. The point is simply that threads aren't a panacea; although they solve some development problems, they invariably introduce others. What's more, bugs because of threading problems are also much, much harder to debug because threading problems are often time sensitive. Designing and implementing thread-safe code is also more difficult because you have a lot more factors to consider.

The TThread Object

Delphi encapsulates the API thread object into an Object Pascal object called TThread. Although TThread encapsulates almost all the commonly used thread API functions into one discrete object, there are some points—particularly those dealing with thread synchronization—in which you have to use the API. In this section, you learn how the TThread object works and how to use it in your applications.

TThread Basics

The TThread object is found in the Classes unit and is defined as follows:

```
  TThread = class
  private
    FHandle: THandle;
{$IFDEF MSWINDOWS}
    FThreadID: THandle;
{$ENDIF}
{$IFDEF LINUX}
    // ** FThreadID is not THandle in Linux **
    FThreadID: Cardinal;
    FCreateSuspendedSem: TSemaphore;
    FInitialSuspendDone: Boolean;
{$ENDIF}
    FCreateSuspended: Boolean;
    FTerminated: Boolean;
    FSuspended: Boolean;
    FFreeOnTerminate: Boolean;
    FFinished: Boolean;
    FReturnValue: Integer;
    FOnTerminate: TNotifyEvent;
    FMethod: TThreadMethod;
    FSynchronizeException: TObject;
    FFatalException: TObject;
```

```
    procedure CheckThreadError(ErrCode: Integer); overload;
    procedure CheckThreadError(Success: Boolean); overload;
    procedure CallOnTerminate;
{$IFDEF MSWINDOWS}
    function GetPriority: TThreadPriority;
    procedure SetPriority(Value: TThreadPriority);
    procedure SetSuspended(Value: Boolean);
{$ENDIF}
{$IFDEF LINUX}
    // ** Priority is an Integer value in Linux
    function GetPriority: Integer;
    procedure SetPriority(Value:  Integer);
    function GetPolicy: Integer;
    procedure SetPolicy(Value: Integer);
    procedure SetSuspended(Value: Boolean);
{$ENDIF}
  protected
    procedure DoTerminate; virtual;
    procedure Execute; virtual; abstract;
    procedure Synchronize(Method: TThreadMethod);
    property ReturnValue: Integer read FReturnValue write FReturnValue;
    property Terminated: Boolean read FTerminated;
  public
    constructor Create(CreateSuspended: Boolean);
    destructor Destroy; override;
    procedure AfterConstruction; override;
    procedure Resume;
    procedure Suspend;
    procedure Terminate;
    function WaitFor: LongWord;
    property FatalException: TObject read FFatalException;
    property FreeOnTerminate: Boolean read FFreeOnTerminate
      write FFreeOnTerminate;
    property Handle: THandle read FHandle;
{$IFDEF MSWINDOWS}
    property Priority: TThreadPriority read GetPriority write SetPriority;
{$ENDIF}
{$IFDEF LINUX}
    // ** Priority is an Integer **
    property Priority: Integer read GetPriority write SetPriority;
    property Policy: Integer read GetPolicy write SetPolicy;
{$ENDIF}
    property Suspended: Boolean read FSuspended write SetSuspended;
{$IFDEF MSWINDOWS}
    property ThreadID: THandle read FThreadID;
{$ENDIF}
```

```
{$IFDEF LINUX}
    // ** ThreadId is Cardinal **
    property ThreadID: Cardinal read FThreadID;
{$ENDIF}
    property OnTerminate: TNotifyEvent read FOnTerminate write FOnTerminate;
  end;
```

As you can tell from the declaration, TThread is a direct descendant of TObject and therefore isn't a component. Looking at all the IFDEFs in the code, you can also tell that TThread is designed to be fairly compatible between Delphi and Kylix, albeit with a few differences. You might further notice that the TThread.Execute() method is abstract. This means that the TThread class itself is abstract, so you will never create an instance of TThread itself. You will only create instances of TThread descendants. Speaking of which, the most straightforward way to create a TThread descendant is to select Thread Object from the New Items dialog box provided by the File, New Menu option. The New Items dialog box is shown in Figure 5.1.

FIGURE 5.1
The Thread Object item in the New Items dialog box.

After choosing Thread Object from the New Items dialog box, you'll be presented with a dialog box that prompts you to enter a name for the new object. You could enter **TTestThread**, for example. Delphi will then create a new unit that contains your object. Your object will initially be defined as follows:

```
type
  TTestThread = class(TThread)
  private
    { Private declarations }
  protected
    procedure Execute; override;
  end;
```

As you can see, the only method that you *must* override in order to create a functional descendant of TThread is the Execute() method. Suppose, for example, that you want to perform a complex calculation within TTestThread. In that case, you could define its Execute() method as follows:

```
procedure TTestThread.Execute;
var
  i, Answer: integer;
begin
  Answer := 0;
  for i := 1 to 2000000 do
    inc(Answer, Round(Abs(Sin(Sqrt(i)))));
end;
```

Admittedly, the equation is contrived, but it still illustrates the point in this case because the sole purpose of this equation is to take a relatively long time to execute.

You can now execute this sample thread by calling its Create() constructor. For now, you can do this from a button click in the main form, as shown in the following code (remember to include the unit containing TTestThread in the uses clause of the unit containing TForm1 to avoid a compiler error):

```
procedure TForm1.Button1Click(Sender: TObject);
var
  NewThread: TTestThread;
begin
  NewThread := TTestThread.Create(False);
end;
```

If you run the application and click the button, you'll notice that you can still manipulate the form by moving it or resizing it while the calculation goes on in the background.

> **NOTE**
>
> The single Boolean parameter passed to TThread's Create() constructor is called CreateSuspended, and it indicates whether to start the thread in a suspended state. If this parameter is False, the object's Execute() method will automatically be called following Create(). If this parameter is True, you must call TThread's Resume() method at some point to actually start the thread running. This will cause the Execute() method to be invoked at that time. You would set CreateSuspended to True if you needed to set additional properties on your thread object before allowing it to run. Setting the properties after the thread is running would be asking for trouble.
>
> To go a little deeper, the constructor of Create() calls the BeginThread() Delphi Runtime Library (RTL) function, which calls the CreateThread() API function in order to create the new thread. The value of the CreateSuspended parameter indicates whether to pass the CREATE_SUSPENDED flag to CreateThread().

Thread Instances

Going back to the `Execute()` method for the `TTestThread` object, notice that it contains a local variable called i. Consider what might happen to i if you create two instances of `TTestThread`. Does the value for one thread overwrite the value for the other? Does the first thread take precedence? Does it blow up? The answers are no, no, and no. Win32 maintains a separate stack for each thread executing in the system. This means that as you create multiple instances of the `TTestThread` object, each one keeps its own copy of i on its own stack. Therefore, all the threads will operate independently of one another in that respect.

An important distinction to make, however, is that this notion of the same variable operating independently in each thread doesn't carry over to global variables. This topic is explored in detail in the "Thread-Local Storage" and "Thread Synchronization" sections, later in this chapter.

Thread Termination

A `TThread` is considered terminated when the `Execute()` method has finished executing. At that point, the `EndThread()` Delphi standard procedure is called, which in turn calls the `ExitThread()` API procedure. `ExitThread()` properly disposes of the thread's stack and deallocates the API thread object. This cleans up the thread as far as the API is concerned.

You also need to ensure that the Object Pascal object is destroyed when you're finished using a `TThread` object. This will ensure that all memory occupied by that object has been properly disposed of. Although this will automatically happen when your process terminates, you might want to dispose of the object earlier so that your application doesn't leak memory as it runs. The easiest way to ensure that the `TThread` object is disposed of is to set its `FreeOnTerminate` property to `True`. This can be done any time before the `Execute()` method finishes executing. For example, you could do this for the `TTestThread` object by setting the property in the `Execute()` method as follows:

```
procedure TTestThread.Execute;
var
  i: integer;
begin
  FreeOnTerminate := True;
  for i := 1 to 2000000 do
    inc(Answer, Round(Abs(Sin(Sqrt(i)))));
end;
```

The `TThread` object also has an `OnTerminate` event that's called when the thread terminates. It's also acceptable to free the `TThread` object from within a handler for this event.

The OnTerminate event of TThread is called from the context of your application's main thread. This means that you can feel free to access VCL properties and methods from within a handler for this event without using the Synchronize() method, as described in the following section.

It's also important to note that your thread's Execute() method is responsible for checking the status of the Terminated property to determine the need to make an earlier exit. Although this means one more thing you must worry about when working with threads, the flip side is that this type of architecture ensures that the rug isn't pulled out from under you, and that you'll be able to perform any necessary cleanup on thread termination. To add this code to the Execute() method of TTestThread is rather simple, and the addition is shown here:

```
procedure TTestThread.Execute;
var
  i: integer;
begin
  FreeOnTerminate := True;
  for i := 1 to 2000000 do begin
    if Terminated then Break;
    inc(Answer, Round(Abs(Sin(Sqrt(i)))));
  end;
end;
```

In case of emergency, you can also use the Win32 API TerminateThread() function to terminate an executing thread. You should do this only when no other options exist, such as when a thread gets caught in an endless loop and stops responding. This function is defined as follows:

```
function TerminateThread(hThread: THandle; dwExitCode: DWORD);
```

The Handle property of TThread provides the API thread handle, so you could call this function with syntax similar to that shown here:

```
TerminateThread(MyHosedThread.Handle, 0);
```

If you choose to use this function, you should be wary of the negative side effects it will cause. First, this function behaves differently under Windows NT/2000 and Windows 95/98. Under Windows 95/98, TerminateThread() disposes of the stack

continues

associated with the thread; under Windows NT/2000, the stack sticks around until the process is terminated. Second, on all Win32 operating systems, TerminateThread() simply halts execution, wherever it might be, and doesn't allow try..finally blocks to clean up resources. This means that files opened by the thread wouldn't be closed, memory allocated by the thread wouldn't be freed, and so forth. Also, DLLs loaded by your process won't be notified when a thread destroyed with TerminateThread() goes away, and this might cause problems when the DLL closes. See Chapter 6, "Dynamic Link Libraries," for more information on thread notifications in DLLs.

Synchronizing with VCL

As mentioned several times earlier in this chapter, you should only access VCL properties or methods from the application's primary thread. This means that any code that accesses or updates your application's user interface should be executed from the context of the primary thread. The disadvantages of this architecture are obvious, and this requirement might seem rather limiting on the surface, but it actually has some redeeming advantages that you should know about.

Advantages of a Single-Threaded User Interface

First, it greatly reduces the complexity of your application to have only one thread accessing the user interface. Win32 requires that each thread that creates a window have its own message loop using the GetMessage() function. As you might imagine, having messages coming into your application from a variety of sources can make it extremely difficult to debug. Because an application's message queue provides a means for serializing input—fully processing one condition before moving on to the next—you can depend in most cases on certain messages coming before or after others. Adding another message loop throws this serialization of input out the door, thereby opening you up to potential synchronization problems and possibly introducing a need for complex synchronization code.

Additionally, because VCL can depend on the fact that it will be accessed by only one thread at any given time, the need for code to synchronize multiple threads inside VCL is obviated. The net result of this is better overall performance of your application due to a more streamlined architecture.

The Synchronize() Method

TThread provides a method called Synchronize() that allows for some of its own methods to be executed from the application's primary thread. Synchronize() is defined as follows:

```
procedure Synchronize(Method: TThreadMethod);
```

Its `Method` parameter is of type `TThreadMethod` (which means a procedural method that takes no parameter), which is defined as follows:

```
type
  TThreadMethod = procedure of object;
```

The method you pass as the `Method` parameter is the one that's then executed from the application's primary thread. Going back to the `TTestThread` example, suppose you want to display the result in an edit control on the main form. You could do this by introducing to `TTestThread` a method that makes the necessary change to the edit control's `Text` property and calling that method by using `Synchronize()`.

In this case, suppose this method is called `GiveAnswer()`. Listing 5.1 shows the complete source code for this unit, called `ThrdU`, which includes the code to update the edit control on the main form.

LISTING 5.1   The `ThrdU.PAS` Unit

```
unit ThrdU;

interface

uses
  Classes;

type
  TTestThread = class(TThread)
  private
    Answer: integer;
  protected
    procedure GiveAnswer;
    procedure Execute; override;
  end;

implementation

uses SysUtils, Main;

{ TTestThread }

procedure TTestThread.GiveAnswer;
begin
  MainForm.Edit1.Text := InttoStr(Answer);
end;

procedure TTestThread.Execute;
```

LISTING 5.1 Continued

```
var
  I: Integer;
begin
  FreeOnTerminate := True;
  for I := 1 to  2000000 do
  begin
    if Terminated then Break;
    Inc(Answer, Round(Abs(Sin(Sqrt(I)))));
    Synchronize(GiveAnswer);
  end;
end;

end.
```

You already know that the Synchronize() method enables you to execute methods from the context of the primary thread, but up to this point you've treated Synchronize() as sort of a mysterious black box. You don't know *how* it works—you only know that it does. If you'd like to take a peek at the man behind the curtain, read on.

The first time you create a secondary thread in your application, VCL creates and maintains a hidden *thread window* from the context of its primary thread. The sole purpose of this window is to serialize procedure calls made through the Synchronize() method.

The Synchronize() method stores the method specified in its Method parameter in a private field called FMethod and sends a VCL-defined CM_EXECPROC message to the thread window, passing Self (Self being the TThread object in this case) as the lParam of the message. When the thread window's window procedure receives this CM_EXECPROC message, it calls the method specified in FMethod through the TThread object instance passed in the lParam. Remember, because the thread window was created from the context of the primary thread, the window procedure for the thread window is also executed by the primary thread. Therefore, the method specified in the FMethod field is also executed by the primary thread.

To see a more visual illustration of what goes on inside Synchronize(), look at Figure 5.2.

Using Messages for Synchronization

As an alternative to the TThread.Synchronize() method, another technique for thread synchronization is to use messages to communicate between threads. You can use the SendMessage() or PostMessage() API function to send or post messages to windows operating in the context of another thread. For example, the following code could be used to set the text in an edit control residing in another thread:

```
var
  S: string;
begin
  S := 'hello from threadland';
  SendMessage(SomeEdit.Handle, WM_SETTEXT, 0, Integer(PChar(S)));
end;
```

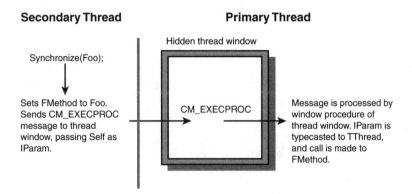

FIGURE 5.2

A road map of the Synchronize() *method.*

A Demo Application

To fully illustrate how multithreading in Delphi works, you can save the current project as **EZThrd**. Then you can also put a memo control on the main form so that it resembles what's shown in Figure 5.3.

FIGURE 5.3

The main form of the EZThrd *demo.*

The source code for the main unit is shown in Listing 5.2.

LISTING 5.2   The MAIN.PAS Unit for the EZThrd Demo

```
unit Main;

interface

uses
  Windows, Messages, SysUtils, Classes, Graphics, Controls, Forms,
    Dialogs, StdCtrls, ThrdU;

type
  TMainForm = class(TForm)
    Edit1: TEdit;
    Button1: TButton;
    Memo1: TMemo;
    Label1: TLabel;
    Label2:  TLabel;
    procedure Button1Click(Sender: TObject);
  private
    { Private declarations }
  public
    { Public declarations }
  end;

var
  MainForm: TMainForm;

implementation

{$R *.DFM}

procedure TMainForm.Button1Click(Sender: TObject);
var
  NewThread:  TTestThread;
begin
  NewThread := TTestThread.Create(False);
end;

end.
```

Notice that after you click the button to invoke the secondary thread, you can still type in the memo control as if the secondary thread doesn't exist. When the calculation is completed, the result will be displayed in the edit control.

Priorities and Scheduling

As mentioned earlier, the operating system is in charge of scheduling each thread some CPU cycles in which it might execute. The amount of time scheduled for a particular thread depends on the priority assigned to the thread. An individual thread's overall priority is determined by a combination of the priority of the process that created the thread—called the *priority class*—and the priority of the thread itself—called the *relative priority*.

Process Priority Class

The *process priority class* describes the priority of a particular process running on the system. Win32 supports four distinct priority classes: Idle, Normal, High, and Realtime. The default priority class for any process, of course, is Normal. Each of these priority classes has a corresponding flag defined in the Windows unit. You can or any of these flags with the dwCreationFlags parameter of CreateProcess() in order to spawn a process with a specific priority. Additionally, you can use these flags to dynamically adjust the priority class of a given process, as shown in a moment. Furthermore, each priority class can also be represented by a numeric priority level, which is a value between 4 and 24 (inclusive).

> **NOTE**
>
> Modifying a process's priority class requires special process privileges under Windows NT/2000. The default settings allow processes to set their priority classes, but these can be turned off by system administrators, particularly on high-load Windows NT/2000 servers.

Table 5.1 shows each priority class and its corresponding flag and numeric value.

TABLE 5.1 Process Priority Classes

Class	Flag	Value
Idle	IDLE_PRIORITY_CLASS	$40
Below Normal*	BELOW_NORMAL_PRIORITY_CLASS	$4000
Normal	NORMAL_PRIORITY_CLASS	$20
Above Normal*	ABOVE_NORMAL_PRIORITY_CLASS	$8000
High	HIGH_PRIORITY_CLASS	$80
Realtime	REALTIME_PRIORITY_CLASS	$100

Available only on Windows 2000 and higher, and flag constant is not present in Delphi 6 version of Windows.pas.

5

To get and set the priority class of a given process dynamically, Win32 provides the GetPriorityClass() and SetPriorityClass() functions, respectively. These functions are defined as follows:

```
function GetPriorityClass(hProcess: THandle): DWORD; stdcall;

function SetPriorityClass(hProcess: THandle; dwPriorityClass: DWORD): BOOL;
  stdcall;
```

The hProcess parameter in both cases represents a handle to a process. In most cases, you'll be calling these functions in order to access the priority class of your own process. In that case, you can use the GetCurrentProcess() API function. This function is defined as follows:

```
function GetCurrentProcess: THandle; stdcall;
```

The return value of these functions is a pseudo-handle for the current process. We say *pseudo* because the function doesn't create a new handle, and the return value doesn't have to be closed with CloseHandle(). It merely provides a handle that can be used to reference an existing handle.

To set the priority class of your application to High, use code similar to the following:

```
if not SetPriorityClass(GetCurrentProcess, HIGH_PRIORITY_CLASS) then
  ShowMessage('Error setting priority class.');
```

> **CAUTION**
>
> In almost all cases, you should avoid setting the priority class of any process to Realtime. Because most of the operating system threads run in a priority class lower than Realtime, your thread will receive more CPU time than the OS itself, and that could cause some unexpected problems.
>
> Even bumping the priority class of the process to High can cause problems if the threads of the process don't spend most of their time idle or waiting for external events (such as file I/O). One high-priority thread is likely to drain all CPU time away from lower-priority threads and processes until it blocks on an event, goes idle, or processes messages. Preemptive multitasking can easily be defeated by abusing scheduler priorities.

Relative Priority

The other thing that goes into determining the overall priority of a thread is the *relative priority* of a particular thread. The important distinction to make is that the priority class is associated with a process and the relative priority is associated with individual threads within a process. A thread can have any one of seven possible relative priorities: Idle, Lowest, Below Normal, Normal, Above Normal, Highest, or Time Critical.

TThread exposes a `Priority` property of an enumerated type `TThreadPriority`. There's an enumeration in this type for each relative priority:

```
type
  TThreadPriority = (tpIdle, tpLowest, tpLower, tpNormal, tpHigher,
    tpHighest, tpTimeCritical);
```

You can get and set the priority of any `TThread` object simply by reading from or writing to its `Priority` property. The following code sets the priority of a `TThread` descendant instance called `MyThread` to Highest:

```
MyThread.Priority := tpHighest.
```

Like priority classes, each relative priority is associated with a numeric value. The difference is that relative priority is a signed value that, when added to a process's class priority, is used to determine the overall priority of a thread within the system. For this reason, relative priority is sometimes called *delta priority*. The overall priority of a thread can be any value from 1 to 31 (1 being the lowest). Constants are defined in the `Windows` unit that represent the signed value for each priority. Table 5.2 shows how each enumeration in `TThreadPriority` maps to an API constant.

TABLE 5.2 Relative Priorities for Threads

TThreadPriority	Constant	Value
tpIdle	THREAD_PRIORITY_IDLE	-15*
tpLowest	THREAD_PRIORITY_LOWEST	-2
tpBelow Normal	THREAD_PRIORITY_BELOW_NORMAL	-1
tpNormal	THREAD_PRIORITY_NORMAL	0
tpAbove Normal	THREAD_PRIORITY_ABOVE_NORMAL	1
tpHighest	THREAD_PRIORITY_HIGHEST	2
tpTimeCritical	THREAD_PRIORITY_TIME_CRITICAL	15*

The reason the values for the `tpIdle` and `tpTimeCritical` priorities are marked with asterisks is that, unlike the others, these relative priority values are not truly added to the class priority to determine overall thread priority. Any thread that has the `tpIdle` relative priority, regardless of its priority class, has an overall priority of 1. The exception to this rule is the `Realtime` priority class, which, when combined with the `tpIdle` relative priority, has an overall value of 16. Any thread that has a priority of `tpTimeCritical`, regardless of its priority class, has an overall priority of 15. The exception to this rule is the `Realtime` priority class, which, when combined with the `tpTimeCritical` relative priority, has an overall value of 31.

5

MULTITHREADED
TECHNIQUES

Suspending and Resuming Threads

Recall when you learned about TThread's Create() constructor earlier in this chapter. At the time, you discovered that a thread could be created in a suspended state, and that you must call its Resume() method in order for the thread to begin execution. As you might guess, a thread can also be suspended and resumed dynamically. You accomplish this using the Suspend() method in conjunction with the Resume() method.

Timing a Thread

Back in the 16-bit days when we programmed under Windows 3.*x*, it was pretty common to wrap some portion of code with calls to GetTickCount() or timeGetTime() to determine how much time a particular calculation would take (something like the following, for example):

```
var
  StartTime, Total: Longint;
begin
  StartTime := GetTickCount;
  { Do some calculation here }
  Total := GetTickCount - StartTime;
```

In a multithreaded environment, this is much more difficult to do because your application might be preempted by the operating system in the middle of the calculation in order to provide CPU cycles to other processes. Therefore, any timing you do that relies on the system time can't provide a true measure of how long it spends crunching the calculation in your thread.

To avoid such problems, Win32 under Windows NT/2000 provides a function called GetThreadTimes(), which provides quite detailed information on thread timing. This function is declared as follows:

```
function GetThreadTimes(hThread: THandle; var lpCreationTime, lpExitTime,
    lpKernelTime, lpUserTime: TFileTime): BOOL; stdcall;
```

The hThread parameter is the handle to the thread for which you want to obtain timing information. The other parameters for this function are passed by reference and are filled in by the function. Here's an explanation of each:

- lpCreationTime—The time when the thread was created.
- lpExitTime—The time when the thread was exited. If the thread is still running, this value is undefined.
- lpKernelTime—The amount of time the thread has spent executing operating system code.
- lpUserTime—The amount of time the thread has spent executing application code.

Each of the last four parameters is of type `TFileTime`, which is defined in the `Windows` unit as follows:

```
type
  TFileTime = record
    dwLowDateTime: DWORD;
    dwHighDateTime: DWORD;
  end;
```

The definition of this type is a bit unusual, but it's a part of the Win32 API, so here goes: `dwLowDateTime` and `dwHighDateTime` are combined into a quad word (64-bit) value that represents the number of 100-nanosecond intervals that have passed since January 1, 1601. This means, of course, that if you wanted to write a simulation of English fleet movements as they defeated the Spanish Armada in 1588, the `TFileTime` type would be a wholly inappropriate way to keep track of time. . . but we digress.

TIP

Because the `TFileTime` type is 64 bits in size, you can typecast a `TFileTime` to an `Int64` type in order to perform arithmetic on `TFileTime` values. The following code demonstrates how to quickly tell whether one `TFileTime` is greater than another:

```
if Int64(UserTime) > Int64(KernelTime) then Beep;
```

In order to help you work with `TFileTime` values in a manner more native to Delphi, the following functions allow you to convert back and forth between `TFileTime` and `TDateTime` types:

```
function FileTimeToDateTime(FileTime: TFileTime): TDateTime;
var
  SysTime: TSystemTime;
begin
  if not FileTimeToSystemTime(FileTime, SysTime) then
    raise EConvertError.CreateFmt('FileTimeToSystemTime failed. ' +
      'Error code %d', [GetLastError]);
  with SysTime do
    Result := EncodeDate(wYear, wMonth, wDay)  +
      EncodeTime(wHour, wMinute, wSecond, wMilliseconds)
end;

function DateTimeToFileTime(DateTime: TDateTime): TFileTime;
var
  SysTime: TSystemTime;
```

```
begin
  with SysTime do
  begin
    DecodeDate(DateTime, wYear, wMonth, wDay);
    DecodeTime(DateTime, wHour, wMinute, wSecond, wMilliseconds);
    wDayOfWeek := DayOfWeek(DateTime);
  end;
  if not SystemTimeToFileTime(SysTime, Result) then
    raise EConvertError.CreateFmt('SystemTimeToFileTime failed. ' +
      + 'Error code %d', [GetLastError]);
end;
```

> **CAUTION**
>
> Remember that the `GetThreadTimes()` function is implemented only under Windows NT/2000. The function always returns `False` when called under Windows 95 or 98. Unfortunately, Windows 95/98 doesn't provide any mechanism for retrieving thread-timing information.

Managing Multiple Threads

As indicated earlier, although threads can solve a variety of programming problems, they're also likely to introduce new types of problems that you must deal with in your applications. Most commonly, these problems revolve around multiple threads accessing global resources, such as global variables or handles. Additionally, problems can arise when you need to ensure that some event in one thread always occurs before or after some other event in another thread. In this section, you learn how to tackle these problems by using the facilities provided by Delphi for thread-local storage and those provided by the API for thread synchronization.

Thread-Local Storage

Because each thread represents a separate and distinct path of execution within a process, it logically follows that you will at some point want to have a means for storing data associated with each thread. There are three techniques for storing data unique to each thread: the first and most straightforward involves local (stack-based) variables. Because each thread gets its own stack, each thread executing within a single procedure or function will have its own copy of local variables. The second technique is to store local information in your `TThread` descendant object. Finally, you can also use Object Pascal's `threadvar` reserved word to take advantage of operating-system–level thread-local storage.

TThread Storage

Storing pertinent data in the TThread descendant object should be your technique of choice for thread-local storage. It's both more straightforward and more efficient than using threadvar (described later). To declare thread-local data in this manner, simply add it to the definition of your TThread descendant, as shown here:

```
type
  TMyThread = class(TThread)
  private
    FLocalInt: Integer;
    FLocalStr: String;
    .
    .
    .
  end;
```

> **TIP**
>
> It's about 10 times faster to access a field of an object than to access a threadvar variable, so you should store your thread-specific data in your TThread descendant, if possible. Data that doesn't need to exist for more than the lifetime of a particular procedure or function should be stored in local variables because those are faster still than the fields of a TThread object.

threadvar: API Thread-Local Storage

Earlier we mentioned that each thread is provided with its own stack for storing local variables, whereas global data has to be shared by all threads within an application. For example, say you have a procedure that sets or displays the value of a global variable. When you call the procedure passing a text string, the global variable is set, and when you call the procedure passing an empty string, the global variable is displayed. Such a procedure might look like this:

```
var
  GlobalStr: String;
procedure SetShowStr(const S: String);
begin
  if S = '' then
    MessageBox(0, PChar(GlobalStr), 'The string is...', MB_OK)
  else
    GlobalStr := S;
end;
```

If this procedure is called from within the context of one thread only, there wouldn't be any problems. You'd call the procedure once to set the value of GlobalStr and call it again to display the value. However, consider what can happen if two or more threads call this procedure at any given time. In such a case, it's possible that one thread could call the procedure to set the string and then get preempted by another thread that might also call the function to set the string. By the time the operating system gives CPU time back to the first thread, the value of GlobalStr for that thread will be hopelessly lost.

For situations such as these, Win32 provides a facility known as *thread-local storage* that enables you to create separate copies of global variables for each running thread. Delphi nicely encapsulates this functionality with the threadvar clause. Just declare any global variables you want to exist separately for each thread within a threadvar (as opposed to var) clause, and the work is done. A redeclaration of the GlobalStr variable is as simple as this:

```
threadvar
  GlobalStr: String;
```

The unit shown in Listing 5.3 illustrates this very problem. It represents the main unit to a Delphi application that contains only a button on a form. When the button is clicked, the procedure is called to set and then to show GlobalStr. Next, another thread is created, and the value internal to the thread is set and shown again. After the thread creation, the primary thread again calls SetShowStr to display GlobalStr.

Try running this application with GlobalStr declared as a var and then as a threadvar. You'll see a difference in the output.

LISTING 5.3 The MAIN.PAS Unit for Thread-Local Storage Demo

```
unit Main;

interface

uses
  Windows, Messages, SysUtils, Classes, Graphics, Controls, Forms,
  Dialogs, StdCtrls;

type
  TMainForm = class(TForm)
    Button1: TButton;
    procedure Button1Click(Sender: TObject);
  private
    { Private declarations }
  public
    { Public declarations }
```

LISTING 5.3 Continued

```
  end;

var
  MainForm: TMainForm;

implementation

{$R *.DFM}

{ NOTE: Change GlobalStr from var to threadvar to see difference }
var
//threadvar
  GlobalStr: string;

type
  TTLSThread = class(TThread)
  private
    FNewStr: String;
  protected
    procedure Execute; override;
  public
    constructor Create(const ANewStr: String);
  end;

procedure SetShowStr(const S: String);
begin
  if S = '' then
    MessageBox(0, PChar(GlobalStr), 'The string is...', MB_OK)
  else
    GlobalStr := S;
end;

constructor TTLSThread.Create(const ANewStr: String);
begin
  FNewStr := ANewStr;
  inherited Create(False);
end;

procedure TTLSThread.Execute;
begin
  FreeOnTerminate := True;
  SetShowStr(FNewStr);
  SetShowStr('');
end;
```

LISTING 5.3 Continued

```
procedure TMainForm.Button1Click(Sender: TObject);
begin
  SetShowStr('Hello world');
  SetShowStr('');
  TTLSThread.Create('Dilbert');
  Sleep(100);
  SetShowStr('');
end;

end.
```

> **NOTE**
>
> The demo program calls the Win32 API `Sleep()` procedure after creating the thread. `Sleep()` is declared as follows:
>
> ```
> procedure Sleep(dwMilliseconds: DWORD); stdcall;
> ```
>
> The `Sleep()` procedure tells the operating system that the current thread doesn't need any more CPU cycles for another `dwMilliseconds` milliseconds. Inserting this call into the code has the effect of simulating system conditions where more multitasking is occurring and introducing a bit more "randomness" into the application as to which threads will be executing when.
>
> It's often acceptable to pass zero in the `dwMilliseconds` parameter. Although that doesn't prevent the current thread from executing for any specific amount of time, it does cause the operating system to give CPU cycles to any waiting threads of equal or greater priority.
>
> Be careful of using `Sleep()` to work around mysterious timing problems. `Sleep()` might work around a particular problem on your machine, but timing problems that aren't solved conclusively will pop up again on somebody else's machine, especially when the machine is significantly faster or slower or has a different number of processors than your machine.

Thread Synchronization

When working with multiple threads, you'll often need to synchronize the access of threads to some particular piece of data or resource. For example, suppose you have an application that uses one thread to read a file into memory and another thread to count the number of characters in the file. It goes without saying that you can't count all the characters in the file until the entire file has been loaded into memory. However, because each operation occurs in its own thread, the operating system would like to treat them as two completely unrelated tasks. To fix this problem, you must synchronize the two threads so that the counting thread doesn't execute until the loading thread finishes.

These are the types of problems that thread synchronization addresses, and Win32 provides a variety of ways to synchronize threads. In this section, you'll see examples of thread synchronization techniques using critical sections, mutexes, semaphores, and events.

In order to examine these techniques, first take a look at a problem involving threads that need to be synchronized. For the purpose of illustration, suppose you have an array of integers that needs to be initialized with ascending values. You want to first go through the array and set the values from 1 to 128 and then reinitialize the array with values from 128 to 255. You'll then display the final thread in a list box. An approach to this might be to perform the initializations in two separate threads. Consider the code in Listing 5.4 for a unit that attempts to perform this task.

LISTING 5.4 A Unit That Attempts to Initialize an Array in Threads

```
unit Main;

interface

uses
  Windows, Messages, SysUtils, Classes, Graphics, Controls, Forms,
  Dialogs, StdCtrls;

type
  TMainForm = class(TForm)
    Button1: TButton;
    ListBox1: TListBox;
    procedure Button1Click(Sender: TObject);
  private
    procedure ThreadsDone(Sender: TObject);
  end;

  TFooThread = class(TThread)
  protected
    procedure Execute; override;
  end;

var
  MainForm: TMainForm;

implementation
```

LISTING 5.4   Continued

```
{$R *.DFM}

const
  MaxSize = 128;

var
  NextNumber: Integer = 0;
  DoneFlags: Integer = 0;
  GlobalArray: array[1..MaxSize] of Integer;

function GetNextNumber: Integer;
begin
  Result := NextNumber;  // return global var
  Inc(NextNumber);       // inc global var
end;

procedure TFooThread.Execute;
var
  i: Integer;
begin
  OnTerminate := MainForm.ThreadsDone;
  for i := 1 to MaxSize do
  begin
    GlobalArray[i] := GetNextNumber;  // set array element
    Sleep(5);                         // let thread intertwine
  end;
end;

procedure TMainForm.ThreadsDone(Sender: TObject);
var
  i: Integer;
begin
  Inc(DoneFlags);
  if DoneFlags = 2 then        // make sure both threads finished
    for i := 1 to MaxSize do
      { fill listbox with array contents }
      Listbox1.Items.Add(IntToStr(GlobalArray[i]));
end;

procedure TMainForm.Button1Click(Sender: TObject);
begin
  TFooThread.Create(False);  // create threads
  TFooThread.Create(False);
end;

end.
```

Because both threads will execute simultaneously, what happens is that the contents of the array are corrupted as it's initialized. As proof, take a look at the output of this code, as shown in Figure 5.4.

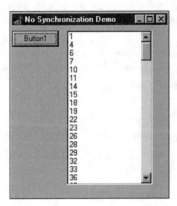

FIGURE 5.4
Output from unsynchronized array initialization.

The solution to this problem is to synchronize the two threads as they access the global array so that they don't both dive in at the same time. You can take any of a number of valid approaches to this problem.

Critical Sections

Critical sections provide one of the most straightforward ways to synchronize threads. A *critical section* is some section of code that allows for only one thread to execute through it at a time. If you wrap the code used to initialize the array in a critical section, other threads will be blocked from entering the code section until the first finishes.

Prior to using a critical section, you must initialize it using the InitializeCriticalSection() API procedure, which is declared as follows:

```
procedure InitializeCriticalSection(var lpCriticalSection:
  TRTLCriticalSection); stdcall;
```

lpCriticalSection is a TRTLCriticalSection record that's passed by reference. The exact definition of TRTLCriticalSection is unimportant because you'll rarely (if ever) actually look at the contents of one. You'll pass an uninitialized record in the lpCriticalSection parameter, and the record will be filled by the procedure.

When the record is filled, you can create a critical section in your application by wrapping some block of code with calls to EnterCriticalSection() and LeaveCriticalSection(). These procedures are declared as follows:

```
procedure EnterCriticalSection(var lpCriticalSection:
  TRTLCriticalSection); stdcall;
procedure LeaveCriticalSection(var lpCriticalSection:
  TRTLCriticalSection); stdcall;
```

As you might guess, the lpCriticalSection parameter you pass these guys is the same one that's filled in by the InitializeCriticalSection() procedure.

When you're finished with the TRTLCriticalSection record, you should clean up by calling the DeleteCriticalSection() procedure, which is declared as follows:

```
procedure DeleteCriticalSection(var lpCriticalSection:
  TRTLCriticalSection); stdcall;
```

Listing 5.5 demonstrates the technique for synchronizing the array-initialization threads with critical sections.

LISTING 5.5 Using Critical Sections

```
unit Main;

interface

uses
  Windows, Messages, SysUtils, Classes, Graphics, Controls, Forms,
    Dialogs, StdCtrls;

type
  TMainForm = class(TForm)
    Button1: TButton;
```

LISTING 5.5 Continued

```
    ListBox1: TListBox;
    procedure Button1Click(Sender: TObject);
  private
    procedure ThreadsDone(Sender: TObject);
  end;

  TFooThread = class(TThread)
  protected
    procedure Execute; override;
  end;

var
  MainForm: TMainForm;

implementation

{$R *.DFM}

const
  MaxSize = 128;

var
  NextNumber: Integer = 0;
  DoneFlags: Integer = 0;
  GlobalArray: array[1..MaxSize] of Integer;
  CS: TRTLCriticalSection;

function GetNextNumber: Integer;
begin
  Result := NextNumber;   // return global var
  inc(NextNumber);        // inc global var
end;

procedure TFooThread.Execute;
var
  i: Integer;
begin
  OnTerminate := MainForm.ThreadsDone;
  EnterCriticalSection(CS);           // CS begins here
  for i := 1 to MaxSize do
  begin
    GlobalArray[i] := GetNextNumber;  // set array element
    Sleep(5);                         // let thread intertwine
  end;
  LeaveCriticalSection(CS);           // CS ends here
```

LISTING 5.5   Continued

```
end;

procedure TMainForm.ThreadsDone(Sender: TObject);
var
  i: Integer;
begin
  inc(DoneFlags);
  if DoneFlags = 2 then
  begin // make sure both threads finished
    for i := 1 to MaxSize do
      { fill listbox with array contents }
      Listbox1.Items.Add(IntToStr(GlobalArray[i]));
    DeleteCriticalSection(CS);
  end;
end;

procedure TMainForm.Button1Click(Sender: TObject);
begin
  InitializeCriticalSection(CS);
  TFooThread.Create(False);  // create threads
  TFooThread.Create(False);
end;

end.
```

After the first thread passes through the call to EnterCriticalSection(), all other threads are prevented from entering that block of code. The next thread that comes along to that line of code is put to sleep until the first thread calls LeaveCriticalSection(). At that point, the second thread is awakened and allowed to take control of the critical section. Figure 5.5 shows the output of this application when the threads are synchronized.

Mutexes

Mutexes work very much like critical sections except for two key differences: First, mutexes can be used to synchronize threads across process boundaries. Second, mutexes can be given a string name, and additional handles to existing mutex objects can be created by referencing that name.

FIGURE 5.5

Output from synchronized array initialization.

> **TIP**
>
> Semantics aside, the biggest difference between critical sections and event objects such as mutexes is performance: Critical sections are very lightweight—as few as 10–15 clock cycles to enter or leave the critical section when there are no thread collisions. As soon as there is a thread collision for that critical section, the system creates an event object (a mutex, probably). The cost of using event objects such as mutexes is that it requires a roundtrip into the kernel, which requires a process context switch and a change of ring levels, which piles up to 400 to 600 clock cycles each way. All this overhead is incurred even if your app doesn't currently have multiple threads, or if no other threads are contending for the resource you're protecting.

The function used to create a mutex is appropriately called CreateMutex(). This function is declared as follows:

```
function CreateMutex(lpMutexAttributes: PSecurityAttributes;
  bInitialOwner: BOOL; lpName: PChar): THandle; stdcall;
```

lpMutexAttributes is a pointer to a TSecurityAttributes record. It's common to pass nil in this parameter, in which case the default security attributes will be used.

bInitialOwner indicates whether the thread creating the mutex should be considered the owner of the mutex when it's created. If this parameter is False, the mutex is unowned.

lpName is the name of the mutex. This parameter can be nil if you don't want to name the mutex. If this parameter is non-nil, the function will search the system for an existing mutex with the same name. If an existing mutex is found, a handle to the existing mutex is returned. Otherwise, a handle to a new mutex is returned.

When you're finished using a mutex, you should close it using the `CloseHandle()` API function.

Listing 5.6 again demonstrates the technique for synchronizing the array-initialization threads, except this time it uses mutexes.

LISTING 5.6   Using Mutexes for Synchronization

```
unit Main;

interface

uses
  Windows, Messages, SysUtils, Classes, Graphics, Controls, Forms,
    Dialogs, StdCtrls;

type
  TMainForm = class(TForm)
    Button1: TButton;
    ListBox1: TListBox;
    procedure Button1Click(Sender: TObject);
  private
    procedure ThreadsDone(Sender: TObject);
  end;

  TFooThread = class(TThread)
  protected
    procedure Execute; override;
  end;

var
  MainForm: TMainForm;

implementation

{$R *.DFM}

const
  MaxSize = 128;

var
  NextNumber: Integer = 0;
  DoneFlags: Integer = 0;
```

LISTING 5.6   Continued

```
  GlobalArray: array[1..MaxSize] of Integer;
  hMutex: THandle = 0;

function GetNextNumber: Integer;
begin
  Result := NextNumber;   // return global var
  Inc(NextNumber);        // inc global var
end;

procedure TFooThread.Execute;
var
  i: Integer;
begin
  FreeOnTerminate := True;
  OnTerminate := MainForm.ThreadsDone;
  if WaitForSingleObject(hMutex, INFINITE) = WAIT_OBJECT_0 then
  begin
    for i := 1 to MaxSize do
    begin
      GlobalArray[i] := GetNextNumber;   // set array element
      Sleep(5);                          // let thread intertwine
    end;
  end;
  ReleaseMutex(hMutex);
end;

procedure TMainForm.ThreadsDone(Sender:  TObject);
var
  i: Integer;
begin
  Inc(DoneFlags);
  if DoneFlags = 2 then     // make sure both threads finished
  begin
    for i := 1 to MaxSize do
      { fill listbox with array contents }
      Listbox1.Items.Add(IntToStr(GlobalArray[i]));
    CloseHandle(hMutex);
  end;
end;

procedure TMainForm.Button1Click(Sender: TObject);
begin
  hMutex := CreateMutex(nil, False, nil);
  TFooThread.Create(False);  // create threads
```

LISTING 5.6 Continued

```
  TFooThread.Create(False);
end;

end.
```

You'll notice that in this case the `WaitForSingleObject()` function is used to control thread entry into the synchronized block of code. This function is declared as follows:

```
function WaitForSingleObject(hHandle: THandle; dwMilliseconds: DWORD):
  DWORD; stdcall;
```

The purpose of this function is to sleep the current thread up to `dwMilliseconds` milliseconds until the API object specified in the `hHandle` parameter becomes signaled. *Signaled* means different things for different objects. A mutex becomes signaled when it's not owned by a thread, whereas a process, for example, becomes signaled when it terminates. Apart from an actual period of time, the `dwMilliseconds` parameter can also have the value `0`, which means to check the status of the object and return immediately, or `INFINITE`, which means to wait forever for the object to become signaled. The return value of this function can be any one of the values shown in Table 5.3.

TABLE 5.3 WAIT Constants Used by `WaitForSingleObject()` API Function

Value	Meaning
WAIT_ABANDONED	The specified object is a mutex object, and the thread owning the mutex was exited before it freed the mutex. This circumstance is referred to as an abandoned mutex; in such a case, ownership of the mutex object is granted to the calling thread, and the mutex is set to nonsignaled.
WAIT_OBJECT_0	The state of the specified object is signaled.
WAIT_TIMEOUT	The timeout interval elapsed, and the object's state is nonsignaled.

Again, when a mutex isn't owned by a thread, it's in the signaled state. The first thread to call `WaitForSingleObject()` on this mutex is given ownership of the mutex, and the state of the mutex object is set to nonsignaled. The thread's ownership of the mutex is severed when the thread calls the `ReleaseMutex()` function, passing the mutex handle as the parameter. At that point, the state of the mutex again becomes signaled.

NOTE

In addition to `WaitForSingleObject()`, the Win32 API also has functions called `WaitForMultipleObjects()` and `MsgWaitForMultipleObjects()`, which enable you to wait for the state of one or more objects to become signaled. These functions are documented in the Win32 API online help.

Semaphores

Another technique for thread synchronization involves using semaphore API objects. *Semaphores* build on the functionality of mutexes while adding one important feature: They offer the capability of resource counting so that a predetermined number of threads can enter synchronized pieces of code at one time. The function used to create a semaphore is `CreateSemaphore()`, and it's declared as follows:

```
function CreateSemaphore(lpSemaphoreAttributes: PSecurityAttributes;
  lInitialCount, lMaximumCount: Longint; lpName: PChar): THandle;stdcall;
```

Like `CreateMutex()`, the first parameter to `CreateSemaphore()` is a pointer to a `TSecurityAttributes` record to which you can pass `Nil` for the defaults.

`lInitialCount` is the initial count of the semaphore object. This is a number between 0 and `lMaximumCount`. A semaphore is signaled as long as this parameter is greater than zero. The count of a semaphore is decremented whenever `WaitForSingleObject()` (or one of the other wait functions) releases a thread. A semaphore's count is increased by using the `ReleaseSemaphore()` function.

`lMaximumCount` specifies the maximum count value of the semaphore object. If the semaphore is used to count some resources, this number should represent the total number of resources available.

`lpName` is the name of the semaphore. This parameter behaves the same as the parameter of the same name in `CreateMutex()`.

Listing 5.7 demonstrates using semaphores to perform synchronization of the array-initialization problem.

LISTING 5.7 Using Semaphores for Synchronization

```
unit Main;

interface
```

LISTING 5.7   Continued

```pascal
uses
  Windows, Messages, SysUtils, Classes, Graphics, Controls, Forms,
    Dialogs, StdCtrls;

type
  TMainForm = class(TForm)
    Button1: TButton;
    ListBox1: TListBox;
    procedure Button1Click(Sender: TObject);
  private
    procedure ThreadsDone(Sender: TObject);
  end;

  TFooThread = class(TThread)
  protected
    procedure Execute; override;
  end;

var
  MainForm: TMainForm;

implementation

{$R *.DFM}

const
  MaxSize = 128;

var
  NextNumber: Integer = 0;
  DoneFlags: Integer = 0;
  GlobalArray: array[1..MaxSize] of Integer;
  hSem: THandle = 0;

function GetNextNumber: Integer;
begin
  Result := NextNumber;   // return global var
  Inc(NextNumber);        // inc global var
end;

procedure TFooThread.Execute;
```

LISTING 5.7 Continued

```
var
  i: Integer;
  WaitReturn: DWORD;
begin
  OnTerminate := MainForm.ThreadsDone;
  WaitReturn := WaitForSingleObject(hSem, INFINITE);
  if WaitReturn = WAIT_OBJECT_0 then
  begin
    for i := 1 to MaxSize do
    begin
      GlobalArray[i] := GetNextNumber;  // set array element
      Sleep(5);                         // let thread intertwine
    end;
  end;
  ReleaseSemaphore(hSem, 1, nil);
end;

procedure TMainForm.ThreadsDone(Sender:  TObject);
var
  i: Integer;
begin
  Inc(DoneFlags);
  if DoneFlags = 2 then       // make sure both threads finished
  begin
    for i := 1 to MaxSize do
      { fill listbox with array contents }
      Listbox1.Items.Add(IntToStr(GlobalArray[i]));
    CloseHandle(hSem);
  end;
end;

procedure TMainForm.Button1Click(Sender: TObject);
begin
  hSem := CreateSemaphore(nil, 1, 1, nil);
  TFooThread.Create(False);  // create threads
  TFooThread.Create(False);
end;

end.
```

Because you allow only one thread to enter the synchronized portion of code, the maximum count for the semaphore is 1 in this case.

The `ReleaseSemaphore()` function is used to increase the count for the semaphore. Notice that this function is a bit more involved than its cousin, `ReleaseMutex()`. The declaration for `ReleaseSemaphore()` is as follows:

```
function ReleaseSemaphore(hSemaphore: THandle; lReleaseCount: Longint;
    lpPreviousCount: Pointer): BOOL; stdcall;
```

The `lReleaseCount` parameter enables you to specify the number by which the count of the semaphore will be increased. The old count will be stored in the `longint` pointed to by the `lpPreviousCount` parameter if its value is not `Nil`. A subtle implication of this capability is that a semaphore is never really owned by any thread in particular. For example, suppose that the maximum count of a semaphore is `10`, and 10 threads call `WaitForSingleObject()` to set the count of the thread to `0` and put the thread in a nonsignaled state. All it takes is one of those threads to call `ReleaseSemaphore()` with `10` as the `lReleaseCount` parameter in order not only to make the thread signaled again, but also to increase the count back to `10`. This powerful capability can introduce some hard-to-track-down bugs into your applications, so you should use it with care.

Be sure to use the `CloseHandle()` function to free the semaphore handle allocated with `CreateSemaphore()`.

A Sample Multithreaded Application

To demonstrate the usage of `TThread` objects within the context of a real-world application, this section focuses on creating a file-search application that performs its searches in a specialized thread. The project is called `DelSrch`, which stands for *Delphi Search*, and the main form for this utility is shown in Figure 5.6.

FIGURE 5.6

The Main form for the `DelSrch` project.

The application works like this. The user chooses a path through which to search and provides a file specification to indicate the types of files to be searched. The user also enters a token to search for in the appropriate edit control. Some option check boxes on one side of the form enable the user to tailor the application to suit his needs for a particular search. When the user clicks the Search button, a search thread is created and the appropriate search information—such as token, path, and file specification—is passed to the TThread descendant object. When the search thread finds the search token in certain files, information is appended to the list box. Finally, if the user double-clicks a file in the list box, he can browse it with a text editor or view it from its desktop association.

Although this is a fairly full-featured application, we'll focus mainly on explaining the application's key search features and how they relate to multithreading.

The User Interface

The main unit for the application is called Main.pas. Shown in Listing 5.8, this unit is responsible for managing the main form and the overall user interface. In particular, this unit contains the logic for owner-drawing the list box, invoking a viewer for files in the list box, invoking the search thread, printing the list box contents, and reading and writing UI settings to an INI file.

LISTING 5.8   The Main.pas Unit for the DelSrch Project

```
unit Main;

interface

uses
  SysUtils, WinTypes, WinProcs, Messages, Classes, Graphics, Controls,
  Forms, Dialogs, StdCtrls, Buttons, ExtCtrls, Menus, SrchIni,
  SrchU, ComCtrls, AppEvnts;


type
  TMainForm = class(TForm)
    lbFiles: TListBox;
    StatusBar: TStatusBar;
    pnlControls: TPanel;
    PopupMenu: TPopupMenu;
    FontDialog: TFontDialog;
    pnlOptions: TPanel;
    gbParams: TGroupBox;
    LFileSpec: TLabel;
    LToken: TLabel;
    lPathName: TLabel;
```

LISTING 5.8   Continued

```
  edtFileSpec: TEdit;
  edtToken: TEdit;
  btnPath: TButton;
  edtPathName: TEdit;
  gbOptions: TGroupBox;
  cbCaseSensitive: TCheckBox;
  cbFileNamesOnly: TCheckBox;
  cbRecurse: TCheckBox;
  cbRunFromAss: TCheckBox;
  pnlButtons: TPanel;
  btnSearch: TBitBtn;
  btnClose: TBitBtn;
  btnPrint:  TBitBtn;
  btnPriority: TBitBtn;
  Font1: TMenuItem;
  Clear1: TMenuItem;
  Print1: TMenuItem;
  N1: TMenuItem;
  Exit1: TMenuItem;
  ApplicationEvents: TApplicationEvents;
  procedure btnSearchClick(Sender: TObject);
  procedure btnPathClick(Sender: TObject);
  procedure lbFilesDrawItem(Control: TWinControl; Index: Integer;
   Rect: TRect; State: TOwnerDrawState);
  procedure Font1Click(Sender: TObject);
  procedure FormDestroy(Sender: TObject);
  procedure FormCreate(Sender: TObject);
  procedure btnPrintClick(Sender: TObject);
  procedure btnCloseClick(Sender: TObject);
  procedure lbFilesDblClick(Sender: TObject);
  procedure FormResize(Sender: TObject);
  procedure btnPriorityClick(Sender: TObject);
  procedure edtTokenChange(Sender: TObject);
  procedure Clear1Click(Sender: TObject);
  procedure ApplicationEventsHint(Sender: TObject);
private
  procedure ReadIni;
  procedure WriteIni;
public
  Running: Boolean;
  SearchPri: Integer;
  SearchThread: TSearchThread;
  procedure EnableSearchControls(Enable: Boolean);
end;
```

LISTING 5.8   Continued

```delphi
var
  MainForm: TMainForm;

implementation

{$R *.DFM}

uses Printers, ShellAPI, StrUtils, FileCtrl, PriU;

procedure PrintStrings(Strings: TStrings);
{ This procedure prints all of the strings in the Strings parameter }
var
  Prn: TextFile;
  I: Integer;
begin
  if Strings.Count = 0 then // Are there strings?
    raise Exception.Create('No text to print!');
  AssignPrn(Prn);                        // assign Prn to printer
  try
    Rewrite(Prn);                        // open printer
    try
      for I := 0 to Strings.Count - 1 do // iterate over all strings
        WriteLn(Prn, Strings.Strings[I]); // write to printer
    finally
      CloseFile(Prn);                    // close printer
    end;
  except
    on EInOutError do
      MessageDlg('Error Printing text.', mtError, [mbOk], 0);
  end;
end;

procedure TMainForm.EnableSearchControls(Enable: Boolean);
{ Enables or disables certain controls so options can't be modified }
{ while search is executing. }
begin
  btnSearch.Enabled := Enable;           // enable/disable proper controls
  cbRecurse.Enabled := Enable;
  cbFileNamesOnly.Enabled := Enable;
  cbCaseSensitive.Enabled := Enable;
  btnPath.Enabled := Enable;
  edtPathName.Enabled := Enable;
  edtFileSpec.Enabled := Enable;
  edtToken.Enabled := Enable;
```

LISTING 5.8   Continued

```
  Running := not Enable;                    // set Running flag
  edtTokenChange(nil);
  with btnClose do
  begin
    if Enable then
    begin                    // set props of Close/Stop button
      Caption := '&Close';
      Hint := 'Close Application';
    end
    else begin
      Caption := '&Stop';
      Hint := 'Stop Searching';
    end;
  end;
end;

procedure TMainForm.btnSearchClick(Sender: TObject);
{ Called when Search button is clicked.  Invokes search thread.  }
begin
  EnableSearchControls(False);            // disable controls
  lbFiles.Clear;                          // clear listbox
  { start thread }
  SearchThread := TSearchThread.Create(cbCaseSensitive.Checked,
      cbFileNamesOnly.Checked, cbRecurse.Checked, edtToken.Text,
      edtPathName.Text, edtFileSpec.Text);
end;

procedure TMainForm.edtTokenChange(Sender: TObject);
begin
  btnSearch.Enabled := not Running and (edtToken.Text <> '');
end;

procedure TMainForm.btnPathClick(Sender: TObject);
{ Called when Path button is clicked.  Allows user to choose new path. }
var
  ShowDir: string;
begin
  ShowDir := edtPathName.Text;
  if SelectDirectory('Choose a search path...', '', ShowDir) then
    edtPathName.Text := ShowDir;
end;

procedure TMainForm.lbFilesDrawItem(Control: TWinControl;
  Index: Integer; Rect: TRect; State: TOwnerDrawState);
```

LISTING 5.8 Continued

```
{ Called in order to owner draw listbox. }
var
  CurStr: string;
begin
  with lbFiles do
  begin
    CurStr := Items.Strings[Index];
    Canvas.FillRect(Rect);                    // clear out rect
    if not cbFileNamesOnly.Checked then       // if not filename only...
      { if current line is filename... }
      if (Pos('File ', CurStr) = 1) and
        (CurStr[Length(CurStr)] = ':') then
        with Canvas.Font do
        begin
          Style := [fsUnderline]; // underline font
          Color := clRed;          // paint red
        end
      else
        Rect.Left := Rect.Left + 15;          // otherwise, indent
    DrawText(Canvas.Handle, PChar(CurStr), Length(CurStr), Rect,
      DT_SINGLELINE);
  end;
end;

procedure TMainForm.Font1Click(Sender: TObject);
{ Allows user to pick new font for listbox }
begin
  { Pick new listbox font }
  if FontDialog.Execute then
    lbFiles.Font := FontDialog.Font;
end;

procedure TMainForm.FormDestroy(Sender: TObject);
{ OnDestroy event handler for form }
begin
  WriteIni;
end;

procedure TMainForm.FormCreate(Sender: TObject);
{ OnCreate event handler for form }
begin
  ReadIni;                               // read INI file
end;
```

LISTING 5.8 Continued

```
procedure TMainForm.btnPrintClick(Sender: TObject);
{ Called when Print button is clicked. }
begin
  if MessageDlg('Send search results to printer?', mtConfirmation,
    [mbYes, mbNo], 0) = mrYes then
    PrintStrings(lbFiles.Items);
end;

procedure TMainForm.btnCloseClick(Sender: TObject);
{ Called to stop thread or close application }
begin
  // if thread is running then terminate thread
  if Running then SearchThread.Terminate
  // otherwise close app
  else Close;
end;

procedure TMainForm.lbFilesDblClick(Sender: TObject);
{ Called when user double-clicks in listbox. Invokes viewer for }
{ highlighted file. }
var
  ProgramStr, FileStr: string;
  RetVal:  THandle;
begin
  { if user clicked on a file.. }
  if (Pos('File ', lbFiles.Items[lbFiles.ItemIndex]) = 1) then
  begin
    { load text editor from INI file.  Notepad is default. }
    ProgramStr := SrchIniFile.ReadString('Defaults', 'Editor', 'notepad');
    FileStr := lbFiles.Items[lbFiles.ItemIndex];      // Get selected file
    FileStr := Copy(FileStr, 6, Length(FileStr) - 5); // Remove prefix
    if FileStr[Length(FileStr)] = ':' then            // Remove ":"
      DecStrLen(FileStr, 1);
    if cbRunFromAss.Checked then
      { Run file from shell association }
      RetVal := ShellExecute(Handle, 'open', PChar(FileStr), nil, nil,
        SW_SHOWNORMAL)
    else
      { View file using text editor }
      RetVal := ShellExecute(Handle, 'open', PChar(ProgramStr),
        PChar(FileStr), nil, SW_SHOWNORMAL);
    { Check for error }
    if RetVal < 32 then RaiseLastWin32Error;
  end;
end;
```

LISTING 5.8 Continued

```
procedure TMainForm.FormResize(Sender: TObject);
{ OnResize event handler. Centers controls in form. }
begin
 { divide status bar into two panels with a 1/3 - 2/3 split }
  with StatusBar do
  begin
    Panels[0].Width := Width div 3;
    Panels[1].Width := Width * 2 div 3;
  end;
end;

procedure TMainForm.btnPriorityClick(Sender: TObject);
{ Show thread priority form }
begin
  ThreadPriWin.Show;
end;

procedure TMainForm.ReadIni;
{ Reads default values from Registry }
begin
  with SrchIniFile do
  begin
    edtPathName.Text := ReadString('Defaults', 'LastPath', 'C:\');
    edtFileSpec.Text := ReadString('Defaults', 'LastFileSpec', '*.*');
    edtToken.Text := ReadString('Defaults', 'LastToken', '');
    cbFileNamesOnly.Checked := ReadBool('Defaults', 'FNamesOnly', False);
    cbCaseSensitive.Checked := ReadBool('Defaults', 'CaseSens', False);
    cbRecurse.Checked := ReadBool('Defaults', 'Recurse', False);
    cbRunFromAss.Checked := ReadBool('Defaults', 'RunFromAss', False);
    Left := ReadInteger('Position', 'Left', Left);
    Top := ReadInteger('Position', 'Top', Top);
    Width := ReadInteger('Position', 'Width', Width);
    Height := ReadInteger('Position', 'Height', Height);
  end;
end;

procedure TMainForm.WriteIni;
{ writes current settings back to Registry }
begin
  with SrchIniFile do
  begin
    WriteString('Defaults', 'LastPath', edtPathName.Text);
    WriteString('Defaults', 'LastFileSpec', edtFileSpec.Text);
x'Defaults', 'LastToken', edtToken.Text);
```

LISTING 5.8   Continued

```
    WriteBool('Defaults', 'CaseSens', cbCaseSensitive.Checked);
    WriteBool('Defaults', 'FNamesOnly', cbFileNamesOnly.Checked);
    WriteBool('Defaults', 'Recurse', cbRecurse.Checked);
    WriteBool('Defaults', 'RunFromAss', cbRunFromAss.Checked);
    WriteInteger('Position', 'Left', Left);
    WriteInteger('Position', 'Top', Top);
    WriteInteger('Position', 'Width', Width);
    WriteInteger('Position', 'Height', Height);
  end;
end;

procedure TMainForm.Clear1Click(Sender: TObject);
begin
  lbFiles.Items.Clear;
end;

procedure TMainForm.ApplicationEventsHint(Sender: TObject);
{ OnHint event handler for Application }
begin
  { Display application hints on status bar }
  StatusBar.Panels[0].Text :=  Application.Hint;
end;

end.
```

Several things worth mentioning happen in this unit. First, you'll notice the fairly small PrintStrings() procedure that's used to send the contents of TStrings to the printer. To accomplish this, the procedure takes advantage of Delphi's AssignPrn() standard procedure, which assigns a TextFile variable to the printer. That way, any text written to the TextFile is automatically written to the printer. When you're finished writing to the printer, be sure to use the CloseFile() procedure to close the connection to the printer.

Also of interest is the use of the ShellExecute() Win32 API procedure to launch a viewer for a file that will be shown in the list box. ShellExecute() not only enables you to invoke executable programs but also to invoke associations for registered file extensions. For example, if you try to invoke a file with a .pas extension using ShellExecute(), it will automatically load Delphi to view the file.

> **TIP**
>
> If `ShellExecute()` returns a value indicating an error, the application calls `RaiseLastWin32Error()`. This procedure, located in the `SysUtils` unit, calls the `GetLastError()` API function and Delphi's `SysErrorMessage()` in order to obtain more detailed information about the error and to format that information into a string. You can use `RaiseLastWin32Error()` in this manner in your own applications if you want your users to obtain detailed error messages on API failures.

The Search Thread

The searching engine is contained within a unit called `SrchU.pas`, which is shown in Listing 5.9. This unit does a number of interesting things, including copying an entire file into a string, recursing subdirectories, and communicating information back to the main form.

LISTING 5.9   The `SrchU.pas` Unit

```
unit SrchU;

interface

uses Classes, StdCtrls;

type
  TSearchThread = class(TThread)
  private
    LB: TListbox;
    CaseSens: Boolean;
    FileNames: Boolean;
    Recurse: Boolean;
    SearchStr: string;
    SearchPath: string;
    FileSpec: string;
    AddStr: string;
    FSearchFile: string;
    procedure AddToList;
    procedure DoSearch(const Path: string);
    procedure FindAllFiles(const Path: string);
    procedure FixControls;
```

LISTING 5.9   Continued

```
    procedure ScanForStr(const FName: string; var FileStr: string);
    procedure SearchFile(const FName: string);
    procedure SetSearchFile;
  protected
    procedure Execute; override;
  public
    constructor Create(CaseS, FName, Rec: Boolean; const Str, SPath,
      FSpec: string);
    destructor Destroy; override;
  end;

implementation

uses SysUtils, StrUtils, Windows, Forms, Main;

constructor TSearchThread.Create(CaseS, FName, Rec: Boolean; const Str,
  SPath, FSpec: string);
begin
  CaseSens := CaseS;
  FileNames := FName;
  Recurse := Rec;
  SearchStr := Str;
  SearchPath := AddBackSlash(SPath);
  FileSpec := FSpec;
  inherited Create(False);
end;

destructor TSearchThread.Destroy;
begin
  FSearchFile := '';
  Synchronize(SetSearchFile);
  Synchronize(FixControls);
  inherited Destroy;
end;

procedure TSearchThread.Execute;
begin
  FreeOnTerminate := True;      // set up all the fields
  LB := MainForm.lbFiles;
  Priority := TThreadPriority(MainForm.SearchPri);
  if not CaseSens then SearchStr := UpperCase(SearchStr);
  FindAllFiles(SearchPath);     // process current directory
  if Recurse then               // if subdirs, then...
    DoSearch(SearchPath);       // recurse, otherwise...
end;
```

LISTING 5.9 Continued

```
procedure TSearchThread.FixControls;
{ Enables controls in main form. Must be called through Synchronize }
begin
  MainForm.EnableSearchControls(True);
end;

procedure TSearchThread.SetSearchFile;
{ Updates status bar with filename. Must be called through Synchronize }
begin
  MainForm.StatusBar.Panels[1].Text := FSearchFile;
end;

procedure TSearchThread.AddToList;
{ Adds string to main listbox. Must be called through Synchronize }
begin
  LB.Items.Add(AddStr);
end;

procedure TSearchThread.ScanForStr(const FName: string;
  var FileStr: string);
{ Scans a FileStr of file FName for SearchStr }
var
  Marker: string[1];
  FoundOnce: Boolean;
  FindPos: integer;
begin
  FindPos := Pos(SearchStr, FileStr);
  FoundOnce := False;
  while (FindPos <> 0) and not Terminated do
  begin
    if not FoundOnce then
    begin
      { use ":" only if user doesn't choose "filename only" }
      if FileNames then
        Marker := ''
      else
        Marker := ':';
      { add file to listbox }
      AddStr := Format('File %s%s', [FName, Marker]);
      Synchronize(AddToList);
      FoundOnce := True;
    end;
    { don't search for same string in same file if filenames only }
    if FileNames then Exit;
```

5

LISTING 5.9   Continued

```
      { Add line if not filename only }
      AddStr := GetCurLine(FileStr, FindPos);
      Synchronize(AddToList);
      FileStr := Copy(FileStr, FindPos + Length(SearchStr),
        Length(FileStr));
      FindPos := Pos(SearchStr, FileStr);
    end;
end;


procedure TSearchThread.SearchFile(const FName: string);
{ Searches file FName for SearchStr }
var
  DataFile: THandle;
  FileSize: Integer;
  SearchString:  string;
begin
  FSearchFile := FName;
  Synchronize(SetSearchFile);
  try
    DataFile := FileOpen(FName, fmOpenRead or fmShareDenyWrite);
    if DataFile = 0 then raise Exception.Create('');
    try
      { set length of search string }
      FileSize := GetFileSize(DataFile, nil);
      SetLength(SearchString, FileSize);
      { Copy file data to string }
      FileRead(DataFile, Pointer(SearchString)^, FileSize);
    finally
      CloseHandle(DataFile);
    end;
    if not CaseSens then SearchString := UpperCase(SearchString);
    ScanForStr(FName, SearchString);
  except
    on Exception do
    begin
      AddStr := Format('Error reading file: %s', [FName]);
      Synchronize(AddToList);
    end;
  end;
end;


procedure TSearchThread.FindAllFiles(const Path: string);
{ procedure searches Path subdir for files matching filespec }
var
  SR: TSearchRec;
```

LISTING 5.9   Continued

```
begin
  { find first file matching spec }
  if FindFirst(Path + FileSpec, faArchive, SR) = 0 then
    try
      repeat
        SearchFile(Path + SR.Name);               // process file
      until (FindNext(SR) <> 0) or Terminated; // find next file
    finally
      SysUtils.FindClose(SR);                     // clean up
    end;
end;

procedure TSearchThread.DoSearch(const Path: string);
{ procedure recurses through a subdirectory tree starting at Path }
var
  SR: TSearchRec;
begin
  { look for directories }
  if FindFirst(Path + '*.*', faDirectory, SR) = 0 then
    try
      repeat
        { if it's a directory and not '.' or '..' then... }
        if ((SR.Attr and faDirectory) <> 0) and (SR.Name[1] <> '.') and
          not Terminated then
        begin
          FindAllFiles(Path + SR.Name + '\');  // process directory
          DoSearch(Path + SR.Name + '\');       // recurse
        end;
      until (FindNext(SR) <> 0) or Terminated;        // find next directory
    finally
      SysUtils.FindClose(SR);                         // clean up
    end;
end;

end.
```

When created, this thread first calls its FindAllFiles() method. This method uses FindFirst() and FindNext() to search for all files in the current directory matching the file specification indicated by the user. If the user has chosen to recurse subdirectories, the DoSearch() method is then called in order to traverse down a directory tree. This method again makes use of FindFirst() and FindNext() to find directories, but the twist is that it calls itself recursively in order to traverse the tree. As each directory is found, FindAllFiles() is called to process all matching files in the directory.

TIP

The recursion algorithm used by the DoSearch() method is a standard technique for traversing a directory tree. Because recursive algorithms are notoriously difficult to debug, the smart programmer will make use of ones that are already known to work. It's a good idea to save this method so that you can use it with other applications in the future.

To process each file, you'll notice that the algorithm for searching for a token within a file involves using the TMemMapFile object, which encapsulates a Win32 memory-mapped file. This object is discussed in detail in the electronic version of *Delphi 5 Developer's Guide* in Chapter 12, "Working with Files," which is on this book's CD-ROM, but for now you can just assume that this provides an easy way to map the contents of a file into memory. The entire algorithm works like this:

1. When a file matching the file spec is found by the FindAllFiles() method, the SearchFile() method is called and the file contents are copied into a string.

2. The ScanForStr() method is called for each file-string. ScanForStr() searches for occurrences of the search token within each string.

3. When an occurrence is found, the filename and/or the line of text is added to the list box. The line of text is added only when the user unchecks the File Names Only check box.

Note that all the methods in the TSearchThread object periodically check the status of the StopIt flag (which is tripped when the thread is told to stop) and the Terminated flag (which is tripped when the TThread object is to terminate).

CAUTION

Remember that any methods within a TThread object that modify the application's user interface in any way must be called through the Synchronize() method, or the user interface must be modified by sending messages.

Adjusting the Priority

Just to add yet another feature, DelSrch enables the user to adjust the priority of the search thread dynamically. The form used for this purpose is shown in Figure 5.7, and the unit for this form, PRIU.PAS, is shown in Listing 5.10.

FIGURE 5.7

The thread priority form for the DelSrch *project.*

LISTING 5.10   The PriU.pas Unit

```
unit PriU;

interface

uses
  Windows, Messages, SysUtils, Classes, Graphics, Controls, Forms,
  Dialogs, StdCtrls, ComCtrls, Buttons, ExtCtrls;

type
  TThreadPriWin = class(TForm)
    tbrPriTrackBar: TTrackBar;
    Label1: TLabel;
    Label2: TLabel;
    Label3: TLabel;
    btnOK: TBitBtn;
    btnRevert: TBitBtn;
    Panel1: TPanel;
    procedure tbrPriTrackBarChange(Sender: TObject);
    procedure btnRevertClick(Sender: TObject);
    procedure FormClose(Sender: TObject; var Action: TCloseAction);
    procedure FormShow(Sender: TObject);
    procedure btnOKClick(Sender: TObject);
    procedure FormCreate(Sender: TObject);
  private
    { Private declarations }
    OldPriVal: Integer;
  public
    { Public declarations }
  end;

var
  ThreadPriWin: TThreadPriWin;
```

LISTING 5.10   Continued

```
implementation

{$R *.DFM}

uses Main, SrchU;

procedure TThreadPriWin.tbrPriTrackBarChange(Sender: TObject);
begin
  with MainForm do
  begin
    SearchPri := tbrPriTrackBar.Position;
    if Running then
      SearchThread.Priority := TThreadPriority(tbrPriTrackBar.Position);
  end;
end;

procedure TThreadPriWin.btnRevertClick(Sender: TObject);
begin
  tbrPriTrackBar.Position := OldPriVal;
end;

procedure TThreadPriWin.FormClose(Sender: TObject;
  var Action: TCloseAction);
begin
  Action := caHide;
end;

procedure TThreadPriWin.FormShow(Sender: TObject);
begin
  OldPriVal := tbrPriTrackBar.Position;
end;

procedure TThreadPriWin.btnOKClick(Sender: TObject);
begin
  Close;
end;

procedure TThreadPriWin.FormCreate(Sender: TObject);
begin
  tbrPriTrackBarChange(Sender);            // initialize thread priority
end;

end.
```

The code for this unit is fairly straightforward. All it does is set the value of the `SearchPri` variable in the main form to match that of the track bar position. If the thread is running, it also sets the priority of the thread. Because `TThreadPriority` is an enumerated type, a straight typecast maps the values 1 to 5 in the track bar to enumerations in `TThreadPriority`.

Multithreading BDE Access

Although database programming isn't really discussed until later in the book, this section is intended to give you some tips on how to use multiple threads in the context of BDE database development. If you're unfamiliar with database programming under Delphi, you might want to look through the later database chapters prior to reading on in this section.

The most common request for database applications developers in Win32 is for the capability to perform complex queries or stored procedures in a background thread. Thankfully, this type of thing is supported by the 32-bit Borland Database Engine (BDE) and is fairly easy to do in Delphi.

There are really only two requirements for running a background query through, for example, a `TQuery` component:

- Each threaded query must reside within its own session. You can provide a `TQuery` with its own session by placing a `TSession` component on your form and assigning its name to the `TQuery`'s `SessionName` property. This also implies that, if your `TQuery` uses a `TDatabase` component, a unique `TDatabase` must also be used for each session.

- The `TQuery` must not be attached to any `TDataSource` components at the time the query is opened from the secondary thread. When the query is attached to a `TDataSource`, it must be done through the context of the primary thread. `TDataSource` is only used to connect datasets to user interface controls, and user interface manipulation must be performed in the main thread.

To illustrate the techniques for background queries, Figure 5.8 shows the main form for a demo project called `BDEThrd`. This form enables you to specify a BDE alias, username, and password for a particular database and to enter a query against the database. When the Go! button is clicked, a secondary thread is spawned to process the query and the results are displayed in a child form.

The child form, `TQueryForm`, is shown in Figure 5.9. Notice that this form contains one each of a `TQuery`, `TDatabase`, `TSession`, `TDataSource`, and `TDBGrid` component. Therefore, each instance of `TQueryForm` has its own instances of these components.

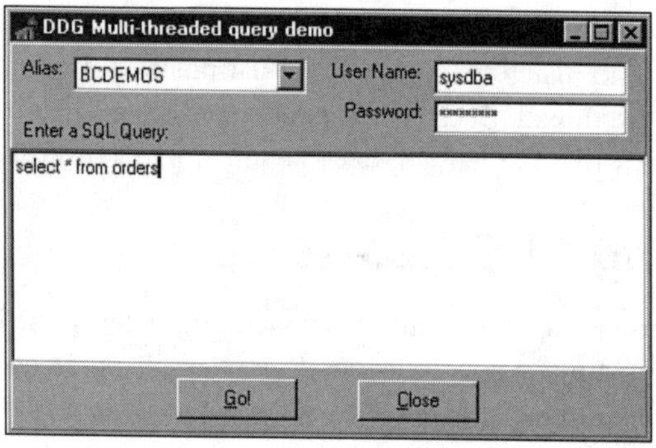

FIGURE 5.8

The main form for the BDEThrd *demo.*

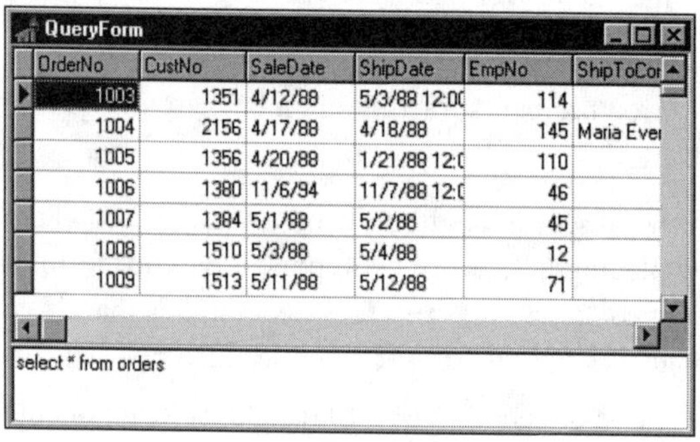

FIGURE 5.9

The child query form for the BDEThrd *demo.*

Listing 5.11 shows Main.pas, the application's main unit.

LISTING 5.11   The Main.pas Unit for the BDEThrd Demo

```
unit Main;

interface

uses
  Windows, Messages, SysUtils, Classes, Graphics, Controls, Forms,
  Dialogs, Grids, StdCtrls, ExtCtrls;

type
  TMainForm = class(TForm)
    pnlBottom: TPanel;
```

LISTING 5.11   Continued

```
    pnlButtons: TPanel;
    GoButton: TButton;
    Button1: TButton;
    memQuery: TMemo;
    pnlTop: TPanel;
    Label1: TLabel;
    AliasCombo: TComboBox;
    Label3: TLabel;
    UserNameEd: TEdit;
    Label4: TLabel;
    PasswordEd: TEdit;
    Label2: TLabel;
    procedure Button1Click(Sender: TObject);
    procedure GoButtonClick(Sender: TObject);
    procedure FormCreate(Sender: TObject);
  private
    { Private declarations }
  public
    { Public declarations }
  end;

var
  MainForm: TMainForm;

implementation

{$R *.DFM}

uses QryU, DB, DBTables;

var
  FQueryNum: Integer = 0;

procedure TMainForm.Button1Click(Sender: TObject);
begin
  Close;
end;

procedure TMainForm.GoButtonClick(Sender: TObject);
begin
  Inc(FQueryNum);    // keep querynum unique
  { invoke new query }
  NewQuery(FQueryNum, memQuery.Lines, AliasCombo.Text, UserNameEd.Text,
    PasswordEd.Text);
```

LISTING 5.11   Continued

```
end;

procedure TMainForm.FormCreate(Sender: TObject);
begin
  { fill drop-down list with BDE Aliases }
  Session.GetAliasNames(AliasCombo.Items);
end;

end.
```

As you can see, there's not much to this unit. The `AliasCombo` combobox is filled with BDE aliases in the `OnCreate` handler for the main form using `TSession`'s `GetAliasNames()` method. The handler for the Go! button `OnClick` event is in charge of invoking a new query by calling the `NewQuery()` procedure that lives in a second unit, `QryU.pas`. Notice that it passes a new unique number, `FQueryNum`, to the `NewQuery()` procedure with every button click. This number is used to create a unique session and database name for each query thread.

Listing 5.12 shows the code for the `QryU` unit.

LISTING 5.12   The `QryU.pas` Unit

```
unit QryU;

interface

uses
  Windows, Messages, SysUtils, Classes, Graphics, Controls, Forms,  Grids,
  DBGrids, DB, DBTables, StdCtrls;

type
  TQueryForm = class(TForm)
    Query: TQuery;
    DataSource: TDataSource;
    Session: TSession;
    Database: TDatabase;
    dbgQueryGrid: TDBGrid;
    memSQL: TMemo;
    procedure FormClose(Sender: TObject; var Action: TCloseAction);
  private
    { Private declarations }
  public
    { Public declarations }
  end;
```

LISTING 5.12 Continued

```
procedure NewQuery(QryNum: integer; Qry: TStrings; const Alias, UserName,
  Password: string);

implementation

{$R *.DFM}

type
  TDBQueryThread = class(TThread)
  private
    FQuery: TQuery;
    FDataSource: TDataSource;
    FQueryException: Exception;
    procedure HookUpUI;
    procedure QueryError;
  protected
    procedure Execute; override;
  public
    constructor Create(Q: TQuery; D: TDataSource); virtual;
  end;

constructor TDBQueryThread.Create(Q: TQuery; D: TDataSource);
begin
  inherited Create(True);        // create suspended thread
  FQuery := Q;                   // set parameters
  FDataSource := D;
  FreeOnTerminate := True;
  Resume;                        // thread that puppy!
end;

procedure TDBQueryThread.Execute;
begin
  try
    FQuery.Open;                 // open the query
    Synchronize(HookUpUI);       // update UI from main thread
  except
    FQueryException := ExceptObject as Exception;
    Synchronize(QueryError);     // show exception from main thread
  end;
end;

procedure TDBQueryThread.HookUpUI;
begin
  FDataSource.DataSet := FQuery;
end;
```

5

MULTITHREADED
TECHNIQUES

LISTING 5.12   Continued

```pascal
procedure TDBQueryThread.QueryError;
begin
  Application.ShowException(FQueryException);
end;

procedure NewQuery(QryNum: integer; Qry: TStrings; const Alias, UserName,
  Password: string);
begin
  { Create a new Query form to show query results }
  with TQueryForm.Create(Application) do
  begin
    { Set a unique session name }
    Session.SessionName := Format('Sess%d', [QryNum]);
    with Database do
    begin
      { set a unique database name }
      DatabaseName := Format('DB%d', [QryNum]);
      { set alias parameter }
      AliasName := Alias;
      { hook database to session }
      SessionName := Session.SessionName;
      { user-defined username and password }
      Params.Values['USER NAME'] := UserName;
      Params.Values['PASSWORD'] := Password;
    end;
    with Query do
    begin
      { hook query to database and session }
      DatabaseName := Database.DatabaseName;
      SessionName := Session.SessionName;
      { set up the query strings }
      SQL.Assign(Qry);
    end;
    { display query strings in SQL Memo }
    memSQL.Lines.Assign(Qry);
    { show query form }
    Show;
    { open query in its own thread }
    TDBQueryThread.Create(Query, DataSource);
  end;
end;

procedure TQueryForm.FormClose(Sender: TObject; var Action: TCloseAction);
begin
```

```
  Action := caFree;
end;

end.
```

The NewQuery() procedure creates a new instance of the child form TQueryForm, sets up the properties for each of its data-access components, and creates unique names for its TDatabase and TSession components. The query's SQL property is filled from the TStrings passed in the Qry parameter, and the query thread is then spawned.

The code inside the TDBQueryThread itself is rather sparse. The constructor merely sets up some instance variables, and the Execute() method opens the query and calls the HookupUI() method through Synchronize() to attach the query to the data source. You should also take note of the try..except block inside the Execute() procedure, which uses Synchronize() to show exception messages from the context of the primary thread.

Multithreaded Graphics

We mentioned earlier that VCL isn't designed to be manipulated simultaneously by multiple threads, but this statement isn't entirely accurate. VCL has the capability to have multiple threads manipulate individual graphics objects. Thanks to new Lock() and Unlock() methods introduced in TCanvas, the entire Graphics unit has been made thread-safe. This includes the TCanvas, TPen, TBrush, TFont, TBitmap, TMetafile, TPicture, and TIcon classes.

The code for these Lock() methods is similar in that it uses a critical section and the EnterCriticalSection() API function (described earlier in this chapter) to guard access to the canvas or graphics object. After a particular thread calls a Lock() method, that thread is free to exclusively manipulate the canvas or graphics object. Other threads waiting to enter the portion of code following the call to Lock() will be put to sleep until the thread owning the critical section calls Unlock(), which calls LeaveCriticalSection() to release the critical section and lets the next waiting thread (if any) into the protected portion of code. The following portion of code shows how these methods can be used to control access to a canvas object:

```
Form.Canvas.Lock;
// code which manipulates canvas goes here
Form.Canvas.Unlock;
```

To further illustrate this point, Listing 5.13 shows the unit Main of the MTGraph project—an application that demonstrates multiple threads accessing a form's canvas.

LISTING 5.13   The `Main.pas` Unit of the `MTGraph` Project

```pascal
unit Main;

interface

uses
  Windows, Messages, SysUtils, Classes, Graphics, Controls, Forms,  Menus;

type
  TMainForm = class(TForm)
    MainMenu1: TMainMenu;
    Options1: TMenuItem;
    AddThread: TMenuItem;
    RemoveThread: TMenuItem;
    ColorDialog1: TColorDialog;
    Add10: TMenuItem;
    RemoveAll: TMenuItem;
    procedure FormCreate(Sender: TObject);
    procedure FormDestroy(Sender: TObject);
    procedure AddThreadClick(Sender: TObject);
    procedure RemoveThreadClick(Sender: TObject);
    procedure Add10Click(Sender: TObject);
    procedure RemoveAllClick(Sender: TObject);
  private
    ThreadList: TList;
  public
    { Public declarations }
  end;

  TDrawThread = class(TThread)
  private
    FColor: TColor;
    FForm: TForm;
  public
    constructor Create(AForm: TForm; AColor: TColor);
    procedure Execute; override;
  end;

var
  MainForm: TMainForm;

implementation

{$R *.DFM}
```

LISTING 5.13 Continued

```
{ TDrawThread }

constructor TDrawThread.Create(AForm: TForm; AColor: TColor);
begin
  FColor := AColor;
  FForm := AForm;
  inherited Create(False);
end;

procedure TDrawThread.Execute;
var
  P1, P2: TPoint;

  procedure GetRandCoords;
  var
    MaxX, MaxY: Integer;
  begin
    // initialize P1 and P2 to random points within Form bounds
    MaxX := FForm.ClientWidth;
    MaxY := FForm.ClientHeight;
    P1.x := Random(MaxX);
    P2.x := Random(MaxX);
    P1.y := Random(MaxY);
    P2.y := Random(MaxY);
  end;

begin
  FreeOnTerminate := True;
  // thread runs until it or the application is terminated
  while not (Terminated or Application.Terminated) do
  begin
    GetRandCoords;          // initialize P1 and P2
    with FForm.Canvas do
    begin
      Lock;                 // lock canvas
      // only one thread at a time can execute the following code:
      Pen.Color := FColor;  // set pen color
      MoveTo(P1.X, P1.Y);   // move to canvas position P1
      LineTo(P2.X, P2.Y);   // draw a line to position P2
      // after the next line executes, another thread will be allowed
      // to enter the above code block
      Unlock;               // unlock canvas
    end;
  end;
end;
```

LISTING 5.13   Continued

```
{ TMainForm }

procedure TMainForm.FormCreate(Sender: TObject);
begin
  ThreadList := TList.Create;
end;

procedure TMainForm.FormDestroy(Sender: TObject);
begin
  RemoveAllClick(nil);
  ThreadList.Free;
end;

procedure TMainForm.AddThreadClick(Sender: TObject);
begin
  // add a new thread to the list... allow user to choose color
  if ColorDialog1.Execute then
    ThreadList.Add(TDrawThread.Create(Self, ColorDialog1.Color));
end;

procedure TMainForm.RemoveThreadClick(Sender: TObject);
begin
  // terminate the last thread in the list and remove it from list
  TDrawThread(ThreadList[ThreadList.Count - 1]).Terminate;
  ThreadList.Delete(ThreadList.Count - 1);
end;

procedure TMainForm.Add10Click(Sender: TObject);
var
  i: Integer;
begin
  // create 10 threads, each with a random color
  for i := 1 to 10 do
    ThreadList.Add(TDrawThread.Create(Self, Random(MaxInt)));
end;

procedure TMainForm.RemoveAllClick(Sender: TObject);
var
  i: Integer;
begin
  Cursor := crHourGlass;
  try
```

LISTING 5.13 Continued

```
    for i := ThreadList.Count - 1 downto 0 do
    begin
      TDrawThread(ThreadList[i]).Terminate; // terminate thread
      TDrawThread(ThreadList[i]).WaitFor;   // make sure thread terminates
    end;
    ThreadList.Clear;
  finally
    Cursor:= crDefault;
  end;
end;

initialization
  Randomize;  // seed random number generator
end.
```

This application has a main menu containing four items, as shown in Figure 5.10. The first item, Add Thread, creates a new TDrawThread instance, which paints random lines on the main form. This option can be selected repeatedly in order to throw more and more threads into the mix of threads accessing the main form. The next item, Remove Thread, removes the last thread added. The third item, Add 10, creates 10 new TDrawThread instances. Finally, the fourth item, Remove All, terminates and destroys all TDrawThread instances. Figure 5.10 also shows the results of 10 threads simultaneously drawing to the form's canvas.

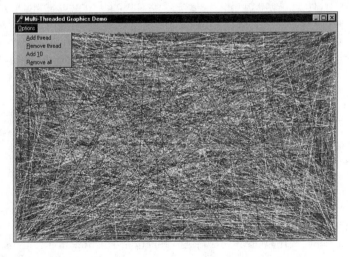

FIGURE 5.10
The MTGraph *main form.*

Canvas-locking rules dictate that as long as every user of a canvas locks it before drawing and unlocks it afterwards, multiple threads using that canvas won't interfere with each other. Note that all `OnPaint` events and `Paint()` method calls initiated by VCL automatically lock and unlock the canvas for you; therefore, existing, normal Delphi code can coexist with new background thread graphics operations.

Using this application as an example, examine the consequences or symptoms of thread collisions if you fail to properly perform canvas locking. If thread 1 sets a canvas's pen color to red and then draws a line, and thread 2 sets the pen color to blue and draws a circle, and these threads don't lock the canvas before starting these operations, the following thread collision scenario is possible: Thread 1 sets the pen color to red. The OS scheduler switches execution to thread 2. Thread 2 sets the pen color to blue and draws a circle. Execution switches to thread 1. Thread 1 draws a line. However, the line isn't red, it is blue because thread 2 had the opportunity to slip in between the operations of thread 1.

Note also that it only takes one errant thread to cause problems. If thread 1 locks the canvas and thread 2 doesn't, the scenario just described is unchanged. Both threads must lock the canvas around their canvas operations to prevent that thread collision scenario.

Fibers

Fibers are a sort of schedule-your-own thread. Like threads, fibers provide state information and execution context in the form their own stack and CPU registers. Unlike threads, however, fibers aren't preemptively scheduled by the operating system. Instead, it is the developer's responsibility to switch between multiple fibers of execution. From an application design point of view, there are probably few occasions when you will elect to use fibers instead of a multi-threaded architecture, except in the infrequent case in which you want to receive the context benefits of multiple stack and CPU register states without having to worry about thread synchronization issues.

> **NOTE**
>
> Fibers are available on Windows NT 3.51 SP3 and higher, Windows 2000, Windows XP, Windows 98, and Windows ME.

Fibers are designed to run within the context of a thread, so one thread might host multiple fibers. Before you can begin using fibers within a thread, the thread itself must be converted to as fiber using the `ConvertThreadToFiber()` API function. This function is defined in the `Windows` unit as

```
function ConvertThreadToFiber(lpParameter: Pointer): BOOL; stdcall;
```

The lone parameter, lpParameter, enables you to pass 32-bits of fiber-specific data, in much the same manner you would pass data to a thread in the BeginThread() or CreateThread() functions. The return value definition is defined incorrectly in the Windows unit. Although listed as a BOOL, the return value is actually a pointer to the fiber object. As you will see, you will need to typecast the return value to use it.

Once a thread has been converted to a fiber, you will be able to create other fibers and begin scheduling between the fibers. You can create additional fibers using the CreateFiber() API function, which is defined in the Windows unit as

```
function CreateFiber(dwStackSize: DWORD; lpStartAddress: TFNFiberStartRoutine;
  lpParameter: Pointer): BOOL; stdcall;
```

The dwStackSize parameter specifies the initial size (in bytes) of the fiber's stack, or you can pass 0 to set it to the default stack size. The lpStartAddress specifies the address of the procedure the fiber should begin executing when execution begins. lpParameter specifies any 32-bits of fiber-specific data you might want to pass. The return value for this function, like ConvertThreadToFiber(), is also incorrect as defined; it is really a pointer to the created fiber object and will need to be typecast to be used (more on this later).

After creating the fibers, you can switch between them using the SwitchToFiber() API function. This function is defined in the Windows unit as

```
function SwitchToFiber(lpFiber: Pointer): BOOL; stdcall;
```

Calling this method with a fiber object pointer in the lpFiber parameter is all you need to do to jump from one fiber's execution context to another. The operating system handles the internal details associated with the context switch, such as modifying the stack pointer and CPU registers. The return value for this function, defined as a BOOL, is again incorrect; this should be defined as a procedure with no return value. You therefore shouldn't expect a valid return value from this function.

When you're ready to do away with a particular fiber, just pass the fiber object pointer to the DeleteFiber API function:

```
function DeleteFiber(lpFiber: Pointer): BOOL; stdcall;
```

By the way, like SwitchToFiber(), the return value for this function is defined incorrectly as well; it should also be a procedure returning no value, so don't expect a valid return value.

CAUTION

Calling DeleteFiber() on the currently executing fiber will result in a call to ExitThread(), which will terminate the entire thread. Unless you mean to terminate the thread, you should only call DeleteFiber() on fibers other than the one currently executing.

5

MULTITHREADED TECHNIQUES

Most of the work you'll need to do with fibers can be accomplished with the four preceding functions. The Win32 header files additionally define a couple of additional helper functions and types not present in Delphi, but we have provided them for your convenience in the following. Listing 5.14 contains the Fiber unit, which provides additional definitions not present in the Windows unit.

LISTING 5.14 The Fiber.pas Unit

```
unit Fibers;

interface

uses Windows;

// type defn for fiber start routine from winbase.h:
type
  PFIBER_START_ROUTINE = procedure (lpFiberParameter: Pointer); stdcall;
  LPFIBER_START_ROUTINE = PFIBER_START_ROUTINE;
  TFiberFunc = PFIBER_START_ROUTINE;

function GetCurrentFiber: Pointer;
function GetFiberData: Pointer;

implementation

// x86-specific fiber inline routines from winnt.h:

function GetCurrentFiber: Pointer;
asm
  mov eax, fs:[$10]
end;

function GetFiberData: Pointer;
asm
  mov eax, fs:[$10]
  mov eax, [eax]
end;

end.
```

To provide an example of fibers in action, we will create a test program that creates a handful of fibers and switches between them to do what we'll pretend is useful work. The main form for this application is shown in Figure 5.11.

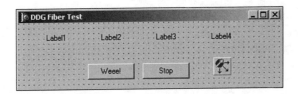

FIGURE 5.11
The FibTest *main form.*

The main unit for this form is shown in Listing 5.15.

LISTING 5.15 FibMain.pas—the Main Unit for FibTest

```
unit FibMain;

interface

uses
  Windows, Messages, SysUtils, Variants, Classes, Graphics, Controls, Forms,
  Dialogs, StdCtrls, AppEvnts;

type
  TForm1 = class(TForm)
    BtnWee: TButton;
    BtnStop: TButton;
    Label1: TLabel;
    Label2: TLabel;
    Label3: TLabel;
    Label4: TLabel;
    AppEvents: TApplicationEvents;
    procedure BtnWeeClick(Sender: TObject);
    procedure AppEventsMessage(var Msg: tagMSG;
      var Handled: Boolean);
    procedure BtnStopClick(Sender: TObject);
  private
    { Private declarations }
    FThreadID: LongWord;
    FThreadHandle: Integer;
  public
    { Public declarations }
  end;

var
  Form1:  TForm1;
```

LISTING 5.15   Continued

```
implementation

uses Fibers;

{$R *.dfm}

const
  DDG_THREADMSG = WM_USER;

var
  FFibers: array[0..3] of Pointer;
  StopIt: Boolean;

procedure FiberFunc(Param: Pointer); stdcall;
var
  J, FibNum, NextNum: Integer;
  I: Cardinal;
  Fiber: Pointer;
begin
  try
    I := 0;
    FibNum := 1;                // suppress compiler warning
    Fiber := GetCurrentFiber; // save away our fiber ptr for later
    // figure out where current fiber is in the array and save for later
    for J := Low(FFibers) to High(FFibers) do
      if FFibers[J] = Fiber then
      begin
        FibNum := J;
        Break;
      end;
    // HIGH TECH: count from zero to really, really high
    while not StopIt do
    begin
      // send the number to the main thread for display every 100
      if I mod 100 = 0 then
        PostMessage(Application.Handle, DDG_THREADMSG,
          Integer(GetFiberData), I);
      // switch fibers every 1000
      if I mod 1000 = 0 then
      begin
        if FibNum = High(FFibers) then NextNum := Low(FFibers)
        else NextNum := FibNum + 1;
        SwitchToFiber(FFibers[NextNum]);
      end;
```

LISTING 5.15   Continued

```
      Inc(I);
    end;
  except
    // stifle all unhandled exceptions
  end;
end;

function ThreadFunc(Param: Pointer): Integer;
var
  I: Integer;
begin
  Result := 0;
  // convert this thread to a fiber
  FFibers[0] := Pointer(ConvertThreadToFiber(Pointer(1)));
  // create the other fibers
  FFibers[1] := Pointer(CreateFiber(0, @FiberFunc, Pointer(2)));
  FFibers[2] := Pointer(CreateFiber(0, @FiberFunc, Pointer(3)));
  FFibers[3] := Pointer(CreateFiber(0,  @FiberFunc, Pointer(4)));
  // join in the fun
  FiberFunc(Pointer(1));
  // when done, kill all the fibers
  // killing the current fiber calls ExitThread
  for I := High(FFibers) downto Low(FFibers) do
    DeleteFiber(FFibers[I]);
end;

procedure TForm1.BtnWeeClick(Sender: TObject);
begin
  BtnWee.Enabled := False;  // pressing the button twice will cause grief
  FThreadHandle := BeginThread(nil, 0, @ThreadFunc, nil, 0, FThreadID);
end;

procedure TForm1.AppEventsMessage(var Msg: tagMSG;
  var Handled: Boolean);
begin
  if Msg.message = DDG_THREADMSG then
  begin
    // The wParam tells us which fiber is sending the message,
    // and therefore which label to update
    case Msg.wParam of
      1: Label1.Caption := IntToStr(Msg.lParam);
      2: Label2.Caption := IntToStr(Msg.lParam);
      3: Label3.Caption := IntToStr(Msg.lParam);
      4: Label4.Caption := IntToStr(Msg.lParam);
```

5

MULTITHREADED TECHNIQUES

Listing 5.15   Continued

```
    end;
    Handled := True;
  end;
end;

procedure TForm1.BtnStopClick(Sender:  TObject);
begin
  StopIt := True;
end;

end.
```

The most interesting work in this example is done in ThreadFunc(), which is the thread function for secondary thread created in response to the button click. This function calls ConvertThreadToFiber() to fiber-ize the thread and then calls CreateFiber() multiple times to create three additional fibers. All the fibers are then prepared to execute FiberFunc(), which simply counts up from 0 to infinity and sends a message every 100 counts to display the value in the UI and switches to the next fiber every 1000 counts.

The application uses the simple and reliable technique of communicating with the main thread by posting a message to the Application window handle. Each fiber holds a value between 1 and 4 because its fiber data and the message handler in the main thread uses this to determine which fiber sent the message.

Figure 5.12 shows the FibTest application in action. The fact that the number in each of the labels is very close in value illustrates that each of the fibers are executing using their own stack.

Figure 5.12
FibTest *in action.*

Summary

By now you've had a thorough introduction to threads and how to use them properly in the Delphi environment. You've learned several techniques for synchronizing multiple threads, and you've learned how to communicate between secondary threads and a Delphi application's primary thread. Additionally, you've seen examples of using threads within the context of a real-world file-search application, you've gotten the lowdown on how to leverage threads in database applications, and you've learned about drawing to a TCanvas with multiple threads. Finally, you've learned about the nifty fiber, which provide bring-your-own-scheduler functionality. In Chapter 6, "Dynamic Link Libraries," you'll learn everything you need to know about creating and using DLLs in Delphi.

Dynamic Link Libraries

IN THIS CHAPTER

This chapter discusses Win32 dynamic link libraries, otherwise known as *DLLs*. DLLs are a key component to writing any Windows application. This chapter discusses several aspects of using and creating DLLs. It gives you an overview of how DLLs work and discusses how to create and use DLLs. You learn different methods of loading DLLs and linking to the procedures and functions they export. This chapter also covers the use of callback functions and illustrates how to share DLL data among different calling processes.

What Exactly Is a DLL?

Dynamic link libraries are program modules that contain code, data, or resources that can be shared among many Windows applications. One of the primary uses of DLLs is to enable applications to load code to execute at runtime instead of linking that code to the application at compile time. Therefore, multiple applications can simultaneously use the same code provided by the DLL. In fact, the files `Kernel32.dll`, `User32.dll`, and `GDI32.dll` are three DLLs on which Win32 relies heavily. `Kernel32.dll` is responsible for memory, process, and thread management. `User32.dll` contains routines for the user interface that deal with the creation of windows and the handling of Win32 messages. `GDI32.dll` deals with graphics. You'll also hear of other system DLLs, such as `AdvAPI32.dll` and `ComDlg32.dll`, which deal with object security/Registry manipulation and common dialog boxes, respectively.

Another advantage to using DLLs is that your applications become modular. This simplifies updating your applications because you need to replace only DLLs instead of replacing the entire application. The Windows environment presents a typical example of this type of modularity. Each time you install a new device, you also install a device driver DLL to enable that device to communicate with Windows. The advantage to modularity becomes obvious when you imagine having to reinstall Windows each time you install a new device to your system.

On disk, a DLL is basically the same as a Windows EXE file. One major difference is that a DLL isn't an independently executable file, although it might contain executable code. The most common DLL file extension is `.dll`. Other file extensions are `.drv` for device drivers, `.sys` for system files, and `.fon` for font resources, which contain no executable code.

> **NOTE**
>
> Delphi introduces a special-purpose DLL known as a *package*, which is used in the Delphi and C++Builder environments. We'll go into greater depth on packages in Chapter 14, "Packages to the Max."

DLLs share their code with other applications through a process called *dynamic linking*, which is discussed later in this chapter. In general, when an application uses a DLL, the Win32 system ensures that only one copy of that DLL resides in memory. It does this by using *memory-mapped files*. The DLL is first loaded into the Win32 system's global heap. It's then mapped into the address space of the calling process. In the Win32 system, each process is given its own 32-bit linear address space. When the DLL is loaded by multiple processes, each process receives its own image of the DLL. Therefore, processes don't share the same physical code, data, or resources, as was the case in 16-bit Windows. In Win32, the DLL appears as though it's actually code belonging to the calling process. For more information on Win32 constructs, you can refer to Chapter 3 of *Delphi 5 Developer's Guide*, "The Win32 API," on this book's CD-ROM.

This doesn't mean that when multiple processes load a DLL, the physical memory is consumed by each usage of the DLL. The DLL image is placed into each process's address space by mapping its image from the system's global heap to the address space of each process that uses the DLL, at least in the ideal scenario (see the following sidebar).

Setting a DLL's Preferred Base Address

DLL code is only shared between processes if the DLL can be loaded into the process address space of all interested clients at the DLL's preferred base address. If the preferred base address and range of the DLL overlaps with something already allocated in a process, the Win32 loader has to relocate the entire DLL image to some other base address. When that happens, none of the relocated DLL image is shared with any other process in the system—each relocated DLL instance consumes its own chunk of physical memory and swap file space.

It's critical that you set the base address of every DLL you produce to a value that doesn't conflict with or overlap other address ranges used by your application by using the $IMAGEBASE directive.

If your DLL will be used by multiple applications, choose a unique base address that's unlikely to collide with application addresses at the low end of the process virtual address range or common DLLs (such as VCL packages) at the high end of the address range. The default base address for all executable files (EXEs and DLLs) is $400000, which means that unless you change your DLL base address, it will always collide with the base address of its host EXE and therefore never be shared between processes.

There's another side benefit to base address loading. Because the DLL doesn't require relocation or fixes (which is usually the case) and because it's stored on a local disk drive, the DLL's memory pages are mapped directly onto the DLL file on disk. The DLL code doesn't consume any space in the system's page file (called a *swap file*). This is why the system's total committed page count and size statistics can be much larger than the system swap file plus RAM.

You'll find detailed information on using the $IMAGEBASE directive by looking up "Image Base Address" in the Delphi 6 online help.

Following are some terms you'll need to know in regard to DLLs:

- Application—A Windows program residing in an `.exe` file.
- Executable—A file containing executable code. Executable files include `.dll` and `.exe` files.
- Instance—When referring to applications and DLLs, an *instance* is the occurrence of an executable. Each instance can be referred to by an *instance handle*, which is assigned by the Win32 system. When an application is run twice, for example, there are two instances of that application and, therefore, two instance handles. When a DLL is loaded, there's an instance of that DLL as well as a corresponding instance handle. The term *instance*, as used here, shouldn't be confused with the instance of a class.
- Module—In 32-bit Windows, *module* and *instance* can be used synonymously. This differs from 16-bit Windows, in which the system maintains a database to manage modules and provides a module handle for each module. In Win32, each instance of an application gets its own address space; therefore, there's no need for a separate module identifier. However, Microsoft still uses the term in its own documentation. Just be aware that *module* and *instance* are one and the same.
- Task—Windows is a multitasking (or task-switching) environment. It must be able to allocate system resources and time to the various instances running under it. It does this by maintaining a task database that maintains instance handles and other necessary information to enable it to perform its task-switching functions. The *task* is the element to which Windows grants resources and time blocks.

Static Linking Versus Dynamic Linking

Static linking refers to the method by which the Delphi compiler resolves a function or procedure call to its executable code. The function's code can exist in the application's `.dpr` file or in a unit. When linking your applications, these functions and procedures become part of the final executable file. In other words, on disk, each function will reside at a specific location in the program's `.exe` file.

A function's location also is predetermined at a location relative to where the program is loaded in memory. Any calls to that function cause program execution to jump to where the function resides, execute the function, and then return to the location from which it was called. The relative address of the function is resolved during the linking process.

This is a loose description of a more complex process that the Delphi compiler uses to perform static linking. However, for the purpose of this book, you don't need to understand the underlying operations that the compiler performs to use DLLs effectively in your applications.

> **NOTE**
>
> Delphi implements a *smart linker* that automatically removes functions, procedures, variables, and typed constants that never get referenced in the final project. Therefore, functions residing in large units that never get used don't become a part of your EXE file.

Suppose you have two applications that use the same function that resides in a unit. Both applications, of course, would have to include the unit in their uses statements. If you ran both applications simultaneously in Windows, the function would exist twice in memory. If you had a third application, there would be a third instance of the function in memory, and you would be using up three times its memory space. This small example illustrates one of the primary reasons for dynamic linking. Through dynamic linking, this function resides in a DLL. Then, when an application loads the function into memory, all other applications that need to reference it can share its code by mapping the image of the DLL into their own process memory space. The end result is that the DLL's function exists only once in memory—theoretically.

With *dynamic linking*, the link between a function call and its executable code is resolved at runtime by using an external reference to the DLL's function. These references can be declared in the application, but usually they're placed in a separate import unit. The import unit declares the imported functions and procedures and defines the various types required by DLL functions.

For example, suppose you have a DLL named MaxLib.dll that contains a function:

```
function Max(i1, I2: integer): integer;
```

This function returns the higher of the two integers passed to it. A typical import unit would look like this:

```
unit MaxUnit;
interface
function Max(I1, I2: integer): integer;
implementation
function Max; external 'MAXLIB';
end.
```

You'll notice that although this looks somewhat like a typical unit, it doesn't define the function Max(). The keyword external simply says that the function resides in the DLL of the name that follows it. To use this unit, an application would simply place MaxUnit in its uses statement. When the application runs, the DLL is loaded into memory automatically, and any calls to Max() are linked to the Max() function in the DLL.

This illustrates one of two ways to load a DLL; it's called *implicit loading*, which causes Windows to automatically load the DLL when the application loads. Another method is to *explicitly load* the DLL; this is discussed later in this chapter.

Why Use DLLs?

There are several reasons for using DLLs, some of which were mentioned earlier. In general, you use DLLs to share code or system resources, to hide your code implementation or low-level system routines, or to design custom controls. We discuss these topics in the following sections.

Sharing Code, Resources, and Data with Multiple Applications

Earlier in this chapter, you learned that the most common reason for creating a DLL is to share code. Unlike units, which enable you to share code with different Delphi applications, DLLs enable you to share code with any Windows application that can call functions from DLLs.

Additionally, DLLs provide a way for you to share resources such as bitmaps, fonts, icons, and so on that you normally would put into a resource file and link directly into your application. If you place these resources into a DLL, many applications can make use of them without using up the memory required to load them more often.

Back in 16-bit Windows, DLLs had their own data segment, so all applications that used a DLL could access the same data—global and static variables. In the Win32 system, this is a different story. Because the DLL image is mapped to each process's address space, all data in the DLL belongs to that process. One thing worth mentioning here is that although the DLL's data isn't shared between different processes, it's shared by multiple threads within the same process. Because threads execute independently of one another, you must take precautions not to cause conflicts when accessing a DLL's global data.

This doesn't mean that there aren't ways to make multiple processes share data made accessible through a DLL. One technique would be to create a shared memory area (using a memory-mapped file) from within the DLL. Each application using that DLL would be able to read the data stored in the shared memory area. This technique is shown later in the chapter.

Hiding Implementation

In some cases, you might want to hide the details of the routines that you make available from a DLL. Regardless of your reason for deciding to hide your code's implementation, a DLL provides a way for you to make your functions available to the public and not give away your source code in doing so. All you need to do is provide an interface unit to enable others to access your DLL. If you're thinking that this is already possible with Delphi compiled units (DCUs), consider that DCUs apply only to other Delphi applications that are created with the same version of Delphi. DLLs are language independent, so you can create a DLL that can be used by C++, VB, or any other language that supports DLLs.

The Windows unit is the interface unit to the Win32 DLLs. The Win32 API unit source files are included with Delphi 6. One of the files you get is Windows.pas, the source to the Windows unit. In Windows.pas, you find function definitions such as the following in the interface section:

```
function ClientToScreen(Hwnd: HWND; var lpPoint: TPoint): BOOL; stdcall;
```

The corresponding link to the DLL is in the implementation section, as in the following example:

```
function ClientToScreen; external user32 name 'ClientToScreen';
```

This basically says that the procedure ClientToScreen() exists in the dynamic link library User32.dll, and its name is ClientToScreen.

Creating and Using DLLs

The following sections take you through the process of actually creating a DLL with Delphi. You'll see how to create an interface unit so that you can make your DLLs available to other programs. You'll also learn how to incorporate Delphi forms into DLLs before going on to using DLLs in Delphi.

Counting Your Pennies (A Simple DLL)

The following DLL example illustrates placing a routine that's a favorite of many computer science professors into a DLL. The routine converts a monetary amount in pennies to the minimum number of nickels, dimes, or quarters needed to match the total number of pennies.

A Basic DLL

The library contains the PenniesToCoins() method. Listing 6.1 shows the complete DLL project.

Listing 6.1   PenniesLib.dpr—A DLL to Convert Pennies to Other Coins

```
library PenniesLib;
{$DEFINE PENNIESLIB}
uses
  SysUtils,
  Classes,
  PenniesInt;
```

LISTING 6.1   Continued

```
function PenniesToCoins(TotPennies: word;
   CoinsRec: PCoinsRec): word; StdCall;
begin
  Result := TotPennies;  // Assign value to Result
  { Calculate the values for quarters, dimes, nickels, pennies }
  with CoinsRec^ do
  begin
    Quarters     := TotPennies div 25;
    TotPennies   := TotPennies - Quarters * 25;
    Dimes        := TotPennies div 10;
    TotPennies   := TotPennies - Dimes * 10;
    Nickels      := TotPennies div 5;
    TotPennies   := TotPennies - Nickels * 5;
    Pennies      := TotPennies;
  end;
end;

{ Export the function by name }
exports
  PenniesToCoins;
end.
```

Notice that this library uses the unit PenniesInt. We'll discuss this in more detail momentarily.

The exports clause specifies which functions or procedures in the DLL get exported and made available to calling applications.

Defining an Interface Unit

Interface units enable users of your DLL to statically import your DLL's routines into their applications by just placing the import unit's name in their module's uses statement. Interface units also allow the DLL writer to define common structures used by both the library and the calling application. We demonstrate that here with the interface unit. Listing 6.2 shows the source code to PenniesInt.pas.

LISTING 6.2   PenniesInt.pas—The interface Unit for PenniesLib.Dll

```
unit PenniesInt;
{ Interface routine for PENNIES.DLL }

interface
type
```

LISTING 6.2 Continued

6

```
{ This record will hold the denominations after the conversions have
  been made }
PCoinsRec = ^TCoinsRec;
TCoinsRec = record
  Quarters,
  Dimes,
  Nickels,
  Pennies: word;
end;

{$IFNDEF PENNIESLIB}
{ Declare function with export keyword }

function PenniesToCoins(TotPennies: word;
  CoinsRec: PCoinsRec): word; StdCall;
{$ENDIF}

implementation

{$IFNDEF PENNIESLIB}
{ Define the imported function }
function PenniesToCoins; external 'PENNIESLIB.DLL' name 'PenniesToCoins';
{$ENDIF}

end.
```

In the type section of this project, you declare the record TCoinsRec as well as a pointer to this record. This record will hold the denominations that will make up the penny amount passed into the PenniesToCoins() function. The function takes two parameters—the total amount of money in pennies and a pointer to a TCoinsRec variable. The result of the function is the amount of pennies passed in.

PenniesInt.pas declares the function that the PenniesLib.dll exports in its interface section. The definition of the PenniesToCoins() function is placed in the implementation section. This definition specifies that the function is an external function existing in the DLL file PenniesLib.dll. It links to the DLL function by the name of the function. Notice that you used a compiler directive PENNIESLIB to conditionally compile the declaration of the PenniesToCoins() function. You do this because it's not necessary to link this declaration when compiling the interface unit for the library. This allows you to share the interface unit's type definitions with both the library and any applications that intend to use the library. Any changes to the structures used by both only have to be made in the interface unit.

TIP

To define an application-wide conditional directive, specify the conditional in the Directories/Conditionals page of the Project, Options dialog box. Note that you must rebuild your project for changes to conditional defines to take effect because Make logic doesn't reevaluate conditional defines.

NOTE

The following definition shows one of two ways to import a DLL function:

```
function PenniesToCoins; external 'PENNIESLIB.DLL' index 1;
```

This method is called *importing by ordinal*. The other method by which you can import DLL functions is *by name*:

```
function PenniesToCoins; external 'PENNIESLIB.DLL' name 'PenniesToCoins';
```

The by-name method uses the name specified after the name keyword to determine which function to link to in the DLL.

The by-ordinal method reduces the DLL's load time because it doesn't have to look up the function name in the DLL's name table. However, this isn't the preferred method in Win32. Importing by name is the preferred technique so that applications won't be hypersensitive to relocation of DLL entry points as DLLs get updated over time. When you import by ordinal, you are binding to a place in the DLL. When you import by name, you're binding to the function name, regardless of where it happens to be placed in the DLL.

If this were an actual DLL that you planned to deploy, you would provide both PenniesLib.dll and PenniesInt.pas to your users. This would enable them to use the DLL by defining the types and functions in PenniesInt.pas that PenniesLib.dll requires. Additionally, programmers using different languages, such as C++, could convert PenniesInt.pas to their languages, thus enabling them to use your DLL in their development environments. You'll find a sample project that uses PenniesLib.dll on the CD that accompanies this book.

Displaying Modal Forms from DLLs

This section shows you how to make modal forms available from a DLL. Placing commonly used forms in a DLL is beneficial because it enables you to extend your forms for use with any Windows application or development environment, such as C++ and Visual Basic.

To do this, remove your DLL-based form from the list of autocreated forms.

We've created such a form that contains a TCalendar component on the main form. The calling application will call a DLL function that will invoke this form. When the user selects a day on the calendar, the date will be returned to the calling application.

Listing 6.3 shows the source for CalendarLib.dpr, the DLL project file. Listing 6.4, in the section, "Displaying Modeless Forms from DLLs," shows the source code for DllFrm.pas, the DLL form's unit, which illustrates how to encapsulate the form into a DLL.

LISTING 6.3 Library Project Source—CalendarLib.dpr

```
unit DLLFrm;

interface

uses
  SysUtils, WinTypes, WinProcs, Messages, Classes, Graphics, Controls,
  Forms, Dialogs, Grids, Calendar;

type

  TDLLForm = class(TForm)
    calDllCalendar: TCalendar;
    procedure calDllCalendarDblClick(Sender: TObject);
  end;

{ Declare the export function }
function ShowCalendar(AHandle: THandle; ACaption: String):
  TDateTime; StdCall;

implementation
{$R *.DFM}

function ShowCalendar(AHandle: THandle; ACaption: String): TDateTime;
var
  DLLForm: TDllForm;
begin
  // Copy application handle to DLL's TApplication object
  Application.Handle := AHandle;
  DLLForm := TDLLForm.Create(Application);
  try
    DLLForm.Caption := ACaption;
    DLLForm.ShowModal;
    // Pass the date back in Result
    Result := DLLForm.calDLLCalendar.CalendarDate;
```

LISTING 6.3 Continued

```
finally
    DLLForm.Free;
  end;
end;

procedure TDLLForm.calDllCalendarDblClick(Sender: TObject);
begin
  Close;
end;

end.
```

The main form in this DLL is incorporated into the exported function. Notice that the DLLForm declaration was removed from the interface section and declared inside the function instead.

The first thing that the DLL function does is to assign the AHandle parameter to the Application.Handle property. Delphi projects, including library projects, contain a global Application object. In a DLL, this object is separate from the Application object that exists in the calling application. For the form in the DLL to truly act as a modal form for the calling application, you must assign the handle of the calling application to the DLL's Application.Handle property, as has been illustrated. Not doing so will result in erratic behavior, especially when you start minimizing the DLL's form. Also, as shown, you must make sure not to pass nil as the owner of the DLL's form.

After the form is created, you assign the ACaption string to the Caption of the DLL form. It's then displayed modally. When the form closes, the date selected by the user in the TCalendar component is passed back to the calling function. The form closes after the user double-clicks the TCalendar component.

> **CAUTION**
>
> ShareMem must be the first unit in your library's uses clause and your project's (select View, Project Source) uses clause if your DLL exports any procedures or functions that pass strings or dynamic arrays as parameters or function results. This applies to all strings passed to and from your DLL—even those nested in records and classes. ShareMem is the interface unit to the Borlndmm.dll shared memory manager, which must be deployed along with your DLL. To avoid using Borlndmm.dll, pass string information using PChar or ShortString parameters.
>
> ShareMem is only required when heap-allocated strings or dynamic arrays are passed between modules, and such transfers also assign ownership of that string memory.
>
> *continues*

> Typecasting an internal string to a `PChar` and passing it to another module as a `PChar` doesn't transfer ownership of the string memory to the calling module, so `ShareMem` isn't required.
>
> Note that this `ShareMem` issue applies only to Delphi/C++Builder DLLs that pass strings or dynamic arrays to other Delphi/BCB DLLs or EXEs. You should never expose Delphi strings or dynamic arrays (as parameters or function results of DLL exported functions) to non-Delphi DLLs or host apps. They won't know how to dispose of the Delphi items correctly.
>
> Also, `ShareMem` is never required between modules built with packages. The memory allocator is implicitly shared between packaged modules.

This is all that's required when encapsulating a modal form into a DLL. In the next section, we'll discuss displaying a modeless form in a DLL.

Displaying Modeless Forms from DLLs

To illustrate placing modeless forms in a DLL, we'll use the same calendar form as the previous section.

When displaying modeless forms from a DLL, the DLL must provide two routines. The first routine must take care of creating and displaying the form. A second routine is required to free the form. Listing 6.4 displays the source code for the illustration of a modeless form in a DLL.

LISTING 6.4 A Modeless Form in a DLL

```
unit DLLFrm;

interface

uses
  SysUtils, WinTypes, WinProcs, Messages, Classes, Graphics, Controls,
  Forms, Dialogs, Grids, Calendar;

type

  TDLLForm = class(TForm)
    calDllCalendar: TCalendar;
  end;

{ Declare the export function }
function ShowCalendar(AHandle: THandle; ACaption: String):
  Longint; stdCall;
```

LISTING 6.4 Continued

```
procedure CloseCalendar(AFormRef: Longint); stdcall;


implementation
{$R *.DFM}

function ShowCalendar(AHandle: THandle; ACaption: String): Longint;
var
  DLLForm: TDllForm;
begin
  // Copy application handle to DLL's TApplication object
  Application.Handle := AHandle;
  DLLForm := TDLLForm.Create(Application);
  Result := Longint(DLLForm);
  DLLForm.Caption := ACaption;
  DLLForm.Show;
end;

procedure CloseCalendar(AFormRef: Longint);
begin
  if AFormRef > 0 then
    TDLLForm(AFormRef).Release;
end;

end.
```

This listing displays the routines ShowCalendar() and CloseCalendar(). ShowCalendar() is similar to the same function in the modal form example in that it makes the assignment of the calling application's application handle to the DLL's application handle and creates the form. Instead of calling ShowModal(), however, this routine calls Show(). Notice that it doesn't free the form. Also, the function returns a longint value to which you assign the DLLForm instance because a reference of the created form must be maintained, and it's best to have the calling application maintain this instance. This would take care of any issues regarding other applications calling this DLL and creating another instance of the form.

In the CloseCalendar() procedure, you simply check for a valid reference to the form and invoke its Release() method. Here, the calling application should pass back the same reference that was returned to it from ShowCalendar().

When using such a technique, you must be careful that your DLL never frees the form independently of the host. If it does (for example, returning caFree in CanClose()), the call to CloseCalendar() will crash.

Demos of both the model and modeless forms are on the CD that accompanies this book.

Using DLLs in Your Delphi Applications

Earlier in this chapter, you learned that there are two ways to load or import DLLs: implicitly and explicitly. Both techniques are illustrated in this section with the DLLs just created.

The first DLL created in this chapter included an `interface` unit. You'll use this `interface` unit in the following example to illustrate implicit linking of a DLL. The sample project's main form has a `TMaskEdit`, `TButton`, and nine `TLabel` components.

In this application, the user enters an amount of pennies. Then, when the user clicks the button, the labels will show the breakdown of denominations of change adding up to that amount. This information is obtained from the `PenniesLib.dll` exported function `PenniesToCoins()`.

The main form is defined in the unit `MainFrm.pas` shown in Listing 6.5.

LISTING 6.5   Main Form for the Pennies Demo

```
unit MainFrm;

interface

uses
  SysUtils, WinTypes, WinProcs, Messages, Classes, Graphics, Controls,
  Forms, Dialogs, StdCtrls, Mask;

type

  TMainForm = class(TForm)
    lblTotal: TLabel;
    lblQlbl: TLabel;
    lblDlbl: TLabel;
    lblNlbl: TLabel;
    lblPlbl: TLabel;
    lblQuarters: TLabel;
    lblDimes: TLabel;
    lblNickels: TLabel;
    lblPennies: TLabel;
    btnMakeChange: TButton;
    meTotalPennies: TMaskEdit;
    procedure btnMakeChangeClick(Sender: TObject);
  end;

var
  MainForm: TMainForm;

implementation
```

LISTING 6.5   Continued

```
uses PenniesInt;  // Use an interface unit

{$R *.DFM}

procedure TMainForm.btnMakeChangeClick(Sender: TObject);
var
  CoinsRec: TCoinsRec;
  TotPennies: word;
begin
  { Call the DLL function to determine the minimum coins required
    for the amount of pennies specified. }
  TotPennies := PenniesToCoins(StrToInt(meTotalPennies.Text), @CoinsRec);
  with CoinsRec do
  begin
    { Now display the coin information }
    lblQuarters.Caption := IntToStr(Quarters);
    lblDimes.Caption    := IntToStr(Dimes);
    lblNickels.Caption  := IntToStr(Nickels);
    lblPennies.Caption  := IntToStr(Pennies);
  end
end;

end.
```

Notice that MainFrm.pas uses the unit PenniesInt. Recall that PenniesInt.pas includes the external declarations to the functions existing in PenniesLib.dpr. When this application runs, the Win32 system automatically loads PenniesLib.dll and maps it to the process address space for the calling application.

Usage of an import unit is optional. You can remove PenniesInt from the uses statement and place the external declaration to PenniesToCoins() in the implementation section of MainFrm.pas, as in the following code:

```
implementation

function PenniesToCoins(TotPennies: word; ChangeRec: PChangeRec): word;
  ⮕StdCall external 'PENNIESLIB.DLL';
```

You also would have to define PChangeRec and TChangeRec again in MainFrm.pas, or you can compile your application using the compiler directive PENNIESLIB. This technique is fine in the case where you only need access to a few routines from a DLL. In many cases, you'll find that you require not only the external declarations to the DLL's routines but also access to the types defined in the interface unit.

> **NOTE**
>
> Many times, when using another vendor's DLL, you won't have a Pascal `interface` unit; instead, you'll have a C/C++ import library. In this case, you have to translate the library to a Pascal equivalent `interface` unit.

You'll find this demo on the accompanying CD.

Loading DLLs Explicitly

Although loading DLLs implicitly is convenient, it isn't always the most desired method. Suppose you have a DLL that contains many routines. If it's likely that your application will never call any of the DLL's routines, it would be a waste of memory to load the DLL every time your application runs. This is especially true when using multiple DLLs with one application. Another example is when using DLLs as large objects: a standard list of functions that are implemented by multiple DLLs but do slightly different things, such as printer drivers and file format readers. In this situation, it would be beneficial to load the DLL when specifically requested to do so by the application. This is referred to as *explicitly loading* a DLL.

To illustrate explicitly loading a DLL, we return to the sample DLL with a modal form. Listing 6.6 shows the code for the main form of the application that demonstrates explicitly loading this DLL. The project file for this application is on the accompanying CD.

LISTING 6.6 Main Form for Calendar DLL Demo Application

```
unit MainFfm;

interface

uses
  SysUtils, WinTypes, WinProcs, Messages, Classes, Graphics, Controls,
  Forms, Dialogs, StdCtrls;

type
  { First, define a procedural data type, this should reflect the
    procedure that is exported from the DLL. }
  TShowCalendar = function (AHandle: THandle; ACaption: String):
    TDateTime; StdCall;

  { Create a new exception class to reflect a failed DLL load }
  EDLLLoadError = class(Exception);
```

LISTING 6.6 Continued

```delphi
TMainForm = class(TForm)
  lblDate: TLabel;
  btnGetCalendar: TButton;
  procedure btnGetCalendarClick(Sender: TObject);
end;

var
  MainForm: TMainForm;

implementation

{$R *.DFM}

procedure TMainForm.btnGetCalendarClick(Sender: TObject);
var
  LibHandle  : THandle;
  ShowCalendar: TShowCalendar;
begin

  { Attempt to load the DLL }
  LibHandle := LoadLibrary('CALENDARLIB.DLL');
  try
    { If the load failed, LibHandle will be zero.
      If this occurs, raise an exception. }
    if LibHandle = 0 then
      raise EDLLLoadError.Create('Unable to Load DLL');
    { If the code makes it here, the DLL loaded successfully, now obtain
      the link to the DLL's exported function so that it can be called. }
    @ShowCalendar := GetProcAddress(LibHandle, 'ShowCalendar');
    { If the function is imported successfully, then set
      lblDate.Caption to reflect the returned date from
      the function. Otherwise, show the return raise an exception. }
    if not (@ShowCalendar = nil) then
      lblDate.Caption := DateToStr(ShowCalendar(Application.Handle, Caption))
    else
      RaiseLastWin32Error;
  finally
    FreeLibrary(LibHandle); // Unload the DLL.
  end;
end;

end.
```

This unit first defines a procedural data type, TShowCalendar, that reflects the definition of the function it will be using from CalendarLib.dll. It then defines a special exception, which is raised when there's a problem loading the DLL. In the btnGetCalendarClick() event handler, you'll notice the use of three Win32 API functions: LoadLibrary(), FreeLibrary(), and GetProcAddress().

LoadLibrary() is defined this way:

```
function LoadLibrary(lpLibFileName: PChar): HMODULE; stdcall;
```

This function loads the DLL module specified by lpLibFileName and maps it into the address space of the calling process. If this function succeeds, it returns a handle to the module. If it fails, it returns the value 0, and an exception is raised. You can look up LoadLibrary() in the online help for detailed information on its functionality and possible return error values.

FreeLibrary() is defined like this:

```
function FreeLibrary(hLibModule: HMODULE): BOOL; stdcall;
```

FreeLibrary() decrements the instance count of the library specified by LibModule. It removes the library from memory when the library's instance count is zero. The instance count keeps track of the number of tasks using the DLL.

Here's how GetProcAddress() is defined:

```
function GetProcAddress(hModule: HMODULE; lpProcName: LPCSTR):
  FARPROC; stdcall
```

GetProcAddress() returns the address of a function within the module specified in its first parameter, hModule. hModule is the THandle returned from a call to LoadLibrary(). If GetProcAddress() fails, it returns nil. You must call GetLastError() for extended error information.

In Button1's OnClick event handler, LoadLibrary() is called to load CALDLL. If it fails to load, an exception is raised. If the call is successful, a call to the window's GetProcAddress() is made to get the address of the function ShowCalendar(). Prepending the procedural data type variable ShowCalendar with the address of operator (@) character prevents the compiler from issuing a type mismatch error due to its strict type-checking. After obtaining the address of ShowCalendar(), you can use it as defined by TShowCalendar. Finally, FreeLibrary() is called within the finally block to ensure that the library is freed from memory when no longer required.

You can see that the library is loaded and freed each time this function is called. If this function was called only once during the run of an application, it becomes apparent how explicit loading can save much-needed and often limited memory resources. On the other hand, if this function were called frequently, the DLL loading and unloading would add a lot of overhead.

The Dynamically Linked Library Entry/Exit Function

You can provide optional entry and exit code for your DLLs when required under various initialization and shutdown operations. These operations can occur during process or thread initialization/termination.

Process/Thread Initialization and Termination Routines

Typical initialization operations include registering Windows classes, initializing global variables, and initializing an entry/exit function. This occurs during the method of entry for the DLL, which is referred to as the DLLEntryPoint function. This function is actually represented by the begin..end block of the DLL project file. This is the location where you would set up an entry/exit procedure. This procedure must take a single parameter of the type DWord.

The global DLLProc variable is a procedural pointer to which you can assign the entry/exit procedure. This variable is initially nil unless you set up your own procedure. By setting up an entry/exit procedure, you can respond to the events listed in Table 6.1.

TABLE 6.1 DLL Entry/Exit Events

Event	Purpose
DLL_PROCESS_ATTACH	The DLL is attaching to the address space of the current process when the process starts up or when a call to LoadLibrary() is made. DLLs initialize any instance data during this event.
DLL_PROCESS_DETACH	The DLL is detaching from the address space of the calling process. This occurs during a clean process exit or when a call to FreeLibrary() is made. The DLL can uninitialize any instance data during this event.
DLL_THREAD_ATTACH	This event occurs when the current process creates a new thread. When this occurs, the system calls the entry-point function of any DLLs attached to the process. This call is made in the context of the new thread and can be used to allocate any thread-specific data.
DLL_THREAD_DETACH	This event occurs when the thread is exiting. During this event, the DLL can free any thread-specific initialized data.

> **NOTE**
>
> Threads terminated abnormally—by calling `TerminateThread()`—are not guaranteed to call `DLL_THREAD_DETACH`.

DLL Entry/Exit Example

Listing 6.7 illustrates how you would install an entry/exit procedure to the DLL's `DLLProc` variable.

LISTING 6.7 The Source Code for `DllEntry.dpr`

```
library DllEntry;
uses
  SysUtils,
  Windows,
  Dialogs,
  Classes;
procedure DLLEntryPoint(dwReason: DWord);
begin
  case dwReason of
    DLL_PROCESS_ATTACH: ShowMessage('Attaching to process');
    DLL_PROCESS_DETACH: ShowMessage('Detaching from process');
    DLL_THREAD_ATTACH:  MessageBeep(0);
    DLL_THREAD_DETACH:  MessageBeep(0);
  end;
end;
begin
  { First, assign the procedure to the DLLProc variable }
  DllProc := @DLLEntryPoint;
  { Now invoke the procedure to reflect that the DLL is attaching to the
    process }
  DLLEntryPoint(DLL_PROCESS_ATTACH);
end.
```

The entry/exit procedure is assigned to the DLL's `DLLProc` variable in the `begin..end` block of the DLL project file. This procedure, `DLLEntryPoint()`, evaluates its word parameter to determine which event is being called. These events correspond to the events listed in Table 6.1. For illustration purposes, we have each event display a message box when the DLL is being loaded or destroyed. When a thread in the calling application is being created or destroyed, a message beep occurs.

To illustrate the use of this DLL, examine the code shown in Listing 6.8.

LISTING 6.8   Sample Code for DLL Entry/Exit Demo

```pascal
unit MainFrm;

interface

uses
  Windows, Messages, SysUtils, Classes, Graphics, Controls,
  Forms, Dialogs, StdCtrls, ComCtrls, Gauges;

type

  { Define a TThread descendant }

TTestThread = class(TThread)
    procedure Execute; override;
    procedure SetCaptionData;
  end;

  TMainForm = class(TForm)
    btnLoadLib: TButton;
    btnFreeLib: TButton;
    btnCreateThread: TButton;
    btnFreeThread: TButton;
    lblCount: TLabel;
    procedure btnLoadLibClick(Sender: TObject);
    procedure btnFreeLibClick(Sender: TObject);
    procedure btnCreateThreadClick(Sender: TObject);
    procedure btnFreeThreadClick(Sender: TObject);
    procedure FormCreate(Sender: TObject);
  private
    LibHandle  : THandle;
    TestThread : TTestThread;
    Counter    : Integer;
    GoThread   : Boolean;
  end;

var
  MainForm: TMainForm;

implementation

{$R *.DFM}
```

LISTING 6.8 Continued

```
procedure TTestThread.Execute;
begin
  while MainForm.GoThread do
  begin
    Synchronize(SetCaptionData);
    Inc(MainForm.Counter);
  end;
end;

procedure TTestThread.SetCaptionData;
begin
  MainForm.lblCount.Caption := IntToStr(MainForm.Counter);
end;

procedure TMainForm.btnLoadLibClick(Sender: TObject);
{ This procedure loads the library DllEntryLib.DLL }
begin
  if LibHandle = 0 then
  begin
    LibHandle := LoadLibrary('DLLENTRYLIB.DLL');
    if LibHandle = 0 then
      raise Exception.Create('Unable to Load DLL');
  end
  else
    MessageDlg('Library already loaded', mtWarning, [mbok], 0);
end;

procedure TMainForm.btnFreeLibClick(Sender: TObject);
{ This procedure frees the library }
begin
  if not (LibHandle = 0) then
  begin
    FreeLibrary(LibHandle);
    LibHandle := 0;
  end;
end;

procedure TMainForm.btnCreateThreadClick(Sender: TObject);
{ This procedure creates the TThread instance. If the DLL is loaded a
  message beep will occur. }
begin
  if TestThread = nil then
  begin
    GoThread    := True;
```

LISTING 6.8   Continued

```
    TestThread := TTestThread.Create(False);
  end;
end;

procedure TMainForm.btnFreeThreadClick(Sender: TObject);
{ In freeing the TThread a message beep will occur if the DLL is loaded. }
begin
  if not (TestThread = nil) then
  begin
    GoThread    := False;
    TestThread.Free;
    TestThread := nil;
    Counter     := 0;
  end;

end;

procedure TMainForm.FormCreate(Sender: TObject);
begin
  LibHandle   := 0;
  TestThread := nil;
end;

end.
```

This project consists of a main form with four TButton components. BtnLoadLib loads the DLL DllEntryLib.dll. BtnFreeLib frees the library from the process. BtnCreateThread creates a TThread descendant object, which in turn creates a thread. BtnFreeThread destroys the TThread object. The lblCount is used just to show the thread execution.

The btnLoadLibClick() event handler calls LoadLibrary() to load DllEntryLib.dll. This causes the DLL to load and be mapped to the process's address space. Additionally, the initialization code in the DLL gets executed. Again, this is the code that appears in the begin..end block of the DLL, which performs the following to set up an entry/exit procedure for the DLL:

```
begin
  { First, assign the procedure to the DLLProc variable }
  DllProc := @DLLEntryPoint;
  { Now invoke the procedure to reflect that the DLL is attaching to the
    process }
  DLLEntryPoint(DLL_PROCESS_ATTACH);
end.
```

This initialization section will only be called once per process. If another process loads this DLL, this section will be called again, except in the context of the separate process—processes don't share DLL instances.

The `btnFreeLibClick()` event handler unloads the DLL by calling `FreeLibrary()`. When this happens, the procedure to which the `DLLProc` points, `DLLEntryProc()`, gets called with the value of `DLL_PROCESS_DETACH` passed as the parameter.

The `btnCreateThreadClick()` event handler creates the `TThread` descendant object. This causes the `DLLEntryProc()` to get called, and the `DLL_THREAD_ATTACH` value is passed as the parameter. The `btnFreeThreadClick()` event handler invokes `DLLEntryProc` again but passes `DLL_THREAD_DETACH` as the value to the procedure.

Although you invoke only a message box when the events occur, you'll use these events to perform any process or thread initialization or cleanup that might be necessary for your application. Later, you'll see an example of using this technique to set up sharable DLL global data. You can look at the demo of this DLL in the project `DLLEntryTest.dpr` on the CD.

Exceptions in DLLs

This section discusses issues regarding DLLs and Win32 exceptions.

Capturing Exceptions in 16-Bit Delphi

Back in the 16-bit days with Delphi 1, Delphi exceptions were language specific. Therefore, if exceptions were raised in a DLL, you were required to capture the exception before it escaped from the DLL so that it wouldn't creep up the calling modules stack, causing it to crash. You had to wrap every DLL entry point with an exception handler, like this:

```
procedure SomeDLLProc;
begin
  try
    { Do your stuff }
  except
    on Exception do
        { Don't let it get away, handle it and don't re-raise it }
  end;
end;
```

This is no longer the case as of Delphi 2. Delphi 6 exceptions map themselves to Win32 exceptions. Exceptions raised in DLLs are no longer a compiler/language feature of Delphi but rather a feature of the Win32 system.

For this to work, however, you must make sure that SysUtils is included in the DLL's uses clause. Not including SysUtils disables Delphi's exception support inside the DLL.

CAUTION

Most Win32 applications aren't designed to handle exceptions, so even though Delphi language exceptions get turned into Win32 exceptions, exceptions that you let escape from a DLL into the host application are likely to shut down the application.

If the host application is built with Delphi or C++Builder, this shouldn't be much of an issue, but there's still a lot of raw C and C++ code out there that doesn't like exceptions.

Therefore, to make your DLLs bulletproof, you might still consider using the 16-bit method of protecting DLL entry points with try..except blocks to capture exceptions raised in your DLLs.

NOTE

When a non-Delphi application uses a DLL written in Delphi, it won't be able to utilize the Delphi language-specific exception classes. However, it can be handled as a Win32 system exception given the exception code of $0EEDFACE. The exception address will be the first entry in the ExceptionInformation array of the Win32 system EXCEPTION_RECORD. The second entry contains a reference to the Delphi exception object. Look up EXCEPTION_RECORD in the Delphi online help for additional information.

Exceptions and the Safecall Directive

Safecall functions are used for COM and exception handling. They guarantee that any exception will propagate to the caller of the function. A Safecall function converts an exception into an HResult return value. Safecall also implies the StdCall calling convention. Therefore, a Safecall function declared as

```
function Foo(i: integer): string; Safecall;
```

really looks like this according to the compiler:

```
function Foo(i: integer): string; HResult; StdCall;
```

The compiler then inserts an implicit try..except block that wraps the entire function contents and catches any exceptions raised. The except block invokes a call to SafecallExceptionHandler() to convert the exception into an HResult. This is somewhat similar to the 16-bit method of capturing exceptions and passing back error values.

Callback Functions

A *callback function* is a function in your application called by Win32 DLLs or other DLLs. Basically, Windows has several API functions that require a callback function. When calling these functions, you pass in an address of a function defined by your application that Windows can call. If you're wondering how this all relates to DLLs, remember that the Win32 API is really several routines exported from system DLLs. Essentially, when you pass a callback function to a Win32 function, you're passing this function to a DLL.

One such function is the EnumWindows() API function, which enumerates through all top-level windows. This function passes the handle of each window in the enumeration to your application-defined callback function. You're required to define and pass the callback function's address to the EnumWindows() function. The callback function that you must provide to EnumWindows() is defined this way:

```
function EnumWindowsProc(Hw: HWnd; lp: lParam): Boolean; stdcall;
```

We illustrate the use of the EnumWindows() function in the CallBack.dpr project on the CD and shown in Listing 6.9.

LISTING 6.9 MainForm.pas—Source to Callback Example

```
unit MainFrm;

interface

uses
  Windows, Messages, SysUtils, Classes, Graphics, Controls,
  Forms, Dialogs, StdCtrls, ComCtrls;

type

  { Define a record/class to hold the window name and class name for
    each window. Instances of this class will get added to ListBox1 }
  TWindowInfo = class
    WindowName,          // The window name
    WindowClass: String; // The window's class name
  end;

  TMainForm = class(TForm)
    lbWinInfo: TListBox;
    btnGetWinInfo: TButton;
    hdWinInfo: THeaderControl;
    procedure btnGetWinInfoClick(Sender: TObject);
```

LISTING 6.9   Continued

```
    procedure FormDestroy(Sender: TObject);
    procedure lbWinInfoDrawItem(Control: TWinControl; Index: Integer;
      Rect: TRect; State: TOwnerDrawState);
    procedure hdWinInfoSectionResize(HeaderControl: THeaderControl;
      Section: THeaderSection);
  end;

var
  MainForm: TMainForm;

implementation

{$R *.DFM}
function EnumWindowsProc(Hw: HWnd; AMainForm: TMainForm):
  Boolean; stdcall;
{ This procedure is called by the User32.DLL library as it enumerates
  through windows active in the system. }
var
  WinName, CName: array[0..144] of char;
  WindowInfo: TWindowInfo;
begin
  { Return true by default which indicates not to stop enumerating
    through the windows }
  Result := True;
  GetWindowText(Hw, WinName, 144); // Obtain the current window text
  GetClassName(Hw, CName, 144);    // Obtain the class name of the window
  { Create a TWindowInfo instance and set its fields with the values of
    the window name and window class name. Then add this object to
    ListBox1's Objects array. These values will be displayed later by
    the listbox }
  WindowInfo := TWindowInfo.Create;
  with WindowInfo do
  begin
    SetLength(WindowName, strlen(WinName));
    SetLength(WindowClass, StrLen(CName));
    WindowName := StrPas(WinName);
    WindowClass := StrPas(CName);
  end;
  // Add to Objects array
  MainForm.lbWinInfo.Items.AddObject('', WindowInfo); end;

procedure TMainForm.btnGetWinInfoClick(Sender: TObject);
```

LISTING 6.9 Continued

```
begin
  { Enumerate through all top-level windows being displayed. Pass in the
    call back function EnumWindowsProc which will be called for each
    window }
  EnumWindows(@EnumWindowsProc, 0);
end;


procedure TMainForm.FormDestroy(Sender: TObject);
var
  i: integer;
begin
  { Free all instances of TWindowInfo }
  for i := 0 to lbWinInfo.Items.Count - 1 do
    TWindowInfo(lbWinInfo.Items.Objects[i]).Free
end;


procedure TMainForm.lbWinInfoDrawItem(Control: TWinControl;
  Index: Integer;Rect: TRect; State: TOwnerDrawState);
begin
  { First, clear the rectangle to which drawing will be performed }
  lbWinInfo.Canvas.FillRect(Rect);
  { Now draw the strings of the TWindowInfo record stored at the
    Index'th position of the listbox. The sections of HeaderControl
    will give positions to which to draw each string }
  with TWindowInfo(lbWinInfo.Items.Objects[Index]) do
  begin
    DrawText(lbWinInfo.Canvas.Handle, PChar(WindowName),
      Length(WindowName), Rect,dt_Left or dt_VCenter);
    { Shift the drawing rectangle over by using the size
      HeaderControl1's sections to determine where to draw the next
      string }
    Rect.Left := Rect.Left + hdWinInfo.Sections[0].Width;
    DrawText(lbWinInfo.Canvas.Handle, PChar(WindowClass),
      Length(WindowClass), Rect, dt_Left or dt_VCenter);
  end;
end;


procedure TMainForm.hdWinInfoSectionResize(HeaderControl:
  THeaderControl; Section: THeaderSection);
begin
  lbWinInfo.Invalidate; // Force ListBox1 to redraw itself.
end;


end.
```

This application uses the EnumWindows() function to extract the window name and classname of all top-level windows and adds them to the owner-draw list box on the main form. The main form uses an owner-draw list box to make both the window name and window classname appear in a columnar fashion. First we'll explain the use of the callback function. Then we'll explain how we created the columnar list box.

Using the Callback Function

You saw in Listing 6.9 that we defined a procedure, EnumWindowsProc(), that takes a window handle as its first parameter. The second parameter is user-defined data, so you can pass whatever data you deem necessary as long as its size is the equivalent to an integer data type.

EnumWindowsProc() is the callback procedure that you'll pass to the EnumWindows() Win32 API function. It must be declared with the StdCall directive to specify that it uses the Win32 calling convention. When passing this procedure to EnumWindows(), it will get called for each top-level window whose window handle gets passed as the first parameter. You use this window handle to obtain both the window name and classname of each window. You then create an instance of the TWindowInfo class and set its fields with this information. The TWindowInfo class instance is then added to the lbWinInfo.Objects array. The data in this list box will be used when the list box is drawn to show this data in a columnar fashion.

Notice that, in the main form's OnDestroy event handler, you make sure to clean up any allocated instances of the TWindowInfo class.

The btnGetWinInfoClick()event handler calls the EnumWindows() procedure and passes EnumWindowsProc() as its first parameter.

When you run the application and click the button, you'll see that the information is obtained from each window and is shown in the list box.

Drawing an Owner-Draw List Box

The window names and classnames of top-level windows are drawn in a columnar fashion in lbWinInfo from the previous project. This was done by using a TListBox with its Style property set to lbOwnerDraw. When this style is set as such, the TListBox.OnDrawItem event is called each time the TListBox is to draw one of its items. You're responsible for drawing the items as illustrated in the example.

In Listing 6.9, the event handler lbWinInfoDrawItem() contains the code that performs the drawing of list box items. Here, you draw the strings contained in the TWindowInfo class instances, which are stored in the lbWinInfo.Objects array. These values are obtained from the callback function EnumWindowsProc(). You can refer to the code commentary to determine what this event handler does.

Calling Callback Functions from Your DLLs

Just as you can pass callback functions to DLLs, you can also have your DLLs call callback functions. This section illustrates how you can create a DLL whose exported function takes a callback procedure as a parameter. Then, based on whether the user passes in a callback procedure, the procedure gets called. Listing 6.10 contains the source code to this DLL.

LISTING 6.10   Calling a Callback Demo—Source Code for `StrSrchLib.dll`

```
library StrSrchLib;

uses
  Wintypes,
  WinProcs,
  SysUtils,
  Dialogs;

type
  { declare the callback function type }
  TFoundStrProc = procedure(StrPos: PChar); StdCall;

function SearchStr(ASrcStr, ASearchStr: PChar;  AProc: TFarProc):
  Integer; StdCall;
{ This function looks for ASearchStr in ASrcStr. When founc ASearchStr,
  the callback procedure referred to by AProc is called if one has been
  passed in. The user may pass nil as this parameter. }
var
  FindStr: PChar;
begin
  FindStr := ASrcStr;
  FindStr := StrPos(FindStr, ASearchStr);
  while FindStr <> nil do
  begin
    if AProc <> nil then
      TFoundStrProc(AProc)(FindStr);
    FindStr := FindStr + 1;
    FindStr := StrPos(FindStr, ASearchStr);
  end;
end;

exports
  SearchStr;
begin

end.
```

The DLL also defines a procedural type, TFoundStrProc, for the callback function, which will be used to typecast the callback function when it's called.

The exported procedure SearchStr() is where the callback function is called. The commentary in the listing explains what this procedure does.

An example of this DLL's usage is given in the project CallBackDemo.dpr in the \DLLCallBack directory on the CD. The source for the main form of this demo is shown in Listing 6.11.

LISTING 6.11   The Main Form for the DLL Callback Demo

```
unit MainFrm;

interface

uses
  Windows, Messages, SysUtils, Classes, Graphics, Controls,
  Forms, Dialogs, StdCtrls;

type
  TMainForm = class(TForm)
    btnCallDLLFunc: TButton;
    edtSearchStr: TEdit;
    lblSrchWrd: TLabel;
    memStr: TMemo;
    procedure btnCallDLLFuncClick(Sender: TObject);
  end;

var
  MainForm: TMainForm;
  Count: Integer;

implementation

{$R *.DFM}

{ Define the DLL's exported procedure }
function SearchStr(ASrcStr, ASearchStr: PChar; AProc: TFarProc):
  Integer; StdCall external
  'STRSRCHLIB.DLL';

{ Define the callback procedure, make sure to use the StdCall directive }
procedure StrPosProc(AStrPsn: PChar); StdCall;
begin
  inc(Count); // Increment the Count variable.
end;
```

LISTING 6.11 Continued

```
procedure TMainForm.btnCallDLLFuncClick(Sender: TObject);
var
  S: String;
  S2: String;
begin
  Count := 0; // Initialize Count to zero.
  { Retrieve the length of the text on which to search. }
  SetLength(S, memStr.GetTextLen);
  { Now copy the text to the variable S }
  memStr.GetTextBuf(PChar(S), memStr.GetTextLen);
  { Copy Edit1's Text to a string variable so that it can be passed to
    the DLL function }
  S2 := edtSearchStr.Text;
  { Call the DLL function }
  SearchStr(PChar(S), PChar(S2), @StrPosProc);
  { Show how many times the word occurs in the string. This has been
    stored in the Count variable which is used by the callback function }
  ShowMessage(Format('%s %s %d %s', [edtSearchStr.Text,
    'occurs', Count, 'times.']));
end;

end.
```

This application contains a TMemo control. EdtSearchStr.Text contains a string that will be searched for in memStr's contents. memStr's contents are passed as the source string to the DLL function SearchStr(), and edtSearchStr.Text is passed as the search string.

The function StrPosProc() is the actual callback function. This function increments the value of the global variable Count, which you use to hold the number of times the search string occurs in memStr's text.

Sharing DLL Data Across Different Processes

Back in the world of 16-bit Windows, DLL memory was handled differently than it is in the 32-bit world of Win32. One often-used trait of 16-bit DLLs is that they share global memory among different applications. In other words, if you declare a global variable in a 16-bit DLL, any application using that DLL will have access to that variable, and changes made to that variable by an application will be seen by other applications.

In some ways, this behavior can be dangerous because one application can overwrite data on which another application is dependent. In other ways, developers have made use of this characteristic.

In Win32, this sharing of DLL global data no longer exists. Because each application process maps the DLL to its own address space, the DLL's data also gets mapped to that same address space. This results in each application getting its own instance of DLL data. Changes made to the DLL global data by one application won't be seen from another application.

If you're planning on porting a 16-bit application that relies on the sharable behavior of DLL global data, you can still provide a means for applications to share data in a DLL with other applications. The process isn't automatic, and it requires the use of memory-mapped files to store the shared data. Memory-mapped files are covered in Chapter 12 of *Delphi 5 Developer's Guide*, "Working with Files," on the CD. We'll use them here to illustrate this method.

Creating a DLL with Shared Memory

Listing 6.12 shows a DLL project file that contains the code to allow applications using this DLL to share its global data. This global data is stored in the variable appropriately named GlobalData.

LISTING 6.12 ShareLib—A DLL That Illustrates Sharing Global Data

```
library ShareLib;

uses
  ShareMem,
  Windows,
  SysUtils,
  Classes;
const

  cMMFileName: PChar = 'SharedMapData';

{$I DLLDATA.INC}

var
  GlobalData : PGlobalDLLData;
  MapHandle  : THandle;

{ GetDLLData will be the exported DLL function }
procedure GetDLLData(var AGlobalData: PGlobalDLLData); StdCall;
begin
  { Point AGlobalData to the same memory address referred to by GlobalData. }
  AGlobalData := GlobalData;
end;

procedure OpenSharedData;
```

LISTING 6.12 Continued

```
var
   Size: Integer;
begin
  { Get the size of the data to be mapped. }
  Size := SizeOf(TGlobalDLLData);

  { Now get a memory-mapped file object. Note the first parameter passes
    the value $FFFFFFFF or DWord(-1) so that space is allocated from
    the system's
    paging file. This requires that a name for the memory-mapped
    object get passed as the last parameter. }

  MapHandle := CreateFileMapping(DWord(-1), nil, PAGE_READWRITE, 0,
    Size, cMMFileName);

  if MapHandle = 0 then
    RaiseLastWin32Error;
  { Now map the data to the calling process's address space and get a
    pointer to the beginning of this address }
  GlobalData := MapViewOfFile(MapHandle, FILE_MAP_ALL_ACCESS, 0, 0, Size);
  { Initialize this data }
  GlobalData^.S := 'ShareLib';
  GlobalData^.I := 1;
  if GlobalData = nil then
  begin
    CloseHandle(MapHandle);
    RaiseLastWin32Error;
  end;
end;

procedure CloseSharedData;
{ This procedure un-maps the memory-mapped file and releases the memory-mapped
  file handle }
begin
  UnmapViewOfFile(GlobalData);
  CloseHandle(MapHandle);
end;

procedure DLLEntryPoint(dwReason: DWord);
begin
  case dwReason of
    DLL_PROCESS_ATTACH: OpenSharedData;
    DLL_PROCESS_DETACH: CloseSharedData;
  end;
```

LISTING 6.12   Continued

```
end;

exports
  GetDLLData;

begin
  { First, assign the procedure to the DLLProc variable }
  DllProc := @DLLEntryPoint;
  { Now invoke the procedure to reflect that the DLL is attaching
    to the process }
  DLLEntryPoint(DLL_PROCESS_ATTACH);
end.
```

GlobalData is of the type PGlobalDLLData, which is defined in the include file DllData.inc. This include file contains the following type definition (note that the include file is linked by using the include directive $I):

```
type

  PGlobalDLLData = ^TGlobalDLLData;
  TGlobalDLLData = record
    S: String[50];
    I: Integer;
  end;
```

In this DLL, you use the same process discussed earlier in the chapter to add entry and exit code to the DLL in the form of an entry/exit procedure. This procedure is called DLLEntryPoint(), as shown in the listing. When a process loads the DLL, the OpenSharedData() method gets called. When a process detaches from the DLL, the CloseSharedData() method is called.

Memory-mapped files provide a means for you to reserve a region of address space in the Win32 system to which physical storage gets committed. This is similar to allocating memory and referring to that memory with a pointer. With memory-mapped files, however, you can map a disk file to this address space and refer to the space within the file as though you were just referencing an area of memory with a pointer.

With memory-mapped files, you must first get a handle to an existing file on disk to which a memory-mapped object will be mapped. You then map the memory-mapping object to that file. At the beginning of the chapter, we told you how the system shares DLLs with multiple applications by first loading the DLL into memory and then giving each application its own image of the DLL so that it appears that each application has loaded a separate instance of the DLL.

In reality, however, the DLL exists in memory only once. This is done by using memory-mapped files. You can use the same process to give access to data files. You just make necessary Win32 API calls that deal with creating and accessing memory-mapped files.

Now, consider this scenario: Suppose an application, which we'll call App1, creates a memory-mapped file that gets mapped to a file on disk, MyFile.dat. App1 can now read and write data in that file. If, while App1 is running, App2 also maps to that same file, changes made to the file by App1 will be seen by App2. Actually, it's a bit more complex; certain flags must be set so that changes to the file are immediately set and so forth. For this discussion, it suffices to say that changes will be realized by both applications because this is possible.

One of the ways in which memory-mapped files can be used is to create a file mapping from the Win32 paging file rather than an existing file. This means that instead of mapping to an existing file on disk, you can reserve an area of memory to which you can refer as though it were a disk file. This prevents you from having to create and destroy a temporary file if all you want to do is to create an address space that can be accessed by multiple processes. The Win32 system manages its paging file, so when memory is no longer required of the paging file, this memory gets released.

In the preceding paragraphs, we presented a scenario that illustrated how two applications can access the same file data by using a memory-mapped file. The same can be done between an application and a DLL. In fact, if the DLL creates the memory-mapped file when it's loaded by an application, it will use the same memory-mapped file when loaded by another application. There will be two images of the DLL, one for each calling application, both of which use the same memory-mapped file instance. The DLL can make the data referred to by the file mapping available to its calling application. When one application makes changes to this data, the second application will see these changes because they're referring to the same data, mapped by two different memory-mapped object instances. We use this technique in the example.

In Listing 6.12, OpenSharedData() is responsible for creating the memory-mapped file. It uses the CreateFileMapping() function to first create the file-mapping object, which it then passes to the MapViewOfFile() function. The MapViewOfFile() function maps a view of the file into the address space of the calling process. The return value of this function is the beginning of that address space. Now remember, this is the address space of the calling process. For two different applications using this DLL, this address location might be different, although the data to which they refer will be the same.

> **NOTE**
>
> The first parameter to `CreateFileMapping()` is a handle to a file to which the memory-mapped file gets mapped. However, if you're mapping to an address space of the system paging file, pass the value `$FFFFFFFF` (which is the same as `DWord(-1)`) as this parameter value. You must also supply a name for the file-mapping object as the last parameter to `CreateFileMapping()`. This is the name that the system uses to refer to this file mapping. If multiple processes create a memory-mapped file using the same name, the mapping objects will refer to the same system memory.

After the call to `MapViewOfFile()`, the variable `GlobalData` refers to the address space for the memory-mapped file. The exported function `GetDLLData()` assigns that memory to which `GlobalData` refers to the `AGlobalData` parameter. `AGlobalData` is passed in from the calling application; therefore, the calling application has read/write access to this data.

The `CloseSharedData()` procedure is responsible for unmapping the view of the file from the calling process and releasing the file-mapping object. This doesn't affect other file-mapping objects or file mappings from other applications.

Using a DLL with Shared Memory

To illustrate the use of the shared memory DLL, we've created two applications that make use of it. The first application, `App1.dpr`, allows you to modify the DLL's data. The second application, `App2.dpr`, also refers to the DLL's data and continually updates a couple of `TLabel` components by using a `TTimer` component. When you run both applications, you'll be able to see the sharable access to the DLL data—`App2` will reflect changes made by `App1`.

Listing 6.13 shows the source code for the `App1` project.

LISTING 6.13   The Main Form for `App1.dpr`

```
unit MainFrmA1;

interface

uses
  Windows, Messages, SysUtils, Classes, Graphics, Controls,
  Forms, Dialogs, StdCtrls, ExtCtrls, Mask;

{$I DLLDATA.INC}

type
```

LISTING 6.13 Continued

```
  TMainForm = class(TForm)
    edtGlobDataStr: TEdit;
    btnGetDllData: TButton;
    meGlobDataInt: TMaskEdit;
    procedure btnGetDllDataClick(Sender: TObject);
    procedure edtGlobDataStrChange(Sender: TObject);
    procedure meGlobDataIntChange(Sender: TObject);
    procedure FormCreate(Sender: TObject);
  public
    GlobalData: PGlobalDLLData;
  end;

var
  MainForm: TMainForm;

{ Define the DLL's exported procedure }
procedure GetDLLData(var AGlobalData: PGlobalDLLData);
  StdCall External 'SHARELIB.DLL';

implementation

{$R *.DFM}

procedure TMainForm.btnGetDllDataClick(Sender: TObject);
begin
  { Get a pointer to the DLL's data }
  GetDLLData(GlobalData);
  { Now update the controls to reflect GlobalData's field values }
  edtGlobDataStr.Text := GlobalData^.S;
  meGlobDataInt.Text  := IntToStr(GlobalData^.I);
end;

procedure TMainForm.edtGlobDataStrChange(Sender: TObject);
begin
  { Update the DLL data with the changes }
  GlobalData^.S := edtGlobDataStr.Text;
end;

procedure TMainForm.meGlobDataIntChange(Sender: TObject);
begin
  { Update the DLL data with the changes }
  if meGlobDataInt.Text = EmptyStr then
    meGlobDataInt.Text := '0';
  GlobalData^.I := StrToInt(meGlobDataInt.Text);
end;
```

LISTING 6.13 Continued

```
procedure TMainForm.FormCreate(Sender: TObject);
begin
  btnGetDllDataClick(nil);
end;

end.
```

This application also links in the include file DllData.inc, which defines the TGlobalDLLData data type and its pointer. The btnGetDllDataClick() event handler gets a pointer to the DLL's data, which is accessed by a memory-mapped file in the DLL. It does this by calling the DLL's GetDLLData() function. It then updates its controls with the value of this pointer, GlobalData. The OnChange event handlers for the edit controls change the values of GlobalData. Because GlobalData refers to the DLL's data, it modifies the data referred to by the DLL's memory-mapped file.

Listing 6.14 shows the source code for the main form for App2.dpr.

LISTING 6.14 The Source Code for Main Form for App2.dpr

```
unit MainFrmA2;

interface

uses
  Windows, Messages, SysUtils, Classes, Graphics, Controls, Forms, Dialogs,
  ExtCtrls, StdCtrls;

{$I DLLDATA.INC}

type

  TMainForm = class(TForm)
    lblGlobDataStr: TLabel;
    tmTimer: TTimer;
    lblGlobDataInt: TLabel;
    procedure tmTimerTimer(Sender: TObject);
  public
    GlobalData: PGlobalDLLData;
  end;

{ Define the DLL's exported procedure }
procedure GetDLLData(var AGlobalData: PGlobalDLLData);
  StdCall External 'SHARELIB.DLL';
```

LISTING 6.14   Continued

```
var
  MainForm: TMainForm;

implementation

{$R *.DFM}

procedure TMainForm.tmTimerTimer(Sender: TObject);
begin
  GetDllData(GlobalData);  // Get access to the data
  { Show the contents of GlobalData's fields.}
  lblGlobDataStr.Caption := GlobalData^.S;
  lblGlobDataInt.Caption := IntToStr(GlobalData^.I);
end;

end.
```

This form contains two TLabel components, which get updated during the tmTimer's OnTimer event. When the user changes the values of the DLL's data from App1, App2 will reflect these changes.

You can run both applications to experiment with them. You'll find them on this book's CD.

Exporting Objects from DLLs

It's possible to access an object and its methods even if that object is contained within a DLL. There are some requirements, however, to how that object is defined within the DLL as well as some limitations as to how the object can be used. The technique we illustrate here is useful in very specific situations. Typically, you can achieve the same functionality by using packages or interfaces.

The following list summarizes the conditions and limitations to exporting an object from a DLL:

- The calling application can only use methods of the object that have been declared as virtual.
- The object instances must be created only within the DLL.
- The object must be defined in both the DLL and calling application with methods defined in the same order.
- You cannot create a descendant object from the object contained within the DLL.

Some additional limitations might exist, but the ones listed are the primary limitations.

To illustrate this technique, we've created a simple, yet illustrative example of an object that we export. This object contains a function that returns the uppercase or lowercase value of a string based on the value of a parameter indicating either uppercase or lowercase. This object is defined in Listing 6.15.

LISTING 6.15 Object to Be Exported from a DLL

```
type

  TConvertType = (ctUpper, ctLower);

  TStringConvert = class(TObject)
{$IFDEF STRINGCONVERTLIB}
  private
    FPrepend: String;
    FAppend : String;
{$ENDIF}
  public
    function ConvertString(AConvertType: TConvertType; AString: String):
String;
      virtual; stdcall; {$IFNDEF STRINGCONVERTLIB} abstract; {$ENDIF}
{$IFDEF STRINGCONVERTLIB}
    constructor Create(APrepend, AAppend: String);
    destructor Destroy; override;
{$ENDIF}
  end;

{ For any application using this class, STRINGCONVERTLIB is not defined and
  therefore, the class definition will be equivalent to:

  TStringConvert = class(TObject)
  public
    function ConvertString(AConvertType: TConvertType; AString: String):
String;
      virtual; stdcall; abstract;
  end;
}
```

Listing 6.15 is actually an include file named StrConvert.inc. This object is placed in an include file to meet the third requirement in the preceding list—that the object be equally defined in both the DLL and in the calling application. By placing the object in an include file, both the calling application and DLL can include this file. If changes are made to the object, you only have to compile both projects instead of typing the changes twice—once in the calling application and once in the DLL, which is error prone.

Observe the following definition of the `ConvertSring()` method:

```
function ConvertString(AConvertType: TConvertType; AString: String):
  ➡String; virtual; stdcall;
```

The reason you declare this method as virtual isn't so that one can create a descendant object that can then override the `ConvertString()` method. Instead, it's declared as virtual so that an entry to the `ConvertString()` method is made in the *Virtual Method Table (VMT)*. Think of the VMT as a block of memory that holds pointers to virtual methods of an object. Because of the VMT, the calling application can obtain a pointer to the method of the object. Without declaring the method as virtual, the VMT wouldn't have an entry for the method, and the calling application would have no way of obtaining the pointer to the method. So really, what you have in the calling application is a pointer to the function. Because you've based this pointer on a method type defined in an object, Delphi automatically handles any fix-ups, such as passing the implicit `self` parameter to the method.

> **NOTE**
>
> The Virtual Method Table is covered in greater detail in Chapter 13 of *Delphi 5 Developer's Guide*, "Hard Core Techniques," on the CD.

Note the conditional define `STRINGCONVERTLIB`. When you're exporting the object, the only methods that need redefinition in the calling application are the methods to be accessed externally from the DLL. Also, these methods can be defined as abstract methods to avoid generating a compile-time error. This is valid because at runtime, these methods will be implemented in the DLL code. The source code comments show what the `TStringConvert` object looks like on the application side.

Listing 6.16 shows the implementation of the `TStringConvert` object.

LISTING 6.16 Implementation of the `TStringConvert` Object

```
unit StringConvertImp;
{$DEFINE STRINGCONVERTLIB}S
interface
uses SysUtils;
{$I StrConvert.inc}

function InitStrConvert(APrepend, AAppend: String): TStringConvert; stdcall;

implementation
```

LISTING 6.16   Continued

```
constructor TStringConvert.Create(APrepend, AAppend: String);
begin
  inherited Create;
  FPrepend := APrepend;
  FAppend  := AAppend;
end;

destructor TStringConvert.Destroy;
begin
  inherited Destroy;
end;

function TStringConvert.ConvertString(AConvertType:
  TConvertType; AString: String): String;
begin
  case AConvertType of
    ctUpper: Result := Format('%s%s%s', [FPrepend, UpperCase(AString),
    FAppend]);
    ctLower: Result := Format('%s%s%s', [FPrepend, LowerCase(AString),
    FAppend]);
  end;
end;

function InitStrConvert(APrepend, AAppend: String): TStringConvert;
begin
  Result := TStringConvert.Create(APrepend, AAppend);
end;

end.
```

As stated in the conditions, the object must be created in the DLL. This is done in a standard DLL exported function `InitStrConvert()`, which takes two parameters that are passed to the constructor. We added this to illustrate how you would pass information to an object's constructor through an interface function.

Also, notice that in this unit you declare the conditional directive `STRINGCONVERTLIB`. The rest of this unit is self-explanatory. Listing 6.17 shows the DLL's project file.

LISTING 6.17   The Project File for `StringConvertLib.dll`

```
library StringConvertLib;
uses
  ShareMem,
  SysUtils,
```

LISTING 6.17   Continued

```
  Classes,
  StringConvertImp in 'StringConvertImp.pas';

exports
  InitStrConvert;
end.
```

Generally, this library doesn't contain anything we haven't already covered. Do note, however, that you used the ShareMem unit. This unit must be the first unit declared in the library project file as well as in the calling application's project file. This is an extremely important thing to remember.

Listing 6.18 shows an example of how to use the exported object to convert a string to both uppercase and lowercase. You'll find this demo project on the CD as StrConvertTest.dpr.

LISTING 6.18   The Demo Project for the String Conversion Object

```
unit MainFrm;

interface

uses
  Windows, Messages, SysUtils, Classes, Graphics, Controls, Forms, Dialogs,
  StdCtrls;

{$I strconvert.inc}

type


  TMainForm = class(TForm)
    btnUpper: TButton;
    edtConvertStr: TEdit;
    btnLower: TButton;
    procedure btnUpperClick(Sender: TObject);
    procedure btnLowerClick(Sender: TObject);
  private
  public
  end;

var
  MainForm: TMainForm;
```

LISTING 6.18 Continued

```pascal
function InitStrConvert(APrepend, AAppend: String): TStringConvert; stdcall;
  external 'STRINGCONVERTLIB.DLL';

implementation

{$R *.DFM}

procedure TMainForm.btnUpperClick(Sender: TObject);
var
  ConvStr: String;
  FStrConvert: TStringConvert;
begin
  FStrConvert := InitStrConvert('Upper ', ' end');
  try
      ConvStr := edtConvertStr.Text;
      if ConvStr <> EmptyStr then
        edtConvertStr.Text := FStrConvert.ConvertString(ctUpper, ConvStr);
  finally
    FStrConvert.Free;
  end;
end;

procedure TMainForm.btnLowerClick(Sender: TObject);
var
  ConvStr: String;
  FStrConvert: TStringConvert;
begin
  FStrConvert := InitStrConvert('Lower ', ' end');
  try
      ConvStr := edtConvertStr.Text;
      if ConvStr <> EmptyStr then
        edtConvertStr.Text := FStrConvert.ConvertString(ctLower, ConvStr);
  finally
    FStrConvert.Free;
  end;
end;

end.
```

6

Summary

DLLs are an essential part of creating Windows applications while focusing in on code reusability. This chapter covered the reasons for creating or using DLLs. The chapter illustrated how to create and use DLLs in your Delphi applications and showed different methods of loading DLLs. The chapter discussed some of the special considerations you must take when using DLLs with Delphi and showed you how to make DLL data sharable with different applications.

With this knowledge under your belt, you should be able to create DLLs with Delphi and use them in your Delphi applications with ease.

Database Development

PART

III

IN THIS PART

Delphi Database Architecture

IN THIS CHAPTER

In this chapter, you'll learn the art and science of accessing external database files from your Delphi applications. If you're new to database programming, we do assume a bit of database knowledge, but this chapter will get you started on the road to creating high-quality database applications. If database applications are "old hat" to you, you'll benefit from the chapter's demonstration of Delphi's spin on database programming. Delphi 6 offers several mechanisms for accessing data, which we will cover in this chapter, and then in more detail in chapters to follow. This chapter discusses the architecture upon which all data access mechanisms in Delphi 6 are built.

Types of Databases

The following list is taken from Delphi's online help under "Using Databases." The references mentioned in the list are also found in the online help. We'll refer to this information here because we felt that Borland described the types of database supported by Delphi's architecture best:

- The BDE page of the Component Palette contains components that use the Borland Database Engine (BDE). The BDE defines a large API for interacting with databases. Of all the data access mechanisms, the BDE supports the broadest range of functions and comes with the most supporting utilities. It is the best way to work with data in Paradox or dBASE tables. However, it is also the most complicated mechanism to deploy. For more information about using the BDE components, see "Using the Borland Database Engine."

- The ADO page of the Component Palette contains components that use ActiveX Data Objects (ADO) to access database information through OLEDB. ADO is a Microsoft Standard. A broad range of ADO drivers is available for connecting to different database servers. Using ADO-based components lets you integrate your application into an ADO-based environment (for example, making use of ADO-based application servers). For more information about using the ADO components, see "Working with ADO Components."

- The dbExpress page of the Component Palette contains components that use dbExpress to access database information. dbExpress is a lightweight set of drivers that provide the fastest access to database information. In addition, dbExpress components support cross-platform development because they are also available on Linux. However, dbExpress database components also support the narrowest range of data manipulation functions. For more information about using the dbExpress components, see "Using Unidirectional Datasets."

- The InterBase page of the Component Palette contains components that access InterBase databases directly, without going through a separate engine layer. For more information about using the InterBase components, see "Getting Started with InterBase Express."

Database Architecture

Delphi's database architecture is made up of components that represent and properly encapsulate database information. Figure 7.1 represents this relationship as defined by Delphi 6's online help under "Database Architecture."

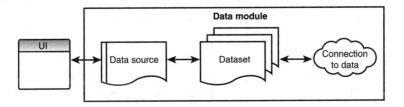

FIGURE 7.1
Delphi database architecture.

Figure 7.1 shows the database architecture in its simplest form. That is, a user interface interacts with data through a data source, which connects to the dataset that encapsulates the data. In the prior section, we discussed different types of databases with which Delphi can work. These different data repositories require different types of datasets. The dataset shown in Figure 7.1 represents an abstract dataset from which others will descend to provide access to different types of data.

Connecting to Database Servers

Okay, so you want to be a database developer. Naturally, the first thing you'll want to do is learn how to make a connection from Delphi to the database of your choice. In this section, you'll learn a number of ways Delphi enables you to make connections to servers.

Overview of Database Connectivity

Datasets must connect to database servers. This is typically done through a connection component. Connection components encapsulate the connectivity to a database server and serve as a single connection point for all datasets in the application.

Connection components are encapsulated in the TCustomConnection component. TCustomConnection is descended from to create components to encapsulate specific data repository types. Among the different types of data access components are the following for each type of data repository:

- TDatabase is the connection component for BDE based datasets. Such datasets are TTable, TQuery, and TStoreproc. BDE database connectivity is covered in Chapter 28 in the CD copy of *Delphi 5 Developer's Guide*.

- `TADOConnection` is the connection component for ADO databases such as Microsoft Access and Microsoft SQL. Such datasets are `TADODataset`, `TADOTable`, `TADOQuery`, and `TADOStoredProc`. ADO database connectivity is covered in Chapter 9, "Database Development with dbGo for ADO."

- `TSQLConnection` is the connection component for dbExpress based datasets. DbExpress datasets are special lightweight unidirectional datasets. These are `TSQLDataset`, `TSQLTable`, `TSQLQuery` and `TSQLStoredProc`. DbExpress is covered in Chapter 8, "Database Development with dbExpress."

- `TIBDatabase` is the connection component for Interbase Express datasets. The datasets are `TIBDataSet`, `TIBTable`, `TIBQuery`, and `TIBStoredProc`. Interbase Express isn't covered in this book because much of the functionality mimics the other connection methods.

Each of these datasets provides the common functionality contained in the `TCustomConnection` component. This common functionality includes methods, properties, and events related to

- Connecting and disconnecting to the data repository
- Login and support for establishing secure connections
- Dataset management

Establishing a Database Connection

Although each connection component surfaces many of the same methods for database connectivity, there are some differences. The reason for this is that each connection component provides the connection functionality of its underlying data repository. Therefore, the `TADOConnection` might function slightly differently from the `TDatabase` connection. The connection methods for `TSQLConnection` and `TADOConnection` are covered in their respective chapters (Chapters 8 and 9). Connecting to a BDE based dataset is covered in Chapter 28 in the CD copy of *Delphi 5 Developer's Guide*.

Working with Datasets

A *dataset* is a collection of rows and columns of data. Each *column* is of some homogeneous data type, and each *row* is made up of a collection of data of each column data type. Additionally, a column is also known as a *field*, and a row is sometimes called a *record*. VCL encapsulates a dataset into an abstract component called `TDataSet`. `TDataSet` introduces many of the properties and methods necessary for manipulating and navigating a dataset and serves as the component from which special types of different datasets descend.

To help keep the nomenclature clear and to cover some of the basics, the following list explains some of the common database terms that are used in this and other database-oriented chapters:

- A *dataset* is a collection of discrete data records. Each record is made up of multiple fields. Each field can contain a different type of data (integer number, string, decimal number, graphic, and so on).

- A *table* is a special type of dataset. A table is generally a file containing records that are physically stored on a disk somewhere. `TTable`, `TADOTable`, `TSQLTable`, and `TIBTable` components encapsulate this functionality.

- A *query* is also a special type of dataset. Think of queries as commands that are executed against a database server. Such commands might result in resultsets (memory tables). These resultsets are the special datasets that are encapsulated by `TQuery`, `TADOQuery`, `TSQLQuery`, and `TIBQuery` components.

> **NOTE**
>
> We mentioned earlier that this chapter assumes a bit of database knowledge. This chapter isn't intended to be a primer on database programming, and we expect that you're already familiar with the items in this list. If terms such as *database*, *table*, and *index* sound foreign to you, you might want to obtain an introductory text on database concepts.

Opening and Closing Datasets

Before you can do anything with a dataset, you must first open it. To open a dataset, simply call its `Open()` method, as shown in this example:

```
Table1.Open;
```

This is equivalent, by the way, to setting a dataset's `Active` property to `True`:

```
Table1.Active := True;
```

There's slightly less overhead in the latter method because the `Open()` method ends up setting the `Active` property to `True`. However, the overhead is so minimal that it's not worth worrying about.

Once the dataset has been opened, you're free to manipulate it, as you'll see in just a moment. When you finish using the dataset, you should close it by calling its `Close()` method, like this:

```
Table1.Close;
```

Alternatively, you could close it by setting its `Active` property to `False`, like this:

```
Table1.Active :=  False;
```

> **TIP**
>
> When you're communicating with SQL servers, a connection to the database must be established when you first open a dataset in that database. When you close the last dataset in a database, your connection is terminated. Opening and closing these connections involves a certain amount of overhead. Therefore, if you find that you open and close the connection to the database often, use a TDatabase component instead to maintain a connection to a SQL server's database throughout many open and close operations. The TDatabase component is explained in more detail in the next chapter.

To illustrate how similar it is to open and close the different type of datasets, we've provide the example shown in Listing 7.1.

LISTING 7.1   Opening and Closing Datasets

```
unit MainFrm;

interface

uses
  Windows, Messages, SysUtils, Variants, Classes, Graphics, Controls, Forms,
  Dialogs, FMTBcd, DBXpress, IBDatabase, ADODB, DBTables, DB, SqlExpr,
  IBCustomDataSet, IBQuery, IBTable, StdCtrls;

type
  TForm1 = class(TForm)
    SQLDataSet1: TSQLDataSet;
    SQLTable1: TSQLTable;
    SQLQuery1: TSQLQuery;

    ADOTable1: TADOTable;
    ADODataSet1: TADODataSet;
    ADOQuery1: TADOQuery;

    IBTable1: TIBTable;
    IBQuery1: TIBQuery;
    IBDataSet1: TIBDataSet;

    Table1: TTable;
    Query1: TQuery;

    SQLConnection1: TSQLConnection;
    Database1: TDatabase;
    ADOConnection1: TADOConnection;
```

LISTING 7.1   Continued

```delphi
    IBDatabase1: TIBDatabase;
    Button1: TButton;
    Label1: TLabel;
    Button2: TButton;
    IBTransaction1: TIBTransaction;
    procedure FormCreate(Sender: TObject);
    procedure Button1Click(Sender: TObject);
    procedure FormClose(Sender: TObject; var Action: TCloseAction);
    procedure Button2Click(Sender: TObject);
  private
    { Private declarations }
    procedure OpenDatasets;
    procedure CloseDatasets;
  public
    { Public declarations }
  end;

var
  Form1: TForm1;

implementation

{$R *.dfm}

procedure TForm1.FormCreate(Sender: TObject);
begin
  IBDatabase1.Connected    := True;
  ADOConnection1.Connected := True;
  Database1.Connected      := True;
  SQLConnection1.Connected := True;
end;

procedure TForm1.Button1Click(Sender: TObject);
begin
  OpenDatasets;
end;

procedure TForm1.FormClose(Sender: TObject; var Action: TCloseAction);
begin
  CloseDatasets;
  IBDatabase1.Connected    := false;
  ADOConnection1.Connected := false;
  Database1.Connected      := false;
  SQLConnection1.Connected := false;
end;
```

LISTING 7.1 Continued

```
procedure TForm1.CloseDatasets;
begin

  // Disconnect from dbExpress datasets
  SQLDataSet1.Close;  // or .Active := false;
  SQLTable1.Close;    // or .Active := false;
  SQLQuery1.Close;    // or .Active := false;

  // Disconnect from ADO datasets
  ADOTable1.Close;    // or .Active := false;
  ADODataSet1.Close;  // or .Active := false;
  ADOQuery1.Close;    // or .Active := false;

  // Disconnect from Interbase Express datasets
  IBTable1.Close;     // or .Active := false;
  IBQuery1.Close;     // or .Active := false;
  IBDataSet1.Close;   // or .Active := false;

  // Disconnect from BDE datasets
  Table1.Close;     // or .Active := false;
  Query1.Close;     // or .Active := false;

  Label1.Caption := 'Datasets are closed.'
end;

procedure TForm1.OpenDatasets;
begin

  // Connect to dbExpress datasets
  SQLDataSet1.Open;  // or .Active := true;
  SQLTable1.Open;    // or .Active := true;
  SQLQuery1.Open;    // or .Active := true;

  // Connect to ADO datasets
  ADOTable1.Open;    // or .Active := true;
  ADODataSet1.Open;  // or .Active := true;
  ADOQuery1.Open;    // or .Active := true;

  // Connect to Interbase Express datasets
  IBTable1.Open;     // or .Active := true;
  IBQuery1.Open;     // or .Active := true;
  IBDataSet1.Open;   // or .Active := true;

  // Connect to BDE datasets
  Table1.Open;     // or .Active := true;
```

LISTING 7.1 Continued

```
  Query1.Open;      // or .Active := true;

  Label1.Caption := 'Datasets are open.';
end;

procedure TForm1.Button2Click(Sender: TObject);
begin
  CloseDatasets;
end;

end.
```

This example is provided on the CD. You might have some problems setting up the database connections because the example was created on our development machine. You'll have to set up connections based on your machine. Nevertheless, the purpose of showing you this example was to illustrate the similarities of the different datasets.

Navigating Datasets

TDataSet provides some simple methods for basic record navigation. The First() and Last() methods move you to the first and last records in the dataset, respectively, and the Next() and Prior() methods move you either one record forward or back in the dataset. Additionally, the MoveBy() method, which accepts an Integer parameter, moves you a specified number of records forward or back.

BOF, EOF, and Looping

BOF and EOF are Boolean properties of TDataSet that reveal whether the current record is the first or last record in the dataset. For example, you might need to iterate through each record in a dataset until reaching the last record. The easiest way to do so would be to employ a while loop to keep iterating over records until the EOF property returns True, as shown here:

```
Table1.First;                    // go to beginning of data set
while not Table1.EOF do          // iterate over table
begin
  // do some stuff with current record
  Table1.Next;                   // move to next record
end;
```

> **CAUTION**
>
> Be sure to call the Next() method inside your while-not-EOF loop; otherwise, your application will get caught in an endless loop.

Avoid using a `repeat..until` loop to perform actions on a dataset. The following code might look okay on the surface, but bad things might happen if you try to use it on an empty dataset because the `DoSomeStuff()` procedure will always execute at least once, regardless of whether the dataset contains records:

```
repeat
  DoSomeStuff;
  Table1.Next;
until Table1.EOF;
```

Because the `while-not-EOF` loop performs the check up front, you won't encounter such a problem with this construct.

To illustrate how similar it is to navigate among the different type of datasets, we've provided the example shown in Listing 7.2.

LISTING 7.2   Navigation with the Different Datasets

```
unit MainFrm;

interface

uses
  Windows, Messages, SysUtils, Variants, Classes, Graphics, Controls, Forms,
  Dialogs, FMTBcd, DBXpress, IBDatabase, ADODB, DBTables, DB, SqlExpr,
  IBCustomDataSet, IBQuery, IBTable, StdCtrls, Grids, DBGrids, ExtCtrls;

type
  TForm1 = class(TForm)
    SQLTable1: TSQLTable;
    ADOTable1: TADOTable;
    IBTable1: TIBTable;
    Table1: TTable;

    SQLConnection1: TSQLConnection;
    Database1: TDatabase;
    ADOConnection1: TADOConnection;
    IBDatabase1: TIBDatabase;
    Button1: TButton;
    Label1: TLabel;
    Button2: TButton;
    IBTransaction1: TIBTransaction;
    DBGrid1: TDBGrid;
    DataSource1: TDataSource;
    RadioGroup1: TRadioGroup;
    btnFirst: TButton;
```

7

LISTING 7.2 Continued

```
    btnLast: TButton;
    btnNext: TButton;
    btnPrior: TButton;
    procedure FormCreate(Sender: TObject);
    procedure Button1Click(Sender: TObject);
    procedure FormClose(Sender: TObject; var Action: TCloseAction);
    procedure Button2Click(Sender: TObject);
    procedure RadioGroup1Click(Sender: TObject);
    procedure btnFirstClick(Sender: TObject);
    procedure btnLastClick(Sender: TObject);
    procedure btnNextClick(Sender: TObject);
    procedure btnPriorClick(Sender: TObject);
    procedure DataSource1DataChange(Sender: TObject; Field: TField);
  private
    { Private declarations }
    procedure OpenDatasets;
    procedure CloseDatasets;
  public
    { Public declarations }
  end;

var
  Form1: TForm1;

implementation

{$R *.dfm}

procedure TForm1.FormCreate(Sender: TObject);
begin
  IBDatabase1.Connected    := True;
  ADOConnection1.Connected := True;
  Database1.Connected      := True;
  SQLConnection1.Connected := True;

  Datasource1.DataSet := IBTable1;
  OpenDatasets;
end;

procedure TForm1.Button1Click(Sender: TObject);
begin
  OpenDatasets;
end;
```

LISTING 7.2 Continued

```
procedure TForm1.FormClose(Sender: TObject; var Action: TCloseAction);
begin
  CloseDatasets;
  IBDatabase1.Connected   := false;
  ADOConnection1.Connected := false;
  Database1.Connected      := false;
  SQLConnection1.Connected := false;
end;

procedure TForm1.CloseDatasets;
begin

  // Disconnect from dbExpress dataset
  SQLTable1.Close;     // or .Active := false;

  // Disconnect from ADO dataset
  ADOTable1.Close;     // or .Active := false;

  // Disconnect from Interbase Express dataset
  IBTable1.Close;     // or .Active := false;

  // Disconnect from BDE datasets
  Table1.Close;     // or .Active := false;

  Label1.Caption := 'Datasets are closed.'
end;

procedure TForm1.OpenDatasets;
begin

  // Connect to dbExpress dataset
  SQLTable1.Open;     // or .Active := true;

  // Connect to ADO dataset
  ADOTable1.Open;     // or .Active := true;

  // Connect to Interbase Express dataset
  IBTable1.Open;     // or .Active := true;

  // Connect to BDE dataset
  Table1.Open;     // or .Active := true;

  Label1.Caption := 'Datasets are open.';
end;
```

LISTING 7.2   Continued

```
procedure TForm1.Button2Click(Sender: TObject);
begin
  CloseDatasets;
end;

procedure TForm1.RadioGroup1Click(Sender: TObject);
begin
  case RadioGroup1.ItemIndex of
    0: Datasource1.DataSet := IBTable1;
    1: Datasource1.DataSet := Table1;
    2: Datasource1.DataSet := ADOTable1;
  end; // case
end;

procedure TForm1.btnFirstClick(Sender: TObject);
begin
  DataSource1.DataSet.First;
end;

procedure TForm1.btnLastClick(Sender: TObject);
begin
  DataSource1.DataSet.Last;
end;

procedure TForm1.btnNextClick(Sender: TObject);
begin
  DataSource1.DataSet.Next;
end;

procedure TForm1.btnPriorClick(Sender: TObject);
begin
  DataSource1.DataSet.Prior;
end;

procedure TForm1.DataSource1DataChange(Sender: TObject; Field: TField);
begin
  btnLast.Enabled := not DataSource1.DataSet.Eof;
  btnNext.Enabled := not DataSource1.DataSet.Eof;
  btnFirst.Enabled := not DataSource1.DataSet.Bof;
  btnPrior.Enabled := not DataSource1.DataSet.Bof;
end;

end.
```

In this example, a TRadioGroup is used to allow the user to select from three of the database types. Additionally, the OnDataChange event handler shows how to evaluate the BOF and EOF properties to properly enable or disable the buttons when one of the two are true. You should notice that the same methods are invoked to navigate through the dataset regardless of which dataset is selected.

> **NOTE**
>
> You'll notice that we did not include the dbExpress component as part of this example. This is because dbExpress datasets are unidirectional datasets. That is, they can only navigate in one direction and are treated as read-only. In fact, if you attempt to connect a navigable component such as a TDBGrid to a dbExpress dataset, you will get an error. Navigating through unidirectional datasets requires some specific setup, which is discussed in Chapter 8.

Manipulating Datasets

A database application isn't really a database application unless you can manipulate its data. Fortunately, datasets provide methods that allow you to do this. With datasets, you are able to add, edit, and delete records from the underlying table. The methods to do this are appropriately named Insert(), Edit(), and Delete().

Listing 7.3 shows a simple application illustrating how to use these methods.

LISTING 7.3 MainFrm.pas—Showing Simple Data Manipulation

```
unit MainFrm;

interface

uses
  Windows, Messages, SysUtils, Variants, Classes, Graphics, Controls, Forms,
  Dialogs, StdCtrls, Mask, DBCtrls, DB, Grids, DBGrids, ADODB;

type
  TMainForm = class(TForm)
    ADOConnection1: TADOConnection;
    adodsCustomer: TADODataSet;
    dtsrcCustomer: TDataSource;
    DBGrid1: TDBGrid;
    adodsCustomerCustNo: TAutoIncField;
    adodsCustomerCompany: TWideStringField;
    adodsCustomerAddress1: TWideStringField;
```

LISTING 7.3 Continued

```
    adodsCustomerAddress2: TWideStringField;
    adodsCustomerCity: TWideStringField;
    adodsCustomerStateAbbr: TWideStringField;
    adodsCustomerZip: TWideStringField;
    adodsCustomerCountry: TWideStringField;
    adodsCustomerPhone: TWideStringField;
    adodsCustomerFax: TWideStringField;
    adodsCustomerContact: TWideStringField;
    Label1: TLabel;
    dbedtCompany: TDBEdit;
    Label2: TLabel;
    dbedtAddress1: TDBEdit;
    Label3: TLabel;
    dbedtAddress2: TDBEdit;
    Label4: TLabel;
    dbedtCity: TDBEdit;
    Label5: TLabel;
    dbedtState: TDBEdit;
    Label6: TLabel;
    dbedtZip: TDBEdit;
    Label7: TLabel;
    dbedtPhone: TDBEdit;
    Label8: TLabel;
    dbedtFax: TDBEdit;
    Label9: TLabel;
    dbedtContact: TDBEdit;
    btnAdd: TButton;
    btnEdit: TButton;
    btnSave: TButton;
    btnCancel: TButton;
    Label10: TLabel;
    dbedtCountry: TDBEdit;
    btnDelete: TButton;
    procedure btnAddClick(Sender: TObject);
    procedure btnEditClick(Sender: TObject);
    procedure btnSaveClick(Sender: TObject);
    procedure btnCancelClick(Sender: TObject);
    procedure FormCreate(Sender: TObject);
    procedure FormClose(Sender: TObject; var Action: TCloseAction);
    procedure btnDeleteClick(Sender: TObject);
  private
    { Private declarations }
    procedure SetButtons;
  public
```

LISTING 7.3 Continued

```
  { Public declarations }
  end;

var
  MainForm: TMainForm;

implementation

{$R *.dfm}

procedure TMainForm.btnAddClick(Sender: TObject);
begin
  adodsCustomer.Insert;
  SetButtons;
end;

procedure TMainForm.btnEditClick(Sender: TObject);
begin
  adodsCustomer.Edit;
  SetButtons;
end;

procedure TMainForm.btnSaveClick(Sender: TObject);
begin
  adodsCustomer.Post;
  SetButtons;
end;

procedure TMainForm.btnCancelClick(Sender: TObject);
begin
  adodsCustomer.Cancel;
  SetButtons;
end;

procedure TMainForm.SetButtons;
begin
  btnAdd.Enabled   := adodsCustomer.State = dsBrowse;
  btnEdit.Enabled := adodsCustomer.State = dsBrowse;
  btnSave.Enabled := (adodsCustomer.State = dsInsert) or
    (adodsCustomer.State = dsEdit);
  btnCancel.Enabled := (adodsCustomer.State = dsInsert) or
    (adodsCustomer.State = dsEdit);
  btnDelete.Enabled := adodsCustomer.State = dsBrowse;
end;
```

LISTING 7.3 Continued

```
procedure TMainForm.FormCreate(Sender: TObject);
begin
  adodsCustomer.Open;
  SetButtons;

end;

procedure TMainForm.FormClose(Sender: TObject; var Action: TCloseAction);
begin
  adodsCustomer.Close;
  ADOConnection1.Connected := False;
end;

procedure TMainForm.btnDeleteClick(Sender: TObject);
begin
  adodsCustomer.Delete;
end;

end.
```

Figure 7.2 illustrates a simple data manipulation application.

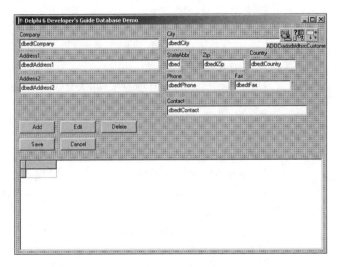

FIGURE 7.2

Main form for the data manipulation application.

This application manipulates data in the simplest form. You'll see the use of the manipulation methods listed as follows:

- `Insert()` allows the user to insert a new record.
- `Edit()` allows the user to modify the active record.
- `Post()` saves changes to a new or existing record to the table.
- `Cancel()` cancels any changes made to the record.
- `Delete()` deletes the active record from the table.

Dataset States

Listing 7.3 also shows how we referred to the `TDataSet.State` property to examine the dataset's state so that we could enable or disable our buttons appropriately. This allows us to do things such as disable our Add button when the dataset is already in Insert or Edit mode. Other states are shown in Table 7.1.

TABLE 7.1   Values for `TDataset.State`

Value	Meaning
dsBrowse	The dataset is in Browse (normal) mode.
dsCalcFields	The `OnCalcFields` event has been called, and a record value calculation is in progress.
dsEdit	The dataset is in Edit mode. This means that the `Edit()` method has been called, but the edited record hasn't yet been posted.
dsInactive	The dataset is closed.
dsInsert	The dataset is in Insert mode. This typically means that `Insert()` has been called but changes haven't been posted.
dsSetKey	The dataset is in SetKey mode, meaning that `SetKey()` has been called but `GotoKey()` hasn't yet been called.
dsNewValue	The dataset is in a temporary state where the `NewValue` property is being accessed.
dsOldValue	The dataset is in a temporary state where the `OldValue` property is being accessed.
dsCurValue	The dataset is in a temporary state where the `OldValue` property is being accessed.
dsFilter	The dataset is currently processing a record filter, lookup, or some other operation that requires a filter.
dsBlockRead	Data is being buffered en masse, so data-aware controls are not updated and events are not triggered when the cursor moves while this member is set.

TABLE 7.1   Continued

Value	Meaning
dsInternalCalc	A field value is currently being calculated for a field that has a FieldKind of fkInternalCalc.
dsOpening	The dataSet is in the process of opening but has not finished. This state occurs when the dataset is opened for asynchronous fetching.

Working with Fields

Delphi enables you to access the fields of any dataset through the TField object and its descendants. Not only can you get and set the value of a given field of the current record of a dataset, but you can also change the behavior of a field by modifying its properties. You can also modify the dataset, itself, by changing the visual order of fields, removing fields, or even creating new calculated or lookup fields.

Field Values

It's very easy to access field values from Delphi. TDataSet provides a default array property called FieldValues[] that returns the value of a particular field as a Variant. Because FieldValues[] is the default array property, you don't need to specify the property name to access the array. For example, the following piece of code assigns the value of Table1's CustName field to String S:

```
S := Table1['CustName'];
```

You could just as easily store the value of an integer field called CustNo in an integer variable called I:

```
I := Table1['CustNo'];
```

A powerful corollary to this is the capability to store the values of several fields into a Variant array. The only catches are that the Variant array index must be zero based and the Variant array contents should be varVariant. The following code demonstrates this capability:

```
const
  AStr = 'The %s is of the %s category and its length is %f in.';
var
  VarArr: Variant;
  F: Double;
begin
  VarArr := VarArrayCreate([0, 2], varVariant);
  { Assume Table1 is attached to Biolife table }
```

```
    VarArr := Table1['Common_Name;Category;Length_In'];
    F := VarArr[2];
    ShowMessage(Format(AStr, [VarArr[0], VarArr[1], F]));
end;
```

You can also use the `TDataset.Fields[]` array property or `FieldsByName()` function to access individual `TField` objects associated with the dataset. The `TField` component provides information about a specific field.

`Fields[]` is a zero-based array of `TField` objects, so `Fields[0]` returns a `TField` representing the first logical field in the record. `FieldsByName()` accepts a string parameter that corresponds to a given field name in the table; therefore, `FieldsByName('OrderNo')` would return a `TField` component representing the `OrderNo` field in the current record of the dataset.

Given a `TField` object, you can retrieve or assign the field's value using one of the `TField` properties shown in Table 7.2.

TABLE 7.2 Properties to Access `TField` Values

Property	Return Type
AsBoolean	Boolean
AsFloat	Double
AsInteger	Longint
AsString	String
AsDateTime	TDateTime
Value	Variant

If the first field in the current dataset is a string, you can store its value in the `String` variable S, like this:

```
S := Table1.Fields[0].AsString;
```

The following code sets the integral variable I to contain the value of the `'OrderNo'` field in the current record of the table:

```
I := Table1.FieldsByName('OrderNo').AsInteger;
```

Field Data Types

If you want to know the type of a field, look at `TField`'s `DataType` property, which indicates the data type with respect to the database table (irrespective of a corresponding Object Pascal type). The `DataType` property is of `TFieldType`, and `TFieldType` is defined as follows:

```
type
  TFieldType = (ftUnknown, ftString, ftSmallint, ftInteger, ftWord,
    ftBoolean, ftFloat, ftCurrency, ftBCD, ftDate, ftTime, ftDateTime,
    ftBytes, ftVarBytes, ftAutoInc, ftBlob, ftMemo, ftGraphic, ftFmtMemo,
    ftParadoxOle, ftDBaseOle, ftTypedBinary, ftCursor, ftFixedChar,
    ftWideString, ftLargeint, ftADT, ftArray, ftReference, ftDataSet,
    ftOraBlob, ftOraClob, ftVariant, ftInterface, ftIDispatch, ftGuid);
```

Descendants of TField are designed to work specifically with many of the preceding data types. These are covered a bit later in this chapter.

Field Names and Numbers

To find the name of a specified field, use the TField.FieldName property. For example, the following code places the name of the first field in the current table in the String variable S:

```
var
  S: String;
begin
  S := Table1.Fields[0].FieldName;
end;
```

Likewise, you can obtain the number of a field you know only by name by using the FieldNo property. The following code stores the number of the OrderNo field in the Integer variable I:

```
var
  I: integer;
begin
  I := Table1.FieldsByName('OrderNo').FieldNo;
end;
```

NOTE

To determine how many fields a dataset contains, use TDataset's FieldList property. FieldList represents a flattened view of all the nested fields in a table containing fields that are abstract data types.

For backward compatibility, the FieldCount property still works, but it will skip over any ADT fields.

Manipulating Field Data

Here's a three-step process for editing one or more fields in the current record:

1. Call the dataset's Edit() method to put the dataset into Edit mode.
2. Assign new values to the fields of your choice.

3. Post the changes to the dataset either by calling the `Post()` method or by moving to a new record, which will automatically post the edit.

For instance, a typical record edit looks like this:

```
Table1.Edit;
Table1['Age'] := 23;
Table1.Post;
```

> **TIP**
>
> Sometimes you work with datasets that contain read-only data. Examples of this would include a table located on a CD-ROM drive or a query with a non-live resultset. Before attempting to edit data, you can determine whether the dataset contains read-only data before you try to modify it by checking the value of the `CanModify` property. If `CanModify` is `True`, you have the green light to edit the dataset.

The Fields Editor

Delphi gives you a great degree of control and flexibility when working with dataset fields through the Fields Editor. You can view the Fields Editor for a particular dataset in the Form Designer, either by double-clicking the `TTable`, `TQuery`, or `TStoredProc` or by selecting Fields Editor from the dataset's local menu. The Fields Editor window enables you to determine which of a dataset's fields you want to work with and create new calculated or lookup fields. You can use a local menu to accomplish these tasks. The Fields Editor window with its local menu deployed is shown in Figure 7.3.

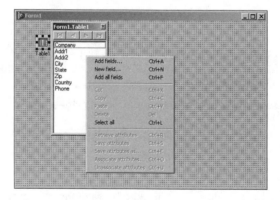

FIGURE 7.3
The Fields Editor's local menu.

To demonstrate the usage of the Fields Editor, open a new project and drop a TTable component onto the main form. Set the Table1.DatabaseName property to DBDEMOS (this is the alias that points to the Delphi sample tables) and set the TableName property to ORDERS.DB. To provide some visual feedback, also drop a TDataSource and TDBGrid component on the form. Hook DataSource1 to Table1 and then hook DBGrid1 to DataSource1. Now set Table1's Active property to True, and you'll see Table1's data in the grid.

Adding Fields

Invoke the Fields Editor by double-clicking Table1, and you'll see the Fields Editor window, as shown in Figure 7.3. Let's say that you want to limit your view of the table to only a few fields. Select Add Fields from the Fields Editor local menu. This will invoke the Add Fields dialog box. Highlight the OrderNo, CustNo, and ItemsTotal fields in this dialog box and click OK. The three selected fields will now be visible in the Fields Editor and in the grid.

Delphi creates TField descendant objects, which map to the dataset fields you select in the Fields Editor. For example, for the three fields mentioned in the preceding paragraph, Delphi adds the following declarations of TField descendants to the source code for your form:

```
Table1OrderNo: TFloatField;
Table1CustNo: TFloatField;
Table1ItemsTotal: TCurrencyField;
```

Notice that the name of the field object is the concatenation of the TTable name and the field name. Because these fields are created in code, you can also access TField descendant properties and methods in your code rather than solely at design time.

TField Descendants

There are one or more different TField descendant objects for each field type. (Field types are described in the "Field Data Types" section, earlier in this chapter.) Many of these field types also map to Object Pascal data types. Table 7.3 shows the various classes in the TField hierarchy, their ancestor classes, their field types, and the Object Pascal types to which they equate.

TABLE 7.3 TField Descendants and Their Field Types

Field Class	Ancestor	Field Type	Object Pascal Type
TStringField	TField	ftString	String
TWideStringField	TStringField	ftWideString	WideString
TGuidField	TStringField	ftGuid	TGUID
TNumericField	TField	*	*
TIntegerField	TNumericField	ftInteger	Integer
TSmallIntField	TIntegerField	ftSmallInt	SmallInt

TABLE 7.3 Continued

Field Class	Ancestor	Field Type	Object Pascal Type
TLargeintField	TNumericField	ftLargeint	Int64
TWordField	TIntegerField	ftWord	Word
TAutoIncField	TIntegerField	ftAutoInc	Integer
TFloatField	TNumericField	ftFloat	Double
TCurrencyField	TFloatField	ftCurrency	Currency
TBCDField	TNumericField	ftBCD	Double
TBooleanField	TField	ftBoolean	Boolean
TDateTimeField	TField	ftDateTime	TDateTime
TDateField	TDateTimeField	ftDate	TDateTime
TTimeField	TDateTimeField	ftTime	TDateTime
TBinaryField	TField	*	*
TBytesField	TBinaryField	ftBytes	*none*
TVarBytesField	TBytesField	ftVarBytes	*none*
TBlobField	TField	ftBlob	*none*
TMemoField	TBlobField	ftMemo	*none*
TGraphicField	TBlobField	ftGraphic	*none*
TObjectField	TField	*	*
TADTField	TObjectField	ftADT	*none*
TArrayField	TObjectField	ftArray	*none*
TDataSetField	TObjectField	ftDataSet	TDataSet
TReferenceField	TDataSetField	ftReference	
TVariantField	TField	ftVariant	OleVariant
TInterfaceField	TField	ftInterface	IUnknown
TIDispatchField	TInterfaceField	ftIDispatch	IDispatch
TAggregateField	TField	*none*	*none*

*Denotes an abstract base class in the TField hierarchy

As Table 7.3 shows, BLOB and Object field types are special in that they don't map directly to native Object Pascal types. BLOB fields are discussed in more detail later in this chapter.

Fields and the Object Inspector

When you select a field in the Fields Editor, you can access the properties and events associated with that `TField` descendant object in the Object Inspector. This feature enables you to modify field properties such as minimum and maximum values, display formats, and whether the field is required as well as whether it's read-only. Some of these properties, such as `ReadOnly`, are obvious in their purpose, but some aren't quite as intuitive.

Switch to the Events page of the Object Inspector, and you'll see that there are also events associated with field objects. The events `OnChange`, `OnGetText`, `OnSetText`, and `OnValidate` are all well-documented in the online help. Simply click to the left of the event in the Object Inspector and press F1. Of these, `OnChange` is probably the most common to use. It enables you to perform some action whenever the contents of the field change (moving to another record or adding a record, for example).

Calculated Fields

You can also add calculated fields to a dataset using the Fields Editor. Let's say, for example, that you wanted to add a field that figures the wholesale total for each entry in the `ORDERS` table, and the wholesale total was 32% of the normal total. Select New Field from the Fields Editor local menu, and you'll be presented with the New Field dialog box, as shown in Figure 7.4. Enter the name, `WholesaleTotal`, for the new field in the Name edit control. The type of this field is Currency, so enter that in the Type edit control. Make sure that the Calculated radio button is selected in the Field Type group; then press OK. Now the new field will show up in the grid, but it won't yet contain any data.

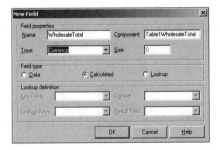

FIGURE 7.4

Adding a calculated field with the New Field dialog box.

To cause the new field to become populated with data, you must assign a method to the `Table1.OnCalcFields` event. The code for this event simply assigns the value of the `WholesaleTotal` field to be 32% of the value of the existing `SalesTotal` field. This method, which handles `Table1.OnCalcFields`, is shown here:

```
procedure TForm1.Table1CalcFields(DataSet: TDataSet);
begin
  DataSet['WholesaleTotal'] := DataSet['ItemsTotal'] * 0.68;
end;
```

Figure 7.5 shows that the WholesaleTotal field in the grid now contains the correct data.

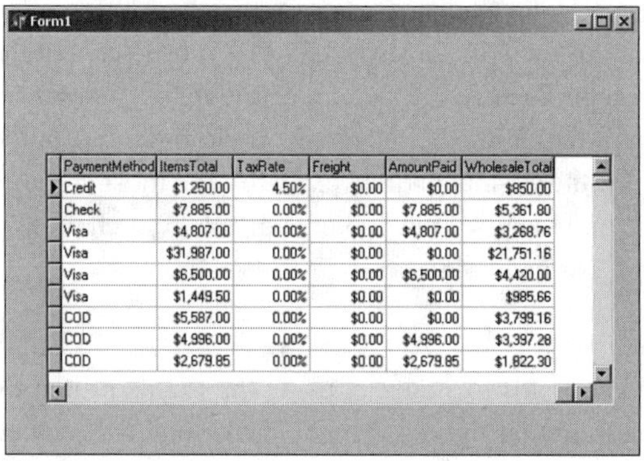

FIGURE 7.5
The calculated field has been added to the table.

Lookup Fields

Lookup fields enable you to create fields in a dataset that actually look up their values from another dataset. To illustrate this, you'll add a lookup field to the current project. The CustNo field of the ORDERS table doesn't mean anything to someone who doesn't have all the customer numbers memorized. You can add a lookup field to Table1 that looks into the CUSTOMER table and then, based on the customer number, retrieves the name of the current customer.

First, you should drop in a second TTable object, setting its DatabaseName property to DBDEMOS and its TableName property to CUSTOMER. This is Table2. Then you once again select New Field from the Fields Editor local menu to invoke the New Field dialog box. This time, you'll call the field CustName, and the field type will be a String. The size of the string is 15 characters. Don't forget to select the Lookup button in the Field Type radio group. The Dataset control in this dialog box should be set to Table2—the dataset you want to look into. The Key Fields and Lookup Keys controls should be set to CustNo—this is the common field upon which the lookup will be performed. Finally, the Result field should be set to Contact—this is the field you want displayed. Figure 7.6 shows the New Field dialog box for the new lookup field. The new field will now display the correct data, as shown in the completed project in Figure 7.7.

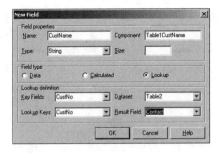

FIGURE 7.6

Adding a lookup field with the New Field dialog box.

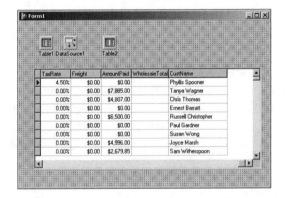

FIGURE 7.7

Viewing the table containing a lookup field.

Drag-and-Drop Fields

Another less obvious feature of the Fields Editor is that it enables you to drag fields from its
Fields list box and drop them onto your forms. We can easily demonstrate this feature by starting a new project that contains only a TTable on the main form. Assign Table1.DatabaseName
to DBDEMOS and assign Table1.TableName to BIOLIFE.DB. Invoke the Fields Editor for this
table and add all the fields in the table to the Fields Editor list box. You can now drag one or
more of the fields at a time from the Fields Editor window and drop them on your main form.

You'll notice a couple of cool things happening here: First, Delphi senses what kind of field
you're dropping onto your form and creates the appropriate data-aware control to display the
data (that is, a TDBEdit is created for a string field, whereas a TDBImage is created for a graphic
field). Second, Delphi checks to see if you have a TDataSource object connected to the dataset;
it hooks to an existing one if available or creates one if needed. Figure 7.8 shows the result of
dragging and dropping the fields of the BIOLIFE table onto a form.

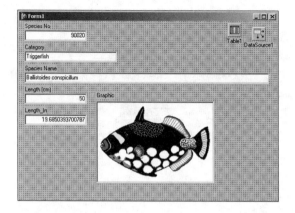

FIGURE 7.8

Dragging and dropping fields on a form.

Working with BLOB Fields

A BLOB (Binary Large Object) field is a field that's designed to contain an indeterminate amount of data. A BLOB field in one record of a dataset might contain three bytes of data, whereas the same field in another record of that dataset might contain 3KB. Blobs are most useful for holding large amounts of text, graphic images, or raw data streams such as OLE objects.

TBlobField and Field Types

As discussed earlier, VCL includes a TField descendant called TBlobField, which encapsulates a BLOB field. TBlobField has a BlobType property of type TBlobType, which indicates what type of data is stored in the BLOB field. TBlobType is defined in the DB unit as follows:

```
TBlobType = ftBlob..ftOraClob;
```

All these field types and the type of data associated with these field types are listed in Table 7.4.

TABLE 7.4 TBlobField Field Types

Field Type	Type of Data
ftBlob	Untyped or user-defined data
ftMemo	Text
ftGraphic	Windows bitmap
ftFmtMemo	Paradox formatted memo
ftParadoxOle	Paradox OLE object
ftDBaseOLE	dBASE OLE object

TABLE 7.4 Continued

Field Type	Type of Data
ftTypedBinary	Raw data representation of an existing type
ftCursor..ftDataSet	Not valid BLOB types
ftOraBlob	BLOB fields in Oracle8 tables
ftOraClob	CLOB fields in Oracle8 tables

You'll find that most of the work you need to do in getting data in and out of TBlobField components can be accomplished by loading or saving the BLOB to a file or by using a TBlobStream. TBlobStream is a specialized descendant of TStream that uses the BLOB field inside the physical table as the stream location. To demonstrate these techniques for interacting with TBlobField components, you'll create a sample application.

BLOB Field Example

This project creates an application that enables the user to store WAV files in a database table and play them directly from the table. Start the project by creating a main form with the components shown in Figure 7.9. The TTable component can map to the Wavez table in the DDGData alias or your own table of the same structure. The structure of the table is as follows:

Field Name	Field Type	Size
WaveTitle	Character	25
FileName	Character	25
Wave	BLOB	

FIGURE 7.9
Main form for Wavez, the BLOB field example.

The Add button is used to load a WAV file from disk and add it to the table. The method assigned to the OnClick event of the Add button is shown here:

```
procedure TMainForm.sbAddClick(Sender: TObject);
begin
  if OpenDialog.Execute then
  begin
    tblSounds.Append;
```

```
    tblSounds['FileName'] := ExtractFileName(OpenDialog.FileName);
    tblSoundsWave.LoadFromFile(OpenDialog.FileName);
    edTitle.SetFocus;
  end;
end;
```

The code first attempts to execute OpenDialog. If it's successful, tblSounds is put into Append mode, the FileName field is assigned a value, and the Wave BLOB field is loaded from the file specified by OpenDialog. Notice that TBlobField's LoadFromFile method is very handy here, and the code is very clean for loading a file into a BLOB field.

Similarly, the Save button saves the current WAV sound found in the Wave field to an external file. The code for this button is as follows:

```
procedure TMainForm.sbSaveClick(Sender: TObject);
begin
  with SaveDialog do
  begin
    FileName := tblSounds['FileName'];    // initialize file name
    if Execute then                       // execute dialog
      tblSoundsWave.SaveToFile(FileName); // save blob to file
  end;
end;
```

There's even less code here. SaveDialog is initialized with the value of the FileName field. If SaveDialog's execution is successful, the tblSoundsWave.SaveToFile() method is called to save the contents of the BLOB field to the file.

The handler for the Play button does the work of reading the WAV data from the BLOB field and passing it to the PlaySound() API function to be played. The code for this handler, shown next, is a bit more complex than the code shown thus far:

```
procedure TMainForm.sbPlayClick(Sender: TObject);
var
  B: TBlobStream;
  M: TMemoryStream;
begin
  B := TBlobStream.Create(tblSoundsWave, bmRead); // create blob stream
  Screen.Cursor := crHourGlass;                   // wait hourglass
  try
    M := TMemoryStream.Create;                     // create memory stream
    try
      M.CopyFrom(B, B.Size);              // copy from blob to memory stream
      // Attempt to play sound. Raise exception if something goes wrong
      Win32Check(PlaySound(M.Memory, 0, SND_SYNC or SND_MEMORY));
```

```
   finally
     M.Free;
   end;
 finally
   Screen.Cursor := crDefault;
   B.Free;                                    // clean up
 end;
end;
```

The first thing this method does is to create an instance of `TBlobStream`, B, using the `tblSoundsWave` BLOB field. The first parameter passed to `TBlobStream.Create()` is the BLOB field object, and the second parameter indicates how you want to open the stream. Typically, you'll use `bmRead` for read-only access to the BLOB stream or `bmReadWrite` for read/write access.

TIP

The dataset must be in Edit, Insert, or Append mode to open a `TBlobStream` with `bmReadWrite` privilege.

An instance of `TMemoryStream`, M, is then created. At this point, the cursor shape is changed to an hourglass to let the user know that the operation may take a couple of seconds. The stream B is then copied to the stream M. The function used to play a WAV sound, `PlaySound()`, requires a filename or a memory pointer as its first parameter. `TBlobStream` doesn't provide pointer access to the stream data, but `TMemoryStream` does through its `Memory` property. Given that, you can successfully call `PlaySound()` to play the data pointed at by `M.Memory`. Once the function is called, it cleans up by freeing the streams and restoring the cursor. The complete code for the main unit of this project is shown in Listing 7.4.

LISTING 7.4   The Main Unit for the Wavez Project

```
unit Main;

interface

uses
  Windows, Messages, SysUtils, Classes, Graphics, Controls, Forms, Dialogs,
  ExtCtrls, DBCtrls, DB, DBTables, StdCtrls, Mask, Buttons, ComCtrls;

type
  TMainForm = class(TForm)
    tblSounds: TTable;
    dsSounds: TDataSource;
```

LISTING 7.4 Continued

```
    tblSoundsWaveTitle: TStringField;
    tblSoundsWave: TBlobField;
    edTitle: TDBEdit;
    edFileName: TDBEdit;
    Label1: TLabel;
    Label2: TLabel;
    OpenDialog: TOpenDialog;
    tblSoundsFileName: TStringField;
    SaveDialog: TSaveDialog;
    pnlToobar: TPanel;
    sbPlay: TSpeedButton;
    sbAdd: TSpeedButton;
    sbSave: TSpeedButton;
    sbExit: TSpeedButton;
    Bevel1: TBevel;
    dbnNavigator: TDBNavigator;
    stbStatus: TStatusBar;
    procedure sbPlayClick(Sender: TObject);
    procedure sbAddClick(Sender: TObject);
    procedure sbSaveClick(Sender: TObject);
    procedure sbExitClick(Sender: TObject);
    procedure FormCreate(Sender: TObject);
    procedure FormClose(Sender: TObject; var Action: TCloseAction);
  private
    procedure OnAppHint(Sender: TObject);
  end;

var
  MainForm: TMainForm;

implementation

{$R *.DFM}

uses MMSystem;

procedure TMainForm.sbPlayClick(Sender: TObject);
var
  B: TBlobStream;
  M: TMemoryStream;
begin
  B := TBlobStream.Create(tblSoundsWave, bmRead); // create blob stream
  Screen.Cursor := crHourGlass;                   // wait hourglass
  try
```

LISTING 7.4 Continued

```delphi
    M := TMemoryStream.Create;                    // create memory stream
    try
      M.CopyFrom(B, B.Size);                // copy from blob to memory stream
      // Attempt to play sound. Raise exception if something goes wrong
      Win32Check(PlaySound(M.Memory, 0, SND_SYNC or SND_MEMORY));
    finally
      M.Free;
    end;
  finally
    Screen.Cursor := crDefault;
    B.Free;                                 // clean up
  end;
end;

procedure TMainForm.sbAddClick(Sender: TObject);
begin
  if OpenDialog.Execute then
  begin
    tblSounds.Append;
    tblSounds['FileName'] := ExtractFileName(OpenDialog.FileName);
    tblSoundsWave.LoadFromFile(OpenDialog.FileName);
    edTitle.SetFocus;
  end;
end;

procedure TMainForm.sbSaveClick(Sender: TObject);
begin
  with SaveDialog do
  begin
    FileName := tblSounds['FileName'];     // initialize file name
    if Execute then                        // execute dialog
      tblSoundsWave.SaveToFile(FileName);  // save blob to file
  end;
end;

procedure TMainForm.sbExitClick(Sender: TObject);
begin
  Close;
end;

procedure TMainForm.FormCreate(Sender: TObject);
begin
  Application.OnHint := OnAppHint;
  tblSounds.Open;
end;
```

LISTING 7.4   Continued

```
procedure TMainForm.OnAppHint(Sender: TObject);
begin
  stbStatus.SimpleText := Application.Hint;
end;

procedure TMainForm.FormClose(Sender: TObject; var Action: TCloseAction);
begin
  tblSounds.Close;
end;

end.
```

Filtering Data

Filters enable you to do simple dataset searching or filtering using only Object Pascal code. The primary advantage of using filters is that they don't require an index or any other preparation on the datasets with which they're used. In many cases, filters can be a bit slower than index-based searching (which is covered later in this chapter), but they're still very usable in almost any type of application.

Using TDataset's Filtering Capabilities

One of the more common uses of Delphi's filtering mechanism is to limit a view of a dataset to some specific records only. This is a simple two-step process:

1. Assign a procedure to the dataset's OnFilterRecord event. Inside of this procedure, you should write code that accepts records based on the values of one or more fields.

2. Set the dataset's Filtered property to True.

As an example, Figure 7.10 shows a form containing TDBGrid, which displays an unfiltered view of Delphi's CUSTOMER table.

In step 1, you write a handler for the table's OnFilterRecord event. In this case, we'll accept only records whose Company field starts with the letter S. The code for this procedure is shown here:

```
procedure TForm1.Table1FilterRecord(DataSet: TDataSet;
  var Accept: Boolean);
var
  FieldVal: String;
begin
  FieldVal := DataSet['Company'];  // Get the value of the Company field
  Accept := FieldVal[1] = 'S';     // Accept record if field starts with 'S'
end;
```

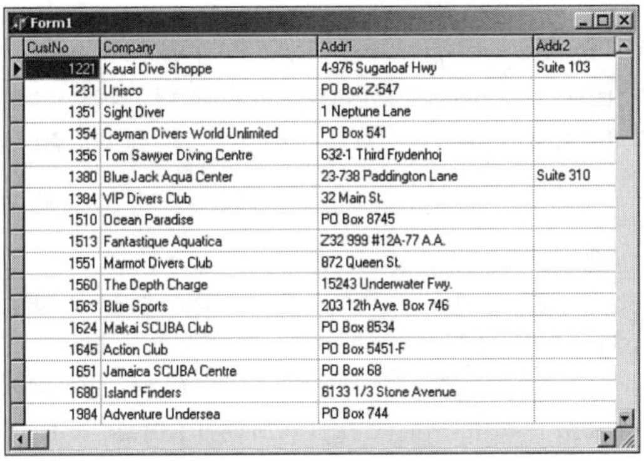

CustNo	Company	Addr1	Addr2
1221	Kauai Dive Shoppe	4-976 Sugarloaf Hwy	Suite 103
1231	Unisco	PO Box Z-547	
1351	Sight Diver	1 Neptune Lane	
1354	Cayman Divers World Unlimited	PO Box 541	
1356	Tom Sawyer Diving Centre	632-1 Third Frydenhoj	
1380	Blue Jack Aqua Center	23-738 Paddington Lane	Suite 310
1384	VIP Divers Club	32 Main St.	
1510	Ocean Paradise	PO Box 8745	
1513	Fantastique Aquatica	Z32 999 #12A-77 A.A.	
1551	Marmot Divers Club	872 Queen St.	
1560	The Depth Charge	15243 Underwater Fwy.	
1563	Blue Sports	203 12th Ave. Box 746	
1624	Makai SCUBA Club	PO Box 8534	
1645	Action Club	PO Box 5451-F	
1651	Jamaica SCUBA Centre	PO Box 68	
1680	Island Finders	6133 1/3 Stone Avenue	
1984	Adventure Undersea	PO Box 744	

FIGURE 7.10
An unfiltered view of the `CUSTOMER` *table.*

After following step 2 and setting the table's `Filtered` property to `True`, you can see in Figure 7.11 that the grid displays only those records that meet the filter criteria.

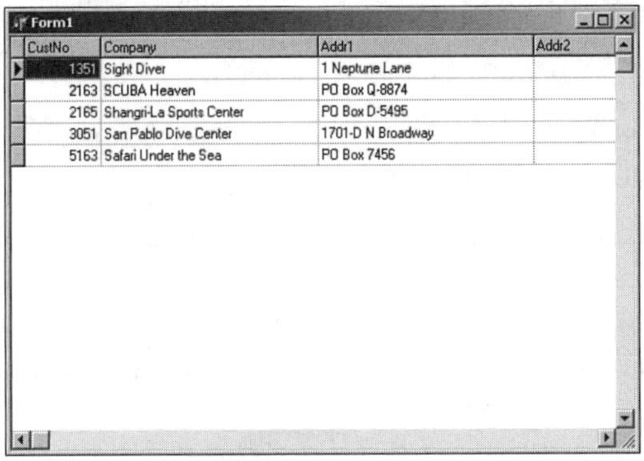

CustNo	Company	Addr1	Addr2
1351	Sight Diver	1 Neptune Lane	
2163	SCUBA Heaven	PO Box Q-8874	
2165	Shangri-La Sports Center	PO Box D-5495	
3051	San Pablo Dive Center	1701-D N Broadway	
5163	Safari Under the Sea	PO Box 7456	

FIGURE 7.11
A filtered view of the `CUSTOMER` *table.*

NOTE

The `OnFilterRecord` event should only be used in cases where the filter cannot be expressed in the `Filter` property. The reason for this is that it can provide significant performance benefits. On SQL databases, for example, the `TTable` component will pass the contents of the `FILTER` property in a `WHERE` clause to the database, which is generally much faster than the record-by-record search performed in `OnFilterRecord`.

Searching Datasets

Datasets provide variations on how to search through datasets. The coverage here shows only the non-SQL type searching techniques. SQL based techniques are covered in Chapter 29 on the CD copy of *Delphi 5 Developer's Guide*.

FindFirst() and FindNext()

TDataSet also provides methods called FindFirst(), FindNext(), FindPrior(), and FindLast() that employ filters to find records that match a particular search criteria. All these functions work on unfiltered datasets by calling that dataset's OnFilterRecord event handler. Based on the search criteria in the event handler, these functions will find the first, next, previous, or last match, respectively. Each of these functions accepts no parameters and returns a Boolean, which indicates whether a match was found.

Locating a Record Using the Locate() Method

Not only are filters useful for defining a subset view of a particular dataset, but they can also be used to search for records within a dataset based on the value of one or more fields. For this purpose, TDataSet provides a method called Locate(). Once again, because Locate() employs filters to do the searching, it will work irrespective of any index applied to the dataset. The Locate() method is defined as follows:

```
function Locate(const KeyFields: string; const KeyValues: Variant;
  Options: TLocateOptions): Boolean;
```

The first parameter, KeyFields, contains the name of the field(s) on which you want to search. The second parameter, KeyValues, holds the field value(s) you want to locate. The third and last parameter, Options, allows you to customize the type of search you want to perform. This parameter is of type TLocateOptions, which is a set type defined in the DB unit as follows:

```
type
  TLocateOption = (loCaseInsensitive, loPartialKey);
  TLocateOptions = set of TLocateOption;
```

If the set includes the loCaseInsensitive member, a not case sensitive search of the data will be performed. If the set includes the loPartialKey member, the values contained in KeyValues will match even if they're substrings of the field value.

Locate() will return True if it finds a match. For example, to search for the first occurrence of the value 1356 in the CustNo field of Table1, use the following syntax:

```
Table1.Locate('CustNo', 1356, []);
```

> **TIP**
>
> You should use Locate() whenever possible to search for records because it will always attempt to use the fastest method possible to find the item, switching indexes temporarily if necessary. This makes your code independent of indexes. Also, if you determine that you no longer need an index on a particular field or if adding one will make your program faster, you can make that change on the data without having to recode the application.

Table Key Searching

This section describes the common properties and methods of the TTable component and how to use them. In particular, you learn how to search for records, filter records using ranges, and create tables. This section also contains a discussion of TTable events.

TTable Record Searching

When you need to search for records in a table, VCL provides several methods to help you out. When you're working with dBASE and Paradox tables, Delphi assumes that the fields on which you search are indexed. For SQL tables, the performance of your search will suffer if you search on non-indexed fields.

Say, for example, you have a table that's keyed on field 1, which is numeric, and on field 2, which is alphanumeric. You can search for a specific record based on those two criteria in one of two ways: using the FindKey() technique or the SetKey()..GotoKey() technique.

FindKey()

TTable's FindKey() method enables you to search for a record matching one or more keyed fields in one function call. FindKey() accepts an array of const (the search criteria) as a parameter and returns True when it's successful. For example, the following code causes the dataset to move to the record where the first field in the index has the value 123 and the second field in the index contains the string Hello:

```
if not Table1.FindKey([123, 'Hello']) then MessageBeep(0);
```

If a match isn't found, FindKey() returns False and the computer beeps.

SetKey()..GotoKey()

Calling TTable's SetKey() method puts the table in a mode that prepares its fields to be loaded with values representing search criteria. Once the search criteria have been established, use the

GotoKey() method to do a top-down search for a matching record. The previous example can be rewritten with SetKey()..GotoKey(), as follows:

```
with Table1 do begin
  SetKey;
  Fields[0].AsInteger := 123;
  Fields[1].AsString := 'Hello';
  if not GotoKey then MessageBeep(0);
end;
```

The Closest Match

Similarly, you can use FindNearest() or the SetKey..GotoNearest methods to search for a value in the table that's the closest match to the search criteria. To search for the first record in which the value of the first indexed field is closest to (greater than or equal to) 123, use the following code:

```
Table1.FindNearest([123]);
```

Once again, FindNearest() accepts an array of const as a parameter that contains the field values for which you want to search.

To search using the longhand technique provided by SetKey()..GotoNearest(), you can use this code:

```
with Table1 do begin
  SetKey;
  Fields[0].AsInteger := 123;
  GotoNearest;
end;
```

If the search is successful and the table's KeyExclusive property is set to False, the record pointer will be on the first matching record. If KeyExclusive is True, the current record will be the one immediately following the match.

TIP

If you want to search on the indexed fields of a table, use FindKey() and FindNearest()—rather than SetKey()..GotoX()—whenever possible because you type less code and leave less room for human error.

Which Index?

All these searching methods assume that you're searching under the table's primary index. If you want to search using a secondary index, you need to set the table's IndexName parameter to the desired index. For instance, if your table had a secondary index on the Company field called ByCompany, the following code would enable you to search for the company "Unisco":

```
with Table1 do begin
  IndexName := 'ByCompany';
  SetKey;
  FieldValues['Company'] := 'Unisco';
  GotoKey;
end;
```

> **NOTE**
>
> Keep in mind that some overhead is involved in switching indexes while a table is opened. You should expect a delay of a second or more when you set the IndexName property to a new value.

Ranges enable you to filter a table so that it contains only records with field values that fall within a certain scope you define. Ranges work similarly to key searches, and as with searches, there are several ways to apply a range to a given table—either using the SetRange() method or the manual SetRangeStart(), SetRangeEnd(), and ApplyRange() methods.

> **CAUTION**
>
> If you are working with dBASE or Paradox tables, ranges only work with indexed fields. If you're working with SQL data, performance will suffer greatly if you don't have an index on the ranged field.

SetRange()

Like FindKey() and FindNearest(), SetRange() enables you to perform a fairly complex action on a table with one function call. SetRange() accepts two array of const variables as parameters: The first represents the field values for the start of the range, and the second represents the field values for the end of the range. As an example, the following code filters through only those records where the value of the first field is greater than or equal to 10 but less than or equal to 15:

```
Table1.SetRange([10], [15]);
```

ApplyRange()

To use the `ApplyRange()` method of setting a range, follow these steps:

1. Call the `SetRangeStart()` method and then modify the `Fields[]` array property of the table to establish the starting value of the keyed field(s).

2. Call the `SetRangeEnd()` method and modify the `Fields[]` array property once again to establish the ending value of the keyed field(s).

3. Call `ApplyRange()` to establish the new range filter.

The preceding range example could be rewritten using this technique:

```
with Table1 do begin
  SetRangeStart;
  Fields[0].AsInteger := 10;      // range starts at 10
  SetRangeEnd;
  Fields[0].AsInteger := 15;      // range ends at 15
  ApplyRange;
end;
```

> **TIP**
>
> Use `SetRange()` whenever possible to filter records—your code will be less prone to error when doing so.

To remove a range filter from a table and restore the table to the state it was in before you called `ApplyRange()` or `SetRange()`, just call TTable's `CancelRange()` method.

```
Table1.CancelRange;
```

Using Data Modules

Data modules enable you to keep all your database rules and relationships in one central location to be shared across projects, groups, or enterprises. Data modules are encapsulated by VCL's `TDataModule` component. Think of `TDataModule` as an invisible form on which you can drop data-access components to be used throughout a project. Creating a `TDataModule` instance is simple: Select File, New from the main menu and then select Data Module from the Object Repository.

The simple justification for using `TDataModule` over just putting data-access components on a form is that it's easier to share the same data across multiple forms and units in your project. In a more complex situation, you would have an arrangement of multiple `TTable`, `TQuery`, and/or `TStoredProc` components. You might have relationships defined between the components and perhaps rules enforced on the field level, such as minimum/maximum values or display formats. Perhaps this assortment of data-access components models the business rules of your enterprise.

After taking great pains to set up something so impressive, you wouldn't want to have to do it again for another application, would you? Of course you wouldn't. In such cases, you would want to save your data module to the Object Repository for later use. If you work in a team environment, you might even want to keep the Object Repository on a shared network drive for the use of all the developers on your team.

In the example that follows, you'll create a simple instance of a data module so that many forms have access to the same data. In the database applications shown in several of the later chapters, you'll build more complex relationships into data modules.

The Search, Range, Filter Demo

Now it's time to create a sample application to help drive home some of the key concepts that were covered in this chapter. In particular, this application will demonstrate the proper use of filters, key searches, and range filters in your applications. This project, called SRF, contains multiple forms. The main form consists mainly of a grid for browsing a table, and other forms demonstrate the different concepts mentioned earlier. Each of these forms will be explained in turn.

The Data Module

Although we're starting a bit out of order, the data module for this project will be covered first. This data module, called DM, contains only a TTable and a TDataSource component. The TTable, called Table1, is hooked to the CUSTOMERS.DB table in the DBDEMOS alias. The TDataSource, DataSource1, is wired to Table1. All the data-aware controls in this project will use DataSource1 as their DataSource. DM is contained in a unit called DataMod.

The Main Form

The main form for SRF, appropriately called MainForm, is shown in Figure 7.12. This form is contained in a unit called Main. As you can see, it contains a TDBGrid control, DBGrid1, for browsing a table, and it contains a radio button that enables you to switch between different indexes on the table. DBGrid1, as explained earlier, is hooked to DM.DataSource1 as its data source.

> **NOTE**
>
> In order for DBGrid1 to be able to hook to DM.DataSource1 at design time, the DataMod unit must be in the uses clause of the Main unit. The easiest way to do this is to bring up the Main unit in the Code Editor and select File, Use Unit from the main menu. You'll then be presented with a list of units in your project from which you can select DataMod. You must do this for each of the units from which you want to access the data contained within DM.

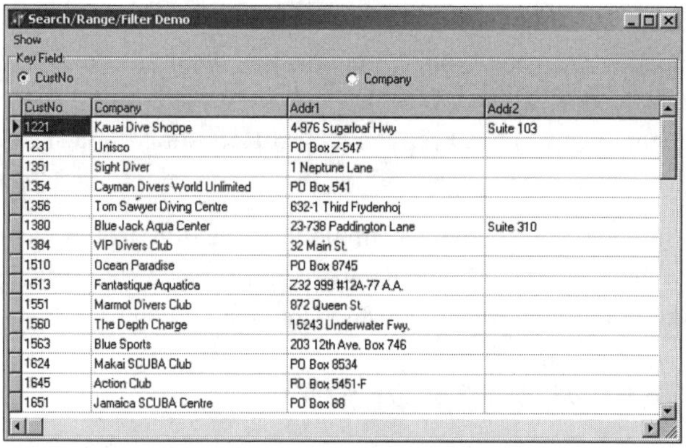

FIGURE 7.12

`MainForm` *in the SRF project.*

The radio group, called `RGKeyField`, is used to determine which of the table's two indexes is currently active. The code attached to the `OnClick` event for `RGKeyField` is shown here:

```
procedure TMainForm.RGKeyFieldClick(Sender: TObject);
begin
  case RGKeyField.ItemIndex of
    0: DM.Table1.IndexName := '';              // primary index
    1: DM.Table1.IndexName := 'ByCompany';     // secondary, by company
  end;
end;
```

`MainForm` also contains a `TMainMenu` component, `MainMenu1`, which enables you to open and close each of the other forms. The items on this menu are Key Search, Range, Filter, and Exit. The `Main` unit, in its entirety, is shown in Listing 7.5.

NOTE

In order for `DBGrid1` to be able to hook to `DM.DataSource1` at design time, the `DataMod` unit must be in the uses clause of the `Main` unit. The easiest way to do this is to bring up the `Main` unit in the Code Editor and select File, Use Unit from the main menu. You'll then be presented with a list of units in your project from which you can select `DataMod`. You must do this for each of the units from which you want to access the data contained within `DM`.

The radio group, called `RGKeyField`, is used to determine which of the table's two indexes is currently active. The code attached to the `OnClick` event for `RGKeyField` is shown here:

```
procedure TMainForm.RGKeyFieldClick(Sender: TObject);
begin
  case RGKeyField.ItemIndex of
    0: DM.Table1.IndexName := '';              // primary index
    1: DM.Table1.IndexName := 'ByCompany';     // secondary, by company
  end;
end;
```

MainForm also contains a `TMainMenu` component, `MainMenu1`, which enables you to open and close each of the other forms. The items on this menu are Key Search, Range, Filter, and Exit. The `Main` unit, in its entirety, is shown in Listing 7.5.

LISTING 7.5   Main.pas—Demonstrating Dataset Ranges

```
unit Main;

interface

uses
  SysUtils, WinTypes, WinProcs, Messages, Classes, Graphics, Controls,
  Forms, Dialogs, StdCtrls, ExtCtrls, Grids, DBGrids, DB, DBTables,
  Buttons, Mask, DBCtrls, Menus, KeySrch, Rng, Fltr;

type
  TMainForm = class(TForm)
    DBGrid1: TDBGrid;
    RGKeyField: TRadioGroup;
    MainMenu1: TMainMenu;
    Forms1: TMenuItem;
    KeySearch1: TMenuItem;
    Range1: TMenuItem;
    Filter1: TMenuItem;
    N1: TMenuItem;
    Exit1: TMenuItem;
    procedure RGKeyFieldClick(Sender: TObject);
    procedure KeySearch1Click(Sender: TObject);
    procedure Range1Click(Sender: TObject);
    procedure Filter1Click(Sender: TObject);
    procedure Exit1Click(Sender: TObject);
  private
    { Private declarations }
  public
    { Public declarations }
  end;
```

LISTING 7.5   Continued

```
var
  MainForm: TMainForm;

implementation

uses DataMod;

{$R *.DFM}

procedure TMainForm.RGKeyFieldClick(Sender: TObject);
begin
  case RGKeyField.ItemIndex of
    0: DM.Table1.IndexName := '';            // primary index
    1: DM.Table1.IndexName := 'ByCompany';   // secondary, by company
  end;
end;

procedure TMainForm.KeySearch1Click(Sender: TObject);
begin
  KeySearch1.Checked := not KeySearch1.Checked;
  KeySearchForm.Visible := KeySearch1.Checked;
end;

procedure TMainForm.Range1Click(Sender: TObject);
begin
  Range1.Checked := not Range1.Checked;
  RangeForm.Visible := Range1.Checked;
end;

procedure TMainForm.Filter1Click(Sender: TObject);
begin
  Filter1.Checked := not Filter1.Checked;
  FilterForm.Visible := Filter1.Checked;
end;

procedure TMainForm.Exit1Click(Sender: TObject);
begin
  Close;
end;

end.
```

> **NOTE**
>
> Pay close attention to the following line of code from the Rng unit:
>
> ```
> DM.Table1.SetRange([StartEdit.Text], [EndEdit.Text]);
> ```
>
> You might find it strange that although the keyed field can be of either a Numeric type or Text type, you're always passing strings to the SetRange() method. Delphi allows this because SetRange(), FindKey(), and FindNearest() will perform the conversion from String to Integer, and vice versa, automatically.
>
> What this means to you is that you shouldn't bother calling IntToStr() or StrToInt() in these situations—it will be taken care of for you.

The Key Search Form

KeySearchForm, contained in the KeySrch unit, provides a means for the user of the application to search for a particular key value in the table. The form enables the user to search for a value in one of two ways. First, when the Normal radio button is selected, the user can search by typing text into the Search For edit control and pressing the Exact or Nearest button to find an exact match or closest match in the table. Second, when the Incremental radio button is selected, the user can perform an incremental search on the table every time he or she changes the text in the Search For edit control. The code for the KeySrch unit is shown in Listing 7.6.

LISTING 7.6 The Source Code for KeySrch.PAS

```
unit KeySrch;

interface

uses
  Windows, Messages, SysUtils, Classes, Graphics, Controls, Forms, Dialogs,
  StdCtrls, ExtCtrls;

type
  TKeySearchForm = class(TForm)
    Panel1: TPanel;
    Label3: TLabel;
    SearchEdit: TEdit;
    RBNormal: TRadioButton;
    Incremental: TRadioButton;
    Label6: TLabel;
    ExactButton: TButton;
    NearestButton: TButton;
    procedure ExactButtonClick(Sender: TObject);
```

LISTING 7.6 Continued

```
    procedure NearestButtonClick(Sender: TObject);
    procedure RBNormalClick(Sender: TObject);
    procedure IncrementalClick(Sender: TObject);
    procedure FormClose(Sender: TObject; var Action: TCloseAction);
  private
    procedure NewSearch(Sender: TObject);
  end;

var
  KeySearchForm: TKeySearchForm;

implementation

uses DataMod, Main;

{$R *.DFM}

procedure TKeySearchForm.ExactButtonClick(Sender: TObject);
begin
  { Try to find record where key field matches SearchEdit's Text value. }
  { Notice that Delphi handles the type conversion from the string      }
  { edit control to the numeric key field value.                        }
  if not DM.Table1.FindKey([SearchEdit.Text]) then
    MessageDlg(Format('Match for "%s" not found.', [SearchEdit.Text]),
               mtInformation, [mbOk], 0);
end;

procedure TKeySearchForm.NearestButtonClick(Sender: TObject);
begin
  { Find closest match to SearchEdit's Text value. Note again the }
  { implicit type conversion.                                     }
  DM.Table1.FindNearest([SearchEdit.Text]);
end;

procedure TKeySearchForm.NewSearch(Sender: TObject);
{ This is the method which is wired to the SearchEdit's OnChange }
{ event whenever the Incremental radio is selected. }
begin
  DM.Table1.FindNearest([SearchEdit.Text]); // search for text
end;

procedure TKeySearchForm.RBNormalClick(Sender: TObject);
begin
```

LISTING 7.6 Continued

```
  ExactButton.Enabled := True;    // enable search buttons
  NearestButton.Enabled := True;
  SearchEdit.OnChange := Nil;     // unhook the OnChange event
end;

procedure TKeySearchForm.IncrementalClick(Sender: TObject);
begin
  ExactButton.Enabled := False;       // disable search buttons
  NearestButton.Enabled := False;
  SearchEdit.OnChange := NewSearch;   // hook the OnChange event
  NewSearch(Sender);                  // search current text
end;

procedure TKeySearchForm.FormClose(Sender: TObject;
  var Action: TCloseAction);
begin
  Action := caHide;
  MainForm.KeySearch1.Checked := False;
end;

end.
```

The code for the KeySrch unit should be fairly straightforward to you. You might notice that, once again, we can safely pass text strings to the FindKey() and FindNearest() methods with the knowledge that they will do the right thing with regard to type conversion. You might also appreciate the small trick that's employed to switch to and from incremental searching on-the-fly. This is accomplished by either assigning a method to or assigning Nil to the OnChange event of the SearchEdit edit control. When assigned a handler method, the OnChange event will fire whenever the text in the control is modified. By calling FindNearest() inside that handler, an incremental search can be performed as the user types.

The Filter Form

The purpose of FilterForm, found in the Fltr unit, is two-fold. First, it enables the user to filter the view of the table to a set where the value of the State field matches that of the current record. Second, this form enables the user to search for a record where the value of any field in the table is equal to some value she has specified.

The record-filtering functionality actually involves very little code. First, the state of the check box labeled Filter on This State (called cbFiltered) determines the setting of

DM.Table1's Filtered property. This is accomplished with the following line of code attached to cbFiltered.OnClick:

```
DM.Table1.Filtered := cbFiltered.Checked;
```

When DM.Table1.Filtered is True, Table1 filters records using the following OnFilterRecord method, which is actually located in the DataMod unit:

```
procedure TDM.Table1FilterRecord(DataSet: TDataSet;
  var Accept: Boolean);
begin
  { Accept record as a part of the filter if the value of the State }
  { field is the same as that of DBEdit1.Text.                      }
  Accept := Table1State.Value = FilterForm.DBEdit1.Text;
end;
```

To perform the filter-based search, the Locate() method of TTable is employed:

```
DM.Table1.Locate(CBField.Text, EValue.Text, LO);
```

The field name is taken from a combo box called CBField. The contents of this combo box are generated in the OnCreate event of this form using the following code to iterate through the fields of Table1:

```
procedure TFilterForm.FormCreate(Sender: TObject);
var
  i: integer;
begin
  with DM.Table1 do begin
    for i := 0 to FieldCount - 1 do
      CBField.Items.Add(Fields[i].FieldName);
  end;
end;
```

TIP

The preceding code will only work when DM is created prior to this form. Otherwise, any attempts to access DM before it's created will probably result in an Access Violation error. To make sure that the data module, DM, is created prior to any of the child forms, we manually adjusted the creation order of the forms in the Autocreate Forms list on the Forms page of the Project Options dialog (found under Options, Project on the main menu).

The main form must, of course, be the first one created, but other than that, this little trick ensures that the data module gets created prior to any other form in the application.

The complete code for the `Fltr` unit is shown in Listing 7.7.

LISTING 7.7   The Source Code for `Fltr.pas`

```
unit Fltr;

interface

uses
  Windows, Messages, SysUtils, Classes, Graphics, Controls, Forms, Dialogs,
  StdCtrls, Buttons, Mask, DBCtrls, ExtCtrls;

type
  TFilterForm = class(TForm)
    Panel1: TPanel;
    Label4: TLabel;
    DBEdit1: TDBEdit;
    cbFiltered: TCheckBox;
    Label5: TLabel;
    SpeedButton1: TSpeedButton;
    SpeedButton2: TSpeedButton;
    SpeedButton3: TSpeedButton;
    SpeedButton4: TSpeedButton;
    Panel2: TPanel;
    EValue: TEdit;
    LocateBtn: TButton;
    Label1: TLabel;
    Label2: TLabel;
    CBField: TComboBox;
    MatchGB: TGroupBox;
    RBExact: TRadioButton;
    RBClosest: TRadioButton;
    CBCaseSens: TCheckBox;
    procedure cbFilteredClick(Sender: TObject);
    procedure FormCreate(Sender: TObject);
    procedure LocateBtnClick(Sender: TObject);
    procedure SpeedButton1Click(Sender: TObject);
    procedure SpeedButton2Click(Sender: TObject);
    procedure SpeedButton3Click(Sender: TObject);
    procedure SpeedButton4Click(Sender: TObject);
    procedure FormClose(Sender: TObject; var Action: TCloseAction);
  end;

var
  FilterForm: TFilterForm;
```

LISTING 7.7   Continued

```
implementation

uses DB, DataMod, Main;

{$R *.DFM}

procedure TFilterForm.cbFilteredClick(Sender: TObject);
begin
  { Filter table if checkbox is checked }
  DM.Table1.Filtered := cbFiltered.Checked;
end;

procedure TFilterForm.FormCreate(Sender: TObject);
var
  i: integer;
begin
  with DM.Table1 do begin
    for i := 0 to FieldCount - 1 do
      CBField.Items.Add(Fields[i].FieldName);
  end;
end;

procedure TFilterForm.LocateBtnClick(Sender: TObject);
var
  LO: TLocateOptions;
begin
  LO := [];
  if not CBCaseSens.Checked then Include(LO, loCaseInsensitive);
  if RBClosest.Checked then Include(LO, loPartialKey);
  if not DM.Table1.Locate(CBField.Text, EValue.Text, LO) then
    MessageDlg('Unable to locate match', mtInformation, [mbOk], 0);
end;

procedure TFilterForm.SpeedButton1Click(Sender: TObject);
begin
  DM.Table1.FindFirst;
end;

procedure TFilterForm.SpeedButton2Click(Sender: TObject);
begin
  DM.Table1.FindNext;
end;

procedure TFilterForm.SpeedButton3Click(Sender: TObject);
```

LISTING 7.7 Continued

```
begin
  DM.Table1.FindPrior;
end;

procedure TFilterForm.SpeedButton4Click(Sender: TObject);
begin
  DM.Table1.FindLast;
end;

procedure TFilterForm.FormClose(Sender: TObject; var Action: TCloseAction);
begin
  Action := caHide;
  MainForm.Filter1.Checked := False;
end;

end.
```

Bookmarks

Bookmarks enable you to save your place in a dataset so that you can come back to the same spot at a later time. Bookmarks are very easy to use in Delphi because you only have one property to remember.

Delphi represents a bookmark as type TBookmarkStr. TTable has a property of this type called Bookmark. When you read from this property, you obtain a bookmark, and when you write to this property, you go to a bookmark. When you find a particularly interesting place in a dataset that you'd like to be able to get back to easily, here's the syntax to use:

```
var
  BM: TBookmarkStr;
begin
  BM := Table1.Bookmark;
```

When you want to return to the place in the dataset you marked, just do the reverse—set the Bookmark property to the value you obtained earlier by reading the Bookmark property:

```
Table1.Bookmark := BM;
```

TBookmarkStr is defined as an AnsiString, so memory is automatically managed for bookmarks (you never have to free them). If you'd like to clear an existing bookmark, just set it to an empty string:

```
BM := '';
```

Note that `TBookmarkStr` is an `AnsiString` for storage convenience. You should consider it an opaque data type and not depend on the implementation because the bookmark data is completely determined by BDE and the underlying data layers.

> **NOTE**
>
> Although 32-bit Delphi still supports `GetBookmark()`, `GotoBookmark()`, and `FreeBookmark()` from Delphi 1.0, because the 32-bit Delphi technique is a bit cleaner and less prone to error, you should use this newer technique unless you have to maintain compatibility with 16-bit projects.

You'll find an example of using bookmarks with an ADO dataset on the CD in the `\Bookmark` subdirectory for this chapter.

Summary

After reading this chapter, you should be ready for just about any type of database programming with Delphi. You learned the ins and outs of Delphi's `TDataSet` component, which is the ancestor of the different types of datasets. You also learned techniques for manipulating datasets, how to manage fields, and how to work with text tables.

In the following chapters, you will learn about dbExpress, Delphi's lightweight database development technology and about dbGo, Delphi's connectivity to ADO data in greater depth.

Database Development with dbExpress

IN THIS CHAPTER

dbExpress is Borland's new technology that provides lightweight database development to Delphi 6 developers.

dbExpress is important for three reasons. First, it is much lighter from a deployment standpoint than its predecessor, the BDE. Second, it is the cross-platform technology that you should use if developing applications intended for the Linux platform using Kylix. Third, it is extensible. To develop dbExpress drivers, one simply implements the required interfaces and provides the resulting database access library.

dbExpress's underlying architecture consists of drivers for supported databases, each of which implement a set of interfaces enabling access to server specific data. These drivers interact with applications through DataCLX connection components in much the same way a TDatabase component interacts with the BDE—minus the extra overhead.

Using dbExpress

dbExpress is designed to efficiently access data and to carry little overhead. To accomplish this, dbExpress uses *unidirectional* datasets.

Unidirectional, Read-Only Datasets

The nature of unidirectional datasets means that they don't buffer records for navigation or modification. This is where the efficiency is gained against the bi-directional BDE datasets that do buffer data in memory. Some limitations that result are

- Unidirectional datasets only support the First() and Next() navigational methods. Attempts to call other methods—such as Last() or Prior()—will result in an exception.

- Unidirectional dataset records aren't editable because there is no buffer support for editing. Note, however, that you would use other components (TClientDataset, TSQLClientDataset) for editing, which we'll discuss later.

- Unidirectional datasets don't support filtering because this is a multirecord feature and unidirectional datasets don't buffer multiple records.

- Unidirectional datasets don't support lookup fields.

dbExpress Versus the Borland Database Engine (BDE)

dbExpress offers several advantages over the BDE, which we'll briefly go over.

Unlike the BDE, dbExpress doesn't consume server resources with metadata queries or other extraneous requests when user-defined queries are executed against the database server.

dbExpress doesn't consume as many client resources as the BDE. Because of the unidirectional cursor, no caching is done. dbExpress doesn't cache metadata on the client either. Metadata definition is handled through the data-access interface DLLs.

Unlike the BDE, dbExpress doesn't generate internal queries for things like navigation and BLOB retrieval. This makes dbExpress much more efficient at runtime in that only those queries specified by the user are executed against the database server. dbExpress is far simpler than the BDE.

dbExpress for Cross-Platform Development

A key advantage to dbExpress is that it is cross-platform between Windows (using Delphi 6) and Linux (using Kylix). By using the CLX components for dbExpress, you can compile your application with Kylix and have the same application running in Linux. In fact, dbExpress can use a cross-platform database such as MySQL or InterBase.

> **NOTE**
>
> At the time of this writing, support for the latest version of mySQL was limited to an earlier version (3.22). However, Delphi 6 can work with the latest version of the database (3.23) by using the shipping version of the dbExpress DLL. Borland is working on an update of the library.

dbExpress Components

All the dbExpress components appear on the dbExpress tab of the Component Palette.

TSQLConnection

For those who have done BDE development, the TSQLConnection will appear very similar to the TDatabase component. In fact, the purpose is the same in that they both encapsulate the database connection. It is through the TSQLConnection that dbExpress datasets access server data.

TSQLConnection relies on two configuration files, dbxdrivers.ini and dbxconnections.ini. These files are installed to the "\Program Files\Common Files\Borland Shared\DbExpress" directory. dbxdrivers.ini contains a listing of all dbExpress supported drivers and driver specific settings. Dbxconnections.ini contains a listing of "*named connections*"—which can be considered similar in nature to a BDE alias—and any specific settings for these connections. It is possible not to use the default dbxconnections.ini file at runtime by setting the TSQLConnection.LoadParamsOnConnect property to true. We'll show an example of doing this momentarily.

A `TSQLConnection` component must use a dbExpress driver specific to the type of database that you are using. This driver is specified in the `dbxdrivers.ini` file.

The `TSQLConnection`'s methods and properties are adequately covered in the online help. As always, we direct you to the online help for detailed information. In this book, we will walk you through establishing a database connection and in creating a new connection.

Establishing a Database Connection

To establish a connection with an existing database, simply drop a `TSQLConnection` on a form and specify a `ConnectionName` by selecting one from the drop-down list in the Object Inspector. When doing so, you should see at least four different connections: IBLocal, DB2Connection, MSConnection, and Oracle. If you didn't install a version of InterBase when you installed Delphi, do so now. You'll need one for this example. Once you have one installed, select the IBLocal connection because Local InterBase should have been installed with your Delphi 6 installation.

Upon selecting a `ConnectionName`, you'll see that other properties such as `DriverName`, `GetDriverFunc`, `LibraryName`, and `VendorLib` are automatically filled in. These default values are specified in the `dbxdrivers.ini` file. You can examine and modify other driver specific properties from the Params property's editor, shown in Figure 8.1.

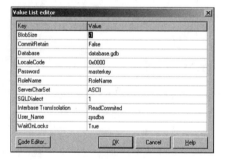

FIGURE 8.1

`TSQLConnection.Params` *property editor.*

> **NOTE**
>
> The default value in the "Database" key in the Params property editor is simply "database.gdb". This refers to an nonexistent database. You can change this value to the "Employee.gdb" example database that should exist in a subdirectory of your InterBase installation. On our machine, this is "...\Program Files\Borland\ InterBase6\examples\Database\Employee.gdb".

Once you have the TSQLConnection component referring to a valid database, you can change the Connected property value to True. You'll be prompted for a username and password, which are "**sysdba**" and "**masterkey**", respectively. This should connect you to the database. It would be a good idea to refer to the help files for each of the TSQLConnection properties at this point.

Creating a New Database Connection

You can create additional "named" connections that refer to databases that you specify. For instance, this would be helpful if you were creating an application that used two separate databases such as a live and a test database. To create a new connection, simply double-click on the TSQLConnection component to bring up the Connection Editor (see Figure 8.2). You can also right-click and select "Edit Connection Properties" from the TSQLConnection local menu to invoke this editor.

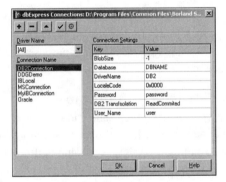

FIGURE 8.2

The TSQLConnection *Connection Editor.*

You'll see that there are five speed buttons on this editor. We'll examine the "Add" button now. When pressed, you are asked to provide a Driver Name and a Connection Name. The Driver Name drop-down will be one of the four supported database drivers. You can select InterBase in this example. You can specify any name for the Connection Name such as "**MyIBConnection**". When you select "OK", you'll see the Connection Settings grid display the driver settings for your specific connection. These are the same as the TSQLConnection.Params property values. Again, you'll need to change the "Database" setting to a valid InterBase database. At this point, you should be able to close the editor and set the Connected property to True by specifying the proper username and password.

Bypassing/Replacing the Login Prompt

Bypassing the login prompt is easy. Simply set the LoginPrompt property to False. You'll have to make sure that the UserName and Password settings in the Params property have a valid user name and password, respectively.

To replace the login prompt with your own login dialog, the `LoginPrompt` property must be set to `True`. Then, you must add an event handler to the `OnLogin` event. For instance, the following code illustrates how this might look:

```
procedure TMainForm.SQLConnection1Login(Database: TSQLConnection;
  LoginParams: TStrings);
var
  UserName: String;
  Password: String;
begin
  if InputQuery('Get UserName', 'Enter UserName', UserName) then
  if InputQuery('Get Password', 'Enter Password', Password) then
  begin
    LoginParams.Values['UserName'] := UserName;
    LoginParams.Values['Password'] := Password;
  end;
end;
```

In this example, we're using a call to the `InputQuery()` function to retrieve the values needed. You would be able to use your own dialog for the same purpose. You'll find this example on the CD that also demonstrates the use of the `AfterConnect` and `AfterDisconnect` events.

Loading Connection Settings at Runtime

The connection settings that you see from the Connection Editor or the `Params` property editor are defaults that get loaded at design time from the dbxconnections.ini file. It is possible for you to load these at runtime. You might do this, for example, if you needed to provide a separate `dbxconnections.ini` file than that provided with Delphi. Of course, you must remember to deploy this new file with your application installation.

To enable your application to load these settings at runtime, you must set the `LoadParamsOn Connect` property to `True`. When your application launches, the `TSQLConnection` component will look to the registry for the "Connection Registry File" key in "`HKEY_CURRENT_USER\ Software\Borland\DBExpress`". You must modify this value to point to the location of your own `dbxconnections.ini` file. This is something that you would probably do in the installation of your application.

TSQLDataset

`TSQLDataset` is the unidirectional dataset used for retrieving data from a dbExpress supported server. This dataset can be used to represent data in a database table, a selection query, or the results of a stored procedure. It can also execute a stored procedure.

TSQLDataset's key properties are CommandType and CommandText. The value selected for CommandType determines how the content of CommandText will be used. Possible values for CommandType are listed in Table 8.1 and in the Delphi help file.

TABLE 8.1 CommandType Values (from Delphi Online Help)

CommandType	*Corresponding* CommandText
ctQuery	An SQL statement that the dataset executes.
ctStoredProc	The name of a stored procedure.
ctTable	The name of a table on the database server. The SQL dataset automatically generates a SELECT statement to fetch all the records of all the fields in this table.

When the CommandType property contains the ctQuery value, CommandText is an SQL statement. This statement might be a SELECT statement that returns a resultset such as the following SQL statement: "SELECT * FROM CUSTOMER".

If CommandType is ctTable, CommandText refers to a table name on the database server. The CommandText property will change to a drop down. If this is an SQL database, any SQL statements needed to retrieve data are automatically generated.

If CommandType has the value ctStoredProc, CommentText will then contain the name of a stored procedure to execute. This would be executed by calling the TSQLDataSet.ExecSQL() method rather then by setting the Active property to True. Note, that ExecSQL() should be used if CommandType is ctQuery and the SQL statement doesn't result in a resultset.

Retrieving Table Data

To extract table data using the TSQLDataset, you simply set the TSQLDataSet.CommandType property to ctTable. The CommandText property will change to a drop down from which you can select the table name. You can look at an example on the CD in the "TableData" directory.

Displaying Query Results

To extract data from a query select statement, simply set the TSQLDataSet.CommandType property to ctQuery. In the CommandText property, you can enter a query select statement such as "Select * from Country". This is demonstrated in the example on the CD under the "QueryData" directory.

Displaying Stored Procedure Results

Given a stored procedure that returns a resultset such as the InterBase procedure that follows, you can extract the resultset using a `TSQLDataset` component:

```
CREATE PROCEDURE SELECT_COUNTRIES  RETURNS (
  RCOUNTRY VARCHAR(15),
  RCURRENCY VARCHAR(10)
) AS
BEGIN
  FOR SELECT
    COUNTRY, CURRENCY FROM COUNTRY
  INTO
    :rCOUNTRY, :rCURRENCY
  DO
    SUSPEND;
END
```

To do this, set the `TSQLDataset.CommandType` property to `ctQuery` and add the following to its `CommandText` property: `Select * from SELECT_COUNTRIES`. Note that we use the stored procedure name as though it were a table.

Executing a Stored Procedure

Using the `TSQLDataset` component, you can execute a stored procedure that does not return a resultset. To do this, set the `TSQLDataSet.CommandType` property to `ctStoredProc`. The `TSQLDataset.CommandText` property will become a drop down that displays a list of stored procedures on the database. You must select one of the stored procedures that doesn't return a resultset. For example, the example on the CD under the directory "ExecSProc" executes the following stored procedure:

```
CREATE PROCEDURE ADD_COUNTRY (
  ICOUNTRY VARCHAR(15),
  ICURRENCY VARCHAR(10)
)  AS
BEGIN
  INSERT INTO COUNTRY(COUNTRY, CURRENCY)
  VALUES (:iCOUNTRY, :iCURRENCY);
  SUSPEND;
END
```

This procedure is a simple insert statement into the country table. To execute the procedure, you must call the `TSQLDataset.ExecSQL()` method as shown in the following code:

```
procedure TForm1.btnAddCurrencyClick(Sender: TObject);
begin
  sqlDSAddCountry.ParamByName('ICountry').AsString := edtCountry.Text;
```

```
  sqlDSAddCountry.ParamByName('ICURRENCY').AsString := edtCurrency.Text;
  sqlDSAddCountry.ExecSQL(False);
end;
```

The first thing you must do is to set the parameter values. Then, by calling ExecSQL(), the specified procedure will be executed with the values you've added. Note that ExecSQL() takes a Boolean parameter. This parameter is used to determine whether any parameters need to be prepared. By default, this parameter should be true.

Metadata Representation

You can retrieve information about a database using the TSQLDataset component. To do this, you use the TSQLDataset.SetSchemaInfo() procedure to specify the type of schema information you desire. SetSchemaInfo is defined as

```
procedure SetSchemaInfo( SchemaType: TSchemaType;
➥SchemaObjectName, SchemaPattern: string );
```

The SchemaType parameter specifies the type of schema information that you are requesting. SchemaObjectName holds the name of a table or procedure in the case of a request for parameter, column, or index information. SchemaPattern is an SQL pattern mask used for filtering the resultset.

Table 8.2 is taken from the Delphi online help for the SetSchemaInfo() procedure and describes the types of schema information that you can retrieve.

TABLE 8.2 SchemaType Values (from Delphi Online Help)

SchemaType *Value*	*Description*
stNoSchema	No schema information. The SQL dataset is populated with the results of its query or stored procedure rather than metadata from the server.
stables	Information about all the data tables on the database server that match the criteria specified by the SQL connection's TableScope property.
stSysTables	Information about all the system tables on the database server. Not all servers use system tables to store metadata. Requesting a list of system tables from a server that doesn't use them results in an empty dataset.
stProcedures	Information about all the stored procedures on the database server.
stColumns	Information about all the columns (fields) in a specified table.
stProcedureParams	Information about all the parameters of a specified stored procedure.
stIndexes	Information about all the indexes defined for a specified table.

We've provided an example of using the SetSchemaInfo() procedure on the CD under the directory "SchemaInfo". Listing 8.1 shows some of the code for this procedure from this example.

LISTING 8.1   Example of TSQLDataset.SetSchemaInfo()

```
procedure TMainForm.Button1Click(Sender: TObject);
begin
  sqldsSchemaInfo.Close;
  cdsSchemaInfo.Close;

  case RadioGroup1.ItemIndex of
  0: sqldsSchemaInfo.SetSchemaInfo(stSysTables, '', '');
  1: sqldsSchemaInfo.SetSchemaInfo(stTables, '', '');
  2: sqldsSchemaInfo.SetSchemaInfo(stProcedures, '', '');
  3: sqldsSchemaInfo.SetSchemaInfo(stColumns, 'COUNTRY', '');
  4: sqldsSchemaInfo.SetSchemaInfo(stProcedureParams, 'ADD_COUNTRY', '');
  5: sqldsSchemaInfo.SetSchemaInfo(stIndexes, 'COUNTRY', '');
  end; // case

  sqldsSchemaInfo.Open;
  cdsSchemaInfo.Open;
end;
```

In the example, we use the selection in TRadioGroup component to determine which type of schema information we want. We then call the SetSchemaInfo() procedure using the proper SchemaType parameter before opening the dataset. The values are stored in a TDBGrid in the example.

Backward Compatibility Components

You'll find three components on the dbExpress tab in the Component Palette that are synonymous with the BDE dataset components. These are TSQLTable, TSQLQuery, and TSQLStoredProc. These components are used very much in the same manner as their BDE counterparts except that they cannot be used in a bidirectional manner. For the most part, you will be using the TSQLDataset components.

TSQLMonitor

The TSQLMonitor component is useful for debugging SQL applications. TSQLMonitor logs the SQL commands being communicated through a TSQLConnection component. To use this, you simply set the TSQLMonitor.SQLConnection parameter to a valid TSQLConnection component.

The `TSQLMonitor.Tracelist` property will then log the commands being passed between the client and the database server. `TraceList` is a simple `TStrings` descendant, so you can save this information to a file or add it to a memo component for viewing the information.

> **NOTE**
>
> You can use the `FileName` and `AutoSave` properties to automatically store the `TraceList` contents.

The example code provided on the CD in the `SQLMon` directory shows how to add the contents of the `TraceList` to a memo control. The resulting SQL tracelist is shown in Figure 8.3.

FIGURE 8.3
Results of the `TSQLMonitor` *component.*

Designing Editable dbExpress Applications

Up to now, we have discussed dbExpress in the context of unidirectional/read-only datasets. The only exception is the example using a `TSQLDataset` component to execute a stored procedure that adds data to a table. Another method to make datasets editable as with a bidirectional dataset is to use cached updates. To do so, this requires the use of another component, `TSQLClientDataset`.

TSQLClientDataset

`TSQLClientDataset` is a component that contains an internal `TSQLDataset` and `TProvider` component. The internal `TSQLDataset` gives the `TSQLClientDataset` the fast data access benefits of dbExpress. The internal `TSQLProvider` gives the `TSQLClientDataset` the bidirectional navigation and ability to edit data.

Using the `TSQLClientDataset` is very much the same as using the standard `TClientDataset`. This information is covered in Chapter 21, "DataSnap Development."

Setting up an application using `TSQLClientDataset` is relatively simple. You'll need a `TSQLConnection`, a `TSQLClientDataset`, and a `TDatasource` component if you intend to display the data. An example is provided on the CD under the directory "`Editable`".

The `TSQLClientDataset.DBConnection` property must be set to the `TSQLConnection` component. Use the `CommandType` and `CommandText` properties as previously discussed for the `TSQLDataset` component.

Now, when running this application, you will note that it is navigable in both directions and it is possible to add, edit, and delete records from the dataset. However, when you close the dataset, none of your changes will persist because you are actually editing the in-memory buffer held by the `TSQLClientDataset` component. Any changes you make are cached in memory. To save your changes to the database server, you must call the `TSQLClientDataset.ApplyUpdates()` method. In the sample provided on the CD, we've added the `ApplyUpdates()` call to the `AfterDelete` and `AfterPost` events of the `TSQLClientDataset` component. This gives us a row-by-row update of server data. For further information on using `TSQLClientDataset`, refer to Chapter 21, or Chapters 32 and 34 in *Delphi 5 Developer's Guide,* which is provided on the CD.

NOTE

The `TSQLClientDataset` contains a `TSQLDataSet` and `TProvider` component. However, it doesn't expose all the properties and events of these two components. If access to these events are needed, you can use the regular `TClientDataset` and `TDatasetProvider` components in lieu of the `TSQLClientDataset` component.

Deploying dbExpress Applications

You can deploy dbExpress applications as a standalone executable or by providing the required dbExpress driver DLLs. To compile as a standalone, you'll need to add the units listed in Table 8.3 to the uses clause of your application as described in the Delphi online help.

TABLE 8.3   Units Required for dbExpress Standalone Application

Database unit	When to Include
dbExpInt	Applications connecting to InterBase databases
dbExpOra	Applications connecting to Oracle databases
dbExpDb2	Applications connecting to DB2 databases
dbExpMy	Applications connecting to MySQL databases
Crtl, MidasLib	Required by dbExpress executables that use client datasets such as `TSQLClientDataSet`

If you want to deploy the DLLs along with your application, you will have to deploy the DLLs specified in Table 8.4.

TABLE 8.4 DLLs to Deploy with a dbExpress Application

Database DLL	When to Deploy
dbexpint.dll	Applications connecting to InterBase databases
dbexpora.dll	Applications connecting to Oracle databases
dbexpdb2.dll	Applications connecting to DB2 databases
dbexpmy.dll	Applications connecting to MySQL databases
Midas.dll	Required by database applications that use client datasets

Summary

With dbExpress, it will be possible to develop robust and lightweight applications not otherwise possible using the BDE. Combined with the caching mechanisms built into TSQLClientDataset and TClientDataset, developers can develop complete cross-platform database applications.

8

DATABASE DEVELOPMENT WITH DBEXPRESS

Database Development with dbGo for ADO

IN THIS CHAPTER

Introduction to dbGo

This chapter will get you programming using Microsoft's ActiveX Data Objects (ADO), which are encapsulated by Delphi's dbGo for ADO components.

dbGo for ADO is represented by those components residing on the ADO tab of the Component Palette and provide data access through the ADO framework.

Overview of Microsoft's Universal Data Access Strategy

Microsoft's strategy for Universal Data Access is to provide access to a wide range of data through a single access model. This data might consist of both relational and non-relational data. Microsoft accomplishes this through the *Microsoft Data Access Components (MDAC)*, which comes installed in all Windows 2000 systems or can be downloaded from `http://www.microsoft.com/data/`.

MDAC is comprised of three elements: OLE DB, Microsoft ActiveX Data Objects (ADO), and Open Database Connectivity (ODBC).

Overview of OLE DB, ADO, and ODBC

OLE DB is a system level interface that uses COM to provide access to many sorts of data including relational and non-relational formats. It is possible to write code that directly interfaces with the OLE DB layer; although with ADO, it's much more complex and in most cases, unnecessary.

Many OLE DB providers are implementations of the OLE DB interfaces for providing access to specific vendor data. For instance, some OLE DB providers give access to data from Paradox, Oracle, Microsoft SQL Server, the Microsoft Jet Engine, and ODBC just to name a few.

ADO is the application level interface that developers use to access data. Whereas OLE DB consists of many (more than 60) different interfaces, ADO only consists of few with which developers must concern themselves. ADO actually uses OLE DB as the underlying technology for accessing data.

ODBC was the precursor to OLE DB and is still a very useful mechanism by which developers can gain access to relational, and some non-relational, data. In fact, one of the OLE DB providers goes through the ODBC layer.

Using dbGo for ADO

dbGo for ADO is made up of the set of Delphi components that encapsulate the ADO inter-faces and adapt them to the abstract way of doing database development that is common in Delphi.

The following sections will show you how to use these components. For this chapter, we will primarily use a Microsoft Access database through an ODBC provider.

Establishing an OLE DB Provider for ODBC

To establish a connection to the database, you must create an ODBC *Data Source Name (DSN)*. DSNs are similar to BDE aliases in that they allow you to provide system-level connec-tion points with connection information for databases centrally accessible on your system. To create DSNs you must use the ODBC Administrator that ships with Windows. On Windows 2000, this is accessed via Control Panel under the Administrative Tools subdirectory. When launching this application, you'll get the dialog box shown in Figure 9.1.

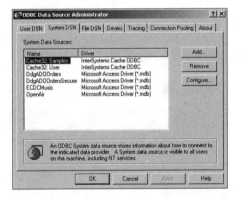

FIGURE 9.1
ODBC Administrator.

There are three types of DSNs:

- User DSN—User data sources are local to a computer and are accessible only when logged in as the current user.
- System DSN—System data sources are local to a computer and are accessible to any user. These are available systemwide to all users with appropriate privileges.
- File DSN—File data sources are available to all users who have the appropriate file dri-vers installed.

For this example, you will create a System DSN. First, launch the ODBC Administrator. Then, select the System DSN tab and click the Add button. This launches the Create New Data Source dialog box shown in Figure 9.2.

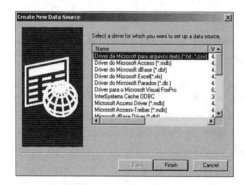

FIGURE 9.2

The Create New Data Source dialog box.

In this dialog box, you are presented a list of available drivers. The driver you need is the Microsoft Access Driver (*.mdb). When you click Finish, you will be shown the ODBC Microsoft Access Setup dialog box (see Figure 9.3).

FIGURE 9.3

The ODBC Microsoft Access Setup dialog box.

Here, you must provide a DSN that will be referenced from within your Delphi application. Again, this is similar to a BDE alias. You may also provide a description if you like. Next, you must select a database by clicking Select. This will launch a File Open dialog box from which you must select a valid *.mdb file. The file that you'll use is ddgADO.mdb and should be installed in the ..\Delphi Developer's Guide\Data directory where you installed the files from this book. When you click OK, your DSN will appear in the list of available System Data Sources. You can now click OK to finish working with the ODBC Administrator.

The Access Database

The database for which you just created a DSN is shown in Figure 9.4.

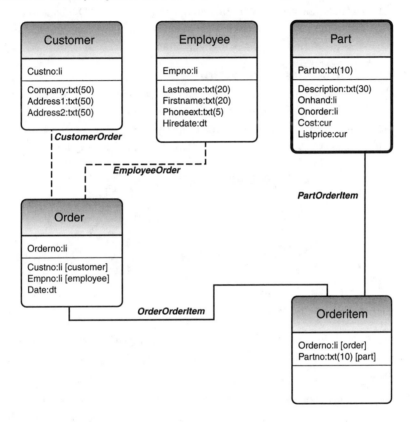

FIGURE 9.4

The sample database.

This is a simple order entry database that you'll use for the purpose of this chapter. There's nothing complicated about this database and frankly, it's not really complete. We simply put a few tables together with some meaningful relationships to show you how to use the dbGo for ADO components.

dbGo for ADO Components

All the dbGo for ADO components appear on the ADO tab of the Component Palette.

TADOConnection

TADOConnection encapsulates the ADO connection object. You use this component to connect to ADO provided data and through which other components hook to ADO data sources. This component is similar to the TDatabase component for BDE database connections. Similar to TDatabase, it handles functionality such as login and transactions.

Establishing a Database Connection

You can create a new application if you want or just read on to learn how to establish a database connection. You'll start with a form containing a TADOConnection component. You must modify the TADOConnection.ConnectionString property by clicking the ellipsis button on this property, which launches the ConnectionString Property Editor (see Figure 9.5).

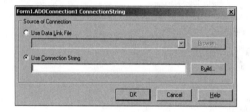

FIGURE 9.5

The TADOConnection.ConnectionString *Property Editor.*

The ConnectionString contains one or more arguments that ADO requires to establish a connection with the database. The arguments required depend on the type of OLE DB Provider that you are using.

The ConnectionString Property Editor asks for the connection source from either a Data Link File (file containing the connection string) or by building the connection string, which you can later save to a file. You've already created a DSN, so you'll build a connection string that references your DSN. Click the Build button to launch the Data Link Properties dialog box (see Figure 9.6).

The first page in this dialog box allows you to select an OLE DB provider. In this case, you'll select Microsoft OLE DB Provider For ODBC Drivers as shown in Figure 9.6. Clicking the Next button takes you to the Connection Page from which you can select our DSN in the drop-down list for a Data Source Name (see Figure 9.7).

You didn't provide any security for your database, so you should be able to click Text Connection to obtain a successful connection to your database. Click OK twice to return to the main form. The connection string that results is shown here:

```
Provider=MSDASQL.1;Persist Security Info=False;Data Source=DdgADOOrders
```

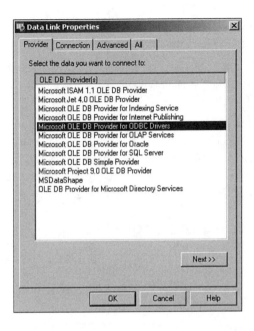

FIGURE 9.6

The Data Link Properties dialog box.

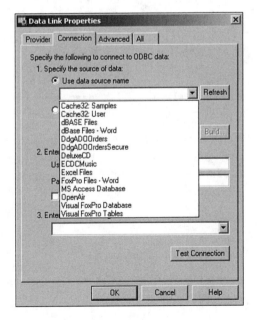

FIGURE 9.7

Selecting a data source name.

Had you used a different OLE DB provider, the connection string would have been completely different. For instance, had you used the Microsoft Jet 4.0 OLE DB Provider, your connection string would be the following:

```
Provider=Microsoft.Jet.OLEDB.4.0;Data Source="C:\Program Files\Delphi '
➥Developer's Guide\Data\ddgADO.mdb";Persist Security Info=False
```

At this point, you should be able to connect to our database by setting the TADO Connection.Connected property to True. You'll be presented with a Login prompt; simply click OK to connect without entering any login information. The next section will show you how to bypass this login dialog, or to replace it with your own. The example shown here is on the CD-ROM under the ADOConnect directory.

Bypassing/Replacing the Login Prompt

To bypass the Login prompt, you simply have to set the TADOConnection.LoginPrompt property to False. If there are no login settings, nothing else needs to be done. However, if a username and password are required, you'll need to do some extra work.

TIP

You can test this by adding a password to the database. You can use Microsoft Access to do this; however, to add a password, you must open the database exclusively, which is a setting in the Tools, Options, Advanced Page in Microsoft Access. Otherwise, you can simply use the ddgADOPW.mdb file provided on the CD-ROM. The password for this database is ddg—go figure.

For this exercise, we've created a new DSN, DdgADOOrdersSecure, which refers to our database, ddgADOPW.mdb. If you'd like to try this example, you must create this DSN.

To bypass the login prompt on a secure database, you must provide a valid username and password in the ConnectionString. This can be done manually or by invoking the ConnectionString property editor, adding the correct username and password, and checking the Allow Saving Password check box (see Figure 9.8).

Now the ConnectionString appears as follows:

```
Provider=MSDASQL.1;Password=ddg;Persist Security Info=True;
➥User ID=Admin;Data Source=DdgADOOrdersSecure
```

Note the presence of the password and username (ID). Now, you should be able to set the Connected property to True while the LoginPrompt property is False.

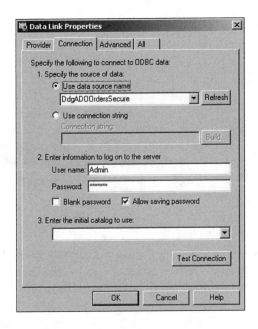

FIGURE 9.8
Adding a username and password to the ConnectionString.

Suppose, however, that you want to provide another login dialog. In this case, you'll want to remove the password from the ConnectionString property and create an event handler for the TADOConnection.OnWillConnect event such as that shown in Listing 9.1.

LISTING 9.1 OnWillConnect Event Handler

```
procedure TForm1.ADOConnection1WillConnect(Connection: TADOConnection;
  var ConnectionString, UserID, Password: WideString;
  var ConnectOptions: TConnectOption; var EventStatus: TEventStatus);
var
  vUserID,
  vPassword: String;
begin
  if InputQuery('Provide User name', 'Enter User name', vUserID) then
    if InputQuery('Provide Password', 'Enter Password', vPassword) then
    begin
      UserID := vUserID;
      Password := vPassword;
    end;
end;
```

9

DATABASE
DEVELOPMENT

This simplified exchange represents the hand off of the username and password. A production application will likely be slightly more complex.

Note

It might seem that the TADOConnection.OnLogin event is where you would provide a username and password to stay with the TDatabase paradigm. However, the TADOConnection.OnWillConnnect event wraps the standard ADO event for this purpose. OnLogin is provided to be used by the TDispatchConnection class, which has to do with providing multitier support.

TADOCommand

The TADOCommand component encapsulates the ADO Command object. This component is used for executing statements that don't return resultsets such as Data Definition Language (DDL) or SQL statements. You would use this component for executing SQL statements such as INSERT, DELETE, or UPDATE. For instance, you'll find an example on the CD-ROM under the directory ADOCommand. This is a simple example that illustrates how to insert and delete a record from the employee table by using the INSERT and DELETE SQL statements. In the example, the TADOCommand.CommandText for the component to insert a record contains the SQL statement:

```
DELETE FROM EMPLOYEE WHERE
FirstName='Rob' AND LastName='Smith
```

The CommandText for the inserting TADOCommand component contains the SQL statement:

```
INSERT INTO EMPLOYEE (
LastName,
FirstName,
PhoneExt,
HireDate)

VALUES
(
'Smith',
 'Rob',
  '123',
  '12/28/1998')
```

To run the SQL statement, you would invoke the TADOCommand.Execute() method.

TADODataset

The TADODataset component retrieves data from one or more tables in a database. This component can also run SQL statements that don't return resultsets and can run user-defined stored procedures.

Much like the TADOCommand component, TADODataset can execute statements such as INSERT, DELETE, and UPDATE. However, TADODataset can also retrieve resultsets by issuing the SELECT statement. The example on the CD-ROM named ADODataset illustrates the use of the TADODataSet component. This example performs the following SELECT statement against the database:

```
SELECT * FROM Customer
```

This statement returns the entire resultset from the Customer table. You can also use SQL filtering schemes such as the WHERE clause if you need to.

In the example, we've connected a TDBNavigator component to the TADODataSet component to illustrate the ability to edit and navigate the component.

Later in this chapter, we'll further illustrate the use of TADODataSet in a sample order entry application.

BDE-Like Dataset Components

The ADO tab in the Component Palette contains three components that have been included to make transitioning from BDE applications to ADO applications easier. These components are TADOTable, TADOQuery, and TADOStoredProc. There's no reason that you can't use only the TADODataSet component when developing ADO applications. However, if it makes it easier, you can use these alternative components that are very similar to their BDE counterparts: TTable, TQuery, and TStoredProc.

TADOTable

TADOTable is a direct descendant of TCustomADODataSet. TADOTable allows you to work on a single table in the database. It operates very similar to the BDE TTable component. In fact, TADOTable adds a drop-down TableName property. Some advantages to a table type of dataset is that they support indexes. Indexes allow for sorting and quick searching. This is particularly true with non-SQL databases such as Microsoft Access. However, when using an SQL type of database, it is best to sort, filter, and so on through the SQL language. To find out more about table-type datasets, look up "Overview of ADO components" in the Delphi online help.

CAUTION

According to the Delphi online help, one of the advantages for using table-type datasets is the ease in emptying tables. The example given uses the `TCustomADODataSet.DeleteRecords()` method as the means to do this. However, a problem exists in the ADO `RecordSet` object that prevents this from working. In fact, a call to

```
TCustomADODataSet.Supports([coDelete])
```

will return `True`, yet the `DeleteRecords()` call will still fail with an exception. Therefore, to empty a table, you must use a `DELETE FROM TableName` statement, or you must loop through each record and delete it individually.

The example on the CD-ROM, `ADOTableIndex`, illustrates the use of the `TADOTable` component with an index. Additionally, it illustrates how to perform a search on the table using the `TADOTable.Locate()` function. Listing 9.2 shows partial source for this demo.

LISTING 9.2   Using the `TADOTable` Component

```
procedure TForm1.FormCreate(Sender: TObject);
var
  i: integer;
begin
  adotblCustomer.Open;
  for i := 0 to adotblCustomer.FieldCount - 1 do
    ListBox1.Items.Add(adotblCustomer.Fields[i].FieldName);
end;

procedure TForm1.ListBox1Click(Sender: TObject);
begin
  adotblCustomer.IndexFieldNames := ListBox1.Items[ListBox1.ItemIndex];
end;

procedure TForm1.Button1Click(Sender: TObject);
begin
  adotblCustomer.Locate('Company', Edit1.Text, [loPartialKey]);
end;
```

In the `FormCreate()` event handler, you open the table and populate a `TListBox` control with all the table's field names. Then, in the `TListBox.OnClick` event handler, you set the `TADOTable.IndexFieldName` property to the field name on which we want to sort out table.

Finally, the `Button1Click()` event illustrates performing a search on the table using the `Locate()` method.

`TADOTable` is useful for those accustomed to using a `TTable` component. However, when using SQL databases, it is more efficient to use either the `TADODataSet` or `TADOQuery` components.

TADOQuery

`TADOQuery`, also a descendant of `TCustomADODataSet`, is very similar to `TADODataSet`. `TADOQuery` has a SQL property into which you would place your SQL statement. On the `TADODataSet` component, this would go in the `CommandText` property as long as `TADODataSet.CommandType` is set to `cmdText`.

We won't cover this component in great depth because most everything that applies to the `TADODataSet` component also applies to `TADOQuery`.

TADOStoredProc

The `TADOStoredProc` component allows you to use a stored procedure that exists on a database server. This is no different from using the `TADOCommand` component with its `CommandType` property set to `cmdStoredProc`. Its use is pretty much the same as `TStoredProc` discussed in Chapter 29, "Developing Client/Server Applications" of *Delphi 5 Developer's Guide*, which you'll find on the CD-ROM.

Transaction Processing

ADO supports transaction processing, and this is handled through the `TADOConnection` component. As an example, the code in Listing 9.3 is taken from our simple order entry application.

LISTING 9.3   Transaction Processing with `TADOConnection`

```
procedure TMainForm.Button1Click(Sender: TObject);
begin
  if TNewOrderForm.Execute then
  begin
    ADOConnection1.BeginTrans;
    try
      // First Create an Orders Record
      adodsOrders.Insert;
      adodsOrders.FieldByName('CustNo').Value :=
        adodsCustomer.FieldByName('CustNo').Value;
      adodsOrders.FieldByName('EmpNo').Value :=
        adodsEmployee.FieldByName('EmpNo').Value;
      adodsOrders.FieldByName('Date').Value := Date;
```

LISTING 9.3   Continued

```
      ShowMessage(IntToStr(adodsOrders.FieldByName('OrderNo').AsInteger));
      adodsOrders.Post;

      // Now create the Order Line Items.

      cdsPartList.First;
      while not cdsPartList.Eof do
      begin
        adocmdInsertOrderItem.Parameters.ParamByName('iOrderNo').Value :=
          adodsOrders.FieldByName('OrderNo').Value;
        adocmdInsertOrderItem.Parameters.ParamByName('iPartNo').Value :=
          cdsPartListPartNo.Value;
        adocmdInsertOrderItem.Execute;
        cdsPartList.Next;
      end;
      adodsOrderItemList.Requery([]);
      ADOConnection1.CommitTrans;
      cdsPartList.EmptyDataSet;
    except
      ADOConnection1.RollbackTrans;
      raise;
    end;
  end;
end;
```

The method in Listing 9.3 is responsible for creating a customer order. There are two parts to this transaction. First, the order record must be created in the Order table. Second, the order line items must be added to the OrderItem table. Because there are two table updates, it makes sense to place this into a single transaction.

Here is a skeleton of our transaction:

```
begin
    ADOConnection1.BeginTrans;
    try
      // First Create an Orders Record
      // Now create the Order Line Items.
      ADOConnection1.CommitTrans;
    except
      ADOConnection1.RollbackTrans;
      raise;
    end;
  end;
end;
```

You'll see that we encapsulate our transaction inside of a `try...except` block. `ADO Connection1.BeginTrans()` method starts the transaction. The `ADOConnection1.Commit Trans()` method commits the transaction. If there are any failures, an exception occurs and the `ADOConnection1.RollbackTrans()` method will roll back any changes that were made to any tables.

Summary

This chapter got you started working with Borland's dbGo for ADO components. These components give you the ability to use Microsoft's ADO technology for accessing both relational and non-relational data.

Component-Based Development

IN THIS PART

Component Architecture: VCL and CLX

IN THIS CHAPTER

Few will recall Borland's first *Object Windows Library (OWL)*, which was introduced with Turbo Pascal for Windows. OWL ushered in a drastic simplification over traditional Windows programming. OWL objects automated and streamlined many tedious tasks you otherwise were required to code yourself. No longer did you have to write huge case statements to capture messages or big chunks of code to manage Windows classes; OWL did this for you. On the other hand, you had to learn a new programming methodology—object-oriented programming.

Then, with Delphi 1, Borland introduced *Visual Component Library (VCL)*. The VCL was based on an object model similar to OWL's in principle but radically different in implementation. The VCL in Delphi 6 is pretty much the same as its predecessors in all previous versions of Delphi.

With Delphi 6, Borland, once again, introduced a new technology, *Component Library for Cross-Platform (CLX)*. According to Borland, CLX is "the next-generation component library and framework for developing native Linux and Windows applications and reusable components."

Both the VCL and CLX are designed specifically to work within Delphi's visual environment. Instead of creating a window or dialog box and adding its behavior in code, you modify the behavioral and visual characteristics of components as you design your program visually.

The level of knowledge required about the VCL/CLX really depends on how you use them. First, you must realize that there are two types of Delphi developers: applications developers and visual component writers. *Applications developers* create complete applications by interacting with the Delphi visual environment (a concept nonexistent in many other frameworks). These people use the VCL/CLX to create their GUI and other elements of their application such as database connectivity. *Component writers*, on the other hand, expand the existing VCL/CLX by developing more components. Such components are made available through third-party companies.

Whether you plan to create applications with Delphi or to create Delphi components, understanding the VCL/CLX is essential. An applications developer should know which properties, events, and methods are available for each component. Additionally, it's advantageous to fully understand the object model inherent in a Delphi application that's provided by the VCL/CLX. A common problem we see with Delphi developers is that they tend to fight the tool—a symptom of not understanding it completely. Component writers take this knowledge one step further to determine whether to write a new component or to extend an existing one by knowing how VCL/CLX works internally: how they handle messages, notifications, component ownership, parenting/ownership issues, property editors, and so on.

This chapter introduces you to the VCL/CLX. It discusses the component hierarchy and explains the purpose of the key levels within the hierarchy. It also discusses the purposes of the common properties, methods, and events that appear at the different component levels. Finally, we complete this chapter by covering *Runtime Type Information (RTTI)*.

More on the New CLX

CLX, the new cross platform library, is actually composed of four pieces. These are explained in Table 10.1.

TABLE 10.1 CLX Parts (from Delphi 6 Online Help)

Part	Description
VisualCLX	Native cross-platform GUI components and graphics. The components in this area might differ on Linux and Windows.
DataCLX	Client data-access components. The components in this area are a subset of the local, client/server, and n-tier based on client datasets. The code is the same on Linux and Windows.
NetCLX	Internet components including Apache DSO and CGI Web Broker. These are the same on Linux and Windows.
RTL	Runtime Library up to and including Classes.pas. The code is the same on Linux and Windows. Under Linux, this file is `BaseRTL`.

VisualCLX sits on top of the Qt framework from Trolltech. Qt is pronounced "cute" by most people, although Trolltech will tell you that it's pronounced "kyu-tee." This framework currently runs under Linux and Windows. VisualCLX is discussed in this chapter, and we cover the other CLX elements in other chapters.

What Is a Component?

Components are the building blocks developers use to design the user interface and provide some non-visual capability to their applications. As far as applications developers are concerned, a component is something developers get from the Component Palette and place on their forms. From there, they can manipulate the various properties and add event handlers to give the component a specific appearance or behavior. From the perspective of a component writer, components are objects in Object Pascal code. These objects can encapsulate the behavior of elements provided by the system (such as the standard Windows controls). Other objects can introduce entirely new visual or non-visual elements; in which case a component's code makes up the entire behavior of the component.

The complexity of components varies widely. Some components are simple; others encapsulate elaborate tasks. There's no limit to what a component can do or be made up of. You can have a simple component such as a `TLabel`, or you can have a much more complex component that encapsulates the complete functionality of a spreadsheet.

The key to understanding the VCL/CLX is to know what types of components exist. You should understand the common elements of components. You should also understand the component hierarchy and the purpose of each level within the hierarchy. The following sections provide this information.

Component Hierarchy

Figures 10.1 and 10.2 show the VCL and CLX hierarchies, respectively. You'll see that there are many similarities between both the VCL and CLX.

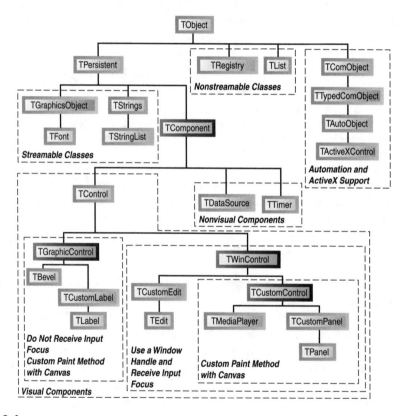

FIGURE 10.1

The VCL hierarchy.

Two types of components exist: nonvisual and visual.

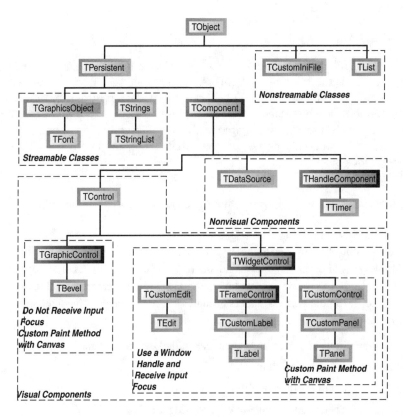

FIGURE 10.2
The CLX hierarchy.

Nonvisual Components

Nonvisual components aren't visible to the end user. These components encapsulate behavior and allow the developer to modify certain characteristics of that component through the Object Inspector at design time by modifying its properties and providing event handlers for its events. Examples of such components are TOpenDialog, TTable, and TTimer. As Figures 10.1 and 10.2 indicate, these nonvisual components descend directly from TComponent.

Visual Components

Visual components, as the name implies, are components that the end user sees. Visual components add visibility and behavior, but not necessarily interaction. These components directly descend from TControl. In fact, TControl is the class that introduces properties and methods that have to do with visibility such as Top, Left, Color, and so forth.

> **NOTE**
>
> You'll often see the terms *component* and *control* used interchangeably, although they're not always the same. A *control* refers to a visual user-interface element. In Delphi, controls are always components because they descend from the TComponent class. *Components* are the objects whose basic behavior allows them to appear on the Component Palette and be manipulated in the form designer. Components are of the type TComponent and aren't always controls—that is, they aren't always visual user-interface elements.

Visual components come in two flavors—those that can have focus and those that cannot.

Visible Controls That Gain Focus

Certain types of controls gain user focus. By this, we mean that the user can manipulate such controls. These types of controls are descendants of TWinControl (VCL) or TWidgetControl (CLX). TWinControl descendants are wrappers around Windows controls, whereas TWidgetControl descendants are wrappers around Qt screen objects. Characteristics of these controls are as follows:

- They can get focus and do things such as handle keyboard events.
- The user can interact with them.
- They can be containers (parents) to other controls.
- They have an associated handle (VCL) or widget (CLX).

> **NOTE**
>
> Both TWinControl and TWidgetControl have a property named Handle. TWinControl's Handle refers to the underlying Windows Handle for the control. TWidgetControl's Handle refers to the underlying Qt object pointer (widget). Both are named Handle for backward compatibility and cross compilation between CLX and VCL applications.

In Chapters 11–14, you'll learn much more about TWinControls and TWidgetControls as you learn how to create components for both VCL and CLX.

> ## Handles
>
> *Handles* are 32-bit numbers issued by Win32 that refer to certain object instances. The term *objects* here refers to Win32 objects, not Delphi objects. There are different types of objects under Win32: kernel objects, user objects, and GDI objects. Kernel objects apply to items such as events, file-mapping objects, and processes. User objects refer to window objects such as edit controls, list boxes, and buttons. GDI objects refer to bitmaps, brushes, fonts, and so on.
>
> In the Win32 environment, every window has a unique handle. Many Windows API functions require a handle so that they know the window on which they are to perform the operation. Delphi encapsulates much of the Win32 API and performs handle management. If you want to use a Windows API function that requires a window handle, you must use descendants of `TWinControl` and `TCustomControl`, which both have a `Handle` property.

Visible Controls That Do Not Gain Focus

Other controls, although visible, don'tave the same characteristics as Windowed controls. These controls are for visibility only and are frequently referred to as *graphical* controls, which descend directly from `TGraphicControl` (see Figures 10.1 and 10.2).

Unlike windowed controls, graphical controls don't receive the input focus from the user. They are useful when you want to display something to the user but don't want the component to use up resources such as windowed controls. Graphical controls don't use Windows resources because they require no window handle (or CLX Gadget), which is also the reason they can't get focus. Examples of graphical controls are `TLabel` and `TShape`. Such controls can't serve as containers either; that is, they can't parent other controls placed on top of them. Other examples of graphical controls are `TImage`, `TBevel`, and `TPaintBox`.

The Component Structure

As we mentioned earlier, components are Object Pascal classes that encapsulate the functionality and behavior of elements developers use to add visual and behavioral characteristics to their programs. All components have a certain structure. The following sections discuss the makeup of Delphi components.

> **NOTE**
>
> Understand the distinction between a component and a class. A *component* is a class that can be manipulated within the Delphi environment. A *class* is an Object Pascal structure, as explained in Chapter 2, "The Object Pascal Language."

10

COMPONENT
ARCHITECTURE:
VCL AND CLX

Properties

Chapter 2 introduced you to properties. Properties give the user an interface to a component's internal storage fields. Using properties, the component user can modify or read storage field values. Typically, the user doesn't have direct access to component storage fields because they're declared in the private section of a component's class definition.

Properties: Storage Field Accessors

Properties provide access to storage fields by either accessing the storage fields directly or through *access methods*. Take a look at the following property definition:

```
TCustomEdit = class(TWinControl)
private
  FMaxLength: Integer;
protected
  procedure SetMaxLength(Value: Integer);
...
published
  property MaxLength: Integer read FMaxLength write SetMaxLength default 0;
...
end;
```

The property MaxLength is the access to the storage field FMaxLength. The parts of a property definition consist of the property name, the property type, a read declaration, a write declaration, and an optional default value. The read declaration specifies how the component's storage fields are read. The MaxLength property directly reads the value from the FMaxLength storage field. The write declaration specifies the method by which the storage fields are assigned values. For the property MaxLength, the writer access method SetMaxLength() is used to assign the value to the storage field FMaxLength. A property can also contain a reader access method; in which case the MaxLength property would be declared as this:

```
property MaxLength: Integer read GetMaxLength write SetMaxLength default 0;
```

The reader access method GetMaxLength() would be declared as follows:

```
function GetMaxLength: Integer;
```

Property Access Methods

Access methods take a single parameter of the same type as the property. The purpose of the writer access method is to assign the value of the parameter to the internal storage field to which the property refers. The reason for using the method layer to assign values is to protect the storage field from receiving erroneous data as well as to perform various side effects, if required. For example, examine the implementation of the following SetMaxLength() method:

```
procedure TCustomEdit.SetMaxLength(Value: Integer);
begin
  if FMaxLength <> Value then
  begin
    FMaxLength := Value;
    if HandleAllocated then SendMessage(Handle, EM_LIMITTEXT, Value, 0);
  end;
end;
```

This method first checks to verify that the component user isn't attempting to assign the same value as that which the property already holds. If not, it makes the assignment to the internal storage field FMaxLength and then calls the SendMessage() function to pass the EM_LIMITTEXT Windows message to the window that the TCustomEdit encapsulates. This message limits the amount of text that a user can enter into an edit control. Calling SendMessage() in the property's writer access method is known as a *side effect* when assigning property values.

Side effects are any actions affected by the assignment of a value to a property. In assigning a value to the MaxLength property of TCustomEdit, the side effect is that the encapsulated edit control is given an entry limit. Side effects can be much more sophisticated than this.

One key advantage to providing access to a component's internal storage fields through properties is that the component writer can change the implementation of the field access without affecting the behavior for the component user.

A reader access method, for example, can change the type of the returned value to something different from the type of the storage field to which the property refers.

Another fundamental reason for the use of properties is to make modifications available to them during design time. When a property appears in the published section of a component's declaration, it also appears in the Object Inspector so that the component user can make modifications to this property.

You learn more about properties and how to create them and their access methods in Chapters 11, "VCL Component Building," and 13, "CLX Component Development," for VCL and CLX, respectively.

Types of Properties

The standard rules that apply to Object Pascal data types apply to properties as well. The important point about properties is that their types also determine how they're edited in the Object Inspector. Properties can be of the types shown in Table 10.2. For more detailed information, look up "properties" in the online help.

TABLE 10.2 Property Types

Property Type	Object Inspector Treatment
Simple	Numeric, character, and string properties appear in the Object Inspector as numbers, characters, and strings, respectively. The user can type and edit the value of the property directly.
Enumerated	Properties of enumerated types (including Boolean) display the value as defined in the source code. The user can cycle through the possible values by double-clicking the Value column. There's also a drop-down list that shows all possible values of the enumerated type.
Set	Properties of set types appear in the Object Inspector grouped as a set. By expanding the set, the user can treat each element of the set as a Boolean value: True if the element is included in the set and False if it's not included.
Object	Properties that are themselves objects often have their own property editors. However, if the object that's a property also has published properties, the Object Inspector allows the user to expand the list of object properties and edit them individually. Object properties must descend from TPersistent.
Array	Array properties must have their own property editors. The Object Inspector has no built-in support for editing array properties.

Methods

Because components are objects, they can therefore have methods. You've already seen information on object methods in Chapter 2 (that information is not repeated here). The later section "The Visual Component Hierarchy" describes some of the key methods of the different component levels in the component hierarchy.

Events

Events are occurrences of an action, typically a system action such as a button control click or a keypress on a keyboard. Components contain special properties called *events*; component users can plug code into the event (called *event handlers*) that executes when the event is invoked.

Plugging Code into Events at Design Time

If you look at the events page of a TEdit component, you'll find events such as OnChange, OnClick, and OnDblClick. To component writers, events are really pointers to methods. When users of a component assign code to an event, they create an *event handler*. For example, when you double-click an event in the Object Inspector's events page for a component, Delphi generates a method to which you add your code, such as the following code for the OnClick event of a TButton component:

```
TForm1 = class(TForm)
  Button1: Tbutton;
  procedure Button1Click(Sender: TObject);
end;
...
procedure TForm1.Button1Click(Sender: TObject);
begin
  { Event code goes here }
end;
```

This code is generated by Delphi.

Plugging Code into Events at Runtime

It becomes clear how events are method pointers when you assign an event handler to an event programmatically. For example, to link your own event handler to an OnClick event of a TButton component, you first declare and define the method you intend to assign to the button's OnClick event. This method might belong to the form that owns the TButton component, as shown here:

```
TForm1 = class(TForm)
  Button1: TButton;
...
private
  MyOnClickEvent(Sender: TObject); // Your method declaration
end;
...
{ Your method definition below }
procedure TForm1.MyOnClickEvent(Sender: TObject);
begin
  { Your code goes here }
end;
```

The preceding example shows a user-defined method called MyOnClickEvent() that serves as the event handler for Button1.OnClick. The following line shows how you assign this method to the Button1.OnClick event in code, which is usually done in the form's OnCreate event handler:

```
procedure TForm1.FormCreate(Sender: TObject);
begin
  Button1.OnClick := MyOnClickEvent;
end;
```

This technique can be used to add different event handlers to events, based on various conditions in your code. Additionally, you can disable an event handler from an event by assigning nil to the event, as shown here:

```
Button1.OnClick := nil;
```

Assigning event handlers at runtime is essentially what happens when you create an event handler through Delphi's Object Inspector—except that Delphi generates the method declaration. You can't just assign any method to a particular event handler. Because event properties are method pointers, they have specific method signatures, depending on the type of event. For example, an OnMouseDown method is of the type TMouseEvent, a procedure definition shown here:

```
TMouseEvent = procedure (Sender: TObject; Button: TMouseButton; Shift:
  TShiftState; X, Y: Integer) of object;
```

Therefore, the methods that become event handlers for certain events must follow the same signature as the event types. They must contain the same type, number, and order of parameters.

Earlier, we said that events are properties. Similar to data properties, events refer to private data fields of a component. This data field is of the procedure type, such as TMouseEvent. Examine this code:

```
TControl = class(TComponent)
private
  FOnMouseDown: TMouseEvent;
protected
  property OnMouseDown: TMouseEvent read FOnMouseDown write FOnMouseDown;
public
end;
```

Recall the discussion of properties and how they refer to private data fields of a component. You can see how events, being properties, refer to private method pointer fields of a component.

You learn more about creating events and event handlers in Chapters 11 and 13.

Streamability

One characteristic of components is that they must have the capability to be streamed. *Streaming* is a way to store a component and information regarding its properties' values to a file. Delphi's streaming capabilities take care of all this for you. In fact, the DFM file created by Delphi is nothing more than a resource file containing the streamed information on the form and its components as an RCDATA resource. As a component writer, however, you must sometimes go beyond what Delphi can do automatically. The streaming mechanism of Delphi is explained in greater depth in Chapter 12, "Advanced VCL Component Building."

Ownership

Components have the capability of owning other components. A component's owner is specified by its `Owner` property. When a component owns other components, it's responsible for freeing the components it owns when it's destroyed. Typically, the form owns all components that appear on it. When you place a component on a form in the form designer, the form automatically becomes the component's owner. When you create a component at runtime, you must pass the ownership of the component to the component's `Create` constructor; it's assigned to the new component's `Owner` property. The following line shows how to pass the form's implicit `Self` variable to a `TButton.Create()` constructor, thus making the form the owner of the newly created component:

```
MyButton := TButton.Create(self);
```

When the form is destroyed, the `TButton` instance to which `MyButton` refers is also destroyed. This is handled internally in the VCL. Essentially, the form iterates through the components referred to by its `Components` array property (explained in more detail shortly) and destroys them.

It's possible to create a component without an owner by passing `nil` to the component's `Create()` method. However, when this is done, it's your responsibility to destroy the component programmatically. The following code shows this technique:

```
MyTable := TTable.Create(nil)
try
  { Do stuff with MyTable }
finally
  MyTable.Free;
end;
```

When using this technique, you should use a `try..finally` block to ensure that you free up any allocated resources if an exception is raised. You wouldn't use this technique except in specific circumstances when it's impossible to pass an owner to the component.

Another property associated with ownership is the `Components` property. The `Components` property is an array property that maintains a list of all components belonging to a component. For example, to loop through all the components on a form to show their classnames, execute the following code:

```
var
  i: integer;
begin
  for i := 0 to ComponentCount - 1 do
    ShowMessage(Components[i].ClassName);
end;
```

10

Obviously, you'll probably perform a more meaningful operation on these components. The preceding code merely illustrates the technique.

Parenthood

Not to be confused with ownership is the concept of *parenthood*. Components can be *parents* to other components. Only windowed components such as TWinControl and TWidgetControl descendants can serve as parents to other components. Parent components are responsible for calling the child component methods to force them to draw themselves. Parent components are responsible for the proper painting of child components. A component's parent is specified through its Parent property.

A component's parent doesn't necessarily have to be its owner. It's perfectly legal for a component to have different parents and owners.

The Visual Component Hierarchy

Remember from Chapter 2 that the abstract class TObject is the base class from which all classes descend (see Figures 10.1 and 10.2).

As a component writer, you don't descend your components directly from TObject. The VCL already has TObject class descendants from which your new components can be derived. These existing classes provide much of the functionality you require for your own components. Only when you create noncomponent classes do your classes descend from TObject.

TObject's Create() and Destroy() methods are responsible for allocating and deallocating memory for an object instance. In fact, the TObject.Create() constructor returns a reference to the object being created. TObject has several functions that return useful information about a specific object.

The VCL uses most of TObject's methods internally. You can obtain useful information about an instance of a TObject or TObject descendant such as the instance's class type, classname, and ancestor classes.

CAUTION

Use TObject.Free instead of TObject.Destroy. The free method calls destroy for you but first checks to see whether the object is nil before calling destroy. This method ensures that you won't generate an exception by attempting to destroy an invalid object.

The TPersistent Class

The TPersistent class descends directly from TObject. The special characteristic of TPersistent is that objects descending from it can read their properties from and write them to a stream after they're created. Because all components are descendants of TPersistent, they are all streamable. TPersistent defines no special properties or events, although it does define some methods that are useful to both the component user and writer.

TPersistent Methods

Table 10.3 lists some methods of interest defined by the TPersistent class.

TABLE 10.3 Methods of the TPersistent Class

Method	Purpose
Assign()	This public method allows a component to assign to itself the data associated with another component.
AssignTo()	This protected method is where TPersistent descendants must implement the VCL definition for AssignTo(). TPersistent raises an exception when this method is called. AssignTo() is where a component can assign its data values to another instance or class—the reverse of Assign().
DefineProperties()	This protected method allows component writers to define how the component stores extra or unpublished properties. This method is typically used to provide a way for a component to store data that's not of a simple data type, such as binary data.

The streamability of components is described in greater depth in Chapter 12, "Working with Files," from *Delphi 5 Developer's Guide* on the CD-ROM. For now, it's enough to know that components can be stored and retrieved from a disk file by means of streaming.

The TComponent Class

The TComponent class descends directly from TPersistent. TComponent's special characteristics are that its properties can be manipulated at design time through the Object Inspector and that it can own other components.

Nonvisual components also descend from TComponent so that they inherit the capability to be manipulated at design time. A good example of a nonvisual TComponent descendant is the TTimer component. TTimer components aren't visual controls, but they are still available on the Component Palette.

TComponent defines several properties and methods of interest, as described in the following sections.

TComponent Properties

The properties defined by TComponent and their purposes are shown in Table 10.4.

TABLE 10.4 The Special Properties of TComponent

Property Name	Purpose
Owner	Points to the component's owner.
ComponentCount	Holds the number of components that the component owns.
ComponentIndex	The position of this component in its owner's list of components. The first component in this list has the value 0.
Components	A property array containing a list of components owned by this component. The first component in this list has the value 0.
ComponentState	This property holds the current state of a component of the type TComponentState. Additional information about TComponentState can be found in the online help and in Chapter 11.
ComponentStyle	Governs various behavioral characteristics of the component. csInheritable and csCheckPropAvail are two values that can be assigned to this property; both values are explained in the online help.
Name	Holds the name of a component.
Tag	An integer property that has no defined meaning. This property shouldn't be used by component writers—it's intended to be used by application writers. Because this value is an integer type, pointers to data structures—or even object instances—can be referred to by this property.
DesignInfo	Used by the form designer. Do not access this property.

TComponent Methods

TComponent defines several methods having to do with its capacity to own other components and to be manipulated on the form designer.

TComponent defines the component's Create() constructor, which was discussed earlier in this chapter. This constructor is responsible for creating an instance of the component and giving it an owner based on the parameter passed to it. Unlike TObject.Create(), TComponent.Create() is virtual. TComponent descendants that implement a constructor must declare the Create() constructor with the override directive. Although you can declare other constructors on a component class, `TComponent.Create()` is the only constructor VCL will use to create an instance of the class at design time and at runtime when loading the component from a stream.

The `TComponent.Destroy()` destructor is responsible for freeing the component and any resources allocated by the component.

The `TComponent.Destroying()` method is responsible for setting a component and its owned components to a state indicating that they are being destroyed; the `TComponent.Destroy Components()` method is responsible for destroying the components. You probably won't have to deal with these methods.

The `TComponent.FindComponent()` method is handy when you want to refer to a component for which you know only the name. Suppose you know that the main form has a `TEdit` component named `Edit1`. When you don't have a reference to this component, you can retrieve a pointer to its instance by executing the following code:

```
EditInstance := FindComponent.('Edit1');
```

In this example, `EditInstance` is a `TEdit` type. `FindComponent()` will return `nil` if the name doesn't exist.

The `TComponent.GetParentComponent()` method retrieves an instance to the component's parent component. This method can return `nil` if there is no parent to a component.

The `TComponent.HasParent()` method returns a Boolean value indicating whether the component has a parent component. Note that this method doesn't refer to whether this component has an owner.

The `TComponent.InsertComponent()` method adds a component so that it's owned by the calling component; `TComponent.RemoveComponent()` removes an owned component from the calling component. You wouldn't normally use these methods because they're called automatically by the component's `Create()` constructor and `Destroy()` destructor.

The `TControl` Class

The `TControl` class defines many properties, methods, and events commonly used by visual components. For example, `TControl` introduces the capability for a control to display itself. The `TControl` class includes position properties such as `Top` and `Left` as well as size properties such as `Width` and `Height`, which hold the horizontal and vertical sizes. Other properties include `ClientRect`, `ClientWidth`, and `ClientHeight`.

`TControl` also introduces properties regarding appearances and accessibility, such as `Visible`, `Enabled`, and `Color`. You can even specify a font for the text of a `TControl` through its `Font` property. This text is provided through the `TControl` properties `Text` and `Caption`.

TControl also introduces some standard events, such as the mouse events OnClick, OnDblClick, OnMouseDown, OnMouseMove, and OnMouseUp. It also introduces drag events such as OnDragOver, OnDragDrop, and OnEndDrag.

TControl isn't very useful at the TControl level. You'll never create descendants of TControl.

Another concept introduced by TControl is that it can have a parent component. Although TControl might have a parent, its parent must be a TWinControl (VCL) or a TWidgetControl (CLX). Parent controls must be *windowed* controls. The TControl introduces the Parent property.

Most of Delphi's controls are derived from TControl's descendants: TWinControl and TWidgetControl.

The TWinControl and TWidgetControl

Standard controls descend from the classes TWinControl for VCL controls and TWidgetControl for CLX controls. These controls are the user-interface objects you see in most applications. Items such as edit controls, list boxes, combo boxes, and buttons are examples of these controls. Because Delphi encapsulates the behavior of standard controls instead of using Windows or Qt API level functions to manipulate them, you use the properties provided by each of the various control components.

The three basic characteristics of these controls are that they have a Windows handle, can receive input focus, and can be parents to other controls. CLX controls don't have a window handle; rather, they have an object pointer that accomplished the same thing. You'll find that the properties, methods, and events belonging to these controls support focus changing, keyboard events, drawing of controls, and other necessary functions.

An applications developer primarily uses TWinControl/TWidgetControl descendants. A component writer must understand these controls and their descendants in much greater depth.

TWinControl/TWidgetControl Properties

TWinControl and TWidgetControl define several properties applicable to changing the focus and appearance of the control. In the remaining text, we'll refer only to TWinControl although it will also be applicable to TWidgetControl.

The TWinControl.Brush property is used to draw the patterns and shapes of the control (See Chapter 8, "Graphics Programming with GDI and Fonts," in *Delphi 5 Developer's Guide* on this book's CD-ROM.)

TWinControl.Controls is an array property that maintains a list of all controls to which the calling TWinControl is a parent.

The `TWinControl.ControlCount` property holds the count of controls to which it is a parent.

`TWinControl.Ctl3D` is a property that specifies whether to draw the control using a three-dimensional appearance.

The `TWinControl.Handle` property corresponds to the handle of the Windows object that the `TWinControl` encapsulates. This is the handle you would pass to Win32 API functions requiring a window handle parameter.

`TWinControl.HelpContext` holds a help context number that corresponds to a help screen in a help file. This is used to provide context-sensitive help for individual controls.

`TWinControl.Showing` indicates whether a control is visible.

The `TWinControl.TabStop` property holds a Boolean value to determine whether a user can tab to the said control. The `TWinControl.TabOrder` property specifies where in the parent's list of tabbed controls the control exists.

TWinControl Methods

The `TWinControl` component also offers several methods that have to do with window creation, focus control, event dispatching, and positioning. There are too many methods to discuss in depth in this chapter; however, they're all documented in Delphi's online help. We'll list only those methods of particular interest in the following paragraphs.

Methods that relate to window creation, re-creation, and destruction apply mainly to component writers and are discussed in Chapter 11. These methods are `CreateParams()`, `CreateWnd()`, `CreateWindowHandle()`, `DestroyWnd()`, `DestroyWindowHandle()`, and `RecreateWnd()` for VCL. For CLX's `TWidgetControl`, these methods are `CreateWidget()`, `DestroyWidget()`, `CreateHandle()`, and `DestroyHandle()`.

Methods having to do with window focusing, positioning, and alignment are `CanFocus()`, `Focused()`, `AlignControls()`, `EnableAlign()`, `DisableAlign()`, and `ReAlign()`.

TWinControl Events

`TWinControl` introduces events for keyboard interaction and focus change. Keyboard events are `OnKeyDown`, `OnKeyPress`, and `OnKeyUp`. Focus-change events are `OnEnter` and `OnExit`. All these events are documented in Delphi's online help.

The TGraphicControl Class

`TGraphicControls`, unlike `TWinControls`, don't have a window handle and therefore can't receive input focus. They also can't be parents to other controls. `TGraphicControls` are used when you want to display something to the user on the form, but you don't want this control to function as a regular user-input control. The advantage of `TGraphicControls` is that they don't request a handle from Windows that uses up system resources. Additionally, not having a window handle means that TGraphicControls don't have to go through the convoluted Windows paint process. This makes drawing with TGraphicControls much faster than using the TWinControl equivalents.

TGraphicControls can respond to mouse events. Actually, the TGraphicControl parent processes the mouse message and sends it to its child controls.

TGraphicControl allows you to paint the control and therefore provides the property Canvas, which is of the type TCanvas. TGraphicControl also provides a Paint() method that its descendants must override.

The TCustomControl Class

You might have noticed that the names of some TWinControl descendants begin with TCustom, such as TCustomComboBox, TCustomControl, TCustomEdit, and TCustomListBox.

Custom controls have the same functionality as other TWinControl descendants, except that with specialized visual and interactive characteristics, custom controls provide you with a base from which you can derive and create your own customized components. You provide the functionality for the custom control to draw itself if you're a component writer.

Other Classes

Several classes aren't components but serve as supporting classes to the existing component. These classes are typically properties of other components and descend directly from TPersistent. Some of these classes are of the type TStrings, TCanvas, and TCollection.

The TStrings and TStringLists Classes

The TStrings abstract class gives you the capability to manipulate lists of strings that belong to a component such as a TListBox. TStrings doesn't actually maintain the memory for the strings (that's done by the native control that owns the TStrings class). Instead, TStrings defines the methods and properties to access and manipulate the control's strings without having to use the control's set of API level functions and messages.

Notice that we said TStrings is an abstract class. This means that TStrings doesn't really implement the code required to manipulate the strings—it just defines the methods that must be there. It's up to the descendant components to implement the actual string-manipulation methods.

To explain this point further, some examples of components and their TStrings properties are TListBox.Items, TMemo.Lines, and TComboBox.Items. Each of these properties is of the type

TStrings. You might wonder, if their properties are TStrings, how can you call methods of these properties when these methods have yet to be implemented in code? That's a good question. The answer is that, even though each of these properties is defined as TStrings, the variable to which the property refers (TListBox.FItems, for example) was instantiated as a descendant class. To clarify this, FItems is the private storage field for the Items property of TListBox:

```
TCustomListBox = class(TWinControl)
 private
   FItems: TStrings;
```

> **NOTE**
>
> Although the class type shown in the preceding code snippet is a TCustomListBox, the TListBox descends directly from TCustomListBox in the same unit and therefore has access to its private fields.

The unit StdCtrls.pas, which is part of the Delphi VCL, defines a descendant class TListBoxStrings, which is a descendant of TStrings. Listing 10.1 shows its definition.

LISTING 10.1 The Declaration of the TListBoxStrings Class

```
TListBoxStrings = class(TStrings)
  private
    ListBox: TCustomListBox;
  protected
    procedure Put(Index: Integer; const S: string); override;
    function Get(Index: Integer): string; override;
    function GetCount: Integer; override;
    function GetObject(Index: Integer): TObject; override;
    procedure PutObject(Index: Integer; AObject: TObject); override;
    procedure SetUpdateState(Updating: Boolean); override;
  public
    function Add(const S: string): Integer; override;
    procedure Clear; override;
    procedure Delete(Index: Integer); override;
    procedure Exchange(Index1, Index2: Integer); override;
    function IndexOf(const S: string): Integer; override;
    procedure Insert(Index: Integer; const S: string); override;
    procedure Move(CurIndex, NewIndex: Integer); override;
end;
```

StdCtrls.pas then defines the implementation of each method of this descendant class. When TListBox creates its class instances for its FItems variable, it actually creates an instance of this descendant class and refers to it with the FItems property:

```
constructor TCustomListBox.Create(AOwner: TComponent);
begin
  inherited Create(AOwner);
  ...
  // An instance of TListBoxStrings is created
  FItems := TListBoxStrings.Create;
  ...
end;
```

We want to make it clear that although the TStrings class defines its methods, it doesn't implement these methods to manipulate strings. The TStrings descendant class does the implementation of these methods. This is important if you're a component writer because you must know how to perform this technique as the Delphi components did it. It's always good to refer to the VCL or CLX source code to see how Borland performs these techniques when you're unsure.

If you're not a component writer but want to manipulate a list of strings, you can use the TStringList class, another descendant of TStrings, with which you can instantiate a completely self-contained class. TStringList maintains a list of strings external to components. The best part is that TStringList is totally compatible with TStrings, which means that you can directly assign a TStringList instance to a control's TStrings property. The following code shows how you can create an instance of TStringList:

```
var
  MyStringList: TStringList;
begin
  MyStringList := TStringList.Create;
```

To add strings to this TStringList instance, do the following:

```
MyStringList.Add('Red');
MyStringList.Add('White');
MyStringList.Add('Blue');
```

If you want to add these same strings to both a TMemo component and a TListBox component, all you have to do is take advantage of the compatibility between the different components' TStrings properties and make the assignments in one line of code each:

```
Memo1.Lines.Assign(MyStringList);
ListBox1.Items.Assign(MyStringList);
```

You use the Assign() method to copy TStrings instances instead of making a direct assignment such as Memo1.Lines := MyStringList.

Table 10.5 shows some common methods of TStrings classes.

TABLE 10.5 Some Common TStrings Methods

TStrings *Method*	*Description*
Add(const S: String): Integer	Adds the string S to the string's list and returns the string's position in the list.
AddObject(const S: string; AObject: TObject): Integer	Appends both a string and an object to a string or string list object.
AddStrings(Strings: TStrings)	Copies strings from one TStrings to the end of its existing list of strings.
Assign(Source: TPersistent)	Replaces the existing strings with those specified by the Source parameter.
Clear	Removes all strings from the list.
Delete(Index: Integer)	Removes the string at the location specified by Index.
Exchange(Index1, Index2: Integer)	Switches the location of the two strings specified by the two index values.
IndexOf(const S: String): Integer	Returns the position of the string S on the list.
Insert(Index: Integer; const S: String)	Inserts the string S into the position in the list specified by Index.
Move(CurIndex, NewIndex: Integer)	Moves the string at the position CurIndex to the position NewIndex.
LoadFromFile(const FileName: String)	Reads the text file, FileName, and places its lines into the string list.
SaveToFile(const FileName: string)	Saves the string list to the text file, FileName.

The TCanvas Class

The Canvas property, of type TCanvas, is provided for windowed controls and represents the drawing surface of the control. TCanvas encapsulates what's called the *device context* of a window. It provides many of the functions and objects required for drawing to the window's surface. (Chapter 8, "Graphics Programming with GDI and Fonts," of *Delphi 5 Developer's Guide* on this book's CD-ROM goes into detail about the TCanvas class.)

Runtime Type Information

Back in Chapter 2 you were introduced to Runtime Type Information (RTTI). This chapter delves much deeper into the RTTI innards that will allow you to take advantage of RTTI beyond what you get in the normal usage of the Object Pascal language. In other words, we're going to show you how to obtain type information on objects and data types much similar to the way the Delphi IDE obtains the same information.

So how does RTTI manifest itself? You'll see RTTI at work in at least two areas with which you normally work. The first place is right in the Delphi IDE, as stated earlier. Through RTTI, the IDE magically knows everything about the object and components with which you work (see the Object Inspector). Actually, there's more to it than just RTTI. But for the sake of this discussion, we're covering only the RTTI aspect. The second area is in the runtime code that you write. Already, in Chapter 2 you read about the is and as operators.

Let's examine the is operator to illustrate typical usage of RTTI.

Suppose that you need to make all TEdit components read-only on a given form. This is simple enough—just loop through all components, use the is operator to determine whether the component is a TEdit class, and then set the ReadOnly property accordingly. Here's an example:

```
for i := 0 to ComponentCount - 1 do
    if Components[i] is TEdit then
      TEdit(Components[i]).ReadOnly := True;
```

A typical usage for the as operator would be to perform an action on the Sender parameter of an event handler, where the handler is attached to several different components. Assuming that you know that all components are derived from a common ancestor whose property you want to access, the event handler can use the as operator to safely typecast Sender as the desired descendant, thus surfacing the wanted property. Here's an example:

```
procedure TForm1.ControlOnClickEvent(Sender: TObject);
var
  i: integer;
begin
  (Sender as TControl).Enabled := False;
end;
```

These examples of *typesafe programming* illustrate enhancements to the Object Pascal language that indirectly use RTTI. Now let's look at a problem that would call for direct usage of RTTI.

Suppose you have a form containing components that are data aware and components that aren't data aware. However, you need to perform some action on the data-aware components only. Certainly you could loop through the Components array for the form and test for each data-aware component type. However, this could get messy to maintain because you would have to test against every type of data-aware component. Also, you don't have a base class to test against that's common to only data-aware components. For instance, something such as TDataAwareControl would have been nice, but it doesn't exist.

A clean way to determine whether a component is data aware is to test for the existence of a `DataSource` property. You are sure that this property exists for all data-aware components. To do this, however, you need to use RTTI directly.

The following sections discuss RTTI in more depth to give you the background knowledge needed to solve problems such as the one mentioned earlier.

The `TypInfo.pas` Unit: Definer of Runtime Type Information

Type information exists for any object (a descendant of `TObject`). This information exists in memory and is queried by the IDE and the Runtime Library to obtain information about objects. The `TypInfo.pas` unit defines the structures that allow you to query for type information. The `TObject` methods shown in Table 10.6 are repeated from Chapter 2.

TABLE 10.6 `TObject` Methods

Function	Return Type	Returns
ClassName()	string	The name of the object's class
ClassType()	TClass	The object's type
InheritsFrom()	Boolean	Boolean to indicate whether the class descends from a given class
ClassParent()	TClass	The object Cancestor's type
InstanceSize()	word	The size, in bytes, of an instance
ClassInfo()	Pointer	A pointer to the object's in-memory RTTI

For now, we want to focus on the `ClassInfo()` function, which is defined as follows:

```
class function ClassInfo: Pointer;
```

This function returns a pointer to the RTTI for the calling class. The structure to which this pointer refers is of the type `PTypeInfo`. This type is defined in the `TypInfo.pas` unit as a pointer to a `TTypeInfo` structure. Both definitions are given in the following code as they appear in `TypInfo.pas`:

```
PPTypeInfo = ^PTypeInfo;
  PTypeInfo = ^TTypeInfo;
  TTypeInfo = record
    Kind: TTypeKind;
    Name: ShortString;
   {TypeData: TTypeData}
  end;
```

The commented field, TypeData, represents the actual reference to the type information for the given class. The type to which it actually refers depends on the value of the Kind field. Kind can be any of the enumerated values defined in the TTypeKind:

```
TTypeKind = (tkUnknown, tkInteger, tkChar, tkEnumeration, tkFloat,
    tkString, tkSet, tkClass, tkMethod, tkWChar, tkLString, tkWString,
    tkVariant, tkArray, tkRecord, tkInterface);
```

Take a look at the TypInfo.pas unit at this time to examine the subtypes to some of the preceding enumerated values to get yourself familiar with them. For example, the tkFloat value can be further broken down into one of the following:

```
TFloatType = (ftSingle, ftDouble, ftExtended, ftComp, ftCurr);
```

Now you know that Kind determines to which type TypeData refers. The TTypeData structure is defined in TypInfo.pas, as shown in Listing 10.2.

LISTING 10.2 The TTypeData Structure

```
PTypeData = ^TTypeData;
TTypeData = packed record
  case TTypeKind of
    tkUnknown, tkLString, tkWString, tkVariant: ();
    tkInteger, tkChar, tkEnumeration, tkSet, tkWChar: (
        OrdType: TOrdType;
        case TTypeKind of
          tkInteger, tkChar, tkEnumeration, tkWChar: (
            MinValue: Longint;
            MaxValue: Longint;
            case TTypeKind of
              tkInteger, tkChar, tkWChar: ();
              tkEnumeration: (
                BaseType: PPTypeInfo;
                NameList: ShortStringBase));
          tkSet: (
            CompType: PPTypeInfo));
    tkFloat: (FloatType: TFloatType);
    tkString: (MaxLength: Byte);
    tkClass: (
        ClassType: TClass;
        ParentInfo: PPTypeInfo;
        PropCount: SmallInt;
        UnitName: ShortStringBase;
      {PropData: TPropData});
    tkMethod: (
      MethodKind: TMethodKind;
      ParamCount: Byte;
```

LISTING 10.2 Continued

```
    ParamList: array[0..1023] of Char
    {ParamList: array[1..ParamCount] of
      record
        Flags: TParamFlags;
        ParamName: ShortString;
        TypeName: ShortString;
      end;
      ResultType: ShortString});
  tkInterface: (
      IntfParent : PPTypeInfo; { ancestor }
      IntfFlags : TIntfFlagsBase;
      Guid : TGUID;
      IntfUnit : ShortStringBase;
    {PropData: TPropData});
  tkInt64: (
      MinInt64Value, MaxInt64Value: Int64);
end;
```

As you can see, the TTypeData structure is really just a big variant record. If you're familiar with working with variant records and pointers, you'll see that dealing with RTTI is really simple. It just seems complex because it's an undocumented feature.

NOTE

Often, Borland doesn't document a feature because it might change between versions. When using features such as the undocumented RTTI, realize that your code might not be fully portable between versions of Delphi.

At this point, we're ready to demonstrate how to use these structures of RTTI to obtain type information.

Obtaining Type Information

To demonstrate how to obtain Runtime Type Information on an object, we've created a project whose main form is defined in Listing 10.3.

LISTING 10.3 Main Form for ClassInfo.dpr

```
unit MainFrm;

interface
```

LISTING 10.3 Continued

```
uses
  Windows, Messages, SysUtils, Classes, Graphics, Controls, Forms, Dialogs,
  StdCtrls, ExtCtrls, DBClient, MidasCon, MConnect;

type

  TMainForm = class(TForm)
    pnlTop: TPanel;
    pnlLeft: TPanel;
    lbBaseClassInfo: TListBox;
    spSplit: TSplitter;
    lblBaseClassInfo: TLabel;
    pnlRight: TPanel;
    lblClassProperties: TLabel;
    lbPropList: TListBox;
    lbSampClasses: TListBox;
    procedure FormCreate(Sender: TObject);
    procedure lbSampClassesClick(Sender: TObject);
  private
    { Private declarations }
  public
    { Public declarations }
  end;

var
  MainForm: TMainForm;

implementation
uses TypInfo;

{$R *.DFM}

function CreateAClass(const AClassName: string): TObject;
{ This method illustrates how you can create a class from the class name. Note
  that this requires that you register the class using RegisterClasses() as
  shown in the initialization method of this unit. }
var
  C : TFormClass;
  SomeObject: TObject;
begin
  C := TFormClass(FindClass(AClassName));
  SomeObject := C.Create(nil);
  Result := SomeObject;
end;
```

LISTING 10.3   Continued

```pascal
procedure GetBaseClassInfo(AClass: TObject; AStrings: TStrings);
{ This method obtains some basic RTTI data from the given object and adds that
  information to the AStrings parameter. }
var
  ClassTypeInfo: PTypeInfo;
  ClassTypeData: PTypeData;
  EnumName: String;
begin
  ClassTypeInfo := AClass.ClassInfo;
  ClassTypeData := GetTypeData(ClassTypeInfo);
  with AStrings do
  begin
    Add(Format('Class Name:     %s', [ClassTypeInfo.Name]));
    EnumName := GetEnumName(TypeInfo(TTypeKind), Integer(ClassTypeInfo.Kind));
    Add(Format('Kind:           %s', [EnumName]));
    Add(Format('Size:           %d', [AClass.InstanceSize]));
    Add(Format('Defined in:     %s.pas', [ClassTypeData.UnitName]));
    Add(Format('Num Properties: %d',[ClassTypeData.PropCount]));
  end;
end;

procedure GetClassAncestry(AClass: TObject; AStrings: TStrings);
{ This method retrieves the ancestry of a given object and adds the
  class names of the ancestry to the AStrings parameter. }
var
  AncestorClass: TClass;
begin
  AncestorClass := AClass.ClassParent;
  { Iterate through the Parent classes starting with Sender's
    Parent until the end of the ancestry is reached. }
  AStrings.Add('Class Ancestry');
  while AncestorClass <> nil do
  begin
    AStrings.Add(Format('    %s',[AncestorClass.ClassName]));
    AncestorClass := AncestorClass.ClassParent;
  end;
end;

procedure GetClassProperties(AClass: TObject; AStrings: TStrings);
{ This method retrieves the property names and types for the given object
  and adds that information to the AStrings parameter. }
var
  PropList: PPropList;
```

LISTING 10.3   Continued

```
  ClassTypeInfo: PTypeInfo;
  ClassTypeData: PTypeData;
  i: integer;
  NumProps: Integer;
begin

  ClassTypeInfo := AClass.ClassInfo;
  ClassTypeData := GetTypeData(ClassTypeInfo);

  if ClassTypeData.PropCount <> 0 then
  begin
    // allocate the memory needed to hold the references to the TPropInfo
    // structures on the number of properties.
    GetMem(PropList, SizeOf(PPropInfo) * ClassTypeData.PropCount);
    try
      // fill PropList with the pointer references to the TPropInfo structures
      GetPropInfos(AClass.ClassInfo, PropList);
      for i := 0 to ClassTypeData.PropCount - 1 do
        // filter out properties that are events ( method pointer properties)
        if not (PropList[i]^.PropType^.Kind = tkMethod) then
          AStrings.Add(Format('%s: %s', [PropList[i]^.Name,
          PropList[i]^.PropType^.Name]));

      // Now get properties that are events (method pointer properties)
      NumProps := GetPropList(AClass.ClassInfo, [tkMethod], PropList);
      if NumProps <> 0 then begin
        AStrings.Add('');
        AStrings.Add('   EVENTS   =============== ');
        AStrings.Add('');
      end;
      // Fill the AStrings with the events.
      for i := 0 to NumProps - 1 do
          AStrings.Add(Format('%s: %s', [PropList[i]^.Name,
          PropList[i]^.PropType^.Name]));

    finally
      FreeMem(PropList, SizeOf(PPropInfo) * ClassTypeData.PropCount);
    end;
  end;

end;

procedure TMainForm.FormCreate(Sender: TObject);
begin
```

LISTING 10.3 Continued

```pascal
  // Add some example classes to the list box.
  lbSampClasses.Items.Add('TApplication');
  lbSampClasses.Items.Add('TButton');
  lbSampClasses.Items.Add('TForm');
  lbSampClasses.Items.Add('TListBox');
  lbSampClasses.Items.Add('TPaintBox');
  lbSampClasses.Items.Add('TMidasConnection');
  lbSampClasses.Items.Add('TFindDialog');
  lbSampClasses.Items.Add('TOpenDialog');
  lbSampClasses.Items.Add('TTimer');
  lbSampClasses.Items.Add('TComponent');
  lbSampClasses.Items.Add('TGraphicControl');
end;

procedure TMainForm.lbSampClassesClick(Sender: TObject);
var
  SomeComp: TObject;
begin
  lbBaseClassInfo.Items.Clear;
  lbPropList.Items.Clear;

  // Create an instance of the selected class.
  SomeComp := CreateAClass(lbSampClasses.Items[lbSampClasses.ItemIndex]);
  try
    GetBaseClassInfo(SomeComp, lbBaseClassInfo.Items);
    GetClassAncestry(SomeComp, lbBaseClassInfo.Items);
    GetClassProperties(SomeComp, lbPropList.Items);
  finally
    SomeComp.Free;
  end;
end;

initialization
begin
  RegisterClasses([TApplication, TButton, TForm, TListBox, TPaintBox,
    TMidasConnection, TFindDialog, TOpenDialog, TTimer, TComponent,
    TGraphicControl]);
end;

end.
```

This main form contains three list boxes. lbSampClasses contains classnames for a few sample objects whose type information we'll retrieve. On selecting an object from lbSampClasses, lbBaseClassInfo will be populated with basic information about the selected object, such as its size and ancestry. lbPropList will display the properties belonging to the selected object from lbSampClasses.

Three helper procedures are used to obtain class information:

- GetBaseClassInfo()—Populates a string list with basic information about an object, such as its type, size, defining unit, and number of properties
- GetClassAncestry()—Populates a string list with the object names of a given object's ancestry
- GetClassProperties()—Populates a string list with the properties and their types for a given class

Each procedure takes an object instance and a string list as parameters.

As the user selects one of the classes from lbSampClasses, its OnClick event, lbSampClassesClick(), calls a helper function, CreateAClass(), which creates an instance of a class given the name of the class type. It then passes the object instance and the appropriate TListBox.Items property to be populated.

Obtaining Runtime Type Information for Objects

GetBaseClassInfo() passes the return value from TObject.ClassInfo() to the function GetTypeData(). GetTypeData() is defined in TypInfo.pas. Its purpose is to return a pointer to the TTypeData structure based on the class whose PTypeInfo structure was passed to it (see Listing 10.2). GetBaseClassInfo() simply refers to the various fields of both the TTypeInfo and TTypeData structures to populate the AStrings string list. Note the use of the function

GetEnumName() to return the string for an enumerated type. This is also a function of RTTI defined in TypInfo.pas. Type information on enumerated types is discussed in a later section.

> **TIP**
>
> Use the GetTypeData() function defined in TypInfo.pas to return a pointer to the TTypeInfo structure for a given class. You must pass the result of TObject.ClassInfo() to GetTypeData().

> **TIP**
>
> You can use the GetEnumName() function to obtain the name of an enumeration value as a string. GetEnumValue() returns the enumeration value given its name.

Obtaining the Ancestry for an Object

The GetClassAncestry() procedure populates a string list with the classnames of the given object's ancestry. This is a simple operation that uses the ClassParent() class procedure on the given object. ClassParent() will return a TClass reference to the given class's parent or nil if the top of the ancestry is reached. GetClassAncestry() simply walks up the ancestry and adds each classname to the string list until the top is reached.

Obtaining Type Information on Object Properties

If an object has properties, its TTypeData.PropCount value will contain the number of properties it has. There are several approaches you can use to obtain the property information for a given class—we demonstrate two.

The GetClassProperties() procedure begins much like the previous two methods in that it passes the ClassInfo() result to GetTypeData() to obtain the reference to the TTypeData structure for the class. It then allocates memory for the PropList variable based on the value of ClassTypeData.PropCount. PropList is defined as the type PPropList. PPropList is defined in TypInfo.pas as follows:

```
type
  PPropList = ^TPropList;
  TPropList = array[0..16379] of PPropInfo;
```

The TPropList array stores pointers to the TPropInfo data for each property. TPropInfo is defined in TypInfo.pas as follows:

```
  PPropInfo = ^TPropInfo;
  TPropInfo = packed record
```

10

COMPONENT ARCHITECTURE: VCL AND CLX

```
      PropType: PPTypeInfo;
      GetProc: Pointer;
      SetProc: Pointer;
      StoredProc: Pointer;
      Index: Integer;
      Default: Longint;
      NameIndex: SmallInt;
      Name: ShortString;
    end;
```

TPropInfo is the Runtime Type Information for a property.

GetClassProperties() uses the GetPropInfos() function to fill this array with pointers to the RTTI information for all properties for the given object. It then loops through the array and writes out the name and type for the property by accessing that property's type information. Note the following line:

```
if not (PropList[i]^.PropType^.Kind = tkMethod) then
```

This is used to filter out properties that are events (method pointers). We populate these properties last, which allows us to demonstrate an alternative method for retrieving property RTTI. In the final part of the GetClassProperties() method, we use the GetPropList() function to return the TPropList for properties of a specific type. In this case, we want only properties of the type tkMethod. GetPropList() is also defined in TypInfo.pas. Refer to the source commentary for additional information.

TIP

Use GetPropInfos() when you want to retrieve a pointer to the property Runtime Type Information for *all* properties of a given object. Use GetPropList() if you want to retrieve the same information, except for properties of a specific type.

Figure 10.3 shows the output of the main form with Runtime Type Information for a selected class.

Checking for the Existence of a Property for an Object

Earlier we presented the problem of needing to check for the existence of a property for a given object. Specifically, we were referring to the DataSource property. Using functions defined in TypInfo.pas, we could write the following function to determine whether a control is data aware:

```
function IsDataAware(AComponent: TComponent): Boolean;
var
  PropInfo: PPropInfo;
```

```
begin
  // Find the property named datasource.
  PropInfo := GetPropInfo(AComponent.ClassInfo, 'DataSource');
  Result := PropInfo <> nil;

  // Double check, make sure it descends from TDataSource
  if Result then
    if not ((PropInfo^.Proptype^.Kind = tkClass) and
        (GetTypeData(PropInfo^.PropType^).ClassType.InheritsFrom(TDataSource)))
      then
    Result := False;
end;
```

Here, we're using the GetPropInfo() function to return the TPropInfo pointer on a given property. This function returns nil if the property doesn't exist. As an additional check, we make sure that the property named DataSource is actually a descendant of TDataSource.

We also could have written this function more generically to check for the existence of any property by its name, like this:

```
function HasProperty(AComponent: TComponent; APropertyName: String): Boolean;
var
  PropInfo: PPropInfo;
begin
  PropInfo := GetPropInfo(AComponent.ClassInfo, APropertyName);
  Result := PropInfo <> nil;
end;
```

Note, however, that this works only on published properties. RTTI doesn't exist for unpublished properties.

FIGURE 10.3

Output of a class's Runtime Type Information.

Obtaining Type Information on Method Pointers

Runtime Type Information can be obtained on method pointers. For example, you can determine the type of method (procedure, function, and so on) and its parameters. Listing 10.4 demonstrates how to obtain Runtime Type Information for a selected group of methods.

LISTING 10.4 Obtaining Runtime Type Information for Methods

```
unit MainFrm;

interface

uses
  Windows, Messages, SysUtils, Classes, Graphics, Controls, Forms, Dialogs,
  StdCtrls, ExtCtrls, DBClient, MidasCon, MConnect;

type

  TMainForm = class(TForm)
    lbSampMethods: TListBox;
    lbMethodInfo: TMemo;
    lblBasicMethodInfo: TLabel;
    procedure FormCreate(Sender: TObject);
    procedure lbSampMethodsClick(Sender: TObject);
  private
    { Private declarations }
  public
    { Public declarations }
  end;

var
  MainForm: TMainForm;

implementation
uses TypInfo, DBTables, Provider;

{$R *.DFM}

type
  // It is necessary to redefine this record as it is commented out in
  // typinfo.pas.

  PParamRecord = ^TParamRecord;
  TParamRecord = record
    Flags:     TParamFlags;
    ParamName: ShortString;
```

LISTING 10.4 Continued

```
  TypeName:  ShortString;
end;

procedure GetBaseMethodInfo(ATypeInfo: PTypeInfo; AStrings: TStrings);
{ This method obtains some basic RTTI data from the TTypeInfo and adds that
  information to the AStrings parameter. }
var
  MethodTypeData: PTypeData;
  EnumName: String;
begin
  MethodTypeData := GetTypeData(ATypeInfo);
  with AStrings do
  begin
    Add(Format('Class Name:    %s', [ATypeInfo^.Name]));
    EnumName := GetEnumName(TypeInfo(TTypeKind), Integer(ATypeInfo^.Kind));
    Add(Format('Kind:          %s', [EnumName]));
    Add(Format('Num Parameters: %d',[MethodTypeData.ParamCount]));
  end;
end;

procedure GetMethodDefinition(ATypeInfo: PTypeInfo; AStrings: TStrings);
{ This method retrieves the property info on a method pointer. We use this
  information to reconstruct the method definition. }
var
  MethodTypeData: PTypeData;
  MethodDefine:   String;
  ParamRecord:    PParamRecord;
  TypeStr:        ^ShortString;
  ReturnStr:      ^ShortString;
  i: integer;
begin
  MethodTypeData := GetTypeData(ATypeInfo);

  // Determine the type of method
  case MethodTypeData.MethodKind of
    mkProcedure:      MethodDefine := 'procedure ';
    mkFunction:       MethodDefine := 'function ';
    mkConstructor:    MethodDefine := 'constructor ';
    mkDestructor:     MethodDefine := 'destructor ';
    mkClassProcedure: MethodDefine := 'class procedure ';
    mkClassFunction:  MethodDefine := 'class function ';
  end;
```

LISTING 10.4 Continued

```
// point to the first parameter
ParamRecord    := @MethodTypeData.ParamList;
i := 1; // first parameter

// loop through the method's parameters and add them to the string list as
// they would be normally defined.
while i <= MethodTypeData.ParamCount do
begin
  if i = 1 then
    MethodDefine := MethodDefine+'(';

  if pfVar in ParamRecord.Flags then
    MethodDefine := MethodDefine+('var ');
  if pfconst in ParamRecord.Flags then
    MethodDefine := MethodDefine+('const ');
  if pfArray in ParamRecord.Flags then
    MethodDefine := MethodDefine+('array of ');
// we won't do anything for the pfAddress but know that the Self parameter
// gets passed with this flag set.
{
  if pfAddress in ParamRecord.Flags then
    MethodDefine := MethodDefine+('*address* ');
}
  if pfout in ParamRecord.Flags then
    MethodDefine := MethodDefine+('out ');


  // Use pointer arithmetic to get the type string for the parameter.
  TypeStr := Pointer(Integer(@ParamRecord^.ParamName) +
    Length(ParamRecord^.ParamName)+1);

  MethodDefine := Format('%s%s: %s', [MethodDefine, ParamRecord^.ParamName,
    TypeStr^]);

  inc(i); // Increment the counter.

  // Go the next parameter. Notice that use of pointer arithmetic to
  // get to the appropriate location of the next parameter.
  ParamRecord := PParamRecord(Integer(ParamRecord) + SizeOf(TParamFlags) +
    (Length(ParamRecord^.ParamName) + 1) + (Length(TypeStr^)+1));

  // if there are still parameters then setup
  if i <= MethodTypeData.ParamCount then
```

LISTING 10.4 Continued

```
  begin
    MethodDefine := MethodDefine + '; ';
  end
  else
    MethodDefine := MethodDefine + ')';
end;

// If the method type is a function, it has a return value. This is also
// placed in the method definition string. The return value will be at the
// location following the last parameter.
if MethodTypeData.MethodKind = mkFunction then
begin
  ReturnStr := Pointer(ParamRecord);
  MethodDefine := Format('%s: %s;', [MethodDefine, ReturnStr^])
end
else
  MethodDefine := MethodDefine+';';

// finally, add the string to the listbox.
with AStrings do
begin
  Add(MethodDefine)
end;
end;

procedure TMainForm.FormCreate(Sender: TObject);
begin
  { Add some method types to the list box. Also, store the pointer to the RTTI
    data in listbox's Objects array }
  with lbSampMethods.Items do
  begin
    AddObject('TNotifyEvent', TypeInfo(TNotifyEvent));
    AddObject('TMouseEvent', TypeInfo(TMouseEvent));
    AddObject('TBDECallBackEvent', TypeInfo(TBDECallBackEvent));
    AddObject('TDataRequestEvent', TypeInfo(TDataRequestEvent));
    AddObject('TGetModuleProc', TypeInfo(TGetModuleProc));
    AddObject('TReaderError', TypeInfo(TReaderError));
  end;
end;

procedure TMainForm.lbSampMethodsClick(Sender: TObject);
begin
  lbMethodInfo.Lines.Clear;
  with lbSampMethods do
```

LISTING 10.4   Continued

```
begin
  GetBaseMethodInfo(PTypeInfo(Items.Objects[ItemIndex]), lbMethodInfo.Lines);
  GetMethodDefinition(PTypeInfo(Items.Objects[ItemIndex]),
    lbMethodInfo.Lines);
  end;
end;

end.
```

In Listing 10.4, we populate a list box, `lbSampMethods`, with some sample method names. We also store the references to those methods' RTTI data in the `Objects` array of the list box. We do this by using the `TypeInfo()` function, which is a special function that can retrieve a pointer to Runtime Type Information for a given type identifier. When the user selects one of these methods, we use that RTTI data from the `Objects` array to retrieve and reconstruct the method definition from the information we have about the method and its parameters in the RTTI data. Refer to the listing's commentary for further information.

> **TIP**
>
> Use the `TypeInfo()` function to retrieve a pointer to the compiler-generated Runtime Type Information for a given type identifier. For example, the following line retrieves a pointer to the RTTI for the `TButton` type:
>
> ```
> TypeInfoPointer := TypeInfo(TButton);
> ```

Obtaining Type Information for Ordinal Types

We've already covered the more difficult pieces to RTTI. However, you can also obtain RTTI for ordinal types. The following sections illustrate how to obtain RTTI data on integer, enumerated, and set types.

Type Information for Integer Types

Obtaining type information for integer types is simple. Listing 10.5 illustrates this process.

LISTING 10.5   Obtaining Runtime Type Information for Integers

```
procedure TMainForm.lbSampsClick(Sender: TObject);
var
  OrdTypeInfo: PTypeInfo;
  OrdTypeData: PTypeData;
```

LISTING 10.5 Continued

```
  TypeNameStr: String;
  TypeKindStr: String;
  MinVal, MaxVal: Integer;
begin
  memInfo.Lines.Clear;
  with lbSamps do
  begin

    // Get the TTypeInfo pointer
    OrdTypeInfo := PTypeInfo(Items.Objects[ItemIndex]);
    // Get the TTypeData pointer
    OrdTypeData := GetTypeData(OrdTypeInfo);

    // Get the type name string
    TypeNameStr := OrdTypeInfo.Name;
    // Get the type kind string
    TypeKindStr := GetEnumName(TypeInfo(TTypeKind),
Integer(OrdTypeInfo^.Kind));

    // Get the minimum and maximum values for the type
    MinVal := OrdTypeData^.MinValue;
    MaxVal := OrdTypeData^.MaxValue;

    // Add the information to the memo
    with memInfo.Lines do
    begin
      Add('Type Name: '+TypeNameStr);
      Add('Type Kind: '+TypeKindStr);

      Add('Min Val: '+IntToStr(MinVal));
      Add('Max Val: '+IntToStr(MaxVal));
    end;
  end;
end;
```

Here, we use the `TypeInfo()` function to obtain a pointer to the `TTypeInfo` structure for the `Integer` data type. We then pass that reference to the `GetTypeData()` function to obtain a pointer to the `TTypeData` structure. We use both those structures to populate a list box with the integer's RTTI. See the demo named `IntegerRTTI.dpr` in the directory for this chapter on the CD-ROM accompanying this book for a more detailed demonstration.

Type Information for Enumerated Types

Obtaining RTTI for enumerated types is just as easy as it is for integers. In fact, you'll see that
Listing 10.6 is almost identical to Listing 10.5, with the exception of the additional `for` loop to
show the values of the enumeration type.

LISTING 10.6   Obtaining RTTI for an Enumerated Type

```
procedure TMainForm.lbSampsClick(Sender: TObject);
var
  OrdTypeInfo: PTypeInfo;
  OrdTypeData: PTypeData;

  TypeNameStr: String;
  TypeKindStr: String;
  MinVal, MaxVal: Integer;
  i: integer;
begin
  memInfo.Lines.Clear;
  with lbSamps do
  begin

    // Get the TTypeInfo pointer
    OrdTypeInfo := PTypeInfo(Items.Objects[ItemIndex]);
    // Get the TTypeData pointer
    OrdTypeData := GetTypeData(OrdTypeInfo);

    // Get the type name string
    TypeNameStr := OrdTypeInfo.Name;
    // Get the type kind string
    TypeKindStr := GetEnumName(TypeInfo(TTypeKind),
Integer(OrdTypeInfo^.Kind));

    // Get the minimum and maximum values for the type
    MinVal := OrdTypeData^.MinValue;
    MaxVal := OrdTypeData^.MaxValue;

    // Add the information to the memo
    with memInfo.Lines do
    begin
      Add('Type Name: '+TypeNameStr);
      Add('Type Kind: '+TypeKindStr);

      Add('Min Val: '+IntToStr(MinVal));
      Add('Max Val: '+IntToStr(MaxVal));
```

LISTING 10.6 Continued

```
      // Show the values and names of the enumerated types
      if OrdTypeInfo^.Kind = tkEnumeration then
        for i := MinVal to MaxVal do
          Add(Format('  Value: %d    Name: %s', [i,
            GetEnumName(OrdTypeInfo, i)]));

    end;
  end;
end;
```

You'll find a more detailed demo named EnumRTTI.dpr on the CD-ROM in the directory for this chapter.

Type Information for Set Types

Obtaining RTTI for set types is only slightly more complex than the two previous techniques. Listing 10.7 is the main form for the project SetRTTI.dpr, which you'll find on the CD-ROM in the directory for this chapter.

LISTING 10.7 Obtaining RTTI for Set Types

```
unit MainFrm;

interface

uses
  Windows, Messages, SysUtils, Classes, Graphics, Controls, Forms, Dialogs,
  StdCtrls, Grids;

type
  TMainForm = class(TForm)
    lbSamps: TListBox;
    memInfo: TMemo;
    procedure FormCreate(Sender: TObject);
    procedure lbSampsClick(Sender: TObject);
  private
    { Private declarations }
  public
    { Public declarations }
  end;

var
  MainForm: TMainForm;
```

LISTING 10.7   Continued

```
implementation
uses TypInfo, Buttons;

{$R *.DFM}


procedure TMainForm.FormCreate(Sender: TObject);
begin
  // Add some example enumerated types
  with lbSamps.Items do
  begin
    AddObject('TBorderIcons', TypeInfo(TBorderIcons));
    AddObject('TGridOptions', TypeInfo(TGridOptions));
  end;
end;

procedure GetTypeInfoForOrdinal(AOrdTypeInfo: PTypeInfo; AStrings: TStrings);
var
//  OrdTypeInfo: PTypeInfo;
  OrdTypeData: PTypeData;

  TypeNameStr: String;
  TypeKindStr: String;
  MinVal, MaxVal: Integer;
  i: integer;
begin

  // Get the TTypeData pointer
  OrdTypeData := GetTypeData(AOrdTypeInfo);

  // Get the type name string
  TypeNameStr := AOrdTypeInfo.Name;
  // Get the type kind string
  TypeKindStr := GetEnumName(TypeInfo(TTypeKind), Integer(AOrdTypeInfo^.Kind));

  // Get the minimum and maximum values for the type
  MinVal := OrdTypeData^.MinValue;
  MaxVal := OrdTypeData^.MaxValue;


  // Add the information to the memo
  with AStrings do
  begin
    Add('Type Name: '+TypeNameStr);
    Add('Type Kind: '+TypeKindStr);
```

LISTING 10.7 Continued

```
    // Call this function recursively to show the enumeration
    // values for this set type.
    if AOrdTypeInfo^.Kind = tkSet then
    begin
      Add('==========');
      Add('');
      GetTypeInfoForOrdinal(OrdTypeData^.CompType^, AStrings);
    end;

    // Show the values and names of the enumerated types belonging to the
    // set.
    if AOrdTypeInfo^.Kind = tkEnumeration then
    begin
      Add('Min Val: '+IntToStr(MinVal));
      Add('Max Val: '+IntToStr(MaxVal));

      for i := MinVal to MaxVal do
        Add(Format('  Value: %d    Name: %s', [i,
          GetEnumName(AOrdTypeInfo, i)]));
    end;
  end;

end;

procedure TMainForm.lbSampsClick(Sender: TObject);
begin
  memInfo.Lines.Clear;
  with lbSamps do
    GetTypeInfoForOrdinal(PTypeInfo(Items.Objects[ItemIndex]), memInfo.Lines);
end;
end.
```

In this demo, we set up two set types in a list box. We add the pointer to the TTypeInfo structures for these two types to the Objects array of the list box by using the TypeInfo() function.
When the user selects one of the items in the list box, the GetTypeInfoForOrdinal() procedure is called, passing both the PTypeInfo pointer and the memInfo.Lines property that's populated with the RTTI data.

The GetTypeInfoForOrdinal() procedure goes through the same steps you've already seen
for getting the pointer to the type's TTypeData structure. This initial type information is stored
to the TStrings parameter and then the GetTypeInfoForOrdinal() is called recursively, passing OrdTypeData^.CompType^, which refers to the enumerated data type for the set. This RTTI
data is also added to the same TStrings property.

Assigning Values to Properties Through RTTI

Now that we've shown you how to find and determine which published properties exist for components, we ought to show you how to assign values to properties through RTTI. This task is simple. The TypInfo.pas unit contains many helper routines to allow you to interrogate and manipulate component-published properties. These are the same helper routines used by the Delphi IDE (Object Inspector). It would be a good idea to open TypInfo.pas and to familiarize yourself with these routines. We'll demonstrate a few of them here.

Suppose that you want to assign an integer value to a property for a given component. Also suppose that you don't know whether this property exists on that component. Here's a procedure that assigns an integer value to a property for a given component, only if that property exists:

```
procedure SetIntegerPropertyIfExists(AComp: TComponent; APropName: String;
  AValue: Integer);
var
  PropInfo: PPropInfo;
begin
  PropInfo := GetPropInfo(AComp.ClassInfo, APropName);
  if PropInfo <> nil then
  begin
    if PropInfo^.PropType^.Kind = tkInteger then
      SetOrdProp(AComp, PropInfo, Integer(AValue));
  end;
end;
```

This procedure takes three parameters. The first, AComp, is the component whose property you want to modify. The second parameter, APropName, is the name of the property to which you want to assign the value of the third parameter, AValue. This procedure uses the GetPropInfo() function to retrieve the TPropInfo pointer on the specified property. GetPropInfo() will return nil if the property doesn't exist. If the property does exist, the second if clause determines whether the property is of the correct type. The property type tkInteger is defined in the TypInfo.pas unit along with other possible property types, as shown here:

```
TTypeKind = (tkUnknown, tkInteger, tkChar, tkEnumeration, tkFloat,
    tkString, tkSet, tkClass, tkMethod, tkWChar, tkLString, tkWString,
    tkVariant, tkArray, tkRecord, tkInterface, tkInt64, tkDynArray);
```

Finally, the assignment is made to the property using the SetOrdProp() procedure, another helper routine from TypInfo.pas used to set values to ordinal-type properties. The call to this procedure might look something like the following:

```
SetIntegerPropertyIfExists(Button2, 'Width', 50);
```

SetOrdProp() is referred to as a *setter* method, a method used to set a value to a property. There is also a *getter* method, which retrieves the property value. Several of these

Component Architecture: VCL and CLX
Chapter 10

Set*XXX*Prop() helper routines are in the TypInfo.pas unit for the possible property types, as shown in Table 10.7.

TABLE 10.7 Getter and Setter Methods

Property Type	Setter Method	Getter Method
Ordinal	SetOrdProp()	GetOrdProp()
Enumerated	SetEnumProp()	GetEnumProp()
Objects	SetObjectProp()	GetObjectProp()
String	SetStrProp()	GetStrProp()
Floating Point	SetFloatProp()	GetFloatProp()
Variant	SetVariantProp()	GetVariantProp()
Methods (Events)	SetMethodProp()	GetMethodProp()
Int64	SetInt64Prop()	GetInt64Prop()

Again, there are many other helper routines you'll find useful in TypInfo.pas.

The following code shows how to assign an object property:

```
procedure SetObjectPropertyIfExists(AComponent: TComponent; APropName: String;
  AValue: TObject);
var
  PropInfo: PPropInfo;
begin
  PropInfo := GetPropInfo(AComponent.ClassInfo, APropName);
  if PropInfo <> nil then
  begin
    if PropInfo^.PropType^.Kind = tkClass then
      SetObjectProp(AComponent, PropInfo, AValue);
  end;
end;
```

This method might be called as follows:

```
var
  F: TFont;
begin
  F := TFont.Create;
  F.Name   := 'Arial';
  F.Size   := 24;
  F.Color  := clRed;
  SetObjectPropertyIfExists(Panel1, 'Font', F);
end;
```

10

COMPONENT
ARCHITECTURE:
VCL AND CLX

The following code shows how to assign a method property:

```
procedure SetMethodPropertyIfExists(AComp: TComponent; APropName: String;
  AMethod: TMethod);
var
  PropInfo: PPropInfo;
begin
  PropInfo := GetPropInfo(AComp.ClassInfo, APropName);
  if PropInfo <> nil then
  begin
    if PropInfo^.PropType^.Kind = tkMethod then
      SetMethodProp(AComp, PropInfo, AMethod);
  end;
end;
```

This method requires the use of the TMethod type, which is defined in the System.pas unit. To call this method to assign an event handler from one component to another, you can use GetMethodProp to retrieve the TMethod value from the source component, as shown here:

```
SetMethodPropertyIfExists(Button5, 'OnClick',
    GetMethodProp(Panel1, 'OnClick'));
```

The accompanying CD-ROM has a project, SetProperties.dpr, that demonstrates these routines.

Summary

This chapter introduced you to the Visual Component Library (VCL) and Component Library for Cross Platform (CLX). We discussed the hierarchies and the special characteristics of components at different levels in each hierarchy. We also covered Runtime Type Information in depth. This chapter prepared you for the following chapters, which cover component writing.

VCL Component Building

IN THIS CHAPTER

The ability to easily write custom components in Delphi 6 is a chief productivity advantage that you wield over other programmers. In most other environments, folks are stuck using the standard controls available through Windows or else have to use an entirely different set of complex controls that were developed by somebody else. Being able to incorporate your custom components into your Delphi applications means that you have complete control over the application's user interface. Custom controls give you the final say in your application's look and feel.

In Delphi 6, you have the option of writing components for the Delphi VCL, which has existed since Delphi 1. You can also write components for Delphi's CLX architecture, which will be covered in Chapter 13, "CLX Component Development."

If your forte is component design, you will appreciate all the information this chapter has to offer. You will learn about all aspects of component design from concept to integration into the Delphi environment. You will also learn about the pitfalls of component design, as well as some tips and tricks to developing highly functional and extensible components.

Even if your primary interest is application development and not component design, you will get a great deal out of this chapter. Incorporating a custom component or two into your programs is an ideal way to spice up and enhance the productivity of your applications. Invariably, you will get caught in a situation while writing your application where, of all the components at your disposal, none is quite right for some particular task. That's where component design comes in. You will be able to tailor a component to meet your exact needs, and hopefully design it smart enough to use again and again in subsequent applications.

Component Building Basics

The following sections teach you the basic skills required to get you started in writing components. Then, we show you how to apply those skills by demonstrating how we designed some useful components.

Deciding Whether to Write a Component

Why go through the trouble of writing a custom control in the first place when it's probably less work to make do with an existing component or hack together something quick and dirty that "will do"? There are a number of reasons to write your own custom control:

- You want to design a new user-interface element that can be used in more than one application.
- You want to make your application more robust by separating its elements into logical object-oriented classes.

- You cannot find an existing Delphi component or ActiveX control that suits your needs for a particular situation.
- You recognize a market for a particular component, and you want to create a component to share with other Delphi developers for fun or profit.
- You want to increase your knowledge of Delphi, VCL internals, and the Win32 API.

One of the best ways to learn how to create custom components is from the people who invented them. Delphi's VCL source code is an invaluable resource for component writers, and it is highly recommended for anyone who is serious about creating custom components. The VCL source code is included in the Enterprise and Professional versions of Delphi.

Writing custom components can seem like a pretty daunting task, but don't believe the hype. Writing a custom component is only as hard or as easy as you make it. Components can be tough to write, of course, but you also can create very useful components fairly easily.

Component Writing Steps

Assuming that you have already defined a problem and have a component-based solution, here are the important points in creating a component from concept to deployment:

- First, you need an idea for a useful and hopefully unique component.
- Next, sit down and map out the algorithm for how the component will work.
- Start with the preliminaries—don't jump right into the component. Ask yourself, "What do I need up front to make this component work?"
- Try to break up the construction of your component into logical portions. This will not only modularize and simplify the creation of the component, but it also will help you to write cleaner, more organized code. Design your component with the thought that someone else might try to create a descendant component.
- Test your component in a test project first. You will be sorry if you immediately add it to the Component Palette.
- Finally, add the component and an optional bitmap to the Component Palette. After a little fine-tuning, it will be ready for you to drop into your Delphi applications.

The six basic steps to writing your Delphi component are as follows:

1. Deciding on an ancestor class.
2. Creating the Component Unit.
3. Adding properties, methods, and events to your new component.
4. Testing your component.

5. Registering your component with the Delphi environment.

6. Creating a help file for your component.

In this chapter, we will discuss the first five steps; however, it is beyond the scope of this chapter to get into the topic of writing help files. However, this doesn't mean that this step is any less important than the others. We recommend that you look into some of the third-party tools available that simplify writing help files. Also, Borland provides information on how to do this in its online help. Look up "Providing Help for Your Component" in the online help for more information.

Deciding on an Ancestor Class

In Chapter 10, "Component Architecture: VCL and CLX," we discussed the VCL hierarchy and the special purposes of the different classes at the different hierarchical levels. We wrote about four basic components from which your components will descend: standard controls, custom controls, graphical controls, and non-visual components. For instance, if you need to simply extend the behavior of an existing Win32 control such as TMemo, you'll be extending a standard control. If you need to define an entirely new component class, you'll be dealing with a custom control. Graphical controls let you create components that have a visual effect, but don't take up Win32 resources. Finally, if you want to create a component that can be edited from Delphi's Object Inspector but doesn't necessarily have a visual characteristic, you'll be creating a non-visual component. Different VCL classes represent these diverse types of components. You might want to review Chapter 10 unless you're quite comfortable with these concepts. Table 11.1 gives you a quick reference.

TABLE 11.1   VCL Classes as Component Base Classes

VCL Class	Types of Custom Controls
TObject	Although classes descending directly from TObject aren't components, strictly speaking, they do merit mention. You will use TObject as a base class for many things that you don't need to work with at design time. A good example is the TIniFile object.
TComponent	This is a starting point for many non-visual components. Its forte is that it offers built-in streaming capability to load and save itself in the IDE at design time.
TGraphicControl	Use this class when you want to create a custom component that has no window handle. TGraphicControl descendants are drawn on their parent's client surface, so they are easier on resources.
TWinControl	This is the base class for all components that require a window handle. It provides you with common properties and events specific to windowed controls.

TABLE 11.1 Continued

VCL Class	Types of Custom Controls
TCustomControl	This class descends from TWinControl. It introduces the concepts of a canvas and a Paint() method to give you greater control over the component's appearance. Use this class for most of your window-handled custom component needs.
TCustom*ClassName*	The VCL contains several classes that don't publish all their properties; they leave it up to descendant classes to do. This allows component developers to create custom components from the same base class and to publish only the predefined properties required for each customized class.
T*ComponentName*	This is an existing class such as TEdit, TPanel, or TScrollBox. Use an already established component as a base class for your class (such as TEdit), and custom components when you want to extend them rather than create a new one from scratch. Many of your custom components will fall into this category.

It is extremely important that you understand these various classes and also the capabilities of the existing components. The majority of the time, you'll find that an existing component already provides most of the functionality you require of your new component. Only by knowing the capabilities of existing components will you be able to decide from which component to derive your new component. We can't inject this knowledge into your brain from this book. What we can do is to tell you that you must make every effort to learn about each component and class within Delphi's VCL, and the only way to do that is to use it, even if only experimentally.

Creating a Component Unit

When you have decided on a component from which your new component will descend, you can go ahead and create a unit for your new component. We're going to go through the steps of designing a new component in the next several sections. Because we want to focus on the steps, and not on component functionality, this component will do nothing other than to illustrate these necessary steps.

The component is appropriately named TddgWorthless. TddgWorthless will descend from TCustomControl and will therefore have both a window handle and the capability to paint itself. This component will also inherit several properties, methods, and events already belonging to TCustomControl.

The easiest way to get started is to use the Component Expert, shown in Figure 11.1, to create a component unit.

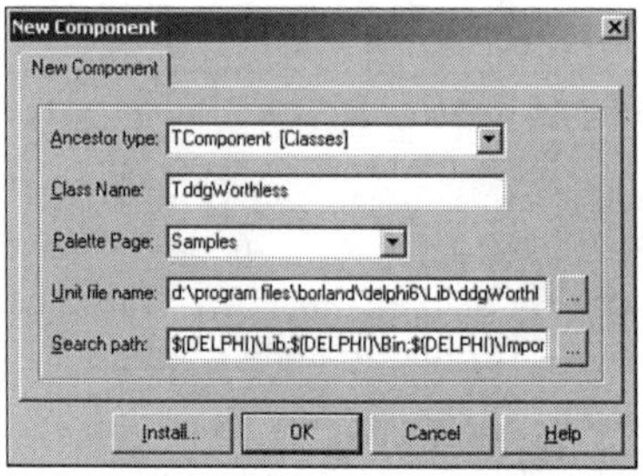

FIGURE 11.1

The Component Expert.

You invoke the Component Expert by selecting Component, New Component. In the Component Expert, you enter the component's ancestor classname, the component's classname, the palette page on which you want the component to appear, and the unit name for the component. When you click OK, Delphi automatically creates the component unit that has the component's type declaration and a register procedure. Listing 11.1 shows the unit created by Delphi.

LISTING 11.1   Worthless.pas—A Sample Delphi Component

```
unit Worthless;
interface
uses
  Windows, Messages, SysUtils, Classes, Graphics, Controls, Forms, Dialogs;
type
  TddgWorthless = class(TCustomControl)
  private
    { Private declarations }
  protected
    { Protected declarations }
  public
    { Public declarations }
  published
    { Published declarations }
  end;
procedure Register;
implementation
procedure Register;
begin
  RegisterComponents('DDG', [TddgWorthless]);
end;
end.
```

At this point, you can see that `TddgWorthless` is nothing more than a skeleton component. In the following sections, you'll add properties, methods, and events to `TddgWorthless`.

Creating Properties

In Chapter 10, we discussed using properties with your components. This section shows you how to add the various types of properties to your components.

Types of Properties

In Chapter 10, we listed the various property types. We're going to add properties of each of these types to the `TddgWorthless` component to illustrate the differences between each type. Each type of property is edited a bit differently from the Object Inspector. You will examine each of these types and how they are edited.

Adding Simple Properties to Components

Simple properties refer to numbers, strings, and characters. They can be edited directly by the user from within the Object Inspector and require no special access method. Listing 11.2 shows the `TddgWorthless` component with three simple properties.

LISTING 11.2 Simple Properties

```
TddgWorthless = class(TCustomControl)
  private
    // Internal Data Storage
    FIntegerProp: Integer;
    FStringProp: String;
    FCharProp: Char;
published
    // Simple property types
    property IntegerProp: Integer read FIntegerProp write FIntegerProp;
    property StringProp: String read FStringProp write FStringProp;
    property CharProp: Char read FCharProp write FCharProp;
  end;
```

You should already be familiar with the syntax used here because it was discussed previously in Chapter 10. Here, you have your internal data storage for the component declared in the `private` section. The properties that refer to these storage fields are declared in the `published` section, meaning that when you install the component in Delphi, you can edit the properties in the Object Inspector.

> **NOTE**
>
> When writing components, the convention is to make private field names begin with the letter *F*. For components and types in general, give the object or type a name starting with the letter *T*. Your code will be much more clear if you follow these simple conventions.

Adding Enumerated Properties to Components

You can edit user-defined enumerated properties and Boolean properties in the Object Inspector by double-clicking in the Value section or by selecting the property value from a drop-down list. An example of such a property is the Align property that exists on most visual components. To create an enumerated property, you must first define the enumerated type as follows:

```
TEnumProp = (epZero, epOne, epTwo, epThree);
```

You then define the internal storage field to hold the value specified by the user. Listing 11.3 shows two enumerated property types for the TddgWorthless component.

LISTING 11.3   Enumerated Properties

```
TddgWorthless = class(TCustomControl)
  private
    // Enumerated data types
    FEnumProp: TEnumProp;
    FBooleanProp: Boolean;
published
    property EnumProp: TEnumProp read FEnumProp write FEnumProp;
    property BooleanProp: Boolean read FBooleanProp write FBooleanProp;
  end;
```

We've excluded the other properties for illustrative purposes. If you were to install this component, its enumerated properties would appear in the Object Inspector as shown in Figure 11.2.

Adding Set Properties to Components

Set properties, when edited in the Object Inspector, appear as a set in Pascal syntax. An easier way to edit them is to expand the properties in the Object Inspector. Each set item then works in the Object Inspector like a Boolean property. To create a set property for the TddgWorthless component, we must first define a set type as follows:

```
TSetPropOption = (poOne, poTwo, poThree, poFour, poFive);
TSetPropOptions = set of TSetPropOption;
```

FIGURE 11.2
The Object Inspector showing enumerated properties for TddgWorthless.

Here, you first define a range for the set by defining an enumerated type, TSetPropOption.
Then you define the set TSetPropOptions.

You can now add a property of TSetPropOptions to the TddgWorthless component as follows:

```
TddgWorthless = class(TCustomControl) s
 private
  FOptions: TSetPropOptions;
published
  property Options: TSetPropOptions read FOptions write FOptions;
end;
```

Figure 11.3 shows how this property looks when expanded in the Object Inspector.

FIGURE 11.3
The set property in the Object Inspector.

Adding Object Properties to Components

Properties can also be objects or other components. For example, the TBrush and TPen properties of a TShape component are also objects. When a property is an object, it can be expanded
in the Object Inspector so its own properties can also be modified. Properties that are objects
must be descendants of TPersistent so that their published properties can be streamed and
displayed in the Object Inspector.

To define an object property for the TddgWorthless component, you must first define an object
that will serve as this property's type. This object is shown in Listing 11.4.

LISTING 11.4   TSomeObject Definition

```
TSomeObject = class(TPersistent)
  private
    FProp1: Integer;
    FProp2: String;
  public
    procedure Assign(Source: TPersistent);
  published
    property Prop1: Integer read FProp1 write FProp1;
    property Prop2: String read FProp2 write FProp2;
  end;
```

The TSomeObject class descends directly from TPersistent, although it doesn't have to. As
long as the object from which the new class descends is, itself, a descendant of TPersistent, it
can be used as another object's property.

We've given this class two properties of its own: Prop1 and Prop2, which are both simple
property types. We've also added a procedure, Assign(), to TSomeObject, which we'll discuss
momentarily.

Now, you can add a field of the type TSomeObject to the TddgWorthless component. However,
because this property is an object, it must be created. Otherwise, when the user places a
TddgWorthless component on the form, there won't be an instance of TSomeObject that the
user can edit. Therefore, it is necessary to override the Create() constructor for
TddgWorthless to create an instance of TSomeObject. Listing 11.5 shows the declaration of
TddgWorthless with its new object property.

LISTING 11.5—Adding Object Properties

```
TddgWorthless = class(TCustomControl)
private
  FSomeObject: TSomeObject;
  procedure SetSomeObject(Value: TSomeObject);
```

LISTING 11.5—Continued

```
public
  constructor Create(AOwner: TComponent); override;
  destructor Destroy; override;
published
  property SomeObject: TSomeObject read FSomeObject write SetSomeObject;
end;
```

Notice that we've included the overridden Create() constructor and Destroy() destructor.
We've also declared a write access method, SetSomeObject(), for the SomeObject property. A
write access method is often referred to as a *writer method* or *setter* method. Read access
methods are called *reader* or *getter methods*. As you might recall from Chapter 10, writer
methods must have one parameter of the same type as the property to which they belong. By
convention, the name of the writer method usually begins with Set.

We've defined the TddgWorthless.Create() constructor as follows:

```
constructor TddgWorthless.Create(AOwner: TComponent);
begin
  inherited Create(AOwner);
  FSomeObject := TSomeObject.Create;
end;
```

Here, we first call the inherited Create() constructor and then create the instance of the
TSomeObject class. Because Create() is called both when the user drops the component on
the form at design time and when the application is run, you can be assured that FSomeObject
will always be valid.

You must also override the Destroy() destructor to free the object before you free the
TddgWorthless component. The code to do this follows:

```
destructor TddgWorthless.Destroy;
begin
  FSomeObject.Free;
  inherited Destroy;
end;
```

Now that we've shown how to create the instance of TSomeObject, consider what would happen if the user executes the following code at runtime:

```
var
  MySomeObject: TSomeObject;
begin
  MySomeObject := TSomeObject.Create;
  ddgWorthless.SomeObjectj := MySomeObject;
end;
```

If the `TddgWorthless.SomeObject` property were defined without a writer method like the following, when the user assigns her own object to the `SomeObject` field, the previous instance to which `FSomeObject` referred would be lost:

```
property SomeObject: TSomeObject read FSomeObject write FSomeObject;
```

As you might recall from Chapter 2, "The Object Pascal Language," object instances are really pointer references to the actual object. When you make an assignment as shown in the preceding example, you refer the pointer to another object instance while the previous object instance still hangs around. When designing components, you want to avoid having to place conditions on your users when accessing properties. To prevent this pitfall, foolproof your component by creating access methods for properties that are objects. These access methods can then ensure that no resources get lost when the user assigns new values to these properties. The access method for `SomeObject` does just that and is shown here:

```
procedure TddgWorthLess.SetSomeObject(Value: TSomeObject);
begin
  if Assigned(Value) then
    FSomeObject.Assign(Value);
end;
```

The `SetSomeObject()` method calls the `FSomeObject.Assign()`, passing it the new `TSomeObject` reference. `TSomeObject.Assign()` is implemented as follows:

```
procedure TSomeObject.Assign(Source: TPersistent);
begin
  if Source is TSomeObject then
  begin
    FProp1 := TSomeObject(Source).Prop1;
    FProp2 := TSomeObject(Source).Prop2;
    inherited Assign(Source);
  end;
end;
```

In `TSomeObject.Assign()`, you first ensure that the user has passed in a valid `TSomeObject` instance. If so, you then copy the property values from `Source` accordingly. This illustrates another technique you'll see throughout the VCL for assigning objects to other objects. If you have the VCL source code, you might take a look at the various `Assign()` methods such as `TBrush` and `TShape` to see how they are implemented. This would give you some ideas on how to implement them in your components.

CAUTION

Never make an assignment to a property in a property's writer method. For example, examine the following property declaration:

```
property SomeProp: integer read FSomeProp write SetSomeProp;
  ....
procedure SetSomeProp(Value:integer);
begin
  SomeProp := Value;  // This causes infinite recursion }
end;
```

Because you are accessing the property itself (not the internal storage field), you cause the SetSomeProp() method to be called again, which results in a recursive loop. Eventually, the program will crash with a stack overflow. Always access the internal storage field in the writer methods of properties.

Adding Array Properties to Components

Some properties lend themselves to being accessed as though they were arrays. That is, they contain a list of items that can be referenced with an index value. The actual items referenced can be of any object type. Examples of such properties are TScreen.Fonts, TMemo.Lines, and TDBGrid.Columns. Such properties require their own property editors. We will get into creating property editors in Chapter 12, "Advanced VCL Component Building." Therefore, we will not go into detail on creating array properties with a list of different object types until later. For now, we'll show a simple method for defining a property that can be indexed as though it were an array of items, yet contains no list at all. We're going to put aside the TddgWorthless component for a moment and instead look at the TddgPlanets component. TddgPlanets contains two properties: PlanetName and PlanetPosition. PlanetName will be an array property that returns the name of the planet based on the value of an integer index. PlanetPosition won't use an integer index, but rather a string index. If this string is one of the planet names, the result will be the planet's position in the solar system.

For example, the following statement will display the string "Neptune" by using the TddgPlanets.PlanetName property:

```
ShowMessage(ddgPlanets.PlanetName[8]);
```

Compare the difference when the sentence From the sun, Neptune is planet number: 8 is generated from the following statement:

```
ShowMessage('From the sun, Neptune is planet number: '+
  IntToStr(ddgPlanets.PlanetPosition['Neptune']));
```

Before we show you this component, we'll list some key characteristics of array properties that differ from the other properties we've mentioned:

- Array properties are declared with one or more index parameters. These indexes can be of any simple type. For example, the index can be an integer or a string, but not a record or a class.

- Both the `read` and `write` property access directives must be methods. They cannot be one of the component's fields.

- If the array property is indexed by multiple index values, that is, the property represents a multidimensional array, the access method must include parameters for each index in the same order as defined by the property.

Now, we'll get to the actual component shown in Listing 11.6.

LISTING 11.6   Using `TddgPlanets` to Illustrate Array Properties

```
unit planets;

interface

uses
  Classes, SysUtils;

type

  TddgPlanets = class(TComponent)
  private
    // Array property access methods
    function GetPlanetName(const AIndex: Integer): String;
    function GetPlanetPosition(const APlanetName: String): Integer;
  public
    { Array property indexed by an integer value. This will be the default
      array property.  }
    property PlanetName[const AIndex: Integer]: String
        read GetPlanetName; default;
    // Array property index by a string value
    property PlanetPosition[const APlantetName: String]: Integer
        read GetPlanetPosition;
  end;

implementation

const
```

LISTING 11.6 Continued

```
// Declare a constant array containing planet names
PlanetNames: array[1..9] of String[7] =
  ('Mercury', 'Venus', 'Earth', 'Mars', 'Jupiter', 'Saturn',
   'Uranus', 'Neptune', 'Pluto');

function TddgPlanets.GetPlanetName(const AIndex: Integer): String;
begin
  { Return the name of the planet specified by Index. If Index is
    out of the range, then raise an exception }
  if (AIndex < 0) or (AIndex > 9) then
    raise Exception.Create('Wrong Planet number, enter a number 1-9')
  else
    Result := PlanetNames[AIndex];
end;

function TddgPlanets.GetPlanetPosition(const APlanetName: String): Integer;
var
  i: integer;
begin
  Result := 0;
  i := 0;
  { Compare PName to each planet name and return the index of the
    appropriate position where PName appears in the constant array.
    Otherwise return zero. }
  repeat
    inc(i);
  until (i = 10) or (CompareStr(UpperCase(APlanetName),
        UpperCase(PlanetNames[i])) = 0);

  if i <> 10 then // A Planet name was found
    Result := i;
end;

end.
```

This component gives you an idea of how you would create an array property with both an
integer and string being used as an index. Notice how the value returned from reading the
property's value is based on the function return value and not a value from a storage field, as is
the case with the other properties. You can refer to the code's comments for additional explanation on this component.

Default Values

You can give a property a default value by assigning a value to the property in the component's constructor. Therefore, if we added the following statement to the constructor of the TddgWorthless component, its FIntegerProp property would always default to 100 when the component is first placed onto the form:

```
FIntegerProp := 100;
```

This is probably the best place to mention the Default and NoDefault directives for property declarations. If you've looked at Delphi's VCL source code, you've probably noticed that some property declarations contain the Default directive, as is the case with the TComponent.FTag property:

```
property Tag: Longint read FTag write FTag default 0;
```

Don't confuse this statement with the default value specified in the component's constructor that actually sets the property value. For example, change the declaration of the IntegerProp property for the TddgWorthless component to read as follows:

```
property IntegerProp: Integer read FIntegerProp write FIntegerProp default 100;
```

This statement doesn't set the value of the property to 100. This only affects whether the property value is saved when you save a form containing the TddgWorthless component. If IntegerProp's value isn't 100, the value will be saved to the DFM file. Otherwise, it doesn't get saved because 100 is what the property value will be in a newly constructed object prior to reading its properties from the stream. It is recommended that you use the Default directive whenever possible because it might speed up the load time of your forms. It is important for you to realize that the Default directive doesn't set the value of the property. You must do that in the component's constructor as was shown previously.

The NoDefault directive is used to redeclare a property that specifies a default value, so it will always be written to the stream regardless of its value. For example, you can redeclare your component to not specify a default value for the Tag property:

```
TSample = class(TComponent)
published
  property Tag NoDefault;
```

Note that you should never declare anything NoDefault unless you have a specific reason. An example of such a property is TForm.PixelsPerInch, which must always be stored so that scaling will work right at runtime. Also, string, floating point, and int64 type properties cannot declare default values.

To change a property's default value, you redeclare it by using the new default value (but no reader or writer methods).

Default Array Properties

You can declare an array property so that it is the default property for the component to which it belongs. This allows the component user to implement the object instance as though it were an array variable. For example, using the TddgPlanets component, we declared the TddgPlanets.PlanetName property with the default keyword. By doing this, the component user isn't required to use the property name, PlanetName, in order to retrieve a value. One simply has to place the index next to the object identifier. Therefore, the following two lines of code will produce the same result:

```
ShowMessage(ddgPlanets.PlanetName[8]);
ShowMessage(ddgPlanets[8]);
```

Only one default array property can be declared for an object, and it cannot be overridden in descendants.

Creating Events

In Chapter 10, we introduced events and told you that events were special properties linked to code that get executed whenever a particular action occurs. In this section, we're going to discuss events in more detail. We'll show you how events are generated and how you can define your own event properties for your custom components.

Where Do Events Come From?

The general definition of an event is basically any type of occurrence that might result from user interaction, the system, or from code logic. The event is linked to some code that responds to that occurrence. The linkage of the event to code that responds to an event is called an *event property* and is provided in the form of a method pointer. The method to which an event property points is called an *event handler*.

For example, when the user clicks the mouse button, a WM_MOUSEDOWN message is sent to the Win32 system. Win32 passes that message to the control for which the message was intended. This control can then respond to the message. The control can respond to this event by first checking to see whether there is any code to execute. It does this by checking to see whether the event property points to any code. If so, it executes that code, or rather, the event handler.

The OnClick event is just one of the standard event properties defined by Delphi. OnClick and other event properties each have a corresponding *event-dispatching method*. This method is typically a protected method of the component to which it belongs. This method performs the logic to determine whether the event property refers to any code provided by the user of the component. For the OnClick property, this would be the Click() method. Both the OnClick property and the Click() method are defined by TControl as follows:

```
TControl = class(TComponent)
private
  FOnClick: TNotifyEvent;
protected
  procedure Click; dynamic;
  property OnClick: TNotifyEvent read FOnClick write FOnClick;
end;
```

Here is the TControl.Click() method:

```
procedure TControl.Click;
begin
  if Assigned(FOnClick) then FOnClick(Self);
end;
```

One bit of essential information that you must understand is that event properties are nothing more than method pointers. Notice that the FOnClick property is defined to be a TNotifyEvent. TNotifyEvent is defined as follows:

```
TNotifyEvent = procedure(Sender: TObject) of object;
```

This says that TNotifyEvent is a procedure that takes one parameter, Sender, which is of the type TObject. The directive, of object, is what makes this procedure become a method. This means that an additional *implicit* parameter that you don't see in the parameter list also gets passed to this procedure. This is the Self parameter that refers to the object to which this method belongs. When the Click() method of a component is called, it checks to see if FOnClick actually points to a method, and if so, calls that method.

As a component writer, you write all the code that defines your event, your event property, and your dispatching methods. The component user will provide the event handler when using your component. Your event-dispatching method will check to see whether the user has assigned any code to your event property and then execute it when code exists.

In Chapter 10, we discussed how event handlers are assigned to event properties either at runtime or at design time. In the following section, we show you how to create your own events, event properties, and dispatching methods.

Defining Event Properties

Before you define an event property, you need to determine whether you need a special event type. It helps to be familiar with the common event properties that exist in the Delphi VCL. Most of the time, you'll be able to have your component descend from one of the existing components and just use its event properties, or you might have to surface a protected event property. If you determine that none of the existing events meet your need, you can define your own.

As an example, consider the following scenario. Suppose you want a component containing an event that gets called every half-minute based on the system clock. That is, it gets invoked on the minute and on the half minute. Well, you can certainly use a TTimer component to check the system time and then perform some action whenever the time is at the minute or half minute. However you might want to incorporate this code into your own component and then make that component available to your users so that all they have to do is add code to your OnHalfMinute event.

The TddgHalfMinute component shown in Listing 11.7 illustrates how you would design such a component. More importantly, it shows how you would go about creating your own event type.

LISTING 11.7   TddgHalfMinute—Event Creation

```
unit halfmin;

interface

uses
  Windows, Messages, SysUtils, Classes, Graphics, Controls,
  Forms, Dialogs, ExtCtrls;

type
  { Define a procedure for the event handler. The event property will
    be of this procedure type. This type will take two parameters, the
    object that invoked the event and a TDateTime value to represent
    the time that the event occurred. For our component this will be
    every half-minute. }
  TTimeEvent = procedure(Sender: TObject; TheTime: TDateTime) of object;

  TddgHalfMinute = class(TComponent)
  private
    FTimer: TTimer;
    { Define a storage field to point to the user's event handler.
      The user's event handler must be of the procedural type
      TTimeEvent. }
    FOnHalfMinute: TTimeEvent;
    FOldSecond, FSecond: Word; // Variables used in the code
    { Define a procedure, FTimerTimer that will be assigned to
      FTimer.OnClick. This procedure must be of the type TNotifyEvent
      which is the type of TTimer.OnClick. }
```

LISTING 11.7 Continued

```
    procedure FTimerTimer(Sender: TObject);
  protected
    { Define the dispatching method for the OnHalfMinute event. }
    procedure DoHalfMinute(TheTime: TDateTime); dynamic;
  public
    constructor Create(AOwner: TComponent); override;
    destructor Destroy; override;
  published
    // Define the actual property that will show in the Object Inspector
    property OnHalfMinute: TTimeEvent read FOnHalfMinute write FOnHalfMinute;
  end;

implementation

constructor TddgHalfMinute.Create(AOwner: TComponent);
{ The Create constructor, creates the TTimer instanced for FTimer. It
  then sets up the various properties of FTimer, including its OnTimer
  event handler which is TddgHalfMinute's FTimerTimer() method. Notice
  that FTimer.Enabled is set to true only if the component is running
  and not while the component is in design mode. }
begin
  inherited Create(AOwner);
  // If the component is in design mode, do not enable FTimer.
  if not (csDesigning in ComponentState) then
  begin
    FTimer := TTimer.Create(self);
    FTimer.Enabled := True;
    // Set up the other properties, including the FTimer.OnTimer event handler
    FTimer.Interval := 500;
    FTimer.OnTimer := FTimerTimer;
  end;
end;

destructor TddgHalfMinute.Destroy;
begin
  FTimer.Free;
  inherited Destroy;
end;

procedure TddgHalfMinute.FTimerTimer(Sender: TObject);
{ This method serves as the FTimer.OnTimer event handler and is assigned
  to FTimer.OnTimer at run-time in TddgHalfMinute's constructor.
```

Listing 11.7 Continued

```
  This method gets the system time, and then determines whether or not
  the time is on the minute, or on the half-minute. If either of these
  conditions are true, it calls the OnHalfMinute dispatching method,
  DoHalfMinute. }
var
  DT: TDateTime;
  Temp: Word;
begin
  DT := Now; // Get the system time.
  FOldSecond := FSecond; // Save the old second.
  // Get the time values, needed is the second value
  DecodeTime(DT, Temp, Temp, FSecond, Temp);

  { If not the same second when this method was last called, and if
    it is a half minute, call DoOnHalfMinute. }
  if FSecond <> FOldSecond then
    if ((FSecond = 30) or (FSecond = 0)) then
      DoHalfMinute(DT)
end;

procedure TddgHalfMinute.DoHalfMinute(TheTime: TDateTime);
{ This method is the dispatching method for the OnHalfMinute event.
  it checks to see if the user of the component has attached an
  event handler to OnHalfMinute and if so, calls that code. }
begin
  if Assigned(FOnHalfMinute) then
    FOnHalfMinute(Self, TheTime);
end;

end.
```

When creating your own events, you must determine what information you want to provide to users of your component as a parameter in the event handler. For example, when you create an event handler for the TEdit.OnKeyPress event, your event handler looks like the following code:

```
procedure TForm1.Edit1KeyPress(Sender: TObject; var Key: Char);
begin
end;
```

Not only do you get a reference to the object that caused the event, but you also get a Char parameter specifying the key that was pressed. Deep in the Delphi VCL, this event occurred as a result of a WM_CHAR Win32 message that drags along some additional information relating to the key pressed. Delphi takes care of extracting the necessary data and making it available to component users as event handler parameters. One of the nice things about the whole scheme is that it enables component writers to take information that might be somewhat complex to understand and make it available to component users in a much more understandable and easy-to-use format.

Notice the var parameter in the preceding Edit1KeyPress() method. You might be wondering why this method wasn't declared as a function that returns a Char type instead of a procedure. Although method types can be functions, you shouldn't declare events as functions because it will introduce ambiguity; when you refer to a method pointer that is a function, you can't know whether you're referring to the function result or to the function pointer value itself. By the way, one function event in the VCL slipped past the developers from the Delphi 1 days, and now it must remain. This event is the TApplication.OnHelp event.

Looking at Listing 11.7, you'll see that we've defined the procedure type TOnHalfMinute as this:

```
TTimeEvent = procedure(Sender: TObject; TheTime: TDateTime) of object;
```

This procedure type defines the procedure type for the OnHalfMinute event handler. Here, we decided that we want the user to have a reference to the object causing the event to occur and the TDateTime value of when the event occurred.

The FOnHalfMinute storage field is the reference to the user's event handler and is surfaced to the Object Inspector at design time through the OnHalfMinute property.

The basic functionality of the component uses a TTimer object to check the seconds value every half second. If the seconds value is 0 or 30, it invokes the DoHalfMinute() method, which is responsible for checking for the existence of an event handler and then calling it. Much of this is explained in the code's comments, which you should read over.

After installing this component to Delphi's Component Palette, you can place the component on the form and add the following event handler to the OnHalfMinute event:

```
procedure TForm1.ddgHalfMinuteHalfMinute(Sender: TObject; TheTime: TDateTime);
begin
  ShowMessage('The Time is '+TimeToStr(TheTime));
end;
```

This should illustrate how your newly defined event type becomes an event handler.

Creating Methods

Adding methods to components is no different from adding methods to other objects. However, there are a few guidelines that you should always take into account when designing components.

No Interdependencies!

One of the key goals behind creating components is to simplify the use of the component for the end user. Therefore, you will want to avoid any method interdependencies as much as possible. For example, you never want to force the user to have to call a particular method in order to use the component, and methods shouldn't have to be called in any particular order. Also, methods called by the user shouldn't place the component in a state that makes other events or methods invalid. Finally, you will want to give your methods meaningful names so that the user doesn't have to try to guess what a method does.

Method Exposure

Part of designing a component is to know what methods to make private, public, or protected. You must take into account not only users of your component, but also those who might use your component as an ancestor for yet another custom component. Table 11.2 will help you decide what goes where in your custom component.

TABLE 11.2 Private, Protected, Public, or Published?

Directive	What Goes There?
Private	Instance variables and methods that you don't want the descendant type to be able to access or modify. Typically, you will give access to some private instance variables through properties that have read and write directives set in such a way as to help prevent users from shooting themselves in the foot. Therefore, you want to avoid giving access to any methods that are property-implementation methods.
Protected	Instance variables, methods, and properties that you want descendant classes to be able to access and modify—but not users of your class. It is a common practice to place properties in the protected section of a base class for descendant classes to publish at their discretion.
Public	Methods and properties that you want to have accessible to any user of your class. If you have properties that you want to be accessible at runtime, but not at design time, this is the place to put them.
Published	Properties that you want to be placed on the Object Inspector at design time. *Runtime Type Information (RTTI)* is generated for all properties in this section.

Constructors and Destructors

When creating a new component, you have the option of overriding the ancestor component's constructor and defining your own. You should keep a few precautions in mind when doing so.

Overriding Constructors

Always make sure to include the `override` directive when declaring a constructor on a TComponent descendant class. Here's an example:

```
TSomeComopnent = class(TComponent)
private
  { Private declarations }
protected
  { Protected declarations }
public
  constructor Create(AOwner: TComponent); override;
published
  { Published declarations }
end;
```

> **NOTE**
>
> The `Create()` constructor is made virtual at the TComponent level. Non-component classes have static constructors that are invoked from within the constructor of TComponent classes. Therefore, if you are creating a non-component, descendant class such as the following, the constructor cannot be overridden because it is not virtual:
>
> ```
> TMyObject = class(TPersistant)
> ```
>
> You simply redeclare the constructor in this instance.

Although not adding the override directive is syntactically legal, it can cause problems when using your component. This is because when you use the component (both at design time and at runtime), the non-virtual constructor won't be called by code that creates the component through a class reference (such as the streaming system).

Also, be sure that you call the inherited constructor inside your constructor's code:

```
constructor TSomeComponent.Create(AOwner: TComponent);
begin
  inherited Create(AOwner);
  // Place your code here.
end;
```

Design-Time Behavior

Remember that your component's constructor is called whenever the component is created. This includes the component's design-time creation—when you place it on the form. You might want to prevent certain actions from occurring when the component is being designed. For example, in the TddgHalfMinute component, you created a TTimer component inside the component's constructor. Although it doesn't hurt to do this, it can be avoided by making sure that the TTimer is only created at runtime.

You can check the ComponentState property of a component to determine its current state. Table 11.3 lists the various component states as shown in Delphi 6's online help.

TABLE 11.3 Component State Values

Flag	Component State
csAncestor	Set if the component was introduced in an ancestor form. Only set if csDesigning is also set.
csDesigning	Design mode, meaning that it is in a form being manipulated by a form designer.
csDestroying	The component is about to be destroyed.
csFixups	Set if the component is linked to a component in another form that hasn't yet been loaded. This flag is cleared when all pending fixups are resolved.
csLoading	Loading from a filer object.
csReading	Reading its property values from a stream.
csUpdating	The component is being updated to reflect changes in an ancestor form. Only set if csAncestor is also set.
csWriting	Writing its property values to a stream.

You will mostly use the csDesigning state to determine whether your component is in design mode. You can do this with the following statement:

```
inherited Create(AOwner);
if  csDesigning in ComponentState then
  { Do your stuff }
```

You should note that the csDesigning state is uncertain until after the inherited constructor has been called and the component is being created with an owner. This is almost always the case in the IDE form designer.

Overriding Destructors

The general guideline to follow when overriding destructors is to make sure that you call the inherited destructor only after you free up resources allocated by your component, not before. The following code illustrates this:

```
destructor TMyComponent.Destroy;
begin
  FTimer.Free;
  MyStrings.Free;
  inherited Destroy;
end;
```

> **TIP**
>
> As a rule of thumb, when you override constructors, you usually call the inherited constructor first, and when you override destructors, you usually call the inherited destructor last. This ensures that the class has been set up before you modify it and that all dependent resources have been cleaned up before you dispose of a class.
>
> There are exceptions to this rule, but you generally should stick with it unless you have a good reason not to.

Registering Your Component

Registering the component tells Delphi which component to place on the Component Palette. If you used the Component Expert to design your component, you don't have to do anything here because Delphi has already generated the code for you. However, if you are creating your component manually, you'll need to add the `Register()` procedure to your component's unit.

All you have to do is add the procedure `Register()` to the `interface` section of the component's unit.

The `Register` procedure simply calls the `RegisterComponents()` procedure for every component that you are registering in Delphi. The `RegisterComponents()` procedure takes two parameters: the name of the page on which to place the components, and an array of component types. Listing 11.8 shows how to do this.

LISTING 11.8 Registering Components

```
Unit MyComp;
interface
type
  TMyComp = class(TComponent)
  ...
  end;
```

LISTING 11.8   Continued

```
  TOtherComp = class(TComponent)
  ...
  end;
procedure Register;
implementation
{ TMyComp methods }
{ TOtherCompMethods }
procedure Register;
begin
  RegisterComponents('DDG', [TMyComp, TOtherComp]);
end;
end.
```

The preceding code registers the components TMyComp and TOtherComp and places them on Delphi's Component Palette on a page labeled DDG.

The Component Palette

In Delphi 1 and 2, Delphi maintained a single component library file that stored all components, icons, and editors for design-time usage. Although it was sometimes convenient to have everything dealing with design in one file, it could easily get unwieldy when many components were placed in the component library. Additionally, the more components you added to the palette, the longer it would take to rebuild the component library when adding new components.

Thanks to packages, introduced with Delphi 3, you can split up your components into several design packages. Although it's slightly more complex to deal with multiple files, this solution is significantly more configurable. The time required to rebuild a package after adding a component is a fraction of the time it took to rebuild the component library.

By default, new components are added to a package called DclUser6, but you can create and install new design packages using the File, New, Package menu item. The CD-ROM accompanying this book contains a pre-built design package called DdgDT6.dpk, which includes the components from this book. The runtime package is named DdgRT6.dpk.

If your design-time support involves anything more than a call to RegisterComponents() (like property editors or component editors or expert registrations), you should move the Register() procedure and the information it registers into a unit separate from your component. The reason for this is that if you compile your all-in-one unit into a runtime package, and your all-in-one unit's Register procedure refers to classes or procedures that exist only in design-time IDE packages, your runtime package is unusable. Design-time support should be packaged separately from runtime material.

Testing the Component

Although it's very exciting when you finally write a component and are in the testing stages, don't get carried away by trying to add your component to the Component Palette before it has been debugged sufficiently. You should do all preliminary testing with your component by creating a project that creates and uses a dynamic instance of the component. The reason for this is that your component lives inside the IDE when it is used at design time. If your component contains a bug that corrupts memory, for example, it might crash the IDE as well. Listing 11.9 depicts a unit for testing the TddgExtendedMemo component that will be created later in this chapter. This project can be found on the CD in the project TestEMem.dpr.

LISTING 11.9   Testing the TddgExtendedMemo Component

```
unit MainFrm;

interface

uses
  Windows, Messages, SysUtils, Classes, Graphics, Controls,
  Forms, Dialogs, StdCtrls, exmemo, ExtCtrls;

type

  TMainForm = class(TForm)
    btnCreateMemo: TButton;
    btnGetRowCol: TButton;
    btnSetRowCol: TButton;
    edtColumn: TEdit;
    edtRow: TEdit;
    Panel1: TPanel;
    procedure btnCreateMemoClick(Sender: TObject);
    procedure btnGetRowColClick(Sender: TObject);
    procedure btnSetRowColClick(Sender: TObject);
  public
    EMemo: TddgExtendedMemo;  // Declare the component.
    procedure OnScroll(Sender: TObject);
  end;

var
  MainForm: TMainForm;

implementation

{$R *.DFM}
```

LISTING 11.9 Continued

```
procedure TMainForm.btnCreateMemoClick(Sender: TObject);
begin
  { Dynamically create the component. Make sure to make the appropriate
    property assignments so that the component can be used normally.
    These assignments depend on the component being tested }
  if not Assigned(EMemo) then
  begin
    EMemo := TddgExtendedMemo.Create(self);
    EMemo.Parent := Panel1;
    EMemo.ScrollBars := ssBoth;
    EMemo.WordWrap := True;
    EMemo.Align := alClient;
    // Assign event handlers to untested events.
    EMemo.OnVScroll := OnScroll;
    EMemo.OnHScroll := OnScroll;
  end;
end;

{ Write whatever methods are required to test the run-time behavior
  of the component. This includes methods to access each of the
  new properties and methods belonging to the component.

  Also, create event handlers for user-defined events so that you can
  test them. Since you're creating the comoponent at run-time, you
  have to manually assign the event handlers as was done in the
  above Create() constructor.
}
procedure TMainForm.btnGetRowColClick(Sender: TObject);
begin
  if Assigned(EMemo) then
    ShowMessage(Format('Row: %d  Column: %d', [EMemo.Row, EMemo.Column]));
  EMemo.SetFocus;
end;

procedure TMainForm.btnSetRowColClick(Sender: TObject);
begin
  if Assigned(EMemo) then
  begin
    EMemo.Row := StrToInt(edtRow.Text);
    EMemo.Column := StrToInt(edtColumn.Text);
    EMemo.SetFocus;
  end;
end;
```

LISTING 11.9   Continued

```
procedure TMainForm.OnScroll(Sender: TObject);
begin
  MessageBeep(0);
end;

end.
```

Keep in mind that even testing the component at design time doesn't mean that your component is foolproof. Some design-time behavior can still raise havoc with the Delphi IDE, such as not calling the inherited Create() constructor.

> **NOTE**
>
> You cannot assume that your component has been created and set up by the design-time environment. Your component must be fully usable after only the Create() constructor has executed. Therefore, you shouldn't treat the Loaded() method as part of the component construction process. The Loaded() method is called only when the component is loaded from a stream—such as when it is placed in a form built at design time. Loaded() marks the end of the streaming process. If your component was simply created (not streamed), Loaded() isn't called.

Providing a Component Icon

No custom component would be complete without its own icon for the Component Palette. To create one of these icons, use Delphi's Image Editor (or your favorite bitmap editor) to create a 24×24 bitmap on which you will draw the component's icon. This bitmap must be stored within a DCR file. A file with a .dcr extension is nothing more than a renamed RES file. Therefore, if you store your icon in a RES file, you can simply rename it to a DCR file.

> **TIP**
>
> Even if you have a 256 or higher color driver, save your Component Palette icon as a 16-color bitmap if you plan on releasing the component to others. Your 256-color bitmaps most likely will look awful on machines running 16-color drivers.

After you create the bitmap in the DCR file, give the bitmap the same name as the classname of your component—in all capital letters. Save the resource file as the same name as your component's unit with a .dcr extension. Therefore, if your component is named TXYZComponent, the bitmap name is TXYZCOMPONENT. If the component's unit name is XYZCOMP.PAS, name the resource file XYZCOMP.DCR. Place this file in the same directory as the unit, and when you recompile the unit, the bitmap is linked into the component library automatically.

Sample Components

The remaining sections of this chapter give some real examples of component creation. The components created here serve two primary purposes. First, they illustrate the techniques explained in the first part of this chapter. Second, you can actually use these components in your applications. You might even decide to extend their functionality to meet your needs.

Extending Win32 Component Wrapper Capabilities

In some cases, you might want to extend the functionality of existing components, especially those components that wrap the Win32 control classes. We're going to show you how to do this by creating two components that extend the behavior of the TMemo control and the TListBox control.

TddgExtendedMemo: Extending the TMemo Component

Although the TMemo component is quite robust, there are a few features it doesn't make available that would be useful. For starters, it's not capable of providing the caret position in terms of the row and column on which the caret sits. We'll extend the TMemo component to provide these as public properties.

Additionally, it is sometimes convenient to perform some action whenever the user touches the TMemo's scrollbars. You'll create events to which the user can attach code whenever these scrolling events occur.

The source code for the TddgExtendedMemo component is shown in Listing 11.10.

LISTING 11.10   ExtMemo.pas—The Source for the TddgExtendedMemo Component

```
unit ExtMemo;

interface

uses
  Windows, Messages, Classes, StdCtrls;

type

  TddgExtendedMemo = class(TMemo)
  private
    FRow: Longint;
```

Listing 11.10   Continued

```delphi
    FColumn: Longint;
    FOnHScroll: TNotifyEvent;
    FOnVScroll: TNotifyEvent;
    procedure WMHScroll(var Msg: TWMHScroll); message WM_HSCROLL;
    procedure WMVScroll(var Msg: TWMVScroll); message WM_VSCROLL;
    procedure SetRow(Value: Longint);
    procedure SetColumn(Value: Longint);
    function GetRow: Longint;
    function GetColumn: Longint;
  protected
    // Event dispatching methods
    procedure HScroll; dynamic;
    procedure VScroll; dynamic;
  public
    property Row: Longint read GetRow write SetRow;
    property Column: Longint read GetColumn write SetColumn;
  published
    property OnHScroll: TNotifyEvent read FOnHScroll write FOnHScroll;
    property OnVScroll: TNotifyEvent read FOnVScroll write FOnVScroll;
  end;


implementation

procedure TddgExtendedMemo.WMHScroll(var Msg: TWMHScroll);
begin
  inherited;
  HScroll;
end;

procedure TddgExtendedMemo.WMVScroll(var Msg: TWMVScroll);
begin
  inherited;
  VScroll;
end;

procedure TddgExtendedMemo.HScroll;
{ This is the OnHScroll event dispatch method. It checks to see
  if OnHScroll points to an event handler and calls it if it does. }
begin
  if Assigned(FOnHScroll) then
    FOnHScroll(self);
end;
```

LISTING 11.10 Continued

```
procedure TddgExtendedMemo.VScroll;
{ This is the OnVScroll event dispatch method. It checks to see
  if OnVScroll points to an event handler and calls it if it does. }
begin
  if Assigned(FOnVScroll) then
    FOnVScroll(self);
end;

procedure TddgExtendedMemo.SetRow(Value: Longint);
{ The EM_LINEINDEX returns the character position of the first
  character in the line specified by wParam. The Value is used for
  wParam in this instance. Setting SelStart to this return value
  positions the caret on the line specified by Value. }
begin
  SelStart := Perform(EM_LINEINDEX, Value, 0);
  FRow := SelStart;
end;

function TddgExtendedMemo.GetRow: Longint;
{ The EM_LINEFROMCHAR returns the line in which the character specified
  by wParam sits. If -1 is passed as wParam, the line number at which
  the caret sits is returned. }
begin
  Result := Perform(EM_LINEFROMCHAR, -1, 0);
end;

procedure TddgExtendedMemo.SetColumn(Value: Longint);
begin
  { Get the length of the current line using the EM_LINELENGTH
    message. This message takes a character position as WParam.
    The length of the line in which that character sits is returned. }
  FColumn := Perform(EM_LINELENGTH, Perform(EM_LINEINDEX, GetRow, 0), 0);
  { If the FColumn is greater than the value passed in, then set
    FColumn to the value passed in }
  if FColumn > Value then
    FColumn := Value;
  // Now set SelStart to the newly specified position
  SelStart := Perform(EM_LINEINDEX, GetRow, 0) + FColumn;
end;

function TddgExtendedMemo.GetColumn: Longint;
begin
  { The EM_LINEINDEX message returns the line index of a specified
    character passed in as wParam. When wParam is -1 then it
```

LISTING 11.10 Continued

```
    returns the index of the current line. Subtracting SelStart from this
    value returns the column position }
  Result := SelStart - Perform(EM_LINEINDEX, -1, 0);
end;

end.
```

We'll discuss adding the capability to provide row and column information to TddgExtendedMemo. Notice that we've added two private fields to the component, FRow and FColumn. These fields will hold the row and column of the TddgExtendedMemo's caret position. We've also provided the Row and Column public properties. These properties are made public because there's really no use for them at design time. The Row and Column properties have both reader and writer access methods. For the Row property, these access methods are GetRow() and SetRow(). The Column access methods are GetColumn() and SetColumn(). For all practical purposes, you probably could do away with the FRow and FColumn storage fields because the values for Row and Column are provided through access methods. However, we've left them there because it offers the opportunity to extend this component.

The four access methods make use of various EM_*XXXX* Messages. The code comments explain what is going on in each method and how these messages are used to provide Row and Column information for the component. The TddgExtendedMemo component also provides two new events: OnHScroll and OnVScroll. The OnHScroll event occurs whenever the user clicks the horizontal scrollbar of the control. Likewise, the OnVScroll occurs when the user clicks the vertical scrollbar. To surface such events, you have to capture the WM_HSCROLL and WM_VSCROLL Win32 messages that are passed to the control whenever the user clicks either scrollbar. Thus, you've created the two message handlers: WMHScroll() and WMVScroll(). These two message handlers call the event-dispatching methods HScroll() and VScroll(). These methods are responsible for checking whether the component user has provided event handlers for the OnHScroll and OnVScroll events and then calling those event handlers. If you're wondering why we didn't just perform this check in the message handler methods, it's because often times you want to be able to invoke an event handler as a result of a different action, such as when the user changes the caret position.

You can install and use the TddgExtendedMemo with your applications. You might even consider extending this component; for example, whenever the user changes the caret position, a WM_COMMAND message is sent to the control's owner. The HiWord(wParam) carries a notification code indicating the action that occurred. This code would have the value of EN_CHANGE, which stands for edit-notification message change. It is possible to have your component subclass its parent and capture this message in the parent's window procedure. It can then automatically update the FRow and FColumn fields. Subclassing is an altogether different and advanced topic that is discussed later.

TddgTabbedListBox—Extending the TListBox Component

VCL's TListbox component is merely an Object Pascal wrapper around the standard Win32 API LISTBOX control. Although it does a fair job encapsulating most of that functionality, there is a little bit of room for improvement. This section takes you through the steps in creating a custom component based on TListbox.

The Idea

The idea for this component, like most, was born out of necessity. A list box was needed with the capability to use tab stops (which is supported in the Win32 API, but not in a TListbox), and a horizontal scrollbar was needed to view strings that were longer than the list box width (also supported by the API but not a TListbox). This component will be called a TddgTabListbox.

The plan for the TddgTabListbox component isn't terribly complex; We did this by creating a TListbox descendant component containing the correct field properties, overridden methods, and new methods to achieve the desired behavior.

The Code

When creating a scrollable list box with tab stops you must include specific window styles in the TddgTabListbox's style when the listbox window is created. The window styles needed are lbs_UseTabStops for tabs and ws_HScroll to allow a horizontal scrollbar. Whenever you add window styles to a descendant of TWinControl, do so by overriding the CreateParams() method, as shown in the following code:

```
procedure TddgTabListbox.CreateParams(var Params: TCreateParams);
begin
  inherited CreateParams(Params);
  Params.Style := Params.Style or lbs_UseTabStops or ws_HScroll;
end;
```

To set the tab stops, the TddgTabListbox performs an lb_SetTabStops message, passing the number of tab stops and a pointer to an array of tabs as the wParam and lParam (these two variables will be stored in the class as FNumTabStops and FTabStops). The only catch is that listbox tab stops are handled in a unit of measure called *dialog box units*. Because dialog box units don't make sense for the Delphi programmer, you will surface tabs only in pixels. With the help of the PixDlg.pas unit shown in Listing 11.11, you can convert back and forth between dialog box units and screen pixels in both the X and Y planes.

CreateParams()

Whenever you need to modify any of the parameters—such as style or window class—that are passed to the CreateWindowEx() API function, you should do so in the CreateParams() method. CreateWindowEx() is the function used to create the window handle associated with a TWinControl descendant. By overriding CreateParams(), you can control the creation of a window on the API level.

CreateParams accepts one parameter of type TCreateParams, which follows:

```
TCreateParams = record
    Caption: PChar;
    Style: Longint;
    ExStyle: Longint;
    X, Y: Integer;
    Width, Height: Integer;
    WndParent: HWnd;
    Param: Pointer;
    WindowClass: TWndClass;
    WinClassName: array[0..63] of Char;
end;
```

As a component writer, you will override CreateParams() frequently—whenever you need to control the creation of a component on the API level. Make sure that you call the inherited CreateParams() first in order to fill up the Params record for you.

LISTING 11.11   The Source Code for PixDlg.pas

```
unit Pixdlg;

interface

function DialogUnitsToPixelsX(DlgUnits: word): word;
function DialogUnitsToPixelsY(DlgUnits: word): word;
function PixelsToDialogUnitsX(PixUnits: word): word;
function PixelsToDialogUnitsY(PixUnits: word): word;


implementation
uses WinProcs;

function DialogUnitsToPixelsX(DlgUnits: word): word;
begin
  Result := (DlgUnits * LoWord(GetDialogBaseUnits)) div 4;
end;
```

LISTING 11.11 Continued

```
function DialogUnitsToPixelsY(DlgUnits: word): word;
begin
  Result := (DlgUnits * HiWord(GetDialogBaseUnits)) div 8;
end;

function PixelsToDialogUnitsX(PixUnits: word): word;
begin
  Result := PixUnits * 4 div LoWord(GetDialogBaseUnits);
end;

function PixelsToDialogUnitsY(PixUnits: word): word;
begin
  Result := PixUnits * 8 div HiWord(GetDialogBaseUnits);
end;

end.
```

When you know the tab stops, you can calculate the extent of the horizontal scrollbar. The scrollbar should extend at least to the end of the longest string in the listbox. Luckily, the Win32 API provides a function called GetTabbedTextExtent() that retrieves just the information you need. When you know the length of the longest string, you can set the scrollbar range by performing the lb_SetHorizontalExtent message, passing the desired extent as the wParam.

You also need to write message handlers for some special Win32 messages. In particular, you need to handle the messages that control inserting and deleting because you need to be able to measure the length of any new string or know when a long string has been deleted. The messages you're concerned with are lb_AddString, lb_InsertString, and lb_DeleteString. Listing 11.12 contains the source code for the LbTab.pas unit, which contains the TddgTabListbox component.

LISTING 11.12 LbTab.pas—The TddgTabListBox

```
unit Lbtab;

interface

uses
  SysUtils, Windows, Messages, Classes, Controls, StdCtrls;

type

  EddgTabListboxError = class(Exception);
```

LISTING 11.12   Continued

```
TddgTabListBox = class(TListBox)
private
  FLongestString: Word;
  FNumTabStops: Word;
  FTabStops: PWord;
  FSizeAfterDel: Boolean;
  function GetLBStringLength(S: String): word;
  procedure FindLongestString;
  procedure SetScrollLength(S: String);
  procedure LBAddString(var Msg: TMessage); message lb_AddString;
  procedure LBInsertString(var Msg: TMessage); message lb_InsertString;
  procedure LBDeleteString(var Msg: TMessage); message lb_DeleteString;
protected
  procedure CreateParams(var Params: TCreateParams); override;
public
  constructor Create(AOwner: TComponent); override;
  procedure SetTabStops(A: array of word);
published
  property SizeAfterDel: Boolean read FSizeAfterDel
      write FSizeAfterDel default True;
  end;

implementation

uses PixDlg;

constructor TddgTabListBox.Create(AOwner: TComponent);
begin
  inherited Create(AOwner);
  FSizeAfterDel := True;
  { set tab stops to Windows defaults... }
  FNumTabStops := 1;
  GetMem(FTabStops, SizeOf(Word) * FNumTabStops);
  FTabStops^ := DialogUnitsToPixelsX(32);
end;

procedure TddgTabListBox.SetTabStops(A: array of word);
{ This procedure sets the listbox's tabstops to those specified
  in the open array of word, A.  New tabstops are in pixels, and must
  be in ascending order.  An exception will be raised if new tabs
  fail to set. }
var
  i: word;
  TempTab: word;
  TempBuf: PWord;
```

LISTING 11.12 Continued

```pascal
begin
  { Store new values in temps in case exception occurs in setting tabs }
  TempTab := High(A) + 1;        // Figure number of tabstops
  GetMem(TempBuf, SizeOf(A));   // Allocate new tabstops
  Move(A, TempBuf^, SizeOf(A));// copy new tabstops }
  { convert from pixels to dialog units, and... }
  for i := 0 to TempTab - 1 do
    A[i] := PixelsToDialogUnitsX(A[i]);
  { Send new tabstops to listbox.  Note that we must use dialog units. }
  if Perform(lb_SetTabStops, TempTab, Longint(@A)) = 0 then
  begin
    { if zero, then failed to set new tabstops, free temp
      tabstop buffer and raise an exception }
    FreeMem(TempBuf, SizeOf(Word) * TempTab);
    raise EddgTabListboxError.Create('Failed to set tabs.')
  end
  else begin
    { if nonzero, then new tabstops set okay, so
      Free previous tabstops }
    FreeMem(FTabStops, SizeOf(Word) * FNumTabStops);
    { copy values from temps... }
    FNumTabStops := TempTab;  // set number of tabstops
    FTabStops := TempBuf;     // set tabstop buffer
    FindLongestString;        // reset scrollbar
    Invalidate;               // repaint
  end;
end;

procedure TddgTabListBox.CreateParams(var Params: TCreateParams);
{ We must OR in the styles necessary for tabs and horizontal scrolling
  These styles will be used by the API CreateWindowEx() function. }
begin
  inherited CreateParams(Params);
  { lbs_UseTabStops style allows tabs in listbox
    ws_HScroll style allows horizontal scrollbar in listbox }
  Params.Style := Params.Style or lbs_UseTabStops or ws_HScroll;
end;

function TddgTabListBox.GetLBStringLength(S: String): word;
{ This function returns the length of the listbox string S in pixels }
var
  Size: Integer;
begin
```

LISTING 11.12   Continued

```
  // Get the length of the text string
   Canvas.Font := Font;
  Result := LoWord(GetTabbedTextExtent(Canvas.Handle, PChar(S),
        StrLen(PChar(S)), FNumTabStops, FTabStops^));
  // Add a little bit of space to the end of the scrollbar extent for looks
  Size := Canvas.TextWidth('X');
  Inc(Result, Size);
end;

procedure TddgTabListBox.SetScrollLength(S: String);
{ This procedure resets the scrollbar extent if S is longer than the }
{ previous longest string                                            }
var
  Extent: Word;
begin
  Extent := GetLBStringLength(S);
  // If this turns out to be the longest string...
  if Extent > FLongestString then
  begin
    // reset longest string
    FLongestString := Extent;
    //reset scrollbar extent
    Perform(lb_SetHorizontalExtent, Extent, 0);
  end;
end;

procedure TddgTabListBox.LBInsertString(var Msg: TMessage);
{ This procedure is called in response to a lb_InsertString message.
  This message is sent to the listbox every time a string is inserted.
  Msg.lParam holds a pointer to the null-terminated string being
  inserted.  This will cause the scrollbar length to be adjusted if
  the new string is longer than any of the existing strings. }
begin
  inherited;
  SetScrollLength(PChar(Msg.lParam));
end;

procedure TddgTabListBox.LBAddString(var Msg: TMessage);
{ This procedure is called in response to a lb_AddString message.
  This message is sent to the listbox every time a string is added.
  Msg.lParam holds a pointer to the null-terminated string being
  added.  This Will cause the scrollbar length to be ajdusted if the
  new string is longer than any of the existing strings.}
```

LISTING 11.12 Continued

```
begin
  inherited;
  SetScrollLength(PChar(Msg.lParam));
end;

procedure TddgTabListBox.FindLongestString;
var
  i: word;
  Strg: String;
begin
  FLongestString := 0;
  { iterate through strings and look for new longest string }
  for i := 0 to Items.Count - 1 do
  begin
    Strg := Items[i];
    SetScrollLength(Strg);
  end;
end;

procedure TddgTabListBox.LBDeleteString(var Msg: TMessage);
{ This procedure is called in response to a lb_DeleteString message.
  This message is sent to the listbox everytime a string is deleted.
  Msg.wParam holds the index of the item being deleted.  Note that
  by setting the SizeAfterDel property to False, you can cause the
  scrollbar update to not occur.  This will improve performance
  if you're deleting often. }
var
  Str: String;
begin
  if FSizeAfterDel then
  begin
    Str := Items[Msg.wParam]; // Get string to be deleted
    inherited;                // Delete string
    { Is deleted string the longest? }
    if GetLBStringLength(Str) = FLongestString then
      FindLongestString;
  end
  else
    inherited;
end;

end.
```

One particular point of interest in this component is the SetTabStops() method, which accepts an open array of word as a parameter. This enables users to pass in as many tabstops as they want. Here is an example:

```
ddgTabListboxInstance.SetTabStops([50, 75, 150, 300]);
```

If the text in the listbox extends beyond the viewable window, the horizontal scrollbar will appear automatically.

TddgRunButton—Creating Properties

If you wanted to run another executable program in 16-bit Windows, you could use the WinExec() API function. Although these functions still work in Win32, it isn't the recommended approach. Now, you should use the CreateProcess() or ShellExecute() functions to launch another application. CreateProcess() can be a somewhat daunting task when needed just for that purpose. Therefore, we've provided the ProcessExecute() method, which we'll show in a moment.

To illustrate the use of ProcessExecute(), we've created the component TddgRunButton. All that is required of the user is to click the button and the application executes.

The TddgRunButton component is an ideal example of creating properties, validating property values, and encapsulating complex operations. Additionally, we'll show you how to grab the application icon from an executable file and how to display it in the TddgRunButton at design time. There's one other thing; TddgRunButton descends from TSpeedButton. Because TSpeed Button contains certain properties that you don't want accessible at design time through the Object Inspector, we'll show you how you can hide (sort of) existing properties from the component user. Admittedly, this technique isn't exactly the cleanest approach to use. Typically, you would create a component of your own if you want to take the purist approach—of which the authors are advocates. However, this is one of those instances in which Borland, in all its infinite wisdom, didn't provide an intermediate component in between TSpeedButton and TCustomControl (from which TSpeedButton descends), as Borland did with its other components. Therefore, the choice was either to roll our own component that pretty much duplicates the functionality you get from TSpeedButton, or borrow from TSpeedButton's functionality and hide a few properties that aren't applicable for your needs. We opted for the latter, but only out of necessity. However, this should clue you in to practice careful forethought as to how component writers might want to extend your own components.

The code to TddgRunButton is shown in Listing 11.13.

LISTING 11.13   RunBtn.pas—The Source to the TddgRunButton Component

```pascal
unit RunBtn;

interface

uses
  Windows, Messages, SysUtils, Classes, Graphics, Controls,
  Forms, Dialogs, StdCtrls, Buttons;

type

  TCommandLine = type string;

  TddgRunButton = class(TSpeedButton)
  private
    FCommandLine: TCommandLine;
    // Hiding Properties from the Object Inspector
    FCaption: TCaption;
    FAllowAllUp: Boolean;
    FFont: TFont;
    FGroupIndex: Integer;
    FLayOut: TButtonLayout;
    procedure SetCommandLine(Value: TCommandLine);
  public
    constructor Create(AOwner: TComponent); override;
    procedure Click; override;
  published
    property CommandLine: TCommandLine read FCommandLine write SetCommandLine;
    // Read only properties are hidden
    property Caption: TCaption read FCaption;
    property AllowAllUp: Boolean read FAllowAllUp;
    property Font: TFont read FFont;
    property GroupIndex: Integer read FGroupIndex;
    property LayOut: TButtonLayOut read FLayOut;
  end;

implementation

uses ShellAPI;

const
  EXEExtension = '.EXE';
```

LISTING 11.13 Continued

```
function ProcessExecute(CommandLine: TCommandLine; cShow: Word): Integer;
{ This method encapsulates the call to CreateProcess() which creates
  a new process and its primary thread. This is the method used in
  Win32 to execute another application, This method requires the use
  of the TStartInfo and TProcessInformation structures. These structures
  are not documented as part of the Delphi 6 online help but rather
  the Win32 help as STARTUPINFO and PROCESS_INFORMATION.

  The CommandLine parameter specifies the pathname of the file to
  execute.

  The cShow parameter specifies one of the SW_XXXX constants which
  specifies how to display the window. This value is assigned to the
  sShowWindow field of the TStartupInfo structure. }
var
  Rslt: LongBool;
  StartUpInfo: TStartUpInfo;  // documented as STARTUPINFO
  ProcessInfo: TProcessInformation; // documented as PROCESS_INFORMATION
begin
  { Clear the StartupInfo structure }
  FillChar(StartupInfo, SizeOf(TStartupInfo), 0);
  { Initialize the StartupInfo structure with required data.
    Here, we assign the SW_XXXX constant to the wShowWindow field
    of StartupInfo. When specifying a value to this field the
    STARTF_USESSHOWWINDOW flag must be set in the dwFlags field.
    Additional information on the TStartupInfo is provided in the Win32
    online help under STARTUPINFO. }
  with StartupInfo do
  begin
    cb := SizeOf(TStartupInfo); // Specify size of structure
    dwFlags := STARTF_USESHOWWINDOW or STARTF_FORCEONFEEDBACK;
    wShowWindow := cShow
  end;

  { Create the process by calling CreateProcess(). This function
    fills the ProcessInfo structure with information about the new
    process and its primary thread. Detailed information is provided
    in the Win32 online help for the TProcessInfo structure under
    PROCESS_INFORMATION. }
  Rslt := CreateProcess(PChar(CommandLine), nil, nil, nil, False,
    NORMAL_PRIORITY_CLASS, nil, nil, StartupInfo, ProcessInfo);
  { If Rslt is true, then the CreateProcess call was successful.
    Otherwise, GetLastError will return an error code representing the
    error which occurred. }
```

LISTING 11.13 Continued

```
  if Rslt then
    with ProcessInfo do
    begin
      { Wait until the process is in idle. }
      WaitForInputIdle(hProcess, INFINITE);
      CloseHandle(hThread); // Free the hThread  handle
      CloseHandle(hProcess);// Free the hProcess handle
      Result := 0;          // Set Result to 0, meaning successful
    end
  else Result := GetLastError; // Set result to the error code.
end;

function IsExecutableFile(Value: TCommandLine): Boolean;
{ This method returns whether or not the Value represents a valid
  executable file by ensuring that its file extension is 'EXE' }
var
  Ext: String[4];
begin
  Ext := ExtractFileExt(Value);
  Result := (UpperCase(Ext) = EXEExtension);
end;

constructor TddgRunButton.Create(AOwner: TComponent);
{ The constructor sets the default height and width properties
  to 45x45 }
begin
  inherited Create(AOwner);
  Height := 45;
  Width  := 45;
end;

procedure TddgRunButton.SetCommandLine(Value: TCommandLine);
{ This write access method sets the FCommandLine field to Value, but
  only if Value represents a valid executable file name. It also
  set the icon for the TddgRunButton to the application icon of the
  file specified by Value. }
var
  Icon: TIcon;
begin
  { First check to see that Value *is* an executable file and that
    it actually exists where specified. }
  if not IsExecutableFile(Value) then
    Raise Exception.Create(Value+' is not an executable file.');
```

LISTING 11.13   Continued

```
if not FileExists(Value) then
  Raise Exception.Create('The file: '+Value+' cannot be found.');

FCommandLine := Value;   // Store the Value in FCommandLine

{ Now draw the application icon for the file specified by Value
  on the TddgRunButton icon. This requires us to create a TIcon
  instance to which to load the icon. It is then copied from this
  TIcon instance to the TddgRunButton's Canvas.

  We must use the Win32 API function ExtractIcon() to retrieve the
  icon for the application. }
Icon := TIcon.Create; // Create the TIcon instance
try
  { Retrieve the icon from the application's file }
  Icon.Handle := ExtractIcon(hInstance, PChar(FCommandLine), 0);
  with Glyph do
  begin
    { Set the TddgRunButton properties so that the icon held by Icon
      can be copied onto it. }
    { First, clear the canvas. This is required in case another
      icon was previously drawn on the canvas }
    Canvas.Brush.Style := bsSolid;
    Canvas.FillRect(Canvas.ClipRect);
    { Set the Icon's width and height }
    Width := Icon.Width;
    Height := Icon.Height;
    Canvas.Draw(0, 0, Icon); // Draw the icon to TddgRunButton's Canvas
  end;
finally
  Icon.Free; // Free the TIcon instance.
end;
end;

procedure TddgRunButton.Click;
var
  WERetVal: Word;
begin
  inherited Click; // Call the inherited Click method
  { Execute the ProcessExecute method and check it's return value.
    if the return value is <> 0 then raise an exception because
    an error occurred. The error code is shown in the exception }
  WERetVal := ProcessExecute(FCommandLine, sw_ShowNormal);
  if WERetVal <> 0 then begin
```

LISTING 11.13 Continued

```
    raise Exception.Create('Error executing program. Error Code:; '+
        IntToStr(WERetVal));
  end;
end;

end.
```

TddgRunButton has one property, CommandLine, which is defined to be of the type String. The private storage field for CommandLine is FCommandLine.

> **TIP**
>
> It is worth discussing the special definition of TCommandLine. Here is the syntax used:
>
> ```
> TCommandLine = type string;
> ```
>
> By defining TCommandLine as such, you tell the compiler to treat TCommandLine as a unique type that is still compatible with other string types. The new type will get its own runtime type information and therefore can have its own property editor. This same technique can be used with other types as well. Here is an example:
>
> ```
> TMySpecialInt = type Integer;
> ```
>
> We will show you how we use this to create a property editor for the CommandLine property in the next chapter. We don't show you this technique in this chapter because creating property editors is an advanced topic that we want to talk about in more depth.

The write access method for CommandLine is SetCommandLine(). We've provided two helper functions: IsExecutableFile() and ProcessExecute().

IsExecutableFile() is a function that determines whether a filename passed to it is an executable file based on the file's extension.

Creating and Executing a Process

ProcessExecute() is a function that encapsulates the CreateProcess() Win32 API function that enables you to launch another application. The application to launch is specified by the CommandLine parameter, which holds the filename path. The second parameter contains one of the SW_XXXX constants that indicate how the process's main windows is to be displayed. Table 11.4 lists the various SW_XXXX constants and their meanings as explained in the online help.

TABLE 11.4 SW_XXXX Constants

SW_XXXX *Constant*	*Meaning*
SW_HIDE	Hides the window. Another window will become active.
SW_MAXIMIZE	Displays the window as maximized.
SW_MINIMIZE	Minimizes the window.
SW_RESTORE	Displays a window at its size before it was maximized/minimized.
SW_SHOW	Displays a window at its current size/position.
SW_SHOWDEFAULT	Shows a window at the state specified by the TStartupInfo structure passed to CreateProcess().
SW_SHOWMAXIMIZED	Activates/displays the window as maximized.
SW_SHOWMINIMIZED	Activates/displays the window as minimized.
SW_SHOWMINNOACTIVE	Displays the window as minimized, but the currently active window remains active.
SW_SHOWNA	Displays the window at its current state. The currently active window remains active.
SW_SHOWNOACTIVATE	Displays the window at the most recent size/position. The currently active window remains active.
SW_SHOWNORMAL	Activates/displays the window at its more recent size/position. This position is restored if the window was previously maximized/minimized.

ProcessExecute() is a handy utility function that you might want to keep around in a separate unit that can be shared by other applications.

TddgRunButton Methods

The TddgRunButton.Create() constructor simply sets a default size for itself after calling the inherited constructor.

The SetCommandLine() method, which is the writer access method for the CommandLine parameter, performs several tasks. It determines whether the value being assigned to CommandLine is a valid executable filename. If not, it raises an exception.

If the entry is valid, it is assigned to the FCommandLine field. SetCommandLine() then extracts the icon from the application file and draws it to TddgRunButton's canvas. The Win32 API function ExtractIcon() is used to do this. The technique used is explained in the source code comments.

TddgRunButton.Click() is the event-dispatching method for the TSpeedButton.OnClick event. It is necessary to call the inherited Click() method that will invoke the OnClick event handler if assigned. After calling the inherited `Click()`, you call `ProcessExecute()` and examine its result value to determine whether the call was successful. If not, an exception is raised.

TddgButtonEdit—Container Components

Occasionally you might like to create a component that is composed of one or more other components. Delphi's `TDBNavigator` is a good example of such a component because it consists of a `TPanel` and a number of `TSpeedButton` components. Specifically, this section illustrates this concept by creating a component that is a combination of a `TEdit` and a `TSpeedButton` component. We will call this component `TddgButtonEdit`.

Design Decisions

Considering that Object Pascal is based on a single-inheritance object model, `TddgButtonEdit` will need to be a component in its own right, which must contain both a `TEdit1` and a `TSpeedButton`. Furthermore, because it's necessary that this component contain windowed controls, it will need to be a windowed control itself. For these reasons, we chose to descend `TddgButtonEdit` from `TWinControl`. We created both the `TEdit` and `TSpeedButton` in `TddgButtonEdit`'s constructor using the following code:

```
constructor TddgButtonEdit.Create(AOwner: TComponent);
begin
  inherited Create(AOwner);
  FEdit        := TEdit.Create(Self);
  FEdit.Parent := self;
  FEdit.Height := 21;

  FSpeedButton := TSpeedButton.Create(Self);
  FSpeedButton.Left := FEdit.Width;
  FSpeedButton.Height := 19; // two less then TEdit's Height
  FSpeedButton.Width  := 19;
  FSpeedButton.Caption := '...';
  FSpeedButton.Parent := Self;

  Width  := FEdit.Width+FSpeedButton.Width;
  Height := FEdit.Height;
end;
```

When creating a component that contains other components, The challenge is surfacing the properties of the "inner" components from the container component. For example, the `TddgButtonEdit` will need a `Text` property. You also might want to be able to change the font for the text in the control, therefore, a `Font` property is needed. Finally, there needs to be an `OnClick` event for the button in the control. You wouldn't want to attempt to implement this yourself in the container component when it is already available from the inner components.

The goal, then, is to surface the appropriate properties of the inner controls without rewriting the interfaces to these controls.

Surfacing Properties

This usually boils down to the simple but time-consuming task of writing reader and writer methods for each of the inner component properties you want to resurface through the container component. In the case of the Text property, for example, you might give the TddgButtonEdit a Text property with read and write methods:

```
TddgButtonEdit = class(TWinControl)
private
  FEdit: TEdit;
  protected
  procedure SetText(Value: String);
    function  GetText: String;
published
    property Text: String read GetText write SetText;
end;
```

The SetText() and GetText() methods directly access the Text property of the contained TEdit control, as shown in the following:

```
function TddgButtonEdit.GetText: String;
begin
  Result := FEdit.Text;
end;

procedure TddgButtonEdit.SetText(Value: String);
begin
  FEdit.Text := Value;
end;
```

Surfacing Events

In addition to properties, it's also quite likely that you might want to resurface events that exist in the inner components. For example, when the user clicks the TSpeedButton control, you would want to surface its OnClick event. Resurfacing events is just as straightforward as resurfacing properties—after all, events are properties.

You need to first give the TddgButtonEdit its own OnClick event. For clarity, we named this event OnButtonClick. The read and write methods for this event simply redirect the assignment to the OnClick event of the internal TSpeedButton.

Listing 11.14 shows the TddgButtonEdit container component.

LISTING 11.14 TddgButtonEdit—A Container Component

```
unit ButtonEdit;

interface

uses
  Windows, Messages, SysUtils, Classes, Graphics, Controls, Forms, Dialogs,
  StdCtrls, Buttons;

type
  TddgButtonEdit = class(TWinControl)
  private
    FSpeedButton: TSpeedButton;
    FEdit: TEdit;
  protected
    procedure WMSize(var Message: TWMSize); message WM_SIZE;
    procedure SetText(Value: String);
    function  GetText: String;
    function GetFont: TFont;
    procedure SetFont(Value: TFont);
    function GetOnButtonClick: TNotifyEvent;
    procedure SetOnButtonClick(Value: TNotifyEvent);
  public
    constructor Create(AOwner: TComponent); override;
    destructor  Destroy; override;
  published
    property Text: String read GetText write SetText;
    property Font: TFont read GetFont write SetFont;
    property OnButtonClick: TNotifyEvent read GetOnButtonClick
        write SetOnButtonClick;
  end;

implementation

procedure TddgButtonEdit.WMSize(var Message: TWMSize);
begin
  inherited;
  FEdit.Width := Message.Width-FSpeedButton.Width;
  FSpeedButton.Left := FEdit.Width;
end;

constructor TddgButtonEdit.Create(AOwner: TComponent);
begin
  inherited Create(AOwner);
  FEdit         := TEdit.Create(Self);
```

LISTING 11.14 Continued

```
  FEdit.Parent := self;
  FEdit.Height := 21;

  FSpeedButton := TSpeedButton.Create(Self);
  FSpeedButton.Left := FEdit.Width;
  FSpeedButton.Height := 19; // two less than TEdit's Height
  FSpeedButton.Width  := 19;
  FSpeedButton.Caption := '...';
  FSpeedButton.Parent := Self;

  Width  := FEdit.Width+FSpeedButton.Width;
  Height := FEdit.Height;
end;

destructor  TddgButtonEdit.Destroy;
begin
  FSpeedButton.Free;
  FEdit.Free;
  inherited Destroy;
end;

function TddgButtonEdit.GetText: String;
begin
  Result := FEdit.Text;
end;

procedure TddgButtonEdit.SetText(Value: String);
begin
  FEdit.Text := Value;
end;

function TddgButtonEdit.GetFont: TFont;
begin
  Result := FEdit.Font;
end;

procedure TddgButtonEdit.SetFont(Value: TFont);
begin
  if Assigned(FEdit.Font) then
    FEdit.Font.Assign(Value);
end;

function TddgButtonEdit.GetOnButtonClick: TNotifyEvent;
```

LISTING 11.14   Continued

```
begin
  Result := FSpeedButton.OnClick;
end;

procedure TddgButtonEdit.SetOnButtonClick(Value: TNotifyEvent);
begin
  FSpeedButton.OnClick := Value;
end;

end.
```

TddgDigitalClock—Creating Component Events

TddgDigitalClock illustrates the process of creating and making available user-defined events. We will use the same technique that was discussed earlier when we illustrated creating events with the TddgHalfMinute component.

TddgDigitalClock descends from TPanel. We decided that TPanel was an ideal component from which TddgDigitalClock could descend because TPanel has the BevelXXXX properties. This enables you to give the TddgDigitalClock a pleasing visual appearance. Also, you can use the TPanel.Caption property to display the system time.

TddgDigitalClock contains the following events to which the user can assign code:

OnHour	Occurs on the hour, every hour.
OnHalfPast	Occurs on the half hour.
OnMinute	Occurs on the minute.
OnHalfMinute	Occurs every 30 seconds, on the minute and on the half minute.
OnSecond	Occurs on the second.

TddgDigitalClock uses a TTimer component internally. Its OnTimer event handler performs the logic to paint the time information and to invoke the event-dispatching methods for the previously listed events accordingly. Listing 11.15 shows the source code for DdgClock.pas.

LISTING 11.15   DdgClock.pas—Source for the TddgDigitalClock Component

```
{$IFDEF VER110}
{$OBJEXPORTALL ON}
{$ENDIF}

unit DDGClock;
```

LISTING 11.15 Continued

```
interface

uses
  Windows, Messages, Controls, Forms, SysUtils, Classes, ExtCtrls;

type

  { Declare an event type which takes the sender of the event, and
    a TDateTime variable as parameters }
  TTimeEvent = procedure(Sender: TObject; DDGTime: TDateTime) of object;

  TddgDigitalClock = class(TPanel)
  private
    { Data fields }
    FHour,
    FMinute,
    FSecond: Word;
    FDateTime: TDateTime;
    FOldMinute,
    FOldSecond: Word;
    FTimer: TTimer;
    { Event handlers }
    FOnHour: TTimeEvent;        // Occurs on the hour
    FOnHalfPast: TTimeEvent;    // Occurs every half-hour
    FOnMinute: TTimeEvent;      // Occurs on the minute
    FOnSecond: TTimeEvent;      // Occurs every second
    FOnHalfMinute: TTimeEvent;  // Occurs every 30 seconds
    { Define OnTimer event handler for internal TTimer, FTimer }
    procedure TimerProc(Sender: TObject);
  protected
    { Override the Paint methods }
    procedure Paint; override;

    { Define the various event dispatching methods }
    procedure DoHour(Tm: TDateTime); dynamic;
    procedure DoHalfPast(Tm: TDateTime); dynamic;
    procedure DoMinute(Tm: TDateTime); dynamic;
    procedure DoHalfMinute(Tm: TDateTime); dynamic;
    procedure DoSecond(Tm: TDateTime); dynamic;

  public
    { Override the Create constructor and Destroy destructor }
    constructor Create(AOwner: TComponent); override;
    destructor Destroy; override;
```

LISTING 11.15 Continued

```pascal
published
  { Define event properties }
  property OnHour: TTimeEvent read FOnHour write FOnHour;
  property OnHalfPast: TTimeEvent read FOnHalfPast write FOnHalfPast;
  property OnMinute: TTimeEvent read FOnMinute write FOnMinute;
  property OnHalfMinute: TTimeEvent read FOnHalfMinute
          write FOnHalfMinute;
  property OnSecond: TTimeEvent read FOnSecond write FOnSecond;
end;

implementation

constructor TddgDigitalClock.Create(AOwner: TComponent);
begin
  inherited Create(AOwner); // Call the inherited constructor
  Height := 25; // Set default width and height properties
  Width := 120;
  BevelInner := bvLowered; // Set Default bevel properties
  BevelOuter := bvLowered;
  { Set the inherited Caption property to an empty string }
  inherited Caption := '';
  { Create the TTimer instance and set both its Interval property and
    OnTime event handler. }
  FTimer:= TTimer.Create(self);
  FTimer.interval:= 200;
  FTimer.OnTimer:= TimerProc;
end;


destructor TddgDigitalClock.Destroy;
begin
  FTimer.Free; // Free the TTimer instance.
  inherited Destroy; // Call inherited Destroy method
end;

procedure TddgDigitalClock.Paint;
begin
  inherited Paint; // Call the inherited Paint method
  { Now set the inherited Caption property to current time. }
  inherited Caption := TimeToStr(FDateTime);
end;

procedure TddgDigitalClock.TimerProc(Sender: TObject);
var
```

LISTING 11.15   Continued

```pascal
  HSec: Word;
begin
  { Save the old minute and second for later use }
  FOldMinute := FMinute;
  FOldSecond := FSecond;
  FDateTime := Now; // Get the current time.
  { Extract the individual time elements }
  DecodeTime(FDateTime, FHour, FMinute, FSecond, Hsec);

  refresh; // Redraw the component so that the new time is displayed.

  { Now call the event handlers depending on the time }
  if FMinute = 0 then
    DoHour(FDateTime);
  if FMinute = 30 then
    DoHalfPast(FDateTime);
  if (FMinute <> FOldMinute) then
    DoMinute(FDateTime);
  if FSecond <> FOldSecond then
    if ((FSecond = 30) or (FSecond = 0)) then
      DoHalfMinute(FDateTime)
    else
      DoSecond(FDateTime);
end;

{ The event dispatching methods below determine if component user has
  attached event handlers to the various clock events and calls them
  if they exist }
procedure TddgDigitalClock.DoHour(Tm: TDateTime);
begin
  if Assigned(FOnHour) then
    TTimeEvent(FOnHour)(Self, Tm);
end;

procedure TddgDigitalClock.DoHalfPast(Tm: TDateTime);
begin
  if Assigned(FOnHalfPast) then
    TTimeEvent(FOnHalfPast)(Self, Tm);
end;

procedure TddgDigitalClock.DoMinute(Tm: TDateTime);
begin
  if Assigned(FOnMinute) then
    TTimeEvent(FOnMinute)(Self, Tm);
end;
```

LISTING 11.15 Continued

```
procedure TddgDigitalClock.DoHalfMinute(Tm: TDateTime);
begin
  if Assigned(FOnHalfMinute) then
    TTimeEvent(FOnHalfMinute)(Self, Tm);
end;

procedure TddgDigitalClock.DoSecond(Tm: TDateTime);
begin
  if Assigned(FOnSecond) then
    TTimeEvent(FOnSecond)(Self, Tm);
end;

end.
```

The logic behind this component is explained in the source commentary. The methods used are no different from those that were previously explained when we discussed creating events. `TddgDigitalClock` only adds more events and contains logic to determine when each event is invoked.

Adding Forms to the Component Palette

Adding forms to the Object Repository is a convenient way to give forms a starting point. But what if you develop a form that you reuse often that doesn't need to be inherited and doesn't require added functionality? Delphi 6 provides a way you can reuse your forms as components on the Component Palette. In fact, the `TFontDialog` and `TOpenDialog` components are examples of forms that are accessible from the Component Palette. Actually, these dialogs aren't Delphi forms; these are dialogs provided by the `CommDlg.dll`. Nevertheless, the concept is the same.

To add forms to the Component Palette, you must wrap your form with a component to make it a separate, installable component. The process as described here uses a simple password dialog whose functionality will verify your password automatically. Although this is a very simple project, the purpose of this discussion is not to show you how to install a complex dialog as a component, but rather to show you the general method for adding dialog boxes to the Component Palette. The same method applies to dialog boxes of any complexity.

You must create the form that is going to be wrapped by the component. The form we used is defined in the file `PwDlg.pas`. This unit also shows a component wrapper for this form.

Listing 11.16 shows the unit defining the `TPasswordDlg` form and its wrapper component, `TddgPasswordDialog`.

LISTING 11.16 *PwDlg.pas*—TPasswordDlg Form and Its Component Wrapper
TddgPasswordDialog

```
unit PwDlg;

interface

uses Windows, SysUtils, Classes, Graphics, Forms, Controls, StdCtrls,
  Buttons;

type

  TPasswordDlg = class(TForm)
    Label1: TLabel;
    Password: TEdit;
    OKBtn: TButton;
    CancelBtn: TButton;
  end;

  { Now declare the wrapper component. }
  TddgPasswordDialog = class(TComponent)
  private
    PassWordDlg: TPasswordDlg; // TPassWordDlg instance
    FPassWord: String;          // Place holder for the password
  public
    function Execute: Boolean; // Function to launch the dialog
  published
    property PassWord: String read FPassword write FPassword;
  end;

implementation
{$R *.DFM}

function TddgPasswordDialog.Execute: Boolean;
begin
  { Create a TPasswordDlg instance }
  PasswordDlg := TPasswordDlg.Create(Application);
  try
    Result := False;  // Initialize the result to false
    { Show the dialog and return true if the password
      is correct. }
    if PasswordDlg.ShowModal = mrOk then
      Result := PasswordDlg.Password.Text = FPassword;
```

LISTING **11.16** Continued

```
finally
  PasswordDlg.Free;   // Free instance of PasswordDlg
end;
end;

end.
```

The TddgPasswordDialog is called a *wrapper* component because it wraps the form with a component that can be installed into Delphi 6's Component Palette.

TddgPasswordDialog descends directly from TComponent. You might recall from the last chapter that TComponent is the lowest-level class that can be manipulated by the Form Designer in the IDE. This class has two private variables: PasswordDlg of type TPasswordDlg and FPassWord of type string. PasswordDlg is the TPasswordDlg instance that this wrapper component displays. FPassWord is an *internal storage field* that holds a password string.

FPassWord gets its data through the property PassWord. Thus, PassWord doesn't actually store data; rather, it serves as an interface to the storage variable FPassWord.

TddgPassWordDialog's Execute() function creates a TPasswordDlg instance and displays it as a modal dialog box. When the dialog box terminates, the string entered in the password TEdit control is compared against the string stored in FPassword.

The code here is contained within a try..finally construct. The finally portion ensures that the TPasswordDlg component is disposed of regardless of any error that might occur.

After you have added TddgPasswordDialog to the Component Palette, you can create a project that uses it. As with any other component, you select TddgPasswordDialog from the Component Palette and place it on your form. The project created in the preceding section contains a TddgPasswordDialog and one button whose OnClick event handler does the following:

```
procedure TForm1.Button1Click(Sender: TObject);
begin
  if ddgPasswordDialog.Execute then      // Launch the PasswordDialog
    ShowMessage('You got it!')           // Correct password
  else
    ShowMessage('Sorry, wrong answer!'); // Incorrect password
end;
```

The Object Inspector contains three properties for the TddgPasswordDialog component: Name, Password, and Tag. To use the component, you must set the Password property to some string value. When you run the project, `TddgPasswordDialog` prompts the user for a password and compares it against the password you entered for the `Password` property.

Summary

Knowing how components work is fundamental to understanding Delphi, and you work with many more custom components later in the book. Now that you can see what happens behind the scenes, components will no longer seem like just a black box. The next chapter goes beyond component creation into more advanced component building techniques.

Advanced VCL Component Building

IN THIS CHAPTER

The last chapter broke into writing Delphi custom components, and it gave you a solid intro-duction to the basics. In this chapter, you'll learn how to take component writing to the next level by incorporating advanced design techniques into your Delphi custom components. This chapter provides examples of advanced techniques such as pseudo-visual components, detailed property editors, component editors, and collections.

Pseudo-Visual Components

You've learned about visual components such as `TButton` and `TEdit`, and you've learned about nonvisual components such as `TTable` and `TTimer`. In this section, you'll also learn about a type of component that kind of falls in between visual and nonvisual components—we'll call these components *pseudo-visual components*.

Extending Hints

Specifically, the pseudo-visual component shown in this section is an extension of a Delphi pop-up hint window. We call this a *pseudo-visual* component because it's not a component that's used visually from the Component Palette at design time, but it does represent itself visu-ally at runtime in the body of pop-up hints.

Replacing the default style hint window in a Delphi application requires that you complete the following four steps:

1. Create a descendant of `THintWindow`.
2. Destroy the old hint window class.
3. Assign the new hint window class.
4. Create the new hint window class.

Creating a `THintWindow` Descendant

Before you write the code for a `THintWindow` descendant, you must first decide how you want your new hint window class to behave differently from the default one. In this case, you'll cre-ate an elliptical hint window rather than the default square one. This actually demonstrates another cool technique: creating nonrectangular windows! Listing 12.1 shows the `RndHint.pas` unit, which contains the `THintWindow` descendant `TDDGHintWindow`.

LISTING 12.1   `RndHint.pas`—Illustrates an Elliptical Hint

```
unit RndHint;

interface

uses Windows, Classes, Controls, Forms, Messages, Graphics;
```

LISTING 12.1   Continued

```
type
  TDDGHintWindow = class(THintWindow)
  private
    FRegion: THandle;
    procedure FreeCurrentRegion;
  public
    destructor Destroy; override;
    procedure ActivateHint(Rect: TRect; const AHint: string); override;
    procedure Paint; override;
    procedure CreateParams(var Params: TCreateParams); override;
  end;

implementation

destructor TDDGHintWindow.Destroy;
begin
  FreeCurrentRegion;
  inherited Destroy;
end;

procedure TDDGHintWindow.FreeCurrentRegion;
{ Regions, like other API objects, should be freed when you are  }
{ through using them.  Note, however, that you cannot delete a   }
{ region which is currently set in a window, so this method sets }
{ the window region to 0 before deleting the region object.      }
begin
  if FRegion <> 0 then begin         // if Region is alive...
    SetWindowRgn(Handle, 0, True);   // set win region to 0
    DeleteObject(FRegion);           // kill the region
    FRegion := 0;                    // zero out field
  end;
end;

procedure TDDGHintWindow.ActivateHint(Rect: TRect; const AHint: string);
{ Called when the hint is activated by putting the mouse pointer }
{ above a control. }
begin
  with Rect do
    Right := Right + Canvas.TextWidth('WWWW');  // add some slop
  BoundsRect := Rect;
  FreeCurrentRegion;
  with BoundsRect do
    { Create a round rectangular region to display the hint window }
    FRegion := CreateRoundRectRgn(0, 0, Width, Height, Width, Height);
```

LISTING 12.1 Continued

```
  if FRegion <> 0 then
    SetWindowRgn(Handle, FRegion, True);        // set win region
  inherited ActivateHint(Rect, AHint);          // call inherited
end;

procedure TDDGHintWindow.CreateParams(var Params: TCreateParams);
{ We need to remove the border created on the Windows API-level }
{ when the window is created. }
begin
  inherited CreateParams(Params);
  Params.Style := Params.Style and not ws_Border;  // remove border
end;

procedure TDDGHintWindow.Paint;
{ This method gets called by the WM_PAINT handler.  It is }
{ responsible for painting the hint window. }
var
  R: TRect;
begin
  R := ClientRect;                    // get bounding rectangle
  Inc(R.Left, 1);                     // move left side slightly
  Canvas.Font.Color := clInfoText;    // set to proper color
  { paint string in the center of the round rect }
  DrawText(Canvas.Handle, PChar(Caption), Length(Caption), R,
           DT_NOPREFIX or DT_WORDBREAK or DT_CENTER or DT_VCENTER);
end;

initialization
  Application.ShowHint := False;      // destroy old hint window
  HintWindowClass := TDDGHintWindow;  // assign new hint window
  Application.ShowHint := True;       // create new hint window
end.
```

The overridden CreateParams() and Paint() methods are fairly straightforward. CreateParams() provides an opportunity to adjust the structure of the window styles before the hint window is created on an API level. In this method, the WS_BORDER style is removed from the window class in order to prevent a rectangular border from being drawn around the window. The Paint() method is responsible for rendering the window. In this case, the method must paint the hint's Caption property into the center of the caption window. The color of the text is set to clInfoText, which is the system-defined color of hint text.

An Elliptical Window

The `ActivateHint()` method contains the magic for creating the nonrectangular hint window. Well, it's not really magic. Actually, two API calls make it happen: `CreateRoundRectRgn()` and `SetWindowRgn()`.

`CreateRoundRectRgn()` defines a rounded rectangular region within a particular window. A *region* is a special API object that allows you to perform special painting, hit testing, filling, and clipping in one area. In addition to `CreateRoundRectRgn()`, a number of other Win32 API functions create different types of regions, including the following:

- `CreateEllipticRgn()`
- `CreateEllipticRgnIndirect()`
- `CreatePolygonRgn()`
- `CreatePolyPolygonRgn()`
- `CreateRectRgn()`
- `CreateRectRgnIndirect()`
- `CreateRoundRectRgn()`
- `ExtCreateRegion()`

Additionally, the `CombineRgn()` function can be used to combine multiple regions into one complex region. All these functions are described in detail in the Win32 API online help.

`SetWindowRgn()` is then called, passing the recently created region handle as a parameter. This function causes the operating system to take ownership of the region, and all subsequent drawing in the specified window will occur only within the region. Therefore, if the region defined is a rounded rectangle, painting will occur only within that rounded rectangular region.

12

ADVANCED VCL COMPONENT BUILDING

> **CAUTION**
>
> You need to be aware of two side effects when using `SetWindowRgn()`. First, because only the portion of the window within the region is painted, your window probably won't have a frame or title bar. You must be prepared to provide the user with an alternative way to move, size, and close the window without the aid of a frame or title bar. Second, because the operating system takes ownership of the region specified in `SetWindowRgn()`, you must be careful not to manipulate or delete the region while it's in use. The `TDDGHintWindow` component handles this by calling its `FreeCurrentRegion()` method before the window is destroyed or a new window is created.

Enabling the `THintWindow` Descendant

The initialization code for the RndHint unit does the work of making the TDDGHintWindow component the application-wide active hint window. Setting Application.ShowHint to False causes the old hint window to be destroyed. At that point, you must assign your THintWindow descendant class to the HintWindowClass global variable. Then, setting Application.ShowHint back to True causes a new hint window to be created—this time it will be an instance of your descendant class.

Deploying `TDDGHintWindow`

Deploying this pseudo-visual component is different from normal visual and non-visual components. Because all the work for instantiating the component is performed in the initialization part of its unit, the unit shouldn't be added to a design package for use on the Component Palette but merely added to the uses clause of one of the source files in your project.

Animated Components

Once upon a time while writing a Delphi application, we thought to ourselves, "This is a really cool application, but our About dialog is kind of boring. We need something to spice it up a little." Suddenly, a light bulb came on and an idea for a new component was born We would create a scrolling credits marquee window to incorporate into our About dialogs.

The Marquee Component

Let's take a moment to analyze how the marquee component works. The marquee control: is able to take a bunch of strings and scroll them across the component on command, like a real-life marquee. You'll use TCustomPanel as the base class for this TddgMarquee component because it already has the basic built-in functionality you need, including a pretty 3D, beveled border.

TddgMarquee paints some text strings to a bitmap residing in memory and then copies portions of the memory bitmap to its own canvas to simulate a scrolling effect. It does this using the BitBlt() API function to copy a component-sized portion of the memory canvas to the component, starting at the top. Then, it moves down a couple pixels on the memory canvas and copies that image to the control. It moves down again, copies again, and repeats the process over and over so that the entire contents of the memory canvas appear to scroll through the component.

Now is the time to identify any additional classes you might need to integrate into the TddgMarquee component in order to bring it to life. There are really only two such classes. First, you need the TStringList class to hold all the strings you want to scroll. Second, you

Advanced VCL Component Building

CHAPTER 12

495

12

ADVANCED VCL
COMPONENT
BUILDING

must have a memory bitmap on which you can render all the text strings. VCL's own `TBitmap` component will work nicely for this purpose.

Writing the Component

As with the previous components in this chapter, the code for `TddgMarquee` should be approached with a logical plan of attack. In this case, we break up the code work into reasonable parts. The `TddgMarquee` component: can be divided into five major parts:

- The mechanism that renders the text onto the memory canvas
- The mechanism that copies the text from the memory canvas to the marquee window
- The timer that keeps track of when and how to scroll the window to perform the animation
- The class constructor, destructor, and associated methods
- The finishing touches, such as various helper properties and methods

Drawing on an Offscreen Bitmap

When creating an instance of `TBitmap`, you need to know how big it must be to hold the entire list of strings in memory. You do this by first figuring out how high each line of text will be and then multiplying by the number of lines. To find the height and spacing of a line of text in a particular font, use the `GetTextMetrics()` API function by passing it the canvas's handle. A `TTextMetric` record to be filled in by the function:

```
var
  Metrics: TTextMetric;
begin
  GetTextMetrics(Canvas.Handle, Metrics);
```

NOTE

The `GetTextMetrics()` API function modifies a `TTextMetric` record that contains a great deal of quantitative information about a device context's currently selected font. This function gives you information not only on font height and width but also on whether the font is boldfaced, italicized, struck out, or even what the character set name is.

The `TextHeight()` method of `TCanvas` won't work here. That method only determines the height of a specific line of text rather than the spacing for the font in general.

The `tmHeight` field of the Metrics record gives the height of a character cell in the canvas's current font. If you add to that value the `tmInternalLeading` field—to allow for some space between lines—you get the height for each line of text to be drawn on the memory canvas:

```
LineHi := Metrics.tmHeight + Metrics.tmInternalLeading;
```

The height necessary for the memory canvas then can be determined by multiplying LineHi by the number of lines of text and adding that value to two times the height of the TddgMarquee control (to create the blank space at the beginning and end of the marquee). Suppose that the TStringList in which all the strings live is called FItems; now place the memory canvas dimensions in a TRect structure:

```
var
  VRect: TRect;
begin
  { VRect rectangle represents entire memory bitmap }
  VRect := Rect(0, 0, Width, LineHi * FItems.Count + Height * 2);
end;
```

After being instantiated and sized, the memory bitmap is initialized further by setting the font to match the Font property of TddgMarquee, filling the background with a color determined by the Color property of TddgMarquee, and setting the Style property of Brush to bsClear.

TIP

When you render text on TCanvas, the text background is filled with the current color of TCanvas.Brush. To cause the text background to be invisible, set TCanvas.Brush.Style to bsClear.

Most of the preliminary work is now in place, so it's time to render the text on the memory bitmap. The most straightforward way to output the text onto a canvas is to use the TextOut() method of TCanvas; however, you have more control over the formatting of the text when you use the more complex DrawText() API function. Because it requires control over justification, TddgMarquee will use the DrawText() function. An enumerated type is ideal to represent the text justification:

```
type
  TJustification = (tjCenter, tjLeft, tjRight);
```

The following code shows the PaintLine() method for TddgMarquee, which makes use of DrawText() to render text onto the memory bitmap. In this method, FJust represents an instance variable of type TJustification. Here's the code:

```
procedure TddgMarquee.PaintLine(R: TRect; LineNum: Integer);
{ this method is called to paint each line of text onto MemBitmap }
const
  Flags: array[TJustification] of DWORD = (DT_CENTER, DT_LEFT, DT_RIGHT);
var
  S: string;
```

```
begin
  { Copy next line to local variable for clarity }
  S := FItems.Strings[LineNum];
  { Draw line of text onto memory bitmap }
  DrawText(MemBitmap.Canvas.Handle, PChar(S), Length(S), R,
    Flags[FJust] or DT_SINGLELINE or DT_TOP);
end;
```

Painting the Component

Now that you know how to create the memory bitmap and paint text onto it, the next step is learning how to copy that text to the TddgMarquee canvas.

The Paint() method of a component is invoked in response to a Windows WM_PAINT message. The Paint() method is what gives your component life; you use the Paint() method to paint, draw, and fill to determine the graphical appearance of your components.

The job of TddgMarquee.Paint() is to copy the strings from the memory canvas to the canvas of TddgMarquee. This feat is accomplished by the BitBlt() API function, which copies the bits from one device context to another.

To determine whether TddgMarquee is currently running, the component will maintain a Boolean instance variable called FActive that reveals whether the marquee's scrolling capability has been activated. Therefore, the Paint() method paints differently depending on whether the component is active:

```
procedure TddgMarquee.Paint;
{ this virtual method is called in response to a }
{ Windows paint message }
begin
  if FActive then
    { Copy from memory bitmap to screen }
    BitBlt(Canvas.Handle, 0, 0, InsideRect.Right, InsideRect.Bottom,
      MemBitmap.Canvas.Handle, 0, CurrLine, srcCopy)
  else
    inherited Paint;
end;
```

If the marquee is active, the component uses the BitBlt() function to paint a portion of the memory canvas onto the TddgMarquee canvas. Notice the CurrLine variable, which is passed as the next-to-last parameter to BitBlt(). The value of this parameter determines which portion of the memory canvas to transfer onto the screen. By continuously incrementing or decrementing the value of CurrLine, you can give TddgMarquee the appearance that the text is scrolling up or down.

Animating the Marquee

The visual aspects of the TddgMarquee component are now in place. The rest of the work involved in getting the component working is just hooking up the plumbing, so to speak. At this point, TddgMarquee requires some mechanism to change the value of CurrLine every so often and to repaint the component. This trick can be accomplished fairly easily using Delphi's TTimer component.

Before you can use TTimer, of course, you must create and initialize the class instance. TddgMarquee will have a TTimer instance called FTimer, and you'll initialize it in a procedure called DoTimer:

```
procedure DoTimer;
{ procedure sets up TddgMarquee's timer }
begin
  FTimer := TTimer.Create(Self);
  with FTimer do
  begin
    Enabled := False;
    Interval := TimerInterval;
    OnTimer := DoTimerOnTimer;
  end;
end;
```

In this procedure, FTimer is created, and it's disabled initially. Its Interval property then is assigned to the value of a constant called TimerInterval. Finally, the OnTimer event for FTimer is assigned to a method of TddgMarquee called DoTimerOnTimer. This is the method that will be called when an OnTimer event occurs.

> **NOTE**
>
> When assigning values to events in your code, you need to follow two rules:
>
> - The procedure you assign to the event must be a method of some object instance. It can't be a standalone procedure or function.
> - The method you assign to the event must accept the same parameter list as the event type. For example, the OnTimer event for TTimer is of type TNotifyEvent. Because TNotifyEvent accepts one parameter, Sender, of type TObject, any method you assign to OnTimer must also take one parameter of type TObject.

The DoTimerOnTimer() method is defined as follows:

```
procedure TddgMarquee.DoTimerOnTimer(Sender:  TObject);
{ This method is executed in response to a timer event }
```

Advanced VCL Component Building

499

CHAPTER 12

12

ADVANCED VCL
COMPONENT
BUILDING

```
begin
  IncLine;
  { only repaint within borders }
  InvalidateRect(Handle, @InsideRect, False);
end;
```

In this method, a procedure named IncLine() is called; this procedure increments or decrements the value of CurrLine as necessary. Then the InvalidateRect() API function is called to "invalidate" (or *repaint*) the interior portion of the component. We chose to use InvalidateRect() rather than the Invalidate() method of TCanvas because Invalidate() causes the entire canvas to be repainted rather than just the portion within a defined rectangle, as is the case with InvalidateRect(). This method, because it doesn't continuously repaint the entire component, eliminates much of the flicker that would otherwise occur. Remember: Flicker is bad.

The IncLine() method, which updates the value of CurrLine and detects whether scrolling has completed, is defined as follows:

```
procedure TddgMarquee.IncLine;
{ this method is called to increment a line }
begin
  if not FScrollDown then        // if Marquee is scrolling upward
  begin
    { Check to see if marquee has scrolled to end yet }
    if FItems.Count * LineHi + ClientRect.Bottom -
      ScrollPixels  >= CurrLine then
      { not at end, so increment current line }
      Inc(CurrLine, ScrollPixels)
    else SetActive(False);
  end
  else begin                     // if Marquee is scrolling downward
    { Check to see if marquee has scrolled to end yet }
    if CurrLine >= ScrollPixels then
      { not at end, so decrement current line }
      Dec(CurrLine, ScrollPixels)
    else SetActive(False);
  end;
end;
```

The constructor for TddgMarquee is actually quite simple. It calls the inherited Create() method, creates a TStringList instance, sets up FTimer, and then sets all the default values for the instance variables. Once again, you must remember to call the inherited Create() method in your components. Failure to do so means your components will miss out on important and useful functionality, such as handle and canvas creation, streaming, and Windows message response. The following code shows the TddgMarquee constructor, Create():

```
constructor TddgMarquee.Create(AOwner: TComponent);
{ constructor for TddgMarquee class }

  procedure DoTimer;
  { procedure sets up TddgMarquee's timer }
  begin
    FTimer := TTimer.Create(Self);
    with FTimer do
    begin
      Enabled := False;
      Interval := TimerInterval;
      OnTimer := DoTimerOnTimer;
    end;
  end;

begin
  inherited Create(AOwner);
  FItems := TStringList.Create;  { instantiate string list }
  DoTimer;                       { set up timer }
  { set instance variable default values }
  Width := 100;
  Height := 75;
  FActive := False;
  FScrollDown := False;
  FJust := tjCenter;
  BevelWidth := 3;
end;
```

The TddgMarquee destructor is even simpler: The method deactivates the component by passing False to the SetActive() method, frees the timer and the string list, and then calls the inherited Destroy() method:

```
destructor TddgMarquee.Destroy;
{ destructor for TddgMarquee class }
begin
  SetActive(False);
  FTimer.Free;              // free allocated objects
  FItems.Free;
  inherited Destroy;
end;
```

> **TIP**
>
> As a rule of thumb, when you override constructors, you usually call `inherited` first, and when you override destructors, you usually call `inherited` last. It might help to remember "first in, last out." This ensures that the class has been set up before you modify it and that all dependent resources have been cleaned up before you dispose of the class.
>
> Exceptions to this rule exist; however, you should generally stick to it unless you have good reason not to.

The `SetActive()` method, which is called by both the `IncLine()` method and the destructor (in addition to serving as the writer for the `Active` property), serves as a vehicle that starts and stops the marquee scrolling up the canvas:

```
procedure TddgMarquee.SetActive(Value: Boolean);
{ called to activate/deactivate the marquee }
begin
  if Value and (not FActive) and (FItems.Count > 0) then
  begin
    FActive := True;                 // set active flag
    MemBitmap := TBitmap.Create;
    FillBitmap;                      // Paint Image on bitmap
    FTimer.Enabled := True;          // start timer
  end
  else if (not Value) and FActive then
  begin
    FTimer.Enabled := False;    // disable timer,
    if Assigned(FOnDone)        // fire OnDone event,
      then FOnDone(Self);
    FActive := False;           // set FActive to False
    MemBitmap.Free;             // free memory bitmap
    Invalidate;                 // clear control window
  end;
end;
```

An important feature of `TddgMarquee` that's lacking thus far is an event that tells the user when scrolling is complete. Never fear—this feature is very straightforward to add by way of an event: `FOnDone`. The first step to adding an event to your component is to declare an instance variable of some event type in the `private` portion of the class definition. You'll use the `TNotifyEvent` type for the `FOnDone` event:

```
FOnDone: TNotifyEvent;
```

The event should then be declared in the published part of the class as a property:

```
property OnDone: TNotifyEvent read FOnDone write FOnDone;
```

Recall that the read and write directives specify from which function or variable a given property should get or set its value.

Taking just these two small steps will cause an entry for OnDone to be displayed in the Events page of the Object Inspector at design time. The only other thing that needs to be done is to call the user's handler for OnDone (if a method is assigned to OnDone), as demonstrated by TddgMarquee with this line of code in the Deactivate() method:

```
if Assigned(FOnDone) then FOnDone(Self); // fire OnDone event
```

This line basically reads, "If the component user has assigned a method to the OnDone event, call that method and pass the TddgMarquee class instance (Self) as a parameter."

Listing 12.2 shows the completed source code for the Marquee unit. Notice that because the component descends from a TCustom*XXX* class, you need to publish many of the properties provided by TCustomPanel.

Listing 12.2 Marquee.pas—Illustrates the TddgMarquee Component

```
unit Marquee;

interface

uses
  SysUtils, Windows, Classes, Forms, Controls, Graphics,
  Messages, ExtCtrls, Dialogs;

const
  ScrollPixels = 3;      // num of pixels for each scroll
  TimerInterval = 50;    // time between scrolls in ms

type
  TJustification = (tjCenter, tjLeft, tjRight);

  EMarqueeError = class(Exception);

  TddgMarquee = class(TCustomPanel)
  private
    MemBitmap: TBitmap;
    InsideRect: TRect;
    FItems: TStringList;
    FJust: TJustification;
```

LISTING 12.2   Continued

```
    FScrollDown: Boolean;
    LineHi : Integer;
    CurrLine : Integer;
    VRect: TRect;
    FTimer: TTimer;
    FActive: Boolean;
    FOnDone: TNotifyEvent;
    procedure SetItems(Value: TStringList);
    procedure DoTimerOnTimer(Sender:  TObject);
    procedure PaintLine(R: TRect; LineNum: Integer);
    procedure SetLineHeight;
    procedure SetStartLine;
    procedure IncLine;
    procedure SetActive(Value: Boolean);
  protected
    procedure Paint; override;
    procedure FillBitmap; virtual;
  public
    property Active: Boolean read FActive write SetActive;
    constructor Create(AOwner: TComponent); override;
    destructor Destroy; override;
  published
    property ScrollDown: Boolean read FScrollDown write FScrollDown;
    property Justify: TJustification read FJust write FJust default tjCenter;
    property Items: TStringList read FItems write SetItems;
    property OnDone: TNotifyEvent read FOnDone write FOnDone;
    { Publish inherited properties: }
    property Align;
    property Alignment;
    property BevelInner;
    property BevelOuter;
    property BevelWidth;
    property BorderWidth;
    property BorderStyle;
    property Color;
    property Ctl3D;
    property Font;
    property Locked;
    property ParentColor;
    property ParentCtl3D;
    property ParentFont;
    property Visible;
    property OnClick;
    property OnDblClick;
```

LISTING 12.2 Continued

```
    property OnMouseDown;
    property OnMouseMove;
    property OnMouseUp;
    property OnResize;
  end;

implementation

constructor TddgMarquee.Create(AOwner: TComponent);
{ constructor for TddgMarquee class }

  procedure DoTimer;
  { procedure sets up TddgMarquee's timer }
  begin
    FTimer := TTimer.Create(Self);
    with FTimer do
    begin
      Enabled := False;
      Interval := TimerInterval;
      OnTimer := DoTimerOnTimer;
    end;
  end;

begin
  inherited Create(AOwner);
  FItems := TStringList.Create;  { instantiate string list }
  DoTimer;                       { set up timer }
  { set instance variable default values }
  Width := 100;
  Height := 75;
  FActive := False;
  FScrollDown := False;
  FJust := tjCenter;
  BevelWidth := 3;
end;

destructor TddgMarquee.Destroy;
{ destructor for TddgMarquee class }
begin
  SetActive(False);
  FTimer.Free;             // free allocated objects
  FItems.Free;
  inherited Destroy;
end;
```

LISTING 12.2 Continued

```pascal
procedure TddgMarquee.DoTimerOnTimer(Sender: TObject);
{ This method is executed in response to a timer event }
begin
  IncLine;
  { only repaint within borders }
  InvalidateRect(Handle, @InsideRect, False);
end;

procedure TddgMarquee.IncLine;
{ this method is called to increment a line }
begin
  if not FScrollDown then        // if Marquee is scrolling upward
  begin
    { Check to see if marquee has scrolled to end yet }
    if FItems.Count * LineHi + ClientRect.Bottom -
      ScrollPixels  >= CurrLine then
      { not at end, so increment current line }
      Inc(CurrLine, ScrollPixels)
    else SetActive(False);
  end
  else begin                     // if Marquee is scrolling downward
    { Check to see if marquee has scrolled to end yet }
    if CurrLine >= ScrollPixels then
      { not at end, so decrement current line }
      Dec(CurrLine, ScrollPixels)
    else SetActive(False);
  end;
end;

procedure TddgMarquee.SetItems(Value: TStringList);
begin
  if FItems <> Value then
    FItems.Assign(Value);
end;

procedure TddgMarquee.SetLineHeight;
{ this virtual method sets the LineHi instance variable }
var
  Metrics : TTextMetric;
begin
  { get metric info for font }
  GetTextMetrics(Canvas.Handle, Metrics);
  { adjust line height }
  LineHi := Metrics.tmHeight + Metrics.tmInternalLeading;
end;
```

LISTING 12.2   Continued

```
procedure TddgMarquee.SetStartLine;
{ this virtual method initializes the CurrLine instance variable }
begin
  // initialize current line to top if scrolling up, or...
  if not FScrollDown then CurrLine := 0
  // bottom if scrolling down
  else CurrLine := VRect.Bottom - Height;
end;

procedure TddgMarquee.PaintLine(R: TRect; LineNum: Integer);
{ this method is called to paint each line of text onto MemBitmap }
const
  Flags: array[TJustification] of DWORD = (DT_CENTER, DT_LEFT, DT_RIGHT);
var
  S: string;
begin
  { Copy next line to local variable for clarity }
  S := FItems.Strings[LineNum];
  { Draw line of text onto memory bitmap }
  DrawText(MemBitmap.Canvas.Handle, PChar(S), Length(S), R,
    Flags[FJust] or DT_SINGLELINE or DT_TOP);
end;

procedure TddgMarquee.FillBitmap;
var
  y, i : Integer;
  R: TRect;
begin
  SetLineHeight;                 // set height of each line
  { VRect rectangle represents entire memory bitmap }
  VRect := Rect(0, 0, Width, LineHi * FItems.Count + Height * 2);
  { InsideRect rectangle represents interior of beveled border }
  InsideRect := Rect(BevelWidth, BevelWidth, Width - (2 * BevelWidth),
    Height - (2 * BevelWidth));
  R := Rect(InsideRect.Left, 0, InsideRect.Right, VRect.Bottom);
  SetStartLine;
  MemBitmap.Width := Width;      // initialize memory bitmap
  with MemBitmap do
  begin
    Height := VRect.Bottom;
    with Canvas do
    begin
      Font := Self.Font;
```

LISTING 12.2   Continued

```
      Brush.Color := Color;
      FillRect(VRect);
      Brush.Style := bsClear;
    end;
  end;
  y := Height;
  i := 0;
  repeat
    R.Top := y;
    PaintLine(R, i);
    { increment y by the height (in pixels) of a line }
    inc(y, LineHi);
    inc(i);
  until i >= FItems.Count;       // repeat for all lines
end;

procedure TddgMarquee.Paint;
{ this virtual method is called in response to a }
{ Windows paint message }
begin
  if FActive then
    { Copy from memory bitmap to screen }
    BitBlt(Canvas.Handle, 0, 0, InsideRect.Right, InsideRect.Bottom,
      MemBitmap.Canvas.Handle, 0, CurrLine, srcCopy)
  else
    inherited Paint;
end;

procedure TddgMarquee.SetActive(Value: Boolean);
{ called to activate/deactivate the marquee }
begin
  if Value and (not FActive) and (FItems.Count > 0) then
  begin
    FActive := True;               // set active flag
    MemBitmap := TBitmap.Create;
    FillBitmap;                     // Paint Image on bitmap
    FTimer.Enabled := True;         // start timer
  end
  else if (not Value) and FActive then
  begin
    FTimer.Enabled := False;    // disable timer,
    if Assigned(FOnDone)        // fire OnDone event,
      then FOnDone(Self);
    FActive := False;           // set FActive to False
```

Listing 12.2   Continued

```
    MemBitmap.Free;          // free memory bitmap
    Invalidate;              // clear control window
  end;
end;

end.
```

Tip

Notice the `default` directive and value used with the `Justify` property of `TddgMarquee`. This use of `default` optimizes streaming of the component, which improves the component's design-time performance. You can give default values to properties of any ordinal type (`Integer`, `Word`, `Longint`, as well as enumerated types, for example), but you can't give them to nonordinal property types such as strings, floating-point numbers, arrays, records, and classes.

You also need to initialize the default values for the properties in your constructor. Failure to do so will cause streaming problems.

Testing `TddgMarquee`

Although it's very exciting to finally have this component written and in the testing stages, don't get carried away by trying to add it to the Component Palette just yet. It has to be debugged first. You should do all preliminary testing with the component by creating a project that creates and uses a dynamic instance of the component. Listing 12.3 depicts the main unit for a project called `TestMarq`, which is used to test the `TddgMarquee` component. This simple project consists of a form that contains two buttons.

Listing 12.3   TestU.pas—Tests the `TddgMarquee` Component

```
unit Testu;

interface

uses
  SysUtils, WinTypes, WinProcs, Messages, Classes, Graphics, Controls,
  Forms, Dialogs, Marquee, StdCtrls, ExtCtrls;

type
  TForm1 = class(TForm)
    Button1: TButton;
    Button2: TButton;
```

Listing 12.3   Continued

```
    procedure FormCreate(Sender: TObject);
    procedure Button1Click(Sender: TObject);
    procedure Button2Click(Sender: TObject);
  private
    Marquee1: TddgMarquee;
    procedure MDone(Sender: TObject);
  public
    { Public declarations }
  end;

var
  Form1: TForm1;

implementation

{$R *.DFM}

procedure TForm1.MDone(Sender: TObject);
begin
  Beep;
end;

procedure TForm1.FormCreate(Sender:  TObject);
begin
  Marquee1 := TddgMarquee.Create(Self);
  with Marquee1 do
  begin
    Parent := Self;
    Top := 10;
    Left := 10;
    Height := 200;
    Width := 150;
    OnDone := MDone;
    Show;
    with Items do
    begin
      Add('Greg');
      Add('Peter');
      Add('Bobby');
      Add('Marsha');
      Add('Jan');
      Add('Cindy');
    end;
  end;
end;
```

LISTING 12.3   Continued

```
procedure TForm1.Button1Click(Sender: TObject);
begin
  Marquee1.Active := True;
end;

procedure TForm1.Button2Click(Sender: TObject);
begin
  Marquee1.Active :=  False;
end;

end.
```

> **TIP**
>
> *Always* create a test project for your new components. *Never* try to do initial testing on a component by adding it to the Component Palette. By trying to debug a component that resides on the palette, not only will you waste time with a lot of gratuitous package rebuilding, but it's possible to crash the IDE as a result of a bug in your component.

After you squash all the bugs you find in this program, it's time to add it to the Component Palette. As you might recall, doing so is easy: Simply choose Component, Install Component. . . from the main menu and then fill in the unit filename and package name in the Install Component dialog. Click OK and Delphi will rebuild the package to which the component was added and update the Component Palette. Of course, your component will need to expose a Register() procedure in order to be placed on the Component Palette. The TddgMarquee component is registered in the DDGReg.pas unit of the DDGDsgn package on the CD-ROM accompanying this book.

Writing Property Editors

Chapter 11, "VCL Component Building," shows how properties are edited in the Object Inspector for most of the common property types. The means by which a property is edited is determined by its *property editor*. Several predefined property editors are used for the existing properties. However, there might be a situation in which none of the predefined editors meet your needs, such as when you've created a custom property. Given this situation, you'll need to create your own editor for that property.

You can edit properties in the Object Inspector in two ways. One is to allow the user to edit the value as a text string. The other is to use a dialog that performs the editing of the property. In some cases, you'll want to allow both editing capabilities for a single property.

Here are the steps required for writing a property editor:

1. Create a descendant property editor object.
2. Edit the property as text.
3. Edit the property as a whole with a dialog (optional).
4. Specify the property editor's attributes.
5. Register the property editor.

The following sections cover each of these steps.

Creating a Descendant Property Editor Object

Delphi defines several property editors in the unit `DesignEditors.pas`, all of which descend from the base class `TPropertyEditor`. When you create a property editor, your property editor must descend from `TPropertyEditor` or one of its descendants. Table 12.1 shows the `TPropertyEditor` descendants that are used with the existing properties.

TABLE 12.1 Property Editors Defined in `DesignEditors.pas`

Property Editor	*Description*
`TOrdinalProperty`	The base class for all ordinal property editors, such as `TIntegerProperty`, `TEnumProperty`, `TCharProperty`, and so on.
`TIntegerProperty`	The default property editor for integer properties of all sizes.
`TCharProperty`	The property editor for properties that are a char type and a subrange of char; that is, `'A'..'Z'`.
`TEnumProperty`	The default property for all user-defined enumerated types.
`TFloatProperty`	The default property editor for floating-point numeric properties.
`TStringProperty`	The default property editor for string type properties.
`TSetElementProperty`	The default property editor for individual set elements. Each element in the set is displayed as an individual Boolean option.

TABLE 12.1 Continued

Property Editor	Description
TSetProperty	The default property editor for set properties. The set expands into separate set elements for each element in the set.
TClassProperty	The default property editor for properties that are, themselves, objects.
TMethodProperty	The default property editor for properties that are method pointers—that is, *events*.
TComponentProperty	The default property editor for properties that refer to a component. This isn't the same as the TClassProperty editor. Instead, this editor allows the user to specify a component to which the property refers—that is, ActiveControl.
TColorProperty	The default property editor for properties of the type TColor.
TFontNameProperty	The default property editor for font names. This editor displays a drop-down list of fonts available on the system.
TFontProperty	The default property editor for properties of type TFont, which allows the editing of subproperties. TFontProperty allows the editing of subproperties because it derives from TClassProperty.
TInt64Property	The default property editor for all Int64 and its derivatives.
TNestedProperty	This property editor uses its parent's property editor.
TClassProperty	The default property editor for objects.
TMethodProperty	The default property editor for methods.
TInterfaceProperty	The default property editor for interface references.
TComponentNameProperty	Property editor for the Name property. It restricts the Name property from being displayed when more than one component is selected.
TDateProperty	The default property editor for the date portion of a TDateTime type property.
TTimePropery	The property editor for the time portion of a TDateTime property.
TDateTimeProperty	The property editor for a TDateTime property type.
TVariantProperty	The property editor for variant types.

The property editor from which your property editor must descend depends on how the property is going to behave when it's edited. In some cases, for example, your property might require the same functionality as TIntegerProperty, but it might also require additional logic in the editing process. Therefore, it would be logical that your property editor descend from TIntegerProperty.

> **TIP**
>
> Bear in mind that there are cases in which you don't need to create a property editor that depends on your property type. For example, subrange types are checked automatically (for example, 1..10 is checked for by TIntegerProperty), enumerated types get drop-down lists automatically, and so on. You should try to use type definitions instead of custom property editors because they're enforced by the language at compile time as well as by the default property editors.

Editing the Property As Text

The property editor has two basic purposes: One is to provide a means for the user to edit the property; this is obvious. The other not-so-obvious purpose is to provide the string representation of the property value to the Object Inspector so that it can be displayed accordingly.

When you create a descendant property editor class, you must override the GetValue() and SetValue() methods. GetValue() returns the string representation of the property value for the Object Inspector to display. SetValue() sets the value based on its string representation as it's entered in the Object Inspector.

As an example, examine the definition of the TIntegerProperty class type as it's defined in DSGNINTF.PAS:

```
TIntegerProperty = class(TOrdinalProperty)
public
  function GetValue: string; override;
  procedure SetValue(const Value: string); override;
end;
```

Here, you see that the GetValue() and SetValue() methods have been overridden. The GetValue() implementation is as follows:

```
function TIntegerProperty.GetValue: string;
begin
  Result :=  IntToStr(GetOrdValue);
end;
```

Here's the `SetValue()` implementation:

```
procedure TIntegerProperty.SetValue(const Value: String);
var
  L: Longint;
begin
  L := StrToInt(Value);
  with GetTypeData(GetPropType)^ do
    if (L < MinValue) or (L > MaxValue) then
      raise EPropertyError.CreateResFmt(SOutOfRange, [MinValue, MaxValue]);
  SetOrdValue(L);
end;
```

`GetValue()` returns the string representation of an integer property. The Object Inspector uses this value to display the property's value. `GetOrdValue()` is a method defined by `TPropertyEditor` and is used to retrieve the value of the property referenced by the property editor.

`SetValue()` takes the string value entered by the user and assigns it to the property in the correct format. `SetValue()` also performs some error checking to ensure that the value is within a specified range of values. This illustrates how you might perform error checking with your descendant property editors. The `SetOrdValue()` method assigns the value to the property referenced by the property editor.

`TPropertyEditor` defines several methods similar to `GetOrdValue()` for getting the string representation of various types. Additionally, `TPropertyEditor` contains the equivalent "set" methods for setting the values in their respective format. `TPropertyEditor` descendants inherit these methods. These methods are used for getting and setting the values of the properties that the property editor references. Table 12.2 shows these methods.

TABLE 12.2 Read/Write Property Methods for `TPropertyEditor`

Property Type	"Get" Method	"Set" Method
Floating point	GetFloatValue()	SetFloatValue()
Event	GetMethodValue()	SetMethodValue()
Ordinal	GetOrdValue()	SetOrdValue()
String	GetStrValue()	SetStrValue()
Variant	GetVarValue()	SetVarValue(), SetVarValueAt()

To illustrate creating a new property editor, we'll have some more fun with the solar system example introduced in the last chapter. This time, we've created a simple component, `TPlanet`, to represent a single planet. `TPlanet` contains the property `PlanetName`. Internal storage for

`PlanetName` is going to be of type integer and will hold the planet's position in the solar system. However, it will be displayed in the Object Inspector as the name of the planet.

So far this sounds easy, but here's the catch: We want to enable the user to type two values to represent the planet. The user should be able to type the planet name as a string, such as `Venus`, `VENUS`, or `VeNuS`. He should also be able to type the position of the planet in the solar system. Therefore, for the planet Venus, the user would type the numeric value 2.

The component `TPlanet` is as follows:

```
type
  TPlanetName = type Integer;

  TPlanet = class(TComponent)
  private
    FPlanetName: TPlanetName;
  published
    property PlanetName: TPlanetName read FPlanetName write FPlanetName;
  end;
```

As you can see, there's not much to this component. It has only one property: `PlanetName` of the type `TPlanetName`. Here, the special definition of `TPlanetName` is used so that it's given its own runtime type information, yet it's still treated like an integer type.

This functionality doesn't come from the `TPlanet` component; rather, it comes from the property editor for the `TPlanetName` property type. This property editor is shown in Listing 12.4.

LISTING 12.4 `PlanetPE.PAS`—The Source Code for `TPlanetNameProperty`

```
unit PlanetPE;

interface

uses
  Windows, SysUtils, DsgnIntF;

type
  TPlanetNameProperty = class(TIntegerProperty)
  public
    function GetValue: string; override;
    procedure SetValue(const Value: string); override;
  end;

implementation

const
  { Declare a constant array containing planet names }
```

12

ADVANCED VCL
COMPONENT
BUILDING

LISTING 12.4   Continued

```pascal
  PlanetNames: array[1..9] of String[7] =
    ('Mercury', 'Venus', 'Earth', 'Mars', 'Jupiter', 'Saturn',
     'Uranus', 'Neptune', 'Pluto');


function TPlanetNameProperty.GetValue: string;
begin
  Result := PlanetNames[GetOrdValue];
end;

procedure TPlanetNameProperty.SetValue(const Value: String);
var
  PName: string[7];
  i, ValErr: Integer;
begin
  PName := UpperCase(Value);
  i := 1;
  { Compare the Value with each of the planet names in the PlanetNames
    array. If a match is found, the variable i will be less than 10 }
  while (PName <> UpperCase(PlanetNames[i])) and (i < 10) do
    inc(i);
  { If i is less than 10, a valid planet name was entered. Set the value
    and exit this procedure. }
  if i < 10 then  // A valid planet name was entered.
  begin
    SetOrdValue(i);
    Exit;
  end
  { If i was greater than 10, the user might have typed in a planet number, or
    an invalid planet name. Use the Val function to test if the user typed in
    a number, if an ValErr is non-zero, an invalid name was entered,
    otherwise, test the range of the number entered for (0 < i < 10). }
  else begin
    Val(Value, i, ValErr);
    if ValErr <> 0 then
      raise Exception.Create(Format('Sorry, Never heard of the planet %s.',
        [Value]));
    if (i <= 0) or (i >= 10) then
      raise Exception.Create('Sorry, that planet is not in OUR solar
system.');
    SetOrdValue(i);
  end;
end;

end.
```

First, we create our property editor, `TPlanetNameProperty`, which descends from `TIntegerProperty`. By the way, it's necessary to include the `DesignEditors` and `DesignIntf` units in the uses clause of this unit.

We've defined an array of string constants to represent the planets in the solar system by their position from the sun. These strings will be used to display the string representation of the planet in the Object Inspector.

As stated earlier, we have to override the `GetValue()` and `SetValue()` methods. In the `GetValue()` method, we just return the string from the `PlanetNames` array, which is indexed by the property value. Of course, this value must be within the range of 1–9. We handle this by not allowing the user to enter a number out of that range in the `SetValue()` method.

`SetValue()` gets a string as it's entered from the Object Inspector. This string can either be a planet name or a number representing a planet's position. If a valid planet name or planet number is entered, as determined by the code logic, the value assigned to the property is specified by the `SetOrdValue()` method. If the user enters an invalid planet name or planet position, the code raises the appropriate exception.

That's all there is to defining a property editor. Well, not quite; it must still be registered before it becomes known to the property to which you want to attach it.

Registering the New Property Editor

You register a property editor by using the appropriately named procedure `RegisterPropertyEditor()`. This method is declared as follows:

```
procedure RegisterPropertyEditor(PropertyType: PTypeInfo;
  ComponentClass: TClass; const PropertyName: string;
  EditorClass: TPropertyEditorClass);
```

The first parameter, `PropertyType`, is a pointer to the Runtime Type Information of the property being edited. This information is obtained by using the `TypeInfo()` function. `ComponentClass` is used to specify to which class this property editor will apply. `PropertyName` specifies the property name on the component, and the `EditorClass` parameter specifies the type of property editor to use. For the `TPlanet.PlanetName` property, the function looks like this:

```
RegisterPropertyEditor(TypeInfo(TPlanetName), TPlanet, 'PlanetName',
  TPlanetNameProperty);
```

You can register the property editor along with the registration of the component in the component's unit, as shown in Listing 12.5.

LISTING 12.5   Planet.pas—The TPlanet Component

```
unit Planet;

interface

uses
  Classes, SysUtils;

type
  TPlanetName = type Integer;

  TddgPlanet = class(TComponent)
  private
    FPlanetName: TPlanetName;
  published
    property PlanetName: TPlanetName read FPlanetName write FPlanetName;
  end;

implementation

end.
```

Advanced VCL Component Building

CHAPTER 12

519

12

ADVANCED VCL
COMPONENT
BUILDING

everything that's listed in the `interface` section of your component's unit (such as the `Register()` procedure) as well as everything it touches (such as the property editor class type) will tag along with your component when it's compiled into a package. For this reason, you might want to perform registration of your property editor in a separate unit. Furthermore, some component writers choose to create both design-time and runtime packages for their components, whereas the property editors and other design-time tools reside only in the design-time package. You'll note that the packages containing this book's code do this using the `DdgRT6` runtime package and the `DDGDT6` design package.

Editing the Property as a Whole with a Dialog

Sometimes it's necessary to provide more editing capability than the in-place editing of the Object Inspector. This is when it becomes necessary to use a dialog as a property editor. An example of this would be the `Font` property for most Delphi components. Certainly, the makers of Delphi could have forced the user to type the font name and other font-related information. However, it would be unreasonable to expect the user to know this information. It's far easier to provide the user with a dialog where he can set these various attributes related to the font and see an example before selecting it.

To illustrate using a dialog to edit a property, we're going to extend the functionality of the `TddgRunButton` component created in Chapter 11. Now the user will be able to click an ellipsis button in the Object Inspector for the `CommandLine` property, which will invoke an Open File dialog from which the user can select a file for `TddgRunButton` to represent.

Sample Dialog Property Editor: Extending `TddgRunButton`

The `TddgRunButton` component is shown in Listing 11.13 in Chapter 11. We won't show it again here, but there are a few things we want to point out. The `TddgRunButton.CommandLine` property is of type `TCommandLine`, which is defined as follows:

```
TCommandLine = type string;
```

Again, this is a special declaration that attaches unique Runtime Type Information to this special type. This allows you to define a property editor specific to the `TCommandLine` type. Additionally, because `TCommandLine` is treated as a string, the property editor for editing string properties still applies to the `TCommandLine` type as well.

Also, as we illustrate the property editor for the `TCommandLine` type, keep in mind that `TddgRunButton` already has included the necessary error checking of property assignments in the properties' access methods. Therefore, it isn't necessary to repeat this error checking in the property editor's logic.

Listing 12.6 shows the definition of the TCommandLineProperty property editor.

LISTING 12.6   RunBtnPE.pas—The Unit Containing TCommandLineProperty

```
unit runbtnpe;

interface
uses
  Windows, Messages, SysUtils, Classes, Graphics, Controls,
  Forms, Dialogs, StdCtrls, Buttons, DsgnIntF, TypInfo;

type

  { Descend from the TStringProperty class so that this editor
    inherits the string property editing capabilities }
  TCommandLineProperty = class(TStringProperty)
    function GetAttributes: TPropertyAttributes; override;
    procedure Edit; override;
  end;


implementation

function TCommandLineProperty.GetAttributes: TPropertyAttributes;
begin
  Result := [paDialog]; // Display a dialog in the Edit method
end;

procedure TCommandLineProperty.Edit;
{ The Edit method displays a TOpenDialog from which the user obtains
  an executable file name that gets assigned to the property }
var
  OpenDialog: TOpenDialog;
begin
  { Create the TOpenDialog }
  OpenDialog := TOpenDialog.Create(Application);
  try
    { Show only executable files }
    OpenDialog.Filter := 'Executable Files|*.EXE';
    { If the user selects a file, then assign it to the property.  }
    if OpenDialog.Execute then
      SetStrValue(OpenDialog.FileName);
  finally
    OpenDialog.Free // Free the TOpenDialog instance.
  end;
end;


end.
```

Examination of `TCommandLineProperty` shows that the property editor itself is very simple. First, notice that it descends from `TStringProperty` so that the string-editing capabilities are maintained. Therefore, in the Object Inspector, it isn't necessary to invoke the dialog. The user can just type the command line directly. Also, we didn't override the `SetValue()` and `GetValue()` methods because `TStringProperty` already handles this correctly. However, it was necessary to override the `GetAttributes()` method in order for the Object Inspector to know that this property is capable of being edited with a dialog. `GetAttributes()` merits further discussion.

Specifying the Property Editor's Attributes

Every property editor must tell the Object Inspector how a property is to be edited and what special attributes (if any) must be used when editing a property. Most of the time, the inherited attributes from a descendant property editor will suffice. In certain circumstances, however, you must override the `GetAttributes()` method of `TPropertyEditor`, which returns a set of property attribute flags (`TPropertyAttribute` flags) that indicate special property-editing attributes. The various `TPropertyAttribute` flags are shown in Table 12.3.

TABLE 12.3 `TPropertyAttribute` Flags

Attribute	How the Property Editor Works with the Object Inspector
paValueList	Returns an enumerated list of values for the property. The `GetValues()` method populates the list. A drop-down arrow button appears to the right of the property value. This applies to enumerated properties such as `TForm.BorderStyle` and integer `const` groups such as `TColor` and `TCharSet`.
paSubProperties	Subproperties are displayed indented below the current property in outline format. `paValueList` must also be set. This applies to set properties and class properties such as `TOpenDialog.Options` and `TForm.Font`.
paDialog	An ellipsis button is displayed to the right of the property in the Object Inspector, which, when clicked, causes the property editor's `Edit()` method to invoke a dialog. This applies to properties such as `TForm.Font`.
paMultiSelect	Properties are displayed when more than one component is selected on the Form Designer, allowing the user to change the property values for multiple components at once. Some properties aren't appropriate for this capability, such as the `Name` property.
paAutoUpdate	`SetValue()` is called on each change made to the property. If this flag isn't set, `SetValue()` is called when the user presses Enter or moves off the property in the Object Inspector. This applies to properties such as `TForm.Caption`.

TABLE 12.3 Continued

Attribute	How the Property Editor Works with the Object Inspector
paFullWidthName	Tells the Object Inspector that the value doesn't need to be rendered and, as such, the name should be rendered the full width of the inspector.
paSortList	The Object Inspector sorts the list returned by GetValues().
paReadOnly	The property value can't be changed.
paRevertable	The property can be reverted to its original value. Some properties, such as nested properties, shouldn't be reverted. TFont is an example of this.

> **NOTE**
>
> You should take a look at DesignEditors.pas and examine which TPropertyAttribute flags are set for various property editors.

Setting the paDialog Attribute for TCommandLineProperty

Because TCommandLineProperty is to display a dialog, you must tell the Object Inspector to use this capability by setting the paDialog attribute in the TCommandLineProperty.GetAttributes() method. This will place an ellipsis button to the right of the CommandLine property value in the Object Inspector. When the user clicks this button, the TCommandLineProperty.Edit() method will be called.

Registering the TCommandLineProperty

The final step required for implementing the TCommandLineProperty property editor is to register it using the RegisterPropertyEditor() procedure discussed earlier in this chapter. This procedure was added to the Register() procedure in DDGReg.pas in the DDGDsgn package:

```
RegisterComponents('DDG', [TddgRunButton]);
  RegisterPropertyEditor(TypeInfo(TCommandLine), TddgRunButton,
    '', TCommandLineProperty);
```

Also, note that the units DsgnIntf and RunBtnPE had to be added to the uses clause.

Component Editors

Component editors extend the design-time behavior of your components by allowing you to add items to the local menu associated with a particular component and by allowing you to change the default action when a component is double-clicked in the Form Designer. You might already be familiar with component editors without knowing it if you've ever used the fields editor provided with the TTable, TQuery, and TStoredProc components.

Advanced VCL Component Building

CHAPTER 12

523

12

ADVANCED VCL
COMPONENT
BUILDING

TComponentEditor

You might not be aware of this, but a different component editor is created for each component that's selected in the Form Designer. The type of component editor created depends on the component's type, although all component editors descend from TComponentEditor. This class is defined in the DesignEditors unit as follows:

```
TComponentEditor = class(TBaseComponentEditor, IComponentEditor)
private
  FComponent: TComponent;
  FDesigner: IDesigner;
public
  constructor Create(AComponent: TComponent; ADesigner: IDesigner); override;
  procedure Edit; virtual;
  procedure ExecuteVerb(Index: Integer); virtual;
  function GetComponent: TComponent;
  function GetDesigner: IDesigner;
  function GetVerb(Index: Integer): string; virtual;
  function GetVerbCount: Integer; virtual;
  function IsInInlined: Boolean;
procedure Copy; virtual;
  procedure PrepareItem(Index: Integer; const AItem: IMenuItem); virtual;
  property Component: TComponent read FComponent;
  property Designer: IDesigner read GetDesigner;
end;
```

Properties

The Component property of TComponentEditor is the instance of the component you're in the process of editing. Because this property is of the generic TComponent type, you must typecast the property in order to access fields introduced by descendant classes.

The Designer property is the instance of IDesigner that's currently hosting the application at design time. You'll find the complete definition for this class in the DesignEditors.pas unit.

Methods

The Edit() method is called when the user double-clicks the component at design time. Often, this method will invoke some sort of design dialog. The default behavior for this method is to call ExecuteVerb(0) if GetVerbCount() returns a value of 1 or greater. You must call Designer.Modified() if you modify the component from this (or any) method.

The use of the term *verb* as it applies to object methods applies to actions an object can take. Delphi has no knowledge of new objects or components initially, and needs to "learn" about them as they are added. With this in mind, it was designed with several methods that can be used to identify an object's actions. The GetVerbCount, GetVerb, and ExecuteVerb methods are generic methods intended for a wide variety of components, and they are the calls you will use to tell Delphi about your component.

The GetVerbCount() method is called to retrieve the number of items that are to be added to the local menu.

GetVerb() accepts an integer, Index, and returns a string containing the text that should appear on the local menu in the position corresponding to Index.

When an item is chosen from the local menu, the ExecuteVerb() method is called. This method receives the zero-based index of the item selected from the local menu in the Index parameter. You should respond by performing whatever action is necessary based on the verb the user selected from the local. menu.

The Paste() method is called whenever the component is pasted to the Clipboard. Delphi places the component's filed stream image on the Clipboard, but you can use this method to paste data on the Clipboard in a different type of format.

TDefaultEditor

If a custom component editor isn't registered for a particular component, that component will use the default component editor, TDefaultEditor. TDefaultEditor overrides the behavior of the Edit() method so that it searches the properties of the component and generates (or navigates to) the OnCreate, OnChanged, or OnClick event (whichever it finds first). If none of these events exists for this component, the first event defined will be selected.

A Simple Component

Consider the following simple custom component:

```
type
  TComponentEditorSample = class(TComponent)
  protected
    procedure SayHello; virtual;
    procedure SayGoodbye; virtual;
  end;

procedure TComponentEditorSample.SayHello;
begin
  MessageDlg('Hello, there!', mtInformation, [mbOk], 0);
end;

procedure TComponentEditorSample.SayGoodbye;
begin
  MessageDlg('See ya!', mtInformation, [mbOk], 0);
end;
```

As you can see, this little guy doesn't do much: It's a nonvisual component that descends directly from TComponent, and it contains two methods, SayHello() and SayGoodbye(), that simply display message dialogs.

A Simple Component Editor

To make the component a bit more exiting, you'll create a component editor that calls into the component and executes its methods at design time. The minimum TComponentEditor methods that must be overridden are ExecuteVerb(), GetVerb(), and GetVerbCount(). The code for this component editor is as follows:

```
type
  TSampleEditor = class(TComponentEditor)
  private
    procedure ExecuteVerb(Index: Integer); override;
    function GetVerb(Index: Integer): string; override;
    function GetVerbCount: Integer; override;
  end;

procedure TSampleEditor.ExecuteVerb(Index: Integer);
begin
  case Index of
    0: TComponentEditorSample(Component).SayHello;     // call function
    1: TComponentEditorSample(Component).SayGoodbye;   // call function
  end;
end;

function TSampleEditor.GetVerb(Index: Integer): string;
begin
  case Index of
    0: Result := 'Hello';      // return hello string
    1: Result := 'Goodbye';    // return goodbye string
  end;
end;

function TSampleEditor.GetVerbCount: Integer;
begin
  Result := 2;        // two possible verbs
end;
```

The GetVerbCount() method returns 2, indicating that there are two different verbs the component editor is prepared to execute. GetVerb() returns a string for each of these verbs to appear on the local menu. The ExecuteVerb() method calls the appropriate method inside the component, based on the verb index it receives as a parameter.

Registering a Component Editor

Like components and property editors, component editors must also be registered with the IDE within a unit's Register() method. To register a component editor, call the aptly named RegisterComponentEditor() procedure, which is defined as follows:

```
procedure RegisterComponentEditor(ComponentClass: TComponentClass;
  ComponentEditor: TComponentEditorClass);
```

The first parameter to this function is the component type for which you want to register a component editor, and the second parameter is the component editor itself.

Listing 12.7 shows the CompEdit.pas unit, which includes the component, component editor, and registration calls.

LISTING 12.7   CompEdit.pas—Illustrates a Component Editor

```
unit CompEdit;

interface

uses
  SysUtils, Windows, Messages, Classes, Graphics, Controls, Forms, Dialogs,
  DsgnIntf;

type
  TComponentEditorSample = class(TComponent)
  protected
    procedure SayHello; virtual;
    procedure SayGoodbye; virtual;
  end;

  TSampleEditor = class(TComponentEditor)
  private
    procedure ExecuteVerb(Index: Integer); override;
    function GetVerb(Index: Integer): string; override;
    function GetVerbCount: Integer; override;
  end;

implementation

{ TComponentEditorSample }

procedure TComponentEditorSample.SayHello;
begin
  MessageDlg('Hello, there!', mtInformation, [mbOk], 0);
end;
```

LISTING 12.7 Continued

```
procedure TComponentEditorSample.SayGoodbye;
begin
  MessageDlg('See ya!', mtInformation, [mbOk],  0);
end;

{ TSampleEditor }

const
  vHello = 'Hello';
  vGoodbye = 'Goodbye';

procedure TSampleEditor.ExecuteVerb(Index: Integer);
begin
  case Index of
    0: TComponentEditorSample(Component).SayHello;    // call function
    1: TComponentEditorSample(Component).SayGoodbye;  // call function
  end;
end;

function TSampleEditor.GetVerb(Index: Integer): string;
begin
  case Index of
    0: Result := vHello;      // return hello string
    1: Result := vGoodbye;       // return goodbye string
  end;
end;

function TSampleEditor.GetVerbCount: Integer;
begin
  Result := 2;      // two possible verbs
end;

end.
```

Streaming Nonpublished Component Data

Chapter 11 indicates that the Delphi IDE automatically knows how to stream the published properties of a component to and from a DFM file. What happens, however, when you have nonpublished data that you want to be persistent by keeping it in the DFM file? Fortunately, Delphi components provide a mechanism for writing and reading programmer-defined data to and from the DFM file.

Defining Properties

The first step in defining persistent nonpublished "properties" is to override a component's
`DefineProperties()` method. This method is inherited from `TPersistent`, and it's defined as
follows:

```
procedure DefineProperties(Filer: TFiler); virtual;
```

By default, this method handles reading and writing published properties to and from the DFM
file. You can override this method, and, after calling `inherited`, you can call the `TFiler`
method `DefineProperty()` or `DefineBinaryProperty()` once for each piece of data you want
to become part of the DFM file. These methods are defined, respectively, as follows:

```
procedure DefineProperty(const Name: string; ReadData: TReaderProc;
    WriteData: TWriterProc; HasData: Boolean); virtual;

procedure DefineBinaryProperty(const Name: string; ReadData,
    WriteData: TStreamProc; HasData: Boolean); virtual;
```

`DefineProperty()` is used to make standard data types such as strings, integers, Booleans,
chars, floats, and enumerated types persistent. `DefineBinaryProperty()` is used to provide
access to raw binary data, such as a graphic or sound, written to the DFM file.

For both of these functions, the `Name` parameter identifies the property name that should be
written to the DFM file. This doesn't have to be the same as the internal name of the data
field you're accessing. The `ReadData` and `WriteData` parameters differ in type between
`DefineProperty()` and `DefineBinaryProperty()`, but they serve the same purpose: These
methods are called in order to write or read data to or from the DFM file. (We'll discuss these
in more detail in just a moment.) The `HasData` parameter indicates whether the "property" has
data that it needs to store.

The `ReadData` and `WriteData` parameters of `DefineProperty()` are of type `TReaderProc` and
`TWriterProc`, respectively. These types are defined as follows:

```
type
  TReaderProc = procedure(Reader: TReader) of object;
  TWriterProc = procedure(Writer: TWriter) of object;
```

`TReader` and `TWriter` are specialized descendants of `TFiler` that have additional methods for
reading and writing native types. Methods of these types provide the conduit between published component data and the DFM file.

The `ReadData` and `WriteData` parameters of `DefineBinaryProperty()` are of type
`TStreamProc`, which is defined as follows:

```
type
  TStreamProc = procedure(Stream: TStream) of object;
```

Because `TStreamProc` type methods receive only `TStream` as a parameter, this allows you to read and write binary data very easily to and from the stream. Like the other method types described earlier, methods of this type provide the conduit between nonstandard data and the DFM file.

An Example of `DefineProperty()`

In order to bring all this rather technical information together, Listing 12.8 shows the `DefProp.pas` unit. This unit illustrates the use of `DefineProperty()` by providing storage for two private data fields: a string and an integer.

LISTING 12.8   DefProp.pas Illustrated Using the `DefineProperty()` Function

```
unit DefProp;

interface

uses
  Windows, Messages, SysUtils, Classes, Graphics, Controls, Forms, Dialogs;

type
  TDefinePropTest = class(TComponent)
  private
    FString: String;
    FInteger: Integer;
    procedure ReadStrData(Reader: TReader);
    procedure WriteStrData(Writer: TWriter);
    procedure ReadIntData(Reader: TReader);
    procedure WriteIntData(Writer: TWriter);
  protected
    procedure DefineProperties(Filer: TFiler); override;
  public
    constructor Create(AOwner: TComponent); override;
  end;

implementation

constructor TDefinePropTest.Create(AOwner: TComponent);
begin
  inherited Create(AOwner);
  { Put data in private fields }
  FString := 'The following number is the answer...';
  FInteger := 42;
end;
```

LISTING 12.8   Continued

```
procedure TDefinePropTest.DefineProperties(Filer: TFiler);
begin
  inherited DefineProperties(Filer);
  { Define new properties and reader/writer methods }
  Filer.DefineProperty('StringProp', ReadStrData, WriteStrData,
    FString <> '');
  Filer.DefineProperty('IntProp', ReadIntData, WriteIntData, True);
end;

procedure TDefinePropTest.ReadStrData(Reader: TReader);
begin
  FString := Reader.ReadString;
end;

procedure TDefinePropTest.WriteStrData(Writer: TWriter);
begin
  Writer.WriteString(FString);
end;

procedure TDefinePropTest.ReadIntData(Reader: TReader);
begin
  FInteger := Reader.ReadInteger;
end;

procedure TDefinePropTest.WriteIntData(Writer: TWriter);
begin
  Writer.WriteInteger(FInteger);
end;

end.
```

CAUTION

Always use the ReadString() and WriteString() methods of TReader and TWriter to read and write string data. Never use the similar-looking ReadStr() and WriteStr() methods because they'll corrupt your DFM file.

TddgWaveFile: An Example of DefineBinaryProperty()

We mentioned earlier that a good time to use DefineBinaryProperty() is when you need to store graphic or sound information along with a component. In fact, VCL uses this technique for storing images associated with components—the Glyph of a TBitBtn, for example, or the

12

Icon of a TForm. In this section, you'll learn how to use this technique when storing the sound associated with the TddgWaveFile component.

> **NOTE**
>
> TddgWaveFile is quite a full-featured component, complete with a custom property, property editor, and component editor to allow you to play sounds at design time. You'll be able to pick through the code for all this a little later in the chapter, but for now we're going to focus the discussion on the mechanism for storing the binary property.

The DefineProperties() method for TddgWaveFile is as follows:

```
procedure TddgWaveFile.DefineProperties(Filer: TFiler);
{ Defines binary property called "Data" for FData field. }
{ This allows FData to be read from and written to DFM file. }

  function DoWrite: Boolean;
  begin
    if Filer.Ancestor <> nil then
      Result := not (Filer.Ancestor is TddgWaveFile) or
        not Equal(TddgWaveFile(Filer.Ancestor))
    else
      Result := not Empty;
  end;

begin
  inherited DefineProperties(Filer);
  Filer.DefineBinaryProperty('Data', ReadData, WriteData, DoWrite);
end;
```

This method defines a binary property called Data, which is read and written using the component's ReadData() and WriteData() methods. Additionally, data is written only if the return value of DoWrite() is True. (You'll learn more about DoWrite() in just a moment.)

The ReadData() and WriteData() methods are defined as follows:

```
procedure TddgWaveFile.ReadData(Stream: TStream);
{ Reads WAV data from DFM stream. }
begin
  LoadFromStream(Stream);
end;

procedure TddgWaveFile.WriteData(Stream: TStream);
{ Writes WAV data to DFM stream }
```

```
begin
  SaveToStream(Stream);
end;
```

As you can see, there isn't much to these methods; they simply call the LoadFromStream()
and SaveToStream() methods, which are also defined by the TddgWaveFile component. The
LoadFromStream() method is as follows:

```
procedure TddgWaveFile.LoadFromStream(S: TStream);
{ Loads WAV data from stream S.  This procedure will free }
{ any memory previously allocated for FData. }
begin
  if not Empty then
    FreeMem(FData, FDataSize);
  FDataSize := 0;
  FData := AllocMem(S.Size);
  FDataSize := S.Size;
  S.Read(FData^, FDataSize);
end;
```

This method first checks to see whether memory has been previously allocated by testing the
value of the FDataSize field. If it's greater than zero, the memory pointed to by the FData field
is freed. At that point, a new block of memory is allocated for FData, and FDataSize is set to
the size of the incoming data stream. The contents of the stream are then read into the FData
pointer.

The SaveToStream() method is much simpler; it's defined as follows:

```
procedure TddgWaveFile.SaveToStream(S: TStream);
{ Saves WAV data to stream S. }
begin
  if FDataSize > 0 then
    S.Write(FData^, FDataSize);
end;
```

This method writes the data pointed to by pointer FData to TStream S.

The local DoWrite() function inside the DefineProperties() method determines whether the
Data property needs to be streamed. Of course, if FData is empty, there's no need to stream
data. Additionally, you must take extra measures to ensure that your component works correctly with form inheritance: You must check to see whether the Ancestor property for Filer
is non-nil. If it is and it points to an ancestor version of the current component, you must
check to see whether the data you're about to write is different from the ancestor. If you don't
perform these additional tests, a copy of the data (the wave file, in this case) will be written in
each of the descendant forms, and changes to the ancestor's wave file won't be copied to the
descendant forms.

Listing 12.9 shows `Wavez.pas`, which includes the complete source code for the component.

LISTING 12.9   `Wavez.pas`—Illustrates a Component Encapsulating a Wave File

```
unit Wavez;

interface

uses
  SysUtils, Classes;

type
  { Special string "descendant" used to make a property editor. }
  TWaveFileString = type string;

  EWaveError = class(Exception);

  TWavePause = (wpAsync, wpsSync);
  TWaveLoop = (wlNoLoop, wlLoop);

  TddgWaveFile = class(TComponent)
  private
    FData: Pointer;
    FDataSize: Integer;
    FWaveName: TWaveFileString;
    FWavePause: TWavePause;
    FWaveLoop: TWaveLoop;
    FOnPlay: TNotifyEvent;
    FOnStop: TNotifyEvent;
    procedure SetWaveName(const Value: TWaveFileString);
    procedure WriteData(Stream: TStream);
    procedure ReadData(Stream: TStream);
  protected
    procedure DefineProperties(Filer: TFiler); override;
  public
    destructor Destroy; override;
    function Empty: Boolean;
    function Equal(Wav: TddgWaveFile): Boolean;
    procedure LoadFromFile(const FileName: String);
    procedure LoadFromStream(S:  TStream);
    procedure Play;
    procedure SaveToFile(const FileName: String);
    procedure SaveToStream(S: TStream);
    procedure Stop;
  published
    property WaveLoop: TWaveLoop read FWaveLoop write FWaveLoop;
```

LISTING 12.9   Continued

```
    property WaveName: TWaveFileString read FWaveName write SetWaveName;
    property WavePause: TWavePause read FWavePause write FWavePause;
    property OnPlay: TNotifyEvent read FOnPlay write FOnPlay;
    property OnStop: TNotifyEvent read FOnStop write FOnStop;
  end;

implementation

uses MMSystem, Windows;

{ TddgWaveFile }

destructor TddgWaveFile.Destroy;
{ Ensures that any allocated memory is freed }
begin
  if not Empty then
    FreeMem(FData, FDataSize);
  inherited Destroy;
end;

function StreamsEqual(S1, S2: TMemoryStream): Boolean;
begin
  Result := (S1.Size = S2.Size) and CompareMem(S1.Memory, S2.Memory, S1.Size);
end;

procedure TddgWaveFile.DefineProperties(Filer: TFiler);
{ Defines binary property called "Data" for FData field. }
{ This allows FData to be read from and written to DFM file. }

  function DoWrite: Boolean;
  begin
    if Filer.Ancestor <> nil then
      Result := not (Filer.Ancestor is TddgWaveFile) or
        not Equal(TddgWaveFile(Filer.Ancestor))
    else
      Result := not Empty;
  end;

begin
  inherited DefineProperties(Filer);
  Filer.DefineBinaryProperty('Data', ReadData, WriteData, DoWrite);
end;

function TddgWaveFile.Empty: Boolean;
```

LISTING 12.9 Continued

```pascal
begin
  Result := FDataSize = 0;
end;

function TddgWaveFile.Equal(Wav: TddgWaveFile): Boolean;
var
  MyImage, WavImage: TMemoryStream;
begin
  Result := (Wav <> nil) and (ClassType = Wav.ClassType);
  if Empty or Wav.Empty then
  begin
    Result := Empty and Wav.Empty;
    Exit;
  end;
  if Result then
  begin
    MyImage := TMemoryStream.Create;
    try
      SaveToStream(MyImage);
      WavImage := TMemoryStream.Create;
      try
        Wav.SaveToStream(WavImage);
        Result := StreamsEqual(MyImage, WavImage);
      finally
        WavImage.Free;
      end;
    finally
      MyImage.Free;
    end;
  end;
end;

procedure TddgWaveFile.LoadFromFile(const FileName: String);
{ Loads WAV data from FileName. Note that this procedure does }
{ not set the WaveName property. }
var
  F: TFileStream;
begin
  F := TFileStream.Create(FileName, fmOpenRead);
  try
    LoadFromStream(F);
  finally
    F.Free;
  end;
end;
```

12

ADVANCED VCL
COMPONENT
BUILDING

LISTING 12.9   Continued

```
procedure TddgWaveFile.LoadFromStream(S: TStream);
{ Loads WAV data from stream S.  This procedure will free }
{ any memory previously allocated for FData. }
begin
  if not Empty then
    FreeMem(FData, FDataSize);
  FDataSize := 0;
  FData :=  AllocMem(S.Size);
  FDataSize := S.Size;
  S.Read(FData^, FDataSize);
end;

procedure TddgWaveFile.Play;
{ Plays the WAV sound in FData using the parameters found in }
{ FWaveLoop and FWavePause. }
const
  LoopArray: array[TWaveLoop] of DWORD = (0, SND_LOOP);
  PauseArray: array[TWavePause] of DWORD = (SND_ASYNC, SND_SYNC);
begin
  { Make sure component contains data }
  if Empty then
    raise EWaveError.Create('No wave data');
  if Assigned(FOnPlay) then FOnPlay(Self);     // fire event
  { attempt to play wave sound }
  if not PlaySound(FData, 0, SND_MEMORY or PauseArray[FWavePause] or
                  LoopArray[FWaveLoop]) then
    raise EWaveError.Create('Error playing sound');
end;

procedure TddgWaveFile.ReadData(Stream: TStream);
{ Reads WAV data from DFM stream. }
begin
  LoadFromStream(Stream);
end;

procedure TddgWaveFile.SaveToFile(const FileName: String);
{ Saves WAV data to file FileName. }
var
  F: TFileStream;
begin
  F := TFileStream.Create(FileName,  fmCreate);
  try
    SaveToStream(F);
  finally
```

LISTING 12.9   Continued

```
    F.Free;
  end;
end;

procedure TddgWaveFile.SaveToStream(S: TStream);
{ Saves WAV data to stream S. }
begin
  if not Empty then
    S.Write(FData^, FDataSize);
end;

procedure TddgWaveFile.SetWaveName(const Value: TWaveFileString);
{ Write method for WaveName property. This method is in charge of }
{ setting WaveName property and loading WAV data from file Value. }
begin
  if Value <> '' then begin
    FWaveName := ExtractFileName(Value);
    { don't load from file when loading from DFM stream }
    { because DFM stream will already contain data. }
    if (not (csLoading in ComponentState)) and FileExists(Value) then
      LoadFromFile(Value);
  end
  else begin
    { if Value is an empty string, that is the signal to free }
    { memory allocated for WAV data. }
    FWaveName := '';
    if not Empty then
      FreeMem(FData, FDataSize);
    FDataSize := 0;
  end;
end;

procedure TddgWaveFile.Stop;
{ Stops currently playing WAV sound }
begin
  if Assigned(FOnStop) then FOnStop(Self);   // fire event
  PlaySound(Nil, 0, SND_PURGE);
end;

procedure TddgWaveFile.WriteData(Stream: TStream);
{ Writes WAV data to DFM stream }
begin
  SaveToStream(Stream);
end;

end.
```

Property Categories

As you learned back in Chapter 1, "Programming in Delphi," a feature new as of Delphi 5 is *property categories*. This feature provides a means for the properties of VCL components to be specified as belonging to particular categories and for the Object Inspector to be sorted by these categories. Properties can be registered as belonging to a particular category using the `RegisterPropertyInCategory()` and `RegisterPropertiesInCategory()` functions declared in the `DesignIntf` unit. The former enables you to register a single property for a category, whereas the latter allows you to register multiple properties with one call.

`RegisterPropertyInCategory()` is overloaded in order to provide four different versions of this function to suit your exact needs. All the versions of this function take a `TPropertyCategoryClass` as the first parameter, describing the category. From there, each of these versions takes a different combination of property name, property type, and component class to enable you to choose the best method for registering your properties. The various versions of `RegisterPropertyInCategory()` are shown here:

```
function RegisterPropertyInCategory(ACategoryClass: TPropertyCategoryClass;
  const APropertyName: string): TPropertyFilter; overload;
function RegisterPropertyInCategory(ACategoryClass: TPropertyCategoryClass;
  AComponentClass: TClass; const APropertyName: string): TPropertyFilter
  overload;
function RegisterPropertyInCategory(ACategoryClass: TPropertyCategoryClass;
  APropertyType: PTypeInfo; const APropertyName: string): TPropertyFilter;
  overload;
function RegisterPropertyInCategory(ACategoryClass: TPropertyCategoryClass;
  APropertyType: PTypeInfo): TPropertyFilter; overload;
```

These functions are also smart enough to understand wildcard symbols, so you can, for example, add all properties that match `'Data*'` to a particular category. Refer to the online help for the `TMask` class for a complete list of supported wildcard characters and their behavior.

`RegisterPropertiesInCategory()` comes in three overloaded variations:

```
function RegisterPropertiesInCategory(ACategoryClass: TPropertyCategoryClass;
  const AFilters: array of const): TPropertyCategory; overload;
function RegisterPropertiesInCategory(ACategoryClass: TPropertyCategoryClass;
  AComponentClass: TClass; const AFilters: array of string): TPropertyCategory;
  overload;
function RegisterPropertiesInCategory(ACategoryClass: TPropertyCategoryClass;
  APropertyType: PTypeInfo; const AFilters: array of string):
TPropertyCategory;
  overload;
```

Advanced VCL Component Building

CHAPTER 12

539

12

ADVANCED VCL
COMPONENT
BUILDING

Category Classes

The TPropertyCategoryClass type is a class reference for a TPropertyCategory. TPropertyCategory is the base class for all standard property categories in VCL. There are 12 standard property categories, and these classes are described in Table 12.4.

TABLE 12.4 Standard Property Category Classes

Class Name	Description
TactionCategory	Properties related to runtime actions. The Enabled and Hint properties of TControl are in this category.
TDatabaseCategory	Properties related to database operations. The DatabaseName and SQL properties of TQuery are in this category.
TDragNDropCategory	Properties related to drag-and-drop and docking operations. The DragCursor and DragKind properties of TControl are in this category.
THelpCategory	Properties related to using online help and hints. The HelpContext and Hint properties of TWinControl are in this category.
TLayoutCategory	Properties related to the visual display of a control at design time. The Top and Left properties of TControl are in this category.
TLegacyCategory	Properties related to obsolete operations. The Ctl3D and ParentCtl3D properties of TWinControl are in this category.
TLinkageCategory	Properties related to associating or linking one component to another. The DataSet property of TDataSource is in this category.
TLocaleCategory	Properties related to international locales. The BiDiMode and ParentBiDiMode properties of TControl are in this category.
TLocalizableCategory	Properties related to database operations. The DatabaseName and SQL properties of TQuery are in this category.
TMiscellaneousCategory	Properties that either do not fit a category, do not need to be categorized, or are not explicitly registered to a specific category. The AllowAllUp and Name properties of TSpeedButton are in this category.

TABLE 12.4   Continued

Class Name	Description
TVisualCategory	Properties related to the visual display of a control at run-time; the Align and Visible properties of TControl are in this category.
TInputCategory	Properties related to the input of data (they need not be related to database operations). The Enabled and ReadOnly properties of TEdit are in this category.

As an example, let's say that you've written a component called TNeato with a property called Keen, and you want to register the Keen property as a member of the Action category represented by TActionCategory. You could do this by adding a call to RegisterPropertyInCategory() to the Register() procedure for your control, as shown here:

```
RegisterPropertyInCategory(TActionCategory, TNeato, 'Keen');
```

Custom Categories

As you've already learned, a property category is represented in code as a class that descends from TPropertyCategory. How difficult is it, then, to create your own property categories in this way? It's quite easy, actually. In most cases, all you need to do is override the Name() and Description() virtual class functions of TPropertyCategory to return information specific to your category.

As an illustration, we'll create a new Sound category that will be used to categorize some of the properties of the TddgWaveFile component, which you learned about earlier in this chapter. This new category class, called TSoundCategory, is shown in Listing 12.10. This listing contains WavezEd.pas, which is a file that contains the component's category, property editor, and component editor.

LISTING 12.10   WavezEd.pas—Illustrates a Property Editor for the Wave File Component

```
unit WavezEd;

interface

uses DsgnIntf;

type
  { Category for some of TddgWaveFile's properties }
  TSoundCategory = class(TPropertyCategory)
```

LISTING 12.10 Continued

```pascal
public
  class function Name: string; override;
  class function Description: string; override;
end;

{ Property editor for TddgWaveFile's WaveName property }
TWaveFileStringProperty = class(TStringProperty)
public
  procedure Edit; override;
  function GetAttributes: TPropertyAttributes; override;
end;

{ Component editor for TddgWaveFile.  Allows user to play and stop }
{ WAV sounds from local menu in IDE. }
TWaveEditor = class(TComponentEditor)
private
  procedure EditProp(PropertyEditor: TPropertyEditor);
public
  procedure Edit; override;
  procedure ExecuteVerb(Index: Integer); override;
  function GetVerb(Index: Integer): string; override;
  function GetVerbCount: Integer; override;
end;

implementation

uses TypInfo, Wavez, Classes, Controls, Dialogs;

{ TSoundCategory }

class function TSoundCategory.Name: string;
begin
  Result := 'Sound';
end;

class function TSoundCategory.Description: string;
begin
  Result := 'Properties dealing with the playing of sounds'
end;

{ TWaveFileStringProperty }

procedure TWaveFileStringProperty.Edit;
{ Executed when user clicks the ellipses button on the WavName   }
```

LISTING 12.10   Continued

```
{ property in the Object Inspector.  This method allows the user }
{ to pick a file from an OpenDialog and sets the property value. }
begin
  with TOpenDialog.Create(nil) do
    try
      { Set up properties for dialog }
      Filter := 'Wav files|*.wav|All files|*.*';
      DefaultExt := '*.wav';
      { Put current value in the FileName property of dialog }
      FileName := GetStrValue;
      { Execute dialog and set property value if dialog is OK }
      if Execute then
        SetStrValue(FileName);
    finally
      Free;
    end;
end;

function TWaveFileStringProperty.GetAttributes: TPropertyAttributes;
{ Indicates the property editor will invoke a dialog. }
begin
  Result := [paDialog];
end;

{ TWaveEditor }

const
  VerbCount = 2;
  VerbArray: array[0..VerbCount - 1] of string[7] = ('Play', 'Stop');

procedure TWaveEditor.Edit;
{ Called when user double-clicks on the component at design time. }
{ This method calls the GetComponentProperties method in order to }
{ invoke the Edit method of the WaveName property editor. }
var
  Components: TDesignerSelectionList;
begin
  Components := TDesignerSelectionList.Create;
  try
    Components.Add(Component);
    GetComponentProperties(Components, tkAny, Designer, EditProp);
  finally
    Components.Free;
  end;
end;
```

Advanced VCL Component Building

CHAPTER 12

543

12

ADVANCED VCL
COMPONENT
BUILDING

LISTING **12.10** Continued

```
procedure TWaveEditor.EditProp(PropertyEditor: TPropertyEditor);
{ Called once per property in response to GetComponentProperties }
{ call.  This method looks for the WaveName property editor and  }
{ calls its Edit method. }
begin
  if PropertyEditor is TWaveFileStringProperty then begin
    TWaveFileStringProperty(PropertyEditor).Edit;
    Designer.Modified;    // alert Designer to modification
  end;
end;

procedure TWaveEditor.ExecuteVerb(Index: Integer);
begin
  case Index of
    0: TddgWaveFile(Component).Play;
    1: TddgWaveFile(Component).Stop;
  end;
end;

function TWaveEditor.GetVerb(Index: Integer): string;
begin
  Result := VerbArray[Index];
end;

function TWaveEditor.GetVerbCount: Integer;
begin
  Result := VerbCount;
end;

end.
```

With the category class defined, all that needs to be done is register the properties for the category using one of the registration functions. This is done in the `Register()` procedure for `TddgWaveFile` using the following line of code:

```
RegisterPropertiesInCategory(TSoundCategory, TddgWaveFile,
  ['WaveLoop', 'WaveName', 'WavePause']);
```

Lists of Components: `TCollection` and `TCollectionItem`

It's common for components to maintain or own a list of items such as data types, records, objects, or even other components. In some cases, it's suitable to encapsulate this list within its own object and then make this object a property of the owner component. An example of this arrangement is the `Lines` property of a `TMemo` component. `Lines` is a `TStrings` object type that encapsulates a list of strings. With this arrangement, the `TStrings` object is responsible for the streaming mechanism used to store its lines to the form file when the user saves the form.

What if you wanted to save a list of items such as components or objects that weren't already encapsulated by an existing class such as `TStrings`? Well, you could create a class that performs the streaming of the listed items and then make that a property of the owner component. Alternatively, you could override the default streaming mechanism of the owner component so that it knows how to stream its list of items. However, a better solution would be to take advantage of the `TCollection` and `TCollectionItem` classes.

The `TCollection` class is an object used to store a list of `TCollectionItem` objects. `TCollection`, itself, isn't a component but rather a descendant of `TPersistent`. Typically, `TCollection` is associated with an existing component.

To use `TCollection` to store a list of items, you would derive a descendant class from `TCollection`, which you could call `TNewCollection`. `TNewCollection` will serve as a property type for a component. Then, you must derive a class from the `TCollectionItem` class, which you could call `TNewCollectionItem`. `TNewCollection` will maintain a list of `TNewCollectionItem` objects. The beauty of this is that data belonging to `TNewCollectionItem` that needs to be streamed only needs to be published by `TNewCollectionItem`. Delphi already knows how to stream published properties.

An example of where `TCollection` is used is with the `TStatusBar` component. `TStatusBar` is a `TWinControl` descendant. One of its properties is `Panels`. `TStatusBar.Panels` is of type `TStatusPanels`, which is a `TCollection` descendant and defined as follows:

```
type
  TStatusPanels = class(TCollection)
  private
    FStatusBar: TStatusBar;
    function GetItem(Index: Integer): TStatusPanel;
    procedure SetItem(Index: Integer; Value: TStatusPanel);
  protected
    procedure Update(Item: TCollectionItem); override;
  public
    constructor Create(StatusBar: TStatusBar);
    function Add: TStatusPanel;
    property Items[Index: Integer]: TStatusPanel read GetItem write SetItem;
      default;
  end;
```

`TStatusPanels` stores a list of `TCollectionItem` descendants, `TStatusPanel`, as defined here:

```
type
  TStatusPanel = class(TCollectionItem)
  private
    FText: string;
    FWidth: Integer;
    FAlignment: TAlignment;
    FBevel: TStatusPanelBevel;
    FStyle: TStatusPanelStyle;
    procedure SetAlignment(Value: TAlignment);
    procedure SetBevel(Value: TStatusPanelBevel);
    procedure SetStyle(Value: TStatusPanelStyle);
    procedure SetText(const Value: string);
    procedure SetWidth(Value: Integer);
  public
    constructor Create(Collection: TCollection); override;
    procedure Assign(Source: TPersistent); override;
  published
    property Alignment: TAlignment read FAlignment
      write SetAlignment default taLeftJustify;
    property Bevel: TStatusPanelBevel read FBevel
      write SetBevel default pbLowered;
    property Style: TStatusPanelStyle read FStyle write SetStyle
      default psText;
    property Text: string read FText write SetText;
    property Width: Integer read FWidth write SetWidth;
  end;
```

The TStatusPanel properties in the published section of the class declaration will automatically be streamed by Delphi. TStatusPanel takes a TCollection parameter in its Create() constructor, and it associates itself with that TCollection. Likewise, TStatusPanels takes the TStatusBar component in its constructor to which it associates itself. The TCollection engine knows how to deal with the streaming of TCollectionItem components and also defines some methods and properties for manipulating the items maintained in TCollection. You can look these up in the online help.

To illustrate how you might use these two new classes, we've created the TddgLaunchPad component. TddgLaunchPad will enable the user to store a list of TddgRunButton components, which we created in Chapter 11.

TddgLaunchPad is a descendant of the TScrollBox component. One of the properties of TddgLaunchPad is RunButtons, a TCollection descendant. RunButtons maintains a list of TRunBtnItem components. TRunBtnItem is a TCollectionItem descendant whose properties are used to create a TddgRunButton component, which is placed on TddgLaunchPad. In the following sections, we'll discuss how we created this component.

Defining the `TCollectionItem` Class: `TRunBtnItem`

The first step is to define the item to be maintained in a list. For `TddgLaunchPad`, this would be a `TddgRunButton` component. Therefore, each `TRunBtnItem` instance must associate itself with a `TddgRunButton` component. The following code shows a partial definition of the `TRunBtnItem` class:

```
type
  TRunBtnItem = class(TCollectionItem)
  private
    FCommandLine: String;    // Store the command line
    FLeft: Integer;          // Store the positional properties for the
    FTop: Integer;           //    TddgRunButton.
    FRunButton: TddgRunButton; // Reference to a TddgRunButton
    ...
  public
    constructor Create(Collection: TCollection); override;
  published
    { The published properties will be streamed }
    property CommandLine: String read FCommandLine write SetCommandLine;
    property Left: Integer read FLeft write SetLeft;
    property Top: Integer read FTop write SetTop;
  end;
```

Notice that `TRunBtnItem` keeps a reference to a `TddgRunButton` component, yet it only streams the properties required to build a `TddgRunButton`. At first you might think that because `TRunBtnItem` associates itself with a `TddgRunButton`, it could just publish the component and let the streaming engine do the rest. Well, this poses some problems with the streaming engine and how it handles the streaming of `TComponent` classes differently from `TPersistent` classes. The fundamental rule here is that the streaming system is responsible for creating new instances for every `TComponent`-derived classname it finds in a stream, whereas it assumes that `TPersistent` instances already exist and doesn't attempt to instantiate new ones. Following this rule, we stream the information required of the `TddgRunButton` and then we create the `TddgRunButton` in the `TRunBtnItem` constructor, which we'll illustrate shortly.

Defining the `TCollection` Class: `TRunButtons`

The next step is to define the object that will maintain this list of `TRunBtnItem` components. We already said that this object must be a `TCollection` descendant. We call this class `TRunButtons`; its definition is as follows:

```
type
  TRunButtons = class(TCollection)
  private
    FLaunchPad: TddgLaunchPad; // Keep a reference to the TddgLaunchPad
```

```
      function GetItem(Index: Integer): TRunBtnItem;
      procedure SetItem(Index: Integer; Value: TRunBtnItem);
    protected
      procedure Update(Item: TCollectionItem); override;
    public
      constructor Create(LaunchPad: TddgLaunchPad);
      function Add: TRunBtnItem;
      procedure UpdateRunButtons;
      property Items[Index: Integer]: TRunBtnItem read GetItem
        write SetItem; default;
    end;
```

TRunButtons associates itself with a TddgLaunchPad component that we'll show a bit later. It does this in its Create() constructor, which, as you can see, takes a TddgLaunchPad component as its parameter. Notice the various properties and methods that have been added to allow the user to manipulate the individual TRunBtnItem classes. In particular, the Items property is an array to the TRunBtnItem list.

The use of the TRunBtnItem and TRunButtons classes will become clearer as we discuss the implementation of the TddgLaunchPad component.

Implementing the **TddgLaunchPad**, **TRunBtnItem**, and **TRunButtons** Objects

The TddgLaunchPad component has a property of the type TRunButtons. Its implementation, as well as the implementation of TRunBtnItem and TRunButtons, is shown in Listing 12.11.

LISTING 12.11   LnchPad.pas—Illustrates the TddgLaunchPad Implementation

```
unit LnchPad;

interface

uses
  Windows, Messages, SysUtils, Classes, Graphics, Controls,
  Forms, Dialogs, RunBtn, ExtCtrls;

type
  TddgLaunchPad = class;

  TRunBtnItem = class(TCollectionItem)
  private
    FCommandLine: string;    // Store the command line
    FLeft: Integer;          // Store the positional properties for the
    FTop: Integer;           // TddgRunButton.
```

LISTING 12.11   Continued

```
  FRunButton: TddgRunButton; // Reference to a TddgRunButton
  FWidth: Integer;         // Keep track of the width and height
  FHeight: Integer;
  procedure SetCommandLine(const Value: string);
  procedure SetLeft(Value: Integer);
  procedure SetTop(Value: Integer);
public
  constructor Create(Collection: TCollection); override;
  destructor Destroy; override;
  procedure Assign(Source: TPersistent); override;
  property Width: Integer read FWidth;
  property Height: Integer read FHeight;
published
  { The published properties will be streamed }
  property CommandLine: String read FCommandLine
    write SetCommandLine;
  property Left: Integer read FLeft write SetLeft;
  property Top: Integer read FTop write SetTop;
end;

TRunButtons = class(TCollection)
private
  FLaunchPad: TddgLaunchPad; // Keep a reference to the TddgLaunchPad
  function GetItem(Index: Integer): TRunBtnItem;
  procedure SetItem(Index: Integer; Value: TRunBtnItem);
protected
  procedure Update(Item: TCollectionItem); override;
public
  constructor Create(LaunchPad: TddgLaunchPad);
  function Add: TRunBtnItem;
  procedure UpdateRunButtons;
  property Items[Index: Integer]: TRunBtnItem read
    GetItem write SetItem; default;
end;

TddgLaunchPad = class(TScrollBox)
private
  FRunButtons: TRunButtons;
  TopAlign: Integer;
  LeftAlign: Integer;
  procedure SetRunButtons(Value: TRunButtons);
  procedure UpdateRunButton(Index: Integer);
public
  constructor Create(AOwner: TComponent); override;
```

LISTING 12.11 Continued

```
    destructor Destroy; override;
    procedure GetChildren(Proc: TGetChildProc; Root: TComponent); override;
  published
    property RunButtons: TRunButtons read FRunButtons write SetRunButtons;
  end;

implementation

{ TRunBtnItem }

constructor TRunBtnItem.Create(Collection: TCollection);
{ This constructor gets the TCollection that owns this TRunBtnItem.  }
begin
  inherited Create(Collection);
  { Create an FRunButton instance. Make the launch pad the owner
    and parent. Then initialize its various properties. }
  FRunButton := TddgRunButton.Create(TRunButtons(Collection).FLaunchPad);
  FRunButton.Parent := TRunButtons(Collection).FLaunchPad;
  FWidth := FRunButton.Width;   // Keep track of the width and the
  FHeight := FRunButton.Height; //   height.
end;

destructor TRunBtnItem.Destroy;
begin
  FRunButton.Free;   // Destroy the TddgRunButton instance.
  inherited Destroy; // Call the inherited Destroy destructor.
end;

procedure TRunBtnItem.Assign(Source: TPersistent);
{ It is necessary to override the TCollectionItem.Assign method so that
  it knows how to copy from one TRunBtnItem to another. If this is done,
  then don't call the inherited Assign(). }
begin
  if Source is TRunBtnItem then
  begin
    { Instead of assigning the command line to the FCommandLine storage
      field, make the assignment to the property so that the accessor
      method will be called. The accessor method as some side-effects
      that we want to occur. }
    CommandLine := TRunBtnItem(Source).CommandLine;
    { Copy values to the remaining fields. Then exit the procedure. }
    FLeft := TRunBtnItem(Source).Left;
    FTop := TRunBtnItem(Source).Top;
```

12

LISTING 12.11 Continued

```
    Exit;
  end;
  inherited Assign(Source);
end;

procedure TRunBtnItem.SetCommandLine(const Value: string);
{ This is the write accessor method for TRunBtnItem.CommandLine. It
  ensures that the private TddgRunButton instance, FRunButton, gets
  assigned the specified string from Value }
begin
  if FRunButton <> nil then
  begin
    FCommandLine := Value;
    FRunButton.CommandLine := FCommandLine;
    { This will cause the TRunButtons.Update method to be called
      for each TRunBtnItem }
    Changed(False);
  end;
end;

procedure TRunBtnItem.SetLeft(Value: Integer);
{ Access method for the TRunBtnItem.Left property. }
begin
  if FRunButton <> nil then
  begin
    FLeft := Value;
    FRunButton.Left := FLeft;
  end;
end;

procedure TRunBtnItem.SetTop(Value: Integer);
{ Access method for the TRunBtnItem.Top property }
begin
  if FRunButton <> nil then
  begin
    FTop := Value;
    FRunButton.Top := FTop;
  end;
end;

{ TRunButtons }

constructor TRunButtons.Create(LaunchPad: TddgLaunchPad);
{ The constructor points FLaunchPad to the TddgLaunchPad parameter.
  LauchPad is the owner of this collection. It is necessary to keep
```

Advanced VCL Component Building

551

CHAPTER 12

12

ADVANCED VCL
COMPONENT
BUILDING

LISTING 12.11 Continued

```
  a reference to LauchPad as it will be accessed internally. }
begin
  inherited Create(TRunBtnItem);
  FLaunchPad := LaunchPad;
end;

function TRunButtons.GetItem(Index: Integer): TRunBtnItem;
{ Access method for TRunButtons.Items which returns the TRunBtnItem
  instance. }
begin
  Result := TRunBtnItem(inherited GetItem(Index));
end;

procedure TRunButtons.SetItem(Index: Integer; Value: TRunBtnItem);
{ Access method for TddgRunButton.Items which makes the assignment to
  the specified indexed item. }
begin
  inherited SetItem(Index, Value)
end;

procedure TRunButtons.Update(Item: TCollectionItem);
{ TCollection.Update is called by TCollectionItems
  whenever a change is made to any of the collection items. This is
  initially an abstract method. It must be overridden to contain
  whatever logic is necessary when a TCollectionItem has changed.
  We use it to redraw the item by calling TddgLaunchPad.UpdateRunButton.}
begin
  if Item <> nil then
    FLaunchPad.UpdateRunButton(Item.Index);
end;

procedure TRunButtons.UpdateRunButtons;
{ UpdateRunButtons is a public procedure that we made available so that
  users of TRunButtons can force all run-buttons to be re-drawn. This
  method calls TddgLaunchPad.UpdateRunButton for each TRunBtnItem
  instance. }
var
  i: integer;
begin
  for i := 0 to Count - 1 do
    FLaunchPad.UpdateRunButton(i);
end;

function TRunButtons.Add: TRunBtnItem;
```

LISTING 12.11   Continued

```
{ This method must be overridden to return the TRunBtnItem instance when
  the inherited Add method is called. This is done by typcasting the
  original result }
begin
  Result := TRunBtnItem(inherited Add);
end;


{ TddgLaunchPad }

constructor TddgLaunchPad.Create(AOwner: TComponent);
{ Initializes the TRunButtons instance and internal variables
  used for positioning of the TRunBtnItem as they are drawn }
begin
  inherited Create(AOwner);
  FRunButtons := TRunButtons.Create(Self);
  TopAlign := 0;
  LeftAlign := 0;
end;

destructor TddgLaunchPad.Destroy;
begin
  FRunButtons.Free;  // Free the TRunButtons instance.
  inherited Destroy; // Call the inherited destroy method.
end;

procedure TddgLaunchPad.GetChildren(Proc: TGetChildProc; Root: TComponent);
{ Override GetChildren to cause TddgLaunchPad to ignore any TRunButtons
  that it owns since they do not need to be streamed in the context
  TddgLaunchPad. The information necessary for creating the TddgRunButton
  instances is already streamed as published properties of the
  TCollectionItem descendant, TRunBtnItem. This method prevents the
  TddgRunButton's from being streamed twice. }
var
  I: Integer;
begin
  for I := 0 to ControlCount - 1 do
    { Ignore the run buttons and the scrollbox }
    if not (Controls[i] is TddgRunButton) then
      Proc(TComponent(Controls[I]));
end;

procedure TddgLaunchPad.SetRunButtons(Value: TRunButtons);
{ Access method for the RunButtons property }
```

LISTING 12.11 Continued

```
begin
  FRunButtons.Assign(Value);
end;

procedure TddgLaunchPad.UpdateRunButton(Index: Integer);
{ This method is responsible for drawing the TRunBtnItem instances.
  It ensures that the TRunBtnItem's do not extend beyond the width
  of the TddgLaunchPad. If so, it creates rows. This is only in effect
  as the user is adding/removing TRunBtnItems. The user can still
  resize the TddgLaunchPad so that it is smaller than the width of a
  TRunBtnItem }
begin
  { If the first item being drawn, set both positions to zero. }
  if Index = 0 then
  begin
    TopAlign := 0;
    LeftAlign := 0;
  end;
  { If the width of the current row of TRunBtnItems is more than
    the width of the TddgLaunchPad, then start a new row of TRunBtnItems. }
  if (LeftAlign + FRunButtons[Index].Width) > Width then
  begin
    TopAlign := TopAlign + FRunButtons[Index].Height;
    LeftAlign := 0;
  end;
  FRunButtons[Index].Left := LeftAlign;
  FRunButtons[Index].Top := TopAlign;
  LeftAlign := LeftAlign + FRunButtons[Index].Width;
end;

end.
```

Implementing TRunBtnItem

The TRunBtnItem.Create() constructor creates an instance of TddgRunButton. Each
TRunBtnItem in the collection will maintain its own TddgRunButton instance. The following
two lines in TRunBtnItem.Create() require further explanation:

```
FRunButton := TddgRunButton.Create(TRunButtons(Collection).FLaunchPad);
FRunButton.Parent := TRunButtons(Collection).FLaunchPad;
```

The first line creates a TddgRunButton instance, FRunButton. The owner of FRunButton is
FLaunchPad, which is a TddgLaunchPad component and a field of the TCollection object
passed in as a parameter. It's necessary to use the FLaunchPad as the owner of FRunButton.

Neither a TRunBtnItem instance nor a TRunButtons object can be owners because they descend from TPersistent. Remember, an owner must be a TComponent.

We want to point out a problem that arises by making FLaunchPad the owner of FRunButton. By doing this, we effectively make FLaunchPad the owner of FRunButton at design time. The normal behavior of the streaming engine will cause Delphi to stream FRunButton as a component owned by the FLaunchPad instance when the user saves the form. This isn't a desired behavior because FRunButton is already being created in the constructor of TRunBtnItem, based on the information that's also streamed in the context of TRunBtnItem. This is a vital tidbit of information. Later, you'll see how we prevent TddgRunButton components from being streamed by TddgLaunchPad in order to remedy this undesired behavior.

The second line assigns FLaunchPad as the parent to FRunButton so that FLaunchPad can take care of drawing FRunButton.

The TRunBtnItem.Destroy() destructor frees FRunButton before calling its inherited destructor.

Under certain circumstances, it becomes necessary to override the TRunBtnItem.Assign() method that's called. One such instance is when the application is first run and the form is read from the stream. In the Assign() method, we tell the TRunBtnItem instance to assign the streamed values of its properties to the properties of the component (in this case TddgRunButton) that it encompasses.

The other methods are simply access methods for the various properties of TRunBtnItem; they are explained in the code's comments.

Implementing TRunButtons

TRunButtons.Create() simply points FLaunchPad to the TddgLaunchPad parameter passed to it so that LaunchPad can be referred to later.

TRunButtons.Update() is a method that's invoked whenever a change has been made to any of the TRunBtnItem instances. This method contains logic that should occur due to that change. We use it to call the method of TddgLaunchPad that redraws the TRunBtnItem instances. We've also added a public method, UpdateRunButtons(), to allow the user to force a redraw.

The remaining methods of TRunButtons are property access methods, which are explained in the code's comments in Listing 12.11.

Implementing TddgLaunchPad

The constructor and destructor for TddgLaunchPad are simple. TddgLaunchPad.Create() creates an instance of the TRunButtons object and passes itself as a parameter. TddgLaunchPad.Destroy() frees the TRunButtons instance.

The overriding of the `TddgLaunchPad.GetChildren()` method is important to note here. This is where we prevent the `TddgRunButton` instances stored by the collection from being streamed as owned components of `TddgLaunchPad`. Remember that this is necessary because they shouldn't be created in the context of the `TddgLaunchPad` object but rather in the context of the `TRunBtnItem` instances. Because no `TddgRunButton` components are passed to the `Proc` procedure, they won't be streamed or read from a stream.

The `TddgLaunchPad.UpdateRunButton()` method is where the `TddgRunButton` instances maintained by the collection are drawn. The logic in this code ensures that they never extend beyond the width of `TddgLaunchPad`. Because `TddgLaunchPad` is a descendant of `TScrollBox`, scrolling will occur vertically.

The other methods are simply property-access methods and are commented in the code in Listing 12.11.

Finally, we register the property editor for the `TRunButtons` collection class in this unit's `Register()` procedure. The next section discusses this property editor and illustrates how to edit a list of components from a dialog property editor.

Editing the List of `TCollectionItem` Components with a Dialog Property Editor

Now that we've defined the `TddgLaunchPad` component, the `TRunButtons` collection class, and the `TRunBtnItem` collection class, we must provide a way for the user to add `TddgRunButton` components to the `TRunButtons` collection. The best way to do this is through a property editor that manipulates the list maintained by the `TRunButtons` collection.

This dialog directly manipulates the `TRunBtnItem` components maintained by the `RunButtons` collection of `TddgLaunchPad`. The various `CommandLine` strings for each `TddgRunButton` enclosed in `TRunBtnItem` are displayed in `PathListBox`. A `TddgRunButton` component reflects the currently selected item in the list box to allow the user to test the selection. The dialog also contains buttons to allow the user to add or remove an item, accept the changes, and cancel the operation. As the user makes changes in the dialog, the changes are reflected on the `TddgLaunchPad`.

TIP

A convention for property editors is to include an Apply button to invoke changes on the form. We didn't show this here, but you might consider adding such a button to the `RunButtons` property editor as an exercise. To see how an Apply button works, take a look at the property editor for the `Panels` property of the `TStatusBar` component from the Win32 page of the Component Palette.

Listing 12.12 shows the source code for the TddgLaunchPad-RunButtons property editor and its dialog.

LISTING 12.12 LPadPE.pas—The TRunButtons Property Editor

```pascal
unit LPadPE;

interface

uses
  Windows, Messages, SysUtils, Classes, Graphics, Controls, Forms,
  Dialogs, Buttons, RunBtn, StdCtrls, LnchPad, DesignIntf, DesignEditors,
  ExtCtrls, TypInfo;

type

  { First declare the editor dialog }
  TLaunchPadEditor = class(TForm)
    PathListBox: TListBox;
    AddBtn: TButton;
    RemoveBtn: TButton;
    CancelBtn: TButton;
    OkBtn: TButton;
    Label1: TLabel;
    pnlRBtn: TPanel;
    procedure PathListBoxClick(Sender: TObject);
    procedure AddBtnClick(Sender: TObject);
    procedure RemoveBtnClick(Sender: TObject);
    procedure FormCreate(Sender: TObject);
    procedure FormDestroy(Sender: TObject);
    procedure CancelBtnClick(Sender: TObject);
  private
    TestRunBtn: TddgRunButton;
    FLaunchPad: TddgLaunchPad;    // To be used as a backup
    FRunButtons: TRunButtons; // Will refer to the actual TRunButtons
    Modified: Boolean;
    procedure UpdatePathListBox;
  end;

  { Now declare the TPropertyEditor descendant and override the
    required methods }
  TRunButtonsProperty = class(TPropertyEditor)
    function GetAttributes: TPropertyAttributes; override;
    function GetValue: string; override;
    procedure Edit; override;
  end;
```

LISTING 12.12   Continued

```
{ This function will be called by the property editor. }
function EditRunButtons(RunButtons: TRunButtons): Boolean;

implementation

{$R *.DFM}

function EditRunButtons(RunButtons: TRunButtons): Boolean;
{ Instantiates the TLaunchPadEditor dialog which directly modifies
  the TRunButtons collection. }
begin
  with TLaunchPadEditor.Create(Application) do
    try
      FRunButtons := RunButtons; // Point to the actual TRunButtons
      { Copy the TRunBtnItems to the backup FLaunchPad which will be
        used as a backup in case the user cancels the operation }
      FLaunchPad.RunButtons.Assign(RunButtons);
      { Draw the listbox with the list of TRunBtnItems. }
      UpdatePathListBox;
      ShowModal; // Display the form.
      Result := Modified;
    finally
      Free;
    end;
end;

{ TLaunchPadEditor }

procedure TLaunchPadEditor.FormCreate(Sender:  TObject);
begin
  { Created the backup instances of TLaunchPad to be used if the user
    cancels editing the TRunBtnItems }
  FLaunchPad := TddgLaunchPad.Create(Self);

  // Create the TddgRunButton instance and align it to the
  // enclosing panel.
  TestRunBtn := TddgRunButton.Create(Self);
  TestRunBtn.Parent := pnlRBtn;

  TestRunBtn.Width  := pnlRBtn.Width;
  TestRunBtn.Height := pnlRBtn.Height;
end;

procedure TLaunchPadEditor.FormDestroy(Sender: TObject);
```

LISTING 12.12   Continued

```
begin
  TestRunBtn.Free;
  FLaunchPad.Free; // Free the TLaunchPad instance.
end;

procedure TLaunchPadEditor.PathListBoxClick(Sender: TObject);
{ When the user clicks on an item in the list of TRunBtnItems, make
  the test TRunButton reflect the currently selected item }
begin
  if PathListBox.ItemIndex > -1 then
    TestRunBtn.CommandLine := PathListBox.Items[PathListBox.ItemIndex];
end;

procedure TLaunchPadEditor.UpdatePathListBox;
{ Re-initializes the PathListBox so that it reflects the list of
  TRunBtnItems }
var
  i: integer;
begin
  PathListBox.Clear; // First clear the list box.
  for i := 0 to FRunButtons.Count - 1 do
    PathListBox.Items.Add(FRunButtons[i].CommandLine);
end;

procedure TLaunchPadEditor.AddBtnClick(Sender: TObject);
{ When the add button is clicked, launch a TOpenDialog to retrieve
  an executable filename and path. Then add this file to the
  PathListBox. Also, add a new FRunBtnItem. }
var
  OpenDialog: TOpenDialog;
begin
  OpenDialog := TOpenDialog.Create(Application);
  try
    OpenDialog.Filter := 'Executable Files|*.EXE';
    if OpenDialog.Execute then
    begin
      { add to the PathListBox. }
      PathListBox.Items.Add(OpenDialog.FileName);
      FRunButtons.Add; // Create a new TRunBtnItem instance.
      { Set focus to the new item in PathListBox }
      PathListBox.ItemIndex := FRunButtons.Count - 1;
      { Set the command line for the new TRunBtnItem to that of the
        file name gotten as specified by PathListBox.ItemIndex }
      FRunButtons[PathListBox.ItemIndex].CommandLine :=
```

LISTING 12.12 Continued

```
        PathListBox.Items[PathListBox.ItemIndex];
      { Invoke.the PathListBoxClick event handler so that the test
        TRunButton will reflect the newly added item }
      PathListBoxClick(nil);
      Modified := True;
    end;
  finally
    OpenDialog.Free
  end;
end;

procedure TLaunchPadEditor.RemoveBtnClick(Sender: TObject);
{ Remove the selected path/filename from PathListBox as well as the
  corresponding TRunBtnItem from FRunButtons }
var
  i: integer;
begin
  i := PathListBox.ItemIndex;
  if i >= 0 then
  begin
    PathListBox.Items.Delete(i);  // Remove the item from the listbox
    FRunButtons[i].Free;          // Remove the item from the collection
    TestRunBtn.CommandLine := ''; // Erase the test run button
    Modified := True;
  end;
end;

procedure TLaunchPadEditor.CancelBtnClick(Sender: TObject);
{ When the user cancels the operation, copy the backup LaunchPad
  TRunBtnItems back to the original TLaunchPad instance. Then,
  close the form by setting ModalResult to mrCancel. }
begin
  FRunButtons.Assign(FLaunchPad.RunButtons);
  Modified := False;
  ModalResult := mrCancel;
end;

{ TRunButtonsProperty }

function TRunButtonsProperty.GetAttributes: TPropertyAttributes;
{ Tell the Object Inspector that the property editor will use a
  dialog. This will cause the Edit method to be invoked when the user
  clicks the ellipsis button in the Object Inspector.  }
```

LISTING 12.12 Continued

```
begin
  Result := [paDialog];
end;

procedure TRunButtonsProperty.Edit;
{ Invoke the EditRunButton() method and pass in the reference to the
  TRunButton's instance being edited. This reference can be obtain by
  using the GetOrdValue method. Then redraw the LaunchDialog by calling
  the TRunButtons.UpdateRunButtons method. }
begin
  if EditRunButtons(TRunButtons(GetOrdValue)) then
    Modified;
  TRunButtons(GetOrdValue).UpdateRunButtons;
end;

function TRunButtonsProperty.GetValue: string;
{ Override the GetValue method so that the class type of the property
  being edited is displayed in the Object Inspector. }
begin
  Result := Format('(%s)', [GetPropType^.Name]);
end;

end.
```

This unit first defines the TddgLaunchPadEditor dialog and then the TRunButtonsProperty property editor. We're going to discuss the property editor first because it's the property editor that invokes the dialog.

The TRunButtonsProperty property editor isn't much different from the dialog property editor we showed earlier. Here, we override the GetAttributes(), Edit(), and GetValue() methods.

GetAttributes() simply sets the TPropertyAttributes return value to specify that this editor invokes a dialog. Again, this will place an ellipsis button on the Object Inspector.

The GetValue() method uses the GetPropType() function to return a pointer to the Runtime Type Information for the property being edited. It returns the name field of this information that represents the property's type string. The string is displayed in the Object Inspector within parentheses, which is a convention used by Delphi.

Finally, the Edit() method calls a function defined in this unit, EditRunButtons(). As a parameter, it passes the reference to the TRunButtons property by using the GetOrdValue function. When the function returns, the method UpdateRunButton() is invoked to cause RunButtons to be redrawn to reflect any changes.

The `EditRunButtons()` function creates the `TddgLaunchPadEditor` instance and points its `FRunButtons` field to the `TRunButtons` parameter passed to it. It uses this reference internally to make changes to the `TRunButtons` collection. The function then copies the `TRunButtons` collection of the property to an internal `TddgLaunchPad` component, `FLaunchPad`. It uses this instance as a backup in case the user cancels the edit operation.

Earlier we talked about the possibility of adding an Apply button to this dialog. To do so, you can edit the `FLaunchPad` component's `RunButtons` collection instance instead of directly modifying the actual collection. This way, if the user cancels the operation, nothing happens; if the user clicks Apply or OK, the changes are invoked.

The form's `Create()` constructor creates the internal `TddgLaunchPad` instance. The `Destroy()` destructor ensures that it's freed when the form is destroyed.

`PathListBoxClick()` is the `OnClick` event handler for `PathListBox`. This method makes `TestRunBtn` (the test `TddgRunButton`) reflect the currently selected item in `PathListBox`, which displays a path to the executable file. The user can click this `TddgRunButton` instance to launch the application.

`UpdatePathListBox()` initializes `PathListBox` with the items in the collection.

`AddButtonClick()` is the `OnClick` event handler for the Add button. This event handler invokes a File Open dialog to retrieve an executable filename from the user and adds the path of this filename to `PathListBox`. It also creates a `TRunBtnItem` instance in the collection and assigns the path to its `CommandLine` property, which in turn does the same for the `TddgRunButton` component it encloses.

`RemoveBtnClick()` is the `OnClick` event handler for the Remove button. It removes the selected item from `PathListBox` as well as the `TRunBtnItem` instance from the collection.

`CancelBtnClick()` is the `OnClick` event handler for the Cancel button. It copies the backup collection from `FLaunchPad` to the actual `TRunButtons` collection and closes the form.

The `TCollection` and `TCollectionItems` objects are extremely useful and offer themselves to being used for a variety of purposes. Get to know them well, and next time you need to store a list of components, you'll already have a solution.

Summary

This chapter let you in on some of the more advanced tricks and techniques for Delphi component design. Among other things, you learned about extending hints and animating components as well as component editors, property editors, and component collections. Armed with this information, as well as the more conventional information you learned in the preceding chapter, you should be able to write a component to suit just about any of your programming needs.

12

ADVANCED VCL
COMPONENT
BUILDING

CLX Component Development

IN THIS CHAPTER

The last three chapters have focused on creating custom components in Delphi. More precisely, Chapters 11, "VCL Component Building," and 12, "Advanced VCL Component Building," have focused on creating custom VCL components. However, as noted in Chapter 10, "Component Architecture: VCL and CLX," there are two component class hierarchies in Delphi 6: the VCL and CLX. In this chapter, we change our focus slightly to that of creating custom CLX components. Fortunately, much of what you have learned in creating VCL components also applies to creating CLX components.

What Is CLX?

CLX, pronounced "clicks," is an acronym for *Component Library for Cross-Platform*, and was first introduced in Borland's new Linux RAD tool, Kylix. However, CLX isn't just simply the VCL under Linux. That is, the CLX architecture is also available in Delphi 6, and therefore provides the foundation for creating native cross-platform applications using Delphi 6 and Kylix.

In Delphi, the VCL is typically associated with the components that appear on the Component Palette. This isn't surprising because the vast majority of the components appearing on the palette are visual controls. However, CLX encompasses much more than a visual component hierarchy. Specifically, CLX is divided into four separate parts: BaseCLX, VisualCLX, DataCLX, and NetCLX.

BaseCLX, as it is called in Kylix, contains the base units and classes that are shared between Kylix and Delphi 6. For example, the System, SysUtils, and Classes units are part of BaseCLX. VisualCLX is similar to what most people consider the VCL. However, VisualCLX is based on the Qt widget library rather than the standard Windows controls defined in User32.dll or ComCtl32.dll. DataCLX contains the data access components and encompasses the new dbExpress technology. And finally, NetCLX contains the new cross-platform WebBroker technology.

If you are familiar with previous versions of Delphi, you will recognize that the units included in BaseCLX have been available in Delphi since version 1. As such, you could argue that these units are also part of the VCL. In fact, Borland recognized the confusion caused by calling these base units collectively as BaseCLX, and in Delphi 6 these base units are referred to as the RTL.

The point of all this is that even though these base units will be used in both VCL and CLX applications, a CLX application is typically defined as one built using the classes in VisualCLX.

In this chapter, we will be focusing on VisualCLX. In particular, we'll be investigating how to extend the VisualCLX architecture by creating our own custom CLX components. As noted earlier, VisualCLX is based on the Qt widget library, which is produced by Troll Tech. Qt, pronounced "cute," is a platform independent C++ class library of user interface (UI) widgets (or controls).To be precise, Qt currently supports Windows and the X Window System, and thus can be used on both Windows and Linux desktops. In fact, Qt is the most prevalent class library used for Linux GUI development. For instance, Qt is used in the development of the KDE Window Manager.

Other cross-platform class libraries are available, but Borland chose to build VisualCLX on top of Qt for several reasons. First, Qt classes look very much like VCL components. For example, properties are defined as get/set method pairs. Qt also incorporates the notion of events through a mechanism called a signal. Plus, the Qt graphics model is very similar to the one used in the VCL. And finally, the Qt library defines a wide variety of standard user interface controls, which are called widgets in the Qt nomenclature. As a result, the Borland engineers were able to wrap many of the existing Qt widgets with Object Pascal wrappers rather than create the required components from scratch.

The CLX Architecture

As suggested previously, VisualCLX consists of Object Pascal classes that wrap around existing functionality defined in the Qt classes. This is very similar to the way in which the VCL encapsulates the functionality of the Windows API and the Common Controls. One of the design goals in creating CLX was to make it as easy as possible to port existing VCL applications to the CLX architecture. As a result, the class hierarchy in CLX is very similar to the VCL as illustrated in Figures 13.1 and 13.2. The dark gray boxes in Figure 13.1 highlight the principal base classes in the VCL.

However, the class hierarchies aren't identical. In particular, some new classes have been added and some classes have been moved to different branches from their VCL counterparts. Figure 13.2 highlights these differences with light gray boxes. For example, the CLX Timer component does not descend directly from TComponent as it does in the VCL. Instead, it descends from the new THandleComponent, which is a base class that should be used whenever a nonvisual component requires access to the handle of an underlying Qt control. Also, note how the CLX Label component is no longer a graphical control, but rather a descendant of the new TFrameControl class. The Qt library provides a wide variety of bordering options for controls, and the TFrameControl class provides a wrapper around that functionality.

As noted earlier, controls in the Qt library are called widgets. As a result, the TWidgetControl class is the CLX equivalent to the VCL's TWinControl. Why change the classname? Switching to Widget puts the class in line with the base Qt classes, and removing Win further removes the dependency on the Windows controls in VisualCLX.

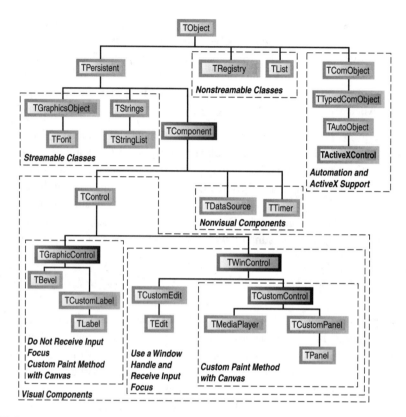

FIGURE 13.1
The VCL Base Class hierarchy.

Surprisingly, Borland also defined the TWinControl class in CLX as an alias for
TWidgetControl. During the development of Kylix and CLX, one of the early ideas that was
promoted was that a single source file could be used to define both a CLX component and a
VCL component. Conditional directives would be used to specify a VCL uses clause when
compiled under Windows and a CLX uses clause when compiled under Linux. However, this
approach is only feasible for very simple components. In practice, there are usually enough
significant changes between the implementations to warrant the creation of separate units.

NOTE

Creating a VCL component and a CLX component in a single source file is different
from creating a CLX component (in a single source file) that can be used in both
Delphi 6 and Kylix. This chapter illustrates how to do the latter.

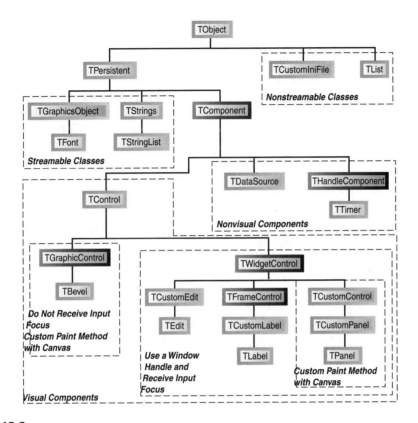

FIGURE 13.2

The CLX Base Class hierarchy.

Fortunately, the changes in the class hierarchy illustrated in Figure 13.2 should have little impact on application developers. That is, most of the VCL components that come with Delphi have VisualCLX equivalents such as TEdit, TListBox, TComboBox, and so on. Unfortunately, component writers aren't so lucky because they will be much more affected by changes to the class hierarchy.

NOTE

The Object Browser in Delphi 6 and Kylix is extremely helpful in learning the structure of the new class hierarchy. However, because of the TWinControl alias to TWidgetControl, you will actually see two identical class hierarchies in the Object Browser.

Fortunately, there are actually quite a few similarities between the VCL and CLX architectures that the figures don't illustrate. For instance, the TCanvas class is very similar in both architectures. Of course, the implementation encapsulated by the class is quite different. Under the VCL, the TCanvas class provides a wrapper around a Windows GDI device context, which is accessible through the TCanvas.Handle property. Under CLX, the TCanvas class provides a wrapper around a Qt painter, which is also accessible through the TCanvas.Handle property. As a result, you can use the Handle property to access any of the low-level GDI functions in a VCL application and the Qt graphics library functions in a CLX application.

The components in CLX were designed to ease porting an existing VCL application to a CLX application. As a result, the public and published interfaces to many of the components are nearly identical in both architectures. This means that events such as OnClick, OnChange, and OnKeyPress as well as their corresponding event dispatch methods—Click(), Change(), and KeyPress()—are implemented in both the VCL and CLX.

Porting Issues

CLX does indeed share many similarities with the VCL. However, many platform differences must be addressed, especially for component writers. You must address Win32 dependencies in your code. For example, any calls to the Win32 API (in Windows.pas) will need to be changed if the component is to operate in Kylix.

> **NOTE**
>
> Building a CLX component implies that you want to use the component in Kylix under Linux and possibly in Delphi 6 under Windows. If you only need to support Windows, create a VCL component and not a CLX component.

In addition, several runtime library (RTL) issues must be handled differently on Linux versus Windows such as case sensitivity for filenames and path delimiters under Linux. For some VCL components, it will simply be impossible to port to Linux. Consider a VCL component that provides a wrapper around the Messaging API (MAPI). Because MAPI doesn't exist under Linux, a different mechanism will need to be used.

In addition to the platform issues described previously, some additional porting issues must be considered when migrating to CLX. For example, COM certainly isn't supported under Linux, but interfaces most certainly are. Owner-Draw techniques available in many VCL wrappers around Windows controls aren't recommended in CLX components. Owner-Draw capabilities have been deprecated in lieu of Qt Styles. Other VCL features that aren't supported under CLX include docking, bi-directional support, the input method editor, and Asian locale support.

One additional change that will certainly cause developers some problems is that the CLX versions of components are located in a different set of units from the VCL controls. For example, the `Controls.pas` unit in the VCL becomes the `QControls.pas` unit in CLX. The problem with this change is that if you are developing a CLX component or application under Delphi 6, the VCL units are still available. As a result, it is quite possible to inadvertently mix CLX and VCL units into your component units. In some cases, your component might run correctly under Windows. However, if you move the component over to Kylix, you will get compiler errors because the VCL units aren't available on Linux.

> **NOTE**
>
> Borland suggests that developers create their CLX components in Kylix on Linux to help prevent the misuse of VCL units in a CLX component. However, many developers will probably opt to develop under Delphi 6, with its new IDE enhancements and the comfort of Windows, and then test their components under Kylix.

Another issue that developers must contend with when writing CLX components (and applications for that matter) is case sensitivity under Linux. In particular because filenames and paths are case sensitive under Linux, the unit names that you specify on your `uses` clause of your own units must be the correct case. This requirement is needed in order for the Kylix compiler to be able to locate the units under Linux. Although Delphi is not case sensitive, this isn't the first time that Delphi requires an element to be case sensitive. The first situation involves the naming of the `Register()` procedure in a unit to be exported from a package.

No More Messages

Linux, or more appropriately XWindows, doesn't implement a messaging architecture like Windows does. As a result, there are no `wm_LButtonDown`, `wm_SetCursor`, or `wm_Char` messages passing around on Linux. When a CLX component is used under Linux, the underlying Qt classes handle the appropriate system events and provide the necessary hooks in order to respond to those events. The bottom line is that system events are handled by the Qt classes even on Windows. Therefore, a CLX component won't be able to hook into a Windows message.

As a result, VCL component message handlers such as `CMTextChanged()` have been replaced with dynamic methods—for example, `TextChanged()`. This will be highlighted in the following section. This also means that implementing certain behaviors, which are easily implemented using messages in the VCL, must be implemented quite differently under CLX.

Sample Components

In this section, we will take a detailed look into several VCL components that have been transformed into CLX components. The first one is a custom spinner component that involves several principle features including custom painting, keyboard handling, focus changes, mouse interactions, and even custom events.

The next three components are successive descendants of the base spinner component—each extending the previous component. The first descendant extends the base spinner by adding support for handling mouse events at design time and displaying custom cursors. The second spinner descendant adds support for displaying images from an ImageList. The final spinner component adds support for connecting the control to a field in a dataset.

> **NOTE**
>
> All the units presented in this chapter can be used in both Delphi 6 and Kylix.

The `TddgSpinner` Component

Figure 13.3 shows three instances of the `TddgSpinner` component being used in a CLX application. Unlike traditional spin-edits, this custom component displays the increment and decrement buttons that change the spinner's value at each end of the spinner rather than on top of one another at one end.

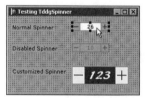

FIGURE 13.3
The `TddgSpinner` CLX component can be used to specify integer values.

Listing 13.1 shows the complete source code for the `QddgSpin.pas` unit, which implements the `TddgSpinner` component. This particular component started out as a custom spinner control that descended from the `TCustomControl` class in the VCL. However, the `TddgSpinner` class now descends from the CLX `TCustomControl` class, and as a result, can be used in both Windows and Linux.

Although classnames rarely change when migrating to CLX, unit names are typically prefixed with the letter Q to indicate their dependency on the Qt library via VisualCLX.

> **NOTE**
>
> Although commented out, each listing includes the original VCL-specific code.
> Comments that start with VCL->CLX: highlight specific issues involved in transforming
> the control from the VCL to CLX.

LISTING 13.1 QddgSpin.pas—Source Code for the TddgSpinner Component

```
unit QddgSpin;

interface

uses
  SysUtils, Classes, Types, Qt, QControls, QGraphics;
  (*
  Windows, Messages, SysUtils, Classes, Graphics, Controls, Forms,
  ImgList;
  *)

type
  TddgButtonType = ( btMinus, btPlus );
  TddgSpinnerEvent = procedure (Sender: TObject; NewValue: Integer;
                               var AllowChange: Boolean ) of object;

  TddgSpinner = class( TCustomControl )
  private
    // Instance Data for Component
    FValue: Integer;
    FIncrement: Integer;
    FButtonColor: TColor;
    FButtonWidth: Integer;
    FMinusBtnDown: Boolean;
    FPlusBtnDown: Boolean;

    // Method Pointers to Hold Custom Events
    FOnChange: TNotifyEvent;
    FOnChanging: TddgSpinnerEvent;

    (*
    // VCL->CLX:  These message handlers are not available in CLX

    // Window Message Handling Method
    procedure WMGetDlgCode( var Msg: TWMGetDlgCode );
      message wm_GetDlgCode;
```

LISTING 13.1   Continued

```
  // Component Message Handling Method
  procedure CMEnabledChanged( var Msg: TMessage );
    message cm_EnabledChanged;
  *)
protected
  procedure Paint; override;
  procedure DrawButton( Button: TddgButtonType; Down: Boolean;
                        Bounds: TRect ); virtual;

  // Support Methods
  procedure DecValue( Amount: Integer ); virtual;
  procedure IncValue( Amount: Integer ); virtual;

  function CursorPosition: TPoint;
  function MouseOverButton( Btn: TddgButtonType ): Boolean;

  // VCL->CLX:  EnabledChanged replaces cm_EnabledChanged
  //            component message handler
  procedure EnabledChanged; override;

  // New Event Dispatch Methods
  procedure Change; dynamic;
  function CanChange( NewValue: Integer ): Boolean; dynamic;

  // Overridden Event Dispatch Methods
  procedure DoEnter; override;
  procedure DoExit; override;
  procedure KeyDown(var Key: Word; Shift: TShiftState); override;

  procedure MouseDown( Button: TMouseButton; Shift: TShiftState;
                       X, Y: Integer ); override;
  procedure MouseUp( Button: TMouseButton; Shift: TShiftState;
                     X, Y: Integer ); override;

  (*
  // VCL->CLX:  These following declarations have changed in CLX

  function DoMouseWheelDown( Shift: TShiftState;
                            MousePos: TPoint ): Boolean; override;

  function DoMouseWheelUp( Shift: TShiftState;
                          MousePos: TPoint ): Boolean; override;
  *)
```

LISTING 13.1   Continued

```
    function DoMouseWheelDown( Shift: TShiftState;
                    const MousePos: TPoint ): Boolean; override;

    function DoMouseWheelUp( Shift: TShiftState;
                    const MousePos: TPoint ): Boolean; override;


    // Access Methods for Properties
    procedure SetButtonColor( Value: TColor ); virtual;
    procedure SetButtonWidth( Value: Integer ); virtual;
    procedure SetValue( Value: Integer ); virtual;
public
    // Don't forget to specify override for constructor
    constructor Create( AOwner: TComponent ); override;
published
    // New Property Declarations
    property ButtonColor: TColor
      read FButtonColor
      write SetButtonColor
      default clBtnFace;

    property ButtonWidth: Integer
      read FButtonWidth
      write SetButtonWidth
      default 18;

    property Increment: Integer
      read FIncrement
      write FIncrement
      default 1;

    property Value: Integer
      read FValue
      write SetValue;

    // New Event Declarations

    property OnChange: TNotifyEvent
      read FOnChange
      write FOnChange;

    property OnChanging: TddgSpinnerEvent
      read FOnChanging
      write FOnChanging;
```

13

CLX COMPONENT DEVELOPMENT

LISTING 13.1   Continued

```
    // Inherited Properties and Events
    property Color;
    (*
    property DragCursor;        // VCL->CLX:  Property not yet in CLX
    *)
    property DragMode;
    property Enabled;
    property Font;
    property Height default 18;
    property HelpContext;
    property Hint;
    property ParentShowHint;
    property PopupMenu;
    property ShowHint;
    property TabOrder;
    property TabStop default True;
    property Visible;
    property Width default 80;

    property OnClick;
    property OnDragDrop;
    property OnDragOver;
    property OnEndDrag;
    property OnEnter;
    property OnExit;
    property OnKeyDown;
    property OnKeyPress;
    property OnKeyUp;
    property OnMouseDown;
    property OnMouseMove;
    property OnMouseUp;
    property OnStartDrag;
  end;


implementation


{========================}
{== TddgSpinner Methods ==}
{========================}

constructor TddgSpinner.Create( AOwner: TComponent );
begin
```

LISTING 13.1 Continued

```
  inherited Create( AOwner );

  // Initialize Instance Data
  FButtonColor := clBtnFace;
  FButtonWidth := 18;
  FValue := 0;
  FIncrement := 1;

  FMinusBtnDown := False;
  FPlusBtnDown := False;

  // Initializing inherited properties
  Width := 80;
  Height := 18;
  TabStop := True;

  // VCL->CLX:  TWidgetControl sets Color property to clNone
  Color := clWindow;

  // VCL->CLX:  InputKeys assignment replaces handling the
  //            wm_GetDlgCode message.
  InputKeys := InputKeys + [ ikArrows ];
end;


{== Property Access Methods ==}

procedure TddgSpinner.SetButtonColor( Value: TColor );
begin
  if FButtonColor <> Value then
  begin
    FButtonColor := Value;
    Invalidate;
  end;
end;

procedure TddgSpinner.SetButtonWidth( Value: Integer );
begin
  if FButtonWidth <> Value then
  begin
    FButtonWidth := Value;
    Invalidate;
  end;
end;
```

13

CLX COMPONENT
DEVELOPMENT

LISTING 13.1 Continued

```
procedure TddgSpinner.SetValue( Value: Integer );
begin
  if FValue <> Value then
  begin
    if CanChange( Value ) then
    begin
      FValue := Value;
      Invalidate;

      // Trigger Change event
      Change;
    end;
  end;
end;


{== Painting Related Methods ==}

procedure TddgSpinner.Paint;
var
  R: TRect;
  YOffset: Integer;
  S: string;
  XOffset: Integer;                // VCL->CLX:  Added for CLX support
begin
  inherited Paint;
  with Canvas do
  begin
    Font := Self.Font;
    Pen.Color := clBtnShadow;

    if Enabled then
      Brush.Color := Self.Color
    else
    begin
      Brush.Color := clBtnFace;
      Font.Color := clBtnShadow;
    end;

    // Display Value
    (*
    // VCL->CLX:  SetTextAlign not available in CLX
    SetTextAlign( Handle, ta_Center or ta_Top );    // GDI function
    *)
```

LISTING 13.1   Continued

```
    R := Rect( FButtonWidth - 1, 0,
              Width - FButtonWidth + 1, Height );
    Canvas.Rectangle( R.Left, R.Top, R.Right, R.Bottom );
    InflateRect( R, -1, -1 );


    S := IntToStr( FValue );
    YOffset := R.Top + ( R.Bottom - R.Top -
                        Canvas.TextHeight( S ) ) div 2;

    // VCL->CLX:  Calculate XOffset b/c no SetTextAlign function
    XOffset := R.Left + ( R.Right - R.Left -
                        Canvas.TextWidth( S ) ) div 2;

    (*
    // VCL->CLX:  Change TextRect call b/c no SetTextAlign function
    TextRect( R, Width div 2, YOffset, S );
    *)
    TextRect( R, XOffset, YOffset, S );

    DrawButton( btMinus, FMinusBtnDown,
              Rect( 0, 0, FButtonWidth, Height ) );
    DrawButton( btPlus, FPlusBtnDown,
              Rect( Width - FButtonWidth, 0, Width, Height ) );

    if Focused then
    begin
      Brush.Color := Self.Color;
      DrawFocusRect( R );
    end;
  end;
end; {= TddgSpinner.Paint =}


procedure TddgSpinner.DrawButton( Button: TddgButtonType;
                                  Down: Boolean; Bounds: TRect );
begin
  with Canvas do
  begin
    if Down then                      // Set background color
      Brush.Color := clBtnShadow
    else
      Brush.Color := FButtonColor;
    Pen.Color := clBtnShadow;
```

13

**CLX COMPONENT
DEVELOPMENT**

LISTING 13.1 Continued

```
    Rectangle( Bounds.Left, Bounds.Top,
               Bounds.Right, Bounds.Bottom );

    if Enabled then
    begin
      (*
      // VCL->CLX: clActiveCaption is set to
      //           clActiveHighlightedText in CLX.
      Pen.Color := clActiveCaption;
      Brush.Color := clActiveCaption;
      *)
      Pen.Color := clActiveBorder;
      Brush.Color := clActiveBorder;
    end
    else
    begin
      Pen.Color := clBtnShadow;
      Brush.Color := clBtnShadow;
    end;

    if Button = btMinus then               // Draw the Minus Button
    begin
      Rectangle( 4, Height div 2 - 1,
                 FButtonWidth - 4, Height div 2 + 1 );
    end
    else                                   // Draw the Plus Button
    begin
      Rectangle( Width - FButtonWidth + 4, Height div 2 - 1,
                 Width - 4, Height div 2 + 1 );
      Rectangle( Width - FButtonWidth div 2 - 1,
                 ( Height div 2 ) - (FButtonWidth div 2 - 4),
                 Width - FButtonWidth div 2 + 1,
                 ( Height div 2 ) + (FButtonWidth div 2 - 4)  );
    end;
    Pen.Color := clWindowText;
    Brush.Color := clWindow;
  end;
end; {= TddgSpinner.DrawButton =}


procedure TddgSpinner.DoEnter;
begin
  inherited DoEnter;
```

LISTING 13.1 Continued

```
  // Controls gets focus--update display to show focus border
  Repaint;
end;

procedure TddgSpinner.DoExit;
begin
  inherited DoExit;
  // Control lost focus--update display to remove focus border
  Repaint;
end;


// VCL->CLX:  EnabledChanged replaces cm_EnabledChanged handler

procedure TddgSpinner.EnabledChanged;
begin
  inherited;
  // Repaint the component so that it reflects the state change
  Repaint;
end;


{== Event Dispatch Methods ==}

{===================================================================
  TddgSpinner.CanChange

  This is the event dispatch method supporting the OnChanging
  event. Notice that this method is a function, rather than the
  common procedure variety. As a function, the Result variable is
  assigned a value before calling the user defined event handler.
====================================================================}

function TddgSpinner.CanChange( NewValue: Integer ): Boolean;
var
  AllowChange: Boolean;
begin
  AllowChange := True;
  if Assigned( FOnChanging ) then
    FOnChanging( Self, NewValue, AllowChange );
  Result := AllowChange;
end;
```

Listing 13.1 Continued

```pascal
procedure TddgSpinner.Change;
begin
  if Assigned( FOnChange ) then
    FOnChange( Self );
end;


// Notice that both DecValue and IncValue assign the new value to
// the Value property (not FValue), which indirectly calls SetValue

procedure TddgSpinner.DecValue( Amount: Integer );
begin
  Value := Value - Amount;
end;

procedure TddgSpinner.IncValue( Amount: Integer );
begin
  Value := Value + Amount;
end;


{== Keyboard Processing Methods ==}

(*
// VCL->CLX:  Replaced with InputKeys assignment in constructor

procedure TddgSpinner.WMGetDlgCode( var Msg: TWMGetDlgCode );
begin
  inherited;
  Msg.Result := dlgc_WantArrows;  // Control will handle arrow keys
end;
*)


procedure TddgSpinner.KeyDown( var Key: Word; Shift: TShiftState );
begin
  inherited KeyDown( Key, Shift );

  // VCL->CLX:  Key constants changed in CLX.
  //            vk_ prefix changed to Key_

  case Key of
    Key_Left, Key_Down:
      DecValue( FIncrement );
```

LISTING 13.1 Continued

```
    Key_Up, Key_Right:
      IncValue( FIncrement );
  end;
end;


{== Mouse Processing Methods ==}

function TddgSpinner.CursorPosition: TPoint;
begin
  GetCursorPos( Result );
  Result := ScreenToClient( Result );
end;


function TddgSpinner.MouseOverButton(Btn: TddgButtonType): Boolean;
var
  R: TRect;
begin
  // Get bounds of appropriate button
  if Btn = btMinus then
    R := Rect( 0, 0, FButtonWidth, Height )
  else
    R := Rect( Width - FButtonWidth, 0, Width, Height );

  // Is cursor position within bounding rectangle?
  Result := PtInRect( R, CursorPosition );
end;


procedure TddgSpinner.MouseDown( Button: TMouseButton;
                                 Shift: TShiftState; X, Y: Integer);
begin
  inherited MouseDown( Button, Shift, X, Y );

  if not ( csDesigning in ComponentState ) then
    SetFocus;                 // Move focus to Spinner only at runtime

  if ( Button = mbLeft ) and
     ( MouseOverButton(btMinus) or MouseOverButton(btPlus) ) then
  begin
    FMinusBtnDown := MouseOverButton( btMinus );
    FPlusBtnDown := MouseOverButton( btPlus );
```

LISTING 13.1   Continued

```
    Repaint;
  end;
end;


procedure TddgSpinner.MouseUp( Button: TMouseButton;
                               Shift: TShiftState; X, Y: Integer );
begin
  inherited MouseUp( Button, Shift, X, Y );

  if Button = mbLeft then
  begin
    if MouseOverButton( btPlus ) then
      IncValue( FIncrement )
    else if MouseOverButton( btMinus ) then
      DecValue( FIncrement );

    FMinusBtnDown := False;
    FPlusBtnDown := False;

    Repaint;
  end;
end;


function TddgSpinner.DoMouseWheelDown( Shift: TShiftState;
                               const MousePos: TPoint ): Boolean;
begin
  inherited DoMouseWheelDown( Shift, MousePos );
  DecValue( FIncrement );
  Result := True;
end;


function TddgSpinner.DoMouseWheelUp( Shift: TShiftState;
                               const MousePos: TPoint ): Boolean;
begin
  inherited DoMouseWheelUp( Shift, MousePos );
  IncValue( FIncrement );
  Result := True;
end;

end.
```

As you can see, the source code for the CLX version is very similar to the VCL edition. However, there are several important differences.

First, notice the inclusion of the Qt specific units: Qt, QControls, and QGraphics. Types is also a new unit that is shared between the VCL and CLX. Fortunately, the majority of the TddgSpinner CLX class declaration looks identical to what you would find in the VCL. That is, instance fields are declared the same way, as are method pointers to hold event handlers, as well as event dispatch methods.

The CMEnabledChanged() and WMGetDlgCode() message handling methods represent the first implementation change that we must handle in migrating to CLX. Specifically, the corresponding cm_EnabledChanged and wm_GetDlgCode messages don't exist in CLX. Therefore the functionality implemented in these message handlers must be moved elsewhere.

As noted earlier, in CLX, component messages such as cm_EnabledChanged have been replaced with appropriate dynamic methods. So instead of sending a cm_EnabledChanged message whenever the Enabled property is changed, the TControl class in CLX simply calls the EnabledChanged() method. Therefore, the code from the old CMEnabledChanged() method is simply moved to the overridden EnabledChanged() method.

A common task in component writing is to handle the arrow keys on the keyboard. For the TddgSpinner component, the arrow keys can be used to increment and decrement the value. In a VCL component, this behavior is accomplished by handling the wm_GetDlgCode message and specifying which keys your control will handle. As noted previously, the wm_GetDlgCode message doesn't exist for a CLX component. Thus a different approach must be taken. Fortunately, the TWidgetControl class defines the InputKeys property, which allows us to specify the keys we want to handle in the constructor of our component.

The constructor code also indicates another change between the VCL and CLX. That is, the TWidgetControl class sets the Color property, which is declared in the TControl class to be clNone. In the VCL, the TWinControl class simply uses the inherited Color value of clWindow. As a result, we need to set the Color property in the constructor to clWindow so that the spinner appears in the correct color.

After these constructor changes, there aren't too many other changes. As you can see, most event dispatch methods are also available under CLX. As a result, it is much easier to migrate to CLX if you are currently overriding event dispatch methods in your VCL components rather than handling specific Windows messages for the underlying window handle.

At the beginning of this chapter, it was noted that all the techniques you learned about VCL component building in the previous chapters also apply to creating CLX components. You will notice that property declarations, access methods, and even custom events are handled the same way in both the VCL and CLX.

13

CLX COMPONENT
DEVELOPMENT

More than any other component method, the Paint() method will probably require the most modifications when transforming a VCL component into a CLX component.

When transforming a VCL control into a CLX component, display methods, such as Paint(), will usually require the most modifications even though the TCanvas classes in both architectures have nearly identical interfaces.

Two display issues needed to be handled in transforming the TddgSpinner component. First, the VCL version of the TddgSpinner used the SetTextAlign GDI function to automatically center the text of the spinner in display area. However, under Linux, this API function doesn't exist. And even under Windows, this function wouldn't work because it expects a handle to a GDI device context, and CLX components don't have access to a device context   the Canvas.Handle property references a Qt Painter object.

Fortunately, most of the TCanvas methods do exist under both Windows and Linux. Therefore, we can circumvent this problem by calculating the center position manually.

The second display problem involves the DrawButton() method. In particular, the plus and minus symbols on the buttons are drawn using the clActiveCaption color in the VCL. Unfortunately, the clActiveCaption identifier is assigned to the clActiveHighlightedText value in the QGraphics.pas unit, which clearly isn't what we want.

> **NOTE**
>
> To perform any painting outside of your CLX component's Paint() method, you must first call the Canvas.Start() method and then call the Canvas.Stop() method when you are finished.

Not everything migrates as easily as you would have expected. The virtual key code constants defined in the VCL, such as vk_Left, aren't available in CLX. Instead, a completely new set of constants is used to determine which key was pressed. It turns out that the virtual key codes are part of the Windows API, and thus aren't available under Linux.

And that's it! We now have a fully functional custom CLX component that can be used in both Windows applications developed with Delphi 6 and Linux applications developed with Kylix. Of course, the most important aspect of this is that the same source code is used for both platforms.

Design-Time Enhancements

All things considered, migrating the TddgSpinner VCL component to CLX was fairly straightforward and not too tricky—although discovering the InputKeys property did take some effort.

However, as you shall see, once you start adding more functionality to our CLX components, the differences between the VCL and CLX will become evident.

Consider the source code displayed in Listing 13.2. This unit implements the TddgDesign Spinner, which is a descendant of TddgSpinner. Figure 13.4 illustrates how this component simply changes the mouse cursor whenever the mouse is positioned over one of the buttons. The descendant component also adds the ability to change the spinner value by clicking the plus or minus buttons directly on the form at design time as illustrated in Figure 13.5.

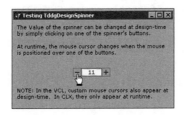

FIGURE 13.4

The TddgDesignSpinner *displays a custom mouse cursor when the mouse is positioned over either button.*

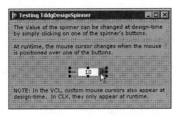

FIGURE 13.5

The TddgDesignSpinner *allows the Value property to be changed at design time by simply clicking on the component's buttons.*

LISTING 13.2 QddgDsnSpin.pas—Source Code for the TddgDesignSpinner Component

```
unit QddgDsnSpn;

interface

uses
  SysUtils, Classes, Qt, QddgSpin;
  (*
  Windows, Messages, SysUtils, Classes, Graphics, Controls, Forms,
  ddgSpin;
  *)
```

LISTING 13.2   Continued

```
type
  TddgDesignSpinner = class( TddgSpinner )
  private
    // VCL->CLX:  Custom cursor stored in QCursorH field
    FThumbCursor: QCursorH;

    (*
    // VCL->CLX:  Custom cursors and design-time interactions are
    //            handled differently under CLX. The following
    //            block is VCL-specific.

    FThumbCursor: HCursor;

    // Window Message Handling Method
    procedure WMSetCursor( var Msg : TWMSetCursor );
      message wm_SetCursor;

    // Component Message Handling Method
    procedure CMDesignHitTest( var Msg: TCMDesignHitTest );
      message cm_DesignHitTest;
    *)
  protected
    procedure Change; override;

    // VCL->CLX:  The following two methods are overridden for CLX
    procedure MouseMove( Shift: TShiftState;
                         X, Y: Integer ); override;
    function DesignEventQuery( Sender: QObjectH;
                              Event: QEventH ): Boolean; override;
  public
    constructor Create( AOwner: TComponent ); override;
    destructor Destroy; override;
  end;

implementation

(*
// VCL->CLX:  CLX does not support cursor resources
{$R DdgDsnSpn.res}                    // Link in custom cursor resource
*)

uses
  Types, QControls, QForms;               // VCL->CLX:  Add CLX units
```

LISTING 13.2 Continued

```
// VCL->CLX:  Two arrays of bytes (one for the image and one for
//            the mask) are used to represent custom cursors in CLX

const
  Bits: array[0..32*4-1] of Byte = (
    $00, $30, $00, $00, $00, $48, $00, $00,
    $00, $48, $00, $00, $00, $48, $00, $00,
    $00, $48, $00, $00, $00, $4E, $00, $00,
    $00, $49, $C0, $00, $00, $49, $30, $00,
    $00, $49, $28, $00, $03, $49, $24, $00,
    $04, $C0, $24, $00, $04, $40, $04, $00,
    $02, $40, $04, $00, $02, $00, $04, $00,
    $01, $00, $04, $00, $01, $00, $04, $00,
    $00, $80, $08, $00, $00, $40, $08, $00,
    $00, $40, $08, $00, $00, $20, $10, $00,
    $00, $20, $10, $00, $00, $7F, $F8, $00,
    $00, $7F, $F8, $00, $00, $7F, $E8, $00,
    $00, $7F, $F8, $00, $00, $00, $00, $00,
    $00, $00, $00, $00, $00, $00, $00, $00,
    $00, $00, $00, $00, $00, $00, $00, $00,
    $00, $00, $00, $00, $00, $00, $00, $00 );

  Mask: array[0..32*4-1] of Byte = (
    $00, $30, $00, $00, $00, $78, $00, $00,
    $00, $78, $00, $00, $00, $78, $00, $00,
    $00, $78, $00, $00, $00, $7E, $00, $00,
    $00, $7F, $C0, $00, $00, $7F, $F0, $00,
    $00, $7F, $F8, $00, $03, $7F, $FC, $00,
    $07, $FF, $FC, $00, $07, $FF, $FC, $00,
    $03, $FF, $FC, $00, $03, $FF, $FC, $00,
    $01, $FF, $FC, $00, $01, $FF, $FC, $00,
    $00, $FF, $F8, $00, $00, $7F, $F8, $00,
    $00, $7F, $F8, $00, $00, $3F, $F0, $00,
    $00, $3F, $F0, $00, $00, $7F, $F8, $00,
    $00, $7F, $F8, $00, $00, $7F, $E8, $00,
    $00, $7F, $F8, $00, $00, $00, $00, $00,
    $00, $00, $00, $00, $00, $00, $00, $00,
    $00, $00, $00, $00, $00, $00, $00, $00,
    $00, $00, $00, $00, $00, $00, $00, $00 );


{===============================}
{== TddgDesignSpinner Methods ==}
{===============================}
```

LISTING 13.2   Continued

```
constructor TddgDesignSpinner.Create( AOwner: TComponent );
var
  BitsBitmap: QBitmapH;
  MaskBitmap: QBitmapH;
begin
  inherited Create( AOwner );

  (*
  // VCL->CLX:  No LoadCursor in CLX
  FThumbCursor := LoadCursor( HInstance, 'DdgDSNSPN_BTNCURSOR' );
  *)

  // VCL->CLX:  Byte arrays are used to create a custom cursor
  BitsBitmap := QBitmap_create( 32, 32, @Bits, False );
  MaskBitmap := QBitmap_create( 32, 32, @Mask, False );
  try
    FThumbCursor := QCursor_create( BitsBitmap, MaskBitmap, 8, 0 );
  finally
    QBitmap_destroy( BitsBitmap );
    QBitmap_destroy( MaskBitmap );
  end;
end;


destructor TddgDesignSpinner.Destroy;
begin
  (*
  VCL->CLX:  In CLX, use QCursor_Destroy instead of DestroyCursor
  DestroyCursor( FThumbCursor );      // Release GDI cursor object
  *)
  QCursor_Destroy( FThumbCursor );
  inherited Destroy;
end;


// If the mouse is over one of the buttons, then change cursor to
// the custom cursor that resides in the DdgDsnSpn.res
// resource file

(*
// VCL->CLX:  There is no wm_SetCursor in CLX
procedure TddgDesignSpinner.WMSetCursor( var Msg: TWMSetCursor );
begin
  if MouseOverButton( btMinus ) or MouseOverButton( btPlus ) then
    SetCursor( FThumbCursor )
```

LISTING 13.2   Continued

```
  else
    inherited;
end;
*)


// VCL->CLX:  Override MouseMove to handle displaying custom cursor

procedure TddgDesignSpinner.MouseMove( Shift: TShiftState;
                                       X, Y: Integer );
begin
  if MouseOverButton( btMinus ) or MouseOverButton( btPlus ) then
    QWidget_setCursor( Handle, FThumbCursor )
  else
    QWidget_UnsetCursor( Handle );
  inherited;
end;



(*
// VCL->CLX:  cm_DesignHitTest does not exist in CLX.  Instead,
//           override the DesignEventQuery method (see below).

procedure TddgDesignSpinner.CMDesignHitTest( var Msg:
                                          TCMDesignHitTest );
begin
  // Handling this component message allows the Value of the
  // spinner to be changed at design-time using the left mouse
  // button.  If the mouse is positioned over one of the buttons,
  // then set the Msg.Result value to 1. This instructs Delphi to
  // allow mouse events to "get through to" the component.

  if MouseOverButton( btMinus ) or MouseOverButton( btPlus ) then
    Msg.Result := 1
  else
    Msg.Result := 0;
end;
*)



function TddgDesignSpinner.DesignEventQuery( Sender: QObjectH;
                                       Event: QEventH ): Boolean;
var
  MousePos: TPoint;
begin
  Result := False;
```

LISTING 13.2 Continued

```
  if ( Sender = Handle ) and
     ( QEvent_type(Event) in [QEventType_MouseButtonPress,
                              QEventType_MouseButtonRelease,
                              QEventType_MouseButtonDblClick]) then
  begin
    // Note: extracting MousePos is not actually needed in this
    //       example, but if you need to get the position of the
    //       mouse, this is how you do it.

    MousePos := Point( QMouseEvent_x( QMouseEventH( Event ) ),
                       QMouseEvent_y( QMouseEventH( Event ) ) );

    if MouseOverButton( btMinus ) or MouseOverButton( btPlus ) then
      Result := True
    else
      Result := False;
  end;
end;


procedure TddgDesignSpinner.Change;
var
  Form: TCustomForm;
begin
  inherited Change;

  // Force the Object Inspector to update what it shows for the
  // Value property of the spinner when changed via the mouse.

  if csDesigning in ComponentState then
  begin
    Form := GetParentForm( Self );

    (*
    // VCL->CLX:  Form.Designer replaced with DesignerHook in CLX
    if ( Form <> nil ) and ( Form.Designer <> nil ) then
      Form.Designer.Modified;
    *)

    if ( Form <> nil ) and ( Form.DesignerHook <> nil ) then
      Form.DesignerHook.Modified;
  end;
end;

end.
```

As you can see from the commented blocks of VCL-based code included in the source code, implementing these two features wasn't trivial because both features use messages in the VCL. As noted earlier, Linux doesn't use a message loop and thus CLX must use a different mechanism to implement these features.

First of all, specifying the mouse cursor to use in the control is much more complicated. In the VCL version, we simply attached a Windows resource file that included a custom cursor, and we then called the `LoadCursor` API function to get a reference to the cursor (a handle). This cursor handle is then used in handling the `wm_SetCursor` message, which Windows sends to any control that needs to have its mouse pointer updated.

Under CLX, this approach cannot be used. First, Qt doesn't support cursor resources. The `Qt.pas` unit defines several `QCursor_create()` methods—each providing a different way to construct a mouse cursor except from a cursor resource. You could specify one of the stock Qt cursors by passing an appropriate integer value to the `QCursor_create()` method. But, to create a custom cursor, you need to create two arrays of bytes that contain the bit layout for the cursor. The first array represents the black or white pixels, whereas the second array represents the mask, which determines which regions in the cursor are transparent.

Next, in order to display the mouse cursor at the appropriate time, we override the `MouseMove()` event dispatch method instead of handling the `wm_SetCursor` message. To change the cursor, the `QWidget_setCursor()` function is called whenever the mouse is positioned over either button. Otherwise, the `QWidget_UnsetCursor()` method is called.

In the VCL, handling the `cm_DesignHitTest` component message allows mouse events to be handled by a component at design-time. Unfortunately, this message doesn't exist in CLX. Instead, to accomplish the same features, we need to override the new `DesignEventQuery()` method. This method provides a way for component writers to become notified when the underlying Qt widget receives an input event at design-time. If the method returns `True`, the control should respond to the event. In our example, we are only concerned with mouse input events. Therefore, we must first determine whether the input event meets our criteria. If so, we must determine whether the mouse is positioned over one of the buttons.

The `Change()` method must be overridden in `TddgDesignSpinner` so that the Object Inspector's display of the `Value` property can remain in-sync with the selected component. If this method isn't overridden, the Object Inspector won't be updated as the user clicks directly on the spinner's button on the Form Designer. As you can see, the only change is the reference of `Form.Designer` to `Form.DesignerHook`.

Component References and Image Lists

The next component once again extends the functionality of the spinner. In particular, the `TddgImgListSpinner` component descends from the `TddgDesignSpinner` and implements a component reference property to allow the user to connect the spinner to an ImageList. The images in the ImageList can then be displayed in place of the plus and minus default symbols as shown in Figure 13.6.

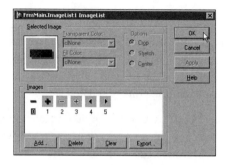

FIGURE 13.6

The `TddgImgListSpinner` *supports displaying images from an ImageList for each button.*

Listing 13.3 shows the complete source code for the `QddgILSpin.pas` unit, which implements the `TddgImgListSpinner` component. Unlike the `TddgDesignSpinner`, this component required very little changes in moving to CLX.

LISTING 13.3   `QddgILSpin.pas`—Source Code for the `TddgImgListSpinner` Component

```
unit QddgILSpin;

interface

uses
  Classes, Types, QddgSpin, QddgDsnSpn, QImgList;
  (*
  Windows, Messages, SysUtils, Classes, Graphics, Controls, Forms,
  ddgSpin, ddgDsnSpn, ImgList;
  *)

type
  TddgImgListSpinner = class( TddgDesignSpinner )
  private
    FImages: TCustomImageList;
    FImageIndexes: array[ 1..2 ] of Integer;
    FImageChangeLink: TChangeLink;

    // Internal Event Handlers
    procedure ImageListChange( Sender: TObject );
  protected
```

LISTING 13.3   Continued

```
    procedure Notification( AComponent : TComponent;
                            Operation : TOperation ); override;

    procedure DrawButton( Button: TddgButtonType; Down: Boolean;
                          Bounds: TRect ); override;
    procedure CalcCenterOffsets( Bounds: TRect; var L, T: Integer);

    procedure CheckMinSize;

    // Property Access Methods
    procedure SetImages( Value: TCustomImageList ); virtual;
    function GetImageIndex( PropIndex: Integer ): Integer; virtual;
    procedure SetImageIndex( PropIndex: Integer;
                             Value: Integer ); virtual;
  public
    constructor Create( AOwner: TComponent ); override;
    destructor Destroy; override;
  published
    property Images: TCustomImageList
      read FImages
      write SetImages;

    property ImageIndexMinus: Integer
      index 1
      read GetImageIndex
      write SetImageIndex;

    property ImageIndexPlus: Integer
      index 2
      read GetImageIndex
      write SetImageIndex;
  end;

implementation

uses
  QGraphics;                        // VCL->CLX:  Added for CLX support


{==============================}
{== TddgImgListSpinner Methods ==}
{==============================}

constructor TddgImgListSpinner.Create( AOwner: TComponent );
```

LISTING 13.3   Continued

```
begin
  inherited Create( AOwner );

  FImageChangeLink := TChangeLink.Create;
  FImageChangeLink.OnChange := ImageListChange;
  // NOTE: Since, the component user does not have direct access to
  // the change link, the user cannot assign custom event handlers.

  FImageIndexes[ 1 ] := -1;
  FImageIndexes[ 2 ] := -1;
end;


destructor TddgImgListSpinner.Destroy;
begin
  FImageChangeLink.Free;
  inherited Destroy;
end;


procedure TddgImgListSpinner.Notification( AComponent: TComponent;
                                          Operation: TOperation );
begin
  inherited Notification( AComponent, Operation );
  if ( Operation = opRemove ) and ( AComponent = FImages ) then
    SetImages( nil );              // Note the call to access method
end;


function TddgImgListSpinner.GetImageIndex( PropIndex:
                                          Integer ): Integer;
begin
  Result := FImageIndexes[ PropIndex ];
end;

procedure TddgImgListSpinner.SetImageIndex( PropIndex: Integer;
                                           Value: Integer );
begin
  if FImageIndexes[ PropIndex ] <> Value then
  begin
    FImageIndexes[ PropIndex ] := Value;
    Invalidate;
  end;
end;
```

LISTING 13.3   Continued

```
procedure TddgImgListSpinner.SetImages( Value: TCustomImageList );
begin
  if FImages <> nil then
    FImages.UnRegisterChanges( FImageChangeLink );

  FImages := Value;

  if FImages <> nil then
  begin
    FImages.RegisterChanges( FImageChangeLink );
    FImages.FreeNotification( Self );
    CheckMinSize;
  end;
  Invalidate;
end;

procedure TddgImgListSpinner.ImageListChange( Sender: TObject );
begin
  if Sender = Images then
  begin
    CheckMinSize;
    // Call Update instead of Invalidate to prevent flicker
    Update;
  end;
end;

procedure TddgImgListSpinner.CheckMinSize;
begin
  // Ensures button area will display entire image
  if FImages.Width > ButtonWidth then
    ButtonWidth := FImages.Width;
  if FImages.Height > Height then
    Height := FImages.Height;
end;


procedure TddgImgListSpinner.DrawButton( Button: TddgButtonType;
                                         Down: Boolean;
                                         Bounds: TRect );
var
  L, T: Integer;
begin
  with Canvas do
  begin
```

LISTING 13.3   Continued

```
Brush.Color := ButtonColor;
Pen.Color := clBtnShadow;
Rectangle( Bounds.Left, Bounds.Top,
           Bounds.Right, Bounds.Bottom );

if Button = btMinus then              // Draw the Minus (-) Button
begin
  if ( Images <> nil ) and ( ImageIndexMinus <> -1 ) then
  begin
    (*
    // VCL->CLX:  DrawingStyle does not exist in CLX TImageList
    //            BkColor is used instead.
    if Down then
      FImages.DrawingStyle := dsSelected
    else
      FImages.DrawingStyle := dsNormal;
    *)
    if Down then
      FImages.BkColor := clBtnShadow
    else
      FImages.BkColor := clBtnFace;

    CalcCenterOffsets( Bounds, L, T );

    (*
    // VCL->CLX:  TImageList.Draw is different in CLX
    FImages.Draw( Canvas, L, T, ImageIndexMinus, Enabled );
    *)
    FImages.Draw( Canvas, L, T, ImageIndexMinus, itImage,
                  Enabled );
  end
  else
    inherited DrawButton( Button, Down, Bounds );
end
else                                  // Draw the Plus (+) Button
begin
  if ( Images <> nil ) and ( ImageIndexPlus <> -1 ) then
  begin
    (*
    // VCL->CLX:  DrawingStyle does not exist in CLX TImageList
    //            BkColor is used instead.
    if Down then
      FImages.DrawingStyle := dsSelected
    else
```

LISTING 13.3   Continued

```
        FImages.DrawingStyle := dsNormal;
      *)
      if Down then
        FImages.BkColor := clBtnShadow
      else
        FImages.BkColor := clBtnFace;

      CalcCenterOffsets( Bounds, L, T );

      (*
      // VCL->CLX:  TImageList.Draw is different in CLX
      FImages.Draw( Canvas, L, T, ImageIndexPlus, Enabled );
      *)
      FImages.Draw( Canvas, L, T, ImageIndexPlus, itImage,
                    Enabled );
    end
    else
      inherited DrawButton( Button, Down, Bounds );
  end;
 end;
end; {= TddgImgListSpinner.DrawButton =}


procedure TddgImgListSpinner.CalcCenterOffsets( Bounds: TRect;
                                        var L, T: Integer );
begin
  if FImages <> nil then
  begin
    L := Bounds.Left + ( Bounds.Right - Bounds.Left ) div 2 -
        ( FImages.Width div 2 );
    T := Bounds.Top + ( Bounds.Bottom - Bounds.Top ) div 2 -
        ( FImages.Height div 2 );
  end;
end;

end.
```

As usual, the uses clause of the unit needs to be changed to include the CLX specific units and to remove the VCL specific ones. In particular, notice that the QImgList unit replaces the ImgList unit. This is significant because under the VCL, the TCustomImageList component is a wrapper around the ImageList common control implemented in the ComCtl32.dll. Borland created a CLX version of the TCustomImageList component that uses the graphics primitives of Qt instead of the ComCtl32.dll.

13

The benefit of this is clearly visible in the class declaration. The declaration of the CLX version of TddgImgListSpinner is identical to the VCL version. Furthermore, the implementations of all but one of the component's methods are also identical.

Of course, it is the single display method, the overridden DrawButton() method, that requires some tweaking. In particular, two issues need to be addressed. The first illustrates a key point in comparing classes that exist in both the VCL and CLX. That is, just because a VCL class has a corresponding class in CLX, it doesn't necessarily mean that all the functionality of the VCL class is also available in the CLX version.

In the case of the TCustomImageList class, the VCL version implements the DrawingStyle property, which is used by the VCL version of the TddgImgListSpinner to display the button's image differently when clicked. The DrawingStyle property doesn't exist in the CLX version, and therefore a different approach must be taken.

The second modification to the DrawButton() method results from the TCustomImageList.Draw() method being different between the two architectures.

Data-Aware CLX Components

In this fourth sample component, data awareness is added to the spinner component. That is, the TddgDBSpinner component can be connected to an integer field in a dataset through its DataSource and DataField properties. Figure 13.7 shows a TddgDBSpinner component connected to the VenueNo field of the Events dataset.

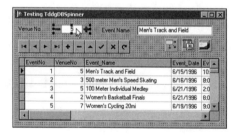

FIGURE 13.7

The TddgDBSpinner *can be used to display and edit integer fields in a dataset.*

Listing 13.4 shows the source code for the QddgDBSpin.pas unit, which implements the TddgDBSpinner component, which in turn descends from TddgImgListSpinner.

LISTING 13.4 QddgDBSpin.pas—Source Code for the TddgDBSpinner Component

```
unit QddgDBSpin;

interface

uses
  SysUtils, Classes, Qt, QddgILSpin, DB, QDBCtrls;
  (*
  Windows, Messages, SysUtils, Classes, Graphics, Controls, Forms,
  ddgILSpin, DB, DBCtrls;
  *)

type
  TddgDBSpinner = class( TddgImgListSpinner )
  private
    FDataLink: TFieldDataLink;          // Provides Access to Data

    // Internal Event Handlers for DataLink Events
    procedure DataChange( Sender: TObject );
    procedure UpdateData( Sender: TObject );
    procedure ActiveChange( Sender: TObject );

    (*
    // VCL->CLX:  Component Message handling methods not in CLX
    procedure CMExit( var Msg: TCMExit ); message cm_Exit;
    procedure CMDesignHitTest( var Msg: TCMDesignHitTest );
      message cm_DesignHitTest;
    *)
  protected
    procedure Notification( AComponent : TComponent;
                            Operation : TOperation ); override;
    procedure CheckFieldType( const Value: string ); virtual;

    // Overridden event dispatch methods
    procedure Change; override;
    procedure KeyPress( var Key : Char ); override;

    // VCL->CLX:  DoExit replaces CMExit
    procedure DoExit; override;
    // VCL->CLX:  DesignEventQuery replaces CMDesignHitTest
    function DesignEventQuery( Sender: QObjectH;
                               Event: QEventH ): Boolean; override;
```

LISTING 13.4   Continued

```pascal
    // Overridden support methods
    procedure DecValue( Amount: Integer ); override;
    procedure IncValue( Amount: Integer ); override;

    // Property Access Methods
    function GetField: TField; virtual;
    function GetDataField: string; virtual;
    procedure SetDataField( const Value: string ); virtual;
    function GetDataSource: TDataSource; virtual;
    procedure SetDataSource( Value: TDataSource ); virtual;
    function GetReadOnly: Boolean; virtual;
    procedure SetReadOnly( Value: Boolean ); virtual;

    // Give Descendants Access to Field object and DataLink
    property Field: TField
      read GetField;

    property DataLink: TFieldDataLink
      read FDataLink;
  public
    constructor Create( AOwner: TComponent ); override;
    destructor Destroy; override;
  published
    property DataField: string
      read GetDataField
      write SetDataField;

    property DataSource: TDataSource
      read GetDataSource
      write SetDataSource;

    // This property controls the ReadOnly state of the DataLink
    property ReadOnly: Boolean
      read GetReadOnly
      write SetReadOnly
      default False;
  end;

type
  EInvalidFieldType = class( Exception );

resourcestring
  SInvalidFieldType = 'DataField can only be connected to ' +
                      'columns of type Integer, Smallint, Word, ' +
                      'and Float';
```

LISTING 13.4   Continued

```
implementation

uses
  Types;                        // VCL->CLX:  Added for CLS support


{===========================}
{== TddgDBSpinner Methods ==}
{===========================}

constructor TddgDBSpinner.Create( AOwner: TComponent );
begin
  inherited Create( AOwner );

  FDataLink := TFieldDataLink.Create;

  // To support the TField.FocusControl method, set the
  // FDataLink.Control property to point to the spinner.
  // The Control property requires a TWinControl component.
  FDataLink.Control := Self;

  // Assign Event Handlers
  FDataLink.OnDataChange := DataChange;
  FDataLink.OnUpdateData := UpdateData;
  FDataLink.OnActiveChange := ActiveChange;

  // NOTE: Since, the component user does not have direct access to
  // the data link, the user cannot assign custom event handlers.
end;


destructor TddgDBSpinner.Destroy;
begin
  FDataLink.Free;
  FDataLink := nil;
  inherited Destroy;
end;


procedure TddgDBSpinner.Notification( AComponent: TComponent;
                                      Operation: TOperation );
begin
  inherited Notification( AComponent, Operation );
  if ( Operation = opRemove ) and
     ( FDataLink <> nil ) and
```

LISTING 13.4   Continued

```pascal
     ( AComponent = FDataLink.DataSource ) then
  begin
    DataSource := nil;              // Indirectly calls SetDataSource
  end;
end;


function TddgDBSpinner.GetField: TField;
begin
  Result := FDataLink.Field;
end;


function TddgDBSpinner.GetDataField: string;
begin
  Result := FDataLink.FieldName;
end;

procedure TddgDBSpinner.SetDataField( const Value: string );
begin
  CheckFieldType( Value );
  FDataLink.FieldName := Value;
end;


function TddgDBSpinner.GetDataSource: TDataSource;
begin
  Result := FDataLink.DataSource;
end;

procedure TddgDBSpinner.SetDataSource( Value: TDataSource );
begin
  if FDatalink.DataSource <> Value then
  begin
    FDataLink.DataSource := Value;

    // FreeNotification must be called b/c DataSource may be
    // located on another form or data module.
    if Value <> nil then
      Value.FreeNotification( Self );
  end;
end;
```

LISTING 13.4 Continued

```
function TddgDBSpinner.GetReadOnly: Boolean;
begin
  Result := FDataLink.ReadOnly;
end;

procedure TddgDBSpinner.SetReadOnly( Value: Boolean );
begin
  FDataLink.ReadOnly := Value;
end;



procedure TddgDBSpinner.CheckFieldType( const Value: string );
var
  FieldType: TFieldType;
begin
  // Make sure the field type corresponding to the column
  // referenced by Value is either ftInteger, ftSmallInt, ftWord,
  // or ftFloat.  If it is not, an EInvalidFieldType exception is
  // raised.

  if ( Value <> '' ) and
     ( FDataLink <> nil ) and
     ( FDataLink.Dataset <> nil ) and
     ( FDataLink.Dataset.Active ) then
  begin
    FieldType := FDataLink.Dataset.FieldByName( Value ).DataType;
    if ( FieldType <> ftInteger ) and
       ( FieldType <> ftSmallInt ) and
       ( FieldType <> ftWord ) and
       ( FieldType <> ftFloat ) then
    begin
      raise EInvalidFieldType.Create( SInvalidFieldType );
    end;
  end;
end;



procedure TddgDBSpinner.Change;
begin
  // Tell the FDataLink that the data has changed
  if FDataLink <> nil then
    FDataLink.Modified;
  inherited Change;                        // Generates OnChange event
end;
```

LISTING 13.4   Continued

```
procedure TddgDBSpinner.KeyPress( var Key: Char );
begin
  inherited KeyPress( Key );

  if Key = #27 then
  begin
    FDataLink.Reset;                            // Esc key pressed
    Key := #0;                  // Set to #0 so Esc won't close dialog
  end;
end;


procedure TddgDBSpinner.DecValue( Amount: Integer );
begin
  if ReadOnly or not FDataLink.CanModify then
  begin
    // Prevent change if FDataLink is ReadOnly
    (*
    // VCL->CLX:  MessageBeep is a Windows API function
    MessageBeep( 0 )
    *)
    Beep;
  end
  else
  begin
    // Try to put Dataset in edit mode--only dec if in edit mode
    if FDataLink.Edit then
      inherited DecValue( Amount );
  end;
end;


procedure TddgDBSpinner.IncValue( Amount: Integer );
begin
  if ReadOnly or not FDataLink.CanModify then
  begin
    // Prevent change if FDataLink is ReadOnly
    (*
    // VCL->CLX:  MessageBeep is a Windows API function
    MessageBeep( 0 )
    *)
    Beep;
  end
  else
```

LISTING 13.4   Continued

```
begin
  // Try to put Dataset in edit mode--only inc if in edit mode
  if FDataLink.Edit then
    inherited IncValue( Amount );
  end;
end;



{=================================================================
  TddgDBSpinner.DataChange

  This method gets called as a result of a number of
  different events:

  1. The underlying field value changes.  Occurs when changing the
     value of the column tied to this control and then move to a
     new column or a new record.
  2. The corresponding Dataset goes into Edit mode.
  3. The corresponding Dataset referenced by DataSource changes.
  4. The current cursor is scrolled to a new record in the table.
  5. The record is reset through a Cancel call.
  6. The DataFields property changes to reference another column.
=================================================================}

procedure TddgDBSpinner.DataChange( Sender: TObject );
begin
  if FDataLink.Field <> nil then
    Value := FDataLink.Field.AsInteger;
end;



{=================================================================
  TddgDBSpinner.UpdateData

  This method gets called when the corresponding field value and
  the contents of the Spinner need to be synchronized.  Note that
  this method only gets called if this control was responsible for
  altering the data.
=================================================================}

procedure TddgDBSpinner.UpdateData( Sender: TObject );
begin
  FDataLink.Field.AsInteger := Value;
end;
```

LISTING 13.4 Continued

```
{===================================================================
   TddgDBSpinner.ActiveChange

   This method gets called whenever the Active property of the
   attached Dataset changes.

   NOTE: You can use the FDataLink.Active property to determine
         the *new* state of the Dataset.
 ===================================================================}

procedure TddgDBSpinner.ActiveChange( Sender: TObject );
begin
  // If the Dataset is becoming Active, then check to make sure the
  // field type of the DataField property is a valid type.

  if ( FDataLink <> nil ) and FDataLink.Active then
    CheckFieldType( DataField );
end;


(*
// VCL->CLX:  CMExit replaced with DoExit (see below)

procedure TddgDBSpinner.CMExit( var Msg: TCMExit );
begin
  try    // Attempt to update the record if focus leaves the spinner
    FDataLink.UpdateRecord;
  except
    SetFocus;       // Keep the focus on the control if Update fails
    raise;                                  // Reraise the exception
  end;
  inherited;
end;
*)

procedure TddgDBSpinner.DoExit;
begin
  try    // Attempt to update the record if focus leaves the spinner
    FDataLink.UpdateRecord;
  except
    SetFocus;       // Keep the focus on the control if Update fails
    raise;                                  // Reraise the exception
  end;
  inherited;
end;
```

LISTING 13.4 Continued

```
(*
// VCL->CLX:  CMDesignHitTest replaced by DesignEventQuery

procedure TddgDBSpinner.CMDesignHitTest(var Msg: TCMDesignHitTest);
begin
  // Ancestor component allows Value to be changed at design-time.
  // This is not valid in a data-aware component because it would
  // put the connected dataset into edit mode.
  Msg.Result := 0;
end;
*)

function TddgDBSpinner.DesignEventQuery( Sender: QObjectH;
                                         Event: QEventH ): Boolean;
begin
  // Ancestor component allows Value to be changed at design-time.
  // This is not valid in a data-aware component because it would
  // put the connected dataset into edit mode.
  Result := False;
end;

end.
```

Fortunately, incorporating data awareness into a CLX component is nearly identical to the VCL implementation. That is, once you have a working nondata-aware CLX component, you simply need to embed a TFieldDataLink object into your CLX component and respond to the DataChange and UpdateData events. Of course, you will need to implement the DataSource, DataField, and ReadOnly properties, but this is no different from doing the same thing in a VCL component.

> **NOTE**
>
> Don't forget to change the DBCtrls unit to QDBCtrls. Although the DB unit is shared between the VCL and CLX, the DBCtrls unit isn't. Both DBCtrls and QDBCtrls define a TFieldDataLink class. Unfortunately, under Delphi 6, you won't receive any errors if you use the VCL version of the TFieldDataLink instead of the CLX version. In fact, the component might even operate correctly under Windows. However, when you try the component under Kylix, you will receive many syntax errors from the compiler.

However, one situation will require your attention. Many data-aware VCL components handle the cm_Exit component message in order to call the UpdateRecord method of the data link.

However, CLX doesn't implement the cm_Exit message, and therefore the DoExit() event dispatch method must be overridden instead.

The TddgDBSpinner is a direct descendant of TddgImgListSpinner, which in turn descends from TddgDesignSpinner. Recall that one of the features of the TddgDesignSpinner was to allow the user to change the value of the spinner using the mouse at design time. This feature is no longer useful in our data-aware component because if the user changes the value of the spinner, the associated dataset will be placed into edit mode. Unfortunately, at design-time there is no way to get out of edit mode once this happens. Therefore, the TddgDBSpinner overrides the DesignEventQuery() method and simply returns False to prevent mouse operations from being handled by the component at design-time.

CLX Design Editors

Design editors for CLX components are implemented in exactly the same way they are for VCL components. However, there are few changes that you must be aware of. The most significant is that the units that implement the base design-time functionality have been broken up and placed into new units. Specifically, the DsgnIntf unit has been renamed to DesignIntf. In most cases, you will also need to add the new DesignEditors unit to your uses clause. The DesignIntf unit defines the interfaces used by the Form Designer and Object Inspector. The DesignEditors unit implements the basic property editor and component editor classes.

Unfortunately, not all the design-time features of the VCL have made it over into CLX. For example, owner-draw property editors are only available in the VCL. As a result, CLX specific editors are implemented in the CLXEditors unit, whereas VCL specific editors are defined in the VCLEditors unit.

Figure 13.8 shows the TddgRadioGroupEditor, a custom component editor for the CLX TRadioGroup component, allowing a user to easily set the ItemIndex property. The TddgRadioGroupEditor is defined in the QddgRgpEdt.pas unit, which appears in Listing 13.5.

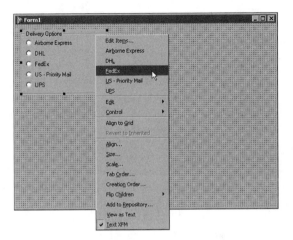

FIGURE 13.8
Selecting an item in the CLX RadioGroup is a snap with this custom component editor.

LISTING 13.5 QddgRgpEdt.pas—Source Code for the TddgRadioGroupEditor Component Editor

```
unit QddgRgpEdt;

interface

uses
  DesignIntf, DesignEditors, QExtCtrls, QDdgDsnEdt;

type
  TddgRadioGroupEditor = class( TddgDefaultEditor )
  protected
    function RadioGroup: TRadioGroup; virtual;
  public
    function GetVerbCount: Integer; override;
    function GetVerb( Index: Integer ) : string; override;
    procedure ExecuteVerb( Index: Integer ); override;
  end;


implementation

uses
  QControls;
```

LISTING 13.5   Continued

```pascal
{==================================}
{== TddgRadioGroupEditor Methods ==}
{==================================}

function TddgRadioGroupEditor.RadioGroup: TRadioGroup;
begin
  // Helper function to provide quick access to component being
  // edited.  Also makes sure Component is a TRadioGroup
  Result := Component as TRadioGroup;
end;

function TddgRadioGroupEditor.GetVerbCount: Integer;
begin
  // Return the number of new menu items to display
  Result := RadioGroup.Items.Count + 1;
end;


function TddgRadioGroupEditor.GetVerb( Index: Integer ): string;
begin
  // Menu item caption for context menu
  if Index = 0 then
    Result := 'Edit Items...'
  else
    Result := RadioGroup.Items[ Index - 1 ];
end;


procedure TddgRadioGroupEditor.ExecuteVerb( Index: Integer );
begin
  if Index = 0 then
    EditPropertyByName( 'Items' )        // Defined in QDdgDsnEdt.pas
  else
  begin
    if RadioGroup.ItemIndex <> Index - 1 then
      RadioGroup.ItemIndex := Index - 1
    else
      RadioGroup.ItemIndex := -1;                // Uncheck all items
    Designer.Modified;
  end;
end;

end.
```

The techniques illustrated in the `TddgRadioGroupEditor` apply to both the VCL and CLX. In this example, the context menu of the `TRadioGroup` component is changed to reflect the items currently in the group. Selecting a group item's corresponding menu item causes the radio group's `ItemIndex` property to be set accordingly. If no items are in the group, only the Edit Items menu item is added.

If the user chooses this menu item, the string list editor is invoked on the Items property for the `TRadioGroup`. The `EditPropertyByName()` method isn't part of CLX or the VCL—it is defined in the `TddgDefaultEditor` class. This method can be used to invoke the currently registered property editor for any named property of a component within the context of a component editor. Listing 13.6 shows the source code for the `QddgDsnEdt.pas` unit, which implements the `TddgDefaultEditor` class.

LISTING 13.6   `QddgDsnEdt.pas`—Source Code for the `TddgDefaultEditor` Component Editor

```
unit QddgDsnEdt;

interface

uses
  Classes, DesignIntf, DesignEditors;

type
  TddgDefaultEditor = class( TDefaultEditor )
  private
    FPropName: string;
    FContinue: Boolean;
    FPropEditor: IProperty;
    procedure EnumPropertyEditors(const PropertyEditor: IProperty);
    procedure TestPropertyEditor( const PropertyEditor: IProperty;
                                  var Continue: Boolean );
  protected
    procedure EditPropertyByName( const APropName: string );
  end;



implementation

uses
  SysUtils, TypInfo;


{==============================}
{== TddgDefaultEditor Methods ==}
{==============================}
```

13

LISTING 13.6 Continued

```
procedure TddgDefaultEditor.EnumPropertyEditors( const
                                     PropertyEditor: IProperty );
begin
  if FContinue then
    TestPropertyEditor( PropertyEditor, FContinue );
end;


procedure TddgDefaultEditor.TestPropertyEditor( const
                                     PropertyEditor: IProperty;
                                     var Continue: Boolean );
begin
  if not Assigned( FPropEditor ) and
     ( CompareText( PropertyEditor.GetName, FPropName ) = 0 ) then
  begin
    Continue := False;
    FPropEditor := PropertyEditor;
  end;
end;


procedure TddgDefaultEditor.EditPropertyByName( const
                                     APropName: string );
var
  Components: IDesignerSelections;
begin
  Components := TDesignerSelections.Create;
  FContinue := True;
  FPropName := APropName;
  Components.Add( Component );
  FPropEditor := nil;
  try
    GetComponentProperties( Components, tkAny, Designer,
                            EnumPropertyEditors );
    if Assigned( FPropEditor ) then
      FPropEditor.Edit;
  finally
    FPropEditor := nil;
  end;
end;

end.
```

Packages

CLX components, like VCL components, need to be placed into a package in order to be installed into the Kylix or Delphi IDEs. However, it is important to note that a compiled Delphi 6 package containing a CLX component cannot be installed into Kylix. This is because packages under Windows are implemented as specially compiled DLLs, whereas packages under Linux are implemented as shared object (.so) files. Fortunately, the format and syntax of package source files under both platforms is identical.

However, the information that you need to provide in the packages will differ between Windows and Linux. For example, the `requires` clause for a Linux runtime package will usually specify the `baseclx` and `visualclx` packages. However, `baseclx` doesn't exist in Delphi 6. Under Windows, a runtime package containing CLX components will only require the `visualclx` package. Of course, as with VCL packages, CLX design packages will require the runtime packages containing your new custom CLX components.

Naming Conventions

The CLX components presented in this chapter are contained in the packages described in Tables 13.1 and 13.2. Table 13.1 shows the BPL files generated under Windows and also lists the packages required for each custom package. Table 13.2 shows the shared object files generated under Linux and likewise lists the required packages. The package source files are the same in both tables. As you can see, we've adopted a specific naming convention for package names.

TABLE 13.1   CLX Packages for Windows (Delphi 6)

Package Source	Compiled Version	Requires
QddgSamples.dpk	QddgSamples60.bpl	visualclx
QddgSamples_Dsgn.dpk	QddgSamples_Dsgn60.bpl	visualclx designide QddgSamples
QddgDBSamples.dpk	QddgDBSamples60.bpl	visualclx dbrtl visualdbclx QddgSamples
QddgDBSamples_Dsgn.dpk	QddgDBSamples_Dsgn60.bpl	visualclx QddgSamples_Dsgn QddgDBSamples

13

CLX COMPONENT DEVELOPMENT

TABLE 13.2   CLX Packages for Linux (Kylix)

Package Source	Compiled Version	Requires
QddgSamples.dpk	bplQddg6Samples.so.6	baseclx visualclx
QddgSamples_Dsgn.dpk	bplQddgSamples_Dsgn.so.6	baseclx visualclx designide QddgSamples
QddgDBSamples.dpk	bplQddgDBSamples.so.6	baseclx visualclx visualdbclx dataclx QddgSamples
QddgDBSamples_Dsgn.dpk	bplQddgDBSamples_Dsgn.so.6	baseclx visualclx QddgSamples_Dsgn QddgDBSamples

CLX packages to be used under Windows typically incorporate the product version in the name. For example, QddgSamples60.bpl indicates that this file is for Delphi 6 and is a Borland Package Library as noted by the .bpl extension. Under Linux, Borland has chosen to follow traditional Linux practices in naming shared objects. For example, rather than use an extension to indicate the type of file, a bpl prefix is used to indicate a package. Borland will occasionally name some of its design packages with the dcl prefix. However, we discourage this practice because design packages are more clearly identified by the _Dsgn suffix. In addition, all packages (runtime and design) under Windows use a .bpl extension. Using a bpl prefix for all packages under Linux establishes a certain level of consistency. The suffix used for a Linux shared object is typically .so followed by a version number. The prefix and suffix used in generating a compiled package are controlled through the package options.

You will also note that the package source files don't specify a version number. In previous versions of Delphi, it was common practice to add a suffix to the package name to indicate which version of the VCL the package required. However, starting in Kylix and Delphi 6, Borland has added several new options controlling the names used when compiling package. In the Delphi 6 examples in Table 13.1, the new {$LIBSUFFIX} option is used to specify 60. When Delphi compiles the package, the suffix is automatically added to the end of the bpl file. In the Kylix examples in Table 13.2, the {$SOPREFIX} directive specifies bpl, whereas the {$SOVERSION} directive specifies 6.

Runtime Packages

Listings 13.7 and 13.8 show the source code for the nondata-aware and data-aware runtime packages containing the components presented in this chapter. Note the use of the conditional symbols MSWINDOWS and LINUX to specify the appropriate directives and to include the appropriate packages in the requires clause. MSWINDOWS is defined when compiling under Delphi 6, whereas LINUX is defined when compiling under Kylix.

LISTING 13.7 QddgSamples.dpk—Source Code for the NonData-Aware CLX Runtime Package

```
package QddgSamples;

{$R *.res}
{$ALIGN 8}
{$ASSERTIONS ON}
{$BOOLEVAL OFF}
{$DEBUGINFO ON}
{$EXTENDEDSYNTAX ON}
{$IMPORTEDDATA ON}
{$IOCHECKS ON}
{$LOCALSYMBOLS ON}
{$LONGSTRINGS ON}
{$OPENSTRINGS ON}
{$OPTIMIZATION ON}
{$OVERFLOWCHECKS OFF}
{$RANGECHECKS OFF}
{$REFERENCEINFO OFF}
{$SAFEDIVIDE OFF}
{$STACKFRAMES OFF}
{$TYPEDADDRESS OFF}
{$VARSTRINGCHECKS ON}
{$WRITEABLECONST ON}
{$MINENUMSIZE 1}
{$IMAGEBASE $400000}
{$DESCRIPTION 'DDG: CLX Components'}
 b
{$IFDEF MSWINDOWS}
{$LIBSUFFIX '60'}
{$ENDIF}

{$IFDEF LINUX}
{$SOPREFIX 'bpl'}
{$SOVERSION '6'}
{$ENDIF}
```

LISTING 13.7   Continued

```
{$RUNONLY}
{$IMPLICITBUILD OFF}

requires
  {$IFDEF LINUX}
  baseclx,
  {$ENDIF}
  visualclx;

contains
  QddgSpin in 'QddgSpin.pas',
  QddgDsnSpn in 'QddgDsnSpn.pas',
  QddgILSpin in 'QddgILSpin.pas';

end.
```

> **NOTE**
>
> When specifying platform specific blocks of code, use separate {$IDFEF}..{$ENDIF} blocks for each platform as illustrated in the package source files. In particular, you want to avoid constructs such as the following:
>
> ```
> {$IFDEF MSWINDOWS}
> // Windows specific code here
> {$ELSE}
> // Linux specific code here
> {$ENDIF}
> ```
>
> If Borland ever decides to support another platform, the preceding construct will cause the Linux specific code to be used as long as the platform isn't Windows.

LISTING 13.8   QddgDBSamples.dpk—Source Code for the Data-Aware CLX Runtime Package

```
package QddgDBSamples;

{$R *.res}
{$ALIGN 8}
{$ASSERTIONS ON}
{$BOOLEVAL OFF}
{$DEBUGINFO ON}
{$EXTENDEDSYNTAX ON}
{$IMPORTEDDATA ON}
{$IOCHECKS ON}
```

LISTING 13.8   Continued

```
{$LOCALSYMBOLS ON}
{$LONGSTRINGS ON}
{$OPENSTRINGS ON}
{$OPTIMIZATION ON}
{$OVERFLOWCHECKS OFF}
{$RANGECHECKS OFF}
{$REFERENCEINFO OFF}
{$SAFEDIVIDE OFF}
{$STACKFRAMES OFF}
{$TYPEDADDRESS OFF}
{$VARSTRINGCHECKS ON}
{$WRITEABLECONST ON}
{$MINENUMSIZE 1}
{$IMAGEBASE $400000}
{$DESCRIPTION 'DDG: CLX Components (Data-Aware)'}

{$IFDEF MSWINDOWS}
{$LIBSUFFIX '60'}
{$ENDIF}

{$IFDEF LINUX}
{$SOPREFIX 'bpl'}
{$SOVERSION '6'}
{$ENDIF}

{$RUNONLY}
{$IMPLICITBUILD OFF}

requires
  {$IFDEF MSWINDOWS}
  dbrtl,
  {$ENDIF}

  {$IFDEF LINUX}
  baseclx,
  dataclx,
  {$ENDIF}

  visualclx,
  visualdbclx,
  QddgSamples;

contains
  QddgDBSpin in 'QddgDBSpin.pas';

end.
```

Design-Time Packages

Although it is possible to put your custom components into a combination runtime/design package, this approach isn't recommended. In fact, this approach only works if you don't have any design editors included in your package. If you do, your package will require the `designide` package, which cannot be redistributed.

The solution is to create separate design packages that handle registering the components contained in your runtime packages. Listings 13.9 and 13.10 show the source code for the nondata-aware and data-aware design packages, respectively. Again note the use of the conditional symbols `MSWINDOWS` and `LINUX` to specify the appropriate directives and to include the appropriate packages in the `requires` clause.

LISTING 13.9   `QddgSamples_Dsgn.dpk`—Source Code for the Nondata-Aware CLX Design-Time Package

```
package QddgSamples_Dsgn;

{$R *.res}
{$R 'QddgSamples_Reg.dcr'}
{$ALIGN 8}
{$ASSERTIONS OFF}
{$BOOLEVAL OFF}
{$DEBUGINFO OFF}
{$EXTENDEDSYNTAX ON}
{$IMPORTEDDATA ON}
{$IOCHECKS ON}
{$LOCALSYMBOLS OFF}
{$LONGSTRINGS ON}
{$OPENSTRINGS ON}
{$OPTIMIZATION ON}
{$OVERFLOWCHECKS OFF}
{$RANGECHECKS OFF}
{$REFERENCEINFO OFF}
{$SAFEDIVIDE OFF}
{$STACKFRAMES OFF}
{$TYPEDADDRESS OFF}
{$VARSTRINGCHECKS ON}
{$WRITEABLECONST ON}
{$MINENUMSIZE 1}
{$IMAGEBASE $400000}
{$DESCRIPTION 'DDG: CLX Components'}

{$IFDEF MSWINDOWS}
{$LIBSUFFIX '60'}
{$ENDIF}
```

LISTING 13.9 Continued

```
{$IFDEF LINUX}
{$SOPREFIX 'bpl'}
{$SOVERSION '6'}
{$ENDIF}

{$DESIGNONLY}
{$IMPLICITBUILD OFF}

requires
  {$IFDEF LINUX}
  baseclx,
  {$ENDIF}
  visualclx,
  designide,
  QddgSamples;

contains
  QddgSamples_Reg in 'QddgSamples_Reg.pas',
  QddgDsnEdt in 'QddgDsnEdt.pas',
  QddgRgpEdt in 'QddgRgpEdt.pas';

end.
```

> **NOTE**
>
> In order to support both Kylix and Delphi 6 with the same package source files, the names specified in the requires and contains clauses must match the case of the actual filename. For example, in the VCL it is common to specify the DesignIDE package in mixed case. However, under Linux, the designide package uses all lowercase letters. If mixed case is used in the source file, Kylix won't be able to locate the designide.dcp file because DesignIDE.dcp is different from designide.dcp on Linux.

LISTING 13.10 QddgDBSamples_Dsgn.dpk—Source Code for the Data-Aware CLX Design-Time Package

```
package QddgDBSamples_Dsgn;

{$R *.res}
{$ALIGN 8}
{$ASSERTIONS OFF}
{$BOOLEVAL OFF}
{$DEBUGINFO OFF}
```

LISTING 13.10 Continued

```
{$EXTENDEDSYNTAX ON}
{$IMPORTEDDATA ON}
{$IOCHECKS ON}
{$LOCALSYMBOLS OFF}
{$LONGSTRINGS ON}
{$OPENSTRINGS ON}
{$OPTIMIZATION ON}
{$OVERFLOWCHECKS OFF}
{$RANGECHECKS OFF}
{$REFERENCEINFO OFF}
{$SAFEDIVIDE OFF}
{$STACKFRAMES OFF}
{$TYPEDADDRESS OFF}
{$VARSTRINGCHECKS ON}
{$WRITEABLECONST ON}
{$MINENUMSIZE 1}
{$IMAGEBASE $400000}
{$DESCRIPTION 'DDG: CLX Components (Data-Aware)'}

{$IFDEF MSWINDOWS}
{$LIBSUFFIX '60'}
{$ENDIF}

{$IFDEF LINUX}
{$SOPREFIX 'bpl'}
{$SOVERSION '6'}
{$ENDIF}

{$DESIGNONLY}
{$IMPLICITBUILD OFF}

requires
  {$IFDEF LINUX}
  baseclx,
  {$ENDIF}
  visualclx,
  QddgSamples_Dsgn,
  QddgDBSamples;

contains
  QddgDBSamples_Reg in 'QddgDBSamples_Reg.pas';

end.
```

Registration Units

As you can see from the source listings for the design packages, registration units are used to handle registering all components. As is customary when creating VCL components, these registration units (QddgSamples_Reg and QddgDBSamples_Reg) are only contained within a design package. Listing 13.11 shows the source code for the QddgSamples_Reg.pas unit, which is responsible for registering the nondata-aware components and the TddgRadioGroupEditor component editor.

LISTING 13.11 QddgSamples_Reg.pas—Registration Unit for Nondata-Aware CLX Sample Components

```
{==================================================================
  QddgSamples_Reg Unit

  Registration Unit for all non-data-aware DDG-CLX components.

  Copyright © 2001 by Ray Konopka
==================================================================}

unit QddgSamples_Reg;

interface

procedure Register;

implementation

uses
  Classes, DesignIntf, DesignEditors, QExtCtrls,
  QddgSpin, QddgDsnSpn, QddgILSpin,
  QddgRgpEdt;


{========================}
{== Register Procedure ==}
{========================}

procedure Register;
begin
  {== Register Components ==}

  RegisterComponents( 'DDG-CLX',
                      [ TddgSpinner,
                        TddgDesignSpinner,
                        TddgImgListSpinner ] );
```

LISTING 13.11 Continued

```
{== Register Component Editors ==}

RegisterComponentEditor( TRadioGroup, TddgRadioGroupEditor );
end;


end.
```

Component Bitmaps

In order to identify your newly created custom CLX component on the Component Palette, you should create a component bitmap, which is a 16-color bitmap that is 24x24 pixels in size. The online help for Kylix and Delphi suggest that you create a separate resource file for each component unit.

However, the Package Editor searches for a matching .dcr file whenever you add a unit to a package. Unfortunately, the Package Editor does this for both runtime and design packages, and linking palette bitmaps into a runtime package is pointless because the bitmaps will go unused and simply waste space.

Therefore, instead of creating separate .dcr files for each component unit, simply create a single .dcr file containing all the component bitmaps. Fortunately, resources in Kylix are the same as those used in Delphi. That is, even though Kylix generates native Linux executables, the format used to attach resources is the Win32 resource format. As a result, we can use any resource editor that can create Windows .res files and then simply rename the file with a .dcr extension. For example, Figure 13.9 shows the QddgSamples_Reg.dcr file being edited in the Image Editor.

Notice that the name of the resource file is the same as the registration unit. As a result, when the registration unit is added to the design package, the component resource file is also added. Furthermore, because the registration unit isn't used in the runtime packages, the component bitmaps won't be linked into them.

As a final comment, don't underestimate the importance of well-designed bitmaps to represent your components. The component bitmaps are the first impression users will have of your components. Unprofessional bitmaps give the impression of unprofessional components. If you build components for the commercial market, you might want to get a professional graphics artist to design the bitmaps.

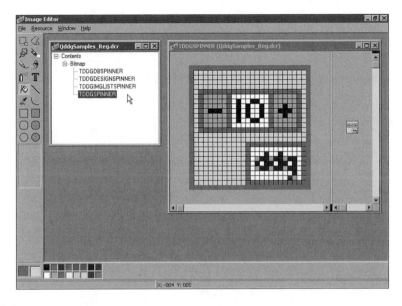

13

CLX COMPONENT
DEVELOPMENT

FIGURE 13.9
The Image Editor can be used to create DCR files for CLX components.

Summary

You can do several things in your current VCL-based components to aid in porting them to CLX in the future. First, use existing VCL wrappers wherever possible. For example, use the TCanvas methods instead of calling GDI functions directly. Override existing event dispatch methods such as MouseDown() instead of handling the wm_LButtonDown window message. Linux doesn't use messages; therefore, the wm_LButtonDown message doesn't even exist under Linux. Another helpful technique is to create your own abstraction classes to help isolate platform dependent code.

Although CLX was modeled after the VCL, migrating your existing VCL components to CLX will definitely require some effort. Platform specific calls such as calls to the Win32 API or to libc must be eliminated or at least wrapped within platform conditional compilation directives. However, it is indeed possible to create a custom CLX component using a single source file that will operate under both Delphi/Windows and Kylix/Linux.

Packages to the Max

IN THIS CHAPTER

Delphi 3 introduced *packages*, which enable you to place portions of your application into separate modules that can be shared across multiple applications. Packages are simply special *dynamic link libraries (DLLs)* that contain additional Delphi specific information. They differ from DLLs in how they are used. Packages are primarily used to store collections of components in a separate, sharable module (a Borland Package Library, or `.bpl` file). As you or other developers create Delphi applications, the packages you create can be used by the application at runtime instead of being directly linked at compile/link time. Because the code for these units resides in the `.bpl` file rather than in your `.exe` or `.dll`, the size of your `.exe` or `.dll` can become very small.

Packages are specific to the VCL; that is, applications written in other languages can't use packages created by Delphi (with the exception of C++Builder). One of the reasons behind packages was to get around a limitation of Delphi 1 and 2. In these prior versions of Delphi, the VCL added a minimum of 150KB to 200KB of code to every executable. Therefore, even if you were to separate a piece of your application into a DLL, both the DLL and the application would contain redundant code. This was especially a problem if you were providing a suite of applications on one machine. Packages allow you to reduce the footprint of your applications and provide a convenient way for you to distribute your component collections.

Why Use Packages?

There are several reasons why you might want to use packages. Three important reasons are discussed in the following sections: code reduction, application partitioning, and component containment.

Code Reduction

A primary reason behind using packages is to reduce the size of your applications and DLLs. Delphi already ships with several predefined packages that break up the VCL into logical groupings. In fact, you can choose to compile your application so that it assumes the existence of many of these Delphi packages.

A Smaller Distribution of Applications— Application Partitioning

You'll find that many programs are available over the Internet as full-blown applications, downloadable demos, or updates to existing applications. Consider the benefit of giving users the option of downloading smaller versions of the application when pieces of the application might already exist on their system, such as when they have a prior installation.

By partitioning your applications using packages, you also allow your users to obtain updates to only those parts of the application that they need. Note, however, that there are some versioning issues that you'll have to take into account. We'll cover these versioning issues in this chapter.

Component Containment

Probably one of the most common reasons for using packages is the distribution of third-party components. If you are a component vendor, you must know how to create packages because certain design-time elements—such as component and property editors, wizards, and experts—are all provided by packages.

Packages Versus DLLs

Using DLLs to host administrative forms for their server applications results in the DLL having its own copy of Forms.pas. This will cause a weird error involving Windows' handling of the window handles generated within the DLL—when the DLL is unloaded, the Window handle isn't dereferenced by the operating system. The next message that crosses the queue for all top-level windows causes a fault at the application, which the operating system then shuts down because the application is in an invalid state. Using packages instead of DLLs overcomes this problem because the packages refer to the main application's copy of Forms.pas, and the message queue can broadcast successfully to the application.

Why Not Use Packages?

You shouldn't use runtime packages unless you are sure that other applications will be using these packages. Otherwise, these packages will end up using more disk space than if you were to just compile the source code into your final executable. Why is this so? If you create a packaged application resulting in a code reduction from 200KB to roughly 30KB, it might seem like you've saved quite a bit of space. However, you still have to distribute your packages and possibly even the Vcl60.dcp package, which is roughly 2MB in size. You can see that this isn't quite the saving you had hoped for. Our point is that you should use packages to share code when that code will be used by multiple executables. Note that this only applies to runtime packages. If you are a component writer, you must provide a design package that contains the component you want to make available to the Delphi IDE.

Types of Packages

Four types of packages are available for you to create and use:

- Runtime package—Runtime packages contain code, components, and so on needed by an application at runtime. If you write an application that depends on a particular runtime package, the application won't run in the absence of that package.

- Design package—Design packages contain components, property/component editors, experts, and so on necessary for application design in the Delphi IDE. This type of package is used only by Delphi and is never distributed with your applications.

- Runtime and design package—A package that is both design- and runtime-enabled is typically used when there are no design-specific elements such as property/component editors and experts. You can create this type of package to simplify application development and deployment. However, if this package does contain design elements, its runtime use will carry the extra baggage of the design support in your deployed applications. In the event of many design time elements, we recommend creating both a design and runtime package to separate design-specific elements when they are present.

- Neither runtime nor design package—This rare breed of package is intended to be used only by other packages and isn't intended to be referenced directly by an application or used in the design environment. This implies that packages can use or include other packages.

Package Files

Table 14.1 lists and describes the types of package-specific files based on their file extensions.

TABLE 14.1 Package Files

File Extension	File Type	Description
.dpk	Package source file	This file is created when you invoke the Package Editor. You can think of this as you might think of the .dpr file for a Delphi project.
.dcp	Runtime/Design package symbol file	This is the compiled version of the package that contains the symbol information for the package and its units. Additionally, there is header information required by the Delphi IDE.
.dcu	Compiled unit	A compiled version of a unit contained in a package. One .dcu file will be created for each unit contained in the package.

TABLE 14.1 Continued

File Extension	File Type	Description
`.bpl`	Runtime/Design	This is the runtime or design package library package, equivalent to a Windows DLL. If this is a runtime package, you will distribute the file along with your applications (if they are enabled for runtime packages). If this file represents a design package, you will distribute it along with its runtime partner to programmers that will use it to write programs. Note that if you aren't distributing source code, you must distribute the corresponding `.dcp` files.

Using Runtime Packages

To use runtime packages in your Delphi applications, simply check the Build With Runtime Packages check box found in the Project, Options dialog on the Packages page. The next time you build your application after this option is selected, your application will be linked dynamically to runtime packages instead of having units linked statically into your `.exe` or `.dll`. The result will be a much more svelte application (although bear in mind that you will have to deploy the necessary packages with your application).

Installing Packages into the Delphi IDE

It's sometimes necessary to install a package into the Delphi IDE. This would be the case if you were to acquire a third-party component set or Delphi add-in that didn't do this during the install.

This being the case, you must first place the package files in their appropriate location. Table 14.2 shows where package files are typically located.

TABLE 14.2 Package File Locations

Package File	Location
Runtime packages (*.bpl)	Runtime package files should be placed in the `\Windows\System\` directory (Windows 95/98) or `\WinNT\System32\` directory (Windows NT/2000).
Design packages (*.bpl)	Because it is possible that you will obtain several packages from various vendors, design packages should be placed in a common directory where they can be properly managed. For example, create a `\PKG` directory off your `\Delphi 6\` directory and place design packages in that location.

TABLE 14.2   Continued

Package File	Location
Package symbol files (*.dcp)	You can place package symbol files in the same location as design package files (*.bpl).
Compiled units (*.dcu)	You must distribute compiled units if you are distributing design packages without source. We recommend keeping DCUs from third-party vendors in a directory similar to the \Delphi 6\Lib directory. For example, you can create the directory \Delphi 6\3PrtyLib in which third-party components' *.dcus will reside. Your search path will have to include this directory.

To install a package, you simply invoke the Packages page of the Project Options dialog box by selecting Component, Install Packages from the Delphi 6 menu.

By clicking the Add button, you can select the specific .bpl file. Upon doing so, this file will become the selected file on the Project page. When you click OK, the new package is installed into the Delphi IDE. If this package contains components, you will see the new component page on the Component Palette along with any newly installed components.

Creating Packages

Before creating a package, you'll need to decide on a few things. First, you need to know what type of package you're going to create (runtime, design, and so on). This will be based on one or more of the scenarios that we present momentarily. Second, you need to know what you intend on naming your newly created package and where you want to store the package project. Keep in mind that the directory where your deployed package exists will probably not be the same as where you create your package. Finally, you need to know which units your package will contain and which other packages your new package will require.

The Package Editor

Packages are most commonly created using the Package Editor, which you invoke by selecting the Packages icon from the Object Repository. (Select File, New, Other from the Delphi main menu.) You'll notice that the Package Editor contains two folders: Contains and Requires.

The Contains Folder

In the Contains folder, you specify units that need to be compiled into your new package. There are a few rules for placing units into the Contains page of a package:

- The unit must not be listed in the contains clause of another package or uses clause of a unit within another package, which will be loaded concurrently with the package the unit is to be contained in.

- The units listed in the contains clause of a package, either directly or indirectly (they exist in uses clauses of units listed in the package's contains clause), cannot be listed in the package's requires clause. This is because these units are already bound to the package when it is compiled.

- You cannot list a unit in a package's contains clause if it is already listed in the con-tains clause of another package used by the sameapplication.

The Requires Folder

In the Requires folder, you specify other packages that are required by the new package. This is similar to the uses clause of a Delphi unit. In most cases, any packages you create will have VCL60—the package that hosts Delphi's standard VCL components—in its requires clause. The typical arrangement here, for example, is that you place all your components into a runtime package. Then you create a design package that includes the runtime package in its requires clause. There are a few rules for placing packages on the Requires folder of another package:

- Avoid circular references—Package1 cannot have Package1 in its requires clause, nor can it contain another package that has Package1 in its requires clause.

- The chain of references must not refer back to a package previously referenced in the chain.

The Package Editor has a toolbar and context-sensitive menus. Refer to the Delphi 6 online help under "Package Editor" for an explanation of what these buttons do. We won't repeat that information here.

Package Design Scenarios

Earlier we said that you must know what type of package you want to create based on a partic-ular scenario. In this section, we're going to present four possible scenarios in which you would use design and/or runtime packages.

Scenario 1—Design and Runtime Packages for Components

The Design and Runtime Packages for Components scenario is the case in which you are a component writer and one or both of the following conditions apply:

- You want Delphi programmers to be able to compile/link your components right into their applications or to distribute them separately along with their applications.

- You have a component package, and you don't want to force your users to have to com-pile design features (component/property editors and so on) into their application code.

Given this scenario, you would create both a design and runtime package. Figure 14.1 depicts this arrangement. As the figure illustrates, the design package (ddgDT60.dpk) encompasses both the design features (property and component editors) and the runtime package (ddgRT60.dpk). The runtime package (ddgRT60.dpk) includes only your components. This arrangement is accomplished by listing the runtime package into the requires section of the design package, as shown in Figure 14.1.

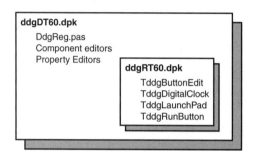

FIGURE 14.1

Design packages hosts design elements and runtime packages.

You must also apply the appropriate usage options for each package before compiling that package. You do this from the Package Options dialog box. (You access the Package Options dialog box by right-clicking within the Package Editor to invoke the local menu. Select Options to get to the dialog box.) For the runtime package, DdgRT60.dpk, the usage option should be set to Runtime Only. This ensures that the package cannot be installed into the IDE as a design package (see the sidebar "Component Security" later in this chapter). For the design package, DdgDT60.dpk, the usage option Design Time Only should be selected. This enables users to install the package into the Delphi IDE, yet prevents them from using the package as a runtime package.

Adding the runtime package to the design package doesn't make the components contained in the runtime package available to the Delphi IDE yet. You must still register your components with the IDE. As you already know, whenever you create a component, Delphi automatically inserts a Register() procedure into the component unit, which in turn calls the RegisterComponents() procedure. RegisterComponents() is the procedure that actually registers your component with the Delphi IDE when you install the component. When working with packages, the recommended approach is to move the Register() procedure from the component unit into a separate registration unit. This registration unit registers all your components by calling RegisterComponents(). This not only makes it easier for you to manage the registration of your components, but it also prevents anyone from being able to install and use your runtime package illegally because the components won't be available to the Delphi IDE.

As an example, the components used in this book are hosted by the runtime package
DdgRT60.dpk. The property editors, component editors, and registration unit (DdgReg.pas)
for our components exist in the design package DdgDT60.dpk. DdgDT60.dpk also includes
DdgRT60.dpk in its requires clause. Listing 14.1 shows what our registration unit looks like.

LISTING 14.1   Registration Unit for Delphi 6 Developer's Guide Components

```
unit DDGReg;

interface

procedure Register;

implementation

uses Classes, ExptIntf, DsgnIntf, TrayIcon, AppBars, ABExpt, Worthless,
  RunBtn, PwDlg, Planets, LbTab, HalfMin, DDGClock, ExMemo, MemView,
  Marquee, PlanetPE, RunBtnPE, CompEdit, DefProp, Wavez,
  WavezEd, LnchPad, LPadPE, Cards, ButtonEdit, Planet, DrwPnel;

procedure Register;
begin

  // Register the components.
  RegisterComponents('DDG',
  [ TddgTrayNotifyIcon, TddgDigitalClock, TddgHalfMinute, tddgButtonEdit,
    TddgExtendedMemo, TddgTabListbox, TddgRunButton, TddgLaunchPad,
    TddgMemView, TddgMarquee, TddgWaveFile, TddgCard, TddgPasswordDialog,
    TddgPlanet, TddgPlanets, TddgWorthLess, TddgDrawPanel,
    TComponentEditorSample, TDefinePropTest]);


  // Register any property editors.
  RegisterPropertyEditor(TypeInfo(TRunButtons), TddgLaunchPad, '',
    TRunButtonsProperty);
  RegisterPropertyEditor(TypeInfo(TWaveFileString), TddgWaveFile, 'WaveName',
    TWaveFileStringProperty);
  RegisterComponentEditor(TddgWaveFile, TWaveEditor);
  RegisterComponentEditor(TComponentEditorSample, TSampleEditor);
  RegisterPropertyEditor(TypeInfo(TPlanetName), TddgPlanet,
   'PlanetName', TPlanetNameProperty);
  RegisterPropertyEditor(TypeInfo(TCommandLine), TddgRunButton, '',
    TCommandLineProperty);
```

Listing 14.1 Continued

```
// Register any custom modules, library experts.
RegisterCustomModule(TAppBar, TCustomModule);
RegisterLibraryExpert(TAppBarExpert.Create);

end;

end.
```

Component Security

It is possible for someone to register your components, even though he has only your runtime package. He would do this by creating his own registration unit in which he would register your components. He would then add this unit to a separate package that would also have your runtime package in the `requires` clause. After he installs this new package into the Delphi IDE, your components will appear on the Component Palette. However, it is still not possible to compile any applications using your components because the required `*.dcu` files for your component units will be missing.

Package Distribution

When distributing your packages to component writers without the source code, you must distribute both compiled packages, DdgDT6.bpl and DdgRT6.bpl, both *.dcp files, and any compiled units (*.dcu) necessary to compile your components. Programmers using your components who want their applications' runtime packages enabled must distribute the DdgRT6.bpl package along with their applications and any other runtime package that they might be using.

Scenario 2—Design Package Only for Components

The Design Package Only for Components scenario is the case in which you want to distribute components that you don't want to be distributed in runtime packages. In this case, you will include the components, component editors, property editors, component registration unit, and so on in one package file.

Package Distribution

When distributing your package to component writers without the source code, you must distribute the compiled package, DdgDT6.bpl, the DdgDT6.dcp file, and any compiled units (*.dcu) necessary to compile your components. Programmers using your components must compile your components into their applications. They will not be distributing any of your components as runtime packages.

Scenario 3—Design Features Only (No Components)
IDE Enhancements

The Design Features Only (No Components) IDE Enhancements scenario is the case in which you are providing enhancements to the Delphi IDE, such as experts. For this scenario, you will register your expert with the IDE in your registration unit. The distribution for this scenario is simple; you only have to distribute the compiled `*.bpl` file.

Scenario 4—Application Partitioning

The Application Partitioning scenario is the case in which you want to partition your application into logical pieces, each of which can be distributed separately. You might want to do this for several reasons:

- This scenario is easier to maintain.

- Users can purchase only the needed functionality when they need it. Later, when they need added functionality, they can download the necessary package only, which will be much smaller than downloading the entire application.

- You can provide fixes (patches) to parts of the application more easily without requiring users to obtain a new version of the application altogether.

In this scenario, you will provide only the `*.bpl` files required by your application. This scenario is similar to the last with the difference being that instead of providing a package for the Delphi IDE, you will be providing a package for your own application. When partitioning your applications as such, you must pay attention to the issues regarding package versioning that we discuss in the next section.

Package Versioning

Package versioning is a topic that isn't well understood. You can think of package versioning in much the same way as you think of unit versioning. That is, any package you provide for your application must be compiled using the same Delphi version used to compile the application. Therefore, you cannot provide a package written in Delphi 6 to be used by an application written in Delphi 5. The Borland developers refer to the version of a package as a *code base*. So a package written in Delphi 6 has a code base of 6.0. This concept should influence the naming convention that you use for your package files.

Package Compiler Directives

There are some specific compiler directives that you can insert into the source code of your packages. Some of these directives are specific to units that are being packaged; others are specific to the package file. These directives are listed and described in Tables 14.3 and 14.4.

TABLE 14.3   Compiler Directives for Units Being Packaged

Directive	Meaning
{$G} or {IMPORTEDDATA OFF}	Use this when you want to prevent the unit from being packaged—when you want it to be linked directly to the application. Contrast this to the {$WEAKPACKAGEUNIT} directive, which allows a unit to be included in a package but whose code gets statically linked to the application.
{$DENYPACKAGEUNIT}	Same as {$G}.
{$WEAKPACKAGEUNIT}	See the section "More on {$WEAKPACKAGEUNIT}."

TABLE 14.4   Compiler Directives for the Package .dpk File

Directive	Meaning
{$DESIGNONLY ON}	Compiles the package as a design-time only package.
{$RUNONLY ON}	Compiles the package as a runtime only package.
{$IMPLICITBUILD OFF}	Prevents the package from being rebuilt later. Use this option when the package isn't changed frequently.

More on {$WEAKPACKAGEUNIT}

The concept of a weak package is simple. Basically, it is used where your package might be referencing libraries (DLLs) that might not be present. For example, the package Vcl60 makes calls to the core Win32 API included with the Windows operating system. Many of these calls exist in DLLs that aren't present on every machine. These calls are exposed by units that contain the {$WEAKPACKAGEUNIT} directive. By including this directive, you keep the unit's source code in the package but place it into the DCP file rather than in the BPL file (think of a DCP as a DCU and a BPL as a DLL). Therefore, any references to functions of these weakly packaged units get statically linked to the application rather than dynamically referenced through the package.

The {$WEAKPACKAGEUNIT} directive is one that you will rarely use, if at all. It was created out of necessity by the Delphi developers to handle a specific situation. The problem exists if there are two components, each in a separate package and referencing the same interface unit of a DLL. When an application uses both of the components, this causes two instances of the DLL to be loaded, which raises havoc with initialization and global variable referencing. The solution was to provide the interface unit into one of the standard Delphi packages such as Vcl60.bpl. However, this raises the other problem for specialized DLLs that may not be present such as PENWIN.DLL. If Vcl60.bpl contains the interface unit for a DLL that isn't present, it will render

`Vcl60.bpl`, and Delphi for that matter, unusable. The Delphi developers addressed this by allowing `Vcl60.bpl` to contain the interface unit in a single package, but to make it statically linked when used and not dynamically loaded whenever `Vcl60` is used with the Delphi IDE.

You'll most likely never have to use this directive, unless you anticipate a similar scenario that the Delphi developers faced or if you want to make certain that a particular unit is included with a package but statically linked to the using application. A reason for the latter might be for optimization purposes. Note that any units that are weakly packaged cannot have global variables or code in their initialization/finalization sections. You must also distribute any `*.dcu` files for weakly packaged units along with your packages.

Package Naming Conventions

Earlier we said that the package versioning issue should influence how you name your packages. There isn't a set rule for how to name your packages, but we suggest using a naming convention that incorporates the code base into the package's name. For example, the components for this book are contained in a runtime package whose name contains the 6 qualifier for Delphi 6 (`DdgRT6.dpk`). The same goes for the design package (`DdgDT6.dpk`). A previous version of the package would be `DdgRT5.dpk`. By using such a convention, you will prevent any confusion for your package users as to which version of the package they have and as to which version of the Delphi compiler applies to them. Note that our package name starts with a 3-character author/company identifier, followed by `RT` to indicate a runtime package and `DT` to signify a design time package. You can follow whatever naming convention you like. Just be consistent and use the recommended inclusion of the Delphi version into your package name.

Extensible Applications Using Runtime (Add-In) Packages

Add-in packages allow you to partition your applications into modules and to distribute those modules separately from the main application. This is useful because it allows you to extend the functionality of your application without having to recompile/redesign the entire application. This, however, requires careful architectural design planning. Although it is beyond the scope of this book to go into such design issues, our discussion will illustrate how to take advantage of this powerful capability.

Generating Add-In Forms

The application is partitioned into three logical pieces: the main application (`ChildTest.exe`), the `TChildForm` package (`AIChildFrm6.bpl`), and the concrete `TChildForm` descendant classes, each residing in its own package.

The package `AIChildFrm6.bpl` contains the base `TChildForm` class. The other packages contain descendant `TChildForm` classes or *concrete* `TChildForms`. We will refer to these packages as the base package and concrete packages, respectively.

The main application uses the abstract package (`AIChildFrm6.bpl`). Each concrete package also uses the abstract package. In order for this to work properly the main application must be compiled with runtime packages including the `AIChildFrm6.dcp` package. Likewise, each concrete package must require the `AIChildFrm6.dcp` package. We will not list the `TChildForm` source nor the concrete descendants to each `TChildForm` descendant unit, which must include `initialization` and `finalization` blocks that look like this:

```
initialization
  RegisterClass(TCF2Form);
finalization
  UnRegisterClass(TCF2Form);
```

The call to `RegisterClass()` is necessary to make the `TChildForm` descendant class available to the main application's streaming system when the main application loads its package. This is similar to how `RegisterComponents()` makes available components to the Delphi IDE. When the package is unloaded, the call to `UnRegisterClass()` is required to remove the registered class. Note, however, that `RegisterClass()` only makes the class available to the main application. The main application still doesn't know of the classname. So how does the main application create an instance of a class whose classname is unknown? Isn't the intent of this exercise to make these forms available to the main application without having to hard-code their classnames into the main applications source? Listing 14.2 shows the source code to the main application's main form where we will highlight how we accomplish add-in forms with add-in packages.

LISTING 14.2   Main Form to the Main Application Using Add-In Packages

```
unit MainFrm;

interface

uses
  Windows, Messages, SysUtils, Classes, Graphics, Controls, Forms, Dialogs,
  StdCtrls, ExtCtrls, ChildFrm, Menus;

const
  { Child form registration location in the Windows Registry. }
  cAddInIniFile  = 'AddIn.ini';
  cCFRegSection  = 'ChildForms';  // Module initialization data section

  FMainCaption   = 'Delphi 6 Developer''s Guide Child Form Demo';
```

LISTING 14.2 Continued

```
type

  TChildFormClass = class of TChildForm;

  TMainForm = class(TForm)
    pnlMain: TPanel;
    Splitter1: TSplitter;
    pnlParent: TPanel;
    mmMain: TMainMenu;
    mmiFile: TMenuItem;
    mmiExit: TMenuItem;
    mmiHelp: TMenuItem;
    mmiForms: TMenuItem;
    procedure mmiExitClick(Sender: TObject);
    procedure FormCreate(Sender: TObject);
    procedure FormDestroy(Sender: TObject);
  private
    // reference to the child form.
    FChildForm: TChildForm;
    // a list of available child forms used to build a menu.
    FChildFormList: TStringList;
    // Index to the Close Form menu which shifts position.
    FCloseFormIndex: Integer;
    // Handle to the currently loaded package.
    FCurrentModuleHandle: HModule;
    // method to create menus for available child forms.
    procedure CreateChildFormMenus;
    // Handler to load a child form and its package.
    procedure LoadChildFormOnClick(Sender: TObject);
    // Handler to unload a child form and its package.
    procedure CloseFormOnClick(Sender: TObject);
    // Method to retrieve the classname for a TChildForm descendant
    function GetChildFormClassName(const AModuleName: String): String;
  public
    { Public declarations }
  end;

var
  MainForm: TMainForm;

implementation
uses IniFiles;

{$R *.DFM}
```

LISTING 14.2   Continued

```
function RemoveExt(const AFileName: String): String;
{ Helper function to remove the extension from a file name. }
begin
  if Pos('.', AFileName) <> 0 then
    Result := Copy(AFileName, 1,  Pos('.', AFileName)-1)
  else
    Result := AFileName;
end;

procedure TMainForm.mmiExitClick(Sender: TObject);
begin
  Close;
end;

procedure TMainForm.FormCreate(Sender: TObject);
begin
  FChildFormList := TStringList.Create;
  CreateChildFormMenus;
end;

procedure TMainForm.FormDestroy(Sender: TObject);
begin
  FChildFormList.Free;
  // Unload any loaded child forms.
  if FCurrentModuleHandle <> 0 then
    CloseFormOnClick(nil);
end;

procedure TMainForm.CreateChildFormMenus;
{ All available child forms are registered in the Windows Registry.
  Here, we use this information to create menu items for loading each of the
  child forms. }
var
  IniFile: TIniFile;
  MenuItem: TMenuItem;
  i:  integer;
begin
  inherited;

  { Retrieve a list of all child forms and build a menu based on the
    entries in the registry. }
  IniFile :=
TIniFile.Create(ExtractFilePath(Application.ExeName)+cAddInIniFile);
  try
```

LISTING 14.2   Continued

```
      IniFile.ReadSectionValues(cCFRegSection, FChildFormList);
    finally
      IniFile.Free;
    end;

    { Add Menu items for each module. Note the mmMain.AutoHotKeys property must
      bet set to maAutomatic }

    for i := 0 to FChildFormList.Count - 1 do
    begin
      MenuItem := TMenuItem.Create(mmMain);
      MenuItem.Caption := FChildFormList.Names[i];
      MenuItem.OnClick := LoadChildFormOnClick;
      mmiForms.Add(MenuItem);
    end;

    // Create Separator
    MenuItem := TMenuItem.Create(mmMain);
    MenuItem.Caption := '-';
    mmiForms.Add(MenuItem);

    // Create Close Module menu item
    MenuItem := TMenuItem.Create(mmMain);
    MenuItem.Caption := '&Close Form';
    MenuItem.OnClick := CloseFormOnClick;
    MenuItem.Enabled := False;
    mmiForms.Add(MenuItem);

    { Save a reference to the index of the menu item required to
      close a child form. This will be referred to in another method. }
    FCloseFormIndex := MenuItem.MenuIndex;
  end;

procedure TMainForm.LoadChildFormOnClick(Sender: TObject);
var
  ChildFormClassName: String;
  ChildFormClass: TChildFormClass;
  ChildFormName: String;
  ChildFormPackage: String;
begin

  // The menu caption represents the module name.
  ChildFormName := (Sender as TMenuItem).Caption;
  // Get the actual Package file name.
  ChildFormPackage := FChildFormList.Values[ChildFormName];
```

14

LISTING 14.2   Continued

```
// Unload any previously loaded packages.
if FCurrentModuleHandle <> 0 then
  CloseFormOnClick(nil);

try
  // Load the specified package
  FCurrentModuleHandle := LoadPackage(ChildFormPackage);

  // Return the classname that needs to be created
  ChildFormClassName :=  GetChildFormClassName(ChildFormPackage);

  { Create an instance of the class using the FindClass() procedure. Note,
    this requires that the class already be registered with the streaming
    system using RegisterClass(). This is done in the child form
    initialization section for each child form package. }
  ChildFormClass := TChildFormClass(FindClass(ChildFormClassName));
  FChildForm := ChildFormClass.Create(self, pnlParent);
  Caption := FChildForm.GetCaption;

  { Merge child form menus with the main menu }
  if FChildForm.GetMainMenu <> nil then
    mmMain.Merge(FChildForm.GetMainMenu);

  FChildForm.Show;

  mmiForms[FCloseFormIndex].Enabled := True;
except
  on E: Exception do
  begin
    CloseFormOnClick(nil);
    raise;
  end;
end;
end;

function TMainForm.GetChildFormClassName(const AModuleName: String): String;
{ The Actual class name of the TChildForm implementation resides in the
  registry. This method retrieves that class name. }
var
  IniFile:  TIniFile;
begin
  IniFile :=
TIniFile.Create(ExtractFilePath(Application.ExeName)+cAddInIniFile);
  try
```

LISTING 14.2   Continued

```
    Result := IniFile.ReadString(RemoveExt(AModuleName), 'ClassName',
      EmptyStr);
  finally
    IniFile.Free;
  end;
end;

procedure TMainForm.CloseFormOnClick(Sender: TObject);
begin
  if FCurrentModuleHandle <> 0 then
  begin
    if FChildForm <> nil then
    begin
      FChildForm.Free;
      FChildForm := nil;
    end;

    // Unregister any classes provided by the module
    UnRegisterModuleClasses(FCurrentModuleHandle);
    // Unload the child form package
    UnloadPackage(FCurrentModuleHandle);

    FCurrentModuleHandle := 0;
    mmiForms[FCloseFormIndex].Enabled := False;
    Caption := FMainCaption;
  end;
end;

end.
```

The application's logic is actually very simple. It uses the system registry to determine which packages are available, the menu captions to use when building menus for loading each package, and the classname of the form contained in each package.

The `LoadChildFormOnClick()` event handler is where most of the work is performed. After determining the package filename, the method loads the package using the `LoadPackage()` function. The `LoadPackage()` function is basically the same thing as `LoadLibrary()` for DLLs. The method then determines the classname for the form contained in the loaded package.

In order to create a class, you require a class reference like `TButton` or `TForm1`. However, this main application doesn't have the hard-coded classname of the concrete `TChildForms`, so this is why we retrieve the classname from the system registry. The main application can pass this classname to the `FindClass()` function to return a class reference for the specified class that has already been registered with the streaming system. Remember, we did this in the initialization section of the concrete form's unit that is called when the package is loaded. We then create the class with the lines:

```
ChildFormClass := TChildFormClass(FindClass(ChildFormClassName));
FChildForm := ChildFormClass.Create(self, pnlParent);
```

> **NOTE**
>
> A class reference is simply an area in memory that contains information about a class. This is the same as a type-definition for a class. It gets into memory when the class is registered with the VCL streaming system; when the `RegisterClass()` function is called. The `FindClass()` function locates the area of memory for a class of a specified name and returns a pointer to that location. This isn't the same as a class instance. Class instances are usually created when the constructor, a class function (see Chapter 2, "The Object Pascal Language"), is called.

The variable `ChildFormClass` is a pre-declared class reference to `TChildForm` and can polymorphically refer to a class reference for a `TChildForm` descendant.

The `CloseFormOnClick()` event handler simply closes the child form and unloads its package. The rest of the code is basically set up code to create the package menus and to read the information from the INI file.

Using this technique, you can create very extensible and loosely coupled application frameworks.

Exporting Functions from Packages

Given that packages are simply enhanced DLLs, it seems that you should be able to export functions and procedures from packages just as you can from DLLs. Well, you can. In this section, we'll show you how to use packages in the same way.

Launching a Form from a Package Function

Listing 14.3 is a unit contained inside of a package.

LISTING 14.3   Package Unit with Two Exported Functions

```
unit FunkFrm;

interface
```

LISTING 14.3   Continued

```
uses
  Windows, Messages, SysUtils, Variants, Classes, Graphics, Controls, Forms,
  Dialogs, StdCtrls;

type

  TFunkForm = class(TForm)
    Label1: TLabel;
    Button1: TButton;
  private
    { Private declarations }
  public
    { Public declarations }
  end;

// Declare the package functions using the StdCall calling convention
procedure FunkForm; stdcall;
function AddEm(Op1, Op2: Integer): Integer; stdcall;

// Export the functions.
exports
  FunkForm,
  AddEm;

implementation

{$R *.dfm}

procedure FunkForm;
var
  FunkForm: TFunkForm;
begin
  FunkForm := TFunkForm.Create(Application);
  try
    FunkForm.ShowModal;
  finally
    FunkForm.Free;
  end;
end;

function AddEm(Op1, Op2: Integer): Integer;
begin
  Result := Op1+Op2;
end;

end.
```

14

PACKAGES
TO THE MAX

The procedure `FunkForm()` simply displays the form declared in the unit as a modal form; nothing clever here. `AdEm()` is a function that takes two operands and returns their sum. Notice that the functions are declared in the interface section of this unit using the `StdCall` calling convention.

Listing 14.4 is an application that demonstrates how to invoke a function from a package.

LISTING 14.4 Demo Application

```
unit MainFrm;

interface

uses
  Windows, Messages, SysUtils, Variants, Classes, Graphics, Controls, Forms,
  Dialogs, StdCtrls, Mask;

const
  cFunkForm = 'FunkForm';
  cAddEm    = 'AddEm';

type
  TForm1 = class(TForm)
    btnPkgForm: TButton;
    meOp1: TMaskEdit;
    meOp2: TMaskEdit;
    btnAdd: TButton;
    lblPlus: TLabel;
    lblEquals: TLabel;
    lblResult: TLabel;
    procedure btnAddClick(Sender: TObject);
    procedure btnPkgFormClick(Sender: TObject);
  private
    { Private declarations }
  public
    { Public declarations }
  end;

  // Defined the method signatures
  TAddEmProc = function(Op1, Op2: Integer): integer; stdcall;
  TFunkFormProc = procedure; stdcall;

var
  Form1: TForm1;

implementation
```

LISTING 14.4 Continued

```
{$R *.dfm}

procedure TForm1.btnAddClick(Sender: TObject);
var
  PackageModule: THandle;
  AddEmProc: TAddEmProc;
  Rslt: Integer;
  Op1, Op2: integer;
begin
  PackageModule := LoadPackage('ddgPackFunk.bpl');
  try

    @AddEmProc := GetProcAddress(PackageModule, PChar(cAddEm));
    if not (@AddEmProc = nil) then
    begin
      Op1 := StrToInt(meOp1.Text);
      Op2 := StrToInt(meOp2.Text);

      Rslt := AddEmProc(Op1, Op2);
      lblResult.Caption := IntToStr(Rslt);
    end;

  finally
    UnloadPackage(PackageModule);
  end;
end;

procedure TForm1.btnPkgFormClick(Sender: TObject);
var
  PackageModule: THandle;
  FunkFormProc: TFunkFormProc;
begin
  PackageModule := LoadPackage('ddgPackFunk.bpl');
  try
    @FunkFormProc := GetProcAddress(PackageModule, PChar(cFunkForm));
    if not (@FunkFormProc = nil) then
      FunkFormProc;
  finally
    UnloadPackage(PackageModule);
  end;
end;

end.
```

First notice that we had to declare the two procedural types, `TAddEmProc` and `TFunkFormProc`. These are declared exactly as they exist in the package.

We'll discuss the `btnPkgFormClick()` event handler first. This code should look familiar from Chapter 6, "Dynamic Link Libraries." Instead of making a `LoadLibrary()` call, we're using `LoadPackage()`. In fact, `LoadPackage()` ends up calling `LoadLibrary()`. Next, we retrieve the reference to the procedure using the `GetProcAddress()` function. You can refer back to Chapter 6 if you need to know more about this function. The `cFunkForm` constant is the same name as the function name in the package.

You can see that the method of exporting functions and procedures from packages is almost exactly the same as exporting from dynamic link libraries.

Obtaining Information About a Package

It is possible to query a package for information about which units it contains and which packages it requires. Two functions are used to do this: `EnumModules()` and `GetPackageInfo()`. Both of these functions require callback functions. Listing 14.5 illustrates the use of these functions. You'll find this demo on the CD.

LISTING 14.5   Package Information Demo

```
unit MainFrm;

interface

uses
  Windows, Messages, SysUtils, Variants, Classes, Graphics, Controls, Forms,
  Dialogs, StdCtrls, ComCtrls, DBXpress, DB, SqlExpr, DBTables;

type
  TForm1 = class(TForm)
    Button1: TButton;
    TreeView1: TTreeView;
    Table1: TTable;
    SQLConnection1: TSQLConnection;
    procedure Button1Click(Sender: TObject);
  private
    { Private declarations }
  public
    { Public declarations }
  end;

var
  Form1: TForm1;
```

Listing 14.5   Continued

```pascal
implementation

{$R *.dfm}

type
  TNodeHolder = class
    ContainsNode: TTreeNode;
    RequiresNode: TTreeNode;
  end;

procedure RealizeLength(var S: string);
begin
  SetLength(S, StrLen(PChar(S)));
end;

procedure PackageInfoProc(const Name: string; NameType:
  TNameType; Flags: Byte; Param: Pointer);
var
  NodeHolder: TNodeHolder;
  TempStr: String;
begin
  with Form1.TreeView1.Items do
  begin

    TempStr := EmptyStr;

    if (Flags and ufMainUnit) <> 0 then
      TempStr := 'Main unit'
    else if (Flags and ufPackageUnit) <> 0 then
      TempStr := 'Package unit' else
    if (Flags and ufWeakUnit) <> 0 then
      TempStr := 'Weak unit';

    if TempStr <> EmptyStr then
      TempStr := Format(' (%s)', [TempStr]);

    NodeHolder := TNodeHolder(Param);
    case NameType of
      ntContainsUnit: AddChild(NodeHolder.ContainsNode,
        Format('%s %s', [Name,TempStr]));
      ntRequiresPackage: AddChild(NodeHolder.RequiresNode, Name);
    end; // case
  end;
end;
```

LISTING 14.5   Continued

```
function EnumModuleProc(HInstance: integer; Data: Pointer): Boolean;
var
  ModFileName: String;
  ModNode: TTreeNode;
  ContainsNode: TTreeNode;
  RequiresNode: TTreeNode;
  ModDesc: String;
  Flags: Integer;
  NodeHolder: TNodeHolder;

begin
  with Form1.TreeView1 do
  begin
    SetLength(ModFileName, 255);
    GetModuleFileName(HInstance, PChar(ModFileName), 255);
    RealizeLength(ModFileName);
    ModNode := Items.Add(nil, ModFileName);

    ModDesc := GetPackageDescription(PChar(ModFileName));
    ContainsNode := Items.AddChild(ModNode, 'Contains');
    RequiresNode := Items.Addchild(ModNode, 'Requires');


    if ModDesc <> EmptyStr then
    begin

      NodeHolder := TNodeHolder.Create;
      try
        NodeHolder.ContainsNode := ContainsNode;
        NodeHolder.RequiresNode := RequiresNode;

        GetPackageInfo(HInstance, NodeHolder, Flags, PackageInfoProc);
      finally
        NodeHolder.Free;
      end;

      Items.AddChild(ModNode, ModDesc);

      if Flags and pfDesignOnly = pfDesignOnly then
        Items.AddChild(ModNode, 'Design-time package');
      if Flags and pfRunOnly = pfRunOnly then
        Items.AddChild (ModNode, 'Run-time package');

    end;
```

LISTING 14.5   Continued

```
  end;
  Result := True;
end;

procedure TForm1.Button1Click(Sender: TObject);
begin
  EnumModules(EnumModuleProc, nil);
end;

end.
```

EnumModules() is first called. It enumerates the executable and any packages in the executable. The callback function passed to EnumModules() is EnumModuleProc(). This function populates a TTreeview component with information about each package in the application. Much of the code is setup code for the TTreeView component. The function GetPackageDescription() returns the description string contained in the packages resource. The call to GetPackageInfo() passes the callback function PackageInfoProc().

In PackageInfoProc(), we are able to process the information in the package's information table. This function is called for every unit included in the package and for every package required by the package. Here, we again populate the TTreeview component with this information by examining the values of the Flags parameter and the NameType parameter. For additional information, both of these are explained in the online help under "TPackageInfoProc."

This code demonstration is a modification of a demo from Marco Cantu's excellent book *Mastering Delphi 5*, a must for every Delphi library.

Summary

Packages are a key part of the Delphi/VCL architecture. By learning how to use packages for more then just component containment, you can develop very elegantly designed and loosely bound architectures.

14

PACKAGES TO THE MAX

COM Development

IN THIS CHAPTER

Robust support for COM-based technologies is one of the marquee features of Delphi. This chapter covers COM and the various sundry technologies that rely on COM as their foundation. These technologies include (but definitely aren't limited to) COM servers and clients, ActiveX controls, *object linking and embedding (OLE)*, and Automation. However, all this new technology at your fingertips can be a bit perplexing, if not daunting. This chapter is designed to give you a complete overview of the technologies that make up COM, ActiveX, and OLE and help you leverage these technologies in your own applications. In earlier days, this topic referred primarily to OLE, which provides a method for sharing data among different applications, dealing primarily with linking or embedding data associated with one type of application to data associated with another application (such as embedding a spreadsheet into a word processor document). However, there's a lot more to COM than just OLE-based word processor tricks!

In this chapter, you'll first get a solid background in the basics of COM-based technologies in general and extensions to Object Pascal and VCL added to support COM. You'll learn how to apply this knowledge in order to control Automation servers from your Delphi applications and write Automation servers of your own. You'll also learn about more sophisticated COM topics, such as advanced Automation techniques and MTS. Finally, this chapter covers VCL's `TOleContainer` class, which encapsulates ActiveX containers. This chapter doesn't teach you everything there is to know about COM—that could take volumes—but it does cover all the important features of COM, particularly as they apply to Delphi.

COM Basics

First things first. Before we jump into the topic at hand, it's important that you understand the basic concepts and terminology associated with the technology. This section introduces you to basic ideas and terms behind the COM-based technologies.

COM: The Component Object Model

The *Component Object Model (COM)* forms the foundation upon which OLE and ActiveX technology is built. COM defines an API and a binary standard for communication between objects that's independent of any particular programming language or (in theory) platform. COM objects are similar to the VCL objects you're familiar with—except that they have only methods and properties associated with them, not data fields.

A COM object consists of one or more *interfaces* (described in the "Interfaces" section later in this chapter), which are essentially tables of functions associated with that object. You can call an interface's methods just like the methods of a Delphi object.

The component objects you use can be implemented from any EXE or DLL, although the implementation is transparent to you as a user of the object because of a service provided by

COM called *marshaling*. The COM marshaling mechanism handles all the intricacies of calling functions across process—and even machine—boundaries, which makes it possible to use a 32-bit object from a 16-bit application or access an object located on machine A from an application running on machine B. This intermachine communication is known as *Distributed COM (DCOM)* and is described in greater detail in the "Distributed COM" section later in this chapter.

COM Versus ActiveX Versus OLE

"So, what's the difference between COM, OLE, and ActiveX, anyway?" That's one of the most common (and reasonable) questions developers ask as they get into this technology. It's a reasonable question because it seems that the purveyor of this technology, Microsoft, does little to clarify the matter. You've already learned that COM is the API and binary standard that forms the building blocks of the other technologies. In the old days (like 1995), *OLE* was the blanket term used to describe the entire suite of technologies built on the COM architecture. These days, OLE refers only to those technologies associated specifically with linking and embedding, such as containers, servers, in-place activation, drag-and-drop, and menu merging. In 1996, Microsoft embarked on an aggressive marketing campaign in an attempt to create brand recognition for the term *ActiveX*, which became the blanket term used to describe non-OLE technologies built on top of COM. ActiveX technologies include Automation (formerly called *OLE Automation*) controls, documents, containers, scripting, and several Internet technologies. Because of the confusion created by using the term *ActiveX* to describe everything short of the family pet, Microsoft has backed off a bit and now sometimes refers to non-OLE COM technologies simply as *COM-based* technologies.

Those with a more cynical view of the industry might say that the term *OLE* became associated with adjectives such as *slow* and *bloated*, and marketing-savvy Microsoft needed a new term for those APIs on which it planned to base its future operating system and Internet technologies. Also amusing is the fact that Microsoft now claims OLE no longer stands for *object linking and embedding*—it's just a word that's pronounced *Oh-lay*.

Terminology

COM technologies bring with them a great deal of new terminology, so some terms are presented here before going any deeper into the guts of ActiveX and OLE.

Although an instance of a COM object is usually referred to simply as an *object*, the type that identifies that object is usually referred to as a *component class* or *coclass*. Therefore, to create an instance of a COM *object*, you must pass the CLSID of the COM *class* you want to create.

The chunk of data that's shared between applications is referred to as an *OLE object*. Applications that have the capability to contain OLE objects are referred to as *OLE containers*.

Applications that have the capability to have their data contained within an OLE container are called *OLE servers*.

A document that contains one or more OLE objects is usually referred to as a *compound document*. Although OLE objects can be contained within a particular document, full-scale applications that can be hosted within the context of another document are known as *ActiveX documents*.

As the name implies, an OLE object can be *linked* or *embedded* into a compound document. Linked objects are stored in a file on disk. With object linking, multiple containers—or even the server application—can link to the same OLE object on disk. When one application modifies the linked object, the modification is reflected in all the other applications maintaining a link to that object. Embedded objects are stored by the OLE container application. Only the container application is able to edit the OLE object. Embedding prevents other applications from accessing (and therefore modifying or corrupting) your data, but it does put the burden of managing the data on the container.

Another facet of ActiveX that you'll learn more about in this chapter is *Automation*, which is a means by which you can allow applications (called *Automation controllers*) to manipulate objects associated with other applications or libraries (called an *Automation server*). Automation enables you to manipulate objects in another application and, conversely, to expose elements of your application to other developers.

What's So Great About ActiveX?

The coolest thing about ActiveX is that it enables you to easily build the capability to manipulate many types of data into your applications. You might snicker at the word *easily*, but it's true. It is much easier, for example, to give your application the capability to contain ActiveX objects than it is to build word processing, spreadsheet, or graphics-manipulation capabilities into your application.

ActiveX fits very well with Delphi's tradition of maximum code reuse. You don't have to write code to manipulate a particular kind of data if you already have an OLE server application that does the job. As complicated as OLE can be, it often makes more sense than the alternatives.

It also is no secret that Microsoft has a large investment in ActiveX technology, and serious developers for Windows 95, NT, and other upcoming operating systems will have to become familiar with using ActiveX in their applications. So, like it or not, COM is here for a while, and it behooves you, as a developer, to become comfortable with it.

OLE 1 Versus OLE 2

One of the primary differences between OLE objects associated with 16-bit OLE version 1 servers and those associated with OLE version 2 servers is in how they activate themselves. When you activate an object created with an OLE 1 server, the server application starts up and receives focus, and then the OLE object appears in the server application, ready for editing. When you activate an OLE 2 object, the OLE 2 server application becomes active "inside" your container application. This is known as *in-place activation* or *visual editing*.

When an OLE 2 object is activated, the menus and toolbars of the server application replace or merge with those of the client application, and a portion of the client application's window essentially becomes the window of the server application. This process is demonstrated in the sample application in the "TOleContainer" section later in this chapter.

Structured Storage

OLE 2 defines a system for storing information on disk known as *structured storage*. This system basically does on a file level what DOS does on a disk level. A storage object is one physical file on a disk, but it equates with the DOS concept of a directory, and it's made up of multiple storages and streams. A *storage* equates to a subdirectory, and a *stream* equates to a DOS file. You'll often hear this implementation referred to as *compound files*.

Uniform Data Transfer

OLE 2 also has the concept of a *data object*, which is the basic object used to exchange data under the rules of uniform data transfer. *Uniform data transfer* (UDT) governs data transfers through the Clipboard, drag-and-drop, DDE, and OLE. Data objects allow for a greater degree of description about the kind of data they contain than previously was practical given the limitations of those transfer media. In fact, UDT is destined to replace DDE. A data object can be aware of its important properties, such as size, color, and even what device it's designed to be rendered on. Try doing that on the Windows Clipboard!

Threading Models

Every COM object operates in a particular threading model that dictates how an object can be manipulated in a multithreaded environment. When a COM server is registered, each of the COM objects contained in that server should register the threading model they support. For COM objects written in Delphi, the threading model chosen in the Automation, ActiveX control, or COM object wizards dictates how a control is registered. The COM threading models include the following:

- Single—The entire COM server runs on a single thread.

15

COM
DEVELOPMENT

- Apartment—Also known as *single-threaded apartment (STA)*. Each COM object executes within the context of its own thread, and multiple instances of the same type of COM object can execute within separate threads. Because of this, any data that's shared between object instances (such as global variables) must be protected by thread synchronization objects when appropriate.

- Free—Also known as *multithreaded apartment (MTA)*. A client can call a method of an object on any thread at any time. This means that the COM object must protect even its own instance data from simultaneous access by multiple threads.

- Both—Both the apartment and free threading models are supported.

Keep in mind that merely selecting the desired threading model in the wizard doesn't guarantee that your COM object will be safe for that threading model. You must write the code to ensure that your COM servers operate correctly for the threading model you want to support. This most often includes using thread synchronization objects to protect access to global or instance data in your COM objects. For more information on multithreaded development in Delphi, see Chapter 5, "Multithreaded Techniques."

COM+

As a part of the Windows 2000 release, Microsoft has provided the most significant update to COM in recent memory with the release of a new iteration called *COM+*. The goal of COM+ is the simplification of the COM development process through the integration of several satellite technologies, most notably MTS and Microsoft Message Queue (MSMQ). The integration of these technologies into the standard COM+ runtime means that all COM+ developers will be able to take advantage of features such as transaction control, security, administration, queued components, and publish and subscribe event services. Because COM+ consists mostly of off-the-shelf parts, this means complete backward compatibility, such that all existing COM and MTS applications automatically become COM+ applications. You can learn more about COM+ and MTS technologies in Chapter 18, "Transactional Development with COM+/MTS."

COM Meets Object Pascal

Now that you understand the basic concepts and terms behind COM, ActiveX, and OLE, it's time to discuss how the concepts are implemented in Delphi. This section goes into more detail on COM and gives you a look at how it fits into the Object Pascal language and VCL.

Interfaces

COM defines a standard map for how an object's functions are laid out in memory. Functions are arranged in virtual tables (called *vtables*)—tables of function addresses identical to Delphi class *virtual method tables (VMTs)*. The programming language description of each vtable is referred to as an *interface*.

Think of an interface as a facet of a particular class. Each facet represents a specific set of functions or procedures that you can use to manipulate the class. For example, a COM object that represents a bitmap image might support two interfaces: one containing methods that enable the bitmap to render itself to the screen or printer and another interface to manage storing and retrieving the bitmap to and from a file on disk.

An interface really has two parts: The first part is the interface definition, which consists of a collection of one or more function declarations in a specific order. The interface definition is shared between the object and the user of the object. The second part is the interface implementation, which is the actual implementation of the functions described in the interface declaration. The interface definition is like a contract between the COM object and a client of that object—a guarantee to the client that the object will implement specific methods in a specific order.

Introduced in Delphi 3, the `interface` keyword in Object Pascal enables you to easily define COM interfaces. An interface declaration is semantically similar to a class declaration, with a few exceptions. Interfaces can consist only of properties and methods—no data. Because interfaces cannot contain data, their properties must write and read to and from methods. Most important, interfaces have no implementation because they only define a contract.

IUnknown

Just as all Object Pascal classes implicitly descend from `TObject`, all COM interfaces (and therefore all Object Pascal interfaces) implicitly derive from `IUnknown`, which is defined in the `System` unit as follows:

```
type
  IUnknown = interface
    ['{00000000-0000-0000-C000-000000000046}']
    function QueryInterface(const IID: TGUID; out Obj): Integer; stdcall;
    function _AddRef: Integer; stdcall;
    function _Release: Integer; stdcall;
  end;
```

Aside from the use of the `interface` keyword, another obvious difference between an interface and class declaration that you'll notice from the preceding code is the presence of a globally unique identifier (GUID).

TIP

You can generate a new GUID in the Delphi IDE using the Ctrl+Shift+G keystroke in the Code Editor.

Globally Unique Identifiers (GUIDs)

A GUID (pronounced *goo-id*) is a 128-bit integer used in COM to uniquely identify an interface, coclass, or other entity. Because of their large size and the hairy algorithm used to generate these numbers, GUIDs are almost guaranteed to be globally unique (hence the name). GUIDs are generated using the CoCreateGUID() API function, and the algorithm employed by this function to generate new GUIDs combines information such as the current date and time, CPU clock sequence, network card number, and the balance of Bill Gates's bank accounts. (Okay, so we made up the last one.) If you have a network card installed on a particular machine, a GUID generated on that machine is guaranteed to be unique because every network card has an internal ID that's globally unique. If you don't have a network card, it will synthesize a close approximation using other hardware information.

Because there's no language type that holds something as large as 128 bits in size, GUIDs are represented by the TGUID record, which is defined as follows in the System unit:

```
type
  PGUID = ^TGUID;
  TGUID = record
    D1: LongWord;
    D2: Word;
    D3: Word;
    D4: array[0..7] of Byte;
  end;
```

Because it can be a pain to assign GUID values to variables and constants in this record format, Object Pascal also allows a TGUID to be represented as a string with the following format:

```
'{xxxxxxxx-xxxx-xxxx-xxxx-xxxxxxxxxxxx}'
```

Thanks to this, the following declarations are equivalent as far as the Delphi compiler is concerned:

```
MyGuid: TGUID = (
  D1:$12345678;D2:$1234;D3:$1234;D4:($01,$02,$03,$04,$05,$06,$07,$08));

MyGuid: TGUID = '{12345678-1234-1234-12345678}';
```

In COM, every interface or class has an accompanying GUID that uniquely defines that interface. In this way, two interfaces or classes having the same name defined by two different people will never conflict because their respective GUIDs will be different. When used to represent an interface, a GUID is normally referred to as an *interface ID (IID)*. When used to represent a class, a GUID is referred to as a *class ID (CLSID)*.

In addition to its IID, IUnknown declares three methods: QueryInterface(), _AddRef(), and _Release(). Because IUnknown is the base interface for COM, all interfaces must implement IUnknown and its methods. The _AddRef() method should be called when a client obtains and wants to use a pointer to a given interface, and a call to _AddRef() must have an accompanying call to _Release() when the client is finished using the interface. In this way, the object that implements the interfaces can maintain a count of clients that are keeping a reference to the object, or *reference count*. When the reference count reaches zero, the object should free itself from memory. The QueryInterface() function is used to query whether an object supports a given interface and, if so, to return a pointer to that interface. For example, suppose that object O supports two interfaces, I1 and I2, and you have a pointer to O's I1 interface. To obtain a pointer to O's I2 interface, you would call I1.QueryInterface().

> **NOTE**
>
> If you're an experienced COM developer, you might have noticed that the underscore in front of the _AddRef() and _Release() methods isn't consistent with other COM programming languages or even with Microsoft's COM documentation. Because Object Pascal is "IUnknown aware," you won't normally call these methods directly (more on this in a moment), so the underscores exist primarily to make you think before calling these methods.

Because every interface in Delphi implicitly descends from IUnknown, every Delphi class that implements interfaces must also implement the three IUnknown methods. You can do this yourself manually, or you can let VCL do the dirty work for you by descending your class from TInterfacedObject, which implements IUnknown for you.

Using Interfaces

Chapter 2, "The Object Pascal Language," and Delphi's own "Object Pascal Language Guide" documentation cover the semantics of using interface instances, so we won't rehash that material here. Instead, we'll discuss how IUnknown is seamlessly integrated into the rules of Object Pascal.

When an interface variable is assigned a value, the compiler automatically generates a call to the interface's _AddRef() method so that the reference count of the object is incremented. When an interface variable falls out of scope or is assigned the value nil, the compiler automatically generates a call to the interface's _Release() method. Consider the following piece of code:

```
var
  I: ISomeInteface;
```

```
begin
  I := FunctionThatReturnsAnInterface;
  I.SomeMethod;
end;
```

Now take a look at the following code snippet, which shows the code you would type (in bold) and an approximate Pascal version of the code the compiler generates (in normal font):

```
var
  I: ISomeInterface;
begin
  // interface is automatically initialized to nil
  I := nil;
  try
    // your code goes here
    I := FunctionThatReturnsAnInterface;
    // _AddRef() is called implicitly when I is assigned
    I._AddRef;
    I.SomeMethod;
  finally
    // implicit finally block ensures that the reference to the
    // interface is released
    if I <> nil I._Release;
  end;
end;
```

The Delphi compiler is also smart enough to know when to call _AddRef() and _Release() as interfaces are reassigned to other interface instances or assigned the value nil. For example, consider the following code block:

```
var
  I: ISomeInteface;
begin
  // assign I
  I := FunctionThatReturnsAnInterface;
  I.SomeMethod;
  // reassign I
  I := OtherFunctionThatReturnsAnInterface;
  I.OtherMethod;
  // set I to nil
  I := nil;
end;
```

Again, here's a composite of the user-written (bold) code and the approximate compiler-generated (normal) code:

```
var
  I: ISomeInterface;
begin
  // interface is automatically initialized to nil
  I := nil;
  try
    // your code goes here
    // assign I
    I := FunctionThatReturnsAnInterface;
    // _AddRef() is called implicitly when I is assigned
    I._AddRef;
    I.SomeMethod;
    // reassign I
    I._Release;
    I := OtherFunctionThatReturnsAnInterface;
    I._AddRef;
    I.OtherMethod;
    // set I to nil
    I._Release;
    I := nil;
  finally
    // implicit finally block ensures that the reference to the
    // interface is released
    if I <> nil I._Release;
  end;
end;
```

The preceding code example also helps to illustrate why Delphi prepends the underscore to the _AddRef() and _Release() methods. Forgetting to increment or decrement the reference of an interface was one of the classic COM programming bugs in the pre-interface days. Delphi's interface support is designed to alleviate these problems by handling the housekeeping details for you, so there's rarely ever a reason to call these methods directly.

Because the compiler knows how to generate calls to _AddRef() and _Release(), wouldn't it make sense if the compiler had some inherent knowledge of the third IUnknown method, QueryInterface()? It would, and it does. Given an interface pointer for an object, you can use the as operator to "typecast" the interface to another interface supported by the COM object. We say *typecast* because this application of the as operator isn't really a typecast in the strict sense but rather an internal call to the QueryInterface() method. The following sample code demonstrates this:

```
var
  I1: ISomeInterface;
  I2: ISomeOtherInterface;
begin
```

```
  // assign to I1
  I1 := FunctionThatReturnsAnInterface;
  // QueryInterface I1 for an I2 interface
  I2 := I1 as ISomeOtherInterface;
end;
```

In the preceding example, if the object referenced by I1 doesn't support the ISomeOtherInterface interface, an exception will be raised by the as operator.

One additional language rule pertaining to interfaces is that an interface variable is assignment compatible with an Object Pascal class that implements that interface. For example, consider the following interface and class declarations:

```
type
  IFoo = interface
    // definition of IFoo
  end;

  IBar = interface(IFoo)
    // definition of IBar
  end;

  TBarClass = class(TObject, IBar)
    // definition of TBarClass
  end;
```

Given the preceding declarations, the following code is correct:

```
var
  IB: IBar;
  TB: TBarClass;
begin
  TB := TBarClass.Create;
  try
    // obtain TB's IBar interface pointer:
    IB := TB;
    // use TB and IB
  finally
    IB := nil;  // explicitly release IB
    TB.Free;
  end;
end;
```

Although this feature seems to violate traditional Pascal assignment-compatibility rules, it does make interfaces feel more natural and easier to work with.

An important but nonobvious corollary to this rule is that interfaces are only assignment compatible with classes that explicitly support the interface. For example, the TBarClass class defined earlier declares explicit support for the IBar interface. Because IBar descends from

IFoo, conventional wisdom might indicate that TBarClass also directly supports IFoo. This isn't the case, however, as the following sample code illustrates:

```
var
  IF: IFoo;
  TB: TBarClass;
begin
  TB := TBarClass.Create;
  try
    // compiler error raised on the next line because TBarClass
    // doesn't explicitly support IFoo.
    IF := TB;
    // use TB and IF
  finally
    IF := nil;  // expicitly release IF
    TB.Free;
  end;
end;
```

Interfaces and IIDs

Because the interface ID is declared as a part of an interface declaration, the Object Pascal compiler knows how to obtain the IID from an interface. Therefore, you can pass an interface type to a procedure or function that requires a TIID or TGUID as a parameter. For example, suppose that you have a function like this:

```
procedure TakesIID(const IID: TIID);
```

The following code is syntactically correct:

```
TakesIID(IUnknown);
```

This capability obviates the need for IID_*InterfaceType* constants defined for each interface type that you might be familiar with if you've done COM development in C++.

Method Aliasing

A problem that occasionally arises when you implement multiple interfaces in a single class is that there can be a collision of method names in two or more interfaces. For example, consider the following interfaces:

```
type
  IIntf1 = interface
    procedure AProc;
  end;

  IIntf2 = interface
    procedure AProc;
  end;
```

15

COM
DEVELOPMENT

Given that each of the interfaces contains a method called AProc(), how can you declare a class that implements both interfaces? The answer is *method aliasing*. Method aliasing enables you to map a particular interface method to a method of a different name in a class. The following code example demonstrates how to declare a class that implements IIntf1 and IIntf2:

```
type
  TNewClass = class(TInterfacedObject, IIntf1, IIntf2)
  protected
    procedure IIntf2.AProc = AProc2;
    procedure AProc;    // binds to IIntf1.AProc
    procedure AProc2;   // binds to IIntf2.AProc
  end;
```

In this declaration, the AProc() method of IIntf2 is mapped to a method with the name AProc2(). Creating aliases in this way enables you to implement any interface on any class without fear of method name collisions.

The HResult Return Type

You might notice that the QueryInterface() method of IUnknown returns a result of type HResult. HResult is a very common return type for many ActiveX and OLE interface methods and COM API functions. HResult is defined in the System unit as a type LongWord. Possible HResult values are listed in the Windows unit. (If you have the VCL source code, you can find them under the heading { HRESULT value definitions }.) An HResult value of S_OK or NOERROR (0) indicates success, whereas if the high bit of the HResult value is set, it indicates failure or some type of error condition. Two functions in the Windows unit, Succeeded() and Failed(), take an HResult as a parameter and return a BOOL, indicating success or failure. Here's the syntax for calling these methods:

```
if Succeeded(FunctionThatReturnsHResult) then
  \\ continue as normal

if Failed(FunctionThatReturnsHResult) then
  \\ error condition code
```

Of course, checking the return value of every single function call can become tedious. Also, dealing with errors returned by functions undermines Delphi's exception-handling methods for error detection and recovery. For these reasons, the ComObj unit defines a procedure called OleCheck() that converts HResult errors to exceptions. The syntax for calling this method is

```
OleCheck(FunctionThatReturnsHResult);
```

This procedure can be quite handy, and it will clean up your ActiveX code considerably.

COM Objects and Class Factories

In addition to supporting one or more interfaces that descend from IUnknown and implementing reference counting for lifetime management, COM objects also have another special feature: They are created through special objects called *class factories*. Each COM class has an associated class factory that's responsible for creating instances of that COM class. Class factories are special COM objects that support the IClassFactory interface. This interface is defined in the ActiveX unit as follows:

```
type
  IClassFactory = interface(IUnknown)
    ['{00000001-0000-0000-C000-000000000046}']
    function CreateInstance(const unkOuter: IUnknown; const iid: TIID;
      out obj): HResult; stdcall;
    function LockServer(fLock: BOOL): HResult; stdcall;
  end;
```

The CreateInstance() method is called to create an instance of the class factory's associated COM object. The unkOuter parameter of this method references the controlling IUnknown if the object is being created as a part of an aggregate (aggregation is explained a bit later). The iid parameter contains the IID of the interface by which you want to manipulate the object. Upon return, the obj parameter will hold a pointer to the interface indicated by iid.

The LockServer() method is called to keep a COM server in memory, even though no clients might be referencing the server. The fLock parameter, when True, should increment the server's lock count. When False, fLock should decrement the server's lock count. When the server's lock count is 0 and no clients are referencing the server, COM will unload the server.

TComObject and TComObjectFactory

Delphi provides two classes that encapsulate COM objects and class factories: TComObject and TComObjectFactory, respectively. TComObject contains the necessary infrastructure for supporting IUnknown and creation via TComObjectFactory. Likewise, TComObjectFactory supports IClassFactory and has the capability to create TComObject objects. You can easily generate a COM object using the COM Object Wizard found on the ActiveX page of the New Items dialog box. Listing 15.1 shows pseudocode for the unit generated by this wizard, which illustrates the relationship between these classes. Note that the wizard's Include Type Library check box is unchecked; type libraries are discussed in the "Automation" section later in this chapter.

LISTING 15.1 COM Server Unit Pseudocode

```
unit ComDemo;

{$WARN SYMBOL_PLATFORM OFF}

interface

uses
  Windows, ActiveX, Classes, ComObj;
type
  TSomeComObject = class(TComObject, interfaces supported)
    class and interface methods declared here
  end;

const
  Class_SomeObject: TGUID = '{CB11BA07-735D-4937-885A-1CFB5312AEC8}';

implementation

uses ComServ;

TSomeComObject implementation here

initialization
  TComObjectFactory.Create(ComServer, TSomeObject, Class_SomeObject,
    'SomeObject', 'The SomeObject class', ciMultiInstance, tmApartment);end;
```

The TComServer descendant is declared and implemented like most VCL classes. What binds it to its corresponding TComObjectFactory object is the parameters passed to TComObjectFactory's constructor Create(). The first constructor parameter is a TComServer object. You almost always will pass the global ComServer object declared in the ComServ unit in this parameter. The second parameter is the TComObject class you want to bind to the class factory. The third parameter is the CLSID of the TComObject's COM class. The fourth and fifth parameters are the class name and description strings used to describe the COM class in the System Registry. The sixth parameter indicates the instancing of the COM object, and the final parameter indicates the threading model of the object.

The TTypedComObjectFactory instance is created in the initialization of the unit in order to ensure that the class factory will be available to create instances of the COM object as soon as the COM server is loaded. Exactly how the COM server is loaded depends on whether the COM server is an in-process server (a DLL) or an out-of-process server (an application).

In-Process COM Servers

In-process (or *in-proc*, for short) COM servers are DLLs that can create COM objects for use by the host application. This type of COM server is called *in-process* because, as a DLL, it resides in the same process as the calling application. An in-proc server must export four standard entry-point functions:

```
function DllRegisterServer: HResult; stdcall;
function DllUnregisterServer: HResult; stdcall;
function DllGetClassObject (const CLSID, IID: TGUID; var Obj): HResult;
  stdcall;
function DllCanUnloadNow: HResult; stdcall;
```

Each of these functions is already implemented by the ComServ unit, so the only work to be done for your Delphi COM servers is to ensure that these functions are added to an exports clause in your project.

> **NOTE**
>
> A good example of a real-world application of in-process COM servers can be found in Chapter 16, "Windows Shell Programming," which demonstrates how to create shell extensions.

DllRegisterServer()

The DllRegisterServer() function is called to register a COM server DLL with the System Registry. If you simply export this method from your Delphi application, as described earlier, VCL will iterate over all the COM objects in your application and register them with the System Registry. When a COM server is registered, it will make a key entry in the System Registry under

```
HKEY_CLASSES_ROOT\CLSID\{xxxxxxxx-xxxx-xxxx-xxxx-xxxxxxxx}
```

for each COM class, where the *X*s denote the CLSID of the COM class. For in-proc servers, an additional entry is created as a subkey of the preceding key called InProcServer32. The default value for this key is the full path to the in-proc server DLL. Figure 15.1 shows a COM server registered with the System Registry.

DllUnregisterServer()

The DllUnregisterServer() function's job is simply to undo what is done by the DllRegisterServer() function. When called, it should remove all the entries in the System Registry made by DllRegisterServer().

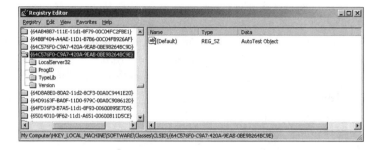

FIGURE 15.1

A COM server as shown in the Registry Editor.

DllGetClassObject()

DllGetClassObject() is called by the COM engine in order to retrieve a class factory for a particular COM class. The CLSID parameter of this method is the CLSID of the type of COM class you want to create. The IID parameter holds the IID of the interface instance pointer you want to obtain for the class factory object (usually, IClassFactory's interface ID is passed here). Upon successful return, the Obj parameter contains a pointer to the class factory interface denoted by IID that's capable of creating COM objects of the class type denoted by CLSID.

DllCanUnloadNow()

DllCanUnloadNow() is called by the COM engine to determine whether the COM server DLL is capable of being unloaded from memory. If there are references to any COM object within the DLL, this function should return S_FALSE, indicating that the DLL shouldn't be unloaded. If none of the DLL's COM objects are in use, this method should return S_TRUE.

TIP

Even after all references to an in-proc server's COM objects have been freed, COM might not necessarily call DllCanUnloadNow() to begin the process of releasing the in-proc server DLL from memory. If you want to ensure that all unused COM server DLLs have been released from memory, call the CoFreeUnusedLibraries() API function, which is defined in the ActiveX units as follows:

```
procedure CoFreeUnusedLibraries; stdcall;
```

Creating an Instance of an In-Proc COM Server

To create an instance of a COM server in Delphi, use the CreateComObject() function, which is defined in the ComObj unit as follows:

```
function CreateComObject(const ClassID: TGUID): IUnknown;
```

The `ClassID` parameter holds the CLSID, which identifies the type of COM object you want to create. The return value of this function is the `IUnknown` interface of the requested COM object, or the function raises an exception if the COM object cannot be created.

`CreateComObject()` is a wrapper around the `CoCreateInstance()` COM API function. Internally, `CoCreateInstance()` calls the `CoGetClassObject()` API function to obtain an `IClassFactory` for the specified COM object. `CoCreateInstance()` does this by looking in the Registry for the COM class's `InProcServer32` entry in order to find the path to the in-proc server DLL, calling `LoadLibrary()` on the in-proc server DLL, and then calling the DLL's `DllGetClassObject()` function. After obtaining the `IClassFactory` interface pointer, `CoCreateInstance()` calls `IClassFactory.CreateInstance()` to create an instance of the specified COM class.

TIP

`CreateComObject()` can be inefficient if you need to create multiple objects from a class factory because it disposes of the `IClassFactory` interface pointer obtained by `CoGetClassObject()` after creating the requested COM object. In cases where you need to create multiple instances of the same COM object, you should call `CoGetClassObject()` directly and use `IClassFactory.CreateInstance()` to create multiple instances of the COM object.

NOTE

Before you can use any COM or OLE API functions, you must initialize the COM library using the `CoInitialize()` function. The single parameter to this function must be nil. To properly shut down the COM library, you should call the `CoUninitialize()` function as the last call to the OLE library. Calls are cumulative, so each call to `CoInitialize()` in your application must have a corresponding call to `CoUninitialize()`.

For applications, `CoInitialize()` is called automatically from `Application.Initialize()`, and `CoUninitialize()` is called automatically from the finalization of `ComObj`.

It's not necessary to call these functions from in-process libraries because their client applications are required to perform the initialization and uninitialization for the process.

Out-of-Process COM Servers

Out-of-process servers are executables that can create COM objects for use by other applications. The name comes from the fact that they do not execute from within the same process of the client but instead are executables that operate within the context of their own processes.

Registration

Similar to their in-proc cousins, out-of-process servers must also be registered with the System Registry. Out-of-process servers must make an entry under

```
HKEY_CLASSES_ROOT\CLSID\{xxxxxxxx-xxxx-xxxx-xxxx-xxxxxxxx}
```

called `LocalServer32`, which identifies the full pathname of the out-of-process server executable.

Delphi applications' COM servers are registered in the `Application.Initialize()` method, which is usually the first line of code in an application's project file. If the `/regserver` command-line switch is passed to your application, `Application.Initialize()` will register the COM classes with the System Registry and immediately terminate the application. Likewise, if the `/unregserver` command-line switch is passed, `Application.Initialize()` will unregister the COM classes with the System Registry and immediately terminate the application. If neither of these switches are passed, `Application.Initialize()` will register the COM classes with the System Registry and continue to run the application normally.

Creating an Instance of an Out-of-Proc COM Server

On the surface, the method for creating instances of COM objects from out-of-process servers is the same as for in-proc servers: Just call `ComObj`'s `CreateComObject()` function. Behind the scenes, however, the process is quite different. In this case, `CoGetClassObject()` looks for the `LocalServer32` entry in the System Registry and invokes the associated application using the `CreateProcess()` API function. When the out-of-proc server application is invoked, the server must register its class factories using the `CoRegisterClassObject()` COM API function. This function adds an `IClassFactory` pointer to COM's internal table of active registered class objects. `CoGetClassObject()` can then obtain the requested COM class's `IClassFactory` pointer from this table to create an instance of the COM object.

Aggregation

You know now that interfaces are the basic building blocks of COM as well as that inheritance is possible with interfaces, but interfaces are entities without implementation. What happens, then, when you want to recycle the implementation of one COM object within another? COM's answer to this question is a concept called *aggregation*. Aggregation means that the containing (outer) object creates the contained (inner) object as part of its creation process, and the interfaces of the inner object are exposed by the outer. An object has to allow itself to operate as an aggregate by providing a means to forward all calls to its IUnknown methods to the containing object. For an example of aggregation within the context of VCL COM objects, you should take a look at the TAggregatedObject class in the AxCtrls unit.

Distributed COM

Introduced with Windows NT 4, Distributed COM (or *DCOM*) provides a means for accessing COM objects located on other machines on a network. In addition to remote object creation, DCOM also provides security facilities that allow servers to specify which clients have rights to create instances of which servers and what operations they might perform. Windows NT 4 and Windows 98 have built-in DCOM capability, but Windows 95 requires an add-on available on Microsoft's Web site (http://www.microsoft.com) to serve as a DCOM client.

You can create remote COM objects using the CreateRemoteComObject() function, which is declared in the ComObj unit as follows:

```
function CreateRemoteComObject(const MachineName: WideString;
  const ClassID: TGUID): IUnknown;
```

The first parameter, MachineName, to this function is a string representing the network name of the machine containing the COM class. The ClassID parameter specifies the CLSID of the COM class to be created. The return value for this function is the IUnknown interface pointer for the COM object specified in CLSID. An exception will be raised if the object cannot be created.

CreateRemoteComObject() is a wrapper around the CoCreateInstanceEx() COM API function, which is an extended version of CoCreateInstance() that knows how to create objects remotely.

Automation

Automation (formerly known as *OLE Automation*) provides a means for applications or DLLs to expose programmable objects for use by other applications. Applications or DLLs that expose programmable objects are referred to as *Automation servers*. Applications that access and manipulate the programmable objects contained within Automation servers are known as *Automation controllers*. Automation controllers are able to program the Automation server using a macro-like language exposed by the server.

Among the chief advantages to using Automation in your applications is its language-independent nature. An Automation controller is able to manipulate a server regardless of the programming language used to develop either component. Additionally, because Automation is supported at the operating system level, the theory is that you'll be able to leverage future

15

COM DEVELOPMENT

advancements in this technology by using Automation today. If these things sound good to you, read on. What follows is information on creating Automation servers and controllers in Delphi.

CAUTION

If you have an Automation project from Delphi 2 that you want to migrate to the current version of Delphi, you should be forewarned that the techniques for Automation changed drastically starting with Delphi 3. In general, you shouldn't mix Delphi 2's Automation unit, OleAuto, with the newer ComObj or ComServ units. If you want to compile a Delphi 2 Automation project in Delphi 5, the OleAuto unit remains in the \Delphi5\lib\Delphi2 subdirectory for backward compatibility.

IDispatch

Automation objects are essentially COM objects that implement the IDispatch interface. IDispatch is defined in the System unit as shown here:

```
type
  IDispatch = interface(IUnknown)
    ['{00020400-0000-0000-C000-000000000046}']
    function GetTypeInfoCount(out Count: Integer): Integer; stdcall;
    function GetTypeInfo(Index, LocaleID: Integer; out TypeInfo):
      Integer; stdcall;
    function GetIDsOfNames(const IID: TGUID; Names: Pointer;
      NameCount, LocaleID: Integer; DispIDs: Pointer): Integer; stdcall;
    function Invoke(DispID: Integer; const IID: TGUID; LocaleID: Integer;
      Flags: Word; var Params; VarResult, ExcepInfo, ArgErr: Pointer): Integer;
  end;
```

The first thing you should know is that you don't have to understand the ins and outs of the IDispatch interface to take advantage of Automation in Delphi, so don't let this complicated interface alarm you. You generally don't have to interact with this interface directly because Delphi provides an elegant encapsulation of Automation, but the description of IDispatch in this section should provide you with a good foundation for understanding Automation.

Central to the function of IDispatch is the Invoke() method, so we'll start there. When a client obtains an IDispatch pointer for an Automation server, it can call the Invoke() method to execute a particular method on the server. The DispID parameter of this method holds a number, called a *dispatch ID*, that indicates which method on the server should be invoked. The IID parameter is unused. The LocaleID parameter contains language information. The Flags parameter describes what kind of method is to be invoked and whether it's a normal method or a put or get method for a property. The Params property contains a pointer to an array of TDispParams, which holds the parameters passed to the method. The VarResult parameter is a pointer to an OleVariant, which will hold the return value of the method that's invoked. ExcepInfo is a pointer to a TExcepInfo record that will contain error information if Invoke() returns DISP_E_EXCEPTION. Finally, if Invoke() returns DISP_E_TYPEMISMATCH or DISP_E_PARAMNOTFOUND, the ArgError parameter is a pointer to an integer that will contain the index of the offending parameter in the Params array.

The GetIDsOfName() method of IDispatch is called to obtain the dispatch ID of one or more method names given strings identifying those methods. The IID parameter of this method is unused. The Names parameter points to an array of PWideChar method names. The NameCount parameter holds the number of strings in the Names array. LocaleID contains language information. The last parameter, DispIDs, is a pointer to an array of NameCount integers, which GetIDsOfNames() will fill in with the dispatch IDs for the methods listed in the Names parameter.

GetTypeInfo() retrieves the type information (type information is described next) for the Automation object. The Index parameter represents the type of information to obtain and should normally be 0. The LCID parameter holds language information. Upon successful return, the TypeInfo parameter will hold an ITypeInfo pointer for the Automation object's type information.

The GetTypeInfoCount() method retrieves the number of type information interfaces supported by the Automation object in the Count parameter. Currently, Count will only contain two possible values: 0, meaning the Automation object doesn't support type information, and 1, meaning the Automation object does support type information.

Type Information

After you've spent a great deal of time carefully crafting an Automation server, it would be a shame if potential users of your server couldn't exploit its capabilities to the fullest because of lack of documentation on the methods and properties provided. Fortunately, Automation provides a means for helping avoid this problem by allowing developers to associate type information with Automation objects. This type information is stored in something called a *type library*, and an Automation server's type library can be linked to the server application or library as a resource or stored in an external file. Type libraries contain information about classes, interfaces, types, and other entities in a server. This information provides clients of the Automation server with the information needed to create instances of each of its classes and properly call methods on each interface.

Delphi generates type libraries for you when you add Automation objects to applications and libraries. Additionally, Delphi knows how to translate type library information into Object Pascal so that you can easily control Automation servers from your Delphi applications.

15

Late Versus Early Binding

The elements of Automation that you've learned about so far in this chapter deal with what's called *late binding*. Late binding is a fancy way to say that a method is called through IDispatch's Invoke() method. It's called *late binding* because the method call isn't resolved until runtime. At compile time, an Automation method call resolves into a call to IDispatch.Invoke() with the proper parameters, and at runtime, Invoke() executes the Automation method. When you call an Automation method via a Delphi Variant or OleVariant type, you're using late binding because Delphi must call IDispatch.GetIDs OfNames() to convert the method name into a DispID, and then it can invoke the method by calling IDispatch.Invoke() with the DispID.

A common optimization of early binding is to resolve the DispIDs of methods at compile time and therefore avoid the runtime calls to GetIDsOfNames() in order to invoke a method. This optimization is often referred to as *ID binding*, and it's the convention used when you invoke methods via a Delphi dispinterface type.

Early binding occurs when the Automation object exposes methods by means of a custom interface descending from IDispatch. This way, controllers can call Automation objects directly through the vtable without going through IDispatch.Invoke(). Because the call is direct, a call to such as method will generally occur faster than a call through late binding. Early binding is used you when call a method using a Delphi interface type.

An Automation object that allows methods to be called both from Invoke() and directly from an IDispatch descendant interface is said to support a *dual interface*. Delphi-generated Automation objects always support a dual interface, and Delphi controllers allow methods to be called both through Invoke() and directly through an interface.

Registration

Automation objects must make all the same Registry entries as regular COM objects, but Automation servers typically also make an additional entry under

HKEY_CLASSES_ROOT\CLSID\{xxxxxxxx-xxxx-xxxx-xxxx-xxxxxxxx}

called ProgID, which provides a string identifier for the Automation class. Yet another Registry entry under HKEY_CLASSES_ROOT*(ProgID string)* is made, which contains the CLSID of the Automation class in order to cross-reference back to the first Registry entry under CLSID.

Creating Automation Servers

Delphi makes it a fairly simple chore to create both out-of-process and in-process Automation servers. The process for creating an Automation server can be boiled down into four steps:

1. Create the application or DLL you want to automate. You can even use one of your existing applications as a starting point in order to spice it up with some automation. This is

the only step in which you'll see a real difference between creating in-process and out-of-process servers.

2. Create the Automation object and add it to your project. Delphi provides an Automation Object Expert to help this step go smoothly.

3. Add properties and methods to the Automation object by means of the type library. These are the properties and methods that will be exposed to Automation controllers.

4. Implement the methods generated by Delphi from your type library in your source code.

Creating an Out-of-Process Automation Server

This section walks you through the creation of a simple out-of-process Automation server. Start by creating a new project and placing a TShape and a TEdit component on the main form, as shown in Figure 15.2. Save this project as Srv.dpr.

FIGURE 15.2

The main form of the Srv project.

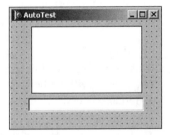

Now add an Automation object to the project by selecting File, New from the main menu and choosing Automation Object from the ActiveX page of the New Items dialog box, as shown in Figure 15.3. This will invoke the Automation Object Wizard shown in Figure 15.4.

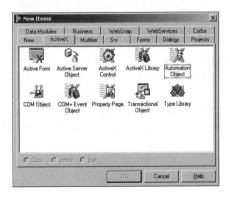

FIGURE 15.3

Adding a new Automation object.

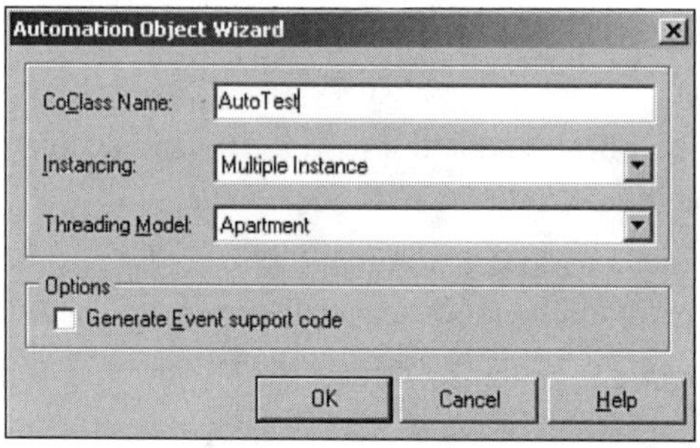

FIGURE 15.4
The Automation Object Wizard.

In the Class Name field of the Automation Object Wizard dialog box, you should enter the name you want to give the COM class for this Automation object. The wizard will automatically prepend a *T* to the classname when creating the Object Pascal class for the Automation object and an *I* to the classname when creating the primary interface for the Automation object. The Instancing combo box in the wizard can hold any one of these three values:

Value	Description
Internal	This OLE object will be used internal to the application only, and it will not be registered with the System Registry. External processes cannot access internal instanced Automation servers.
Single Instance	Each instance of the server can export only one instance of the OLE object. If a controller application requests another instance of the OLE object, Windows will start a new instance of the server application.
Multiple Instance	Each server instance can create and export multiple instances of the OLE object. In-process servers are always multiple instance.

When you complete the wizard's dialog, Delphi will create a new type library for your project (if one doesn't already exist) and add an interface and a coclass to the type library. Additionally, the wizard will generate a new unit in your project that contains the implementation of the Automation interface added to the type library. Figure 15.5 shows the type library editor immediately after the wizard's dialog is dismissed, and Listing 15.2 shows the implementation unit for the Automation object.

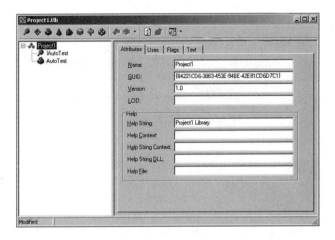

Figure 15.5

A new Automation project as shown in the type library editor.

Listing 15.2   Automation Object Implementation Unit

```
unit TestImpl;

interface

uses
  ComObj, ActiveX, Srv_TLB;

type
  TAutoTest = class(TAutoObject, IAutoTest)
  protected
    { Protected declarations }
  end;

implementation

uses ComServ;

initialization
  TAutoObjectFactory.Create(ComServer, TAutoTest, Class_AutoTest,
    ciMultiInstance, tmApartment);
end.
```

The Automation object, `TAutoTest`, is a class that descends from `TAutoObject`. `TAutoObject` is the base class for all Automation servers. As you add methods to your interface by using the type library editor, new method skeletons will be generated in this unit that you'll implement, thus forming the innards of your Automation object.

15

COM
DEVELOPMENT

> **CAUTION**
>
> Again, be careful not to confuse Delphi 2's `TAutoObject` (from the `OleAuto` unit) with Delphi 5's `TAutoObject` (from the `ComObj` unit). The two aren't compatible.
>
> Similarly, the `automated` visibility specifier introduced in Delphi 2 is now mostly obsolete.

When the Automation object has been added to the project, you must add one or more properties or methods to the primary interface using the type library editor. For this project, the type library will contain properties to get and set the shape, color, and type as well as the edit control's text. For good measure, you'll also add a method that displays the current status of these properties in a dialog. Figure 15.6 shows the completed type library for the Srv project. Note especially the enumeration added to the type library (whose values are shown in the right pane) to support the `ShapeType` property.

> **NOTE**
>
> As you add properties and methods to Automation objects in the type library, keep in mind that the parameters and return values used for these properties and methods must be of Automation-compatible types. Types compatible with Automation include `Byte`, `SmallInt`, `Integer`, `Single`, `Double`, `Currency`, `TDateTime`, `WideString`, `WordBool`, `PSafeArray`, `TDecimal`, `OleVariant`, `IUnknown`, and `IDispatch`.

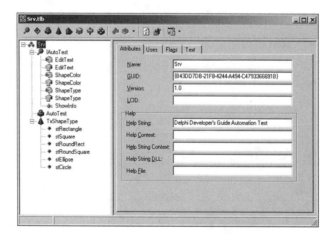

FIGURE 15.6

The completed type library.

When the type library has been completed, all that is left to do is fill in the implementation for each of the method stubs created by the type library editor. This unit is shown in Listing 15.3.

LISTING 15.3 The Completed Implementation Unit

```
unit TestImpl;

interface

uses
  ComObj, ActiveX, Srv_TLB;

type
  TAutoTest = class(TAutoObject, IAutoTest)
  protected
    function Get_EditText: WideString; safecall;
    function Get_ShapeColor: OLE_COLOR; safecall;
    procedure Set_EditText(const Value: WideString); safecall;
    procedure Set_ShapeColor(Value: OLE_COLOR); safecall;
    function Get_ShapeType: TxShapeType; safecall;
    procedure Set_ShapeType(Value: TxShapeType); safecall;
    procedure ShowInfo; safecall;
  end;

implementation

uses ComServ, SrvMain, TypInfo, ExtCtrls, Dialogs, SysUtils, Graphics;

function TAutoTest.Get_EditText: WideString;
begin
  Result := FrmAutoTest.Edit.Text;
end;

function TAutoTest.Get_ShapeColor: OLE_COLOR;
begin
  Result := ColorToRGB(FrmAutoTest.Shape.Brush.Color);
end;

procedure TAutoTest.Set_EditText(const Value: WideString);
begin
  FrmAutoTest.Edit.Text := Value;
end;

procedure TAutoTest.Set_ShapeColor(Value: OLE_COLOR);
begin
  FrmAutoTest.Shape.Brush.Color := Value;
end;
```

15

COM
DEVELOPMENT

LISTING 15.3   Continued

```
function TAutoTest.Get_ShapeType: TxShapeType;
begin
  Result := TxShapeType(FrmAutoTest.Shape.Shape);
end;

procedure TAutoTest.Set_ShapeType(Value: TxShapeType);
begin
  FrmAutoTest.Shape.Shape := TShapeType(Value);
end;

procedure TAutoTest.ShowInfo;
const
  SInfoStr = 'The Shape''s color is %s, and it''s shape is %s.'#13#10 +
    'The Edit''s text is "%s."';
begin
  with FrmAutoTest do
    ShowMessage(Format(SInfoStr, [ColorToString(Shape.Brush.Color),
      GetEnumName(TypeInfo(TShapeType), Ord(Shape.Shape)), Edit.Text]));
end;

initialization
  TAutoObjectFactory.Create(ComServer, TAutoTest, Class_AutoTest,
    ciMultiInstance, tmApartment);
end.
```

The uses clause for this unit contains a unit called Srv_TLB. This unit is the Object Pascal translation of the project type library, and it's shown in Listing 15.4.

LISTING 15.4   Srv_TLB—The Type Library File

```
unit Srv_TLB;

// ************************************************************************ //
// WARNING
// -------
// The types declared in this file were generated from data read from a
// Type Library. If this type library is explicitly or indirectly (via
// another type library referring to this type library) re-imported, or the
// 'Refresh' command of the Type Library Editor activated while editing the
// Type Library, the contents of this file will be regenerated and all
// manual modifications will be lost.
// ************************************************************************ //
```

LISTING 15.4 Continued

```
// PASTLWTR : $Revision:   1.130  $
// File generated on 8/27/2001 1:23:58 AM from Type Library described below.

// ********************************************************************** //
// Type Lib: C:\ D6DG\Source\Ch15\Automate\Srv.tlb (1)
// LIBID: {B43DD7DB-21F8-4244-A494-C4793366691B}
// LCID: 0
// Helpfile:
// DepndLst:
//   (1) v2.0 stdole, (C:\WINNT\System32\stdole2.tlb)
//   (2) v4.0 StdVCL, (C:\WINNT\System32\stdvcl40.dll)
// ********************************************************************** //
{$TYPEDADDRESS OFF} // Unit must be compiled without type-checked pointers.
{$WARN SYMBOL_PLATFORM OFF}
{$WRITEABLECONST ON}

interface

uses ActiveX, Classes, Graphics, StdVCL, Variants, Windows;


// **********************************************************************//
// GUIDS declared in the TypeLibrary. Following prefixes are used:
//   Type Libraries     : LIBID_xxxx
//   CoClasses          : CLASS_xxxx
//   DISPInterfaces     : DIID_xxxx
//   Non-DISP interfaces: IID_xxxx
// **********************************************************************//
const
  // TypeLibrary Major and minor versions
  SrvMajorVersion = 1;
  SrvMinorVersion = 0;

  LIBID_Srv: TGUID = '{B43DD7DB-21F8-4244-A494-C4793366691B}';

  IID_IAutoTest: TGUID = '{C16B6A4C-842C-417F-8BF2-2F306F6C6B59}';
  CLASS_AutoTest: TGUID = '{64C576F0-C9A7-420A-9EAB-0BE98264BC9E}';

// **********************************************************************//
// Declaration of Enumerations defined in Type Library
// **********************************************************************//
// Constants for enum TxShapeType
type
  TxShapeType = TOleEnum;
```

LISTING 15.4   Continued

```
const
  stRectangle = $00000000;
  stSquare = $00000001;
  stRoundRect = $00000002;
  stRoundSquare = $00000003;
  stEllipse = $00000004;
  stCircle = $00000005;

type

// ********************************************************************//
// Forward declaration of types defined in TypeLibrary
// ********************************************************************//
  IAutoTest = interface;
  IAutoTestDisp = dispinterface;

// ********************************************************************//
// Declaration of CoClasses defined in Type Library
// (NOTE: Here we map each CoClass to its Default Interface)
// ********************************************************************//
  AutoTest = IAutoTest;


// ********************************************************************//
// Interface: IAutoTest
// Flags:     (4416) Dual OleAutomation Dispatchable
// GUID:      {C16B6A4C-842C-417F-8BF2-2F306F6C6B59}
// ********************************************************************//
  IAutoTest = interface(IDispatch)
    ['{C16B6A4C-842C-417F-8BF2-2F306F6C6B59}']
    function  Get_EditText: WideString; safecall;
    procedure Set_EditText(const Value: WideString); safecall;
    function  Get_ShapeColor: OLE_COLOR; safecall;
    procedure Set_ShapeColor(Value: OLE_COLOR); safecall;
    function  Get_ShapeType: TxShapeType; safecall;
    procedure Set_ShapeType(Value: TxShapeType); safecall;
    procedure ShowInfo; safecall;
    property EditText: WideString read Get_EditText write Set_EditText;
    property ShapeColor: OLE_COLOR read Get_ShapeColor write Set_ShapeColor;
    property ShapeType: TxShapeType read Get_ShapeType write Set_ShapeType;
  end;

// ********************************************************************//
// DispIntf:  IAutoTestDisp
```

LISTING 15.4 Continued

```
// Flags:      (4416) Dual OleAutomation Dispatchable
// GUID:       {C16B6A4C-842C-417F-8BF2-2F306F6C6B59}
// **********************************************************************//
  IAutoTestDisp = dispinterface
    ['{C16B6A4C-842C-417F-8BF2-2F306F6C6B59}']
    property EditText: WideString dispid 1;
    property ShapeColor: OLE_COLOR dispid 2;
    property ShapeType: TxShapeType dispid 3;
    procedure ShowInfo; dispid 4;
  end;


// **********************************************************************//
// The Class CoAutoTest provides a Create and CreateRemote method to
// create instances of the default interface IAutoTest exposed by
// the CoClass AutoTest. The functions are intended to be used by
// clients wishing to automate the CoClass objects exposed by the
// server of this typelibrary.
// **********************************************************************//
  CoAutoTest = class
    class function Create: IAutoTest;
    class function CreateRemote(const MachineName: string): IAutoTest;
  end;

implementation

uses ComObj;

class function CoAutoTest.Create: IAutoTest;
begin
  Result := CreateComObject(CLASS_AutoTest) as IAutoTest;
end;

class function CoAutoTest.CreateRemote(const MachineName: string): IAutoTest;
begin
  Result := CreateRemoteComObject(MachineName, CLASS_AutoTest) as IAutoTest;
end;

end.
```

Looking at this unit from the top down, you'll notice that the type library version is specified first and then the GUID for the type library, LIBID_Srv, is declared. This GUID will be used when the type library is registered with the System Registry. Next, the values for the TxShapeType enumeration are listed. What's interesting about the enumeration is that the values are declared as constants rather than as an Object Pascal enumerated type. This is because type library enums are like C/C++ enums (and unlike Object Pascal) in that they don't have to start at the ordinal value zero or be sequential in value.

Next, in the Srv_TLB unit the IAutoTest interface is declared. In this interface declaration you'll see the properties and methods you created in the type library editor. Additionally, you'll see the Get_*XXX* and Set_*XXX* methods generated as the read and write methods for each of the properties.

Safecall

Safecall is the default calling convention for methods entered into the type library editor, as you can see from the IAutoTest declaration earlier. Safecall is actually more than a calling convention because it implies two things: First, it means that the method will be called using the safecall calling convention. Second, it means that the method will be encapsulated so that it returns an HResult value to the caller. For example, suppose that you have a method that looks like this in Object Pascal:

```
function Foo(W: WideString): Integer; safecall;
```

This method actually compiles to code that looks something like this:

```
function Foo(W: WideString; out RetVal: Integer): HResult; stdcall;
```

The advantage of safecall is that it catches all exceptions before they flow back into the caller. When an unhandled exception is raised in a safecall method, the exception is handled by the implicit wrapper and converted into an HResult, which is returned to the caller.

Next in Srv_TLB is the dispinterface declaration for the Automation object: IAutoTestDisp. A dispinterface signals to the caller that Automation methods might be executed by Invoke() but doesn't imply a custom interface through which methods can be executed. Although the IAutoTest interface can be used by development tools that support early-binding Automation, IAutoTestDisp's dispinterface can be used by tools that support late binding.

The Srv_TLB unit then declares a class called CoAutoTest, which makes creation of the Automation object easy; just call CoAutoTest.Create() to create an instance of the Automation object.

Finally, Srv_TLB creates a class called TAutoTest that wraps the server into a component that can be placed on the palette. This feature, new in Delphi 5, is targeted more toward Automation servers that you import rather than new Automation servers that you create.

As mentioned earlier, you must run this application once to register it with the System Registry. Later, in the "Automation" section of this chapter, you'll learn about the controller application used to manipulate this server.

Creating an In-Process Automation Server

Just as out-of-process servers start out as applications, in-process servers start out as DLLs. You can begin with an existing DLL or with a new DLL, which you can create by selecting DLL from the New Items dialog found under the File, New menu.

> **NOTE**
>
> If you're not familiar with DLLs, they're covered in depth in Chapter 6, "Dynamic Link Libraries." This chapter assumes that you have some knowledge of DLL programming.

As mentioned earlier, in order to serve as an in-process Automation server, a DLL must export four functions that are defined in the ComServ unit: DllGetClassObject(), DllCanUnloadNow(), DllRegisterServer(), and DllUnregisterServer(). Do this by adding these functions to the exports clause in your project file, as shown in the project file IPS.dpr in Listing 15.5.

LISTING 15.5 IPS.dpr—The Project File for an In-Process Server

```
library IPS;

uses
  ComServ;

exports
  DllRegisterServer,
  DllUnregisterServer,
  DllGetClassObject,
  DllCanUnloadNow;

begin
end.
```

The Automation object is added to the DLL project in the same manner as an executable project: through the Automation Object Wizard. For this project, you'll add only one property and one method, as shown in the type library editor in Figure 15.7. The Object Pascal version of the type library, IPS_TLB, is shown in Listing 15.6.

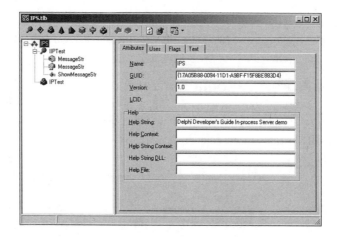

FIGURE 15.7

The IPS project in the type library editor.

LISTING 15.6   IPS_TLB.pas—The Type Library Import File for the In-Process Server Project

```
unit IPS_TLB;

// ************************************************************************ //
// WARNING
// -------
// The types declared in this file were generated from data read from a
// Type Library. If this type library is explicitly or indirectly (via
// another type library referring to this type library) re-imported, or the
// 'Refresh' command of the Type Library Editor activated while editing the
// Type Library, the contents of this file will be regenerated and all
// manual modifications will be lost.
// ************************************************************************ //

// PASTLWTR : $Revision:   1.130  $
// File generated on 8/27/2001 1:27:45 AM from Type Library described below.

// ************************************************************************ //
// Type Lib: C:\ D6DG\Source\Ch15\Automate\IPS.tlb (1)
// LIBID: {17A05B88-0094-11D1-A9BF-F15F8BE883D4}
// LCID: 0
// Helpfile:
// DepndLst:
//    (1) v1.0 stdole, (C:\WINNT\System32\stdole32.tlb)
//    (2) v2.0 StdType, (C:\WINNT\System32\olepro32.dll)
//    (3) v1.0 StdVCL, (C:\WINNT\System32\STDVCL32.DLL)
// ************************************************************************ //
```

LISTING 15.6 Continued

```
{$TYPEDADDRESS OFF} // Unit must be compiled without type-checked pointers.
{$WARN SYMBOL_PLATFORM OFF}
{$WRITEABLECONST ON}


interface

uses ActiveX, Classes, Graphics, StdVCL, Variants, Windows;


// *********************************************************************//
// GUIDS declared in the TypeLibrary. Following prefixes are used:
//   Type Libraries     : LIBID_xxxx
//   CoClasses          : CLASS_xxxx
//   DISPInterfaces     : DIID_xxxx
//   Non-DISP interfaces: IID_xxxx
// *********************************************************************//
const
  // TypeLibrary Major and minor versions
  IPSMajorVersion = 1;
  IPSMinorVersion = 0;

  LIBID_IPS: TGUID = '{17A05B88-0094-11D1-A9BF-F15F8BE883D4}';

  IID_IIPTest: TGUID = '{17A05B89-0094-11D1-A9BF-F15F8BE883D4}';
  CLASS_IPTest: TGUID = '{17A05B8A-0094-11D1-A9BF-F15F8BE883D4}';
type

// *********************************************************************//
// Forward declaration of types defined in TypeLibrary
// *********************************************************************//
  IIPTest = interface;
  IIPTestDisp = dispinterface;

// *********************************************************************//
// Declaration of CoClasses defined in Type Library
// (NOTE: Here we map each CoClass to its Default Interface)
// *********************************************************************//
  IPTest = IIPTest;


// *********************************************************************//
// Interface: IIPTest
// Flags:     (4432) Hidden Dual OleAutomation Dispatchable
// GUID:      {17A05B89-0094-11D1-A9BF-F15F8BE883D4}
```

LISTING 15.6   Continued

```
// *********************************************************************//
  IIPTest = interface(IDispatch)
    ['{17A05B89-0094-11D1-A9BF-F15F8BE883D4}']
    function  Get_MessageStr: WideString; safecall;
    procedure Set_MessageStr(const Value: WideString); safecall;
    function  ShowMessageStr: Integer; safecall;
    property MessageStr: WideString read Get_MessageStr write Set_MessageStr;
  end;


// *********************************************************************//
// DispIntf:  IIPTestDisp
// Flags:     (4432) Hidden Dual OleAutomation Dispatchable
// GUID:      {17A05B89-0094-11D1-A9BF-F15F8BE883D4}
// *********************************************************************//
  IIPTestDisp = dispinterface
    ['{17A05B89-0094-11D1-A9BF-F15F8BE883D4}']
    property MessageStr: WideString dispid 1;
    function  ShowMessageStr: Integer; dispid 2;
  end;


// *********************************************************************//
// The Class CoIPTest provides a Create and CreateRemote method to
// create instances of the default interface IIPTest exposed by
// the CoClass IPTest. The functions are intended to be used by
// clients wishing to automate the CoClass objects exposed by the
// server of this typelibrary.
// *********************************************************************//
  CoIPTest = class
    class function Create: IIPTest;
    class function CreateRemote(const MachineName: string): IIPTest;
  end;

implementation

uses ComObj;

class function CoIPTest.Create: IIPTest;
begin
  Result := CreateComObject(CLASS_IPTest) as IIPTest;
end;

class function CoIPTest.CreateRemote(const MachineName: string): IIPTest;
```

LISTING 15.6   Continued

```
begin
  Result := CreateRemoteComObject(MachineName, CLASS_IPTest) as IIPTest;
end;


end.
```

Clearly, this is a pretty simple Automation server, but it serves to illustrate the point. The
`MessageStr` property can be set to a value and then shown with the `ShowMessageStr()` function. The implementation of the `IIPTest` interface resides in the unit `IPSMain.pas`, which is
shown in Listing 15.7.

LISTING 15.7   IPSMain.pas—The Main Unit for the In-Process Server Project

```
unit IPSMain;

interface

uses
  ComObj, IPS_TLB;

type
  TIPTest = class(TAutoObject, IIPTest)
  private
    MessageStr: string;
  protected
    function Get_MessageStr: WideString; safecall;
    procedure Set_MessageStr(const Value: WideString); safecall;
    function ShowMessageStr: Integer; safecall;
  end;

implementation

uses Windows, ComServ;

function TIPTest.Get_MessageStr: WideString;
begin
  Result := MessageStr;
end;

function TIPTest.ShowMessageStr: Integer;
begin
  MessageBox(0, PChar(MessageStr), 'Your string is...', MB_OK);
  Result := Length(MessageStr);
end;
```

LISTING 15.7   Continued

```
procedure TIPTest.Set_MessageStr(const Value: WideString);
begin
  MessageStr := Value;
end;

initialization
  TAutoObjectFactory.Create(ComServer, TIPTest, Class_IPTest, ciMultiInstance,
    tmApartment);
end.
```

As you learned earlier in this chapter, in-process servers are registered differently than out-of-process servers; an in-process server's `DllRegisterServer()` function is called to register it with the System Registry. The Delphi IDE makes this very easy: Select Run, Register ActiveX server from the main menu.

Creating Automation Controllers

Delphi makes it extremely easy to control Automation servers in your applications. Delphi also gives you a great amount of flexibility in how you want to control Automation servers: with options for early binding using interfaces or late binding using dispinterfaces or variants.

Controlling Out-of-Process Servers

The Control project is an Automation controller that demonstrates all three types of Automation (interfaces, dispinterface, and variants). Control is the controller for the Srv Automation server application from earlier in this chapter. The main form for this project is shown in Figure 15.8.

When the Connect button is clicked, the Control application connects to the server in several different ways with the following code:

```
FIntf := CoAutoTest.Create;
FDispintf := CreateComObject(Class_AutoTest) as IAutoTestDisp;
FVar := CreateOleObject('Srv.AutoTest');
```

This code shows `interface`, `dispinterface`, and `OleVariant` variables, each creating an instance of the Automation server in different ways. What's interesting about these different techniques is that they're almost totally interchangeable. For example, the following code is also correct:

```
FIntf := CreateComObject(Class_AutoTest) as IAutoTest;
FDispintf := CreateOleObject('Srv.AutoTest') as IAutoTestDisp;
FVar := CoAutoTest.Create;
```

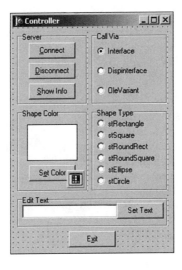

FIGURE 15.8

The main form for the Control project.

Listing 15.8 shows the Ctrl unit, which contains the rest of the source code for the Automation controller. Notice that the application allows you to manipulate the server using either the interface, dispinterface, or OleVariant.

LISTING 15.8   Ctrl.pas—The Main Unit for the Controller Project for the Out-of-Process Server Project

```
unit Ctrl;

interface

uses
  Windows, Messages, SysUtils, Classes, Graphics, Controls, Forms, Dialogs,
  StdCtrls, ColorGrd, ExtCtrls, Srv_TLB, Buttons;

type
  TControlForm = class(TForm)
    CallViaRG: TRadioGroup;
    ShapeTypeRG: TRadioGroup;
    GroupBox1: TGroupBox;
    GroupBox2: TGroupBox;
    Edit: TEdit;
    GroupBox3: TGroupBox;
    ConBtn: TButton;
    DisBtn: TButton;
    InfoBtn: TButton;
```

LISTING 15.8 Continued

```
    ColorBtn: TButton;
    ColorDialog: TColorDialog;
    ColorShape: TShape;
    ExitBtn: TButton;
    TextBtn: TButton;
    procedure ConBtnClick(Sender: TObject);
    procedure DisBtnClick(Sender: TObject);
    procedure ColorBtnClick(Sender: TObject);
    procedure ExitBtnClick(Sender: TObject);
    procedure TextBtnClick(Sender: TObject);
    procedure InfoBtnClick(Sender: TObject);
    procedure ShapeTypeRGClick(Sender: TObject);
  private
    { Private declarations }
    FIntf: IAutoTest;
    FDispintf: IAutoTestDisp;
    FVar: OleVariant;
    procedure SetControls;
    procedure EnableControls(DoEnable: Boolean);
  public
    { Public declarations }
  end;

var
  ControlForm: TControlForm;

implementation

{$R *.DFM}

uses ComObj;

procedure TControlForm.SetControls;
// Initializes the controls to the current server values
begin
  case CallViaRG.ItemIndex of
    0:
      begin
        ColorShape.Brush.Color := FIntf.ShapeColor;
        ShapeTypeRG.ItemIndex := FIntf.ShapeType;
        Edit.Text := FIntf.EditText;
      end;
    1:
      begin
        ColorShape.Brush.Color := FDispintf.ShapeColor;
```

LISTING 15.8 Continued

```pascal
        ShapeTypeRG.ItemIndex := FDispintf.ShapeType;
        Edit.Text := FDispintf.EditText;
      end;
    2:
      begin
        ColorShape.Brush.Color := FVar.ShapeColor;
        ShapeTypeRG.ItemIndex := FVar.ShapeType;
        Edit.Text := FVar.EditText;
      end;
  end;
end;

procedure TControlForm.EnableControls(DoEnable: Boolean);
begin
  DisBtn.Enabled := DoEnable;
  InfoBtn.Enabled := DoEnable;
  ColorBtn.Enabled := DoEnable;
  ShapeTypeRG.Enabled := DoEnable;
  Edit.Enabled := DoEnable;
  TextBtn.Enabled := DoEnable;
end;

procedure TControlForm.ConBtnClick(Sender: TObject);
begin
  FIntf := CoAutoTest.Create;
  FDispintf := CreateComObject(Class_AutoTest) as IAutoTestDisp;
  FVar := CreateOleObject('Srv.AutoTest');
  EnableControls(True);
  SetControls;
end;

procedure TControlForm.DisBtnClick(Sender: TObject);
begin
  FIntf := nil;
  FDispintf := nil;
  FVar := Unassigned;
  EnableControls(False);
end;

procedure TControlForm.ColorBtnClick(Sender: TObject);
var
  NewColor: TColor;
begin
  if ColorDialog.Execute then
```

LISTING 15.8   Continued

```pascal
  begin
    NewColor := ColorDialog.Color;
    case CallViaRG.ItemIndex of
      0: FIntf.ShapeColor := NewColor;
      1: FDispintf.ShapeColor := NewColor;
      2: FVar.ShapeColor := NewColor;
    end;
    ColorShape.Brush.Color := NewColor;
  end;
end;


procedure TControlForm.ExitBtnClick(Sender: TObject);
begin
  Close;
end;


procedure TControlForm.TextBtnClick(Sender: TObject);
begin
  case CallViaRG.ItemIndex of
    0: FIntf.EditText := Edit.Text;
    1: FDispintf.EditText := Edit.Text;
    2: FVar.EditText := Edit.Text;
  end;
end;


procedure TControlForm.InfoBtnClick(Sender: TObject);
begin
  case CallViaRG.ItemIndex of
    0: FIntf.ShowInfo;
    1: FDispintf.ShowInfo;
    2: FVar.ShowInfo;
  end;
end;


procedure TControlForm.ShapeTypeRGClick(Sender: TObject);
begin
  case CallViaRG.ItemIndex of
    0: FIntf.ShapeType := ShapeTypeRG.ItemIndex;
    1: FDispintf.ShapeType := ShapeTypeRG.ItemIndex;
    2: FVar.ShapeType := ShapeTypeRG.ItemIndex;
  end;
end;

end.
```

Another interesting thing this code illustrates is how easy it is to disconnect from an Automation server: Interfaces and dispinterfaces can be set to `nil`, and variants can be set to `Unassigned`. Of course, the Automation server will also be released when the `Control` application is closed, as a part of the normal finalization of these lifetime-managed types.

TIP

Interfaces will almost always perform better than dispinterfaces and variants, so you should always use interfaces to control Automation servers when available.

Variants rank last in terms of performance because, at runtime, an Automation call through a variant must call `GetIDsOfNames()` to convert a method name into a dispatch ID before it can execute the method with a call to `Invoke()`.

The performance of dispinterfaces is in between that of an interface and that of a variant. "But why," you might ask, "is the performance different if variants and dispinterfaces both use late binding?" The reason for this is that dispinterfaces take advantage of an optimization called *ID binding*, which means that the dispatch IDs of methods are known at compile time, so the compiler doesn't need to generate a runtime call to `GetIDsOfName()` prior to calling `Invoke()`. Another, perhaps more obvious, advantage of dispinterfaces over variants is that dispinterfaces allow for the use of CodeInsight for easier coding, whereas this is not possible using variants.

Figure 15.9 shows the Control application controlling the Srv server.

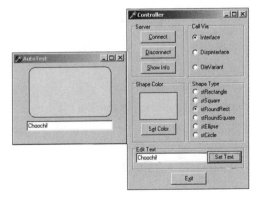

FIGURE 15.9

Automation controller and server.

Controlling In-Process Servers

The technique for controlling an in-process server is no different from that for controlling its
out-of-process counterpart. Just keep in mind that the Automation controller is now executing
within your own process space. This means that performance will be a bit better than with out-
of-process servers, but it also means that a crash in the Automation server can take down your
application.

Now you'll look at a controller application for the in-process Automation server created earlier
in this chapter. In this case, we'll use only the interface for controlling the server. This is a
pretty simple application, and Figure 15.10 shows the main form for the IPCtrl project. The
code in Listing 15.9 is IPCMain.pas, the main unit for the IPCtrl project.

FIGURE 15.10

The IPCtrl project's main form.

LISTING 15.9 IPCMain.pas—The Main Unit for the Controller Project for the In-Process
Server Project

```
unit IPCMain;

interface

uses
  Windows, Messages, SysUtils, Classes, Graphics, Controls, Forms, Dialogs,
  StdCtrls, ExtCtrls, IPS_TLB;

type
  TIPCForm = class(TForm)
    ExitBtn: TButton;
    Panel1: TPanel;
    ConBtn: TButton;
    DisBtn: TButton;
    Edit: TEdit;
    SetBtn: TButton;
    ShowBtn: TButton;
    procedure ConBtnClick(Sender: TObject);
```

LISTING 15.9 Continued

```
    procedure DisBtnClick(Sender: TObject);
    procedure SetBtnClick(Sender: TObject);
    procedure ShowBtnClick(Sender: TObject);
    procedure ExitBtnClick(Sender: TObject);
  private
    { Private declarations }
    IPTest: IIPTest;
    procedure EnableControls(DoEnable: Boolean);
  public
    { Public declarations }
  end;

var
  IPCForm: TIPCForm;

implementation

uses ComObj;

{$R *.DFM}

procedure TIPCForm.EnableControls(DoEnable: Boolean);
begin
  DisBtn.Enabled := DoEnable;
  Edit.Enabled := DoEnable;
  SetBtn.Enabled := DoEnable;
  ShowBtn.Enabled := DoEnable;
end;

procedure TIPCForm.ConBtnClick(Sender: TObject);
begin
  IPTest := CreateComObject(CLASS_IPTest) as IIPTest;
  EnableControls(True);
end;

procedure TIPCForm.DisBtnClick(Sender: TObject);
begin
  IPTest := nil;
  EnableControls(False);
end;

procedure TIPCForm.SetBtnClick(Sender: TObject);
begin
  IPTest.MessageStr := Edit.Text;
end;
```

LISTING 15.9   Continued

```
procedure TIPCForm.ShowBtnClick(Sender: TObject);
begin
  IPTest.ShowMessageStr;
end;

procedure TIPCForm.ExitBtnClick(Sender: TObject);
begin
  Close;
end;

end.
```

Remember to ensure that the server has been registered prior to attempting to run IPCtrl. You can do this in several ways: Using Run, Register ActiveX Server from the main menu while the IPS project is loaded, using the Windows `RegSvr32.exe` utility, and using the `TRegSvr.exe` tool that comes with Delphi. Figure 15.11 shows this project in action controlling the IPS server.

FIGURE 15.11
IPCtrl controlling the IPS server.

Advanced Automation Techniques

In this section, our goal is to get you up to speed on some of the more advanced features of Automation that the wizards never told you about. Topics such as Automation events, collections, type library gotchas, and low-level language support for COM are all covered. Rather than devote more time to talking about this stuff, let's jump right in and do it!

Automation Events

We Delphi programmers have long taken events for granted. You drop a button, you double-click OnClick in the Object Inspector, and you write some code. It's no big deal. Even from the control writer's point of view, events are a snap. You create a new method type, add a field and published property to your control, and you're good to go. For Delphi COM developers, however, events can be scary. Many Delphi COM developers avoid events altogether simply because they "don't have time to learn all that mumbo jumbo." If you fall into that group, you'll be happy to know that working with events actually isn't very difficult thanks to some nice built-in support provided by Delphi. Although all the new terms associated with Automation events can add an air of complexity, in this section I hope to demystify events to the point where you think, "Oh, is that all they are?"

What Are Events?

Put simply, events provide a means for a server to call back into a client to provide some information. Under a traditional client/server model, the client calls the server to perform an action or obtain some data, the server executes the action or obtains the data, and control returns to the client. This model works fine for most things, but it breaks down when the event in which the client is interested is asynchronous in nature or is driven by a user interface entry. For example, if the client sends the server a request to download a file, the client probably doesn't want to sit around and wait for the thing to download before it can continue processing (especially over a high-latency connection such as a modem). A better model would be for the client to issue the instruction to the server and continue to go about its business until the server notifies the client about the completion of the file download. Similarly, a user interface entry, such as a button click, is a good example of when the server needs to notify the client using an event mechanism. The client obviously can't call a method on the server that waits around until some button is clicked.

Generally speaking, the server is responsible for defining and firing events, whereas the client is normally responsible for connecting itself to and implementing events. Of course, given such a loose definition, there's room to haggle, and consequently Delphi and Automation provide two very different approaches to the idea of events. Drilling down into each of these models will help put things into perspective.

Events in Delphi

Delphi follows the KISS (keep it simple, stupid!) methodology when it comes to events. Events are implemented as method pointers—these pointers can be assigned to some method in the application and are executed when such a method is called via the method pointer. As an illustration, consider the everyday application-development scenario of an application that needs to handle an event on a component. If you look at the situation abstractly, the "server" in this case would be a component, which defines and fires the event. The "client" is the application that employs the component because it connects to the event by assigning some specific method name to the event method pointer.

Although this simple event model is one of the things that makes Delphi elegant and easy to use, it definitely sacrifices some power for the sake of usability. For example, there's no built-in way to allow multiple clients to listen for the same event (this is called *multicasting*). Also, there's no way to dynamically obtain a type description for an event without writing some RTTI code (which you probably shouldn't be using in a application anyway because of its version-specific nature).

Events in Automation

Whereas the Delphi event model is simple yet limited, the Automation event model is powerful but more complex. As a COM programmer, you might have guessed that events are implemented in Automation using interfaces. Rather than existing on a per-method basis, events exist only as part of an interface. This interface is often called an *events interface* or an *outgoing interface*. It's called *outgoing* because it's not implemented by the server like other interfaces but is instead implemented by clients of the server, and methods of the interface will be called outward from the server to the client. Like all interfaces, event interfaces have associated with them corresponding interface identifications (IIDs) that uniquely identify them. Also, the description of the events interface is found in the type library of an Automation object, tied to the Automation object's coclass like other interfaces.

Servers needing to surface event interfaces to clients must implement the IConnectionPoint Container interface. This interface is defined in the ActiveX unit as follows:

```
type
  IConnectionPointContainer = interface
    ['{B196B284-BAB4-101A-B69C-00AA00341D07}']
    function EnumConnectionPoints(out Enum: IEnumConnectionPoints):
      HResult; stdcall;
    function FindConnectionPoint(const iid: TIID;
      out cp: IConnectionPoint): HResult; stdcall;
  end;
```

In COM parlance, a *connection point* describes the entity that provides programmatic access to an outgoing interface. If a client needs to determine whether a server supports events, all it has to do is QueryInterface for the IConnectionPointContainer interface. If this interface is present, the server is capable of surfacing events. The EnumConnectionPoints() method of IConnectionPointContainer enables clients to iterate over all the outgoing interfaces supported by the server. Clients can use the FindConnectionPoint() method to obtain a specific outgoing interface.

You'll notice that FindConnectionPoint() provides an IConnectionPoint that represents an outbound interface. IConnectionPoint is also defined in the ActiveX unit, and it looks like this:

```
type
  IConnectionPoint = interface
    ['{B196B286-BAB4-101A-B69C-00AA00341D07}']
```

```
    function GetConnectionInterface(out iid: TIID): HResult; stdcall;
    function GetConnectionPointContainer(
      out cpc: IConnectionPointContainer): HResult; stdcall;
    function Advise(const unkSink: IUnknown; out dwCookie: Longint):
      HResult; stdcall;
    function Unadvise(dwCookie: Longint): HResult; stdcall;
    function EnumConnections(out Enum: IEnumConnections): HResult;
      stdcall;
  end;
```

The `GetConnectionInterface()` method of `IConnectionPoint` provides the IID of the outgoing interface supported by this connection point. The `GetConnectionPointContainer()` method provides the `IConnectionPointContainer` (described earlier), which manages this connection point. The `Advise` method is the interesting one. `Advise()` is the method that actually does the magic of hooking up the outgoing events on the server to the `events` interface implemented by the client. The first parameter to this method is the client's implementation of the `events` interface, and the second parameter will receive a cookie that identifies this particular connection. `Unadvise()` simply disconnects the client/server relationship established by `Advise()`. `EnumConnections` enables the client to iterate over all currently active connections (that is, all connections that have called `Advise()`).

Because of the obvious confusion that can arise if we describe the participants in this relationship as simply *client* and *server*, Automation defines some different nomenclature that enables us to unambiguously describe who is who. The implementation of the outgoing interface contained within the client is called a *sink*, and the server object that fires events to the client is referred to as the *source*.

What is hopefully clear in all this is that Automation events have a couple of advantages over Delphi events. Namely, they can be multicast because `IConnectionPoint.Advise()` can be called more than once. Also, Automation events are self-describing (via the type library and the enumeration methods), so they can be manipulated dynamically.

Automation Events in Delphi

Okay, all this technical stuff is well and good, but how do we actually make Automation events work in Delphi? I'm glad you asked. At this point, we'll create an Automation server application that exposes an outgoing interface and a client that implements a sink for the interface. Bear in mind, too, that you don't need to be an expert in connection points, sinks, sources, and whatnot in order to get Delphi to do what you want. However, it does help you in the long run when you understand what goes on behind the wizard's curtain.

The Server

The first step in creating the server is to create a new application. For purposes of this demo, we'll create a new application containing one form with a client-aligned `TMemo`, as shown in Figure 15.12.

FIGURE 15.12

Automation Server with the Events main form.

Next, we'll add an Automation object to this application by selecting File, New, ActiveX, Automation Object from the main menu. This invokes the Automation Object Wizard (refer to Figure 15.4).

Note the Generate Event Support Code option on the Automation Object Wizard. This box must be selected because it will generate the code necessary to expose an outgoing interface on the Automation object. It will also create the outgoing interface in the type library. After selecting OK in this dialog box, we're presented with the Type Library Editor window. Both the Automation interface and the outgoing interface are already present in the type library (named IServerWithEvents and IServerWithEventsEvents, respectively). AddText() and Clear() methods have been added to the IServerWithEvents interface, and OnTextChanged() and OnClear() methods have been added to the IServerWithEventsEvents interface.

As you might guess, Clear() will clear the contents of the memo, and AddText() will add another line of text to the memo. The OnTextChanged() event will fire when the contents of the memo change, and the OnClear() event will fire when the memo is cleared. Notice also that AddText() and OnTextChanged() each have one parameter of type WideString.

The first thing to do is implement the AddText() and Clear() methods. The implementation for these methods is shown here:

```
procedure TServerWithEvents.AddText(const NewText: WideString);
begin
  MainForm.Memo.Lines.Add(NewText);
end;

procedure TServerWithEvents.Clear;
begin
  MainForm.Memo.Lines.Clear;
  if FEvents <> nil then FEvents.OnClear;
end;
```

You should be familiar with all this code except perhaps the last line of Clear(). This code ensures that there's a client sink advised on the event by checking for nil; then it first fires the event simply by calling OnClear().

To set up the OnTextChanged() event, we first have to handle the OnChange event of the memo. We'll do this by inserting a line of code into the Initialized() method of TServerWithEvents that points the event to the method in TServerWithEvents:

```
MainForm.Memo.OnChange := MemoChange;
```

The MemoChange() method is implemented as follows:

```
procedure TServerWithEvents.MemoChange(Sender: TObject);
begin
  if FEvents <> nil then FEvents.OnTextChanged((Sender as TMemo).Text);
end;
```

This code also checks to ensure that a client is listening; then it fires the event, passing the memo's text as the parameter.

Believe it or not, that sums the implementation of the server! Now we'll move on to the client.

The Client

The client is an application with one form that contains a TEdit, TMemo, and three TButton components, as shown in Figure 15.13.

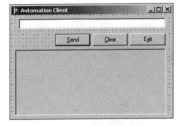

FIGURE 15.13

The Automation Client main form.

In the main unit for the client application, the Server_TLB unit has been added to the uses clause so that we have access to the types and methods contained within that unit. The main form object, TMainForm, of the client application will contain a field that references the server called FServer of type IServerWithEvents. We'll create an instance of the server in TMainForm's constructor using the helper class found in Server_TLB, like this:

```
FServer := CoServerWithEvents.Create;
```

The next step is to implement the event sink class. Because this class will be called by the server via Automation, it must implement IDispatch (and therefore IUnknown). The type declaration for this class is shown here:

```
type
  TEventSink = class(TObject, IUnknown, IDispatch)
  private
    FController: TMainForm;
    { IUnknown }
    function QueryInterface(const IID: TGUID; out Obj): HResult; stdcall;
    function _AddRef: Integer; stdcall;
    function _Release: Integer; stdcall;
    { IDispatch }
    function GetTypeInfoCount(out Count: Integer): HResult; stdcall;
    function GetTypeInfo(Index, LocaleID: Integer; out TypeInfo):
      HResult; stdcall;
    function GetIDsOfNames(const IID: TGUID; Names: Pointer;
      NameCount, LocaleID: Integer; DispIDs: Pointer): HResult; stdcall;
    function Invoke(DispID: Integer; const IID: TGUID; LocaleID: Integer;
      Flags: Word; var Params; VarResult, ExcepInfo, ArgErr: Pointer):
      HResult; stdcall;
  public
    constructor Create(Controller: TMainForm);
  end;
```

Most of the methods of IUnknown and IDispatch aren't implemented, with the notable exceptions of IUnknown.QueryInterface() and IDispatch.Invoke(). These will be discussed in turn.

The QueryInterface() method for TEventSink is implemented as shown here:

```
function TEventSink.QueryInterface(const IID: TGUID; out Obj): HResult;
begin
  // First look for my own implementation of an interface
  // (I implement IUnknown and IDispatch).
  if GetInterface(IID, Obj) then
    Result := S_OK
  // Next, if they are looking for outgoing interface, recurse to return
  // our IDispatch pointer.
  else if IsEqualIID(IID, IServerWithEventsEvents) then
    Result := QueryInterface(IDispatch, Obj)
  // For everything else, return an error.
  else
    Result := E_NOINTERFACE;
end;
```

Essentially, this method returns an instance only when the requested interface is IUnknown, IDispatch, or IServerWithEventsEvents.

Here's the Invoke method for TEventSink:

```
function TEventSink.Invoke(DispID: Integer; const IID: TGUID;
  LocaleID: Integer; Flags: Word; var Params; VarResult, ExcepInfo,
  ArgErr: Pointer): HResult;
var
  V: OleVariant;
begin
  Result := S_OK;
  case DispID of
    1:
      begin
        // First parameter is new string
        V := OleVariant(TDispParams(Params).rgvarg^[0]);
        FController.OnServerMemoChanged(V);
      end;
    2: FController.OnClear;
  end;
end;
```

TEventSink.Invoke() is hard-coded for methods having DispID 1 or DispID 2, which happen to be the DispIDs chosen for OnTextChanged() and OnClear(), respectively, in the server application. OnClear() has the most straightforward implementation: It simply calls the client main form's OnClear() method in response to the event. The OnTextChanged() event is a little trickier: This code pulls the parameter out of the Params.rgvarg array, which is passed in as a parameter to this method, and passes it through to the client main form's OnServerMemoChanged() method. Note that because the number and type of parameters is known, we're able to make simplifying assumptions in the source code. If you're clever, it's possible to implement Invoke() in a generic manner such that it figures out the number and types of parameters and pushes them onto the stack and/or into registers prior to calling the appropriate function. If you'd like to see an example of this, take a look at the TOleControl.InvokeEvent() method in the OleCtrls unit. This method represents the event-sinking logic for the ActiveX control container.

The implementation for OnClear() and OnServerMemoChanged() manipulate the contents of the client's memo. They're shown here:

```
procedure TMainForm.OnServerMemoChanged(const NewText: string);
begin
  Memo.Text := NewText;
end;
```

```
procedure TMainForm.OnClear;
begin
  Memo.Clear;
end;
```

The final piece of the puzzle is to connect the event sink to the server's source interface. This is easily accomplished using the `InterfaceConnect()` function found in the `ComObj` unit, which we'll call from the main form's constructor, like so:

```
InterfaceConnect(FServer, IServerWithEventsEvents, FEventSink, FCookie);
```

The first parameter to this function is a reference to the source object. The second parameter is the IID of the outgoing interface. The third parameter holds the event sink interface. The fourth and final parameter is the cookie, and it's a reference parameter that will be filled in by the callee.

To be a good citizen, you should also clean up properly by calling `InterfaceDisconnect()` when you're finished playing with events. This is done in the main form's destructor:

```
InterfaceDisconnect(FEventSink, IServerWithEventsEvents, FCookie);
```

The Demo

Now that the client and server are written, we can see them in action. Be sure to run and close the server once (or run it with the /regserver switch) to ensure that it's registered before attempting to run the client. Figure 15.14 shows the interactions between client, server, source, and sink.

FIGURE 15.14
The Automation client manipulating the server and receiving events.

Events with Multiple Sinks

Although the technique just described works great for firing events back to a single client, it doesn't work so well when multiple clients are involved. You'll often find yourself in situations where multiple clients are connecting to your server, and you need to fire events back to all clients. Fortunately, you need just a little bit more code to add this type of functionality. In order to fire events back to multiple clients, you must write code that enumerates over each advised connection and calls the appropriate method on the sink. This can be done by making several modifications to the previous example.

First things first. In order to support multiple client connections on a connection point, we must pass `ckMulti` in the `Kind` parameter of `TConnectionPoints.CreateConnectionPoint()`. This method is called from the Automation object's `Initialize()` method, as shown here:

```
FConnectionPoints.CreateConnectionPoint(AutoFactory.EventIID, ckMulti,
  EventConnect);
```

Before connections can be enumerated, we need to obtain a reference to `IConnection PointContainer`. From `IConnectionPointContainer`, we can obtain the `IConnectionPoint` representing the outgoing interface, and using the `IConnectionPoint.EnumConnections()` method, we can obtain an `IEnumConnections` interface that can be used to enumerate the connections. All this logic is encapsulated into the following method:

```
function TServerWithEvents.GetConnectionEnumerator: IEnumConnections;
var
  Container: IConnectionPointContainer;
  CP: IConnectionPoint;
begin
  Result := nil;
  OleCheck(QueryInterface(IConnectionPointContainer, Container));
  OleCheck(Container.FindConnectionPoint(AutoFactory.EventIID, CP));
  CP.EnumConnections(Result);
end;
```

After the enumerator interface has been obtained, calling the sink for each client is just a matter of iterating over each connection. This logic is demonstrated in the following code, which fires the `OnTextChanged()` event:

```
procedure TServerWithEvents.MemoChange(Sender: TObject);
var
  EC: IEnumConnections;
  ConnectData: TConnectData;
  Fetched: Cardinal;
begin
  EC := GetConnectionEnumerator;
  if EC <> nil then
  begin
    while EC.Next(1, ConnectData, @Fetched) = S_OK do
      if ConnectData.pUnk <> nil then
        (ConnectData.pUnk as IServerWithEventsEvents).OnTextChanged(
➥(Sender as TMemo).Text);
  end;
end;
```

Finally, in order to enable clients to connect to a single active instance of the Automation object, we must call the `RegisterActiveObject()` COM API function. This function accepts as parameters an `IUnknown` for the object, the CLSID of the object, a flag indicating whether the registration is strong (the server should be `AddRef`-ed) or weak (do not `AddRef` the server), and a handle that's returned by reference:

```
RegisterActiveObject(Self as IUnknown, Class_ServerWithEvents,
    ACTIVEOBJECT_WEAK, FObjRegHandle);
```

Listing 15.10 shows the complete source code for the `ServAuto` unit, which ties all these tidbits together.

LISTING 15.10   ServAuto.pas

```
unit ServAuto;

interface

uses
  ComObj, ActiveX, AxCtrls, Server_TLB;

type
  TServerWithEvents = class(TAutoObject, IConnectionPointContainer,
    IServerWithEvents)
  private
    { Private declarations }
    FConnectionPoints: TConnectionPoints;
    FObjRegHandle: Integer;
    procedure MemoChange(Sender: TObject);
  protected
    { Protected declarations }
    procedure AddText(const NewText: WideString); safecall;
    procedure Clear; safecall;
    function GetConnectionEnumerator: IEnumConnections;
    property ConnectionPoints: TConnectionPoints read FConnectionPoints
      implements IConnectionPointContainer;
  public
    destructor Destroy; override;
    procedure Initialize; override;
  end;

implementation

uses Windows, ComServ, ServMain, SysUtils, StdCtrls;

destructor TServerWithEvents.Destroy;
```

Listing 15.10 Continued

```
begin
  inherited Destroy;
  RevokeActiveObject(FObjRegHandle, nil);  // Make sure I'm removed from ROT
end;

procedure TServerWithEvents.Initialize;
begin
  inherited Initialize;
  FConnectionPoints := TConnectionPoints.Create(Self);
  if AutoFactory.EventTypeInfo <> nil then
    FConnectionPoints.CreateConnectionPoint(AutoFactory.EventIID, ckMulti,
      EventConnect);
  // Route main form memo's OnChange event to MemoChange method:
  MainForm.Memo.OnChange := MemoChange;
  // Register this object with COM's Running Object Table (ROT) so other
  // clients can connect to this instance.
  RegisterActiveObject(Self as IUnknown, Class_ServerWithEvents,
    ACTIVEOBJECT_WEAK, FObjRegHandle);
end;

procedure TServerWithEvents.Clear;
var
  EC: IEnumConnections;
  ConnectData: TConnectData;
  Fetched: Cardinal;
begin
  MainForm.Memo.Lines.Clear;
  EC := GetConnectionEnumerator;
  if EC <> nil then
  begin
    while EC.Next(1, ConnectData, @Fetched) = S_OK do
      if ConnectData.pUnk <> nil then
        (ConnectData.pUnk as IServerWithEventsEvents).OnClear;
  end;
end;

procedure TServerWithEvents.AddText(const NewText: WideString);
begin
  MainForm.Memo.Lines.Add(NewText);
end;

procedure TServerWithEvents.MemoChange(Sender: TObject);
var
  EC: IEnumConnections;
```

15

LISTING 15.10   Continued

```pascal
  ConnectData: TConnectData;
  Fetched: Cardinal;
begin
  EC := GetConnectionEnumerator;
  if EC <> nil then
  begin
    while EC.Next(1, ConnectData, @Fetched) = S_OK do
      if ConnectData.pUnk <> nil then
        (ConnectData.pUnk as IServerWithEventsEvents).OnTextChanged(
➥(Sender as TMemo).Text);
  end;
end;

function TServerWithEvents.GetConnectionEnumerator: IEnumConnections;
var
  Container: IConnectionPointContainer;
  CP: IConnectionPoint;
begin
  Result := nil;
  OleCheck(QueryInterface(IConnectionPointContainer, Container));
  OleCheck(Container.FindConnectionPoint(AutoFactory.EventIID, CP));
  CP.EnumConnections(Result);
end;

initialization
  TAutoObjectFactory.Create(ComServer, TServerWithEvents,
    Class_ServerWithEvents, ciMultiInstance, tmApartment);
end.
```

On the client side, a small adjustment needs to be made in order to enable clients to connect to an active instance if it's already running. This is accomplished using the `GetActiveObject` COM API function, as shown here:

```pascal
procedure TMainForm.FormCreate(Sender: TObject);
var
  ActiveObj: IUnknown;
begin
  // Get active object if it's available, or create anew if not
  GetActiveObject(Class_ServerWithEvents, nil, ActiveObj);
  if ActiveObj <> nil then FServer := ActiveObj as IServerWithEvents
  else FServer := CoServerWithEvents.Create;
  FEventSink := TEventSink.Create(Self);
  InterfaceConnect(FServer, IServerWithEventsEvents, FEventSink, FCookie);
end;
```

Figure 15.15 shows several clients receiving events from a single server.

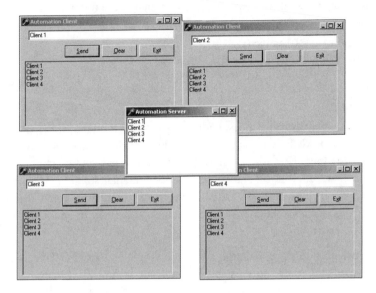

FIGURE 15.15
Several clients manipulating the same server and receiving events.

Automation Collections

Let's face it: We programmers are obsessed with bits of software code that serve as containers for other bits of software code. Think about it—whether it's an array, a TList, a TCollection, a template container class for you C++ folks, or a Java vector, it seems that we're always in search of the proverbial better mousetrap for software objects that hold other software objects. If you consider the time invested over the years in this pursuit for the perfect container class, it's clear that this is an important problem in the minds of developers. And why not? This logical separation of container and contained entities helps us better organize our algorithms and maps to the real world rather nicely (a basket can contain eggs, a pocket can contain coins, a parking lot can contain autos, and so on). Whenever you learn a new language or development model, you have to learn "their way" of managing groups of entities. This leads to my point: Like any other software development model, COM also has its ways for managing these kinds of groups of entities, and to be an effective COM developer, we must learn how to master these things.

When we work with the IDispatch interface, COM specifies two primary methods by which we represent the notion of containership: arrays and collections. If you've done a bit of Automation or ActiveX control work in Delphi, you'll probably already be familiar with

arrays. You can easily create automation arrays in Delphi by adding an array property to your
IDispatch descendant interface or dispinterface, as shown in the following example:

```
type
  IMyDisp = interface(IDispatch)
    function GetProp(Index: Integer): Integer; safecall;
    procedure SetProp(Index, Value: Integer); safecall;
    property Prop[Index: Integer]: Integer read GetProp write SetProp;
  end;
```

Arrays are useful in many circumstances, but they pose some limitations. For example, arrays
make sense when you have data that can be accessed in a logical, fixed-index manner, such as
the strings in an IStrings. However, if the nature of the data is such that individual items are
frequently deleted, added, or moved, an array is a poor container solution. The classic example
is a group of active windows. Because windows are constantly being created, destroyed, and
changing z-order, there's no solid criteria for determining the order in which the windows
should appear in the array.

Collections are designed to solve this problem by allowing you to manipulate a series of elements in a manner that doesn't imply any particular order or number of items. Collections are
unusual because there isn't really a *collection* object or interface, but a collection is instead
represented as a custom IDispatch that follows a number of rules and guidelines. The following rules must be adhered to in order for an IDispatch to qualify as a collection:

- Collections must contain a _NewEnum property that returns the IUnknown for an object
  that supports the IEnumVARIANT interface, which will be used to enumerate the items in
  the collection. Note that the name of this property must be preceded with an underscore,
  and this property must be marked as *restricted* in the type library. The DispID for the
  _NewEnum property must be DISPID_NEWENUM (-4), and it will be defined as follows in the
  Delphi type library editor:

  ```
  function _NewEnum: IUnknown [propget, dispid $FFFFFFFC, restricted];
  safecall;
  ```

- Languages that support the For Each construct, such as Visual Basic, will use this
  method to obtain the IEnumVARIANT interface needed to enumerate collection items. More
  on this is discussed later.

- Collections must contain an Item() method that returns an element from the collection
  based on the index. The DispID for this method must be 0, and it should be marked with
  the *default collection element* flag. If we were to implement a collection of IFoo interface pointers, the definition for this method in the type library editor might look something like this:

  ```
  function Item(Index: Integer): IFoo [propget, dispid $00000000,
    defaultcollelem]; safecall;
  ```

Note that it's also acceptable for the `Index` parameter to be an `OleVariant` so that an `Integer`, `WideString`, or some other type of value can index the item in question.

- Collections must contain a `Count` property that contain returns the number of items in the collection. This method would typically be defined in the type library editor as this:

```
function Count: Integer [propget, dispid $00000001]; safecall;
```

In addition to the aforementioned rules, you should also follow these guidelines when creating your own collection contain objects:

- The property or method that returns a collection should be named with the plural of the name of the items in the collection. For example, if you had a property that returned a collection of listview items, the property name would probably be `Items`, whereas the name of the item in the collection would be `Item`. Likewise, an item called `Foot` would be contained in a collection property called `Feet`. In the rare case that the plural and singular of a word are the same (a collection of fish or deer, for example), the collection property name should be the name of the item with `Collection` tacked on the end (`FishCollection` or `DeerCollection`).

- Collections that support the addition of items should do so using a method called `Add()`. The parameters for this method vary depending on the implementation, but you might want to pass parameters that indicate the initial position of the new item within the collection. The `Add()` method normally returns a reference to the item added to the collection.

- Collections that support the deletion of items should do so using a method called `Remove()`. This method should take one parameter that identifies the index of the item being deleted, and this index should behave semantically in the same manner as the `Item()` method.

A Delphi Implementation

If you've ever created ActiveX controls in Delphi, you might have noticed that fewer controls are listed in the combo box in the ActiveX Control Wizard than there are on the IDE's Component Palette. This is because Borland prevents some controls showing in the list using the `RegisterNonActiveX()` function. One such control that's available on the palette but not in the wizard is the `TListView` control found on the Win32 page of the palette. The `TListView` control isn't shown in the wizard because the wizard doesn't know what to do with its `Items` property, which is of type `TListItems`. Because the wizard doesn't know how to wrap this property type in an ActiveX control, the control is simply excluded from the wizard's list rather than allowing the user to create an utterly useless ActiveX control wrapper of a control.

However, in the case of `TListView`, `RegisterNonActiveX()` is called with the `axrComponentOnly` flag, which means that a descendent of `TListView` will show up in the ActiveX Control Wizard's list. By taking the minor detour of creating a do-nothing descendent of `TListView` called `TListView2` and adding it to the palette, we can then create an ActiveX control that encapsulates the listview control. Of course, then we're faced with the same problem of the wizard not generating wrappers for the `Items` property and having a useless ActiveX control. Fortunately, ActiveX control writing doesn't have to stop at the wizard-generated code, and we're free to wrap the `Items` property ourselves at this point in order to make the control useful. As you might be beginning to suspect, a collection is the perfect way to encapsulate the `Items` property of the `TListView`.

In order to implement this collection of listview items, we must create new objects representing the item and the collection and add a new property to the ActiveX control default interface that returns a collection. We'll begin by defining the object representing an item, which we'll call `ListItem`. The first step to creating the `ListItem` object is to create a new Automation object using the icon found on the ActiveX page of the New Items dialog box. After creating the object, we can fill out the properties and methods for this object in the type library editor. For the purposes of this demonstration, we'll add properties for the `Caption`, `Index`, `Checked`, and `SubItems` properties of a listview item. Similarly, we'll create yet another new Automation object for the collection itself. This Automation object is called `ListItems`, and it's provided with the `_NewEnum`, `Item()`, `Count()`, `Add()`, and `Remove()` methods mentioned earlier. Finally, we'll add a new property to the default interface of the ActiveX control called `Items` that returns a collection.

After the interfaces for `IListItem` and `IListItems` are completely defined in the type library editor, there's a little manual tweaking to be done in the implementation files generated for these objects. Specifically, the default parent class for a new automation object is `TAutoObject`; however, these objects will only be created internally (that is, not from a factory), so we'll manually change the ancestor to `TAutoIntfObject`, which is more appropriate for internally created automation objects. Also, because these objects won't be created from a factory, we'll remove from the units the initialization code that creates the factories because it's not needed.

Now that the entire infrastructure is properly set up, it's time to implement the `ListItem` and `ListItems` objects. The `ListItem` object is the most straightforward because it's a pretty simple wrapper around a listview item. The code for the unit containing this object is shown in Listing 15.11.

LISTING 15.11   The Listview Item Wrapper

```
unit LVItem;

interface

uses
   ComObj, ActiveX, ComCtrls, LVCtrl_TLB, StdVcl, AxCtrls;
```

LISTING 15.11 Continued

```
type
  TListItem = class(TAutoIntfObject, IListItem)
  private
    FListItem: ComCtrls.TListItem;
  protected
    function Get_Caption: WideString; safecall;
    function Get_Index: Integer; safecall;
    function Get_SubItems: IStrings; safecall;
    procedure Set_Caption(const Value: WideString); safecall;
    procedure Set_SubItems(const Value: IStrings); safecall;
    function Get_Checked: WordBool; safecall;
    procedure Set_Checked(Value: WordBool); safecall;
  public
    constructor Create(AOwner: ComCtrls.TListItem);
  end;

implementation

uses ComServ;

constructor TListItem.Create(AOwner: ComCtrls.TListItem);
begin
  inherited Create(ComServer.TypeLib, IListItem);
  FListItem := AOwner;
end;

function TListItem.Get_Caption: WideString;
begin
  Result := FListItem.Caption;
end;

function TListItem.Get_Index: Integer;
begin
  Result := FListItem.Index;
end;

function TListItem.Get_SubItems: IStrings;
begin
  GetOleStrings(FListItem.SubItems, Result);
end;

procedure TListItem.Set_Caption(const Value: WideString);
begin
  FListItem.Caption := Value;
end;
```

LISTING 15.11 Continued

```
procedure TListItem.Set_SubItems(const Value: IStrings);
begin
  SetOleStrings(FListItem.SubItems, Value);
end;

function TListItem.Get_Checked: WordBool;
begin
  Result := FListItem.Checked;
end;

procedure TListItem.Set_Checked(Value: WordBool);
begin
  FListItem.Checked := Value;
end;

end.
```

Note that `ComCtrls.TListItem()` is being passed into the constructor to serve as the listview item to be manipulated by this Automation object.

The implementation for the `ListItems` collection object is just a bit more complex. First, because the object must be able to provide an object supporting `IEnumVARIANT` in order to implement the `_NewEnum` property, `IEnumVARIANT` is supported directly in this object. Therefore, the `TListItems` class supports both `IListItems` and `IEnumVARIANT`. `IEnumVARIANT` contains four methods, which are described in Table 15.1.

TABLE 15.1 `IEnumVARIANT` Methods

Method	Purpose
Next	Retrieves the next *n* number of items in the collection
Skip	Skips over *n* items in the collection
Reset	Resets current item back to the first item in the collection
Clone	Creates a copy of this `IEnumVARIANT`

The source code for the unit containing the `ListItems` object is shown in Listing 15.12.

LISTING 15.12 The Listview Items Wrapper

```
unit LVItems;

interface
```

LISTING 15.12 Continued

```
uses
  ComObj, Windows, ActiveX, ComCtrls, LVCtrl_TLB;

type
  TListItems = class(TAutoIntfObject, IListItems, IEnumVARIANT)
  private
    FListItems: ComCtrls.TListItems;
    FEnumPos: Integer;
  protected
    { IListItems methods }
    function Add: IListItem; safecall;
    function Get_Count: Integer; safecall;
    function Get_Item(Index: Integer): IListItem; safecall;
    procedure Remove(Index: Integer); safecall;
    function Get__NewEnum: IUnknown; safecall;
    { IEnumVariant methods }
    function Next(celt: Longint; out elt;  pceltFetched: PLongint): HResult;
      stdcall;
    function Skip(celt: Longint): HResult; stdcall;
    function Reset: HResult; stdcall;
    function Clone(out Enum: IEnumVariant): HResult; stdcall;
  public
    constructor Create(AOwner: ComCtrls.TListItems);
  end;

implementation

uses ComServ, LVItem;

{ TListItems }

constructor TListItems.Create(AOwner: ComCtrls.TListItems);
begin
  inherited Create(ComServer.TypeLib, IListItems);
  FListItems := AOwner;
end;

{ TListItems.IListItems }

function TListItems.Add: IListItem;
begin
  Result := LVItem.TListItem.Create(FListItems.Add);
end;
```

LISTING 15.12 Continued

```
function TListItems.Get__NewEnum: IUnknown;
begin
  Result := Self;
end;

function TListItems.Get_Count: Integer;
begin
  Result := FListItems.Count;
end;

function TListItems.Get_Item(Index: Integer): IListItem;
begin
  Result := LVItem.TListItem.Create(FListItems[Index]);
end;

procedure TListItems.Remove(Index: Integer);
begin
  FListItems.Delete(Index);
end;

{ TListItems.IEnumVariant }

function TListItems.Clone(out Enum: IEnumVariant): HResult;
begin
  Enum := nil;
  Result := S_OK;
  try
    Enum := TListItems.Create(FListItems);
  except
    Result := E_OUTOFMEMORY;
  end;
end;

function TListItems.Next(celt: Integer; out elt; pceltFetched: PLongint):
  HResult;
var
  V: OleVariant;
  I: Integer;
begin
  Result := S_FALSE;
  try
    if pceltFetched <> nil then pceltFetched^ := 0;
    for I := 0 to celt - 1 do
    begin
      if FEnumPos >= FListItems.Count then Exit;
```

LISTING 15.12   Continued

```
      V := Get_Item(FEnumPos);
      TVariantArgList(elt)[I] := TVariantArg(V);
      // trick to prevent variant from being garbage collected, since it needs
      // to stay alive because it is party of the elt array
      TVarData(V).VType := varEmpty;
      TVarData(V).VInteger := 0;
      Inc(FEnumPos);
      if pceltFetched <> nil then Inc(pceltFetched^);
    end;
  except
  end;
  if (pceltFetched = nil) or ((pceltFetched <> nil) and
    (pceltFetched^ = celt)) then
    Result := S_OK;
end;

function TListItems.Reset: HResult;
begin
  FEnumPos := 0;
  Result := S_OK;
end;

function TListItems.Skip(celt: Integer): HResult;
begin
  Inc(FEnumPos, celt);
  Result := S_OK;
end;

end.
```

The only method in this unit with a nontrivial implementation is the Next() method. The celt parameter of the Next() method indicates how many items should be retrieved. The elt parameter contains an array of TVarArgs with at least elt elements. Upon return, pceltFetched (if not nil) should hold the actual number of items fetched. This method returns S_OK when the number of items returned is the same as the number requested; it returns S_FALSE otherwise. The logic for this method iterates over the array in elt and assigns a TVarArg representing a collection item to an element of the array. Note the little trick we're performing to clear out the OleVariant after assigning it to the array. This ensures that the array won't be garbage collected. Were we not to do this, the contents of elt could potentially become stale if the objects referenced by V are freed when the OleVariant is finalized.

Similar to TListItem, the constructor for TListItems takes ComCtrls.TListItems as a parameter and manipulates that object in the implementation of its methods.

Finally, we complete the implementation of the ActiveX control by adding the logic to manage the Items property. First, we must add a field to the object to hold the collection:

```
type
  TListViewX = class(TActiveXControl, IListViewX)
  private
    ...
    FItems: IListItems;
    ...
  end;
```

Next, we assign FItems to a new TListItems instance in the InitializeControl() method:

```
FItems := LVItems.TListItems.Create(FDelphiControl.Items);
```

Last, the Get_Items() method can be implemented to simply return FItems:

```
function TListViewX.Get_Items: IListItems;
begin
  Result := FItems;
end;
```

The real test to see whether this collection works is to load the control in Visual Basic 6 and try to use the For Each construct with the collection. Figure 15.16 shows a simple VB test application running.

FIGURE 15.16

A Visual Basic application to test our collection.

Of the two command buttons you see in Figure 15.16, Command1 adds items to the listview, whereas Command2 iterates over all the items in the listview using For Each and adds exclamation points to each caption. The code for these methods is shown here:

```
Private Sub Command1_Click()
  ListViewX1.Items.Add.Caption = "Delphi"
End Sub
```

```
Private Sub Command2_Click()
  Dim Item As ListItem
  Set Items = ListViewX1.Items
  For Each Item In Items
   Item.Caption = Item.Caption + " Rules!!"
  Next
End Sub
```

Despite the feelings that some of the Delphi faithful have toward VB, we must remember that VB is the primary consumer of ActiveX controls, and it's very important to ensure that our controls function properly in that environment.

Collections provide powerful functionality that can enable your controls and Automation servers to function more smoothly in the world of COM. Because collections are terribly difficult to implement, it's worth your while to get in the habit of using them when appropriate. Unfortunately, once you become comfortable with collections, it's very likely that someone will soon come along and create yet a newer and better container object for COM.

New Interface Types in the Type Library

As every well-behaved Delphi developer should, we've used the type library editor to define new interfaces for our Automation objects. However, it's not unusual to occasionally run into a situation whereby one of the methods for a new interface includes a parameter of a COM interface type that isn't supported by default in the type library editor. Because the type library editor doesn't let you work with types that it doesn't know about, how do you complete such a method definition?

Before this is explained, it's important that you understand why the type library editor behaves the way it does. If you create a new method in the type library editor and take a look at the types available in the Type column of the Parameters page, you'll see a number of interfaces, including IDataBroker, IDispatch, IEnumVARIANT, IFont, IPicture, IProvider, IStrings, and IUnknown. Why are these the only interfaces available? What makes them so special? They're not special, really—they just happen to be types defined in type libraries that are used by this type library. By default, a Delphi type library automatically uses the Borland Standard VCL type library and the OLE Automation type library. You can configure which type libraries are used by your type library by selecting the root node in the tree view in the left pane of the type library editor and choosing the Uses tab in the page control in the right pane. The types contained in the type libraries used by your type library will automatically become available in the drop-down list shown in the type library editor.

Armed with this knowledge, you've probably already figured out that if the interface you want to use as the method parameter in question is defined in a type library, you can simply use that type library, and the problem is solved. But what if the interface isn't defined in a type library?

There are certainly quite a few COM interfaces that are defined only by SDK in header or IDL files and aren't found in type libraries. If this is the case, the best course is to define the method parameter as being of type IUnknown. This IUnknown can be QueryInterfaced in your method implementation for the specific interface type you want to work with. You should also be sure to document this method parameter as an IUnknown that must support the appropriate interface. The following code shows an example of how such a method could be implemented:

```
procedure TSomeClass.SomeMethod(SomeParam: IUnknown);
var
  Intf: ISomeComInterface;
begin
  Intf := SomeParam as ISomeComInterface;
  // remainder of method implementation
end;
```

You should also be aware of the fact that the interface to which you cast the IUnknown must be an interface that COM knows how to marshal. This means that it must either be defined in a type library somewhere, must be a type compatible with the standard Automation marshaler, or the COM server in question must provide a proxy/stub DLL capable of marshaling the interface.

Exchanging Binary Data

Occasionally you might want to exchange a block of binary data between an Automation client and server. Because COM doesn't support the exchange of raw pointers, you can't simply pass pointers around. However, the solution isn't much more difficult than that. The easiest way to exchange binary data between Automation clients and servers is to use safearrays of bytes. Delphi encapsulates safearrays nicely in OleVariants. The admittedly contrived example shown in Listings 15.13 and 15.14 depicts client and server units that use memo text to demonstrate how to transfer binary data using safearrays of bytes.

LISTING 15.13   The Server Unit

```
unit ServObj;

interface

uses
  ComObj, ActiveX, Server_TLB;

type
  TBinaryData = class(TAutoObject, IBinaryData)
  protected
    function Get_Data: OleVariant; safecall;
```

LISTING 15.13   Continued

```
    procedure Set_Data(Value: OleVariant); safecall;
  end;

implementation

uses ComServ, ServMain;

function TBinaryData.Get_Data: OleVariant;
var
  P: Pointer;
  L: Integer;
begin
  // Move data from memo into array
  L := Length(MainForm.Memo.Text);
  Result := VarArrayCreate([0, L - 1], varByte);
  P := VarArrayLock(Result);
  try
    Move(MainForm.Memo.Text[1], P^, L);
  finally
    VarArrayUnlock(Result);
  end;
end;

procedure TBinaryData.Set_Data(Value: OleVariant);
var
  P: Pointer;
  L: Integer;
  S: string;
begin
  // Move data from array into memo
  L := VarArrayHighBound(Value, 1) - VarArrayLowBound(Value, 1) + 1;
  SetLength(S, L);
  P := VarArrayLock(Value);
  try
    Move(P^, S[1], L);
  finally
    VarArrayUnlock(Value);
  end;
  MainForm.Memo.Text := S;
end;

initialization
  TAutoObjectFactory.Create(ComServer, TBinaryData, Class_BinaryData,
    ciSingleInstance, tmApartment);
end.
```

Listing 15.14   The Client Unit

```
unit CliMain;

interface

uses
  Windows, Messages, SysUtils, Classes, Graphics, Controls, Forms, Dialogs,
  StdCtrls, ExtCtrls, Server_TLB;

type
  TMainForm = class(TForm)
    Memo: TMemo;
    Panel1: TPanel;
    SetButton: TButton;
    GetButton: TButton;
    OpenButton: TButton;
    OpenDialog: TOpenDialog;
    procedure OpenButtonClick(Sender: TObject);
    procedure FormCreate(Sender: TObject);
    procedure SetButtonClick(Sender: TObject);
    procedure GetButtonClick(Sender: TObject);
  private
    FServer: IBinaryData;
  end;

var
  MainForm: TMainForm;

implementation

{$R *.DFM}

procedure TMainForm.FormCreate(Sender: TObject);
begin
  FServer := CoBinaryData.Create;
end;

procedure TMainForm.OpenButtonClick(Sender: TObject);
begin
  if OpenDialog.Execute then
    Memo.Lines.LoadFromFile(OpenDialog.FileName);
end;

procedure TMainForm.SetButtonClick(Sender: TObject);
var
  P: Pointer;
```

LISTING **15.14**   Continued

```
  L: Integer;
  V: OleVariant;
begin
  // Send memo data to server
  L := Length(Memo.Text);
  V := VarArrayCreate([0, L - 1], varByte);
  P := VarArrayLock(V);
  try
    Move(Memo.Text[1], P^, L);
  finally
    VarArrayUnlock(V);
  end;
  FServer.Data := V;
end;

procedure TMainForm.GetButtonClick(Sender: TObject);
var
  P: Pointer;
  L: Integer;
  S: string;
  V: OleVariant;
begin
  // Get server's memo data
  V := FServer.Data;
  L := VarArrayHighBound(V, 1) - VarArrayLowBound(V, 1) + 1;
  SetLength(S, L);
  P := VarArrayLock(V);
  try
    Move(P^, S[1], L);
  finally
    VarArrayUnlock(V);
  end;
  Memo.Text := S;
end;

end.
```

Behind the Scenes: Language Support for COM

One thing often heard when folks talk about COM development in Delphi is what great language support Object Pascal provides for COM. (You won't get any static from us on that point.) With features such as interfaces, variants, and wide strings built right into the language, it's hardly a point to be argued. However, what does it mean to have these things built into the language? How do these features work, and what's the nature of their dependence on the COM APIs? In this section, we'll take a low-level look at how all the pieces fit together to form Object Pascal's COM support and dig into some of the implementation details of the language features.

As I mentioned, Object Pascal's COM language features can basically be summed up into three categories:

- Variant and OleVariant, which encapsulate COM's variant record, safearrays, and late-bound Automation.

- WideString, which encapsulates COM's BSTR.

- Interface and dispinterface, which encapsulate COM interfaces and early- and ID-bound Automation.

You crusty old OLE developers from the Delphi 2 days might have noticed the automated reserved word, although which late-bound Automation servers could be created is conveniently ignored. Because this feature was superceded by the "real" Automation support first introduced in Delphi 3 and remains only for backward compatibility, it won't be discussed here.

Variants

Variants are the oldest form of COM support in Delphi, dating back to Delphi 2. As you likely already know, a Variant is really just a big record that's used to pass around some bit of data that can be any one of a number of types. If you're interested in what this record looks like, it's defined in the System unit as TVarData:

```
type
  PVarData = ^TVarData;
  TVarData = record
    VType: Word;
    Reserved1, Reserved2, Reserved3: Word;
    case Integer of
      varSmallint: (VSmallint: Smallint);
      varInteger:  (VInteger: Integer);
      varSingle:   (VSingle: Single);
      varDouble:   (VDouble: Double);
      varCurrency: (VCurrency: Currency);
      varDate:     (VDate: Double);
      varOleStr:   (VOleStr: PWideChar);
      varDispatch: (VDispatch: Pointer);
      varError:    (VError: LongWord);
      varBoolean:  (VBoolean: WordBool);
      varUnknown:  (VUnknown: Pointer);
      varByte:     (VByte: Byte);
      varString:   (VString: Pointer);
```

```
        varAny:        (VAny: Pointer);
        varArray:      (VArray: PVarArray);
        varByRef:      (VPointer: Pointer);
   end;
```

The value of the VType field of this record indicates the type of data contained in the Variant, and it can be any of the variant type codes found at the top of the System unit and listed in the variant portion of this record (within the case statement). The only difference between Variant and OleVariant is that Variant supports all the type codes, whereas OleVariant only supports those types compatible in Automation. For example, an attempt to assign a Pascal string (varString) to a Variant is an acceptable practice, but assigning the same string to an OleVariant will cause it to be converted to an Automation-compatible WideString (varOleStr).

When you work with the Variant and OleVariant types, what the compiler is really manipulating and passing around is instances of this TVarData record. In fact, you can safely typecast a Variant or OleVariant to a TVarData if you for some reason need to manipulate the innards of the record (although we don't recommend this practice unless you really know what you're doing).

In the harsh world of COM programming in C and C++ (without a class framework such as Microsoft's Active Template Library), variants are represented with the VARIANT struct defined in oaidl.h. When working with variants in this environment, you have to manually initialize and manage them using VariantXXX() API functions found in oleaut32.dll, such as VariantInit(), VariantCopy(), VariantClear(), and so on. This makes working with variants in straight C and C++ a high-maintenance task.

With support for variants built into Object Pascal, the compiler generates the necessary calls to the API's variant-support routines automatically as you use instances of the Variant and OleVariant types. This nicety in the language does saddle you with one bit of baggage you should know about, however. If you inspect the import table of a "do-nothing" Delphi EXE using a tool such as Borland's TDUMP.EXE or Microsoft's DUMPBIN.EXE, you'll notice a few suspicious imports from oleaut32.dll: VariantChangeTypeEx(), VariantCopyInd(), VariantCopy(), VariantClear(), and VariantInit(). What this means is that even in an application in which you do not explicitly employ Variant or OleVariant types, your Delphi EXE still has a dependence on these COM API functions in oleaut32.dll.

Variant Arrays

Variant arrays in Delphi are designed to encapsulate COM safearrays, which are a type of record used to encapsulate an array of data in Automation. They're called *safe* because they're self-describing; in addition to array data, the record contains information regarding the number of dimensions, the size of an element, and the number of elements in the array. Variant arrays are created and managed in Delphi using the VarArray*XXX*() functions and procedures found in the System unit and documented in the online help. These functions and procedures are essentially wrappers around the API's SafeArray*XXX*() functions. Once a Variant contains a variant array, standard array subscript syntax is used to access array elements. Once again, comparing this to manually coding safearrays as you would in C and C++, Object Pascal's language encapsulation is clean and much less cumbersome and error prone.

Late-Binding Automation

As you learned earlier in this chapter, Variant and OleVariant types enable you to write late-binding Automation clients. (*Late-binding* means that functions are called at runtime using the Invoke method of the IDispatch interface.) That's all pretty easy to take at face value, but the question is "Where's the magic connection between calling a method of an Automation server from a Variant and IDispatch.Invoke() somehow getting called with the right parameters?" The answer is more low tech than you might expect.

When a method call is made on a Variant or OleVariant containing an IDispatch, the compiler simply generates a call to the _DispInvoke helper function declared in the System unit, which jumps to a function pointer called VarDispProc. By default, the VarDispProc pointer is assigned to a method that simply returns an error when it's called. However, if you include the ComObj unit in your uses clause, the initialization section for the ComObj unit redirects VarDispProc to another method with a line of code that looks like this:

```
VarDispProc := @VarDispInvoke;
```

VarDispInvoke is a procedure in the ComObj unit with the following declaration:

```
procedure VarDispInvoke(Result: PVariant; const Instance: Variant;
  CallDesc: PCallDesc; Params: Pointer); cdecl;
```

The implementation of the procedure handles the complexity of calling IDispatch.GetIDsOfNames() to obtain a DispID from the method name, setting up the parameters correctly, and making the call to IDispatch.Invoke(). What's interesting about this is that the compiler in this instance doesn't have any inherent knowledge of IDispatch or how the Invoke() call is made; it simply passes a bunch of stuff through a function pointer. Also interesting is the fact that because of this architecture, you could reroute this function pointer to your own procedure if you wanted to handle all Automation calls through Variant and OleVariant types yourself. You would only have to ensure that your function declaration matched that of VarDispInvoke. Certainly, this would be a task reserved for experts, but it's interesting to know that the flexibility is there when you need it.

WideString

The WideString data type was added in Delphi 3 to serve the dual purpose of providing a native double-byte, Unicode character string and a character string compatible with the COM BSTR string. The WideString type differs from its cousin AnsiString in a few keys respects:

- The characters comprising a WideString string are all two bytes in size.
- WideString types are always allocated using SysAllocStringLen() and therefore are fully compatible with BSTRs.
- WideString types are never reference-counted and therefore are always copied on assignment.

Like variants, BSTRs can be cumbersome to work with using standard API functions, so the native Object Pascal support via WideString is certainly a welcome language addition. However, because they consume twice the memory and aren't reference-counted, they are much more inefficient than AnsiStrings, and you should therefore be judicious about their use.

Like the Pascal Variant, WideString causes a number of functions to be imported from oleaut32.dll. Inspecting the import table of a Delphi application that employs WideStrings reveals that functions such as SysStringLen(), SysFreeString(), SysReAllocStringLen(), and SysAllocStringLen() are all pulled in by the Delphi RTL in order to provide WideString support.

Interfaces

Perhaps the most important big-ticket COM feature in the Object Pascal language is the native support for interfaces. Somewhat ironically, although arguably smaller features such as Variants and WideStrings pull in functions from the COM API for implementation, Object Pascal's implementation of interfaces doesn't require COM at all. That is, Object Pascal provides a completely self-contained implementation of interfaces that adheres to the COM specification, but it doesn't necessarily require any COM API functions.

As a part of adhering to the COM spec, all interfaces in Delphi implicitly descend from IUnknown. As you might know, IUnknown provides the identity and reference-counting support that's the root of COM. This means that knowledge of IUnknown is built into the compiler, and IUnknown is defined in the System unit. By making IUnknown a first-class citizen in the language, Delphi is able to provide the automatic reference counting by having the compiler generate the calls to IUnknown.AddRef() and IUnknown.Release() at the appropriate times. Additionally, the as operator can be used as a shortcut for interface identity normally obtained via QueryInterface(). The root support for IUnknown, however, is almost incidental when you consider the low-level support that the language and compiler provide for interfaces in general.

Figure 15.17 shows a simplified diagram of how classes internally support interfaces. A Delphi object is really a reference that points to the physical instance. The first four bytes of an object instance are a pointer to the object's virtual method table (VMT). At a positive offset from the VMT are all the object's virtual methods. At a negative offset are pointers to methods and data that are important to the internal function of the object. In particular, offset -72 from the VMT contains a pointer to the object's interface table. The interface table is a list of `PInterfaceEntry` records (defined in the `System` unit) that essentially contain the IID and information on where to find the vtable pointer for that IID.

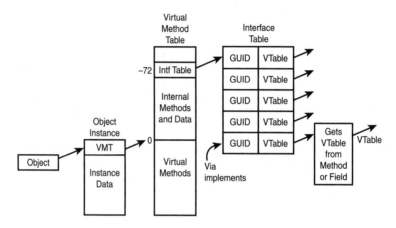

FIGURE 15.17

How interfaces are supported internally in Object Pascal.

After you have a moment to reflect on the diagram in Figure 15.17 and understand how things are put together, the details surrounding the implementation of interfaces just kind of fall into place. For example, `QueryInterface()` is normally implemented on Object Pascal objects by calling `TObject.GetInterface()`. `GetInterface()` walks the interface table looking for the IID in question and returns the vtable pointer for that interface. This also illustrates why new interface types must be defined with a GUID; otherwise, there would be no way for `GetInterface()` to walk the interface table, and therefore there would be no identity via `QueryInterface()`. Typecasting of interfaces using the as operator simply generates a call to `QueryInterface()`, so the same rules apply there.

The last entry in the interface table in Figure 15.17 illustrates how an interface is implemented internally using the `implements` directive. Rather than providing a direct pointer for the vtable, the interface table entry provides the address of a little compiler-generated getter function that gets the interface vtable from the property upon which the implements directive was used.

Dispinterfaces

A dispinterface provides an encapsulation of a non–dual `IDispatch`. That is, an `IDispatch` in which methods can be called via `Invoke()` but not via a vtable. In this respect, a dispinterface is similar to Automation with variants. However, dispinterfaces are slightly more efficient than variants because `dispinterface` declarations contain the DispID for each of the properties or methods supported. This means that `IDispatch.Invoke()` can be called directly without first calling `IDispatch.GetIDsOfNames()`, as must be done with a variant. The mechanism behind dispinterfaces is similar to that of variants: When you call a method via a dispinterface, the compiler generates a call to `_IntfDispCall` in the `System` unit. This method jumps through the `DispCallByIDProc` pointer, which by default only returns an error. However, when the `ComObj` unit is included, `DispCallByIDProc` is routed to the `DispCallByID()` procedure, which is declared in `ComObj` as follows:

```
procedure DispCallByID(Result: Pointer; const Dispatch: IDispatch;
  DispDesc: PDispDesc; Params: Pointer); cdecl;
```

TOleContainer

Now that you have some ActiveX OLE background under your belt, take a look at Delphi's `TOleContainer` class. `TOleContainer` is located in the `OleCntrs` unit, and it encapsulates the complexities of an OLE Document and ActiveX Document container into an easily digestible VCL component.

> **NOTE**
>
> If you were familiar with using Delphi 1.0's `TOleContainer` component, you can pretty much throw that knowledge out the window. The 32-bit version of this component was redesigned from the ground up (as they say in the car commercials), so any knowledge you have of the 16-bit version of this component might not be applicable to the 32-bit version. Don't let that scare you, though; the 32-bit version of this component is of a much cleaner design, and you'll find that the code you must write to support the object is perhaps a quarter of what it used to be.

A Small Sample Application

Now let's jump right in and create an OLE container application. Create a new project and drop a `TOleContainer` object (found on the System page of the Component Palette) on the form. Right-click the object in the Form Designer and select Insert Object from the local menu. This invokes the Insert Object dialog box, as shown in Figure 15.18.

Embedding a New OLE Object

By default, the Insert Object dialog box contains the names of OLE server applications registered with Windows. To embed a new OLE object, you can select a server application from the Object Type list box. This causes the OLE server to execute in order to create a new OLE object to be inserted into `TOleContainer`. When you close the server application, the `TOleContainer` object is updated with the embedded object. For this example, we'll create a new MS Word 2000 document, as shown in Figure 15.19.

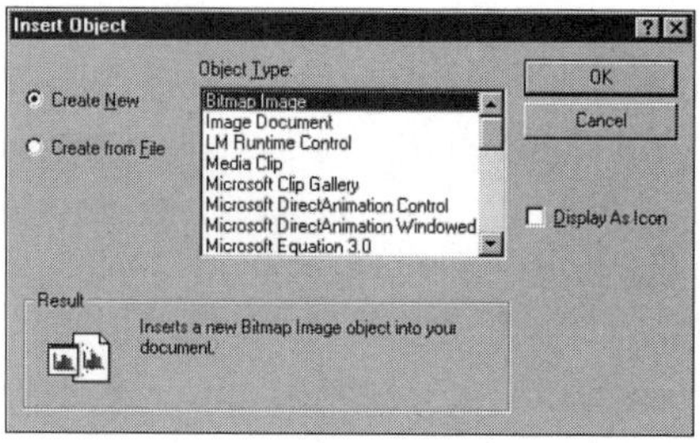

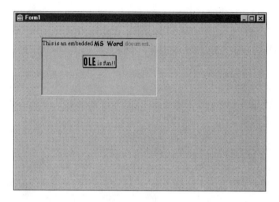

FIGURE 15.18

The Insert Object dialog box.

FIGURE 15.19

An embedded MS Word 2000 document.

> **NOTE**
>
> An OLE object won't activate in place at design time. You'll only be able to take advantage of the in-place activation capability of TOleContainer at runtime.

If you want to invoke the Insert Object dialog box at runtime, you can call the InsertObjectDialog() method of TOleContainer, which is defined as follows:

```
function InsertObjectDialog: Boolean;
```

This function returns True if a new type of OLE object was successfully chosen from the dialog box.

Embedding or Linking an Existing OLE File

To embed an existing OLE file into the TOleContainer, select the Create From File radio button on the Insert Object dialog box. This enables you to pick an existing file, as shown in Figure 15.20. After you choose the file, it behaves much the same as a new OLE object.

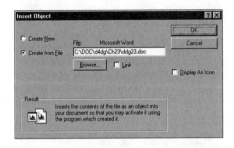

FIGURE 15.20
Inserting an object from a file.

To embed a file at runtime, call the CreateObjectFromFile() method of TOleContainer, which is defined as follows:

```
procedure CreateObjectFromFile(const FileName: string; Iconic: Boolean);
```

To link (rather than embed) the OLE object, simply check the Link check box in the Insert Object dialog box shown in Figure 15.20. As described earlier, this creates a link from your application to the OLE file so that you can edit and view the same linked object from multiple applications.

To link to a file at runtime, call the CreateLinkToFile() method of TOleContainer, which is defined as follows:

```
procedure CreateLinkToFile(const FileName: string; Iconic: Boolean);
```

A Bigger Sample Application

Now that you have the basics of OLE and the TOleContainer class behind you, we'll create a more sizable application that truly reflects the usage of OLE in realistic applications.

Start by creating a new project based on the MDI application template. The main form makes only a few modifications to the standard MDI template, and it's shown in Figure 15.21.

The MDI child form is shown in Figure 15.22. It's simply an fsMDIChild-style form with a TOleContainer component aligned to alClient.

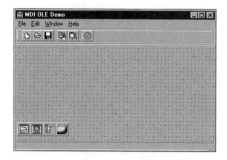

FIGURE 15.21
The MDI OLE Demo main window.

FIGURE 15.22
The MDI OLE Demo child window.

Listing 15.15 shows ChildWin.pas, the source code unit for the MDI child form. Note that this unit is fairly standard except for the addition of the OLEFileName property and the associated method and private instance variable. This property stores the path and filename of the OLE file, and the property accessor sets the child form's caption to the filename.

LISTING 15.15   The Source Code for ChildWin.pas

```
unit Childwin;

interface

uses WinTypes, WinProcs, Classes, Graphics, Forms, Controls, OleCtnrs;

type
  TMDIChild = class(TForm)
    OleContainer: TOleContainer;
    procedure FormClose(Sender: TObject; var Action: TCloseAction);
  private
    FOLEFilename: String;
    procedure SetOLEFileName(const Value: String);
```

LISTING 15.15   Continued

```
  public
    property OLEFileName: String read FOLEFileName write SetOLEFileName;
  end;

implementation

{$R *.DFM}

uses Main, SysUtils;

procedure TMDIChild.SetOLEFileName(const Value: String);
begin
  if Value <> FOLEFileName then begin
    FOLEFileName := Value;
    Caption := ExtractFileName(FOLEFileName);
  end;
end;

procedure TMDIChild.FormClose(Sender: TObject; var Action: TCloseAction);
begin
  Action := caFree;
end;

end.
```

Creating a Child Form

When a new MDI child form is created from the File, New menu of the MDI OLE Demo application, the Insert Object dialog box is invoked using the `InsertObjectDialog()` method mentioned earlier. Additionally, a caption is assigned to the MDI child form using a global variable called `NumChildren` to provide a unique number. The following code shows the main form's `CreateMDIChild()` method:

```
procedure TMainForm.FileNewItemClick(Sender: TObject);
begin
  inc(NumChildren);
  { create a new MDI child window }
  with TMDIChild.Create(Application) do
  begin
    Caption := 'Untitled' + IntToStr(NumChildren);
    { bring up insert OLE object dialog and insert into child }
    OleContainer.InsertObjectDialog;
  end;
end;
```

15

COM
DEVELOPMENT

Saving to and Reading from Files

As discussed earlier in this chapter, OLE objects lend themselves to the capability of being written to and read from streams and, therefore, files. The `TOleContainer` component has the methods `SaveToStream()`, `LoadFromStream()`, `SaveToFile()`, and `LoadFromFile()`, which make saving an OLE object out to a file or stream very easy.

The `MDIOLE` application's main form contains methods for saving and opening OLE object files. The following code shows the `FileOpenItemClick()` method, which is called in response to choosing File, Open from the main form. In addition to loading a saved OLE object from a file specified by `OpenDialog`, this method also assigns the `OleFileName` field of the `TMDIChild` instance to the filename provided by `OpenDialog`. If an error occurs loading the file, the form instance is freed. Here's the code:

```
procedure TMainForm.FileOpenItemClick(Sender: TObject);
begin
  if OpenDialog.Execute then
    with TMDIChild.Create(Application) do
    begin
      try
        OleFileName := OpenDialog.FileName;
        OleContainer.LoadFromFile(OleFileName);
        Show;
      except
        Release;  // free form on error
        raise;    // reraise exception
      end;
    end;
end;
```

The following code handles the File, Save As and File, Save menu items. Note that the `FileSaveItemClick()` method invokes `FileSaveAsItemClick()` when the active MDI child doesn't have a name specified. Here's the code:

```
procedure TMainForm.FileSaveAsItemClick(Sender: TObject);
begin
  if (ActiveMDIChild <> Nil) and (SaveDialog.Execute) then
    with TMDIChild(ActiveMDIChild) do
    begin
      OleFileName := SaveDialog.FileName;
      OleContainer.SaveToFile(OleFileName);
    end;
end;

procedure TMainForm.FileSaveItemClick(Sender: TObject);
begin
  if ActiveMDIChild <> Nil then
```

```
    { if no name is assigned, then do a "save as" }
    if TMDIChild(ActiveMDIChild).OLEFileName = '' then
      FileSaveAsItemClick(Sender)
    else
      { otherwise save under current name }
      with TMDIChild(ActiveMDIChild) do
        OleContainer.SaveToFile(OLEFileName);
end;
```

Using the Clipboard to Copy and Paste

Thanks to the universal data-transfer mechanism described earlier, it's also possible to use the Windows Clipboard to transfer OLE objects. Again, the TOleContainer component automates these tasks to a great degree.

Copying an OLE object from a TOleContainer to the Clipboard, in particular, is a trivial task. Simply call the Copy() method:

```
procedure TMainForm.CopyItemClick(Sender: TObject);
begin
  if ActiveMDIChild <> Nil then
    TMDIChild(ActiveMDIChild).OleContainer.Copy;
end;
```

After you think you have an OLE object on the Clipboard, only one additional step is required to properly read it out into a TOleContainer component. Prior to attempting to paste the contents of the Clipboard into a TOleContainer, you should first check the value of the CanPaste property to ensure that the data on the Clipboard is a suitable OLE object. After that, you can invoke the Paste Special dialog box to paste the object into the TOleContainer by calling its PasteSpecialDialog() method, as shown in the following code (the Paste Special dialog box is shown in Figure 15.23):

```
procedure TMainForm.PasteItemClick(Sender: TObject);
begin
  if ActiveMDIChild <> nil then
    with TMDIChild(ActiveMDIChild).OleContainer do
      { Before invoking dialog, check to be sure that there }
      { are valid OLE objects on the clipboard. }
      if CanPaste then PasteSpecialDialog;
end;
```

When the application is run, the server controlling the OLE object in the active MDI child merges with or takes control of the application's menu and toolbar. Figures 15.24 and 15.25 show OLE's in-place activation feature—the MDI OLE application is controlled by two different OLE servers.

15

COM DEVELOPMENT

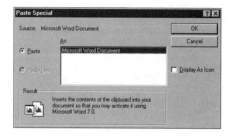

FIGURE 15.23
The Paste Special dialog box.

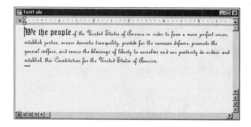

FIGURE 15.24
Editing an embedded Word 2000 document.

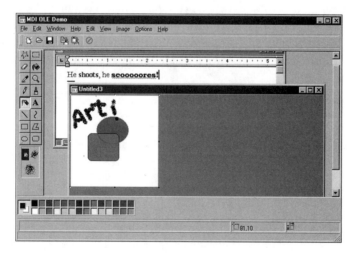

FIGURE 15.25
Editing an embedded Paint graphic.

The complete listing for Main.pas, the MDI OLE application's main unit, is shown in
Listing 15.16.

LISTING 15.16 The Source Code for Main.pas

```
unit Main;

interface

uses WinTypes, WinProcs, SysUtils, Classes, Graphics, Forms, Controls, Menus,
  StdCtrls, Dialogs, Buttons, Messages, ExtCtrls, ChildWin, ComCtrls,
  ToolWin;

type
  TMainForm = class(TForm)
    MainMenu1: TMainMenu;
    File1: TMenuItem;
    FileNewItem: TMenuItem;
    FileOpenItem: TMenuItem;
    FileCloseItem: TMenuItem;
    Window1: TMenuItem;
    Help1: TMenuItem;
    N1: TMenuItem;
    FileExitItem: TMenuItem;
    WindowCascadeItem: TMenuItem;
    WindowTileItem: TMenuItem;
    WindowArrangeItem: TMenuItem;
    HelpAboutItem: TMenuItem;
    OpenDialog: TOpenDialog;
    FileSaveItem: TMenuItem;
    FileSaveAsItem: TMenuItem;
    Edit1: TMenuItem;
    PasteItem: TMenuItem;
    WindowMinimizeItem: TMenuItem;
    SaveDialog: TSaveDialog;
    CopyItem: TMenuItem;
    CloseAll1: TMenuItem;
    StatusBar: TStatusBar;
    CoolBar1: TCoolBar;
    ToolBar1: TToolBar;
    OpenBtn: TToolButton;
    SaveBtn: TToolButton;
    ToolButton3: TToolButton;
    CopyBtn: TToolButton;
    PasteBtn: TToolButton;
    ToolButton6: TToolButton;
```

LISTING 15.16   Continued

```
    ExitBtn: TToolButton;
    ImageList1: TImageList;
    procedure FormCreate(Sender: TObject);
    procedure FileNewItemClick(Sender: TObject);
    procedure WindowCascadeItemClick(Sender: TObject);
    procedure UpdateMenuItems(Sender: TObject);
    procedure WindowTileItemClick(Sender: TObject);
    procedure WindowArrangeItemClick(Sender: TObject);
    procedure FileCloseItemClick(Sender: TObject);
    procedure FileOpenItemClick(Sender: TObject);
    procedure FileExitItemClick(Sender: TObject);
    procedure FileSaveItemClick(Sender: TObject);
    procedure FileSaveAsItemClick(Sender: TObject);
    procedure PasteItemClick(Sender: TObject);
    procedure WindowMinimizeItemClick(Sender: TObject);
    procedure FormDestroy(Sender: TObject);
    procedure HelpAboutItemClick(Sender: TObject);
    procedure CopyItemClick(Sender: TObject);
    procedure CloseAll1Click(Sender: TObject);
  private
    procedure ShowHint(Sender: TObject);
  end;

var
  MainForm: TMainForm;

implementation

{$R *.DFM}

uses About;

var
  NumChildren: Cardinal = 0;

procedure TMainForm.FormCreate(Sender: TObject);
begin
  Application.OnHint := ShowHint;
  Screen.OnActiveFormChange := UpdateMenuItems;
end;

procedure TMainForm.ShowHint(Sender: TObject);
begin
  { Show hints on status bar }
```

LISTING 15.16 Continued

```
  StatusBar.Panels[0].Text := Application.Hint;
end;

procedure TMainForm.FileNewItemClick(Sender: TObject);
begin
  inc(NumChildren);
  { create a new MDI child window }
  with TMDIChild.Create(Application) do
  begin
    Caption := 'Untitled' + IntToStr(NumChildren);
    { bring up insert OLE object dialog and insert into child }
    OleContainer.InsertObjectDialog;
  end;
end;

procedure TMainForm.FileOpenItemClick(Sender: TObject);
begin
  if OpenDialog.Execute then
    with TMDIChild.Create(Application) do
    begin
      try
        OleFileName := OpenDialog.FileName;
        OleContainer.LoadFromFile(OleFileName);
        Show;
      except
        Release;  // free form on error
        raise;    // reraise exception
      end;
    end;
end;

procedure TMainForm.FileCloseItemClick(Sender: TObject);
begin
  if ActiveMDIChild <> nil then
    ActiveMDIChild.Close;
end;

procedure TMainForm.FileSaveAsItemClick(Sender: TObject);
begin
  if (ActiveMDIChild <> nil) and (SaveDialog.Execute) then
    with TMDIChild(ActiveMDIChild) do
    begin
      OleFileName := SaveDialog.FileName;
      OleContainer.SaveToFile(OleFileName);
    end;
end;
```

LISTING 15.16   Continued

```
procedure TMainForm.FileSaveItemClick(Sender: TObject);
begin
  if ActiveMDIChild <> nil then
    { if no name is assigned, then do a "save as" }
    if TMDIChild(ActiveMDIChild).OLEFileName = '' then
      FileSaveAsItemClick(Sender)
    else
      { otherwise save under current name }
      with TMDIChild(ActiveMDIChild) do
        OleContainer.SaveToFile(OLEFileName);
end;

procedure TMainForm.FileExitItemClick(Sender: TObject);
begin
  Close;
end;

procedure TMainForm.PasteItemClick(Sender: TObject);
begin
  if ActiveMDIChild <> nil then
    with TMDIChild(ActiveMDIChild).OleContainer do
      { Before invoking dialog, check to be sure that there }
      { are valid OLE objects on the clipboard. }
      if CanPaste then PasteSpecialDialog;
end;

procedure TMainForm.WindowCascadeItemClick(Sender: TObject);
begin
  Cascade;
end;

procedure TMainForm.WindowTileItemClick(Sender: TObject);
begin
  Tile;
end;

procedure TMainForm.WindowArrangeItemClick(Sender: TObject);
begin
  ArrangeIcons;
end;

procedure TMainForm.WindowMinimizeItemClick(Sender: TObject);
var
  I: Integer;
```

LISTING 15.16 Continued

```pascal
begin
  { Must be done backwards through the MDIChildren array }
  for I := MDIChildCount - 1 downto 0 do
    MDIChildren[I].WindowState := wsMinimized;
end;

procedure TMainForm.UpdateMenuItems(Sender: TObject);
var
  DoIt: Boolean;
begin
  DoIt := MDIChildCount > 0;
  { only enable options if there are active children }
  FileCloseItem.Enabled := DoIt;
  FileSaveItem.Enabled := DoIt;
  CloseAll1.Enabled := DoIt;
  FileSaveAsItem.Enabled := DoIt;
  CopyItem.Enabled := DoIt;
  PasteItem.Enabled := DoIt;
  CopyBtn.Enabled := DoIt;
  SaveBtn.Enabled := DoIt;
  PasteBtn.Enabled := DoIt;
  WindowCascadeItem.Enabled := DoIt;
  WindowTileItem.Enabled := DoIt;
  WindowArrangeItem.Enabled := DoIt;
  WindowMinimizeItem.Enabled := DoIt;
end;

procedure TMainForm.FormDestroy(Sender: TObject);
begin
  Screen.OnActiveFormChange := nil;
end;

procedure TMainForm.HelpAboutItemClick(Sender: TObject);
begin
  with TAboutBox.Create(Self) do
  begin
    ShowModal;
    Free;
  end;
end;

procedure TMainForm.CopyItemClick(Sender: TObject);
begin
  if ActiveMDIChild <> nil then
```

LISTING 15.16   Continued

```
      TMDIChild(ActiveMDIChild).OleContainer.Copy;
end;

procedure TMainForm.CloseAll1Click(Sender: TObject);
begin
  while ActiveMDIChild <> nil do
  begin
    ActiveMDIChild.Release;          // use Release, not Free!
    Application.ProcessMessages;     // let Windows take care of business
  end;
end;

end.
```

Summary

That wraps up this chapter on COM, OLE, and ActiveX. This chapter covers an enormous amount of information! First, you received a solid foundation in COM-based technologies, which should help you understand what goes on behind the scenes. Next, you got some insight and information on various types of COM clients and servers. Following that, you were immersed in various advanced techniques for Automation in Delphi. In addition to in-depth coverage of COM and Automation, you should now be familiar with the workings of VCL's TOleContainer component.

If you'd like to know more about COM, you'll find what you're looking for in several other areas of this book. Chapter 16 shows real-world examples of COM server creation, and Chapter 18 discusses development with some of the more enterprise-targeted features of COM+ in Delphi.

Windows Shell Programming

IN THIS CHAPTER

First introduced in Windows 95, the Windows shell is also supported on all subsequent Windows versions (NT 3.51 and higher, 98, 2000, Me, and XP). A far cry from the old Program Manger, the Windows shell includes some great features for extending the shell to meet your needs. The problem is, many of these nifty extensible features are some of the most poorly documented subjects of Win32 development. This chapter is intended to give you the information and examples you need to tap into shell features such as tray-notification icons, application desktop toolbars, shell links, and shell extensions.

A Tray-Notification Icon Component

This section illustrates a technique for encapsulating the Windows shell tray-notification icon cleanly into a Delphi component. As you build the component—called TTrayNotifyIcon—you'll learn about the API requirements for creating a tray-notification icon as well as how to tackle some of the hairy problems you'll come across as you work to embed all the icon's functionality within the component. If you're unfamiliar with what a tray-notification icon is, it's one of those little icons that appear in the bottom-right corner of the Windows system taskbar (assuming that your taskbar is aligned to the bottom of your screen), as shown in Figure 16.1.

Tray-notification icons

FIGURE 16.1
Tray-notification icons.

The API

Believe it or not, only one API call is involved in creating, modifying, and removing tray-notification icons from the notification tray. The function is called Shell_NotifyIcon().This and other functions dealing with the Windows shell are contained in the ShellAPI unit. Shell_NotifyIcon() is defined as follows:

```
function Shell_NotifyIcon(dwMessage: DWORD; lpData:
    PNotifyIconData): BOOL; stdcall;
```

The dwMessage parameter describes the action to be taken for the icon. This can be any one of the values shown in Table 16.1.

TABLE 16.1 Values for the dwMessage Parameter

Constant	Value	Meaning
NIM_ADD	0	Adds an icon to the notification tray
NIM_MODIFY	1	Modifies the properties of an existing icon
NIM_DELETE	2	Removes an icon from the notification tray

The lpData parameter is a pointer to a TNotifyIconData record. This record is defined as follows:

```
type
  TNotifyIconData = record
    cbSize: DWORD;
    Wnd: HWND;
    uID: UINT;
    uFlags: UINT;
    uCallbackMessage: UINT;
    hIcon: HICON;
    szTip: array [0..63] of AnsiChar;
  end;
```

The cbSize field holds the size of the record, and it should be initialized to SizeOf(TNotifyIconData).

Wnd is the handle of the window to which tray-notification "callback" messages should be sent. (*Callback* is in quotes here because it's not really a callback in the strict sense; however, the Win32 documentation uses this terminology for messages sent to a window on behalf of a tray-notification icon.)

uID is a programmer-defined unique ID number. If you have an application with several icons, you'll need to identify each one by a placing a different number in this field.

uFlags describes which of the fields of the TNotifyIconData record should be considered live by the Shell_NotifyIcon() function, and, therefore, which of the icon properties are to be affected by the action specified by the dwMessage parameter. This parameter can be any combination of the flags (using or to join them) shown in Table 16.2.

TABLE 16.2 Possible Flags to Be Included in uFlags

Constant	Value	Meaning
NIF_MESSAGE	0	The uCallbackMessage field is live.
NIF_ICON	2	The hIcon field is live.
NIF_TIP	4	The szTip field is live.

uCallbackMessage contains the value of the Windows message to be sent to the window identified by the Wnd field. Generally, the value of this field is obtained by calling RegisterWindowMessage() or by using an offset from WM_USER. The lParam of this message will be the same value as the uID field, and the wParam will hold the mouse message generated over the notification icon.

hIcon identifies the handle to the icon that will be placed in the notification tray.

szTip holds a null-terminated string that will appear in the hint window displayed when the mouse pointer is held above the notification icon.

The TTrayNotifyIcon component encapsulates the Shell_NotifyIcon() into a method called SendTrayMessage(), which is shown here:

```
procedure TTrayNotifyIcon.SendTrayMessage(Msg: DWORD; Flags: UINT);
{ This method wraps up the call to the API's Shell_NotifyIcon }
begin
  { Fill up record with appropriate values }
  with Tnd do
  begin
    cbSize := SizeOf(Tnd);
    StrPLCopy(szTip, PChar(FHint), SizeOf(szTip));
    uFlags := Flags;
    uID := UINT(Self);
    Wnd := IconMgr.HWindow;
    uCallbackMessage := Tray_Callback;
    hIcon  := ActiveIconHandle;
  end;
  Shell_NotifyIcon(Msg, @Tnd);
end;
```

In this method, szTip is copied from a private string field called FHint.

uID is used to hold a reference to Self. Because this data will be included in subsequent notification tray messages, correlating notification tray messages for multiple icons to individual components will be easy.

Wnd is assigned the value of IconMgr.HWindow. IconMgr is a global variable of type TIconMgr. You'll see the implementation of this object in a moment, but for now you only need know that it's through this component that all notification tray messages will be sent.

uCallbackMessage is assigned from DDGM_TRAYICON. DDGM_TRAYICON obtains its value from the RegisterWindowMessage() API function. This ensures that DDGM_TRAYICON is a systemwide unique message ID. The following code accomplishes this task:

```
const
  { String to identify registered window message }
```

```
   TrayMsgStr = 'DDG.TrayNotifyIconMsg';

initialization
   { Get a unique windows message ID for tray callback }
   DDGM_TRAYICON := RegisterWindowMessage(TrayMsgStr);
```

hIcon takes on the return value provided by the `ActiveIconHandle()` method. This method returns the handle for the icon currently selected in the component's `Icon` property.

Handling Messages

We mentioned earlier that all notification tray messages are sent to a window maintained by the global `IconMgr` object. This object is constructed and freed in the `initialization` and `finalization` sections of the component's unit, as shown here:

```
initialization
   { Get a unique windows message ID for tray callback }
   DDGM_TRAYICON := RegisterWindowMessage(TrayMsgStr);
   IconMgr := TIconManager.Create;
finalization
   IconMgr.Free;
```

This object is fairly small. Here's its definition:

```
type
   TIconManager = class
   private
      FHWindow: HWnd;
      procedure TrayWndProc(var Message: TMessage);
   public
      constructor Create;
      destructor Destroy; override;
      property HWindow: HWnd read FHWindow write FHWindow;
   end;
```

The window to which notification tray messages will be sent is created in the constructor for this object using the `AllocateHWnd()` function:

```
constructor TIconManager.Create;
begin
   FHWindow := AllocateHWnd(TrayWndProc);
end;
```

The `TrayWndProc()` method serves as the window procedure for the window created in the constructor. More about this method will be discussed in a moment.

Icons and Hints

The most straightforward way to surface icons and hints for the component's end user is through properties. Additionally, creating an `Icon` property of type `TIcon` means that it can automatically take advantage of Delphi's property editor for icons, which is a nice touch. Because the tray icon is visible even at design time, you need to ensure that the icon and tip can change dynamically. Doing this really isn't a lot of extra work; it's just a matter of making sure that the `SendTrayMessage()` method is called (using the `NIM_MODIFY` message) in the `write` method of the `Hint` and `Icon` properties.

Here are the `write` methods for those properties:

```
procedure TTrayNotifyIcon.SetIcon(Value: TIcon);
{ Write method for Icon property. }
begin
  FIcon.Assign(Value);   // set new icon
  if FIconVisible then
    { Change icon on notification tray }
    SendTrayMessage(NIM_MODIFY, NIF_ICON);
end;

procedure TTrayNotifyIcon.SetHint(Value: String);
{ Set method for Hint property }
begin
  if FHint <> Value then
  begin
    FHint := Value;
    if FIconVisible then
      { Change hint on icon on notification tray }
      SendTrayMessage(NIM_MODIFY, NIF_TIP);
  end;
end;
```

Mouse Clicks

One of the most challenging parts of this component is ensuring that the mouse clicks are handled properly. You might have noticed that many tray-notification icons perform three different actions because of mouse clicks:

- Brings up a window on a single-click
- Brings up a different window (usually a properties sheet) on a double-click
- Invokes a local menu with a right-click

The challenge comes in creating an event that represents the double-click without also firing the single-click event.

In Windows message terms, when the user double-clicks with the left mouse button, the window with focus will receive both the WM_LBUTTONDOWN message and the WM_LBUTTONDBLCLK message. In order to allow a double-click message to be processed independently of a single-click, some mechanism is required to delay the handling of the single-click message long enough to ensure that a double-click message isn't forthcoming.

The amount of time to wait before you can be sure that a WM_LBUTTONDBLCLK message isn't following a WM_LBUTTONDOWN message is actually pretty easy to determine. The API function GetDoubleClickTime(), which takes no parameters, returns the maximum amount of time (in milliseconds) that the Control Panel will allow between the two clicks of a double-click. The obvious choice for a mechanism to allow you to wait the number of milliseconds specified by GetDoubleClickTime() to ensure that a double-click isn't following a click is the TTimer component. Therefore, a TTimer component is created and initialized in the TTrayNotifyIcon component's constructor with the following code:

```
FTimer := TTimer.Create(Self);
with FTimer do
begin
  Enabled := False;
  Interval := GetDoubleClickTime;
  OnTimer := OnButtonTimer;
end;
```

OnButtonTimer() is a method that will be called when the timer interval expires. We'll show you this method in just a moment.

Earlier, we mentioned that notification tray messages are filtered through the TrayWndProc() method of the IconMgr. Now it's time to spring this method on you, so here it is:

```
procedure TIconManager.TrayWndProc(var Message: TMessage);
{ This allows us to handle all tray callback messages }
{ from within the context of the component. }
var
  Pt: TPoint;
  TheIcon: TTrayNotifyIcon;
begin
  with Message do
  begin
    { if it's the tray callback message }
    if (Msg = DDGM_TRAYICON) then
    begin
      TheIcon := TTrayNotifyIcon(WParam);
      case lParam of
        { enable timer on first mouse down. }
        { OnClick will be fired by OnTimer method, provided }
```

```
          { double click has not occurred. }
          WM_LBUTTONDOWN: TheIcon.FTimer.Enabled := True;
          { Set no click flag on double click.  This will suppress }
          { the single click. }
          WM_LBUTTONDBLCLK:
            begin
              TheIcon.FNoShowClick := True;
              if Assigned(TheIcon.FOnDblClick) then TheIcon.FOnDblClick(Self);
            end;
          WM_RBUTTONDOWN:
            begin
              if Assigned(TheIcon.FPopupMenu) then
              begin
                { Call to SetForegroundWindow is required by API }
                SetForegroundWindow(IconMgr.HWindow);
                { Popup local menu at the cursor position. }
                GetCursorPos(Pt);
                TheIcon.FPopupMenu.Popup(Pt.X, Pt.Y);
                { Message post required by API to force task switch }
                PostMessage(IconMgr.HWindow, WM_USER, 0, 0);
              end;
            end;
      end;
    end
    else
      { If it isn't a tray callback message, then call DefWindowProc }
      Result := DefWindowProc(FHWindow, Msg, wParam, lParam);
  end;
end;
```

What makes this all work is that the single-click message merely enables the timer, whereas the double-click message sets a flag to indicate that the double-click has occurred before firing its OnDblClick event. The right-click, incidentally, invokes the pop-up menu given by the component's PopupMenu property. Now take a look at the OnButtonTimer method:

```
procedure TTrayNotifyIcon.OnButtonTimer(Sender: TObject);
begin
  { Disable timer because we only want it to fire once. }
  FTimer.Enabled := False;
  { if double click has not occurred, then fire single click. }
  if (not FNoShowClick) and Assigned(FOnClick) then
    FOnClick(Self);
  FNoShowClick := False;    // reset flag
end;
```

This method first disables the timer to ensure that the event fires only once per mouse click. The method then checks the status of the FNoShowClick flag. Remember that this flag will be set by the double-click message in the OwnerWndProc() method. Therefore, the OnClick event will be fired only when OnDblClk isn't.

Hiding the Application

Another aspect of tray-notification applications is that they don't appear as buttons in the system taskbar. To provide this functionality, the TTrayNotifyIcon component surfaces a HideTask property that allows the user to decide whether the application should be visible in the taskbar. The write method for this property is shown in the following code. The line of code that does the work is the call to the ShowWindow() API procedure, which passes the Handle property of Application and a constant to indicate whether the application is to be shown normally or hidden. Here's the code:

```
procedure TTrayNotifyIcon.SetHideTask(Value: Boolean);
{ Write method for HideTask property }
const
  { Flags to show application normally or hide it }
  ShowArray: array[Boolean] of integer = (sw_ShowNormal, sw_Hide);
begin
  if FHideTask <> Value then begin
    FHideTask := Value;
    { Don't do anything in design mode }
    if not (csDesigning in ComponentState) then
      ShowWindow(Application.Handle, ShowArray[FHideTask]);
  end;
end;
```

Listing 16.1 shows the TrayIcon.pas unit, which contains the complete source code for the TTrayNotifyIcon component.

LISTING 16.1   TrayIcon.pas—Source Code for the TTrayNotifyIcon Component

```
unit TrayIcon;

interface

uses Windows, SysUtils, Messages, ShellAPI, Classes, Graphics, Forms, Menus,
  StdCtrls, ExtCtrls;

type
  ENotifyIconError = class(Exception);

  TTrayNotifyIcon = class(TComponent)
```

LISTING 16.1   Continued

```
private
  FDefaultIcon: THandle;
  FIcon: TIcon;
  FHideTask: Boolean;
  FHint: string;
  FIconVisible: Boolean;
  FPopupMenu: TPopupMenu;
  FOnClick: TNotifyEvent;
  FOnDblClick: TNotifyEvent;
  FNoShowClick: Boolean;
  FTimer: TTimer;
  Tnd: TNotifyIconData;
  procedure SetIcon(Value: TIcon);
  procedure SetHideTask(Value: Boolean);
  procedure SetHint(Value: string);
  procedure SetIconVisible(Value: Boolean);
  procedure SetPopupMenu(Value: TPopupMenu);
  procedure SendTrayMessage(Msg: DWORD; Flags: UINT);
  function ActiveIconHandle: THandle;
  procedure OnButtonTimer(Sender: TObject);
protected
  procedure Loaded; override;
  procedure LoadDefaultIcon; virtual;
  procedure Notification(AComponent: TComponent;
    Operation: TOperation); override;
public
  constructor Create(AOwner: TComponent); override;
  destructor Destroy; override;
published
  property Icon: TIcon read FIcon write SetIcon;
  property HideTask: Boolean read FHideTask write SetHideTask default False;
  property Hint: String read FHint write SetHint;
  property IconVisible: Boolean read FIconVisible write SetIconVisible
    default False;
  property PopupMenu: TPopupMenu read FPopupMenu write SetPopupMenu;
  property OnClick: TNotifyEvent read FOnClick write FOnClick;
  property OnDblClick: TNotifyEvent read FOnDblClick write FOnDblClick;
end;

implementation

{ TIconManager }
{ This class creates a hidden window which handles and routes }
{ tray icon messages }
```

LISTING 16.1 Continued

```pascal
type
  TIconManager = class
  private
    FHWindow: HWnd;
    procedure TrayWndProc(var Message: TMessage);
  public
    constructor Create;
    destructor Destroy; override;
    property HWindow: HWnd read FHWindow write FHWindow;
  end;

var
  IconMgr: TIconManager;
  DDGM_TRAYICON: Integer;

constructor TIconManager.Create;
begin
  FHWindow := AllocateHWnd(TrayWndProc);
end;

destructor TIconManager.Destroy;
begin
  if FHWindow <> 0 then DeallocateHWnd(FHWindow);
  inherited Destroy;
end;

procedure TIconManager.TrayWndProc(var Message: TMessage);
{ This allows us to handle all tray callback messages }
{ from within the context of the component. }
var
  Pt: TPoint;
  TheIcon: TTrayNotifyIcon;
begin
  with Message do
  begin
    { if it's the tray callback message }
    if (Msg = DDGM_TRAYICON) then
    begin
      TheIcon := TTrayNotifyIcon(WParam);
      case lParam of
        { enable timer on first mouse down. }
        { OnClick will be fired by OnTimer method, provided }
        { double click has not occurred. }
        WM_LBUTTONDOWN: TheIcon.FTimer.Enabled := True;
```

LISTING 16.1   Continued

```pascal
          { Set no click flag on double click.  This will suppress }
          { the single click. }
          WM_LBUTTONDBLCLK:
            begin
              TheIcon.FNoShowClick := True;
              if Assigned(TheIcon.FOnDblClick) then TheIcon.FOnDblClick(Self);
            end;
          WM_RBUTTONDOWN:
            begin
              if Assigned(TheIcon.FPopupMenu) then
              begin
                { Call to SetForegroundWindow is required by API }
                SetForegroundWindow(IconMgr.HWindow);
                { Popup local menu at the cursor position. }
                GetCursorPos(Pt);
                TheIcon.FPopupMenu.Popup(Pt.X, Pt.Y);
                { Message post required by API to force task switch }
                PostMessage(IconMgr.HWindow, WM_USER, 0, 0);
              end;
            end;
        end;
    end
    else
      { If it isn't a tray callback message, then call DefWindowProc }
      Result := DefWindowProc(FHWindow, Msg, wParam, lParam);
  end;
end;


{ TTrayNotifyIcon }

constructor TTrayNotifyIcon.Create(AOwner: TComponent);
begin
  inherited Create(AOwner);
  FIcon := TIcon.Create;
  FTimer := TTimer.Create(Self);
  with FTimer do
  begin
    Enabled := False;
    Interval := GetDoubleClickTime;
    OnTimer := OnButtonTimer;
  end;
  { Keep default windows icon handy... }
  LoadDefaultIcon;
end;
```

LISTING 16.1 Continued

```
destructor TTrayNotifyIcon.Destroy;
begin
  if FIconVisible then SetIconVisible(False);     // destroy icon
  FIcon.Free;                                      // free stuff
  FTimer.Free;
  inherited Destroy;
end;

function TTrayNotifyIcon.ActiveIconHandle: THandle;
{ Returns handle of active icon }
begin
  { If no icon is loaded, then return default icon }
  if (FIcon.Handle <> 0) then
    Result := FIcon.Handle
  else
    Result := FDefaultIcon;
end;

procedure TTrayNotifyIcon.LoadDefaultIcon;
{ Loads default window icon to keep it handy. }
{ This will allow the component to use the windows logo }
{ icon as the default when no icon is selected in the }
{ Icon property. }
begin
  FDefaultIcon := LoadIcon(0, IDI_WINLOGO);
end;

procedure TTrayNotifyIcon.Loaded;
{ Called after component is loaded from stream }
begin
  inherited Loaded;
  { if icon is supposed to be visible, create it. }
  if FIconVisible then
    SendTrayMessage(NIM_ADD, NIF_MESSAGE or NIF_ICON or NIF_TIP);
end;

procedure TTrayNotifyIcon.Notification(AComponent: TComponent;
  Operation: TOperation);
begin
  inherited Notification(AComponent, Operation);
  if (Operation = opRemove) and (AComponent = PopupMenu) then
    PopupMenu := nil;
end;
```

LISTING 16.1 Continued

```
procedure TTrayNotifyIcon.OnButtonTimer(Sender: TObject);
{ Timer used to keep track of time between two clicks of a }
{ double click. This delays the first click long enough to }
{ ensure that a double click hasn't occurred.  The whole   }
{ point of these gymnastics is to allow the component to    }
{ receive OnClicks and OnDblClicks independently. }
begin
  { Disable timer because we only want it to fire once. }
  FTimer.Enabled := False;
  { if double click has not occurred, then fire single click. }
  if (not FNoShowClick) and Assigned(FOnClick) then
    FOnClick(Self);
  FNoShowClick := False;    // reset flag
end;


procedure TTrayNotifyIcon.SendTrayMessage(Msg: DWORD; Flags: UINT);
{ This method wraps up the call to the API's Shell_NotifyIcon }
begin
  { Fill up record with appropriate values }
  with Tnd do
  begin
    cbSize := SizeOf(Tnd);
    StrPLCopy(szTip, PChar(FHint), SizeOf(szTip));
    uFlags := Flags;
    uID := UINT(Self);
    Wnd := IconMgr.HWindow;
    uCallbackMessage := DDGM_TRAYICON;
    hIcon  := ActiveIconHandle;
  end;
  Shell_NotifyIcon(Msg, @Tnd);
end;


procedure TTrayNotifyIcon.SetHideTask(Value: Boolean);
{ Write method for HideTask property }
const
  { Flags to show application normally or hide it }
  ShowArray: array[Boolean] of integer = (sw_ShowNormal, sw_Hide);
begin
  if FHideTask <> Value then
  begin
    FHideTask := Value;
    { Don't do anything in design mode }
    if not (csDesigning in ComponentState) then
      ShowWindow(Application.Handle, ShowArray[FHideTask]);
  end;
end;
```

LISTING 16.1 Continued

```pascal
procedure TTrayNotifyIcon.SetHint(Value: string);
{ Set method for Hint property }
begin
  if FHint <> Value then
  begin
    FHint := Value;
    if FIconVisible then
      { Change hint on icon on notification tray }
      SendTrayMessage(NIM_MODIFY, NIF_TIP);
  end;
end;

procedure TTrayNotifyIcon.SetIcon(Value: TIcon);
{ Write method for Icon property. }
begin
  FIcon.Assign(Value);  // set new icon
  { Change icon on notification tray }
  if FIconVisible then SendTrayMessage(NIM_MODIFY, NIF_ICON);
end;

procedure TTrayNotifyIcon.SetIconVisible(Value: Boolean);
{ Write method for IconVisible property }
const
  { Flags to add or delete a tray-notification icon }
  MsgArray: array[Boolean] of DWORD = (NIM_DELETE, NIM_ADD);
begin
  if FIconVisible <> Value then
  begin
    FIconVisible := Value;
    { Set icon as appropriate }
    SendTrayMessage(MsgArray[Value], NIF_MESSAGE or NIF_ICON or NIF_TIP);
  end;
end;

procedure TTrayNotifyIcon.SetPopupMenu(Value: TPopupMenu);
{ Write method for PopupMenu property }
begin
  FPopupMenu := Value;
  if Value <> nil then Value.FreeNotification(Self);
end;

const
  { String to identify registered window message }
  TrayMsgStr = 'DDG.TrayNotifyIconMsg';
```

LISTING 16.1   Continued

```
initialization
  { Get a unique windows message ID for tray callback }
  DDGM_TRAYICON := RegisterWindowMessage(TrayMsgStr);
  IconMgr := TIconManager.Create;
finalization
  IconMgr.Free;
end.
```

Figure 16.2 shows a picture of the icon generated by TTrayNotifyIcon in the notification tray.

FIGURE 16.2
The TTrayNotifyIcon *component in action.*

By the way, because the tray icon is initialized inside the component's constructor and because constructors are executed at design time, this component displays the tray-notification icon even at design time!

Sample Tray Application

In order to provide you with a better overall feel for how the TTrayNotifyIcon component works within the context of an application, Figure 16.3 shows the main window of this application, and Listing 16.2 shows the fairly minimal code for the main unit for this application.

FIGURE 16.3
Notification icon application.

LISTING 16.2   Main.pas—the Main Unit for the Notification Icon Demo Application

```
unit main;

interface

uses
```

LISTING 16.2 Continued

```pascal
Windows, Messages, SysUtils, Classes, Graphics, Controls, Forms, Dialogs,
StdCtrls, ShellAPI, TrayIcon, Menus, ComCtrls;

type
  TMainForm = class(TForm)
    pmiPopup: TPopupMenu;
    pgclPageCtl: TPageControl;
    TabSheet1: TTabSheet;
    btnClose: TButton;
    btnTerm: TButton;
    Terminate1: TMenuItem;
    Label1: TLabel;
    N1: TMenuItem;
    Propeties1: TMenuItem;
    TrayNotifyIcon1: TTrayNotifyIcon;
    procedure NotifyIcon1Click(Sender: TObject);
    procedure NotifyIcon1DblClick(Sender: TObject);
    procedure FormClose(Sender: TObject; var Action: TCloseAction);
    procedure btnTermClick(Sender: TObject);
    procedure btnCloseClick(Sender: TObject);
    procedure FormCreate(Sender: TObject);
  end;

var
  MainForm: TMainForm;

implementation

{$R *.DFM}

procedure TMainForm.NotifyIcon1Click(Sender: TObject);
begin
  ShowMessage('Single click');
end;

procedure TMainForm.NotifyIcon1DblClick(Sender: TObject);
begin
  Show;
end;

procedure TMainForm.FormClose(Sender: TObject; var Action: TCloseAction);
begin
  Action := caNone;
  Hide;
end;
```

LISTING 16.2   Continued

```
procedure TMainForm.btnTermClick(Sender: TObject);
begin
  Application.Terminate;
end;

procedure TMainForm.btnCloseClick(Sender: TObject);
begin
  Hide;
end;

procedure TMainForm.FormCreate(Sender: TObject);
begin
  TrayNotifyIcon1.IconVisible := True;
end;

end.
```

Application Desktop Toolbars

Application desktop toolbars, also known as *AppBars*, are windows that can dock to one of the edges of your screen. You're already familiar with AppBars, even though you might not know it; the shell's taskbar, which you probably work with every day, is an example of an AppBar. As shown in Figure 16.4, the taskbar is really little more than an AppBar window containing a Start button, notification tray, and other controls.

FIGURE 16.4
The shell's taskbar.

Apart from docking to screen edges, AppBars can, optionally, employ taskbar-like features, such as auto-hide and drag-and-drop functionality. What you might find surprising, however, is how small the API is (just one function). As its small size might imply, the API doesn't provide a whole lot. The role of the API is more advisory than functional. That is, rather than controlling the AppBar with "do this, do that" command types, you interrogate the AppBar with "can I do this, can I do that?" command types.

The API

Just like tray-notification icons, AppBars have only one API function that you'll work with—SHAppBarMessage(), in this case. Here's how SHAppBarMessage() is defined in the ShellAPI unit:

```
function SHAppBarMessage(dwMessage: DWORD; var pData: TAppBarData): UINT;
  stdcall;
```

The first parameter to this function, dwMessage, can contain any one of the values described in
Table 16.3.

TABLE 16.3 AppBar Messages

Constant	Value	Meaning
ABM_NEW	$0	Registers a new AppBar and specifies a new callback message
ABM_REMOVE	$1	Unregisters an existing AppBar
ABM_QUERYPOS AppBar	$2	Requests a new position and size for an
ABM_SETPOS	$3	Sets a new position and size of an AppBar
ABM_GETSTATE	$4	Gets the auto-hide and always-on-top states of the shell taskbar
ABM_GETTASKBARPOS	$5	Gets the position of the shell taskbar
ABM_ACTIVATE	$6	Notifies the shell that a new AppBar has been created
ABM_GETAUTOHIDEBAR	$7	Gets the handle of an auto-hide AppBar docked to a particular edge of the screen
ABM_SETAUTOHIDEBAR	$8	Registers an auto-hide AppBar for a particular screen edge
ABM_WINDOWPOSCHANGED	$9	Notifies the shell that the position of an AppBar has changed

The pData parameter of SHAppBarMessage() is a record of type TAppBarData, which is defined
in ShellAPI as follows:

```
type
  PAppBarData = ^TAppBarData;
  TAppBarData = record
    cbSize: DWORD;
    hWnd: HWND;
    uCallbackMessage: UINT;
    uEdge: UINT;
    rc: TRect;
    lParam: LPARAM; { message specific }
  end;
```

In this record, the cbSize field holds the size of the record, the hWnd field holds the window handle of the specified AppBar, uCallbackMessage holds the message value that will be sent to the AppBar window along with notification messages, rc holds the bounding rectangle of the AppBar in question, and lParam holds some additional message-specific information.

> **TIP**
>
> You'll find more information on the SHAppBarMessage() API function and the TAppBarData type in the Win32 online help.

TAppBar: The AppBar Form

Given this fairly small API, it's not terribly difficult to encapsulate an AppBar in a VCL form. This section explains the techniques used to wrap the AppBar API into a control descending from TCustomForm. Because TCustomForm is a form, you'll interact with the control as a top-level form in the Form Designer rather than as a component on a form.

Most of the work in an AppBar is done by sending a TAppBarData record to the shell using the SHAppBarMessage() API function. The TAppBar component maintains an internal TAppBarData record called FABD. FABD is set up for the call to SendAppBarMsg() in the constructor and the CreateWnd() methods in order to create the AppBar. In particular, the cbSize field is initialized, the uCallbackMessage field is set to a value obtained from the RegisterWindowMessage() API function, and the hWnd field is set to the current window handle of the form. SendAppBarMessage() is a simple wrapper for SHAppBarMessage() and is defined as follows:

```
function TAppBar.SendAppBarMsg(Msg: DWORD): UINT;
begin
  Result := SHAppBarMessage(Msg, FABD);
end;
```

If the AppBar is created successfully, the SetAppBarEdge() method is called to set the AppBar to its initial position. This method, in turn, calls the SetAppBarPos() method, passing the appropriate API-defined flag that indicates the requested screen edge. As you would expect, the ABE_TOP, ABE_BOTTOM, ABE_LEFT, and ABE_RIGHT flags represent each of the screen edges. This is shown in the following code snippet:

```
procedure TAppBar.SetAppBarPos(Edge: UINT);
begin
  if csDesigning in ComponentState then Exit;
  FABD.uEdge := Edge;        // set edge
  with FABD.rc do
```

```
begin
  // set coordinates to full-screen
  Top := 0;
  Left := 0;
  Right := Screen.Width;
  Bottom := Screen.Height;
  // Send ABM_QUERYPOS to obtain proper rect on edge
  SendAppBarMsg(ABM_QUERYPOS);
  // re-adjust rect based on that modified by ABM_QUERYPOS
  case Edge of
    ABE_LEFT: Right := Left + FDockedWidth;
    ABE_RIGHT: Left := Right - FDockedWidth;
    ABE_TOP: Bottom := Top + FDockedHeight;
    ABE_BOTTOM: Top := Bottom - FDockedHeight;
  end;
  // Set the app bar position.
  SendAppBarMsg(ABM_SETPOS);
end;
// Set the BoundsRect property so that it conforms to the
// bounding rectangle passed to the system.
BoundsRect := FABD.rc;
end;
```

This method first sets the uEdge field of FABD to the value passed via the Edge parameter. It then sets the rc field to the full-screen coordinates and sends the ABM_QUERYPOS message. This message resets the rc field so that it contains the correct bounding rectangle for the edge indicated by uEdge. Once the proper bounding rectangle has been obtained, rc is again adjusted so that it's a reasonable height or width. At this point, rc holds the final bounding rectangle for the AppBar. The ABM_SETPOS message is then sent to inform the shell of the new rectangle, and the rectangle is set using the control's BoundsRect property.

We mentioned earlier that AppBar notification messages will be sent to the window indicated by FABD.hWnd using the message identifier held in FABD.uCallbackMessage. These notification messages are handled in the WndProc() method shown here:

```
procedure TAppBar.WndProc(var M: TMessage);
var
  State: UINT;
  WndPos: HWnd;
begin
  if M.Msg = AppBarMsg then
  begin
    case M.WParam of
      // Sent when always on top or auto-hide state has changed.
      ABN_STATECHANGE:
```

```
      begin
        // Check to see whether the access bar is still ABS_ALWAYSONTOP.
        State := SendAppBarMsg(ABM_GETSTATE);
        if ABS_ALWAYSONTOP and State = 0 then
          SetTopMost(False)
        else
          SetTopMost(True);
      end;
    // A full screen application has started, or the last
    // full-screen application has closed.
    ABN_FULLSCREENAPP:
      begin
        // Set the access bar's z-order appropriately.
        State := SendAppBarMsg(ABM_GETSTATE);
        if M.lParam <> 0 then begin
          if ABS_ALWAYSONTOP and State = 0 then
            SetTopMost(False)
          else
            SetTopMost(True);
        end
        else
          if State and ABS_ALWAYSONTOP <> 0 then
            SetTopMost(True);
      end;
    // Sent when something happened which may effect the AppBar position.
    ABN_POSCHANGED:
      begin
        // The taskbar or another access bar
        // has changed its size or position.
        SetAppBarPos(FABD.uEdge);
      end;
    end;
  end
  else
    inherited WndProc(M);
end;
```

This method handles some notification messages that permit the AppBar to respond to changes that might occur in the shell while the application is running. The remainder of the AppBar component code is shown in Listing 16.3.

LISTING 16.3   AppBars.pas—Unit Containing Base Class for AppBar Support

```
unit AppBars;

interface
```

LISTING 16.3 Continued

```delphi
uses Windows, Messages, SysUtils, Forms, ShellAPI, Classes, Controls;

type
  TAppBarEdge = (abeTop, abeBottom, abeLeft, abeRight);

  EAppBarError = class(Exception);

  TAppBar = class(TCustomForm)
  private
    FABD: TAppBarData;
    FDockedHeight: Integer;
    FDockedWidth: Integer;
    FEdge: TAppBarEdge;
    FOnEdgeChanged: TNotifyEvent;
    FTopMost: Boolean;
    procedure WMActivate(var M: TMessage); message WM_ACTIVATE;
    procedure WMWindowPosChanged(var M: TMessage); message WM_WINDOWPOSCHANGED;
    function SendAppBarMsg(Msg: DWORD): UINT;
    procedure SetAppBarEdge(Value: TAppBarEdge);
    procedure SetAppBarPos(Edge: UINT);
    procedure SetTopMost(Value: Boolean);
    procedure SetDockedHeight(const Value: Integer);
    procedure SetDockedWidth(const Value: Integer);
  protected
    procedure CreateParams(var Params: TCreateParams); override;
    procedure CreateWnd; override;
    procedure DestroyWnd; override;
    procedure WndProc(var M: TMessage); override;
  public
    constructor CreateNew(AOwner: TComponent; Dummy: Integer = 0); override;
    property DockManager;
  published
    property Action;
    property ActiveControl;
    property AutoScroll;
    property AutoSize;
    property BiDiMode;
    property BorderWidth;
    property Color;
    property Ctl3D;
    property DockedHeight: Integer read FDockedHeight write SetDockedHeight
      default 35;
    property DockedWidth: Integer read FDockedWidth write SetDockedWidth
      default 40;
```

Listing 16.3   Continued

```
property UseDockManager;
property DockSite;
property DragKind;
property DragMode;
property Edge: TAppBarEdge read FEdge write SetAppBarEdge default abeTop;
property Enabled;
property ParentFont default False;
property Font;
property HelpFile;
property HorzScrollBar;
property Icon;
property KeyPreview;
property ObjectMenuItem;
property ParentBiDiMode;
property PixelsPerInch;
property PopupMenu;
property PrintScale;
property Scaled;
property ShowHint;
property TopMost: Boolean read FTopMost write SetTopMost default False;
property VertScrollBar;
property Visible;
property OnActivate;
property OnCanResize;
property OnClick;
property OnClose;
property OnCloseQuery;
property OnConstrainedResize;
property OnCreate;
property OnDblClick;
property OnDestroy;
property OnDeactivate;
property OnDockDrop;
property OnDockOver;
property OnDragDrop;
property OnDragOver;
property OnEdgeChanged: TNotifyEvent read FOnEdgeChanged
  write FOnEdgeChanged;
property OnEndDock;
property OnGetSiteInfo;
property OnHide;
property OnHelp;
property OnKeyDown;
property OnKeyPress;
```

LISTING 16.3 Continued

```pascal
    property OnKeyUp;
    property OnMouseDown;
    property OnMouseMove;
    property OnMouseUp;
    property OnMouseWheel;
    property OnMouseWheelDown;
    property OnMouseWheelUp;
    property OnPaint;
    property OnResize;
    property OnShortCut;
    property OnShow;
    property OnStartDock;
    property OnUnDock;
  end;

implementation

var
  AppBarMsg: UINT;

constructor TAppBar.CreateNew(AOwner: TComponent; Dummy: Integer);
begin
  FDockedHeight := 35;
  FDockedWidth := 40;
  inherited CreateNew(AOwner, Dummy);
  ClientHeight := 35;
  Width := 100;
  BorderStyle := bsNone;
  BorderIcons := [];
  // set up the TAppBarData record
  FABD.cbSize := SizeOf(FABD);
  FABD.uCallbackMessage := AppBarMsg;
end;

procedure TAppBar.WMWindowPosChanged(var M: TMessage);
begin
  inherited;
  // Must inform shell that the AppBar position has changed
  SendAppBarMsg(ABM_WINDOWPOSCHANGED);
end;

procedure TAppBar.WMActivate(var M: TMessage);
begin
  inherited;
```

LISTING 16.3 Continued

```
// Must inform shell that the AppBar window was activated
  SendAppBarMsg(ABM_ACTIVATE);
end;

procedure TAppBar.WndProc(var M: TMessage);
var
  State: UINT;
begin
  if M.Msg = AppBarMsg then
  begin
    case M.WParam of
      // Sent when always on top or auto-hide state has changed.
      ABN_STATECHANGE:
        begin
          // Check to see whether the access bar is still ABS_ALWAYSONTOP.
          State := SendAppBarMsg(ABM_GETSTATE);
          if ABS_ALWAYSONTOP and State = 0 then
            SetTopMost(False)
          else
            SetTopMost(True);
        end;
      // A full screen application has started, or the last
      // full-screen application has closed.
      ABN_FULLSCREENAPP:
        begin
          // Set the access bar's z-order appropriately.
          State := SendAppBarMsg(ABM_GETSTATE);
          if M.lParam <> 0 then begin
            if ABS_ALWAYSONTOP and State = 0 then
              SetTopMost(False)
            else
              SetTopMost(True);
          end
          else
            if State and ABS_ALWAYSONTOP <> 0 then
              SetTopMost(True);
        end;
      // Sent when something happened which may effect the AppBar position.
      ABN_POSCHANGED:
        // The taskbar or another access bar
        // has changed its size or position.
        SetAppBarPos(FABD.uEdge);
    end;
  end
```

LISTING 16.3   Continued

```
  else
    inherited WndProc(M);
end;

function TAppBar.SendAppBarMsg(Msg: DWORD): UINT;
begin
  // Don't do AppBar stuff at design time... too funky
  if csDesigning in ComponentState then Result := 0
  else Result := SHAppBarMessage(Msg, FABD);
end;

procedure TAppBar.SetAppBarPos(Edge:  UINT);
begin
  if csDesigning in ComponentState then Exit;
  FABD.uEdge := Edge;        // set edge
  with FABD.rc do
  begin
    // set coordinates to full-screen
    Top := 0;
    Left := 0;
    Right := Screen.Width;
    Bottom := Screen.Height;
    // Send ABM_QUERYPOS to obtain proper rect on edge
    SendAppBarMsg(ABM_QUERYPOS);
    // re-adjust rect based on that modified by ABM_QUERYPOS
    case Edge of
      ABE_LEFT: Right := Left + FDockedWidth;
      ABE_RIGHT: Left := Right - FDockedWidth;
      ABE_TOP: Bottom := Top + FDockedHeight;
      ABE_BOTTOM: Top := Bottom - FDockedHeight;
    end;
    // Set the app bar position.
    SendAppBarMsg(ABM_SETPOS);
  end;
  // Set the BoundsRect property so that it conforms to the
  // bounding rectangle passed to the system.
  BoundsRect := FABD.rc;
end;

procedure TAppBar.SetTopMost(Value: Boolean);
const
  WndPosArray: array[Boolean] of HWND = (HWND_BOTTOM, HWND_TOPMOST);
begin
  if FTopMost <> Value then
```

LISTING 16.3 Continued

```
  begin
    FTopMost := Value;
    if not (csDesigning in ComponentState) then
      SetWindowPos(Handle, WndPosArray[Value], 0, 0, 0, 0, SWP_NOMOVE or
        SWP_NOSIZE or SWP_NOACTIVATE);
  end;
end;

procedure TAppBar.CreateParams(var Params: TCreateParams);
begin
  inherited CreateParams(Params);
  if not (csDesigning in ComponentState) then
  begin
    Params.ExStyle := Params.ExStyle or WS_EX_TOPMOST or WS_EX_WINDOWEDGE;
    Params.Style := Params.Style or WS_DLGFRAME;
  end;
end;

procedure TAppBar.CreateWnd;
begin
  inherited CreateWnd;
  FABD.hWnd := Handle;
  if not (csDesigning in ComponentState) then
  begin
    if SendAppBarMsg(ABM_NEW) = 0 then
      raise EAppBarError.Create('Failed to create AppBar');
    // Initialize the position
    SetAppBarEdge(FEdge);
  end;
end;

procedure TAppBar.DestroyWnd;
begin
  // Must inform shell that the AppBar is going away
  SendAppBarMsg(ABM_REMOVE);
  inherited DestroyWnd;
end;

procedure TAppBar.SetAppBarEdge(Value: TAppBarEdge);
const
  EdgeArray: array[TAppBarEdge] of UINT =
    (ABE_TOP, ABE_BOTTOM, ABE_LEFT, ABE_RIGHT);
begin
  SetAppBarPos(EdgeArray[Value]);
```

LISTING 16.3 Continued

```
  FEdge := Value;
  if Assigned(FOnEdgeChanged) then FOnEdgeChanged(Self);
end;

procedure TAppBar.SetDockedHeight(const Value: Integer);
begin
  if FDockedHeight <> Value then
  begin
    FDockedHeight := Value;
    SetAppBarEdge(FEdge);
  end;
end;

procedure TAppBar.SetDockedWidth(const Value: Integer);
begin
  if FDockedWidth <> Value then
  begin
    FDockedWidth := Value;
    SetAppBarEdge(FEdge);
  end;
end;

initialization
  AppBarMsg := RegisterWindowMessage('DDG AppBar Message');
end.
```

Using TAppBar

If you installed the software found on the CD-ROM accompanying this book, using a TAppBar should be a snap: just select the AppBar option from the DDG page of the File, New dialog box. This invokes a wizard that will generate a unit containing a TAppBar component.

> **NOTE**
>
> Chapter 17, "Using the Open Tools API," demonstrates how to create a wizard that automatically generates a TAppBar. For the purposes of this chapter, you can ignore the wizard implementation for the time being. Just understand that some work is being done behind the scenes to generate the AppBar's form and unit for you.

In this small sample application, TAppBar is used to create an application toolbar that contains buttons for various editing commands: Open, Save, Cut, Copy, and Paste. The buttons will manipulate a TMemo component found on the main form. The source code for this unit is shown in Listing 16.4, and Figure 16.5 shows the application in action with the AppBar control docked at the bottom of the screen.

LISTING 16.4   ApBarFrm.pas—Main Unit for AppBar Demo Application

```
unit ApBarFrm;

interface

uses
  Windows, Messages, SysUtils, Classes, Graphics, Controls, Forms, Dialogs,
  AppBars, Menus, Buttons;

type
  TAppBarForm = class(TAppBar)
    sbOpen: TSpeedButton;
    sbSave: TSpeedButton;
    sbCut: TSpeedButton;
    sbCopy: TSpeedButton;
    sbPaste: TSpeedButton;
    OpenDialog: TOpenDialog;
    pmPopup: TPopupMenu;
    Top1: TMenuItem;
    Bottom1: TMenuItem;
    Left1: TMenuItem;
    Right1: TMenuItem;
    N1: TMenuItem;
    Exit1: TMenuItem;
    procedure Right1Click(Sender: TObject);
    procedure sbOpenClick(Sender: TObject);
    procedure sbSaveClick(Sender: TObject);
    procedure sbCutClick(Sender: TObject);
    procedure sbCopyClick(Sender: TObject);
    procedure sbPasteClick(Sender: TObject);
    procedure Exit1Click(Sender: TObject);
    procedure FormCreate(Sender: TObject);
    procedure FormEdgeChanged(Sender: TObject);
  private
    FLastChecked: TMenuItem;
    procedure MoveButtons;
  end;
```

LISTING 16.4   Continued

```
var
  AppBarForm: TAppBarForm;

implementation

uses Main;

{$R *.DFM}

{ TAppBarForm }

procedure TAppBarForm.MoveButtons;
// This method looks complicated, but it really just arranges the buttons
// properly depending on what side the AppBar is docked.
var
  DeltaCenter, NewPos: Integer;
begin
  if Edge in [abeTop, abeBottom] then
  begin
    DeltaCenter := (ClientHeight - sbOpen.Height) div 2;
    sbOpen.SetBounds(10, DeltaCenter, sbOpen.Width, sbOpen.Height);
    NewPos := sbOpen.Width + 20;
    sbSave.SetBounds(NewPos, DeltaCenter, sbOpen.Width, sbOpen.Height);
    NewPos := NewPos + sbOpen.Width + 10;
    sbCut.SetBounds(NewPos, DeltaCenter, sbOpen.Width, sbOpen.Height);
    NewPos := NewPos + sbOpen.Width + 10;
    sbCopy.SetBounds(NewPos, DeltaCenter, sbOpen.Width, sbOpen.Height);
    NewPos := NewPos + sbOpen.Width + 10;
    sbPaste.SetBounds(NewPos, DeltaCenter, sbOpen.Width, sbOpen.Height);
  end
  else
  begin
    DeltaCenter := (ClientWidth - sbOpen.Width) div 2;
    sbOpen.SetBounds(DeltaCenter, 10, sbOpen.Width, sbOpen.Height);
    NewPos := sbOpen.Height + 20;
    sbSave.SetBounds(DeltaCenter, NewPos, sbOpen.Width, sbOpen.Height);
    NewPos := NewPos + sbOpen.Height + 10;
    sbCut.SetBounds(DeltaCenter, NewPos, sbOpen.Width, sbOpen.Height);
    NewPos := NewPos + sbOpen.Height + 10;
    sbCopy.SetBounds(DeltaCenter, NewPos, sbOpen.Width, sbOpen.Height);
    NewPos := NewPos + sbOpen.Height + 10;
    sbPaste.SetBounds(DeltaCenter, NewPos, sbOpen.Width, sbOpen.Height);
  end;
end;
```

LISTING 16.4   Continued

```
procedure TAppBarForm.Right1Click(Sender: TObject);
begin
  FLastChecked.Checked := False;
  (Sender as TMenuItem).Checked := True;
  case TMenuItem(Sender).Caption[2] of
    'T': Edge := abeTop;
    'B': Edge := abeBottom;
    'L': Edge := abeLeft;
    'R': Edge := abeRight;
  end;
  FLastChecked := TMenuItem(Sender);
end;

procedure TAppBarForm.sbOpenClick(Sender: TObject);
begin
  if OpenDialog.Execute then
    MainForm.FileName := OpenDialog.FileName;
end;

procedure TAppBarForm.sbSaveClick(Sender: TObject);
begin
  MainForm.memEditor.Lines.SaveToFile(MainForm.FileName);
end;

procedure TAppBarForm.sbCutClick(Sender: TObject);
begin
  MainForm.memEditor.CutToClipboard;
end;

procedure TAppBarForm.sbCopyClick(Sender: TObject);
begin
  MainForm.memEditor.CopyToClipboard;
end;

procedure TAppBarForm.sbPasteClick(Sender: TObject);
begin
  MainForm.memEditor.PasteFromClipboard;
end;

procedure TAppBarForm.Exit1Click(Sender: TObject);
begin
  Application.Terminate;
end;
```

LISTING 16.4 Continued

```
procedure TAppBarForm.FormCreate(Sender: TObject);
begin
  FLastChecked := Top1;
end;

procedure TAppBarForm.FormEdgeChanged(Sender: TObject);
begin
  MoveButtons;
end;

end.
```

FIGURE 16.5

TAppBar *in action.*

Shell Links

The Windows shell exposes a series of interfaces that can be employed to manipulate different aspects of the shell. These interfaces are defined in the ShlObj unit. Discussing in depth all the objects in that unit could take a book in its own right, so for now we'll focus on one of the most useful (and most used) interfaces: IShellLink.

`IShellLink` is an interface that permits the creating and manipulating of shell links in your applications. In case you're unsure, most of the icons on your desktop are probably shell links. Additionally, each item in the shell's local Send To menu or the Documents menu (off of the Start menu) are all shell links. The `IShellLink` interface is defined as follows:

```
const

type
  IShellLink = interface(IUnknown)
    ['{000214EE-0000-0000-C000-000000000046}']
    function GetPath(pszFile: PAnsiChar; cchMaxPath: Integer;
      var pfd: TWin32FindData; fFlags: DWORD): HResult; stdcall;
    function GetIDList(var ppidl: PItemIDList): HResult; stdcall;
    function SetIDList(pidl: PItemIDList): HResult; stdcall;
    function GetDescription(pszName: PAnsiChar; cchMaxName: Integer): HResult;
      stdcall;
    function SetDescription(pszName: PAnsiChar): HResult; stdcall;
    function GetWorkingDirectory(pszDir: PAnsiChar; cchMaxPath: Integer):
      HResult;
      stdcall;
    function SetWorkingDirectory(pszDir: PAnsiChar): HResult; stdcall;
    function GetArguments(pszArgs: PAnsiChar; cchMaxPath: Integer): HResult;
      stdcall;
    function SetArguments(pszArgs: PAnsiChar): HResult; stdcall;
    function GetHotkey(var pwHotkey: Word): HResult; stdcall;
    function SetHotkey(wHotkey: Word): HResult; stdcall;
    function GetShowCmd(out piShowCmd: Integer): HResult; stdcall;
    function SetShowCmd(iShowCmd: Integer): HResult; stdcall;
    function GetIconLocation(pszIconPath: PAnsiChar; cchIconPath: Integer;
      out piIcon: Integer): HResult; stdcall;
    function SetIconLocation(pszIconPath: PAnsiChar; iIcon: Integer): HResult;
      stdcall;
    function SetRelativePath(pszPathRel: PAnsiChar; dwReserved: DWORD):
      HResult;
      stdcall;
    function Resolve(Wnd: HWND; fFlags: DWORD): HResult; stdcall;
    function SetPath(pszFile: PAnsiChar): HResult; stdcall;
  end;
```

NOTE

`IShellLink` and all its methods are described in detail in the Win32 online help, so we won't cover them here.

Obtaining an `IShellLink` Instance

Unlike working with shell extensions, which you'll learn about later in this chapter, you don't implement the `IShellLink` interface. Instead, this interface is implemented by the Windows shell, and you use the `CoCreateInstance()` COM function to create an instance. Here's an example:

```
var
  SL: IShellLink;
begin
  OleCheck(CoCreateInstance(CLSID_ShellLink, nil, CLSCTX_INPROC_SERVER,
    IShellLink, SL));
  // use SL here
end;
```

> **NOTE**
>
> Don't forget that before you can use any OLE functions, you must initialize the COM library using the `CoInitialize()` function. When you're through using COM, you must clean up by calling `CoUninitialize()`. These functions will be called for you by Delphi in an application that uses `ComObj` and contains a call to `Application.Initialize()`. Otherwise, you'll have to call these functions yourself.

Using `IShellLink`

Shell links seem kind of magical: you right-click on the desktop, create a new shortcut, and *something* happens that causes an icon to appear on the desktop. That *something* is actually a pretty mundane occurrence once you know what's going on. A *shell link* is actually just a file with an `.LNK` extension that lives in some particular directory. When Windows starts up, it looks in certain directories for LNK files, which represent links residing in different *shell folders*. These shell folders, or *special folders*, include items such as Network Neighborhood, Send To, Startup, the Desktop, and so on. The shell stores the link/folder correspondence in the System Registry—they're found mostly under the following key if you're interested in looking:

```
HKEY_CURRENT_USER\Software\Microsoft\Windows\CurrentVersion\Explorer
➥\Shell Folders
```

Creating a shell link in a special folder, then, is just a matter of placing a link file in a particular directory. Rather than spelunking through the Registry, you can use the `SHGetSpecialFolderPath()` to obtain the directory path for the various special folders. This method is defined as follows:

```
function SHGetSpecialFolderPath(hwndOwner: HWND; lpszPath: PChar;
  nFolder: Integer; fCreate: BOOL): BOOL; stdcall;
```

`hwndOwner` contains the handle of a window that will serve as the owner to any dialogs the function might invoke.

`lpszPath` is a pointer to a buffer to receive the path. This buffer must be at least MAX_PATH characters in length.

`nFolder` identifies the special folder for which you want to obtain the path. Table 16.4 shows the possible values for this parameter and a description for each.

`fCreate` indicates whether a folder should be created if it doesn't exist.

TABLE 16.4 Possible Values for `nFolder`

Flag	Description
CSIDL_ALTSTARTUP	The directory that corresponds to the user's non-localized Startup program group.
CSIDL_APPDATA	The directory that serves as a common repository for application-specific data.
CSIDL_BITBUCKET	The directory containing file objects in the user's Recycle Bin. The location of this directory isn't in the Registry; it's marked with the hidden and system attributes to prevent the user from moving or deleting it.
CSIDL_COMMON_ALTSTARTUP	The directory that corresponds to the nonlocalized Startup program group for all users.
CSIDL_COMMON_DESKTOPDIRECTORY	The directory that contains files and folders that appear on the desktop for all users.
CSIDL_COMMON_FAVORITES	The directory that serves as a common repository for all users' favorite items.
CSIDL_COMMON_PROGRAMS	The directory that contains the directories for the common program groups that appear on the Start menu for all users.
CSIDL_COMMON_STARTMENU	The directory that contains the programs and folders that appear on the Start menu for all users.
CSIDL_COMMON_STARTUP	The directory that contains the programs that appear in the Startup folder for all users.
CSIDL_CONTROLS	A virtual folder containing icons for the Control Panel applications.
CSIDL_COOKIES	The directory that serves as a common repository for Internet cookies.

TABLE 16.4 Continued

Flag	Description
CSIDL_DESKTOP	The Windows Desktop virtual folder at the root of the namespace.
CSIDL_DESKTOPDIRECTORY	The directory used to physically store file objects on the desktop (not to be confused with the Desktop folder, itself).
CSIDL_DRIVES	The My Computer virtual folder containing everything on the local computer: storage devices, printers, and the Control Panel. The folder might also contain mapped network drives.
CSIDL_FAVORITES	The directory that serves as a common repository for the user's favorite items.
CSIDL_FONTS	A virtual folder containing fonts.
CSIDL_HISTORY	The directory that serves as a common repository for Internet history items.
CSIDL_INTERNET	A virtual folder representing the Internet.
CSIDL_INTERNET_CACHE	The directory that serves as a common repository for temporary Internet files.
CSIDL_NETHOOD	The directory that contains objects that appear in the Network Neighborhood.
CSIDL_NETWORK	The Network Neighborhood virtual folder representing the top level of the network hierarchy.
CSIDL_PERSONAL	The directory that serves as a common repository for documents.
CSIDL_PRINTERS	A virtual folder containing installed printers.
CSIDL_PRINTHOOD	The directory that serves as a common repository for printer links.
CSIDL_PROGRAMS	The directory that contains the user's program groups (which are also directories).
CSIDL_RECENT	The directory that contains the user's most recently used documents.
CSIDL_SENDTO	The directory that contains Send To menu items.
CSIDL_STARTMENU	The directory that contains Start menu items.

TABLE 16.4   Continued

Flag	Description
CSIDL_STARTUP	The directory that corresponds to the user's Startup program group. The system starts these programs whenever any user logs onto Windows NT or starts Windows 95 or 98.
CSIDL_TEMPLATES	The directory that serves as a common repository for document templates.

Creating a Shell Link

The IShellLink interface is an encapsulation of a shell link object, but it has no concept of how to read or write itself to a file on disk. However, implementers of the IShellLink interface are also required to support the IPersistFile interface in order to provide file access. IPersistFile is an interface that provides methods for reading and writing to and from disk, and it's defined as follows:

```
type
  IPersistFile = interface(IPersist)
    ['{0000010B-0000-0000-C000-000000000046}']
    function IsDirty: HResult; stdcall;
    function Load(pszFileName: POleStr; dwMode: Longint): HResult;
      stdcall;
    function Save(pszFileName: POleStr; fRemember: BOOL): HResult;
      stdcall;
    function SaveCompleted(pszFileName: POleStr): HResult;
      stdcall;
    function GetCurFile(out pszFileName: POleStr): HResult;
      stdcall;
  end;
```

> **NOTE**
>
> You'll find a complete description of IPersistFile and its methods in the Win32 online help.

Because the class that implements IShellLink is also required to implement IPersistFile, you can QueryInterface the IShellLink instance for an IPersistFile instance using the as operator, as shown here:

```
var
  SL: IShellLink;
  PF: IPersistFile;
```

```
begin
  OleCheck(CoCreateInstance(CLSID_ShellLink, nil, CLSCTX_INPROC_SERVER,
    IShellLink, SL));
  PF := SL as IPersistFile;
  // use PF and SL
end;
```

As mentioned earlier, using COM interface objects works the same as using normal Object Pascal objects. The following code, for example, creates a desktop shell link to the Notepad application:

```
procedure MakeNotepad;
const
  // NOTE: Assumed location for Notepad:
  AppName = 'c:\windows\notepad.exe';
var
  SL: IShellLink;
  PF: IPersistFile;
  LnkName: WideString;
begin
  OleCheck(CoCreateInstance(CLSID_ShellLink, nil, CLSCTX_INPROC_SERVER,
    IShellLink, SL));
  { IShellLink implementers are required to implement IPersistFile }
  PF := SL as IPersistFile;
  OleCheck(SL.SetPath(PChar(AppName)));    // set link path to proper file
  { create a path location and filename for link file }
  LnkName := GetFolderLocation('Desktop') + '\' +
    ChangeFileExt(ExtractFileName(AppName), '.lnk');
  PF.Save(PWideChar(LnkName), True);       // save link file
end;
```

In this procedure, the SetPath() method of IShellLink is used to point the link to an executable file or document (Notepad in this case). Then, a path and filename for the link is created using the path returned by GetFolderLocation('Desktop') (described earlier in this section) and by using the ChangeFileExt() function to change the extension of Notepad from .EXE to .LNK. This new filename is stored in LnkName. After that, the Save() method saves the link to a disk file. As you've learned, when the procedure terminates and the SL and PF interface instances fall out of scope, their respective references will be released.

Getting and Setting Link Information

As you can see from the definition of the IShellLink interface, it contains a number of GetXXX() and SetXXX() methods that allow you to get and set different aspects of the shell link. Consider the following record declaration, which contains fields for each of the possible values that can be set or retrieved:

```
type
  TShellLinkInfo = record
    PathName: string;
    Arguments: string;
    Description: string;
    WorkingDirectory: string;
    IconLocation: string;
    IconIndex: Integer;
    ShowCmd: Integer;
    HotKey: Word;
  end;
```

Given this record, you can create functions that retrieve the settings of a given shell link to the record or that set a link's values to those indicated by the record's contents. Such functions are shown in Listing 16.5; WinShell.pas is a unit that contains the complete source for these functions.

LISTING 16.5   WinShell.pas—Unit Containing Functions That Operate on Shell Links

```
unit WinShell;

interface

uses SysUtils, Windows, Registry, ActiveX, ShlObj;

type
  EShellOleError = class(Exception);

  TShellLinkInfo = record
    PathName: string;
    Arguments: string;
    Description: string;
    WorkingDirectory: string;
    IconLocation: string;
    IconIndex: integer;
    ShowCmd: integer;
    HotKey: word;
  end;

  TSpecialFolderInfo = record
    Name: string;
    ID: Integer;
  end;

const
  SpecialFolders: array[0..29] of TSpecialFolderInfo = (
```

LISTING 16.5 Continued

```pascal
    (Name: 'Alt Startup'; ID: CSIDL_ALTSTARTUP),
    (Name: 'Application Data'; ID: CSIDL_APPDATA),
    (Name: 'Recycle Bin'; ID: CSIDL_BITBUCKET),
    (Name: 'Common Alt Startup'; ID: CSIDL_COMMON_ALTSTARTUP),
    (Name: 'Common Desktop'; ID: CSIDL_COMMON_DESKTOPDIRECTORY),
    (Name: 'Common Favorites'; ID: CSIDL_COMMON_FAVORITES),
    (Name: 'Common Programs'; ID: CSIDL_COMMON_PROGRAMS),
    (Name: 'Common Start Menu'; ID: CSIDL_COMMON_STARTMENU),
    (Name: 'Common Startup'; ID: CSIDL_COMMON_STARTUP),
    (Name: 'Controls'; ID: CSIDL_CONTROLS),
    (Name: 'Cookies'; ID: CSIDL_COOKIES),
    (Name: 'Desktop'; ID: CSIDL_DESKTOP),
    (Name: 'Desktop Directory'; ID: CSIDL_DESKTOPDIRECTORY),
    (Name: 'Drives'; ID: CSIDL_DRIVES),
    (Name: 'Favorites'; ID: CSIDL_FAVORITES),
    (Name: 'Fonts'; ID: CSIDL_FONTS),
    (Name: 'History'; ID: CSIDL_HISTORY),
    (Name: 'Internet'; ID: CSIDL_INTERNET),
    (Name: 'Internet Cache'; ID: CSIDL_INTERNET_CACHE),
    (Name: 'Network Neighborhood'; ID: CSIDL_NETHOOD),
    (Name: 'Network Top'; ID: CSIDL_NETWORK),
    (Name: 'Personal'; ID: CSIDL_PERSONAL),
    (Name: 'Printers'; ID: CSIDL_PRINTERS),
    (Name: 'Printer Links'; ID: CSIDL_PRINTHOOD),
    (Name: 'Programs'; ID: CSIDL_PROGRAMS),
    (Name: 'Recent Documents'; ID: CSIDL_RECENT),
    (Name: 'Send To'; ID: CSIDL_SENDTO),
    (Name: 'Start Menu'; ID: CSIDL_STARTMENU),
    (Name: 'Startup'; ID: CSIDL_STARTUP),
    (Name: 'Templates'; ID: CSIDL_TEMPLATES));

function CreateShellLink(const AppName, Desc: string; Dest: Integer): string;
function GetSpecialFolderPath(Folder: Integer; CanCreate: Boolean): string;
procedure GetShellLinkInfo(const LinkFile: WideString;
  var SLI: TShellLinkInfo);
procedure SetShellLinkInfo(const LinkFile: WideString;
  const SLI: TShellLinkInfo);

implementation

uses ComObj;

function GetSpecialFolderPath(Folder: Integer; CanCreate: Boolean): string;
var
  FilePath: array[0..MAX_PATH] of char;
```

LISTING 16.5   Continued

```
begin
  { Get path of selected location }
  SHGetSpecialFolderPathW(0, FilePath, Folder, CanCreate);
  Result := FilePath;
end;

function CreateShellLink(const AppName, Desc: string; Dest: Integer): string;
{ Creates a shell link for application or document specified in  }
{ AppName with description Desc.  Link will be located in folder }
{ specified by Dest, which is one of the string constants shown  }
{ at the top of this unit.  Returns the full path name of the    }
{ link file. }
var
  SL: IShellLink;
  PF: IPersistFile;
  LnkName: WideString;
begin
  OleCheck(CoCreateInstance(CLSID_ShellLink, nil, CLSCTX_INPROC_SERVER,
    IShellLink, SL));
  { The IShellLink implementer must also support the IPersistFile }
  { interface. Get an interface pointer to it. }
  PF := SL as IPersistFile;
  OleCheck(SL.SetPath(PChar(AppName)));  // set link path to proper file
  if Desc <> '' then
    OleCheck(SL.SetDescription(PChar(Desc))); // set description
  { create a path location and filename for link file }
  LnkName := GetSpecialFolderPath(Dest, True) + '\' +
             ChangeFileExt(AppName, 'lnk');
  PF.Save(PWideChar(LnkName), True);              // save link file
  Result := LnkName;
end;

procedure GetShellLinkInfo(const LinkFile: WideString;
  var SLI: TShellLinkInfo);
{ Retrieves information on an existing shell link }
var
  SL: IShellLink;
  PF: IPersistFile;
  FindData: TWin32FindData;
  AStr: array[0..MAX_PATH] of char;
begin
  OleCheck(CoCreateInstance(CLSID_ShellLink, nil, CLSCTX_INPROC_SERVER,
    IShellLink, SL));
  { The IShellLink implementer must also support the IPersistFile }
```

LISTING 16.5 Continued

```pascal
    { interface. Get an interface pointer to it. }
    PF := SL as IPersistFile;
    { Load file into IPersistFile object }
    OleCheck(PF.Load(PWideChar(LinkFile), STGM_READ));
    { Resolve the link by calling the Resolve interface function. }
    OleCheck(SL.Resolve(0, SLR_ANY_MATCH or SLR_NO_UI));
    { Get all the info! }
    with SLI do
    begin
      OleCheck(SL.GetPath(AStr, MAX_PATH, FindData, SLGP_SHORTPATH));
      PathName := AStr;
      OleCheck(SL.GetArguments(AStr, MAX_PATH));
      Arguments := AStr;
      OleCheck(SL.GetDescription(AStr, MAX_PATH));
      Description := AStr;
      OleCheck(SL.GetWorkingDirectory(AStr, MAX_PATH));
      WorkingDirectory := AStr;
      OleCheck(SL.GetIconLocation(AStr, MAX_PATH, IconIndex));
      IconLocation := AStr;
      OleCheck(SL.GetShowCmd(ShowCmd));
      OleCheck(SL.GetHotKey(HotKey));
    end;
end;

procedure SetShellLinkInfo(const LinkFile: WideString;
  const SLI: TShellLinkInfo);
{ Sets information for an existing shell link }
var
  SL: IShellLink;
  PF: IPersistFile;
begin
  OleCheck(CoCreateInstance(CLSID_ShellLink, nil, CLSCTX_INPROC_SERVER,
    IShellLink, SL));
  { The IShellLink implementer must also support the IPersistFile }
  { interface. Get an interface pointer to it. }
  PF := SL as IPersistFile;
  { Load file into IPersistFile object }
  OleCheck(PF.Load(PWideChar(LinkFile), STGM_SHARE_DENY_WRITE));
  { Resolve the link by calling the Resolve interface function. }
  OleCheck(SL.Resolve(0, SLR_ANY_MATCH or SLR_UPDATE or SLR_NO_UI));
  { Set all the info! }
  with SLI, SL do
  begin
    OleCheck(SetPath(PChar(PathName)));
```

LISTING 16.5   Continued

```
    OleCheck(SetArguments(PChar(Arguments)));
    OleCheck(SetDescription(PChar(Description)));
    OleCheck(SetWorkingDirectory(PChar(WorkingDirectory)));
    OleCheck(SetIconLocation(PChar(IconLocation), IconIndex));
    OleCheck(SetShowCmd(ShowCmd));
    OleCheck(SetHotKey(HotKey));
  end;
  PF.Save(PWideChar(LinkFile), True);    // save file
end;

end.
```

One method of IShellLink that has yet to be explained is the Resolve() method. Resolve() should be called after the IPersistFile interface of IShellLink is used to load a link file. This searches the specified link file and fills the IShellLink object with values specified in the file.

> **TIP**
>
> In the GetShellLinkInfo() function shown in Listing 16.5, notice the use of the AStr local array into which values are retrieved. This technique is used rather than using the SetLength() to allocate space for the strings—using SetLength() on so many strings would cause fragmentation of the application's heap. Using AStr as an intermediate prevents this from occurring. Additionally, because the length of the strings needs to be set only once, using AStr ends up being slightly faster.

A Sample Application

These functions and interfaces might be fun and all, but they're nothing without a nifty application in which to show them off. The Shell Link project allows you to do just that. The main form of this project is shown in Figure 16.6.

Listing 16.6 shows the main unit for this project, Main.pas. Listings 16.7 and 16.8 show NewLinkU.pas and PickU.pas, two supporting units for the project.

FIGURE 16.6

The Shell Link main form, showing one of the desktop links.

LISTING 16.6 Main.pas—Main for Shell Link Project

```
unit Main;

interface

uses
  Windows, Messages, SysUtils, Classes, Graphics, Controls, Forms, Dialogs,
  StdCtrls, ComCtrls, ExtCtrls, Spin, WinShell, Menus;

type
  TMainForm = class(TForm)
    Panel1: TPanel;
    btnOpen: TButton;
    edLink: TEdit;
    btnNew: TButton;
    btnSave: TButton;
    Label3: TLabel;
    Panel2: TPanel;
    Label1: TLabel;
    Label2: TLabel;
    Label4: TLabel;
    Label5: TLabel;
    Label6: TLabel;
    Label7: TLabel;
    Label8: TLabel;
    Label9: TLabel;
    edIcon: TEdit;
    edDesc: TEdit;
    edWorkDir: TEdit;
    edArg: TEdit;
```

LISTING 16.6   Continued

```
    cbShowCmd: TComboBox;
    hkHotKey: THotKey;
    speIcnIdx: TSpinEdit;
    pnlIconPanel: TPanel;
    imgIconImage: TImage;
    btnExit: TButton;
    MainMenu1: TMainMenu;
    File1: TMenuItem;
    Open1: TMenuItem;
    Save1: TMenuItem;
    NewLInk1: TMenuItem;
    N1: TMenuItem;
    Exit1: TMenuItem;
    Help1: TMenuItem;
    About1: TMenuItem;
    edPath: TEdit;
    procedure btnOpenClick(Sender: TObject);
    procedure btnNewClick(Sender: TObject);
    procedure edIconChange(Sender: TObject);
    procedure btnSaveClick(Sender: TObject);
    procedure btnExitClick(Sender: TObject);
    procedure About1Click(Sender: TObject);
  private
    procedure GetControls(var SLI: TShellLinkInfo);
    procedure SetControls(const SLI: TShellLinkInfo);
    procedure ShowIcon;
    procedure OpenLinkFile(const LinkFileName: String);
  end;

var
  MainForm: TMainForm;

implementation

{$R *.DFM}

uses PickU, NewLinkU, AboutU, CommCtrl, ShellAPI;

type
  THotKeyRec = record
    Char, ModCode: Byte;
  end;

procedure TMainForm.SetControls(const SLI: TShellLinkInfo);
```

LISTING 16.6 Continued

```pascal
{ Sets values of UI controls based on contents of SLI }
var
  Mods: THKModifiers;
begin
  with SLI do
  begin
    edPath.Text := PathName;
    edIcon.Text := IconLocation;
    { if icon name is blank and link is to exe, use exe name for icon }
    { path.  This is done because the icon index is ignored if the    }
    { icon path is blank, but an exe may contain more than one icon.  }
    if (IconLocation = '') and
      (CompareText(ExtractFileExt(PathName), 'EXE') = 0) then
      edIcon.Text := PathName;
    edWorkDir.Text := WorkingDirectory;
    edArg.Text := Arguments;
    speIcnIdx.Value := IconIndex;
    edDesc.Text := Description;
    { SW_* constants start at 1 }
    cbShowCmd.ItemIndex := ShowCmd - 1;
    { Hot key char in low byte }
    hkHotKey.HotKey := Lo(HotKey);
    { Figure out which modifier flags are in high byte }
    Mods := [];
    if (HOTKEYF_ALT and Hi(HotKey)) <> 0 then include(Mods, hkAlt);
    if (HOTKEYF_CONTROL and Hi(HotKey)) <> 0 then include(Mods, hkCtrl);
    if (HOTKEYF_EXT and Hi(HotKey)) <> 0 then include(Mods, hkExt);
    if (HOTKEYF_SHIFT and Hi(HotKey)) <> 0 then include(Mods, hkShift);
    { Set modifiers set }
    hkHotKey.Modifiers := Mods;
  end;
  ShowIcon;
end;

procedure TMainForm.GetControls(var SLI: TShellLinkInfo);
{ Gets values of UI controls and uses them to set values of SLI }
var
  CtlMods: THKModifiers;
  HR: THotKeyRec;
begin
  with SLI do
  begin
    PathName := edPath.Text;
    IconLocation := edIcon.Text;
```

LISTING 16.6   Continued

```
      WorkingDirectory := edWorkDir.Text;
      Arguments := edArg.Text;
      IconIndex := speIcnIdx.Value;
      Description := edDesc.Text;
      { SW_* constants start at 1 }
      ShowCmd := cbShowCmd.ItemIndex + 1;
      { Get hot key character }
      word(HR) := hkHotKey.HotKey;
      { Figure out which modifier keys are being used }
      CtlMods := hkHotKey.Modifiers;
      with HR do begin
        ModCode := 0;
        if (hkAlt in CtlMods) then ModCode := ModCode or HOTKEYF_ALT;
        if (hkCtrl in CtlMods) then ModCode := ModCode or HOTKEYF_CONTROL;
        if (hkExt in CtlMods) then ModCode := ModCode or HOTKEYF_EXT;
        if (hkShift in CtlMods) then ModCode := ModCode or HOTKEYF_SHIFT;
      end;
      HotKey := word(HR);
    end;
end;

procedure TMainForm.ShowIcon;
{ Retrieves icon from appropriate file and shows in IconImage }
var
  HI: THandle;
  IcnFile: string;
  IconIndex: word;
begin
  { Get name of icon file }
  IcnFile := edIcon.Text;
  { If blank, use the exe name }
  if IcnFile = '' then
    IcnFile := edPath.Text;
  { Make sure file exists }
  if FileExists(IcnFile) then
  begin
    IconIndex := speIcnIdx.Value;
    { Extract icon from file }
    HI := ExtractAssociatedIcon(hInstance, PChar(IcnFile), IconIndex);
    { Assign icon handle to IconImage }
    imgIconImage.Picture.Icon.Handle := HI;
  end;
end;
```

LISTING 16.6 Continued

```pascal
procedure TMainForm.OpenLinkFile(const LinkFileName: string);
{ Opens a link file, get info, and displays info in UI }
var
  SLI: TShellLinkInfo;
begin
  edLink.Text := LinkFileName;
  try
    GetShellLinkInfo(LinkFileName, SLI);
  except
    on EShellOleError do
      MessageDlg('Error occurred while opening link', mtError, [mbOk], 0);
  end;
  SetControls(SLI);
end;

procedure TMainForm.btnOpenClick(Sender: TObject);
{ OnClick handler for OpenBtn }
var
  LinkFile: String;
begin
  if GetLinkFile(LinkFile) then
    OpenLinkFile(LinkFile);
end;

procedure TMainForm.btnNewClick(Sender: TObject);
{ OnClick handler for NewBtn }
var
  FileName: string;
  Dest: Integer;
begin
  if GetNewLinkName(FileName, Dest) then
    OpenLinkFile(CreateShellLink(FileName, '', Dest));
end;

procedure TMainForm.edIconChange(Sender: TObject);
{ OnChange handler for IconEd and IcnIdxEd }
begin
  ShowIcon;
end;

procedure TMainForm.btnSaveClick(Sender: TObject);
{ OnClick handler for SaveBtn }
var
  SLI: TShellLinkInfo;
```

LISTING 16.6   Continued

```
begin
  GetControls(SLI);
  try
    SetShellLinkInfo(edLink.Text, SLI);
  except
    on EShellOleError do
      MessageDlg('Error occurred while setting info', mtError, [mbOk], 0);
  end;
end;

procedure TMainForm.btnExitClick(Sender: TObject);
{ OnClick handler for ExitBtn }
begin
  Close;
end;

procedure TMainForm.About1Click(Sender: TObject);
{ OnClick handler for Help|About menu item }
begin
  AboutBox;
end;

end.
```

LISTING 16.7   NewLinkU.pas—Unit with Form That Helps Create New Link

```
unit NewLinkU;

interface

uses
  Windows, Messages, SysUtils, Classes, Graphics, Controls, Forms, Dialogs,
  Buttons, StdCtrls;

type
  TNewLinkForm = class(TForm)
    Label1: TLabel;
    Label2: TLabel;
    edLinkTo: TEdit;
    btnOk: TButton;
    btnCancel: TButton;
    cbLocation: TComboBox;
    sbOpen: TSpeedButton;
    OpenDialog: TOpenDialog;
```

LISTING 16.7   Continued

```delphi
    procedure sbOpenClick(Sender: TObject);
    procedure FormCreate(Sender: TObject);
  end;

function GetNewLinkName(var LinkTo: string; var Dest: Integer): Boolean;

implementation

uses WinShell;

{$R *.DFM}

function GetNewLinkName(var LinkTo: string; var Dest: Integer): Boolean;
{ Gets file name and destination folder for a new shell link. }
{ Only modifies params if Result = True. }
begin
  with TNewLinkForm.Create(Application) do
  try
    cbLocation.ItemIndex := 0;
    Result := ShowModal = mrOk;
    if Result then
    begin
      LinkTo := edLinkTo.Text;
      Dest := cbLocation.ItemIndex;
    end;
  finally
    Free;
  end;
end;

procedure TNewLinkForm.sbOpenClick(Sender: TObject);
begin
  if OpenDialog.Execute then
    edLinkTo.Text := OpenDialog.FileName;
end;

procedure TNewLinkForm.FormCreate(Sender: TObject);
var
  I: Integer;
begin
  for I := Low(SpecialFolders) to High(SpecialFolders) do
    cbLocation.Items.Add(SpecialFolders[I].Name);
end;

end.
```

LISTING 16.8   PickU.pas—Unit with Form that Enables User to Choose Link Location

```
unit PickU;

interface

uses
  Windows, Messages, SysUtils, Classes, Graphics, Controls, Forms, Dialogs,
  StdCtrls, FileCtrl;

type
  TLinkForm = class(TForm)
    lbLinkFiles: TFileListBox;
    btnOk: TButton;
    btnCancel: TButton;
    cbLocation: TComboBox;
    Label1: TLabel;
    procedure lbLinkFilesDblClick(Sender: TObject);
    procedure cbLocationChange(Sender: TObject);
    procedure FormCreate(Sender: TObject);
  end;

function GetLinkFile(var S: String): Boolean;

implementation

{$R *.DFM}

uses WinShell, ShlObj;

function GetLinkFile(var S: String): Boolean;
{ Returns link file name in S. }
{ Only modifies S when Result is True. }
begin
  with TLinkForm.Create(Application) do
    try
      { Make sure location is selected }
      cbLocation.ItemIndex := 0;
      { Get path of selected location }
      cbLocationChange(nil);
      Result := ShowModal = mrOk;
      { Return full pathname for link file }
      if Result then
        S := lbLinkFiles.Directory + '\' +
          lbLinkFiles.Items[lbLinkFiles.ItemIndex];
    finally
```

LISTING 16.8   Continued

```
      Free;
    end;
end;

procedure TLinkForm.lbLinkFilesDblClick(Sender: TObject);
begin
  ModalResult := mrOk;
end;

procedure TLinkForm.cbLocationChange(Sender: TObject);
var
  Folder: Integer;
begin
  { Get path of selected location }
  Folder := SpecialFolders[cbLocation.ItemIndex].ID;
  lbLinkFiles.Directory := GetSpecialFolderPath(Folder, False);
end;

procedure TLinkForm.FormCreate(Sender: TObject);
var
  I: Integer;
begin
  for I := Low(SpecialFolders) to High(SpecialFolders) do
    cbLocation.Items.Add(SpecialFolders[I].Name);
end;

end.
```

Shell Extensions

For the ultimate in extensibility, the Windows shell provides a means for you to develop code that executes from within the shell's own process and namespace. *Shell extensions* are implemented as in-process COM servers that are created and used by the shell.

> **NOTE**
>
> Because shell extensions are COM servers at heart, understanding them requires a basic understand of COM. If your COM knowledge needs brushing up, Chapter 15, "COM Development," provides this foundation.

Several types of shell extensions are available to deal with a variety of the shell's aspects. Also known as a *handler*, a shell extension must implement one or more COM interfaces. The shell supports the following types of shell extensions:

- *Copy hook handlers* implement the `ICopyHook` interface. These shell extensions allow you to receive notifications whenever a folder is copied, deleted, moved, or renamed and to optionally prevent the operation from occurring.

- *Context menu handlers* implement the `IContextMenu` and `IShellExtInit` interfaces. These shell extensions enable you to add items to the context menu of a particular file object in the shell.

- *Drag-and-drop handlers* also implement the `IContextMenu` and `IShellExtInit` interfaces. These shell extensions are almost identical in implementation to context menu handlers, except that they're invoked when a user drags an object and drops it to a new location.

- *Icon handlers* implement the `IExtractIcon` and `IPersistFile` interfaces. Icon handlers allow you to provide different icons for multiple instances of the same type of file object.

- *Property sheet handlers* implement the `IShellPropSheetExt` and `IShellExtInit` interfaces, and they allow you to add pages to the properties dialog associated with a file type.

- *Drop target handlers* implement the `IDropTarget` and `IPersistFile` interfaces. These shell extensions allow you to control what happens when you drop one shell object on another.

- *Data object handlers* implement the `IDataObject` and `IPersistFile` interfaces, and they supply the data object used when files are being dragged and dropped or copied and pasted.

Debugging Shell Extensions

Before we get into the subject of actually writing shell extensions, consider the question of debugging shell extensions. Because shell extensions execute from within the shell's own process, how is it possible to "hook into" the shell in order to debug your shell extension?

The solution to the problem is based on the fact that the shell is an executable (not very different from any other application) called explorer.exe. Explorer.exe has a property, however, that is kind of unique: The first instance of explorer.exe will invoke the shell. Subsequent instances will simply invoke additional "Explorer" windows in the shell.

Using a little-known trick in the shell, it's possible to close the shell without closing Windows. Follow these steps to debug your shell extensions in Delphi:

1. Make `explorer.exe` the host application for your shell extension in the Run, Parameters dialog box. Be sure to include the full path (that is, `c:\windows\explorer.exe`).

2. From the shell's Start menu, select Shut Down. This will invoke the Shut Down Windows dialog box.

3. In the Shut Down Windows dialog box, hold down Ctrl+Alt+Shift and click the No button. This will close the shell without closing Windows.

4. Using Alt+Tab, switch back to Delphi and run the shell extension. This will invoke a new copy of the shell running under the Delphi debugger. You can now set breakpoints in your code and debug as usual.

5. When you're ready to close Windows, you can still do so properly without the use of the shell: Use Ctrl+Esc to invoke the Tasks window and then select Windows, Shutdown Windows to close Windows.

The remainder of this chapter is dedicated to showing a cross section of the shell extensions just described. You'll learn about copy hook handlers, context menu handlers, and icon handlers.

The COM Object Wizard

Before discussing each of the shell extension DLLs, we should first mention a bit about how they're created. Because shell extensions are in-process COM servers, you can let the Delphi IDE do most of the grunt work in creating the source code for you. Work begins for all the shell extensions with the same two steps:

1. Select ActiveX Library from the ActiveX page of the New Items dialog box. This will create a new COM server DLL into which you can insert COM objects.

2. Select COM Object from the ActiveX page of the New Items dialog boxes. This will invoke the COM Server Wizard. In the wizard's dialog box, enter a name and description for your shell extension and select the Apartment threading model. Click OK, and a new unit containing the code for your COM object will be generated.

Copy Hook Handlers

As mentioned earlier, copy hook shell extensions allow you to install a handler that receives notifications whenever a folder is copied, deleted, moved, or renamed. After receiving this notification, the handler can optionally prevent the operation from occurring. Note that the handler is only called for folder and printer objects; it's not called for files and other objects.

The first step in creating a copy hook handler is to create an object that descends from
TComObject and implements the ICopyHook interface. This interface is defined in the ShlObj
unit as follows:

```
type
  ICopyHook = interface(IUnknown)
    ['{000214EF-0000-0000-C000-000000000046}']
    function CopyCallback(Wnd: HWND; wFunc, wFlags: UINT;
      pszSrcFile: PAnsiChar; dwSrcAttribs: DWORD; pszDestFile: PAnsiChar;
      dwDestAttribs: DWORD): UINT; stdcall;
  end;
```

The CopyCallback() Method

As you can see, ICopyHook is a pretty simple interface, and it implements only one function:
CopyCallback(). This function will be called whenever a shell folder is manipulated. The following paragraphs describe the parameters for this function.

Wnd is the handle of the window the copy hook handler should use as the parent for any windows it displays. wFunc indicates the operation being performed. This can be any one of the
values shown in Table 16.5.

TABLE 16.5   The wFunc Values for CopyCallback()

Constant	Value	Meaning
FO_COPY	$2	Copies the file specified by pszSrcFile to the location specified by pszDestFile.
FO_DELETE	$3	Deletes the file specified by pszSrcFile.
FO_MOVE	$1	Moves the file specified by pszSrcFile to the location specified by pszDestFile.
FO_RENAME	$4	Renames the file specified by pszSrcFile.
PO_DELETE	$13	Deletes the printer specified by pszSrcFile.
PO_PORTCHANGE	$20	Changes the printer port. The pszSrcFile and pszDestFile parameters contain double null-terminated lists of strings. Each list contains the printer name followed by the port name. The port name in pszSrcFile is the current printer port, and the port name in pszDestFile is the new printer port.
PO_RENAME	$14	Renames the printer specified by pszSrcFile.
PO_REN_PORT	$34	A combination of PO_RENAME and PO_PORTCHANGE.

wFlags holds the flags that control the operation. This parameter can be a combination of the values shown in Table 16.6.

TABLE 16.6 The wFlags Values for CopyCallback()

Constant	Value	Meaning
FOF_ALLOWUNDO	$40	Preserves undo information (when possible).
FOF_MULTIDESTFILES	$1	The SHFileOperation() function specifies multiple destination files (one for each source file) rather than one directory where all the source files are to be deposited. A copy hook handler typically ignores this value.
FOF_NOCONFIRMATION	$10	Responds with "Yes to All" for any dialog box that's displayed.
FOF_NOCONFIRMMKDIR	$200	Does not confirm the creation of any needed directories if the operation requires a new directory to be created.
FOF_RENAMEONCOLLISION	$8	Gives the file being operated on a new name (such as "Copy #1 of. . .") in a copy, move, or rename operation when a file with the target name already exists.
FOF_SILENT	$4	Does not display a progress dialog box.
FOF_SIMPLEPROGRESS	$100	Displays a progress dialog box, but the dialog box doesn't show the names of the files.

pszSourceFile is the name of the source folder, dwSrcAttribs holds the attributes of the source folder, pszDestFile is the name of the destination folder, and dwDestAttribs holds the attributes of the destination folder.

Unlike most methods, this interface doesn't return an OLE result code. Instead, it must return one of the values listed in Table 16.7, as defined in the Windows unit.

TABLE 16.7 The wFlags Values for CopyCallback()

Constant	Value	Meaning
IDYES	6	Allows the operation
IDNO	7	Prevents the operation on this file but continues with any other operations (for example, a batch copy operation)

TABLE 16.7 Continued

Constant	Value	Meaning
IDCANCEL	2	Prevents the current operation and cancels any pending operations

TCopyHook Implementation

Being an object that implements one interface with one method, there isn't much to
TCopyHook:

```
type
  TCopyHook = class(TComObject, ICopyHook)
  protected
    function CopyCallback(Wnd: HWND; wFunc, wFlags: UINT;
      pszSrcFile: PAnsiChar;
      dwSrcAttribs: DWORD; pszDestFile: PAnsiChar; dwDestAttribs: DWORD): UINT;
      stdcall;
  end;
```

The implementation of the CopyCallback() method is also small. The MessageBox() API
function is called to confirm whatever operation is being attempted. Conveniently, the return
value for MessageBox() will be the same as the return value for this method:

```
function TCopyHook.CopyCallback(Wnd: HWND; wFunc, wFlags: UINT;
  pszSrcFile: PAnsiChar; dwSrcAttribs: DWORD; pszDestFile: PAnsiChar;
  dwDestAttribs: DWORD): UINT;
const
  MyMessage: string = 'Are you sure you want to mess with "%s"?';
begin
  // confirm operation
  Result := MessageBox(Wnd,  PChar(Format(MyMessage, [pszSrcFile])),
    'DDG Shell Extension', MB_YESNO);
end;
```

> **TIP**
>
> You might wonder why the MessageBox() API function is used to display a message
> rather than using a Delphi function such as MessageDlg() or ShowMessage(). The rea-
> son is simple: size and efficiency. Calling any function out of the Dialogs or Forms
> unit would cause a great deal of VCL to be linked into the DLL. By keeping these
> units out of the uses clause, the shell extension DLL weighs in at a svelte 70KB.

Believe it or not, that's all there is to the TCopyHook object itself. However, there's still one major detail to work through before calling it a day: The shell extension must be registered with the System Registry before it will function.

Registration

In addition to the normal registration required of any COM server, a copy hook handler must have an additional Registry entry under

```
HKEY_CLASSES_ROOT\directory\shellex\CopyHookHandlers
```

Furthermore, Windows NT requires that all shell extensions be registered as approved shell extensions under

```
HKEY_LOCAL_MACHINE\ SOFTWARE\Microsoft\Windows\CurrentVersion
➥\Shell Extensions\Approved
```

You can take several approaches to registering shell extensions: They can be registered via a REG file or through an installation program. The shell extension DLL, itself, can be self-registering. Although it might be just a bit more work, the best solution is to make each shell extension DLL self-registering. This is cleaner because it makes your shell extension a one-file, self-contained package.

As you learned in Chapter 15, COM objects are always created from class factories. Within the VCL framework, class factory objects are also responsible for registering the COM object they will create. If a COM object requires custom Registry entries (as is the case with a shell extension), setting up these entries is just a matter of overriding the class factory's UpdateRegistry() method. Listing 16.9 shows the completed CopyMain unit, which includes a specialized class factory used to perform custom registration.

LISTING 16.9 CopyMain.pas—Main Unit for Copy Hook Implementation

```
unit CopyMain;

interface

uses Windows, ComObj, ShlObj;

type
  TCopyHook = class(TComObject, ICopyHook)
  protected
    function CopyCallback(Wnd: HWND; wFunc, wFlags: UINT;
      pszSrcFile: PAnsiChar; dwSrcAttribs: DWORD;
      pszDestFile: PAnsiChar; dwDestAttribs: DWORD): UINT; stdcall;
  end;
```

LISTING 16.9   Continued

```
TCopyHookFactory = class(TComObjectFactory)
protected
  function GetProgID: string; override;
  procedure ApproveShellExtension(Register: Boolean; const ClsID: string);
    virtual;
public
  procedure UpdateRegistry(Register: Boolean); override;
end;

implementation

uses ComServ, SysUtils, Registry;

{ TCopyHook }

// This is the method which is called by the shell for folder operations
function TCopyHook.CopyCallback(Wnd: HWND; wFunc, wFlags: UINT;
  pszSrcFile: PAnsiChar; dwSrcAttribs: DWORD; pszDestFile: PAnsiChar;
  dwDestAttribs: DWORD): UINT;
const
  MyMessage: string = 'Are you sure you want to mess with "%s"?';
begin
  // confirm operation
  Result := MessageBox(Wnd,  PChar(Format(MyMessage, [pszSrcFile])),
    'DDG Shell Extension', MB_YESNO);
end;

{ TCopyHookFactory }

function TCopyHookFactory.GetProgID: string;
begin
  // ProgID not needed for shell extension
  Result := '';
end;

procedure TCopyHookFactory.UpdateRegistry(Register: Boolean);
var
  ClsID: string;
begin
  ClsID := GUIDToString(ClassID);
  inherited UpdateRegistry(Register);
  ApproveShellExtension(Register, ClsID);
  if Register then
    // add shell extension clsid to CopyHookHandlers Reg entry
    CreateRegKey('directory\shellex\CopyHookHandlers\' + ClassName, '',
      ClsID)
```

LISTING 16.9 Continued

```
  else
    DeleteRegKey('directory\shellex\CopyHookHandlers\' + ClassName);
end;

procedure TCopyHookFactory.ApproveShellExtension(Register: Boolean;
  const ClsID: string);
// This registry entry is required in order for the extension to
// operate correctly under Windows NT.
const
  SApproveKey = 'SOFTWARE\Microsoft\Windows\CurrentVersion\Shell
➥Extensions\Approved';

begin
  with TRegistry.Create do
    try
      RootKey := HKEY_LOCAL_MACHINE;
      if not OpenKey(SApproveKey, True) then Exit;
      if Register then WriteString(ClsID, Description)
      else DeleteValue(ClsID);
    finally
      Free;
    end;
end;

const
  CLSID_CopyHook: TGUID = '{66CD5F60-A044-11D0-A9BF-00A016E3867F}';

initialization
  TCopyHookFactory.Create(ComServer, TCopyHook, CLSID_CopyHook,
    'DDG_CopyHook', 'DDG Copy Hook Shell Extension Example',
    ciMultiInstance, tmApartment);
end.
```

What makes the TCopyHookFactory class factory work is the fact that an instance of it, rather than the usual TComObjectFactory, is being created in the initialization part of the unit. Figure 16.7 shows what happens when you try to rename a folder in the shell after the copy hook shell extension DLL is installed.

FIGURE 16.7

The copy hook handler in action.

Context Menu Handlers

Context menu handlers enable you to add items to the local menu that are associated with file objects in the shell. A sample local menu for an EXE file is shown in Figure 16.8.

FIGURE 16.8
The shell local menu for an EXE file.

Context menu shell extensions work by implementing the IShellExtInit and IContextMenu interfaces. In this case, we'll implement these interfaces to create a context menu handler for Borland Package Library (BPL) files; the local menu for package files in the shell will provide an option for obtaining package information. This context menu handler object will be called TContextMenu, and, like the copy hook handler, TContextMenu will descend from TComObject.

IShellExtInit

The IShellExtInit interface is used to initialize a shell extension. This interface is defined in the ShlObj unit as follows:

```
type
  IShellExtInit = interface(IUnknown)
    ['{000214E8-0000-0000-C000-000000000046}']
    function Initialize(pidlFolder: PItemIDList; lpdobj: IDataObject;
      hKeyProgID: HKEY): HResult; stdcall;
  end;
```

Initialize(), being the only method of this interface, is called to initialize the context menu handler. The following paragraphs describe the parameters for this method.

pidlFolder is a pointer to a PItemIDList (item identifier list) structure for the folder that contains the item whose context menu is being displayed. lpdobj holds the IDataObject interface object used to retrieve the objects being acted upon. hkeyProgID contains the Registry key for the file object or folder type.

The implementation for this method is shown in the following code. Upon first glance, the code might look complex, but it really boils down to three things: a call to lpobj.GetData() to obtain data from IDataObject and two calls to DragQueryFile() (one call to obtain the number of files and the other to obtain the filename). The filename is stored in the object's FFileName field. Here's the code:

```
function TContextMenu.Initialize(pidlFolder: PItemIDList; lpdobj: IDataObject;
  hKeyProgID: HKEY): HResult;
var
  Medium: TStgMedium;
  FE: TFormatEtc;
begin
  try
    // Fail the call if lpdobj is nil.
    if lpdobj = nil then
    begin
      Result := E_FAIL;
      Exit;
    end;
    with FE do
    begin
      cfFormat := CF_HDROP;
      ptd := nil;
      dwAspect := DVASPECT_CONTENT;
      lindex := -1;
      tymed := TYMED_HGLOBAL;
    end;
    // Render the data referenced by the IDataObject pointer to an HGLOBAL
    // storage medium in CF_HDROP format.
    Result := lpdobj.GetData(FE, Medium);
    if Failed(Result) then Exit;
    try
      // If only one file is selected, retrieve the file name and store it in
      // szFile. Otherwise fail the call.
      if DragQueryFile(Medium.hGlobal, $FFFFFFFF, nil, 0) = 1 then
      begin
        DragQueryFile(Medium.hGlobal, 0, FFileName, SizeOf(FFileName));
        Result := NOERROR;
      end
      else
        Result := E_FAIL;
```

```
    finally
      ReleaseStgMedium(medium);
    end;
  except
    Result := E_UNEXPECTED;
  end;
end;
```

IContextMenu

The IContextMenu interface is used to manipulate the pop-up menu associated with a file in the shell. This interface is defined in the ShlObj unit as follows:

```
type
  IContextMenu = interface(IUnknown)
    ['{000214E4-0000-0000-C000-000000000046}']
    function QueryContextMenu(Menu: HMENU;
      indexMenu, idCmdFirst, idCmdLast, uFlags: UINT): HResult; stdcall;
    function InvokeCommand(var lpici: TCMInvokeCommandInfo): HResult; stdcall;
    function GetCommandString(idCmd, uType: UINT; pwReserved: PUINT;
      pszName: LPSTR; cchMax: UINT): HResult; stdcall;
  end;
```

After the handler has been initialized through the IShellExtInit interface, the next method to be called is IContextMenu.QueryContextMenu(). The parameters passed to this method include a menu handle, the index at which to insert the first menu item, the minimum and maximum values for menu item IDs, and flags that indicate menu attributes. The following TContextMenu implementation of this method adds a menu item with the text "Package Info. . ." to the menu handle passed in the Menu parameter (note that the return value for QueryContextMenu() is the index of the last menu item inserted plus one):

```
function TContextMenu.QueryContextMenu(Menu: HMENU; indexMenu, idCmdFirst,
  idCmdLast, uFlags: UINT): HResult;
begin
  FMenuIdx := indexMenu;
  // Add one menu item to context menu
  InsertMenu (Menu, FMenuIdx, MF_STRING or MF_BYPOSITION, idCmdFirst,
    'Package Info...');
  // Return index of last inserted item + 1
  Result := FMenuIdx + 1;
end;
```

The next method called by the shell is GetCommandString(). This method is intended to retrieve the language-independent command string or help string for a particular menu item. The parameters for this method include the menu item offset, flags indicating the type of information to receive, a reserved parameter, and a string buffer and buffer size. The following TContextMenu implementation of this method only needs to deal with providing the help string for the menu item:

```
function TContextMenu.GetCommandString(idCmd, uType: UINT; pwReserved: PUINT;
  pszName: LPSTR; cchMax: UINT): HRESULT;
begin
  Result := S_OK;
  try
    // make sure menu index is correct, and shell is asking for help string
    if (idCmd = FMenuIdx) and ((uType and GCS_HELPTEXT) <> 0) then
      // return help string for menu item
      StrLCopy(pszName, 'Get information for the selected package.', cchMax)
    else
      Result := E_INVALIDARG;
  except
    Result := E_UNEXPECTED;
  end;
end;
```

When you click the new item in the context menu, the shell will call the InvokeCommand()
method. The method accepts a TCMInvokeCommandInfo record as a parameter. This record is
defined in the ShlObj unit as follows:

```
type
  PCMInvokeCommandInfo = ^TCMInvokeCommandInfo;
  TCMInvokeCommandInfo = packed record
    cbSize: DWORD;          { must be SizeOf(TCMInvokeCommandInfo) }
    fMask: DWORD;           { any combination of CMIC_MASK_* }
    hwnd: HWND;             { might be NULL (indicating no owner window) }
    lpVerb: LPCSTR;         { either a string of MAKEINTRESOURCE(idOffset) }
    lpParameters: LPCSTR;   { might be NULL (indicating no parameter) }
    lpDirectory: LPCSTR;    { might be NULL (indicating no specific directory) }
    nShow: Integer;         { one of SW_ values for ShowWindow() API }
    dwHotKey: DWORD;
    hIcon: THandle;
  end;
```

The low word or the lpVerb field will contain the index of the menu item selected. Here's the
implementation of this method:

```
function TContextMenu.InvokeCommand(var lpici: TCMInvokeCommandInfo): HResult;
begin
  Result := S_OK;
  try
    // Make sure we are not being called by an application
    if HiWord(Integer(lpici.lpVerb)) <> 0 then
    begin
      Result := E_FAIL;
      Exit;
    end;
    // Execute the command specified by lpici.lpVerb.
    // Return E_INVALIDARG if we are passed an invalid argument number.
```

```
    if LoWord(lpici.lpVerb) = FMenuIdx then
      ExecutePackInfoApp(FFileName, lpici.hwnd)
    else
      Result := E_INVALIDARG;
  except
    MessageBox(lpici.hwnd, 'Error obtaining package information.', 'Error',
      MB_OK or MB_ICONERROR);
    Result := E_FAIL;
  end;
end;
```

If all goes well, the ExecutePackInfoApp() function is called to invoke the PackInfo.exe application, which displays various information about a package. We won't go into the particulars of that application right now; however, it's discussed in detail on the electronic version of *Delphi 5 Developer's Guide* on the CD accompanying this book in Chapter 13, "Hard-Core Techniques."

Registration

Context menu handlers must be registered under

```
HKEY_CLASSES_ROOT\<file type>\shellex\ContextMenuHandlers
```

in the System Registry. Following the model of the copy hook extension, registration capability is added to the DLL by creating a specialized TComObject descendant. The object is shown in Listing 16.10 along with the complete source code for the unit containing TContextMenu. Figure 16.9 shows the local menu for the BPL file with the new item, and Figure 16.10 shows the PackInfo.exe window as invoked by the context menu handler.

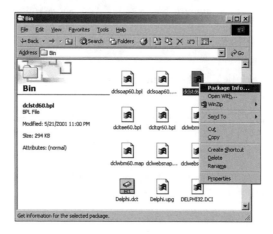

FIGURE 16.9

The context menu handler in action.

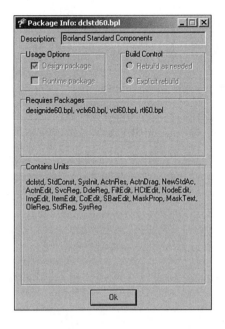

FIGURE 16.10

Obtaining package information from the context menu handler.

LISTING 16.10 ContMain.pas—Main Unit for Context Menu Handler Implementation

```pascal
unit ContMain;

interface

uses Windows, ComObj, ShlObj, ActiveX;

type
  TContextMenu = class(TComObject, IContextMenu, IShellExtInit)
  private
    FFileName: array[0..MAX_PATH] of char;
    FMenuIdx: UINT;
  protected
    // IContextMenu methods
    function QueryContextMenu(Menu: HMENU; indexMenu, idCmdFirst, idCmdLast,
      uFlags: UINT): HResult; stdcall;
    function InvokeCommand(var lpici: TCMInvokeCommandInfo): HResult; stdcall;
    function GetCommandString(idCmd, uType: UINT; pwReserved: PUINT;
      pszName: LPSTR; cchMax: UINT): HResult; stdcall;
    // IShellExtInit method
    function Initialize(pidlFolder: PItemIDList; lpdobj: IDataObject;
```

LISTING 16.10   Continued

```pascal
        hKeyProgID: HKEY): HResult; reintroduce; stdcall;
  end;

  TContextMenuFactory = class(TComObjectFactory)
  protected
    function GetProgID: string; override;
    procedure ApproveShellExtension(Register: Boolean; const ClsID: string);
      virtual;
  public
    procedure UpdateRegistry(Register: Boolean); override;
  end;

implementation

uses ComServ, SysUtils, ShellAPI, Registry;

procedure ExecutePackInfoApp(const FileName: string; ParentWnd: HWND);
const
  SPackInfoApp = '%sPackInfo.exe';
  SCmdLine = '"%s" %s';
  SErrorStr = 'Failed to execute PackInfo:'#13#10#13#10;
var
  PI: TProcessInformation;
  SI: TStartupInfo;
  ExeName, ExeCmdLine: string;
  Buffer: array[0..MAX_PATH] of char;
begin
  // Get directory of this DLL.  Assume EXE being executed is in same dir.
  GetModuleFileName(HInstance, Buffer, SizeOf(Buffer));
  ExeName := Format(SPackInfoApp, [ExtractFilePath(Buffer)]);
  ExeCmdLine := Format(SCmdLine, [ExeName, FileName]);
  FillChar(SI, SizeOf(SI), 0);
  SI.cb := SizeOf(SI);
  if not CreateProcess(PChar(ExeName), PChar(ExeCmdLine), nil, nil, False,
    0, nil, nil, SI, PI) then
    MessageBox(ParentWnd, PChar(SErrorStr + SysErrorMessage(GetLastError)),
      'Error', MB_OK or MB_ICONERROR);
end;

{ TContextMenu }

{ TContextMenu.IContextMenu }

function TContextMenu.QueryContextMenu(Menu: HMENU; indexMenu, idCmdFirst,
  idCmdLast, uFlags: UINT): HResult;
```

LISTING 16.10 Continued

```pascal
begin
  FMenuIdx := indexMenu;
  // Add one menu item to context menu
  InsertMenu (Menu, FMenuIdx, MF_STRING or MF_BYPOSITION, idCmdFirst,
    'Package Info...');
  // Return index of last inserted item + 1
  Result := FMenuIdx + 1;
end;

function TContextMenu.InvokeCommand(var lpici: TCMInvokeCommandInfo): HResult;
begin
  Result := S_OK;
  try
    // Make sure we are not being called by an application
    if HiWord(Integer(lpici.lpVerb)) <> 0 then
    begin
      Result := E_FAIL;
      Exit;
    end;
    // Execute the command specified by lpici.lpVerb.
    // Return E_INVALIDARG if we are passed an invalid argument number.
    if LoWord(lpici.lpVerb) = FMenuIdx then
      ExecutePackInfoApp(FFileName, lpici.hwnd)
    else
      Result := E_INVALIDARG;
  except
    MessageBox(lpici.hwnd, 'Error obtaining package information.', 'Error',
      MB_OK or MB_ICONERROR);
    Result := E_FAIL;
  end;
end;

function TContextMenu.GetCommandString(idCmd, uType: UINT; pwReserved: PUINT;
  pszName: LPSTR; cchMax: UINT): HRESULT;
begin
  Result := S_OK;
  try
    // make sure menu index is correct, and shell is asking for help string
    if (idCmd = FMenuIdx) and ((uType and GCS_HELPTEXT) <> 0) then
      // return help string for menu item
      StrLCopy(pszName, 'Get information for the selected package.', cchMax)
    else
      Result := E_INVALIDARG;
  except
```

LISTING 16.10   Continued

```
    Result := E_UNEXPECTED;
  end;
end;


{ TContextMenu.IShellExtInit }

function TContextMenu.Initialize(pidlFolder: PItemIDList; lpdobj: IDataObject;
  hKeyProgID: HKEY): HResult;
var
  Medium: TStgMedium;
  FE: TFormatEtc;
begin
  try
    // Fail the call if lpdobj is nil.
    if lpdobj = nil then
    begin
      Result := E_FAIL;
      Exit;
    end;
    with FE do
    begin
      cfFormat := CF_HDROP;
      ptd := nil;
      dwAspect := DVASPECT_CONTENT;
      lindex := -1;
      tymed := TYMED_HGLOBAL;
    end;
    // Render the data referenced by the IDataObject pointer to an HGLOBAL
    // storage medium in CF_HDROP format.
    Result := lpdobj.GetData(FE, Medium);
    if Failed(Result) then Exit;
    try
      // If only one file is selected, retrieve the file name and store it in
      // szFile. Otherwise fail the call.
      if DragQueryFile(Medium.hGlobal, $FFFFFFFF, nil, 0) = 1 then
      begin
        DragQueryFile(Medium.hGlobal, 0, FFileName, SizeOf(FFileName));
        Result := NOERROR;
      end
      else
        Result := E_FAIL;
    finally
      ReleaseStgMedium(medium);
    end;
```

LISTING 16.10 Continued

```
  except
    Result := E_UNEXPECTED;
  end;
end;


{ TContextMenuFactory }

function TContextMenuFactory.GetProgID: string;
begin
  // ProgID not required for context menu shell extension
  Result := '';
end;

procedure TContextMenuFactory.UpdateRegistry(Register: Boolean);
var
  ClsID: string;
begin
  ClsID := GUIDToString(ClassID);
  inherited UpdateRegistry(Register);
  ApproveShellExtension(Register, ClsID);
  if Register then
  begin
    // must register .bpl as a file type
    CreateRegKey('.bpl', '', 'DelphiPackageLibrary');
    // register this DLL as a context menu handler for .bpl files
    CreateRegKey('BorlandPackageLibrary\shellex\ContextMenuHandlers\' +
      ClassName, '', ClsID);
  end
  else begin
    DeleteRegKey('.bpl');
    DeleteRegKey('BorlandPackageLibrary\shellex\ContextMenuHandlers\' +
      ClassName);
  end;
end;

procedure TContextMenuFactory.ApproveShellExtension(Register: Boolean;
  const ClsID: string);
// This registry entry is required in order for the extension to
// operate correctly under Windows NT.
const
  SApproveKey = 'SOFTWARE\Microsoft\Windows\CurrentVersion\
➥Shell Extensions\Approved';

begin
  with TRegistry.Create do
```

LISTING 16.10   Continued

```
    try
      RootKey := HKEY_LOCAL_MACHINE;
      if not OpenKey(SApproveKey, True) then Exit;
      if Register then WriteString(ClsID, Description)
      else DeleteValue(ClsID);
    finally
      Free;
    end;
end;

const
  CLSID_CopyHook: TGUID = '{7C5E74A0-D5E0-11D0-A9BF-E886A83B9BE5}';

initialization
  TContextMenuFactory.Create(ComServer, TContextMenu, CLSID_CopyHook,
    'DDG_ContextMenu', 'DDG Context Menu Shell Extension Example',
    ciMultiInstance, tmApartment);
end.
```

Icon Handlers

Icon handlers enable you to cause different icons to be used for multiple instances of the same type of file. In this example, the TIconHandler icon handler object provides different icons for different types of Borland Package (BPL) files. Depending on whether a package is runtime, design time, both, or none, a different icon will be displayed in a shell folder.

Package Flags

Before getting into the implementations of the interfaces necessary for this shell extension, take a moment to examine the method that determines the type of a particular package file. The method returns TPackType, which is defined as follows:

```
TPackType = (ptDesign, ptDesignRun, ptNone, ptRun);
```

Now here's the method:

```
function TIconHandler.GetPackageType: TPackType;
var
  PackMod: HMODULE;
  PackFlags: Integer;
begin
  // Since we only need to get into the package's resources,
  // LoadLibraryEx with LOAD_LIBRARY_AS_DATAFILE provides a speed-
  // efficient means for loading the package.
```

```
PackMod := LoadLibraryEx(PChar(FFileName), 0, LOAD_LIBRARY_AS_DATAFILE);
if PackMod = 0 then
begin
  Result := ptNone;
  Exit;
end;
try
  GetPackageInfo(PackMod, nil, PackFlags, PackInfoProc);
finally
  FreeLibrary(PackMod);
end;
// mask off all but design and run flags, and return result
case PackFlags and (pfDesignOnly or pfRunOnly) of
  pfDesignOnly: Result := ptDesign;
  pfRunOnly: Result := ptRun;
  pfDesignOnly or pfRunOnly: Result := ptDesignRun;
else
  Result := ptNone;
  end;
end;
```

This method works by calling the GetPackageInfo() method from the SysUtils unit to obtain
the package flags. An interesting point to note concerning performance optimization is that the
LoadLibraryEx() API function is called rather than Delphi's LoadPackage() procedure to load
the package library. Internally, the LoadPackage() procedure calls the LoadLibrary() API to
load the BPL and then calls InitializePackage() to execute the initialization code for each
of the units in the package. Because all we want to do is get the package flags and they reside
in a resource linked to the BPL, we can safely load the package with LoadLibraryEx() using
the LOAD_LIBRARY_AS_DATAFILE flag.

Icon Handler Interfaces

As mentioned earlier, icon handlers must support both the IExtractIcon (defined in ShlObj)
and IPersistFile (defined in the ActiveX unit) interfaces. These interfaces are shown here:

```
type
  IExtractIcon = interface(IUnknown)
    ['{000214EB-0000-0000-C000-000000000046}']
    function GetIconLocation(uFlags: UINT; szIconFile: PAnsiChar; cchMax: UINT;
      out piIndex: Integer; out pwFlags: UINT): HResult; stdcall;
    function Extract(pszFile: PAnsiChar; nIconIndex: UINT;
      out phiconLarge, phiconSmall: HICON; nIconSize: UINT): HResult; stdcall;
  end;

  IPersistFile = interface(IPersist)
    ['{0000010B-0000-0000-C000-000000000046}']
```

```
  function IsDirty: HResult; stdcall;
  function Load(pszFileName: POleStr; dwMode: Longint): HResult; stdcall;
  function Save(pszFileName: POleStr; fRemember: BOOL): HResult; stdcall;
  function SaveCompleted(pszFileName: POleStr): HResult; stdcall;
  function GetCurFile(out pszFileName: POleStr): HResult; stdcall;
end;
```

Although this might look like a lot of work, it's really not; only two of these methods actually have to be implemented. The first file that must be implemented is `IPersistFile.Load()`. This is the method that's called to initialize the shell extension, and in it, you must save the filename passed via the `pszFileName` parameter. Here's the `TExtractIcon` implementation of this method:

```
function TIconHandler.Load(pszFileName: POleStr; dwMode: Longint): HResult;
begin
  // this method is called to initialized the icon handler shell
  // extension.  We must save the file name which is passed in pszFileName
  FFileName := pszFileName;
  Result := S_OK;
end;
```

The other method that must be implemented is `IExtractIcon.GetIconLocation()`. The parameters for this method are discussed in the following paragraphs.

`uFlags` indicates the type of icon to be displayed. This parameter can be `0`, `GIL_FORSHELL`, or `GIL_OPENICON`. `GIL_FORSHELL` means that the icon is to be displayed in a shell folder. `GIL_OPENICON` means that the icon should be in the "open" state if images for both the open and closed states are available. If this flag isn't specified, the icon should be in the normal, or "closed," state. This flag is typically used for folder objects.

`szIconFile` is the buffer to receive the icon location, and `cchMax` is the size of the buffer. `piIndex` is an integer that receives the icon index, which further describes the icon location. `pwFlags` receives zero or more of the values shown in Table 16.8.

TABLE 16.8   The `pwFlags` Values for `GetIconLocation()`

Flag	Meaning
GIL_DONTCACHE	The physical image bits for this icon shouldn't be cached by the caller. This distinction is important to consider because a `GIL_DONTCACHELOCATION` flag might be introduced in future versions of the shell.
GIL_NOTFILENAME	The location isn't a filename/index pair. Callers that decide to extract the icon from the location must call this object's `IExtractIcon.Extract()` method to obtain the desired icon images.

TABLE 16.8 Continued

Flag	Meaning
GIL_PERCLASS	All objects of this class have the same icon. This flag is used internally by the shell. Typical implementations of IExtractIcon don't require this flag because it implies that an icon handler is not required to resolve the icon on a per-object basis. The recommended method for implementing per-class icons is to register a default icon for the class.
GIL_PERINSTANCE	Each object of this class has its own icon. This flag is used internally by the shell to handle cases such as setup.exe, where more than one object with identical names might be known to the shell and use different icons. Typical implementations of IExtractIcon don't require this flag.
GIL_SIMULATEDOC	The caller should create a document icon using the specified icon.

The TIconHandler implementation of GetIconLocation() is shown here:

```
function TIconHandler.GetIconLocation(uFlags: UINT; szIconFile: PAnsiChar;
  cchMax: UINT; out piIndex: Integer; out pwFlags: UINT): HResult;
begin
  Result := S_OK;
  try
    // return this DLL for name of module to find icon
    GetModuleFileName(HInstance, szIconFile, cchMax);
    // tell shell not to cache image bits, in case icon changes
    // and that each instance may have its own icon
    pwFlags := GIL_DONTCACHE or GIL_PERINSTANCE;
    // icon index coincides with TPackType
    piIndex := Ord(GetPackageType);
  except
    // if there's an error, use the default package icon
    piIndex := Ord(ptNone);
  end;
end;
```

The icons are linked into the shell extension DLL as a resource file, so the name of the current file, as returned by GetModuleFileName(), is written to the szIconFile buffer. Also, the icons are arranged in such a way that the index of an icon for a package type corresponds to the package type's index into the TPackType enumeration, so the return value of GetPackageType() is assigned to piIndex.

Registration

Icon handlers must be registered under the

```
HKEY_CLASSES_ROOT\<file type>\shellex\IconHandler
```

key in the Registry. Again, a descendant of `TComObjectFactory` is created to deal with the registration of this shell extension. This is shown in Listing 16.11 along with the rest of the source code for the icon handler.

Figure 16.11 shows a shell folder containing packages of different types. Notice the different icons for different types of packages.

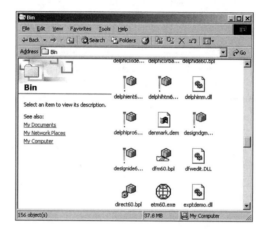

FIGURE 16.11
The result of using the icon handler.

LISTING 16.11 IconMain.pas—Main Unit for Icon Handler Implementation

```
unit IconMain;

interface

uses Windows, ActiveX, ComObj, ShlObj;

type
  TPackType = (ptDesign, ptDesignRun, ptNone, ptRun);

  TIconHandler = class(TComObject, IExtractIcon, IPersistFile)
  private
    FFileName: string;
    function GetPackageType: TPackType;
```

LISTING 16.11   Continued

```pascal
protected
  // IExtractIcon methods
  function GetIconLocation(uFlags: UINT; szIconFile: PAnsiChar; cchMax: UINT;
    out piIndex: Integer; out pwFlags: UINT): HResult; stdcall;
  function Extract(pszFile: PAnsiChar; nIconIndex: UINT;
    out phiconLarge, phiconSmall: HICON; nIconSize: UINT): HResult; stdcall;
  // IPersist method
  function GetClassID(out classID: TCLSID): HResult; stdcall;
  // IPersistFile methods
  function IsDirty: HResult; stdcall;
  function Load(pszFileName: POleStr; dwMode: Longint): HResult; stdcall;
  function Save(pszFileName: POleStr; fRemember: BOOL): HResult; stdcall;
  function SaveCompleted(pszFileName: POleStr): HResult; stdcall;
  function GetCurFile(out pszFileName: POleStr): HResult; stdcall;
end;

TIconHandlerFactory = class(TComObjectFactory)
protected
  function GetProgID: string; override;
  procedure ApproveShellExtension(Register: Boolean; const ClsID: string);
    virtual;
public
  procedure UpdateRegistry(Register: Boolean); override;
end;

implementation

uses SysUtils, ComServ, Registry;

{ TIconHandler }

procedure PackInfoProc(const Name: string; NameType: TNameType; Flags: Byte;
  Param: Pointer);
begin
  // we don't need to implement this procedure because we are only
  // interested in package flags, not contained units and required pkgs.
end;

function TIconHandler.GetPackageType: TPackType;
var
  PackMod: HMODULE;
  PackFlags: Integer;
begin
  // Since we only need to get into the package's resources,
```

LISTING 16.11   Continued

```pascal
  // LoadLibraryEx with LOAD_LIBRARY_AS_DATAFILE provides a speed-
  // efficient means for loading the package.
  PackMod := LoadLibraryEx(PChar(FFileName), 0, LOAD_LIBRARY_AS_DATAFILE);
  if PackMod = 0 then
  begin
    Result := ptNone;
    Exit;
  end;
  try
    GetPackageInfo(PackMod, nil, PackFlags, PackInfoProc);
  finally
    FreeLibrary(PackMod);
  end;
  // mask off all but design and run flags, and return result
  case PackFlags and (pfDesignOnly or pfRunOnly) of
    pfDesignOnly: Result := ptDesign;
    pfRunOnly: Result := ptRun;
    pfDesignOnly or pfRunOnly: Result := ptDesignRun;
  else
    Result := ptNone;
  end;
end;


{ TIconHandler.IExtractIcon }

function TIconHandler.GetIconLocation(uFlags: UINT; szIconFile: PAnsiChar;
  cchMax: UINT; out piIndex: Integer; out pwFlags: UINT): HResult;
begin
  Result := S_OK;
  try
    // return this DLL for name of module to find icon
    GetModuleFileName(HInstance, szIconFile, cchMax);
    // tell shell not to cache image bits, in case icon changes
    // and that each instance may have its own icon
    pwFlags := GIL_DONTCACHE or GIL_PERINSTANCE;
    // icon index coincides with TPackType
    piIndex := Ord(GetPackageType);
  except
    // if there's an error, use the default package icon
    piIndex := Ord(ptNone);
  end;
end;


function TIconHandler.Extract(pszFile: PAnsiChar; nIconIndex: UINT;
  out phiconLarge, phiconSmall: HICON; nIconSize: UINT): HResult;
```

LISTING 16.11   Continued

```pascal
begin
  // This method only needs to be implemented if the icon is stored in
  // some type of user-defined data format.  Since our icon is in a
  // plain old DLL, we just return S_FALSE.
  Result := S_FALSE;
end;

{ TIconHandler.IPersist }

function TIconHandler.GetClassID(out classID: TCLSID): HResult;
begin
  // this method is not called for icon handlers
  Result := E_NOTIMPL;
end;

{ TIconHandler.IPersistFile }

function TIconHandler.IsDirty: HResult;
begin
  // this method is not called for icon handlers
  Result := S_FALSE;
end;

function TIconHandler.Load(pszFileName: POleStr; dwMode: Longint): HResult;
begin
  // this method is called to initialized the icon handler shell
  // extension.  We must save the file name which is passed in pszFileName
  FFileName := pszFileName;
  Result := S_OK;
end;

function TIconHandler.Save(pszFileName: POleStr; fRemember: BOOL): HResult;
begin
  // this method is not called for icon handlers
  Result := E_NOTIMPL;
end;

function TIconHandler.SaveCompleted(pszFileName: POleStr): HResult;
begin
  // this method is not called for icon handlers
  Result := E_NOTIMPL;
end;

function TIconHandler.GetCurFile(out pszFileName: POleStr): HResult;
```

LISTING 16.11   Continued

```pascal
begin
  // this method is not called for icon handlers
  Result := E_NOTIMPL;
end;


{ TIconHandlerFactory }

function TIconHandlerFactory.GetProgID: string;
begin
  // ProgID not required for context menu shell extension
  Result := '';
end;

procedure TIconHandlerFactory.UpdateRegistry(Register: Boolean);
var
  ClsID: string;
begin
  ClsID := GUIDToString(ClassID);
  inherited UpdateRegistry(Register);
  ApproveShellExtension(Register, ClsID);
  if Register then
  begin
    // must register .bpl as a file type
    CreateRegKey('.bpl', '', 'BorlandPackageLibrary');
    // register this DLL as an icon handler for .bpl files
    CreateRegKey('BorlandPackageLibrary\shellex\IconHandler', '', ClsID);
  end
  else begin
    DeleteRegKey('.bpl');
    DeleteRegKey('BorlandPackageLibrary\shellex\IconHandler');
  end;
end;

procedure TIconHandlerFactory.ApproveShellExtension(Register: Boolean;
  const ClsID: string);
// This registry entry is required in order for the extension to
// operate correctly under Windows NT.
const
  SApproveKey = 'SOFTWARE\Microsoft\Windows\CurrentVersion\
➥Shell Extensions\Approved';

begin
  with TRegistry.Create do
    try
      RootKey := HKEY_LOCAL_MACHINE;
```

LISTING 16.11 Continued

```
      if not OpenKey(SApproveKey, True) then Exit;
      if Register then WriteString(ClsID, Description)
      else DeleteValue(ClsID);
    finally
      Free;
    end;
end;

const
  CLSID_IconHandler: TGUID = '{ED6D2F60-DA7C-11D0-A9BF-90D146FC32B3}';

initialization
  TIconHandlerFactory.Create(ComServer, TIconHandler, CLSID_IconHandler,
    'DDG_IconHandler', 'DDG Icon Handler Shell Extension Example',
    ciMultiInstance, tmApartment);
end.
```

InfoTip Handlers

Introduced in the Windows 2000 shell, InfoTip handlers provide the ability to create custom pop-up *InfoTips* (also called *ToolTips* in Delphi) when the mouse is placed over the icon representing a file in the shell. The default InfoTip displayed by the shell contains the name of the file, the type of file (as determined based on its extension), and the file size. InfoTip handlers are handy when you want to display more than this rather limited and generic bit of file information to the user at a glance.

For Delphi developers, a great case in point is package files. Although we all know that package files are composed of one or more units, it's impossible to know at a glance exactly which units are contained within. Earlier in this chapter, you saw a context menu handler that provides this information by choosing an option from a local menu, causing an external application to be launched. Now you'll see how to get this information even more easily, without the use of an external program.

InfoTip Handler Interfaces

InfoTip handlers must implement the IQueryInfo and IPersistFile interfaces. You already learned about IPersistFile in the discussions on shell links and icon handlers earlier in this chapter, and it is used in this case to obtain the name of the file in question. IQueryInfo is a relatively simple interface containing two methods, and it is defined in the ShlObj unit as shown here:

```
type
  IQueryInfo = interface(IUnknown)
```

```
[SID_IQueryInfo]
function GetInfoTip(dwFlags: DWORD; var ppwszTip: PWideChar): HResult;
  stdcall;
function GetInfoFlags(out pdwFlags: DWORD): HResult; stdcall;
end;
```

The GetInfoTip() method is called by the shell to retrieve the InfoTip for a given file. The dwFlags parameter is currently unused. The InfoTip string is returned in the ppwszTip parameter.

NOTE

The ppwszTip parameter points to a wide character string. Memory for this string must be allocated within the InfoTip handler using the shell's memory allocator. The shell is responsible for freeing this memory.

Implementation

Like the other shell extensions, the InfoTip handler is implemented as a simple COM server DLL. The COM object contained within implements the IQueryInfo and IPersistFile methods. Listing 16.12 shows the contents of InfoMain.pas, the main unit for the DDGInfoTip project, which contains the Delphi implementation of an InfoTip handler.

LISTING 16.12   InfoMain.pas—Main Unit for InfoTip Handler

```
unit InfoMain;

{$WARN SYMBOL_PLATFORM OFF}

interface

uses
  Windows, ActiveX, Classes, ComObj, ShlObj;

type
  TInfoTipHandler = class(TComObject, IQueryInfo, IPersistFile)
  private
    FFileName: string;
    FMalloc: IMalloc;
  protected
    { IQueryInfo }
    function GetInfoTip(dwFlags: DWORD; var ppwszTip: PWideChar): HResult;
      stdcall;
    function GetInfoFlags(out pdwFlags: DWORD): HResult; stdcall;
    {IPersist}
    function GetClassID(out classID: TCLSID): HResult; stdcall;
```

LISTING 16.12 Continued

```delphi
    { IPersistFile }
    function IsDirty: HResult; stdcall;
    function Load(pszFileName: POleStr; dwMode: Longint): HResult; stdcall;
    function Save(pszFileName: POleStr; fRemember: BOOL): HResult; stdcall;
    function SaveCompleted(pszFileName: POleStr): HResult; stdcall;
    function GetCurFile(out pszFileName: POleStr): HResult; stdcall;
  public
    procedure Initialize; override;
  end;

  TInfoTipFactory = class(TComObjectFactory)
  protected
    function GetProgID: string; override;
    procedure ApproveShellExtension(Register: Boolean; const ClsID: string);
      virtual;
  public
    procedure UpdateRegistry(Register: Boolean); override;
  end;

const
  Class_InfoTipHandler: TGUID = '{5E08F28D-A5B1-4996-BDF1-5D32108DB5E5}';

implementation

uses ComServ, SysUtils, Registry;

const
  TipBufLen = 1024;

procedure PackageInfoCallback(const Name: string; NameType: TNameType;
  Flags: Byte; Param: Pointer);
var
  S: string;
begin
  // if we are being passed the name of a contained unit, then
  // concatenate it to the list of units, which is passed in Param.
  if NameType = ntContainsUnit then
  begin
    S := Name;
    if PChar(Param)^ <> #0 then
      S := ', ' + S;
    StrLCat(PChar(Param), PChar(S), TipBufLen);
  end;
end;
```

LISTING 16.12   Continued

```pascal
function TInfoTipHandler.GetClassID(out classID: TCLSID): HResult;
begin
  classID := Class_InfoTipHandler;
  Result := S_OK;
end;

function TInfoTipHandler.GetCurFile(out pszFileName: POleStr): HResult;
begin
  Result := E_NOTIMPL;
end;

function TInfoTipHandler.GetInfoFlags(out pdwFlags: DWORD): HResult;
begin
  Result := E_NOTIMPL;
end;

function TInfoTipHandler.GetInfoTip(dwFlags: DWORD;
  var ppwszTip: PWideChar): HResult;
var
  PackMod: HModule;
  TipStr: PChar;
  Size, Flags, TipStrLen: Integer;
begin
  Result := S_OK;
  if (CompareText(ExtractFileExt(FFileName), '.bpl') = 0) and
    Assigned(FMalloc) then
  begin
    // Since we only need to get into the package's resources,
    // LoadLibraryEx with LOAD_LIBRARY_AS_DATAFILE provides a speed-
    // efficient means for loading the package.
    PackMod := LoadLibraryEx(PChar(FFileName), 0, LOAD_LIBRARY_AS_DATAFILE);
    if PackMod <> 0 then
      try
        TipStr := StrAlloc(TipBufLen);
        try
          FillChar(TipStr^, TipBufLen, 0);  // zero out string memory
          // Fill up TipStr with contained units
          GetPackageInfo(PackMod, TipStr, Flags, PackageInfoCallback);
          TipStrLen := StrLen(TipStr);
          Size := (TipStrLen + 1) * SizeOf(WideChar);
          ppwszTip := FMalloc.Alloc(Size); // use shell's allocator
          // copy PAnsiChar to PWideChar
          MultiByteToWideChar(0, 0, TipStr, TipStrLen, ppwszTip, Size);
        finally
```

LISTING 16.12 Continued

```
          StrDispose(TipStr);
        end;
      finally
        FreeLibrary(PackMod);
      end;
  end;
end;

procedure TInfoTipHandler.Initialize;
begin
  inherited;
  // shells shell's memory allocator and save it away
  SHGetMalloc(FMalloc);
end;

function TInfoTipHandler.IsDirty: HResult;
begin
  Result := E_NOTIMPL;
end;

function TInfoTipHandler.Load(pszFileName: POleStr;
  dwMode: Integer): HResult;
begin
  // This is the only important IPersistFile method -- we need to save
  // away the file name
  FFileName := pszFileName;
  Result := S_OK;
end;

function TInfoTipHandler.Save(pszFileName: POleStr;
  fRemember: BOOL): HResult;
begin
  Result := E_NOTIMPL;
end;

function TInfoTipHandler.SaveCompleted(pszFileName: POleStr): HResult;
begin
  Result := E_NOTIMPL;
end;

{ TInfoTipFactory }

function TInfoTipFactory.GetProgID: string;
begin
  // ProgID not required for IntoTip handler shell extension
```

LISTING 16.12   Continued

```
  Result := '';
end;

procedure TInfoTipFactory.UpdateRegistry(Register: Boolean);
var
  ClsID: string;
begin
  ClsID := GUIDToString(ClassID);
  inherited UpdateRegistry(Register);
  ApproveShellExtension(Register, ClsID);
  if Register then
  begin
    // register this DLL as the InfoTip handler for .bpl files
    CreateRegKey('.bpl\shellex\{00021500-0000-0000-C000-000000000046}',
      '', ClsID);
  end
  else begin
    DeleteRegKey('.bpl\shellex\{00021500-0000-0000-C000-000000000046}');
  end;
end;

procedure TInfoTipFactory.ApproveShellExtension(Register: Boolean;
  const ClsID: string);
// This registry entry is required in order for the extension to
// operate correctly under Windows NT.
const
  SApproveKey = 'SOFTWARE\Microsoft\Windows\CurrentVersion\' +
    'Shell Extensions\Approved';
begin
  with TRegistry.Create do
    try
      RootKey := HKEY_LOCAL_MACHINE;
      if not OpenKey(SApproveKey, True) then Exit;
      if Register then WriteString(ClsID, Description)
      else DeleteValue(ClsID);
    finally
      Free;
    end;
end;

initialization
  TInfoTipFactory.Create(ComServer, TInfoTipHandler, Class_InfoTipHandler,
    'InfoTipHandler', 'DDG sample InfoTip handler', ciMultiInstance,
    tmApartment);
end.
```

There are a couple of interesting points in this implementation. Notice that the shell's memory allocator is retrieved and stored in the `Initialize()` method. The allocator is later used to allocate memory for the InfoTip string in the `GetInfoTip()` method. The name of the file in question is passed to the handler in the `Load()` method. The work is done in the `GetInfoTip()` method, which gets package information using the `GetPackageInfo()` function that you learned about earlier in this chapter. As the `PackageInfoCallback()` callback function is called repeatedly from within `GetPackageInfo()`, the IntoTip string is concatenated together file-by-file.

Registration

The technique used for registration of the COM server DLL is almost identical to that of the other shell extensions in this chapter, as you can see in Listing 16.12. The key difference is the key under which InfoTip handlers are registered; these are always registered under `HKEY_CLASSES_ROOT\<file extension>\shellex\{00021500-0000-0000-C000-000000000046}`, where `<file extension>` is the file extension name, including the preceding dot.

Figure 16.12 shows this InfoTip handler in action.

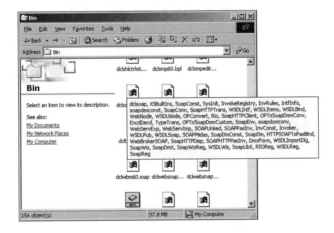

The Delphi InfoTip handler shell extension.

Summary

This chapter covers all the different aspects of extending the Windows shell: tray-notification icons, AppBars, shell links, and a variety of shell extensions. It builds upon some of the knowledge you obtained in the last chapter when working with COM. In Chapter 17, you'll learn more about component-based development using interfaces.

Using the Open Tools API

IN THIS CHAPTER

Have you ever thought to yourself, "Delphi is great, but why doesn't the IDE perform this little task that I'd like it to?" If you have, the Open Tools API is for you. The Delphi Open Tools API provides you with the capability of integrating your own tools that work closely with Delphi's IDE. In this chapter, you'll learn about the different interfaces that make up the Open Tools API, how to use the interfaces, and also how to leverage your newly found expertise to write a fully featured wizard.

Open Tools Interfaces

The Open Tools API is composed of 14 units, each containing one or more objects that provide interfaces to a variety of facilities in the IDE. Using these interfaces enables you to write your own Delphi wizards, version control managers, and component and property editors. You'll also gain a window into Delphi's IDE and editor through any of these add-ons.

With the exception of the interfaces designed for component and property editors, the Open Tools interface objects provide an all-virtual interface to the outside world—meaning that using these interface objects involves working only with the objects' virtual functions. You can't access the objects' data fields, properties, or static functions. Because of this, the Open Tools interface objects follow the COM standard (see Chapter 15, "COM Development"). With a little work on your part, these interfaces can be used in any programming language that supports COM interfaces. In this chapter, you'll work only with Delphi, but you should know that the capacity for using other languages is available (in case you just can't get enough of C++).

> **NOTE**
>
> The complete Open Tools API is available only with Delphi Professional and Enterprise. Delphi Personal has the capability to use add-ons created with the Open Tools API, but it cannot create add-ons because it contains only the units for creating component and property editors. You can find the source code for the Open Tools interfaces in the `\Delphi 6\Source\ToolsAPI` subdirectory.

Table 17.1 shows the units that make up the Open Tools API and the classes and interfaces they provide. Table 17.2 lists obsolete Open Tools API units that remain only for backward compatibility with experts written in Delphi 4 or earlier. Because the obsolete units pre-date the native `interface` type, they employ regular Delphi classes with virtual abstract methods as a substitute for true interfaces. The use of true interfaces has been phased into the Open Tools API over the past few versions of Delphi, and the current incarnation of the Open Tools API is primarily `interface`-based.

TABLE 17.1 Units in the Open Tools API

Unit Name	Purpose
ToolsAPI	Contains the latest interface-based Open Tools API elements. The contents of this unit essentially supersede the pre-Delphi 5 Open Tools API units that use abstract classes to manipulate menus, notifications, the filesystem, the editor, and wizard add-ins. It also contains new interfaces for manipulating the debugger, IDE key mappings, projects, project groups, packages, and the To Do list.
VCSIntf	Defines the TIVCSClient class, which enables the Delphi IDE to communicate with version-control software.
DesignConst	Contains strings used by the Open Tools API.
DesignEditors	Provides property editor support.
DesignIntf	This unit replaces the DsgnIntf unit from previous versions and provides core support for design-time IDE interfaces. The IProperty interface is used by the IDE to edit properties. IDesignerSelections is used to manipulate the form designer's selected objects list (replaces TDesignerSelectionList used in previous Delphi versions). IDesigner is one of the primary interfaces used by wizards for general IDE services. IDesignNotification provides notification of designer events such as items being inserted, deleted, or modified. The IComponentEditor interface is implemented by component editors to provide design time component editing, and ISelectionEditor provides the same functionality for a group of selected components. The TBaseComponentEditor class is the class from which all component editors should be derived. ICustomModule and TBaseCustomModule are provided in order to install modules that can be edited in the IDE's form designer.
DesignMenus	Contains the IMenuItems, IMenuItem, and related interfaces for design-time manipulation of the IDE's menus.
DesignWindows	Declares the TDesignWindow class, which would serve as the base class for any new design windows one might want to add to the IDE.
PropertyCategories	Contains the classes to support the categorization of custom component properties. Used by the Object Inspector's category view.
TreeIntf	Provides TSprig and related classes and interfaces to support custom *sprigs*, or nodes in the IDE's Object TreeView.
VCLSprigs	Sprig implementations for VCL components.

TABLE 17.1   Continued

Unit Name	Purpose
VCLEditors	Declares base ICustomPropertyDrawing and ICustomPropertyListDrawing to handle custom drawing of properties and property lists in the IDE's Object Inspector. Also declares custom property drawing objects for common VCL properties.
ClxDesignWindows	Declares the TClxDesignWindow class, which is the CLX equivalent of the TDesignWindow class.
ClxEditors	CLX equivalent of the VCLEditors unit, which includes property editors for CLX components.
ClxSprigs	Sprig implementations for CLX components.

TABLE 17.2   Obsolete Open Tools API units

Unit Name	Purpose
FileIntf	Defines the TIVirtualFileSystem class, which the Delphi IDE uses for filing. Wizards, version-control managers, and property and component editors can use this interface to hook into Delphi's own file system to perform special file operations.
EditIntf	Defines classes necessary for manipulating the Delphi Code Editor and Form Designer. The TIEditReader class provides read access to an editor buffer. TIEditWriter provides write access to the same. TIEditView is defined as an individual view of an edit buffer. TIEditInterface is the base interface to the editor, which can be used to obtain the previously mentioned editor interfaces. The TIComponentInterface class is an interface to an individual component sitting on a form at design time. TIFormInterface is the base interface to a design-time form or data module. TIResourceEntry is an interface for the raw data in a project's resource (*.res) file. TIResourceFile is a higher-level interface to the project resource file. TIModuleNotifier is a class that provides notifications when various events occur for a particular module. Finally, TIModuleInterface is the interface for any file or module open in the IDE.
ExptIntf	Defines the abstract TIExpert class from which all experts descend.

TABLE 17.2 Continued

Unit Name	Purpose
VirtIntf	Defines the base TInterface class from which other interfaces are derived. This unit also defines TIStream class, which is a wrapper around a VCL TStream.
IStreams	Defines TIMemoryStream, TIFileStream, and TIVirtualStream classes, which are descendants of TIStream. These interfaces can be used to hook into the IDE's own streaming mechanism.
ToolIntf	Defines TIMenuItemIntf and TIMainMenuIntf classes, which enable the Open Tools developer to create and modify menus in the Delphi IDE. This unit also defines the TIAddInNotifier class, which allows add-in tools to be notified of certain events within the IDE. Most importantly, this unit defines the TIToolServices class, which provides an interface into various portions of the Delphi IDE (such as the editor, component library, Code Editor, Form Designer, and filesystem).

NOTE

You might wonder where all this wizard stuff is documented in Delphi. We assure you that it is documented, but the documentation isn't easy to find. Each of these units contains complete documentation for the interface, classes, methods, and procedures declared within. We won't regurgitate the same information that these units contain, so we urge you to take a look at the units for complete documentation.

Using the Open Tools API

Now that you know what's what, it's time to get your hands dirty and look at some actual code. This section focuses primarily on writing wizards by using the Open Tools API. We won't discuss the building of version-control systems because the interest for such a topic is arguably limited. For examples of component and property editors, you should look at Chapter 11, "VCL Component Building," and Chapter 12, "Advanced VCL Component Building."

A Dumb Wizard

To start out, you'll create a very simple wizard appropriately dubbed the Dumb Wizard. The minimum requirement to create a wizard is to create a class that implements the IOTAWizard interface. For reference, IOTAWizard is defined in the ToolsAPI unit as follows:

```
type
  IOTAWizard = interface(IOTANotifier)
```

```
['{B75C0CE0-EEA6-11D1-9504-00608CCBF153}']
{ Expert UI strings }
function GetIDString: string;
function GetName: string;
function GetState: TWizardState;
{ Launch the AddIn }
procedure Execute;
end;
```

This interface consists mainly of some GetXXX() functions that are designed to be overridden
by the descendant classes in order to provide specific information for each wizard. The
Execute() method is the business end of IOTAWizard. Execute() is called by the IDE when
the user selects your wizard from the main menu or the New Items menu, and it's in this
method that the wizard should be created and invoked.

If you've got a keen eye, you might have noticed that IOTAWizard descends from another interface, called IOTANotifier. IOTANotifier is an interface defined in the ToolsAPI unit that contains methods that can be called by the IDE to notify a wizard of various goings on. This
interface is defined as

```
type
  IOTANotifier = interface(IUnknown)
  ['{F17A7BCF-E07D-11D1-AB0B-00C04FB16FB3}']
  { This procedure is called immediately after the item is successfully
    saved. This is not called for IOTAWizards }
  procedure AfterSave;
  { This function is called immediately before the item is saved. This is not
    called for IOTAWizard }
  procedure BeforeSave;
  { The associated item is being destroyed so all references should be
    dropped. Exceptions are ignored. }
  procedure Destroyed;
  { This associated item was modified in some way. This is not called for
    IOTAWizards }
  procedure Modified;
  end;
```

As the comments in the source code indicate, most of these methods aren't called for simple
IOTAWizard wizards. Because of this, ToolsAPI provides a class called TNotifierObject that
provides empty implementations for IOTANotifier methods. You might choose to descend
your wizards from this class to take advantage of the convenience of having the IOTANotifier
methods implemented for you.

Wizards are not much use without a means to invoke them, and one of the simplest ways to do that is through a menu pick. If you want to place your wizard on Delphi's main menu, you need only implement the IOTAMenuWizard interface, which is defined in all its complexity in ToolsAPI as

```
type
  IOTAMenuWizard = interface(IOTAWizard)
    ['{B75C0CE2-EEA6-11D1-9504-00608CCBF153}']
    function GetMenuText: string;
  end;
```

As you can see, this interface descends from IOTAWizard and adds only one additional method to return the menu text string.

To jump right in and pull together your knowledge thus far, Listing 17.1 shows the DumbWiz.pas unit, which contains the source code for TDumbWizard.

LISTING 17.1 DumbWiz.pas—a Simple Wizard Implementation

```
unit DumbWiz;

interface

uses
  ShareMem, SysUtils, Windows, ToolsAPI;

type
  TDumbWizard = class(TNotifierObject, IOTAWizard, IOTAMenuWizard)
    // IOTAWizard methods
    function GetIDString: string;
    function GetName: string;
    function GetState: TWizardState;
    procedure Execute;
    // IOTAMenuWizard method
    function GetMenuText: string;
  end;

implementation

uses Dialogs;

function TDumbWizard.GetName: string;
begin
  Result := 'Dumb Wizard';
end;
```

LISTING 17.1   Continued

```
function TDumbWizard.GetState: TWizardState;
begin
  Result := [wsEnabled];
end;

function TDumbWizard.GetIDString: String;
begin
  Result := 'DDG.DumbWizard';
end;

procedure TDumbWizard.Execute;
begin
  MessageDlg('This is a dumb wizard.', mtInformation, [mbOk], 0);
end;

function TDumbWizard.GetMenuText: string;
begin
  Result := 'Dumb Wizard';
end;

end.
```

The IOTAWizard.GetName() function should return a unique name for this wizard.

IOTAWizard.GetState() returns the state of an wsStandard wizard on the main menu. The return value of this function is a set that can contain wsEnabled and/or wsChecked, depending on how you want the menu item to appear in the IDE. This function is called every time the wizard is shown in order to determine how to paint the menu.

IOTAWizard.GetIDString() should return a globally unique string identifier for the wizard. Convention dictates that the return value of this string should be in the following format:

CompanyName.WizardName

IOTAWizard.Execute() invokes the wizard. As Listing 17.1 shows, the Execute() method for TDumbWizard doesn't do much. However, later in this chapter you'll see some wizards that actually do perform stuff.

IOTAMenuWizard.GetMenuText() returns the text that should appear on the main menu. This function is called every time the user pulls down the Help menu, so it's possible to dynamically change the value of the menu text as your wizard runs.

Take a look at the call to RegisterPackageWizard() inside the Register() procedure. You might notice that this is very similar to the syntax used for registering components, component editors, and property editors for inclusion in the component library, as described in Chapters 11 and 12. The reason for this similarity is that this type of wizard is stored in a package that's part of the component library, along with components and the like. You can also store wizards in a standalone DLL, as you'll see in the next example.

This wizard is installed just like a component: Select the Components, Install Component option from the main menu and add the unit to a new or existing package. Once this is installed, the menu choice to invoke the wizard appears under the Help menu, as shown in Figure 17.1. You can see the outstanding output of this wizard in Figure 17.2.

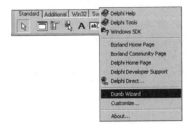

FIGURE 17.1

The Dumb Wizard on the main menu.

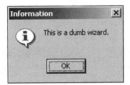

FIGURE 17.2

The Dumb Wizard in action.

The Wizard Wizard

There's just a little bit more work involved in creating a DLL-based wizard (as opposed to a component-library–based wizard). In addition to demonstrating the creation of a DLL-based wizard, the Wizard Wizard example has a couple of ulterior motives, including illustrating how DLL wizards relate to the Registry and how to maintain one source code base that targets either an EXE or a DLL wizard.

> **NOTE**
>
> If you're unfamiliar with the ins and outs of Windows DLLs, take a look at Chapter 9, "Dynamic Link Libraries," in the electronic version of *Delphi 5 Developer's Guide* on the CD accompanying this book.

> **TIP**
>
> There's no hard-and-fast rule that dictates whether a wizard should reside in a pack-age in the component library or a DLL. From a user's perspective, the primary differ-ence between the two is that component library wizards require a simple package installation to be rebuilt, whereas DLL wizards require a Registry entry, and Delphi must be exited and restarted for changes to take effect. However, as a developer, you'll find package wizards a bit easier to deal with for a number of reasons. Namely, exceptions propagate between your wizard and the IDE automatically, you don't have to use sharemem.dll for memory management, you don't have to do anything special to initialize the DLL's application variable, and pop-up hints and mouse enter/exit messages will work properly.
>
> With this in mind, you should consider using a DLL wizard when you want the wizard to install with a minimum amount of work on the part of the end user.

For Delphi to recognize a DLL wizard, it must have an entry in the system Registry under the following key:

HKEY_CURRENT_USER\Software\Borland\Delphi\5.0\Experts

Figure 17.3 shows sample entries using the Windows RegEdit application.

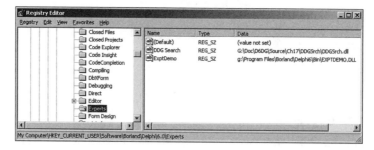

FIGURE 17.3
Delphi wizard entries viewed with RegEdit.

Wizard Interface

The purpose of the Wizard Wizard is to provide an interface to add, modify, and delete DLL wizard entries from the Registry without having to use the cumbersome RegEdit application. First, let's examine InitWiz.pas, the unit containing the wizard class (see Listing 17.2).

LISTING 17.2   InitWiz.pas—Unit Containing DLL Wizard Class

```
unit InitWiz;

interface

uses Windows, ToolsAPI;

type
  TWizardWizard = class(TNotifierObject, IOTAWizard, IOTAMenuWizard)
    // IOTAWizard methods
    function GetIDString: string;
    function GetName: string;
    function GetState: TWizardState;
    procedure Execute;
    // IOTAMenuWizard method
    function GetMenuText: string;
  end;

function InitWizard(const BorlandIDEServices: IBorlandIDEServices;
  RegisterProc: TWizardRegisterProc;
  var Terminate: TWizardTerminateProc): Boolean stdcall;

var
  { Registry key where Delphi 6 wizards are kept.  EXE version uses default, }
  { whereas DLL version gets key from ToolServices.GetBaseRegistryKey }
  SDelphiKey: string = '\Software\Borland\Delphi\6.0\Experts';

implementation

uses SysUtils, Forms, Controls, Main;
function TWizardWizard.GetName: string;
{ Return name of expert }
begin
  Result := 'WizardWizard';
end;

function TWizardWizard.GetState: TWizardState;
{ This expert is always enabled }
begin
  Result := [wsEnabled];
end;

function TWizardWizard.GetIDString: String;
{ "Vendor.AppName" ID string for expert }
```

Listing 17.2 Continued

```
begin
  Result := 'DDG.WizardWizard';
end;

function TWizardWizard.GetMenuText: string;
{ Menu text for expert }
begin
  Result := 'Wizard Wizard';
end;

procedure TWizardWizard.Execute;
{ Called when expert is chosen from the main menu. }
{ This procedure creates, shows, and frees the main form. }
begin
  MainForm := TMainForm.Create(Application);
  try
    MainForm.ShowModal;
  finally
    MainForm.Free;
  end;
end;

function InitWizard(const BorlandIDEServices: IBorlandIDEServices;
  RegisterProc: TWizardRegisterProc;
  var Terminate: TWizardTerminateProc): Boolean stdcall;
var
  Svcs: IOTAServices;
begin
  Result := BorlandIDEServices <> nil;
  if Result then
  begin
    Svcs := BorlandIDEServices as IOTAServices;
    ToolsAPI.BorlandIDEServices := BorlandIDEServices;
    Application.Handle := Svcs.GetParentHandle;
    SDelphiKey := Svcs.GetBaseRegistryKey + '\Experts';
    RegisterProc(TWizardWizard.Create);
  end;
end;

end.
```

You should notice a couple of differences between this unit and the one used to create the Dumb Wizard. Most importantly, an initialization function of type `TWizardInitProc` is required as an entry point for the IDE into the wizard DLL. In this case, that function is called `InitWizard()`. This function performs a number of wizard initialization tasks, including the following:

- Obtaining a `IOTAServices` interface from the `BorlandIDEServices` parameter.
- Saving the `BorlandIDEServices` interface pointer for use at a later time.
- Setting the handle of the DLL's `Application` variable to the value returned by `IOTAServices.GetParentHandle()`. `GetParentHandle()` returns the window handle of the window that must serve as the parent to all top-level windows created by the wizard.
- Passing the newly created instance of the wizard to the `RegisterProc()` procedure in order to register the wizard with the IDE. `RegisterProc()` will be called once for each wizard instance the DLL registers with the IDE.
- Optionally, `InitWizard()` can also assign a procedure of type `TWizardTerminateProc` to the `Terminate` parameter to serve as an exit procedure for the wizard. This procedure will be called immediately before the wizard is unloaded by the IDE, and in it you can perform any necessary cleanup. This parameter is initially `nil`, so if you don't need to perform any special cleanup, leave its value as `nil`.

> **CAUTION**
>
> The wizard initialization method must use the `stdcall` calling convention.

> **CAUTION**
>
> Any DLL wizards calling Open Tools API functions that have string parameters must have the `ShareMem` unit in their uses clause; otherwise, Delphi will raise an access violation when the wizard instance is freed.

The Wizard User Interface

The `Execute()` method is a bit more complex this time around. It creates an instance of the wizard's `MainForm`, shows it modally, and then frees the instances. Figure 17.4 shows this form, and Listing 17.3 shows the `Main.pas` unit in which `MainForm` exists.

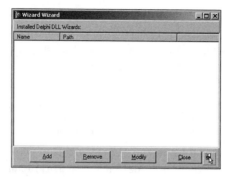

FIGURE 17.4

MainForm *in the Wizard Wizard.*

LISTING 17.3   Main.pas—Main Unit of Wizard Wizard

```pascal
unit Main;

interface

uses
  Windows, Messages, SysUtils, Classes, Graphics, Controls, Forms, Dialogs,
  StdCtrls, ExtCtrls, Registry, AddModU, ComCtrls, Menus;

type
  TMainForm = class(TForm)
    TopPanel: TPanel;
    Label1: TLabel;
    BottomPanel: TPanel;
    WizList: TListView;
    PopupMenu1: TPopupMenu;
    Add1: TMenuItem;
    Remove1: TMenuItem;
    Modify1: TMenuItem;
    AddBtn: TButton;
    RemoveBtn: TButton;
    ModifyBtn: TButton;
    CloseBtn: TButton;
    procedure RemoveBtnClick(Sender: TObject);
    procedure CloseBtnClick(Sender: TObject);
    procedure AddBtnClick(Sender: TObject);
    procedure ModifyBtnClick(Sender: TObject);
    procedure FormCreate(Sender: TObject);
  private
    procedure DoAddMod(Action: TAddModAction);
```

LISTING 17.3 Continued

```
    procedure RefreshReg;
  end;

var
  MainForm: TMainForm;

implementation

uses InitWiz;

{$R *.DFM}

var
  DelReg: TRegistry;

procedure TMainForm.RemoveBtnClick(Sender: TObject);
{ Handler for Remove button click. Removes selected item from registry. }
var
  Item: TListItem;
begin
  Item := WizList.Selected;
  if Item <> nil then
  begin
    if MessageDlg(Format('Remove item "%s"', [Item.Caption]), mtConfirmation,
      [mbYes, mbNo], 0) = mrYes then
      DelReg.DeleteValue(Item.Caption);
    RefreshReg;
  end;
end;

procedure TMainForm.CloseBtnClick(Sender: TObject);
{ Handler for Close button click. Closes app. }
begin
  Close;
end;

procedure TMainForm.DoAddMod(Action: TAddModAction);
{ Adds a new expert item to registry or modifies existing one. }
var
  OrigName, ExpName, ExpPath: String;
  Item: TListItem;
begin
  if Action = amaModify then              // if modify...
  begin
    Item := WizList.Selected;
```

LISTING 17.3   Continued

```
    if Item = nil then Exit;          // make sure item is selected
    ExpName := Item.Caption;          // init variables
    if Item.SubItems.Count > 0 then
      ExpPath := Item.SubItems[0];
    OrigName := ExpName;                   // save original name
  end;
  { Invoke dialog which allows user to add or modify entry }
  if AddModWiz(Action, ExpName, ExpPath) then
  begin
    { if action is Modify, and the name was changed, handle it }
    if (Action = amaModify) and (OrigName <> ExpName) then
      DelReg.RenameValue(OrigName, ExpName);
    DelReg.WriteString(ExpName, ExpPath);  // write new value
  end;
  RefreshReg;                              // update listbox
end;

procedure TMainForm.AddBtnClick(Sender: TObject);
{ Handler for Add button click }
begin
  DoAddMod(amaAdd);
end;

procedure TMainForm.ModifyBtnClick(Sender: TObject);
{ Handler for Modify button click }
begin
  DoAddMod(amaModify);
end;

procedure TMainForm.RefreshReg;
{ Refreshes listbox with contents of registry }
var
  i: integer;
  TempList: TStringList;
  Item: TListItem;
begin
  WizList.Items.Clear;
  TempList := TStringList.Create;
  try
    { Get expert names from registry }
    DelReg.GetValueNames(TempList);
    { Get path strings for each expert name }
    for i := 0 to TempList.Count - 1 do
    begin
      Item := WizList.Items.Add;
```

LISTING 17.3 Continued

```
      Item.Caption := TempList[i];
      Item.SubItems.Add(DelReg.ReadString(TempList[i]));
    end;
  finally
    TempList.Free;
  end;
end;

procedure TMainForm.FormCreate(Sender: TObject);
begin
  RefreshReg;
end;

initialization
  DelReg := TRegistry.Create;              // create registry object
  DelReg.RootKey := HKEY_CURRENT_USER;     // set root key
  DelReg.OpenKey(SDelphiKey, True);        // open/create Delphi expert key
finalization
  Delreg.Free;                             // free registry object
end.
```

This is the unit responsible for providing the user interface for adding, removing, and modifying DLL wizard entries in the Registry. In the `initialization` section of this unit, a `TRegistry` object called `DelReg` is created. The `RootKey` property of `DelReg` is set to `HKEY_CURRENT_USER`, and it opens the `\Software\Borland\Delphi\6.0\Experts` key—the key used to keep track of DLL wizards—using its `OpenKey()` method.

When the wizard first comes up, a `TListView` component called `ExptList` is filled with the items and values from the previously mentioned Registry key. This is accomplished by first calling `DelReg.GetValueNames()` to retrieve the names of the items into a `TStringList`. A `TListItem` component is added to `ExptList` for each element in the string list, and the `DelReg.ReadString()` method is used to read the value for each item, which is placed in the `SubItems` list of `TListItem`.

The Registry work is done in the `RemoveBtnClick()` and `DoAddMod()` methods. `RemoveBtnClick()` is in charge of removing the currently selected wizard item from the Registry. It first checks to ensure that an item is highlighted; then it throws up a confirmation dialog box. Finally, it does the deed by calling the `DelReg.DeleteValue()` method and passing `CurrentItem` as the parameter.

`DoAddMod()` accepts a parameter of type `TAddModAction`. This type is defined as follows:

```
type
  TAddModAction = (amaAdd, amaModify);
```

17

USING THE OPEN
TOOLS API

As the values of the type imply, this variable indicates whether a new item is to be added or an existing item modified. This function first checks to see that there's a currently selected item or, if there isn't, that the Action parameter holds the value amaAdd. After that, if Action is amaModify, the existing wizard item and value are copied to the local variables ExpName and ExpPath. These values are then passed to a function called AddModExpert(), which is defined in the AddModU unit shown in Listing 17.4. This function invokes a dialog box in which the user can enter new or modified name or path information for a wizard (see Figure 17.5). It returns True when the user exits the dialog with the OK button. At that point, an existing item is modified using DelReg.RenameValue(), and a new or modified value is written with DelReg.WriteString().

FIGURE 17.5

AddModForm *in the Wizard Wizard.*

LISTING 17.4 AddModU.pas—Unit That Adds and Modifies Wizard Entries in the Registry

```
unit AddModU;

interface

uses
  Windows, Messages, SysUtils, Classes, Graphics, Controls, Forms, Dialogs,
  StdCtrls, ExtCtrls;

type
  TAddModAction = (amaAdd, amaModify);

  TAddModForm = class(TForm)
    OkBtn: TButton;
    CancelBtn: TButton;
    OpenDialog: TOpenDialog;
    Panel1: TPanel;
    Label1: TLabel;
    Label2: TLabel;
    PathEd: TEdit;
    NameEd: TEdit;
    BrowseBtn: TButton;
    procedure BrowseBtnClick(Sender: TObject);
  private
```

LISTING 17.4   Continued

```
    { Private declarations }
  public
    { Public declarations }
  end;

function AddModWiz(AAction: TAddModAction; var WizName,
  WizPath: String): Boolean;

implementation

{$R *.DFM}

function AddModWiz(AAction: TAddModAction; var WizName,
  WizPath: String): Boolean;
{ called to invoke dialog to add and modify registry entries }
const
  CaptionArray: array[TAddModAction] of string[31] =
    ('Add new expert', 'Modify expert');
begin
  with TAddModForm.Create(Application) do      // create dialog
  begin
    Caption := CaptionArray[AAction];           // set caption
    if AAction = amaModify then                 // if modify...
    begin
      NameEd.Text := WizName;                   // init name and
      PathEd.Text := WizPath;                   // path
    end;
    Result := ShowModal = mrOk;                 // show dialog
    if Result then                              // if Ok...
    begin
      WizName := NameEd.Text;                   // set name and
      WizPath := PathEd.Text;                   // path
    end;
    Free;
  end;
end;

procedure TAddModForm.BrowseBtnClick(Sender: TObject);
begin
  if OpenDialog.Execute then
    PathEd.Text := OpenDialog.FileName;
end;


end.
```

Dual Targets: EXE and DLL

As mentioned earlier, it's possible to maintain one set of source code modules that target both a DLL wizard and a standalone executable. This is possible through the use of compiler directives in the project file. Listing 17.5 shows WizWiz.dpr, the project file source code for this project.

LISTING 17.5   WizWiz.dpr—Main Project File for the WizWiz Project

```
{$ifdef BUILD_EXE}
program WizWiz;      // Build as EXE
{$else}
library WizWiz;      // Build as DLL
{$endif}

uses
{$ifndef BUILD_EXE}
  ShareMem,                    // ShareMem required for DLL
  InitWiz in 'InitWiz.pas',  // Wizard stuff
{$endif}
  ToolsAPI,
  Forms,
  Main in 'Main.pas' {MainForm},
  AddModU in 'AddModU.pas' {AddModForm};

{$ifdef BUILD_EXE}
{$R *.RES}                              // required for EXE
{$else}
exports                                 // required for DLL
  InitWizard name WizardEntryPoint;    // required entry point
{$endif}

begin
{$ifdef BUILD_EXE}                      // required for EXE...
  Application.Initialize;
  Application.CreateForm(TMainForm, MainForm);
  Application.Run;
{$endif}
end.
```

As the code shows, this project will build an executable if the BUILD_EXE conditional is defined. Otherwise, it will build a DLL-based wizard. You can define a conditional under Conditional Defines in the Directories/Conditionals page of the Project Options dialog box, which is shown in Figure 17.6.

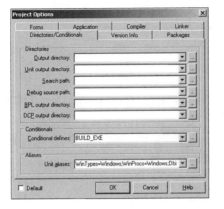

FIGURE 17.6
The Project Options dialog box.

One final note concerning this project: Notice that the InitWizard() function from the
InitWiz unit is being exported in the exports clause of the project file. You must export this
function with the name WizardEntryPoint, which is defined in the ToolsAPI unit.

> **CAUTION**
>
> Borland doesn't provide a ToolsAPI.dcu file, meaning that EXEs or DLLs containing a
> reference to ToolsAPI in a uses clause can only be built *with packages*. It isn't cur-
> rently possible to build wizards without packages.

DDG Search

Remember the nifty little Delphi Search program you developed back in Chapter 5, " Multithreaded
Techniques"? In this section, you'll learn how you can turn that useful application into an even
more useful Delphi wizard with just a little bit of code. This wizard is called DDG Search.

First, the unit that interfaces DDG Search to the IDE, InitWiz.pas, is shown in Listing 17.6.
You'll notice that this unit is very similar to the unit of the same name in the previous example.
That's on purpose. This unit is just a copy of the previous one with some necessary changes
involving the name of the wizard and the Execute() method. Copying and pasting is what we
call "old-fashioned inheritance." After all, why do more typing than you have to?

LISTING 17.6 InitWiz.pas—Unit Containing Wizard Logic for the DDGSrch Wizard

```
unit InitWiz;

interface
```

LISTING 17.6   Continued

```pascal
uses
  Windows, ToolsAPI;

type
  TSearchWizard = class(TNotifierObject, IOTAWizard, IOTAMenuWizard)
    // IOTAWizard methods
    function GetIDString: string;
    function GetName: string;
    function GetState: TWizardState;
    procedure Execute;
    // IOTAMenuWizard method
    function GetMenuText: string;
  end;

function InitWizard(const BorlandIDEServices: IBorlandIDEServices;
  RegisterProc: TWizardRegisterProc;
  var Terminate: TWizardTerminateProc): Boolean stdcall;

var
  ActionSvc: IOTAActionServices;

implementation

uses SysUtils, Dialogs, Forms, Controls, Main, PriU;

function TSearchWizard.GetName: string;
{ Return name of expert }
begin
  Result := 'DDG Search';
end;

function TSearchWizard.GetState: TWizardState;
{ This expert is always enabled on the menu }
begin
  Result := [wsEnabled];
end;

function TSearchWizard.GetIDString: String;
{ Return the unique Vendor.Product name of expert }
begin
  Result := 'DDG.DDGSearch';
end;

function TSearchWizard.GetMenuText: string;
{ Return text for Help menu }
```

LISTING 17.6 Continued

```pascal
begin
  Result := 'DDG Search Expert';
end;

procedure TSearchWizard.Execute;
{ Called when expert name is selected from Help menu of IDE. }
{ This function invokes the expert }
begin
  // if not created, created it and show it
  if MainForm = nil then
  begin
    MainForm := TMainForm.Create(Application);
    ThreadPriWin := TThreadPriWin.Create(Application);
    MainForm.Show;
  end
  else
  // if created then restore window and show it
    with MainForm do
    begin
      if not Visible then Show;
      if WindowState = wsMinimized then WindowState := wsNormal;
      SetFocus;
    end;
end;

function InitWizard(const BorlandIDEServices: IBorlandIDEServices;
  RegisterProc: TWizardRegisterProc;
  var Terminate: TWizardTerminateProc): Boolean stdcall;
var
  Svcs: IOTAServices;
begin
  Result := BorlandIDEServices <> nil;
  if Result then
  begin
    Svcs := BorlandIDEServices as IOTAServices;
    ActionSvc := BorlandIDEServices as IOTAActionServices;
    ToolsAPI.BorlandIDEServices := BorlandIDEServices;
    Application.Handle := Svcs.GetParentHandle;
    RegisterProc(TSearchWizard.Create);
  end;
end;

end.
```

The Execute() function of this wizard shows you something a bit different from what you've seen so far: The wizard's main form, MainForm, is being shown modelessly rather than modally. Of course, this requires a bit of extra housekeeping because you have to know when a form is created and when the form variable is invalid. This can be accomplished by making sure that the MainForm variable is set to nil when the wizard is inactive. More on this is discussed a bit later.

One other aspect of this project that has changed significantly since Chapter 5 is that the project file is now called DDGSrch.dpr. This file is shown in Listing 17.7.

LISTING 17.7   DDGSrch.dpr—Project File for the DDGSrch Project

```
{$IFDEF BUILD_EXE}
program DDGSrch;
{$ELSE}
library DDGSrch;
{$ENDIF}

uses
{$IFDEF BUILD_EXE}
  Forms,
{$ELSE}
  ShareMem,
  ToolsAPI,
  InitWiz in 'InitWiz.pas',
{$ENDIF}
  Main in 'MAIN.PAS' {MainForm},
  SrchIni in 'SrchIni.pas',
  SrchU in 'SrchU.pas',
  PriU in 'PriU.pas' {ThreadPriWin},
  MemMap in '..\..\Utils\MemMap.pas',
  DDGStrUtils in '..\..\Utils\DDGStrUtils.pas';

{$R *.RES}

{$IFNDEF BUILD_EXE}
exports
  { Entry point which is called by Delphi IDE }
  InitWizard name WizardEntryPoint;
{$ENDIF}

begin
{$IFDEF BUILD_EXE}
  Application.Initialize;
```

LISTING 17.7   Continued

```
  Application.CreateForm(TMainForm, MainForm);
  Application.Run;
{$ENDIF}
end.
```

Once again, you can see that this project is designed to be compiled as a standalone EXE or a DLL-based wizard. When compiled as a wizard, it uses the `library` header to indicate that it's a DLL, and it exports the `InitWiz()` function for initialization by the Delphi IDE.

We made only a couple of changes to the Main unit in this project. As mentioned earlier, the `MainForm` variable must be set to `nil` when the wizard isn't active. As you learned in Chapter 2, "The Object Pascal Language," the `MainForm` instance variable will automatically have the value `nil` upon application startup. Also, in the `OnClose` event handler for the form, the form instance is released and the `MainForm` global is reset to `nil`. Here's the method:

```
procedure TMainForm.FormClose(Sender: TObject; var Action: TCloseAction);
begin
  Action := caFree;
  Application.OnShowHint := FOldShowHint;
  MainForm := nil;
end;
```

The finishing touch for this wizard is to bring up files in the IDE's Code Editor when they're double-clicked in the list box in the main form. This logic is handled by a new `FileLBDblClick()` method, as follows:

```
procedure TMainForm.FileLBDblClick(Sender: TObject);
{ Called when user double-clicks in listbox. Loads file into IDE }
var
  FileName: string;
  Len: Integer;
begin
  { make sure user clicked on a file... }
  if Integer(FileLB.Items.Objects[FileLB.ItemIndex]) > 0 then
  begin
    FileName := FileLB.Items[FileLB.ItemIndex];
    { Trim "File " and ":" from string }
    FileName := Copy(FileName, 6, Length(FileName));
    Len := Length(FileName);
    if FileName[Len] = ':' then SetLength(FileName, Len - 1);
    { Open the project or file }
{$IFNDEF BUILD_EXE}
    if CompareText(ExtractFileExt(FileName), '.DPR') = 0 then
      ActionSvc.OpenProject(FileName, True)
```

```
    else
      ActionSvc.OpenFile(FileName);
{$ELSE}
    ShellExecute(0, 'open', PChar(FileName), nil, nil, SW_SHOWNORMAL);
{$ENDIF}
  end;
end;
```

When compiled as a wizard, this method employs the OpenFile() and OpenProject() methods of the IOTAActionServices in order to open a particular file. As a standalone EXE, this method calls the ShellExecute() API function to open the file using the default application associated with the file extension.

Listing 17.8 shows the complete source code for the Main unit in the DDGSrch project, and Figure 17.7 shows the DDG Search Wizard doing its thing inside the IDE.

LISTING 17.8   Main.pas—the Main Unit for the DDGSrch Project

```
unit Main;

interface

{$WARN UNIT_PLATFORM OFF}

uses
  SysUtils, WinTypes, WinProcs, Messages, Classes, Graphics, Controls,
  Forms, Dialogs, StdCtrls, Buttons, ExtCtrls, Menus, SrchIni,
  SrchU, ComCtrls;

type
  TMainForm = class(TForm)
    FileLB: TListBox;
    PopupMenu1: TPopupMenu;
    Font1: TMenuItem;
    N1: TMenuItem;
    Exit1: TMenuItem;
    FontDialog1: TFontDialog;
    StatusBar: TStatusBar;
    AlignPanel: TPanel;
    ControlPanel: TPanel;
    ParamsGB: TGroupBox;
    LFileSpec: TLabel;
    LToken: TLabel;
    lPathName: TLabel;
    EFileSpec: TEdit;
    EToken: TEdit;
```

LISTING 17.8 Continued

```pascal
    PathButton: TButton;
    OptionsGB: TGroupBox;
    cbCaseSensitive: TCheckBox;
    cbFileNamesOnly: TCheckBox;
    cbRecurse: TCheckBox;
    SearchButton: TBitBtn;
    CloseButton: TBitBtn;
    PrintButton: TBitBtn;
    PriorityButton: TBitBtn;
    View1: TMenuItem;
    EPathName: TEdit;
    procedure SearchButtonClick(Sender: TObject);
    procedure PathButtonClick(Sender: TObject);
    procedure FileLBDrawItem(Control: TWinControl; Index: Integer;
      Rect: TRect; State: TOwnerDrawState);
    procedure Font1Click(Sender: TObject);
    procedure FormDestroy(Sender: TObject);
    procedure FormCreate(Sender: TObject);
    procedure PrintButtonClick(Sender: TObject);
    procedure CloseButtonClick(Sender: TObject);
    procedure FileLBDblClick(Sender: TObject);
    procedure FormResize(Sender: TObject);
    procedure PriorityButtonClick(Sender: TObject);
    procedure ETokenChange(Sender: TObject);
    procedure FormClose(Sender: TObject; var Action: TCloseAction);
  private
    FOldShowHint: TShowHintEvent;
    procedure ReadIni;
    procedure WriteIni;
    procedure DoShowHint(var HintStr: string; var CanShow: Boolean;
      var HintInfo: THintInfo);
  protected
    procedure WndProc(var Message: TMessage); override;
  public
    Running: Boolean;
    SearchPri: integer;
    SearchThread: TSearchThread;
    procedure EnableSearchControls(Enable: Boolean);
  end;

var
  MainForm: TMainForm;

implementation
```

LISTING 17.8   Continued

```
{$R *.DFM}

uses Printers, ShellAPI, MemMap, FileCtrl, PriU;

procedure PrintStrings(Strings: TStrings);
{ This procedure prints all of the string in the Strings parameter }
var
  Prn: TextFile;
  i: word;
begin
  if Strings.Count = 0 then // Are there strings?
  begin
    MessageDlg('No text to print!', mtInformation, [mbOk], 0);
    Exit;
  end;
  AssignPrn(Prn);                        // assign Prn to printer
  try
    Rewrite(Prn);                        // open printer
    try
      for i := 0 to Strings.Count - 1 do   // iterate over all strings
        WriteLn(Prn, Strings.Strings[i]);  // write to printer
    finally
      CloseFile(Prn);                    // close printer
    end;
  except
    on EInOutError do
      MessageDlg('Error Printing text.', mtError, [mbOk], 0);
  end;
end;

procedure TMainForm.EnableSearchControls(Enable: Boolean);
{ Enables or disables certain controls so options can't be modified }
{ while search is executing. }
begin
  SearchButton.Enabled := Enable;        // enabled/disable proper controls
  cbRecurse.Enabled := Enable;
  cbFileNamesOnly.Enabled := Enable;
  cbCaseSensitive.Enabled := Enable;
  PathButton.Enabled := Enable;
  EPathName.Enabled := Enable;
  EFileSpec.Enabled := Enable;
  EToken.Enabled := Enable;
  Running := not Enable;                  // set Running flag
  ETokenChange(nil);
```

LISTING 17.8 Continued

```
  with CloseButton do
  begin
    if Enable then
    begin                       // set props of Close/Stop button
      Caption := '&Close';
      Hint := 'Close Application';
    end
    else begin
      Caption := '&Stop';
      Hint := 'Stop Searching';
    end;
  end;
end;

procedure TMainForm.SearchButtonClick(Sender: TObject);
{ Called when Search button is clicked.  Invokes search thread. }
begin
  EnableSearchControls(False);      // disable controls
  FileLB.Clear;                     // clear listbox
  { start thread }
  SearchThread := TSearchThread.Create(cbCaseSensitive.Checked,
    cbFileNamesOnly.Checked, cbRecurse.Checked, EToken.Text,
    EPathName.Text, EFileSpec.Text, Handle);
end;

procedure TMainForm.ETokenChange(Sender: TObject);
begin
  SearchButton.Enabled := not Running and (EToken.Text <> '');
end;

procedure TMainForm.PathButtonClick(Sender: TObject);
{ Called when Path button is clicked.  Allows user to choose new path. }
var
  ShowDir: string;
begin
  ShowDir := EPathName.Text;
  if SelectDirectory(ShowDir, [], 0) then
    EPathName.Text := ShowDir;
end;

procedure TMainForm.FileLBDblClick(Sender: TObject);
{ Called when user double-clicks in listbox. Loads file into IDE }
var
  FileName: string;
  Len: Integer;
```

LISTING 17.8   Continued

```pascal
begin
  { make sure user clicked on a file... }
  if Integer(FileLB.Items.Objects[FileLB.ItemIndex]) > 0 then
  begin
    FileName := FileLB.Items[FileLB.ItemIndex];
    { Trim "File " and ":" from string }
    FileName := Copy(FileName, 6, Length(FileName));
    Len := Length(FileName);
    if FileName[Len] = ':' then SetLength(FileName, Len - 1);
    { Open the project or file }
{$IFNDEF BUILD_EXE}
    if CompareText(ExtractFileExt(FileName), '.DPR') = 0 then
      ActionSvc.OpenProject(FileName, True)
    else
      ActionSvc.OpenFile(FileName);
{$ELSE}
    ShellExecute(0, 'open', PChar(FileName), nil, nil, SW_SHOWNORMAL);
{$ENDIF}
  end;
end;


procedure TMainForm.FileLBDrawItem(Control: TWinControl;
  Index: Integer; Rect: TRect; State: TOwnerDrawState);
{ Called in order to owner draw listbox. }
var
  CurStr: string;
begin
  with FileLB do
  begin
    CurStr := Items.Strings[Index];
    Canvas.FillRect(Rect);                    // clear out rect
    if not cbFileNamesOnly.Checked then       // if not filename only...
    begin
      { if current line is file name... }
      if Integer(Items.Objects[Index]) > 0 then
        Canvas.Font.Style := [fsBold]; // bold font
      end
    else
      Rect.Left := Rect.Left + 15;            // otherwise, indent
    DrawText(Canvas.Handle, PChar(CurStr), Length(CurStr), Rect,
dt_SingleLine);
  end;
end;
```

LISTING 17.8 Continued

```pascal
procedure TMainForm.Font1Click(Sender: TObject);
{ Allows user to pick new font for listbox }
begin
  { Pick new listbox font }
  if FontDialog1.Execute then
    FileLB.Font := FontDialog1.Font;
end;


procedure TMainForm.FormDestroy(Sender: TObject);
{ OnDestroy event handler for form }
begin
  WriteIni;
end;

procedure TMainForm.FormCreate(Sender: TObject);
{ OnCreate event handler for form }
begin
  Application.HintPause := 0;                 // don't wait to show hints
  FOldShowHint := Application.OnShowHint; // set up hints
  Application.OnShowHint := DoShowHint;
  ReadIni;                                    // read reg INI file
end;

procedure TMainForm.DoShowHint(var HintStr: string; var CanShow: Boolean;
  var HintInfo: THintInfo);
{ OnHint event handler for Application }
begin
  { Display application hints on status bar }
  StatusBar.Panels[0].Text := HintStr;
  { Don't show tool tip if we're over our own controls }
  if (HintInfo.HintControl <> nil) and
    (HintInfo.HintControl.Parent <> nil) and
    ((HintInfo.HintControl.Parent = ParamsGB) or
    (HintInfo.HintControl.Parent = OptionsGB) or
    (HintInfo.HintControl.Parent = ControlPanel)) then
    CanShow := False;
  if Assigned(FOldShowHint) then
    FOldShowHint(HintStr, CanSHow, HintInfo);
end;

procedure TMainForm.PrintButtonClick(Sender: TObject);
{ Called when Print button is clicked. }
begin
  if MessageDlg('Send search results to printer?', mtConfirmation,
```

LISTING 17.8   Continued

```
    [mbYes, mbNo], 0) = mrYes then
    PrintStrings(FileLB.Items);
end;

procedure TMainForm.CloseButtonClick(Sender: TObject);
{ Called to stop thread or close application }
begin
  // if thread is running then terminate thread
  if Running then SearchThread.Terminate
  // otherwise close app
  else Close;
end;


procedure TMainForm.FormResize(Sender: TObject);
{ OnResize event handler. Centers controls in form. }
begin
 { divide status bar into two panels with a 1/3 - 2/3 split }
  with StatusBar do
  begin
    Panels[0].Width := Width div 3;
    Panels[1].Width := Width * 2 div 3;
  end;
  { center controls in the middle of the form }
  ControlPanel.Left := (AlignPanel.Width div 2) - (ControlPanel.Width div 2);
end;

procedure TMainForm.PriorityButtonClick(Sender: TObject);
{ Show thread priority form }
begin
  ThreadPriWin.Show;
end;

procedure TMainForm.ReadIni;
{ Reads default values from Registry }
begin
  with SrchIniFile do
  begin
    EPathName.Text := ReadString('Defaults', 'LastPath', 'C:\');
    EFileSpec.Text := ReadString('Defaults', 'LastFileSpec', '*.*');
    EToken.Text := ReadString('Defaults', 'LastToken', '');
    cbFileNamesOnly.Checked := ReadBool('Defaults', 'FNamesOnly', False);
    cbCaseSensitive.Checked := ReadBool('Defaults', 'CaseSens', False);
    cbRecurse.Checked := ReadBool('Defaults', 'Recurse', False);
```

LISTING 17.8 Continued

```pascal
      Left := ReadInteger('Position', 'Left', 100);
      Top := ReadInteger('Position', 'Top', 50);
      Width := ReadInteger('Position', 'Width', 510);
      Height := ReadInteger('Position', 'Height', 370);
    end;
end;

procedure TMainForm.WriteIni;
{ writes current settings back to Registry }
begin
  with SrchIniFile do
  begin
    WriteString('Defaults', 'LastPath', EPathName.Text);
    WriteString('Defaults', 'LastFileSpec', EFileSpec.Text);
    WriteString('Defaults', 'LastToken', EToken.Text);
    WriteBool('Defaults', 'CaseSens', cbCaseSensitive.Checked);
    WriteBool('Defaults', 'FNamesOnly', cbFileNamesOnly.Checked);
    WriteBool('Defaults', 'Recurse', cbRecurse.Checked);
    WriteInteger('Position', 'Left', Left);
    WriteInteger('Position', 'Top', Top);
    WriteInteger('Position', 'Width', Width);
    WriteInteger('Position', 'Height', Height);
  end;
end;

procedure TMainForm.FormClose(Sender: TObject; var Action: TCloseAction);
begin
  Action := caFree;
  Application.OnShowHint := FOldShowHint;
  MainForm := nil;
end;

procedure TMainForm.WndProc(var Message: TMessage);
begin
  if Message.Msg = DDGM_ADDSTR then
  begin
    FileLB.Items.AddObject(PChar(Message.WParam), TObject(Message.LParam));
    StrDispose(PChar(Message.WParam));
  end
  else
    inherited WndProc(Message);
end;

end.
```

> **TIP**
>
> Note the following line from Listing 17.8:
>
> ```
> {$WARN UNIT_PLATFORM OFF}
> ```
>
> This compiler directive is used to silence the compile-time warning that is generated because Main.pas uses the FileCtrl unit, which is a Windows platform specific unit. FileCtrl is marked as such using the platform directive.

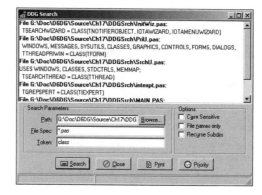

FIGURE 17.7
The DDG Search wizard in action.

Form Wizards

Yet another type of wizard supported by the Open Tools API is the form wizard. Once installed, form wizards are accessed from the New Items dialog box; they generate new forms and units for the user. Chapter 16, "Windows Shell Programming," employs this type of wizard to generate new AppBar forms; however, you didn't get to see the code that made the wizard tick.

Creating a form wizard is fairly straightforward, although there a good number of interface methods that you must implement. Creation of a form wizard can be boiled down to five basic steps:

1. Create a class that descends from TCustomForm, TDataModule, or any TWinControl that will be used as the base form class. This class will typically reside in a separate unit from the wizard. In this case, TAppBar will serve as the base class.

2. Create a TNotifierObject descendent that implements the following interfaces: IOTAWizard, IOTARepositoryWizard, IOTAFormWizard, IOTACreator, and IOTAModuleCreator.

3. In your `IOTAWizard.Execute()` method, you will typically call `IOTAModule Services.GetNewModuleAndClassName()` to obtain a new unit and classname for your wizard and `IOTAModuleServices.CreateModule()` to instruct the IDE to begin creation of the new module.

4. Many of the method implementations for the aforementioned interfaces are one-liners. The non-trivial ones include `IOTAModuleCreator`'s `NewFormFile()` and `NewImplFile()` methods, which will return the code for the form and unit, respectively. The `IOTACreator.GetOwner()` method can also be a little tricky, but the example that follows gives you a good technique for adding the unit to the current project (if any).

5. Complete the `Register()` procedure for the wizard by registering a handler for your new form class using the `RegisterCustomModule()` procedure in the `DsgnIntf` unit and creating your wizard by calling the `RegisterPackageWizard()` procedure in the `ToolsAPI` unit.

Listing 17.9 shows the source code for `ABWizard.pas`, which is the `AppBar` wizard.

LISTING 17.9 `ABWizard.pas`—The Unit Containing the Implementation of the AppBar Wizard

```
unit ABWizard;

interface

uses Windows, Classes, ToolsAPI;

type
  TAppBarWizard = class(TNotifierObject, IOTAWizard, IOTARepositoryWizard,
    IOTAFormWizard, IOTACreator, IOTAModuleCreator)
  private
    FUnitIdent: string;
    FClassName: string;
    FFileName: string;
  protected
    // IOTAWizard methods
    function GetIDString: string;
    function GetName: string;
    function GetState: TWizardState;
    procedure Execute;
    // IOTARepositoryWizard / IOTAFormWizard methods
    function GetAuthor: string;
    function GetComment: string;
    function GetPage: string;
    function GetGlyph: HICON;
```

LISTING 17.9   Continued

```
    // IOTACreator methods
    function GetCreatorType: string;
    function GetExisting: Boolean;
    function GetFileSystem: string;
    function GetOwner: IOTAModule;
    function GetUnnamed: Boolean;
    // IOTAModuleCreator methods
    function GetAncestorName: string;
    function GetImplFileName: string;
    function GetIntfFileName: string;
    function GetFormName: string;
    function GetMainForm: Boolean;
    function GetShowForm: Boolean;
    function GetShowSource: Boolean;
    function NewFormFile(const FormIdent, AncestorIdent: string): IOTAFile;
    function NewImplSource(const ModuleIdent, FormIdent,
      AncestorIdent: string): IOTAFile;
    function NewIntfSource(const ModuleIdent, FormIdent,
      AncestorIdent: string): IOTAFile;
    procedure FormCreated(const FormEditor: IOTAFormEditor);
  end;

implementation

uses Forms, AppBars, SysUtils, DsgnIntf;

{$R CodeGen.res}

type
  TBaseFile = class(TInterfacedObject)
  private
    FModuleName: string;
    FFormName: string;
    FAncestorName: string;
  public
    constructor Create(const ModuleName, FormName, AncestorName: string);
  end;

  TUnitFile = class(TBaseFile, IOTAFile)
  protected
    function GetSource: string;
    function GetAge: TDateTime;
  end;
```

LISTING 17.9   Continued

```
TFormFile = class(TBaseFile, IOTAFile)
protected
  function GetSource: string;
  function GetAge: TDateTime;
end;

{ TBaseFile }

constructor TBaseFile.Create(const ModuleName, FormName,
  AncestorName: string);
begin
  inherited Create;
  FModuleName := ModuleName;
  FFormName := FormName;
  FAncestorName := AncestorName;
end;

{ TUnitFile }

function TUnitFile.GetSource: string;
var
  Text: string;
  ResInstance: THandle;
  HRes: HRSRC;
begin
  ResInstance := FindResourceHInstance(HInstance);
  HRes := FindResource(ResInstance, 'CODEGEN', RT_RCDATA);
  Text := PChar(LockResource(LoadResource(ResInstance, HRes)));
  SetLength(Text, SizeOfResource(ResInstance, HRes));
  Result := Format(Text, [FModuleName, FFormName, FAncestorName]);
end;

function TUnitFile.GetAge: TDateTime;
begin
  Result := -1;
end;

{ TFormFile }

function TFormFile.GetSource: string;
const
  FormText =
    'object %0:s: T%0:s'#13#10'end';
```

LISTING 17.9   Continued

```delphi
begin
  Result := Format(FormText, [FFormName]);
end;

function TFormFile.GetAge: TDateTime;
begin
  Result := -1;
end;

{ TAppBarWizard }

{ TAppBarWizard.IOTAWizard }

function TAppBarWizard.GetIDString: string;
begin
  Result := 'DDG.AppBarWizard';
end;

function TAppBarWizard.GetName: string;
begin
  Result := 'DDG AppBar Wizard';
end;

function TAppBarWizard.GetState: TWizardState;
begin
  Result := [wsEnabled];
end;

procedure TAppBarWizard.Execute;
begin
  (BorlandIDEServices as IOTAModuleServices).GetNewModuleAndClassName(
    'AppBar', FUnitIdent, FClassName, FFileName);
  (BorlandIDEServices as IOTAModuleServices).CreateModule(Self);
end;

{ TAppBarWizard.IOTARepositoryWizard / TAppBarWizard.IOTAFormWizard }

function TAppBarWizard.GetGlyph: HICON;
begin
  Result := 0;   // use standard icon
end;

function TAppBarWizard.GetPage: string;
```

LISTING 17.9   Continued

```
begin
  Result := 'DDG';
end;

function TAppBarWizard.GetAuthor: string;
begin
  Result := 'Delphi 5 Developer''s Guide';
end;

function TAppBarWizard.GetComment: string;
begin
  Result := 'Creates a new AppBar form.'
end;

{ TAppBarWizard.IOTACreator }

function TAppBarWizard.GetCreatorType: string;
begin
  Result := '';
end;

function TAppBarWizard.GetExisting: Boolean;
begin
  Result := False;
end;

function TAppBarWizard.GetFileSystem: string;
begin
  Result := '';
end;

function TAppBarWizard.GetOwner: IOTAModule;
var
  I: Integer;
  ModServ: IOTAModuleServices;
  Module: IOTAModule;
  ProjGrp: IOTAProjectGroup;
begin
  Result := nil;
  ModServ := BorlandIDEServices as IOTAModuleServices;
  for I := 0 to ModServ.ModuleCount - 1 do
  begin
    Module := ModSErv.Modules[I];
    // find current project group
```

Listing 17.9   Continued

```
    if CompareText(ExtractFileExt(Module.FileName), '.bpg') = 0 then
      if Module.QueryInterface(IOTAProjectGroup, ProjGrp) = S_OK then
      begin
        // return active project of group
        Result := ProjGrp.GetActiveProject;
        Exit;
      end;
  end;
end;


function TAppBarWizard.GetUnnamed: Boolean;
begin
  Result := True;
end;


{ TAppBarWizard.IOTAModuleCreator }

function TAppBarWizard.GetAncestorName: string;
begin
  Result := 'TAppBar';
end;


function TAppBarWizard.GetImplFileName: string;
var
  CurrDir: array[0..MAX_PATH] of char;
begin
  // Note: full path name required!
  GetCurrentDirectory(SizeOf(CurrDir), CurrDir);
  Result := Format('%s\%s.pas', [CurrDir, FUnitIdent, '.pas']);
end;


function TAppBarWizard.GetIntfFileName: string;
begin
  Result := '';
end;


function TAppBarWizard.GetFormName: string;
begin
  Result := FClassName;
end;


function TAppBarWizard.GetMainForm: Boolean;
begin
  Result := False;
end;
```

LISTING 17.9   Continued

```pascal
function TAppBarWizard.GetShowForm: Boolean;
begin
  Result := True;
end;

function TAppBarWizard.GetShowSource: Boolean;
begin
  Result := True;
end;

function TAppBarWizard.NewFormFile(const FormIdent,
  AncestorIdent: string): IOTAFile;
begin
  Result := TFormFile.Create('', FormIdent, AncestorIdent);
end;

function TAppBarWizard.NewImplSource(const ModuleIdent, FormIdent,
  AncestorIdent: string): IOTAFile;
begin
  Result := TUnitFile.Create(ModuleIdent, FormIdent, AncestorIdent);
end;

function TAppBarWizard.NewIntfSource(const ModuleIdent, FormIdent,
  AncestorIdent: string): IOTAFile;
begin
  Result := nil;
end;

procedure TAppBarWizard.FormCreated(const FormEditor: IOTAFormEditor);
begin
  // do nothing
end;

end.
```

This unit employs an interesting trick for source code generation: The unformatted source code is stored in an RES file that's linked in with the $R directive. This is a very flexible way to store a wizard's source code so that it can be readily modified. The RES file is built by including a text file and RCDATA resource in an RC file and then compiling that RC file with BRCC32. Listings 17.10 and 17.11 show the contents of CodeGen.txt and CodeGen.rc.

LISTING 17.10 CodeGen.txt—the Resource Template for the AppBar Wizard

```
unit %0:s;

interface

uses
  Windows, Messages, SysUtils, Classes, Graphics, Controls, Forms,
  Dialogs, AppBars;

type
  T%1:s = class(%2:s)
  private
    { Private declarations }
  public
    { Public declarations }
  end;

var
  %1:s: T%1:s;

implementation

{$R *.DFM}

end.
```

LISTING 17.11 CODEGEN.RC

```
CODEGEN RCDATA CODEGEN.TXT
```

Registration of the custom module and wizard occurs inside of a `Register()` procedure in the design package containing the wizard using the following two lines:

```
RegisterCustomModule(TAppBar, TCustomModule);
RegisterPackageWizard(TAppBarWizard.Create);
```

Summary

After reading this chapter, you should have a greater understanding of the various units and interfaces involved in the Delphi Open Tools API. In particular, you should know and understand the issues involved in creating wizards that plug into the IDE. This chapter completes the "Component-Based Development" section of the book. In the next section, "Enterprise Development," you will learn techniques for building enterprise-grade applications, starting with those based on COM+ and MTS.

Enterprise Development

PART

V

IN THIS PART

Transactional Development with COM+/MTS

IN THIS CHAPTER

The release of Windows 2000 brought with it perhaps the largest single step forward for COM since its inception as the underpinnings of OLE 2.0: COM+. COM+ is the latest iteration of COM, and it ships as a standard part of Windows 2000 and Windows XP. This chapter is intended to bring you up to speed on all the various aspects of COM+ and how you can leverage its power in your Delphi applications.

What Is COM+?

Before we progress any further into describing COM+, allow us to set your mind at ease by saying this: Almost everything you know about COM still applies. After all, COM definitely takes no small degree of dedication to learn well, and it would be very disheartening to have to ride the same learning curve once again. The interesting thing about COM+ is that it isn't this strange, new monster, but merely some nice evolutionary changes to COM exist combined with the integration of some of Microsoft's COM-based services that you might already be familiar with. In plain English, COM+ can be boiled down to this: COM with a few new features, integrated with *Microsoft Transaction Server (MTS)* and *Microsoft Message Queue (MSMQ)*.

Because COM+ is based on and fully backward compatible with COM, you have no worries from a Delphi perspective. Delphi works just as great with COM+ as it does with COM. To build optimized COM+ components, there are certainly a few fundamental additions you'll need to know about, particularly with regard to a new type of components called configured that we'll discuss later. But, it's important for you to know that the entire world of COM+ is available to you as a Delphi developer.

Why COM?

Why did Microsoft choose to base COM+ on COM, rather than moving it to some completely different direction? This is a fair question, especially in light of some of the negative comments we all might hear about COM in its skirmishes with competing technologies such as CORBA and *Enterprise Java Beans (EJB)* in the battlefields of the industry tabloids. Not only is COM a good foundation to build on technologically, but also a business case around COM is very compelling when you consider that

- COM is programming language independent.
- COM is supported by every major Windows development tool.
- Every 32-bit Windows user is already running COM, which puts the installed base at somewhere around 150 million users (according to Microsoft).
- The Giga Information Group recently reported that COM is a $670 million market (not including Microsoft).

Probably the biggest drawback of COM is its reputation for being difficult to scale to large numbers of users involved in large numbers of transactions. In Microsoft fashion, a major intent of COM+ is to leverage the assets s, while attempting to eliminate the liabilities.

We can classify COM+ features into three distinct categories: administration, services, and runtime. Administration is primarily handled in the Component Services administration tool, which is discussed throughout this chapter. We will tackle the discussion of services and runtime in turn. Because services make up the bulk of the new features in COM+, we'll discuss those first.

Services

COM+ services are the things that we today consider to be add-ons to COM. Technology currently found in MTS and MSMQ, for example, make up some of the services found in COM+. Think of services as systems built by Microsoft on top of COM+ designed to somehow add value to component-based development. As we mentioned, some services, such as transactions and queued components, are present thanks to off-the-shelf technology. Consequently, if you have experience with these technologies already, you'll have an advantage as you begin to write COM+ applications. Other services, however, such as object pooling and late-bound-events are probably new to you and might take some getting used to.

Transactions

As the "T" in MTS, it should be no surprise to find transactions playing a major role in COM+. COM+ implements the MTS model for transactions, which is described in greater detail later in this chapter. Without transaction support, there is no way that collection objects would be able to support a complicated business application. For example, a transaction involving an online purchase of some item might involve the participation of several objects communicating with one or more databases to receive the request, check inventory, debit the credit card, update the accounting ledger, and issue a ship order. All these things needs to happen in concert; if something goes wrong in any of these processes, the state of all objects and data needs to be rolled back to the state they were in before the entire transaction began. As you can imagine, this process of managing transactions is even more complicated when the objects involved are spread across multiple machines.

Transactions are controlled centrally by the MS *Distributed Transaction Coordinator (DTC)*. When a COM+ application calls for transactions, the DTC will enlist the assistance of and coordinate other software elements, including transaction managers, resource managers, and resource dispensers. Each computer participating in a transaction has a transaction manager that tracks transaction activity on that specific machine. Transaction managers, however, are ignorant of data because persistent information such as database data or message queue messages are managed by a resource manager. A resource dispenser manages non-persistent state information, such as database connections. Each of these specialized elements managed by the DTC knows how to commit and recover its specific resource.

Security

As the introduction of one new technology quickly follows another in today's insanely paced world of software development, we occasionally reflect with fond remembrance on the olden days of PC software development, when applications consisted of a .EXE or a .COM file and a network was a place to share data files with your co-workers. Business applications today often consist of multiple types of user interfaces (Windows, Web-based, Java, and so on) communicating with software components distributed across a network, which in turn communicates with one or more database servers on the network. Our success as developers is now linked not only to our ability to tie disparate application elements together, but also to provide a means by which they can communicate in privacy. This means building security into distributed applications that enables components to authenticate one another, determine what services they should offer one another, and provide a means for private communication between one another.

The notion of security has become common sense at this point. We all understand that most data needs to be protected; for example, human resources data shouldn't be accessible to all employees, sales data shouldn't be accessible to your competitors, and so on. Equally, component functionality also needs to be secure; perhaps only administrators should have the right to use certain objects or only department managers should have access to a particular business rules engine. In practice, however, building this type of security into distributed applications can be a time-consuming process, and security features naturally take a backseat to core functionality in project schedules.

COM+ provides a well-constructed set of security features that addresses many of these issues. COM+ makes security more of an administrative issue than a programmatic one, and therefore helps you to spend your time developing application logic and less time writing security code. Configuring COM+ application security in the Component Services administration tool is a one-time process, and your application can remain free of security-specific code. At the same time, COM+ does provide APIs for accessing security information for cases in which you do need to go beyond the provided functionality. My goal here is to provide you with an overview of security architecture for COM+ server applications and how to use security in your COM+ applications.

Role-Based Security

COM+'s security architecture is often referred to as role-based. Rather than managing accounts for individual users, COM+ applications rely on categories or groups of users referred to as roles. Roles work hand-in-hand with the operating system-based security because the members of roles are the user accounts on the Windows 2000 server or domain. Roles can be created on an application-by-application basis using the Component Services administration tool, and the process is rather straightforward. This is done by right-clicking on the Roles node of the COM+ application in the treeview on the left in the Component Services administration tool. After a role has been added, another right-click can add users to the role. Figure 18.1 illustrates the process of adding users to a role.

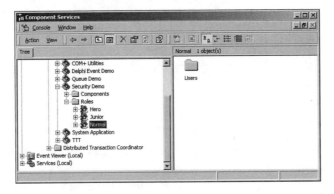

FIGURE 18.1
Using the Component Services administration tools to configure roles.

You can see from Figure 18.1 that in this example, the COM+ application has three roles: Junior, Normal, and Hero. These are simply names made up to indicate three different groups of users we plan to provide differing functionality for in our COM+ application. Noteworthy is the fact that the actual authentication is handled automatically by the OS, and COM+ builds on top of those services.

Role-Based Security Configuration

Arguably the slickest aspect of COM+'s role-based security system is that security can be established at the application, component, interface, or even method level! This means that you can control which roles have access to which methods without writing a line of code.

The first step to configuring COM+ application security is to enable security at the application level. This is done by editing the properties of the application in the Component Services administration tool and switching to the Security tab, which is shown in Figure 18.2.

Application security is enabled when the Enforce Access Checks For This Application check box is checked. This dialog also enables selection of the security level, which can be set to perform security checking at the process level only or at the process and component level.

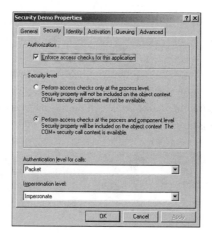

FIGURE 18.2

Configuring COM+ application security.

Enabling security only at the process level has the effect of locking the front door to the COM+ application, where all members of roles assigned to the application have the key to that door. When this option is selected, no security checking will be performed on the component, interface, or method level, and security context information will not be maintained for objects running in the application. This type of security is useful when you don't need granular security control, but simply want to limit overall access to the COM+ application to a specific group of users. This type of security also has the advantage in increased performance because security checks don't need to be made by COM+ during execution of the application.

Enabling security at the process and component level ensures that role-based security checks will be made at the component, interface, and method level and security context information will be available to objects in the application. Although this provides maximum control and flexibility, note that a performance of your COM+ application will suffer slightly because of the increased level of management that COM+ will need to perform during execution.

The security properties dialog box shown in the Figure 18.2 also provides for configuration of the authentication level of the COM+ application. The authentication level determines the degree to which authentication is performed on client calls into the application. Each successive authentication level option provides for a greater level of security, and the options are shown in Table 18.1.

TABLE 18.1 COM+ Authentication Levels

Level	Description
None	No authentication occurs.
Connect	Authenticates credentials only when the connection is made.
Call	Authenticates credentials at the beginning of every call.
Packet	Authenticates credentials and verifies that all call data is received. This is the default setting for COM+ server applications.
Packet Integrity	Authenticates credentials and verifies that no call data has been modified in transit.
Packet Privacy	Authenticates credentials and encrypts the packet, including the data and the sender's identity and signature.

Note that authentication requires the participation of the client as well as the server. COM+ will examine the client and the server preference for authentication and will use the maximum of the two. The client authentication preference can be set using any one of the following techniques:

- The machine-wide setting specified in the Component Services administration tool (or DCOMCNFG on non-Windows 2000/XP machines)
- The application-level setting specified in the Component Services administration tool (or DCOMCNFG on non-Windows 2000/XP machines)
- The process-level setting specified programmatically using the `CoInitializeSecurity()` COM API call
- An on-the-fly setting that can be specified programmatically using the `CoSetProxyBlanket()` API

Finally, the properties security dialog box shown in Figure 18.2 allows configuration of the application impersonation level. The impersonation level setting dictates to what degree the server application might impersonate its client in order to access other resources on behalf of clients. Table 18.2 explains the options for impersonation level.

TABLE 18.2 COM+ Impersonation Levels

Level	Description
Anonymous	The client is anonymous to the server.
Identify	The server can obtain the client's identity, and can impersonate the client only to perform Access Control checking.

18

TRANSACTIONAL
DEVELOPMENT

TABLE 18.2   Continued

Level	Description
Impersonate	The server can impersonate the client while acting on its behalf, although with restrictions. The server can access resources on the same computer as the client. If the server is on the same computer as the client, it can access network resources as the client. If the server is on a computer different from the client, it can only access resources that are on the same computer as the server. This is the default setting for COM+ server applications.
Delegate	The server can impersonate the client while acting on its behalf, whether or not on the same computer as the client. During impersonation, the client's credentials can be passed to any number of machines. This is the broadest permission that can be granted.

Like authentication, impersonation can also only be accomplished with the consent of the client. The client's consent and preferences can be established exactly the same as authentication, using Component Services administration tool, DCOMCNFG, or the CoInitializeSecurity() and CoSetProxyBlanket() APIs.

After application security has been configured, security can then be configured for components, interfaces, and methods of the application. This is done in a similar manner by editing the properties of the item in the tree and choosing the Security tab. This will invoke a dialog box with a page similar to that shown in Figure 18.3.

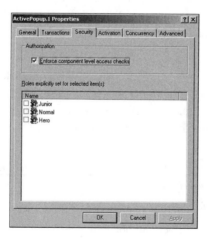

FIGURE 18.3

Configuring COM+ component security.

The dialog box shown in Figure 18.3 is fairly straightforward; it enables you to specify whether security checks should be enabled for the item and which roles are to be allowed access to the item.

Multitier Performance

When designing multitier applications that employ COM+ security, there are a number of performance considerations you should weigh. First and foremost, always bear in mind that one of the primary goals of a multitier system is to improve overall system scalability. One mistake that often compromises scalability and performance is over securing an application by implementing security at multiple tiers. A better solution would be to leverage COM+ services by implementing security only or mostly at the middle tier. For example, rather than impersonating the client in order to gain access to a database, it is more efficient to access the database using a common connection that can be pooled among multiple clients.

Programmatic Security

Up until now, we've focused primarily on declarative (or administration-driven) security; however we did mention that it is also possible to program security into COM+ applications. The most common thing you might want to do is determine whether the caller of a particular method belongs to a specific role. This enables you to control not only method access, but also method behavior, based on the role of the client. To serve this purpose, COM+ provides not one but two means for making this determination. There is a method of IObjectContext called IsCallerInRole(), which is defined as

```
function IsCallerInRole(const bstrRole: WideString): Bool; safecall;
```

This function is used by passing the name of the role in the bstrRole parameter, and it will return a Boolean value indicating whether the current caller belongs to the specified role. A reference to the current object context can be found by calling the GetObjectContext() API, which is defined as

```
function GetObjectContext: IObjectContext;
```

The following code checks to see if the caller is in the Hero role prior to performing a task:

```
var
  Ctx: IObjectContext;
begin
  Ctx := GetObjectContext;
  if (Ctx <> nil) and (Ctx.IsCallerInRole('Hero')) then
  begin
    // do something interesting
  end;
end;
```

Similarly, an `IsCallerInRole()` method is also found on the `ISecurityCallContext` interface, a reference that can be obtained using the `CoGetCallContext()` API. This version of the method is actually preferred, simply because `ISecurityCallContext` makes handy a lot of other security information, such as the caller and its authentication and impersonation level.

Just-In-Time Activation

Just-In-Time (JIT) activation refers to functionality already present in COM+ that enables an object to be transparently destroyed and re-created without the knowledge of the client application. JIT activation potentially enables a server to handle a higher volume of clients because resources used by an object can be reclaimed by the system when it is deactivated.

The object developers has full control over when an object is deactivated, and objects should only be deactivated when they have no state to maintain. An object can be deactivated using the `SetComplete()` or `SetAbort()` methods of `IObjectContext` or the `SetDeactivateOnReturn()` method of `IContextState`.

Queued Components

Delphi developers normally don't have to be lectured on the benefits of briefcase model applications. When MIDAS was introduced in Delphi 3, the barrier of entry was forever lowered for creating applications having the capability to operate even when the client is disconnected from the server. Delphi developers quickly realized the power of enabling their users to work with their data in a disconnected, briefcase model, and embraced MIDAS as well as other technologies that provide this capability. Rather than having to write complicated code to, for example, enable a salesman to edit his customer database on his laptop while on the road and synchronize when he gets back into the office, this functionality is now easily accessible simply by dropping a few components and writing a few lines of code.

This is all really great if you happen to be data, but what to do if you're an object? As object remoting technologies such as DCOM, MTS/COM+, and CORBA become easier to implement in our tools, our reliance on such technologies increases as we build solutions for our companies and clients. Consequently, this reliance increases as we employ object remoting technologies to build ever-more-complex distributed applications. As a result of all this, distributed component applications—like data applications—also have the need to function when disconnected from servers.

Queued Components: The Object Briefcase

COM+ queued components answer this need. Based on *MSMQ (Microsoft Message Queue)* technology, queued components provide a means for COM+ clients to asynchronously invoke methods of COM+ server components. In essence, this means that clients can create instances of server objects and invoke their methods without regard to whether the server is actually accessible to the client. COM+ manages this by storing the method invocations in a queue and executing the methods at a later time when the server is accessible. What's more, the server objects likewise have little reason to know or care whether their methods are being invoked directly or via a COM+ queue. Our goal here is to cover the essential elements of working with COM+ queued components.

Figure 18.4 illustrates how queued components are internally implemented. When the client makes a method call on a queued component, that method call is captured by the recorder, which packages up the call and parameters and places it into a queue. Because the client has no knowledge that it isn't actually communicating with the server, you can see that the recorder server as a sort of a proxy for the server. The recorder knows how to behave because it obtains information on the server from its type library and its configuration or registration information. The listener removes the message, which contains the call information, from the queue and passes it on to the player. Finally, the player unpackages the call information (along with related information, such as the client's security context) and executes the method call on the server.

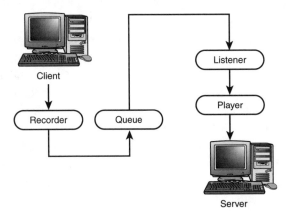

FIGURE 18.4
COM+ queued component architecture.

"All this sounds cool," you might be saying to yourself, "but I'll bet implementing it requires a degree in some new variety of non-Newtonian physics." If you did say that to yourself, you're only half right; it is cool, but it's also very easy to do, as you will soon see.

Why Queued Components?

Before jumping into implementation, however, we'd like to address some of the specific reasons for using queued components.

- System scalability—In a non-queued system, there will be a finite number of server objects capable of handling requests from clients at any given time. When all these objects become tied up handling client calls, other incoming client calls will be blocked until an object finishes and again becomes available. In a system having a large number of simultaneous transactions, this can seriously limit the number of concurrent clients that can be serviced. Using queues, the call always returns immediately to the client after being queued and played back to servers in the servers' own time. This enables the system to handle a greater number of concurrent transactions.

  Scalability is also increased on the back end because the client doesn't manage the lifetime of the server. Rather than being active while the client carries on with its processing and various method calls, a queued server only needs to be active while calls are being played back by the recorder. Reducing the amount of time a server needs to remain in memory means that a greater number of servers can be activated over a given period of time with a given amount of RAM.

- Briefcase model—As we mentioned, COM+ enables queued components to behave in a disconnected manner in much the same way MIDAS does for data. This enables clients to work without being connected to their network and method calls to be played back to the server when the client connects to the network at a later time.

- Fail-safety—If you are creating a mission-critical application that requires a high degree of availability, such as an e-commerce storefront, the last thing you want to happen is for the system to go down because your front end is having trouble communicating with server objects. Queued components provide an ideal safety net to prevent this problem because they will queue method calls intended for servers if the servers become unavailable and play them back when the server again comes online.

- Load scheduling—Rather than having your servers work like rented mules during their peak hours of activity and sit nearly dormant during the other hours of the day, using queued components you can spread processing throughout the day to even the workflow and place less demand on your servers at any specific time.

Creating a Server

There's little difference between creating a queued component and a creating normal COM/COM+ component. The biggest adjustment you will need to make is that all methods on queued interfaces must accept only in parameters and must not make use of return values. Of course, these limitations make perfect sense when you consider the fact that the client won't be sitting around waiting for the server to return any values or out parameters. Also, you will need to perform a few extra steps as far as component configuration at install time.

To illustrate, we will create a Delphi server that contains one COM+ class with one interface with one method. To make life easier, we'll get started using the Automation Object Wizard accessible via the File, New Main menu item. We call this object QTest, and the wizard automatically names the primary interface IQTest. (Don't worry, it's easier than it sounds.) To the IQTest interface we add one method, which is defined in the type library editor as follows:

```
procedure SendText(Value: WideString; Time: TDateTime) [dispid $00000001];
  safecall;
```

The idea is that this method takes two parameters: the first a string message and the second the time on the client when the method was called. Our implementation of this method simply writes this information, in addition to the time the message was processed by the server, to a log file we create called c:\queue.txt. The implementation file for this Automation object is shown Listing 18.1.

LISTING 18.1 TestImpl.pas—Implementation of Queued Object

```
unit TestImpl;

interface

uses
  Windows, ComObj, ActiveX, Srv_TLB, StdVcl;

type
  TQTest = class(TAutoObject, IQTest)
  protected
    procedure SendText(const Value: WideString; Time: TDateTime); safecall;
  end;

implementation

uses ComServ, SysUtils;

procedure TQTest.SendText(const Value: WideString; Time: TDateTime);
const
  SFileName = 'c:\queue.txt';
  SEntryFormat = 'Send time: %s'#13#10'Write time: %s'#13#10 +
    'Message: %s'#13#10#13#10;
var
  F: THandle;
  WriteStr: string;
begin
  F := CreateFile(SFileName, GENERIC_WRITE, FILE_SHARE_READ, nil, OPEN_ALWAYS,
    FILE_ATTRIBUTE_NORMAL, 0);
  if F = INVALID_HANDLE_VALUE then RaiseLastWin32Error;
  try
```

LISTING 18.1 Continued

```
    FileSeek(F, 0, 2);  // go to EOF
    WriteStr := Format(SEntryFormat, [DateTimeToStr(Time),
      DateTimeToStr(Now), Value]);
    FileWrite(F, WriteStr[1], Length(WriteStr));
  finally
    CloseHandle(F);
  end;
end;

initialization
  TAutoObjectFactory.Create(ComServer, TQTest, Class_QTest,
    ciMultiInstance, tmApartment);
end.
```

After the server has been created, it needs to be installed into a new COM+ application using either the Component Services management tool or the COM+ Administration Library API. Using the Component Services tool, the first step is to create a new empty application by selecting that option from the local menu of the COM+ Applications node in the tree and following the prompts. Once the application has been created, the next step is to edit the application's properties to mark the application as queued, as shown in Figure 18.5. We also chose to enable queue listening on this application so that it would immediately play any incoming messages on its queue when it is active. The configuration is shown in Figure 18.5.

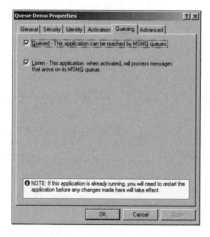

FIGURE 18.5
Configuring a queued COM+ application.

To install the server into the COM+ application, select New, Component from the local menu of the Component node of the application in the tree. This invokes the COM Component Install Wizard, which can install a new component using the defaults and select the name of the COM+ server DLL created earlier. After installation into the application, edit the properties of the IQTest interface on this object to support queuing as shown in Figure 18.6.

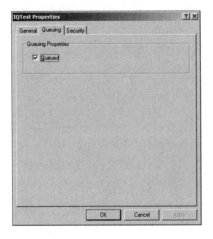

FIGURE 18.6

Specifying an interface as queued.

Note that COM+ requires that queuing be enabled on both the COM+ application and the interface level.

Creating a Client

The workflow for creating a queued component client is identical to creating a client of any old Automation client. In this case, create an application with a main form as shown in Figure 18.7.

FIGURE 18.7

A client application for a queued component.

When the Send button is clicked, the contents of the edit is sent to the server via its SendText() method. The code for this unit corresponding to this form is shown in Listing 18.2.

LISTING 18.2   Ctrl.pas—The Main Unit for a Queued Component Client

```pascal
unit Ctrl;

interface

uses
  Windows, Messages, SysUtils, Classes, Graphics, Controls, Forms, Dialogs,
  StdCtrls, ColorGrd, ExtCtrls, Srv_TLB, Buttons;

type
  TControlForm = class(TForm)
    BtnExit: TButton;
    Edit: TEdit;
    BtnSend: TButton;
    procedure BtnExitClick(Sender: TObject);
    procedure BtnSendClick(Sender: TObject);
    procedure FormCreate(Sender: TObject);
  private
    FIntf: IQTest;
  end;

var
  ControlForm: TControlForm;

implementation

{$R *.DFM}

uses ComObj, ActiveX;

// Need to import CoGetObject because import in the ActiveX unit is incorrect:
function MyCoGetObject(pszName: PWideChar; pBindOptions: PBindOpts;
  const iid: TIID; out ppv): HResult; stdcall;
  external 'ole32.dll' name 'CoGetObject';

procedure TControlForm.BtnExitClick(Sender: TObject);
begin
  Close;
end;

procedure TControlForm.BtnSendClick(Sender: TObject);
begin
  FIntf.SendText(Edit.Text, Now);
  Edit.Clear;
end;
```

LISTING 18.2   Continued

```
procedure TControlForm.FormCreate(Sender: TObject);
const
  SMoniker: PWideChar = 'queue:/new:{64C576F0-C9A7-420A-9EAB-0BE98264BC9D}';
begin
  // Create object using a moniker that specifies queued creation
  OleCheck(MyCoGetObject(SMoniker, nil, IQTest, FIntf));
end;

end.
```

The only element in this unit that sets it apart from a standard Automation controller is the means by which it creates the server object instance. Rather than using, for example, the `CoCreateInstance()` COM API function, this client uses the `CoGetObject()` API. `CoGetObject()` enables an object to be created via a moniker, and COM+ allows a special string moniker syntax that can be used to invoke components in a queued manner. The general syntax of this moniker is `queue:/new:` followed by the CLSID or program ID of the server object. The following are all examples of properly formatted queue monikers:

```
queue:/new:Srv.IQTest
queue:/new:{64C576F0-C9A7-420A-9EAB-0BE98264BC9D}
queue:/new:64C576F0-C9A7-420A-9EAB-0BE98264BC9D
```

There are also a number of queue moniker parameters that you can incorporate into the string to modify the destination queue or queue behavior. The following list describes these moniker parameters:

- `ComputerName`—The parameter's value is the string name of the computer containing the queue. Specifies the computer name portion of a queue pathname. If not specified, the computer name associated with the configured application is used.

- `QueueName`—The parameter's value is the string name of the queue on the target server machine. Specifies the queue name. If not specified, the queue name associated with the configured application is used.

- `PathName`—The queue pathname must be formatted as `ComputerName\QueueName`. Specifies the complete queue pathname. If not specified, the queue pathname associated with the configured application is used.

- `FormatName`—The parameter's value is the format name of queue, for example, `DIRECT=9CA3600F-7E8F-11D2-88C5-00A0C90AB40E`. Specifies the queue format name.

- `AppSpecific`—For example, `AppSpecific=8675309`. An unsigned integer design for application-specific use.

- AuthLevel—MQMSG_AUTH_LEVEL_NONE (0) or MQMSG_AUTH_LEVEL_ALWAYS (1). Specifies the message authentication level. An authenticated message is digitally signed and requires a certificate for the user sending the message.

- Delivery—MQMSG_DELIVERY_EXPRESS (0) or MQMSG_DELIVERY_RECOVERABLE (1). Specifies the message delivery option. Ignored for transacted queues.

- EncryptAlgorithm—CALG_RC2, CALG_RC4, or other integer value recognized by COM+ as an identifier representing an acceptable encryption algorithm. Specifies the encryption algorithm to be used by COM+ to encrypt and decrypt the message.

- HashAlgorithm—CALG_MD2, CALG_MD4, CALG_MD5, CALG_SHA, CALG_SHA1, CALG_MAC, CALG_SSL3_SHAMD5, CALG_HMAC, CALG_TLS1PRF, or other integer value recognized by COM+ as acceptable. Specifies a cryptographic hash function.

- Journal—MQMSG_JOURNAL_NONE (0), MQMSG_DEADLETTER (1), or MQMSG_JOURNAL (2). Specifies the COM+ queue message journal option.

- Label—Any string. Specifies a message label string up to MQ_MAX_MSG_LABEL_LEN characters.

- MaxTimeToReachQueue—INFINITE, LONG_LIVED, or an integer value indicating a specific number of seconds. Specifies a maximum time, in seconds, for the message to reach the queue.

- MaxTimeToReceive—INFINITE, LONG_LIVED, or an integer value indicating a specific number of seconds. Specifies a maximum time, in seconds, for the message to be received by the target application.

- Priority—MQ_MIN_PRIORITY (0), Q_MAX_PRIORITY (7), MQ_DEFAULT_PRIORITY (3), or any integer between 0 and 7. Specifies a message priority level, within the MSMQ values permitted.

- PrivLevel—MQMSG_PRIV_LEVEL_NONE, NONE, MQMSG_PRIV_LEVEL_BODY, BODY, MQMSG_PRIV_LEVEL_BODY_BASE, BODY_BASE, MQMSG_PRIV_LEVEL_BODY_ENHANCED, or BODY_ENHANCED. Specifies the privacy level that is used to encrypt messages.

- Trace—MQMSG_TRACE_NONE (0) or QMSG_SEND_ROUTE_TO_REPORT_QUEUE (1). Specifies trace options, used in tracing COM+ queue routing.

Using some of these options, other valid queue monikers might be

```
queue:Priority=6,ComputerName=foo/new:{64C576F0-C9A7-420A-9EAB-0BE98264BC9D}
queue:PathName=drevil\myqueue/new:{64C576F0-C9A7-420A-9EAB-0BE98264BC9D}
```

Running the Server

After invoking the client and typing a few strings into the edit, you can check for yourself on your hard disk, and you will see that the file c:\queue.txt isn't present on your hard disk.

That is because the server application needs to start running before queued messages will be played back. Three ways to start the server are as follows:

1. Manually—Using the Component Services tool. This can be done simply by selecting Start from the local menu of the application node in the tree.

2. Programmatically—Using the COM+ Administration Library API.

3. Scheduled—Using scripting. This can be done using a script similar to the following in the task scheduler:

```
dim cat
set cat = CreateObject("COMAdmin.COMAdminCatalog");
cat.StartApplication("YourApplication");
```

After starting the application, you will see the `c:\queue.txt` file present on your hard disk. Its contents will look something like this:

```
Send time:  7/6/2001 7:15:08 AM
Write time: 7/6/2001 7:15:18 AM
Message: this is a test

Send time:  7/6/2001 7:15:10 AM
Write time: 7/6/2001 7:15:18 AM
Message: this is another
```

Object Pooling

You might remember that wacky `CanBePooled()` method of `IObjectControl` that MTS simply ignored. The good news is that `CanBePooled()` is no longer ignored, and COM+ does support object pooling. Object pooling provides the ability to keep a pool of some particular number of instances of a particular object, and have the objects in this pool used by multiple clients. Similar to JIT activation, the goal is to increase overall throughput of the system. However, JIT activation carries the assumption that objects aren't expensive to create or destroy (because it is done frequently). If an object is expensive to create or destroy, it makes more sense to keep instances around after their creation by pooling them.

A number of limitations are imposed on objects that want to support pooling. These include

- The object must be stateless so that it maintains no instance-specific data between method calls.

- The object must have no thread affinity. That is, they shouldn't be bound to any particular thread and they shouldn't use thread local storage (TLS, or "threadvar" variables in the Delphi world).

- The object must be aggregatable.

- Resources must be manually enlisted in transactions. The resource manager cannot automatically enlist resources on the object's behalf.
- The object must implement `IObjectControl`.

Events

Delphi developers don't need to be sold on the importance of events. How else would we know when a button was clicked or a record posted? However, although COM developers have also been aware of the importance of events, they often avoided them because of the complexity of implementation. COM+ introduces a new event model, which—thank heavens—isn't tied to the Byzantine connection points model that has been common in COM to this point.

The typical picture we imagine when we think about the relationship between COM client and server objects is fairly linear; clients invoke methods on servers and servers do useful things in response to the client call and optionally provide some data back to the client in the form of a return value and out parameters. It's probably true that this relationship is an accurate representation of probably more than 90% of COM client/server interactions, but you don't have to be a COM guru to realize that this model is limited, particularly with regard to clients having the ability to be quickly updated when some server data changes.

The simplest way to obtain such a notification would be for clients to poll servers on a periodic basis in order to check whether the information in which they're interested changes. However, the disadvantages of polling are pretty self-evident; clients waste a lot of cycles sending polls, servers likewise waste a lot of clocks responding to polls, extraneous network traffic can be generated, and the overall scalability of the system is diminished to the sum of all this increased load on client, server, and wire.

More desirable, but still low tech, is a system whereby clients can pass servers one or more predefined interfaces to call back on when the information in question changes. However, this system essentially has to be re-invented for every different interface you want to use, and it is incumbent upon the server to write specialized code to track multiple client connections.

Traditional COM provides a more efficient and structured solution to this problem, called events. This solution involves the use of the connection points, which provide servers with the capability to track clients that want to be notified of information changes as well as the means for servers to call client methods to make the notifications. Connection points are an example of what is known as a *tightly coupled event (TCE)* system. In a TCE system, clients and servers are mutually aware of the other's identity. Additionally, TCE systems require that clients and servers be running simultaneously, and they provide no means for filtering of events. The connection point system also has the inherent disadvantages because it is rather complex to implement and use, and clients are forced to implement entire event interfaces, even if they are only interested in a single method of the interface.

COM+ contains a new event system that solves some of these problems and adds some nice additional features. The COM+ event model is known as a *Loosely Coupled Event (LCE)* system. It is referred to as such because there is no hard connection between servers (known as *event publishers*) and clients (known as *event subscribers*). Instead, publishers register with the COM+ catalog the events they want to publish, and subscribers separately register with the COM+ catalog the events in which they are interested. When a publisher fires an event, the COM+ runtime reviews its database to determine which clients should receive an event notification and sends the notification to those clients. What's more, clients don't even have to be running when the event is fired; COM will activate clients upon invocation of the event. Additionally, the event registration model supports method-level granularity. This means that subscribers aren't forced to implement methods for events for which they have no interest. Figure 18.8 provides an illustration of the COM+ event system.

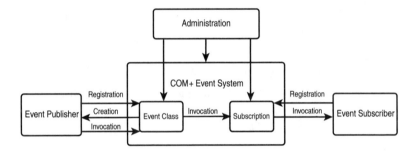

FIGURE 18.8

The COM+ event system architecture.

As Figure 18.8 shows, the process begins when the publisher registers a new event class. This can be done using the Component Services administration tool or using the `ICOMAdminCatalog.InstallEventClass()` method. Once registered, the object that implements the event class will reside in the COM+ runtime. The publisher or another object can then call the `CoCreateInstance()` COM API call to create an instance of this object and call methods on this object to fire events.

On the subscriber side, the subscriber can register for an event class permanently, using the Component Services administration tool, or in a transient manner using the COM admin catalog API. Permanent subscription means that the subscribing component doesn't need to be active when the event fires; the COM+ runtime will automatically create the component before invoking the event. Transient subscriptions are intended for already active components that want to receive event notifications only temporarily. When the publisher fires an event, COM+ will iterate over all the registered subscribers, invoking the event on each. Note that it isn't possible to determine the order in which COM+ will iterate over the clients when invoking an event. However, it is possible to gain some control over the firing of events using event filters, which we describe in more detail later.

Speaking practically, creating a COM+ event can be boiled down to a five-step process:

1. Creating an event class server
2. Registering and configuring the event class server
3. Creating a subscriber server
4. Registering and configuring the subscriber servers
5. Publishing of events

We'll take these steps one at a time to demonstrate a Delphi implementation of COM+ events.

Creating an Event Class Server

The first step to creating an event class server is to create an in-process COM server to which you will add a COM object. The important distinction to bear in mind between creating an event class server and creating a regular COM server is that an event class server carries with it no implementation—it only serves as a vehicle for definition of the event class.

You create an event class server in Delphi by using the ActiveX Library wizard to create a new COM server DLL and the Automation Object wizard to generate the event class and interface. Call this object EventObj. The wizards leave you off in the Type Library Editor in order to complete the definition of the server, where you add a method called MyEvent to the IEventObj interface that will serve as the event method. The implementation file produced for this type library is shown in Listing 18.3.

LISTING 18.3   PubMain.pas—The Main Unit for an Event Class Server

```
unit PubMain;

interface

uses
  ComObj, ActiveX, Publisher_TLB, StdVcl;

type
  TEventObj = class(TAutoObject, IEventObj)
  protected
    function MyEvent(const EventParam: WideString): HResult; safecall;
  end;

implementation
```

LISTING 18.3 Continued

```
uses ComServ;

function TEventObj.MyEvent(const EventParam: WideString): HResult;
begin

end;

initialization
  TAutoObjectFactory.Create(ComServer, TEventObj, Class_EventObj,
    ciMultiInstance, tmApartment);
end.
```

That's all there is to creating the event class server. Note that it's not necessary to register this server. Registration is handled specially, and we discuss it in the next step.

Registration and Configuration of the Event Class Server

In this phase, we will again make use of the Component Services administration tool. You'll use this tool often as you develop COM+ applications. You'll find this tool in the Administrative Tools group of the Programs section of the Start menu. The first thing you'll need to do in the Component Services administration tool is create a new COM+ application. You can do this by selecting New, Application from the local menu of the COM+ Applications node in the tree view on the left. This will invoke the COM+ Application Install Wizard as shown in Figure 18.9. In this wizard, I choose to create a new application from scratch and call it Delphi Event Demo.

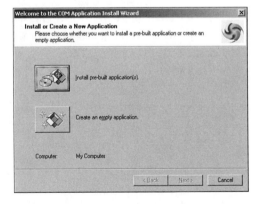

FIGURE 18.9
Using the Component Services tool to add a COM+ application.

After the COM+ application has been installed, you can install the event class server into the application. This is done by selecting New, Component from the local menu of the Components node under the new application in the tree. This invokes the COM Component Install Wizard, a frame of which is shown in Figure 18.10.

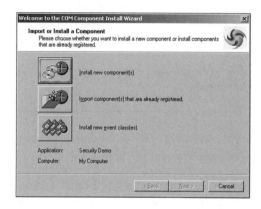

FIGURE 18.10
Using the Component Services tool to add a COM+ component.

In this wizard, install a new event class, and select the filename of the event class server that was just created. With that done, it's time to move on to the creation of the subscriber server.

Creation of a Subscriber Server

A subscriber server is essentially a standard Delphi Automation server. The only catch is that you need to implement the event interface that you defined when creating the event class server. We accomplish this by using the type library from the event class server in the subscriber server and adding the IEventObj interface to the implements list of the co-class. Figure 18.11 shows the SubObj coclass, containing both ISubObj and IEventObj, and the implementation file for this type library is shown in Listing 18.4.

LISTING 18.4   SubMain.pas—The Implementation Unit for the Event Server

```
unit SubMain;

interface

uses
  ComObj, ActiveX, Subscriber_TLB, StdVcl, Publisher_TLB;

type
  TSubObj = class(TAutoObject, ISubObj, IEventObj)
  protected
```

LISTING 18.4   Continued

```
  function MyEvent(const EventParam: WideString): HResult; safecall;
  { Protected declarations }
end;

implementation

uses ComServ, Windows;

function TSubObj.MyEvent(const EventParam: WideString): HResult;
begin
  MessageBox(0, PChar(string(EventParam)), 'COM+ Event!', MB_OK);
  Result := S_OK;
end;

initialization
  TAutoObjectFactory.Create(ComServer, TSubObj, Class_SubObj,
    ciMultiInstance, tmApartment);
end.
```

FIGURE 18.11
The IEventObj *interface in the type library editor.*

You can see that the implementation of the event is quite earth shattering; a message box is
displayed showing a real, live text string! Again, there is no need to register this server as you
would a standard COM server. That housekeeping is handled in the next step.

Registration and Configuration of the Subscriber Servers

To register the subscriber server, reopen the Component Services administration tool, and
choose New, Component from the local menu just as you did for the event class server. The

difference is that this time you should choose to install a new component in the COM
Component Install Wizard and select the subscriber DLL.

After the subscriber server is installed, you can create a new subscription for the subscriber
server by selecting New, Subscription from the Subscriptions node under your new subscriber
server. This brings up the New Subscription Wizard, which allows you to define the correlation
between the publisher and subscriber interfaces or methods. In this case, select IEventObj for
the subscriber method(s) and Publisher.EventObj for the event class. Enter **Subscription of**
Doom as the name of this subscription and choose to enable the server immediately, as shown in
Figure 18.12.

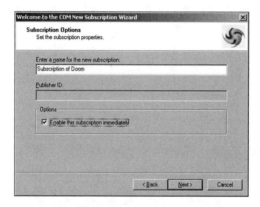

FIGURE 18.12
Subscription wizard in the Component Services tool.

Figure 18.13 shows the complete COM+ application definition as shown in the Component
Services administration tool.

Publishing of Events

The setup is now complete, so all that is left is to publish the event by creating an instance of
the EventObj class and calling the IEventObj.MyEvent method. The simplest way to do this is
in a simple test application, as shown in Listing 18.5.

LISTING 18.5   TestU.pas—Unit to Fire the Loosely Coupled Event

```
unit TestU;

interface
```

LISTING 18.5 Continued

```
uses
  Windows, Messages, SysUtils, Classes, Graphics, Controls, Forms, Dialogs,
  Publisher_TLB, StdCtrls;

type
  TForm1 = class(TForm)
    Button1: TButton;
    procedure Button1Click(Sender: TObject);
  private
    FEvent: IEventObj;
  end;

var
  Form1: TForm1;

implementation

uses ComObj, ActiveX;

{$R *.DFM}

procedure TForm1.Button1Click(Sender: TObject);
begin
  OleCheck(CoCreateInstance(CLASS_EventObj, nil, CLSCTX_ALL, IEventObj,
    FEvent));
  FEvent.MyEvent('This is a clever string');
end;

end.
```

Figure 18.14 shows the result of pushing the magic button. Note that the event subscriber is created automatically by COM+ and the event handler code is executed.

You might notice that COM+ takes a few moments to invoke the event the first time through. This is because of the fairly substantial amount of internal infrastructure that needs to be loaded in order to fire COM+ events. The bottom line here is that you shouldn't depend on events being fired back to subscribers in real time. They'll get there soon, but not instantly.

18

TRANSACTIONAL
DEVELOPMENT

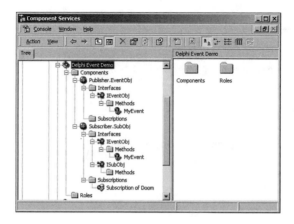

FIGURE 18.13
Event demo application in the Component Services tool.

FIGURE 18.14
Event demo application in action.

Beyond the Basics

Although this information provides a solid grounding in the fundamentals of the COM+ event model, there are a couple of powerful features that a we'd like to mention. The first is queued events. Queued events are the synthesis of COM+ events and queued components (MSMQ components in pre-COM+ days). Essentially, this functionality provides the capability to fire events to disconnected components, and those events can be played back at a later time. The other advanced topic worthy of mention is event filters, which come in two flavors: publisher filters and parameter filters. *Publisher* filters provide a means for publishers to control the order and firing of an event method by an event class. *Parameter* filters enable the publisher to intercept events based on the value of the parameters of that event.

Runtime

You can think of the COM+ runtime a as essentially the COM you already know and love. The COM+ runtime is comprised of all the various COM API functions (you know, all those functions that start with Co...) and the underlying code that makes those functions go. The runtime handles things like object creation and lifetime, marshaling, proxies, memory management, and all the other low-level things that make up the foundation of COM+. In order to support many of the nifty services you just learned about, Microsoft has added a number of new features to the COM+ runtime, including configured components, a registration database, the promotion of the contexts concept, and a new neutral threading model.

Registration Database (RegDB)

In COM, the attributes of a particular COM object are generally kept in two places: the system registry and a type library. COM+ now introduces the concept of a registration database that will be used to hold attribute information for COM+ object. Type libraries will continue to be used, but the system registry has distinctly fallen out of favor as the place to store object attributes, and use of the registry for this purpose is supported only for the sake of backward compatibility. Common attributes stored in the RegDB include the transaction level supported by an object and whether it supports JIT activation.

Configured Components

Components that store attributes in RegDB are referred to as configured components, whereas components that don't are called non-configured. The best example of a non-configured component is a COM or MTS component that you are using unchanged in the COM+ environment. In order to participate in most of the services we mentioned earlier, your components will need to be configured.

Contexts

Contexts is a term originally introduced in MTS that described the state of the current execution environment of a given component. Not only has this term moved forward in COM+, but also it has been promoted. In COM, an apartment is the most granular description of the runtime context of a given object, referring to an execution context bounded by a thread or process. In COM+ that honor goes to a context, which runs within some particular apartment. A context implies a description on a more granular level than an apartment, such as transaction and activation state.

Neutral Threading

COM+ introduces a new threading model, known as *Thread Neutral Apartment (TNA)*. TNA is designed to provide the performance and scalability benefits of a free threaded object without the programming problems of dealing with interlocking access to shared data and resources within the server. TNA is the preferred threading model for COM+ components that don't surface UI elements. Components containing UI should continue to use apartment threading because window handles are tied to a specific thread. There is a limitation of one TNA per process.

Creating COM+ Applications

With all the knowledge of individual COM+ features under your belt, now is a good time to learn more about creating applications that leverage COM+ features such as transactions, lifetime management, and shared resources.

The Goal: Scale

The magic word of system design these days is scalability. With the hyper-growth of the Internet (intranets, extranet, and all other things net), the consolidation of corporate data into centrally-located data stores, and the need for everyone and their cousin to get at the data, it's absolutely crucial that systems be able to scale to ever larger numbers of concurrent users. It's definitely a challenge, especially considering the rather unforgiving limitations we must deal with, such as finite database connections, network bandwidth, server load, and so on. In the good old days of the early 90s, client/server computing was all the rage and considered "The Way" to write scalable applications. However, as databases were bogged down with triggers and stored procedures and clients were complicated with various bits of code here and there in an effort to implement business rules, it shortly became obvious that such systems would never scale to a large number of users. The multitier architecture soon became popular as a way to scale a system to a greater number of users. By placing application logic and sharing database connections in the middle tier, database and client logic could be simplified and resource usage optimized for an overall higher-bandwidth system.

NOTE

The added infrastructure introduced in a multitier environment tends to increase latency as it increases bandwidth. In other words, you might very well need to sacrifice the performance of the system in order to improve scalability!

Execution Context

It's important to bear in mind that because COM+ object don't run directly within the context of a client like other COM objects, clients never really obtain interface pointers directly to an object instance. Instead, COM+ inserts a proxy between the client and the COM+ object such that the proxy is identical to the object from the client's point of view. However, because COM+ has complete control over the proxy, it can control access to interface methods of the object for purposes such as lifetime management and security, as you will soon learn.

Stateful Versus Stateless

The number one topic of conversation among folks looking at, playing with, and working on COM+ technology seems to be the discussion of stateful versus stateless objects. Although COM itself doesn't give a whit as to the state of an object, in practice most traditional COM objects are stateful. That is, they continuously maintain state information from the time that they're created, while they're being used, and up until the time that they're destroyed. The problem with stateful objects is that they aren't particularly scalable because state information would have to be maintained for every object being accessed by every client. A stateless object is one that generally doesn't maintain state information between method calls. COM+ prefers stateless objects because they enable COM+ to play some optimization tricks. If an object doesn't maintain any state between method calls, COM+ could theoretically make the object go away between calls without causing any harm. Furthermore because the client maintains pointers only to COM+'s internal proxy for the object, COM+ could do so without the client being any the wiser. It's more than a theory; this is actually how COM+ works. COM+ will destroy the instances of the object between calls in order to free up resources associated with the object. When the client makes another call to that object, the COM+ proxy will intercept it and a new instance of the object will be created automatically. This helps the system scale to a larger number of users because there will likely be comparatively few active instances of a class at any given time.

Writing interfaces to behave in a stateless manner will probably require a slight departure from your usual way of thinking for interface design. For example, consider the following classic COM-style interface:

```
ICheckbook = interface
['{2CCF0409-EE29-11D2-AF31-0000861EF0BB}']
  procedure SetAccount(AccountNum: WideString); safecall;
  procedure AddActivity(Amount: Integer); safecall;
end;
```

As you might imagine, you would use this interface in a manner something like this:

```
var
  CB: ICheckbook;
begin
  CB := SomehowGetInstance;
  CB.SetAccount('12345ABCDE');  // open my checking account
  CB.AddActivity(-100);         // add a debit for $100
  ...
end;
```

The problem with this style is that the object isn't stateless between method calls because state information regarding the account number must be maintained across the call. A better approach to this interface for use in COM+ would be to pass all the necessary information to the AddActivity() method so that the object could behave in a stateless manner:

```
procedure AddActivity(AccountNum: WideString; Amount: Integer); safecall;
```

The particular state of an active object is also referred to as a context. COM+ maintains a context for each active object that tracks things like security and transaction information for the object. An object can at any time call GetObjectContext() to obtain an IObjectContext interface pointer for the object's context. IObjectContext is defined in the Mtx unit as

```
IObjectContext = interface(IUnknown)
    ['{51372AE0-CAE7-11CF-BE81-00AA00A2FA25}']
    function CreateInstance(const cid, rid: TGUID; out pv): HResult; stdcall;
    procedure SetComplete; safecall;
    procedure SetAbort; safecall;
    procedure EnableCommit; safecall;
    procedure DisableCommit; safecall;
    function IsInTransaction: Bool; stdcall;
    function IsSecurityEnabled: Bool; stdcall;
    function IsCallerInRole(const bstrRole: WideString): Bool; safecall;
end;
```

The two most important methods in this interface are SetComplete() and SetAbort(). If either of these methods are called, the object is telling COM+ that it no longer has any state to maintain. COM+ will therefore destroy the object (unbeknown to the client, of course), thereby freeing up resources for other instances. If the object is participating in a transaction, SetComplete() and SetAbort() also have effect of a commit or rollback for the transaction, respectively.

Lifetime Management

From the time we were tiny COM programmers, we were taught to hold on to interface pointers only for as long as necessary and to release them as soon as they are unneeded. In traditional COM, this makes a lot of sense because we don't want to occupy the system with maintaining resources that aren't being used. However, because COM+ will automatically free up stateless objects after they call SetComplete() or SetAbort(), there is no expense associated with holding a reference to such an object indefinitely. Furthermore, because the client never knows that the object instance might have been deleted under the sheets, clients don't have to be rewritten to take advantage of this feature.

COM+ Application Organization

Remember that a collection of COM+ components that share common configuration and attributes are referred to in the Component Services tools as an *application*. Prior to COM+ MTS, used the word *package* to refer to what we now call applications, but we are happy with the change in terminology—the term *package* was already overloaded enough, with Delphi packages, C++Builder packages, Oracle packages, and holiday gifts all coming to mind as examples of the overuse of this word.

By default, COM+ will run all components within a package in the same process. This enables you to configure well behaved and error-free packages that are insulated from the potential problems that could be caused by faults or errors in other packages. It is also interesting to note that the physical location of components has no bearing on eligibility for package inclusion; a single COM+ server can contain several COM+ objects, each in a separate package.

Applications can be created and manipulated using either the Run, Install COM+ Objects menu in Delphi or the Component Services tool.

Thinking About Transactions

And of course, COM+ also does transactions. You might be thinking to yourself, "big deal, my database server already supports transactions. Why do I need my components to support them as well?" A fair question, and luckily we're equipped with good answers. Transaction support in COM+ can enable you to perform transactions across multiple databases or can even make a single atomic action out of some set of operations having nothing to do with databases. In order to support transactions on your COM+ objects, you must either set the correct transaction flag on your object's coclass in the type library during development (this is what the Delphi Transactional Object wizard does) or after deployment in the Transaction Server Explorer.

When should you use transactions in your objects? That's easy: you should use transactions whenever you have a process involving multiple steps that you want to make into a single, atomic transaction. In doing so, the entire process can be either committed or rolled back, but you will never leave your logic or data in an incorrect or indeterminate state somewhere in between. For example, if you are writing software for a bank and you want to handle the case in which a client bounces a check, there would likely be several steps involved in handling that, including

- debiting the account for amount of check
- debiting the account for bounced check service charge
- sending a letter to the client

In order to properly process the bounced check, each of these things must happen. Therefore, wrapping them in a single transaction would ensure that all will occur if no errors are encountered. All will roll back to their original pre-transaction state if an error occurs.

Resources

With objects being created and destroyed all the time and transactions happening everywhere, it's important for COM+ to provide a means for sharing certain finite or expensive resources (such as database connections) across multiple objects. COM+ does this using resource managers and resource dispensers. A resource manager is a service that manages some type of durable data, such as account balance or inventory. Microsoft provides a resource manager in MS SQL Server. A resource dispenser manages non-durable resources, such as database connections. Microsoft provides a resource dispenser for ODBC database connections, and Borland provides a resource dispenser for BDE database connections.

When a transaction makes use of some type of resource, it enlists the resource to become a part of the transaction so that all changes made to the resource during the transaction will participate in the commit or rollback of the transaction.

COM+ in Delphi

Now that you've got the "what" and "why" down, it's time to talk about the "how." In particular we intend to focus on Delphi's support of COM+ and how to build COM+ solutions in Delphi. Before we jump right in, however, you should first know that COM+ support is built only into the Client/Server version of Delphi. Although it's technically possible to create COM+ components using the facilities available in the Standard and Professional versions, we wouldn't consider it the most productive use of your time, so we intend to help you leverage the features of Delphi to build COM+ applications.

COM+ Wizards

Delphi provides two wizards for building COM+ components: the Transactional Data Module Wizard found on the Multitier tab of the New Items dialog box and the Transactional Object Wizard found on the ActiveX tab. The Transactional Data Module Wizard enables you to build MIDAS servers that operate in the COM+ environment. The Transactional Object Wizard will serve as the starting point for your COM+ transactional objects, and it is this wizard upon which I will focus my discussion. Upon invoking this wizard, you will be presented with the dialog box shown in Figure 18.15.

This dialog box is similar to the Automation Object Wizard with which you are probably already familiar based on your previous COM development experience in Delphi. The obvious difference is the facility provided by this wizard to select the transaction model supported by your COM+ component. The available transaction models are as follows:

- Requires a Transaction—The component will always be created within the context of a transaction. It will inherit the transaction of its creator if one exists, or it will otherwise create a new one.

- Requires a New Transaction—A new transaction will always be created for the component to execute within.

- Supports Transactions—The component will inherit the transaction of its creator if one exists, or it will execute without a transaction otherwise.

- Does Not Support Transactions—The component will never be created within a transaction.

- Ignores Transactions—The component doesn't care about the transaction context.

The transaction model information is stored along with the component's co-class in the type library.

FIGURE 18.15
COM+ Transactional Object Wizard.

After you click OK to dismiss the dialog box, the wizard will generate an empty definition for a class that descends from TMtsAutoObject and it will present the Type Library Editor in order to define your COM+ components by adding properties, methods, interfaces, and so on. This should be familiar territory because the workflow is identical at this point to developing automation objects in Delphi. It's interesting to note that, although the Delphi wizard-created COM+ objects are automation objects (that is, COM objects that implement IDispatch), COM+ doesn't technically require this. However, because COM inherently knows how to marshal IDispatch interfaces accompanied by type libraries, employing this type of object in COM+ enables you to concentrate more on your components' functionality and less on how they integrate with COM+. You should also be aware that COM+ components must reside in in-process COM servers (.DLLs); COM+ components aren't supported in out-of-process servers (.EXEs).

COM+ Framework

The aforementioned TMtsAutoObject class, which is the base class for all Delphi wizard-created COM+ objects, is defined in the MtsObj unit. TMtsAutoObject is a relatively straightforward class that is defined as follows:

```
type
  TMtsAutoObject = class(TAutoObject, IObjectControl)
  private
    FObjectContext: IObjectContext;
  protected
    { IObjectControl }
    procedure Activate; safecall;
    procedure Deactivate; stdcall;
    function CanBePooled: Bool; stdcall;

    procedure OnActivate; virtual;
    procedure OnDeactivate; virtual;
    property ObjectContext: IObjectContext read FObjectContext;
  public
    procedure SetComplete;
    procedure SetAbort;
    procedure EnableCommit;
    procedure DisableCommit;
    function IsInTransaction: Bool;
    function IsSecurityEnabled: Bool;
    function IsCallerInRole(const Role: WideString): Bool;
  end;
```

TMtsAutoObject is essentially a TAutoObject that adds functionality to manage initialization, cleanup, and context.

TMtsAutoObject implements the IObjectControl interface, which manages initialization and cleanup of COM+ components. The methods of this interface are as follows:

Activate()—Allows an object to perform context-specific initialization when activated. This method will be called by COM+ prior to any custom methods on your COM+ component.

Deactivate()—Enables you to perform context-specific cleanup when an object is deactivated.

CanBePooled()—Was unused in MTS, but is supported in COM+, as described earlier in this chapter.

TMtsAutoObject provides virtual OnActivate() and OnDeactivate() methods, which are fired from the private Activate() and Deactivate() methods. Simply override these to create special context-specific activation or deactivation logic.

TMtsAutoObject also maintains a pointer to COM+'s IObjectContext interface in the form of the ObjectContext property. As a shortcut for users of this class, TMtsAutoObject also surfaces each of IObjectContext's methods, which are implemented to simply call into

`ObjectContext`. For example, the implementation of `TMtsAutoObject`'s `SetComplete()` method simply checks `FObjectContext` for `nil` and then calls `FObjectContext.SetComplete()`.

The following is a list of `IObjectContext`'s methods and a brief explanation of each:

> `CreateInstance()`—Creates an instance of another COM+ object. You can think of this method as performing the same task for COM+ objects as `IClassFactory.CreateInstance()` does for normal COM objects.

> `SetComplete()`—Signals to COM+ that the component has completed whatever work it needs to do and no longer has any internal state to maintain. If the component is transactional, it also indicates that the current transactions can be committed. After the method calling this function returns, COM+ might deactivate the object, thereby freeing up resources for greater scalability.

> `SetAbort()`—Similar to `SetComplete()`, this method signals to COM+ that the component has completed work and no longer has state information to maintain. However, calling this method also means that the component is in an error or indeterminate state and any pending transactions must be aborted.

> `EnableCommit()`—Indicates that the component is in a "committable" state, such that transactions can be committed when the component calls `SetComplete()`. This is the default state of a component.

> `DisableCommit()`—Indicates that the component is in an inconsistent state, and further method invocations are necessary before the component will be prepared to commit transactions.

> `IsInTransaction()`—Enables the component to determine whether it is executing within the context of a transaction.

> `IsSecurityEnabled()`—Allows a component to determine whether COM+ security is enabled. This method always returns `True` unless the component is executing in the client's process space.

> `IsCallerInRole()`—Provides a means by which a component can determine whether the user serving as the client for the component is a member of a specific COM+ role. This method is the heart of COM+'s easy-to-use, role-based security system. We'll speak more on roles later.

The `Mtx` unit contains the core COM+ support. It is the Pascal translation of the `mtx.h` header file, and it contains the types (such as `IObjectControl` and `IObjectContext`) and functions that make up the COM+ API.

18

TRANSACTIONAL DEVELOPMENT

Tic-Tac-Toe: A Sample Application

That's enough theory. Now it's time to write some code and see how all this COM+ stuff performs on the open road. COM+ ships with a sample tic-tac-toe application that's a bit on the ugly side, so it inspired me to implement the classic game from the ground up in Delphi. To start, you use the Transactional Object Wizard to create a new object called GameServer. Using the Type Library Editor, add to the default interface for this object, IGameServer, three methods, NewGame(), ComputerMove(), and PlayerMove(). Additionally, add two new enums, SkillLevels and GameResults, that are used by these methods. Figure 18.16 shows all these items displayed in the Type Library Editor.

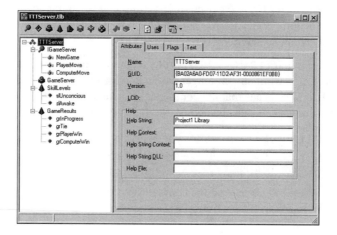

FIGURE 18.16

Tic-Tac-Toe server in the Type Library Editor.

The logic behind the three methods of this interface is simple, and they make up the requirements to support a game of human versus computer tic-tac-toe. NewGame initializes a new game for the client. ComputerMove analyzes the available moves and makes a move for the computer. PlayerMove enables the client to let the computer know how he has chosen to move. Earlier, we mentioned that COM+ component development requires a frame of mind different from the development of standard COM components. This component offers a nice opportunity to illustrate this fact.

If this were your average, everyday, run-of-the-mill COM component, you might approach the design of the object by initializing some data structure to maintain game state in the NewGame() method. That data structure would probably be an instance field of the object, which the other methods would access and manipulate throughout the life of the object.

What's the problem with this approach for a COM+ component? One word: state. As you learned earlier, object must be stateless in order to realize the full benefit of COM+. However, a component architecture that depends on instance data to be maintained across method calls is far from stateless. A better design for COM+ would be to return a handle identifying a game from the NewGame() method and using that handle to maintain per-game data structures in some type of shared resource facility. This shared resource facility would need to be maintained outside the context of a specific object instance because COM+ might activate and deactivate object instances with each method call. Each of the other methods of the component could accept this handle as a parameter, enabling it to retrieve game data from the shared resource facility. This is a stateless design because it doesn't require the object to remain activated between method calls and because each method is a self-contained operation that gets all the data it needs from parameters and a shared data facility.

This shared data facility is known as a *resource dispenser* in COM+. Specifically, the Shared Property Manager is the COM+ resource dispenser used to maintain component-defined, process-wide shared data. The Shared Property Manager is represented by the ISharedPropertyGroupManager interface. The Shared Property Manager is the top level of a hierarchical storage system, maintaining any number of shared property groups, which are represented by the ISharedPropertyGroup interface. In turn, each shared property group can contain any number of shared properties, represented by the ISharedProperty interface. Shared properties are convenient because they exist within COM+, outside the context of any specific object instance, and access to them is controlled by locks and semaphores managed by the Shared Property Manager.

With all that in mind, the implementation of the NewGame() method is shown in the following listing:

```
procedure TGameServer.NewGame(out GameID: Integer);
var
  SPG: ISharedPropertyGroup;
  SProp: ISharedProperty;
  Exists: WordBool;
  GameData: OleVariant;
begin
  // Use caller's role to validate security
  CheckCallerSecurity;
  // Get shared property group for this object
  SPG := GetSharedPropertyGroup;
  // Create or retrieve NextGameID shared property
  SProp := SPG.CreateProperty('NextGameID', Exists);
  if Exists then GameID := SProp.Value
  else GameID := 0;
  // Increment and store NextGameID shared property
```

18

TRANSACTIONAL
DEVELOPMENT

```
    SProp.Value := GameID + 1;
    // Create game data array
    GameData := VarArrayCreate([1, 3, 1, 3], varByte);
    SProp := SPG.CreateProperty(Format(GameDataStr, [GameID]), Exists);
    SProp.Value := GameData;
    SetComplete;
  end;
```

This method first checks to ensure that the caller is in the proper role to invoke this method
(more on this in a moment). It then uses a shared property to obtain an ID number for the next
game. Next, this method creates a variant array into which to store game data and saves that
data as a shared property. Finally, this method calls SetComplete() so that COM+ knows it's
okay to deactivate this instance after the method returns.

This leads us to the number one rule of COM+ development: call SetComplete() or SetAbort()
as often as possible. Ideally, you will call SetComplete() or SetAbort() in every method so
that COM+ can reclaim resources previously consumed by your component instance after the
method returns. A corollary to this rule is that object activation and deactivation shouldn't be
expensive because that code is likely to be called quite frequently.

The implementation of the CheckCallerSecurity() method illustrates how easy it is to take
advantage of role-based security in COM+:

```
procedure TGameServer.CheckCallerSecurity;
begin
  // Just for fun, only allow those in the "TTT" role to play the game.
  if IsSecurityEnabled and not IsCallerInRole('TTT') then
    raise Exception.Create('Only those in the TTT role can play tic-tac-toe');
end;
```

This code raises the obvious question, "how does one establish the TTT role and determine
what users belong to that role?" Although it's possible to define roles programmatically, the
most straightforward way to add and configure roles is using the Transaction Server Explorer.
After the component is installed (you'll learn how to install the component shortly), you can
set up roles using the Roles node found under each package node in the Explorer. It's important to note that roles-based security is supported only for components running on Windows
NT. For components running on Windows 9x/Me, IsCallerInRole() will always return True.

The ComputerMove() and PlayerMove() methods are shown here:

```
procedure TGameServer.ComputerMove(GameID: Integer;
  SkillLevel: SkillLevels; out X, Y: Integer; out GameRez: GameResults);
var
  Exists: WordBool;
  PropVal: OleVariant;
```

```
    GameData: PGameData;
    SProp: ISharedProperty;
begin
  // Get game data shared property
  SProp := GetSharedPropertyGroup.CreateProperty(Format(GameDataStr, [GameID]),
    Exists);
  // Get game data array and lock it for more efficient access
  PropVal := SProp.Value;
  GameData := PGameData(VarArrayLock(PropVal));
  try
    // If game isn't over, then let computer make a move
    GameRez := CalcGameStatus(GameData);
    if GameRez = grInProgress then
    begin
      CalcComputerMove(GameData, SkillLevel, X, Y);
      // Save away new game data array
      SProp.Value := PropVal;
      // Check for end of game
      GameRez := CalcGameStatus(GameData);
    end;
  finally
    VarArrayUnlock(PropVal);
  end;
  SetComplete;
end;

procedure TGameServer.PlayerMove(GameID, X, Y: Integer;
  out GameRez: GameResults);
var
  Exists: WordBool;
  PropVal: OleVariant;
  GameData: PGameData;
  SProp: ISharedProperty;
begin
  // Get game data shared property
  SProp := GetSharedPropertyGroup.CreateProperty(Format(GameDataStr, [GameID]),
    Exists);
  // Get game data array and lock it for more efficient access
  PropVal := SProp.Value;
  GameData := PGameData(VarArrayLock(PropVal));
  try
    // Make sure game isn't over
    GameRez := CalcGameStatus(GameData);
    if GameRez = grInProgress then
    begin
      // If spot isn't empty, raise exception
```

18

TRANSACTIONAL
DEVELOPMENT

```
      if GameData[X, Y] <> EmptySpot then
        raise Exception.Create('Spot is occupied!');
      // Allow move
      GameData[X, Y] := PlayerSpot;
      // Save away new game data array
      SProp.Value := PropVal;
      // Check for end of game
      GameRez := CalcGameStatus(GameData);
    end;
  finally
    VarArrayUnlock(PropVal);
  end;
  SetComplete;
end;
```

These methods are similar in that they both obtain the game data from the shared property based on the GameID parameter, manipulate the data to reflect the current move, save the data away again, and check to see if the game is over. The ComputerMove() method also calls CalcComputerMove() to analyze the game and make a move. If you're interested in seeing this and the other logic of this COM+ component, take a look at Listing 18.6, which contains the entire source code for the ServMain unit.

LISTING 18.6 ServMain.pas—Containing TGameServer

```
unit ServMain;

interface

uses
  ActiveX, MtsObj, Mtx, ComObj, TTTServer_TLB;

type
  PGameData = ^TGameData;
  TGameData = array[1..3, 1..3] of Byte;

  TGameServer = class(TMtsAutoObject, IGameServer)
  private
    procedure CalcComputerMove(GameData: PGameData; Skill: SkillLevels;
      var X, Y: Integer);
    function CalcGameStatus(GameData: PGameData): GameResults;
    function GetSharedPropertyGroup: ISharedPropertyGroup;
    procedure CheckCallerSecurity;
  protected
    procedure NewGame(out GameID: Integer); safecall;
```

LISTING 18.6   Continued

```pascal
    procedure ComputerMove(GameID: Integer; SkillLevel: SkillLevels; out X,
      Y: Integer; out GameRez: GameResults); safecall;
    procedure PlayerMove(GameID, X, Y: Integer; out GameRez: GameResults);
      safecall;
  end;

implementation

uses ComServ, Windows, SysUtils;

const
  GameDataStr = 'TTTGameData%d';
  EmptySpot = 0;
  PlayerSpot = $1;
  ComputerSpot = $2;

function TGameServer.GetSharedPropertyGroup: ISharedPropertyGroup;
var
  SPGMgr: ISharedPropertyGroupManager;
  LockMode, RelMode: Integer;
  Exists: WordBool;
begin
  if ObjectContext = nil then
    raise Exception.Create('Failed to obtain object context');
  // Create shared property group for this object
  OleCheck(ObjectContext.CreateInstance(CLASS_SharedPropertyGroupManager,
    ISharedPropertyGroupManager, SPGMgr));
  LockMode := LockSetGet;
  RelMode := Process;
  Result := SPGMgr.CreatePropertyGroup('DelphiTTT', LockMode, RelMode, Exists);
  if Result = nil then
    raise Exception.Create('Failed to obtain property group');
end;

procedure TGameServer.NewGame(out GameID: Integer);
var
  SPG: ISharedPropertyGroup;
  SProp: ISharedProperty;
  Exists: WordBool;
  GameData: OleVariant;
begin
  // Use caller's role to validate security
  CheckCallerSecurity;
```

LISTING 18.6   Continued

```
  // Get shared property group for this object
  SPG := GetSharedPropertyGroup;
  // Create or retrieve NextGameID shared property
  SProp := SPG.CreateProperty('NextGameID', Exists);
  if Exists then GameID := SProp.Value
  else GameID := 0;
  // Increment and store NextGameID shared property
  SProp.Value := GameID + 1;
  // Create game data array
  GameData := VarArrayCreate([1, 3, 1, 3], varByte);
  SProp := SPG.CreateProperty(Format(GameDataStr, [GameID]), Exists);
  SProp.Value := GameData;
  SetComplete;
end;


procedure TGameServer.ComputerMove(GameID: Integer;
  SkillLevel: SkillLevels; out X, Y: Integer; out GameRez: GameResults);
var
  Exists: WordBool;
  PropVal: OleVariant;
  GameData: PGameData;
  SProp: ISharedProperty;
begin
  // Get game data shared property
  SProp := GetSharedPropertyGroup.CreateProperty(Format(GameDataStr, [GameID]),
    Exists);
  // Get game data array and lock it for more efficient access
  PropVal := SProp.Value;
  GameData := PGameData(VarArrayLock(PropVal));
  try
    // If game isn't over, then let computer make a move
    GameRez := CalcGameStatus(GameData);
    if GameRez = grInProgress then
    begin
      CalcComputerMove(GameData, SkillLevel, X, Y);
      // Save away new game data array
      SProp.Value := PropVal;
      // Check for end of game
      GameRez := CalcGameStatus(GameData);
    end;
  finally
    VarArrayUnlock(PropVal);
  end;
  SetComplete;
end;
```

LISTING 18.6 Continued

```
procedure TGameServer.PlayerMove(GameID, X, Y: Integer;
  out GameRez: GameResults);
var
  Exists: WordBool;
  PropVal: OleVariant;
  GameData: PGameData;
  SProp: ISharedProperty;
begin
  // Get game data shared property
  SProp := GetSharedPropertyGroup.CreateProperty(Format(GameDataStr, [GameID]),
    Exists);
  // Get game data array and lock it for more efficient access
  PropVal := SProp.Value;
  GameData := PGameData(VarArrayLock(PropVal));
  try
    // Make sure game isn't over
    GameRez := CalcGameStatus(GameData);
    if GameRez = grInProgress then
    begin
      // If spot isn't empty, raise exception
      if GameData[X, Y] <> EmptySpot then
        raise Exception.Create('Spot is occupied!');
      // Allow move
      GameData[X, Y] := PlayerSpot;
      // Save away new game data array
      SProp.Value := PropVal;
      // Check for end of game
      GameRez := CalcGameStatus(GameData);
    end;
  finally
    VarArrayUnlock(PropVal);
  end;
  SetComplete;
end;

function TGameServer.CalcGameStatus(GameData: PGameData): GameResults;
var
  I, J: Integer;
begin
  // First check for a winner
  if GameData[1, 1] <> EmptySpot then
  begin
    // Check top row, left column, and top left to bottom right diagonal for win
```

18

LISTING 18.6   Continued

```
    if ((GameData[1, 1] = GameData[1, 2]) and
      (GameData[1, 1] = GameData[1, 3])) or
      ((GameData[1, 1] = GameData[2, 1]) and
      (GameData[1, 1] = GameData[3, 1])) or
      ((GameData[1, 1] = GameData[2, 2]) and
      (GameData[1, 1] = GameData[3, 3])) then
    begin
      Result := GameData[1, 1] + 1; // Game result is spot ID + 1
      Exit;
    end;
  end;
  if GameData[3, 3] <> EmptySpot then
  begin
    // Check bottom row and right column for win
    if ((GameData[3, 3] = GameData[3, 2]) and
      (GameData[3, 3] = GameData[3, 1])) or
      ((GameData[3, 3] = GameData[2, 3]) and
      (GameData[3, 3] = GameData[1, 3])) then
    begin
      Result := GameData[3, 3] + 1; // Game result is spot ID + 1
      Exit;
    end;
  end;
  if GameData[2, 2] <> EmptySpot then
  begin
    // Check middle row, middle column, and bottom left to top right
    // diagonal for win
    if ((GameData[2, 2] = GameData[2, 1]) and
      (GameData[2, 2] = GameData[2, 3])) or
      ((GameData[2, 2] = GameData[1, 2]) and
      (GameData[2, 2] = GameData[3, 2])) or
      ((GameData[2, 2] = GameData[3, 1]) and
      (GameData[2, 2] = GameData[1, 3])) then
    begin
      Result := GameData[2, 2] + 1; // Game result is spot ID + 1
      Exit;
    end;
  end;
  // Finally, check for game still in progress
  for I := 1 to 3 do
    for J := 1 to 3 do
      if GameData[I, J] = 0 then
      begin
        Result := grInProgress;
        Exit;
      end;
```

LISTING 18.6 Continued

```pascal
  // If we get here, then we've tied
  Result := grTie;
end;

procedure TGameServer.CalcComputerMove(GameData: PGameData;
  Skill: SkillLevels; var X, Y: Integer);
type
  // Used to scan for possible moves by either row, column, or diagonal line
  TCalcType = (ctRow, ctColumn, ctDiagonal);
  // mtWin = one move away from win, mtBlock = opponent is one move away from
  // win, mtOne = I occupy one other spot in this line, mtNew = I occupy no
  // spots on this line
  TMoveType = (mtWin, mtBlock, mtOne, mtNew);
var
  CurrentMoveType: TMoveType;

  function DoCalcMove(CalcType: TCalcType; Position: Integer): Boolean;
  var
    RowData, I, J, CheckTotal: Integer;
    PosVal, Mask: Byte;
  begin
    Result := False;
    RowData := 0;
    X := 0;
    Y := 0;
    if CalcType = ctRow then
    begin
      I := Position;
      J := 1;
    end
    else if CalcType = ctColumn then
    begin
      I := 1;
      J := Position;
    end
    else begin
      I := 1;
      case Position of
        1: J := 1; // scanning from top left to bottom right
        2: J := 3; // scanning from top right to bottom left
      else
        Exit;   // bail; only 2 diagonal scans
      end;
    end;
```

18

LISTING 18.6 Continued

```
// Mask masks off Player or Computer bit, depending on whether we're
//thinking
// offensively or defensively. Checktotal determines whether that is a row
// we need to move into.
case CurrentMoveType of
  mtWin:
    begin
      Mask := PlayerSpot;
      CheckTotal := 4;
    end;
  mtNew:
    begin
      Mask := PlayerSpot;
      CheckTotal := 0;
    end;
  mtBlock:
    begin
      Mask := ComputerSpot;
      CheckTotal := 2;
    end;
else
  begin
    Mask := 0;
    CheckTotal := 2;
  end;
end;
// loop through all lines in current CalcType
repeat
  // Get status of current spot (X, O, or empty)
  PosVal := GameData[I, J];
  // Save away last empty spot in case we decide to move here
  if PosVal = 0 then
  begin
    X := I;
    Y := J;
  end
  else
    // If spot isn't empty, then add masked value to RowData
    Inc(RowData, (PosVal and not Mask));
  if (CalcType = ctDiagonal) and (Position = 2) then
  begin
    Inc(I);
    Dec(J);
  end
```

LISTING 18.6   Continued

```
      else begin
        if CalcType in [ctRow, ctDiagonal] then Inc(J);
        if CalcType in [ctColumn, ctDiagonal] then Inc(I);
      end;
    until (I > 3) or (J > 3);
    // If RowData adds up, then we must block or win, depending on whether
    // we're thinking offensively or defensively.
    Result := (X <> 0) and (RowData = CheckTotal);
    if Result then
    begin
      GameData[X, Y] := ComputerSpot;
      Exit;
    end;
  end;

var
  A, B, C: Integer;
begin
  if Skill = slAwake then
  begin
    // First look to win the game, next look to block a win
    for A := Ord(mtWin) to Ord(mtBlock) do
    begin
      CurrentMoveType := TMoveType(A);
      for B := Ord(ctRow) to Ord(ctDiagonal) do
        for C := 1 to 3 do
          if DoCalcMove(TCalcType(B), C) then Exit;
    end;
    // Next look to take the center of the board
    if GameData[2, 2] = 0 then
    begin
      GameData[2, 2] := ComputerSpot;
      X := 2;
      Y := 2;
      Exit;
    end;
    // Next look for the most advantageous position on a line
    for A := Ord(mtOne) to Ord(mtNew) do
    begin
      CurrentMoveType := TMoveType(A);
      for B := Ord(ctRow) to Ord(ctDiagonal) do
        for C := 1 to 3 do
```

18

TRANSACTIONAL
DEVELOPMENT

LISTING 18.6   Continued

```
        if DoCalcMove(TCalcType(B), C) then Exit;
    end;
  end;
  // Finally (or if skill level is unconscious), just find the first open place
  for A := 1 to 3 do
    for B := 1 to 3 do
      if GameData[A, B] = 0 then
      begin
        GameData[A, B] := ComputerSpot;
        X := A;
        Y := B;
        Exit;
      end;
end;

procedure TGameServer.CheckCallerSecurity;
begin
  // Just for fun, only allow those in the "TTT" role to play the game.
  if IsSecurityEnabled and not IsCallerInRole('TTT') then
    raise Exception.Create('Only those in the TTT role can play tic-tac-toe');
end;

initialization
  TAutoObjectFactory.Create(ComServer, TGameServer, Class_GameServer,
    ciMultiInstance, tmApartment);
end.
```

Installing the Server

Once the server has been written, and you're ready to install it into COM+, Delphi makes your life very easy. Simple select Run, Install COM+ Objects from the main menu, and you will invoke the Install COM+ Objects dialog box. This dialog box enables you to install your object(s) into a new or existing package, and it is shown in Figure 18.17.

FIGURE 18.17
Installing a COM+ object via the Delphi IDE.

Select the component(s) to be installed, specify whether the package is new or existing, click OK, and that's it; the component is installed. Alternatively, you can also install COM+ components via the Transaction Server Explorer application. Note that this installation procedure is markedly different from that of standard COM objects, which typically involves using the RegSvr32 tool from the command line to register a COM server. Transaction Server Explorer also make it similarly easy to set up COM+ components on remote machines, providing a welcome alternative to the configuration hell experienced by many of those trying to configure DCOM connectivity.

The Client Application

Listing 18.7 shows the source code for the client application for this COM+ component. Its purpose is to essentially map the engine provided by the COM+ component to a Tic-Tac-Toe–looking user interface.

LISTING 18.7   UiMain.pas—The Main Unit for the Client Application

```
unit UiMain;

interface

uses
  Windows, Messages, SysUtils, Classes, Graphics, Controls, Forms, Dialogs,
  Buttons, ExtCtrls, Menus, TTTServer_TLB, ComCtrls;

type
  TRecord = record
    Wins, Loses, Ties: Integer;
  end;

  TFrmMain = class(TForm)
    SbTL: TSpeedButton;
    SbTM: TSpeedButton;
    SbTR: TSpeedButton;
    SbMM: TSpeedButton;
    SbBL: TSpeedButton;
    SbBR: TSpeedButton;
    SbMR: TSpeedButton;
    SbBM: TSpeedButton;
    SbML: TSpeedButton;
    Bevel1: TBevel;
    Bevel2: TBevel;
    Bevel3: TBevel;
    Bevel4: TBevel;
    MainMenu1: TMainMenu;
```

LISTING 18.7   Continued

```
    FileItem: TMenuItem;
    HelpItem: TMenuItem;
    ExitItem: TMenuItem;
    AboutItem: TMenuItem;
    SkillItem: TMenuItem;
    UnconItem: TMenuItem;
    AwakeItem: TMenuItem;
    NewGameItem: TMenuItem;
    N1: TMenuItem;
    StatusBar: TStatusBar;
    procedure FormCreate(Sender: TObject);
    procedure ExitItemClick(Sender: TObject);
    procedure SkillItemClick(Sender: TObject);
    procedure AboutItemClick(Sender: TObject);
    procedure SBClick(Sender: TObject);
    procedure NewGameItemClick(Sender: TObject);
  private
    FXImage: TBitmap;
    FOImage: TBitmap;
    FCurrentSkill: Integer;
    FGameID: Integer;
    FGameServer: IGameServer;
    FRec: TRecord;
    procedure TagToCoord(ATag: Integer; var Coords: TPoint);
    function CoordToCtl(const Coords: TPoint): TSpeedButton;
    procedure DoGameResult(GameRez: GameResults);
  end;

var
  FrmMain: TFrmMain;

implementation

uses UiAbout;

{$R *.DFM}

{$R xo.res}

const
  RecStr = 'Wins: %d, Loses: %d, Ties: %d';

procedure TFrmMain.FormCreate(Sender: TObject);
begin
```

LISTING 18.7 Continued

```
// load "X" and "O" images from resource into TBitmaps
FXImage := TBitmap.Create;
FXImage.LoadFromResourceName(MainInstance, 'x_img');
FOImage := TBitmap.Create;
FOImage.LoadFromResourceName(MainInstance, 'o_img');
// set default skill
FCurrentSkill := slAwake;
// init record UI
with FRec do
  StatusBar.SimpleText := Format(RecStr, [Wins, Loses, Ties]);
// Get server instance
FGameServer := CoGameServer.Create;
// Start a new game
FGameServer.NewGame(FGameID);
end;

procedure TFrmMain.ExitItemClick(Sender: TObject);
begin
  Close;
end;

procedure TFrmMain.SkillItemClick(Sender: TObject);
begin
  with Sender as TMenuItem do
  begin
    Checked := True;
    FCurrentSkill := Tag;
  end;
end;

procedure TFrmMain.AboutItemClick(Sender: TObject);
begin
  // Show About box
  with TFrmAbout.Create(Application) do
    try
      ShowModal;
    finally
      Free;
    end;
end;

procedure TFrmMain.TagToCoord(ATag: Integer; var Coords: TPoint);
begin
  case ATag of
```

LISTING 18.7   Continued

```
    0: Coords := Point(1, 1);
    1: Coords := Point(1, 2);
    2: Coords := Point(1, 3);
    3: Coords := Point(2, 1);
    4: Coords := Point(2, 2);
    5: Coords := Point(2, 3);
    6: Coords := Point(3, 1);
    7: Coords := Point(3, 2);
  else
    Coords := Point(3, 3);
  end;
end;

function TFrmMain.CoordToCtl(const Coords: TPoint): TSpeedButton;
begin
  Result := nil;
  with Coords do
    case X of
      1:
        case Y of
          1: Result := SbTL;
          2: Result := SbTM;
          3: Result := SbTR;
        end;
      2:
        case Y of
          1: Result := SbML;
          2: Result := SbMM;
          3: Result := SbMR;
        end;
      3:
        case Y of
          1: Result := SbBL;
          2: Result := SbBM;
          3: Result := SbBR;
        end;
    end;
end;

procedure TFrmMain.SBClick(Sender: TObject);
var
  Coords: TPoint;
  GameRez: GameResults;
  SB: TSpeedButton;
```

LISTING 18.7 Continued

```
begin
  if Sender is TSpeedButton then
  begin
    SB := TSpeedButton(Sender);
    if SB.Glyph.Empty then
    begin
      with SB do
      begin
        TagToCoord(Tag, Coords);
        FGameServer.PlayerMove(FGameID, Coords.X, Coords.Y, GameRez);
        Glyph.Assign(FXImage);
      end;
      if GameRez = grInProgress then
      begin
        FGameServer.ComputerMove(FGameID, FCurrentSkill, Coords.X, Coords.Y,
          GameRez);
        CoordToCtl(Coords).Glyph.Assign(FOImage);
      end;
      DoGameResult(GameRez);
    end;
  end;
end;

procedure TFrmMain.NewGameItemClick(Sender: TObject);
var
  I: Integer;
begin
  FGameServer.NewGame(FGameID);
  for I := 0 to ControlCount - 1 do
    if Controls[I] is TSpeedButton then
      TSpeedButton(Controls[I]).Glyph := nil;
end;

procedure TFrmMain.DoGameResult(GameRez: GameResults);
const
  EndMsg: array[grTie..grComputerWin] of string = (
    'Tie game', 'You win', 'Computer wins');
begin
  if GameRez <> grInProgress then
  begin
    case GameRez of
      grComputerWin: Inc(FRec.Loses);
      grPlayerWin: Inc(FRec.Wins);
      grTie: Inc(FRec.Ties);
    end;
```

18

TRANSACTIONAL
DEVELOPMENT

LISTING 18.7   Continued

```
    with FRec do
      StatusBar.SimpleText := Format(RecStr, [Wins, Loses, Ties]);
    if MessageDlg(Format('%s! Play again?', [EndMsg[GameRez]]), mtConfirmation,
      [mbYes, mbNo], 0) = mrYes then
      NewGameItemClick(nil);
  end;
end;

end.
```

Figure 18.18 shows this application in action. Human is X and computer is O.

FIGURE 18.18
Playing tic-tac-toe.

Debugging COM+ Applications

Because COM+ components run within COM+'s process space rather than the client's, you might think that they would be difficult to debug. However, COM+ provides a side door for debugging purposes that makes debugging a snap. Just load the server project, and use the Run Parameters dialog box to specify mtx.exe as the host application. As a parameter to mtx.exe, you must pass /p:{package guid}, where *package guid* is the GUID of the package as shown in the Component Services tool. This dialog box is shown in Figure 18.19. Next, set your desired breakpoints and run the application. You won't see anything happen initially because the client application isn't yet running. Now you can run the client from Windows Explorer or a command prompt, and you will be off and debugging.

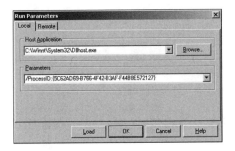

FIGURE 18.19
The Run Parameters dialog box.

Summary

COM+ is a powerful addition to the COM family of technologies. By adding services such as lifetime management, transaction support, security, and transactions to COM objects without requiring significant changes to existing source code, Microsoft has leveraged COM into a more scalable technology, suitable for large-scale distributed development. This chapter took you through a tour of the basics of COM+ and on to the specifics of Delphi's support for COM+ and how to create COM+ applications in Delphi. What's more, you've hopefully caught a few tips and tricks along the way for developing optimized and well-behaved COM+ components. COM+ packs a wallop out of the box by providing services such as lifetime management, transaction support, security, all in a familiar framework. COM+ and Delphi combine to provide you with a great way to leverage your COM experience into creating scalable multi-tier applications. Just don't forget those differences in design nuances between normal COM components and COM+ components!

CORBA Development

by David Sampson

IN THIS CHAPTER

CORBA stands for *Common Object Request Broker Architecture*. Its purpose is to facilitate distributed object computing. Unlike a proprietary approach such as DCOM, CORBA is an open standard that isn't under the control of any single company. An organization called the Object Management Group (OMG), which is made up of more than 800 industry representatives, controls the CORBA specification. The OMG meets periodically to issue updates or amendments to the standard and to resolve any outstanding issues.

The OMG specifies what CORBA will do and to a certain degree, how it will do it. Beyond that, each CORBA vendor is free to come up with its own implementation and method of complying with the CORBA specification. This freedom has a price. For example, the OMG doesn't specify how different CORBA implementations locate objects when using two different *ORBs (Object Request Brokers)*. So in the past, it has been a struggle to get applications to bootstrap together when they were written with different vendor's products. This is one area that has received a lot of attention and is continuing to improve as the CORBA specification evolves.

More information on the OMG is available at its Web site (www.omg.org). You'll find a wealth of information about CORBA, including the latest specifications, tutorials, Web links to vendors, and so on.

One thing you'll discover is that many free CORBA implementations are available on the internet. This chapter deals with the Borland CORBA implementation bundled with Delphi 6 Enterprise edition. The CORBA product is called VisiBroker, and is arguably the most widely used ORB in the world. Delphi 6 contains all the runtime library files needed to use CORBA. In addition, wizards are integrated into the IDE that make application development relatively straightforward.

CORBA Features

CORBA has several features that make it beneficial for use in distributed enterprise environments:

- CORBA is an object-oriented approach. Each CORBA server publishes an interface that lists the methods and data types it supports. The implementation details are hidden from the caller.

- Location Transparency. The real power in CORBA is that objects can be located anywhere. When a CORBA client application calls a server object, it doesn't know where the server resides. In fact, CORBA presents the client application with an image of the server application. The client then operates as if the server object is running locally in its own process space. This will be discussed in more detail in the CORBA Architecture section.

- Programming Language Independence. A major benefit is that objects can be written in a variety of different languages. Java and C++ are the leaders, but Delphi is gaining much wider acceptance because of all the features available in the product. To make sure that these languages can interoperate, CORBA objects interact with each other through their published interfaces. Each server object must comply with its interface definition. Because of the differences in programming languages, clients cannot know about or compensate for any of the implementation details on the server side. Strict object-oriented design is enforced in the CORBA world.

- Multi Platform/Multi Operating Systems. CORBA implementations exist for different platforms and operating systems. It isn't unusual for a deployment to use Java on the back-end mainframe computer and Delphi on the middle tier or client side. Developers can write powerful applications that tap into legacy systems and present information to end users with feature-rich clients built in Delphi.

CORBA Architecture

Figure 19.1 shows a block diagram of the CORBA architecture. The common piece to both the client and the server is the ORB. The ORB handles all communications between objects. It does this using the *Internet Inter-ORB Protocol (IIOP)* that is layered on TCP/IP. This guarantees reliable end-to-end message delivery and usage anywhere TCP/IP is deployed. In addition to handling all message traffic, the ORB also corrects for platform variations.

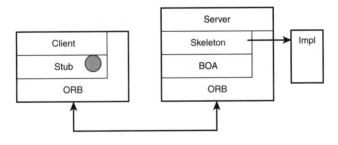

FIGURE 19.1
The CORBA Architecture.

19

CORBA
DEVELOPMENT

For example, if the number 123 is originated on an Intel based machine and is sent to a Sun workstation, the number won't be processed correctly without some sort of intervention. This is because the two processors use different layouts for their registers.

This is referred to as the Big-Endian/Little-Endian problem. Because the ORB knows what platform it is running on, it will set a flag in the CORBA message to indicate whether it originated on a big-endian or little-endian machine. The receiving side will read this flag and automatically process the data correctly. This ensures that the number 123 is processed correctly on both ends.

> **NOTE**
>
> According to Rhu, Herron, and Klinker in *IIOP Complete* (Addison Wesley), p.65, "The terms *little endian* and *big endian* are an analogy drawn by Cohen from *Gulliver's Travels*, in which the islands of Lilliput and Blefescua feuded over which end of an egg to crack, the little end or the big end."

The client side consists of two additional layers. The client block is the application that is written by the developer. The more interesting piece is the stub. The stub is a file that is automatically generated by a tool that is included in the Delphi Enterprise edition. This tool is called the IDL2Pas compiler. Its purpose is to take files that describe the server interfaces and generate Delphi Pascal that can interact with the CORBA ORB. The IDL2Pas compiler is documented in a set of HTML files on the Delphi 6 CD-ROM (Delphi6\Doc\Corba).

The stub file contains one or more classes that "mirror" the CORBA server. The classes contain the same published interfaces and data types that are exposed by the server. The client calls the stub classes in order to communicate with the server. The stub classes act as a proxy for the server objects. The symbol in the stub block represents a connection to the server. The connection is established through a *bind* call that is issued by the client. The stub is said to have an *object reference* to the server (represented by the symbol). Once the connection is made to the server, the client invokes a method call on the stub class. The stub packs the request and any required method arguments into a buffer for transmission to the server. This is referred to as *marshaling* the data. The stub invokes the call through its server object reference via the ORB. When the server responds, the stub class receives the message from the ORB and hands the response back to the client.

The client can also call some utility type functions directly in the ORB. The block diagram shows this logical connection.

The server side contains an ORB interface called the *Basic Object Adaptor (BOA)*. The BOA is responsible for routing messages from the ORB to the skeleton interface (described next). In the future, Delphi will also provide a *Portable Object Adaptor (POA)*, which will offer more flexibility and customization of the server interface.

The skeleton is a class that is generated by the IDL2Pas compiler, just like the stub. The skeleton contains one or more classes that publish the server side CORBA interfaces. In the Delphi CORBA implementation, the skeleton doesn't contain any implementation details of the server-side interfaces. Instead, there is another file (also generated by IDL2Pas) that contains the classes which represent the functional details of the server. This is referred to as the IMPL file (short for Implementation).

The classes in the Impl file aren't tied to CORBA. The same implementation classes can be used to provide interfaces for CORBA, COM, or anything else.

When a message arrives on the server side, the ORB passes a message buffer to the BOA, which in turn, passes the buffer to the skeleton class. The skeleton un-marshals the data from the buffer and determines which method should be called in the IMPL file. After the IMPL file class method is called, the skeleton takes any return results and parameter values and marshals them into a buffer for transmission back to the client. The response buffer is handed back to the BOA and ORB, and is sent back to the client-side ORB.

OSAgent

CORBA objects need a way of locating one another. The OMG provides a solution for this with the Naming Service that is described in the CORBA specification. The Naming Service is a program that runs somewhere on the network. Server-side objects register with the Naming Service so that client applications have a method of locating specific objects. The Naming Service requires additional code on both the client and server sides. The location of the Naming Service process has to be known in advance before a client application can request a connection to a server object.

This is a fairly complicated way of letting clients and servers connect. VisiBroker has a utility that makes object location much easier than using the Naming Service. This program is called OSAgent. It isn't part of the CORBA specification. OSAgent is a proprietary utility that is only available with the Borland ORB. As long as the VisiBroker ORB is used within a CORBA implementation, the OSAgent is the preferred method of locating and binding to objects.

Before running CORBA applications created with VisiBroker, start OSAgent. When the server application starts, it will register itself with the agent. The client application will connect to the server by first contacting the OSAgent, requesting the address of the server, and then connecting directly to the server process.

Interfaces

All CORBA objects are described by their interfaces. This is pure object-oriented design. A server application will publish specific type declarations, interfaces, and methods that any client might call. Once these interfaces are published, they are immutable. That is, they should never change. To add additional features to an object, the best approach is to derive a new server from the old one and enhance the new object. That way, a new interface can be published without creating backward compatibility problems for deployed applications.

To describe interfaces, the OMG has published an *Interface Definition Language (IDL)*. IDL is programming language independent, but looks like C or Java. Each ORB vendor supplies an IDL compiler to translate IDL files into code for a specific language. The term *IDL compiler* is a misnomer. It doesn't actually compile the IDL file into an executable file. It is more of a code generator because the output is a set of source code files in the target language.

The OMG has specified language mappings for some languages like C++ and Java. A C++ ORB will have an IDL2CPP compiler. Java ORBs have an IDL2Java compiler.

The files generated by the IDL2 whatever compilers are the stub and skeleton class files that were discussed in the CORBA Architecture section. Delphi contains an IDL2Pas compiler that can be executed from the command line or launched through the IDE CORBA wizards.

Interface Definition Language (IDL)

IDL is an extensive subject. The Delphi 6 Enterprise CD-ROM contains a PDF document (Delphi6\Doc\CORBA) that describes the Object Pascal mapping for IDL. This document contains all the details about each data type, modules, inheritance, and user-defined types. This section highlights some of the notable aspects of IDL; however, to gain more insight into the details, refer to the mapping document.

There are a few rules that an IDL file must follow. The first is that an IDL file must have .idl as the file extension. This can be upper- or lowercase. Other file extensions won't be accepted.

The contents of an IDL file are relatively free flowing but do follow a certain structure. The interface descriptions are case sensitive. In C++ and Java, two interfaces named Foo and foo are considered different. However, in Delphi, they will create a problem because it will appear that the same interface has been created twice.

Comments in an IDL file are the same as C and C++. These are valid comments:

```
// This is a single line comment.
/* This is an example of a block comment
   that can be spread
   over several lines */
```

All IDL keywords must be written in lowercase, or the IDL2Pas compiler will reject them. Avoid using Delphi keywords if possible. The Delphi mapping specification states that all Delphi keywords will be prepended with the underscore (_) character. It is a good practice to avoid the use of Delphi reserved words.

An IDL file can include another IDL file with the #include pragma statement. This facilitates organizing large IDL files into smaller groups.

Basic Types

IDL has a number of basic types that can be used in interface descriptions. Table 19.1 shows a list of the basic types and shows how they are mapped to Object Pascal.

TABLE 19.1   Basic IDL Types

IDL Type	Pascal Type
boolean	Boolean
Char	Char
wchar	Wchar
octet	Byte
string	AnsiString
wstring	WideString
short	SmallInt
unsigned short	Word
long	Integer
unsigned long	Cardinal
long long	Int64
unsigned long long	Int64
float	Single
double	Double
long double	Extended
fixed	not implemented—no corresponding type

IDL doesn't have a type called int. Instead, the short, long, unsigned short, and unsigned long are used to specify the integer type. Characters correspond to the ISO Latin-1 type, which is equivalent to the ASCII table. The only exception is the NUL character (#0). C and C++ programmers asked the OMG to make that an illegal character because it represents the termination character in a string in those languages.

The implementation of Booleans is vendor specific. The Boolean mapping corresponds to a Boolean type in Delphi. The Any type is mapped to a Variant in Delphi.

User-Defined Types

You can define your own types in IDL. The syntax is similar to the way data structures are specified in C. Common user-defined types include aliases, enumerations, structures, arrays, and sequences.

Aliases

Aliases are used to give data types more meaningful names. For example, a year type can be created like this:

```
typedef short YearType;
```

Enumerations

IDL enumerations are mapped to an enumeration type in Delphi. An enumeration of some color values would look like this:

```
enum Color(red, white, blue, green, black);
```

Structures

Structures are similar to records in Pascal. Here's an example of a structure that represents a time value:

```
struct TimeOfDay {
    short hour;
    short minute;
    short seconds;
};
```

Arrays

Arrays can be single or multi dimensional. Specify an array with a typedef. Here are some examples:

```
typedef Color ColorArray[4];   // single dimensional array of the Color enum
typedef string StringArray[10][20];   //10 strings of max length 20
```

Sequences

Sequences are used heavily in IDL. They map to a variable length array in Delphi. Sequences can be bounded or unbounded.

```
typedef sequence<Color> Colors;
typedef sequence<long, 1000> NumSeq;
```

The first argument in the sequence specification is the base type of the variable array. The second argument is optional and specifies the length in a bounded sequence.

The most common use of sequences in CORBA programming is to pass database records between servers and clients. When the client application receives a sequence, it has to loop through it to extract all the fields in a record. Then it populates the user interface database controls with the information. MIDAS and CORBA can be used together to provide a friendlier approach.

Method Arguments

All arguments that are specified in a method have to be declared with one of three attributes. These attributes are in, out, or inout.

A parameter declared as an in type has its values set by the client. This is mapped as a const parameter in Delphi.

An out parameter has its value set by the server. It is mapped as a var parameter.

An inout parameter has its initial value set by the client. The server receives the data and changes it before returning the variable to the client. An inout parameter is mapped as a var' parameter in Delphi.

Modules

The keyword module is used to group interfaces and types. The module name will be used by IDL2Pas to name the Delphi unit. Interfaces and types defined within a module are local in scope. A module named Foo that contained an interface named Bar would be referenced outside the module with the module name and the interface name like this: Foo::Bar.

IDL doesn't support the idea of private or protected types and methods. All interfaces and methods are considered public. This makes sense when you consider that the IDL file represents the interfaces that the server exposes to the world. It wouldn't make sense to hide or protect something in this context.

One of the best ways to learn how to write IDL is to look at examples other people have written. The VisiBroker directory (c:\Inprise, by default) has a subdirectory called IDL that contains the IDL files for the various CORBA interfaces such as the ORB and the various services. These files are a good starting point and are full of examples of type declarations and interface definitions. These files contain examples of nested modules and references to outer scoped types.

19

CORBA DEVELOPMENT

With this basic understanding of IDL, several CORBA examples can be developed to demonstrate the power of distributed object computing. The remainder of the chapter covers the development of several CORBA servers and clients.

The Bank Example

CORBA has a traditional example that is the equivalent of "Hello, world" in C. It's known as the Bank Example and consists of a simple method call that returns a bank balance. We're going to add some additional capabilities such as a deposit and withdraw method. It would also be a good idea to prohibit overdrafts on the account, so an exception will be used to block drawing out more than the account contents. The IDL for this example is in Listing 19.1.

LISTING 19.1   Bank.idl

```
module Bank {
    exception WithdrawError {
        float current_balance;
    };

    interface Account {
        void deposit(in float amount);
        void withdraw(in float amount) raises (WithdrawError);
        float balance();
    };
};
```

The exception is declared with one data member. If the client attempts to withdraw more money than the account contains, the exception will be raised with the current account balance stored in the data member. Client applications can trap the exception and display a message to the user. In this case, a warning will be displayed along with the current balance.

The deposit and withdraw methods are equivalent to procedures, so they have a return type of void. Each takes one argument: the amount to add to or subtract from the account. The amount is a floating point number that will be mapped to a single in Delphi. Notice that the arguments for deposit and withdraw are declared as in parameters because the methods are passing the value from the client to the server. The balance method is a function that returns a floating point value that contains the current balance of the account.

The Delphi 6 IDE contains a set of wizards that make creating CORBA clients and servers pretty easy. We'll start by creating the server side of our application. To bring up the wizard, go to File, New, Other and select the CORBA tab in the dialog box. Then double-click on the CORBA server icon. The main wizard screen will appear as shown in Figure 19.2.

FIGURE 19.2
The CORBA Wizard in Delphi 6.

This window contains a list of all the IDL files that will be processed to generate the application. Initially, it is empty. To add one or more files, click the Add' button. This brings up a standard file open dialog. Change to the directory where the `Bank.idl` file is located, select that file, and then click OK. The `Bank.idl` file will be added to the list of files that will be processed by the IDL2Pas compiler. Because this is the only IDL file in the application, click on Generate to create the server application.

The IDL2Pas compiler will process the IDL file, and the wizard will create an application with the generated files. For server applications, four files are generated:

- `Bank_I.pas`—This file contains all the interfaces and type definitions.
- `Bank_C.pas`—This contains any user-defined types, exceptions, and client stub classes. In addition, all user-defined types and stub classes will have a helper class. The helper class assists in reading and writing data to the CORBA buffers.
- `Bank_S.pas`—This has the server-side skeleton class definitions.
- `Bank_Impl.pas`—This has a general class definition for an implementation on the server side. You can add code to the methods to perform the actions you want the server to complete. You don't have to use this file, but it's a handy starting point.

From this list of files, you can see that the client-side stub shown in the CORBA architecture is in the `Bank_C.pas` file, whereas the server-side skeleton is in `Bank_S.pas`. A sample implementation for the server side is stored in the `Bank_Impl.pas` file.

Listing 19.2 shows the interface definitions for the application. There is only one interface named `Account`, and it contains the three methods that were declared in the IDL file.

LISTING 19.2   Bank_I.pas

```pascal
unit Bank_i;
 interface

uses
  CORBA;

type
  Account = interface;

  Account = interface
    ['{99FCA96D-77B2-4A99-7677-E1E0C32F8C67}']
    procedure deposit (const amount : Single);
    procedure withdraw (const amount : Single);
    function  balance : Single;
  end;

implementation

initialization

end.
```

Listing 19.3 shows the source for the Bank_C.pas file. This file contains the declaration of the Overdrawn exception. It is derived from a class called UserException that is also defined in that file.

LISTING 19.3   The Bank_C.pas File

```pascal
unit Bank_c;

interface

uses
  CORBA, Bank_i;

type
  EWithdrawError = class;
  TAccountHelper = class;
  TAccountStub = class;

  EWithdrawError = class(UserException)
  private
    Fcurrent_balance : Single;
```

LISTING 19.3   Continued

```
protected
  function  _get_current_balance : Single; virtual;
public
  property  current_balance : Single read _get_current_balance;
  constructor Create; overload;
  constructor Create(const current_balance : Single); overload;
  procedure Copy(const _Input : InputStream); override;
  procedure WriteExceptionInfo(var _Output : OutputStream); override;
end;


TAccountHelper = class
  class procedure Insert (var _A: CORBA.Any; const _Value : Bank_i.Account);
  class function  Extract(var _A: CORBA.Any) : Bank_i.Account;
  class function  TypeCode     : CORBA.TypeCode;
  class function  RepositoryId : string;
  class function  Read (const _Input  : CORBA.InputStream) : Bank_i.Account;
  class procedure Write(const _Output : CORBA.OutputStream;
      const _Value : Bank_i.Account);
  class function  Narrow(const _Obj   : CORBA.CORBAObject; _
      IsA : Boolean = False) : Bank_i.Account;
  class function  Bind(const _InstanceName : string = ''; _
      HostName : string = '') : Bank_i.Account; overload;
  class function  Bind(_Options : BindOptions;
      const _InstanceName : string = ''; _HostName: string = '') :
      Bank_i.Account; overload;
  end;

TAccountStub = class(CORBA.TCORBAObject, Bank_i.Account)
public
  procedure deposit ( const amount : Single); virtual;
  procedure withdraw ( const amount : Single); virtual;
  function  balance : Single; virtual;
end;

implementation

var

  WithdrawErrorDesc : PExceptionDescription;

function  EWithdrawError._get_current_balance : Single;
begin
  Result := Fcurrent_balance;
end;
```

LISTING 19.3   Continued

```
constructor EWithdrawError.Create;
begin
  inherited Create;
end;

constructor EWithdrawError.Create(const current_balance : Single);
begin
  inherited Create;
  Fcurrent_balance := current_balance;
end;

procedure EWithdrawError.Copy(const _Input: InputStream);
begin
  _Input.ReadFloat(Fcurrent_balance);
end;

procedure EWithdrawError.WriteExceptionInfo(var _Output : OutputStream);
begin
  _Output.WriteString('IDL:Bank/WithdrawError:1.0');
  _Output.WriteFloat(Fcurrent_balance);
end;

function  WithdrawError_Factory: PExceptionProxy; cdecl;
begin
  with Bank_c.EWithdrawError.Create() do Result := Proxy;
end;

class procedure TAccountHelper.Insert(var _A : CORBA.Any;
➥     const _Value : Bank_i.Account);
begin
  _A := Orb.MakeObjectRef( TAccountHelper.TypeCode, _
➥        Value as CORBA.CORBAObject);
end;

class function TAccountHelper.Extract(var _A : CORBA.Any): Bank_i.Account;
var
  _obj : Corba.CorbaObject;
begin
  _obj := Orb.GetObjectRef(_A);
  Result := TAccountHelper.Narrow(_obj, True);
end;

class function TAccountHelper.TypeCode : CORBA.TypeCode;
```

LISTING 19.3 Continued

```
begin
  Result := ORB.CreateInterfaceTC(RepositoryId, 'Account');
end;

class function TAccountHelper.RepositoryId : string;
begin
  Result := 'IDL:Bank/Account:1.0';
end;

class function TAccountHelper.Read(const _Input : CORBA.InputStream)
➥    : Bank_i.Account;
var
  _Obj : CORBA.CORBAObject;
begin
  _Input.ReadObject(_Obj);
  Result := Narrow(_Obj, True)
end;

class procedure TAccountHelper.Write(const _Output : CORBA.OutputStream;
➥    const _Value : Bank_i.Account);
begin
  _Output.WriteObject(_Value as CORBA.CORBAObject);
end;

class function TAccountHelper.Narrow(const _Obj : CORBA.CORBAObject; _
➥    IsA : Boolean) : Bank_i.Account;
begin
  Result := nil;
  if (_Obj = nil) or (_Obj.QueryInterface(Bank_i.Account, Result) = 0) then
    exit;
  if _IsA and _Obj._IsA(RepositoryId) then
    Result := TAccountStub.Create(_Obj);
end;

class function TAccountHelper.Bind(const _InstanceName : string = ''; _
➥    HostName: string = '') : Bank_i.Account;
begin
  Result := Narrow(ORB.bind(RepositoryId, _InstanceName, _HostName), True);
end;

class function TAccountHelper.Bind(_Options : BindOptions;
➥    const_InstanceName : string = ''; HostName : string = '') :
➥    Bank_i.Account;
```

LISTING 19.3   Continued

```pascal
begin
  Result := Narrow(ORB.bind(RepositoryId, _Options, _InstanceName, _
➡      HostName), True);
end;

procedure TAccountStub.deposit ( const amount : Single);
var
  _Output: CORBA.OutputStream;
  _Input : CORBA.InputStream;
begin
  inherited _CreateRequest('deposit',True, _Output);
  _Output.WriteFloat(amount);
  inherited _Invoke(_Output, _Input);
end;

procedure TAccountStub.withdraw ( const amount : Single);
var
  _Output: CORBA.OutputStream;
  _Input : CORBA.InputStream;
begin
  inherited _CreateRequest('withdraw',True, _Output);
  _Output.WriteFloat(amount);
  inherited _Invoke(_Output, _Input);
end;

function  TAccountStub.balance : Single;
var
  _Output: CORBA.OutputStream;
  _Input : CORBA.InputStream;
begin
  inherited _CreateRequest('balance',True, _Output);
  inherited _Invoke(_Output, _Input);
  _Input.ReadFloat(Result);
end;

initialization

Bank_c.WithdrawErrorDesc := RegisterUserException('WithdrawError',
➡      'IDL:Bank/WithdrawError:1.0', @Bank_c.WithdrawError_Factory);

finalization

UnRegisterUserException(Bank_c.WithdrawErrorDesc);

end.
```

Listing 19.4 shows the definition for the Account implementation class. This class isn't tied to CORBA, so it can be reused for other applications or interfaces. The Account class contains the methods that were declared in the Bank.idl file. Code has been added to the TAccount methods to implement the full server.

LISTING 19.4 The Implementation Class for the Bank Server

```
unit Bank_impl;

interface

uses
  SysUtils, CORBA, Bank_i, Bank_c;

type
  TAccount = class;

 unit Bank_impl;

interface

uses
  SysUtils, CORBA, Bank_i, Bank_c;

type

TAccount = class(TInterfacedObject, Bank_i.Account)
  protected
    _balance : Single;
  public
    constructor Create;
    procedure deposit (const amount : Single);
    procedure withdraw (const amount : Single);
    function  balance : Single;
  end;


implementation

constructor TAccount.Create;
begin
  inherited;
  _balance := random(10000);
end;
```

LISTING 19.4   Continued

```
procedure TAccount.deposit(const amount : Single);
begin
  if amount > 0 then
    _balance := _balance + amount;
end;

procedure TAccount.withdraw(const amount : Single);
begin
  if amount < _balance then
    _balance := _balance - amount
  else
    raise EWithdrawError.Create(_balance);
end;

function  TAccount.balance : Single;
begin
  result := _balance;
end;

initialization
  randomize;

end.
```

The TAccount object is derived from TInterfacedObject, so it will be reference counted auto-matically. It implements the Account interface that was contained in the Bank_I.pas file. The deposit method does a simple check to make sure that the user hasn't passed a negative number to the application. The withdraw method performs a check on the amount passed by the client. If it is less than the balance, the exception is raised with the current account balance as the exception argument. The client can process the exception to display information to the end user. The balance method returns the current balance on the server.

Listing 19.5 shows the stub class that is used as the proxy object for the client application. Like the server skeleton, it has the three methods defined in the Account interface in the IDL file.

LISTING 19.5   Client-Side Stub Class

```
TAccountStub = class(CORBA.TCORBAObject, Bank_i.Account)  public

public

public
```

LISTING 19.5 Continued

```
  procedure deposit ( const amount : Single); virtual;
  procedure withdraw ( const amount : Single); virtual;
  function  balance : Single; virtual;
end;
```

Listing 19.6 shows the deposit() method in detail. Two CORBA buffer streams are declared as local variables. The CreateRequest() method is a call into the ORB that asks for a valid output buffer so that information can be written into it. The stub passes the name of the method that will be called on the server side and specifies whether to wait for the server to complete its task before continuing. This is referred to as a one-way call or a two-way call.

LISTING 19.6 The Stub Class Deposit Method

```
procedure TAccountStub.deposit(const amount : Single);
var
  _Output: CORBA.OutputStream;
  _Input : CORBA.InputStream;
begin
  inherited _CreateRequest('deposit', True, Output);
  _Output.WriteFloat(amount);
  inherited _Invoke(Output, Input);
end;
```

The next step is to write any data values that need to be passed to the server into the output buffer. In this case, the amount to deposit is stored in the buffer. The final call is the Invoke method. This is another call to the ORB that sends the request and output buffer to the server side. After the server has finished processing, execution continues on the client side. In situations where the method call is a function (such as the balance method), the input buffer contains the returned result. IDL2Pas would have generated the code to read the values from the input buffer. However, in this case it was a call to a procedure, so no return value is present.

All of the stub code is generated automatically by IDL2Pas, so you should never have to edit it yourself. However, it is helpful to understand what this generated code does.

The final part of the code for the application is in the client GUI. The client will contain three push buttons, two edit controls, and one label control as shown in Figure 19.3. All CORBA interface variables are declared as interface types. In this case, the Account interface is declared as type Account. This establishes a variable from the type defined in the Bank_i.pas file that has the three methods defined in the Bank.idl file. The other benefit to having interface type variables is the automatic reference counting that takes place behind the scenes. All the CORBA objects should be reference counted. The IDL2Pas compiler automatically generates the code to facilitate this.

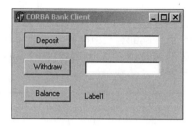

FIGURE 19.3
The CORBA Client Application.

The most interesting part of the code is the Withdraw OnClick event. Listing 19.7 contains the client-side source. The call to the Withdraw() method checks to make sure that the client isn't attempting to take more than the account holds. If this is the case, an exception is raised. Notice that raising an exception in CORBA is identical to raising an exception in Delphi. The Delphi exception gets translated to a CORBA exception automatically.

LISTING 19.7   The Client Source

```
unit ClientMain;

interface

uses
  Windows, Messages, SysUtils, Classes, Graphics, Controls, Forms, Dialogs,
  Corba, Bank_c, Bank_i, StdCtrls;

type
  TForm1 = class(TForm)
    btnDeposit: TButton;
    btnWithdraw: TButton;
    btnBalance: TButton;
    Edit1: TEdit;
    Edit2: TEdit;
    Label1: TLabel;
    procedure btnDepositClick(Sender: TObject);
    procedure btnWithdrawClick(Sender: TObject);
    procedure btnBalanceClick(Sender: TObject);
    procedure FormCreate(Sender: TObject);
  private
  { private declarations }
  protected
    Acct : Account;
    procedure InitCorba;
  { protected declarations }
```

LISTING 19.7   Continued

```
public
{ public declarations }
end;

var
  Form1: TForm1;

implementation

{$R *.DFM}

procedure TForm1.InitCorba;
begin
  CorbaInitialize;
  // Bind to the Corba server
  Acct := TAccountHelper.bind;
end;

procedure TForm1.btnDepositClick(Sender: TObject);
begin
  Acct.deposit(StrToFloat(Edit1.text));
end;

procedure TForm1.btnWithdrawClick(Sender: TObject);
begin
  try
    Acct.withdraw(StrToFloat(Edit2.Text));
  except
    on e: EWithdrawError do
      ShowMessage('Withdraw Error. The balance = ' +
      FormatFloat('$##,##0.00', E.current_balance));
  end;
end;

procedure TForm1.btnBalanceClick(Sender: TObject);
begin
  label1.caption := FormatFloat('Balance = $##,##0.00', acct.balance);
end;

procedure TForm1.FormCreate(Sender: TObject);
begin
 InitCorba;
end;

end.
```

19

CORBA
DEVELOPMENT

After the client and server applications are compiled, OSAgent needs to be started. On a Windows NT machine, the VisiBroker OSAgent can be installed as a service. On other operating systems, it has to be started manually. To start OSAgent manually on any MS Windows platform, choose the Start, Run menu and type **OSAgent -C**. This starts OSAgent in console mode. The agent will appear as an icon on the taskbar.

The server application is started next, followed by the client. The client GUI is shown in Figure 19.3. It has three buttons, two edit boxes, and a label control to display the balance. Click the Balance button to get the initial value from the server. Then add some money. Click Balance again to refresh the value on the client side. (Balance can also be called as part of the deposit and withdraw methods to automatically update the client.) After trying a few values, try to withdraw more than the balance. You should see the exception message.

Complex Data Types

This next example won't do much as a practical application. However, it illustrates how to use some of the complex data types that are available in CORBA IDL. Listing 19.8 shows the IDL for the *Advanced Data Types (ADTs)*.

LISTING 19.8   ADT.idl

```
// ADT IDL file
//
// Demonstrates various data structures in IDL
//

// use an alias for string types

typedef string Identifier;

enum EnumType
{
  first,
  second,
  third
};

struct StructType
{
  short s;
  long l;
  Identifier i;
};
```

LISTING 19.8   Continued

```
const unsigned long ArraySize = 3;

typedef StructType StructArray[ArraySize];

typedef sequence<StructType> StructSequence;


interface ADT
{

  void Test1(in Identifier st, in EnumType myEnum, inout StructType myStruct);

  void Test2(out StructType myStruct, in StructArray myStructArray,
➥        out StructSequence myStructSeq);

};
```

The first data type shows the use of an alias to remap the string type. All strings in this example will be of type Identifier. The EnumType consists of three values: first, second, and third.

The StructType is similar to a record in Pascal. This data structure consists of a short, a long, and a string (mapped to the Identifier alias). The ArraySize is mapped as a constant.

The next two items in the IDL file declare types based on the previous definitions. The StructArray is declared as an array of three elements maximum (zero based). A sequence is a dynamic array. The last typedef declares a sequence of StructTypes.

Finally, the ADT interface is defined with two methods: Test1 and Test2. The arguments to these methods are designed to show the different directions data can take. In parameters are created and initialized on the client side. Out parameters are created and initialized on the server side. InOut parameters are created and initialized on the client side, but typically are modified on the server side and returned to the client with new values in the data members.

Listing 19.9 shows the ADT_I.pas interface file. Notice that the typedefs are defined in this file. Also an interface is created for the StructType. All complex types are mapped to objects in Object Pascal with the appropriate get and set methods and a Helper class to facilitate marshaling the data in a CORBA buffer.

LISTING 19.9   The ADT_I.pas File

```
unit adt_i;

interface
```

LISTING 19.9   Continued

```
uses
  CORBA;

type

  EnumType = (first, second, third);

const
  { (Do not edit the values assigned to these constants.) }

  ArraySize : Cardinal = 3;

type
  StructType = interface;
  ADT = interface;

  Identifier = AnsiString;

  StructArray = array[0..2] of adt_i.StructType;

  StructSequence = array of adt_i.StructType;

  StructType = interface
    ['{B4A1845D-4DB0-9B2E-A2E3-001F2D6B8C81}']
    function _get_s : SmallInt;
    procedure _set_s (const s : SmallInt);
    function _get_l : Integer;
    procedure _set_l (const l : Integer);
    function _get_i : adt_i.Identifier;
    procedure _set_i (const i : adt_i.Identifier);
    property  s : SmallInt read _get_s write _set_s;
    property  l : Integer read _get_l write _set_l;
    property  i : adt_i.Identifier read _get_i write _set_i;
  end;

  ADT = interface
    ['{203B9E07-735F-2980-CB02-353A7C6A5B68}']
    procedure Test1 (const st : adt_i.Identifier;
                     const myEnum : adt_i.EnumType;
                     var   myStruct : adt_i.StructType);
    procedure Test2 (out   myStruct : adt_i.StructType;
                     const myStructArray : adt_i.StructArray;
                     out   myStructSeq : adt_i.StructSequence);
  end;
```

LISTING 19.9 Continued

```
implementation

initialization

end.
```

Listing 19.10 shows the implementation of the server side. When you read the method parameter lists in IDL, the direction is applicable to the server, or receiving side. So an out parameter means that it is out relative to the server. An in parameter is in relative to the server, and so on.

All the out parameters on the server side need to have their data structures created and initialized before the data can be passed back to the client. Any parameter defined as a const or var parameter will have an existing data structure associated with it.

LISTING 19.10 The ADT Implementation File for the Server

```
unit adt_impl;

interface

uses
  SysUtils, CORBA, adt_i, adt_c;

type
  TADT = class;

  TADT = class(TInterfacedObject, adt_i.ADT)
  public
    constructor Create;
    procedure Test1 ( const st : adt_i.Identifier;
                      const myEnum : adt_i.EnumType;
                      var   myStruct : adt_i.StructType);
    procedure Test2 ( out   myStruct : adt_i.StructType;
                      const myStructArray : adt_i.StructArray;
                      out   myStructSeq : adt_i.StructSequence);
  end;

implementation

uses ServerMain;

constructor TADT.Create;
```

LISTING 19.10   Continued

```
begin
  inherited;
end;

procedure TADT.Test1 ( const st : adt_i.Identifier;
                       const myEnum : adt_i.EnumType;
                       var   myStruct : adt_i.StructType);
begin
  Form1.Memo1.Lines.Add('String from Client : ' + st);

  case myEnum of
    first : Form1.Memo1.Lines.Add('Enum value is "first"');
    second: Form1.Memo1.Lines.Add('Enum value is "second"');
    third:  Form1.Memo1.Lines.Add('Enum value is "third"');
  end;

  Form1.Memo1.Lines.Add(Format('myStruct.s = %d', [myStruct.s]));
  Form1.Memo1.Lines.Add(Format('myStruct.l = %d', [myStruct.l]));
  Form1.Memo1.Lines.Add(Format('myStruct.i = %s', [myStruct.i]));

  myStruct.s := 10;
  myStruct.l := 1000;
  myStruct.i := 'This is the return string from the Server';
end;

procedure TADT.Test2 ( out   myStruct : adt_i.StructType;
                       const myStructArray : adt_i.StructArray;
                       out   myStructSeq : adt_i.StructSequence);
var
  k : integer;
  tempSeq : StructSequence;
begin
  myStruct := TStructType.Create(20, 2000,
➡       'Hello from the server structType Test 2');

  for k := 0 to ArraySize - 1 do
    With Form1.Memo1.Lines do
    begin
      Add(Format('myStructArray[%d].s = %d', [k, myStructArray[k].s]));
      Add(Format('myStructArray[%d].l = %d', [k, myStructArray[k].l]));
      Add(Format('myStructArray[%d].i = %s', [k, myStructArray[k].i]));
    end;

  SetLength(tempSeq, 2);
```

LISTING 19.10   Continued

```
  for k := 0 to 1 do
    tempSeq[k] := TStructType.Create(k + 100, k + 1000, Format('k = %d', [k]));
  myStructSeq := tempSeq;
end;


initialization

end.
```

The client application user interface has two buttons and a memo control. Each button is mapped to one of the ADT test methods. The results of the calls are written to the memo control. Listing 19.11 shows the client file.

LISTING 19.11   The ADT Client Side

```
unit ClientMain;

interface

uses
  Windows, Messages, SysUtils, Classes, Graphics, Controls, Forms, Dialogs,
  Corba, adt_c, adt_i, StdCtrls;

type
  TForm1 = class(TForm)
    Button1: TButton;
    Button2: TButton;
    Memo1: TMemo;
    procedure FormCreate(Sender: TObject);
    procedure Button1Click(Sender: TObject);
    procedure Button2Click(Sender: TObject);
  private
  { private declarations }
  protected
    myADT : ADT;
    procedure InitCorba;
  { protected declarations }
  public
  { public declarations }
  end;

var
  Form1: TForm1;
```

LISTING 19.11   Continued

```
implementation

{$R *.DFM}

procedure TForm1.InitCorba;
begin
  CorbaInitialize;
  myADT := TADTHelper.bind;
end;

procedure TForm1.FormCreate(Sender: TObject);
begin
  initCorba;
end;

procedure TForm1.Button1Click(Sender: TObject);
var
  temp : StructType;
begin
  temp := TStructType.Create(50, 500, 'This is the client struct in Test 1');
  myADT.Test1('Hello from the Test1 Client', first, temp);

  with Memo1.Lines do
  begin
    Add('Response from server inout struc var:');
    Add(Format('myStruct.s = %d', [temp.s]));
    Add(Format('myStruct.l = %d', [temp.l]));
    Add(Format('myStruct.i = %s', [temp.i]));
  end;
end;

procedure TForm1.Button2Click(Sender: TObject);
var
  I: Integer;
  temp : StructType;
  tempSeq : StructSequence;
  tempArray : StructArray;
begin
  temp := TStructType.Create(0,0,'test');
  SetLength(tempSeq, 2);

  for I := 0 to ArraySize -1 do
    tempArray[I] := TStructType.Create(200 + I, 2000 + I,
        Format('Stuct %d in Array', [I]) );
```

LISTING 19.11 Continued

```
  myADT.Test2(temp, tempArray, tempSeq);

  with Memo1.Lines do
  begin
    Add(Format('struct.s = %d', [temp.s]) );
    Add(Format('struct.l = %d', [temp.l]) );
    Add(Format('struct.i = %s', [temp.i]) );
  end;

  for I := 0 to 1 do
  with Memo1.Lines do
  begin
    Add( Format('tempSeq[%d].s = %d', [I, tempSeq[I].s]) );
    Add( Format('tempSeq[%d].l = %d', [I, tempSeq[I].l]) );
    Add( Format('tempSeq[%d].i = %s', [I, tempSeq[I].i]) );
  end;
end;

end.
```

To run this example, compile the code and make sure that the OSAgent is running. When you click on either of the test buttons on the data, structures are exchanged between the client and server. The data that is received on each side is written to the respective memo control in the application's window.

Delphi, CORBA, and Enterprise Java Beans (EJBs)

This section shows you how to make a Delphi CORBA application connect to EJBs that are deployed under the Borland Application Server. To construct and deploy the EJB for this demo, you'll need Borland JBuilder 5 and Borland Application Server 4.51. Both of these products are available as a free trial download edition from the Borland Web site (www.borland.com).

A Crash Course in EJBs for Delphi Programmers

Several years ago, Sun Microsystems came out with their J2EE platform. This was an enhancement to the Java environment to add enterprise level distributed object computing. The specification for J2EE is fairly complex, but from an application developer's point of view, it can be broken down into a few straightforward concepts.

One key piece of the J2EE platform is an *Enterprise Java Bean (EJB)*. An EJB is (usually) a small, portable and scaleable object that is designed to do a specific job. The idea is that many

19

CORBA
DEVELOPMENT

EJBs can be scattered around the enterprise to perform various functions. At some central point, an application is deployed that will contact an EJB only when it needs the functionality that EJB provides.

An EJB Is a Specialized Component

In terms of Delphi, think of an EJB as a component. One example of an EJB would be a component that connects to a database and provides records to any application that requests them. Another EJB might perform a calculation based on information supplied to it, such as calculating sales tax for a purchase.

EJBs Live Within a Container

In Delphi, components are put into a package and are installed into the IDE. The IDE manages the components on the palette. The hooks are there to create the component when you drop one on a form. If you delete the component from the form, it is destroyed within the IDE.

A similar approach is taken for EJBs only not through the Delphi IDE. The J2EE specification describes an entity known as the *EJB container*. The container is the host for all EJBs. This is a similar concept to the way the IDE manages components within Delphi. The container manages the process of creating and destroying EJBs.

EJBs Have Predefined APIs

Borland AppServer has an EJB container embedded within itself. Just like the Delphi IDE and its components, the EJB container and all EJBs must have a predefined set of APIs that let the EJB live within the container. The EJB developer adds additional methods to the EJB to give it specific functionality. However, the predefined APIs must be there for the EJB to be managed correctly by the container.

In addition to creating and destroying the EJB, there are specific APIs for message routing and callbacks to an EJB. The container also performs numerous other features described in the specification, but those details are beyond the scope of this book.

The Home and Remote Interfaces

As part of the predefined API set, all EJBs must have two interfaces. One is called the Home interface, and the other is the Remote interface. The Home interface is the initial method that an application calls to get an instance of the EJB. The Home interface is a factory that creates instances of the Remote interface and hands them back to the calling application.

The Remote interface has all the methods that the calling program wants to use. These are equivalent to the interfaces declared in an IDL file. So the process is that a client application will call the EJB `Home` interface to get an instance of the `Remote` interface. Once it has the `Remote` interface, the client can call any method published by that interface.

Types of EJBs

All EJBs can be divided into one of two groups:

- Session beans
- Entity beans

A session bean is (typically) a stateless EJB. *Stateless* means that between calls, the session bean doesn't store any information about the calling application. It is said to be nonpersistent. It doesn't keep track of where the client might be in a calling sequence, so it doesn't have the equivalent of a state machine. It is possible to have a stateful session bean, but the developer has to write all the logic to implement that.

An entity bean generally wraps a database record. This type of bean is said to have state because the information it processes (the database record) is stored between calls.

There is another key difference between a session and entity bean. When a client connects to a session bean, one instance of the session bean is created specifically for the calling client. If another client calls the session bean, another instance is created. So each client will get its own instance of a session bean.

When a client calls an entity bean, one instance of the entity bean is created. If another client calls the entity bean, it will share the same entity bean instance. Each entity bean is managed by the container in a connection pool.

Configuring JBuilder 5 for EJB Development

The easiest way to create EJBs is with Borland's JBuilder 5. To connect Delphi to an EJB, the EJB needs to be deployed with Borland's Application Server (version 4.51 or higher). Both JBuilder 5 and Borland AppServer are available on the Borland Web site as trial edition downloads. Typically, AppServer should be installed, followed by JBuilder.

Before starting JBuilder, it is a good idea to set up a projects directory for all your JBuilder applications. Typically, this will be something similar to `c:\MyProjects`.

When you start JBuilder 5 and try to create an EJB using the wizards built into the IDE, you might see them grayed out. If this is the case, it is because JBuilder needs to be configured to point to the AppServer. This is a configuration setting in a JBuilder dialog box.

To configure JBuilder 5 for EJB support,

1. Start JBuilder 5, go to the Tools menu, and select Enterprise Setup. This opens a dialog box to set the CORBA configuration.

2. On the CORBA tab, select VisiBroker. JBuilder ships with VisiBroker for Java.

3. Click on the Edit button. The Edit Configuration dialog box appears. Enter the path to the ORB. This is where IDL2Java resides (typically, `c:\Borland\AppServer\bin`).

4. Select that Application server tab. This is used to tell JBuilder which Application Server to use. Select BAS 4.5 and make sure that it is pointing to the AppServer directory (that is, `c:\Borland\AppServer`).

5. Under Projects, Default Project Proprieties, select the Servers tab. Then make sure that the Borland Application Server is selected. If not, click on the ellipse button and add it to the configuration.

That should configure JBuilder for EJBs. Now we can create our first EJB.

Building a Simple `"Hello, world"` EJB

Borrowing from the C world, the EJB application we'll build is one that returns the string `"Hello, world"`. This example guides you through the process of making an EJB. More complex EJBs can be developed by following the same process and adding more methods to the Remote interface.

First start Borland AppServer, and then JBuilder. When you become more proficient in Java and JBuilder, you can eventually develop and test your EJBs totally within the JBuilder environment. In this section, we'll develop the EJB and deploy it to the Borland AppServer. Then we'll make a Delphi client that will connect to the EJB. This is a more realistic scenario for real-world development and deployment.

To build the `"Hello, world"` EJB,

1. Close down all projects within JBuilder. Then choose File, New Project. Give this project the name `"HelloWorld"`. This will also be the name of the project file when JBuilder saves it to disk.

2. Next we need to add an EJB Group. Choose File, New, Enterprise and select the Empty EJB Group icon. When prompted for a name, give it **HelloGroup**. Notice that there is an edit control that specifies the name of the jar file that this application will be built into. A jar file is similar to a zip file. You archive all the Java byte code files into a jar file so that you only have one file to deploy. In this case, rename the jar file to `HelloWorld.jar`.

3. Next add a new EJB by selecting File, New, Enterprise and select Enterprise Java Bean. When prompted for a name, enter **HelloBean**. JBuilder 5 will automatically create the bean and all the required interfaces.

4. Select the `HelloBean.java` file in the project window and click on the Source tab. Make sure that your source code resembles Listing 19.12.

LISTING 19.12 The JavaBean Source

```java
package helloworld;
import java.rmi.*;
import javax.ejb.*;
import java.lang.String;
public class HelloBean implements SessionBean
{
    private SessionContext sessionContext;
    public void ejbCreate()
    {
    }
    public void ejbRemove() throws RemoteException
    {
    }
    public void ejbActivate() throws RemoteException
    {
    }
    public void ejbPassivate() throws RemoteException
    {
    }
    public void setSessionContext(SessionContext sessionContext) throws
    RemoteException
    {
        this.sessionContext = sessionContext;
    }
    public String sayHello() {
        return "Hello, world";
    }
}
```

5. You need to enter the last method in the code block (`sayHello()`). This method returns a string, so it must include the `java.lang.String` package as shown near the top of the file.

6. Now we need to expose the `sayHello()` method through the `Remote` interface. To do that, select the Bean tab at the bottom of the code window. Then select the Methods tab at the bottom of the Bean tab window. You'll see the `sayHello()` method listed with an unchecked check box next to it. Check the box. That exposes the method through the Remote interface. To verify this, double-click on the `Hello.java` file in the project window. This brings up the source for the Remote interface. Notice that `sayHello()` is there now.

7. Save your work and build the project. You should have no errors.

Building a Client Test Application in JBuilder

JBuilder lets you build a client-side Java application to test your EJB. To do this,

1. Choose File, New, Enterprise and select EJB Test Client. Name this `HelloTestClient1.java`.

2. JBuilder will automatically create the file. Go to the bottom of it, and you will see a main program. Make yours resemble Listing 19.13.

LISTING 19.13   EJB Java Test Client Application

```
public static void main(String[] args) {
   HelloTestClient1 client = new HelloTestClient1();
   client.create();   //add these two lines
   client.sayHello();
   // Use the client object to call one of the Home interface wrappers
   // above, to create a Remote interface reference to the bean.
   // If the return value is of the Remote interface type, you can use it
   // to access the remote interface methods. You can also just use the
   // client object to call the Remote interface wrappers.
}
```

You add the `create()` and `sayHello()` methods to the main program.

Building the Client and Testing the EJB

Now build the test client. Follow these steps:

1. Run the EJB by selecting the HelloGroup entity in the project window and right-clicking on it. Then choose Run. Soon you should see messages in the JBuilder message pane indicating that the EJB is running. This might take 20 or 30 seconds depending on the speed and memory of your machine. Remember, Java is a resource hog.

2. Select the client application and right-click on it. Choose Run from the menu. You'll see it start up and eventually print `"Hello, world"` to the message window. This means that our EJB works correctly.

3. You can stop the EJB group by clicking on the red Stop button at the bottom of the message window.

Deploying the EJB to AppServer

To deploy the EJB to AppServer, follow these steps:

1. Select Tools, EJB Deployment. Follow the wizard, and it will deploy the EJB.

2. Once the EJB is deployed, AppServer will automatically start it. Click on the Next button until you reach step 4.

3. In step 4 of the wizard, you must select an EJB container. Make sure that Borland AppServer is running. Then click on the Add EJB Container button, and you'll see the AppServer container. Select it and click OK. Then continue with the wizard until it completes.

Generating the SIDL File

Borland has developed a proprietary technique to remap EJBs to an AppServer interface called *Simplified IDL (SIDL)*. This remapping makes sure that older CORBA applications can call EJBs by using the CORBA 2.1 standard (or higher). There is a tool that ships with AppServer called the SIDL compiler that can take a Remote interface and generate conventional IDL files.

Borland provides a free plug-in for JBuilder that facilitates converting the EJB interfaces to IDL with the SIDL compiler. The plug-in can be found on the CD-ROM in the same directory as the source code for this chapter. The plug-in is a Java jar file called `otSIDL.jar`. Copy it to the `c:\ JBuilder5\lib\ext` directory (or the equivalent path where you installed JBuilder). You'll have to restart JBuilder to activate the tool.

When the JBuilder IDE comes up, choose Tools, IDE Options, and you'll see a dialog box with a tab for SIDL. Select the SIDL tab and specify an output directory. In this case, enter `c:\MyProjects\HelloWorld` (or where ever you stored the HelloWorld project).

This tool adds a pop-up menu to the EJB Remote interface.

Select the `HelloHome.java` file from the project list and right-click on it. You'll see a menu item called Generate Simplified IDL. Choose that, and it will run the SIDL compiler. The output will be in the `classes` directory for the project.

Developing the EJB Client in Delphi

Now that we have a complete EJB, we can take the IDL file generated by the SIDL compiler and create a Delphi CORBA client to talk to the EJB. If you look under the EJB project's `classes` directory, you'll see a file called `HelloHome.idl`. You will need this and a copy of the `sidl.idl` file that is found on the `Delphi6\Demos\Corba\Idl2pas\EJB\EuroConverter` directory. Put those two files in a new directory. Then, follow these steps:

1. Start Delphi and choose File, New, Other, CORBA, CORBA Client Application.

2. Add the `HelloHome.idl` file to the list of files that will be processed. You don't need to add the `sidl.idl` file because it is included automatically in `HelloHome.idl` via the `include` pragma.

3. The wizard will create a new CORBA client. Save the project and call it `HelloClient`. Many file windows will be displayed after the wizard runs. Other than the `Unit1.pas` file, the only two that need to be displayed are `HelloHome_HelloWorld_i.pas` and `HelloHome_HelloWorld_c.pas`. All the rest can be closed.

4. On the main form, drop a button and label control. Make your application resemble Figure 19.4.

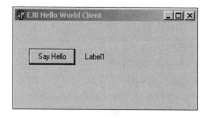

FIGURE 19.4

The EJB Delphi Client.

5. In the form's OnCreate() method, enter **initCorba**.

6. Modify the initCorba() method to resemble the code block shown in Listing 19.14. You'll have to add two variables to the class definition. One is for the Home interface, and the other one is for the Remote interface. The Home interface is a factory that creates Remote interfaces. Once you have an instance of the Remote interface, you can call the methods on the EJB. So the initCorba() method will contain the code that binds to the Home interface and generates a Remote interface object.

7. Add a button OnClick event and make it resemble the button OnClick code block shown in Listing 19.14.

8. Build the client application. See the note if you get errors.

LISTING 19.14 The EJB Client Main Application File

```
unit ClientMain;

interface

uses
  Windows, Messages, SysUtils, Classes, Graphics, Controls, Forms, Dialogs,
  Corba, HelloHome_c, HelloHome_helloworld_c, HelloHome_helloworld_i,
  HelloHome_i, HelloHome_sidl_javax_ejb_c, HelloHome_sidl_javax_ejb_i,
  HelloHome_sidl_java_lang_c, HelloHome_sidl_java_lang_i,
  HelloHome_sidl_java_math_c, HelloHome_sidl_java_math_i,
  HelloHome_sidl_java_sql_c, HelloHome_sidl_java_sql_i,
  HelloHome_sidl_java_util_c, HelloHome_sidl_java_util_i,
  StdCtrls;

type
  TForm1 = class(TForm)
```

LISTING **19.14**   Continued

```pascal
    Button1: TButton;
    Label1: TLabel;
    procedure FormCreate(Sender: TObject);
    procedure Button1Click(Sender: TObject);
  private
  { private declarations }
  protected
    myHome : HelloHome;
    myRemote : Hello;
    procedure InitCorba;
  { protected declarations }
  public
  { public declarations }
  end;

var
  Form1: TForm1;

implementation

{$R *.DFM}

procedure TForm1.InitCorba;
begin
   CorbaInitialize;

   myHome := THelloHomeHelper.Bind;
   myRemote := myHome._create;
end;

procedure TForm1.FormCreate(Sender: TObject);
begin
   initCorba;
end;

procedure TForm1.Button1Click(Sender: TObject);
begin
   Label1.Caption := myRemote.sayHello;
end;

end.
```

> **NOTE**
>
> You'll encounter two possible errors with the original Delphi 6 distribution. These errors were fixed in the Service Pack 1 update. The first error is that the compiler will complain about a unit not being included. It will point you to the particular unit name. When it does, just add the unit name to the uses clause in the file with the error.
>
> The second error occurs at runtime. This is related to the Home interface create() method. *Create* was originally on the reserved word list for IDL2Pas. So when it encounters that word, it puts an underscore in front of it. When the EJB gets a request for a method called _create(), it generates an exception because it doesn't publish that method. It publishes a method called create().
>
> To fix this, go to the THelloHomeStub._create() method in HelloHome_helloworld_c.pas (the code snippet follows). The first argument in the _CreateRequest() method tells the CORBA server which method will be called. If you see _create as the first argument, change it to create:
>
> ```
> function  THelloHomeStub._create : HelloHome_helloworld_i.Hello;
> var
>   _Output: CORBA.OutputStream;
>   _Input : CORBA.InputStream;
> begin
>   inherited _CreateRequest('create', True, _Output);
>   inherited _Invoke(_Output, _Input);
>   Result := HelloHome_helloworld_c.THelloHelper.Read(_Input);
> end;
> ```
>
> Both of these errors were fixed in the Delphi 6 update 1, so you should upgrade to that to get around these errors.

Running the Application

To run the application, follow these steps:

1. Start the OSAgent.

2. Make sure that Borland AppServer has started.

3. Start the HelloClient. Click on the button, and you should see the label text change to "Hello, world".

More complex EJBs can be developed by following a similar development process. In Java, you just add more method interfaces to increase the capabilities of the EJB. The client-side process will essentially remain the same as this example. Delphi CORBA clients will be built by gathering the SIDL produced IDL files and processing them through the Delphi CORBA IDE wizard.

CORBA and Web Services

It is fairly straightforward to extend a CORBA application through the Web Services architecture. The SOAP specification doesn't allow object references to be passed between applications, so a little work needs to be done on the middle-tier level to isolate SOAP clients from the details of CORBA applications.

This next example will publish the EJB that was created in the last section so that it can be used by SOAP clients. Figure 19.5 shows the architecture of the application.

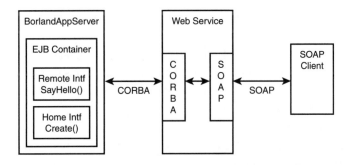

FIGURE 19.5

The CORBA/Web Services example architecture.

The EJB is deployed under the Borland AppServer. It has a published CORBA interface that any CORBA client can call. The Web Service application is both a SOAP server and a CORBA client. The SOAP server portion of the application will wrap the calls the SOAP client makes around the CORBA client interface.

By using this technique, you can harness the power of EJBs and publish the results as SOAP interfaces to clients that only have that capability. This means that a SOAP enabled application can access applications that manipulate EJBs. This brings an enormous capability to the client desktop and gets rid of CORBA ORB deployment issues on the client side as well.

In this example, the EJB will remain exactly as it was in the last section. No modifications to its interface or functionally have to be made. That portion of the application is complete.

Creating the Web Service

To create the Web Service, you need the IDL files from the last section. IDL2Pas can be run in a command window to generate the client-side files. Create a directory for the project and copy the SIDL.idl and HelloHome.idl files into the new directory. Then open a command window and type the following:

```
IDL2Pas HelloHome.idl
```

The IDL2Pas compiler will generate the files for the application. We only need the `HelloHome_I.pas` and `HelloHome_C.pas` files for the CORBA client side.

In order to build this project, you need to install the Invokamatic Wizard, which lets you create a SOAP application in a couple of minutes. When you register Delphi 6, you get access to the Delphi 6 Registered Users' Web site, which contains the Delphi eXtreme Toys downloads. This contains additional tools and freebies for Delphi 6, including the Invokamatic Wizard. Download this wizard from the Borland Web site and install it into the IDE.

Now, to create the Web Service application, follow these steps:

1. Close down all projects in Delphi and select File, New, Other, Web Services. Then choose the Soap Server Application icon.

2. Choose the Web App Debugger Executable for the target application Web server and give it a name such as `coHelloWorld` for the `coClass` name. Make sure that you use a unique name every time you repeat this exercise, or clean the registry by unregistering your application when you are done with it.

3. The wizard will generate a bare bones application. Save it to the project directory that contains the IDL files. Name the module file `ServerMod.pas`, the main form file `ServerMain.pas`, and the application `Server.dpr`.

4. Now select the Files, New, Other, Web Services and choose the Invokamatic Wizard.

5. The dialog box prompts you for a name to use. Name it HelloWorldSoap. This automatically names the interface and files. In the Invokable Class drop-down box, choose TInvokable Class. When you select OK, it creates two new units in your project. One is an interface unit, and the other is an implementation unit.

6. Select the interface unit and add the following method to the `IHelloWorldSoapIntf` interface:

   ```
   function sayHello: string; stdcall;
   ```

   The `stdcall` call tag is required so that the correct calling convention is established.

7. Now copy this method declaration to the implementation unit `THelloWorldSoapIntf` class and make it a public method.

8. Put the cursor anywhere on the method line and press Shift+Control+C to activate the class completion. Just for test purposes, we'll have this method return a hard-wired string to test the client. So type

   ```
   result := 'Hello, world';
   ```

9. Save the program, compile it, and run it. Running it registers the method interface. Make sure you start the Web App Debugger from the Delphi Tools menu. You can start the server and check the interfaces it knows about by clicking on the URL in the Web App Debugger UI.

Creating the SOAP Client Application

To create a SOAP client application,

1. Close down the project and choose File, New, Application.
2. Add one label and one edit control to the main form. Also add the interface files `SoapHTTPClient` and `HelloWorldSoapIntf` to the uses clause.
3. Declare a variable called `mySoap` to be of type `IHelloWorldSoap`.
4. On the button `OnClick` method, make the code resemble Listing 19.15.
5. Save the program and compile the files.
6. Run the application and click on the Say Hello button. After a small delay while the server application is loaded, you should see `"Hello, world"` in the label caption.

This is a preliminary test to show that the SOAP client and server work together. Now we can add the CORBA client to the server project to complete the full application.

LISTING 19.15 SOAP Client Main Form Class

```
unit ClientMain;

interface

uses
  Windows, Messages, SysUtils, Variants, Classes, Graphics, Controls, Forms,
  Dialogs, StdCtrls, SoapHTTPClient, HelloWorldSoapIntf;

type
  TForm1 = class(TForm)
    Button1: TButton;
    Label1: TLabel;
    procedure Button1Click(Sender: TObject);
  private
    { Private declarations }
    mySoap : IHelloWorldSoap;
  public
    { Public declarations }
  end;

var
  Form1: TForm1;

implementation

{$R *.dfm}
```

LISTING 19.15   Continued

```
procedure TForm1.Button1Click(Sender: TObject);
var x : THTTPRio;
begin
   x := THTTPRio.Create(nil);
   x.URL := 'http://localhost:1024/Server.exe/SOAP/';
   mySoap := x as IHelloWorldSoap;
   Label1.Caption := mySoap.sayHello;
end;

end.
```

Adding the CORBA Client Code to the Web Service

To add the CORBA client files to the Web Server project,

1. Copy the *_i.pas and *_c.pas files from the EJB client application developed in the last
   section. The interface file is shown in Listing 19.16.

LISTING 19.16   SOAP Interface File

```
{ Invokable interface declaration unit for IHelloWorldSoap }

unit HelloWorldSoapIntf;

interface

uses
  Types, XSBuiltIns;

type
  IHelloWorldSoap = interface(IInvokable)
    ['{CA738F7B-B111-4F12-BEBD-C2ADDD80C3E2}']
    // Declare your invokable logic here using standard Object Pascal code
    // Remember to include a calling convention! (usually stdcall)
    // For example:
    // function Add(const First, Second: double): double; stdcall;
    // function Subtract(const First, Second: double): double; stdcall;
    // function Multiply(const First, Second: double): double; stdcall;
    // function Divide(const First, Second: double): double; stdcall;
    function sayHello : String; stdcall;
  end;

implementation
```

LISTING 19.16 Continued

```
uses
  InvokeRegistry;

initialization
  InvRegistry.RegisterInterface(TypeInfo(IHelloWorldSoap), '', '');

end.
```

2. Add two public variables to the `Form1` class as shown in Listing 19.17. The variables will be public so that they are exposed to other units in the application.

3. Add an `OnCreate()` method to the main form and make it look like the one in Listing 19.17.

4. Finally, change the `HelloWorldSoapImpl.pas` file `sayHello()` method to look like Listing 19.18.

5. Now save the project and compile the server.

6. Make sure OSAgent, and Borland AppServer are running, then run the client. When you click on the Say Hello button you should see "Hello, world".

This was not a difficult example. However, you can now see the process of exposing EJBs to SOAP clients. This opens up new possibilities for bringing J2EE applications to the desktop and other Delphi application types.

LISTING 19.17 SOAP Server Main Form Class

```
unit ServerMain;

interface

uses
  SysUtils, Classes, Graphics, Controls, Forms, Dialogs, Corba,
  HelloHome_helloworld_i, HelloHome_helloworld_c;

type
  TForm1 = class(TForm)
    procedure FormCreate(Sender: TObject);
  private
    { Private declarations }
  public
    { Public declarations }
    myHome :  HelloHome;
    myRemote : Hello;
  end;
```

19

CORBA DEVELOPMENT

LISTING 19.17 Continued

```
var
  Form1: TForm1;

implementation

uses ComApp;

{$R *.DFM}

const
  CLASS_ComWebApp: TGUID = '{63859D3A-005F-43BB-8E64-85A466D9C364}';

procedure TForm1.FormCreate(Sender: TObject);
begin
  CorbaInitialize;
  myHome := THelloHomeHelper.bind;
  myRemote := myHome._create;
end;

initialization
  TWebAppAutoObjectFactory.Create(Class_ComWebApp,
    'coHelloWorld', 'coHelloWorld Object');

end.
```

LISTING 19.18 SOAP Server Implementation Class

```
{ Invokable implementation declaration unit for THelloWorldSoap,
  which implements IHelloWorldSoap }

unit HelloWorldSoapImpl;

interface

uses
  HelloWorldSoapIntf, InvokeRegistry, ServerMain;

type
  THelloWorldSoap = class(TInvokableClass, IHelloWorldSoap)
    // Make sure you have your invokable logic implemented in IHelloWorldSoap
    // first, save the file, then use CodeInsight(tm) to fill in this
    // implementation section by pressing Ctrl+Space, marking all the interface
    // declarations for IHelloWorldSoap, and pressing Enter.
```

LISTING 19.18 Continued

```
    // Once the declarations are inserted here, use ClassCompletion(tm)
    // to write the implementation stubs by pressing Ctrl+Shift+C
    function sayHello : String; stdcall;
  end;

implementation

{ THelloWorldSoap }

function THelloWorldSoap.sayHello: String;
begin
//  result := 'Hello, world';  //test for soap client
  result := ServerMain.Form1.myRemote.sayHello;
end;

initialization
  InvRegistry.RegisterInvokableClass(THelloWorldSoap);

end.
```

Summary

This chapter provides an introduction to developing CORBA applications in Delphi. We started with the basics of the CORBA architecture and developed a fairly simple Bank application. From there, we looked at more complex data structures.

Then we got into an area that is generating a lot of interest from enterprise developers. We learned how to develop an EJB in JBuilder 5, deploy it to the Borland AppServer, and connect a Delphi CORBA client to the EJB.

From there, we extended the EJB through a combination of CORBA and Web Services using the SOAP protocol. Using this approach, you can now take any EJB, connect it to a Web Service, and expose it to any client that can use the SOAP protocol. The client doesn't have to be aware that CORBA is deployed on the back end. This opens up new possibilities for extending corporate legacy applications.

19

CORBA DEVELOPMENT

BizSnap Development: Writing SOAP-Based Web Services

IN THIS CHAPTER

Developing eBusiness solutions *rapidly* is key to the success of many organizations. Fortunately, Borland has made this rapid development possible through the use of a new Delphi 6 feature called BizSnap. BizSnap is a technology that integrates XML and Web Services using the SOAP protocol into Delphi 6.

What Are Web Services?

Borland describes Web Services as follows:

> Using the Internet and Web infrastructure as the platform, Web Services seamlessly connect applications, business processes, customers, and suppliers—anywhere in the world—with standardized language and machine-independent Internet protocols.

Distributed applications generally consist of servers and clients—servers that provide some functionality to the clients. Any distributed application might contain many servers, and those servers might themselves be clients. Web Services are a new type of server component for applications with a distributed architecture. Web Services are applications that use common Internet protocols to deliver their functionality.

Because Web Services communicate using open standards, they offer the opportunity for many different platforms to interoperate. For instance, from the perspective of a client application, a Web service deployed on a Sun Solaris machine will look (for all intents and purposes) identical to the same service deployed on a Windows NT machine. Prior to Web Services, this type of integration was extremely time-consuming, expensive, and generally proprietary.

This open nature and the ability to use existing network hardware and software position Web Services to be powerful tools for both internal and business-to-business transactions.

What Is SOAP?

SOAP is the acronym for *Simple Object Access Protocol*. SOAP is a lightweight protocol used for exchanging data in a distributed environment, similar to portions of CORBA and DCOM, but with less functionality and resulting overhead. SOAP exchanges data using XML documents, using HTTP (or HTTPS) for its communications. A specification on SOAP is available for reference on the Internet at http://www.w3.org/TR/SOAP/.

Web Services also use a form of XML to instruct users about themselves, called WSDL. WSDL is short for *Web Services Description Language*. WSDL is used by client applications to identify what a Web service can do, where it can be found, and how to call it.

The wonderful thing about BizSnap is that you don't have to learn all the specifics of SOAP, XML, or WSDL in order to create Web Service applications.

In this chapter, we will show you how simple it is to create a Web Service, and then we'll show you how to access this service from a client application.

Writing a Web Service

To demonstrate how to create a Web Service, we'll show you how to create the ever-popular Fahrenheit Celsius converter as a Web Service.

A Web service written in Delphi consists of three main things. The first is a WebModule with a few SOAP components (described in a moment). The module is automatically created for you when you execute the SOAP Server Wizard. The second two components you must build yourself. One of those is a class implementation, which is simply the code that describes what your Web service will actually do. The second thing to create is an interface to that class. The interface will expose only those pieces of the class that you want to offer to the rest of the world through your Web service.

Delphi provides a Web Service Wizard in the WebServices tab of the Object Repository. You will see three items in this tab. At this point, we'll concern ourselves with only the Soap Server Application Wizard. When you click this, you'll be shown the New Soap Server Application dialog box (see Figure 20.1). This dialog box should look familiar if you've done any Web Server development. In fact, Web Services are really Web Servers that handle the specific SOAP response.

FIGURE 20.1
The New Soap Server Application dialog box.

In our example, we chose a CGI Stand-alone Executable. Click OK, and the wizard will generate a TWebModule as shown in Figure 20.2.

A Look at the TWebModule

Three components exist on the TWebModule. The purpose of these components is as follows:

- THTTPSoapDispatcher receives SOAP messages and dispatches them to the appropriate *Invoker* as specified by its Dispatcher property.

20

WRITING SOAP-
BASED WEB
SERVICES

- THTTPSoapPascalInvoker is the component referred to by the THTTPSoap Dispatcher.Dispatcher property. This component receives the SOAP message, interprets it, and then invokes the invokable interface being called by the message.
- TWSDLHTMLPublish is used to publish the list of WSDL documents that contain the information on available invokable interfaces. This allows clients other than Delphi to identify and use the methods made available through a given Web Service.

There is nothing that you have to do with the Web Module at this point. However, you must define and implement an invokable interface.

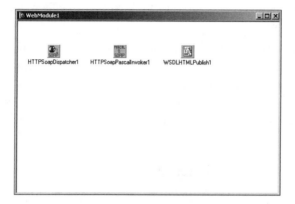

FIGURE 20.2
The Web Module generated from the wizard.

Defining an Invokable Interface

You must create a new unit in which you'll place your interface definition. Listing 20.1 shows the source code for the unit that we've created for our demonstration application, which you'll find on the CD. We've named this unit TempConverterIntf.pas.

LISTING 20.1   TempConverter.pas — Invokable Interface Definition

```
unit TempConverterIntf;

interface

type
  ITempConverter = Interface(IInvokable)
    ['{6D239CB5-6E74-445B-B101-F76F5C0F6E42}']
    function FahrenheitToCelsius(AFValue: double): double; stdcall;
    function CelsiusToFahrenheit(ACValue: double): double; stdcall;
```

LISTING 20.1 Continued

```
    function Purpose: String; stdcall;
  end;

implementation
uses InvokeRegistry;
initialization
  InvRegistry.RegisterInterface(TypeInfo(ITempConverter));

end.
```

This small unit contains only an interface that defines the methods that we intend to publish as part of our Web Service. You'll note that our interface descends from IInvokable. IInvokable is a simple interface compiled with the {M+} compiler option to ensure that RTTI is compiled into all of its descendants. This is necessary to allow the Web Services and Clients to translate code and symbolic information passed to each other.

In our example, we've defined two methods for converting temperatures and a Purpose() method that returns a string. Also, note that we provided a GUID for this interface to give it unique identification (to create a GUID in your own code, simply press Ctrl+Shift+G in the editor).

> **CAUTION**
>
> Note that each method defined in the invokable interface is defined using the std-call calling convention. This convention must be used, or the invokable interface will not work.

Finally, the last items to note are the user of the InvokeRegistry unit and the call to InvRegistry.RegisterInterface(). The THTTPSoapPascalInvoker component must be able to identify the invokable interface when it is passed a SOAP message. The RegisterInterface() method call registers the interface with the invocation registry. When we discuss the client code later, you'll see that the RegisterInterface() call is also made on the client. The server requires the registration so that it can identify the interface implementation to execute on an interface call. On the client, the method is used to allow components to look up information on invokable interfaces and how to call them. By placing the RegisterInterface() call in the initialization block, we ensure that the method is called when the service is run.

Implementing an Invokable Interface

Implementing an invokable interface is no different from implementing any interface. Listing 20.2 shows the source for our temperature conversion interface.

LISTING 20.2   TempConverterImpl.pas—Invokable Interface Implementation

```
unit TempConverterImpl;

interface
uses InvokeRegistry, TempConverterIntf;
type

  TTempConverter = class(TInvokableClass, ITempConverter)
  public
    function FahrenheitToCelsius(AFValue: double): double; stdcall;
    function CelsiusToFahrenheit(ACValue: double): double; stdcall;
    function Purpose: String; stdcall;
  end;

implementation

{ TTempConverter }

function TTempConverter.CelsiusToFahrenheit(ACValue: double): double;
begin
// Tf = (9/5)*Tc+32
  Result := (9/5)*ACValue+32;
end;

function TTempConverter.FahrenheitToCelsius(AFValue: double): double;
begin
// Tc = (5/9)*(Tf-32)

  Result := (5/9)*(AFValue-32);
end;

function TTempConverter.Purpose: String;
begin
  Result := 'Temperature converstions';
end;

initialization
  InvRegistry.RegisterInvokableClass(TTempConverter);
end.
```

First, note that our interface implementation is a descendant of the TInvokableClass object.
There are two primary reasons for doing this. The following reasons are take from the Delphi 6
online help:

- The invocation registry (InvRegistry) knows how to create instances of TInvokableClass and (because it has a virtual constructor) its descendants. This allows the registry to supply an invoker in a Web Service application with an instance of the invokable class that can handle an incoming request.

- TInvokableClass is an interfaced object that frees itself when the reference count on its interface drops to zero. Invoker components do not know when to free the implementation classes of the interfaces they call. Because TInvokableClass knows when to free itself, you do not need to supply your own lifetime management for this object.

Additionally, you'll see that our TTempConverter class implements the ITempConverter interface. The implementation methods for performing temperature conversions are self-explanatory.

In the initialization section, the call to RegisterInvokableClass() registers the TTempConverter class with the invocation registry. This is required only on the server so that the Web Service will be able to invoke the appropriate interface implementation.

That is really all there is to creating a simple Web Service. At this point, you can compile the Web Service and place it into an executable directory of a Web Server such as IIS or Apache. Typically, this would be a \Scripts or \cgi-bin directory.

Testing the Web Service

The URL http://127.0.0.1/cgi-bin/TempConvWS.exe/wsdl/ITempConverter was used to view the WSDL document generated from our Web Service. This service is hosted on an Apache server. To get a list of all the service interfaces available from a Delphi-generated Web service, the URL can be ended at wsdl. To see the specific WSDL document for a service, append the interface name desired—in this case ItempConverter. The resulting WSDL document is shown in Listing 20.3.

LISTING 20.3   Resulting WSDL Document from Web Service

```
<?xml version=”1.0” ?>
- <definitions xmlns="http://schemas.xmlsoap.org/wsdl/"
➥xmlns:xs="http://www.w3.org/2001/XMLSchema" name="ITempConverterservice"
targetNamespace="http://www.borland.com/soapServices/"
➥xmlns:soap="http://schemas.xmlsoap.org/wsdl/soap"
xmlns:soapenc="http://schemas.xmlsoap.org/soap/encoding/">
- <message name="FahrenheitToCelsiusRequest">
  <part name="AFValue" type="xs:double" />
  </message>
- <message name="FahrenheitToCelsiusResponse">
  <part name="return" type="xs:double" />
  </message>
```

LISTING 20.3   Continued

```xml
- <message name="CelsiusToFahrenheitRequest">
  <part name="ACValue" type="xs:double" />
  </message>
- <message name="CelsiusToFahrenheitResponse">
  <part name="return" type="xs:double" />
  </message>
  <message name="PurposeRequest" />
- <message name="PurposeResponse">
  <part name="return" type="xs:string" />
  </message>
- <portType name="ITempConverter">
- <operation name="FahrenheitToCelsius">
  <input message="FahrenheitToCelsiusRequest" />
  <output message="FahrenheitToCelsiusResponse" />
  </operation>
- <operation name="CelsiusToFahrenheit">
  <input message="CelsiusToFahrenheitRequest" />
  <output message="CelsiusToFahrenheitResponse" />
  </operation>
- <operation name="Purpose">
  <input message="PurposeRequest" />
  <output message="PurposeResponse" />
  </operation>
  </portType>
- <binding name="ITempConverterbinding" type="ITempConverter">
  <soap:binding style="rpc" transport="http://schemas.xmlsoap.org/soap/http" />
- <operation name="FahrenheitToCelsius">
  <soap:operation soapAction="urn:TempConverterIntf-
➥ITempConverter#FahrenheitToCelsius" />
- <input>
  <soap:body use="encoded" encodingStyle="http:
➥//schemas.xmlsoap.org/soap/encoding/"
  namespace="urn:TempConverterIntf-ITempConverter" />
  </input>
- <output>
  <soap:body use="encoded" encodingStyle=
➥"http://schemas.xmlsoap.org/soap/encoding/"
  namespace="urn:TempConverterIntf-ITempConverter" />
  </output>
  </operation>
- <operation name="CelsiusToFahrenheit">
  <soap:operation soapAction="urn:TempConverterIntf-
➥ITempConverter#CelsiusToFahrenheit" />
- <input>
```

LISTING 20.3 Continued

```
  <soap:body use="encoded" encodingStyle="http:
➡//schemas.xmlsoap.org/soap/encoding/"
namespace="urn:TempConverterIntf-ITempConverter" />
  </input>
- <output>
  <soap:body use="encoded" encodingStyle=
➡"http://schemas.xmlsoap.org/soap/encoding/"
namespace="urn:TempConverterIntf-ITempConverter" />
  </output>
  </operation>
- <operation name="Purpose">
  <soap:operation soapAction="urn:TempConverterIntf-ITempConverter#Purpose" />
- <input>
  <soap:body use="encoded" encodingStyle=
➡"http://schemas.xmlsoap.org/soap/encoding/"
namespace="urn:TempConverterIntf-ITempConverter" />
  </input>
- <output>
  <soap:body use="encoded" encodingStyle=
➡"http://schemas.xmlsoap.org/soap/encoding/"
namespace="urn:TempConverterIntf-ITempConverter" />
  </output>
  </operation>
  </binding>
- <service name="ITempConverterservice">
- <port name="ITempConverterPort" binding="ITempConverterbinding">
  <soap:address location="http://127.0.0.1/cgi-bin/TempConvWS.exe
➡/soap/ITempConverter" />
  </port>
  </service>
  </definitions>
```

Now we'll show you how simple it is to invoke a Web Service.

Invoking a Web Service from a Client

To invoke the Web Service, you must know the URL used to retrieve the WSDL document. This is the same URL we used earlier.

To demonstrate this, we used a simple application with single, main form (see Figure 20.3).

This application is straightforward: The user enters a temperature in the edit control, presses the desired conversion button, and the converted value is displayed in the Temperature label. The source for this application is shown in Listing 20.4.

20

WRITING SOAP-
BASED WEB
SERVICES

FIGURE 20.3

The Main Form to the Web Service Client Application.

LISTING 20.4   Web Service Client

```
unit MainFrm;

interface

uses
  Windows, Messages, SysUtils, Variants, Classes, Graphics, Controls, Forms,
  Dialogs, StdCtrls, Rio, SoapHTTPClient;

type
  TMainForm = class(TForm)
    btnFah2Cel: TButton;
    btnCel2Fah: TButton;
    edtArguement: TEdit;
    lblTemperature: TLabel;
    lblResultValue: TLabel;
    lblResult: TLabel;
    HTTPRIO1: THTTPRIO;
  private
    { Private declarations }
  public
    { Public declarations }
  end;

var
  MainForm: TMainForm;

implementation

uses TempConvImport;

{$R *.dfm}

end.
```

On the main form, we've placed a THTTPRIO component. A THTTPRIO represents a remotely invokable object, and acts as a local proxy for a Web service that very likely resides on a remote machine somewhere. The two TButton event handlers perform the code to invoke the remove object from our Web Service. Note that we must cast the THTTPRIO component as ITempConverter to refer to it. Then, we are able to invoke its method call.

Before any of this code will run, we must prepare the THTTPRIO component, which requires a few steps.

Generating an Import Unit for the Remote Invokable Object

Before we are able to use the THTTPRIO component, we need to create an import unit for our invokable object. Fortunately, Borland made this easy by providing a wizard to handle this. This wizard is available on the WebServices page of the Object Repository. When launched, you'll see the dialog box shown in Figure 20.4.

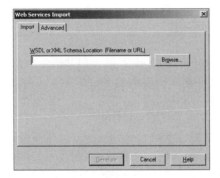

FIGURE 20.4
The Web Services Import Wizard.

In order to import a Web service into a client application, you put the WSDL path (the URL specified earlier) in the Schema Location and then press the Generate button to create the import unit. The import unit for our Web Service is shown in Listing 20.5 and looks almost exactly like our original interface definition unit.

LISTING 20.5   Web Service Import Unit

```
Unit TempConvImport;

interface

uses Types, XSBuiltIns;
```

LISTING 20.5   Continued

```
type

  ITempConverter = interface(IInvokable)
    ['{684379FC-7D4B-4037-8784-B58C63A0280D}']
    function FahrenheitToCelsius(const AFValue: Double): Double;  stdcall;
    function CelsiusToFahrenheit(const ACValue: Double): Double;  stdcall;
    function Purpose: WideString;  stdcall;
  end;


implementation

uses InvokeRegistry;

initialization
  InvRegistry.RegisterInterface(TypeInfo(ITempConverter),
➥ 'urn:TempConverterIntf-ITempConverter', '');

end.
```

Once it has been generated, return to the main form of the client application and use the newly-generated import unit. This will make the main form aware of the new interface.

Using the `THTTPRIO` Component

Three properties must be set for the `THTTPRIO` component. The first, `WSDLLocation`, needs to contain, once again, the path to the WSDL document. Once set, you can drop down the `Service` property to select the only available option. Then, do the same for the `Port` property. At this point, you will be able to run the client.

Putting the Web Service to Work

Now that all the pieces are in place, create an event handler for the button's `OnClick` event by double-clicking on it. The event should look like Listing 20.6.

LISTING 20.6   `OnClick` Event Handler

```
procedure TMainForm.btnFah2CelClick(Sender: TObject);
var
  TempConverter: ITempConverter;
  FloatVal: Double;
begin
  TempConverter := HTTPRIO1 as ITempConverter;
  FloatVal := TempConverter.FahrenheitToCelsius(StrToFloat(edtArguement.Text));
```

LISTING 20.6 Continued

```
  lblResultValue.Caption := FloatToStr(FloatVal);
end;

procedure TMainForm.btnCel2FahClick(Sender: TObject);
var
  TempConverter: ITempConverter;
  FloatVal: Double;
begin
  TempConverter := HTTPRIO1 as ITempConverter;
  FloatVal := TempConverter.CelsiusToFahrenheit(StrToFloat(edtArguement.Text));
  lblResultValue.Caption := FloatToStr(FloatVal);
end;
```

While entering this code, notice that Delphi's CodeInsight is available for the Web service itself. This is because Delphi has adapted the Web service into your application as a native object. The implications here are very broad-ranging: any Web service brought into a Delphi application, regardless of whether that service is deployed on Solaris, Windows, Linux, a mainframe, and independent of what language the service is written in, will benefit from this. In addition to CodeInsight, an application written to use a Web service will also gain compiler typechecking and other debugging features because of this tight integration.

Summary

Web Services are a powerful new tool in distributed computing, using open standards and existing infrastructure to enable interoperation within and between different platforms.

In this chapter, we showed you how to create a simple Web Service and the Client to use this service. We demonstrated the steps required to deploy this server and to set up the client's THTTPRIO component properly. At this point, you should be familiar enough with developing Web Services in greater complexity. You can examine many more examples of Web Services on Borland's community site. One that we highly recommend is "Managing Sessions with Delphi 6 Web Services." This article was written by Daniel Polistchuck (Article ID: 27575) and can be read at http://community.borland.com/article/0,1410,27575,00.html.

DataSnap Development

By Dan Miser

IN THIS CHAPTER

Multitier applications are being talked about as much as any topic in computer programming today. This is happening for good reason. Multitier applications hold many advantages over the more traditional client/server applications. Borland's DataSnap is one way to help you create and deliver a multitier application using Delphi, building on techniques and skills you've accumulated when using Delphi. This chapter walks you through some general information about multitier application design and shows you how to apply those principles to create solid DataSnap applications.

Mechanics of Creating a Multitier Application

Because we'll be talking about a multitier application, it might be helpful to first provide a frame of reference to what a tier really is. A *tier*, in this sense, is a layer of an application that provides some specific set of functionality. Here are the three basic tiers used in database applications:

- Data—The data tier is responsible for storing your data. Typically, this will be an RDBMS such as Microsoft SQL Server, Oracle, or InterBase.

- Business—The business tier is responsible for retrieving data from the data tier in a format appropriate for the application and performing final validation of the data (also known as *enforcing business rules*). This is also the application server layer.

- Presentation—Also known as the *GUI tier*, this tier is responsible for displaying the data in an appropriate format in the client application. The presentation tier always talks to the business tier. It never talks directly to the data tier.

In traditional client/server applications, you have an architecture similar to that shown in Figure 21.1. Notice that the client libraries for data access must be located on every single client machine. This has historically been a trouble spot when deploying client/server applications due to incompatible versions of DLLs and costly configuration management. Also, because most of the business tier is located on each client, you need to update all the clients every single time you need to update a business rule.

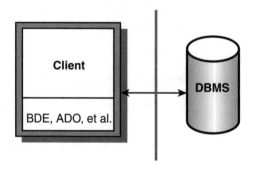

FIGURE 21.1

The traditional client/server architecture.

In multitier applications, the architecture more closely resembles that shown in Figure 21.2 Using this architecture, you'll find many benefits over the equivalent client/server application.

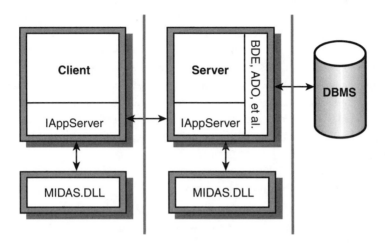

FIGURE 21.2
Multitier architecture.

Benefits of the Multitier Architecture

We list the major benefits of the multitier architecture in the next few sections.

Centralized Business Logic

In most client/server applications, each client application is required to keep track of the individual business rules for a business solution. Not only does this increase the size of the executable, but it also poses a challenge to the software developer to keep strict control over version maintenance. If user A has an older version of the application than user B, the business rules might not be performed consistently, thus resulting in logical data errors. Placing the business rules on the application server requires only one copy of the business rules to be created and maintained. Therefore, everyone using that application server will use the same copy of those business rules. In client/server applications, the RDBMS could address some of the concerns, but not all RDBMS systems provide the same set of features. Also, writing stored procedures makes your application less portable. Using a multitier approach, your business rules are hosted independent of your RDBMS, thus making database independence easier, while still providing some degree of rule enforcement for your data.

Thin-Client Architecture

In addition to the business rules mentioned, the typical client/server application also bears the burden of the majority of the data-access layer. This produces a more sizable executable, more commonly known as a *fat client*. For a Delphi database application accessing a SQL server database, you would need to install the BDE, SQL Links, and/or ODBC to access the database, along with the client libraries necessary to talk to the SQL server. After installing these files, you would then need to configure each piece appropriately. This increases the install footprint considerably. Using DataSnap, the data access is controlled by the application server, whereas the data is presented to the user by the client application. This means that you only need to distribute the client application and one DLL to help your client talk to your server. This is clearly a thin-client architecture.

Automatic Error Reconciliation

Delphi comes with a built-in mechanism to help with error reconciliation. Error reconciliation is necessary in a multitier application for the same reasons it would be necessary with cached updates. The data is copied to the client machine, where changes are made. Multiple clients can be working on the same record. Error reconciliation helps the user determine what to do with records that have changed since the user last downloaded the record. In the true Delphi spirit, if this dialog doesn't suit your needs, you can remove it and create one that does.

Briefcase Model

The briefcase model is based on the metaphor of a physical briefcase. You place your important papers in your briefcase and transport them back and forth, unpacking them when needed. Delphi provides a way to pack up all your data and take it with you on the road without requiring a live connection to the application server or the database server.

Fault Tolerance

If your server machine becomes unavailable due to unforeseen circumstances, it would be nice to dynamically change to a backup server without recompiling your client or server applications. Delphi provides functionality for this out of the box.

Load Balancing

As you deploy your client application to more people, you'll inevitably start to saturate your server's bandwidth. There are two ways to attempt to balance the network traffic: static and dynamic load balancing. For static load balancing, you would add another server machine and have one half of your clients use server A, and the other half would access server B. However, what if the clients who use server A put a greater strain on the server than those who use server

B? Using dynamic load balancing, you could address this issue by telling each client application which server to access. Many different dynamic load-balancing algorithms are available, such as random, sequential, round robin, and least network traffic. Delphi 4 and above address this by providing you with a component to implement sequential load balancing.

Typical DataSnap Architecture

Figure 21.3 shows how a typical DataSnap application looks after it's created. At the heart of this diagram is a Data Module constructed for this task. Several varieties are available. For simplicity, we'll use a COM-based one in this chapter, called the Remote Data Module (RDM). The RDM is a descendant of the classic data module available since Delphi 2. This data module is a special container that only allows non-visual components to be placed on it. The RDM is no different in this respect. In addition, the RDM is actually a COM object—or to be more precise, an *Automation object*. Services that you export from this RDM will be available for use on client machines.

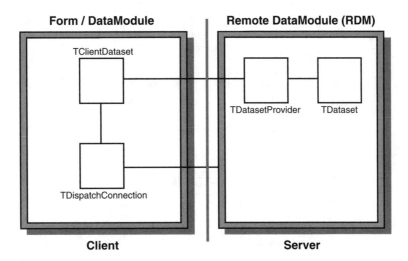

FIGURE 21.3
A typical DataSnap application.

Let's look at some of the options available to you when creating an RDM. Figure 21.4 shows the dialog box that Delphi presents when you select File, New, Remote Data Module.

Server

Now that you've seen how a typical DataSnap application is put together, we will show you how to make that happen in Delphi. We'll begin with a look at some of the choices available when setting up the server.

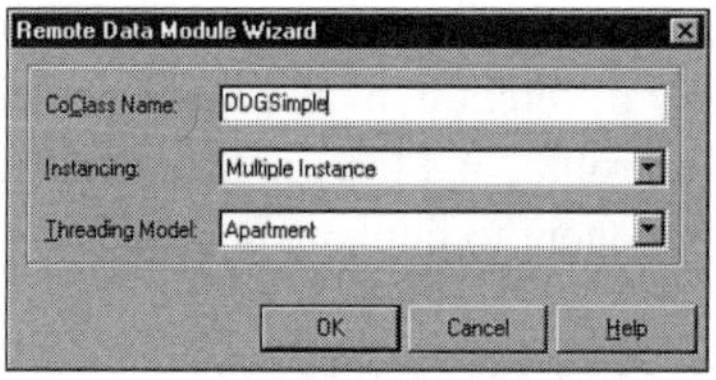

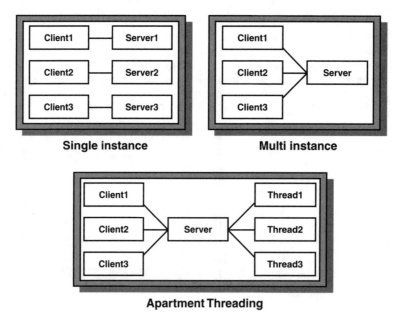

FIGURE 21.4
The New Remote Data Module dialog box.

Instancing Choices

Specifying an instancing choice affects how many copies of the server process that will be launched. Figure 21.5 shows how the choices made here control how your server behaves.

FIGURE 21.5
Server behavior based on instancing options.

Here are the different instancing choices available to a COM server:

- ciMultiInstance—Each client that accesses the COM server will use the same server instance. By default, this implies that one client must wait for another before being allowed to operate on the COM server. See the next section, "Threading Choices," for more detailed information on how the value specified for the Threading Model also affects this behavior. This is equivalent to serial access for the clients. All clients must share one database connection; therefore, the `TDatabase.HandleShared` property must be `True`.

- `ciSingleInstance`—Each client that accesses the COM server will use a separate instance. This implies that each client will consume server resources for each server instance to be loaded. This is equivalent to parallel access for the clients. If you decide to go with this choice, beware of BDE limits that could make this choice less attractive. Specifically, BDE 5.01 has a 48-process limit per machine. Because each client spawns a new server process, you can only have 48 clients connected at one time.

- `ciInternal`—The COM server cannot be created from external applications. This is useful when you want to control access to a COM object through a proxy layer. One example of using this instancing choice can be found in the `<DELPHI>\DEMOS\MIDAS\POOLER` example.

Also note that the configuration of the DCOM object has a direct effect on the object instancing mode. See the "Deploying DataSnap Applications" section for more information on this topic.

Threading Choices

The threading support in Delphi 5 saw a drastic change for the better. In Delphi 4, selecting the threading model for an EXE server was meaningless. The flag merely marked the Registry to tell COM that a DLL was capable of running under the selected threading model. With Delphi 5 and 6, the threading model choice now applies to EXE servers by allowing COM to thread the connections without using any external code. The following is a summary of the threading choices available for an RDM:

- Single—Selecting Single means that the server is only capable of handling one request at a time. When using Single, you need not worry about threading issues because the server runs in one thread and COM handles the details of synchronizing the messages for you. However, this is the worst selection you can make if you plan on having a multiuser system because client B would then need to wait for client A to finish processing before client B could even start working. This obviously isn't a good situation because client A could be doing an end-of-day summary report or some other similar time-intensive operation.

- Apartment—Selecting the Apartment threading model gives you the best of all possible worlds when combined with `ciMultiInstance` instancing. In this scenario, all the clients share one server process because of `ciMultiInstance`, but the work done on the server from one client doesn't block another client from doing work due to the Apartment threading choice. When using apartment threading, you're guaranteed that the instance data of your RDM is safe, but you need to protect access to global variables using some thread synchronization technique, such as `PostMessage()`, critical sections, mutexes, semaphores, or the Delphi wrapper class `TMultiReadExclusiveWriteSynchronizer`. This is the preferred threading model for BDE datasets. Note that if you do use this threading model with BDE datasets, you need to place a `TSession` component on your RDM and set the `AutoSessionName` property to `True` to help the BDE conform to its internal requirements for threading.

- Free—This model provides even more flexibility in server processing by allowing multiple calls to be made from the client to the server simultaneously. However, along with that power comes responsibility. You must take care to protect all data from thread conflicts—both instance data and global variables. This is the preferred threading model when using ADO.

- Both—This setting is effectively the same as the Free setting, with one exception—callbacks are serialized automatically.

Data-Access Choices

Delphi 6 Enterprise comes with many different data-access choices. The BDE continues to be supported, thus allowing you to use `TDBDataset` components, such as `TTable`, `TQuery`, and `TStoredProc`. However, DBExpress provides a more flexible architecture for data access. In addition, you also have the choice of supporting ADO and having direct InterBase access through new `TDataset` components.

Advertising Services

The RDM is responsible for communicating which services will be available to clients. If the RDM is going to make a `TQuery` available for use on the client, you need to place the `TQuery` on the RDM along with a `TDatasetProvider`. The `TDatasetProvider` component is then tied to the `TQuery` via the `TDatasetProvider.Dataset` property. Later, when a client comes along and wants to use the data from the `TQuery`, it can do so by binding to the `TDatasetProvider` you just created. You can control which providers are visible to the client by setting the `TDatasetProvider.Exported` property to `True` or `False`.

If, on the other hand, you don't need an entire dataset exposed from the server and just have a need for the client to make a method call to the server, you can do that, too. While the RDM has focus, select the Edit, Add To Interface menu option and fill in the dialog box with a standard method prototype (which is simply a declaration matching a method you'll create in your implementation). You can then specify the implementation of this method in code as you always have, keeping in mind the implications of your threading model.

Client

After building the server, you need to create a client to use the services provided by the server. Let's take a look at some of the options available when building your DataSnap client.

Connection Choices

Delphi's architecture for connecting the client to the server starts with the TDispatchConnection. This base object is the parent of all the connection types listed later. When the connection type is irrelevant for a specific section, TDispatchConnection will be used to denote that fact.

TDCOMConnection provides core security and authentication by using the standard Windows implementation of these services. This connection type is especially useful if you're using this application in an intranet/extranet setup (that is, where the people using your application are known from the domain's perspective). You can use early binding when using DCOM, and you can use callbacks and ConnectionPoints easily. (You can use callbacks when using sockets, too, but you're limited to using late binding to do so.) The drawbacks of using this connection are as follows:

- Difficult configuration in many cases
- Not a firewall-friendly connection type
- Requires installation of DCOM95 for Windows 95 machines

TSocketConnection is the easiest connection to configure. In addition, it only uses one port for DataSnap traffic, so your firewall administrators will be happier than if they had to make DCOM work through the firewall. You must be running ScktSrvr (found in the <DELPHI>\BIN directory) to make this setup work, so there's one extra file to deploy and run on the server. Delphi 4 required you to have WinSock2 installed when using this connection type, which meant another installation for Windows 9x clients. However, if you're not using callbacks, you might want to consider setting TSocketConnection.SupportCallbacks to False. This allows you to stick with WinSock 1 on the client machines.

You can also use TCORBAConnection if you want to use CORBA as your transport protocol. CORBA can be thought of as the open-standard equivalent of DCOM, and it includes many features for autodiscovery, failover, and load-balancing automatically performed for your application. You'll want to look at CORBA as you migrate your DataSnap applications to allow for cross-platform and cross-language connections.

The TWebConnection component is also available to you. This connection component allows traffic to be transported over HTTP or HTTPS. When using this connection type, some limitations are as follows:

- Callbacks of any type aren't supported.
- The client must have WININET.DLL installed.
- The server machine must be running MS Internet Information Server (IIS) 4.0 or Netscape 3.6 or greater.

However, these limitations seem well worth it when you have to deliver an application across the Internet or through a firewall that's not under your control.

Delphi 6 introduced a new type of connection: the TSOAPConnection. This connection behaves similarly to the WebConnection, but connects to a DataSnap Web service. Unlike when using other DataSnap connection components, you can't use the AppServer property of TSoapConnection to call methods of the application server's interface that aren't IAppServer methods. Instead, to communicate with a SOAP data module on the application interface, use a separate THTTPRIO object.

Note that all these transports assume a valid installation of TCP/IP. The one exception to this is if you're using two Windows NT machines to communicate via DCOM. In that case, you can specify which protocol DCOM will use by running DCOMCNFG and moving the desired protocol to the top of the list on the Default Protocols tab. DCOM for Windows 9*x* only supports TCP/IP.

Connecting the Components

From the diagram in Figure 21.3, you can see how the DataSnap application communicates across tiers. This section points out the key properties and components that give the client the ability to communicate with the server.

To communicate from the client to the server, you need to use one of the TDispatchConnection components listed previously. Each component has properties specific only to that connection type, but all of them allow you to specify where to find the application server. The TDispatchConnection is analogous to the TDatabase component when used in client/server applications because it defines the link to the external system and serves as the conduit for other components when communicating with elements from that system.

Once you have a connection to the server, you need a way to use the services you exposed on the server. This can be accomplished by dropping a TClientDataset on your client and hooking it up to the TDispatchConnection via the RemoteServer property. Once this connection is made, you can view a list of the exported providers on the server by dropping down the list in the ProviderName property. You'll see a list of exported providers that exist on the server. In this way, the TClientDataset component is similar to a TTable in client/server applications.

You also have the ability to call custom methods that exist on the server by using the TDispatchConnection.AppServer property. For example, the following line of code will call the Login function on the server, passing two string parameters and returning a Boolean value:

```
LoginSucceeded := DCOMConnection1.AppServer.Login(UserName, Password);
```

Using DataSnap to Create an Application

Now that we've covered many of the options available when building DataSnap applications, let's use DataSnap to actually create an application to put that theory into practice.

Setting Up the Server

Let's focus on the mechanics of building the application server first. After you have created the server, we will explore how to build the client.

Remote Data Module

The Remote Data Module (RDM) is central to creating an application server. To create an RDM for a new application, select the Remote Data Module icon from the Multitier tab of the Object Repository (available by selecting File, New). A dialog box will be displayed to allow for initial customization of some options that pertain to the RDM.

The name for the RDM is important because the ProgID for this application server will be built using the project name and RDM name. For example, if the project (DPR) is named AppServer and the RDM name is MyRDM, the ProgID will be AppServer.MyRDM. Be sure to select the appropriate instancing and threading options based on the preceding explanations and the behavior desired for this application server.

Both TSocketConnection and TWebConnection bypass Windows' default authentication processing, so it is imperative to make sure that the only objects that run on the server are the ones that you specify. This is accomplished by marking the registry with certain values to let DataSnap know that you intended to allow these objects to run. Fortunately, all that is required to do this is to override the UpdateRegistry class method. See Listing 21.1 for the implementation provided by Delphi automatically when you create a new Remote DataModule.

LISTING 21.1 UpdateRegistry Class Method from a Remote DataModule

```
class procedure TDDGSimple.UpdateRegistry(Register:  Boolean;
 const ClassID, ProgID: string);
begin
  if Register then
  begin
    inherited UpdateRegistry(Register, ClassID, ProgID);
    EnableSocketTransport(ClassID);
    EnableWebTransport(ClassID);
  end else
  begin
    DisableSocketTransport(ClassID);
    DisableWebTransport(ClassID);
```

LISTING 21.1   Continued

```
    inherited UpdateRegistry(Register, ClassID, ProgID);
  end;
end;
```

This method gets called whenever the server gets registered or unregistered. In addition to the COM-specific registry entries that get created in the inherited `UpdateRegistry` call, you can call the `EnableXXXTransport()` and `DisableXXXTransport()` methods to mark this object as secure.

> **NOTE**
>
> `TSocketConnection` will only show registered, secure objects in the `ServerName` property. If you don't want to enforce security at all, uncheck the Connections, Registered Objects Only menu option in the SCKTSRVR.

Providers

The application server will be responsible for providing data to the client, so you must find a way to serve data from the server in a format that's useable on the client. Fortunately, DataSnap provides a `TDatasetProvider` component to make this step easy.

Start by dropping a `TQuery` on the RDM. If you're using a RDBMS, you'll inevitably need a `TDatabase` component set up, too. For now, you'll tie the `TQuery` to the `TDatabase` and specify a simple query in the SQL property, such as `select * from customer`. Last, drop a `TDatasetProvider` component onto the RDM and tie it to the `TQuery` via the `Dataset` property. The `Exported` property on the `DatasetProvider` determines whether this provider will be visible to clients. This property provides the ability to easily control which providers are visible at runtime, as well.

> **NOTE**
>
> Although the discussion in this section focuses on using the BDE-based `TDBDataset`, the same principles apply if you want to use any other `TDataset` descendant for your data access. Several possibilities exist out of the box, such as DBExpress, ADO, and InterBase Express, and several third-party components are available to access specific databases.

Registering the Server

Once the application server is built, it needs to be registered with COM to make it available for the client applications that will connect with it. The Registry entries discussed in Chapter 15, "COM Development" are also used for DataSnap servers. You just need to run the server application, and the Registry setting will be added. However, before registering the server, be sure to save the project first. This ensures that the ProgID will be correct from this point forward.

If you would rather not run the application, you can pass the parameter /regserver on the command line when running the application. This will just perform the registration process and immediately terminate the application. To remove the Registry entries associated with this application, you can use the /unregserver parameter.

Creating the Client

Now that you have a working application server, let's look at how to perform some basic tasks with the client. We will discuss how to retrieve the data, how to edit the data, how to update the database with changes made on the client, and how to handle errors during the database update process.

Retrieving Data

Throughout the course of a database application, it's necessary to bring data from the server to the client to edit that data. By bringing the data to a local cache, you can reduce network traffic and minimize transaction times. In previous versions of Delphi, you would use cached updates to perform this task. However, the same general steps still apply to DataSnap applications.

The client talks to the server via a TDispatchConnection component. Providing the TDispatchConnection the name of the computer where the application server lives accomplishes this task easily. If you use TDCOMConnection, you can specify the fully qualified domain name (FQDN; for example, nt.dmiser.com), the numeric IP address of the computer (for example, 192.168.0.2), or the NetBIOS name of the computer (for example, nt). However, because of a bug in DCOM, you cannot use the name localhost, or even some IP addresses, reliably in all cases. If you use TSocketConnection, you specify numeric IP addresses in the Address property or the FQDN in the Host property. We'll take a look at the options for TWebConnection a little later.

Once you specify where the application server resides, you need to give the TDispatch Connection a way to identify that application server. This is done via the ServerName property. Assigning the ServerName property fills in the ServerGUID property for you. The ServerGUID property is the most important part. As a matter of fact, if you want to deploy your client application in the most generic manner possible, be sure to delete the ServerName property and just use the ServerGUID.

> **NOTE**
>
> If you use `TDCOMConnection`, the <u>ServerName</u> list will only display the list of servers that are registered on the current machine. However, `TSocketConnection` is smart enough to display the list of application servers registered on the remote machine.

At this point, setting `TDispatchConnection.Connected` to `True` will connect you to the application server.

Now that you have the client talking to the server, you need a way to use the provider you created on the server. Do this by using the `TClientDataset` component. A `TClientDataSet` is used to link to a provider (and, thus, the `TQuery` that is linked to the provider) on the server.

First, you must tie the `TClientDataSet` to the `TDispatchConnection` by assigning the `RemoteServer` property of the `TClientDataSet`. Once you've done that, you can get a list of the available providers on that server by looking at the list in the `ProviderName` property.

At this point, everything is now set up properly to open a `ClientDataset`.

Because the `TClientDataSet` is a virtual `TDataset` descendant, you can build on many of the techniques that you've already learned using the `TDBDataset` components in client/server applications. For example, setting `Active` to `True` opens the `TClientDataSet` and displays the data. The difference between this and setting `TTable.Active` to `True` is that the `TClientDataSet` is actually getting its data from the application server.

Editing Data on the Client

All the records passed from the server to the `TClientDataSet` are stored in the `Data` property of the `TClientDataSet`. This property is a variant representation of the DataSnap data packet. The `TClientDataset` knows how to decode this data packet into a more useful format. The reason the property is defined as a variant is because of the limited types available to the COM subsystem when using type library marshaling.

As you manipulate the records in the `TClientDataset`, a copy of the inserted, modified, or deleted records gets placed in the `Delta` property. This allows DataSnap to be extremely efficient when it comes to applying updates back to the application server, and eventually the database. Only the changed records need to be sent back to the application server.

The format of the `Delta` property is also very efficient. It stores one record for every insert or delete, and it stores two records for every update. The updated records are stored in an efficient manner, as well. The unmodified record is provided in the first record, whereas the corresponding modified record is stored next. However, only the changed fields are stored in the modified record to save on storage.

One interesting aspect of the Delta property is that it's compatible with the Data property. In other words, it can be assigned directly to another ClientDataset component's Data property. This will allow you to investigate the current contents of the Delta property at any given time.

Several methods are available to deal with the editing of data on the TClientDataset. We'll refer to these methods as change control methods. The *change control* methods allow you to modify the changes made to the TClientDataset in a variety of ways.

> **NOTE**
>
> TClientDataset has proven useful in more ways than originally intended. It also serves as an excellent method for storing in-memory tables, which has nothing to do with DataSnap specifically. Additionally, because of the way it exposes data through the Data and Delta properties, it has proven useful in a variety of OOP pattern implementations. It is beyond the scope of the chapter to discuss these techniques. However, you will find white papers on these topics at http://www.xapware.com or http://www.xapware.com/ddg.

Undoing Changes

Most users have used a word-processing application that permits the Undo operation. This operation takes your most previous action and rolls it back to the state right before you started. Using TClientDataset, you can call cdsCustomer.UndoLastChange() to simulate that behavior. The undo stack is unlimited, allowing the user to continue to back up all the way to the beginning of the editing session if so desired. The parameter you pass to this method specifies whether the cursor is positioned to the record being affected.

If the user wanted to get rid of all her updates at once, there's an easier way than calling UndoLastChange() repeatedly. You can simply call cdsCustomer.CancelUpdates() to cancel all changes that have been made in a single editing session.

Reverting to the Original Version

Another possibility is to allow the user to restore a specific record back to the state it was in when the record was first retrieved. Do this by calling cdsCustomer.RevertRecord() while the TClientDataset is positioned on the record you intend to restore.

Client-Side Transactions: SavePoint

The ClientDataset.SavePoint property provides the ability to use client-side transactions. This property is ideal for developing what-if scenarios for the user. The act of retrieving the value of the SavePoint property stores a snapshot of the data at that point in time. The user can continue to edit as long as needed. If, at some point, the user decides that the baseline set of data is actually what she wanted, that saved variable can be assigned back to SavePoint and the TClientDataset is returned back to the same state it was in at the time when the initial snapshot was taken. It's worth noting that you can have multiple, nested levels of SavePoint for a complex scenario as well.

> ## CAUTION
>
> A word of caution about SavePoint is in order: You can invalidate a SavePoint by calling UndoLastChange() past the point that's currently saved. For example, assume that the user edits two records and issues a SavePoint. At this point, the user edits another record. However, she uses UndoLastChange() to revert changes twice in a row. Because the TClientDataset state is now in a state prior to the SavePoint, the SavePoint is in an undefined state.

Reconciling Data

After you've finished making changes to the local copy of data in the TClientDataset, you'll need to signal your intent to apply these changes back to the database. This is done by calling cdsCustomer.ApplyUpdates(). At this point, DataSnap will take the Delta from cdsCustomer and pass it to the application server, where DataSnap will apply these changes to the database server using the reconciliation mechanism that you chose for this dataset. All updates are performed inside the context of a transaction. We'll cover how errors are handled during this process shortly.

The parameter you pass into ApplyUpdates() specifies the number of errors the update process will allow before considering the update to be bad, and subsequently, roll back all the changes that have been made. The word *errors* here refers to key violation errors, referential integrity errors, or any other business logic or database errors. If you specify zero for this parameter, you're telling DataSnap that you won't tolerate any errors. Therefore, if an error does occur, all the changes you made will not be committed to the database. This is the setting that you'll use most often because it most closely matches solid database guidelines and principles.

However, if you want, you can specify that a certain number of errors can occur, while still committing all the records that were successful. The ultimate extension of this concept is to pass -1 as the parameter to ApplyUpdates(). This tells DataSnap that it should commit every single record that it can, regardless of the number of errors encountered along the way. In other words, the transaction will always commit when using this parameter.

If you want to take ultimate control over the update process—including changing the SQL that will execute for an insert, update, or delete—you can do so in the TDatasetProvider.Before UpdateRecord() event. For example, when a user wants to delete a record, you might not want to actually perform a delete operation on the database. Instead, a flag is set to tell applications that this record isn't available. Later, an administrator can review these deletions and commit the physical delete operation. The following example shows how to do this:

```
procedure TDataModule1.Provider1BeforeUpdateRecord(Sender: TObject;
  SourceDS: TDataset; DeltaDS: TClientDataset; UpdateKind: TUpdateKind;
  var Applied: Boolean);
begin
  if UpdateKind=ukDelete then
  begin
    Query1.SQL.Text:='update CUSTOMER set STATUS="DEL" where ID=:ID';
    Query1.Params[0].Value:=DeltaDS.FieldByName('ID').OldValue;
    Query1.ExecSQL;
    Applied:=true;
  end;
end;
```

You can create as many queries as you want, controlling the flow and content of the update process based on different factors, such as UpdateKind and values in the Dataset. When inspecting or modifying records of the DeltaDS, be sure to use the OldValue and NewValue properties of the appropriate TField. Using the TField.AsXXX properties will yield unpredictable results.

In addition, you can enforce business rules here or avoid posting a record to the database altogether. Any exception you raise here will wind its way through DataSnap's error-handling mechanism, which we'll cover next.

After the transaction is finished, you get an opportunity to deal with errors. The error stops at events on both the server and the client, giving you a chance to take corrective action, log the error, or do anything else you want to with it.

The first stop for the error is the DatasetProvider.OnUpdateError event. This is a great place to deal with errors that you're expecting or can resolve without further intervention from the client.

The final destination for the error is back on the client, where you can deal with the error by letting the user help determine what to do with the record. You do this by assigning an event handler to the TClientDataset.OnReconcileError event.

This is especially useful because DataSnap is based on an optimistic record-locking strategy. This strategy allows multiple users to work on the same record at the same time. In general, this causes conflicts when DataSnap tries to reconcile the data back to the database because the record has been modified since it was retrieved.

Using Borland's Error Reconciliation Dialog Box

Fortunately, Borland provides a standard error reconciliation dialog box that you can use to display the error to the user. Figure 21.6 shows this dialog box. The source code is also provided for this unit, so you can modify it if it doesn't suit your needs. To use this dialog box, select File, New in Delphi's main menu and then select Reconcile Error Dialog from the Dialogs page. Remember to remove this unit from the Autocreate Forms list; otherwise, you'll receive compile errors.

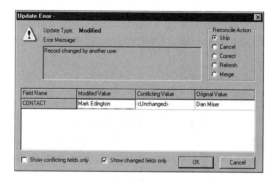

FIGURE 21.6

Reconcile Error dialog box in action.

The main functionality of this unit is wrapped up in the function HandleReconcileError(). A high degree of correlation exists between the OnReconcileError event and the HandleReconcileError function. As a matter of fact, the typical course of action in the OnReconcileError event is to call the HandleReconcileError function. By doing this, the application allows the end user on the client machine to interact with the error reconciliation process on the server machine and specify how these errors should be handled. Here's the code:

```
procedure TMyForm.CDSReconcileError(Dataset: TCustomClientDataset;
  E: EReconcileError; UpdateKind: TUpdateKind;
  var Action: TReconcileAction);
begin
  Action:=HandleReconcileError(Dataset, UpdateKind, E);
end;
```

The value of the Action parameter determines what DataSnap will do with this record. We'll touch on some other factors that affect which actions are valid at this point a little later. The following list shows the valid actions:

- raSkip—Do not update this specific database record. Leave the changed record in the client cache.

- raMerge—Merge the fields from this record into the database record. This record won't apply to records that were inserted.

- raCorrect—Update the database record with the values you specify. When selecting this action in the Reconcile Error dialog box, you can edit the values in the grid. You cannot use this method if another user changed the database record.

- raCancel—Don't update the database record. Remove the record from the client cache.

- raRefresh—Update the record in the client cache with the current record in the database.

- raAbort—Abort the entire update operation.

Not all these options make sense (and therefore won't be displayed) in all cases. One requirement to have the raMerge and raRefresh actions available is that DataSnap can identify the record via the primary key of the database. This is done by setting the TField.ProviderFlags.pfInKey property to True on the TDataset component of the RDM for all fields in your primary key.

More Options to Make Your Application Robust

Once you master these basics, the inevitable question is "What next?" This section is provided to give you some more insight into DataSnap and how you can use these features to make your applications act as you want them to act.

Client Optimization Techniques

The model of retrieving data is fairly elegant. However, because the TClientDataset stores all its records in memory, you need to be very careful about the resultsets you return to the TClientDataSet. The cleanest approach is to ensure that the application server is well designed and only returns the records the user is interested in. Because the real world seldom follows the utopian solution, you can use the following technique to help throttle the number of records you retrieve at one time to the client.

Limiting the Data Packet

When opening a TClientDataSet, the server retrieves the number of records specified in the TClientDataSet.PacketRecords property at one time. However, DataSnap will retrieve enough records to fill all available visual controls with data. For example, if you have a TDBGrid on a form that can display 10 records at once, and you specify a value of 5 for PacketRecords, the initial fetch of data will contain 10 records. After that, the data packet will contain just 5 records per fetch. If you specify -1 for this property (the default), all records will be transferred. If you specify a value greater than zero for PacketRecords, this introduces state to your application. This is because of the requirement that the app server must keep track of each client's cursor position so the app server can return the appropriate packet of records to the client requesting a packet. However, you can keep track of the state on the client, passing the last record position to the server, as appropriate. For a simple example, look at this code, which does exactly that:

```
Server RDM:
procedure TStateless.DataSetProvider1BeforeGetRecords(Sender: TObject;
  var OwnerData: OleVariant);
begin
  with Sender as TDataSetProvider do
  begin
    DataSet.Open;
    if VarIsEmpty(OwnerData) then
      DataSet.First
    else
    begin
      while not DataSet.Eof do
      begin
        if DataSet.FieldByName('au_id').Value = OwnerData then
          break;
      end;
    end;
  end;
end;

procedure TStateless.DataSetProvider1AfterGetRecords(Sender: TObject;
  var OwnerData: OleVariant);
begin
  with Sender as TDataSetProvider do
  begin
    OwnerData := Dataset.FieldValues['au_id'];
    DataSet.Close;
  end;
end;

Client:
procedure TForm1.ClientDataSet1BeforeGetRecords(Sender: TObject;
  var OwnerData:  OleVariant);
begin
  // KeyValue is a private OleVariant variable
  if not (Sender as TClientDataSet).Active then
    KeyValue := Unassigned;
  OwnerData := KeyValue;
end;

procedure TForm1.ClientDataSet1AfterGetRecords(Sender: TObject;
  var OwnerData: OleVariant);
```

```
begin
  KeyValue := OwnerData;
end;
```

One last point when using partial fetching is that executing `TClientDataSet.Last()` retrieves the rest of the records left in the resultset. This can be done innocently by pressing Ctrl+End in the `TDBGrid`. To work around this problem, you should set `TClientDataSet.FetchOnDemand` to `False`. This property controls whether a data packet will be retrieved automatically when the user has read through all the existing records on the client. To emulate that behavior in code, you can use the `GetNextPacket()` method, which will return the next data packet for you.

> **NOTE**
>
> Note that the previous code sample walks through the dataset until it finds the proper record. This is done so that unidirectional datasets such as DBExpress can use this same code without modification. Of course, there are many ways to find the proper record, such as modifying an SQL statement or parameterizing a query, but this sample concentrates on the mechanics of passing around the key between client and server.

Using the Briefcase Model

Another optimization to reduce network traffic is to use the briefcase model support offered with DataSnap. Do this by assigning a filename to the `TClientDataset.Filename` property. If the file specified in this property exists, the `TClientDataSet` will open up the local copy of the file as opposed to reading the data directly from the application server. In addition to allowing users to work with files while disconnected from the network, this is tremendously useful for items that rarely change, such as lookup tables.

> **TIP**
>
> If you specify a `TClientDataset.Filename` that has an `.XML` extension, the data packet will be stored in XML format, enabling you to use any number of XML tools available to work on the briefcase file.

Sending Dynamic SQL to the Server

Some applications require modification to the underlying `TDataset`'s core properties, such as the `SQL` property of the `TQuery`, from the client. As long as solid multitier principles are followed, this can actually be a very efficient and elegant solution. Delphi makes this task trivial to accomplish.

Two steps are required to allow for ad hoc queries. First, you simply assign the query statement to the `TClientDataset.CommandText` property. Second, you must also include the `poAllowCommandText` option in the `DatasetProvider.Options` property. When you open the `TClientDataSet` or call `TClientDataSet.Execute()`, the `CommandText` is passed across to the server. This same technique also works if you want to change the table or stored procedure name on the server.

Application Server Techniques

DataSnap now has many different events for you to customize the behavior of your application. `BeforeXXX` and `AfterXXX` events exist for just about every method on the IAppServer interface. These two events in particular will be useful as you migrate your application server to be completely stateless.

Resolving Record Contention

The preceding discussion of the resolving mechanism included a brief mention that two users working on the same record would cause an error when the second user tried to apply the record back to the database. Fortunately, you have full control over detecting this collision.

The `TDatasetProvider.UpdateMode` property is used to generate the SQL statement that will be used to check whether the record has changed since it was last retrieved. Consider the scenario in which two users edit the same record. Here's how `DatasetProvider.UpdateMode` affects what happens to the record for each user:

- `upWhereAll`—This setting is the most restrictive setting but provides the greatest deal of assurance that the record is the same one the user retrieved initially. If two users edit the same record, the first user will be able to update the record, whereas the second user will receive the infamous `Another user changed the record.` error message. If you want to further refine which fields are used to perform this check, you can remove the `pfInWhere` element from the corresponding `TField.ProviderFlags` property.

- `upWhereChanged`—This setting allows the two users to actually edit the same record at the same time; as long as both users edit different fields in the same record, there will be no collision detection. For example, if user A modifies the `Address` field and updates the record, user B can still modify the `BirthDate` field and update the record successfully.

- `upWhereKeyOnly`—This setting is the most forgiving of all. As long as the record exists on the database, every user's change will be accepted. This will always overwrite the existing record in the database, so it can be viewed as a way to provide "last one in wins" functionality.

Miscellaneous Server Options

Quite a few more options are available in the TDatasetProvider.Options property to control how the DataSnap data packet behaves. For example, adding poReadOnly will make the dataset read-only on the client. Specifying poDisableInserts, poDisableDeletes, or poDisableEdits prevents the client from performing that operation and triggers the corresponding OnEditError or OnDeleteError event to be fired on the client.

When using nested datasets, you can have updates or deletes cascade from the master record to the detail records if you add poCascadeUpdates or poCascadeDeletes to the DatasetProvider.Options property. Using this property requires your back-end database to support cascading referential integrity.

One shortcoming in previous versions of DataSnap was the inability to easily merge changes made on the server into your TClientDataset on the client. The user had to resort to using RefreshRecord (or possibly Refresh to repopulate the entire dataset in some cases) to achieve this.

By setting DatasetProvider.Options to include poPropogateChanges, all the changes made to your data on the application server (for example, in the DatasetProvider.BeforeUpdateRecord event to enforce a business rule) are now automatically brought back into the TClientDataSet. Furthermore, setting TDatasetProvider.Options to include poAutoRefresh will automatically merge AutoIncrement and default values back into the TClientDataSet.

CAUTION

The poAutoRefresh option is non-functional in Delphi 5 and 6. poAutoRefresh will only work with a later version of Delphi that includes the fix for this bug. The workaround in the meantime is to either call Refresh() for your TClientDatasets or take control of the entire process of applying updates yourself.

The entire discussion of the reconciliation process thus far has revolved around the default SQL-based reconciliation. This means that all the events on the underlying TDataset will not be used during the reconciliation process. The TDatasetProvider.ResolveToDataset property was created to use these events during reconciliation. For example, if TDatasetProvider.ResolveToDataset is true, most of the events on the TDataset will be triggered. Be aware that the events used are only called when applying updates back to the server. In other words, if you have a TQuery.BeforeInsert event defined on the server, it will only fire on the server once you call TClientDataSet.ApplyUpdates. The events don't integrate into the corresponding events of the TClientDataSet.

Dealing with Master/Detail Relationships

No discussion of database applications would be complete without at least a mention of master/detail relationships. With DataSnap, you have two choices for dealing with master/detail.

Nested Datasets

One option for master/detail relationships is nested datasets. Nested datasets allow a master table to actually contain detail datasets. In addition to updating master and detail records in one transaction, they allow for storage of all master and detail records to be stored in one briefcase file, and you can use the enhancements to DBGrid to pop up detail datasets in their own windows. A word of caution if you do decide to use nested datasets: All the detail records will be retrieved and brought over to the client when selecting a master record. This will become a possible performance bottleneck if you nest several levels of detail datasets. For example, if you retrieve just one master record that has 10 detail records, and each detail record has three detail records linked to the first level detail, you would retrieve 41 records initially. When using client-side linking, you would only retrieve 14 records initially and obtain the other grandchild records as you scrolled through the detail TClientDataSet.

In order to set up a nested dataset relationship, you need to define the master/detail relationship on the application server. This is done using the same technique you've been using in client/server applications—namely, defining the SQL statement for the detail TQuery, including the link parameter. Here's an example:

```
"select * orders where custno=:custno"
```

You then assign the TQuery.Datasource for the detail TQuery to point to a TDatasource component that's tied to the master TDataset. Once this relationship is set up, you only need to export the TDatasetProvider that's tied to the master dataset. DataSnap is smart enough to understand that the master dataset has detail datasets linked to it and will therefore send the detail datasets across to the client as a TDatasetField.

On the client, you assign the master TClientDataset.ProviderName property to the master provider. Then, you add persistent fields to the TClientDataset. Notice the last field in the Fields Editor. It contains a field named the same as the detail dataset on the server and is declared as a TDatasetField type. At this point, you have enough information to use the nested dataset in code. However, to make things really easy, you can add a detail TClientDataset and assign its DatasetField property to the appropriate TDatasetField from the master. It's important to note here that you didn't set any other properties on the detail TClientDataset, such as RemoteServer, ProviderName, MasterSource, MasterFields, or PacketRecords. The only property you set was the DatasetField property. At this point, you can bind data-aware controls to the detail TClientDataset as well.

After you've finished working with the data in the nested dataset, you need to apply the updates back to the database. This is done by calling the master TClientDataset's ApplyUpdates() method. DataSnap will apply all the changes in the master TClientDataset, which includes the detail datasets, back to the server inside the context of one transaction.

You'll find an example on the book's CD-ROM in the directory for this chapter under \NestCDS.

Client-Side Linking

Recall that some cautions were mentioned earlier regarding using nested datasets. The alternative to using nested datasets is to create the master/detail relationship on the client side. In order to create a master/detail link using this method, you simply create a TDataset and TDatasetProvider for the master and the detail on the server.

On the client, you bind two TClientDataset components to the datasets that you exported on the server. Then, you create the master/detail relationship by assigning the detail TClientDataset.MasterSource property to the TDatasource component that points to the master TClientDataset.

Setting MasterSource on a TClientDataset sets the PacketRecords property to zero. When PacketRecords equals zero, it means that DataSnap should just return the metadata information for this TClientDataset. However, when PacketRecords equals zero in the context of a master/detail relationship, the meaning changes. DataSnap will now retrieve the records for the detail dataset for each master record. In summary, leave the PacketRecords property set to the default value.

In order to reconcile the master/detail data back to the database in one transaction, you need to write your own ApplyUpdates logic. This isn't as simple as most tasks in Delphi, but it does give you full flexible control over the update process.

Applying updates to a single table is usually triggered by a call to TClientDataset.Apply Updates. This method sends the changed records from the ClientDataset to its provider on the middle tier, where the provider will then write the changes to the database. All this is done within the scope of a transaction and is accomplished without any intervention from the programmer. To do the same thing for master/detail tables, you must understand what Delphi is doing for you when you make that call to TClientDataset.ApplyUpdates.

Any changes you make to a TClientDataset are stored in the Delta property. The Delta property contains all the information that will eventually be written to the database. The following code illustrates the update process for applying Delta properties back to the database. Listings 21.2 and 21.3 show the relevant sections of the client and server for applying updates to a master/detail setup.

LISTING 21.2 Client Updates to Master/Detail

```
procedure TClientDM.ApplyUpdates;
var
  MasterVar, DetailVar: OleVariant;
begin
  Master.CheckBrowseMode;
  Detail_Proj.CheckBrowseMode;
  if Master.ChangeCount > 0 then
    MasterVar := Master.Delta else
    MasterVar := NULL;
  if Detail.ChangeCount > 0 then
    DetailVar := Detail.Delta else
    DetailVar := NULL;
  RemoteServer.AppServer.ApplyUpdates(DetailVar, MasterVar);
  { Reconcile the error datapackets. Since we allow 0 errors, only one error
    packet can contain errors. If neither packet contains errors then we
    refresh the data.}
  if not VarIsNull(DetailVar) then
    Detail.Reconcile(DetailVar) else
  if not VarIsNull(MasterVar) then
    Master.Reconcile(MasterVar) else
  begin
    Detail.Reconcile(DetailVar);
    Master.Reconcile(MasterVar);
    Detail.Refresh;
    Master.Refresh;
  end;
end;
```

LISTING 21.3 Server Updates to Master/Detail

```
procedure TServerRDM.ApplyUpdates(var DetailVar, MasterVar: OleVariant);
var
  ErrCount: Integer;
begin
Database.StartTransaction;
  try
    if not VarIsNull(MasterVar) then
    begin
      MasterVar := cdsMaster.Provider.ApplyUpdates(MasterVar, 0, ErrCount);
      if ErrCount > 0 then
        SysUtils.Abort;    // This will cause Rollback
    end;
    if not VarIsNull(DetailVar) then
```

LISTING 21.3   Continued

```
  begin
    DetailVar := cdsDetail.Provider.ApplyUpdates(DetailVar, 0, ErrCount);
    if ErrCount > 0 then
      SysUtils.Abort;     // This will cause Rollback
  end;
  Database.Commit;
except
  Database.Rollback
end;
end;
```

Although this method works quite well, it really doesn't provide for opportunities for code reuse. This would be a good time to extend Delphi and provide easy reuse. Here are the main steps required to abstract the update process:

1. Place the deltas for each CDS in a variant array.
2. Place the providers for each CDS in a variant array.
3. Apply all the deltas in one transaction.
4. Reconcile the error datapackets returned in the previous step and refresh the data.

The result of this abstraction is provided in the utility unit shown in Listing 21.4.

LISTING 21.4   A Unit Providing Utility Routines and Abstraction

```
unit CDSUtil;

interface

uses
  DbClient, DbTables;

function RetrieveDeltas(const cdsArray : array of TClientDataset): Variant;
function RetrieveProviders(const cdsArray : array of TClientDataset): Variant;
procedure ReconcileDeltas(const cdsArray : array of TClientDataset;
                          vDeltaArray: OleVariant);

procedure CDSApplyUpdates(ADatabase : TDatabase; var vDeltaArray: OleVariant;
                          const vProviderArray: OleVariant);

implementation

uses
  SysUtils, Provider, Midas, Variants;
```

LISTING 21.4 Continued

```
type
  PArrayData = ^TArrayData;
  TArrayData = array[0..1000] of Olevariant;

{Delta is the CDS.Delta on input. On return, Delta will contain a data packet}
{containing all of the records that could not be applied to the database.}
{Remember Delphi needs the provider name, so it is passed in the first}
{element of the AProvider variant.}
procedure ApplyDelta(AProvider: OleVariant; var Delta : OleVariant);
var
  ErrCount : integer;
  OwnerData: OleVariant;
begin
  if not VarIsNull(Delta) then
  begin
    // ScktSrvr does not support early-binding
    Delta := (IDispatch(AProvider[0]) as IAppServer).AS_ApplyUpdates(
                AProvider[1], Delta, 0, ErrCount, OwnerData);
    if ErrCount > 0 then
      SysUtils.Abort;  // This will cause Rollback in the calling procedure
  end;
end;

{Server call}
procedure CDSApplyUpdates(ADatabase : TDatabase; var vDeltaArray: OleVariant;
  const vProviderArray: OleVariant);
var
  i : integer;
  LowArr, HighArr: integer;
  P: PArrayData;
begin
  {Wrap the updates in a transaction. If any step results in an error, raise}
  {an exception, which will Rollback the transaction.}
  ADatabase.Connected:=true;
  ADatabase.StartTransaction;
  try
    LowArr:=VarArrayLowBound(vDeltaArray,1);
    HighArr:=VarArrayHighBound(vDeltaArray,1);
    P:=VarArrayLock(vDeltaArray);
    try
      for i:=LowArr to HighArr do
        ApplyDelta(vProviderArray[i], P^[i]);
  finally
      VarArrayUnlock(vDeltaArray);
    end;
```

LISTING 21.4 Continued

```
    ADatabase.Commit;
  except
    ADatabase.Rollback;
  end;
end;

{Client side calls}
function RetrieveDeltas(const cdsArray : array of TClientDataset): Variant;
var
  i : integer;
  LowCDS, HighCDS : integer;
begin
  Result:=NULL;
  LowCDS:=Low(cdsArray);
  HighCDS:=High(cdsArray);
  for i:=LowCDS to HighCDS do
    cdsArray[i].CheckBrowseMode;

  Result:=VarArrayCreate([LowCDS, HighCDS], varVariant);
  {Setup the variant with the changes (or NULL if there are none)}
  for i:=LowCDS to HighCDS do
  begin
    if cdsArray[i].ChangeCount>0 then
      Result[i]:=cdsArray[i].Delta else
      Result[i]:=NULL;
  end;
end;

{If we're using Delphi 5 or greater, then we need to return the provider name
 AND the AppServer from this function. We will use ProviderName to call
 AS_ApplyUpdates in the CDSApplyUpdates function later.}
function RetrieveProviders(const cdsArray : array of TClientDataset): Variant;
var
  i: integer;
  LowCDS, HighCDS: integer;
begin
  Result:=NULL;
  LowCDS:=Low(cdsArray);
  HighCDS:=High(cdsArray);

  Result:=VarArrayCreate([LowCDS, HighCDS], varVariant);
  for i:=LowCDS to HighCDS do
    Result[i]:=VarArrayOf([cdsArray[i].AppServer, cdsArray[i].ProviderName]);
end;
```

LISTING 21.4   Continued

```pascal
procedure ReconcileDeltas(const cdsArray : array of TClientDataset;
  vDeltaArray: OleVariant);
var
  bReconcile : boolean;
  i: integer;
  LowCDS, HighCDS : integer;
begin
  LowCDS:=Low(cdsArray);
  HighCDS:=High(cdsArray);

  {If the previous step resulted in errors, Reconcile the error datapackets.}
  bReconcile:=false;
  for i:=LowCDS to HighCDS do
    if not VarIsNull(vDeltaArray[i]) then begin
      cdsArray[i].Reconcile(vDeltaArray[i]);
      bReconcile:=true;
      break;
    end;

  {Refresh the Datasets if needed}
  if not bReconcile then
    for i:=HighCDS downto LowCDS do begin
      cdsArray[i].Reconcile(vDeltaArray[i]);
      cdsArray[i].Refresh;
    end;
end;

end.
```

Listing 21.5 shows a reworking of the previous example using the CDSUtil unit.

LISTING 21.5   A Rework of the Previous Example Using CDSUtil.pas

```pascal
procedure TForm1.btnApplyClick(Sender: TObject);
var
  vDelta: OleVariant;
  vProvider: OleVariant;
  arrCDS: array[0..1] of TClientDataset;
begin
  arrCDS[0]:=cdsMaster;   // Set up ClientDataset array
  arrCDS[1]:=cdsDetail;

  vDelta:=RetrieveDeltas(arrCDS);              // Step 1
  vProvider:=RetrieveProviders(arrCDS);        // Step 2
```

LISTING 21.5 Continued

```
  DCOMConnection1.ApplyUpdates(vDelta, vProvider); // Step 3
  ReconcileDeltas(arrCDS, vDelta);                 // Step 4
end;

procedure TServerRDM.ApplyUpdates(var vDelta, vProvider: OleVariant);
begin
  CDSApplyUpdates(Database1, vDelta, vProvider);  // Step 3
end;
```

You can use this unit in either two-tier or three-tier applications. To move from a two-tier to a three-tier approach, you would export a function on the server that calls CDSApplyUpdates instead of calling CDSApplyUpdates on the client. Everything else on the client remains the same.

You'll find an example on the book's CD-ROM in the directory for this chapter under \MDCDS.

Real-World Examples

Now that we have the basics out of the way, let's look at how DataSnap can help you by exploring several real-world examples.

Joins

Writing a relational database application depends heavily on walking the relationships between tables. Often, you'll find it convenient to represent your highly normalized data in a view that's more flattened than the underlying data structure. However, updating the data from these joins takes some extra care on your end.

One-Table Update

Applying updates to a joined query is a special case in database programming, and DataSnap is no exception. The problem lies in the join query itself. Although some join queries will produce data that could be automatically updated, others will never conform to rules that will allow automatic retrieval, editing, and updating of the underlying data. To that end, Delphi currently forces you to resolve updates to join queries yourself.

For joins that require only one table to be updated, Delphi can handle most of the updating details for you. Here are the steps required in order to write one table back to the database:

1. Add persistent fields to the joined TQuery.
2. Set TQuery.TField.ProviderFlags=[] for every field of the table that you won't be updating.

3. Write the following code in the `DatasetProvider.OnGetTableName` event to tell
DataSnap which table you want to update. Keep in mind that this event makes it easier to
specify the table name, although you could do the same thing in previous versions of
Delphi by using the `DatasetProvider.OnGetDatasetProperties` event:

```
procedure TJoin1Server.prvJoinGetTableName(Sender: TObject;
  DataSet: TDataSet; var TableName: String);
begin
  TableName := 'Emp';
end;
```

By doing this, you're telling the `ClientDataset` to keep track of the table name for you. Now
when you call `ClientDataset1.ApplyUpdates()`, DataSnap knows to try and resolve to the
table name that you specified, as opposed to letting DataSnap try and figure out what the table
name might be.

An alternative approach would be to use a `TUpdateSQL` component that only updates the table
of interest. This allows the `TQuery.UpdateObject` to be used during the reconciliation process
and more closely matches the process used in traditional client/server applications.

> **NOTE**
>
> Not all `TDatasets` have an `UpdateObject` property. However, you can still use the
> same approach because of the rework done to `TUpdateSQL`. Simply define your SQL
> for each action (delete, insert, modify) and use code similar to the following:
>
> ```
> procedure TForm1.DataSetProvider1BeforeUpdateRecord(Sender: TObject;
>   SourceDS: TDataSet; DeltaDS: TCustomClientDataSet;
>   UpdateKind: TUpdateKind; var Applied: Boolean);
> begin
>   UpdateSQL1.DataSet := DeltaDS;
>   UpdateSQL1.SetParams(UpdateKind);
>   ADOCommand1.CommandText := UpdateSQL1.SQL[UpdateKind].Text;
>   ADOCommand1.Parameters.Assign(UpdateSQL1.Query[UpdateKind].Params);
>   ADOCommand1.Execute;
>   Applied := true;
> end;
> ```

You'll find an example on the book's CD-ROM in the directory for this chapter under \Join1.

Multitable Update

For more complex scenarios, such as allowing the editing and updating of multiple tables, you
need to write some code yourself. There are two approaches to solving this problem:

- The older method of using DatasetProvider.BeforeUpdateRecord() to break the data packet apart and apply the updates to the underlying tables
- The newer method of applying updates by using the UpdateObject property

When using cached updates with a multitable join, you need to configure one TUpdateSQL component for each table that will be updated. Because the UpdateObject property can only be assigned to one TUpdateSQL component, you needed to link all the TUpdateSQL.Dataset properties to the joined dataset programmatically in TQuery.OnUpdateRecord and call TUpdateSQL.Apply to bind the parameters and execute the underlying SQL statement. In this case, the dataset you're interested in is the Delta dataset. This dataset is passed as a parameter into the TQuery.OnUpdateRecord event.

All you need to do is assign the SessionName and DatabaseName properties to allow the update to occur in the same context as other transactions and tie the Dataset property to the Delta that is passed to the event. The resulting code for the TQuery.OnUpdateRecord event is shown in Listing 21.6.

LISTING 21.6   Join Using a TUpdateSQL

```
procedure TJoin2Server.JoinQueryUpdateRecord(DataSet: TDataSet;
  UpdateKind: TUpdateKind; var UpdateAction: TUpdateAction);
begin
  usqlEmp.SessionName := JoinQuery.SessionName;
  usqlEmp.DatabaseName := JoinQuery.DatabaseName;
  usqlEmp.Dataset := Dataset;
  usqlEmp.Apply(UpdateKind);

  usqlFTEmp.SessionName := JoinQuery.SessionName;
  usqlFTEmp.DatabaseName := JoinQuery.DatabaseName;
  usqlFTEmp.Dataset := Dataset;
  usqlFTEmp.Apply(UpdateKind);

  UpdateAction := uaApplied;
end;
```

Because you've complied with the rules of updating data within the DataSnap architecture, the whole update process is seamlessly triggered as it always is in DataSnap, with a call to ClientDataset1.ApplyUpdates(0);.

You'll find an example on the book's CD-ROM in the directory for this chapter under \Join2.

DataSnap on the Web

Even with the introduction of Kylix, Delphi is tied to the Windows platform (or Linux); therefore, any clients you write must run on that type of machine. This isn't always desirable. For example, you might want to provide easy access to the data that exists on your database to anyone who has an Internet connection. Because you've already written an application server that acts as a broker for your data—in addition to housing business rules for that data—it would be desirable to reuse the application server as opposed to rewriting the entire data-access and business rule tier in another environment.

Straight HTML

This section focuses on how to leverage your application server while providing a new presentation tier that will use straight HTML. This section assumes that you're familiar with the material covered in Chapter 31, "Internet-Enabling Your Applications with WebBroker" of *Delphi 5 Developer's Guide*, which is on this book's CD-ROM. Using this method, you're introducing another layer into your architecture. WebBroker acts as the client to the application server and repackages this data into HTML that will be displayed on the browser. You also lose some of the benefits of working with the Delphi IDE, such as the lack of data-aware controls. However, this is a very viable option for allowing access to your data in a simple HTML format.

After creating a WebBroker Application and a WebModule, you simply place a TDispatch Connection and TClientDataset on the WebModule. Once the properties are filled in, you can use a number of different methods to translate this data into HTML that will eventually be seen by the client.

One valid technique would be to add a TDatasetTableProducer linked to the TClientDataset of interest. From there, the user can click a link and go to an edit page, where she can edit the data and apply the updates. See Listings 21.7 and 21.8 for a sample implementation of this technique.

LISTING 21.7   HTML for Editing and Applying Updates

```
<form action="<#SCRIPTNAME>/updaterecord" method="post">
<b>EmpNo: <#EMPNO></b>
<input type="hidden" name="EmpNo" value=<#EMPNO>>
<table cellspacing="2" cellpadding="2" border="0">
<tr>
  <td>Last Name:</td>
  <td><input type="text" name="LastName" value=<#LASTNAME>></td>
</tr>
<tr>
  <td>First Name:</td>
  <td><input type="text" name="FirstName" value=<#FIRSTNAME>></td>
```

LISTING 21.7   Continued

```html
</tr>
<tr>
  <td>Hire Date:</td>
  <td><input type="text" name="HireDate" size="8" value=<#HIREDATE>></td>
</tr>
<tr>
  <td>Salary:</td>
  <td><input type="text" name="Salary" size="8" value=<#SALARY>></td>
</tr>
<tr>
  <td>Vacation:</td>
  <td><input type="text" name="Vacation" size="4" value=<#VACATION>></td>
</tr>
</table>
<input type="submit" name="Submit" value="Apply Updates">
<input type="Reset">
</form>
```

LISTING 21.8   Code for Editing and Applying Updates

```pascal
unit WebMain;

interface

uses
  Windows, Messages, SysUtils, Classes, HTTPApp, DBWeb, Db, DBClient,
  MConnect, DSProd;

type
  TWebModule1 = class(TWebModule)
    dcJoin: TDCOMConnection;
    cdsJoin: TClientDataSet;
    dstpJoin: TDataSetTableProducer;
    dsppJoin: TDataSetPageProducer;
    ppSuccess: TPageProducer;
    ppError: TPageProducer;
    procedure WebModuleBeforeDispatch(Sender: TObject;
      Request: TWebRequest; Response: TWebResponse; var Handled: Boolean);
    procedure WebModule1waListAction(Sender: TObject; Request: TWebRequest;
      Response: TWebResponse; var Handled: Boolean);
    procedure dstpJoinFormatCell(Sender: TObject; CellRow,
      CellColumn: Integer; var BgColor: THTMLBgColor;
      var Align: THTMLAlign; var VAlign: THTMLVAlign; var CustomAttrs,
      CellData: String);
```

LISTING 21.8 Continued

```
    procedure WebModule1waEditAction(Sender: TObject; Request: TWebRequest;
      Response: TWebResponse; var Handled: Boolean);
    procedure dsppJoinHTMLTag(Sender: TObject; Tag: TTag;
      const TagString: String; TagParams: TStrings;
      var ReplaceText: String);
    procedure WebModule1waUpdateAction(Sender: TObject;
      Request: TWebRequest; Response: TWebResponse; var Handled: Boolean);
  private
    { Private declarations }
    DataFields : TStrings;
  public
    { Public declarations }
  end;

var
  WebModule1: TWebModule1;

implementation

{$R *.DFM}

procedure TWebModule1.WebModuleBeforeDispatch(Sender: TObject;
  Request: TWebRequest; Response: TWebResponse; var Handled: Boolean);
begin
  with Request do
    case MethodType of
      mtPost: DataFields:=ContentFields;
      mtGet: DataFields:=QueryFields;
    end;
end;

function LocalServerPath(sFile : string = '') : string;
var
  FN: array[0..MAX_PATH- 1] of char;
  sPath : shortstring;
begin
  SetString(sPath, FN, GetModuleFileName(hInstance, FN, SizeOf(FN)));
  Result := ExtractFilePath( sPath ) + ExtractFileName( sFile );
end;

procedure TWebModule1.WebModule1waListAction(Sender: TObject;
  Request: TWebRequest; Response: TWebResponse; var Handled: Boolean);
begin
  cdsJoin.Open;
  Response.Content :=  dstpJoin.Content;
end;
```

Listing 21.8 Continued

```
procedure TWebModule1.dstpJoinFormatCell(Sender: TObject; CellRow,
  CellColumn: Integer; var BgColor: THTMLBgColor; var Align: THTMLAlign;
  var VAlign: THTMLVAlign; var CustomAttrs, CellData: String);
begin
  if (CellRow > 0) and (CellColumn = 0) then
    CellData := Format('<a href="%s/getrecord?empno=%s">%s</a>',
      [Request.ScriptName, CellData, CellData]);
end;

procedure TWebModule1.WebModule1waEditAction(Sender: TObject;
  Request: TWebRequest; Response: TWebResponse; var Handled: Boolean);
begin
  dsppJoin.HTMLFile := LocalServerPath('join.htm');
  cdsJoin.Filter := 'EmpNo = ' + DataFields.Values['empno'];
  cdsJoin.Filtered := true;
  Response.Content := dsppJoin.Content;
end;

procedure TWebModule1.dsppJoinHTMLTag(Sender: TObject; Tag: TTag;
  const TagString: String; TagParams: TStrings; var ReplaceText: String);
begin
  if CompareText(TagString, 'SCRIPTNAME')=0 then
    ReplaceText:=Request.ScriptName;
end;

procedure TWebModule1.WebModule1waUpdateAction(Sender: TObject;
  Request: TWebRequest; Response: TWebResponse; var Handled: Boolean);
var
  EmpNo, LastName, FirstName, HireDate, Salary, Vacation:  string;
begin
  EmpNo:=DataFields.Values['EmpNo'];
  LastName:=DataFields.Values['LastName'];
  FirstName:=DataFields.Values['FirstName'];
  HireDate:=DataFields.Values['HireDate'];
  Salary:=DataFields.Values['Salary'];
  Vacation:=DataFields.Values['Vacation'];

  cdsJoin.Open;
  if cdsJoin.Locate('EMPNO', EmpNo, []) then
  begin
    cdsJoin.Edit;
    cdsJoin.FieldByName('LastName').AsString:=LastName;
    cdsJoin.FieldByName('FirstName').AsString:=FirstName;
    cdsJoin.FieldByName('HireDate').AsString:=HireDate;
```

LISTING 21.8   Continued

```
    cdsJoin.FieldByName('Salary').AsString:=Salary;
    cdsJoin.FieldByName('Vacation').AsString:=Vacation;
    if cdsJoin.ApplyUpdates(0)=0 then
      Response.Content:=ppSuccess.Content else
      Response.Content:=pPError.Content;
  end;
end;

end.
```

Note that this method requires much custom code to be written, and the full feature set of DataSnap isn't implemented in this example—specifically error reconciliation. You can continue to enhance this example to be more robust if you use this technique extensively.

> **CAUTION**
>
> It's imperative that you consider the concept of state when writing your WebModule and application server. Because HTTP is a stateless protocol, you cannot rely on the values of properties to be the same as you left them when the call was over.

> **TIP**
>
> WebBroker is one way to get your data to Web browsers. Using WebSnap, you can extend the capabilities of your application even further by using the new features WebSnap offers, such as scripting and session support.

To run this sample, be sure to compile and register the Join2 sample application. Next, compile the Web application (either the CGI or ISAPI version), and place the executable in a script-capable directory for your Web server. The code also expects to find the file join.htm in the scripts directory, so copy that too. Then, just point your browser to http://localhost/scripts/WebJoin.exe and see the results of this sample.

You'll find an example on the book's CD-ROM in the directory for this chapter under \WebBrok.

InternetExpress

With InternetExpress, you can enhance the functionality of a straight WebModule approach to allow for a richer experience on the client. This is possible due to the use of open standards such as XML and JavaScript in InternetExpress. Using InternetExpress, you can create a browser-only front end to your DataSnap application server: no ActiveX controls to download; zero client-side install and configuration requirements; nothing but a Web browser hitting a Web server.

In order to use InternetExpress, you will need to have some code running on a Web server. For this example, we will use an ISAPI application, but you could also use CGI or ASP. The purpose of the Web broker is to take requests from the browser and pass those requests on to the app server. Placing InternetExpress components in the Web broker application makes this task very easy.

This example will use a standard DataSnap app server that has Customers, Orders, and Employees. Customers and Orders are linked in a nested dataset relationship (for more information on nested datasets, see the next section), whereas the Employees dataset will serve as a lookup table. See the accompanying source code for the app server definition. After the app server has been built and registered, you can focus on building the Web broker application that will communicate with the app server.

Create a new ISAPI application by selecting File, New, Web Server Application from the Object Repository. Place a `TDCOMConnection` component on the `WebModule`. This will act as the link to the app server, so fill in the `ServerName` property with the ProgID of the app server.

Next, you will place a `TXMLBroker` component from the InternetExpress page of the Component Palette on the WebModule and set the `RemoteServer` and `ProviderName` properties to the CustomerProvider. The `TXMLBroker` component acts in a manner similar to the `TClientDataset`. It is responsible for retrieving data packets from the app server and passing those data packets to the browser. The main difference between the data packet in a `TXMLBroker` and a `TClientDataset` is that the `TXMLBroker` translates the DataSnap data packets into XML. You will also add a `TClientDataset` to the `WebModule` and tie it to the Employees provider on the app server. You will use this as a lookup datasource later.

The `TXMLBroker` component is responsible for communication to the application server and also the navigation of HTML pages. Many properties are available to customize how your InternetExpress application will behave. For example, you can limit the number of records that will be transmitted to the client or specify the number of errors allowed during an update.

You now need a way to move this data to the browser. Using the `TInetXPageProducer` component, you can use the WebBroker technology in Delphi to serve an HTML page up to the browser. However, the `TInetXPageProducer` also allows for visual creation of the Web page via the Web Page Editor.

Double-click on the `TInetXPageProducer` to bring up the Web Page Editor. This visual editor helps you customize what elements are present on a given Web page. One of the most interesting things about InternetExpress is that it is completely extensible. You can create your own components that can be used in the Web Page Editor by following some well-defined rules. For examples of custom InternetExpress components, see the `<DELPHI>\DEMOS\MIDAS\` `INTERNETEXPRESS\INETXCUSTOM` directory.

CAUTION

`TInetXPageProducer` has a property named `IncludePathURL`. It is essential to set this property properly, or your InternetExpress application won't work. Set the value to the virtual directory that contains the InternetExpress JavaScript files. For example, if you place the files in `c:\inetpub\wwwroot\jscript`, the value for this property will be `/jscript/`.

With the Web Page Editor active, click the Insert tool button to display the Add Web Component dialog box (see Figure 21.7). This dialog box contains a list of Web components that can be added to the HTML page. This list is based on which parent component (the section in the upper left) is currently selected. For example, add a DataForm Web component to the root node to allow end users to display and edit database information in a form-like layout.

FIGURE 21.7
The Add Web Component dialog box from the Web Page Editor.

If you then select the DataForm node in the Web Page Editor, you can click the Insert button again. Notice that the list of components available at this point is different from the list displayed from the previous step. After selecting the FieldGroup component, you will see a warning in the preview pane, telling you that the TXMLBroker property for the FieldGroup isn't assigned. By assigning the XMLBroker in the Object Inspector, you will immediately notice the layout of the HTML in the preview pane of the Web Page Editor. As you continue to modify properties or add components, the state of the HTML page will be constantly updated (see Figure 21.8).

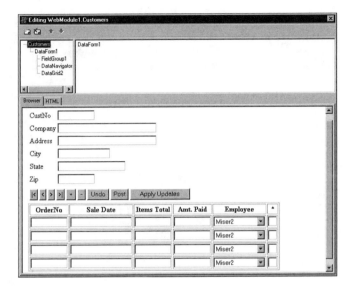

FIGURE 21.8

The Web Page Editor after designing an HTML page.

The level of customization available with the standard Web components is practically limitless. Properties make it easy to change field captions, alignment, colors; add straight custom HTML code; and even use style sheets. Furthermore, if the component doesn't suit your needs exactly, you can always create a descendant component and use that in its place. The framework is truly as extensible as your imagination allows.

In order to call the ISAPI DLL, you need to place it in a virtual directory capable of executing script. You also need to move the JavaScript files found in `<DELPHI>\SOURCE\WEBMIDAS` to a valid location on your Web server and modify the `TInetXPageProducer.IncludePathURL` property to point to the URI of the JavaScript files. After that, the page is ready to be viewed.

To access the page, all you need is a JavaScript-capable browser. Simply point the browser to `http://localhost/inetx/inetxisapi.dll`, and the data will display in the browser. Figure 21.9 shows a screenshot of the application in action.

You can detect reconciliation errors during the ApplyUpdates process as you are already used to doing in a standalone DataSnap application. This capability is made possible when you assign the `TXMLBroker.ReconcileProducer` property to a `TPageProducer`. Whenever an error occurs, the `Content` of the `TPageProducer` assigned to this property will be returned to the end user.

A specialized `TPageProducer`, `TReconcilePageProducer`, is available by installing the `InetXCustom.dpk` package found in `<DELPHI>\DEMOS\MIDAS\INTERNETEXPRESS\INETXCUSTOM`. This PageProducer generates HTML that acts much like the standard DataSnap Reconciliation Error dialog box (see Figure 21.10).

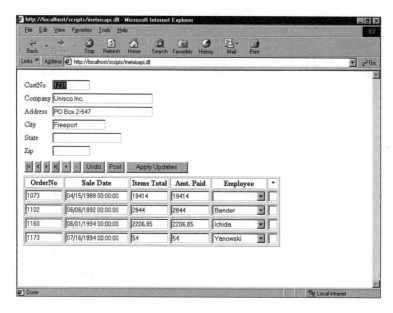

FIGURE 21.9

Internet Explorer accessing the InternetExpress Web page.

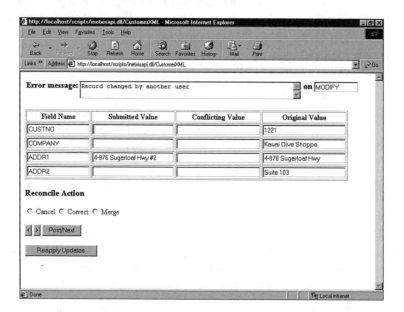

FIGURE 21.10

View of the HTML page generated by TReconcilePageProducer.

You'll find an example on the book's CD-ROM in the directory for this chapter under \InetX.

More Client Dataset Features

Many options are available to control the TClientDataset component. In this section, we will look at ways to use the TClientDataset to make coding easier in complex applications.

Two-Tier Applications

You've seen how to assign the provider—and therefore the data—to the ClientDataset in a three-tier application. However, many times a simple two-tier application is all that's needed. So, how do you use DataSnap in a two-tier application? There are four possibilities:

- Runtime assignment of data
- Design-time assignment of data
- Runtime assignment of a provider
- Design-time assignment of a provider

The two basic choices when using ClientDataset are assigning the AppServer property and assigning the data. If you choose to assign the AppServer, you have a link between the TDatasetProvider and the ClientDataset that will allow you to have communication between the ClientDataset and TDatasetProvider as needed. If, on the other hand, you choose to assign the data, you have effectively created a local storage mechanism for your data and the ClientDataset will not communicate with the TDatasetProvider component for more information or data.

In order to assign the data directly from a TDataset to a TClientDataset at runtime, use the code in Listing 21.9.

LISTING 21.9 Code to Assign Data Directly from a TDataSet

```
function GetData(ADataset: TDataset): OleVariant;
begin
  with TDatasetProvider.Create(nil) do
  try
    Dataset:=ADataset;
    Result:=Data;
  finally
    Free;
  end;
end;
procedure TForm1.Button1Click(Sender: TObject);
begin
  ClientDataset1.Data:=GetData(ADOTable1);
end;
```

This method takes more code and effort than previous versions of Delphi, where you would simply assign the `Table1.Provider.Data` property to the `ClientDataset1.Data` property. However, this function will help make the additional code less noticeable.

You can also use the `TClientDataset` component to retrieve the data from a `TDataset` at design time by selecting the Assign Local Data command from the context menu of the `TClientDataset` component. Then, you specify the `TDataset` component that contains the data you want, and the data is brought to the `TClientDataset` and stored in the `Data` property.

CAUTION

If you were to save the file in this state and compare the size of the DFM file to the size before executing this command, you would notice an increase in the DFM size. This is because Delphi has stored all the metadata and records associated with the `TDataset` in the DFM. Delphi will only stream this data to the DFM if the `TClientDataset` is `Active`. You can also trim this space by executing the Clear Data command on the `TClientDataset` context menu.

If you want the full flexibility that a provider assignment allows, you need to assign the `AppServer` property. At runtime, you can assign the `AppServer` property in code. This can be as simple as the following statement, found in `FormCreate`:

```
ClientDataset1.AppServer:=TLocalAppServer.Create(Table1);
ClientDataset1.Open;
```

You can assign the `AppServer` property at design time. If you leave the `RemoteServer` property blank on a `TClientDataset`, you can assign a `TDatasetProvider` component to the `TClientDataset.ProviderName` property.

One major drawback to using the `TClientDataset.ProviderName` property is that it can't be assigned to providers that reside on another form or `DataModule` at design time. This is why Delphi 6 introduced the `TLocalConnection` component. `TLocalConnection` will autodiscover and expose any `TDatasetProviders` that it finds with the same owner. To use this method of assigning providers, assign the `ClientDataset.RemoteServer` property to be the `LocalConnection` component on the external form or `DataModule`. After doing this, you will have the list of providers for that `LocalConnection` in the `ClientDataset.ProviderName` property.

The major difference between using `TDataset` components and `ClientDataset` is that when you're using `ClientDataset`, you're using the `IAppServer` interface to broker your requests for data to the underlying `TDataset` component. This means that you'll be manipulating the properties, methods, events, and fields of the `TClientDataset` component, not the `TDataset` component. Think of the `TDataset` component as if it were in a separate application and therefore can't be manipulated directly by you in code. Place all your server components on a separate `DataModule`. Placing the `TDatabase`, `TDataset`, and `TLocalConnection` components on a separate `DataModule` effectively prepares your application for an easier transition to a multitier deployment later on. Another benefit of doing this is that it might help you think of the `DataModule` as something that the client cannot touch easily. Again, this is good preparation for your application, and your own mindset, when it comes time to port this application to a multitier deployment.

Classic Mistakes

The most common mistake in creating a multitier application is introducing unnecessary knowledge of the data tier into the presentation tier. Some validation is more suitable in the presentation tier, but it's how that validation is performed that determines its suitability in a multitier application.

For example, if you're passing dynamic SQL statements from the client to the server, this introduces a dependency for the client application to always be synchronized with the data tier. Doing things this way introduces more moving parts that need to be coordinated in the overall multitier application. If you change one of the tables' structures on the data tier, you must update all the client applications that send dynamic SQL so that they can now send the proper SQL statement. This clearly limits the benefit that a properly developed thin-client application holds.

Another example of a classic mistake is when the client application attempts to control the transaction lifetime, as opposed to allowing the business tier to take care of this on the client's behalf. Most of the time, this is implemented by exposing three methods of the `TDataBase` instance on the server—`BeginTransaction()`, `Commit()`, and `Rollback()`—and calling those methods from the client. Doing things in this manner makes the client code much more complicated to maintain and violates the principle that the presentation tier should be the only tier responsible for communication to the data tier. The presentation tier should never have to rely on such an approach. Instead, you should send your updates to the business tier and let that tier deal with updating the data in a transaction.

Deploying DataSnap Applications

After you've built a complete DataSnap application, the last hurdle left to clear is deploying that application. This section outlines what needs to be done in order to make your DataSnap application deployment painless.

Licensing Issues

Licensing has been a tough subject for many people ever since DataSnap was first introduced in Delphi 3. The myriad of options for deploying this technology has contributed to this confusion. This section details the overall requirements of when you need to purchase a DataSnap license. However, the only legally binding document for licensing is in DEPLOY.TXT, located in the Delphi 6 directory. Finally, for the ultimate authority to answer this question for a specific situation, you must contact your local Borland sales office. More guidelines and examples are available at

http://www.borland.com/midas/papers/licensing/

or our Web site at

http://www.xapware.com/ddg

The information from this document was prepared to answer some of the more common scenarios in which DataSnap is used. Pricing information and options are also included in the document.

The key criteria to determine the necessity of a DataSnap license for your application is whether the DataSnap data packet crosses a machine boundary. If it does, and you use the DataSnap components on both machines, you need to purchase a license. If it doesn't (as in the one- and two-tier examples presented earlier), you're using DataSnap technology, but there's no need to purchase a license to use DataSnap in this manner.

DCOM Configuration

DCOM configuration appears to be as much art as it is science. There are many aspects to a complete and secure DCOM configuration, but this section will help you understand some of the basics of this black art.

After registering your application server, your server object is now available for customization in the Microsoft utility DCOMCNFG. This utility is included with NT systems automatically but is a separate download for Win9x machines. As a side note, there are plenty of bugs in DCOMCNFG; the most notable being DCOMCNFG can only be run on Win9x machines that have User-level share enabled. This, of course, requires a domain. This isn't always possible or desirable in a peer-to-peer network, such as two Windows 9x machines. This has led many people to incorrectly assume that an NT machine is required to run DCOM.

If you can run DCOMCNFG, you can select the registered application server and click the Properties button to reveal information about your server. The Identity page is a good place to start in our brief tour of DCOMCNFG. The default setting for a registered server object is Launching User. Microsoft couldn't have made a worse decision for the default if it tried.

When DCOM creates the server, it uses the security context of the user specified on the Identity page. The launching user will spawn one new process of the server object for each and every distinct user login. Many people look at the fact that they selected the `ciMultiple` instancing mode and wonder why multiple copies of their server are being created. For example, if user A connects to the server and then user B connects, DCOM will spawn an entirely new process for user B. Additionally, you won't see the GUI portion of the server for users who log in under an account different from that currently in use on the server machine. This is because of the NT concept known as *Windows stations*. The only Windows station capable of writing to the screen is the Interactive User, which is the user who is currently logged in on the server machine. Furthermore, windows stations are a scarce resource, and you might not be able to run many server processes if you use this setting. In summary, never use the Launching User option as your identity for your server.

The next interesting option on this page is the Interactive User, which means that every single client that creates a server will do so under the context of the user who is logged in to the server at that point in time. This will also allow you to have visual interaction with your application server. Unfortunately, most system administrators don't allow an open login to just sit there idle on an NT machine. In addition, if the logged-in user decides to log out, the application server will no longer work as desired.

For this discussion, this only leaves the last enabled option on the Identity page: This User. Using this setting, all clients will create one application server and use the login credentials and context of the user specified on the Identity page. This also means that the NT machine doesn't require a user to be logged in to use the application server. The one downside to this approach is that there will be no GUI display of the server when using this option. However, it is by far the best of all available options to put your application server in production.

After the server object is configured properly with the right identity, you need to turn your attention to the Security tab. Make sure that the user who will be running this object has the appropriate privileges assigned. Also be sure to grant the SYSTEM user access to the server; otherwise, you'll encounter errors along the way.

Many subtle nuances are strewn throughout the DCOM configuration process. For the latest on DCOM configuration issues, especially as they pertain to Windows 9x, Delphi, and DataSnap, visit the DCOM page of our Web site at

`http://www.DistribuCon.com/dcom95.htm`

Files to Deploy

The requirements for deploying a DataSnap application have changed with each new release of Delphi. Delphi 6 makes deployment easier than any other version.

With Delphi 6, the minimum files needed for deployment of your DataSnap application is shown in the following lists.

Here are the steps for the server (these steps assume a COM server; they will differ slightly for other varieties):

1. Copy the application server to a directory with sufficient NTFS privileges or share level privileges set properly if on a Win9x machine.

2. Install your data access layer to allow the application server to act as a client to the RDBMS (for example, BDE, MDAC, specific client-side database libraries, and so on).

3. Copy `MIDAS.DLL` to the `%SYSTEM%` directory. By default, this would be `C:\Winnt\System32` for NT machines and `C:\Windows\System` for 9x machines.

4. Run the application server once to register it with COM.

Here are the steps for the client:

1. Copy the client to a directory, along with any other external dependency files used by your client (for example, runtime packages, DLLs, ActiveX controls, and so on).

2. Copy `MIDAS.DLL` to the `%SYSTEM%` directory. Note that Delphi 6 can statically link `MIDAS.DLL` into your application, thus making this step unnecessary. To do this, simply add the unit MidasLib to your uses clause and rebuild your application. You will see an increase in the size of the EXE due to the static linking.

3. Optional: If you specify the `ServerName` property in your `TDispatchConnection` or if you employ early binding in your client, you need to register the server's type library (TLB) file. This can be done by using a utility such as `<DELPHI>\BIN\TREGSVR.EXE` (or programmatically if you so choose).

Internet Deployment Considerations (Firewalls)

When deploying your application over a LAN, there's nothing to get in your way. You can choose whatever connection type best suits your application's needs. However, if you need to rely on the Internet as your backbone, many things can go wrong—namely, firewalls.

DCOM isn't the most firewall-friendly protocol. It requires opening multiple ports on a firewall. Most system administrators are wary of opening an entire range of ports (particularly those commonly recognized as DCOM ports) because it invites hackers to come knocking on the door. Using `TSocketConnection`, the story improves somewhat. The firewall only needs one open port. However, the occasional system administrator will even refuse to do that on the grounds that this is a security breach.

`TWebConnection` is similar to `TSocketConnection` in that it permits DataSnap traffic to be bundled up into valid HTTP traffic, and then uses the most open port in the world—the HTTP port (default port 80). Actually, the component even supports SSL, so you can have secure communications. By doing this, all firewall issues are completely eliminated. After all, if a corporation doesn't allow HTTP traffic in or out, nothing can be done to communicate with them anyway.

This bit of magic is accomplished by using the Borland-provided ISAPI extension that translates HTTP traffic into DataSnap traffic, and vice versa. In this regard, the ISAPI DLL does the same work that ScktSrvr does for socket connections. The ISAPI extension `httpsrvr.dll` needs to be placed in a directory capable of executing code. For example, with IIS, the default location for this file would be in `C:\Inetpub\Scripts`.

One more benefit of using `TWebConnection` is that it supports object pooling. Object pooling is used to spare the server the overhead of object creation every time a client connects to the server. Furthermore, the pooling mechanism in DataSnap allows for a maximum number of objects to be created. After this maximum has been reached, an error will be sent to the client saying that the server is too busy to process this request. This is more flexible and scalable than just creating an arbitrary number of threads for every single client that wants to connect to the server.

To take this a step further, building your RDM as a Web Service using a SOAP Data Module will not only provide the benefits of a `TwebConnection`, but will also permit clients using industry-standard SOAP protocols to be constructed. This platform enables your application server for use by .Net, Sun ONE, and other industry-compliant SOAP systems.

In order to tell DataSnap that this RDM will be pooled, you need to call `RegisterPooled` and `UnregisterPooled` in the `UpdateRegistry` method of the RDM. (See Listing 21.1 for a sample implementation of `UpdateRegistry`.) The following is a sample call to the `RegisterPooled` method:

```
RegisterPooled(ClassID, 16, 30);
```

This call tells DataSnap that 16 objects will be available in the pool, and that DataSnap can free any instances of objects that have been created if there has been no activity for 30 minutes. If you never want to free the objects, then you can pass `0` as the timeout parameter.

The client doesn't change that drastically. Simply use a `TWebConnection` as the `TDispatchConnection` for the client and fill in the appropriate properties, and the client will be communicating to the application server over HTTP. The one major difference when using `TWebConnection` is the need to specify the complete URL to the `httpsrvr.dll`, as opposed to just identifying the server computer by name or address. Figure 21.11 shows a screenshot of a typical setup using `TWebConnection`.

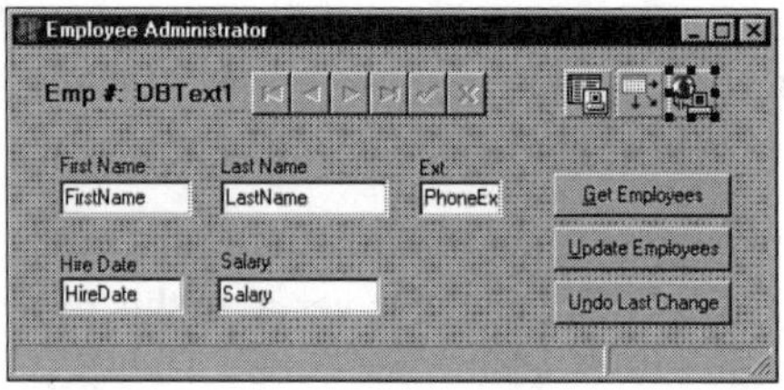

FIGURE 21.11
TWebConnection *setup at design time.*

Another benefit of using HTTP for your transport is that an OS such as NT Enterprise allows you to cluster servers. This provides automated load balancing and fault tolerance for your application server. For more information about clustering, see http://www.microsoft.com/ntserver/ntserverenterprise/exec/overview/clustering.

The limitations of using TWebConnection are fairly trivial, and they're well worth any concession in order to have more clients capable of reaching your application server. The limitations are that you must install wininet.dll on the client, and no callbacks are available when using TWebConnection.

Summary

This chapter provides quite a bit of information on DataSnap. Still, it only scratches the surface of what can be done with this technology—something far beyond the scope of a single chapter. Even after you explore all the nooks and crannies of DataSnap, you can still add to your knowledge and capabilities by using DataSnap with C++Builder and JBuilder. Using JBuilder, you can achieve the nirvana of cross-platform access to an application server while using the same technology and concepts you learned here.

DataSnap is a fast-evolving technology that brings the promise of multitier applications to every programmer. Once you experience the true power of creating an application with DataSnap, you might never return to database application development as you know it today.

Internet Development

IN THIS PART

ASP Development

by Bob Swart

IN THIS CHAPTER

In this chapter, you will learn what Active Server Pages and Active Server Objects are, and how Delphi 6 can support you when creating and deploying Active Server Objects.

Understanding Active Server Objects

Like *CGI (common gateway interface)* and *ISAPI/NSAPI (Internet Server API/Netscape Server API)* extensions, as supported by WebBroker, *ASP (Active Server Pages)* is a server-side Web application solution. This means that you can put Active Server Pages and Active Server Objects on a Web server to let clients connect to the Web server and load the pages and objects. This chapter focuses mainly on Active Server Objects written in Delphi 6 but created and used within Active Server Pages.

Delphi 5 introduced a new wizard that enables you to create Active Server Objects. These Active Server Objects can be used in ASP to dynamically generate HTML code every time the server loads the page. This chapter explains what Active Server Page Objects are, how they are related to CGI, ISAPI, and COM, and how they can be used in the context of Active Server Pages. Further, we will focus on different aspects that are important when creating Active Server Objects. Active Server Objects are server-side components, and differences between operating systems (like Windows NT version 4 and Windows 2000) as well as differences between Internet Information (Web) Servers (IIS 3 and 4 compared to IIS 5) will also affect the way we deal with Active Server Objects.

As an example, we will generate a simple Active Server Object and a template script and then adjust the object and the script for our own needs by adding some methods. Then we will install and register the object on the Web server. Finally, we will examine how to deploy new versions of Active Server Objects and how to test and debug them.

Active Server Pages

Before we start creating our own Active Server Objects, I want to give you an introduction into the technology and syntax of Active Server Pages, which will be the operating environment for our Active Server Objects. Active Server Pages enable you to use a scripting language that is interpreted by the Web server—and not the Web browser. This means that you must have a Web server installed to be able to test the source code listings and examples in this chapter. We've used Microsoft *Internet Information Server (IIS)* version 4 on Windows NT 4 as well as IIS 5 on Windows 2000, but *Personal Web Server (PWS)* on Windows 95 or 98 works just as well. Whereas normal HTML pages have the .htm or .html extension, ASP pages have an .asp extension. In order for the Web server to execute ASP pages, you must place them in a directory that has scripting rights enabled. In your default installation of any of the Microsoft Web servers, you'll have a Scripts directory. But even if you don't have Scripts, it's easy to create a new virtual directory with scripting rights. On Windows NT, start the Internet Service Manager

(Microsoft Management Console), go to your Web service, add a new virtual directory—for example a directory called Scripts or cgi-bin—and make sure that the Scripting option is enabled.

You can change the server-side scripts without having to compile them or restart the Web server. The scripting statements are written between <% and %> tags, and the Active Scripting language is based on JavaScript and VBScript, which isn't hard to learn or understand.

As special support, Active Server Pages get a number of built-in objects that they can use to communicate with the browser and server environment.

The two most useful objects are as follows:

- Request—Implemented for user input. The Request object can access form input variables and check their values.
- Response—Used to generate user output. The Response object has a write method that can be used to generate HTML output.

As a little ASP scripting example, the following script will check the HTML input variable Name, and if the entered value is Bob, Response will write "Hello, Bob!"; otherwise Response will simply write "Hello, User!":

```
<%
  if Request("Name") = "Bob" then
    Response.Write("Hello, Bob!")
  else
    Response.Write("Hello, User!")
  end if
%>
```

If this ASP code is contained in a page called test.asp, the following HTML form can be used to trigger it:

```
<FORM ACTION="test.asp" METHOD=POST>
Name: <INPUT TYPE=text NAME=Name>
<P>
<INPUT TYPE=submit>
</FORM>
```

NOTE

The input variable called Name can be queried using the ASP Request variable.

22

ASP
DEVELOPMENT

Remember that Active Server Pages can only be executed (interpreted) by the Web server if they are actually served by the Web server. This means that the URL used to view them must activate the Web server. So a file test.asp in the \cgi-bin directory shouldn't be activated as file:///d:/www/cgi-bin/test.asp because that won't involve the Web server and will just show the file itself with the ASP source intact. However, the URL http://localhost/cgi-bin/test.asp will activate the Web server (for a local machine), and the result will be the executed output from the Active Server Page.

On the surface, this might seem simple and easy to use. As a Delphi developer however, you wouldn't want to write your entire Internet Web application using server-side ASP scripting. Consider the performance issue when it comes to interpreting ASP scripts that aren't compiled. ASP counts among its advantages the capacity to change its scripts on-the-fly as opposed to recompiling and redeploying them. However, because sites have grown larger and more complex, this advantage is far outweighed by the performance deficits introduced by the use of an interpreter. Fortunately, using the ASP scripting language, you can create and use special Active Server COM Objects that reside on the server. These objects are compiled binaries; therefore, they are faster and more efficient. This is where Delphi comes in, of course because we can make these special Active Server Objects using Delphi 6 Enterprise.

The Active Server Object Wizard

Delphi 6 Enterprise contains wizards that accelerate the creation of Active Server Objects. You can still write Active Server Objects using Delphi 6 Professional, but you'll have to do a lot of the work manually—users would be well-advised to consider moving to the Enterprise edition if development time is at a premium.

The Object Repository of Delphi 6 Enterprise contains a wizard to create new Active Server Objects on the ActiveX tab. To create a new Active Server Object (referred to as ASP Object from now on), you must close all projects (if any are open), and start a new ActiveX Library to contain our ASP Object. This can be done using the following steps:

1. Start Delphi 6 and close the default project.
2. From the menu, choose File, New, Other and select the ActiveX Library icon from the ActiveX tab in the Delphi 6 Object Repository (see Figure 22.1).
3. Save your ActiveX Library project as **D6ASP.dpr**.

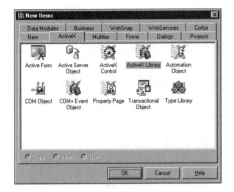

FIGURE 22.1

The ActiveX Library icon on the ActiveX tab.

> **TIP**
>
> If, like me, you grow tired of having to close down the default project every time you start Delphi, you will be happy to learn that there is an easy way to have Delphi start up with no project loaded, using a -np command line option. You have to go to the program group that contains your Delphi 6 shortcut and change the way Delphi 6 is started.
>
> To do so, right-click on the taskbar and select the Properties pop-up menu. Go to Start Menu Programs, and click on the Advanced button. You are now exploring the Start Menu items. Go to the Program group of All Users, which will contain the Borland Delphi 6 group. Select the Delphi 6 item, and right-click to get a pop-up menu in which you can select the Properties option. Click on the tab that says Shortcut, and add the **-np** text right after the current value specified in the Target editbox. For example, a default would look like the following:
>
> ```
> "C:\Program Files\Borland\Delphi6\Bin\delphi32.exe " -np
> ```
>
> This is also a good place to consider the Start In editbox because you might want Delphi 6 to start in a specific default directory.

When you have saved the ActiveX Library you've just created (as D6ASP.dpr), you can add an Active Server Object to it by selecting the Active Server Object icon from the ActiveX tab of the Delphi 6 Object Repository that you also see in Figure 22.1.

This will produce the Delphi 6 New Active Server Object dialog box, shown in Figure 22.2, which needs some explanation if you're seeing it for the first time (especially if you have no or little previous experience with COM or ASP Objects).

FIGURE 22.2

The New Active Server Object dialog box.

The CoClass Name is the internal name of your COM Object. Normally, you can enter anything here. For the example in this chapter, use DrBob42 as the CoClass Name. This will result in the classname TDrBob42, which derives from TASPObject and implements the IDrBob42 interface. The Threading Model is set to Apartment by default, and Instancing is set to Multiple Instance. These are fine for most purposes because you shouldn't have to change these settings generally.

The five Threading Model choices are as follows:

- Single—All client requests are handled in a single thread. This isn't a good idea because others have to wait until the first client is finished.

- Apartment—Every client request runs in its own thread, separated from the others. (No thread can access the state of another.) Class instance data is safe, but we must guard against threading issues when using global variables and the like. This is the preferred threading model that I always use.

- Free—A class instance can be accessed by multiple threads at the same time. Class instance data is no longer thread-safe, so you must take care to avoid multiuser issues here.

- Both—A combination of Apartment and Free because it follows the Free threading model with the exception that callbacks are executed in the same thread. (So parameters in callback functions are safe from multithreading problems.)

- Neutral—COM+ specific, and it defaults to Apartment for COM. Client requests can access object instances on different threads, but COM ensures that the calls won't conflict. Still, you'll have to watch threading issues (see the chapter on multi-threading) with global variables as well as instance data in between method calls.

The Instancing option offers three choices. Note that it doesn't matter what you select, if you're registering the Active Server Object as an in-process server (we'll cover in-process and out-of-process later), but it's good to know what the choices are:

- Internal Instance—This COM object is only instantiated within its own DLL.
- Single Instance—The application can have one client instance.
- Multiple Instance—A single application (ActiveX Library) can instantiate more than one instance of the COM object.

Also found in this dialog box are the Active Server Type options. These are dependent on the version of the IIS installed on your machine. For IIS 3 and IIS 4, the page-level event methods with OnStartPage and OnEndPage are used, whereas IIS 4 and IIS 5 can also use the Object Context method; that is, using *Microsoft Transaction Server (MTS)* or COM+ to manage instance data of the Active Server Object.

Delphi 6 will encapsulate most of the differences, so for this example, select the default Page-Level Event Methods. You can do the same with Active Server Objects if you select the Object Context option. Remember that you need to select an option that's right for (or at least supported by) your Web server.

The last option on the New Active Server Object dialog box is used to generate a very simple HTML test script for this Active Server Object. If you don't know ASP or the ASP scripting language, this is a good way to begin learning. It consists of only two lines, but the template shows you how to call methods of your Active Server Object using script.

Apart from assigning the CoClass Name, you generally don't have to do anything with this dialog box.

Type Library Editor

The Active Server Object has been created, including a type library for it. You end up in the Delphi 6 Type Library Editor for the DrBob42 Active Server Object shown in Figure 22.3.

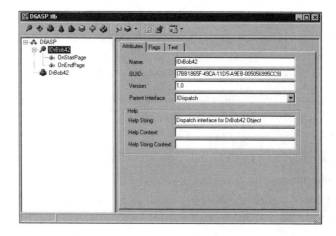

FIGURE 22.3
The Type Library Editor for IDrBob42.

Save the project files again (File, Save All), which first prompts you for a name for Unit1 (the unit containing the Active Server Object itself). I've named this unit DrBob42ASP.pas. Next, you're asked to save the file DrBob42.asp, which contains the ASP HTML template file. This file initially has the following content:

```
<HTML>
<BODY>
<TITLE> Testing Delphi ASP </TITLE>
<CENTER>
<H3> You should see the results of your Delphi Active Server method below </H3>
</CENTER>
<HR>
<% Set DelphiASPObj = Server.CreateObject("D6ASP.DrBob42")
   DelphiASPObj.{Insert Method name here}
%>
<HR>
</BODY>
</HTML>
```

As we've seen earlier in this chapter, ASP tags use % to distinguish themselves from regular HTML tags. In the single ASP tag, you'll see a two-line script. The first line creates an instance of the DrBob42 object from the D6ASP ActiveX Library, and the second line calls an unnamed method.

The second thing that you might have noticed in Figure 22.3 is that you already see the OnStartPage and OnEndPage methods for your IDrBob42 interface. This is a consequence of selecting the Page-Level Event Methods option in the New Active Server Object dialog box.

(You wouldn't have seen them when selecting the Object Context, as you can see in Listing 22.2.) You can see their implementation in the generated DrBob42ASP unit that contains the source code, shown in Listing 22.1, for your Active Server Object.

LISTING 22.1   DrBob42ASP—Active Server Object Source Code

```
unit DrBob42ASP;

{$WARN SYMBOL_PLATFORM OFF}

interface
uses
  ComObj, ActiveX, AspTlb, D6ASP_TLB, StdVcl;

type
  TDrBob42 = class(TASPObject, IDrBob42)
  protected
    procedure OnEndPage; safecall;
    procedure OnStartPage(const AScriptingContext: IUnknown); safecall;
  end;

implementation

uses ComServ;

procedure TDrBob42.OnEndPage;
begin
  inherited OnEndPage;
end;

procedure TDrBob42.OnStartPage(const AScriptingContext: IUnknown);
begin
  inherited OnStartPage(AScriptingContext);
end;

initialization
  TAutoObjectFactory.Create(ComServer, TDrBob42, Class_DrBob42,
    ciMultiInstance, tmApartment);
end.
```

Before you start adding more methods, let's see what an Active Server Object generated with the Object Context would look like. Fortunately, you can add more than one Active Server Object to a single ActiveX Library, so start the New Active Server Object dialog box again—this time specifying Micha42 as CoClass Name and selecting the Object Context option. Save the resulting source code in Micha42ASP.pas and the corresponding ASP file in Micha42.asp.

The source code listing can be seen in Listing 22.2. The differences are minor. (You only lack the OnEndPage and OnStartPage events. More importantly, TDrBob42 is derived from TASPObject whereas TMicha42 is derived from TASPMTSObject.) This is one of the major benefits of creating ASP objects with Delphi: the implementation details, while available, aren't necessary for the creation of robust, fast objects. From now on, you can add the same functionality to DrBob42ASP or Micha42ASP, and they will behave identically while using very different technology behind the scenes.

LISTING 22.2 Micha42ASP—Active Server Object Source Code

```
unit Micha42ASP;

{$WARN SYMBOL_PLATFORM OFF}

interface
uses
  ComObj, ActiveX, AspTlb, D6ASP_TLB, StdVcl;

type
  TMicha42 = class(TASPMTSObject, IMicha42)
  end;

implementation

uses ComServ;

initialization
  TAutoObjectFactory.Create(ComServer, TMicha42, Class_Micha42,
    ciMultiInstance, tmApartment);
end.
```

New Methods

It's now time to add a new method to the IDrBob42 (or IMicha42) interface that can be invoked by the outside world (typically from the .asp Web page).

Apart from the OnEndPage and OnStartPage methods (in the TDrBob42 object), you can also specify one or more custom methods. For example, using the type library, you can add a method called Welcome to the IDrBob42 interface. (Right-click on the IDrBob42 node and select New, Method from the pop-up menu.)

This method can be used to display a dynamic welcome message. After you've added the method and refreshed the implementation, you can write the code for the TDrBob42.Welcome method. To do this, you should know a little bit about the ASP internal objects and functionality made available by Delphi 6. Like ASP scripting, Delphi ASP Objects have access to special `Request` and `Response` objects.

ASP Response Object

The ASP `Response` object is an internal object that is available within methods of your Active Server Object. You should use `Response` whenever you want to generate dynamic output. `Response` has a number of properties and methods to set the content of the response. The most important one by far is the `Write` method. This method takes an `OleVariant` as argument (as you can see from the Code Insight hint in figure 22.4) and makes sure that the argument is written to the dynamic output at the exact location in the ASP script where the call appeared inside the `<%` and `%>` tags.

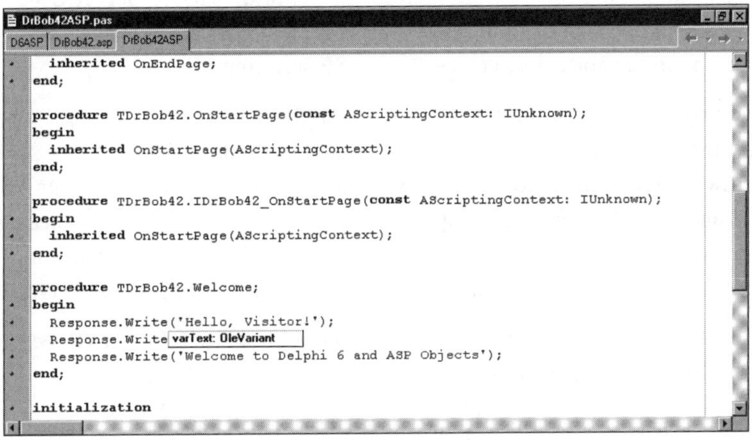

```
DrBob42ASP.pas
D6ASP  DrBob42.asp  DrBob42ASP

    inherited OnEndPage;
  end;

  procedure TDrBob42.OnStartPage(const AScriptingContext: IUnknown);
  begin
    inherited OnStartPage(AScriptingContext);
  end;

  procedure TDrBob42.IDrBob42_OnStartPage(const AScriptingContext: IUnknown);
  begin
    inherited OnStartPage(AScriptingContext);
  end;

  procedure TDrBob42.Welcome;
  begin
    Response.Write('Hello, Visitor!');
    Response.Write varText: OleVariant
    Response.Write('Welcome to Delphi 6 and ASP Objects');
  end;

  initialization
```

FIGURE 22.4
The Code Editor.

To write a welcome message, insert the code in Listing 22.3 within the `TDrBob42.Welcome` method.

LISTING 22.3 Implementation of the `Welcome` Method

```
procedure TDrBob42.Welcome;
begin
  Response.Write('Hello, Visitor!');
  Response.Write('<P>');
  Response.Write('Welcome to Delphi 6 and ASP Objects');
end;
```

The DrBob42.ASP file needs only a single change inside the ASP tags (the method now has a name: Welcome). The new ASP tags are as follows:

```
<% Set DelphiASPObj = Server.CreateObject("D6ASP.DrBob42")
   DelphiASPObj.Welcome
%>
```

Note that the ASP script doesn't need to destroy or free the DelphiASPObj variable: this will automatically be taken care of when the object gets out-of-scope. Apart from the call to Welcome, you can add more methods to the IDrBob42 interface and call these additional methods also from the ASP script as listed earlier. But let's first take the Active Server Object for a test run and worry about extending it later.

First Run

This is all it takes to prepare for the first operational test of the Active Server Object inside an Active Server Page. All you need to do now is register the D6ASP.dll Active Server Object and place DrBob42.asp in the correct directory (with ASP scripting rights).

We mentioned earlier in-process and out-of-process options for running the ASP objects. *In-process* means that your ASP object will be loaded and run alongside your Web server, and only unloaded when the Web server shuts down. *Out-of-process* means that your ASP object will be loaded and unloaded as clients request it from the server. In-process objects generally perform better, whereas out-of-process objects are more easily debugged. You can register Active Server Objects in two ways: either as in-process or as out-of-process servers.

To register D6ASP.dll as an in-process server containing the Active Server Object(s), choose Run, Register ActiveX Server from the Delphi 6 menu.

To unregister the same server, choose Run, Unregister ActiveX Server.

Figure 22.5 shows the confirmation message after you've registered the D6ASP ActiveX Server.

FIGURE 22.5
Registered ActiveX Server.

We'll get back to registering the ActiveX Server as an out-of-process server later in this chapter. But first, let's finish the test run.

After the D6ASP.dll ActiveX Server has been registered on your development machine, you have to move the DrBob42.asp file to a location that has ASP Scripting rights, such as the WWWRoot/Scripts directory.

The requesting URL will be http://localhost/scripts/DrBob42.asp; the result is shown in Figure 22.6.

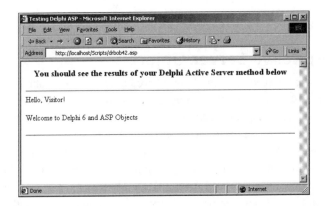

FIGURE 22.6
Running Active Server Object.

Using the Response.Write method, you can put any dynamic text at the location where the Welcome method was called inside the DrBob42.asp Web page.

ASP Request Object

Before we continue, let's consider another very important internal ASP object: Request. Like Response, Request is available within your Active Server Object (interface) methods. Request can be used to obtain all input. There are three different ways in which input can be given: by form variables using the POST method, by "fat" URL variables using the GET method, and using cookies. Each of these possesses a property called Items, which is a stringlist for holding the content of the Response or Request.

A modified Welcome method that obtains the Name value from the input form used to start the ASP script is shown in Listing 22.4.

LISTING 22.4 Definition of the Modified Welcome Method

```
procedure TDrBob42.Welcome;
var
  Str: String;
begin
```

LISTING 22.4   Continued

```
  Str := Request.Form.Item['Name'];
  Response.Write('Hello, '+Str+'!');
  Response.Write('<P>');
  Response.Write('Welcome to Delphi 6 and ASP Objects');
end;
```

The same technique can be used for the QueryString and Cookies objects.

Recompiling Active Server Objects

If you went on and tried to recompile the D6ASP project again, you probably received this
Delphi error message: Could not create output file D6ASP.dll.. You received the error
because the Active Server Object DrBob42 inside D6ASP.dll has been used and is still cached
by the Web server. So, when you try to recompile your Active Server Object, the linker will
give an error message: The file is still in use.. You can try to shut down IIS, but that
won't help. Shutting down the World Wide Web Publishing Service won't help either. You
actually have to shut down the entire IIS Admin Service before the ASP.DLL and all Active
Server Objects are released from memory so that you can recompile any of them. Note that
shutting down IIS Admin Service from the dialog box shown in Figure 22.7 means that all
dependent services (WWW, FTP, and so on) will shut down as well. This isn't something you
want to do on a live Web server, of course.

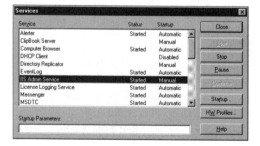

FIGURE 22.7

IIS Admin Service.

If you try to shut down the IIS Admin Service, you will see the Stopping dialog box shown in
Figure 22.8, telling you which sub-services depend on the IIS Admin Service and will also
have to shut down first.

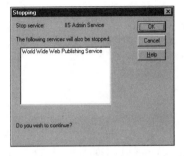

FIGURE 22.8
Stopping World Wide Web Publishing Service.

To simplify the process of shutting down and starting up the required NT services, the following simple batch file, RESTART.BAT, can be used when you want to recompile and redeploy an Active Server Object:

```
net stop "World Wide Web Publishing Service"
net stop "IIS Admin Service"
net start "World Wide Web Publishing Service"
```

> **TIP**
>
> On a machine that will be used for development only, you can specify that your Active Server Object should explicitly not be cached by your web server. Obviously, this should never be used on production machines because it effectively turns Active Server Objects into even slower CGI applications: loading them for each client request. This is equivalent to having an out-of-process Active Server Object that is generally never used, except in this particular development situation.

Running Active Server Pages Again

Although you can load an Active Server Page by itself, it's often more effective if you run it in response to an HTML input form. For this example, you can use the small HTML page that follows:

```
<HTML>
<HEAD>
<TITLE>Dr.Bob's ASP Example</TITLE>
</HEAD>
```

```
<BODY BGCOLOR=FFFFCC>
<FONT FACE="Verdana"SIZE=2>
<FORM ACTION="drbob42.asp" METHOD=POST>
Name: <INPUT TYPE=text NAME=Name>
<P>
<INPUT TYPE=submit>
</FORM>
</BODY>
</HTML>
```

Loaded inside Internet Explorer as page `http://localhost/cgi-bin/drbob42.htm`, this gives
the output shown in Figure 22.9. I've already typed a name in the edit box, and am now ready
to click the Submit Query button.

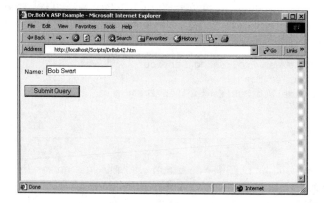

FIGURE 22.9
Internet Explorer with DrBob42.htm.

After you fill your name in the edit box and click Submit Query, the Active Server Page is
loaded. It will create an instance of the DrBob42 Active Server Object and call the Welcome
method as specified in the ASP script. This will result in the dynamic output shown in
Figure 22.10.

This was yet another simple ASP example, using only Request and Response, but you get the
idea. We'll now continue with some more ASP internal objects such as Session, Server, and
Application, and then we will return to Delphi specific Web server application support—such
as WebBroker components—most of which also can be used in combination with Active Server
Objects.

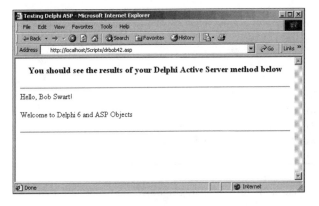

FIGURE 22.10
Internet Explorer with DrBob42.asp *output.*

ASP Session, Server, and Application Objects

Apart from the Request and Response objects, ASP also has access to Session, Server, and Application objects. This is actually one of the benefits of ASP over CGI and ISAPI: An Active Server Object can access session and application information without any further effort on your part (by using cookies, hidden fields, or fat URLs).

Recall from the previous example that your TDrBob42 class was derived from the TASPObject class. In addition to the Request and Response properties, this class introduces the TASPObject.Session, Server, and Application properties. These properties provide direct access to the underlying ASP Session, Server, and Application objects, respectively. You can also use these properties from within your TDrBob42 methods to store the names of each visitor to your Web site, for example. In ASP HTML, this could be done as follows (note the second line):

```
<% Set DelphiASPObj = Server.CreateObject("D6ASP.DrBob42")
Session.Value("Name") = "Bob Swart"
DelphiASPObj.Welcome
%>
```

To obtain this persistent value (persistent among other Active Server Pages that are visited by the same user in the same session), you can use the Session object in your Active Server Object, just like using the Form, QueryString, or Cookies object (see Listing 22.5).

LISTING 22.5   DrBob42ASP—Active Server Object Source Code

```
procedure TDrBob42.Welcome;
var
  Str: String;
begin
  Str := Session.Value['Name'];
  Response.Write('Hello, '+Str+'!');
  Response.Write('<P>');
  Response.Write('Welcome back to Delphi 6 and ASP Objects');
end;
```

The Session object maintains its state using cookies, so make sure that your Web server has cookies enabled.

Active Server Objects and Databases

Now, let's make the example a bit more useful and introduce a database or table in it, so we can demonstrate how to perform a query or open a table on the server and show the results inside an Active Server Page. In order to add this functionality, you should first add a new data module, using File, New, Data Module.

Give the Name property of the data module a new value, say DataModuleASP, and save this new unit in file DataMod.pas. Also choose File, Save All to save the entire project so that your main project file D6ASP.dpr will contain the data module in its uses clause. Inside this data module, you will use a TClientDataSet component from the Data Access tab because this will be the simplest way of providing a dataset, and also the most flexible way. You can replace it with another dataset component later if you want to extend this example.

Drop a TClientDataSet component on the data module. In order to supply it with data, click on the ellipsis button next to the FileName property. Go to the C:\Program Files\Common Files\Borland Shared\Data directory and you'll see all the well-known tables from DBDEMOS in MyBase XML as well as binary ClientDataSet format. Select the biolife.xml file for this example.

Having the data module, you should still worry about sharing it in a multithreading environment! The best way is to create the data module inside your Active Server Object when you need it, either in the BeginPage and EndPage events, or—even more clearly—inside the Welcome method itself.

But you need to add the DataMod unit to the uses clause of the DrBob42ASP unit, so you can actually use it. Then, write the code from Listing 22.6 inside the Welcome method to create, use, and safely destroy the data module.

LISTING 22.6   DrBob42ASP—Active Server Object Source Code

```
procedure TDrBob42.Welcome;
var
  Str: String;
  DM: TDataModuleASP;
begin
  Str := Request.Form.Item['Name'];
  Response.Write('Hello, '+Str+'!');
  Response.Write('<P>');
  Response.Write('Welcome to Delphi 6 and ASP Objects');
  try
    DM := TDataModuleASP.Create(nil);
    // use DM...
  finally
    DM.Free
  end
end;
```

In order to present the information from the dataset to the browser, let's walk through the data inside the `ClientDataSet` and produce a grid-like HTML table that shows the common names, `Common_Name`, and description, `Notes`, of the fish listed in the biolife `dataset`. This only takes a few lines of additional code producing dynamic HTML (see Listing 22.7).

LISTING 22.7   DrBob42ASP—Active Server Object Source Code

```
procedure TDrBob42.Welcome;
var
  Str: String;
  DM: TDataModuleASP;
begin
  Str := Request.Form.Item['Name'];
  Response.Write('Hello, '+Str+'!');
  Response.Write('<P>');
  Response.Write('Welcome to Delphi 6 and ASP Objects');
  try
    Response.Write('<P>');
    DM := TDataModuleASP.Create(nil);
    with DM.ClientDataSet1 do
    try
      Open;
      First;
      Response.Write('<TABLE BORDER=1><TR><TD>Common_Name</TD>');
      Response.Write('<TD>Notes</TD></TR>');
```

22

ASP
DEVELOPMENT

LISTING 22.7   Continued

```
      while not Eof do
      begin
        Response.Write('<TR><TD>');
        Response.Write(FieldByName('Common_Name').AsString);
        Response.Write('</TD><TD>');
        Response.Write(FieldByName('Notes').AsString);
        Response.Write('</TD></TR>');
        Next
      end;
      Close;
    finally
      Response.Write('</TABLE>')
    end;
  finally
    DM.Free
  end
end;
```

The output can be seen in Figure 22.11.

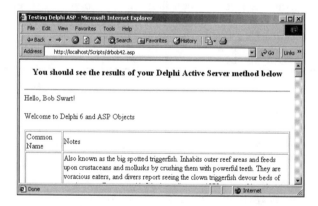

FIGURE 22.11
Dynamic HTML output from Active Server Object.

Delphi already contains a lot of helpful components and techniques to produce dynamic and well-formatted HTML in the NetCLX HTML-producing components called *PageProducers*. Rather than spend a lot of time learning HTML, using PageProducers will generate the HTML needed dynamically.

Active Server Objects and NetCLX Support

If you compare Active Server Objects with the NetCLX architecture, you should notice a lot of similarities. Both use Request and Response objects as the primary means to communicate with the client. From a developer point of view, however, there is much more support for NetCLX with the PageProducer and TableProducer components that were especially written for use inside Web modules. Fortunately, these HTML-producing components aren't limited to use inside Web modules; they can be used anywhere, and you're free to dynamically create a TDataSetTableProducer, assign it to a dataset, and write the resulting HTML back using the Response.Write method. You can drop a TDataSetTableProducer component on the data module you just created and even customize it at design-time!

In fact, it isn't very hard to use the same HTML-producing components, originally written for NetCLX, inside your Active Server Object. The only exceptions are the TQueryTableProducer and TSQLQueryTableProducer components, which rely on input passed on by the NetCLX Request object, not the ASP Request object. All other PageProducers can be used as they are, as the next example will demonstrate.

Drop a TDataSetTableProducer component on the data module, and assign its DataSet property to the ClientDataSet you used in the previous example. In order to customize the settings of the DataSetTableProducer, make sure that the ClientDataSet actually contains data. So, temporarily set the Active property of the ClientDataSet component to True (set it back to False afterward), and then click on the ellipsis next to the Columns property of the DataSetTableProducer (or right-click on the DataSetTableProducer component and select Response Editor). This will give you the Columns property editor shown in Figure 22.12.

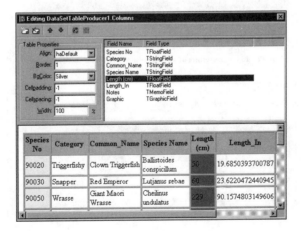

FIGURE 22.12
DataSetTableProducer *Response Editor.*

Back in the Welcome method, call the DataSetTableProducer.Content method as shown in Listing 22.8 to get the dynamic produced HTML output you need (a lot smaller than you had to write yourself, and much easier to customize as well).

LISTING 22.8   DrBob42ASP—Active Server Object Source Code

```
procedure TDrBob42.Welcome;
var
  Str: String;
  DM: TDataModuleASP;
begin
  Str := Request.Form.Item['Name'];
  Response.Write('Hello, '+Str+'!');
  Response.Write('<P>');
  Response.Write('Welcome to Delphi 6 and ASP Objects');
  try
    Response.Write('<P>');
    DM := TDataModuleASP.Create(nil);
    Response.Write(DM.DataSetTableProducer1.Content);
  finally
    DM.Free
  end
end;
```

After you've recompiled your Active Server Object, you can reload the DrBob42.htm file to start the Active Server Page, resulting in the output shown in Figure 22.13.

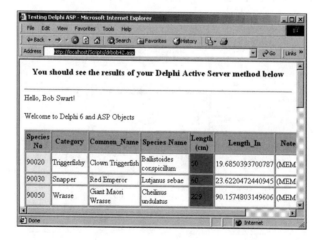

FIGURE 22.13

Internet Explorer with DrBob42.asp *NetCLX output.*

Debugging Active Server Objects

As you saw in the previous section, Active Server Objects are like ISAPI DLLs: After they are loaded, you need to bring down the entire Web server to unload them because Active Server Objects are loaded by the ASP.DLL, which is an ISAPI DLL in itself. However, the advantage of ASP is the fact that for the Active Server Pages themselves, you can update the scripts as much as you want, without having to change, unload, or reload the Active Server Objects themselves. As long as the functionality inside the Active Server Object doesn't change, you need only to update the scripts. Of course, making sure that the Active Server Objects work correctly is another task, which at times requires the capability to debug Active Server Objects.

When it comes to debugging Active Server Objects, a few things can be done right away, such as showing a simple message box or using a debug window to show strings sent from the Active Server Object. In order to get any of these messages, however, you must first specify that the owner of the Active Server Object is indeed qualified to interact with the desktop. Specifically, for the IIS Admin Service, set the Interact with Desktop option in the Services applet (dialog box) of the Control Panel Services dialog box, as shown in Figure 22.14.

FIGURE 22.14
Allow Service to interact with Desktop.

After you've specified that option, you can use almost any means to have your Active Server Objects interact with the desktop. This is still a bit crude, but it can be effective enough at times.

Debugging Active Server Objects with MTS

There is an easier way to manage your Active Server Objects, which also greatly improves your abilities to actually debug Active Server Objects written in Delphi (or C++Builder for that matter). The solution, as the title of this section indicates, involves MTS as host for your Active Server Object.

The first step involves unregistering the Active Server Object you've written in this chapter. This can be done by choosing Run, Unregister ActiveX Server from the Delphi 6 menu.

After the Active Server Object has been successfully unregistered, you can register it again, but this time as an MTS Object. To do this, choose Run, Install MTS Objects. (On Windows 2000, this menu option will be called Install COM+ Object.) The resulting dialog box appears in Figure 22.15.

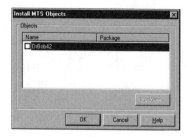

FIGURE 22.15
Install MTS (or COM+) Objects.

In this Install MTS Objects dialog box, select your DrBob42 object by clicking on the check box. This will result in the pop-up dialog box shown in Figure 22.16, which asks for a package name to install the DrBob42 object into. You can either select an existing package, or specify a new package such as DelphiDebugPackage: The COM+ dialog box works in a similar way on Windows 2000.

FIGURE 22.16
Install Object DelphiDebugPackage.

Now, click OK in the Install Object dialog box and click OK again in the Install MTS Objects dialog box.

After having installed the DrBob42 object as an MTS object, you can debug the Active Server Object from within the Delphi IDE itself. For this, you need a host application in order to load the Active Server Object. The steps you must take from this point on differ in Windows NT and Windows 2000. First, I'll show you the steps for Windows NT, followed by the steps for Windows 2000.

Debugging Using Windows NT 4

For Windows NT with the Option Pack installed, you need to specify MTS as the Host Application. MTS will already be running, so you must shut it down first.

> **CAUTION**
>
> As a consequence, you should never try to do this on a real production machine. Only use a development machine in which you can afford to shut down MTS from time to time (when debugging your Active Server Objects that are hosted inside MTS).

In order to shut down MTS, you must start the Internet Service Manager application, which is part of the Windows NT 4 Option Pack. Open the Microsoft Transaction Server node in the treeview until you see Packages Installed under My Computer (which includes the DelphiDebugPackage you just installed).

If you right-click on the My Computer icon, you can shut down all server processes (see Figure 22.17). This won't give you any feedback. You can verify the shutdown by looking at the Processes list of the Windows NT Task Manager. It shouldn't list mtx.exe anymore.

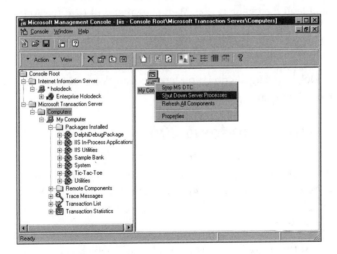

FIGURE 22.17
Shutdown server processes.

Now all you have to do is specify MTS as the Host Application inside the Delphi 6 Run Parameters dialog box, so you can use MTS as host for your DrBob42 Active Server Object. On my NT 4 machine, that's c:\winnt\system32\mtx.exe. You must also specify the package that contains your DrBob42 object using the /p:"DelphiDebugPackage" parameter. In this case, the DrBob42 object is DelphiDebugPackage. Specifying the package brings up a dialog box similar to that shown in Figure 22.18.

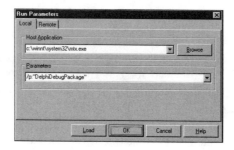

FIGURE 22.18
Run Parameters dialog box.

Now, set a breakpoint in your code by clicking in the left-side gutter or pressing F5 while your cursor is on a line of code and press F9 to run and debug your DrBob42 Active Server Object as hosted inside MTS. Nothing will happen because MTS is running, but your Active Server Object has not been invoked by a browser call yet. You must now restart Internet Explorer (or another browser) and load the DrBob42.asp Web page that will load the Active Server Object.

This will trigger the breakpoint: At which time, you're able to use the Delphi integrated debugger on your Active Server Object.

In order to end the Delphi debug session, you have to shut down MTS again (just as you did when you started to debug using MTS).

Debugging Using Windows 2000

Using Windows 2000, you can no longer use mtx.exe simply because under Windows 2000, MTS is integrated into the operating system. However, you can use dllhost.exe to load the ProcessID of your Active Server Object. This technique will also work on Windows NT. but, it is slightly more complex, which is why I first showed you how to debug using MTS as the Host Application under Windows NT.

You should now use dllhost.exe as the Host Application, which can be specified in the Run, Parameters dialog box. The parameter should be the ProcessID of the DelphiDebugPackage containing your DrBob42 Active Server Object. You can obtain this information using the

Internet Service Manager (Microsoft Management Console) on Windows NT or the Component Services on Windows 2000.

The Package ID of the DelphiDebugPackage in this example is {50AE66A2-349B-11D5-A9F0-005056995CC9}. This ID can be copied from the text label of the Run Properties dialog box shown in Figure 22.19. This is the most convenient way to copy it because you probably don't want to type it in yourself. Figure 22.20 shows the Run Parameters dialog box with the ID pasted into the Parameters text box.

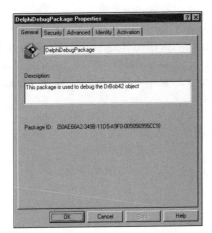

FIGURE 22.19
DelphiDebugPackage *Package ID.*

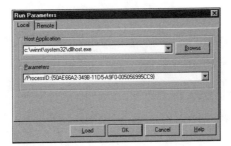

FIGURE 22.20
Run Parameters with ID inserted.

Now, make sure to set a breakpoint and press F9 to run (and debug) your DrBob42 Active Server Object. Similar to the previous example, nothing will happen until the ASP object is invoked through a browser. You must restart Internet Explorer (or another browser) and load the `DrBob42.asp` Web page that will in turn load the Active Server Object. This will trigger the breakpoint; at which time, you're able to use the Delphi integrated debugger on your Active Server Object.

Note that in order to end the Delphi debug session, you have to shut down `DelphiDebug Package` inside MTS again (just as you did when you started to debug using MTS).

Summary

In this chapter, you have learned what Active Server Pages are, what role Active Server Objects play in them, and how Delphi 6 can be used to write these Active Server Objects. You've also seen how you can use internal objects (like Request and Response), how you can add database processing to your Active Server Objects, how you can combine Active Server Objects and NetCLX components, and finally how to debug Active Server Objects with Delphi 6 under Windows NT or Windows 2000.

Building WebSnap Applications

by Nick Hodges

IN THIS CHAPTER

Delphi 6 introduces a new Web application framework called WebSnap that brings the strengths of *Rapid Application Development (RAD)* to Web development. Building on WebBroker and InternetExpress, WebSnap is a big leap forward for Delphi developers who want to use their favorite tool to build Web applications. It provides all the standard nuts and bolts for Web applications, including session management, user login, user preference tracking, and scripting. Naturally, Delphi 6 brings RAD to Web site development, making building robust, dynamic, database-driven Web applications easy and fast.

WebSnap Features

WebSnap isn't a totally new technology, and it doesn't leave behind your WebBroker and InternetExpress applications. WebSnap is compatible with these two older technologies, and it is a relatively straightforward process to integrate your existing code into a new WebSnap application. WebSnap provides several features listed in the following sections.

Multiple Webmodules

In Delphi's previous versions, WebBroker and InternetExpress applications had to do all their work in a single Web module. Multiple webmodules weren't allowed. To add datamodules, they had to be created manually at runtime, rather than automatically. WebSnap eliminates this restriction and allows any number of webmodules and datamodules to be part of a Web application. WebSnap is based on multiple modules, and each module represents a single Web page. This allows different developers to work on different portions of the application without having to worry about modifying each other's code.

Server-side Scripting

WebSnap seamlessly integrates server-side scripting into your applications, and allows you to very easily build powerful scriptable objects that you can use to build and customize your applications and HTML. The TAdapter component and all of its descendents are scriptable components, meaning that they can be called by your server-side script and produce HTML and client-side JavaScript for your applications.

TAdapter Components

TAdapter components define an interface between an application and the server-side scripting. Server-side script only has access to your application via adapters, ensuring that the script doesn't inadvertently change the data in an application or expose functions that aren't intended for public consumption. You can build custom TAdapter descendents that manage content for your specific needs, and that content can even be visible and configurable at design time. TAdapters can hold data and execute actions. For instance, the TDataSetAdapter can display records from a dataset as well as take the normal actions on a dataset such as scroll, add, update, and delete.

Multiple Dispatching Methods

WebSnap provides a number of ways to manage HTTP requests. You can access your Web content by page name, by TAdapter actions, or by simple Web action requests as WebBroker does. This gives you the power and flexibility to display your Web pages based on any number of different kinds of inputs. You might want to display a page in response to a submit button, or you might want to build a set of links into a menu based on the collection of pages in your site.

Page Producer Components

WebBroker introduced TPageProducer, a component for managing HTML and inserting and updating content based on custom tags. InternetExpress advanced this notion with TMidasPage Producers. WebSnap advances the notion of PageProducers even further, adding a number of new and powerful controls that can access TAdapter content, as well as XSL/XML data. The most powerful of these new TPageProducer descendents is TAdapterPageProducer, which knows how to produce HTML based on the actions and fields of TAdapter components.

Session Management

WebSnap applications contain automatic, built-in session management; now you can keep track of user's actions across multiple HTTP requests. Because HTTP is a stateless protocol, your Web applications must keep track of users by leaving something on the client that identifies each user. Normally this is done with cookies, URL references, or hidden field controls. WebSnap provides seamless session support that makes tracking users very easy. WebSnap does this via its SessionsService component. The SessionsService component seamlessly maintains a session identification value for each user, making it a simple task to keep track of each user as she makes individual requests. This is normally a difficult service to manage, but WebSnap handles all the details and makes the session information available both in server-side script and the Web application code itself.

Login Services

Your Web applications will likely need security to be implemented, requiring users to log in to the given application. WebSnap automates this process by providing a specialized login adapter component. This component contains the functions needed to properly query and authenticate users according to the application's chosen security model. It gathers login information, and in conjunction with WebSnap's session management, provides current login credentials for each request. The login components also automate login validation and login expiration. Throughout your application, users who try to access unauthorized pages can be automatically referred to the login page.

User Tracking

The most common function that session tracking provides is the ability to keep track of your users and their preferences for your application. WebSnap provides components that allow you to easily track user information and display it on your site. You can store user login information, and then retrieve user information based on that. You can maintain user access rights and site preferences, as well as things such as shopping cart information.

HTML Management

Often in a dynamic Web application, keeping track of and managing HTML can be difficult. HTML content can reside in any number of places such as files and resources, or they can be dynamically generated. WebSnap provides a means for you to manage this process with its file location services.

File Uploading Services

Managing the uploading of files usually requires a lot of custom code. WebSnap provides a simple adapter solution that manages the multipart forms needed to upload files. You can provide file upload capability in your WebSnap application quickly and easily using the built-in functionality of the TAdapter component.

Building a WebSnap Application

As always, the best way to learn about the new technology in Delphi is to try it out. We'll start by building the "Hello World" version of a WebSnap application.

Designing the Application

First, you'll want to add the WebSnap toolbar to the IDE, so right-click on the speedbutton area of the IDE title bar, and select the Internet toolbar (see Figure 23.1). This adds a toolbar to the IDE main window that makes creating WebSnap applications and adding forms and web-modules easy.

Next, click the speedbutton with the hand holding the globe, and you will see dialog box shown in Figure 23.2.

FIGURE 23.1

Internet toolbar.

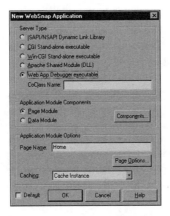

FIGURE 23.2

The New WebSnap Application dialog box.

The dialog box in Figure 23.2 gives you a number of options for setting up your WebSnap application. The first is the type of server that your application is going to run on. You are given five choices:

- ISAPI/NSAPI Dynamic Link Library—This option produces a project that runs under IIS (or under Netscape servers with the appropriate ISAPI adapter installed). The project produces a DLL when compiled, and runs in the same memory space as the Web server. The most common Web server to run ISAPI applications is Microsoft's Internet Information Server, although other Web servers can run ISAPI DLLs.

- CGI Standalone executable—This option creates a project that produces a console executable that reads and writes from the standard input and output ports. It conforms to the CGI specification. Almost all Web servers support CGI.

- Win-CGI Standalone executable—This option produces a Win-CGI project that communicates with a Web server via text-based INI files. Win-CGI is very uncommon and not recommended.

- Apache Shared Module (DLL)—This option produces a project that will run in the Apache Web server. For more information about Apache, see `http://www.apache.org`.

- Web App Debugger Executable—If you select this option, you get an application that will be run by Delphi's Web App Debugger (see Figure 23.3). Your Web application will be an out-of-process COM server, and the Web App Debugger will control and run the application. This type of Web application will allow you to use the full power of Delphi's debugger when debugging it. This means no more hassling with Web servers, turning them on and off in order to load and unload your applications. Instead, debugging your application will be fast and easy.

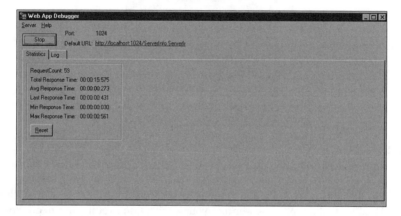

FIGURE 23.3

The Web App Debugger application greatly simplifies debugging your Web applications.

NOTE

The WebApp Debugger can be accessed via the Tools menu in the IDE. In order to work properly, you need to register the application found in the `<Delphi Dir>\bin` directory called `serverinfo.exe`. All you need to do to register it is run it once, and it will register itself. The Web App Debugger is a COM-based application that acts as a Web server to your testing applications. When you create a Web App Debugger Application, your new project will contain a form and a Web module. The form acts as a placeholder for the COM server, and running the application once will register it. After that, the Web App Debugger will control it via the Web browser, and will serve your application in the browser. Because the application is a Delphi executable and not a Web server extension, you can set a breakpoint in it and run it in the Delphi IDE. Then, when you access it through the browser, Delphi's debugger will take over when your breakpoints are reached, and you can debug the application normally.

continues

To access your application via the browser, run the Web App Debugger, and click on the hyperlink labeled Default URL. This will bring up a Web application that lists all the applications registered with the server. You can then select your application and run it. The View Details option will allow you to see more information about the different applications, and to clean them out of the registry when they are no longer needed. Be careful, though, not to delete the ServerInfo application; otherwise, you'll have to go back and register it again.

For the sample application that you will build here, select the Web App Debugger option. This will allow you to debug the application as you build it.

The next option in the wizard allows you to select the type of module you want and the different components that will be included. If you choose the Page Module option, you will get a Web module that represents a page in your application. If you choose the Data Module option, you will get a datamodule that can be used in a WebSnap application. It can perform the same function as datamodules do in traditional client/server applications. For this application, select the Page Module option.

Next, click on the Components button, and you'll see the dialog box shown in Figure 23.4.

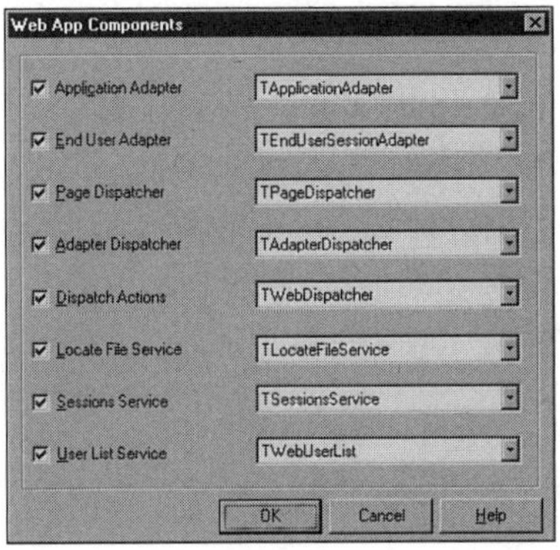

FIGURE 23.4
The Web App Components dialog box allows you to select the components that will be included in your new module.

You have the choice of the following components listed:

- Application Adapter—This component manages the fields and actions available through the Application server-side scripting object. The most common property you'll use in this component is the Title property.

- End User Adapter—This component manages the information about the current user of the application such as the session ID, username, user rights, and other customized user information. It also will manage the user's login and logout actions.

- Page Dispatcher—This component manages and dispatches HTTP requests made by page name. You can create HREF links or actions that call specific pages, and the Page Dispatcher will retrieve the proper response.

- Adapter Dispatcher—The Adapter Dispatcher handles all requests that come as a result of adapter actions. These are generally the result of an HTML form submission.

- Dispatcher Actions—This option adds a `TWebDispatcher` to your applications. Users of WebBroker will remember this component. It handles requests from the application based on URLs, just as WebBroker applications did. You can use this component to add your own custom actions to your application in the same way you did with WebBroker.

- Locate File Service—The events of this component are called whenever a Web module requires HTML input. You can add event handlers that allow you to bypass the default HTML finding mechanism and get HTML from almost any source. This component is used most often for grabbing page content and templates for building standard pages.

- SessionsService—This component manages sessions for users, allowing you to maintain state for individual users between HTTP requests. The SessionsService can store information about users and automatically expire their sessions after a certain period of inactivity. You can add any session-specific information you want to the `Session.Values` property, a string indexed array of variants. By default, the sessions are managed using cookies on the user's machine, although you could build a class to handle them some other way, such as with fat URLs or hidden fields.

- User List Service—This component maintains a list of users who are authorized to log in to the application and information about them.

NOTE

These options each have drop-down boxes that allow you to choose the component that will fulfill each of the preceding roles. You can create your own components that will fulfill these roles and register them with WebSnap. They will then appear as choices in this dialog box. You could, for instance, create a session component that maintains session information in a fat URL rather than with cookies.

For this example, select all the check boxes. Then, for the End User Adapter component, drop down the combo box and select `TEndUserSessionAdapter`. This component will automatically associate a session ID with an end user. Then click OK.

The next option in the wizard is the name of the page. Name this main page **Home**, and then click Page Options. You'll see dialog box shown in Figure 23.5.

FIGURE 23.5

The Application Module Page Options dialog box allows you to select the options for the page in your Web module.

This dialog box allows you to customize the PageProducer component of your Web module and the HTML associated with it. It presents a number of options. The first is the type of page producer. WebSnap includes a number of standard PageProducers that can produce and manage HTML in different ways. To start with, select the default option, a plain PageProducer. You can also select the type of server-side scripting you want to use. Out of the box, Delphi supports JScript and VBScript (as well as XML/XSL, which will be discussed later.) Leave the default value of JScript here.

Each module has an HTML page associated with it. The next option allows you to select what type of HTML you want. By default, Delphi provides a Standard page with a simple scripted navigation menu on it. You can create your own HTML templates, register them with WebSnap, and then select them here. We'll look at how to do that later in this chapter. For now, leave the default value of Standard here.

Name the page **Home** (the Title is automatically filled in the same). Make sure Published is checked, and leave Login Required unchecked. A published page will show up in the list of pages in the application and can be referenced by the Pages scripting object. This is needed to create page-based menus in script using the Pages scripting object.

After you have done this, click OK, and then click OK on the main wizard. The wizard will then create your application for you, and the new Web module will look something like that shown in Figure 23.6.

FIGURE 23.6

The Web module for the demo application as created by the WebSnap Wizard.

We haven't yet discussed the TWebAppComponents control. This control is the *central clearing house* for all the other components. Because many of the components in a WebSnap application work together, the WebAppComponents component is the one that ties them together and allows them to communicate and refer to each other. Its properties consist merely of other components that fill the specific roles discussed previously.

At this point, you should save the project. To keep consistent with the rest of the chapter, name the Web module (unit2) wmHome, name the form (Unit1) ServerForm, and name the project itself DDG6Demo.

By examining the Code Editor, you should see some new, unfamiliar features. First, notice the tabs along the bottom. Each Webmodule—because it represents a page in a Web application—has an associated HTML file that can contain server-side script. The second tab on the bottom shows this page (see Figure 23.7). Because you selected the Standard HTML page template in the wizard, the HTML contains server-side script that will greet the user if she is logged in, and will provide a basic navigation menu that will be automatically built based on all the published pages in the application. As pages get added to this demo application, this menu will grow larger and will allow users to navigate to each of the pages. The default HTML code is shown in Listing 23.1.

FIGURE 23.7
The HTML page associated with the Web module.

LISTING 23.1   Default HTML Code

```html
<html>
<head>
<title>
<%= Page.Title %>
</title>
</head>
<body>
<h1><%= Application.Title %></h1>

<% if (EndUser.Logout != null) { %>
<%    if (EndUser.DisplayName != '') { %>
  <h1>Welcome <%=EndUser.DisplayName %></h1>
<%    } %>
<%    if (EndUser.Logout.Enabled) { %>
  <a href="<%=EndUser.Logout.AsHREF%>">Logout</a>
<%    } %>
<%    if (EndUser.LoginForm.Enabled) { %>
  <a href=<%=EndUser.LoginForm.AsHREF%>>Login</a>
<%    } %>
<% } %>
```

LISTING 23.1   Continued

```
<h2><%= Page.Title %></h2>

<table cellspacing="0" cellpadding="0">
<td>
<%  e = new Enumerator(Pages)
    s = ''
    c = 0
    for (; !e.atEnd(); e.moveNext())
    {
      if (e.item().Published)
      {
        if (c>0) s += ' | '
        if (Page.Name != e.item().Name)
          s += '<a href="' + e.item().HREF + '">' + e.item().Title + '</a>'
        else
          s += e.item().Title
        c++
      }
    }
    if (c>1) Response.Write(s)
%>
</td>
</table>

</body>
</html>
```

This code contains both normal HTML tags as well as server-side JScript.

You should also note that the HTML is syntax-highlighted in the IDE. (You can set the colors to be used in Tools, Editor Options, Color property page.) In addition, you can set your own external HTML editor such as HomeSite and access it via the IDE as well. Set the HTML Editor in Tools, Environment Options, Internet. Select HTML in the listview, and then click Edit. From there, select the appropriate edit action to use your external editor. Then, when you right-click on the HTML page in the Code Editor, you can select the HTML Editor option and call up your editor.

In addition to the HTML viewing tab, the next tab shows the HTML that results from the script being run. The following tab shows a preview of the HTML in an Internet Explorer window. Do note that not all the script will execute and display in this view because some of the code relies on runtime values. However, you can at least get an idea what the page will look like without having to run it in the browser.

Adding Functionality to the Application

Now let's add a little code and make the application do something. First, go to the Home Web module and select the Application adapter. Set the `ApplicationTitle` property to Delphi Developers Guide 6 WebSnap Demo Application. Note that this will immediately show up in the preview tab because the HTML contains the following server-side script as the first thing in the `<BODY>` section:

```
<h1><%= Application.Title %></h1>
```

This causes the Application scripting object to display the value for `ApplicationTitle` in the HTML.

Next, go to the Code Editor, and select the HTML page for the Home Module. Then move the cursor down below the `</table>` tag near the bottom and add a pithy description of the page, which welcomes the user. The code on the CD-ROM has such an entry, adding the following:

```
<P>
<FONT SIZE="+1" COLOR="Red">Welcome to the Delphi 6 Developers Guide WebSnap
➥ Demonstration Application!</FONT>
<P>
This application will demonstrate many of the new features in Delphi 6 and
➥WebSnap. Feel free to browse around and look at the code involved. There is
➥a lot of power, and thus a lot to learn, in WebSnap, so take your time and
don't try to absorb it all at once.
<P>
```

This new code of course immediately shows up in the HTML Preview panel as well.

Next, just to prove that you are actually building a browser application, run the project. The first thing you will see is a blank form. This is the COM server. You can shut it down once it runs, and then start up the Web App Debugger from the Tools menu. After you have done that, click on the Default URL hyperlink (it will be called `DDG6DemoApp.DDG6TestApp`), find the application in the list box in your browser, and click the Go button. Your browser should show your page as illustrated in Figure 23.8.

As you can see, it really is a Web application!

Navigation Menu Bar

Now, you'll add another page that demonstrates the navigation menu. Go to the IDE's main menu bar, and select the second toolbutton on the Internet menu, the one with the little globe and the sheet of paper. This will bring up the New WebSnap Page Module Wizard, which is similar to the dialog box you saw as part of the main wizard. Leave all the options with the default values, except for the Name edit box. Name the page Simple. The result is a Web module with a single PageProducer in it. Note that an HTML page is associated with this page, and it has the same code as the first page you saw. Save the unit as `wmSimple.pas`.

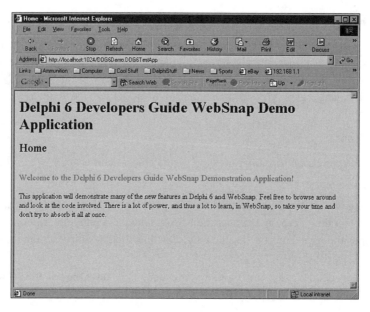

FIGURE 23.8
Results of the first page added to the demo application.

Setting Threading and Caching Options

The New WebSnap Page Module Wizard has two options at the bottom that determine how instances of each Web module are to be handled. The first is the Creation option. Web modules can be created either On Demand or Always. Web modules created On Demand are only instantiated when a request comes in for them. Choose this option for pages that are less frequently used. Choose Always for pages that are created immediately upon application startup. The second option is the Caching Option, and this determines what happens to a Web module when it has finished servicing its request. If Cache Instance is chosen, each Web module created is cached when it is finished providing a request, and it remains in a pool of cached instances, ready to be used again. It is important to note that when it is used again, the field data will be in the same state it was in when it finished its last request. Choose Destroy Instance if you want each instance of the Web module to be destroyed upon completion instead of being cached.

Next, add some simple message in the HTML page in the same spot below the table in the standard page. Then, compile and run the application via the Web App Debugger as you did before. If the page was there from the last time you checked it, all you need to do is click the Refresh button on your browser.

This time when you run the application, you should note that the navigation menu now appears. That menu is a result of the following server-side script:

```
<%  e = new Enumerator(Pages)
    s = ''
    c = 0
    for (; !e.atEnd(); e.moveNext())
    {
      if (e.item().Published)
      {
        if (c>0) s += ' | '
        if (Page.Name != e.item().Name)
          s += '<a href="' + e.item().HREF + '">' + e.item().Title + '</a>'
        else
          s += e.item().Title
        c++
      }
    }
    if (c>1) Response.Write(s)
%>
```

This code simply iterates over the Pages scripting object, building a menu of page names. The code makes a link if the page found isn't the current page. Thus, the current page isn't a link, and all the other page names are, no matter what the current page is. This is a rather simple menu, and of course you could write your own more sophisticated menus for your custom application.

> **NOTE**
>
> If you toggle between the two pages, you might notice that the application's form flashes in the background each time a request is made. That is because the Web App Debugger is calling the application as a COM object for each request, running the application, getting the HTTP response back, and shutting down the application.

Next, you can make part of the application restricted only to users who are logged in. First, add a page that requires a user to be logged in to see it. Click the New WebSnap Page button on the Internet toolbar, and name the page "LoggedIn." Then, select the LoginRequired check box. Click OK to create a Web page that can only be viewed by a user who is logged in. Save the page as wmLoggedIn.pas. Then, add some HTML code to the HTML page letting the user know that only logged in users can view the page. The application on the CD-ROM includes the following:

```
<P>
<FONT COLOR="Green"><B>Congratulations! </B></FONT>
<BR>
You are successfully logged in!  Only logged in users are granted access
➥to this page. All others are sent back to the Login page.
<P>
```

The only difference between the LoggedIn page and the Simple page is a parameter in the code that registers the page with the application manager. Every WebSnap page has an initialization section that looks something like this:

```
initialization
  if WebRequestHandler <> nil then
  WebRequestHandler.AddWebModuleFactory(TWebPageModuleFactory.Create(TLoggedIn,
TWebPageInfo.Create([wpPublished, wpLoginRequired], '.html'),
➥crOnDemand, caCache));
```

This code registers the page with the `WebRequestHandler` object, which manages all the pages and provides their HTML content when needed. `WebRequestHandler` knows how to create, cache, and destroy instances of webmodules as needed. The preceding code is the code for the LoggedIn page, and it has the `wpLoginRequired` parameter, telling the page that only logged in users can access it. By default, the New Page Wizard adds this value, but comments it out. If you want the page to become password protected later, you can simply uncomment the parameter and recompile the application.

Logging In

You need to create a page that lets the user log in. First, however, there is some housekeeping to do on the Home page.

First, create a new page and give it the name Login. Then, select `TAdapterPageProducer` for the page producer type. This time, however, don't publish it by deselecting the Publish check box, and obviously don't require a user to be logged in to view the login page! Deselecting the Publish option will make the page available for use, but it won't be part of the Pages scripting object, and thus it won't show up on the navigation menu. Save it as wmLogin. This time, go to the WebSnap page of the Component Palette and drop a `TLoginAdapter` component on the module.

The `TAdapterPageProducer` is a specialized PageProducer that knows how to display and handle the appropriate HTML fields and controls for a `TAdapter`. In the case of the Demo application, this `TAdapterPageProducer` is going to display the Username and Password edit boxes that the user will need to use to log in. When you begin to understand WebSnap better, you'll quickly want to use `TAdapterPageProducers` in all your pages because they make it very easy to display `TAdapter` information, execute `TAdapter` actions, and build HTML forms based on `TAdapter` fields.

Because the `TLoginFormAdapter` has all the fields needed for this, creating the login page will be very easy, and done with no code at all—that's right, no code. You'll be able to add users, create a login page, and enforce the login on pages you specify, all without a single line of code.

First, to manage logins, you'll need to create some users. Go to the Home Web module and double-click on the `WebUserList` component. This component manages users and passwords. You can easily add users and their passwords. Click on the New button and add two different users. Add whatever passwords you want for each user. The two users on the demo application on the CD-ROM are ddg6 and user. Their passwords are the same as their usernames, as shown in Figure 23.9.

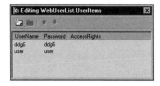

FIGURE 23.9
The component editor for the `WebUserList` *component with two users added.*

Select the `EndUserSessionAdapter` and set the `LoginPage` property to `Login`, that is, the name of the page that has the controls to log in users. Next, go back to the Login Web module and double-click on the `TAdapterPageProducer` component. This will bring up the Web Surface designer, shown in Figure 23.10.

Select the `AdapterPageProducer` in the upper right, and click the New Component button. Select `AdapterForm` and click OK. Then, select the `AdapterForm1`, and click the New Component button again. Select `AdapterErrorList`. Do the same for `AdapterFieldGroup` and `AdapterCommandGroup`. Then set the `Adapter` property for these three components to `LoginFormAdapter1`. Then, select the `AdapterFieldGroup` and add two `AdapterDisplayField` objects. Set the `FieldName` property on the first one to `UserName`, and the second one to `Password`. Select the `AdapterCommandGroup`, and set its `DisplayComponent` property to `AdapterFieldGroup1`. You should then have a form that looks like Figure 23.10. If you close this form, and then go to the Code Editor, you can see that the form now has the login controls in it.

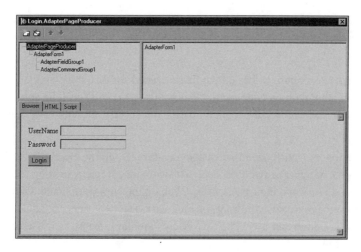

FIGURE 23.10

The TAdapterPageProducer *Web Surface Designer with the LoginFormAdapter components on it.*

That's all you need to do. Run the application and leave it running. Now, because you are rely-ing on session information about the user, you need to leave the application in memory for it to remember that you are logged in. Run the application in the browser, and then try to navigate to the page that requires you to be logged in. It should take you to the Login page. Enter a valid username and password, click the login button, and you will be taken to the page asking you to log in. From now on, any page that you specify as requiring a valid login will only dis-play if you are properly logged in. Otherwise it will send you to the login page. All that hap-pens without writing a single line of Pascal code.

Try this as well: Log out by selecting the Logout link, and then try to login with an invalid username or password. Note that an error message is displayed. That is the AdapterErrorList component at work. It automatically collects login errors and displays them for you.

When you are logged in to the application and navigating around the pages in the application, you will notice that it remembers who you are and displays your login name in the heading for each page. This is a result of the following server-side script in the HTML file for the web-modules:

```
<% if (EndUser.Logout != null) { %>
<%    if (EndUser.DisplayName != '') { %>
  <h1>Welcome <%=EndUser.DisplayName %></h1>
<%    } %>
```

Managing User Preference Data

The next thing you might want to do is to maintain some user preference information. Most dynamic, user-based applications will want to display all different types of user information ranging from items in a shopping cart to a user's color preferences. Of course, WebSnap makes this very easy. But this time, you'll actually have to write a few lines of code.

First, add another page to the application. Give it a TAdapterPageProducer and require the user to be logged in to view it. (By now, you should be able to do this using the toolbar and the resulting wizard.) Save the file as wmPreferenceInput. Add a TAdapter to the Webmodule. Rename the Adapter from Adapter1 to PrefAdapter, as shown in Figure 23.11.

FIGURE 23.11
The PreferenceInput *Web module that will gather up the user's preferences.*

First, double-click on the PrefAdapter component, and then add two AdapterFields and one AdapterBooleanField. Name the two AdapterFields FavoriteMovie and PasswordHint. Name the AdapterBooleanField LikesChocolate. (Notice that when you rename these components, the DisplayLabel and FieldName values change as well.) You can also change the DisplayLabel values that make more sense in your HTML.

The PrefAdapter component will hold the values for these preferences, and they can be accessed from other pages. TAdapters are scriptable components that can hold, manage, and manipulate information for you, but doing that will require some code. Each of the three AdapterFields you created need to be able to retrieve their values when asked for them in script, so each has an OnGetValue event that does just that. Because you want this information to be persistent across requests, you'll store the information in the Session.Values property. The Session.Values variable is a string-indexed array of variants, so you can store almost anything in it, and it will maintain that information as long as the current session is active.

The TAdapter class also allows you to take actions on its data. Most commonly, this will take the form of a Submit button on your HTML form. Select the PrefAdapter component, go to the Object Inspector, and double-click on the Actions property. Add a single action and name it SubmitAction. Change its DisplayLabel property to Submit Information. Then, go to the Events page in the Object Inspector and add this code to the action's OnExecute event as shown in Listing 23.2.

LISTING 23.2   OnExecute Handler

```
procedure TPreferenceInput.SubmitActionExecute(Sender: TObject;
  Params: TStrings);
var
  Value: IActionFieldValue;
begin

  Value := FavoriteMovieField.ActionValue;
  if Value.ValueCount > 0 then
  begin
    Session.Values[sFavoriteMovie] := Value.Values[0];
  end;

  Value := PasswordHintField.ActionValue;
  if Value.ValueCount > 0 then
  begin
    Session.Values[sPasswordHint] := Value.Values[0];
  end;

  Value := LikesChocolateField.ActionValue;
  if Value <> nil then
  begin
    if Value.ValueCount > 0 then
    begin
      Session.Values[sLikesChocolate] := Value.Values[0];
    end;
  end else
  begin
    Session.Values[sLikesChocolate] := 'false';
  end;;
end;
```

This code retrieves the values from the input fields in your HTML when the user clicks the
Submit button, and puts the values in the session variable for later retrieval by the
AdapterFields.

Of course, you need to be able to retrieve those values once they are set, so each field of the
adapter will get its value back from the SessionsService object. For each field in the adapter,
make the OnGetValue event handlers resemble the code in Listing 23.3.

LISTING 23.3   OnGetValue Event Handlers

```
...
const
  sFavoriteMovie = 'FavoriteMovie';
  sPasswordHint = 'PasswordHint';
```

LISTING 23.3 Continued

```
  sLikesChocolate = 'LikesChocolate';
  sIniFileName = 'DDG6Demo.ini';
...

procedure TPreferenceInput.LikesChocolateFieldGetValue(Sender: TObject;
  var Value: Boolean);
var
  S: string;
begin
  S := Session.Values[sLikesChocolate];
  Value := S = 'true';
end;

procedure TPreferenceInput.FavoriteMovieFieldGetValue(Sender: TObject;
  var Value: Variant);
begin
  Value := Session.Values[sFavoriteMovie];
end;

procedure TPreferenceInput.PasswordHintFieldGetValue(Sender: TObject;
  var Value: Variant);
begin
  Value := Session.Values[sPasswordHint];
end;
```

Next, you need to be able to display controls that will actually get the data from the user. You'll do that via the TAdapterPageProducer, just as you did with the Login page. First, double-click on the TAdapterPageProducer, and you will get the Web Surface designer again. Create a new AdapterForm, and then add an AdapterFieldGroup, as well as an AdapterCommandGroup. Set the Adapter property of the AdapterFieldGroup to PrefAdaper, and set the DisplayComponent of the AdapterCommandGroup to AdapterFieldGroup. Then, right-click on the AdapterFieldGroup and select Add All Fields from the menu. For each of the resulting fields, use the Object Inspector to set the FieldName property to the appropriate values. You can also change the Caption properties to more friendly values than the default. Then select the AdapterCommandGroup, right-click on it, and select Add All Commands from the menu. Set the ActionName property of the resulting AdapterActionButton to SubmitAction. Finally, set the AdapterActionButton.PageName property to PreferencesPage. (This is the page that the action will go to once it is done processing the action. You'll create that page in a minute.)

If something isn't hooked up correctly in the Web Surface Designer, you will see an error message in the Browser tab. The message will instruct you on the properties that need to be set for everything to be connected properly and for the HTML to be rendered properly.

After you have done all this, and the HTML looks right, the page is done. Now, if you run the application, you'll see an additional page on the menu. If you log in, you can see the input controls to enter your preference data. Don't click the Submit button just yet because there is no place to go.

Next, create a page to display the user preferences by using the toolbar, and then name it PreferencesPage. Publish the page and require users to be logged in to view it. (Again, the wizard can do all this for you as before.) Save the new unit as wmPreferences.

Then, go the HTML for the page, and in the area just below the table that holds the navigation menu, add the following script:

```
<P>
Favorite Movie: <%= Modules.PreferenceInput.PrefAdapter.FavoriteMovieField.
Value %>
<BR>
Password Hint:  <%= Modules.PreferenceInput.PrefAdapter.PasswordHintField.
Value %>

<BR>
<% s = ''
  if (Modules.PreferenceInput.PrefAdapter.LikesChocolateField.Value)
    s = 'You like Chocolate'
  else
    s = 'You do not like chocolate'
  Response.Write(s);
%>
```

Now, when you compile and run the application, you can enter your preferences and click the Submit button—the application will remember and display your preferences in the Preferences page. You can access those values in the script for any other page as well once they are set. The values are maintained between HTTP requests by the Session object and retrieved from the Adapter component via script.

> **Note**
>
> Each of the pages in a WebSnap application has an associated HTML file, as you have seen. Because these files exist outside of the application, you can edit them, save the changes, refresh the page in your browser, and see the results without recompiling your application. This means that you can update the page itself without having to take down your Web server. You can also easily experiment with your server-side script during development without having to recompile your application. Later in the chapter, you'll look at alternative ways to store and retrieve your HTML.

Persisting Preference Data Between Sessions

There's only one problem now—the user's selections aren't persistent between sessions. The preferences are lost if the user logs out. You can make these values persist even between sessions by storing them each time the session ends and grabbing them each time a user logs in. The demo application reads any stored data in the `LoginFormAdapter.OnLogin` event, and then writes out any data in the `SessionService.OnEndSession` event. The code for those two events is shown in Listing 23.4.

LISTING 23.4   OnLogin and OnEndSession Events

```
procedure TLogin.LoginFormAdapter1Login(Sender: TObject; UserID: Variant);
var
  IniFile: TIniFile;
  TempName: string;
begin
  // Grab session data here
  TempName := Home.WebUserList.UserItems.FindUserID(UserId).UserName;
➡     //WebContext.EndUser.DisplayName;
  Home.CurrentUserName := TempName;

  Lock.BeginRead;
  try
    IniFile := TIniFile.Create(IniFileName);
    try
      Session.Values[sFavoriteMovie] := IniFile.ReadString(TempName,
      ➡sFavoriteMovie, '');
      Session.Values[sPasswordHint] := IniFile.ReadString(TempName,
      ➡sPasswordHint, '');
      Session.Values[sLikesChocolate] := IniFile.ReadString(TempName,
      ➡sLikesChocolate, 'false');
    finally
      IniFile.Free;
    end;
  finally
    Lock.EndRead;
  end;
end;

procedure THome.SessionsServiceEndSession(ASender: TObject;
  ASession: TAbstractWebSession; AReason: TEndSessionReason);
var
  IniFile: TIniFile;
begin
  //Save out the preferences here
```

LISTING 23.4   Continued

```
Lock.BeginWrite;
if FCurrentUserName <> '' then
begin
  try
    IniFile := TIniFile.Create(IniFileName);
    try
      IniFile.WriteString(FCurrentUserName, sFavoriteMovie,
      ➥ASession.Values[sFavoriteMovie]);
      IniFile.WriteString(FCurrentUserName, sPassWordHint,
      ➥ASession.Values[sPasswordHint]);
      IniFile.WriteString(FCurrentUserName, sLikesChocolate,
      ➥ASession.Values[sLikesChocolate]);
    finally
      IniFile.Free;
    end;
  finally
    Lock.EndWrite
  end;
end;
end;
```

These event handlers store the data in an INI file, but there is no reason that you couldn't store the data in a database or any other persistent storage method.

The Lock variable is a global variable of type TMultiReadExclusiveWriteSynchronizer, and it is created in the Home page's initialization section. Because multiple sessions could be reading and writing to the INI file, this component makes reading and writing to the INI file thread-safe. Add the following declaration to the interface portion of your wmHome unit:

```
var
    Lock: TMultiReadExclusiveWriteSynchronizer;
```

And then add this to the initialization and finalization sections for the same unit:

```
Initialization
  ...
  Lock := TMultiReadExclusiveWriteSynchronizer.Create;
finalization
  Lock.Free;
```

This code also uses a function called IniFileName that is declared as follows:

```
const
    sIniFileName = 'DDG6Demo.ini';

...
```

```
function IniFileName: string;
begin
  Result := ExtractFilePath(GetModuleName(HInstance)) + sIniFileName;
end;
```

Add this to your wmHome unit, and you should have a fully functioning Web application that logs in users and tracks their preferences, even between sessions.

Image Handling

Practically every Web application displays graphics. Graphics can enhance your application's appeal and functionality. Naturally, WebSnap makes including images and graphics in your applications as easy as, well, everything else WebSnap does. As you might expect, WebSnap will enable you to use graphics and images from any source you prefer—files, resources, database streams, and so on. If your image data can be put into a stream, it can be used in a WebSnap application.

Use the Internet toolbar to add another page to your application. Use a TAdapterPageProducer, publish the page, and require users to log in to gain access to it. Next name the page Images, and save the resulting unit as wmImages. After this is done, go to the Images Web module, add a TAdapter to the module, and give it the name ImageAdapter. Finally, double-click on ImageAdapter, and add two fields of type TAdapterImageField. Each of these will show a different way to display images.

First, you can display an image based on a URL. Highlight the first AdaperImageField, and set the HREF property to a fully qualified URL that points to an image on your system or anywhere on the Internet for that matter. For instance, if you want to look at the one-year history of Borland's stock price, set the HREF property to http://chart.yahoo.com/c/1y/b/borl.gif.

Double-click on the TAdapterPageProducer in the Images Web module, add an AdapterForm, and then to that add an AdapterFieldGroup. Set the adapter property of this new AdapterFieldGroup to the ImageAdapter. Then right-click again on the AdapterFieldGroup and select Add All Fields. Next, set the ReadOnly field of the AdapterImageField to True. If this property is True, it will display the image on your page. If it is set to False, it will give you an edit box and a button to look up a filename. Obviously, to see images, you should set this property to True. When you first look at the image, you will notice that the image has a pesky little caption. Most often you won't want that, so to get rid of it, set the Caption property to a single space. (Note that it won't accept a blank caption.) You should then see the chart appear in the Web Surface Designer as shown in Figure 23.12.

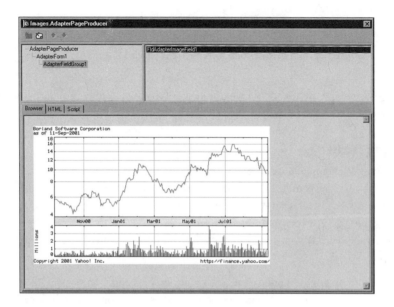

FIGURE 23.12

The Web Surface Designer with a graphic in it from the ImageAdapterField.

NOTE

If you want images referenced by relative links to show up at design time, you must add the directory where they reside to the Search Path on the Options page of the Web App Debugger.

Now you can display images based on a URL. At other times, however, you might want to get an image from a stream. The `AdapterImageField` component provides support for that as well. Select the second `AdapterImageField` from your `ImageAdapter` and open the Object Inspector. Go to the events page, and double-click on the `OnGetImage`. Put a JPG image in the same directory as application (the demo on the CD-ROM uses `athena.jpg`), and make your event handler resemble the following:

```
procedure TImages.AdapterImageField2GetImage(Sender: TObject;
  Params: TStrings; var MimeType: String; var Image: TStream;
  var Owned: Boolean);
begin
  MimeType := 'image\jpg';
  Image := TFileStream.Create('athena.jpg', fmOpenRead);
end;
```

This code is quite simple—Image is a stream variable that you create and fill with an image. Of course, the application needs to know what type of image it is getting, so you can return that information in the `MimeType` parameter. A `TFileStream` is a simple solution, but you could get the image from any source, such as a `BlobStream` from a database, or build the image on-the-fly and return it in a memory stream. Now when you run the application, you should see the JPG you chose right below the stock graphic.

Displaying Data

Of course, you want your application to do more than the simple things it does so far. You'll certainly want to be able to display data from a database, both in tabular form and record by record. Naturally, WebSnap makes this easy, and you can build powerful database applications with only a modicum of code. By using the `TDatasetAdapter` and its built-in fields and actions, you can easily display data, as well as make additions, updates, and deletions to any database.

Actually displaying a dataset on a form is very easy. Add a new unit to your demo app—but this time make it a WebDataModule, using the third button on the Internet toolbar. This wizard is a simple one, so just accept the defaults. Then add a `TDatasetAdapter` from the WebSnap tab on the Component Palette, and a `TTable` from the BDE tab. Point the `TTable` to the DBDemos database, and then to the BioLife table. Then set the `Dataset` property of `DatasetAdapter1` to `Table1`. Finally, set `Table1.Active` to `True` to open the table. Name the Webdatamodule BioLife data, and save the unit as `wdmBioLife`.

23

**BUILDING
WEBSNAP
APPLICATIONS**

> **NOTE**
>
> Your application is using a simple BDE-based Paradox table, but the `TDatasetAdapter` component will display data from any `TDataset` descendent. Note, too, that it isn't really a good idea to use a `TTable` in a Web application without explicit session support. The demo app does this just for ease of use, and to keep attention on the WebSnap features and not the data.

Then, for a change of pace, use the Object Treeview to set the properties of the components. If the Object Treeview isn't visible, select View, Object Treeview from the main menu. Select the DatasetAdapter, right-click on the Actions node, and select Add All Actions. Then, hook the TTable to the `TAdapterDataset` via its `Dataset` property. Select the Fields node and right-click, selecting Add All Fields. Do the same for the `TTable`, adding all the fields in the dataset to the WebDatamodule. Then, because WebSnap builds stateless servers for database operations, you must indicate a primary key for the dataset to enable client-requested navigation and data manipulation. WebSnap will do this all for you automatically after you specify the primary key. Do this by selecting the Species_No Field in the Object Treeview and adding the pfInKey value to its ProviderFlags property.

Next, add a regular page to the application. Make it a Login Required page, give it a TAdapter PageProducer, and name the page Biolife. Save the unit as wmBioLife. Because you want to display the data in this new page, add the wdmBioLife unit name to the uses clause of your wmBioLife unit. Then, give the BioLife Web module the focus, and right-click on the Adapter PageProducer component. Right-click on the WebPageItems node just below it, select New Component, and select an AdapterForm. Select the AdapterForm, right-click it, and add an AdapterErrorList. Then add an AdapterGrid. Set the Adapter property of both components to the DatasetAdapter. Right-click on the AdapterGrid and select Add All Columns. Then select the Actions node under the DatasetAdapter, right-click it, and select Add All Actions. Next, select the Fields node, right-click, and add all the fields as well. You should now have all the properties properly set to display data.

Go to the BioLife Web module and double-click on the AdaperPageProducer. You should see the Web Surface Designer, with live data in it. If not, check to make sure that you have opened the table and hooked up all the Adapter properties for the components within the DatasetAdapter. The Notes field makes the table too long, so select the AdapterGrid in the upper left and the ColNotes component in the panel in the upper right, and then delete it. Now you should have something similar to that shown in Figure 23.13.

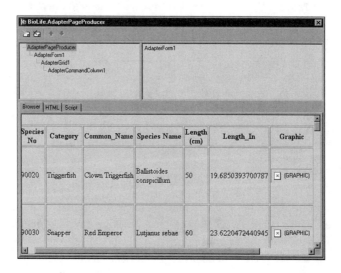

FIGURE 23.13
The BioLife table in the Web Surface designer of a TAdapterPageProducer; *the HTML table is produced by the* TDatasetAdapter *component.*

The graphics don't display at design time, but they will at runtime. Indeed, you can now compile and run the application, and you can view all the data on the BioLife page—all without writing a single line of code.

Of course, simply looking at the data isn't very useful. You'll likely want to manipulate individual records. Naturally, this is easy to do in WebSnap. Go to the Web Surface Designer and select the AdapterGrid. Right-click on it and add an AdapterCommandColumn. Then right-click on this and select the DeleteRow, EditRow, BrowseRow, and NewRow commands, as shown in Figure 23.14.

FIGURE 23.14
Use the Add Commands dialog box to select the actions you want to take on individual rows of the dataset.

Click OK. Then, vertically stack the buttons by setting the DisplayColumns property of the AdapterCommandColumn component to 1. After you do that, you should see a collection of command buttons in the Web Designer (see Figure 23.15).

Currently, those buttons need to do something, and they'll need a page to display the individual record. Add another page to the project with a TAdapterPageProducer and require the user login to see the page. Name the page BioLifeEdit, and save the unit as wmBioLifeEdit. Add wdmBioLife to the uses clause so that you can access the data.

Double-click on the TAdapterPageProducer in the new Web module and add an AdapterForm. Then add an AdapterErrorList, an AdapterFieldGroup, and an AdapterCommandGroup. Right-click on the AdapterFieldGroup and add all the fields and then all the commands to the AdapterCommandGroup. The Web Surface Designer resembles what is shown in Figure 23.16.

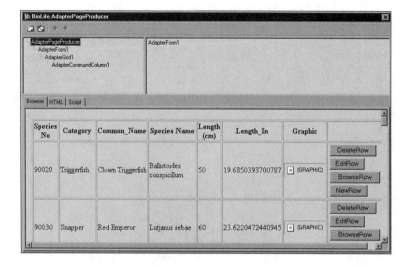

FIGURE 23.15

The Demo application displaying the action buttons.

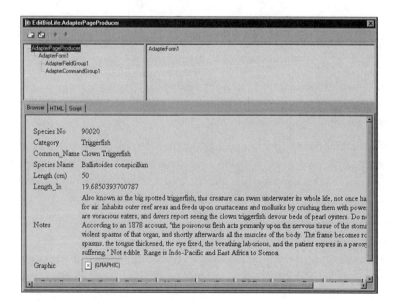

FIGURE 23.16

The BioLifeEdit page with all the fields and actions added to the Web Surface Designer.

Now, in order to use this page to edit a single record, go back to the wmBioLife unit where the grid is, and use the Object TreeView and the shift key to select all four buttons in the

AdapterCommandColumn. Set their page property to EditBioLife—the name of the page that will display a single record. Now, when you click the button in the grid, the EditBioLife page will be displayed. If you ask to browse the record, the data will be displayed as simple text. But if you ask to edit the record, the data will be displayed in edit boxes. The graphic field will even allow you to add a new graphic to the database by browsing for a new file. You can navigate through the dataset using the command buttons. And again, all this was accomplished without writing a single line of code—or script for that matter.

> **NOTE**
>
> You might want to tweak the presentation of the Notes field a little bit. By default, the TextArea control used when the page is in edit mode is quite small and doesn't wrap the text. You can select the FldNotes component and adjust the TextAreaWrap, DisplayRows, and DisplayWidth properties to get better results.

Converting the Application to an ISAPI DLL

Your application has so far been run under the Web App Debugger, making it easy to debug and test. However, you certainly don't want to deploy the application that way. Instead, you'll likely want to make the application an ISAPI DLL so that it will always reside in memory and maintain all the session information needed to keep things in order.

Converting your application from a Web App Debugger based server to an ISAPI server is very straightforward. Simply create a new, blank ISAPI-based project, and remove all the units from it. Then, add in all units from the Web App version except the form. Then compile and run. It's that simple. In fact, you can maintain two projects that use the very same webmodules—one project for testing and another for deploying. Most of the demo applications in the WebSnap directory do this, and the demo application on the CD-ROM has both Web App Server and ISAPI projects. When deploying the new ISAPI DLL, be sure to include any HTML files that will need to be in the same directory as the DLL.

Advanced Topics

So far, you have seen what can be considered the basics. You've created a WebSnap application that manages users, session information about those users, as well as manages and manipulates data. WebSnap does a lot more than that, however, and gives you more control over what your application can do. The next section covers some advanced topics that will allow you to more finely tune your WebSnap applications.

LocateFileServices

The development of WebSnap Web applications usually requires the coordination of differing resources. HTML, server-side script, Delphi code, database access, and graphics all need to be properly tied together into a single application. Most often, many of these resources lie embedded in and are managed via an HTML file. WebSnap provides support for separating HTML from the implementation of a dynamic Web page, meaning that you can edit the HTML files separately from the Web application's binary file. However, by default, that HTML must reside in files in the same location as the binary file does. This isn't always convenient or possible, and there might be times when you want HTML to reside in locations away from your binary. Or it might be that you want to get HTML content from sources other than files, say a database.

WebSnap provides you the ability to get HTML from any source that you want. The `LocateFileService` component allows you to get HTML from any file location, include files, or any `TStream` descendant. Being able to access HTML from a `TStream` means that you can get the HTML from any source as long as it can be placed in a `TStream`.

For example, HTML can be streamed from a RES file embedded in your application's binary file. The demo application can show how this is done. Naturally, you'll need some HTML to embed. Using a text editor or your favorite HTML editor, take the wmLogin.html file as a template and save it in your demo application's directory as `embed.html`. Then, add some text to the file to note that the file is embedded in the RES file. That way, you'll know for sure that you have the right file when it is displayed.

Then, of course, you need to embed this HTML into your application. Delphi easily manages this via RC files, automatically compiling them and adding them to an application. Therefore, use Notepad or some text-handling tool to create a text file, and call it `HTML.RC`. Save it in the same directory as your demo application and add it to your project. Then, add this text to the RC file:

```
#define HTML 23  // HTML resource identifier
EMBEDDEDHTML HTML embed.html
```

When included in a Delphi project, Delphi will compile the RC file into a RES file and include it in your application.

When the HTML is in your app, create a new page with a `TPageProducer` and call it Embedded. Save the file as `wmEmbedded`. Then, go to the Home page and select the `LocateFileServices` component. Go to the Object Inspector Events page and double-click on the `OnFindStream` event. You'll get an event handler similar to this one:

```
procedure THome.LocateFileServiceFindStream(ASender: TObject;
  AComponent: TComponent; const AFileName: String;
  var AFoundStream: TStream; var AOwned, AHandled: Boolean);
```

```
begin

end;
```

The key parameters here are the `AFileName` and `AFoundStream` parameters. You'll use them to get the HTML from the embedded resources. Make your event handler resemble the following:

```
procedure THome.LocateFileServiceFindStream(ASender: TObject;
  AComponent: TComponent; const AFileName: String;
  var AFoundStream: TStream; var AOwned, AHandled: Boolean);
begin
  // we are hunting up the Embedded file
  if Pos('EMBEDDED', UpperCase(AFileName)) > 0 then    begin
    AFoundStream := TResourceStream.Create(hInstance, 'EMBEDDED', 'HTML');
    AHandled := True; // no need to look further
  end;
end;
```

`AFileName` will be the unqualified name of the HTML file that Delphi would use as a default. You can use that name to determine which resource to look up. `AFoundStream` will be `nil` when passed into event handler, so it is up to you to create a stream using the variable. In this case, `AFoundStream` becomes a `TResourceStream`, which grabs the HTML from the resources in the executable. Setting `AHandled` to `True` ensures that the LocateFileServices makes no further effort to find the HTML content.

Run the application, and you will see your HTML show up when you display the Embedded page.

File Uploading

In the past, one of the more challenging tasks for a Web application developer is uploading files from the client to the server. It often involved dealing with the very arcane features of the HTTP specification and counting every byte passed very carefully. As you would expect, WebSnap makes this previously difficult task easy. WebSnap provides all the functionality for uploading a file inside a `TAdapter`, and your part isn't much more difficult than placing a file in a stream.

As usual, create another page in your application that will upload files to the server from the client. Name the page Upload and give it a `TAdapterPageProducer`. Then save the file as `wmUpload`. Then, drop a `TAdapter` on the form. Give the `TAdapter` a new `AdapterFileField`. This field will manage all the uploading of the files selected on the client. In addition, give the `Adapter` a single action and call it `UploadAction`.

Next, give the `AdapterPageProducer` an `AdapterForm` with an `AdapterErrorList`, an `AdapterFieldGroup`, and an `AdapterCommandGroup`. Connect the first two to `Adapter1`, and the

AdapterCommandGroup to the AdapterFieldGroup. Then add all the fields to the
AdapterFieldGroup and all the actions to the AdapterCommandGroup. Change the caption on
the button to Upload File. Figure 23.17 shows what you should see in the Surface Designer.

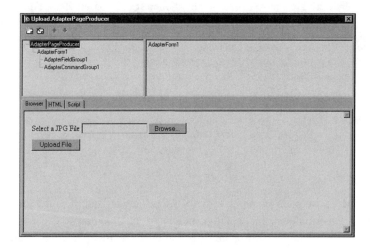

FIGURE 23.17
The Web Surface Designer for the Upload page, with the Browse button automatically added.

Code can be added in two places. The first place is to the Adapter1.AdapterFileField
OnFileUpload event handler. The code there should resemble that in Listing 23.5.

LISTING 23.5   OnFileUpload Event Handler

```
procedure TUpload.AdapterFileField1UploadFiles(Sender: TObject;
  Files: TUpdateFileList);
var
  i: integer;
  CurrentDir: string;
  Filename: string;
  FS: TFileStream;
begin
  // Upload file here
    if Files.Count <= 0 then
    begin
      raise Exception.Create('You have not selected any files to be uploaded');
    end;
    for i := 0 to Files.Count - 1 do
    begin
    // Make sure that the file is a .jpg or .jpeg
    if (CompareText(ExtractFileExt(Files.Files[I].FileName), '.jpg') <> 0)
```

LISTING 23.5 Continued

```
            and (CompareText(ExtractFileExt(Files.Files[I].FileName), '.jpeg')
            ➡<> 0) then
    begin
      Adapter1.Errors.AddError('You must select a JPG or JPEG file to upload');
    end else
    begin
      CurrentDir := ExtractFilePath(GetModuleName(HInstance)) + 'JPEGFiles';
      ForceDirectories(CurrentDir);
      FileName := CurrentDir + '\' + ExtractFileName(Files.Files[I].FileName);
      FS := TFileStream.Create(Filename, fmCreate or fmShareDenyWrite);
      try
        FS.CopyFrom(Files.Files[I].Stream, 0); // 0 = copy all from start
      finally
        FS.Free;
      end;
    end;
  end;
end;
```

This code first checks to make sure that you have selected a file, and then it makes sure that you have selected a JPEG file. After it determines that you have done that, it takes the filename, ensures that the receiving directory exists, and puts the file into a TFileStream. The real work here is done behind the scenes by the TUpdateFileList class that manages all the HTTP esoterica and multi-part form handling needed to upload a file from the client to the server.

The second place to add code is in the OnExecute handler for the UploadAction in Adapter1. It is as follows:

```
procedure TUpload.UploadActionExecute(Sender: TObject; Params: TStrings);
begin
  Adapter1.UpdateRecords;
end;
```

which simply tells the Adapter to update its records and get the files that have been requested.

Including Custom Templates

One thing you have likely noticed is that when you create a new page with the New Page Wizard, you only have two choices for the HTML in your application—the standard template or a blank template. The standard template is nice for things such as the demo application in this chapter, but when you start developing more sophisticated sites, you'll want to be able to automatically include your own HTML templates when adding pages to your applications. WebSnap allows you to do that.

You can add new templates to the selections in the New Page Wizard by creating and register-ing a descendent of TProducerTemplatesList in a design-time package. There is a demo pack-age that does this in the <Delphi>\Demos\WebSnap\Producer Template directory. You can look at that package and add your own HTML/script templates to the RC file included in the package. Note that for this package to compile, you must first have compiled the package <Delphi>\Demos\WebSnap\Util\TemplateRes.dpk. After you compile and install these pack-ages, you will have more templates to choose from in the New Page Wizard.

Custom Components in **TAdapterPageProducer**

Much of the work of displaying HTML throughout this chapter has been done by TAdapter PageProducer components, and the components that are embedded within it. However, you certainly will want to customize the HTML therein beyond the standard code you have seen so far. WebSnap allows you to do this by creating your own components that plug in to the TAdapterPageProducer, allowing you to add your own custom HTML to the mix.

Your custom TAdapterPageProducer components must descend from TWebContainedComponent and implement the IWebContent interface. Because all the compo-nents must do this, it is a perfect opportunity to use an abstract class as in Listing 23.6.

LISTING 23.6   Abstract Descendent Class of TWebContainedComponent

```
type

Tddg6BaseWebSnapComponent = class(TWebContainedComponent, IWebContent)
  protected
    { IWebContent }
    function Content(Options: TWebContentOptions; ParentLayout: TLayout):
    ➥string;
    function GetHTML: string; virtual; abstract;
  end;
```

This class is implemented like so:

```
function Tddg6BaseWebSnapComponent.Content(Options: TWebContentOptions;
  ParentLayout: TLayout): string;
var
  Intf: ILayoutWebContent;
begin
  if Supports(ParentLayout, ILayoutWebContent, Intf) then
    Result := Intf.LayoutField(GetHTML, nil)
  else
    Result := GetHTML;
end;
```

The abstract class implements the Content function only because the GetHTML function is declared as abstract. The Content function basically checks to see whether the containing component is a LayoutGroup. If it is LayoutGroup, the Content function places its content inside the LayoutGroup. Otherwise, Content simply returns the results of GetHTML. Descendent components, therefore, need only implement the GetHTML function, returning the appropriate HTML code, and they can be registered to work inside a TAdapterPageProducer.

The code on the CD-ROM implements two components that allow you to add HTML content to a TAdapterPageProducer, either as a string or as a file. The code for the Tddg6HTMLCode component is as shown in Listing 23.7.

LISTING 23.7   Tddg6HTMLCode Component

```
Tddg6HTMLCode = class(Tddg6BaseWebSnapComponent)
private
  FHTML: TStrings;
  procedure SetHTML(const Value: TStrings);
protected
  function GetHTML: string; override;
public
  constructor Create(AOwner: TComponent); override;
  destructor Destroy; override;
published
  property HTML: TStrings read FHTML write SetHTML;
end;

constructor Tddg6HTMLCode.Create(AOwner: TComponent);
begin
  inherited;
  FHTML := TStringList.Create;
end;

destructor Tddg6HTMLCode.Destroy;
begin
  FHTML.Free;
  inherited;
end;

function Tddg6HTMLCode.GetHTML: string;
begin
  Result := FHTML.Text;
end;

procedure Tddg6HTMLCode.SetHTML(const Value: TStrings);
```

23

LISTING 23.7   Continued

```
begin
  FHTML.Assign(Value);
end;
```

This is a pretty simple class. It merely provides a published property of type TStrings that will take any HTML code and then put it in the TAdapterPageProducer as is. The GetHTML function simply returns the HTML in string form. You can build components to return any HTML code you want to include—images, links, files, and other content. All descendent components have to do is to provide their HTML content in an overridden GetHTML() method. Note that there are supporting registration functions in the unit where the components are implemented. When creating components, be sure to register them in your unit similar to those on the CD-ROM. To use these components, merely install them in a design-time package, and the components will appear in the TAdapterPageProducer's Web Surface Designer (see Figure 23.18).

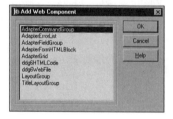

FIGURE 23.18

TAdapterPageProducer *components in the Web Surface Designer.*

Summary

That's a quick overview of the power of WebSnap. This chapter barely scratched the surface of what WebSnap can do. Be sure to check out the numerous demo applications in the <Delphi>\ Demos\WebSnap directory. Many of the demos add functionality to the standard slate of WebSnap components.

Clearly, WebSnap is a powerful technology, but it does take some effort to understand. However, once you get over the initial learning curve, you will soon be building powerful, database driven, dynamic Web sites with ease.

Wireless Development

IN THIS CHAPTER

Without a doubt, two technologies in the past 10 years have touched our lives more than any others: the Internet and mobile devices. Despite the ups and downs of Internet-based businesses, the Internet—and the Web in particular—has permanently changed our lives. It has affected the way we communicate, shop, work, and play. What's more, many of us now shudder at the thought of being caught somewhere without our trusty mobile phone or Personal Digital Assistant (PDA). Given their importance in our lives, it seems natural that these two technologies are now in a state of convergence, with mobile devices becoming wireless tentacles reaching out from the wired Internet to provide us with the services and information to which we've become so addicted.

With mobile information devices becoming more necessity than novelty in today's business and social climate, we developers are faced with the challenge of leveraging this hardware and infrastructure in order to fulfill the ever-growing demand to push data and applications out to mobile devices. With a dizzying array of mobile devices, networks, and technologies on the market, the key questions for developers become: Which of the wireless platforms should you target? What is the most efficient way to target them? What technologies can I leverage to mobilize my data and applications? What are the trade-offs between all these platforms and technologies?

This chapter is by no means intended to serve as an exhaustive how-to, describing how to implement all the various mobile technologies. That would require volumes. We will, however, have done our job if you get two things from this chapter. First, you will hopefully be able to use this chapter as a *cheat sheet* in understanding the role many of the various types of hardware, software, and technologies play in mobile computing from a developer's perspective. Second, you should understand how some of these mobile technologies can be implemented using Delphi.

Evolution of Development—How Did We Get Here?

Before discussing how you might build the applications to harness these emerging trends in information technology, it's important to look back at what brought us here. Here is a rather simplified snapshot of recent trends in information technology.

Pre-1980s: Here There Be Dragons

Before the PC revolution of the 1980s brought information technology to the masses, development for these systems was a jumble of mainframes, terminals, and proprietary systems. Developer tools were generally rudimentary, making application development an expensive and time-consuming process reserved for true bit-heads.

Late 1980s: Desktop Database Applications

After the PC revolution took hold, folks began to leverage the new found power residing on their desktops using desktop database applications such as dBASE, FoxPro, and Paradox. General application development tools also became more mature, making application development a relatively straightforward task using third generation languages such as C, Pascal, and BASIC. DOS was king of the desktop, providing applications with a common platform upon which to build. Local area networks were becoming practical for businesses of all sizes, which provided for centralized storage of data on file servers.

Early 1990s: Client/Server

Corporate networks were now taken for granted; most everyone in the office was connected. The question now was how to bridge the gap between the aging mainframe systems and the non-scalable desktop databases that were both important to business. The answer was client/server systems, the notion of powerful databases from companies such as Oracle, Sybase, and Informix connected to user-interfaces running on PCs. This enabled systems to leverage the power on every desktop while enabling database servers to perform their specialized tasks. Fourth generation development tools such as Visual Basic and Delphi made development easier than ever before, and database support was built in as a first class citizen of the tools.

Late 1990s: Multitier and Internet-Based Transactions

The primary problem with the client/server model is the notion of where the business logic should reside—place it on the database server and you limit scalability; place it on the client and you have a maintenance nightmare. Multitier systems solved this problem by placing the business logic on one or more additional *tiers* logically and/or physically separate from the client and server. This enabled properly written systems to scale to a nearly unlimited extent and paved the way for complex transactions to be served to thousands or millions of clients via the Internet. Development tools extended into the multitier world with technologies such as CORBA, EJB, and COM. Businesses were quick to leverage the Internet to offer information and services to employees, clients, and partners, and industries grew up around the ability to manage, publish, and exchange data between machines over the Internet.

Early 2000s: Application Infrastructure Extends to Wireless Mobile Devices

So, what is the net result of the vast information availability provided by the Internet? The answer is two words: information addiction. The availability of information and services via the Internet has made us dependent on the same in ever increasing aspects of our lives. PDAs and mobile phones have served to scratch that itch, feeding our information addiction while away from our desks. Application servers and development tools are growing in scope to manage the push of functionality to these types of devices. The potential market for applications on mobile devices is mind boggling in size because the projected number of these devices coming into the market over the next few years dwarfs the numbers for PCs.

Mobile Wireless Devices

Between mobile phones, PDAs, and smart pagers, there is no shortage of devices from which to choose should you want to remain connected while away from your desk. Those of us who have trouble choosing sometimes carry all three on belts that cause us to resemble Batman more and more everyday. We are also seeing a convergence of these devices into single, multifunctional devices. Recent examples of this include the mobile phone Springboard module for Handspring handhelds, the Kyocera Smartphone running PalmOS, and Microsoft's Stinger Windows CE-powered mobile phone. In this section, we will call out a few of the leaders in this area.

Mobile Phones

Mobile phones are by far the most pervasive variety of mobile wireless device. Mobile phones have moved beyond the realm of pure voice communication systems into the realm of data communications. Most notably, the majority of new phones coming into the market support text messaging using Short Message Service (SMS) and Web-like browsing using Wireless Application Protocol (WAP). Current data rates are rather paltry at 9.6-14.4k, but new technologies promise to deliver speeds of up to 2Mbits within 2-3 years.

PalmOS Devices

Devices running the Palm Computing's PalmOS operating system have been the market share leader in the PDA space for several years. Some PalmOS devices have wireless capability built in (such as the Palm VII series or the Kyocera Smartphone), and wireless can be added to others through the use of a wireless modem (such as those made by Novatel) or a mobile phone connector available from Palm. A wide range of companies have licensed PalmOS from Palm, Inc. for inclusion in their own devices, including Handspring, Sony, Kyocera, Symbol, Nokia, Samsung, and TRG. Advantages of PalmOS includes the fact that they own the overwhelming share of the market for PDAs, and there is strong developer community with an active third-party market.

Pocket PC

Compaq, HP, Casio, and other manufacturers produce PDAs based on Microsoft's Pocket PC (formerly Windows CE) operating system. To date, none of these devices have built-in wireless capability, but they do support wireless modems in a manner similar to PalmOS devices. Even more, Pocket PC devices tend to be a bit more powerful than their PalmOS counterpart, with some having the capability of accepting standard PC Cards (PCMCIA). This potentially allows an even greater range of expansion to higher-bandwidth wireless networks.

RIM BlackBerry

The BlackBerry provides PDA-type functionality in a pager-sized form factor. With an internal wireless modem and type-with-your-thumbs keyboard, the BlackBerry is especially well suited to mobile e-mail tasks. However, the BlackBerry also supports web browsing via a third-party browser. I have found the BlackBerry to be an outstanding platform for corporate e-mail, thanks to built-in integration with MS Exchange or Lotus Domino, but the device is wanting as a Web appliance because of its screen size and navigation capabilities.

Radio Technologies

Radio technologies provide the connection between mobile devices and the Internet or corporate LAN.

GSM, CDMA, and TDMA

These are the primary technologies used as the transport for mobile phones, and they are often referred to as *2G* because they embody the second generation of mobile communications networks (*1G* being analog service). Most networks in the United States are based on CDMA or TDMA, whereas most of the rest of the world relies on GSM. The details of these technologies are relatively unimportant from a software developer's point of view, except to know that the very existence of these competing standards makes it difficult to create applications that function across the spectrum of phones and networks. Generally, data speeds on these types of networks top out at 9.6-14.4k.

CDPD

Cellular Digital Packet Data (CDPD) is a technology that enables packet-based data transfer over wireless networks, offering increase in bandwidth and "always on" functionality. CDPD is common with aftermarket PDA wireless service in the United States, such as that provided by GoAmerica or OmniSky, and speeds reach about 19.2k.

3G

3G, or third generation, mobile networks are designed from the ground up to handle a variety of different types of media streams and boast bandwidth estimated to be somewhere in the range of 384k-2M. The most likely candidates to be the 3G standard bearers are technologies known as EDGE and UMTS. However, although the technology exists and several carriers own enough spectrum to implement 3G networks, no carrier seems to want to be the first to make the multi-billion dollar investment in network upgrades in order to move forward with 3G.

GPRS

General Packet Radio Service (GPRS) is considered the migration path from 2G to 3G, and is often therefore referred to as *2.5G*. GPRS enables packet-based traffic over existing 2G infra-structure with only relatively minor upgrades. Realized throughput on GPRS networks will likely be in the 20-30k range.

Bluetooth

Devices incorporating Bluetooth radio technology are just now beginning to come available in the market. Bluetooth is an important emerging technology because it permits short range, ad-hoc networking among different types of devices. Because Bluetooth radio modules are very small, have low power, and are relatively inexpensive, they will be embedded in all manner of mobile devices, including phones, PDAs, laptops, and so on. Most Bluetooth radios will have a range of about 10 meters and enjoy about 700k of bandwidth. Potential applications for Bluetooth include synchronizing data between PDA and computer when they come into prox-imity with one another or providing a laptop with Internet connectivity via a mobile phone in one's pocket. A new term, personal area network (PAN), is used to describe this notion of a small wireless network where all of our personal mobile devices regularly communicate with one another.

It's more accurate to think of Bluetooth as a replacement for serial, USB, or IEEE 1394 cables than as a Ethernet-type networking technology. The current iteration of Bluetooth supports only one master device controlling a maximum of seven simultaneous slave devices.

802.11

Although Bluetooth technology is designed as a short-range personal networking technology, 802.11 is intended to be used for LANs. The current generation of this technology, 802.11b or *WiFi*, provides up to 11Mb of bandwidth, with a 45Mb version known as 802.11a on the hori-zon. 802.11 has a range of about 30 meters, with greater ranges possible using special anten-nas. 802.11's power requirements are greater than that of Bluetooth, and the devices are larger in size; the radio device can fit inside a standard PC Card, which is great for laptops, but not convenient for phones or most PDAs.

One important note to keep in mind is that Bluetooth and 802.11 share the same 2.4 GHz spectrum, so it is possible that the two might interfere with one another when occupying the same space. Although it's unlikely that they would completely freeze each other out because of the fact that both use spread spectrum technology to hop frequencies many times per second, it's feasible that performance could suffer on either or both connections because of mutual interference.

Server-Based Wireless Data Technologies

Wireless data technologies ride on top of the radio technology in order to provide data and services to mobile devices. These technologies involve servers generating content, which is sent wirelessly to clients and interpreted by built-in software residing on the client.

SMS

Short Message Service (SMS) technology is used to send short (generally 100 to 160 character maximum) text messages to mobile phones. Aside from the limited message length, SMS technology is limited due to issues of interoperability between network operators and varying SMS protocols employed by operators. However, SMS has become very popular—particularly in Europe—because of its ease-of-use and wide availability.

Because each carrier might employ slight variations on the SMS theme, techniques for developing applications that support SMS can vary depending on the carrier you are targeting. Although GSM has an advantage over other mobile phone networks in that the support for SMS is built into the GSM standard, from an application developer's standpoint, it can still be challenging to send SMS messages from a server connected to the Internet to a mobile client. This is because you have to work with SMS servers on the carrier side, which might involve a varying support of standards and even licensing fees.

We recommend one of two avenues for incorporating SMS support into servers. The first option is to simply use e-mail; most carriers support the sending of an SMS message by sending an e-mail message to a specific e-mail address that contains the number of the recipient's phone. Although this is a relatively simple approach from a technical standpoint, the disadvantage is that support isn't universal and it adds another layer of potential failure. The second option is to purchase any one of many third-party tools that handle the sending of SMS messages on a variety of networks. This is the preferred technique, although it will involve some up-front costs and/or licensing fees.

WAP

Wireless Application Protocol (WAP) was established as a standard means for accessing information from the Internet via a mobile device. The general acceptance of WAP in the market has been mixed. On the one hand, WAP has been well received by network operators and phone manufacturers because it was designed from the beginning to work over any wireless service and network standard on practically any device. However, the user experience with WAP hasn't been positive overall because of limitation in display, data entry capabilities, and wireless bandwidth. Additionally, because WAP sites have little way to generate revenue based on usage, there is not a strong business incentive for developing high-quality WAP sites. Content for WAP systems is developed in an XML-based language known as Wireless Markup Language (WML).

The typical WAP application architecture is illustrated in Figure 24.1.

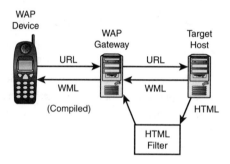

FIGURE 24.1

WAP application architecture.

The mobile device, typically a phone, has a piece of resident software known as a *microbrowser*. As the name implies, this piece of software is similar to a Web browser but designed for devices such as mobile phones with limited memory and processing power. Most mobile phones on the market today use OpenWave's (formerly Phone.com) microbrowser. Additionally, the microbrowser is usually designed to render the WML or HDML languages rather than HTML, as described in the next section.

Because the current generation of mobile phones do not inherently know how to communicate with resources on the Internet, the WAP gateway acts as an intermediary between the mobile device and the public Internet. Most WAP gateways are managed by the wireless service provider, and run software created by companies such as OpenWave, Nokia, or SAS.

The target host is generally just a plain old Web server that simply returns content properly formatted for WAP. Proper formatting means that the content is described using WML or, less optimally, by employing a filter to dynamically convert HTML content to WML.

The chief benefit of WAP is its wide support across pretty much all mobile and wireless devices. What's more, the available functionality in WAP is essentially the lowest common denominator of mobile devices, meaning wider compatibility at the expense of powerful functionality. In addition, between the application server, Web server, WAP gateway, microbrowser, and client device, WAP developers have a lot to worry about in their efforts to create applications that function properly for the greatest number of end users.

The chief drawbacks of WAP include the limited screen size and processing capabilities of the devices, the typical lack of a full keyboard for data entry, the slow download speeds, and the fact that wireless airtime for WAP applications can still be expensive.

WML: The Language of WAP

As we mentioned earlier, information is exchanged in WAP using wireless markup language (WML). WML is in some ways modeled after HTML, but WML has two things going for it when compared to HTML. First, it is made up of a relatively small set of tags and attributes, making it compact enough to be used efficiently with machines with little memory and processor muscle. Second, it is based on Extensible Markup Language (XML), so content is well formed and not as open to browser interpretation as is HTML. This chapter is not intended to present a primer on WAP, but we would like to turn you on to some of the basics.

You probably know that HTML is based on a page metaphor, with each .html file served to a browser generally representing one page of information. WML, on the other hand, is based on a card deck metaphor, with one .wml file representing a deck containing some number of cards. Each card represents one screen of information. In this way, the functionality of an entire WML deck can be sent to a client with only one client-to-server round trip, as opposed to the round-trip-per-page system that is the norm on the Web. A typical .wml file, then, might look something like this:

```
<?xml version="1.0"?>
<!DOCTYPE wml PUBLIC "-//WAPFORUM//DTD WML 1.1//EN"
"http://www.WAPforum.org/DTD/wml_1.1.xml">
<wml>
  <card>
    <do type="accept">
      <go href="#hello"/>
    </do>
    <p>Punch the Button</p>
  </card>
  <card id="hello">
    <p>Hello from WAP!</p>
  </card>
</wml>
```

If you know just a little about HTML and XML, you can probably figure out this code with relative ease. The document prologue, which makes up the first few lines, is standard XML and describes the XML version of this document and the location of the DTD used to describe the tags and attributes contained within. After that, the code goes on to create a deck with two cards, one with an OK button, and one with a greeting.

WML syntax additionally supports things such as events, timers, field sets, lists, and images (although not all devices support images). Some of the later versions of WAP browsers even support a scripting language called WMLScript. We cannot cover the entirety of the WML language here, but if you're interested, you can view the details of the WML spec at `http://www.WAPforum.org`.

If you want to try your hand at developing some WML content, the easiest way to start is to obtain an emulator. You can obtain the emulator from the microbrowser developer at `http://www.openwave.com`, or two other popular emulators come directly from the mobile communications leaders Nokia and Ericsson; visit `http://forum.nokia.com` or `http://www.ericsson.com/developerszone`. It's always a good idea to get things working on the emulators first before moving on to real hardware because the emulators offer much quicker write-run-debug turnaround time. It's also a good idea to test your final product on as many devices as possible prior to release because each device's unique characteristics can cause your deck to behave or display differently from how you intend.

WAP Security

The WAP specification calls for a wireless encryption stack known as Wireless Transport Layer Security (WTLS) to be used for secure connections. Because SSL is too resource intensive to be used with the current generation of mobile devices, WTLS was created to provide encryption and authentication services between the device and the WAP gateway. The gateway is then able to communicate with Internet hosts via the standard SSL protocol. Despite the fact that both WTLS and SSL are quite secure in themselves, the potential for security breaches exists at the WAP gateway at the point where the WTLS data stream is decrypted and re-encrypted with SSL. WTLS architecture is illustrated in Figure 24.2.

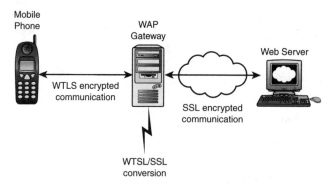

FIGURE 24.2
WAP's Wireless Transport Layer Security.

A Simple WAP Application

Creating a WAP application in Delphi is little different from creating a regular Web application in Delphi. WAP is perhaps even easier to target because the limitations inherent in WAP and the target devices tend to beget simpler applications on the server side than traditional browser-based applications. The opposite side of this coin, however, is that it is more challenging for developers to develop applications that are engaging to useful to end users given these limitations.

For this example, start by creating a normal WebBroker application as you learned in Chapter 23, "Building WebSnap Applications." This application has a single Web module with a single action. This action is marked as default as shown in Figure 24.3.

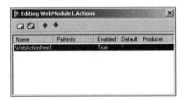

FIGURE 24.3
A simple WebBroker WAP application.

Listing 24.1 shows the source code for the main unit of this application, including the OnAction event handler for the Web module's default action.

LISTING 24.1   Main.pas—The Main Unit for the SimpWap Project

```
unit Main;

interface

uses
  SysUtils, Classes, HTTPApp;

type
  TWebModule1 = class(TWebModule)
    procedure WebModule1WebActionItem1Action(Sender: TObject;
      Request: TWebRequest; Response: TWebResponse; var Handled: Boolean);
  private
    { Private declarations }
  public
    { Public declarations }
  end;
```

LISTING 24.1 Continued

```
var
  WebModule1: TWebModule1;

implementation

{$R *.DFM}

const
  SWMLContent = 'text/vnd.wap.wml';
  SWMLDeck =
    '<?xml version="1.0"?>'#13#10 +
    '<!DOCTYPE wml PUBLIC "-//WAPFORUM//DTD WML 1.1//EN"'#13#10 +
    '"http://www.WAPforum.org/DTD/wml_1.1.xml">'#13#10 +
    '<wml>'#13#10 +
    '  <card>'#13#10 +
    '    <do type="accept">'#13#10 +
    '      <go href="#hello"/>'#13#10 +
    '    </do>'#13#10 +
    '    <p>Punch the Button</p>'#13#10 +
    '  </card>'#13#10 +
    '  <card id="hello">'#13#10 +
    '    <p>Hello from WAP!</p>'#13#10 +
    '  </card>'#13#10 +
    '</wml>'#13#10;


procedure TWebModule1.WebModule1WebActionItem1Action(Sender: TObject;
  Request: TWebRequest; Response: TWebResponse; var Handled: Boolean);
begin
  Response.ContentType := SWMLContent;
  Response.Content := SWMLDeck;
end;

end.
```

When the action is invoked, the event handler responds by setting the ContentType and Content properties of the Response object. ContentType is set to the WML content type string, and the content returned is the same simple WAP deck that was explained earlier in this chapter.

Remember to set the `ContentType` of the `Response` object to the string containing the MIME type of the variety of content you are returning. This sets the content type information in the HTTP header. If you return the incorrect content type, your content will likely be misinterpreted on the target device. Some notable WAP content types include

- `text/vnd.wap.wml` for WML code
- `text/vnd.wap.wmlscript` for WML script code
- `image/vnd.wap.wbmp` for wireless bitmap images

Figure 24.4 shows this simple Delphi WAP application in action.

FIGURE 24.4
Delphi WAP application in action.

Error Reporting

The default exception handler for WebSnap applications sends an HTML message to the client with information on the error. Of course, most WAP devices will not be able to understand an HTML error, so it's important to ensure that any errors that might occur in your WAP application are surfaced as WML messages to the client rather than HTML. This can be done by wrapping each `OnAction` event handler with a `try..except` block that calls out to an error message formatting routine. This is shown in Listing 24.2.

Wireless Bitmaps

Although WAP doesn't yet support the fancy JPEG and GIF graphics common on the Web, most WAP devices support monochrome images in the form of wireless bitmaps (wbmp). Listing 24.2 adds a new action to the Web module to support the generation of a wbmp. This action generates an official-looking but quite random graph for display on the target device. Although we won't delve into the binary format of wbmp files in this text, you can see that it isn't a great deal of work to generate wbmps manually in your WAP applications. Figure 24.5 shows what a WBMP will look like on a phone display.

> **NOTE**
>
> Not all WAP browsers, devices, and emulators support wbmp images. Be sure to test before assuming support.

LISTING 24.2   `Main.pas`—Once More with Feeling

```
unit Main;

interface

uses
  SysUtils, Classes, HTTPApp;

type
  TWebModule1 = class(TWebModule)
    procedure WebModule1WebActionItem1Action(Sender: TObject;
      Request: TWebRequest; Response: TWebResponse; var Handled: Boolean);
    procedure WebModule1GraphActionAction(Sender: TObject;
      Request: TWebRequest; Response: TWebResponse; var Handled: Boolean);
  private
    procedure CreateWirelessBitmap(MemStrm: TMemoryStream);
    procedure HandleException(e: Exception; Response: TWebResponse);
  end;

var
  WebModule1: TWebModule1;

implementation

{$R *.DFM}
```

LISTING 24.2   Continued

```
const
  SWMLContent = 'text/vnd.wap.wml';
  SWBMPContent = 'image/vnd.wap.wbmp';
  SWMLDeck =
    '<?xml version="1.0"?>'#13#10 +
    '<!DOCTYPE wml PUBLIC "-//WAPFORUM//DTD WML 1.1//EN"'#13#10 +
    '"http://www.WAPforum.org/DTD/wml_1.1.xml">'#13#10 +
    '<wml>'#13#10 +
    '  <card>'#13#10 +
    '    <do type="accept">'#13#10 +
    '      <go href="#hello"/>'#13#10 +
    '    </do>'#13#10 +
    '    <p>Punch the Button</p>'#13#10 +
    '  </card>'#13#10 +
    '  <card id="hello">'#13#10 +
    '    <p>Hello from WAP!</p>'#13#10 +
    '  </card>'#13#10 +
    '</wml>'#13#10;

  SWMLError =
    '<?xml version="1.0"?>'#13#10 +
    '<!DOCTYPE wml PUBLIC "-//WAPFORUM//DTD WML 1.1//EN"'#13#10 +
    '"http://www.wapforum.org/DTD/wml_1.1.xml">'#13#10 +
    '<wml>'#13#10 +
    '  <card id="error" title="SimpWAP">'#13#10 +
    '    <p>Error: %s'#13#10 +
    '      <do type="prev" label="Back">'#13#10 +
    '        <prev/>'#13#10 +
    '      </do>'#13#10 +
    '    </p>'#13#10 +
    '  </card>'#13#10 +
    '</wml>'#13#10;

procedure TWebModule1.HandleException(e: Exception; Response: TWebResponse);
begin
  Response.ContentType := SWMLContent;
  Response.Content := Format(SWMLError, [e.Message]);
end;

procedure TWebModule1.WebModule1WebActionItem1Action(Sender: TObject;
  Request: TWebRequest; Response: TWebResponse; var Handled: Boolean);
```

LISTING 24.2   Continued

```
begin
  try
    Response.ContentType := SWMLContent;
    Response.Content := SWMLDeck;
  except
    on e: Exception do
      HandleException(e, Response);
  end;
end;

procedure TWebModule1.WebModule1GraphActionAction(Sender: TObject;
  Request: TWebRequest; Response: TWebResponse; var Handled: Boolean);
var
  MemStream: TMemoryStream;
begin
  try
    MemStream := TMemoryStream.Create;
    try
      CreateWirelessBitmap(MemStream);
      MemStream.Position := 0;
      with Response do
      begin
        ContentType := SWBMPContent;
        ContentStream := MemStream;
        SendResponse;
      end;
    finally
      MemStream.Free;
    end;
  except
    on e: Exception do
      HandleException(e, Response);
  end;
end;

procedure TWebModule1.CreateWirelessBitmap(MemStrm: TMemoryStream);
const
  Header : Array[0..3] of Char = #0#0#104#20;
var
  Bmp: array[1..104,1..20] of Boolean;
  X, Y, Dir, Bit: Integer;
  B: Byte;
```

LISTING 24.2   Continued

```
begin
  { clear the bitmap out }
  FillChar(Bmp,SizeOf(Bmp),0);
  { draw X and Y axis }
  for X := 1 to 104 do Bmp[X, 20] := True;
  for Y := 1 to 20 do Bmp[1, Y] := True;
  { draw random data }
  Y := Random(20) + 1;
  Dir := Random(10);
  for X := 1 to 104 do
  begin
    Bmp[X,Y] := True;
    if (Dir > 4) then Y := Y+Random(2)+1
    else Y := Y - Random(2) - 1;
    if (Y > 20) then Y := 20;
    if (Y < 1) then Y := 1;
    Dir := Random(10);
  end;
  { create WBMP data }
  MemStrm.Write(Header, SizeOf(Header));
  Bit := 7;
  B := 0;
  for Y := 1 to 20 do
  begin
    for X := 1 to 104 do
    begin
      if Bmp[X,Y] = True then
        B := B or (1 shl Bit);
      Dec(Bit);
      if (Bit < 0) then begin
        B := not B;
        MemStrm.Write(B, SizeOf(B));
        Bit := 7;
        B := 0;
      end;
    end;
  end;
end;

initialization
  Randomize;
end.
```

FIGURE 24.5
Viewing the WBMP in the Nokia emulator.

I-mode

I-mode is a proprietary technology for Internet content on mobile phones developed by NTT DoCoMo, Japan's telecommunications behemoth. I-mode is very successful in Japan, with over 20 million subscribers and growing. In many ways, i-mode is everything WAP isn't: It supports rich 256-color graphics, color phone displays, and uses an "always-on" TCP/IP connection. Additionally, DoCoMo has developed a revenue sharing model that enables i-mode sites to get a slice of the financial pie based on usage. However, i-mode is hampered by the "P" word (proprietary) and availability outside Japan is scarce; i-mode services will be rolling out in the United States, United Kingdom, and continental Europe beginning this year.

From a developer's standpoint, targeting i-mode phones isn't much more difficult than generating content for the Web because i-mode content is developed using a subset of HTML known as Compact HTML (cHTML). Supported cHTML tags and rules are available from DoCoMo at `http://www.nttdocomo.com/i/tagindex.html`. Note that in addition to using only cHTML-supported tags, i-mode sites must also ensure that the S-JIS character set is used, images are in GIF format, and pages have no script or Java content.

PQA

Palm Query Applications (PQA) are essentially normal HTML pages stripped of add-ons such as scripting and images that are designed for display on the screen of a wireless PalmOS device. Wireless PalmOS devices, such as Palm VIIx devices or those equipped with Novatel modems, are currently limited to North America. Like i-mode, PQAs are developed using a subset of HTML, except Palm has added a few proprietary extensions. Developers interested in creating PQAs should download the Web Clipping Developer's Guide from Palm at `http://www.palmos.com/dev/tech/docs/`.

In general, the PQA flavor of HTML includes everything in HTML 3.2 with the exception of applets, JavaScript, nested tables, image maps, and the VSPACE, SUB, SUP, LINK, and ISINDEX tags. PQAs also include several interesting additions to HTML. Most notable among these are the `palmcomputingplatform` meta tag and `%zipcode` and `%deviceid` tags. When an HTML document contains the `palmcomputingplatform` meta tag, this serves as an indicator to Palm Computing's Palm.net proxy (which acts as the intermediary between a Web server and Palm device, not unlike a WAP gateway) that the document is optimized for display on a PalmOS handheld and doesn't require parsing to be stripped of invalid content. When the `%zipcode` tag appears in a requested posted by the client, the Palm.net proxy will replace the tag with the ZIP Code where the device is located (based on radio tower information). The `%deviceid` tag similarly sends the PalmOS's device's unique ID to the server. This is particularly handy because PQA HTML does not support cookies, but a similar means of state management can be crafted using the `%deviceid` tag.

With Web clipping, Palm has taken a different approach than most other players in this space. Rather than use a browser-like entity to navigate to a site and pull down content, PQAs exist locally on the PalmOS device. PQAs are built by running a standard .HTML file through a special compiler that links the HTML with referenced graphic files and other dependencies. Users install PQAs like normal PalmOS PRC applications. PQAs gain efficiency by including portions of the application local and only going out to the network for "results" pages.

PQA Client

The first step toward developing a PQA application is to create the piece that will physically reside on the client device. This is done by creating an HTML document and compiling it using Palm Computing's PQA Builder tool. A sample PQA HTML document is shown in Listing 24.3.

LISTING 24.3   An HTML Document for a PQA

```
<html>
<head>
<title>DDG PQA Test</title>
<meta name="palmcomputingplatform" content="true">
</head>
<body>
<p>This is a sample PQA for DDG</p>
<img src="image.gif">
<form method="post" action="http://128.64.162.164/scripts/pqatest.dll">
<input type="hidden" value="%zipcode" name="zip">
```

LISTING 24.3   Continued

```
<input type="hidden" value="%deviceid" name="id">
<input type="submit">
</form>
</body>
```

You can see that this simple HTML document contains a reference to an image, some text, a form with a submit button, and hidden fields used to pass the ZIP Code and device ID to the server.

Figure 24.6 shows this document being compiled in PQA Builder.

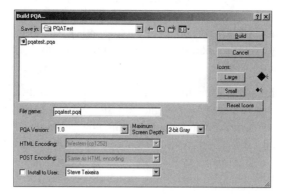

FIGURE 24.6

Compiling with PQA Builder.

Once compiled, a file with a .pqa extension is generated. This file contains the HTML document as well as any referenced images. This file can be installed onto the PalmOS device the same as any other PalmOS application.

PQA Server

The server-side portion, like WAP, is a WebSnap application that handles the page requests from clients and returns pages. Unlike WAP with its WML, however, PQAs communicate using the HTML variant described previously. Listing 24.4 shows the main unit of a WebBroker application designed to fulfill the server role for the PQA client described previously.

LISTING 24.4   Main.pas—the Main Unit for the PQATest Application

```
unit Main;

interface
```

LISTING 24.4   Continued

```
uses
  SysUtils, Classes, HTTPApp;

type
  TWebModule1 = class(TWebModule)
    procedure WebModule1WebActionItem1Action(Sender: TObject;
      Request: TWebRequest; Response: TWebResponse; var Handled: Boolean);
  private
    { Private declarations }
  public
    { Public declarations }
  end;

var
  WebModule1: TWebModule1;

implementation

{$R *.DFM}

const
  SPQAResp =
    '<html><head><meta name="palmcomputingplatform" content="true"></head>'+
    #13#10 +
    '<body>Hello from a Delphi server<br>Your zipcode is: %s<br>'#13#10 +
    'Your device ID is: %s<br><img src="file:pqatest.pqa/image.gif"></body>'+
    '</html>';

procedure TWebModule1.WebModule1WebActionItem1Action(Sender: TObject;
  Request: TWebRequest; Response: TWebResponse; var Handled: Boolean);
begin
  Response.Content := Format(SPQAResp, [Request.ContentFields.Values['zip'],
    Request.ContentFields.Values['id']]);
end;

end.
```

24

WIRELESS
DEVELOPMENT

The server responds to the client by sending the client's ZIP Code and device ID. An interesting technique in the HTML code returned by the server is that it references the same image that was compiled into the .pqa on the client side using the *file:<pqaname>* syntax. This allows you to build rich graphics into your PQAs by compiling them into the client side and referencing them on the server, thereby obviating the need to download any graphics over the wireless modem. Figures 24.7 and 24.8 show this application in action, before and after the submit button is pressed. Note that the ZIP Code and device ID are null values in the emulator.

FIGURE 24.7

PQATest in the PalmOS emulator.

FIGURE 24.8

PQATest in the PalmOS emulator after pressing Submit.

Wireless User Experience

User experience is by far the most important factor in determining whether a mobile system will ultimately prove useful to individuals. However, user experience is all-too-often given short shrift in favor of gratuitous features or technology. Because of inherent limitations in the mobile world—particularly connectivity and device size—there is little room for error in a developer's attempt to provide users with the functionality they need when they need it. The trick is to focus on the user: Determine what information or service the users need and endeavor to get it to them as efficiently as possible.

Circuit-Switched Versus Packet-Switched Networks

When considering the mobile phone as a client platform, one issue that can have a dramatic impact on usability is whether the mobile phone network is circuit-switched or packet-switched. Circuit-switched networks operate like a modem on a conventional phone: you must dial-in to establish a direct connection with the host, and that connection must be maintained while data exchange is taking place. Packet-switched networks behave more like a fixed Ethernet connection: The connection is always active, and data packets can be sent and received out over the connection at any time.

The overhead required to establish connections in circuit-switched networks can often be a major impediment to user satisfaction—particularly if the user is performing a task that should only take a few seconds. After all, who wants to wait up to 20 seconds to connect in order to interact with an application for 3 seconds? Most mobile networks today are still circuit-switched, but notable example of networks utilizing packet-switched technology include NTT DoCoMo's i-mode, Nextel's iDEN, and AT&T's CDPD networks.

Wireless Is Not the Web

A common misconception among purveyors of mobile devices and wireless networks is that people desire to surf the Web on these devices. With their tiny screens and limited bandwidth, mobile devices are an exceedingly inconvenient vehicle for Web surfing. Each page of information can take several seconds to fetch due to network constraints, and entering data can be downright painful—particularly on a mobile phone. Instead, mobile applications need to be optimized to deliver specific information and services with minimal data entry required on the part of the user and as few client-to-server roundtrips as feasible.

The Importance of Form Factor

When designing mobile applications, you must always remain sensitive to the available amount of screen real estate. Whether creating a WAP-based application bound to a microbrowser or a custom user interface in J2ME, application developers have to balance the issues of communicating a sufficient quantity of information in each screen against maintaining a readable and navigable user interface.

Data Entry and Navigation Techniques

Related to form factor is the issue of data entry. Different types of devices rely on different mechanisms for data entry. PalmOS and Pocket PC devices use a combination of a stylus and handwriting recognition (with optional portable keyboards); RIM BlackBerry devices use thumb-size keyboards; mobile phones generally have only a numeric keypad and a few extra buttons. This means that applications designed for one mobile platform might be difficult to use on another. For example, a PDA stylus is great for tapping random areas of the screen, whereas a BlackBerry is better suited toward text data entry, and a phone is best suited for as little data entry as possible!

M-Commerce

Just as e-commerce has come to refer to commercial transactions performed over the Web, *m-commerce* refers to commercial transactions over mobile devices. Developers of mobile commerce sites must understand that m-commerce is fundamentally different from e-commerce. Most conspicuously, it's not feasible for mobile customers to browse for items. In the case of a mobile phone, for instance, it's too time-consuming to enter keystrokes—images either don't exist or are of poor quality, and there isn't enough screen real estate to describe items.

Instead, m-commerce systems should be designed with the notion in mind that the users know what they want; just make it easy for them to give you their money. Remember: if the user wants to buy a television or book, there's little reason why he wouldn't simply wait until he get to his home or office to make the purchase on a full-sized computer. The fact that the user is even willing to engage in m-commerce implies that there is some sense of immediacy or urgency in making the purchase, and winning m-commerce merchants will be the ones who recognize and take advantage of this fact.

For example, one eastern European country allows motorists to pay parking meter tolls using their mobile phone. This seems like a relatively simple application on the surface, but the value proposition for both parties is very compelling. The motorist doesn't have to worry about whether he has enough coins to feed the meters, and the meter operator isn't burdened with collecting coins from dozens or hundreds or thousands of meters and trucking the coins to the bank. Police monitoring the meters can use a mobile device tied to the same system to know at an instance how much time is left for a given space.

Summary

The world of mobile computing has grown dramatically in recent years, and it can be difficult to keep track of emerging trends. Our hope is that at this point, you are now armed with enough information to make some strategic decisions and move forward with a mobility project. In addition, you have seen that Delphi is a very capable tool when it comes to building this next generation of wireless applications.

INDEX

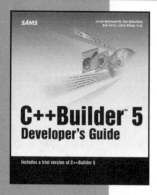

C++Builder™ 5 Developer's Guide

Jarrod Hollingworth, Dan Butterfield, Bob Swart, Jamie Allsop

0-672-31972-1
$59.99 US/$89.95 CAN

C++Builder5 Developer's Guide is your key to unlocking the full potential
C ++Builder. The text provides comprehensive coverage of all major
C++Builder5 features, including InternetExpress™, ADOExpress,
InterBase®, TeamSource™, CodeGuard™, and more. In addition, you'll
discover how to take advantage of enhanced support for MIDAS™,
CORBA™, and COM+.

Kylix™ Developer's Guide

Charlie and Marjorie Calvert, John Kaster, Bob Swart

0-672-32060-6
$59.99 US/$89.95 CAN

The *Kylix™ Developer's Guide* introduces programmers to the new
Borland® Delphi compiler for Linux. The book provides comprehensive
coverage of CLX, a VCL-like visual programming library that runs on
both Windows and Linux. You'll learn the Linux system environment,
development of databases with CLX, and Web development with Kylix.

Pure CORBA®

Fintan Bolton

0-672-31812-1
$49.99 US/$74.95 CAN

Pure CORBA® is a practical guide to writing CORBA-compliant applications in C++ and Java™. This book focuses on the CORBA standard itself
rather than on any particular ORB. Equal priority for C++ and Java is
ensured by presenting code fragments and examples in both languages
throughout. The book is self-contained and requires no previous knowledge of distributed systems or of CORBA application development. *Pure
CORBA®* is for experienced C++ and Java programmers.

What's on the CD-ROM

The companion CD-ROM contains all the code for the examples developed in the book and related software.

Windows Installation Instructions

1. Insert the disc into your CD-ROM drive.
2. From the Windows desktop, double-click the My Computer icon.
3. Double-click the icon representing your CD-ROM drive.
4. Double-click the icon titled start.exe to run the installation program.
5. Follow the onscreen prompts to finish the installation.

> **NOTE**
>
> If you have the AutoPlay feature enabled, the start.exe program starts automatically whenever you insert the disc into your CD-ROM drive.

Read This Before Opening the Software

By opening this package, you are also agreeing to be bound by the following agreement:

You may not copy or redistribute the entire CD-ROM as a whole. Copying and redistribution of individual software programs on the CD-ROM is governed by terms set by individual copyright holders.

The installer and code from the author(s) are copyrighted by the publisher and the author(s). Individual programs and other items on the CD-ROM are copyrighted or are under an Open Source license by their various authors or other copyright holders.

This software is sold as-is without warranty of any kind, either expressed or implied, including but not limited to the implied warranties of merchantability and fitness for a particular purpose. Neither the publisher nor its dealers or distributors assumes any liability for any alleged or actual damages arising from the use of this program. (Some states do not allow for the exclusion of implied warranties, so the exclusion may not apply to you.)

NOTE

Please note that this CD-ROM uses long and mixed-case filenames, requiring the use of a protected-mode CD-ROM Driver.